DEPARTMENT OF ECONOMIC AND SOCIAL AFFAIRS
Statistics Division

ST/ESA/STAT/SER.J/50

DÉPARTEMENT DES AFFAIRES ÉCONOMIQUES ET SOCIALES
Division de statistique

2006
Energy Statistics Yearbook
Annuaire des statistiques
de l'énergie

United Nations
Nations Unies
New York, 2008

The Department of Economic and Social Affairs of the United Nations Secretariat is a vital interface between global policies in the economic, social and environmental spheres and national action. The Department works in three main interlinked areas: (i) it compiles, generates and analyses a wide range of economic, social and environmental data and information on which States Members of the United Nations draw to review common problems and to take stock of policy options; (ii) it facilitates the negotiations of Member States in many intergovernmental bodies on joint courses of action to address ongoing or emerging global challenges; and (iii) it advises interested Governments on the ways and means of translating policy frameworks developed in United Nations conferences and summits into programmes at the country level and, through technical assistance, helps build national capacities.

Le Département des affaires économiques et sociales du Secrétariat de l'Organisation des Nations Unies sert de relais entre les orientations arrêtées au niveau international dans les domaines économiques, sociaux et environnementaux et les politiques exécutées à l'échelon national. Il intervient dans trois grands domaines liés les uns aux autres : i) il compile, produit et analyse une vaste gamme de données et d'éléments d'information sur des questions économiques, sociales et environnementales dont les États Membres de l'Organisation se servent pour examiner des problèmes communs et évaluer les options qui s'offrent à eux; ii) il facilite les négociations entre les États Membres dans de nombreux organes intergouvernementaux sur les orientations à suivre de façon collective afin de faire face aux problèmes mondiaux existants ou en voie d'apparition; iii) il conseille les gouvernements intéressés sur la façon de transposer les orientations politiques arrêtées à l'occasion des conférences et sommets des Nations Unies en programmes exécutables au niveau national et aide à renforcer les capacités nationales au moyen de programmes d'assistance technique.

NOTE

Symbols of United Nations documents are composed of capital letters combined with figures. Mention of such a symbol indicates reference to a United Nations document.

NOTE

Les cotes des documents de l'Organisation des Nations Unies se composent de lettres majuscules et de chiffres. La simple mention d'une cote dans un texte signifie qu'il s'agit d'un document de l'Organisation.

General Disclaimer

The designations employed and the presentation of material in this publication do not imply the expression of any opinion whatsoever on the part of the Secretariat of the United Nations concerning the legal status of any country, territory, city or area, or of its authorities, or concerning the delimitation of its frontiers or boundaries.

Where the designation "country or area" appears in the headings of tables, it covers countries, territories, cities or areas. In prior issues of this publication, where the designation "country" appears in the headings of tables, it should be interpreted to cover countries, territories, cities or areas.

Déni de responsabilité

Les appellations employées dans cette publication et la présentation des données qui y figurent n'impliquent de la part du Secrétariat de l'Organisation des Nations Unies aucune prise de position quant au statut juridique des pays, territoires, villes ou zones, ou de leurs autorités, ni quant au tracé de leurs frontières ou limites.

L'appellation "pays ou zone" figurant dans les titres des rubriques des tableaux désigne des pays, des territoires, des villes ou des zones. L'appellation "pays" figurant dans certaines rubriques des tableaux de numéros antérieurs de cette publication doit être interprétée comme désignant des pays, des territoires, des villes ou des zones.

ST/ESA/STAT/SER.J/50

UNITED NATIONS PUBLICATION
Sales number: E/F 09.XVII.4

PUBLICATION DES NATIONS UNIES
Numéro de vente: E/F 09.XVII.4

ISBN 978-92-1-061261-6
ISSN 0256-6400

CONTENTS

Page

Introduction x
Country nomenclature.......................... xii
Abbreviations and symbols xiv
Definitions.. xv
Units of measurement and conversions xxx
Tables notes xxxi

TABLES

Conversion factors

I.   Coal equivalent coefficients xxxii

II. Specific gravities of crude petroleum xlii
III. Specific gravities of petroleum products xliv
IV. Selected conversion factors for crude petroleum and petroleum products xlv
V.   Heat values of gases xlvi

Commercial energy

1. Production, trade and consumption - Coal equivalent 2
2. Production, trade and consumption - Oil equivalent 37
3. Production, trade and consumption - Terajoules 71
4. Total energy requirement - Terajoules............ 104

Solid Fuels

5. Production, trade and consumption of solid fuels - coal equivalent............................. 122
6. Production, trade and consumption of hard coal 133
7. International trade of hard coal (principal importers and exporters); 2005 and 2006 144
8. Production, trade and consumption of Brown coal/lignite 148
9. Production, trade and consumption of coke 154
10. Production, trade and consumption of hard coal briquettes.................................. 163
11. Production, trade and consumption of briquettes of lignite and peat........................ 166
12. Production, trade and consumption of peat 169
13. Selected series of statistics on renewables and wastes 173

TABLE DES MATIERES

Page

Introduction x
Nomenclature des pays xii
Abréviations et signes conventionnels......xiv
Définitions.. xv
Unités de mesure et conversions xxx
Notes relatives aux tableaux................... xxxi

TABLEAUX

Facteurs de conversion

I.   Facteurs de conversion en équivalent houille xxxii
II. Densités du pétrole brut xlii
III. Densités des produits pétroliers xliv
IV. Quelques facteurs de conversion pour le pétrole et les produits pétroliers............................. xlv
V.   Pouvoirs calorifiques des gaz...................... xlvi

Energie commerciale

1. Production, commerce et consommation - Equivalent houille 2
2. Production, commerce et consommation - Equivalent pétrole 37
3. Production, commerce et consommation - Térajoules 71
4. Montant total des besoins énergétiques - Térajoules 104

Combustibles solides

5.   Production, commerce et consommation de combustibles solides - équivalent houille.......122
6. Production, commerce et consommation de houille 133
7. Commerce international de houille (principaux importateurs et exportateurs) 2005 et 2006...144
8. Production, commerce et consommation de charbon brun/lignite............................148
9. Production, commerce et consommation de coke 154
10. Production, commerce et consommation d'agglomérés (briquettes de houille) 163
11. Production, commerce et consommation de briquettes de lignite et de tourbe 166
12. Production, commerce et consommation de tourbe..169
13. Séries de statistiques des renouvelables et des déchets..173

CONTENTS (continued)

Tables	Page

Liquid fuels

14. Production, trade and consumption of crude petroleum 204
15. International trade of crude petroleum (principal importers and exporters); 2005 and 2006 218
16. Refinery distillation capacity, throughput and output 222
17. Production, trade and consumption of liquefied petroleum gas 234
18. Production, trade and consumption of aviation gasolene 249
19. Production, trade and consumption of motor gasolene 259
20. Production, trade and consumption of kerosene 277
21. Production, trade and consumption of jet fuels 293
22. Production, trade and consumption of gas-diesel oils 309
23. Production, trade and consumption of residual fuel oil 327
24. Production, trade and consumption of energy petroleum products 343
25. Production of non-energy products from refineries - by type 361
26. Production of energy products from refineries - by type 371
27. Capacity and production of natural gas liquid plants - by type 382

Gaseous fuels

28. Production, trade and consumption of natural gas 388
29. International trade of natural gas (principal importers and exporters); 2005 and 2006 398
30. Production of other gases - by type 402
31. Production, trade and consumption of gases 413

TABLE DES MATIERES (suite)

Tableaux	Page

Combustibles liquides

14. Production, commerce et consommation de pétrole brut 204
15. Commerce international du pétrole brut (principaux importateurs et exportateurs); 2005 et 2006 218
16. Capacité de traitement des raffineries, quantités traitées et production totale 222
17. Production, commerce et consommation de gaz de pétrole liquéfié 234
18. Production, commerce et consommation d'essence aviation 249
19. Production, commerce et consommation d'essence auto 259
20. Production, commerce et consommation de pétrole lampant 277
21. Production, commerce et consommation de carburéacteurs 293
22. Production, commerce et consommation de gazole/carburant diesel 309
23. Production, commerce et consommation de mazout résiduel 327
24. Production, commerce et consommation de produits pétroliers énergétiques 343
25. Production des raffineries – produits non énergétiques - par catégorie 361
26. Production des raffineries – produits énergétiques - par catégorie 371
27. Capacité et production des usines d'extraction de liquides de gaz naturel - par catégorie de produits 382

Combustibles gazeux

28. Production, commerce et consommation de gaz naturel 388
29. Commerce international du gaz naturel (principaux importateurs et exportateurs); 2005 et 2006 398
30. Production d'autres gaz - par catégorie 402
31. Production, commerce et consommation de gaz 413

CONTENTS (continued)

Tables	Page

Electricity and heat

32. Net installed capacity of electric generating plants - by type 429
33. Utilization of installed electric generating capacity - by type 463
34. Production of electricity - by type 496
35. Production, trade and consumption of electricity 530
36. Production of heat - by type 548

Nuclear fuels

37. Production of uranium (uranium content) 554

Energy resources

38. Selected energy resources and reserves 556

TABLE DES MATIERES (suite)

Tableaux	Page

Energie électrique et chaleur

32. Puissance nette installée des centrales électriques - par catégorie 429
33. Utilisation de la capacité des centrales électriques - par catégorie 463
34. Production d'électricité - par catégorie 496
35. Production, commerce et consommation d'électricité 530
36. Production de chaleur - par catégorie 548

Combustibles nucléaires

37. Production d'uranium (contenu en uranium) ..554

Ressources énergétiques

38. Ressources et réserves énergétiques choisies 556

FIGURES

Commercial Energy   Production, Trade and Consumption

1. World commercial primary energy production of solids, by region, in 2006 3
2. World commercial primary energy production of liquids, by region, in 2006 3
3. World commercial primary energy production of gas, by region, in 2006.............3
4. World commercial primary electricity production, by region, in 2006....................3
5. Commercial primary energy production, by region, in 2006.........................37
6. Commercial primary energy consumption, by region, in 2006.........................37
7. World commercial primary energy production 1993-2006 71
8. World commercial primary energy production, by type, in 2006 71
9. World commercial primary energy production, by region, in 2006...................71
10. World energy requirement 1993-2006 104
11. World energy requirement, by region, in 2006 104

Solid Fuels

12. World solid fuel production, by region, in 2006 122
13. World solid fuel consumption, by region, in 2006 122
14. World coal production 1993-2006 133
15. Major hard coal producing countries 2006..133
16. Major hard coal consuming countries in 2006 133
17. World brown coal/lignite production 1993-2006 148
18. Major brown coal/lignite producing countries in 2006....................148
19. Major brown coal/lignite consuming countries in 2006....................148
20. World production of coke 1993-2006 154
21. Major coke producing countries in 2006 154
22. Major coke consuming countries in 2006 ...154
23. Major hard coal briquette producing countries in 2006....................163
24. Major hard coal briquette consuming countries in 2006....................163
25. World production of briquettes of lignite and peat 1993-2006 166
26. Major briquettes of lignite and peat producing countries in 2006 166
27. Major briquettes of lignite and peat consuming countries in 2006 166

GRAPHIQUES

Energie commerciale - Production, commerce et consommation

1. Production mondial d'énergie commerciale primaire par région - solides 2006.................. 3
2. Production mondial d'énergie commerciale primaire par région - liquides 2006................. 3
3. Production mondial d'énergie commerciale primaire par région - gaz 2006 3
4. Production mondial d'énergie commerciale primaire par région - électricité 2006............. 3
5. Production d'énergie commerciale primaire par région 2006 37
6. Consommation d'énergie commerciale primaire par région 2006 37
7. Production mondial d'énergie commerciale primaire par catégorie 1993- 2006 71
8. Production d'énergie commerciale primaire par catégorie, 2006 71
9. Production d'énergie commerciale primaire par région, 2006 71
10. Besoins énergétiques mondiales 1993-2006.................. 104
11. Besoins énergétiques mondiales par région 2006 104

Combustibles solides

12. Production de combustibles solides par région 2006 122
13. Consommation de combustibles solides par région 2006 122
14. Production mondial de houille 1993-2006.. 133
15. Pays grands producteurs de houille 2006.. 133
16. Pays grands consommateurs de houille 2006.................... 133
17. Production mondial de charbon brun/lignite 1993-2006...................... 148
18. Pays grands producteurs de charbon brun/lignite 2006...................... 148
19. Pays grands consommateurs de charbon brun/lignite 2006...................... 148
20. Production mondial de coke 1993-2006..... 154
21. Pays grands producteurs de coke 2006..... 154
22. Pays grands consommateurs de coke 2006.................... 154
23. Pays grands producteurs de briquettes de houille 2006 163
24. Pays grands consommateurs de briquettes de houille 2006 163
25. Briquettes de lignite et de tourbe: production mondial 1993-2006.................. 166
26. Pays grands producteurs de briquettes de lignite et de tourbe 2006........................... 166
27. Pays grands consommateurs de briquettes de lignite et de tourbe 2006....... 166

FIGURES (continued)		GRAPHIQUES (suite)	
28.	World production of peat 1993-2006..........169	28.	Production mondial de tourbe 1993-2006 .. 169
29.	Major peat producing countries in 2006......169	29.	Pays grands producteurs de tourbe 2006 .. 169
30.	Major peat consuming countries in 2006 169	30.	Pays grands consommateurs de tourbe 2006 169
31.	World fuelwood production 1993-2006 174	31.	Production mondial de bois de chauffage 1993-2006 174
32.	World charcoal production 1993-2006........174	32.	Production mondial de charbon de bois, 1990-2006 174
33.	Fuelwood production, by region, in 2006....174	33.	Production de bois de chauffage par région 2006 174
34.	Charcoal production, by region, in 2006 174	34.	Production de charbon de bois par région 2006...... 174
35.	World total primary energy production from renewable sources 1993-2006 175	35.	Production mondial d'énergie primaire des ressources d'énergie renouvelable 1993 - 2006...... 175
36.	Bagasse production, by region, in 2006......175	36.	Production de bagasse par région, 2006 ... 175
37.	Liquids and gases production from renewable sources, by region, in 2006 175	37.	Production d'énergie primaire renouvelable de ressources liquides et gazeuses par région, 2006...... 175
38.	Electricity production from renewable sources, by region, in 2006 175	38.	Production d'électricité primaire renouvelable par région, 2006 175
39.	Energy production from wastes, by region, in 2006....................................175	39.	Production d'énergie des déchets par région, 2006 175

Liquid Fuels

Combustibles liquides

40.	World crude petroleum production 1993-2006 204	40.	Production mondiale de pétrole brut 1993-2006...... 204
41.	World crude petroleum export 1993-2006 ..205	41.	Exportation mondiale de pétrole brut 1993-2006 205
42.	Production, trade and consumption of crude petroleum by region 2006 205	42.	Production, commerce et consommation de pétrole brut par région 2006...... 205
43.	Major crude petroleum producing countries in 2006................................205	43.	Pays grands producteurs de pétrole brut 2006...... 205
44.	Major crude petroleum consuming countries in 2006................................205	44.	Pays grands consommateurs de pétrole brut 2006 205
45.	Refinery distillation capacity, throughput and output, by region, in 2006 222	45.	Capacité de traitement des raffineries, quantités traitées et production, par région 2006...... 222
46.	Refinery utilization (expressed as throughput to capacity) 1993-2006, selected regions.................................223	46.	Rapport entre quantités traitées et capacité de traitement des raffineries 1993-2006 223
47.	World total refinery distillation capacity 1993-2006 223	47.	Capacité de traitement des raffineries, total mondial 1993-2006...... 223
48.	World LPG production 1993-2006 234	48.	Production mondial de GPL 1993-2006 234
49.	Major LPG producing countries in 2006......234	49.	Pays grands producteurs de GPL, 2006 234
50.	Major LPG consuming countries in 2006 234	50.	Pays grands consommateurs de GPL, 2006...... 234
51.	World production of aviation gasolene 1993-2006 249	51.	Production mondial d'essence d'aviation 1993-2006 249
52.	Major aviation gasolene producing countries in 2006................................249	52.	Pays grands producteurs d'essence d'aviation, 2006 249
53.	Major aviation gasolene consuming countries in 2006................................249	53.	Pays grands consommateurs d'essence d'aviation, 2006 249
54.	World production of motor gasolene 1993-2006 259	54.	Production mondial d'essence d'auto 1993-2006 259
55.	Major motor gasolene producing countries in 2006................................259	55.	Pays grands producteurs d'essence d'auto, 2006...... 259

FIGURES (continued)

56. Major motor gasolene consuming countries in 2006...............................259
57. World production of kerosene 1993-2006...277
58. Major kerosene producing countries in 2006 277
59. Major kerosene consuming countries in 2006 277
60. World production of jet fuels 1993-2006 293
61. Major jet fuel producing countries in 2006 ..293
62. Major jet fuel consuming countries in 2006.293
63. World production of gas-diesel oils 1993-2006 309
64. Major gas-diesel oils producing countries in 2006..309
65. Major gas-diesel oils consuming countries in 2006..309
66. World production of residual fuel oil 1993-2006...327
67. Major residual fuel oil producing countries in 2006..327
68. Major residual fuel oil consuming countries in 2006..327
69. World production of energy petroleum products 1993-2006 343
70. Production of non-energy products from refineries, by type and region, in 2006........361
71. World production of non-energy products from refineries, by type, in 2006.................361
72. Production of energy products from refineries, by type and region, in 2006........371
73. World production of energy products from refineries, by type, in 2006.........................371
74. World capacity of natural gas liquid plants, by region, in 2006..............................382
75. World production of natural gas liquids, by type, in 2006.................................382

Gaseous fuels

76. World production of natural gas 1993-2006 388
77. Major natural gas producing countries in 2006 388
78. Major natural gas consuming countries in 2006 388
79. Production of other gases by type, by region, 2006 402
80. World production of other gases by type, in 2006..402
81. World production of gases 1993-2006 413

GRAPHIQUES (suite)

56. Pays grands consommateurs d'essence d'auto, 2006 259
57. Production mondial de pétrole lampant 1993-2006 277
58. Pays grands producteurs de pétrole lampant, 2006... 277
59. Pays grands consommateurs de pétrole lampant, 2006... 277
60. Production mondial des carburéacteurs 1993-2006 293
61. Pays grands producteurs des carburéacteurs, 2006 293
62. Pays grands consommateurs des carburéacteurs, 2006 293
63. Production mondial de gazole/ carburant diesel 1993-2006............................ 309
64. Pays grands producteurs de gazole/ carburant diesel, 2006............................ 309
65. Pays grands consommateurs de gazole/ carburant diesel, 2006............................ 309
66. Production mondial de mazout résiduel 1993-2006 327
67. Pays grands producteurs de mazout résiduel, 2006 327
68. Pays grands consommateurs de mazout résiduel, 2006 327
69. Production mondial de produits pétroliers énergétiques 1993-2006 343
70. Production de produits pétroliers non énergétiques des raffineries, par catégorie et par région, 2006 361
71. Production mondial de produits pétroliers non énergétiques des raffineries par catégorie, 2006.. 361
72. Production de produits pétroliers énergétiques des raffineries, par catégorie et par région, 2006 371
73. Production mondial de produits pétroliers énergétiques des raffineries par catégorie, 2006... 371
74. Capacité des usines d'extraction de liquides de gaz naturel, par région, 2006 ... 382
75. Production des liquides de gaz naturel par catégorie, 2006.. 382

Combustibles gazeux

76. Production mondial de gaz naturel 1993-2006.. 388
77. Pays grands producteurs de gaz naturel, 2006.. 388
78. Pays grands consommateurs de gaz naturel, 2006 388
79. Production d'autres gaz par région, par catégorie, 2006 402
80. Production mondial d'autres gaz par catégorie, 2006 402
81. Production mondial de gaz 1993-2006 413

FIGURES (continued)

82. World consumption of gases by region, in 2006 413

Electricity and Heat

83. Net installed capacity of electricity generating plants in 2006 429
84. Utilization of installed electricity generating capacity, by region, by type, in 2006 463
85. World electricity generation by type 1993-2006 496
86. World production of electricity, by type, by region, in 2006 497
87. Major thermal producing countries in 2006.497
88. Major hydro producing countries in 2006 497
89. Major nuclear producing countries in 2006.497
90. Major geothermal producing countries in 2006 497
91. World electricity generation 1993-2006 530
92. Major electricity producing countries in 2006 .530
93. Major electricity consuming countries in 2006 530
94. World heat production 1993-2006 548
95. Major heat producing countries in 2006 548
96. World heat production by type, in 2006 548

Statistics compiled as of November 2008

GRAPHIQUES (suite)

82. Consommation mondial de gaz par région, 2006 413

Energie électrique et chaleur

83. Puissance nette installée des centrales électriques par région par catégorie 2006.. 429
84. Utilisation de la capacité des centrales électriques par catégorie par région 2006.. 463
85. Génération d'électricité par catégorie, total mondial 1993-2006 496
86. Production mondial d'électricité par catégorie par région 2006 497
87. Pays grands producteurs d'électricité thermique, 2006 497
88. Pays grands producteurs d'électricité hydraulique, 2006 497
89. Pays grands producteurs d'électricité nucléaire, 2006 497
90. Pays grands producteurs d'électricité géothermique, 2006 497
91. Génération d'électricité, total mondial 1993-2006 530
92. Pays grands producteurs d'électricité 2006 530
93. Pays grands consommateurs d'électricité, 2006 530
94. Production mondial de chaleur 1993-2006 548
95. Pays grands producteurs de chaleur 2006 548
96. Production mondial de chaleur par catégorie, 2006 548

Statistiques compilées à la fin de novembre 2008

INTRODUCTION

The *Energy Statistics Yearbook 2006* is a comprehensive collection of international energy statistics prepared by the United Nations Statistics Division. It is the fiftieth in a series of annual compilations which commenced under the title *World Energy Supplies in Selected Years, 1929-1950*[1]. It updates the statistical series shown in the previous issue. Supplementary series of monthly and quarterly data on production of energy may be found in the *Monthly Bulletin of Statistics*[2].

The principal objective of the *Yearbook* is to provide a global framework of comparable data on long-term trends in the supply of mainly commercial primary and secondary forms of energy. Data for each type of fuel and aggregate data for the total mix of commercial fuels are shown for individual countries and areas and are summarized into regional and world totals. The data are compiled primarily from the annual energy questionnaire distributed by the United Nations Statistics Division and supplemented by official national statistical publications. Where official data are not available or are inconsistent, estimates are made by the Statistics Division based on governmental, professional or commercial materials. Estimates include, but are not limited to, extrapolated data based on partial year information, use of annual trends, trade data based on partner country reports, breakdowns of aggregated data as well as analysis of current energy events and activities.

This issue of the *Yearbook* contains data in original and common units (coal equivalent, oil equivalent, joules) for the years 2003-2006. By referring to previous volumes of the publication, a time series can be established from 1950 to the present. In addition to the basic tables showing production, trade, stock changes, bunkers, and consumption, information is included on various other topics such as:

L'*Annuaire des statistiques de l'énergie 2006* est une collection complète de statistiques internationales de l'énergie, établie par la Division de statistique de l'Organisation des Nations Unies. La présente édition est la cinquantième d'une série de compilations annuelles dont la première est parue sous le titre *World Energy Supplies in Selected Years, 1929-1950*[1]. Elle constitue une mise à jour des séries statistiques présentées dans l'édition précédente. Des séries additionnelles de données mensuelles ou trimestrielles sur la production d'énergie sont publiées dans le *Bulletin mensuel de statistique*[2].

Le principal objet de l'*Annuaire* est de fournir un cadre global de comparaison des données sur les mouvements à long terme de l'offre des formes primaires et secondaires d'énergie à caractère essentiellement commercial. Les données pour chaque type de combustible et les données agrégées pour l'ensemble des combustibles commerciaux sont présentées pour chaque pays ou zone et sont regroupées en totaux régionaux et mondiaux. Les données, essentiellement rassemblées à partir du questionnaire annuel de l'énergie envoyé par la Division de statistique de l'ONU, sont complétées à l'aide des publications officielles des organismes nationaux de statistique. Lorsque les données officielles ne sont pas disponibles ou ne sont pas cohérentes, la Division de statistique établit des estimations en s'appuyant sur la documentation d'origine gouvernementale, professionnelle ou commerciale. Les estimations comprennent mais ne se limitent pas à l'extrapolation des données basées sur des informations annuelles partielles, à l'utilisation des tendances annuelles, aux données du commerce fournies par les pays partenaires, à la désagrégation de même qu'à l'analyse des activités et développements courants dans le domaine de l'énergie.

La présente édition contient des données exprimées en unités d'origine et en unités communes (équivalent charbon, équivalent pétrole, joules) pour les années 2003 à 2006. En se référant aux éditions antérieures, on peut établir une série allant de 1950 jusqu'à maintenant. En plus des tableaux de base, où apparaissent la production, le commerce, les variations de stocks, les soutes et la consommation, l'*Annuaire* contient des données sur d'autres sujets, par exemple:

[1]Statistical Papers, Series J, No. 1 (United Nations publication, Sales No. 1952.XVII.3).
[2]Statistical Papers, Series Q, *Monthly Bulletin of Statistics*, (United Nations publication).

[1]Etudes statistiques; Séries J No. 1 (publication des Nations Unies, numéro de vente: 1952, XVII.3).
[2]Etudes statistiques, Series Q, Bulletin mensuel de statistique (publication des Nations Unies).

(a) Principal importers and exporters of coal, crude petroleum and natural gas for the years 2005 and 2006;

(b) The capacity of petroleum refineries, natural gas liquids plants and electric generating plants by type;

(c) The ratio of crude petroleum reserves to petroleum production (R/P ratio);

(d) The new and renewable sources of energy: fuelwood, charcoal, bagasse, peat, biodiesel, biogas, alcohol, and electricity generated from hydro, solar, wind, tide, wave and geothermal sources;

(e) Heat produced in combined heat and power plants generating electricity and useful heat in a single installation, district heating plants and geothermal sources and nuclear power plants.

The information contained in the *Yearbook* is also available on CD and in electronic format. Requests for information should be directed to the United Nations Statistics Division.

Acknowledgement is due to the following specialized and intergovernmental agencies whose publications have been utilized in supplementing our statistics: Comité professionnel du pétrole (CPP), Food and Agriculture Organization of the United Nations (FAO), International Atomic Energy Agency (IAEA), International Energy Agency of the Organisation for Economic Co-operation and Development (IEA/OECD), International Sugar Organization (ISO), Organization of Arab Petroleum Exporting Countries (OAPEC), Organization of the Petroleum Exporting Countries (OPEC), Organización Latinoamericana de Energía (OLADE), Interstate Statistical Committee of the Commonwealth of Independent States (STATCIS), Statistical Office of the European Communities (Eurostat), World Energy Council (WEC). Acknowledgement is also made to various governmental, energy and statistical authorities of the member states which have been extremely cooperative in providing data.

(a) Les principaux importateurs et exportateurs de houille, de pétrole brut et de gaz naturel pour les années 2005 et 2006;

(b) La capacité des raffineries de pétrole, des usines d'extraction de liquides de gaz naturel et des centrales électriques, par catégorie;

(c) Le rapport entre réserves brutes de pétrole et production de pétrole (rapport R/P);

(d) Les sources d'énergie nouvelles et renouvelables: le bois de chauffage, le charbon de bois, la bagasse, le biodiesel, le biogaz, l'alcool, la tourbe et l'électricité de source hydraulique, solaire, éolienne, marémotrice, géothermique, et des vagues;

(e) Chaleur en provenance des centrales à cycle mixte produisant dans une même installation de l'électricité et de la chaleur utile, des centrales de chauffage urbain, et des sources géothermiques et des centrales nucléaires.

Les données présentées dans l'*Annuaire* sont également disponibles sur CD et sur le format électronique. On peut les obtenir auprès de la Division de statistique de l'Organisation des Nations Unies.

Nous remercions de leur aide les institutions spécialisées et intergouvernementales énumérées ci-après dont les publications nous ont aidés à complémenter nos statistiques: le Comité professionnel du pétrole (CPP), l'Organisation des Nations Unies pour l'alimentation et l'agriculture (FAO), l'Agence internationale de l'énergie atomique (AIEA), l'Agence internationale de l'énergie, l'Organisation de coopération et de développement économiques (AIE/OCDE), l'Organisation internationale du sucre (OIS), l'Organisation des pays arabes exportateurs de pétrole (OPAEP), l'Organisation des pays exportateurs de pétrole (OPEP), l'Organisation de l'énergie de l'Amérique latine (OLADE), le Comité de statistique de la Communauté d'Etats indépendants (STATCIS), l'Office statistique des Communautés européennes (Eurostat), le Conseil mondiale de l'énergie (CME). Les auteurs de l'*Annuaire des statistiques de l'énergie* remercient les institutions gouvernementales, les agences de l'énergie et les offices de statistiques des États Membres pour leur plus haut degré de coopération.

COUNTRY NOMENCLATURE - NOMENCLATURE DES PAYS

AUSTRALIA - excludes the overseas territories.

CAMBODIA - formerly Democratic Kampuchea.

CHINA - excludes data for Hong Kong and Macao Special Administrative Regions (Hong Kong SAR and Macao SAR) and Taiwan Province.

DEMOCRATIC REPUBLIC OF THE CONGO - formerly Zaire.

DENMARK - excludes Greenland and the Danish Faroes.

FRANCE - excludes the following departments and territories: Guadeloupe, French Guiana, Martinique, New Caledonia, French Polynesia, Réunion and St. Pierre Miquelon.

JAPAN - includes Okinawa.

MALAYSIA - comprises Peninsular Malaysia, Sabah and Sarawak.

MYANMAR - formerly Burma.

NETHERLANDS - excludes Suriname and the Netherlands Antilles.

NETHERLANDS ANTILLES - comprises Bonaire, Curaçao, Saba, St. Eustatius and the Dutch part of St. Martin.

PANAMA - includes Former Panama Canal Zone.

PORTUGAL - includes the Azores and Madeira.

SERBIA - includes Montenegro for the years 2003 and 2004, but not for 2005 and 2006.

SOUTH AFRICA CUSTOMS UNION - includes South Africa, Botswana, Lesotho, Swaziland and Namibia.

AUSTRALIE - ne comprend pas les territoires d'outre-mer.

CAMBODGE – anciennement Kampuchea démocratique.

CHINE - les données ne comprennent pas las Régions administratives spéciales de Hong-Kong et Macao (Hong-Kong RAS et Macao RAS) et la province de Taiwan.

REPUBLIQUE DEMOCRATIQUE DU CONGO - anciennement Zaire.

DANEMARK - le Groenland et les Iles Féroé danoises ne sont pas pris en compte dans les données.

FRANCE - ne comprend pas les territoires d'outre-mer suivants : Guadeloupe, Guyane française, Martinique, Nouvelle-Calédonie, Polynésie française, Ile de la Réunion et Saint-Pierre-et-Miquelon.

JAPON - y compris Okinawa.

MALAISIE - comprend la Malaisie péninsulaire, Sabah et Sarawak.

MYANMAR - anciennement Birmanie.

PAYS-BAS – ni le Suriname ni les Antilles néerlandaises ne sont pris en compte dans les données.

ANTILLES NEERLANDAISES - comprend Bonaire, Curaçao, Saba, Saint-Eustache et la partie néerlandaise de Saint-Martin.

PANAMA - y compris l'ancienne Zone du Canal.

PORTUGAL - englobe les Açores et l'Ile de Madère.

SERBIE - y compris Monténégro pour les données de 2003 et 2004, sans inclure celles de 2005 et 2006.

UNION DOUANIERE D'AFRIQUE MERIDIONALE - comprend l'Afrique du Sud, le Botswana, le Lesotho, la Namibie et le Swaziland.

SPAIN - includes the Canary Islands.

ESPAGNE - englobe les Iles Canaries.

UNITED ARAB EMIRATES - comprises the seven emirates of the former Trucial Oman: Abu Dhabi, Ajman, Dubai, Fujairah, Ras al Khaimah, Sharjah and Umm al Qaiwain.

EMIRATS ARABES UNIS – comprend les sept Emirats de l'ancien Oman sous régime de traité: Abu Dhabi, Ajman, Dubai, Fujairah, Ras al Khaimah, Sharjah et Umm al Qaiwain.

UNITED STATES - includes the 50 states and the District of Columbia. Oil statistics as well as coal trade statistics also include Puerto Rico, Guam, the U.S. Virgin Islands, American Samoa, Johnston Atoll, Midway Islands, Wake Island and the Northern Mariana Islands.

ETATS-UNIS - englobent les 50 Etats fédérés et le District de Columbia. Les statistiques sur le pétrole et sur les échanges de charbon concernent également Porto Rico, l'Ile de Guam, les Iles Vierges des Etats-Unis, le Territoire non incorporé des Samoa américaines, l'Ile Johnston, les Iles Midway, l'Ile de Wake et les Iles Mariannes-du-Nord.

WORLD - comprises the sum of Africa, North America, South America, Asia, Europe and Oceania.

MONDE - comprend Afrique, Amérique du Nord, Amérique du Sud, Asie, Europe et Océanie.

ABBREVIATIONS AND SYMBOLS – ABREVIATIONS ET SIGNES CONVENTIONNELS

The following symbols and abbreviations have been used:

Les abréviations et signes conventionnels utilisés sont les suivants:

C:H	ratio between carbon and hydrogen	C:H	rapport du carbone à l'hydrogène
cSt	centistoke	cSt	centistoke
cu m (or m^3)	cubic metre	MC (ou m^3)	mètre cube
C_3H_8	chemical symbol for propane gas	C_3H_8	symbole chimique du gaz propane
C_4H_{10}	chemical symbol for butane gas	C_4H_{10}	symbole chimique du gaz butane
°C	degree Celsius	°C	degré Celsius
kcal	kilocalorie	kcal	kilocalorie
kg	kilogramme	kg	kilogramme
kg/cm^2	kilogramme per square centimetre	kg/cm^2	kilogramme par centimètre carré
kWh	kilowatt-hour	kWh	kilowatt-heure
LPG	liquefied petroleum gas	GPL	gaz de pétrole liquéfié
mg/g	milligramme per gramme	mg/g	milligramme par gramme
MJ	megajoule (10^6 joules)	MJ	mégajoule (10^6 joules)
NGL	natural gas liquids	LGN	liquides de gaz naturel
RON	research octane number	IOR	indice d'octane recherché
t	metric ton	t	tonne métrique
TCE	ton of coal equivalent	TEC	tonne d'équivalent charbon
TJ	terajoule (10^{12} joules)	TJ	terajoule (10^{12} joules)
TOE	ton of oil equivalent	TEP	tonne d'équivalent pétrole
*	estimate by the Statistics Division of the United Nations Secretariat	*	estimation de la Division de statistique du Secrétariat de l'Organisation des Nations Unies
..	not applicable	..	sans objet
...	not available	...	données non disponibles
0	less than 0.5 of the unit specified or nil.	0	moins de 0,5 de l'unité en question ou nul.

DEFINITIONS

SOLID FUELS

Hard coal – Coal that has a high degree of coalification with a gross calorific value above 23,865 KJ/kg (5,700 kcal/kg) on an ash-free but moist basis, and a mean random reflectance of vitrinite of at least 0.6. Slurries, middlings and other low-grade coal products, which cannot be classified according to the type of coal from which they are obtained, are included under hard coal. There are two sub-categories of hard coal: (i) coking coal and (ii) other bituminous coal and anthracite (also known as steam coal). Coking coal is a hard coal with a quality that allows the production of coke suitable to support a blast furnace charge. Steam coal is coal used for steam raising and space heating purposes and includes all anthracite coals and bituminous coals not classified as coking coal.

Lignite – One of the two sub-categories of brown coal. Brown coal is coal with a low degree of coalification which retained the anatomical structure of the vegetable matter from which it was formed. It has a mean random reflectance of vitrinite of less than 0.6, provided that the gross calorific value (on a moist ash-free basis) is less than 23,865 KJ/kg (5,700 kcal/kg). Brown coal comprises: (i) lignite - non-agglomerating coals with a gross calorific value less than 17,435 KJ/kg (4,165 kcal/kg) and greater than 31 per cent volatile matter on a dry mineral matter free basis and (ii) sub-bituminous coal - non-agglomerating coals with a gross calorific value between 17,435 KJ/kg (4,165 kcal/kg) and 23,865 KJ/kg (5,700 kcal/kg) containing more than 31 per cent volatile matter on a dry mineral matter free basis.

Peat – A solid fuel formed from the partial decomposition of dead vegetation under conditions of high humidity and limited air access (initial stage of coalification). Only peat used as fuel is included. Its principal use is as a household fuel.

Patent fuel (hard coal briquettes) – A composition fuel manufactured from coal fines by shaping with the addition of a binding agent such as pitch.

COMBUSTIBLES SOLIDES

Houille – Charbon à haut degré de houillification et de pouvoir calorifique brut supérieur à 23 865 kJ/kg (5 700 kcal/kg), valeur mesurée pour un combustible exempt de cendres, mais humide et ayant un indice moyen de réflectance de la vitrinite au moins égal à 0,6. Les schlamms, les mixtes et autres produits du charbon de faible qualité qui ne peuvent être classés en fonction du type de charbon dont ils sont dérivés sont inclus dans cette rubrique. Il y a deux sous-catégories de houille: (i) charbon à coke et (ii) autres charbons bitumineux et anthracite (également dénommé charbon vapeur). Le charbon à coke est une houille d'une qualité permettant la production d'un coke susceptible d'être utilisé dans les hauts fourneaux. Le charbon vapeur est utilisé pour la production de vapeur et pour le chauffage des locaux, et comprend tous les charbons anthraciteux et bitumineux autres que ceux classifiés comme charbons à coke.

Lignite – Une des deux sous-catégories du charbon brun. Le charbon brun est un charbon d'un faible degré de houillification qui a gardé la structure anatomique des végétaux dont il est issu. Son indice moyen de réflectance de la vitrinite est inférieur à 0,6, si son pouvoir calorifique brut (sur base humide, cendres déduites) est inférieur à 23 865 kJ/kg (5 700 kcal/kg). Les charbons bruns comprennent: (i) le lignite – charbon non agglutinant dont le pouvoir calorifique brut est inférieur à 17 435 kJ/kg (4 165 kcal/kg) et qui contient plus de 31% de matières volatiles sur produit sec exempt de matières minérales; (ii) le charbon sous-bitumineux - charbon non agglutinant dont le pouvoir calorifique supérieur se situe entre 17 435 kJ/kg (4 165 kcal/kg) et 23 865 kJ/kg (5 700 kcal/kg) et qui contient plus de 31% de matières volatiles sur produit sec exempt de matières minérales.

Tourbe – Combustible solide issu de la décomposition partielle de végétaux morts dans des conditions de forte humidité et de faible circulation d'air (phase initiale de la houillification). N'est prise en considération ici que la tourbe utilisée comme combustible. La tourbe est utilisée principalement comme combustible domestique.

Agglomérés (briquettes de houille) – Combustibles composites fabriqués par moulage au moyen de fines de charbon avec l'addition d'un liant tel que le brai.

Lignite briquettes – A composition fuel manufactured from lignite. The lignite is crushed, dried and molded under high pressure into an even shaped briquette without the addition of binders.

Peat briquettes – A composition fuel manufactured from peat. Raw peat, after crushing and drying, is molded under high pressure into an even-shaped briquette without the addition of binders.

Coke – The solid residue obtained from coal or lignite by heating it to a high temperature in the absence or near absence of air. It is high in carbon and low in moisture and volatile matter. Several categories are distinguished:

a) Coke-oven coke - The solid product obtained from carbonization of coal, principally coking coal, at high temperature. Coke-oven coke is also called metallurgical coke and is used mainly in the iron and steel industry. Semi-coke, the solid product obtained from carbonization of coal at low temperature, is included with coke-oven coke. It is used mainly as a domestic fuel.

b) Gas coke - A by-product of coal used for the production of gas works gas in gasworks. Gas coke is mainly used as a domestic fuel.

c) Brown coal coke – A solid product obtained from carbonization of brown coal briquettes.

Oil shale – A sedimentary rock containing a high proportion of organic matter (kerogen), which can be converted to crude oil or gas by heating.

Bituminous sands – Sands or sandstones containing a high proportion of tarry hydrocarbons, capable of yielding oil through heating or other extractive processes. Heavy oils and tars which are so dense and viscous and lacking in primary energy that they cannot be produced commercially by conventional methods, that is, by natural flow or pumping, are also included.

Briquettes de lignite – Combustibles composites fabriqués au moyen de lignite. Le lignite est broyé, séché et moulé sous pression élevée pour donner une briquette de forme régulière sans l'addition d'un élément liant.

Briquettes de tourbe – Combustibles composites fabriqués au moyen de tourbe. La tourbe brute, après broyage et séchage, est moulée sous pression élevée pour donner une briquette de forme régulière sans l'addition d'un élément liant.

Coke – Résidu solide obtenu lors de la distillation de houille ou de lignite en l'absence totale ou presque totale d'air. Il a une haute teneur en carbone, et une faible teneur en humidité et en matières volatiles. On distingue plusieurs catégories de coke:

a) Coke de four – Produit solide obtenu par carbonisation de charbon, principalement le charbon à coke, à une température élevée. Le coke de four est également connu sous le nom de coke métallurgique et est utilisé principalement dans l'industrie sidérurgique. Le semi-coke, qui est un produit solide obtenu par carbonisation de charbon à basse température, est inclus avec le coke de four. Il est utilisé principalement comme combustible domestique.

b) Coke de gaz – Sous-produit de l'utilisation du charbon pour la production de gaz manufacturé ou gaz de ville dans les usines à gaz. Le coke de gaz est utilisé principalement comme combustible domestique.

c) Coke de lignite – Produit solide obtenu par carbonisation de briquettes de lignite.

Schiste bitumineux – Roche sédimentaire contenant une forte proportion de matières organiques (kérogène), qui peut être transformée en pétrole brut ou en gaz par chauffage.

Sables bitumineux – Sables ou grès contenant une forte proportion d'hydrocarbures goudronneux dont on peut extraire du pétrole par chauffage ou par d'autres procédés d'extraction. Les huiles lourdes et les goudrons qui sont si denses et si visqueux et dépourvus d'énergie primaire qu'ils ne peuvent être extraits commercialement par les méthodes classiques, c'est-à-dire par écoulement naturel ou par pompage, sont aussi inclus dans cette rubrique.

LIQUID FUELS

Crude oil – A mineral oil consisting of a mixture of hydrocarbons of natural origin, yellow to black in color, of variable density and viscosity. Data in this category also includes lease or field condensate (separator liquids) which is recovered from gaseous hydrocarbons in lease separation facilities, as well as synthetic crude oil, mineral oils extracted from bituminous minerals such as shales and bituminous sand, and oils from coal liquefaction.

Natural gas liquids (NGL) – Liquid or liquefied hydrocarbons produced in the manufacture, purification and stabilization of natural gas. NGL's include, but are not limited to, ethane, propane, butane, pentane, natural gasolene, and plant condensate. NGL's are either distilled with crude oil in refineries, blended with refined petroleum products or used directly depending on their characteristics.

Plant condensate – Liquid hydrocarbons condensed from wet natural gas in natural gas processing plants. It is used as a petroleum refinery input.

Natural gasolene - Light spirit extracted from wet natural gas, often in association with crude petroleum. It is used as a petroleum refinery and petrochemical plant input and is also used directly for blending with motor spirit without further processing.

Petroleum products – Comprise the liquid fuels, lubricant oils and solid and semi-solid products obtained by distillation and cracking of crude petroleum, shale oil, or semi-refined and unfinished petroleum products. As far as possible the series include fuels consumed in refining, but exclude oil products obtained from natural gas, coal, lignite and their derivatives.

Aviation gasolene – Motor spirit prepared especially for aviation piston engines, with an octane number varying from 80 to 145 RON and a freezing point of -60°C.

COMBUSTIBLES LIQUIDES

Pétrole brut – Huile minérale constituée d'un mélange d'hydrocarbures d'origine naturelle, de couleur variant du jaune au noir, d'une densité et d'une viscosité variables. Figurent également sous cette rubrique les condensats directement récupérés sur les sites d'exploitation des hydrocarbures gazeux (dans les installations prévues pour la séparation des phases liquide et gazeuse), le pétrole brut synthétique, les huiles minérales brutes extraites des roches bitumineuses telles que schistes et sables asphaltiques et les huiles issues de la liquéfaction du charbon.

Liquides de gaz naturel (LGN) – Hydrocarbures liquides ou liquéfiés produits lors de la fabrication, de la purification et de la stabilisation du gaz naturel. Les liquides de gaz naturel comprennent l'éthane, le propane, le butane, le pentane, l'essence naturelle et les condensats d'usine, sans que la liste soit limitative. Les LGN sont soit distillés avec le pétrole brut dans les raffineries, soit mélangés avec les produits pétroliers raffinés, soit utilisés directement, en fonction de leurs caractéristiques.

Condensat d'usine – Hydrocarbure liquide résultant de la condensation du gaz naturel humide dans les usines de traitement du gaz naturel. Il est utilisé comme charge d'alimentation dans les raffineries de pétrole.

Essence naturelle – Essence légère extraite du gaz naturel humide, souvent en association avec le pétrole brut. Elle est utilisée comme charge dans les raffineries de pétrole et les usines pétrochimiques et est aussi employée directement en mélange avec le carburant auto sans traitement supplémentaire.

Produits pétroliers – Comprennent les combustibles liquides, les huiles lubrifiantes et les produits solides et semi-solides obtenus par distillation et craquage du pétrole brut, de l'huile de schiste ou de dérivés du pétrole semi-raffinés ou non raffinés. Autant que possible, les séries comprennent les combustibles consumés lors du raffinage mais ne comprennent pas les produits oléiques obtenus à partir du gaz naturel, du charbon, du lignite et de leurs dérivés.

Essence d'aviation – Carburant fabriqué spécialement pour les moteurs d'avion à pistons, avec un indice d'octane variant de 80 à 145 IOR et dont le point de congélation est de -60°C.

DEFINITIONS (continued/ suite)

Motor gasolene – Light hydrocarbon oil for use in internal combustion engines such as motor vehicles, excluding aircraft. It distills between 35°C and 200°C, and is treated to reach a sufficiently high octane number of generally between 80 and 100 RON. Treatment may be by reforming, blending with an aromatic fraction, or the addition of benzole or other additives (such as tetraethyl lead).

Jet fuel – Consists of gasolene-type jet fuel and kerosene-type jet fuel.

Gasolene-type jet fuel – All light hydrocarbon oils for use in aviation gas-turbine engines. It distills between 100°C and 250°C with at least 20% of volume distilling at 143°C. It is obtained by blending kerosene and gasolene or naphtha in such a way that the aromatic content does not exceed 25% in volume. Additives are included to reduce the freezing point to -58°C or lower, and to keep the Reid vapour pressure between 0.14 and 0.21 kg/cm^2.

Kerosene-type jet fuel – Medium oil for use in aviation gas-turbine engines with the same distillation characteristics and flash point as kerosene, with a maximum aromatic content of 20% in volume. It is treated to give a kinematic viscosity of less than 15 cSt at -34°C and a freezing point below -50°C.

Kerosene – Medium oil distilling between 150°C and 300°C; at least 65% of volume distills at 250°C. Its specific gravity is roughly 0.80 and its flash point is above 38°C. It is used as an illuminant and as a fuel in certain types of spark-ignition engines, such as those used for agricultural tractors and stationary engines. Other names for this product are burning oil, vaporizing oil, power kerosene and illuminating oil.

Essence auto – Hydrocarbure léger utilisé dans les moteurs à combustion interne, tels que ceux des véhicules à moteur, à l'exception des aéronefs. Sa température de distillation se situe entre 35°C et 200°C et il est traité de façon à atteindre un indice d'octane suffisamment élevé, généralement entre 80 et 100 IOR. Le traitement peut consister en reformage, mélange avec une fraction aromatique, ou adjonction de benzol ou d'autres additifs (tels que du plomb tétraéthyle).

Carburéacteurs – Comprennent les carburéacteurs du type essence et les carburéacteurs du type kérosène.

Les carburéacteurs du type essence comprennent tous les hydrocarbures légers utilisés dans les turboréacteurs d'aviation. Leur température de distillation se situe entre 100°C et 250°C et donne au moins 20% en volume de distillat à 143°C. Ils sont obtenus par mélange de pétrole lampant et d'essence ou de naphta de façon que la teneur en composés aromatiques ne dépasse pas 25% en volume. Des additifs y sont ajoutés afin d'abaisser le point de congélation à -58°C ou au-dessous, et de maintenir la tension de vapeur Reid entre 0,14 et 0,21 kg/cm2.

Les carburéacteurs du type kérosène sont des huiles moyennement visqueuses utilisées dans les turboréacteurs d'aviation, ayant les mêmes caractéristiques de distillation et le même point d'éclair que le pétrole lampant et une teneur en composés aromatiques ne dépassant pas 20% en volume. Elles sont traitées de façon à atteindre une viscosité cinématique de moins de 15 cSt à -34°C et un point de congélation inférieur à -50°C.

Pétrole lampant – Huile moyennement visqueuse dont la température de distillation se situe entre 150°C et 300°C, et qui donne au moins 65% en volume de distillat à 250°C. Sa densité se situe aux alentours de 0,80 et son point d'éclair est supérieur à 38°C. Il sert à l'éclairage et aussi de carburant dans certains moteurs à allumage par étincelle, tels que ceux utilisés dans les tracteurs agricoles et les installations stationnaires. Les données concernent les produits couramment appelés kérosène, pétrole carburant ou "power kerosene", et huile d'éclairage.

Gas-diesel oil (distillate fuel oil) – Heavy oils distilling between 200°C and 380°C, but distilling less than 65% in volume at 250°C, including losses, and 85% or more at 350°C. Its flash point is always above 50°C and its specific gravity is higher than 0.82. Heavy oils obtained by blending are grouped together with gas oils on the condition that their kinematic viscosity does not exceed 27.5 cSt at 38°C. Also included are middle distillates intended for the petrochemical industry. Gas-diesel oils are used as a fuel for internal combustion in diesel engines, as a burner fuel in heating installations, such as furnaces, and for enriching water gas to increase its luminosity. Other names for this product are diesel fuel, diesel oil and gas oil.

Residual fuel oil – A heavy oil that makes up the distillation residue. It comprises all fuels (including those obtained by blending) with a kinematic viscosity above 27.5 cSt at 38°C. Its flash point is always above 50°C and its specific gravity is higher than 0.90. It is commonly used by ships and industrial large-scale heating installations as a fuel in furnaces or boilers.

Liquefied petroleum gas (LPG) – Hydrocarbons which are gaseous under conditions of normal temperature and pressure but are liquefied by compression or cooling to facilitate storage, handling and transportation. They are (i) extracted by stripping of natural gas at crude petroleum and natural gas sources; (ii) extracted by stripping of imported natural gas in installations of the importing country; and (iii) produced both in refineries and outside of refineries in the course of processing crude petroleum or its derivatives. It comprises propane (C_3H_8), butane (C_4H_{10}), or a combination of the two. Also included is ethane (C_2H_6) from petroleum refineries or natural gas producers' separation and stabilization plants.

Gazole/carburant diesel (mazout distillé) – Huiles lourdes dont la température de distillation se situe entre 200°C et 380°C, mais qui donnent moins de 65% en volume de distillat à 250°C (y compris les pertes) et 85% ou davantage à 350°C. Leur point d'éclair est toujours supérieur à 50°C et leur densité supérieure à 0,82. Les huiles lourdes obtenues par mélange sont classées dans la même catégorie que les gazoles à condition que leur viscosité cinématique ne dépasse pas 27,5 cSt à 38°C. Sont compris dans cette rubrique les distillats moyens destinés à l'industrie pétrochimique. Les gazoles servent de carburant pour la combustion interne dans les moteurs diesel, de combustible dans les installations de chauffage telles que les chaudières, et d'additifs destinés à augmenter la luminosité de la flamme du gaz à l'eau. Ce produit est aussi connu sous les appellations de gazole ou gasoil et carburant ou combustible diesel.

Mazout résiduel – Huile lourde constituant le résidu de la distillation. La rubrique comprend tous les combustibles (y compris ceux obtenus par mélange) d'une viscosité supérieure à 27,5 cSt à 38°C. Leur point d'éclair est toujours supérieur à 50°C et leur densité supérieure à 0,90. Ces produits sont couramment utilisés comme combustible dans les chaudières des navires et des grandes installations de chauffage industriel. Ils sont également connus sous le nom de fioul lourd.

Gaz de pétrole liquéfiés (GPL) – Hydrocarbures qui sont à l'état gazeux dans des conditions de température et de pression normales mais qui sont liquéfiés par compression ou refroidissement pour en faciliter l'entreposage, la manipulation et le transport. Ils sont (i) extraits par désessenciement du gaz naturel sur les sites de production de pétrole brut et de gaz naturel; (ii) extraits par désessenciement du gaz naturel importé dans les installations du pays importateur; et (iii) produits aussi bien à l'intérieur qu'en dehors des raffineries, au cours du traitement du pétrole brut ou de ses dérivés. Dans cette rubrique figurent le propane (C_3H_8) et le butane (C_4H_{10}) ou un mélange de ces deux hydrocarbures. Est également inclus l'éthane (C_2H_6) produit dans les raffineries ou dans les installations de séparation et de stabilisation des producteurs de gaz naturel.

Refinery gas – Non-condensable gas obtained during distillation of crude oil or treatment of oil products (e.g. cracking) in refineries. It consists mainly of hydrogen, methane, ethane and olefins, and is used principally as a refinery fuel. Refinery gas is also known as still gas.

Feedstocks – Products or a combination of products derived from crude oil destined for further processing in the refining industry other than blending. They are transformed into one or more components and/or finished products. This definition covers naphtha imported for refinery intake and naphtha returned from the chemical industry to the refining industry.

Naphtha – Light or medium oil distilling between 30°C and 210°C, for which there is no official definition, but which does not meet the standards laid down for motor spirit. The properties depend upon consumer specification. The C:H ratio is usually 84:14 or 84:16, with a very low sulphur content. Naphtha may be further blended or mixed with other materials to make high-grade motor gasolene or jet fuel, or may be used as a raw material for manufactured gas. Naphtha is sometimes used as input to feedstocks to make various kinds of chemical products, or may be used as a solvent.

White spirit/industrial spirit – A highly refined distillate with a boiling point ranging from 135°C to 200°C, which is used as a paint solvent and for dry-cleaning purposes.

Lubricants – Viscous, liquid hydrocarbons rich in paraffin waxes, distilling between 380°C and 500°C, obtained by vacuum distillation of oil residues from atmospheric distillation. Additives may be included to alter their characteristics. Their main characteristics are: a flash point greater than 125°C; a pour point between –25°C and +5°C depending on the grade; a strong acid number (normally 0.5 mg/g); an ash content less than or equal to 0.3%; and a water content less than or equal to 0.2%. Included are cutting oils, white oils, insulating oils, spindle oils and lubricating greases.

Gaz de raffinerie – Comprend les gaz non condensables obtenus dans les raffineries lors de la distillation du pétrole brut ou du traitement des produits pétroliers (par craquage par exemple). Il s'agit principalement d'hydrogène, de méthane, d'éthane et d'oléfines. Ils sont généralement utilisés en totalité comme combustible de raffinerie. Ce produit est également appelé gaz de distillation.

Produits d'alimentation de raffinerie – Produits ou combinaisons de produits dérivés du pétrole brut, destinés à subir dans l'industrie du raffinage un traitement ultérieur autre qu'un mélange. Ils sont transformés en un ou plusieurs constituants et/ou produits finis. Cette rubrique comprend les naphtas importés pour l'alimentation des raffineries et les naphtas retournés par l'industrie chimique à l'industrie du raffinage.

Naphtas – Huiles légères ou moyennes, dont les températures de distillation se situent entre 30°C et 210°C et pour lesquelles il n'existe pas de définition officielle, mais qui ne satisfont pas aux normes fixées pour le carburant auto. Leurs propriétés peuvent être adaptées aux spécifications des utilisateurs; le rapport C/H est habituellement de 84/14 ou 84/16, avec une très faible teneur en soufre. Les naphtas peuvent être coupés ou mélangés avec d'autres produits en vue d'obtenir de l'essence auto de haute qualité ou du carburéacteur, ou peuvent servir de matière première dans la fabrication du gaz de ville. Les naphtas sont souvent utilisés comme charge de départ pour la fabrication de divers produits chimiques, ou encore peuvent être utilisés comme solvant.

White spirit/essences spéciales – Distillats hautement raffinés dont le point d'ébullition se situe entre 135°C et 200°C, utilisés comme diluants pour peinture et comme solvants pour le nettoyage à sec.

Lubrifiants – Hydrocarbures liquides et visqueux, riches en paraffines, dont les températures de distillation se situent entre 380°C et 500°C et qui sont obtenus par distillation sous vide des résidus de la distillation atmosphérique du pétrole. Des additifs peuvent y être incorporés pour modifier leurs caractéristiques. Leurs principales caractéristiques sont les suivantes: point d'éclair supérieur à 125°C; point d'écoulement compris entre -25°C et +5°C selon la qualité; indice d'acide fort (normalement égal à 0,5 mg/g); teneur en cendres inférieure ou égale à 0,3%, et teneur en eau inférieure ou égale à 0,2%. Figurent dans cette rubrique les huiles de coupe, les huiles blanches, les huiles isolantes, les huiles à broches et les graisses lubrifiantes.

Bitumen – Solid or viscous hydrocarbon with a colloidal structure, brown or black in color, which is obtained as a residue by vacuum distillation of oil residues from atmospheric distillation. It is sometimes soluble in carbon bisulphite, non-volatile, thermoplastic (generally between 150°C and 200°C), often with insulating and adhesive properties. It is used mainly in road construction. Natural asphalt is excluded.

Petroleum waxes – Saturated aliphatic hydrocarbons obtained as residues extracted when dewaxing lubricant oils, with a crystalline structure with C greater than 12. Their main characteristics are as follows: they are colorless, in most cases odorless and translucent; they have a melting point above 45°C, a specific gravity of 0.76 to 0.78 at 80°C, and a kinematic viscosity between 3.7 and 5.5 cSt at 99°C. These waxes are used for candle manufacture, polishes and waterproofing of containers, wrappings, etc.

Petroleum coke – A shiny, black solid residue obtained by cracking and carbonization in furnaces. It consists mainly of carbon (90 to 95%) and generally burns without leaving any ash. It is used mainly in metallurgical processes. It excludes those solid residues obtained from carbonization of coal.

Other petroleum products – Products of petroleum origin (including partially refined products) not otherwise specified.

Alcohol – Ethanol (ethyl alcohol) and methanol (methyl alcohol) for use as a fuel. Ethanol can be produced from sugar, starch and cellulose and is used mainly in transport (on its own or blended with gasolene). Methanol can be produced from wood, crop residues, grass, and the like and can be used in internal combustion engines.

Bitume – Hydrocarbure solide ou visqueux de structure colloïdale, de couleur brune ou noire, obtenu comme résidu de la distillation sous vide des résidus de la distillation atmosphérique du pétrole. Il est parfois soluble dans le bisulphite de carbone, non volatil, thermoplastique (généralement entre 150°C et 200°C), ayant souvent des propriétés isolantes et adhésives. Il est utilisé principalement pour la construction des routes. Cette rubrique ne comprend pas l'asphalte naturel.

Cires de pétrole (paraffines) – Hydrocarbures aliphatiques saturés obtenus comme résidus lors du déparaffinage des huiles lubrifiantes et qui ont une structure cristalline, avec un nombre d'atomes de carbone supérieur à 12. Leurs principales caractéristiques sont les suivantes: incolores, la plupart du temps inodores et translucides; point de fusion supérieur à 45°C, densité comprise entre 0,76 et 0,78 à 80°C, et viscosité cinématique comprise entre 3,7 et 5,5 cSt à 99°C. Ces cires servent à la fabrication des bougies et des encaustiques, à l'imperméabilisation de récipients et d'emballages, etc.

Coke de pétrole – Résidu solide d'un noir brillant, obtenu par craquage et carbonisation au four, constitué essentiellement de carbone (90 à 95%) et dont la combustion ne laisse généralement aucune cendre. Il est utilisé surtout en métallurgie. Cette rubrique ne comprend pas les résidus solides obtenus par carbonisation du charbon.

Autres produits pétroliers – Produits d'origine pétrolière (y compris les produits partiellement raffinés) non désignés autrement.

Alcools – Comprennent l'éthanol (alcool éthylique) et le méthanol (alcool méthylique) utilisés comme combustibles. L'éthanol peut être obtenu à partir du sucre, de l'amidon et de la cellulose et est utilisé essentiellement pour les transports (seul ou mélangé avec de l'essence). Le méthanol peut être obtenu à partir du bois, des résidus agricoles et des fourrages verts et peut être utilisé dans les moteurs à combustion interne.

Biodiesel – It refers to oil derived from biological sources and modified chemically so that it can be used as fuel in compression ignition (diesel) internal combustion engines, or for heating. Biological sources of biodiesel include, but are not limited to, vegetable oils made from canola (rapeseed), soybeans, corn, oil palm, peanut, or sunflower. Chemically, biodiesel is a linear alkyl ester made by transesterification of vegetable oils or animal fats with methanol. The transesterification distinguishes biodiesel from straight vegetable and waste oils. Straight oils can be used as fuel only in if the engine is modified; for this reason, it is not recommended to report them as biodiesel. Biodiesel has a flash point of around 150°C and a density of 0.86 kg/liter. When burned, some of the emissions (sulfur, carbon monoxide, and aromatic hydrocarbons) are lower than that of petroleum-derived gas-diesel oil, while some are higher (nitrogen oxides, particulate matter (sooth)). Biodiesel is biodegradable and non-toxic. It has higher cetane rating than petroleum diesel, with which it is often blended. For example, B20 is a fuel containing 20% of biodiesel and 80% of regular diesel; B100 refers to pure biodiesel.

Biodiesel – Le biodiesel fait référence aux huiles dérivées de sources biologiques et modifiées chimiquement pour être utilisées comme carburant pour les moteurs ou comme chauffage. Comme sources biologiques de biodiesel on peut citer: les huiles végétales provenant du canola (colza), du soja, du maïs, du palmier, de la pistache, du tournesol. Chimiquement, le biodiesel est un ester alkyle linéaire obtenu à travers transestérification d'huile végétale ou animale mélangée avec le méthanol. La transestérification distingue le biodiesel des huiles végétales brutes et des huiles déchets. Les huiles végétales à l'état brut peuvent être utilisées comme carburants seulement avec modification du moteur, pour cette raison il n'est pas recommandé de les considérer comme biodiesel. Le biodiesel a un point d'éclair aux environs de 150°C et une densité de 0.86 kg/litre. Les dégagements (sulfure, monoxyde de carbone et hydrocarbonés aromatiques) obtenus du biodiesel chauffé sont inférieurs à ceux dérivés du carburant diesel, alors que d'autres (oxydes de nitrogène, suie) sont supérieurs. Le biodiesel est biodégradable et n'est pas toxique. Son taux de cétane est plus élevé que le pétrodiesel avec lequel il est souvent mélangé. Par exemple, le B20 est un carburant diesel contenant 20% de biodiesel et 80% de gazole ; B100 fait référence au biodiesel vierge.

GASEOUS FUELS

Natural gas – Gases consisting mainly of methane occurring naturally in underground deposits. It includes both non-associated gas (originating from fields producing only hydrocarbons in gaseous form) and associated gas (originating from fields producing both liquid and gaseous hydrocarbons), as well as methane recovered from coal mines. Production of natural gas refers to dry marketable production, measured after purification and extraction of natural gas liquids and sulphur. Extraction losses and the amounts that have been reinjected, flared, and vented are excluded from the data on production.

Gasworks gas – Gas produced by public utilities or private plants whose main activity is the production, transport and distribution of such gas. It includes gas produced by carbonization, by total gasification with or without enrichment with oil products, by cracking of natural gas, and by reforming or mixing gases.

Coke-oven gas – By-product of the carbonization process in the production of coke in coke ovens.

Blast furnace gas – By-product in blast furnaces recovered on leaving the furnace.

Biogas – By-product of the fermentation of biomass, principally animal wastes, by bacteria. It consists mainly of methane gas and carbon dioxide.

ELECTRICITY AND OTHER FORMS OF ENERGY

Electricity production – Refers to gross production, which includes the consumption by station auxiliaries and any losses in the transformers that are considered integral parts of the station. Included also is total electric energy produced by pumping installations without deduction of electric energy absorbed by pumping.

Production data includes Solar, Tide, Wave, Wind, Wastes, Wood and Fuel cell production when reported.

COMBUSTIBLES GAZEUX

Gaz naturel – Est constitué de gaz, méthane essentiellement, extraits de gisements naturels souterrains. Il peut s'agir aussi bien de gaz non associé (provenant de gisements qui produisent uniquement des hydrocarbures gazeux) que de gaz associé (provenant de gisements qui produisent à la fois des hydrocarbures liquides et gazeux) ou de méthane récupéré dans les mines de charbon. La production de gaz naturel se rapporte à la production de gaz commercialisable sec, mesurée après purification et extraction des condensats de gaz naturel et du soufre. Les quantités réinjectées, brûlées à la torchère ou éventées et les pertes d'extraction sont exclus des données sur la production.

Gaz d'usine à gaz – Gaz produit par des entreprises publiques ou privées ayant pour principale activité la production, le transport et la distribution de gaz manufacturé. Il comprend le gaz produit par carbonisation, par gazéification totale avec ou sans enrichissement au moyen de produits pétroliers, par craquage de gaz naturel et par reformage ou mélange de différents gaz.

Gaz de cokerie – Sous-produit du processus de carbonisation dans la production du coke dans les fours à coke.

Gaz de haut-fourneau – Sous-produit du fonctionnement des haut-fourneaux, récupéré à la sortie du gueulard.

Biogaz - Sous-produit de la fermentation bactérienne de la biomasse, principalement des déchets animaux. Il est composé surtout de méthane et de gaz carbonique.

ELECTRICITE ET AUTRES FORMES D'ENERGIE

La production d'électricité – La production brute qui comprend la consommation des équipements auxiliaires des centrales et les pertes au niveau des transformateurs considérés comme faisant partie intégrante de ces centrales, ainsi que la quantité totale d'énergie électrique produite par les installations de pompage sans déduction de l'énergie électrique absorbée par ces dernières.

Les données de production incluent solaire, la marée, la vague, le vent, les déchets, le bois et la production de cellule de carburant quand rapporté.

DEFINITIONS (continued/ suite)

Primary electricity refers to electrical energy of geothermal, hydro, nuclear, tide, wind, wave/ocean and solar origin. Its production is assessed at the heat value of electricity (3.6 TJ/million kWh).

Secondary electricity is defined as thermal electricity, which comprises conventional thermal plants of all types, whether or not equipped for the combined generation of heat and electric energy. Accordingly, they include steam-operated generating plants, with condensation (with or without extraction) or with back-pressure turbines and plants using internal combustion engines or gas turbines whether or not these are equipped for heat recovery.

Public utilities comprise the undertakings whose essential purpose is the production, transmission and distribution of electric energy, primarily for use by the public. These may be private companies, co-operative organizations, local or regional authorities, nationalized undertakings or governmental organizations.

Self-producers include undertakings which, in addition to their main activities, they produce (individually or in combination) electric energy intended, in whole or in part, to meet their own needs. They may be privately or publicly owned.

Net installed capacity is measured at the terminals of the stations, i.e., after deduction of the power absorbed by the auxiliary installations and the losses in the station transformers, if any. Data concerning capacity refer in principle to 31 December of the year under consideration.

Imports and exports – Refer to the amounts of electric energy transferred to and from the country concerned, respectively, which are measured at the metering points on the lines crossing the frontiers. Included are imports and exports of electric energy made by means of high-voltage lines crossing frontiers as well as imports and exports made by means of low-voltage lines for use in the immediate vicinity of the frontier, if the quantities so transferred are known.

Electricité primaire est définie comme électricité d'origine géothermique, hydraulique, nucléaire, marémotrice, éolienne, des vagues/océans et solaire. La production est exprimée en pouvoir calorifique de l'électricité (3,6 TJ par million de kWh).

Electricité secondaire est définie comme électricité d'origine thermique qui comprend les centrales thermiques classiques de tous types, qu'elles soient ou non équipées pour la production combinée de chaleur et d'électricité. Sont incluses en conséquence les centrales à vapeur, avec condensation (avec ou sans extraction) ou avec turbines à contre-pression, et les centrales utilisant des moteurs à combustion interne ou des turbines à gaz, équipées ou non d'un système de récupération thermique.

Les services publics comprennent les entreprises dont l'activité principale est la production, le transport et la distribution de l'énergie électrique, principalement pour l'usage public. Il peut s'agir de sociétés privées, de coopératives, de régies locales ou régionales et d'entreprises nationalisées ou autres organismes étatiques.

Les autoproducteurs comprennent les entreprises qui, en plus de leurs activités principales, produisent elles-mêmes (seules ou en association avec d'autres) de l'énergie électrique destinée en totalité ou en partie à satisfaire leurs besoins propres. Celles-ci peuvent appartenir aussi bien au secteur privé qu'au secteur public.

Puissance nette installée est mesurée au bornes de sortie de la centrale, c'est-à-dire déduction faite de la puissance absorbée par les services auxiliaires et par les pertes dans les transformateurs de la centrale s'il en existe. Les données relatives à la puissance installée se rapportent en principe au 31 décembre de l'année considérée.

Importations et exportations – Se rapportent aux quantités d'énergie électrique transférées respectivement vers le pays concerné ou à partir de ce dernier, mesurées aux compteurs situés sur les lignes électriques qui franchissent les frontières. Sont comprises dans cette rubrique les importations et exportations d'énergie électrique effectuées au moyen de lignes à haute tension traversant les frontières, ainsi que les importations et exportations d'électricité effectuées au moyen des lignes à basse tension desservant les régions frontalières lorsque les quantités ainsi transférées sont connues.

Heat – Heat obtained from (a) combined heat and power (CHP) plants generating electricity and useful heat in a single installation; (b) district heating (DH) plants and (c) nuclear power plants and geothermal sources. The heat may be in the form of steam, hot water or hot air.

Uranium (U) production – Comprises the U content of uranium ores and concentrates intended for treatment for uranium recovery.

TRADITIONAL FUELS

Fuelwood – All wood in the rough used for fuel purposes. Production data include the portion used for charcoal production, using a factor of 6 to convert from a weight basis to the volumetric equivalent (metric tons to cubic metres) of charcoal.

Bagasse – The cellulosic residue left after sugar is extracted from sugar cane. It is often used as a fuel within the sugar milling industry.

Charcoal – Solid residue, consisting mainly of carbon, obtained by the destructive distillation of wood in the absence of air.

Animal wastes – Excreta of cattle, horses, pigs, poultry, etc., and (in principle) excreta of humans, used as a fuel.

Vegetal wastes – Mainly crop residues (cereal straw from maize, wheat, paddy rice, etc.) and food processing wastes (rice hulls, coconut husks, ground-nut shells, etc.) used for fuel. Bagasse is excluded.

Municipal wastes – Consist of products that are combusted directly to produce heat and/or power and comprise wastes produced by the residential, commercial and public services sectors that are collected by local authorities for disposal in a central location. Hospital waste is included in this category.

Chaleur – Chaleur en provenance (a) des centrales à cycle mixte produisant dans une même installation de l'électricité et de chaleur utile, (b) par le chauffage urbain, (c) des centrales nucléaires et des sources géothermiques. La chaleur peut être produite sous forme de vapeur, d'eau chaude ou d'air chaud.

Production d'uranium (U) – Cette rubrique se rapporte à la teneur en U des minerais d'uranium et des concentrés uranifères destinés à être traités en vue de l'extraction de l'uranium.

COMBUSTIBLES TRADITIONNELS

Bois de chauffage – Tous les types de bois à l'état brut non dégrossis utilisés comme combustibles. Les données de production englobent les quantités utilisées pour la production de charbon de bois, utilisant un facteur de 6 pour convertir en volume le poids de charbon de bois (tonnes en mètres cubes).

Bagasse – Le résidu cellulosique de l'extraction du sucre de la canne à sucre. Elle est souvent utilisée comme combustible dans l'industrie sucrière.

Charbon de bois – Résidu solide essentiellement constitué de carbone, obtenu par la pyrogénation du bois en l'absence d'air.

Déchets animaux – Les excréments des bovins, chevaux, porcs, volailles, etc., ainsi que, en principe, les excréments humains, utilisés comme combustible.

Déchets végétaux – Comprennent essentiellement des résidus des récoltes (pailles de blé, de paddy, de maïs, etc.) et des déchets du traitement de produits alimentaires (balle du riz, coques des noix de coco et des arachides, etc.), qui sont utilisés comme combustible. La bagasse n'est pas comprise sous cette rubrique.

Déchets urbains – Correspondent aux produits brûlés directement pour produire de la chaleur et/ou de l'énergie électrique, dont notamment les déchets des secteurs résidentiel et commercial ainsi que du secteur des services publics, qui sont recueillis par les autorités municipales pour leur élimination dans des installations centralisées. Les déchets hospitaliers entrent dans cette catégorie.

Industrial wastes – Consist of solid and liquid products other than solid biomass and animal products mentioned above (e.g. tires) combusted directly, usually in specialised plants, to produce heat and/or power.

Other wastes - Wastes not specifically defined above, such as pulp and paper wastes.

TRANSACTIONS

The data on **production** refer to the first stage of production: accordingly, for hard coal the data refer to mine production; for briquettes to the output of briquetting plants; for crude petroleum and natural gas to production at oil and gas wells; for natural gas liquids to production at wells and processing plants; for refined petroleum products to gross refinery output; for cokes and coke-oven gas to the output of ovens; for other manufactured gas to production at gas works, blast furnaces or refineries; and for electricity to the gross production of generating plants.

The **international trade** of energy commodities is based on the "general trade" system, that is, all goods entering and leaving the national boundary of a country are recorded as imports and exports.

Bunkers refer to fuels supplied to ships and aircraft engaged in international transportation, irrespective of the carrier's flag.

In general, data on **stocks** refer to changes in stocks at producers, importers and/or industrial consumers at the beginning and end of each year. In some cases, however, stock series have been derived on the basis of the difference between gross availabilities for transformation or consumption and official or published data on actual consumption. A positive stock change (+) reflects additions to stocks which in effect decreases "apparent consumption"; while a negative stock change (-) creates exactly the opposite result.

Déchets industriels – Correspondent aux produits liquides et solides autres que la biomasse solide et les produits d'origine animale susmentionnés (pneus par example) brûlés directement, généralement dans des installations spécialisées, pour produire de la chaleur et/ou de l'énergie électrique.

Autres déchets - Tous les autres déchets qui n'ont pas été expressément définis ci-dessus, tels que vieux papiers et rebuts de pâte à papier.

TRANSACTIONS

Les données sur **la production** se rapportent au premier stade de production; il s'agit donc: pour la houille, des quantités extraites des mines; pour les agglomérés, de la production des usines d'agglomération; pour le pétrole brut et le gaz naturel, de la production des puits de pétrole et de gaz; pour les liquides de gaz naturel, de la production des puits et des usines de traitement; pour les produits pétroliers raffinés, de la production brute des raffineries; pour le coke et le gaz de cokerie, de la production des fours; pour les autres gaz manufacturés, de la quantité produite par les usines à gaz, les hauts fourneaux ou les raffineries; et pour l'électricité, de la production brute des centrales génératrices.

Le **commerce international** des produits énergétiques est fondé sur le système du "commerce général", c'est-à-dire que tous les biens entrant sur le territoire national d'un pays ou en sortant sont respectivement enregistrés comme importations et exportations.

Les **soutages** se rapportent aux carburants fournis aux navires et aux avions assurant des transports internationaux, quel que soit leur pavillon.

En général, les **variations de stocks** se rapportent aux différences entre les stocks des producteurs, des importateurs ou des consommateurs industriels au début et à la fin de chaque année. Dans quelques cas cependant, les séries relatives aux stocks ont été calculées d'après la différence entre les disponibilités brutes pour transformation ou consommation et les chiffres officiels ou publiés de la consommation réelle. Une variation positive des stocks (+) correspond à une augmentation de stock qui diminue en fait la "consommation apparente"; alors qu'une variation négative des stocks (-) a un effet exactement opposé.

Data on **consumption** refer to "apparent consumption" and are derived from the formula "production + imports - exports - bunkers +/- stock changes." Accordingly, the series on apparent consumption may occasionally represent only an indication of the magnitude of actual (i.e., "measured") gross inland availability. This statement is particularly suitable either when stock data are unavailable or unreliable, or when apparent consumption is a small residual element derived from calculations between large aggregate series and thus is sensitive to small variations in these series. This latter point is also appropriate with respect to the *per capita* consumption calculations presented in some tables. Where the quantities involved are small, the series tend to exaggerate the effects of such elements as stock additions or withdrawals.

Les données sur la **consommation** se rapportent à la "consommation apparente" et sont obtenues par la formule "production + importations - exportations - soutage +/- variations des stocks". En conséquence, les séries relatives à la consommation apparente peuvent occasionnellement ne donner qu'une indication de l'ordre de grandeur des disponibilités intérieures brutes réelles (c.à.d. mesurées). Il en est ainsi en particulier soit lorsque les données sur les stocks n'existent pas ou sont de valeur douteuse, soit quand la consommation apparente est le reste, relativement peu important, de calculs effectués sur des séries agrégées d'un ordre de grandeur élevé, et est de ce fait sensible à de petites variations de ces séries. Cette dernière considération vaut aussi pour les calculs de consommation par habitant présentés dans certains tableaux. Lorsque les quantités en cause sont petites, les séries tendent à exagérer les effets d'éléments comme les augmentations ou diminutions de stocks.

ENERGY RESOURCES AND RESERVES

RESSOURCES ET RESERVES ENERGETIQUES

Hard Coal, Lignite and Peat

Houille, Lignite et Tourbe

Proved amount in place is the tonnage that has been both carefully measured and assessed as being exploitable under present and expected local economic conditions with existing available technology.

Les quantités avérées en place représentent le tonnage qui a non seulement été soigneusement mesuré, mais dont on a vérifié aussi qu'il était exploitable dans les conditions économiques locales présentes et prévues avec une technologie réellement disponible.

Proved recoverable reserves are the tonnage of the proved amount in place that can be recovered (extracted from the earth in raw form) under present and expected local economic conditions with existing available technology.

Les réserves récupérables avérées représentent le tonnage des quantités avérées en place qui peuvent être récupérées (extraites du sol sous forme primaire) dans les conditions économiques locales présentes et prévues avec une technologie réellement disponible.

Estimated additional amount in place is the indicated and inferred tonnage *additional* to the proved amount in place. It includes estimates of amounts which could exist in unexplored extensions of known deposits (and also in the case of coal, in undiscovered deposits in known coal-bearing areas), as well as amounts inferred through knowledge of favorable geological conditions. Deposits whose existence is entirely speculative are not included.

Les quantités additionnelles estimées en place représentent le tonnage indiqué et inféré *en plus* des quantités avérées en place. Cela comprend des estimations des quantités qui pourraient exister dans les extensions inexplorées des dépôts connus (et aussi dans le cas de la houille dans les dépôts non découverts dans les régions houillères) ainsi que les quantités inférées par la connaissance des conditions géologiques favorables. Les ressources dont l'existence est purement spéculative ne sont pas prises en compte.

Crude Oil and Natural Gas Liquids

Proved recoverable reserves is the tonnage of the proved amount in place that can be recovered (extracted from the earth in raw form) in the future under present and expected economic conditions and existing technological limits.

The ratio of crude oil reserves to production (R/P ratio) is used to show the length of time those reserves would last in years if production continued at the then current level and there were no further increases in the proved recoverable reserves. The ratio is calculated by dividing the proved recoverable crude oil reserves (which for the most part refer to reserves at the end of 1995) by the production. *These R/P ratios should be viewed with extreme caution.* The definition used for proved recoverable reserves is very restrictive and confined to those known reserves which can be recovered with reasonable certainty under existing economic conditions. The R/P ratios, therefore, can frequently give a very pessimistic impression of the expected life of a country's reserves. In addition, for some of those countries whose R/P ratios appear very large, it can reasonably be assumed that the figures for proved recoverable reserves include some unproved reserves.

Oil Shale and Bituminous Sands

Proved recoverable reserves are the amount, expressed as tonnage of recoverable synthetic oil, that has been both carefully measured and has also been assessed as exploitable under present and expected local economic conditions with existing available technology.

Natural Gas

Proved recoverable reserves is the volume of the proved amount in place that can be recovered (in raw form) in the future under local economic conditions with existing available technology.

Pétrole brut et liquides de gaz naturel

Les réserves récupérables avérées représentent les tonnages des quantités avérées en place, récupérables dans l'avenir (par extraction du sol à l'état brut), dans les conditions économiques actuelles, prévues et futures et avec les moyens technologiques disponibles.

Le rapport entre réserves brutes de pétrole et production de pétrole (rapport R/P) est utilisé comme indicateur du nombre d'années que pourraient durer les réserves si la production continuait au rythme actuel et les réserves prouvées récupérables n'augmentent plus. Ce rapport est calculé en divisant les réserves avérées de pétrole (qui se rapportent en général aux réserves à la fin de 1995) par la production. *Il faut toutefois utiliser cet indicateur avec les plus grandes précautions.* La définition utilisée pour les réserves prouvées récupérables est confinée aux réserves connues qui peuvent être récupérées avec une certitude raisonnable dans les conditions économiques actuelles. Le R/P rapport, cependant, peut souvent donner une impression très pessimiste de l'espérance de vie des réserves d'un pays. En plus, pour certains des pays dont le rapport R/P paraît très prononcé, il peut être raisonnable d'admettre que les données concernant les réserves prouvées récupérables comprennent des réserves non prouvées.

Schistes et sables bitumineux

Les réserves récupérables avérées représentent les quantités, en tonnage, de pétrole de synthèse récupérable, minutieusement mesurées et jugées exploitables dans les conditions économiques actuelles et prévues et avec les moyens technologiques disponibles.

Gaz naturel

Les réserves récupérables avérées: volumes des quantités avérées en place, récupérables à l'avenir (à l'état brut), dans les conditions économiques et avec les moyens technologiques disponibles

Uranium

Reasonably assured resources refer to recoverable uranium that occurs in known mineral deposits of such size, grade and configuration that it could be recovered with currently proven mining and processing technology, at a cost of between US $80 and $130 per kilogramme.

Estimated additional resources refers to recoverable uranium, in addition to reasonably assured resources, that is expected to occur, mostly on the basis of direct geological evidence in:

- extensions of well-explored deposits,

- little-explored deposits, and

- undiscovered deposits believed to exist along a well-defined geological trend with known deposits, recoverable at costs of up to US $130.

Hydropower

Gross theoretical capability is the annual energy potentially available in the country if all natural flows were turbined down to sea level or to the water level of the border of the country (if the water course extends into another country) with 100% efficiency from the machinery and driving water-works. Unless otherwise stated, the figures have been estimated on the basis of atmospheric precipitation and water run off.

Uranium

Les ressources raisonnablement assurées se rapportent à l'uranium récupérable qui se trouve dans des dépôts minéraux connus dont la taille, la qualité et la configuration sont telles qu'il pourrait être récupéré avec une technologie d'extraction et de traitement ayant actuellement fait ses preuves, à un coût situé entre 80 et 130 dollars E.-U. le kilogramme.

Les ressources additionnelles estimées se rapportent à l'uranium récupérable, autre que celui des ressources raisonnablement assurées dont on escompte la présence, principalement sur la base de preuves géologiques directes, dans:

- des extensions de gisements déjà bien explorés;

- des gisements peu explorés; et

- des gisements non encore découverts mais que l'on suppose qu'ils existent sur la base d'analogies géologiques bien établies avec des dépôts connus, récupérables à un coût de 130 dollars E.-U. ou moins.

Energie hydraulique

Capacité brute théorique: énergie annuelle potentiellement disponible dans un pays si tous les cours naturels sont refoulés au niveau de la mer ou au niveau des eaux à la frontière (en cas d'acheminement à l'étranger), selon un rendement de 100% de l'installation et du système d'entranement. Sauf indication contraire, les chiffres sont déterminés d'après la précipitation atmosphérique et le ruissellement.

UNITS OF MEASUREMENT AND CONVERSIONS - UNITES DE MESURE ET CONVERSIONS

Metric units of measurement are used throughout the *Yearbook*. **Conversion Factor Tables** I through V provide the necessary factors for converting energy data from one measurement system (mass or weight, volume or heat) to another. Unless otherwise stated in the Table Notes, in the case of solid fuels, liquid fuels and gases, the conversions are based on the net calorific value.

The comparison between different fuels is presented in metric tons of coal equivalent (Tables 1 and 5), oil equivalent (Table 2), and terajoules (Tables 3 and 4) on the basis of the heat energy which may be obtained from each of them. In the case of solids fuels, liquid fuels and gases, this is represented by the heat energy obtained by burning an average grade of the fuel in a bomb calorimeter under ideal conditions.

A unit of primary electricity may be equated theoretically with the amount of coal or oil required to produce an equivalent unit of thermal electricity. In the case of hydro-electricity, the ideal condition (assuming 100% efficiency), is taken to be 3.6 TJ per million kWh which corresponds to 0.123 tons of coal equivalent or 0.086 tons of oil equivalent per 1,000 kWh. In the case of nuclear and geothermal electricity, the average condition is assumed (33 and 10% efficiency respectively) and is taken to be 10.909 and 36 TJ per million kWh which corresponds to 0.372 and 1.228 tons of coal equivalent or 0.261 and 0.860 tons of oil equivalent per 1,000 kWh.

The procedure to convert from original units to common units and from one common unit to another is as follows:

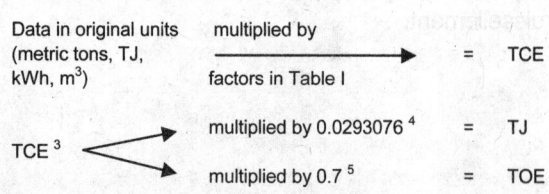

Les unités métriques de mesure sont utilisées dans le présent *Annuaire*. **Les tableaux des facteurs de conversion** I à V fournissent les coefficients nécessaires pour convertir les données relatives à l'énergie d'un système de mesures (masse ou poids, volume ou contenu calorifique) à un autre. Sauf indication contraire dans les Notes relatives aux tableaux, dans le cas des combustibles solides, liquides et gazeux, on utilise pour les conversions la valeur calorifique nette.

La comparaison entre les divers combustibles est présentée en tonnes métriques d'équivalent charbon (Tableaux 1 et 5), d'équivalent pétrole (Table 2), et térajoules (Tableaux 3 et 4) sur la base de l'énergie calorifique que l'on peut obtenir de chacun d'eux. Dans le cas des combustibles solides, liquides et des gaz cela correspond à l'énergie calorifique obtenue en brûlant une qualité moyenne de chacun de ces combustibles dans une bombe calorimétrique dans des conditions idéales.

Une unité d'électricité primaire peut théoriquement équivaloir à la quantité de charbon ou de pétrole nécessaire pour produire une quantité équivalente d'électricité thermique. Dans le cas de l'électricité d'origine hydraulique, le rendement idéal (l'hypothèse d'un rendement de 100%) est défini comme égal à 3,6 TJ par million de kWh, ce qui correspond à un équivalent charbon de 0,123 tonne métrique ou un équivalent pétrole de 0,086 tonne métrique pour 1 000 kWh. Pour l'électricité d'origine nucléaire et géothermique, on assume le rendement moyen, (l'hypothèse d'un rendement de 33 et 10% respectivement) qui est défini comme égal à 10,909 et 36 TJ par million de kWh, ce qui correspond à un équivalent charbon de 0,372 et 1,228 tonne métrique ou un équivalent pétrole de 0,261 et 0,860 tonne métrique pour 1 000 kWh.

La méthode de conversion suivie pour passer des unités de mesure d'origine aux unités de mesure communes et d'une unité commune à une autre est la suivante:

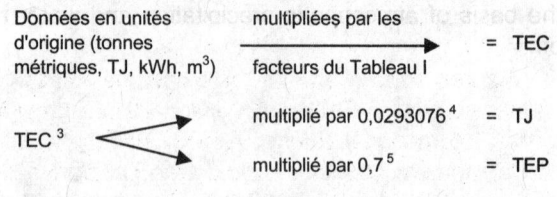

---

[3] The base used for coal equivalency comprises 7,000 calories per gram.

[4] One TCE is defined as 7×10^6 kcal or 0.0293076 TJ.
[5] One TOE is defined as 10.0×10^6 kcal or 0.041868 TJ (1 calorie =4.1868 joules).

---

[3] La base utilisée pour l'équivalence charbon correspond à 7 000 calories par gramme.
[4] Une TEC équivaut par définition à 7×10^6 kcal ou 0,0293076 TJ.
[5] Une TEP équivaut par définition à $10,0 \times 10^6$ kcal ou 0,041868 TJ (1 calorie = 4,1868 joules).

TABLE NOTES - NOTES RELATIVES AUX TABLEAUX

GENERAL NOTES

Consumption

Consumption throughout the *Yearbook* is defined as: production + imports - exports - bunkers +/- stock changes.

Negative Consumption

Consumption for some of the petroleum products is negative due to the exclusion of inter-product transfers from the calculations.

Negative consumption of electricity is due to negligible or no primary electricity production and/or net exports.

Time Period

The period to which the data refer is the calendar year, with the exception of the data of the following countries which refer to the fiscal year:

Afghanistan and Iran (Islamic Rep. of) - beginning 21 March of the year stated;

Australia, Bangladesh, Egypt (electricity only), Nepal, Pakistan - ending June of the year stated;

India, Myanmar and New Zealand - beginning April of the year stated.

Trade data

Figures displayed for international trade by partner country in Tables 7, 15 and 29 are provided by the International Energy Agency (when between OECD-member countries) and by the United Nations Statistics Division COMTRADE (Commodity Trade Statistics). For this reason, the totals (either export to the world or import from the world) may differ from the figures given in other tables.

REMARQUES GENERALES

Consommation

Dans *l'Annuaire*, la consommation est définie comme suit: production + importations - exportations - soutages +/– variations de stocks.

Consommation négative

La consommation de quelques produits pétroliers est négative du fait de l'exclusion des transferts inter-produits des calculs.

La consommation d'électricité apparaît comme un nombre négatif quand la production d'électricité primaire est nulle ou négligeable et/ou quand il y a des exportations nettes.

Période couverte

Les données se rapportent à l'année civile, sauf celles des pays suivants qui se rapportent à l'exercice budgétaire:

Afghanistan et Iran (Rép. islamique) - commençant le 21 mars de l'année indiquée;

L'Australie, le Bangladesh, l'Egypte (pour l'électricité seulement), le Népal, le Pakistan - finissant en juin de l'année indiquée;

L'Inde, le Myanmar et la Nouvelle-Zélande commençant en avril de l'année indiquée.

Données commerciales

Les figures montrées pour le commerce international par le pays d'associé dans les tableaux 7, 15 et 29 sont fournies par l'Agence internationale de l'énergie (quand entre les pays d'OCDE-pays membres) et par la Division de statistiques des Nations Unies – COMTRADE (statistiques commerciales des produits). Pour cette raison, les totaux (exportation vers le monde ou importation du monde) peuvent différer des figures indiquées dans d'autres tables.

Table I

COEFFICIENTS USED TO CONVERT FROM ORIGINAL UNITS
INTO COAL EQUIVALENT

FACTEURS DE CONVERSION DES DIFFERENTES UNITES D'ORIGINE
EN EQUIVALENT CHARBON

PRODUCTION, EXPORTS AND CHANGES IN STOCKS

PRODUCTION, EXPORTATIONS ET VARIATIONS DES STOCKS

HARD COAL	2003	2004	2005	2006	HOUILLE
Standard factor	**1.000**	**1.000**	**1.000**	**1.000**	**Facteur standard**
Albania	0.928	0.928	0.928	0.928	Albanie
Argentina	0.843	0.843	0.843	0.843	Argentine
Australia	0.922	0.923	0.922	0.925	Australie
Bangladesh	0.714	0.714	0.714	0.714	Bangladesh
Belarus	0.871	0.871	0.871	0.871	Bélarus
Belgium	0.860	0.860	0.860	0.860	Belgique
Brazil	0.635	0.635	0.635	0.635	Brésil
Canada	0.982	0.982	0.969	0.969	Canada
Chile	0.970	0.970	0.970	0.970	Chili
China	0.714	0.714	0.714	0.714	Chine
Colombia	0.928	0.928	0.928	0.928	Colombie
Czech Republic	0.836	0.836	0.836	0.836	République tchèque
Denmark	0.851	0.851	0.851	0.851	Danemark
Egypt	0.871	0.871	0.871	0.871	Égypte
France incl. Monaco	0.927	0.927	0.961	0.927	France y comp. Monaco
Germany	0.925	0.925	0.925	0.925	Allemagne
Georgia	0.836	0.836	0.836	0.836	Géorgie
Greece	0.928	0.928	0.928	0.928	Grèce
Hungary	0.480	0.480	0.480	0.480	Hongrie
India	0.829	0.828	0.829	0.829	Inde
Italy and San Marino	0.899	0.899	0.899	0.899	Italie y comp. S. Mrn
Japan	0.828	0.828	0.828	0.828	Japon
Kazakhstan	0.634	0.634	0.634	0.634	Kazakhstan
Korea,Republic of	0.643	0.643	0.643	0.643	Corée, République de
Kyrgyzstan	0.634	0.634	0.634	0.634	Kirghizistan
Mexico	0.698	0.698	0.698	0.698	Mexique
Morocco	0.800	0.800	0.800	0.800	Maroc
New Zealand	0.829	0.829	0.829	0.829	Nouvelle-Zélande
Norway, Svlbd, J.Myn.I.	0.959	0.959	0.959	0.959	Norvège,Svalbd, J.May
Pakistan	0.676	0.676	0.676	0.676	Pakistan
Peru	0.978	0.978	0.978	0.978	Pérou
Philippines	0.675	0.675	0.675	0.675	Philippines
Poland	0.814	0.814	0.814	0.814	Pologne
Portugal	0.586	0.586	0.585	0.585	Portugal
Romania	0.557	0.557	0.557	0.557	Roumanie

Table I (continued - suite)

COEFFICIENTS USED TO CONVERT FROM ORIGINAL UNITS INTO COAL EQUIVALENT

FACTEURS DE CONVERSION DES DIFFERENTES UNITES D'ORIGINE EN EQUIVALENT CHARBON

PRODUCTION, EXPORTS AND CHANGES IN STOCKS
PRODUCTION, EXPORTATIONS ET VARIATIONS DES STOCKS

HARD COAL	2003	2004	2005	2006	HOUILLE
Russian Federation	0.634	0.634	0.634	0.634	Fédération de Russie
S. Africa Customs Un.	0.753	0.753	0.753	0.753	Un. douan. d'Afr. mérid.
Spain	0.731	0.731	0.731	0.731	Espagne
Sweden	0.964	0.964	0.964	0.964	Suède
Turkey	0.819	0.819	0.819	0.819	Turquie
Ukraine	0.737	0.737	0.737	0.737	Ukraine
United Kingdom	0.861	0.861	0.861	0.861	Royaume-Uni
United States	0.831	0.831	0.831	0.831	États-Unis
Uzbekistan	0.634	0.634	0.634	0.634	Ouzbékistan
Venezuela	0.999	0.999	0.999	0.999	Venezuela
Serbia	0.803	0.803	0.803	0.803	Serbie
Zambia	0.843	0.843	0.843	0.843	Zambie

LIGNITE	2003	2004	2005	2006	LIGNITE
Standard factor	**0.385**	**0.385**	**0.385**	**0.385**	**Facteur standard**
Albania	0.336	0.336	0.336	0.336	Albanie
Australia	0.427	0.425	0.423	0.424	Australie
Austria	0.372	0.372	0.372	0.372	Autriche
Bosnia and Herzegovina	0.445	0.445	0.461	0.461	Bosnie-Herzégovine
Brazil	0.553	0.549	0.549	0.549	Brésil
Bulgaria	0.233	0.233	0.233	0.233	Bulgarie
Canada	0.486	0.486	0.486	0.486	Canada
Chile	0.586	0.586	0.586	0.586	Chili
Czech Republic	0.427	0.427	0.427	0.427	République tchèque
Estonia	0.322	0.322	0.322	0.322	Estonie
France incl. Monaco	0.585	0.585	0.585	0.585	France y comp. Monaco
Germany	0.298	0.298	0.298	0.298	Allemagne
Greece	0.171	0.174	0.176	0.176	Grèce
Hungary	0.295	0.277	0.261	0.261	Hongrie
India	0.330	0.330	0.330	0.330	Inde
Italy and San Marino	0.331	0.331	0.331	0.331	Italie y comp. S. Mrn
Japan	0.586	0.586	0.586	0.586	Japon
Kazakhstan	0.500	0.500	0.500	0.500	Kazakhstan
Korea, Dem. Ppl's. Rep.	0.600	0.600	0.600	0.600	Corée, Rép.pop.dém.de
Mongolia	0.330	0.330	0.330	0.330	Mongolie
New Zealand	0.427	0.427	0.427	0.427	Nouvelle-Zélande
Philippines	0.667	0.667	0.667	0.667	Philippines
Poland	0.294	0.294	0.294	0.294	Pologne

Table I (continued - suite)

COEFFICIENTS USED TO CONVERT FROM ORIGINAL UNITS
INTO COAL EQUIVALENT

FACTEURS DE CONVERSION DES DIFFERENTES UNITES D'ORIGINE
EN EQUIVALENT CHARBON

PRODUCTION, EXPORTS AND CHANGES IN STOCKS

PRODUCTION, EXPORTATIONS ET VARIATIONS DES STOCKS

LIGNITE	2003	2004	2005	2006	LIGNITE
Romania	0.247	0.247	0.247	0.247	Roumanie
Russian Federation	0.500	0.500	0.500	0.500	Fédération de Russie
Slovakia	0.418	0.418	0.418	0.418	Slovaquie
Slovenia	0.311	0.311	0.311	0.311	Slovénie
Spain	0.255	0.255	0.255	0.255	Espagne
Thailand	0.628	0.628	0.628	0.628	Thaïlande
Turkey	0.290	0.290	0.290	0.290	Turquie
Ukraine	0.500	0.500	0.500	0.500	Ukraine
United States	0.481	0.481	0.481	0.481	États-Unis
Serbia	0.303	0.303	0.303	0.303	Serbie

COKE-OVEN COKE	2003	2004	2005	2006	COKE DE FOUR
Standard factor	**0.900**	**0.900**	**0.900**	**0.900**	**Facteur standard**
Australia	0.875	0.875	0.875	0.875	Australie
Austria	0.980	0.981	0.989	0.989	Autriche
Belgium	0.945	0.945	0.945	0.945	Belgique
Brazil	1.042	1.042	1.042	1.042	Brésil
Canada	0.934	0.934	0.934	0.934	Canada
China	0.970	0.970	0.970	0.970	Chine
Colombia	0.686	0.686	0.686	0.686	Colombie
Czech Republic	0.905	0.905	0.905	0.905	République tchèque
Denmark	1.000	1.000	1.000	1.000	Danemark
Estonia	0.857	0.857	0.857	0.857	Estonie
France incl. Monaco	0.979	0.979	0.979	0.979	France y comp. Monaco
Germany	0.977	0.977	0.977	0.977	Allemagne
Greece	1.000	1.000	1.000	1.000	Grèce
Hungary	1.005	1.005	1.072	1.072	Hongrie
Italy and San Marino	1.000	1.000	1.000	1.000	Italie y comp. S. Mrn
Mexico	0.952	0.952	0.952	0.952	Mexique
Netherlands	0.972	0.972	0.972	0.972	Pays-Bas
New Zealand	0.927	0.927	0.927	0.927	Nouvelle-Zélande
Norway, Svlbd, J.Myn.I.	0.972	0.972	0.972	0.972	Norvège,Svalbd, J.May
Poland	0.965	0.965	0.965	0.965	Pologne
Portugal	0.957	0.957	0.957	0.957	Portugal
Slovakia	0.921	0.921	0.921	0.921	Slovaquie
S. Africa Customs Un.	0.952	0.952	0.952	0.952	Un. Douan. D'Afr. Mérid.

Table I (continued - suite)

COEFFICIENTS USED TO CONVERT FROM ORIGINAL UNITS INTO COAL EQUIVALENT

FACTEURS DE CONVERSION DES DIFFERENTES UNITES D'ORIGINE EN EQUIVALENT CHARBON

PRODUCTION, EXPORTS AND CHANGES IN STOCKS

PRODUCTION, EXPORTATIONS ET VARIATIONS DES STOCKS

COKE-OVEN COKE	2003	2004	2005	2006	COKE DE FOUR
Spain	1.033	1.033	1.033	1.033	Espagne
Sweden	0.957	0.957	0.957	0.957	Suède
Turkey	1.000	1.000	1.000	1.000	Turquie
United Kingdom	0.911	0.911	0.911	0.911	Royaume-Uni
United States	0.937	0.937	0.937	0.937	États-Unis

BROWN COAL COKE	2003	2004	2005	2006	COKE DE LIGNITE
Standard factor	**0.670**	**0.670**	**0.670**	**0.670**	**Facteur standard**
Germany	0.989	0.989	0.989	0.989	Allemagne

GAS COKE	2003	2004	2005	2006	COKE DE GAZ
Standard factor	**0.900**	**0.900**	**0.900**	**0.900**	**Facteur standard**
Australia	0.875	0.875	0.875	0.875	Australie
Japan	1.028	1.028	1.028	1.028	Japon
S. Africa Customs Un.	0.873	0.873	0.873	0.873	Un. Douan. D'Afr. Mérid.

HARD COAL BRIQUETTES	2003	2004	2005	2006	AGGLOMERES DE HOUILLE
Standard factor	**1.000**	**1.000**	**1.000**	**1.000**	**Facteur standard**
Denmark	1.000	1.000	1.000	1.000	Danemark
France incl. Monaco	1.026	1.026	1.026	1.026	France y comp. Monaco
Germany	1.071	1.071	1.071	1.071	Allemagne
Hungary	0.954	0.954	0.954	0.954	Hongrie
Ireland	0.993	0.933	0.933	0.933	Irlande
Japan	0.814	0.814	0.814	0.814	Japon
Korea,Republic of	0.665	0.665	0.665	0.665	Corée, République de
New Zealand	0.911	0.911	0.911	0.911	Nouvelle-Zélande
Poland	0.771	0.771	0.771	0.771	Pologne
Spain	1.000	1.000	1.000	1.000	Espagne
Russian Federation	1.000	1.000	1.000	1.000	Fédération de Russie
Turkey	0.996	0.996	0.996	0.996	Turquie
Ukraine	1.000	1.000	1.000	1.000	Ukraine
United Kingdom	0.898	0.898	0.898	0.898	Royaume-Uni

Table I (continued – suite)

COEFFICIENTS USED TO CONVERT FROM ORIGINAL UNITS INTO COAL EQUIVALENT

FACTEURS DE CONVERSION DES DIFFERENTES UNITES D'ORIGINE EN EQUIVALENT CHARBON

PRODUCTION, EXPORTS AND CHANGES IN STOCKS

PRODUCTION, EXPORTATIONS ET VARIATIONS DES STOCKS

LIGNITE BRIQUETTES	2003	2004	2005	2006	BRIQUETTES DE LIGNITE
Standard factor	**0.670**	**0.670**	**0.670**	**0.670**	**Facteur standard**
Australia	0.716	0.716	0.716	0.716	Australie
Austria	0.659	0.659	0.659	0.659	Autriche
Denmark	0.624	0.624	0.624	0.624	Danemark
Germany	0.689	0.689	0.689	0.689	Allemagne
Greece	0.521	0.521	0.521	0.521	Grèce
Hungary	0.720	0.720	0.720	0.720	Hongrie
Ireland	0.633	0.633	0.633	0.633	Irlande
Poland	0.607	0.607	0.607	0.607	Pologne
Russian Federation	0.686	0.686	0.686	0.686	Fédération de Russie

PEAT	2003	2004	2005	2006	TOURBE
Standard factor	**0.325**	**0.325**	**0.325**	**0.325**	**Facteur standard**
Burundi	0.500	0.500	0.500	0.500	Burundi
Finland	0.362	0.362	0.362	0.362	Finlande
Denmark	0.286	0.286	0.286	0.286	Danemark
Falkland Is. (Malvinas)	0.325	0.325	0.325	0.325	Iles Falkland (Malvinas)
Germany	0.286	0.286	0.286	0.286	Allemagne
Ireland	0.317	0.317	0.317	0.317	Irlande
Norway, Svlbd, J.Myn.I.	0.300	0.300	0.300	0.300	Norvège,Svalbd, J.May
Poland	0.286	0.286	0.286	0.286	Pologne
Sweden	0.413	0.413	0.413	0.413	Suède
United Kingdom	0.500	0.500	0.500	0.500	Royaume-Uni

Table I (continued – suite)

COEFFICIENTS USED TO CONVERT FROM ORIGINAL UNITS INTO COAL EQUIVALENT

FACTEURS DE CONVERSION DES DIFFERENTES UNITES D'ORIGINE EN EQUIVALENT CHARBON

IMPORTS
IMPORTATIONS

HARD COAL	2003	2004	2005	2006	HOUILLE
Standard factor	**1.000**	**1.000**	**1.000**	**1.000**	**Facteur standard**
Albania	0.928	0.928	0.928	0.928	Albanie
Argentina	1.028	1.028	1.028	1.028	Argentine
Austria	0.963	0.978	0.975	0.976	Autriche
Bangladesh	0.714	0.714	0.714	0.714	Bangladesh
Belarus	0.871	0.871	0.871	0.871	Bélarus
Belgium	0.999	0.999	0.999	0.929	Belgique
Brazil	1.042	1.042	1.042	1.042	Brésil
Bulgaria	0.883	0.883	0.883	0.883	Bulgarie
Canada	0.940	0.940	0.969	0.937	Canada
Chile	0.970	0.970	0.970	0.970	Chili
China, Hong Kong SAR	0.764	0.764	0.764	0.764	Chine, Hong-Kong RAS
Columbia	0.928	0.928	0.928	0.928	Colombie
Czech Republic	0.836	0.836	0.836	0.836	République tchèque
Denmark	0.851	0.851	0.851	0.851	Danemark
Egypt	0.871	0.871	0.871	0.871	Égypte
Estonia	0.634	0.634	0.634	0.634	Estonie
Finland	0.914	0.914	0.914	0.914	Finlande
France incl. Monaco	0.965	0.965	0.965	0.965	France y comp. Monaco
Georgia	0.836	0.836	0.836	0.836	Géorgie
Germany	0.901	0.901	0.901	0.901	Allemagne
Greece	0.928	0.928	0.928	0.928	Grèce
Hungary	0.936	0.936	0.960	0.960	Hongrie
Iceland	0.957	0.957	0.957	0.957	Islande
India	0.829	0.829	0.829	0.829	Inde
Ireland	1.023	1.023	1.023	1.023	Irlande
Italy and San Marino	0.972	0.972	0.972	0.972	Italie y comp. S. Mrn
Japan	0.992	0.992	0.992	0.992	Japon
Kazakhstan	0.634	0.634	0.634	0.634	Kazakhstan
Korea, Republic of	0.943	0.943	0.943	0.943	Corée, République de
Kyrgyzstan	0.634	0.634	0.634	0.634	Kirghizistan
Latvia	0.634	0.634	0.634	0.634	Lettonie
Luxembourg	1.000	1.000	1.000	1.000	Luxembourg
Malta	0.853	0.853	0.853	0.853	Malta
Mexico	1.033	1.033	1.033	1.033	Mexique
Morocco	0.943	0.943	0.943	0.943	Maroc

Table I (continued – suite)

COEFFICIENTS USED TO CONVERT FROM ORIGINAL UNITS INTO COAL EQUIVALENT

FACTEURS DE CONVERSION DES DIFFERENTES UNITES D'ORIGINE EN EQUIVALENT CHARBON

IMPORTS
IMPORTATIONS

HARD COAL	2003	2004	2005	2006	HOUILLE
Netherlands	0.924	0.924	0.924	0.924	Pays-Bas
Norway, Svlbd, J.Myn.l.	0.959	0.959	0.959	0.959	Norvège,Svalbd, J.May
Pakistan	0.989	0.989	0.989	0.989	Pakistan
Peru	0.928	0.928	0.928	0.928	Pérou
Poland	1.010	1.010	1.010	1.010	Pologne
Portugal	0.900	0.900	0.900	0.900	Portugal
Republic of Moldova	0.634	0.634	0.634	0.634	République de Moldova
Romania	0.857	0.857	0.857	0.857	Raumanie
Russian Federation	0.634	0.634	0.634	0.634	Fédération de Russie
Slovakia	0.816	0.816	0.816	0.816	Slovaquie
Slovenia	1.047	1.047	1.047	1.047	Slovénie
Spain	0.904	0.904	0.894	0.894	Espagne
Sweden	0.973	0.973	0.973	0.973	Suède
Switzerland	0.957	0.957	0.957	0.957	Suisse
Tajikistan	0.634	0.634	0.634	0.634	Tadjikistan
Thailand	0.900	0.900	0.900	0.900	Thaïlande
Turkey	1.022	1.022	1.022	1.023	Turquie
Ukraine	0.871	0.871	0.871	0.871	Ukraine
United Kingdom	0.976	0.976	0.976	0.976	Royaume-Uni
United States	0.934	0.934	0.934	0.934	États-Unis
Uzbekistan	0.634	0.634	0.634	0.634	Ouzbékistan
Venezuela	0.911	0.911	0.911	0.911	Venezuela
Uruguay	1.000	1.000	1.000	1.000	Uruguay
Serbia	1.047	1.047	1.047	1.047	Serbie

LIGNITE	2003	2004	2005	2006	LIGNITE
Standard factor	**0.385**	**0.385**	**0.385**	**0.385**	**Facteur standard**
Austria	0.372	0.372	0.372	0.372	Autriche
Croatia	0.498	0.498	0.498	0.498	Croatie
Estonia	0.322	0.322	0.322	0.322	Estonie
France incl. Monaco	0.585	0.585	0.585	0.585	France y comp. Monaco
Germany	0.449	0.449	0.449	0.449	Allemagne

Table I (continued – suite)

COEFFICIENTS USED TO CONVERT FROM ORIGINAL UNITS
INTO COAL EQUIVALENT

FACTEURS DE CONVERSION DES DIFFERENTES UNITES D'ORIGINE
EN EQUIVALENT CHARBON

IMPORTS
IMPORTATIONS

LIGNITE	2003	2004	2005	2006	LIGNITE
Hungary	0.620	0.598	0.615	0.573	Hongrie
Ireland	0.676	0.676	0.676	0.676	Irlande
Italy and San Marino	0.357	0.357	0.357	0.357	Italie y comp. S. Mrn
Japan	0.330	0.330	0.330	0.330	Japon
Netherlands	0.682	0.682	0.682	0.682	Pays-Bas
Poland	0.289	0.289	0.289	0.289	Pologne
Romania	0.247	0.247	0.247	0.247	Roumanie
Singapore	0.330	0.330	0.330	0.330	Singapour
Slovakia	0.416	0.416	0.416	0.416	Slovaquie
Slovenia	0.577	0.577	0.577	0.577	Slovénie
Spain	0.255	0.255	0.255	0.255	Espagne

COKE-OVEN COKE	2003	2004	2005	2006	COKE DE FOUR
Standard factor	**0.900**	**0.900**	**0.900**	**0.900**	**Facteur standard**
Austria	0.980	0.981	0.989	0.989	Autriche
Belgium	0.945	0.945	0.945	0.945	Belgique
Brazil	1.042	1.042	1.042	1.042	Brésil
Canada	0.934	0.934	0.934	0.934	Canada
Denmark	1.000	1.000	1.000	1.000	Danemark
France incl. Monaco	0.979	0.979	0.979	0.979	France y comp. Monaco
Germany	0.977	0.977	0.977	0.977	Allemagne
Greece	1.000	1.000	1.000	1.000	Grèce
Hungary	1.003	1.003	1.003	1.003	Hongrie
Iceland	0.910	0.910	0.910	0.910	Islande
Ireland	1.114	1.114	1.114	1.114	Irlande
Italy and San Marino	1.000	1.000	1.000	1.000	Italie y comp. S. Mrn
Netherlands	0.972	0.972	0.972	0.972	Pays-Bas
Norway, Svlbd, J.Myn.I.	0.972	0.972	0.972	0.972	Norvège,Svalbd, J.May
Peru	0.914	0.914	0.914	0.914	Pérou
Poland	0.983	0.983	0.983	0.983	Pologne
Portugal	0.957	0.957	0.957	0.957	Portugal
Spain	1.033	1.033	1.033	1.033	Espagne
Sweden	0.957	0.957	0.957	0.957	Suède
Switzerland	0.957	0.957	0.957	0.957	Suisse
United Kingdom	0.843	0.843	0.843	0.843	Royaume-Uni
United States	0.937	0.937	0.937	0.937	États-Unis
Uruguay	0.971	0.971	0.971	0.971	Uruguay

Table I (continued – suite)

COEFFICIENTS USED TO CONVERT FROM ORIGINAL UNITS
INTO COAL EQUIVALENT

FACTEURS DE CONVERSION DES DIFFERENTES UNITES D'ORIGINE
EN EQUIVALENT CHARBON

IMPORTS
IMPORTATIONS

HARD COAL BRIQUETTES	2003	2004	2005	2006	AGGLOMERES DE HOUILLE
Standard factor	**1.000**	**1.000**	**1.000**	**1.000**	**Facteur standard**
France incl. Monaco	1.026	1.026	1.026	1.026	France y comp. Monaco
Germany	1.071	1.071	1.071	1.071	Allemagne
Ireland	0.993	0.993	0.993	0.993	Irlande
United Kingdom	0.898	0.898	0.898	0.898	Royaume-Uni

LIGNITE BRIQUETTES	2003	2004	2005	2006	BRIQUETTES DE LIGNITE
Standard factor	**0.670**	**0.670**	**0.670**	**0.670**	**Facteur standard**
Austria	0.659	0.659	0.659	0.659	Autriche
Belgium	0.686	0.686	0.686	0.686	Belgique
Denmark	0.624	0.624	0.624	0.624	Danemark
France incl. Monaco	0.686	0.686	0.686	0.686	France y comp. Monaco
Germany	0.648	0.648	0.648	0.648	Allemagne
Hungary	0.721	0.721	0.721	0.721	Hongrie
Luxembourg	0.686	0.686	0.686	0.686	Luxembourg
Netherlands	0.682	0.682	0.682	0.682	Pays-Bas
Sweden	0.686	0.686	0.686	0.686	Suède
Switzerland	0.686	0.686	0.686	0.686	Suisse

Table I (continued – suite)

COEFFICIENTS USED TO CONVERT FROM ORIGINAL UNITS INTO COAL EQUIVALENT

FACTEURS DE CONVERSION DES DIFFERENTES UNITES D'ORIGINE EN EQUIVALENT CHARBON

OTHERS

AUTRES

Oil shale	0.314	Schiste bitumineux
Fuelwood	0.333	Bois de chauffage
Bagasse	0.264	Bagasse
Peat briquettes	0.500	Briquettes de tourbe
Charcoal	0.986	Charbon de bois
Crude oil	1.429	Pétrole brut
Natural gas liquids (weighted average)	1.542	Liquides de gaz naturel (moyenne pondérée)
Gasolene	1.500	Essences
Kerosene	1.474	Pétrole lampant
Jet fuel	1.474	Carburéacteurs
Gas-Diesel oils	1.450	Gazole/carburant Diesel
Residual fuel oil	1.416	Mazout résiduel
Liquefied petroleum gases	1.554	Gaz de pétrole liquéfié
Natural gasolene	1.532	Essence naturelle
Condensate	1.512	Condensat
Other natural gas liquids	1.512	Autres liquides de gaz naturel
Natural gas (in terajoules)[1]	34.121	Gaz naturel (en térajoules)[1]
Other gases (in terajoules)[1]	34.121	Autres gaz (en térajoules)[1]
Hydro and wind electricity (in 1,000 kWh)	0.123	Electricité hydraulique et éolienne (en 1 000 kWh)
Nuclear electricity (in 1,000 kWh)	0.123	Electricité nucléaire (en 1 000 kWh)
Geothermal electricity (in 1,000 kWh)	0.123	Electricité géothermique (en 1 000 kWh)

[1]The average calorific value of gas is measured in kcal/m^3 (st), i.e., in kcal per cubic metre of gas under standard conditions of 15°C, 1,013.25 mbar, dry.

[1]La valeur calorifique moyenne du gaz est mesurée en kcal/m^3 (n) ; c'est-à-dire en kcal par mètre cube de gaz dans les conditions normales 15°C, 1.013,25 mbar sèc.

Table II

SPECIFIC GRAVITIES OF CRUDE PETROLEUM

DENSITES DU PETROLE BRUT

Country	2003	2004	2005	2006	Pays
Albania	0.940*	0.940*	0.940*	0.940*	Albanie
Algeria	0.795*	0.795	0.795	0.795	Algérie
Angola	0.851*	0.851*	0.851*	0.851*	Angola
Argentina	0.887*	0.887*	0.887*	0.887*	Argentine
Australia	0.880*	0.880*	0.880*	0.880*	Australie
Austria	0.890*	0.890*	0.890*	0.890*	Autriche
Bahrain	0.860	0.860	0.860	0.860	Bahreïn
Bangladesh	0.860*	0.860*	0.860*	0.860*	Bangladesh
Barbados	0.860*	0.860*	0.860*	0.860*	Barbade
Bolivia	0.800*	0.800*	0.800*	0.800*	Bolivie
Brazil	0.876	0.876	0.876	0.876	Brésil
Brunei	0.890	0.890	0.890	0.890	Brunéi
Bulgaria	0.860*	0.860*	0.860*	0.860*	Bulgarie
Cameroon	0.870	0.870	0.870	0.870	Cameroun
Canada	0.847*	0.847*	0.847*	0.847*	Canada
Chile	0.840*	0.840*	0.840*	0.840*	Chili
China	0.860*	0.860*	0.860*	0.860*	Chine
Colombia	0.869*	0.869*	0.869*	0.869*	Colombie
Congo	0.840	0.840	0.840	0.840	Congo
Côte d'Ivoire	0.860	0.860	0.860	0.860	Côte d'Ivoire
Cuba	0.950*	0.950*	0.950*	0.950*	Cuba
Dem. Rep. Of Congo	0.860	0.860	0.860	0.860	Rép. dem. du Congo
Denmark	0.820*	0.820*	0.820*	0.820*	Danemark
Ecuador	0.900*	0.900*	0.900*	0.900*	Équateur
Egypt	0.908*	0.908*	0.908*	0.908*	Égypte
France incl. Monaco	0.860*	0.860*	0.860*	0.860*	France y comp. Monaco
Gabon	0.866	0.866	0.866	0.866	Gabon
Germany	0.870*	0.870*	0.870*	0.870*	Allemagne
Ghana	0.860*	0.860*	0.860*	0.860*	Ghana
Greece	0.880*	0.880*	0.880*	0.880*	Grèce
Guatemala	0.860*	0.860*	0.860*	0.860*	Guatemala
Hungary	0.830*	0.830*	0.830*	0.830*	Hongrie
India	0.840	0.840	0.840	0.840	Inde
Indonesia	0.724	0.724	0.724	0.724	Indonésie
Iran (Islamic Rep. of)	0.730	0.728	0.728	0.728	Iran (Rép. Islamique)
Iraq	0.742	0.742	0.742	0.742	Iraq
Israel	0.870*	0.870*	0.870*	0.870*	Israël
Italy and San Marino	0.920*	0.920*	0.920*	0.920*	Italie y comp. S. Mrn
Japan	0.850	0.850	0.850	0.850	Japon
Kuwait, part Ntl. Zone	0.725	0.726	0.726	0.726	Koweït et prt. Zne. N.
Libyan Arab Jamah.	0.756	0.756	0.756	0.756	Jamah. Arabe libyenne
Malaysia	0.820	0.820	0.820	0.820	Malaisie

Table II (continued – suite)

SPECIFIC GRAVITIES OF CRUDE PETROLEUM

DENSITES DU PETROLE BRUT

Country	2003	2004	2005	2006	Pays
Mexico	0.896*	0.896*	0.896*	0.896*	Mexique
Morocco	0.800*	0.800*	0.800*	0.800*	Maroc
Myanmar	0.890	0.890	0.890	0.890	Myanmar
Netherlands	0.920*	0.920*	0.920*	0.920*	Pays-Bas
New Zealand	0.775*	0.775*	0.775*	0.775*	Nouvelle-Zélande
Nigeria	0.741	0.741	0.741	0.741	Nigéria
Norway, Svlbd, J.Myn I	0.810*	0.810*	0.810*	0.810*	Norvège, Svalbd, J. May
Oman	0.855*	0.855*	0.855*	0.855*	Oman
Pakistan	0.839	0.839	0.839	0.839	Pakistan
Paraguay	0.849	0.849	0.849	0.849	Paraguay
Peru	0.922*	0.922*	0.922*	0.922*	Pérou
Philippines	0.893	0.893	0.893	0.893	Philippines
Poland	0.940	0.940	0.940	0.940	Pologne
Qatar	0.762	0.762	0.762	0.762	Qatar
Romania	0.900	0.900	0.900	0.900	Roumanie
Russian Federation	0.877*	0.877*	0.877*	0.877*	Fédération de Russie
S. Arabia, pt. Ntrl. Zn	0.728	0.728	0.728	0.728	Arab. saoud, p. Zn. neut
Spain	0.840*	0.840*	0.840*	0.840*	Espagne
Suriname	0.961*	0.961*	0.961*	0.961*	Suriname
Sweden	0.870*	0.870*	0.870*	0.870*	Suède
Syrian Arab Republic	0.908	0.908	0.908	0.908	Rép. arabe syrienne
Thailand	0.920	0.920	0.920	0.920	Thaïlande
Trinidad and Tobago	0.890*	0.890*	0.890*	0.890*	Trinité-et-Tobago
Tunisia	0.860*	0.860*	0.860*	0.860*	Tunisie
Turkey	0.880*	0.880*	0.880*	0.880*	Turquie
United Arab Emirates	0.759	0.759	0.759	0.759	Emirats arabes unis
United Kingdom	0.843*	0.843*	0.843*	0.843*	Royaume-Uni
United States	0.869	0.869	0.869	0.869	États-Unis
Venezuela	0.903	0.912	0.912	0.912	Venezuela
Unspecified origin	0.860	0.860	0.860	0.860	De source non spécifiée

Table III

SPECIFIC GRAVITIES OF PETROLEUM PRODUCTS

DENSITES MOYENNES DES PRODUITS PETROLIERS

ENERGY PETROLEUM PRODUCTS		PRODUITS PETROLIERS ENERGETIQUES
Aviation gasolene	0.730	Essence aviation
Fuel oils (undifferentiated)	0.910	Mazouts (non différenciés)
Gas-diesel oil	0.870	Gazole/carburant Diesel
Jet fuel	0.810	Carburéacteurs
Kerosene	0.810	Pétrole lampant
Liquefied petroleum gas	0.540	Gaz de pétrole liquéfié
Motor gasolene	0.740	Essence auto
Residual fuel oil	0.950	Mazout résiduel

NON-ENERGY PETROLEUM PRODUCTS		PRODUITS PETROLIERS NON ENERGETIQUES
Bitumen	1.040	Bitume
Lubricating oils	0.900	Lubrifiants
Naphthas	0.720	Naphtas
Paraffin wax	0.800	Cires de pétrole (paraffines)
Petroleum coke	1.140	Coke de pétrole
White spirit	0.810	White spirit/essences spéciales

Table IV

SELECTED CONVERSION FACTORS FOR CRUDE PETROLEUM AND PETROLEUM PRODUCTS

QUELQUES FACTEURS DE CONVERSION POUR LE PETROLE BRUT ET LES PRODUITS PETROLIERS

(To convert from metric tons into the following units, multiply by the factor in the appropriate column)

(Pour convertir en unite de volume, une quantité exprimée en tonnes métriques, multiplier celle-ci par le facteur qui figure dans la colonne correspondant à l'unité voulue)

Commodity/ Produit	Litre	U.S. Gallon	Imperial Gallon	Barrel	Barrels/ day	Cubic Metre
	Litre	Gallon E.-U.	Gallon brit.	Baril	Barils/ jour	Mètre cube
Crude petroleum (average specific gravity) - Pétrole brut (densité moyenne)	1164	308	256	7.32	0.02005	1.164
Aviation gasolene - Essence aviation	1370	362	301	8.62	0.02362	1.370
Bitumen - Bitume	962	254	212	6.05	0.01658	0.962
Condensate - Condensat	1429	378	253	7.23	0.02463	1.429
Fuel oils (undifferentiated) - Mazouts (non différenciés)	1099	290	242	6.91	0.01893	1.099
Gas-diesel oil - Gazole/carburant Diesel	1149	304	253	7.23	0.01981	1.149
Gasolenes (undifferentiated) - Essences (non différenciés)	1351	357	297	8.50	0.02329	1.351
Jet fuel - Carburéacteurs	1235	326	272	7.77	0.02129	1.235
Kerosene - Pétrole lampant	1235	326	272	7.77	0.02129	1.235
Liquefied petroleum gas - Gaz de pétrole liquéfie	1852	489	407	11.65	0.03192	1.852
Lubricants - Lubrifiants	1111	294	244	6.99	0.01915	1.111
Motor gasolene - Essence auto	1351	357	297	8.50	0.02329	1.351
Naphthas (undifferentiated) - Naphtas (non différenciés)	1389	367	306	8.74	0.02395	1.389
Natural gasolene - Essence naturelle	1590	420	350	10.00	0.02740	1.590
Paraffin wax - Cires de pétrole (paraffines)	1250	330	275	7.86	0.02153	1.250
Petroleum coke - Coke de pétrole	877	232	193	5.52	0.01512	0.877
Residual fuel oil - Mazout résiduel	1053	278	232	6.62	0.01814	1.053
White spirit - White spirit/essences spéciales	1235	326	272	7.77	0.02129	1.235

Table V

HEAT VALUES OF GASES

POUVOIRS CALORIFIQUES DES GAZ

NATURAL GAS - GAZ NATUREL
(Kilojoules/Cubic Metres) - (Kilojoules/Mètres Cubes)

Standard Heat Value	39021	Pouvoir calorifique standard
Albania	35000 (N)	Albanie
Algeria	39565 (N)	Algérie
Argentina	40337* (G)	Argentine
Australia	35658 (G)	Australie
Austria	39600 (G)	Autriche
Bangladesh	35064	Bangladesh
Belarus	34760 (N)	Bélarus
Belgium	39687* (G)	Belgique
Bolivia	37263	Bolivie
Brazil	43740	Brésil
Brunei	43000	Brunéi
Bulgaria	35152* (G)	Bulgarie
Canada	38550* (G)	Canada
Chile	37263	Chili
Colombia	34598	Colombie
Croatia	38000 (G)	Croatie
Denmark	40901 (N)	Danemark
Ecuador	48441* (G)	Équateur
Estonia	33537	Éstonie
Finland	39170 (G)	Finlande
France incl. Monaco	39205* (G)	France y comp. Monaco
Germany	33339 (G)	Allemagne
Greece	57211 (G)	Grèce
Hungary	32456 (N)	Hongrie
India	38586 (N)	Inde
Iran (Islamic Rep. of)	39356*	Iran (Rép. islamique)
Ireland	37604* (G)	Irlande
Israel	38728*	Israël
Italy and San Marino	37306 (G)	Italie y comp. S. Mrn
Japan	41023 (G)	Japon
Kazakhstan	33949 (N)	Kazakhstan
Latvia	33597	Lettonie
Lithuania	33949	Lituanie
Luxembourg	40773 (G)	Luxembourg
Mexico	44257* (G)	Mexique
Netherlands	33320 (G)	Pays-Bas

Table V (continued - suite)

HEAT VALUES OF GASES

POUVOIRS CALORIFIQUES DES GAZ

NATURAL GAS - GAZ NATUREL
(Kilojoules/Cubic Metres) - (Kilojoules/Mètres Cubes)

New Zealand	42537 (G)	Nouvelle-Zélande
Norway, Svlbd, J.Myn I	42091 (G)	Norvège, Svalbd, J. May
Pakistan	34805	Pakistan
Peru	34598	Pérou
Poland	28811 (G)	Pologne
Romania	33514 (N)	Roumanie
Russian Federation	33704 (N)	Fédération de Russie
Slovakia	32663 (N)	Slovaquie
Slovenia	35729 (G)	Slovénie
Spain	42530 (G)	Espagne
Sweden	38880 (G)	Suède
Switzerland, Liechtenst.	40319 (G)	Suisse, Liechtenstein
Thailand	37258 (N)	Thaïlande
Trinidad and Tobago	38937	Trinité-et-Tobago
Tunisia	46055	Tunisie
Turkey	34500 (N)	Turquie
Turkmenistan	33949 (N)	Turkménistan
Ukraine	33949 (N)	Ukraine
United Kingdom	39211 (G)	Royaume-Uni
United States	38304 (N)	États-Unis
Uzbekistan	33949 (N)	Ouzbékistan
Venezuela	44380 (G)	Venezuela
Yugoslavia	35588 (N)	Yougoslavie

COKE-OVEN GAS - GAZ DE COKERIE
(Kilojoules/Cubic Metres) - (Kilojoules/Mètres Cubes)

Standard Heat Value	**17585**	**Pouvoir calorifique standard**
Australia	19890*	Australie
Austria	18500* (N)	Autriche
Belgium	15002 (N)	Belgique
Brazil	18841(G)	Brésil
Bulgaria	16747*	Bulgarie
Canada	18610*	Canada
Chile	19469	Chili
Colombia	20097	Colombie
Czech Republic	15597 (N)	République tchèque
Finland	16400 (N)	Finlande
France incl. Monaco	17640* (G)	France y comp. Monaco
Germany	31736* (N)	Allemagne

Table V (continued - suite)

HEAT VALUES OF GASES

POUVOIRS CALORIFIQUES DES GAZ

COKE-OVEN GAS - GAZ DE COKERIE
(Kilojoules/Cubic Metres) - (Kilojoules/Mètres Cubes)

Hungary	16961 (N)	Hongrie
Indonesia	15072	Indonésie
Italy and San Marino	17791* (G)	Italie y comp. S. Mrn
Japan	22609 (G)	Japon
Netherlands	20290*	Pays-Bas
New Zealand	42538 (G)	Nouvelle-Zélande
Norway, Svlbd, J.Myn I	18020* (N)	Norvège, Svalbd, J. May
Poland	17650 (N)	Pologne
Portugal	20184* (G)	Portugal
Romania	17581* (G)	Roumanie
Russian Federation	16744 (G)	Fédération de Russie
Slovakia	15597 (N)	Slovaquie
South Africa Customs Union	20000*	Un. Douan. d'Afr. mérid.
Spain	18113* (G)	Espagne
Sweden	16747* (N)	Suède
Turkey	18003* (N)	Turquie
United Arab Emirates	39021*	Emirats arabes unis
United Kingdom	19665* (G)	Royaume-Uni
United States	20494 (G)	États-Unis
Yugoslavia	17372* (G)	Yougoslavie

GASWORKS GAS - GAZ D'USINES A GAZ
(Kilojoules/Cubic Metres) - (Kilojoules/Mètres Cubes)

Standard Heat Value	**17585**	**Pouvoir calorifique standard**
Algeria	16747*	Algérie
Australia	19594 (G)	Australie
Austria	27100 (N)	Autriche
Belgium	27214* (G)	Belgique
Brazil	18841 (G)	Brésil
Chile	20138	Chili
China, Hong Kong SAR	16915	Chine, Hong-Kong RAS
Cuba	18464*	Cuba
Czech Republic	14120 (N)	République tchèque
Denmark	17400* (N)	Danemark
Finland	15490 (N)	Finlande
France incl. Monaco	17640* (G)	France y comp. Monaco

Table V (continued - suite)

HEAT VALUES OF GASES

POUVOIRS CALORIFIQUES DES GAZ

GASWORKS GAS - GAZ D'USINES A GAZ
(Kilojoules/Cubic Metres) - (Kilojoules/Mètres Cubes)

Germany	16800* (N)	Allemagne
Greece	38511*	Grèce
Hungary	17765 (N)	Hongrie
India	17585	Inde
Indonesia	15072	Indonésie
Italy and San Marino	17791* (G)	Italie y comp. S. Mrn
Japan	20934 (G)	Japon
New Zealand	16747	Nouvelle-Zélande
Nigeria	39021*	Nigéria
Norway, Svlbd, J.Myn I	17600*	Norvège, Svalbd, J. May
Panama	20327*	Panama
Philippines	22316	Philippines
Poland	17910 (N)	Pologne
Portugal	18550* (G)	Portugal
Singapore	18548	Singapour
South Africa Customs Union	13420*	Un. Douan. d'Afr. mérid.
Spain	17703*	Espagne
Sri Lanka	22353	Sri Lanka
Sweden	16747* (N)	Suède
Switzerland, Liechtenst.	15900 (N)	Suisse, Liechtenstein
Tunisia	18841*	Tunisie
Turkey	14654* (N)	Turquie
United Kingdom	18940*	Royaume-Uni
Uruguay	18003 (G)	Uruguay
Yugoslavia	17713* (N)	Yougoslavie

BLAST FURNACE GAS - GAZ DE HAUT-FOURNEAU
(Kilojoules/Cubic Metres) - (Kilojoules/Mètres Cubes)

Standard Heat Value	**4000**	**Pouvoir calorifique standard**
Austria	3200 (N)	Autriche
Belgium	3521 (N)	Belgique
Colombia	3349	Colombie
Czech Republic	3697 (N)	République tchèque
Finland	3350 (N)	Finlande
France incl. Monaco	3600* (G)	France y comp. Monaco
Germany	4187*	Allemagne
Greece	3200*	Grèce
Hungary	3559 (N)	Hongrie
Italy and San Marino	3767* (G)	Italie y comp. S. Mrn
Japan	3349 (G)	Japon
Luxembourg	4186*	Luxembourg

Table V (continued - suite)

HEAT VALUES OF GASES

POUVOIRS CALORIFIQUES DES GAZ

BLAST FURNACE GAS - GAZ DE HAUT-FOURNEAU
(Kilojoules/Cubic Metres) - (Kilojoules/Mètres Cubes)

Netherlands	3052*	Pays-Bas
Poland	3920 (N)	Pologne
Portugal	2861*	Portugal
Romania	4102 (G)	Roumanie
Russian Federation	4186 (G)	Fédération de Russie
South Africa Customs Union	4777*	Un. douan. d'Afr. mérid.
Spain	3081	Espagne
Sweden	3300* (N)	Suède
Turkey	4186* (N)	Turquie
United Kingdom	3420*	Royaume-Uni
United States	3542*	États-Unis
Yugoslavia	4120* (G)	Yougoslavie

(G) = Gross heat value
(N) = Net heat value

(G) = Pouvoir calorifique supérieur
(N) = Pouvoir calorifique inférieur

TABLES

TABLEAUX

Table 1

Production, trade and consumption of commercial energy
Production, commerce et consommation d'énergie commerciale
Thousand metric tons of coal equivalent and kilograms per capita
Milliers de tonnes métriques d'équivalent houille et kilogrammes par habitant

Table Notes:
For tables 1 to 4
Data on individual energy commodities are aggregated and presented in these tables.

Production
Included in the production of commercial primary energy for **Solids** are hard coal, lignite, peat and oil shale; **Liquids** are comprised of crude petroleum, natural gas liquids, biodiesel and alcohol; **Gas** comprises natural gas and primary steam/heat; and **Electricity** is comprised of primary electricity generation from hydro, nuclear, geothermal, wind, tide, wave and solar sources.

Stocks, International Trade and Bunkers
Changes in stocks, imports and exports refer to all primary and secondary forms of commercial energy (including condensate and feedstocks); **Aviation bunkers** refer to bunkers of aviation gasolene and jet fuel; **Marine bunkers** refer to bunkers of hard coal, gas-diesel oil and residual fuel oil.

Consumption
Included in the consumption of commercial energy for **Solids** are consumption of primary forms of solid fuels, net imports and changes in stocks of secondary fuels; **Liquids** are comprised of consumption of energy petroleum products including feedstocks, natural gasolene, condensate, refinery gas and input of crude petroleum to thermal power plants; **Gases** include the consumption of natural gas, input of heat to thermal power plants, net imports and changes in stocks of gasworks and coke-oven gas; and **Electricity** is comprised of production of primary electricity and net imports of electricity.

Notes relatives aux tableaux:
Pour les tableaux 1 à 4
On trouvera dans ces tableaux les agrégats des données relatifs aux différents produits énergétiques.

Production
Sont compris dans la production d'énergie primaire commerciale: pour **les solides**, la houille, le lignite, la tourbe et le schiste bitumineux; pour **les liquides**, le pétrole brut, les liquides de gaz naturel, l'alcool et le biodiesel; pour **les gaz**, le gaz naturel et la vapeur/chaleur primaire; pour **l'électricité**, l'électricité primaire de source hydraulique, nucléaire, géothermique, éolienne, marémotrice, solaire et des vagues.

Stocks, commerce international et soutages
Les variations de stocks, importations et exportations se réfèrent à toutes les formes primaires et secondaires d'énergie commerciale (y compris le condensat et les charges d'alimentation des usines de traitement). **Les soutes avions** se rapportent aux soutages d'essence aviation et de carburéacteur. **Les soutes maritimes** se rapportent aux soutages de houille, de gazole ou carburant Diesel et de mazout résiduel.

Consommation
Sont compris dans la consommation d'énergie commerciale: pour **les solides**, la consommation de combustibles solides primaires, les importations nettes et les variations de stocks de combustibles solides secondaires; pour **les liquides**, la consommation de produits pétroliers énergétiques y compris les charges d'alimentation des usines de traitement, l'essence naturelle, le condensat et le gaz de raffinerie ainsi que le pétrole brut consommé dans les centrales thermiques pour la production d'électricité; pour **les gaz**, la consommation de gaz naturel, les importations nettes et les variations de stocks de gaz d'usines à gaz et de gaz de cokerie ainsi que la vapeur/chaleur primaire consommée dans les centrales thermiques pour la production d'électricité; pour **l'électricité**, la production d'électricité primaire et les importations nettes d'électricité.

Unallocated

An **unallocated column** has been created in tables 1-3 in order to balance out the difference between the results of the above formula for consumption and the total consumption column. This inequality occurs primarily because of the exclusion of non-energy petroleum products as well as inadequate or unavailable stock data.

Changes in Methodology

Beginning with the forty-eighth edition of this publication, the following products were added: steam/heat, alcohol and biodiesel.

- **Please refer to the Definitions Section on pages xv to xxix for the appropriate product description/ classification.**

Quantités non réparties

La colonne **quantités non réparties** introduite dans les tableaux 1 à 3 a pour objet de compenser la différence entre les résultats de la formule ci-dessus pour la consommation et les chiffres de la colonne consommation totale. Cette inégalité résulte essentiellement de l'exclusion des produits pétroliers non énergétiques et de l'absence ou de l'insuffisance des données concernant les stocks.

Modifications apportées à la méthodologie

A partir de la quarante-huitième édition de cette publication, les produits suivants ont été ajoutés : vapeur/chaleur, alcool et biodiesel.

- **Veuillez consulter la section "définitions" de la page xv à la page xxix pour une description/classification appropriée des produits.**

Figure 1: World commercial primary energy production of solids, by region, in 2006

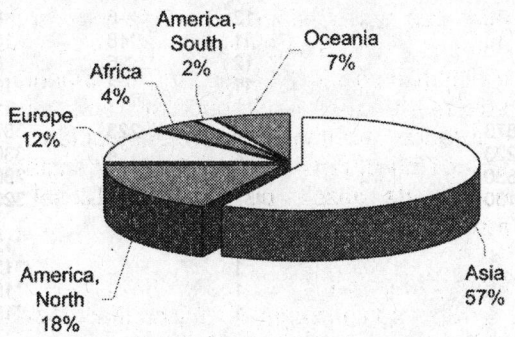

Figure 2: World commercial primary energy production of liquids, by region, in 2006

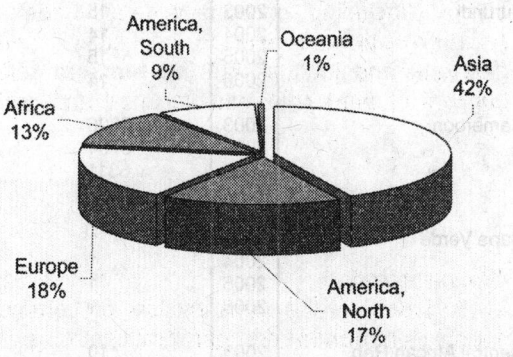

Figure 3: World commercial primary energy production of gas, by region, in 2006

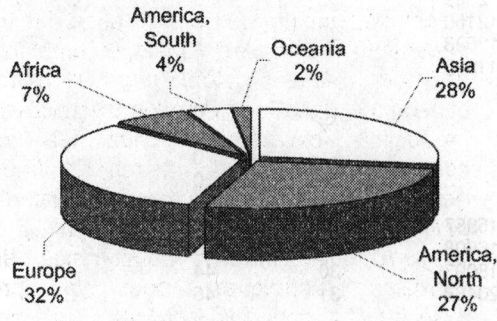

Figure 4: World commercial primary energy production of electricity, by region, in 2006

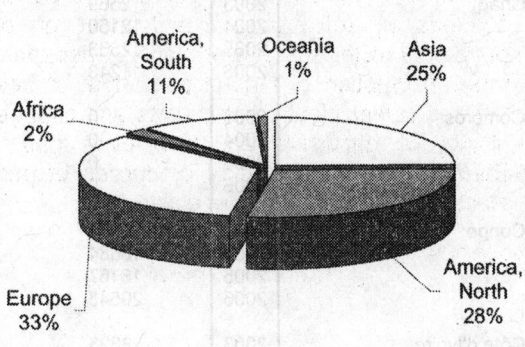

Table 1

Production, trade and consumption of commercial energy
Thousand metric tons of coal equivalent and kilograms per capita

Country or area Pays ou zone	Year Année	Primary energy production Production d'énergie primaire					Changes in stocks Variations des stocks	Imports Importations	Exports Exportations
		Total Totale	Solids Solides	Liquids Liquides	Gas Gaz	Electricity Electricité			
World	**2003**	**13143990**	**3495641**	**5425069**	**3551044**	**672236**	**7716**	**5721168**	**5652431**
	2004	**13764493**	**3786749**	**5630264**	**3639964**	**707516**	**14304**	**6119140**	**6043455**
	2005	**14228728**	**4037026**	**5722351**	**3740643**	**728708**	**2853**	**6280493**	**6265857**
	2006	**14638594**	**4254146**	**5768233**	**3866745**	**749471**	**76965**	**6438266**	**6445575**
Africa	**2003**	**1018406**	**185229**	**627281**	**193771**	**12124**	**2198**	**118625**	**682838**
	2004	**1092799**	**188273**	**685473**	**206259**	**12794**	**-1948**	**125592**	**742637**
	2005	**1172691**	**190156**	**725996**	**243704**	**12835**	**-944**	**141050**	**799854**
	2006	**1198051**	**189914**	**726167**	**268413**	**13557**	**1322**	**142896**	**837316**
Algeria	2003	262704	..	151833	110839	33	-60	1389	194764
	2004	268258	..	158485	109742	31	*219	1765	202525
	2005	285401	..	162965	122367	68	93	1597	206447
	2006	291333	..	160115	131191	27	1024	1936	216884
Angola	2003	62542	..	61547	843	152	310	1047	58990
	2004	71820	..	70632	972	215	1114	1142	67301
	2005	90265	..	89020	972	273	184	1291	86631
	2006	101710	..	100346	1037	327	874	1723	97204
Benin	2003	0	..	..	..	0	16	1618	463
	2004	0	..	..	..	0	31	1851	622
	2005	0	..	..	..	0	-21	1707	444
	2006	0	..	..	..	0	-21	2279	758
Burkina Faso	2003	12	..	..	..	12	57	592	0
	2004	12	..	..	..	12	-28	529	0
	2005	12	..	..	..	12	-9	565	0
	2006	10	..	..	..	10	-123	562	0
Burundi	2003	15	2	..	..	12	-6	80	..
	2004	14	2	..	..	11	*18	103	..
	2005	15	2	..	..	12	*-5	89	..
	2006	14	*2	..	..	11	3	105	..
Cameroon	2003	6306	..	5873	..	433	-223	3875	7881
	2004	6704	..	6223	..	482	4	3306	7827
	2005	6311	..	5830	..	481	-157	2804	7160
	2006	6637	..	6180	..	457	-14	3251	7533
Cape Verde	2003	1	..	..	..	1	..	*128	..
	2004	1	..	..	..	1	..	*137	..
	2005	1	..	..	..	1	..	*155	..
	2006	1	..	..	..	1	..	*159	..
Central African Rep.	2003	*10	..	..	..	*10	..	*150	..
	2004	*10	..	..	..	*10	..	*150	..
	2005	*10	..	..	..	*10	..	*150	..
	2006	*10	..	..	..	*10	..	*160	..
Chad	2003	2569	..	2569	..	..	..	*106	2469
	2004	12150	..	12150	..	..	..	*112	12056
	2005	12583	..	12583	..	..	..	*121	12487
	2006	11248	..	11248	..	..	..	*123	11152
Comoros	2003	0	..	..	..	0	..	*46	..
	2004	0	..	..	..	0	..	*46	..
	2005	0	..	..	..	0	..	*46	..
	2006	0	..	..	..	0	..	*47	..
Congo	2003	16031	..	15967	22	42	..	44	15536
	2004	16684	..	16608	26	49	..	115	15891
	2005	18167	..	18093	30	44	..	166	17592
	2006	20545	..	20468	31	46	..	190	20050
Côte d'Ivoire	2003	3323	..	1468	1630	225	*237	4269	3828
	2004	3894	..	1608	2071	215	-340	5167	4771
	2005	5338	..	2849	2313	176	*-44	6093	6451
	2006	6837	..	4479	2173	185	-292	5320	8158

Table 1

Production, commerce et consommation d'énergie commerciale
Milliers de tonnes métriques d'équivalent houille et kilogrammes par habitant

Bunkers Soutes		Unallocated Quantités non réparties	Consumption Consommation						Year Année	Country or area Pays ou zone
Aviation Avion	Marine Maritime		Per Capita Par habitant	Total Totale	Solids Solides	Liquids Liquides	Gas Gaz	Electricity Electricité		
154560	206364	454267	1974	12374330	3579930	4567000	3555193	672207	2003	Monde
162460	225156	460509	2043	12962439	3879739	4749475	3625636	707588	2004	
173615	240565	456740	2080	13352193	4071848	4815241	3736529	728575	2005	
176436	253820	438680	2098	13670437	4268709	4855563	3797033	749132	2006	
6470	10144	12733	501	422215	137783	174849	97284	12299	2003	Afrique
6388	8676	11175	519	451038	148051	186614	103386	12987	2004	
7179	9155	23226	534	474863	147199	191901	122750	13013	2005	
7252	8043	10254	520	476345	147627	194059	120953	13706	2006	
391	310	7343	1916	61006	1087	29347	30538	34	2003	Algérie
312	474	3896	1923	62250	748	32886	28583	33	2004	
454	472	4321	2276	74881	920	31439	42457	65	2005	
531	452	6409	2020	67633	1048	28543	38006	37	2006	
430	0	304	318	3555	..	2560	843	152	2003	Angola
489	0	369	324	3689	..	2502	972	215	2004	
408	1	360	339	3971	..	2726	972	273	2005	
486	1	461	367	4405	..	3041	1037	327	2006	
37	..	..	139	1103	..	1040	..	63	2003	Bénin
35	..	..	141	1163	..	1092	..	71	2004	
34	..	..	147	1250	..	1177	..	73	2005	
35	..	..	172	1507	..	1434	..	73	2006	
21	..	..	41	526	0	506	..	20	2003	Burkina Faso
24	..	..	42	545	0	521	..	24	2004	
30	..	..	43	557	0	529	..	28	2005	
23	..	..	49	672	0	645	..	27	2006	
6	..	..	13	95	2	74	..	19	2003	Burundi
9	..	..	12	90	2	68	..	19	2004	
10	..	..	13	98	2	75	..	21	2005	
10	..	..	13	107	*2	86	..	19	2006	
102	20	618	105	1784	..	1350	..	433	2003	Cameroun
102	22	226	105	1830	..	1349	..	482	2004	
91	17	153	104	1850	..	1370	..	481	2005	
105	61	326	103	1878	..	1422	..	457	2006	
..	*9	..	*261	*120	..	*120	..	1	2003	Cap-Vert
..	*10	..	*271	*127	..	*126	..	1	2004	
..	*14	..	*297	*142	..	*141	..	1	2005	
..	*14	..	*298	*145	..	*144	..	1	2006	
*38	..	..	*30	*122	..	*112	..	*10	2003	Rép. centrafricaine
*38	..	..	*30	*122	..	*112	..	*10	2004	
*38	..	..	*29	*122	..	*112	..	*10	2005	
*41	..	..	*30	*129	..	*119	..	*10	2006	
*27	..	100	*9	*79	..	*79	..	..	2003	Tchad
*27	..	94	*9	*85	..	*85	..	..	2004	
*28	..	96	*9	*93	..	*93	..	..	2005	
*28	..	96	*9	*94	..	*94	..	..	2006	
..	..	..	*72	*46	..	*46	..	0	2003	Comores
..	..	..	*71	*46	..	*46	..	0	2004	
..	..	..	*69	*46	..	*46	..	0	2005	
..	..	..	*68	*47	..	*47	..	0	2006	
..	..	66	137	473	..	365	22	86	2003	Congo
..	..	361	155	547	..	422	26	98	2004	
..	..	168	159	573	..	448	30	95	2005	
..	..	36	176	649	..	521	31	96	2006	
*155	129	227	171	3016	..	1324	1630	62	2003	Côte d'Ivoire
131	129	622	202	3746	..	1633	2071	42	2004	
131	108	940	201	3846	..	1528	2313	5	2005	
131	93	239	195	3827	..	1600	2173	55	2006	

Table 1

Production, trade and consumption of commercial energy
Thousand metric tons of coal equivalent and kilograms per capita

Country or area Pays ou zone	Year Année	Primary energy production Production d'énergie primaire					Changes in stocks Variations des stocks	Imports Importations	Exports Exportations
		Total Totale	Solids Solides	Liquids Liquides	Gas Gaz	Electricity Electricité			
Dem. Rep. of Congo	2003	2418	105	1547		766	..	732	1718
	2004	2423	108	1476		839	..	984	1662
	2005	2434	120	1406		908	..	985	1634
	2006	2355	124	1266		966	..	1001	1494
Djibouti	2003	..				..	..	410	
	2004	..				..	..	439	
	2005	..				..	..	454	
	2006	..				..	..	473	
Egypt	2003	100164	32	57162	41424	1546	*649	3747	16691
	2004	100604	29	54212	44747	1617	*-569	5573	15493
	2005	119046	29	53241	64155	1621	0	9941	26406
	2006	115480	22	47741	66054	1663	-127	10108	28518
Equatorial Guinea	2003	19707	..	19066	641	0	..	*79	19066
	2004	25871	..	25231	*639	0	..	*69	25231
	2005	26315	..	25676	*639	0	..	*69	25676
	2006	25131	..	24491	*639	0	..	*75	24491
Eritrea	2003	0	..	..		0	16	367	0
	2004	0	..	..		0	-36	333	0
	2005	0	..	..		0	-57	301	0
	2006	0	..	..		0	-42	218	0
Ethiopia	2003	280				280	-388	1820	
	2004	310				310	-567	1927	
	2005	350				350	-299	2149	
	2006	400				400	-312	2394	
Gabon	2003	16056	..	15794	151	111	-319	165	15290
	2004	15614	..	15337	168	110	-272	125	14787
	2005	15539	..	15271	168	100	-271	213	14672
	2006	15621	..	15337	168	116	-378	262	14804
Gambia	2003	..		..		..	..	*154	*
	2004	..		..		..	..	*156	*
	2005	..		..		..	..	*156	*
	2006	..		..		..	..	*163	*
Ghana	2003	477	..	..		477	-9	3789	470
	2004	649	..	..		649	0	3527	649
	2005	691	..	..		691	-9	3894	655
	2006	690	..	..		690	-9	4528	419
Guinea	2003	*52	..	..		*52	..	*578	
	2004	*53	..	..		*53	..	*578	
	2005	*53	..	..		*53	..	*589	
	2006	*53	..	..		*53	..	*590	
Guinea-Bissau	2003	..		..			..	*143	
	2004	..		..			..	*143	
	2005	..		..			..	*143	
	2006	..		..			..	*147	
Kenya	2003	497	..	..		497	0	4274	451
	2004	480	..	..		480	0	5238	605
	2005	481	..	..		481	69	5141	344
	2006	513	..	..		513	-287	5318	319
Liberia	2003	..		..		..	..	*271	*
	2004	..		..		..	..	293	*
	2005	..		..		..	..	338	*
	2006	..		..		..	..	*360	*
Libyan Arab Jamah.	2003	109646	..	101348	8298	..	..	0	82630
	2004	121303	..	110853	10451	..	..	0	92820
	2005	133567	..	118916	14651	..	..	19	106160
	2006	144463	..	125273	19190	..	..	15	117035

Table 1

Production, commerce et consommation d'énergie commerciale
Milliers de tonnes métriques d'équivalent houille et kilogrammes par habitant

Bunkers Soutes		Unallocated Quantités	Consumption Consommation						Year	Country or area
Aviation Avion	Marine Maritime	non réparties	Per Capita Par habitant	Total Totale	Solids Solides	Liquids Liquides	Gas Gaz	Electricity Electricité	Année	Pays ou zone
*139	3	0	24	1291	331	356	..	603	2003	Rép. dem. du Congo
173	3	0	28	1570	358	551	..	661	2004	
171	3	0	28	1611	376	546	..	688	2005	
171	3	0	28	1688	397	546	..	745	2006	
142	*103	..	212	165	..	165	..	..	2003	Djibouti
142	*107	..	241	190	..	190	..	..	2004	
149	*106	..	247	199	..	199	..	..	2005	
149	*120	..	249	204	..	204	..	..	2006	
700	3909	4782	1145	77086	561	34709	40377	1439	2003	Egypte
1017	2633	4142	1171	83381	1276	40605	39969	1532	2004	
1088	2819	8334	1261	90260	1276	43375	44084	1525	2005	
1144	1546	2828	1258	91598	1115	44765	44098	1620	2006	
..	..	0	1558	720	..	*79	641	0	2003	Guinée équatoriale
..	..	0	*1497	*708	..	*69	*639	0	2004	
..	..	0	*1463	*708	..	*69	*639	0	2005	
..	..	0	*1440	*714	..	*75	*639	0	2006	
16	..	..	80	334	..	334	..	0	2003	Erythrée
16	..	..	80	349	..	349	..	0	2004	
13	..	..	76	344	..	344	..	0	2005	
10	..	..	53	250	..	250	..	0	2006	
125	..	..	34	2363	..	2083	..	280	2003	Ethiopie
142	..	..	38	2662	..	2352	..	310	2004	
215	..	..	36	2584	..	2233	..	350	2005	
261	..	..	38	2845	..	2445	..	400	2006	
115	207	70	660	858	..	597	151	111	2003	Gabon
96	213	50	635	866	..	588	168	110	2004	
98	218	35	716	1000	..	732	168	100	2005	
92	221	139	705	1005	..	721	168	116	2006	
..	..	..	*101	*152	..	*152	..	..	2003	Gambie
..	..	..	*99	*153	..	*153	..	..	2004	
..	..	..	*96	*153	..	*153	..	..	2005	
..	..	..	*98	*160	..	*160	..	..	2006	
202	..	-60	174	3657	..	3169	..	488	2003	Ghana
165	..	-113	160	3475	..	2800	..	675	2004	
183	..	-100	174	3857	..	3144	..	713	2005	
232	..	25	198	4551	..	3877	..	675	2006	
*31	..	..	*69	*599	..	*547	..	*52	2003	Guinée
*31	..	..	*68	*601	..	*547	..	*53	2004	
*33	..	..	*68	*609	..	*556	..	*53	2005	
*33	..	..	*67	*611	..	*557	..	*53	2006	
*15	..	..	*101	*128	..	*128	..	..	2003	Guinée-Bissau
*15	..	..	*99	*128	..	*128	..	..	2004	
*15	..	..	*96	*128	..	*128	..	..	2005	
*15	..	..	*98	*132	..	*132	..	..	2006	
..	18	64	129	4229	93	3618	..	518	2003	Kenya
..	53	473	134	4587	108	3989	..	490	2004	
..	60	163	141	4985	108	4398	..	479	2005	
..	67	193	152	5539	120	4914	..	506	2006	
*4	*18	..	*71	*246	..	*246	..	..	2003	Libéria
*4	*18	..	77	269	..	269	..	..	2004	
*4	*18	..	87	313	..	313	..	..	2005	
*4	*18	..	*91	*336	..	*336	..	..	2006	
304	127	3485	3712	23094	..	15768	7326	0	2003	Jamah. arabe libyenne
307	127	3524	3819	24519	..	15625	8895	0	2004	
273	127	3551	3540	23469	..	15813	7650	6	2005	
255	127	3406	3531	23655	..	15366	8285	4	2006	

Table 1

Production, trade and consumption of commercial energy
Thousand metric tons of coal equivalent and kilograms per capita

Country or area Pays ou zone	Year Année	Primary energy production Production d'énergie primaire					Changes in stocks Variations des stocks	Imports Importations	Exports Exportations
		Total Totale	Solids Solides	Liquids Liquides	Gas Gaz	Electricity Electricité			
Madagascar	2003	75	..	..	..	75	..	*1229	*28
	2004	79	..	..	..	79	..	*1320	*28
	2005	*81	..	..	..	*81	..	*1348	*28
	2006	*83	..	..	..	*83	..	*1365	*28
Malawi	2003	207	66	..	..	141	..	387	16
	2004	226	*70	..	..	156	..	*406	*16
	2005	208	45	..	..	163	..	*413	*16
	2006	219	*55	..	..	164	..	*391	*11
Mali	2003	*29	..	..	..	*29	..	287	..
	2004	*31	..	..	..	*31	..	*300	..
	2005	*32	..	..	..	*32	..	*301	..
	2006	*33	..	..	..	*33	..	*301	..
Mauritania	2003	..	..	..	..	..	..	650	
	2004	..	..	..	..	..	..	698	
	2005	..	..	..	..	..	..	726	
	2006	..	..	..	..	..	..	714	
Mauritius	2003	14	..	..	..	14	-43	1692	
	2004	15	..	..	..	15	20	1800	
	2005	14	..	..	..	14	-22	1919	
	2006	9	..	..	..	9	-98	2009	
Morocco	2003	274	..	14	56	204	133	16012	423
	2004	306	..	16	67	223	-277	17840	1112
	2005	271	..	10	61	200	55	21064	823
	2006	324	..	16	89	219	-44	19858	463
Mozambique	2003	1376	37	..	4	1335	60	1823	1199
	2004	3235	17	..	1785	1433	-12	2032	3088
	2005	4636	3	..	3004	1629	-22	1910	4390
	2006	5444	41	..	3595	1808	28	2016	5079
Niger	2003	148	148	..	..	..	..	269	..
	2004	157	157	..	..	..	..	265	..
	2005	143	143	..	..	..	..	263	..
	2006	*144	*144	..	..	..	..	262	..
Nigeria	2003	194833	23	168520	25328	963	-566	10715	177713
	2004	214565	3	183905	29808	849	320	10972	194642
	2005	220937	8	191153	29025	752	-189	11370	193842
	2006	217500	8	178610	37934	948	-60	11070	196095
Réunion	2003	*71	..	..	..	*71	..	*1143	
	2004	*71	..	..	..	*71	..	*1159	
	2005	*71	..	..	..	*71	..	*1160	
	2006	*71	..	..	..	*71	..	*1163	
Rwanda	2003	15	..	..	0	15	..	*280	1
	2004	*16	..	..	*1	*15	..	284	1
	2005	*17	..	..	*1	*16	..	*296	*1
	2006	15	..	..	*1	14	..	*309	*1
Sao Tome and Principe	2003	*1	..	..	..	*1	..	*44	
	2004	*1	..	..	..	*1	..	*44	
	2005	*1	..	..	..	*1	..	*48	
	2006	*1	..	..	..	*1	..	*50	
Senegal	2003	56	..	..	14	42	26	2541	271
	2004	54	..	..	17	36	-60	2390	266
	2005	51	..	..	18	33	118	2788	391
	2006	46	..	..	16	30	-188	1654	206
Seychelles	2003	..	..	..	..	..	..	402	3
	2004	..	..	..	..	..	..	560	3
	2005	..	..	..	..	..	..	511	3
	2006	..	..	..	..	..	..	544	3

Table 1

Production, commerce et consommation d'énergie commerciale

Milliers de tonnes métriques d'équivalent houille et kilogrammes par habitant

Bunkers Soutes		Unallocated Quantités non réparties	Consumption Consommation						Year Année	Country or area Pays ou zone
Aviation Avion	Marine Maritime		Per Capita Par habitant	Total Totale	Solids Solides	Liquids Liquides	Gas Gaz	Electricity Electricité		
*3	*24	*204	*64	*1045	*10	*960	..	75	2003	Madagascar
*3	*24	*208	*66	*1135	*10	*1047	..	79	2004	
*3	*24	*206	*66	*1167	*10	*1076	..	*81	2005	
*3	*24	*209	*65	*1183	*10	*1090	..	*83	2006	
..	..	..	50	579	53	385	..	141	2003	Malawi
..	..	..	*52	*616	*57	*404	..	155	2004	
..	..	..	*49	*605	60	*383	..	162	2005	
..	..	..	*47	*600	*50	*386	..	163	2006	
28	..	..	26	288	..	259	..	*29	2003	Mali
30	..	..	*27	*301	..	*270	..	*31	2004	
30	..	..	*26	*303	..	*272	..	*32	2005	
*30	..	..	*25	*304	..	*272	..	*33	2006	
0	*7	..	224	643	0	633	..	9	2003	Mauritanie
0	*7	..	238	691	0	683	..	8	2004	
0	*7	..	247	719	0	703	..	16	2005	
0	*7	..	236	707	0	692	..	15	2006	
131	193	..	1178	1425	316	1095	..	14	2003	Maurice
130	209	..	1193	1456	289	1152	..	15	2004	
143	274	..	1237	1538	364	1160	..	14	2005	
147	260	..	1364	1708	484	1215	..	9	2006	
430	19	955	497	14324	4611	9280	56	378	2003	Maroc
473	*19	1410	517	15409	5159	9774	67	409	2004	
542	19	1646	605	18250	6364	10985	602	299	2005	
615	19	1422	581	17708	5541	10942	760	465	2006	
56	64	..	97	1819	0	760	4	1055	2003	Mozambique
59	61	..	107	2071	0	773	4	1294	2004	
65	4	..	109	2109	0	678	97	1333	2005	
80	4	..	115	2270	0	716	112	1441	2006	
15	..	..	34	402	148	220	..	34	2003	Niger
17	..	..	33	405	157	211	..	36	2004	
19	..	..	31	387	143	203	..	42	2005	
16	..	..	30	390	*144	203	..	44	2006	
572	898	1000	206	25932	26	15305	9639	963	2003	Nigéria
282	747	1028	221	28519	6	14792	12872	849	2004	
711	680	8678	214	28586	11	14995	12829	752	2005	
336	870	748	218	30581	11	15337	14286	948	2006	
..	*44	..	*1549	*1170	..	*1099	..	*71	2003	Réunion
..	*47	..	*1544	*1183	..	*1112	..	*71	2004	
..	*47	..	*1524	*1184	..	*1113	..	*71	2005	
..	*48	..	*1490	*1186	..	*1115	..	*71	2006	
*18	..	..	*31	*276	..	*244	0	32	2003	Rwanda
*18	..	..	31	281	..	252	*1	29	2004	
*18	..	..	*32	*294	..	*264	*1	*29	2005	
*18	..	..	*33	*305	..	*278	*1	26	2006	
..	..	..	*315	*45	..	*44	..	*1	2003	Sao Tomé-et-Principe
..	..	..	*309	*45	..	*44	..	*1	2004	
..	..	..	*333	*50	..	*48	..	*1	2005	
..	..	..	*337	*51	..	*50	..	*1	2006	
*332	16	7	191	1946	*120	1770	14	42	2003	Sénégal
362	0	37	174	1838	127	1658	17	36	2004	
360	0	13	180	1957	152	1754	18	33	2005	
357	0	-17	122	1342	167	1128	16	30	2006	
*38	*101	..	3130	259	..	262	..	-3	2003	Seychelles
*44	*147	..	4428	365	..	368	..	-3	2004	
*39	*143	..	3932	326	..	329	..	-3	2005	
*42	*151	..	4109	348	..	351	..	-3	2006	

Table 1

Production, trade and consumption of commercial energy
Thousand metric tons of coal equivalent and kilograms per capita

| Country or area
Pays ou zone | Year
Année | Primary energy production
Production d'énergie primaire | | | | | Changes in
stocks
Variations
des stocks | Imports
Importations | Exports
Exportations |
		Total Totale	Solids Solides	Liquids Liquides	Gas Gaz	Electricity Electricité			
Sierra Leone	2003	2	..	..	..	2	..	*525	24
	2004	2	..	..	..	2	..	*648	28
	2005	2	..	..	..	2	..	*656	*31
	2006	*3	..	..	..	*3	..	*635	*33
Somalia	2003	..	..	..	..	..	..	*254	*52
	2004	..	..	..	..	..	..	*263	*52
	2005	..	..	..	..	..	..	*267	*44
	2006	..	..	..	..	..	..	*266	*84
South Africa Customs Un.	2003	185921	181024	990	1713	2194	1690	36511	62544
	2004	191631	184210	2399	2633	2388	-1831	36838	58434
	2005	193077	185904	2221	2831	2121	*-19	42360	64450
	2006	192857	185785	2151	2577	2344	*5	43760	63093
St. Helena and Depend.	2003	..	..	..	..	..	..	*6	..
	2004	..	..	..	..	..	..	4	..
	2005	..	..	..	..	..	..	*5	..
	2006	..	..	..	..	..	..	*5	..
Sudan	2003	19071	..	18929	..	143	193	500	14943
	2004	21558	..	21429	..	130	166	550	16885
	2005	21938	..	21786	..	152	-244	448	17162
	2006	23811	..	23643	..	168	1295	769	17832
Togo	2003	15	..	..	..	15	3	615	..
	2004	10	..	..	..	10	-2	600	..
	2005	9	..	..	..	9	-25	563	..
	2006	11	..	..	..	11	-65	444	..
Tunisia	2003	7489	..	4655	2809	24	317	7976	5046
	2004	7895	..	4908	2962	24	56	8109	5549
	2005	7998	..	4977	2998	23	-161	8172	5647
	2006	8040	..	4804	3221	16	85	8251	5314
Uganda	2003	221	..	..	..	221	..	*697	*20
	2004	238	..	..	..	238	..	740	*21
	2005	225	..	..	..	225	..	947	*20
	2006	152	..	..	..	152	..	1121	6
United Rep.Tanzania	2003	368	55	..	0	313	..	1609	..
	2004	524	65	..	170	289	..	1727	..
	2005	763	75	..	470	218	..	1848	..
	2006	755	80	..	498	176	..	1951	..
Western Sahara	2003	..	..	..	..	..	..	*122	..
	2004	..	..	..	..	..	..	*122	..
	2005	..	..	..	..	..	..	*122	..
	2006	..	..	..	..	..	..	*122	..
Zambia	2003	1201	186	..	..	1014	80	895	77
	2004	1236	196	..	..	1039	79	939	49
	2005	1297	206	..	..	1091	85	988	53
	2006	1352	206	..	..	1146	73	1029	61
Zimbabwe	2003	4208	3550	..	..	658	26	1567	206
	2004	4093	3415	..	..	678	17	1174	206
	2005	4338	3621	..	..	717	6	1382	184
	2006	4129	3447	..	..	682	-5	1327	184
America, North	**2003**	**2903675**	**687690**	**980749**	**1039882**	**195354**	**-9920**	**1285819**	**654821**
	2004	**2926911**	**723632**	**977409**	**1024726**	**201145**	**1289**	**1368696**	**678973**
	2005	**2904270**	**736056**	**949486**	**1013541**	**205187**	**-5533**	**1413688**	**680061**
	2006	**2956255**	**748817**	**952218**	**1045693**	**209526**	**43342**	**1414280**	**701349**
Anguilla	2003	..	..	..	..	..	..	19	..
	2004	..	..	..	..	..	..	20	..
	2005	..	..	..	..	..	..	24	..
	2006	..	..	..	..	..	..	25	..

Table 1

Production, commerce et consommation d'énergie commerciale
Milliers de tonnes métriques d'équivalent houille et kilogrammes par habitant

Bunkers Soutes		Unallocated Quantités	Consumption Consommation						Year	Country or area
Aviation Avion	Marine Maritime	non réparties	Per Capita Par habitant	Total Totale	Solids Solides	Liquids Liquides	Gas Gaz	Electricity Electricité	Année	Pays ou zone
*38	*126	*98	*43	*241	..	*239	..	2	2003	Sierra Leone
38	*130	*134	*56	*319	..	*317	..	2	2004	
*38	*131	*153	*52	*305	..	*303	..	2	2005	
*41	*124	*144	*49	*295	..	*292	..	*3	2006	
*74	*29	*-145	*32	*246	..	*246	..	..	2003	Somalie
*74	*29	*-136	*31	*246	..	*246	..	..	2004	
*74	*30	*-136	*31	*255	..	*255	..	..	2005	
*74	*30	*-178	*30	*255	..	*255	..	..	2006	
1266	3715	-6727	3133	159945	126869	29042	1713	2320	2003	Un.douan.d'Afr.mérid
1115	3415	-5603	3251	172939	136329	29729	4414	2467	2004	
1095	3782	-5881	3212	172012	133714	30177	5766	2355	2005	
1134	3720	-6053	3225	174719	134993	31252	6060	2414	2006	
..	..	..	*797	*6	..	*6	..	..	2003	St-Hélène et dépend
..	..	..	593	4	..	4	..	..	2004	
..	..	..	*648	*5	..	*5	..	..	2005	
..	..	..	*644	*5	..	*5	..	..	2006	
195	12	133	123	4097	..	3955	..	143	2003	Soudan
203	12	303	132	4540	..	4410	..	130	2004	
287	12	268	138	4901	..	4749	..	152	2005	
323	12	-482	154	5601	..	5433	..	168	2006	
38	10	..	116	578	..	507	..	71	2003	Togo
57	7	..	107	546	..	476	..	70	2004	
71	4	..	98	522	..	450	..	72	2005	
50	3	..	87	467	..	394	..	73	2006	
..	0	151	1011	9951	23	5574	4331	22	2003	Tunisie
..	0	90	1038	10311	0	5772	4518	21	2004	
..	0	193	1046	10492	0	5820	4653	19	2005	
..	13	236	1051	10645	0	5845	4783	17	2006	
..	..	..	*35	*898	..	*697	..	200	2003	Ouganda
..	..	..	35	957	..	740	..	217	2004	
..	..	..	41	1152	..	947	..	205	2005	
..	..	..	43	1268	..	1121	..	146	2006	
106	33	..	51	1838	55	1459	0	325	2003	Rép. Unie de Tanzanie
113	33	..	58	2105	65	1567	170	303	2004	
122	33	..	66	2456	75	1676	470	235	2005	
130	33	..	66	2544	80	1774	498	191	2006	
*9	..	..	*430	*113	..	*113	..	..	2003	Sahara occidental
*9	..	..	*421	*113	..	*113	..	..	2004	
*9	..	..	*415	*113	..	*113	..	..	2005	
*9	..	..	*409	*113	..	*113	..	..	2006	
69	..	59	168	1810	121	737	..	952	2003	Zambie
72	..	62	172	1911	129	772	..	1011	2004	
75	..	65	175	2005	136	808	..	1061	2005	
80	..	65	178	2102	144	843	..	1115	2006	
52	..	..	424	5491	3357	1085	..	1050	2003	Zimbabwe
12	..	..	386	5032	3231	872	..	929	2004	
12	..	..	421	5519	3488	948	..	1082	2005	
12	..	..	398	5265	3321	914	..	1030	2006	
29398	34054	51150	6834	3430492	698092	1499940	1037257	195204	2003	Amérique du Nord
29948	41902	48516	6892	3495518	718209	1550067	1026114	201128	2004	
30872	43441	32643	6906	3536992	725222	1579879	1026741	205151	2005	
29256	46271	32040	6811	3518759	714687	1568648	1026071	209354	2006	
..	..	..	1503	19	..	19	..	..	2003	Anguilla
..	..	..	1561	20	..	20	..	..	2004	
..	..	..	1786	24	..	24	..	..	2005	
..	..	..	1774	25	..	25	..	..	2006	

Table 1

Production, trade and consumption of commercial energy
Thousand metric tons of coal equivalent and kilograms per capita

| Country or area Pays ou zone | Year Année | Primary energy production Production d'énergie primaire | | | | | Changes in stocks Variations des stocks | Imports Importations | Exports Exportations |
		Total Totale	Solids Solides	Liquids Liquides	Gas Gaz	Electricity Electricité			
Antigua and Barbuda	2003	..	..	..	..	..	..	*271	*1:
	2004	..	..	..	..	..	..	*280	*1:
	2005	..	..	..	..	..	..	*285	*1:
	2006	..	..	..	..	..	..	*293	*1!
Aruba	2003	*171	..	*171	..	..	..	*15294	1499:
	2004	*171	..	*171	..	..	..	*15294	1499:
	2005	*171	..	*171	..	..	..	15304	1499:
	2006	*171	..	*171	..	..	..	*15304	*1499:
Bahamas	2003	..	..	..	..	..	*72	*4518	*315
	2004	..	..	..	..	..	0	*4585	*321
	2005	..	..	..	..	..	0	*4665	*322
	2006	..	..	..	..	..	0	*4676	*322:
Barbados	2003	142	..	107	35	..	..	462	10(
	2004	127	..	94	33	..	..	501	9:
	2005	129	..	94	35	..	..	521	9:
	2006	110	..	74	36	..	..	531	7:
Belize	2003	*13	..	..	..	*13	..	*429	
	2004	*13	..	..	..	*13	..	*439	
	2005	*13	..	..	..	*13	..	*456	
	2006	*13	..	..	..	*13	..	*460	
Bermuda	2003	..	..	..	..	..	..	*280	
	2004	..	..	..	..	..	..	*290	
	2005	..	..	..	..	..	..	*299	
	2006	..	..	..	..	..	..	*301	
British Virgin Islands	2003	..	..	..	..	..	..	*37	
	2004	..	..	..	..	..	..	*41	
	2005	..	..	..	..	..	..	*43	
	2006	..	..	..	..	..	..	*47	
Canada	2003	537847	43414	203719	239943	50771	-6199	108769	30668(
	2004	550164	46603	210973	239415	53173	-10451	111863	31895
	2005	554684	45582	208328	244616	56158	-8475	111758	31876:
	2006	567350	46749	218698	245887	56016	-2201	106036	32456
Cayman Islands	2003	..	..	..	..	..	..	*257	
	2004	..	..	..	..	..	..	*266	
	2005	..	..	..	..	..	..	*271	
	2006	..	..	..	..	..	..	*278	
Costa Rica	2003	908	..	..	..	908	-140	2871	6:
	2004	977	..	..	..	977	21	3087	12(
	2005	993	..	..	..	993	-23	3008	1:
	2006	994	..	..	..	994	25	3366	4:
Cuba	2003	6193	..	5301	876	16	43	6301	
	2004	5640	..	4691	937	11	*33	6320	
	2005	5163	..	4165	989	8	574	7592	
	2006	5654	..	4198	1445	12	-24	8817	
Dominica	2003	4	..	..	..	4	..	55	
	2004	4	..	..	..	4	..	52	
	2005	3	..	..	..	3	..	*55	
	2006	*4	..	..	..	*4	..	*56	
Dominican Republic	2003	147	..	..	..	147	0	9396	
	2004	194	..	..	..	194	52	8881	
	2005	233	..	..	..	233	-7	8891	
	2006	173	..	..	..	173	-27	9035	
El Salvador	2003	298	..	..	..	298	62	3200	26
	2004	295	..	..	..	295	55	3263	39
	2005	334	..	..	..	334	93	3165	17
	2006	381	..	..	..	381	76	3081	11

Table 1

Production, commerce et consommation d'énergie commerciale
Milliers de tonnes métriques d'équivalent houille et kilogrammes par habitant

Bunkers Soutes		Unallocated Quantités non réparties	Consumption Consommation						Year Année	Country or area Pays ou zone
Aviation Avion	Marine Maritime		Per Capita Par habitant	Total Totale	Solids Solides	Liquids Liquides	Gas Gaz	Electricity Electricité		
*69	*4	..	*2326	*186	..	*186	..	..	2003	Antigua-et-Barbuda
*71	*4	..	*2387	*193	..	*193	..	..	2004	
*71	*4	..	*2370	*196	..	*196	..	..	2005	
*71	*4	..	*2422	*204	..	*204	..	..	2006	
*108	..	*7	3766	358	..	358	..	..	2003	Aruba
*108	..	*7	3666	358	..	358	..	..	2004	
*111	..	7	3631	365	..	365	..	..	2005	
*111	..	*7	*3553	*365	..	*365	..	..	2006	
*62	*348	..	*2772	*884	*3	*881	..	..	2003	Bahamas
*63	*363	..	*3167	*949	*3	*946	..	..	2004	
*66	*380	..	*3080	*995	*3	*992	..	..	2005	
*68	*377	..	*3086	*1009	*4	*1005	..	..	2006	
..	..	0	1835	499	..	464	35	..	2003	Barbade
..	..	0	1965	535	..	502	33	..	2004	
..	..	0	2041	557	..	522	35	..	2005	
..	..	0	2073	568	..	532	36	..	2006	
*31	*17	..	*1437	*393	..	*377	..	*16	2003	Belize
*32	*17	..	*1423	*402	..	*386	..	*16	2004	
*34	*19	..	*1427	*416	..	*399	..	*17	2005	
*34	*19	..	*1381	*420	..	*404	..	*16	2006	
*24	*4	..	*3993	*252	..	*252	..	..	2003	Bermudes
*25	*4	..	*4119	*261	..	*261	..	..	2004	
*25	*4	..	*4235	*269	..	*269	..	..	2005	
*28	*4	..	*4220	*269	..	*269	..	..	2006	
..	..	..	*1725	*37	..	*37	..	..	2003	Iles Vierges britanniques
..	..	..	*1899	*41	..	*41	..	..	2004	
..	..	..	*1939	*43	..	*43	..	..	2005	
..	..	..	*2092	*47	..	*47	..	..	2006	
998	724	3508	10762	340905	37549	126866	126553	49937	2003	Canada
1265	881	7741	10740	343636	36699	131200	123850	51888	2004	
1192	864	7583	10724	346518	35916	129349	128024	53229	2005	
1179	784	5724	10516	343339	35247	128251	126174	53668	2006	
*31	..	..	*5198	*227	..	*227	..	..	2003	Iles Caïmanes
*32	..	..	*5284	*234	..	*234	..	..	2004	
*32	..	..	*4925	*238	..	*238	..	..	2005	
*34	..	..	*4692	*244	..	*244	..	..	2006	
..	..	194	894	3656	143	2614	..	899	2003	Costa Rica
..	..	127	907	3790	118	2723	..	948	2004	
..	..	80	921	3930	86	2850	..	994	2005	
..	..	38	976	4249	117	3128	..	1005	2006	
316	95	1171	961	10869	26	9952	876	16	2003	Cuba
319	102	502	970	11003	26	10028	937	11	2004	
321	104	83	1038	11671	33	10641	989	8	2005	
*302	*78	1614	1112	12500	*29	11014	1445	12	2006	
..	..	..	831	58	..	55	..	4	2003	Dominique
..	..	..	797	56	..	52	..	4	2004	
..	..	..	*841	*58	..	*55	..	3	2005	
..	..	..	*877	*60	..	*56	..	*4	2006	
131	..	900	951	8512	1057	7161	147	147	2003	Rép. dominicaine
144	..	275	947	8605	777	7455	179	194	2004	
143	..	223	950	8765	476	7694	362	233	2005	
142	..	77	964	9016	799	7603	441	173	2006	
100	..	45	455	3022	1	2683	..	338	2003	El Salvador
108	..	-40	451	3044	1	2702	..	342	2004	
112	..	213	423	2907	2	2536	..	369	2005	
108	..	68	443	3100	1	2718	..	381	2006	

Table 1

Production, trade and consumption of commercial energy
Thousand metric tons of coal equivalent and kilograms per capita

Country or area Pays ou zone	Year Année	Primary energy production Production d'énergie primaire					Changes in stocks Variations des stocks	Imports Importations	Exports Exportations
		Total Totale	Solids Solides	Liquids Liquides	Gas Gaz	Electricity Electricité			
Greenland	2003	..	..	..	..	..	..	*279	*10
	2004	..	..	..	..	..	..	*281	*10
	2005	..	..	..	..	..	..	*285	*10
	2006	..	..	..	..	..	..	*291	*10
Grenada	2003	..	..	..	..	..	..	119	..
	2004	..	..	..	..	..	..	118	..
	2005	..	..	..	..	..	..	123	..
	2006	..	..	..	..	..	..	126	..
Guadeloupe	2003	..	..	..	..	..	..	*1060	..
	2004	..	..	..	..	..	..	*1068	..
	2005	..	..	..	..	..	..	*1103	..
	2006	..	..	..	..	..	..	*1116	..
Guatemala	2003	2049	..	1745	..	304	0	4789	1646
	2004	1726	..	1427	..	299	36	5027	1364
	2005	1750	..	1300	..	450	241	5312	1208
	2006	1667	..	1169	..	498	-300	4966	1314
Haiti	2003	31	..	..	..	31	..	768	..
	2004	32	..	..	..	32	..	802	..
	2005	33	..	..	..	33	..	806	..
	2006	33	..	..	..	33	..	829	..
Honduras	2003	267	..	..	..	267	347	3149	26
	2004	288	..	..	..	288	7	3254	39
	2005	211	..	..	..	211	25	3391	36
	2006	238	..	..	..	238	8	3557	54
Jamaica	2003	18	..	..	..	18	50	5431	185
	2004	21	..	..	..	21	16	5311	176
	2005	19	..	..	..	19	37	4902	0
	2006	20	..	..	..	20	-16	5887	0
Martinique	2003	..	..	..	..	..	..	1093	*321
	2004	..	..	..	..	..	..	1133	*321
	2005	..	..	..	..	..	..	1163	*321
	2006	..	..	..	..	..	..	1199	*321
Mexico	2003	334039	4205	271430	53895	4509	-1507	32179	156271
	2004	339872	4348	274141	56343	5040	2347	35063	156058
	2005	337727	4702	268811	58578	5636	636	38432	149005
	2006	337776	5022	262517	64339	5898	888	43635	148734
Montserrat	2003	..	..	..	..	..	..	*35	.
	2004	..	..	..	..	..	..	*35	.
	2005	..	..	..	..	..	..	*35	.
	2006	..	..	..	..	..	..	*35	.
Netherlands Antilles	2003	..	..	..	..	..	..	18263	10976
	2004	..	..	..	..	..	..	19644	11644
	2005	..	..	..	..	..	..	21049	13365
	2006	..	..	..	..	..	..	20241	12400
Nicaragua	2003	70	..	..	..	70	59	1887	7
	2004	71	..	..	..	71	-60	1837	7
	2005	87	..	..	..	87	44	1881	8
	2006	84	..	..	..	84	20	1974	20
Panama	2003	355	..	..	..	355	-28	2934	298
	2004	479	..	..	..	479	-266	2529	31
	2005	476	..	..	..	476	0	2912	323
	2006	479	..	..	..	479	0	3126	327
Puerto Rico	2003	32	..	..	..	32	..	980	..
	2004	17	..	..	..	17	..	905	..
	2005	18	..	..	..	18	..	905	..
	2006	*18	..	..	..	*18	..	905	..

Table 1

Production, commerce et consommation d'énergie commerciale
Milliers de tonnes métriques d'équivalent houille et kilogrammes par habitant

Bunkers Soutes		Unallocated Quantités non réparties	Consumption Consommation						Year Année	Country or area Pays ou zone
Aviation Avion	Marine Maritime		Per Capita Par habitant	Total Totale	Solids Solides	Liquids Liquides	Gas Gaz	Electricity Electricité		
*12	..	..	*4565	*257	..	*257	..	..	2003	Groënland
*12	..	..	*4591	*259	..	*259	..	..	2004	
*12	..	..	*4669	*263	..	*263	..	..	2005	
*13	..	..	*4748	*268	..	*268	..	..	2006	
*12	..	..	1021	107	..	107	..	..	2003	Grenade
*12	..	..	1009	106	..	106	..	..	2004	
*10	..	..	1070	112	..	112	..	..	2005	
*10	..	..	1092	116	..	116	..	..	2006	
*148	..	..	*2078	*912	..	*912	..	..	2003	Guadeloupe
*148	..	..	*2070	*920	..	*920	..	..	2004	
*154	..	..	*2131	*949	..	*949	..	..	2005	
*157	..	..	*2095	*960	..	*960	..	..	2006	
59	174	151	398	4808	369	4183	..	255	2003	Guatemala
63	174	119	403	4996	416	4333	..	247	2004	
55	174	108	415	5275	408	4456	..	411	2005	
55	174	152	403	5240	428	4324	..	488	2006	
39	..	..	91	761	..	729	..	31	2003	Haïti
35	..	..	95	799	..	767	..	32	2004	
34	..	..	95	805	..	773	..	33	2005	
35	..	..	96	826	..	793	..	33	2006	
37	..	..	438	3006	169	2529	..	308	2003	Honduras
41	..	..	492	3455	174	2949	..	332	2004	
40	..	..	486	3501	183	3100	..	218	2005	
43	..	..	501	3690	190	3259	..	241	2006	
279	43	35	1828	4858	85	4755	..	18	2003	Jamaïque
*265	36	84	1776	4753	66	4667	..	21	2004	
261	43	10	1724	4570	60	4491	..	19	2005	
338	43	17	2075	5525	32	5473	..	20	2006	
*4	*63	*-151	*2190	*855	..	*855	..	..	2003	Martinique
*6	*65	*-139	*2235	*880	..	*880	..	..	2004	
*6	*65	*-114	*2228	*886	..	*886	..	..	2005	
*6	*65	*-89	*2240	*896	..	*896	..	..	2006	
3704	1164	10002	1927	196584	8054	117494	66633	4403	2003	Mexique
3558	1106	7592	1983	204274	7243	122724	69386	4922	2004	
3687	1254	10047	2035	211530	8668	127206	70168	5488	2005	
3946	1258	7703	2087	218881	8750	127231	77098	5802	2006	
..	*1	..	*3685	*33	..	*33	..	..	2003	Montserrat
..	*1	..	*3586	*33	..	*33	..	..	2004	
..	*1	..	*3549	*33	..	*33	..	..	2005	
..	*1	..	*3589	*34	..	*34	..	..	2006	
103	2439	2479	12681	2266	..	2266	..	..	2003	Antilles néerlandaises
105	2442	2173	17912	3280	..	3280	..	..	2004	
106	2446	3286	9961	1846	..	1846	..	..	2005	
108	2452	3561	9077	1720	..	1720	..	..	2006	
..	..	50	346	1841	..	1772	..	69	2003	Nicaragua
..	..	43	356	1917	..	1846	..	71	2004	
..	..	50	342	1866	..	1777	..	89	2005	
..	..	68	352	1944	..	1854	..	90	2006	
3	..	0	968	3016	0	2683	..	333	2003	Panama
0	..	0	933	2959	2	2494	..	463	2004	
0	..	0	950	3066	2	2594	..	470	2005	
0	..	0	998	3279	2	2803	..	473	2006	
..	..	..	261	1012	..	..	980	32	2003	Porto Rico
..	..	..	237	922	..	..	905	17	2004	
..	..	..	236	923	..	..	905	18	2005	
..	..	..	235	923	..	..	905	*18	2006	

Table 1

Production, trade and consumption of commercial energy
Thousand metric tons of coal equivalent and kilograms per capita

Country or area Pays ou zone	Year Année	Primary energy production Production d'énergie primaire					Changes in stocks Variations des stocks	Imports Importations	Exports Exportations
		Total Totale	Solids Solides	Liquids Liquides	Gas Gaz	Electricity Electricité			
St. Kitts-Nevis	2003	..		..	..	..	..	*105	..
	2004	..		..	..	..	..	*108	..
	2005	..		..	..	..	..	*112	..
	2006	..		..	..	..	..	*112	..
St. Lucia	2003	..		..	..	..	..	*172	..
	2004	..		..	..	..	..	*182	..
	2005	..		..	..	..	..	*188	..
	2006	..		..	..	..	..	*192	..
St. Pierre-Miquelon	2003	..		..	..	..	..	*39	..
	2004	..		..	..	..	..	*38	..
	2005	..		..	..	..	..	*39	..
	2006	..		..	..	..	..	*39	..
St. Vincent-Grenadines	2003	3		..	..	3	..	*91	..
	2004	3		..	..	3	..	*91	..
	2005	*3		..	..	*3	..	*91	..
	2006	*4		..	..	*4	..	*94	..
Trinidad and Tobago	2003	44549	..	11391	33157	..	463	6717	32054
	2004	45496	..	10550	34946	..	447	4928	30689
	2005	48477	..	12063	36414	..	111	6538	34308
	2006	56977	..	11752	45226	..	-611	6767	41866
United States	2003	1976538	640071	486884	711976	137607	-3143	1053569	127746
	2004	1981321	672681	475361	693051	140228	9049	1131162	140571
	2005	1953747	685772	454553	672909	140512	1211	1168086	144206
	2006	1984108	697046	453639	688762	144661	45504	1166878	153274
America, South	**2003**	**744163**	**56857**	**489654**	**127760**	**69891**	**7293**	**114076**	**341351**
	2004	**761911**	**60283**	**495388**	**134168**	**72072**	**-1652**	**129842**	**376475**
	2005	**797152**	**66600**	**515608**	**138875**	**76069**	**-215**	**126794**	**385202**
	2006	**822742**	**72829**	**523532**	**145820**	**80562**	**-7024**	**130411**	**388214**
Argentina	2003	126120	75	64168	56781	5096	82	2576	36103
	2004	125138	43	61911	58459	4725	-164	4419	31721
	2005	122033	21	59445	57504	5062	210	6552	28689
	2006	126341	360	60119	60221	5640	-221	5062	23454
Bolivia	2003	11828	..	2826	8726	276	*-91	469	6139
	2004	15636	..	3238	12134	264	-729	276	11290
	2005	18886	..	3486	15097	302	-675	365	14702
	2006	20216	..	3791	16159	265	-1322	537	15374
Brazil	2003	179895	2949	124202	13564	39181	935	63684	29695
	2004	182668	3431	124074	14332	40831	-1108	73720	32028
	2005	198605	3970	137332	14641	42662	-322	65973	33290
	2006	208668	3732	145563	14838	44535	-606	68456	42054
Chile	2003	6377	559	528	2514	2776	214	28462	2282
	2004	5627	182	525	2307	2612	144	31304	2108
	2005	7035	528	489	2807	3211	579	32280	2313
	2006	7751	384	472	2688	4207	1048	33703	2774
Colombia	2003	99734	46452	40038	8795	4449	880	477	64848
	2004	102286	49857	38243	9259	4927	11	456	69068
	2005	107034	54845	37573	9715	4901	510	1354	72375
	2006	115582	60911	38431	10977	5264	-1891	983	79525
Ecuador	2003	32148	..	30712	554	882	1619	3024	21750
	2004	41004	..	39237	857	910	435	3011	29050
	2005	39762	..	38009	696	1057	140	3976	27999
	2006	40533	..	38303	1136	1095	-361	4628	2958
Falkland Is. (Malvinas)	2003	*4	*4	..	..	..	..	*17	
	2004	*4	*4	..	..	..	..	*17	
	2005	*4	*4	..	..	..	..	*19	
	2006	*4	*4	..	..	..	..	*19	

Table 1

Production, commerce et consommation d'énergie commerciale

Milliers de tonnes métriques d'équivalent houille et kilogrammes par habitant

Bunkers Soutes		Unallocated Quantités non réparties	Consumption Consommation						Year Année	Country or area Pays ou zone
Aviation Avion	Marine Maritime		Per Capita Par habitant	Total Totale	Solids Solides	Liquids Liquides	Gas Gaz	Electricity Electricité		
..	..	..	*2362	*105	..	*105		..	2003	St-Kitts-Nevis
..	..	..	*2455	*108	..	*108		..	2004	
..	..	..	*2615	*112	..	*112	..	..	2005	
..	..	..	*2615	*112	..	*112	..	..	2006	
..	*7	..	*1028	*165	..	*165	..		2003	St-Lucie
..	*7	..	*1076	*175	..	*175	..		2004	
..	*8	..	*1089	*179	..	*179	..	..	2005	
..	*8	..	*1101	*184	..	*184	..	..	2006	
..	*9	..	*4379	*31	..	*31	..	..	2003	St-Pierre-Miquelon
..	*9	..	*4171	*29	..	*29	..	..	2004	
..	*9	..	*4371	*31	..	*31	..	..	2005	
..	*9	..	*4363	*31	..	*31	..	..	2006	
..	..	..	*894	*94	..	*91	..	3	2003	St. Vincent-Grenadines
..	..	..	*906	*95	..	*91	..	3	2004	
..	..	..	*913	*95	..	*91	..	*3	2005	
..	..	..	*946	*98	..	*94	..	*4	2006	
12	1062	783	12851	16899	..	1048	15851	..	2003	Trinité-et-Tobago
9	1283	408	13340	17595	..	951	16644	..	2004	
85	377	1345	14196	18795	..	1410	17385	..	2005	
108	*357	644	16106	21389	..	1874	19515	..	2006	
23118	27897	31976	9706	2823005	650636	1207792	826181	138396	2003	Etats-Unis
23527	35408	29625	9791	2874834	672684	1246353	814180	141618	2004	
24314	37689	9722	9801	2905202	679386	1273395	808873	143549	2005	
22362	40636	12455	9641	2877228	669088	1260758	800458	146924	2006	
3860	**8674**	**43146**	**1253**	**453816**	**28999**	**227505**	**127633**	**69679**	**2003**	**Amérique du Sud**
4887	**9310**	**24347**	**1302**	**478172**	**30045**	**241747**	**134296**	**72084**	**2004**	
4859	**11039**	**25346**	**1337**	**497548**	**31109**	**251559**	**138628**	**76252**	**2005**	
5529	**10443**	**28030**	**1399**	**527672**	**31048**	**269655**	**146141**	**80828**	**2006**	
..	840	6965	2238	84743	750	30370	47908	5714	2003	Argentine
..	774	7210	2356	90056	828	34246	49831	5151	2004	
..	993	5669	2411	93065	1282	35269	50976	5538	2005	
..	1059	7213	2565	99943	1075	38821	54117	5930	2006	
..	..	506	637	5745	..	2467	3001	277	2003	Bolivie
..	..	574	518	4780	..	2314	2201	265	2004	
..	..	803	469	4423	..	2853	1268	302	2005	
..	..	1464	544	5239	..	3135	1839	266	2006	
1571	4598	9837	1100	196837	19727	113122	20244	43744	2003	Brésil
1557	4782	9256	1155	209643	20518	118684	25017	45424	2004	
1571	4996	9203	1171	215668	19891	121789	26531	47458	2005	
1816	4848	8723	1178	219989	19685	122939	27773	49591	2006	
777	1259	1177	1829	29132	3493	12396	10227	3016	2003	Chili
859	1374	1372	1930	31076	4696	13357	10177	2846	2004	
914	1780	1160	1999	32570	4733	13461	10900	3476	2005	
976	2005	-40	2111	34693	5640	14212	10353	4487	2006	
842	356	2639	688	30648	3923	13619	8795	4312	2003	Colombie
839	564	1413	681	30847	2772	14090	9259	4726	2004	
881	592	1936	697	32094	3857	13835	9715	4687	2005	
947	668	3654	720	33663	3525	14117	10977	5044	2006	
..	368	928	818	10502	..	8929	554	1020	2003	Equateur
..	323	3653	810	10555	..	8586	857	1112	2004	
..	960	1367	1005	13276	..	11313	696	1267	2005	
..	*425	1026	1081	14488	..	12065	1136	1288	2006	
..	..	..	*7303	*21	*4	*17	..	..	2003	Iles Falkland (Malvinas)
..	..	..	*7278	*21	*4	*17	..	..	2004	
..	..	..	*7643	*23	*4	*19	..	..	2005	
..	..	..	*7630	*23	*4	*19	..	..	2006	

Table 1

Production, trade and consumption of commercial energy
Thousand metric tons of coal equivalent and kilograms per capita

| Country or area Pays ou zone | Year Année | Primary energy production Production d'énergie primaire | | | | | Changes in stocks Variations des stocks | Imports Importations | Exports Exportations |
		Total Totale	Solids Solides	Liquids Liquides	Gas Gaz	Electricity Electricité			
French Guiana	2003	..	..	..	..	..	..	*410	..
	2004	..	..	..	..	..	..	*410	..
	2005	..	..	..	..	..	..	*410	..
	2006	..	..	..	..	..	..	*426	..
Guyana	2003	..	..	..	..	..	..	725	..
	2004	..	..	..	..	..	..	702	..
	2005	..	..	..	..	..	..	725	..
	2006	..	..	..	..	..	..	733	..
Paraguay	2003	6359	..	1	..	6358	-101	1752	5549
	2004	6378	..	0	..	6378	-17	1846	5527
	2005	6290	..	6	..	6284	-37	1684	5378
	2006	6612	..	7	..	6605	-18	1773	5613
Peru	2003	10438	16	7265	880	2277	1261	9197	4847
	2004	10839	22	7289	1376	2153	51	9346	4178
	2005	12495	42	7680	2320	2452	-135	9357	4932
	2006	15257	105	9858	2655	2639	1686	9473	4770
Suriname	2003	933	..	840	..	93	..	383	184
	2004	969	..	874	..	95	..	388	202
	2005	1012	..	910	..	102	..	406	211
	2006	1044	..	937	..	107	..	415	218
Uruguay	2003	1048	..	..	..	1048	188	2900	368
	2004	587	..	..	..	587	112	3947	505
	2005	821	..	..	..	821	-184	3694	634
	2006	442	..	..	..	442	56	4203	341
Venezuela(Bolivar. Rep.)	2003	269279	6803	219073	35947	7456	2305	..	169581
	2004	270775	6744	219996	35445	8589	-387	..	190800
	2005	283176	7191	230675	36094	9216	-302	..	194683
	2006	280294	7334	226052	37145	9763	-5394	..	184506
Asia	**2003**	**5045736**	**1781001**	**2232249**	**887567**	**144920**	**-3805**	**1977647**	**2082740**
	2004	**5475260**	**2027049**	**2342230**	**944099**	**161883**	**1284**	**2185839**	**2236472**
	2005	**5849340**	**2240887**	**2422349**	**1012139**	**173966**	**-9040**	**2226416**	**2357626**
	2006	**6161352**	**2442400**	**2469185**	**1065310**	**184455**	**1414**	**2324214**	**2469179**
Afghanistan	2003	123	35	..	8	79	..	*234	..
	2004	109	34	..	4	71	..	281	..
	2005	*109	*33	..	*3	*73	..	*300	..
	2006	*109	*33	..	*3	*73	..	*300	..
Armenia	2003	489	..	..	..	489	..	2100	72
	2004	543	..	..	..	543	..	2265	141
	2005	551	..	..	..	551	..	2749	184
	2006	561	..	..	..	561	..	2755	121
Azerbaijan	2003	28887	..	21988	6596	303	-4	5551	15676
	2004	29224	..	22236	6650	338	60	6944	16293
	2005	39502	..	31759	7373	370	1291	6763	23958
	2006	55140	..	46128	8703	309	-190	6303	39978
Bahrain	2003	23554	..	14553	9000	..	-861	4690	14777
	2004	23886	..	14526	9360	..	-451	4751	14181
	2005	24405	..	14490	9915	..	-357	5686	14404
	2006	24748	..	14243	10505	..	-733	5371	13923
Bangladesh	2003	15130	..	154	14837	138	-191	6039	.
	2004	16248	..	139	15959	151	-80	6098	.
	2005	17464	..	148	17157	159	-466	6422	.
	2006	18845	..	143	18531	171	-167	6482	.
Bhutan	2003	336	66	..	..	270	..	*99	227
	2004	340	30	..	..	310	..	*117	247
	2005	374	85	..	..	289	..	*98	247
	2006	423	98	..	..	325	..	*99	305

Table 1

Production, commerce et consommation d'énergie commerciale

Milliers de tonnes métriques d'équivalent houille et kilogrammes par habitant

Bunkers Soutes		Unallocated Quantités non réparties	Consumption Consommation						Year Année	Country or area Pays ou zone
Aviation Avion	Marine Maritime		Per Capita Par habitant	Total Totale	Solids Solides	Liquids Liquides	Gas Gaz	Electricity Electricité		
*25	..	..	*2126	*385	..	*385	..	..	2003	Guyane française
*25	..	..	*2011	*385	..	*385	..	..	2004	
*25	..	..	*1968	*385	..	*385	..	..	2005	
*28	..	..	*2019	*398	..	*398	..	..	2006	
17	..	..	941	708	..	708	..	..	2003	Guyana
18	..	..	907	685	..	685	..	..	2004	
18	..	..	933	707	..	707	..	..	2005	
18	..	..	940	715	..	715	..	..	2006	
37	..	2	462	2623	..	1814	..	809	2003	Paraguay
27	..	3	463	2683	..	1832	..	851	2004	
28	..	1	442	2605	..	1699	..	906	2005	
35	..	0	459	2756	..	1764	..	992	2006	
199	62	-809	523	14052	1042	9853	880	2277	2003	Pérou
632	81	-838	593	16048	1224	11295	1376	2153	2004	
447	326	369	584	15867	1289	9806	2320	2452	2005	
666	144	-380	650	17796	1064	11437	2655	2639	2006	
..	..	196	1946	936	..	843	..	93	2003	Suriname
..	..	206	1926	949	..	854	..	95	2004	
..	..	214	1991	994	..	892	..	102	2005	
..	..	221	2023	1020	..	913	..	107	2006	
47	452	25	841	2867	2	1826	77	961	2003	Uruguay
65	485	36	1009	3332	2	2322	134	873	2004	
62	509	129	1018	3365	2	2323	128	912	2005	
81	354	148	1105	3664	3	2727	146	788	2006	
344	738	21681	2906	74617	59	31156	35947	7456	2003	Venezuela(Rép. bolivar.)
865	927	1461	2951	77114	0	33079	35445	8589	2004	
914	883	4496	3104	82508	52	37210	36094	9152	2005	
963	940	6001	3451	93287	52	46394	37145	9696	2006	
47864	**82879**	**296885**	**1184**	**4502603**	**1962431**	**1513748**	**881476**	**144948**	**2003**	**Asie**
50278	**89876**	**323805**	**1288**	**4945755**	**2240331**	**1619312**	**924278**	**161835**	**2004**	
54916	**98164**	**320824**	**1349**	**5239204**	**2436191**	**1642261**	**986730**	**174022**	**2005**	
57458	**106038**	**334227**	**1397**	**5503956**	**2622530**	**1643673**	**1053115**	**184638**	**2006**	
*12	..	..	*16	*345	35	*210	8	92	2003	Afghanistan
0	..	..	17	390	34	269	4	83	2004	
*15	..	..	*17	*395	*33	*273	*3	*85	2005	
*15	..	..	*17	*395	*33	*273	*3	*85	2006	
38	..	0	653	2479	27	452	1545	455	2003	Arménie
56	..	0	812	2611	0	445	1716	450	2004	
65	..	0	949	3052	0	475	2125	452	2005	
57	..	0	974	3137	1	445	2179	512	2006	
287	..	700	2159	17779	..	5456	11828	496	2003	Azerbaïdjan
326	..	55	2340	19436	..	6013	12917	506	2004	
612	..	283	2398	20121	..	6682	12921	517	2005	
715	..	223	2442	20716	..	6101	14197	418	2006	
681	..	2404	15878	10946	..	1946	9000	..	2003	Bahreïn
744	..	2456	16139	11413	..	2052	9360	..	2004	
805	..	2648	16932	12269	..	2354	9915	..	2005	
824	..	2573	17798	13216	..	2711	10505	..	2006	
335	51	678	151	20296	500	4820	14837	138	2003	Bangladesh
346	51	614	157	21415	500	4806	15959	151	2004	
398	51	684	168	23218	500	5403	17157	159	2005	
392	51	670	172	24381	500	5180	18531	171	2006	
..	..	..	340	208	56	*71	..	81	2003	Bhoutan
..	..	..	339	211	50	*75	..	86	2004	
..	..	..	353	224	57	*75	..	92	2005	
..	..	..	336	218	52	*75	..	91	2006	

Table 1

Production, trade and consumption of commercial energy
Thousand metric tons of coal equivalent and kilograms per capita

Country or area Pays ou zone	Year Année	Primary energy production Production d'énergie primaire					Changes in stocks Variations des stocks	Imports Importations	Exports Exportations
		Total Totale	Solids Solides	Liquids Liquides	Gas Gaz	Electricity Electricité			
Brunei Darussalam	2003	31451	..	14988	16463	..	*-137	0	28463
	2004	31056	..	14769	16286	..	79	0	27683
	2005	30441	..	14452	15990	..	*-118	37	27347
	2006	32283	..	15476	16807	..	*-303	0	29339
Cambodia	2003	5	..	..	..	5	..	1542	..
	2004	3	..	..	..	3	..	1717	..
	2005	5	..	..	..	5	..	1825	..
	2006	7	..	..	..	7	..	2006	..
China	2003	1568719	1228770	242286	57494	40170	-397	183117	115518
	2004	1774887	1421661	251247	52710	49269	-178	255773	103683
	2005	1952358	1573227	259076	64767	55289	-5946	260165	98280
	2006	2086280	1693300	263951	68088	60941	-4694	290086	90809
China, Hong Kong SAR	2003	..	..	..	..	..	-163	32315	2116
	2004	..	..	..	..	..	-3	35089	2336
	2005	..	..	..	..	..	-774	34495	3852
	2006	..	..	..	..	..	901	36254	2282
China, Macao SAR	2003	..	..	..	..	..	-6	892	..
	2004	..	..	..	..	..	26	1090	..
	2005	..	..	..	..	..	-3	1124	..
	2006	..	..	..	..	..	11	1181	..
Cyprus	2003	0	..	..	..	0	-95	3788	..
	2004	0	..	..	..	0	-88	3426	..
	2005	0	..	..	..	0	102	3999	..
	2006	0	..	..	..	0	172	4228	..
Georgia	2003	1033	7	200	24	802	-33	2163	177
	2004	905	7	140	16	743	0	2427	151
	2005	883	4	96	18	766	0	2953	128
	2006	785	9	91	22	662	0	3347	110
India	2003	408295	308544	53653	34672	11426	1397	158106	18357
	2004	428129	327029	54225	34392	12483	2188	171575	22681
	2005	449124	347183	52359	34986	14596	8565	186484	24280
	2006	472720	367263	54954	34294	16210	9278	209176	34565
Indonesia	2003	285952	105568	81565	96928	1891	9	46920	189832
	2004	305950	127970	75585	100390	2005	825	57904	202539
	2005	327244	155248	71603	98259	2133	815	53895	215505
	2006	373316	204089	68701	98526	2000	749	47051	253719
Iran(Islamic Rep. of)	2003	382779	1232	275121	105063	1363	-188	15107	188157
	2004	405185	1246	285810	116823	1305	0	18315	195746
	2005	440395	1330	310502	126586	1978	0	18296	218990
	2006	451345	1520	308533	139049	2244	0	22908	216803
Iraq	2003	96366	..	94290	2023	53	0	561	59624
	2004	144884	..	141452	3371	61	656	6390	108715
	2005	134594	..	131094	3436	64	639	7332	97905
	2006	141823	..	137226	4538	60	-2499	7589	106685
Israel	2003	158	137	4	11	5	-147	34090	4417
	2004	1633	138	3	1487	5	-288	33211	5128
	2005	2184	130	3	2047	5	783	32698	5609
	2006	3007	142	3	2860	2	-266	33312	4700
Japan	2003	47881	..	957	4120	42804	-637	615621	6922
	2004	53206	..	989	4277	47939	-1621	625690	7267
	2005	54294	..	1048	4593	48653	3493	631553	12858
	2006	55708	..	1037	5066	49605	-1677	625434	14807
Jordan	2003	348	..	3	338	*7	-65	7487	0
	2004	353	..	1	345	7	161	9132	6
	2005	293	..	1	284	7	205	10167	0
	2006	273	..	1	265	7	-9	9918	4

2006 Energy Statistics Yearbook United Nations / 2006 Annuaire des statistiques de l' énergie des Nations Unies

Table 1

Production, commerce et consommation d'énergie commerciale

Milliers de tonnes métriques d'équivalent houille et kilogrammes par habitant

Bunkers Soutes		Unallocated Quantités non réparties	Consumption Consommation						Year Année	Country or area Pays ou zone
Aviation Avion	Marine Maritime		Per Capita Par habitant	Total Totale	Solids Solides	Liquids Liquides	Gas Gaz	Electricity Electricité		
..	..	-511	10377	3628	..	1615	2012	..	2003	Brunéi Darussalam
..	..	-741	11187	4024	..	1775	2249	..	2004	
..	..	-730	10731	3972	..	1694	2277	..	2005	
..	..	-800	10542	4038	..	1790	2247	..	2006	
32	..	..	115	1514	..	1502	..	12	2003	Cambodge
29	..	..	126	1691	..	1680	..	11	2004	
29	..	..	132	1801	..	1786	..	16	2005	
37	..	..	139	1976	..	1956	..	20	2006	
485	3576	92425	1195	1540229	1158507	286927	55530	39266	2003	Chine
184	413	115168	1398	1811389	1368286	344973	49608	48522	2004	
458	1325	111879	1539	2006527	1540508	350497	60993	54529	2005	
626	2057	124132	1646	2163436	1676130	362685	64524	60096	2006	
5068	7730	..	2579	17564	8204	6426	2026	908	2003	Chine, Hong-Kong RAS
4633	11031	..	2520	17093	7492	5845	2927	829	2004	
5376	8167	..	2623	17874	8343	5807	2926	799	2005	
5478	10470	..	2496	17123	8190	5059	3092	782	2006	
..	..	..	2003	898	..	876	..	22	2003	Chine, Macao RAS
..	..	..	2287	1064	..	1046	..	19	2004	
..	..	..	2309	1127	..	1085	..	42	2005	
..	..	..	2330	1170	..	1051	..	119	2006	
472	177	52	4417	3183	53	3130	..	0	2003	Chypre
435	79	8	4061	2993	57	2936	..	0	2004	
429	416	0	4028	3053	52	3000	..	0	2005	
442	423	0	4140	3191	54	3137	..	0	2006	
38	..	77	678	2936	43	755	1224	914	2003	Géorgie
55	..	30	717	3097	10	753	1434	900	2004	
55	..	21	833	3632	27	966	1708	931	2005	
55	..	21	897	3946	26	974	2189	757	2006	
3529	45	47459	464	495643	329009	120328	34672	11634	2003	Inde
4143	10	44791	487	525917	351822	127012	34392	12691	2004	
4857	7	48439	502	549486	371157	128557	34986	14787	2005	
5859	3	49563	521	582654	397011	134806	34294	16543	2006	
1159	700	2274	648	138901	15529	77692	43789	1891	2003	Indonésie
1135	511	1948	723	156898	22162	85023	47708	2005	2004	
1042	534	3426	727	159829	25401	84988	47307	2133	2005	
1024	514	3079	726	161292	31965	77486	49841	2000	2006	
1142	835	708	3118	207224	1838	95778	108175	1433	2003	Iran(Rép. islamique)
1160	884	125	3343	225579	1596	102663	119974	1346	2004	
1257	794	-6270	3562	243913	1810	113031	127178	1893	2005	
1474	656	-7217	3724	262531	1930	118616	139769	2215	2006	
597	..	5212	1196	31503	..	29427	2023	53	2003	Iraq
1714	..	1974	1409	38225	..	34631	3371	222	2004	
1105	..	2339	1453	39947	..	36277	3436	234	2005	
1160	..	2915	1429	41163	..	36405	4538	220	2006	
*6	389	571	4337	29013	12804	16373	11	-175	2003	Israël
*6	327	-343	4408	30013	13014	15686	1487	-174	2004	
*6	370	-1817	4319	29931	12255	15829	2047	-199	2005	
6	374	-588	4554	32093	13134	16324	2860	-224	2006	
9600	7314	27965	4850	612338	164900	291423	113210	42804	2003	Japon
9932	7657	26796	4981	628866	180319	288557	112050	47939	2004	
10000	8606	27270	4941	623622	176027	286901	112042	48653	2005	
9283	8094	29781	4921	620854	178167	270121	122961	49605	2006	
89	11	92	1474	7707	..	7323	338	46	2003	Jordanie
112	68	269	1739	8875	..	6868	1899	108	2004	
*111	113	488	1744	9543	..	7247	2197	98	2005	
109	58	232	1749	9796	..	6869	2862	65	2006	

Table 1

Production, trade and consumption of commercial energy
Thousand metric tons of coal equivalent and kilograms per capita

Country or area Pays ou zone	Year Année	Primary energy production Production d'énergie primaire					Changes in stocks Variations des stocks	Imports Importations	Exports Exportations
		Total Totale	Solids Solides	Liquids Liquides	Gas Gaz	Electricity Electricité			
Kazakhstan	2003	150631	53281	74191	22100	1059	581	17964	98609
	2004	170966	54568	85978	29430	990	572	24595	116718
	2005	177646	54387	89041	33253	965	512	24128	118719
	2006	191391	60387	94921	35129	954	381	27290	128203
Korea, Dem.Ppl's.Rep.	2003	28792	27352	..	..	1440	..	1935	755
	2004	30310	28775	..	..	1535	..	1955	1571
	2005	33125	31512	..	..	1613	..	1718	2804
	2006	33479	31929	..	..	1550	..	1413	2481
Korea, Republic of	2003	18902	2120	3	0	16780	3545	273781	32038
	2004	18843	2051	6	0	16786	1371	287463	36288
	2005	21297	1820	92	699	18685	-6435	284786	42337
	2006	21624	1815	125	738	18946	4204	301641	46242
Kuwait	2003	178175	..	163505	14670	..	..	841	122439
	2004	193248	..	177458	15790	..	..	162	133441
	2005	214378	..	196672	17706	..	..	0	150323
	2006	221568	..	202843	18726	..	..	0	159759
Kyrgyzstan	2003	1971	176	99	36	1660	-33	2351	433
	2004	2069	193	106	39	1731	-14	2558	663
	2005	2032	141	106	33	1752	0	2450	510
	2006	2090	135	101	25	1829	0	2383	457
Lao People's Dem. Rep.	2003	*756	*381	..	..	375	..	*216	455
	2004	*801	*405	..	..	*396	..	*220	*447
	2005	*836	*423	..	..	*413	..	*230	*455
	2006	*854	*428	..	..	*426	..	*224	*454
Lebanon	2003	85	..	..	..	85	-809	7415	..
	2004	138	..	..	..	138	1	7146	..
	2005	129	..	..	..	129	-596	6874	..
	2006	85	..	..	..	85	0	6346	..
Malaysia	2003	127689	153	55859	70970	706	-838	33924	65470
	2004	128761	382	53250	74413	716	567	42224	70183
	2005	137035	682	53753	81964	637	715	39602	74474
	2006	143642	902	52861	89011	869	162	37995	75149
Maldives	2003	..	..	..	..	..	..	284	.
	2004	..	..	..	..	..	..	357	.
	2005	..	..	..	..	..	..	322	.
	2006	..	..	..	..	..	..	412	.
Mongolia	2003	2489	2489	..	..	..	..	774	144
	2004	3016	3016	..	..	..	..	850	516
	2005	3301	3301	..	..	..	..	831	700
	2006	3546	3546	..	..	..	..	956	813
Myanmar	2003	13013	870	1395	10471	276	-125	1395	9127
	2004	17009	921	1466	14326	296	0	1648	13041
	2005	18065	1134	1592	14971	368	0	1812	13791
	2006	18568	1152	1512	15495	408	81	1295	13813
Nepal	2003	289	11	..	..	278	..	1332	25
	2004	304	9	..	..	295	..	1261	14
	2005	330	9	..	..	321	..	1444	16
	2006	337	9	..	..	328	..	1476	17
Occup. Palestinian Terr.	2003	..	..	..	..	..	-2	898	.
	2004	..	..	..	..	..	*-1	1231	21
	2005	..	..	..	..	..	0	1693	2
	2006	..	..	..	..	..	0	*1806	*3
Oman	2003	82279	..	58683	23596	..	-2232	428	67872
	2004	80165	..	56070	24094	..	-1451	603	66242
	2005	80796	..	55541	25254	..	-2122	1002	6663
	2006	84919	..	52884	32035	..	3	1050	6335

Table 1

Production, commerce et consommation d'énergie commerciale

Milliers de tonnes métriques d'équivalent houille et kilogrammes par habitant

Bunkers Soutes		Unallocated Quantités non réparties	Consumption Consommation						Year Année	Country or area Pays ou zone
Aviation Avion	Marine Maritime		Per Capita Par habitant	Total Totale	Solids Solides	Liquids Liquides	Gas Gaz	Electricity Electricité		
245	..	777	4587	68383	38119	10365	19020	879	2003	Kazakhstan
318	..	3064	4988	74888	39404	12832	21929	723	2004	
345	..	414	5399	81783	40310	12775	27663	1035	2005	
366	..	1107	5789	88625	43312	14459	29797	1057	2006	
..	..	21	1276	29951	26950	1561	..	1440	2003	Corée,Rép.pop.dém.de
..	..	19	1299	30675	27565	1574	..	1535	2004	
..	..	15	1356	32024	29089	1322	..	1613	2005	
..	..	10	1367	32401	29839	1012	..	1550	2006	
1680	9257	23517	4653	222646	71189	99745	34932	16780	2003	Corée, République de
1837	10193	33192	4647	223426	74241	92260	40139	16786	2004	
3392	14528	27880	4646	224380	74616	87609	43471	18685	2005	
4130	14546	31431	4611	222712	76575	81484	45707	18946	2006	
1055	795	14134	16692	38816	..	24146	14670	..	2003	Koweït
789	810	14275	17732	42390	..	26600	15790	..	2004	
849	755	14115	19013	46720	..	29015	17706	..	2005	
817	906	12635	18115	45758	..	27032	18726	..	2006	
..	..	7	777	3916	840	640	973	1463	2003	Kirghizistan
..	..	3	781	3976	792	798	1063	1322	2004	
..	..	-12	774	3983	737	844	980	1422	2005	
..	..	-18	777	4035	686	806	1024	1519	2006	
..	..	..	*91	*517	*315	*189	..	13	2003	Rép. dém. pop. lao
..	..	..	*98	*574	*327	*194	..	*54	2004	
..	..	..	*109	*610	*337	*195	..	*79	2005	
..	..	..	*108	*623	*342	*196	..	*85	2006	
184	23	..	2068	8102	200	7817	..	85	2003	Liban
187	24	..	1783	7071	200	6707	..	164	2004	
217	24	..	1835	7359	200	6974	..	185	2005	
152	24	..	1543	6256	200	5856	..	199	2006	
2647	102	15002	3163	79239	7623	27989	42921	706	2003	Malaisie
2963	121	12413	3313	84743	13275	29742	41075	651	2004	
2792	84	12323	3285	85834	10821	30204	44447	363	2005	
2871	72	10673	3463	92267	11143	30089	50477	559	2006	
..	..	..	995	284	..	284	..	..	2003	Maldives
..	..	..	1232	357	..	357	..	..	2004	
..	..	..	1095	322	..	322	..	..	2005	
..	..	..	1378	412	..	412	..	..	2006	
..	..	..	1252	3118	2345	753	..	20	2003	Mongolie
..	..	..	1330	3351	2502	829	..	20	2004	
..	..	..	1347	3433	2603	811	..	19	2005	
..	..	..	1431	3689	2735	936	..	18	2006	
99	4	308	94	4995	138	2460	2120	276	2003	Myanmar
94	4	86	100	5431	146	2567	2424	296	2004	
72	4	81	107	5929	152	2683	2727	368	2005	
111	4	72	103	5782	171	2381	2822	408	2006	
57	..	..	63	1538	291	976	..	271	2003	Népal
77	..	..	59	1474	257	906	..	311	2004	
85	..	..	66	1672	410	932	..	329	2005	
87	..	..	66	1710	420	953	..	337	2006	
..	..	..	256	900	0	615	..	284	2003	Terr. palestiniens occup.
..	..	..	333	1211	*1	890	..	319	2004	
..	..	..	443	1666	0	1315	..	*352	2005	
..	..	..	*455	*1769	0	*1425	..	*344	2006	
528	1	318	6929	16220	..	4729	11492	..	2003	Oman
*285	1	219	6405	15472	..	4794	10678	..	2004	
401	1	592	6493	16291	..	5149	11142	..	2005	
*460	0	1110	8167	21046	..	6187	14860	..	2006	

Table 1

Production, trade and consumption of commercial energy
Thousand metric tons of coal equivalent and kilograms per capita

Country or area Pays ou zone	Year Année	Primary energy production Production d'énergie primaire					Changes in stocks Variations des stocks	Imports Importations	Exports Exportations
		Total Totale	Solids Solides	Liquids Liquides	Gas Gaz	Electricity Electricité			
Other Asia	2003	6742	..	59	1056	5627	-1179	129294	12568
	2004	6823	..	57	1105	5661	3635	145487	17227
	2005	6630	..	41	696	5893	519	148224	19932
	2006	6533	..	30	589	5914	1530	151609	19684
Pakistan	2003	45437	2237	4735	34939	3526	-321	18723	719
	2004	49551	3099	4879	38076	3497	-97	23353	431
	2005	52332	3291	4986	39959	4096	*-24	23806	587
	2006	52054	2461	5057	40330	4206	8	27942	628
Philippines	2003	8725	3070	29	3451	2175	165	27489	1259
	2004	7467	1818	27	3301	2321	-362	29100	876
	2005	8751	2110	41	4353	2247	-1285	27240	1662
	2006	8675	*2169	37	3954	2515	118	26789	2234
Qatar	2003	96791	..	54984	41807	..	3711	..	73301
	2004	110466	..	58314	52152	..	-1097	..	86931
	2005	120213	..	59233	60979	..	-1867	..	90840
	2006	142524	..	76619	65906	..	-59	..	111425
Saudi Arabia	2003	755078	..	687154	67924	..	57	1821	554436
	2004	781533	..	707740	73792	..	-66	2177	565790
	2005	821768	..	740670	81097	..	36	2679	593135
	2006	813779	..	728639	85140	..	-170	5086	579646
Singapore	2003	..	..	..	..	..	-4775	122855	60112
	2004	..	..	..	..	..	-3300	139971	67367
	2005	..	..	..	..	..	-6292	150708	72446
	2006	..	..	..	..	..	-6441	160458	79509
Sri Lanka	2003	407	..	..	..	407	-163	4994	0
	2004	364	..	..	..	364	-3	5837	54
	2005	424	..	..	..	424	58	5733	0
	2006	570	..	..	..	570	171	5962	0
Syrian Arab Republic	2003	49156	..	40000	8812	344	16	1571	24300
	2004	43019	..	33364	9133	522	-28	2014	18014
	2005	40043	..	31773	7847	423	25	2454	14574
	2006	38342	..	29747	8104	491	25	1865	11549
Tajikistan	2003	2113	38	26	43	2007	..	3016	572
	2004	2140	59	27	47	2007	..	3194	552
	2005	2235	82	31	38	2084	..	3309	531
	2006	2202	93	31	26	2051	..	3628	529
Thailand	2003	51318	11841	14447	24133	897	-1337	74559	11243
	2004	52056	12606	14783	23924	742	-1402	83874	12234
	2005	56509	13120	16959	25717	712	-1836	81643	12769
	2006	57326	11941	18400	25987	998	-2812	82938	14731
Timor-Leste	2003	*10453	..	*10453	..	..	..	*132	*10346
	2004	*10524	..	*10524	..	..	..	*138	*10416
	2005	*10563	..	*10563	..	..	..	*140	*10454
	2006	*10581	..	*10581	..	..	..	*141	*10472
Turkey	2003	23634	15185	3359	732	4358	624	89658	5328
	2004	24285	14491	3216	899	5679	-647	93447	6451
	2005	27358	18082	3226	1172	4878	-921	100417	7055
	2006	29611	19878	3088	1183	5462	290	111601	8568
Turkmenistan	2003	91326	..	14843	76482	0	..	124	64878
	2004	90773	..	14497	76275	0	..	124	66705
	2005	95517	..	14070	81447	0	..	124	70095
	2006	96227	..	14457	81770	0	..	124	69743
United Arab Emirates	2003	241873	..	182271	59603	..	..	17797	155272
	2004	251762	..	190163	61599	..	..	19171	162253
	2005	254290	..	192345	61945	..	..	21540	164085
	2006	269264	..	206255	63009	..	..	22560	176265

Table 1

Production, commerce et consommation d'énergie commerciale

Milliers de tonnes métriques d'équivalent houille et kilogrammes par habitant

Bunkers Soutes		Unallocated Quantités	Consumption Consommation						Year	Country or area
Aviation Avion	Marine Maritime	non réparties	Per Capita Par habitant	Total Totale	Solids Solides	Liquids Liquides	Gas Gaz	Electricity Electricité	Année	Pays ou zone
3036	4337	9126	4785	108148	51108	39960	11453	5627	2003	Autre Asie
3423	3504	11683	4973	112837	53176	39890	14110	5661	2004	
3557	3539	12360	5057	114947	55010	40353	13691	5893	2005	
3625	3392	10028	5260	119884	57586	40957	15427	5914	2006	
203	21	1664	424	61875	3799	19594	34947	3535	2003	Pakistan
240	90	1845	473	70396	.6371	22428	38086	3510	2004	
305	114	2467	474	72692	6103	22512	39963	4114	2005	
252	146	2183	490	76782	6668	25552	40335	4227	2006	
840	265	1405	398	32279	6149	20504	3451	2175	2003	Philippines
*884	198	1238	408	33732	7068	21043	3301	2321	2004	
*1032	172	1121	391	33288	6811	19878	4353	2247	2005	
1182	184	986	354	30760	*6946	17344	3954	2515	2006	
879	..	-181	26023	19081	..	2528	16553	..	2003	Qatar
523	..	1627	28936	22482	..	2661	19821	..	2004	
669	..	1675	35549	28895	..	3206	25690	..	2005	
852	..	1140	31150	29166	..	3746	25420	..	2006	
2534	3159	13333	7779	171282	..	103357	67924	..	2003	Arabie saoudite
2422	3213	10379	8438	190405	..	116613	73792	..	2004	
2438	3260	11724	8745	202186	..	121088	81097	..	2005	
2534	3802	9802	8972	212456	..	127316	85140	..	2006	
3457	29517	15433	4566	19112	12	11981	7119	..	2003	Singapour
4257	33422	18935	4552	19291	8	10890	8393	..	2004	
4549	36131	22777	4859	21098	3	11674	9422	..	2005	
4914	39696	22029	4628	20752	6	11185	9561	..	2006	
164	163	187	262	5051	97	4547	..	407	2003	Sri Lanka
189	170	169	289	5624	96	5164	..	364	2004	
192	241	198	278	5468	96	4948	..	424	2005	
175	195	362	283	5629	96	4963	..	570	2006	
143	..	2381	1361	23887	4	14728	8812	344	2003	Rép. arabe syrienne
171	..	1644	1415	25231	4	15573	9133	522	2004	
155	..	2705	1370	25037	4	16764	7847	423	2005	
150	..	2568	1384	25913	4	17315	8104	491	2006	
6	..	19	690	4533	44	1751	730	2008	2003	Tadjikistan
6	..	21	708	4753	64	1884	754	2051	2004	
6	..	24	727	4983	86	2015	766	2115	2005	
6	..	23	739	5271	98	2271	776	2126	2006	
..	..	11486	1631	104427	18973	50147	34141	1165	2003	Thaïlande
..	..	10874	1779	114148	21227	57110	34699	1113	2004	
..	..	12115	1774	115043	20525	55859	37483	1176	2005	
..	..	12847	1768	115431	20771	55013	38107	1540	2006	
..	..	0	*132	*132	..	*132	..	..	2003	Timor-Leste
..	..	0	*136	*138	..	*138	..	..	2004	
..	..	0	*134	*140	..	*140	..	..	2005	
..	..	0	*133	*141	..	*141	..	..	2006	
1291	894	4376	1435	100779	31610	36613	28128	4428	2003	Turquie
1391	1439	4946	1464	104152	32351	36508	29697	5596	2004	
1557	1532	5315	1571	113237	36472	35852	36177	4736	2005	
1409	1416	6513	1686	123015	40839	35692	41227	5258	2006	
..	..	37	5648	26535	..	6291	20375	-130	2003	Turkménistan
..	..	37	5068	24155	..	6071	18229	-144	2004	
..	..	36	5278	25511	..	6201	19464	-154	2005	
..	..	44	5423	26565	..	7188	19542	-164	2006	
4885	13332	5411	22769	80853	..	30765	50088	..	2003	Emirats arabes unis
4680	15475	5493	22100	83118	..	31473	51645	..	2004	
5156	17215	5102	20544	84360	..	31917	52443	..	2005	
5292	18775	5028	20467	86556	..	32968	53588	..	2006	

Table 1

Production, trade and consumption of commercial energy
Thousand metric tons of coal equivalent and kilograms per capita

Country or area Pays ou zone	Year Année	Primary energy production Production d'énergie primaire					Changes in stocks Variations des stocks	Imports Importations	Exports Exportations
		Total Totale	Solids Solides	Liquids Liquides	Gas Gaz	Electricity Electricité			
Uzbekistan	2003	87875	737	11494	74865	779	17	3280	11512
	2004	88913	1039	10761	76308	805	24	3106	14714
	2005	88478	1156	8819	77750	753	27	2789	17720
	2006	91111	1204	8233	80896	778	28	2835	18065
Viet Nam	2003	47804	16700	24473	4299	2332	0	14910	30816
	2004	64772	25500	29777	7324	2170	1000	16465	38597
	2005	72678	32396	27803	9843	2635	904	17638	46102
	2006	77058	37899	26260	10000	2899	1143	17512	48636
Yemen	2003	30428	..	30428	..	..	810	3464	24379
	2004	28643	..	28643	..	..	1297	3911	21926
	2005	28360	..	28360	..	..	1314	4041	21301
	2006	26017	..	26017	..	..	2181	5076	18566
Europe	**2003**	**3055952**	**517567**	**1047997**	**1246051**	**244337**	**11458**	**2170852**	**1646568**
	2004	**3124668**	**509456**	**1087327**	**1274282**	**253602**	**14954**	**2254041**	**1757942**
	2005	**3108467**	**511822**	**1070925**	**1270723**	**254998**	**20090**	**2313594**	**1781158**
	2006	**3101171**	**508170**	**1059992**	**1277465**	**255545**	**40111**	**2363996**	**1785473**
Albania	2003	1219	27	536	21	635	..	1336	91
	2004	1332	37	600	24	671	..	1470	40
	2005	1355	31	639	26	660	..	1364	0
	2006	1392	31	721	26	614	..	1314	0
Austria	2003	9123	429	1476	2836	4382	-97	38368	4664
	2004	9222	88	1569	2664	4901	335	39554	5380
	2005	8502	0	1454	2139	4908	265	42411	6185
	2006	8866	0	1524	2502	4840	1038	43384	7294
Belarus	2003	3524	586	2600	335	3	-271	48368	14111
	2004	3568	648	2577	339	4	290	54106	18132
	2005	3605	750	2550	300	5	-145	56257	21065
	2006	3527	691	2543	289	4	23	60518	22705
Belgium	2003	6042	50	0	..	5992	73	110330	33165
	2004	6096	70	0	..	6027	163	113151	35734
	2005	6131	42	18	..	6071	556	111634	36717
	2006	6017	11	31	..	5975	153	110004	34561
Bosnia and Herzegovina	2003	7827	7274	..	..	553	0	1933	640
	2004	8081	7347	..	..	734	4	2537	826
	2005	8483	7746	..	..	737	-21	2875	973
	2006	8999	8280	..	..	719	-21	3120	1179
Bulgaria	2003	9062	6447	43	44	2528	-474	16439	2984
	2004	9173	6208	43	444	2479	659	17628	4142
	2005	9318	5771	43	631	2873	-10	18703	4722
	2006	9636	6014	48	613	2959	-254	20395	6277
Croatia	2003	5327	..	1882	2839	606	-203	10244	2632
	2004	5537	..	1820	2850	866	-8	10965	3165
	2005	5475	..	1722	2961	792	6	11227	3322
	2006	5938	..	1665	3518	755	98	11193	3721
Czech Republic	2003	34925	30522	797	208	3399	181	28166	10344
	2004	35128	30370	914	294	3550	-63	27706	9557
	2005	34088	29420	973	282	3412	564	29857	9798
	2006	34361	29853	632	270	3606	582	30894	10819
Denmark	2003	38098	..	25975	11437	686	-186	20632	31078
	2004	41895	..	27599	13483	812	184	19675	34849
	2005	42256	..	26542	14898	816	461	18805	35087
	2006	39742	..	24179	14810	753	-745	19633	32526
Estonia	2003	4915	4913	..	..	2	57	2821	361
	2004	4600	4596	..	..	4	-160	3198	357
	2005	4830	4821	..	..	9	1	2899	301
	2006	4714	4703	..	..	11	185	3088	219

Table 1

Production, commerce et consommation d'énergie commerciale

Milliers de tonnes métriques d'équivalent houille et kilogrammes par habitant

Bunkers Soutes		Unallocated Quantités	Consumption Consommation						Year	Country or area
Aviation Avion	Marine Maritime	non réparties	Per Capita Par habitant	Total Totale	Solids Solides	Liquids Liquides	Gas Gaz	Electricity Electricité	Année	Pays ou zone
..	..	-2948	3197	82573	718	13989	67096	769	2003	Ouzbékistan
..	..	-2749	3054	80030	1014	13084	65138	794	2004	
..	..	-2099	2844	75620	1128	10569	63180	743	2005	
..	..	-2045	2887	77898	1174	9952	66004	768	2006	
227	..	0	392	31675	10400	14644	4299	2332	2003	Viet Nam
380	..	0	503	41263	14900	16869	7324	2170	2004	
379	..	0	517	42935	14510	17988	7801	2635	2005	
351	..	0	528	44446	15727	17894	7926	2899	2006	
134	181	968	394	7420	..	7420	..	..	2003	Yémen
150	181	1241	400	7759	..	7759	..	..	2004	
150	181	1235	411	8219	..	8219	..	..	2005	
165	181	1118	431	8882	..	8882	..	..	2006	
62138	**68990**	**53393**	**4652**	**3383003**	**680155**	**1088322**	**1370057**	**244468**	**2003**	**Europe**
66060	**73632**	**56886**	**4681**	**3407643**	**669613**	**1088708**	**1395789**	**253533**	**2004**	
70316	**76960**	**58544**	**4678**	**3411705**	**653592**	**1083971**	**1419658**	**254485**	**2005**	
71866	**80984**	**35311**	**4725**	**3449977**	**673196**	**1114035**	**1407965**	**254781**	**2006**	
69	..	225	615	2170	31	1373	19	747	2003	Albanie
84	..	224	787	2454	40	1696	22	696	2004	
102	..	331	728	2287	36	1522	23	706	2005	
122	..	345	711	2239	35	1492	23	689	2006	
612	..	1562	5052	40751	5957	17732	11991	5071	2003	Autriche
718	..	1585	5007	40757	5692	17690	12095	5280	2004	
809	..	1218	5171	42436	5850	18337	13013	5235	2005	
848	..	1584	5009	41487	5777	18183	11845	5681	2006	
..	..	4919	3356	33132	924	7055	24311	843	2003	Bélarus
..	..	4344	3553	34908	791	7329	26385	404	2004	
..	..	3489	3627	35453	781	7279	26893	501	2005	
..	..	4473	3786	36842	746	8174	27383	540	2006	
2111	10140	6242	6242	64642	8880	26121	22860	6780	2003	Belgique
1943	11397	5494	6206	64516	8745	25662	23127	6982	2004	
1838	11279	5270	5945	62105	7859	24900	22501	6846	2005	
1689	12207	4029	6030	63383	6820	25444	23897	7222	2006	
..	..	6	2378	9114	7042	1377	256	438	2003	Bosnie y Herzégovine
..	..	31	2539	9758	7242	1616	404	496	2004	
..	..	13	2705	10393	7832	1514	480	568	2005	
..	..	13	2849	10947	8377	1603	507	461	2006	
228	199	1521	2690	21043	10299	4921	3969	1854	2003	Bulgarie
220	167	739	2683	20876	9966	5197	3957	1757	2004	
270	159	1158	2807	21722	9772	5558	4451	1942	2005	
258	154	1309	2895	22287	9971	5704	4604	2008	2006	
34	31	-206	2979	13234	1092	7318	3740	1085	2003	Croatie
41	34	341	2900	12876	1165	6492	3902	1317	2004	
57	36	172	2939	13057	1119	6745	3773	1420	2005	
57	29	210	2920	12966	1048	6742	3731	1445	2006	
290	..	2520	4877	49756	26706	9195	12448	1407	2003	République tchèque
416	..	2939	4897	49985	26313	9691	12362	1619	2004	
454	..	3307	4868	49822	25743	9983	12235	1860	2005	
479	..	3193	4878	50183	26174	9934	12021	2054	2006	
1029	1415	-153	4835	25547	8146	10367	7398	-364	2003	Danemark
1173	1151	-126	4506	24338	6283	10241	7355	459	2004	
1234	1191	101	4244	22988	5340	9681	6983	984	2005	
1241	1544	-15	4568	24825	7843	9879	7201	-99	2006	
27	163	..	5267	7129	5053	1227	1079	-231	2003	Estonie
40	218	..	5441	7342	5065	1264	1229	-217	2004	
60	174	..	5344	7193	4840	1272	1269	-188	2005	
41	309	..	5245	7047	4585	1261	1283	-81	2006	

Table 1

Production, trade and consumption of commercial energy
Thousand metric tons of coal equivalent and kilograms per capita

Country or area Pays ou zone	Year Année	Primary energy production Production d'énergie primaire					Changes in stocks Variations des stocks	Imports Importations	Exports Exportations
		Total Totale	Solids Solides	Liquids Liquides	Gas Gaz	Electricity Electricité			
Faeroe Islands	2003	11	..	..	..	11	..	*312	..
	2004	11	..	..	..	11	..	*312	..
	2005	*11	..	..	..	*11	..	*314	..
	2006	*11	..	..	..	*11	..	*314	..
Finland	2003	6624	2642	..	..	3982	712	40436	8118
	2004	5971	1314	..	..	4656	-2004	38079	8207
	2005	7802	3229	..	..	4573	1002	33821	6693
	2006	9032	4787	..	..	4245	803	37268	7518
France incl. Monaco	2003	69119	2076	2811	2034	62197	-1007	239122	37660
	2004	68608	808	2850	1758	63191	-1480	245317	39830
	2005	67238	593	2618	1442	62584	1654	254581	43555
	2006	67764	419	2528	1680	63136	2635	249360	43446
Germany	2003	137269	80048	6302	25284	25635	-2161	344198	41078
	2004	138160	81260	6355	23398	27147	1898	355854	49561
	2005	136438	79013	8019	22594	26813	2280	359045	55316
	2006	135060	74595	10195	22324	27945	1827	365141	59428
Gibraltar	2003	..	..	..	..	..	..	1770	..
	2004	..	..	..	..	..	..	1826	..
	2005	..	..	..	..	..	..	1868	..
	2006	..	..	..	..	..	..	1915	..
Greece	2003	12707	11680	198	49	780	-1223	41315	7565
	2004	13222	12207	192	46	777	1451	43863	7205
	2005	13213	12195	144	29	845	-712	42471	8091
	2006	12579	11338	196	41	1004	546	46144	9736
Hungary	2003	11750	3918	2798	3659	1374	666	29104	3996
	2004	11167	3117	2774	3786	1489	19	28470	3742
	2005	10510	2498	2557	3730	1725	178	32095	4652
	2006	10435	2509	2442	3802	1682	222	32139	5391
Iceland	2003	1351	..	..	308	1043	-75	1315	..
	2004	1375	..	..	317	1058	45	1496	..
	2005	1362	..	..	296	1066	28	1474	..
	2006	1547	..	..	328	1219	-40	1500	..
Ireland	2003	2779	1742	0	863	173	388	21922	2284
	2004	2685	1391	0	1093	201	637	21749	1773
	2005	2241	1252	1	731	256	76	21795	1991
	2006	2158	1169	4	652	333	208	22379	1833
Italy and San Marino	2003	32509	225	7957	18051	6277	-2427	263542	30781
	2004	32106	88	8140	16849	7029	-273	269751	32524
	2005	30979	85	8982	15692	6219	-2316	277793	38293
	2006	29197	19	8523	14273	6382	4512	284045	36286
Latvia	2003	287	3	0	..	284	90	4609	12
	2004	392	4	0	..	388	649	5517	560
	2005	421	4	3	..	414	178	5366	795
	2006	355	5	14	..	337	291	5507	414
Lithuania	2003	2660	15	546	76	2023	185	15095	8925
	2004	2493	16	436	70	1971	223	17539	11070
	2005	1785	23	324	68	1371	121	18326	10854
	2006	1531	18	281	69	1163	197	17817	9846
Luxembourg	2003	116	..	0	..	116	9	6441	361
	2004	113	..	1	..	111	-19	7052	406
	2005	118	..	1	..	117	-26	7161	405
	2006	124	..	1	..	122	41	7234	413
Malta	2003	..	..	..	..	..	..	1298	..
	2004	..	..	..	..	..	..	1367	..
	2005	..	..	..	..	..	..	1349	..
	2006	..	..	..	..	..	..	1311	..

Table 1

Production, commerce et consommation d'énergie commerciale

Milliers de tonnes métriques d'équivalent houille et kilogrammes par habitant

Bunkers Soutes		Unallocated Quantités non réparties	Consumption Consommation						Year Année	Country or area Pays ou zone
Aviation Avion	Marine Maritime		Per Capita Par habitant	Total Totale	Solids Solides	Liquids Liquides	Gas Gaz	Electricity Electricité		
*3	..	..	*6690	*321	..	*310	..	11	2003	Iles Féroé
*3	..	..	*6644	*321	..	*310	..	11	2004	
*3	..	..	*6673	*322	..	*311	..	*11	2005	
*3	..	..	*6672	*322	..	*311	..	*11	2006	
517	929	-1939	7428	38724	11997	15666	6483	4578	2003	Finlande
597	748	-2857	7528	39359	10971	16802	6332	5255	2004	
600	735	-3419	6864	36011	7101	16480	5767	6663	2005	
668	809	-3915	7675	40418	10863	17687	6222	5645	2006	
7255	3847	14079	4094	246409	21150	108811	62410	54039	2003	France y compris Monaco
7753	4358	13809	4123	249655	20382	109959	63728	55587	2004	
7843	3972	15508	4093	249286	21120	107791	65201	55174	2005	
8163	4127	9329	4084	249424	19476	111696	62895	55357	2006	
8195	3772	9219	5106	421363	119203	151323	125605	25233	2003	Allemagne
8859	3862	8989	5101	420846	120178	148873	124970	26825	2004	
9534	3617	9157	5039	415579	114623	146361	128343	26252	2005	
10020	3749	7074	5076	418103	115133	150927	126183	25860	2006	
6	1593	..	6110	171	..	171	..	..	2003	Gibraltar
6	1643	..	6318	177	..	177	..	..	2004	
6	1680	..	6525	183	..	183	..	..	2005	
6	1727	..	6325	183	..	183	..	..	2006	
1122	4625	-1805	3968	43738	12720	26763	3216	1037	2003	Grèce
1156	4662	-999	3942	43610	13038	25911	3538	1124	2004	
1116	4156	-1881	4045	44913	12815	27054	3736	1309	2005	
1338	4487	-2832	4077	45449	11725	27843	4361	1520	2006	
292	..	839	3462	35064	5323	8648	18867	2227	2003	Hongrie
333	..	1057	3412	34490	4820	8672	18591	2407	2004	
386	..	1610	3547	35784	4363	9733	19197	2490	2005	
391	..	1364	3496	35209	4264	10198	18180	2567	2006	
147	97	479	6975	2018	130	845	..	1043	2003	Islande
170	101	497	7035	2058	147	853	..	1058	2004	
192	93	478	6912	2045	142	837	..	1066	2005	
255	51	560	7297	2221	111	891	..	1219	2006	
1044	246	88	5190	20652	4003	10535	5798	316	2003	Irlande
988	216	8	5147	20812	3574	11059	5786	395	2004	
1139	150	194	4959	20486	4167	10304	5507	507	2005	
1163	178	-201	5043	21357	3725	10711	6370	551	2006	
3857	4619	-1528	4527	260749	21817	125409	100986	12538	2003	Italie y comp. St. Marin
3863	4831	2302	4445	258610	24557	116626	104792	12634	2004	
4092	4873	1586	4475	262245	24255	113589	112145	12257	2005	
4360	5022	4093	4394	258969	24505	112727	109828	11908	2006	
57	272	11	1915	4453	91	1616	2139	608	2003	Lettonie
69	293	4	1873	4333	72	1500	2115	645	2004	
84	377	6	1890	4347	86	1427	2155	678	2005	
94	285	29	2076	4749	79	1792	2233	645	2006	
31	159	200	2390	8255	302	3055	3801	1098	2003	Lituanie
16	165	216	2428	8341	294	3172	3788	1087	2004	
66	209	172	2545	8690	323	3364	3996	1006	2005	
75	202	-149	2704	9177	444	3661	3962	1110	2006	
560	..	..	12460	5627	111	3256	1689	571	2003	Luxembourg
610	..	..	13463	6167	134	3603	1904	526	2004	
619	..	..	13504	6281	116	3776	1871	518	2005	
581	..	..	13377	6323	158	3647	1959	559	2006	
113	33	..	2881	1152	..	1152	..	..	2003	Malte
144	33	..	2955	1190	..	1190	..	..	2004	
130	33	..	2931	1187	..	1187	..	..	2005	
111	33	..	2874	1168	..	1168	..	..	2006	

Table 1

Production, trade and consumption of commercial energy
Thousand metric tons of coal equivalent and kilograms per capita

Country or area Pays ou zone	Year Année	Primary energy production Production d'énergie primaire					Changes in stocks Variations des stocks	Imports Importations	Exports Exportations
		Total Totale	Solids Solides	Liquids Liquides	Gas Gaz	Electricity Electricité			
Netherlands	2003	88108	..	4564	82876	668	-335	184510	140412
	2004	102718	..	4250	97754	715	618	186781	153524
	2005	93859	..	3789	89310	760	1683	206003	160858
	2006	91860	..	3088	87993	779	135	217691	173500
Norway,Svlbd.J.Myn. I	2003	341287	2823	220201	105190	13074	1530	8387	307066
	2004	346850	2785	218833	111776	13456	-566	8696	312427
	2005	341745	1410	202416	121080	16838	495	7380	298325
	2006	328623	2296	187060	124468	14798	738	7926	296149
Poland	2003	108904	101618	1134	5732	420	372	46124	25938
	2004	108351	100361	1286	6234	471	487	48845	26093
	2005	105797	97782	1369	6166	481	2792	52279	26152
	2006	103291	95368	1362	6159	402	-411	57917	25783
Portugal	2003	2044	..	0	..	2044	642	33450	2249
	2004	1357	..	0	..	1357	-590	34211	2433
	2005	856	..	0	..	856	593	37132	3069
	2006	1879	..	100	..	1779	79	35190	4551
Republic of Moldova	2003	8	..	0	..	8	74	5056	18
	2004	19	..	11	..	7	-10	5085	61
	2005	15	..	7	..	8	1	5352	30
	2006	15	..	6	..	9	-28	5066	31
Romania	2003	35404	8178	8441	16553	2231	-356	20002	5476
	2004	35220	7860	8178	16473	2710	1443	23405	6618
	2005	34470	7690	8215	15400	3164	-486	24074	8941
	2006	34868	8634	8109	15178	2947	-1196	24800	8195
Russian Federation	2003	1583952	152632	599533	793905	37882	17379	36476	705611
	2004	1657626	155383	653624	808956	39663	9679	31519	778166
	2005	1697417	170011	668313	819237	39856	9799	29053	808170
	2006	1728745	170922	681803	835217	40804	19891	29776	804319
Serbia	2003	15031	12249	1104	468	1210	0	7761	571
	2004	15229	12524	931	408	1366	0	9840	1079
	2005	13509	10742	927	363	1478	0	9546	1347
	2006	13804	11160	923	374	1347	-30	10372	1310
Slovakia	2003	4352	1295	74	338	2645	-78	23547	5978
	2004	4227	1235	76	308	2609	830	24894	6710
	2005	4186	1050	93	281	2761	133	24809	6943
	2006	4158	921	99	364	2774	-251	24526	7273
Slovenia	2003	2534	1500	0	7	1027	57	6078	840
	2004	2674	1494	0	7	1173	57	6289	1053
	2005	2563	1410	0	5	1148	13	6657	1232
	2006	2540	1404	8	5	1123	-133	6839	1444
Spain	2003	25258	9729	735	312	14481	-117	166849	7956
	2004	24621	9474	677	491	13979	-1118	179179	10036
	2005	22384	9045	609	228	12502	2539	192048	10327
	2006	23078	8689	447	87	13855	3993	194808	13163
Sweden	2003	15378	333	97	..	14948	1482	47042	14986
	2004	17589	369	206	..	17014	-621	45712	17288
	2005	18546	292	297	..	17957	1093	45325	16837
	2006	16578	256	390	..	15932	-1044	44742	16646
Switzerland	2003	7946	..	0	38	7907	-228	25894	4948
	2004	7715	..	4	40	7671	21	25679	4233
	2005	6982	..	10	38	6935	197	27487	4614
	2006	7516	..	11	44	7461	105	27159	4592
T.F.Yug.Rep. Macedonia	2003	3011	2842	..	..	169	-53	1966	480
	2004	2971	2789	..	..	182	6	1878	300
	2005	2832	2649	..	..	183	-85	2167	472
	2006	2759	2556	..	..	203	23	2325	514

Table 1

Production, commerce et consommation d'énergie commerciale
Milliers de tonnes métriques d'équivalent houille et kilogrammes par habitant

Bunkers Soutes		Unallocated Quantités non réparties	Consumption Consommation						Year Année	Country or area Pays ou zone
Aviation Avion	Marine Maritime		Per Capita Par habitant	Total Totale	Solids Solides	Liquids Liquides	Gas Gaz	Electricity Electricité		
4698	19677	-23410	8121	131495	12192	59407	57140	2755	2003	Pays-Bas
5026	21379	-20907	7986	129830	11904	56895	58325	2707	2004	
5166	24540	-19555	7788	127093	11417	56197	56472	3007	2005	
5237	25471	-20433	7691	125640	10722	56683	54820	3415	2006	
301	810	558	8354	38260	1127	14600	8492	14041	2003	Norvège,Svalbd,J.May
346	742	2568	8349	38479	1315	14185	8120	14860	2004	
389	1002	6249	8502	39468	1108	14741	8260	15359	2005	
539	725	-3549	8694	40519	1019	17007	7590	14903	2006	
417	414	2489	3283	125398	82855	25498	17874	-828	2003	Pologne
408	368	2744	3329	127096	81462	27447	18858	-671	2004	
463	468	3033	3280	125167	79109	27532	19420	-893	2005	
616	429	3387	3446	131404	83218	29493	19640	-947	2006	
907	842	1782	2784	29073	4830	17671	4185	2388	2003	Portugal
993	956	1574	2876	30201	4886	17917	5244	2153	2004	
1030	841	1754	2910	30700	4869	18184	5953	1694	2005	
1103	924	1372	2744	29040	5023	15793	5777	2447	2006	
18	..	0	1371	4955	128	853	3542	432	2003	Rép. de Moldova
16	..	0	1398	5037	120	913	3636	368	2004	
18	..	0	1479	5319	108	924	3894	394	2005	
18	..	0	1411	5061	130	901	3589	441	2006	
168	..	573	2280	49544	11587	12601	23380	1975	2003	Roumanie
196	..	2193	2223	48175	11608	11880	22123	2565	2004	
159	..	1555	2237	48374	11307	12130	22130	2808	2005	
196	..	2281	2325	50191	12220	12363	23187	2422	2006	
6966	..	14345	6060	876126	129184	166893	543810	36238	2003	Fédération de Russie
6841	..	10981	6143	883479	125020	169476	550255	38727	2004	
7397	..	13720	6201	887385	124268	169751	555031	38335	2005	
7814	..	13187	6410	913311	128299	176773	569377	38862	2006	
91	..	847	2011	21282	12744	4096	2889	1553	2003	Serbie
68	..	1075	2173	22848	13236	4611	3669	1333	2004	
71	..	1009	1970	20629	11472	4844	3073	1239	2005	
77	..	848	2102	21972	12316	5247	3161	1247	2006	
49	..	668	3957	21283	6040	3877	8998	2369	2003	Slovaquie
38	..	184	3968	21359	5875	4376	8728	2380	2004	
56	..	232	4015	21630	5466	4465	9339	2360	2005	
57	..	447	3924	21158	5875	4259	8536	2488	2006	
37	0	6	3846	7672	1892	3294	1439	1047	2003	Slovénie
28	0	75	3882	7750	1915	3330	1427	1078	2004	
32	31	79	3914	7832	1847	3402	1474	1108	2005	
35	42	77	3940	7913	1858	3499	1427	1129	2006	
3997	10214	10998	3787	159058	29113	81416	33894	14636	2003	Espagne
4432	10537	11262	3950	168650	31267	83821	39955	13607	2004	
4447	11563	8419	4082	177137	30422	87006	47372	12337	2005	
4636	12073	7510	4005	176510	27005	86814	49238	13453	2006	
733	2351	3273	4420	39596	3762	17901	1410	16524	2003	Suède
898	2767	2895	4456	40074	4154	17760	1404	16756	2004	
905	2826	2998	4343	39212	3686	17140	1338	17049	2005	
948	3037	2734	4295	39000	3748	17179	1400	16674	2006	
1729	14	38	3724	27339	203	15440	4171	7525	2003	Suisse
1649	13	11	3686	27466	190	15389	4303	7585	2004	
1686	17	9	3746	27945	213	15601	4417	7715	2005	
1782	13	-24	3769	28206	197	15921	4295	7793	2006	
10	..	9	2235	4531	2984	1156	105	286	2003	L'ex-RY Macédoine
9	..	17	2226	4518	2922	1176	93	326	2004	
9	..	15	2253	4589	2895	1213	101	380	2005	
7	..	34	2208	4504	2697	1277	107	423	2006	

Table 1

Production, trade and consumption of commercial energy
Thousand metric tons of coal equivalent and kilograms per capita

Country or area Pays ou zone	Year Année	Primary energy production Production d'énergie primaire					Changes in stocks Variations des stocks	Imports Importations	Exports Exportations
		Total Totale	Solids Solides	Liquids Liquides	Gas Gaz	Electricity Electricité			
Ukraine	2003	89861	47430	5725	25549	11156	0	124888	24421
	2004	89674	44012	6242	27267	12153	440	124792	25941
	2005	91130	44623	6388	27677	12443	-3843	110460	18282
	2006	92933	45574	6592	28079	12688	2458	97904	11189
United Kingdom	2003	335629	24340	152467	147037	11784	-3147	143703	158768
	2004	306889	21601	137140	137152	10996	1727	169052	144919
	2005	276014	17643	121902	125116	11353	1028	180330	126743
	2006	255540	15947	114467	114298	10827	3481	201334	123202
Oceania	**2003**	**376058**	**267297**	**47139**	**56012**	**5610**	**492**	**54148**	**244113**
	2004	**382944**	**278056**	**42437**	**56430**	**6021**	**377**	**55130**	**250956**
	2005	**396807**	**291505**	**37988**	**61661**	**5653**	**-1504**	**58952**	**261956**
	2006	**399023**	**292016**	**37138**	**64044**	**5825**	**-2200**	**62468**	**264044**
Australia	2003	357793	264141	41869	49700	2083	704	39062	237286
	2004	365462	274842	37787	50796	2038	209	39183	244930
	2005	379521	288236	32978	56246	2061	-1457	42759	255121
	2006	380668	288405	31614	58469	2180	-2508	45986	256523
Cook Islands	2003	..	..	..	..	..	..	19	..
	2004	..	..	..	..	..	..	26	..
	2005	..	..	..	..	..	..	29	..
	2006	..	..	..	..	..	..	*31	..
Fiji	2003	*82	..	..	..	*82	..	1461	*169
	2004	*82	..	..	..	*82	..	1523	*192
	2005	*83	..	..	..	*83	..	1358	*177
	2006	*85	..	..	..	*85	..	1406	*170
French Polynesia	2003	15	..	..	..	15	..	446	..
	2004	19	..	..	..	19	..	444	..
	2005	16	..	..	..	16	..	476	..
	2006	19	..	..	..	19	..	466	..
Kiribati	2003	..	..	..	..	..	..	*15	..
	2004	..	..	..	..	..	..	*15	..
	2005	..	..	..	..	..	..	*15	..
	2006	..	..	..	..	..	..	*18	..
Marshall Islands	2003	..	..	..	..	..	..	*39	..
	2004	..	..	..	..	..	..	*41	..
	2005	..	..	..	..	..	..	*41	..
	2006	..	..	..	..	..	..	*43	..
Nauru	2003	..	..	..	..	..	..	*76	..
	2004	..	..	..	..	..	..	*76	..
	2005	..	..	..	..	..	..	*76	..
	2006	..	..	..	..	..	..	*76	..
New Caledonia	2003	40	..	..	..	40	..	1240	42
	2004	41	..	..	..	41	..	1155	42
	2005	44	..	..	..	44	..	1274	*44
	2006	52	..	..	..	52	..	1341	*45
New Zealand	2003	14352	3155	1803	6124	3269	-320	9551	3239
	2004	14021	3214	1602	5481	3723	460	10241	2725
	2005	13165	3269	1492	5070	3333	-47	10128	3061
	2006	13620	3611	1429	5204	3375	-112	10231	3412
Niue	2003	..	..	..	..	..	..	*1	..
	2004	..	..	..	..	..	..	*1	..
	2005	..	..	..	..	..	..	*1	..
	2006	..	..	..	..	..	..	*1	..
Palau	2003	*2	..	..	..	*2	..	*111	..
	2004	*2	..	..	..	*2	..	*110	..
	2005	*2	..	..	..	*2	..	*113	..
	2006	*2	..	..	..	*2	..	*118	..

Table 1

Production, commerce et consommation d'énergie commerciale

Milliers de tonnes métriques d'équivalent houille et kilogrammes par habitant

Bunkers Soutes		Unallocated Quantités non réparties	Consumption Consommation						Year Année	Country or area Pays ou zone
Aviation Avion	Marine Maritime		Per Capita Par habitant	Total Totale	Solids Solides	Liquids Liquides	Gas Gaz	Electricity Electricité		
532	..	4288	3880	185508	53021	18594	103343	10549	2003	Ukraine
539	..	4797	3866	182748	47202	19487	104560	11498	2004	
537	..	-219	3969	186833	48319	20011	107086	11417	2005	
479	..	-706	3794	177417	52388	21161	92463	11406	2006	
13885	2528	648	5169	306671	57520	100781	136320	12050	2003	Royaume-Uni
15369	2989	-1181	5229	312153	57068	104459	138710	11916	2004	
17317	2937	775	5108	307577	58800	101642	134759	12375	2005	
16358	3360	-2348	5164	312852	64621	107811	128670	11750	2006	
4829	**1623**	**-3041**	**5622**	**182201**	**72469**	**62637**	**41486**	**5610**	**2003**	**Océanie**
4899	**1761**	**-4220**	**5605**	**184312**	**73490**	**63029**	**41774**	**6021**	**2004**	
5473	**1807**	**-3843**	**5752**	**191880**	**78535**	**65670**	**42022**	**5653**	**2005**	
5075	**2042**	**-1182**	**5719**	**193727**	**79621**	**65493**	**42788**	**5825**	**2006**	
3209	1048	-2800	7909	157417	70483	49678	35173	2083	2003	Australie
3237	1202	-4004	7899	159079	71531	49405	36106	2038	2004	
3791	1224	-3761	8201	167371	76429	52292	36589	2061	2005	
3409	1411	-1334	8172	169165	77500	52289	37195	2180	2006	
*3	..	..	880	16	..	16	..	..	2003	Iles Cook
0	..	..	1298	26	..	26	..	..	2004	
0	..	..	1448	29	..	29	..	..	2005	
0	..	..	*1441	*31	..	*31	..	..	2006	
*429	*103	..	1017	842	*13	748	..	*82	2003	Fidji
*332	*117	..	1154	964	*13	869	..	*82	2004	
*324	*103	..	993	836	*12	741	..	*83	2005	
*414	*96	..	950	811	*12	714	..	*85	2006	
*9	*52	..	1616	400	..	385	..	15	2003	Polynésie française
*9	*65	..	1550	389	..	370	..	19	2004	
*9	*67	..	1636	416	..	400	..	16	2005	
*9	*71	..	1583	406	..	386	..	19	2006	
*3	..	..	*126	*12	..	*12	..	..	2003	Kiribati
*3	..	..	*117	*12	..	*12	..	..	2004	
*3	..	..	*114	*12	..	*12	..	..	2005	
*3	..	..	*139	*15	..	*15	..	..	2006	
..	..	..	*717	*39	..	*39	..	..	2003	Îles Marshall
..	..	..	*719	*41	..	*41	..	..	2004	
..	..	..	*697	*41	..	*41	..	..	2005	
..	..	..	*719	*43	..	*43	..	..	2006	
*10	..	..	*5226	*66	..	*66	..	..	2003	Nauru
*10	..	..	*5129	*66	..	*66	..	..	2004	
*10	..	..	*5035	*66	..	*66	..	..	2005	
*10	..	..	*4939	*66	..	*66	..	..	2006	
13	..	..	5370	1224	313	871	..	40	2003	Nouvelle-Calédonie
16	..	..	4930	1138	281	815	..	41	2004	
15	..	..	5382	1259	260	956	..	44	2005	
21	..	..	5579	1328	283	992	..	52	2006	
1076	375	-232	4930	19767	1660	8713	6124	3269	2003	Nouvelle-Zélande
1209	330	-411	4912	19951	1665	9048	5515	3723	2004	
1238	368	-528	4685	19202	1834	8947	5088	3333	2005	
1123	418	-171	4630	19181	1826	8758	5222	3375	2006	
..	..	..	*820	*1	..	*1	..	..	2003	Nioué
..	..	..	*823	*1	..	*1	..	..	2004	
..	..	..	*861	*1	..	*1	..	..	2005	
..	..	..	*892	*1	..	*1	..	..	2006	
*22	..	..	*4493	*91	..	*89	..	*2	2003	Palaos
*22	..	..	*4393	*91	..	*88	..	*2	2004	
*22	..	..	*4445	*93	..	*91	..	*2	2005	
*22	..	..	*4525	*98	..	*96	..	*2	2006	

Table 1

Production, trade and consumption of commercial energy
Thousand metric tons of coal equivalent and kilograms per capita

Country or area Pays ou zone	Year Année	Primary energy production Production d'énergie primaire					Changes in stocks Variations des stocks	Imports Importations	Exports Exportations
		Total Totale	Solids Solides	Liquids Liquides	Gas Gaz	Electricity Electricité			
Papua New Guinea	2003	3770	..	3467	189	114	*107	1827	3377
	2004	3311	..	3049	153	110	*-292	2014	3068
	2005	3971	..	3517	345	109	0	2380	3553
	2006	4572	..	4096	370	106	420	2447	3894
Samoa	2003	*4	..	..	..	*4	..	*72	..
	2004	*5	..	..	..	*5	..	*74	..
	2005	*5	..	..	..	*5	..	*75	..
	2006	*5	..	..	..	*5	..	*75	..
Solomon Islands	2003	..	..	..	..	..	..	*88	..
	2004	..	..	..	..	..	..	*88	..
	2005	..	..	..	..	..	..	*88	..
	2006	..	..	..	..	..	..	*89	..
Tonga	2003	..	..	..	..	..	..	84	..
	2004	..	..	..	..	..	..	83	..
	2005	..	..	..	..	..	..	*82	..
	2006	..	..	..	..	..	..	*82	..
Vanuatu	2003	..	..	..	..	..	..	*42	..
	2004	..	..	..	..	..	..	*42	..
	2005	..	..	..	..	..	..	*42	..
	2006	..	..	..	..	..	..	*44	..
Wallis and Futuna Is	2003	..	..	..	..	..	..	*13	..
	2004	..	..	..	..	..	..	14	..
	2005	..	..	..	..	..	..	14	..
	2006	..	..	..	..	..	..	13	..

Table 1

Production, commerce et consommation d'énergie commerciale
Milliers de tonnes métriques d'équivalent houille et kilogrammes par habitant

Bunkers Soutes		Unallocated Quantités non réparties	Consumption Consommation						Year Année	Country or area Pays ou zone
Aviation Avion	Marine Maritime		Per Capita Par habitant	Total Totale	Solids Solides	Liquids Liquides	Gas Gaz	Electricity Electricité		
*48	*46	-10	350	2028	..	1726	189	114	2003	Papouasie-Nvl-Guinée
*54	*46	194	380	2256	..	1993	153	110	2004	
*54	*46	446	371	2252	..	1798	345	109	2005	
*56	*46	323	368	2281	..	1804	370	106	2006	
..	..	..	*425	*76	..	*72	..	*4	2003	Samoa
..	..	..	*433	*79	..	*74	..	*5	2004	
..	..	..	*437	*80	..	*75	..	*5	2005	
..	..	..	*433	*80	..	*75	..	*5	2006	
*4	..	..	*186	*83	..	*83	..	..	2003	Iles Salomon
*4	..	..	*181	*83	..	*83	..	..	2004	
*4	..	..	*177	*83	..	*83	..	..	2005	
*4	..	..	*176	*85	..	*85	..	..	2006	
*1	..	..	818	83	..	83	..	..	2003	Tonga
*1	..	..	803	82	..	82	..	..	2004	
*1	..	..	*790	*81	..	*81	..	..	2005	
*1	..	..	*800	*81	..	*81	..	..	2006	
..	..	..	*200	*42	..	*42	..	..	2003	Vanuatu
..	..	..	*198	*42	..	*42	..	..	2004	
..	..	..	*197	*42	..	*42	..	..	2005	
..	..	..	*199	*44	..	*44	..	..	2006	
*1	..	..	*798	*12	..	*12	..	..	2003	Iles Wallis et Futuna
1	..	..	805	12	..	12	..	..	2004	
1	..	..	793	13	..	13	..	..	2005	
1	..	..	767	12	..	12	..	..	2006	

Table 2

Production, trade and consumption of commercial energy
Production, commerce et consommation d'énergie commerciale
Thousand metric tons of oil equivalent and kilograms per capita
Milliers de tonnes métriques d'équivalent pétrole et kilogrammes par habitant

Table Notes:
Please refer to notes on table 1.

- **Please refer to the Definitions Section on pages xv to xxix for the appropriate product description/ classification.**

Notes relatives aux tableaux:
Veuillez consulter les notes de bas de page au tableau 1.

- **Veuillez consulter la section "définitions" de la page xv à la page xxix pour une description/classification appropriée des produits.**

Figure 5: Commercial primary energy production, by region, in 2006 (in million metric tons of oil equivalent)

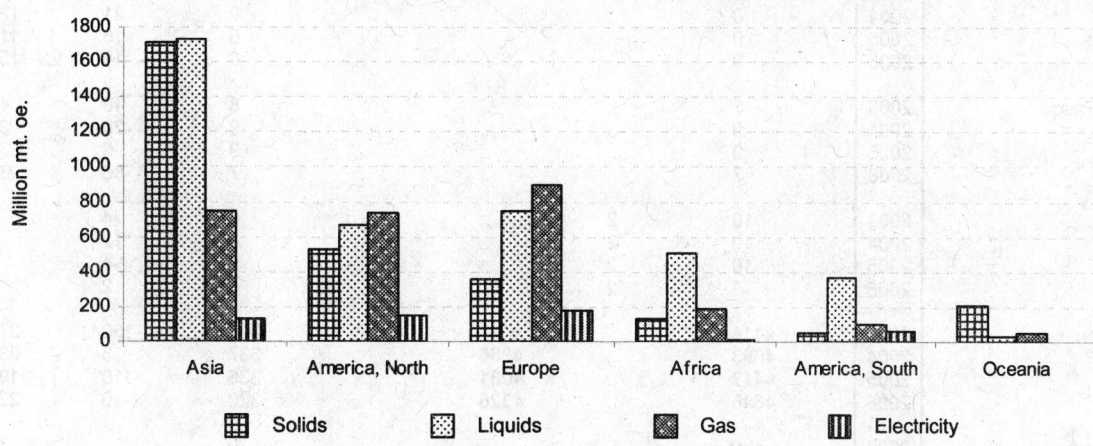

Figure 6: Commercial primary energy consumption, by region, in 2006 (in million metric tons of oil equivalent)

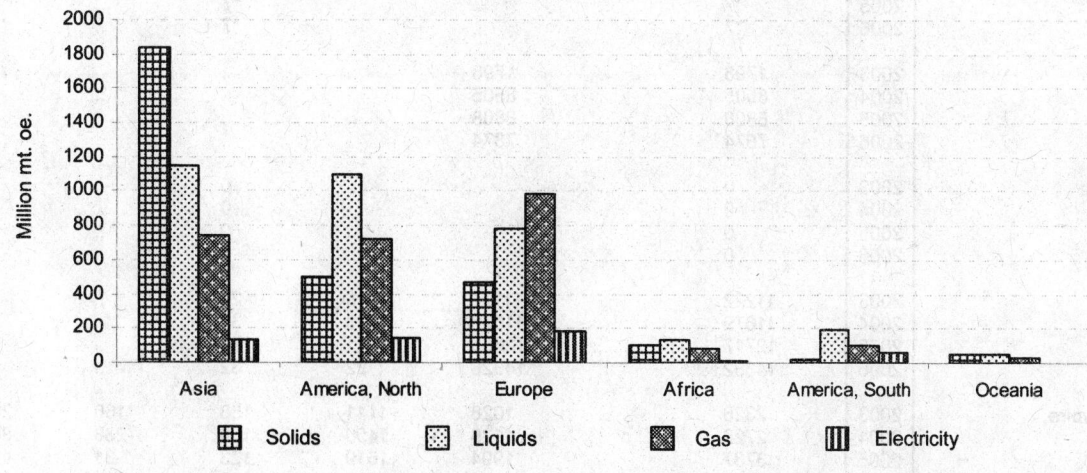

Table 2

Production, trade and consumption of commercial energy

Thousand metric tons of oil equivalent and kilograms per capita

| Country or area Pays ou zone | Year Année | Primary energy production Production d'énergie primaire | | | | | Changes in stocks Variations des stocks | Imports Importations | Exports Exportations |
		Total Totale	Solids Solides	Liquids Liquides	Gas Gaz	Electricity Electricité			
World	2003	9200793	2446949	3797548	2485731	470565	5401	4004817	3956701
	2004	9635145	2650724	3941185	2547975	495261	10013	4283398	4230419
	2005	9960109	2825918	4005646	2618450	510096	1997	4396345	4386100
	2006	10247016	2977902	4037763	2706722	524629	53876	4506786	4511902
Africa	2003	712884	129661	439097	135640	8487	1539	83038	477987
	2004	764959	131791	479831	144381	8956	-1364	87915	519846
	2005	820884	133109	508197	170593	8985	-661	98735	559898
	2006	838636	132940	508317	187889	9490	926	100027	586121
Algeria	2003	183893	..	106283	77587	23	-42	972	136335
	2004	187780	..	110940	76819	22	*153	1235	141768
	2005	199780	..	114076	85657	48	65	1118	144513
	2006	203933	..	112081	91833	19	717	1355	151819
Angola	2003	43780	..	43083	590	107	217	733	41293
	2004	50274	..	49443	681	150	780	800	47110
	2005	63186	..	62314	681	191	129	904	60642
	2006	71197	..	70242	726	229	612	1206	68043
Benin	2003	0	..	..	..	0	11	1133	324
	2004	0	..	..	..	0	21	1296	436
	2005	0	..	..	..	0	-15	1195	311
	2006	0	..	..	..	0	-14	1595	531
Burkina Faso	2003	8	..	..	..	8	40	415	0
	2004	9	..	..	..	9	-20	370	0
	2005	9	..	..	..	9	-6	396	0
	2006	7	..	..	..	7	-86	394	0
Burundi	2003	10	2	..	..	9	-4	56	..
	2004	10	2	..	..	8	*12	72	..
	2005	10	2	..	..	9	*-4	62	..
	2006	10	*2	..	..	8	2	74	..
Cameroon	2003	4414	..	4111	..	303	-156	2713	5517
	2004	4693	..	4356	..	337	3	2314	5479
	2005	4417	..	4081	..	336	-110	1963	5012
	2006	4646	..	4326	..	320	-10	2276	5273
Cape Verde	2003	0	..	..	..	0	..	*90	..
	2004	1	..	..	..	1	..	*96	..
	2005	1	..	..	..	1	..	*109	..
	2006	1	..	..	..	1	..	*111	..
Central African Rep.	2003	*7	..	..	..	*7	..	*105	..
	2004	*7	..	..	..	*7	..	*105	..
	2005	*7	..	..	..	*7	..	*105	..
	2006	*7	..	..	..	*7	..	*112	..
Chad	2003	1798	..	1798	..	..	..	*74	1728
	2004	8505	..	8505	..	..	..	*78	8440
	2005	8808	..	8808	..	..	..	*84	8741
	2006	7874	..	7874	..	..	..	*86	7806
Comoros	2003	0	..	..	..	0	..	*32	..
	2004	0	..	..	..	0	..	*32	..
	2005	0	..	..	..	0	..	*32	..
	2006	0	..	..	..	0	..	*33	..
Congo	2003	11222	..	11177	16	29	..	31	10875
	2004	11679	..	11626	18	34	..	81	11124
	2005	12717	..	12665	21	31	..	116	12314
	2006	14382	..	14328	22	32	..	133	14035
Côte d'Ivoire	2003	2326	..	1028	1141	158	*166	2989	2680
	2004	2726	..	1126	1450	150	-238	3617	3346
	2005	3737	..	1994	1619	123	*-31	4265	4516
	2006	4786	..	3135	1521	130	-204	3724	5711

Table 2

Production, commerce et consommation d'énergie commerciale
Milliers de tonnes métriques d'équivalent pétrole et kilogrammes par habitant

Bunkers Soutes		Unallocated Quantités	Consumption Consommation						Year	Country or area
Aviation Avion	Marine Maritime	non réparties	Per capita Par habitant	Total Totale	Solids Solides	Liquids Liquides	Gas Gaz	Electricity Electricité	Année	Pays ou zone
108192	144455	317987	1382	8662031	2505951	3196900	2488635	470545	2003	Monde
113722	157609	322356	1430	9073707	2715817	3324633	2537945	495312	2004	
121530	168396	319718	1456	9346535	2850293	3370669	2615570	510003	2005	
123505	177674	307076	1469	9569306	2988096	3398894	2657923	524393	2006	
4529	7101	8913	351	295550	96448	122394	68099	8609	2003	Afrique
4471	6073	7823	363	315726	103636	130630	72370	9091	2004	
5025	6408	16258	374	332404	103040	134330	85925	9109	2005	
5076	5630	7178	364	333442	103339	135841	84667	9594	2006	
273	217	5140	1341	42705	761	20543	21377	24	2003	Algérie
219	332	2727	1346	43575	524	23020	20008	23	2004	
318	331	3025	1593	52417	644	22008	29720	45	2005	
371	317	4486	1414	47343	734	19980	26604	26	2006	
301	0	213	222	2489	..	1792	590	107	2003	Angola
343	0	258	227	2583	..	1751	681	150	2004	
286	1	252	237	2780	..	1908	681	191	2005	
340	1	323	257	3084	..	2129	726	229	2006	
26	..	..	97	772	..	728	..	44	2003	Bénin
25	..	..	99	814	..	764	..	50	2004	
24	..	..	103	875	..	824	..	51	2005	
25	..	..	120	1055	..	1004	..	51	2006	
15	..	..	29	368	0	354	..	14	2003	Burkina Faso
17	..	..	29	382	0	365	..	17	2004	
21	..	..	30	390	0	370	..	19	2005	
16	..	..	34	470	0	451	..	19	2006	
4	..	..	9	67	2	52	..	13	2003	Burundi
7	..	..	8	63	2	48	..	13	2004	
7	..	..	9	69	2	53	..	15	2005	
7	..	..	9	75	*2	60	..	13	2006	
71	14	433	73	1249	..	945	..	303	2003	Cameroun
71	15	158	74	1281	..	944	..	337	2004	
64	12	107	73	1295	..	959	..	336	2005	
73	42	228	72	1315	..	995	..	320	2006	
..	*6	..	*183	*84	..	*84	..	0	2003	Cap-Vert
..	*7	..	*190	*89	..	*89	..	1	2004	
..	*10	..	*208	*99	..	*99	..	1	2005	
..	*10	..	*209	*102	..	*101	..	1	2006	
*27	..	..	*21	*85	..	*78	..	*7	2003	Rép. centrafricaine
*27	..	..	*21	*85	..	*78	..	*7	2004	
*27	..	..	*20	*85	..	*78	..	*7	2005	
*29	..	..	*21	*91	..	*83	..	*7	2006	
*19	..	70	*6	*56	..	*56	..	..	2003	Tchad
*19	..	66	*6	*60	..	*60	..	..	2004	
*20	..	67	*6	*65	..	*65	..	..	2005	
*20	..	67	*6	*66	..	*66	..	..	2006	
..	..	..	*51	*32	..	*32	..	0	2003	Comores
..	..	..	*50	*32	..	*32	..	0	2004	
..	..	..	*48	*33	..	*32	..	0	2005	
..	..	..	*47	*33	..	*33	..	0	2006	
..	..	46	96	331	..	256	16	60	2003	Congo
..	..	253	108	383	..	295	18	69	2004	
..	..	118	111	401	..	314	21	66	2005	
..	..	25	123	454	..	365	22	67	2006	
*108	91	159	120	2111	..	927	1141	44	2003	Côte d'Ivoire
92	91	435	141	2623	..	1143	1450	29	2004	
92	75	658	141	2692	..	1069	1619	3	2005	
92	65	168	136	2679	..	1120	1521	38	2006	

Table 2

Production, trade and consumption of commercial energy

Thousand metric tons of oil equivalent and kilograms per capita

Country or area Pays ou zone	Year Année	Primary energy production Production d'énergie primaire					Changes in stocks Variations des stocks	Imports Importations	Exports Exportations
		Total Totale	Solids Solides	Liquids Liquides	Gas Gaz	Electricity Electricité			
Dem. Rep. of Congo	2003	1693	73	1083	..	536	..	513	1202
	2004	1696	76	1033	..	587	..	689	1163
	2005	1704	84	984	..	636	..	689	1144
	2006	1649	87	886	..	676	..	701	1046
Djibouti	2003	..	..	..	..	..	..	287	
	2004	..	..	..	..	..	..	307	
	2005	..	..	..	..	..	..	318	
	2006	..	..	..	..	..	..	331	
Egypt	2003	70115	23	40013	28996	1082	*454	2623	11684
	2004	70423	20	37948	31323	1132	*-398	3901	10845
	2005	83332	20	37269	44908	1135	0	6959	18484
	2006	80836	15	33419	46238	1164	-89	7075	19963
Equatorial Guinea	2003	13795	..	13346	448	0	..	*55	13346
	2004	18110	..	17662	*447	0	..	*48	17662
	2005	18421	..	17973	*447	0	..	*48	17973
	2006	17592	..	17144	*447	0	..	*52	17144
Eritrea	2003	0	..	..	..	0	11	257	0
	2004	0	..	..	..	0	-25	233	3
	2005	0	..	..	..	0	-40	211	0
	2006	0	..	..	..	0	-30	153	0
Ethiopia	2003	196	..	..	..	196	-272	1274	
	2004	217	..	..	..	217	-397	1349	
	2005	245	..	..	..	245	-209	1504	
	2006	280	..	..	..	280	-218	1676	
Gabon	2003	11239	..	11056	106	77	-224	116	1070.
	2004	10930	..	10736	117	77	-190	88	1035
	2005	10877	..	10690	117	70	-190	149	10270
	2006	10935	..	10736	117	81	-265	183	10363
Gambia	2003	..	..	..	..	..	..	*108	*2
	2004	..	..	..	..	..	..	*109	*2
	2005	..	..	..	..	..	..	*109	*2
	2006	..	..	..	..	..	..	*114	*2
Ghana	2003	334	..	..	..	334	-6	2653	33.
	2004	454	..	..	..	454	0	2469	45
	2005	484	..	..	..	484	-6	2726	45
	2006	483	..	..	..	483	-6	3170	29.
Guinea	2003	*36	..	..	..	*36	..	*405	
	2004	*37	..	..	..	*37	..	*405	
	2005	*37	..	..	..	*37	..	*412	
	2006	*37	..	..	..	*37	..	*413	
Guinea-Bissau	2003	..	..	..	..	..	..	*100	
	2004	..	..	..	..	..	..	*100	
	2005	..	..	..	..	..	..	*100	
	2006	..	..	..	..	..	..	*103	
Kenya	2003	348	..	..	..	348	0	2992	32.
	2004	336	..	..	..	336	0	3667	42.
	2005	336	..	..	..	336	48	3599	24
	2006	359	..	..	..	359	-201	3723	22.
Liberia	2003	..	..	..	..	..	..	*190	*
	2004	..	..	..	..	..	..	205	*
	2005	..	..	..	..	..	..	236	*
	2006	..	..	..	..	..	..	*252	*
Libyan Arab Jamah.	2003	76752	..	70943	5809	..	..	0	5784
	2004	84912	..	77597	7315	..	..	0	6497
	2005	93497	..	83241	10256	..	..	13	7431
	2006	101124	..	87691	13433	..	..	11	8192

Table 2

Production, commerce et consommation d'énergie commerciale
Milliers de tonnes métriques d'équivalent pétrole et kilogrammes par habitant

Bunkers Soutes		Unallocated Quantités non réparties	Consumption Consommation						Year Année	Country or area Pays ou zone
Aviation Avion	Marine Maritime		Per capita Par habitant	Total Totale	Solids Solides	Liquids Liquides	Gas Gaz	Electricity Electricité		
*97	2	0	17	904	232	249	..	422	2003	Rép. dem. du Congo
121	2	0	20	1099	251	385	..	463	2004	
120	2	0	20	1128	264	382	..	482	2005	
120	2	0	19	1182	278	382	..	522	2006	
99	*72	..	149	116	..	116	..	..	2003	Djibouti
99	*75	..	169	133	..	133	..	..	2004	
104	*74	..	173	139	..	139	..	..	2005	
104	*84	..	174	143	..	143	..	..	2006	
490	2737	3347	802	53960	392	24296	28264	1007	2003	Egypte
712	1843	2900	819	58366	893	28423	27978	1072	2004	
761	1973	5834	883	63182	893	30363	30859	1068	2005	
801	1082	1980	881	64119	780	31335	30869	1134	2006	
..	..	0	1091	504		*55	448	0	2003	Guinée équatoriale
..	..	0	*1048	*496		*48	*447	0	2004	
..	..	0	*1024	*496		*48	*447	0	2005	
..	..	0	*1008	*500		*52	*447	0	2006	
11	..	..	56	234	..	234	..	0	2003	Erythrée
11	..	..	56	244	..	244	..	0	2004	
9	..	..	53	241	..	241	..	0	2005	
7	..	..	37	175	..	175	..	0	2006	
88	..	..	24	1654	..	1458	..	196	2003	Ethiopie
99	..	..	27	1864	..	1647	..	217	2004	
151	..	..	25	1808	..	1563	..	245	2005	
183	..	..	27	1992	..	1711	..	280	2006	
81	145	49	462	601	..	418	106	77	2003	Gabon
67	149	35	444	606	..	412	117	77	2004	
68	153	25	501	700	..	512	117	70	2005	
64	155	97	493	704	..	505	117	81	2006	
..	..	..	*71	*106	..	*106	..	..	2003	Gambie
..	..	..	*69	*107	..	*107	..	..	2004	
..	..	..	*67	*107	..	*107	..	..	2005	
..	..	..	*68	*112	..	*112	..	..	2006	
141	..	-42	122	2560	..	2219	..	341	2003	Ghana
116	..	-79	112	2433	..	1960	..	472	2004	
128	..	-70	122	2700	..	2201	..	499	2005	
162	..	18	138	3186	..	2714	..	472	2006	
*22	..	..	*48	*419	..	*383	..	*36	2003	Guinée
*22	..	..	*48	*420	..	*383	..	*37	2004	
*23	..	..	*47	*426	..	*389	..	*37	2005	
*23	..	..	*47	*428	..	*390	..	*37	2006	
*10	..	..	*71	*90	..	*90	..	..	2003	Guinée-Bissau
*10	..	..	*69	*90	..	*90	..	..	2004	
*10	..	..	*68	*90	..	*90	..	..	2005	
*10	..	..	*68	*93	..	*93	..	..	2006	
..	13	45	91	2960	65	2532	..	363	2003	Kenya
..	37	331	94	3211	76	2792	..	343	2004	
..	42	114	99	3490	76	3079	..	336	2005	
..	47	135	106	3878	84	3440	..	354	2006	
*3	*13	..	*50	*172	..	*172	..	..	2003	Libéria
*3	*13	..	54	188	..	188	..	..	2004	
*3	*13	..	61	219	..	219	..	..	2005	
*3	*13	..	*64	*235	..	*235	..	..	2006	
213	89	2439	2599	16166	..	11038	5128	0	2003	Jamah. arabe libyenne
215	89	2467	2673	17164	..	10937	6226	0	2004	
191	89	2486	2478	16428	..	11069	5355	4	2005	
179	89	2384	2471	16559	..	10756	5800	3	2006	

Table 2

Production, trade and consumption of commercial energy
Thousand metric tons of oil equivalent and kilograms per capita

| Country or area Pays ou zone | Year Année | Primary energy production Production d'énergie primaire | | | | | Changes in stocks Variations des stocks | Imports Importations | Exports Exportations |
		Total Totale	Solids Solides	Liquids Liquides	Gas Gaz	Electricity Electricité			
Madagascar	2003	52	..	..	..	52	..	*860	*2
	2004	55	..	..	..	55	..	*924	*2
	2005	*57	..	..	..	*57	..	*943	*2
	2006	*58	..	..	..	*58	..	*955	*2
Malawi	2003	145	46	..	..	99	..	271	1
	2004	158	*49	..	..	109	..	*284	*1
	2005	146	31	..	..	114	..	*289	*1
	2006	154	*38	..	..	115	..	*274	*
Mali	2003	*20	..	..	..	*20	..	201	
	2004	*21	..	..	..	*21	..	*210	
	2005	*22	..	..	..	*22	..	*211	
	2006	*23	..	..	..	*23	..	*211	
Mauritania	2003	..	..	..	..	..	..	455	
	2004	..	..	..	..	..	..	489	
	2005	..	..	..	..	..	..	508	
	2006	..	..	..	..	..	..	500	
Mauritius	2003	10	..	..	..	10	-30	1185	
	2004	10	..	..	..	10	14	1260	
	2005	10	..	..	..	10	-15	1343	
	2006	7	..	..	..	7	-68	1406	
Morocco	2003	192	..	10	39	143	93	11208	29
	2004	214	..	11	47	156	-194	12488	77
	2005	190	..	7	43	140	38	14745	57
	2006	226	..	11	62	153	-31	13901	32
Mozambique	2003	963	26	..	3	935	42	1276	84
	2004	2265	12	..	1249	1003	-8	1422	216
	2005	3245	2	..	2103	1140	-15	1337	307
	2006	3811	29	..	2516	1265	19	1412	355
Niger	2003	104	104	..	..	..	..	188	
	2004	110	110	..	..	..	..	185	
	2005	100	100	..	..	..	..	184	
	2006	*101	*101	..	..	..	..	184	
Nigeria	2003	136383	16	117964	17729	674	-396	7501	12439
	2004	150196	2	128734	20866	594	224	7680	13625
	2005	154656	6	133807	20318	526	-133	7959	13569
	2006	152250	6	125027	26554	663	-42	7749	13726
Réunion	2003	*50	..	..	..	*50	..	*800	
	2004	*50	..	..	..	*50	..	*811	
	2005	*50	..	..	..	*50	..	*812	
	2006	*50	..	..	..	*50	..	*814	
Rwanda	2003	10	..	..	0	10	..	*196	
	2004	*11	..	..	0	*11	..	199	
	2005	*12	..	..	*1	*11	..	*207	*
	2006	10	..	..	*1	10	..	*216	*
Sao Tome and Principe	2003	*1	..	..	..	*1	..	*31	
	2004	*1	..	..	..	*1	..	*31	
	2005	*1	..	..	..	*1	..	*34	
	2006	*1	..	..	..	*1	..	*35	
Senegal	2003	39	..	..	10	29	18	1779	19
	2004	38	..	..	12	25	-42	1673	18
	2005	36	..	..	13	23	83	1951	27
	2006	32	..	..	12	21	-132	1158	14
Seychelles	2003	..	..	..	..	..	..	281	
	2004	..	..	..	..	..	..	392	
	2005	..	..	..	..	..	..	357	
	2006	..	..	..	..	..	..	381	

Table 2

Production, commerce et consommation d'énergie commerciale
Milliers de tonnes métriques d'équivalent pétrole et kilogrammes par habitant

Bunkers Soutes		Unallocated Quantités non réparties	Consumption Consommation						Year Année	Country or area Pays ou zone
Aviation Avion	Marine Maritime		Per capita Par habitant	Total Totale	Solids Solides	Liquids Liquides	Gas Gaz	Electricity Electricité		
*2	*17	*142	*44	*731	*7	*672	..	52	2003	Madagascar
*2	*17	*145	*46	*795	*7	*733	..	55	2004	
*2	*17	*144	*46	*817	*7	*753	..	*57	2005	
*2	*17	*146	*45	*828	*7	*763	..	*58	2006	
..	..	..	35	405	37	270	..	98	2003	Malawi
..	..	..	*36	*431	*40	*283	..	109	2004	
..	..	..	*34	*424	*42	*268	..	113	2005	
..	..	..	*33	*420	*35	*271	..	114	2006	
20	..	..	18	201	..	181	..	*20	2003	Mali
21	..	..	*19	*211	..	*189	..	*21	2004	
21	..	..	*18	*212	..	*190	..	*22	2005	
*21	..	..	*18	*213	..	*190	..	*23	2006	
0	*5	..	157	450	0	443	..	7	2003	Mauritanie
0	*5	..	167	484	0	478	..	6	2004	
0	*5	..	173	503	0	492	..	11	2005	
0	*5	..	165	495	0	484	..	11	2006	
92	135	..	825	998	221	766	..	10	2003	Maurice
91	146	..	835	1019	202	806	..	10	2004	
100	192	..	866	1077	255	812	..	10	2005	
103	182	..	955	1196	339	850	..	7	2006	
301	13	669	348	10027	3227	6496	39	264	2003	Maroc
331	*13	987	362	10787	3612	6842	47	286	2004	
380	13	1152	423	12775	4455	7690	421	209	2005	
430	13	995	406	12395	3879	7659	532	325	2006	
39	45	..	68	1273	0	532	3	739	2003	Mozambique
41	43	..	75	1449	0	541	3	906	2004	
45	3	..	76	1476	0	475	68	933	2005	
56	3	..	80	1589	0	501	79	1009	2006	
10	..	..	24	281	104	154	..	24	2003	Niger
12	..	..	23	284	110	148	..	25	2004	
13	..	..	21	271	100	142	..	29	2005	
11	..	..	21	273	*101	142	..	31	2006	
400	628	700	144	18152	18	10713	6747	674	2003	Nigéria
197	523	719	155	19963	4	10354	9011	594	2004	
497	476	6075	150	20011	7	10497	8980	526	2005	
235	609	524	153	21406	7	10736	10000	663	2006	
..	*31	..	*1084	*819	..	*769	..	*50	2003	Réunion
..	*33	..	*1081	*828	..	*778	..	*50	2004	
..	*33	..	*1067	*829	..	*779	..	*50	2005	
..	*34	..	*1043	*830	..	*780	..	*50	2006	
*12	..	..	*22	*193	..	*171	0	22	2003	Rwanda
*12	..	..	22	197	..	176	0	20	2004	
*12	..	..	*22	*206	..	*185	*1	*21	2005	
*12	..	..	*23	*213	..	*194	*1	18	2006	
..	..	..	*221	*32	..	*31	..	*1	2003	Sao Tomé-et-Principe
..	..	..	*216	*32	..	*31	..	*1	2004	
..	..	..	*233	*35	..	*34	..	*1	2005	
..	..	..	*236	*36	..	*35	..	*1	2006	
*233	11	5	134	1362	*84	1239	10	29	2003	Sénégal
253	0	26	122	1287	89	1160	12	25	2004	
252	0	9	126	1370	106	1228	13	23	2005	
250	0	-12	85	939	117	790	12	21	2006	
*27	*71	..	2191	181	..	184	..	-2	2003	Seychelles
*31	*103	..	3100	256	..	258	..	-2	2004	
*27	*100	..	2753	228	..	230	..	-2	2005	
*30	*106	..	2877	243	..	246	..	-2	2006	

Table 2

Production, trade and consumption of commercial energy
Thousand metric tons of oil equivalent and kilograms per capita

Country or area Pays ou zone	Year Année	Primary energy production Production d'énergie primaire					Changes in stocks Variations des stocks	Imports Importations	Exports Exportations
		Total Totale	Solids Solides	Liquids Liquides	Gas Gaz	Electricity Electricité			
Sierra Leone	2003	1	..	..	..	1	..	*368	17
	2004	1	..	..	..	1	..	*454	20
	2005	2	..	..	..	2	..	*459	*2
	2006	*2	..	..	..	*2	..	*444	*2
Somalia	2003	..	..	..	..	..	..	*178	*3
	2004	..	..	..	..	..	..	*184	*3
	2005	..	..	..	..	..	..	*187	*3
	2006	..	..	..	..	..	..	*186	*5
South Africa Customs Un.	2003	130145	126717	693	1199	1536	1183	25557	4378
	2004	134142	128947	1680	1843	1672	-1282	25787	4090
	2005	135154	130133	1555	1982	1485	*-13	29652	4511
	2006	135000	130050	1506	1804	1641	*3	30632	4416
St. Helena and Depend.	2003	..	..	..	..	..	..	*4	
	2004	..	..	..	..	..	..	3	
	2005	..	..	..	..	..	..	*3	
	2006	..	..	..	..	..	..	*3	
Sudan	2003	13350	..	13250	..	100	135	350	1046
	2004	15091	..	15000	..	91	116	385	1182
	2005	15357	..	15250	..	107	-171	314	1201
	2006	16668	..	16550	..	118	907	538	1248
Togo	2003	10	..	..	..	10	2	430	
	2004	7	..	..	..	7	-1	420	
	2005	6	..	..	..	6	-18	394	
	2006	8	..	..	..	8	-46	311	
Tunisia	2003	5242	..	3259	1966	17	222	5583	353
	2004	5526	..	3436	2074	17	39	5677	388
	2005	5598	..	3484	2098	16	-113	5720	395
	2006	5628	..	3363	2254	11	60	5776	371
Uganda	2003	154	..	..	..	154	..	*488	*1
	2004	167	..	..	..	167	..	518	*1
	2005	158	..	..	..	158	..	663	*1
	2006	107	..	..	..	107	..	785	
United Rep.Tanzania	2003	258	38	..	0	219	..	1126	
	2004	367	45	..	119	203	..	1209	
	2005	534	52	..	329	153	..	1293	
	2006	528	56	..	349	123	..	1366	
Western Sahara	2003	..	..	..	..	..	..	*85	
	2004	..	..	..	..	..	..	*85	
	2005	..	..	..	..	..	..	*85	
	2006	..	..	..	..	..	..	*85	
Zambia	2003	840	130	..	..	710	56	627	5
	2004	865	137	..	..	727	56	657	3
	2005	908	144	..	..	764	60	691	3
	2006	946	144	..	..	802	51	720	4
Zimbabwe	2003	2946	2485	..	..	461	18	1097	14
	2004	2865	2390	..	..	475	12	822	14
	2005	3036	2535	..	..	502	4	967	12
	2006	2890	2413	..	..	477	-4	929	12
America, North	**2003**	**2032572**	**481383**	**686524**	**727918**	**136748**	**-6944**	**900074**	**45837**
	2004	**2048838**	**506542**	**684186**	**717308**	**140801**	**902**	**958087**	**47528**
	2005	**2032989**	**515239**	**664640**	**709479**	**143631**	**-3873**	**989581**	**47604**
	2006	**2069379**	**524172**	**666553**	**731985**	**146668**	**30339**	**989996**	**49094**
Anguilla	2003	..	..	..	..	..	..	13	
	2004	..	..	..	..	..	..	14	
	2005	..	..	..	..	..	..	17	
	2006	..	..	..	..	..	..	18	

Table 2

Production, commerce et consommation d'énergie commerciale
Milliers de tonnes métriques d'équivalent pétrole et kilogrammes par habitant

Bunkers Soutes		Unallocated Quantités non réparties	Consumption Consommation						Year Année	Country or area Pays ou zone
Aviation Avion	Marine Maritime		Per capita Par habitant	Total Totale	Solids Solides	Liquids Liquides	Gas Gaz	Electricity Electricité		
*27	*88	*69	*30	*169	..	*168		1	2003	Sierra Leone
27	*91	*94	*39	*223	..	*222		1	2004	
*27	*92	*107	*36	*214	..	*212	..	2	2005	
*29	*87	*101	*34	*207	..	*205		*2	2006	
*52	*20	*-102	*22	*172	..	*172	..	..	2003	Somalie
*52	*20	*-96	*22	*172	..	*172	..	..	2004	
*52	*21	*-96	*22	*179	..	*179	..	..	2005	
*52	*21	*-124	*21	*179	..	*179	..	..	2006	
886	2601	-4709	2193	111961	88808	20330	1199	1624	2003	Un.douan.d'Afr.mérid
781	2390	-3922	2275	121057	95430	20811	3090	1727	2004	
766	2647	-4117	2249	120408	93600	21124	4037	1648	2005	
794	2604	-4237	2257	122303	94495	21876	4242	1690	2006	
..	..	..	*558	*4	..	*4	..	..	2003	St-Hélène et dépend
..	..	..	415	3	..	3	..	..	2004	
..	..	..	*454	*3	..	*3	..	..	2005	
..	..	..	*451	*3	..	*3	..	..	2006	
136	8	93	86	2868	..	2768	..	100	2003	Soudan
142	8	212	92	3178	..	3087	..	91	2004	
201	8	188	97	3431	..	3324	..	107	2005	
226	8	-337	108	3921	..	3803	..	118	2006	
27	7	..	81	405	..	355	..	50	2003	Togo
40	5	..	75	383	..	333	..	49	2004	
50	3	..	68	365	..	315	..	50	2005	
35	2	..	61	327	..	276	..	51	2006	
..	0	106	708	6965	16	3902	3032	15	2003	Tunisie
..	0	63	727	7217	0	4040	3162	15	2004	
..	0	135	732	7344	0	4074	3257	13	2005	
..	9	165	736	7451	0	4092	3348	12	2006	
..	..	..	*25	*628	..	*488	..	140	2003	Ouganda
..	..	..	25	670	..	518	..	152	2004	
..	..	..	29	807	..	663	..	144	2005	
..	..	..	30	887	..	785	..	102	2006	
74	23	..	36	1287	38	1021	0	227	2003	Rép. Unie de Tanzanie
79	23	..	41	1473	45	1097	119	212	2004	
86	23	..	46	1719	52	1173	329	165	2005	
91	23	..	47	1781	56	1242	349	134	2006	
*6	..	..	*301	*79	..	*79	..	..	2003	Sahara occidental
*6	..	..	*294	*79	..	*79	..	..	2004	
*6	..	..	*290	*79	..	*79	..	..	2005	
*6	..	..	*286	*79	..	*79	..	..	2006	
49	..	41	118	1267	85	516	..	667	2003	Zambie
51	..	43	121	1338	90	540	..	708	2004	
53	..	46	122	1404	95	566	..	743	2005	
56	..	46	125	1471	101	590	..	780	2006	
36	..	..	297	3844	2350	760	..	735	2003	Zimbabwe
8	..	..	270	3522	2261	611	..	650	2004	
8	..	..	294	3863	2442	664	..	758	2005	
8	..	..	279	3686	2325	640	..	721	2006	
20579	23838	35805	4784	2401344	488664	1049958	726080	136643	2003	**Amérique du Nord**
20963	29332	33961	4825	2446863	502747	1085047	718280	140790	2004	
21610	30409	22850	4834	2475895	507655	1105916	718719	143605	2005	
20479	32389	22428	4768	2463132	500281	1098054	718250	146548	2006	
..	..	..	1052	13	..	13	..	..	2003	Anguilla
..	..	..	1092	14	..	14	..	..	2004	
..	..	..	1250	17	..	17	..	..	2005	
..	..	..	1242	18	..	18	..	..	2006	

Table 2

Production, trade and consumption of commercial energy
Thousand metric tons of oil equivalent and kilograms per capita

Country or area Pays ou zone	Year Année	Primary energy production Production d'énergie primaire					Changes in stocks Variations des stocks	Imports Importations	Exports Exportations
		Total Totale	Solids Solides	Liquids Liquides	Gas Gaz	Electricity Electricité			
Antigua and Barbuda	2003	..	..	..	..	..	..	*190	*
	2004	..	..	..	..	..	..	*196	*
	2005	..	..	..	..	..	..	*199	*
	2006	..	..	..	..	..	..	*205	*1
Aruba	2003	*120	..	*120	..	..	..	*10706	1049
	2004	*120	..	*120	..	..	..	*10706	1049
	2005	*120	..	*120	..	..	..	10713	1049
	2006	*120	..	*120	..	..	..	*10713	*1049
Bahamas	2003	..	..	..	..	..	*50	*3163	*220
	2004	..	..	..	..	..	0	*3209	*224
	2005	..	..	..	..	..	0	*3265	*225
	2006	..	..	..	..	..	0	*3273	*225
Barbados	2003	99	..	75	24	..	..	324	7
	2004	89	..	65	23	..	..	351	6
	2005	90	..	66	25	..	..	364	6
	2006	77	..	52	25	..	..	372	5
Belize	2003	*9	..	..	..	*9	..	*300	
	2004	*9	..	..	..	*9	..	*307	
	2005	*9	..	..	..	*9	..	*319	
	2006	*9	..	..	..	*9	..	*322	
Bermuda	2003	..	..	..	..	..	..	*196	
	2004	..	..	..	..	..	..	*203	
	2005	..	..	..	..	..	..	*209	
	2006	..	..	..	..	..	..	*211	
British Virgin Islands	2003	..	..	..	..	..	..	*26	
	2004	..	..	..	..	..	..	*29	
	2005	..	..	..	..	..	..	*30	
	2006	..	..	..	..	..	..	*33	
Canada	2003	376493	30390	142603	167960	35540	-4339	76138	21467
	2004	385115	32622	147681	167591	37221	-7315	78304	22326
	2005	388279	31907	145830	171231	39311	-5933	78231	22313
	2006	397145	32724	153089	172121	39211	-1541	74225	22719
Cayman Islands	2003	..	..	..	..	..	..	*180	
	2004	..	..	..	..	..	..	*186	
	2005	..	..	..	..	..	..	*189	
	2006	..	..	..	..	..	..	*195	
Costa Rica	2003	636	..	..	..	636	-98	2010	4
	2004	684	..	..	..	684	15	2161	8
	2005	695	..	..	..	695	-16	2106	
	2006	696	..	..	..	696	17	2356	3
Cuba	2003	4335	..	3711	613	11	30	4411	
	2004	3948	..	3284	656	8	*23	4424	
	2005	3614	..	2916	692	6	402	5314	
	2006	3958	..	2938	1011	8	-17	6172	
Dominica	2003	2	..	..	..	2	..	38	
	2004	3	..	..	..	3	..	36	
	2005	2	..	..	..	2	..	*38	
	2006	*3	..	..	..	*3	..	*39	
Dominican Republic	2003	103	..	..	..	103	0	6577	
	2004	136	..	..	..	136	36	6217	
	2005	163	..	..	..	163	-5	6224	
	2006	121	..	..	..	121	-19	6325	
El Salvador	2003	209	..	..	..	209	44	2240	18
	2004	206	..	..	..	206	38	2284	2
	2005	234	..	..	..	234	65	2215	12
	2006	267	..	..	..	267	53	2157	7

Table 2

Production, commerce et consommation d'énergie commerciale

Milliers de tonnes métriques d'équivalent pétrole et kilogrammes par habitant

Bunkers Soutes		Unallocated Quantités non réparties	Consumption Consommation						Year Année	Country or area Pays ou zone
Aviation Avion	Marine Maritime		Per capita Par habitant	Total Totale	Solids Solides	Liquids Liquides	Gas Gaz	Electricity Electricité		
*48	*3	..	*1628	*130	..	*130	..	..	2003	Antigua-et-Barbuda
*50	*3	..	*1671	*135	..	*135	..	..	2004	
*50	*3	..	*1659	*137	..	*137	..	..	2005	
*50	*3	..	*1695	*143	..	*143	..	..	2006	
*75	..	*5	2636	251	..	251	..	..	2003	Aruba
*75	..	*5	2566	251	..	251	..	..	2004	
*77	..	5	2541	256	..	256	..	..	2005	
*77	..	*5	*2487	*256	..	*256	..	..	2006	
*43	*244	..	*1941	*619	*2	*617	..	..	2003	Bahamas
*44	*254	..	*2217	*664	*2	*662	..	..	2004	
*46	*266	..	*2156	*696	*2	*694	..	..	2005	
*47	*264	..	*2160	*706	*3	*703	..	..	2006	
..	..	0	1285	349	..	325	24	..	2003	Barbade
..	..	0	1376	375	..	352	23	..	2004	
..	..	0	1429	390	..	366	25	..	2005	
..	..	0	1451	398	..	373	25	..	2006	
*22	*12	..	*1006	*275	..	*264	..	*11	2003	Belize
*23	*12	..	*996	*281	..	*270	..	*11	2004	
*24	*13	..	*999	*291	..	*280	..	*12	2005	
*24	*13	..	*966	*294	..	*283	..	*12	2006	
*17	*3	..	*2795	*176	..	*176	..	..	2003	Bermudes
*18	*3	..	*2883	*183	..	*183	..	..	2004	
*18	*3	..	*2964	*188	..	*188	..	..	2005	
*20	*3	..	*2954	*188	..	*188	..	..	2006	
..	..	..	*1208	*26	..	*26	..	..	2003	Iles Vierges britanniques
..	..	..	*1330	*29	..	*29	..	..	2004	
..	..	..	*1357	*30	..	*30	..	..	2005	
..	..	..	*1464	*33	..	*33	..	..	2006	
699	507	2456	7534	238633	26284	88806	88587	34956	2003	Canada
885	617	5419	7518	240545	25689	91840	86695	36321	2004	
835	604	5308	7507	242562	25141	90544	89617	37260	2005	
825	549	4007	7361	240337	24673	89775	88322	37568	2006	
*22	..	..	*3639	*159	..	*159	..	..	2003	Iles Caïmanes
*23	..	..	*3699	*164	..	*164	..	..	2004	
*23	..	..	*3447	*167	..	*167	..	..	2005	
*24	..	..	*3285	*171	..	*171	..	..	2006	
..	..	136	626	2559	100	1830	..	629	2003	Costa Rica
..	..	89	635	2653	83	1906	..	664	2004	
..	..	56	645	2751	60	1995	..	696	2005	
..	..	26	683	2974	82	2189	..	703	2006	
221	67	820	673	7608	18	6966	613	11	2003	Cuba
223	72	351	679	7702	18	7020	656	8	2004	
225	73	58	727	8170	23	7449	692	6	2005	
*212	*55	1130	778	8750	*20	7710	1011	8	2006	
..	..	..	582	41	..	38	..	2	2003	Dominique
..	..	..	558	39	..	36	..	3	2004	
..	..	..	*589	*41	..	*38	..	2	2005	
..	..	..	*614	*42	..	*39	..	*3	2006	
92	..	630	666	5958	740	5012	103	103	2003	Rép. dominicaine
101	..	192	663	6023	544	5218	125	136	2004	
100	..	156	665	6135	333	5386	253	163	2005	
99	..	54	675	6311	560	5322	309	121	2006	
70	..	32	319	2115	1	1878	..	236	2003	El Salvador
75	..	-28	315	2131	1	1891	..	239	2004	
78	..	149	296	2035	1	1775	..	258	2005	
75	..	48	310	2170	1	1903	..	267	2006	

Table 2

Production, trade and consumption of commercial energy
Thousand metric tons of oil equivalent and kilograms per capita

Country or area Pays ou zone	Year Année	Primary energy production Production d'énergie primaire					Changes in stocks Variations des stocks	Imports Importations	Exports Exportations
		Total Totale	Solids Solides	Liquids Liquides	Gas Gaz	Electricity Electricité			
Greenland	2003	..	..	..	..	..	..	*196	*7
	2004	..	..	..	..	..	..	*197	*7
	2005	..	..	..	..	..	..	*200	*7
	2006	..	..	..	..	..	..	*204	*7
Grenada	2003	..	..	..	..	..	..	83	..
	2004	..	..	..	..	..	..	82	..
	2005	..	..	..	..	..	..	86	..
	2006	..	..	..	..	..	..	88	..
Guadeloupe	2003	..	..	..	..	..	..	*742	..
	2004	..	..	..	..	..	..	*748	..
	2005	..	..	..	..	..	..	*772	..
	2006	..	..	..	..	..	..	*781	..
Guatemala	2003	1434	..	1221	..	213	0	3352	1152
	2004	1208	..	999	..	209	25	3519	955
	2005	1225	..	910	..	315	169	3718	846
	2006	1167	..	818	..	349	-210	3477	920
Haiti	2003	22	..	..	..	22	..	538	..
	2004	22	..	..	..	22	..	561	..
	2005	23	..	..	..	23	..	565	..
	2006	23	..	..	..	23	..	580	..
Honduras	2003	187	..	..	..	187	243	2204	18
	2004	202	..	..	..	202	5	2278	27
	2005	148	..	..	..	148	17	2374	25
	2006	167	..	..	..	167	6	2490	38
Jamaica	2003	13	..	..	..	13	35	3802	129
	2004	14	..	..	..	14	12	3717	124
	2005	13	..	..	..	13	26	3431	0
	2006	14	..	..	..	14	-11	4121	0
Martinique	2003	..	..	..	..	..	..	765	*225
	2004	..	..	..	..	..	..	793	*225
	2005	..	..	..	..	..	..	814	*225
	2006	..	..	..	..	..	..	840	*225
Mexico	2003	233827	2944	190001	37726	3157	-1055	22525	109390
	2004	237911	3044	191899	39440	3528	1643	24544	109241
	2005	236409	3292	188168	41004	3945	445	26902	104304
	2006	236443	3516	183762	45037	4128	621	30544	104114
Montserrat	2003	..	..	..	..	..	..	*24	..
	2004	..	..	..	..	..	..	*24	..
	2005	..	..	..	..	..	..	*24	..
	2006	..	..	..	..	..	..	*25	..
Netherlands Antilles	2003	..	..	..	..	..	..	12784	7683
	2004	..	..	..	..	..	..	13751	8151
	2005	..	..	..	..	..	..	14734	9355
	2006	..	..	..	..	..	..	14169	8680
Nicaragua	2003	49	..	..	..	49	41	1321	5
	2004	50	..	..	..	50	-42	1286	5
	2005	61	..	..	..	61	31	1317	6
	2006	59	..	..	..	59	14	1382	18
Panama	2003	248	..	..	..	248	-20	2054	209
	2004	335	..	..	..	335	-186	1770	220
	2005	333	..	..	..	333	0	2038	226
	2006	336	..	..	..	336	0	2188	229
Puerto Rico	2003	22	..	..	..	22	..	686	..
	2004	12	..	..	..	12	..	633	..
	2005	12	..	..	..	12	..	633	..
	2006	*13	..	..	..	*13	..	633	..

Table 2

Production, commerce et consommation d'énergie commerciale

Milliers de tonnes métriques d'équivalent pétrole et kilogrammes par habitant

Bunkers Soutes — Aviation Avion	Bunkers Soutes — Marine Maritime	Unallocated Quantités non réparties	Consumption Consommation — Per capita Par habitant	Consumption Consommation — Total Totale	Consumption Consommation — Solids Solides	Consumption Consommation — Liquids Liquides	Consumption Consommation — Gas Gaz	Consumption Consommation — Electricity Electricité	Year Année	Country or area Pays ou zone
*8	..	..	*3196	*180	..	*180	..	..	2003	Groënland
*8	..	..	*3214	*181	..	*181	..	..	2004	
*8	..	..	*3268	*184	..	*184	..	..	2005	
*9	..	..	*3324	*187	..	*187	..	..	2006	
*8	..	..	715	75	..	75	..	..	2003	Grenade
*8	..	..	707	74	..	74	..	..	2004	
*7	..	..	749	79	..	79	..	..	2005	
*7	..	..	765	81	..	81	..	..	2006	
*103	..	..	*1455	*639	..	*639	..	..	2003	Guadeloupe
*103	..	..	*1449	*644	..	*644	..	..	2004	
*108	..	..	*1491	*664	..	*664	..	..	2005	
*110	..	..	*1467	*672	..	*672	..	..	2006	
41	122	106	278	3365	258	2928	..	179	2003	Guatemala
44	122	83	282	3497	291	3033	..	173	2004	
38	122	76	291	3693	285	3119	..	288	2005	
38	122	106	282	3668	300	3027	..	342	2006	
27	..	..	64	533	..	511	..	22	2003	Haïti
24	..	..	66	559	..	537	..	22	2004	
24	..	..	66	564	..	541	..	23	2005	
25	..	..	67	579	..	555	..	23	2006	
26	..	..	307	2104	118	1770	..	215	2003	Honduras
29	..	..	344	2419	122	2064	..	233	2004	
28	..	..	340	2450	128	2170	..	153	2005	
30	..	..	351	2583	133	2281	..	168	2006	
195	30	24	1279	3400	59	3328	..	13	2003	Jamaïque
*186	25	59	1243	3327	46	3267	..	14	2004	
183	30	7	1207	3199	42	3144	..	13	2005	
236	30	12	1452	3868	22	3831	..	14	2006	
*3	*44	*-106	*1533	*599	..	*599	..	..	2003	Martinique
*4	*45	*-97	*1564	*616	..	*616	..	..	2004	
*4	*45	*-80	*1560	*620	..	*620	..	..	2005	
*4	*45	*-62	*1568	*627	..	*627	..	..	2006	
2593	815	7001	1349	137609	5638	82246	46643	3082	2003	Mexique
2491	774	5314	1388	142992	5070	85907	48570	3445	2004	
2581	877	7033	1424	148071	6068	89044	49117	3842	2005	
2763	880	5392	1461	153217	6125	89062	53968	4062	2006	
..	*1	..	*2580	*23	..	*23	..	..	2003	Montserrat
..	*1	..	*2510	*23	..	*23	..	..	2004	
..	*1	..	*2484	*23	..	*23	..	..	2005	
..	*1	..	*2512	*24	..	*24	..	..	2006	
72	1707	1735	8877	1586	..	1586	..	..	2003	Antilles néerlandaises
73	1709	1521	12538	2296	..	2296	..	..	2004	
74	1712	2300	6972	1293	..	1293	..	..	2005	
75	1716	2493	6354	1204	..	1204	..	..	2006	
..	..	35	243	1289	..	1241	..	48	2003	Nicaragua
..	..	30	249	1342	..	1293	..	50	2004	
..	..	35	239	1306	..	1244	..	62	2005	
..	..	48	246	1361	..	1298	..	63	2006	
2	..	0	677	2111	0	1878	..	233	2003	Panama
0	..	0	653	2071	1	1746	..	324	2004	
0	..	0	665	2146	1	1816	..	329	2005	
0	..	0	699	2295	1	1962	..	331	2006	
..	..	..	183	709	..	..	686	22	2003	Porto Rico
..	..	..	166	645	..	..	633	12	2004	
..	..	..	165	646	..	..	633	12	2005	
..	..	..	165	646	..	..	633	*13	2006	

Table 2

Production, trade and consumption of commercial energy
Thousand metric tons of oil equivalent and kilograms per capita

Country or area Pays ou zone	Year Année	Primary energy production Production d'énergie primaire					Changes in stocks Variations des stocks	Imports Importations	Exports Exportations
		Total Totale	Solids Solides	Liquids Liquides	Gas Gaz	Electricity Electricité			
St. Kitts-Nevis	2003	..	..	..	..	..	..	*74	..
	2004	..	..	..	..	..	..	*76	..
	2005	..	..	..	..	..	..	*79	..
	2006	..	..	..	..	..	..	*79	..
St. Lucia	2003	..	..	..	..	..	..	*121	..
	2004	..	..	..	..	..	..	*127	..
	2005	..	..	..	..	..	..	*132	..
	2006	..	..	..	..	..	..	*135	..
St. Pierre-Miquelon	2003	..	..	..	..	..	..	*28	..
	2004	..	..	..	..	..	..	*27	..
	2005	..	..	..	..	..	..	*28	..
	2006	..	..	..	..	..	..	*28	..
St. Vincent-Grenadines	2003	2	..	..	..	2	..	*64	..
	2004	2	..	..	..	2	..	*64	..
	2005	*2	..	..	..	*2	..	*64	..
	2006	*2	..	..	..	*2	..	*66	..
Trinidad and Tobago	2003	31184	..	7974	23210	..	324	4702	22437
	2004	31847	..	7385	24462	..	313	3449	21483
	2005	33934	..	8444	25490	..	78	4577	24016
	2006	39884	..	8226	31658	..	-427	4737	29306
United States	2003	1383577	448050	340819	498383	96325	-2200	737498	89422
	2004	1386925	470876	332753	485136	98160	6335	791813	98400
	2005	1367623	480041	318187	471037	98358	847	817660	100944
	2006	1388875	487932	317547	482133	101263	31853	816815	107292
America, South	**2003**	**520914**	**39800**	**342758**	**89432**	**48924**	**5105**	**79853**	**238945**
	2004	**533338**	**42198**	**346772**	**93918**	**50450**	**-1156**	**90890**	**263532**
	2005	**558006**	**46620**	**360925**	**97213**	**53248**	**-151**	**88756**	**269641**
	2006	**575920**	**50980**	**366472**	**102074**	**56393**	**-4917**	**91288**	**271750**
Argentina	2003	88284	53	44918	39747	3567	57	1804	25272
	2004	87597	30	43338	40921	3307	-115	3093	22204
	2005	85423	15	41612	40253	3544	147	4587	20082
	2006	88438	252	42083	42155	3948	-155	3544	16418
Bolivia	2003	8279	..	1978	6108	193	*-64	329	4297
	2004	10946	..	2267	8494	185	-510	193	7903
	2005	13220	..	2441	10568	211	-472	255	10291
	2006	14151	..	2654	11312	186	-925	376	10762
Brazil	2003	125927	2064	86941	9495	27427	654	44579	20787
	2004	127868	2402	86852	10032	28582	-775	51604	22419
	2005	139024	2779	96133	10249	29863	-226	46181	23303
	2006	146068	2613	101894	10386	31174	-424	47919	29438
Chile	2003	4464	391	369	1760	1944	150	19923	1597
	2004	3939	128	368	1615	1829	100	21913	1475
	2005	4925	369	343	1965	2248	406	22596	1619
	2006	5425	269	330	1882	2945	734	23592	1942
Colombia	2003	69814	32517	28027	6157	3114	616	334	45393
	2004	71600	34900	26770	6481	3449	8	319	48347
	2005	74924	38391	26301	6800	3430	357	947	50662
	2006	80907	42637	26901	7684	3685	-1324	688	55668
Ecuador	2003	22504	..	21499	388	617	1133	2117	15229
	2004	28703	..	27466	600	637	305	2108	20335
	2005	27834	..	26606	488	740	98	2783	19596
	2006	28373	..	26812	795	766	-253	3240	20709
Falkland Is. (Malvinas)	2003	*3	*3	..	..	..	..	*12	..
	2004	*3	*3	..	..	..	..	*12	..
	2005	*3	*3	..	..	..	..	*13	..
	2006	*3	*3	..	..	..	..	*13	..

Table 2

Production, commerce et consommation d'énergie commerciale
Milliers de tonnes métriques d'équivalent pétrole et kilogrammes par habitant

Bunkers Soutes		Unallocated Quantités non réparties	Consumption Consommation						Year Année	Country or area Pays ou zone
Aviation Avion	Marine Maritime		Per capita Par habitant	Total Totale	Solids Solides	Liquids Liquides	Gas Gaz	Electricity Electricité		
..	..	..	*1654	*74	..	*74	..	..	2003	St-Kitts-Nevis
..	..	..	*1718	*76	..	*76	..	..	2004	
..	..	..	*1830	*79	..	*79	..	..	2005	
..	..	..	*1830	*79	..	*79	..	..	2006	
..	*5	..	*720	*116	..	*116	..	..	2003	St-Lucie
..	*5	..	*753	*122	..	*122	..	..	2004	
..	*6	..	*762	*126	..	*126	..	..	2005	
..	*6	..	*771	*129	..	*129	..	..	2006	
..	*6	..	*3065	*21	..	*21	..	..	2003	St-Pierre-Miquelon
..	*6	..	*2920	*20	..	*20	..	..	2004	
..	*6	..	*3060	*21	..	*21	..	..	2005	
..	*6	..	*3054	*21	..	*21	..	..	2006	
..	..	..	*626	*66	..	*64	..	2	2003	St. Vincent-Grenadines
..	..	..	*634	*66	..	*64	..	2	2004	
..	..	..	*639	*66	..	*64	..	*2	2005	
..	..	..	*662	*69	..	*66	..	*2	2006	
8	744	548	8996	11830		..	734	11096	..	2003	Trinité-et-Tobago
6	898	286	9338	12317	..	666	11651	..	2004	
60	264	942	9937	13157	..	987	12170	..	2005	
75	*250	451	11274	14972	..	1312	13660	..	2006	
16183	19528	22383	6794	1976104	455445	845455	578327	96877	2003	Etats-Unis
16469	24786	20737	6854	2012384	470879	872447	569926	99132	2004	
17020	26383	6805	6861	2033642	475570	891377	566211	100484	2005	
15653	28445	8718	6749	2014060	468361	882531	560321	102847	2006	
2702	**6072**	**30202**	**877**	**317672**	**20300**	**159253**	**89343**	**48775**	**2003**	**Amérique du Sud**
3421	**6517**	**17043**	**912**	**334721**	**21031**	**169223**	**94007**	**50459**	**2004**	
3402	**7727**	**17742**	**936**	**348284**	**21776**	**176091**	**97040**	**53376**	**2005**	
3871	**7310**	**19621**	**979**	**369370**	**21734**	**188758**	**102298**	**56580**	**2006**	
..	588	4875	1566	59320	525	21259	33536	4000	2003	Argentine
..	542	5047	1649	63040	580	23972	34882	3606	2004	
..	695	3968	1688	65145	897	24688	35683	3877	2005	
..	741	5049	1795	69960	753	27175	37882	4151	2006	
..	..	354	446	4021		1727	2101	194	2003	Bolivie
..	..	402	363	3346	..	1619	1541	185	2004	
..	..	562	328	3096	..	1997	887	212	2005	
..	..	1025	381	3668	..	2195	1287	186	2006	
1100	3219	6886	770	137786	13809	79185	14171	30621	2003	Brésil
1090	3348	6479	808	146750	14363	83079	17512	31796	2004	
1100	3497	6442	820	150968	13923	85252	18572	33220	2005	
1271	3393	6106	824	153992	13779	86057	19441	34714	2006	
544	881	824	1280	20392	2445	8677	7159	2111	2003	Chili
602	961	961	1351	21753	3287	9350	7124	1992	2004	
640	1246	812	1399	22799	3313	9423	7630	2433	2005	
683	1404	-28	1478	24285	3948	9948	7247	3141	2006	
589	249	1847	481	21454	2746	9533	6157	3018	2003	Colombie
587	395	989	477	21593	1941	9863	6481	3308	2004	
616	415	1355	488	22466	2700	9685	6800	3281	2005	
663	468	2558	504	23564	2467	9882	7684	3531	2006	
..	258	650	572	7351	..	6250	388	714	2003	Equateur
..	226	2557	567	7389	..	6010	600	779	2004	
..	672	957	703	9293	..	7919	488	887	2005	
..	*297	719	756	10141	..	8445	795	901	2006	
..	..	..	*5112	*15	*3	*12	..	..	2003	Iles Falkland (Malvinas)
..	..	..	*5095	*15	*3	*12	..	..	2004	
..	..	..	*5350	*16	*3	*13	..	..	2005	
..	..	..	*5341	*16	*3	*13	..	..	2006	

Table 2

Production, trade and consumption of commercial energy

Thousand metric tons of oil equivalent and kilograms per capita

Country or area Pays ou zone	Year Année	Primary energy production Production d'énergie primaire					Changes in stocks Variations des stocks	Imports Importations	Exports Exportations
		Total Totale	Solids Solides	Liquids Liquides	Gas Gaz	Electricity Electricité			
French Guiana	2003	..	..	..	..	..	..	*287	..
	2004	..	..	..	..	..	..	*287	..
	2005	..	..	..	..	..	..	*287	..
	2006	..	..	..	..	..	..	*298	..
Guyana	2003	..	..	..	..	..	..	508	..
	2004	..	..	..	..	..	..	492	..
	2005	..	..	..	..	..	..	508	..
	2006	..	..	..	..	..	..	513	..
Paraguay	2003	4451	..	0	..	4451	-71	1226	3884
	2004	4464	..	0	..	4464	-12	1292	3869
	2005	4403	..	5	..	4399	-26	1179	3765
	2006	4628	..	5	..	4624	-13	1241	3929
Peru	2003	7307	11	5086	616	1594	883	6438	3393
	2004	7588	15	5103	963	1507	36	6542	2924
	2005	8746	29	5376	1624	1717	-94	6550	3452
	2006	10680	73	6900	1859	1847	1180	6631	3339
Suriname	2003	653	..	588	..	65	..	268	129
	2004	678	..	612	..	66	..	272	142
	2005	708	..	637	..	71	..	284	148
	2006	731	..	656	..	75	..	290	152
Uruguay	2003	733	..	..	..	733	132	2030	258
	2004	411	..	..	..	411	78	2763	353
	2005	575	..	..	..	575	-129	2586	444
	2006	309	..	..	..	309	39	2942	239
Venezuela(Bolivar. Rep.)	2003	188495	4762	153351	25163	5219	1614	..	118706
	2004	189543	4721	153997	24812	6013	-271	..	133560
	2005	198223	5034	161473	25266	6451	-211	..	136278
	2006	196206	5134	158237	26002	6834	-3776	..	129154
Asia	**2003**	**3532015**	**1246700**	**1562574**	**621297**	**101444**	**-2663**	**1384353**	**1457918**
	2004	**3832682**	**1418934**	**1639561**	**660869**	**113318**	**899**	**1530087**	**1565530**
	2005	**4094538**	**1568621**	**1695644**	**708497**	**121776**	**-6328**	**1558491**	**1650338**
	2006	**4312946**	**1709680**	**1728430**	**745717**	**129119**	**990**	**1626950**	**1728425**
Afghanistan	2003	86	24	..	6	56	..	*164	.
	2004	76	24	..	3	50	..	197	.
	2005	*77	*23	..	*2	*51	..	*210	.
	2006	*77	*23	..	*2	*51	..	*210	.
Armenia	2003	342	..	..	..	342	..	1470	50
	2004	380	..	..	..	380	..	1586	99
	2005	386	..	..	..	386	..	1924	129
	2006	393	..	..	..	393	..	1928	85
Azerbaijan	2003	20221	..	15391	4618	212	-3	3886	10973
	2004	20457	..	15565	4655	237	42	4861	11405
	2005	27652	..	22232	5161	259	904	4734	16771
	2006	38598	..	32289	6092	217	-133	4412	27985
Bahrain	2003	16488	..	10187	6300	..	-603	3283	10344
	2004	16720	..	10168	6552	..	-315	3326	9927
	2005	17083	..	10143	6941	..	-250	3980	10082
	2006	17324	..	9970	7354	..	-513	3760	9740
Bangladesh	2003	10591	..	108	10386	97	-133	4227	.
	2004	11374	..	97	11171	105	-56	4269	.
	2005	12225	..	104	12010	111	-326	4495	.
	2006	13191	..	100	12972	119	-117	4537	.
Bhutan	2003	235	46	..	..	189	..	*69	159
	2004	238	21	..	..	217	..	*82	173
	2005	262	59	..	..	202	..	*68	173
	2006	296	69	..	..	228	..	*69	213

Table 2

Production, commerce et consommation d'énergie commerciale

Milliers de tonnes métriques d'équivalent pétrole et kilogrammes par habitant

Bunkers Soutes		Unallocated Quantités non réparties	Consumption Consommation						Year Année	Country or area Pays ou zone
Aviation Avion	Marine Maritime		Per capita Par habitant	Total Totale	Solids Solides	Liquids Liquides	Gas Gaz	Electricity Electricité		
*18	..	..	*1488	*269	..	*269	..	..	2003	Guyane française
*18	..	..	*1408	*269	..	*269	..	..	2004	
*18	..	..	*1378	*269	..	*269	..	..	2005	
*20	..	..	*1413	*278	..	*278	..	..	2006	
12	..	..	659	496	..	496	..	..	2003	Guyana
12	..	..	635	479	..	479	..	..	2004	
13	..	..	653	495	..	495	..	..	2005	
13	..	..	658	500	..	500	..	..	2006	
26	..	1	323	1836	..	1270	..	567	2003	Paraguay
19	..	2	324	1878	..	1282	..	595	2004	
19	..	1	309	1823	..	1189	..	634	2005	
24	..	0	321	1929	..	1235	..	694	2006	
139	44	-566	366	9837	730	6897	616	1594	2003	Pérou
443	57	-586	415	11233	857	7906	963	1507	2004	
313	228	258	409	11107	902	6864	1624	1717	2005	
466	100	-266	455	12457	745	8006	1859	1847	2006	
..	..	137	1362	655	..	590	..	65	2003	Suriname
..	..	144	1348	664	..	598	..	66	2004	
..	..	149	1394	696	..	624	..	71	2005	
..	..	155	1416	714	..	639	..	75	2006	
33	317	17	589	2007	1	1279	54	673	2003	Uruguay
45	340	25	706	2332	1	1626	94	611	2004	
43	356	91	712	2355	1	1626	89	639	2005	
57	248	104	774	2565	2	1909	102	552	2006	
241	517	15177	2034	52232	41	21809	25163	5219	2003	Venezuela(Rép. bolivar.)
606	649	1023	2066	53980	0	23156	24812	6013	2004	
640	618	3147	2173	57756	36	26047	25266	6406	2005	
674	658	4201	2416	65301	36	32476	26002	6787	2006	
33505	58015	207820	829	3151822	1373702	1059624	617033	101463	2003	**Asie**
35195	62913	226663	902	3462029	1568231	1133518	646995	113284	2004	
38441	68715	224577	944	3667443	1705334	1149583	690711	121815	2005	
40221	74227	233959	978	3852769	1835771	1150571	737180	129247	2006	
*8	..	..	*11	*241	24	*147	6	64	2003	Afghanistan
0	..	..	12	273	24	188	3	58	2004	
*10	..	..	*12	*276	*23	*191	*2	*60	2005	
*10	..	..	*12	*276	*23	*191	*2	*60	2006	
27	..	0	457	1735	19	316	1081	318	2003	Arménie
39	..	0	569	1828	0	311	1201	315	2004	
45	..	0	664	2136	0	333	1488	316	2005	
40	..	0	682	2196	1	312	1525	358	2006	
201	..	490	1511	12445	..	3819	8280	347	2003	Azerbaïdjan
228	..	38	1638	13605	..	4209	9042	354	2004	
428	..	198	1678	14085	..	4678	9045	362	2005	
500	..	156	1709	14501	..	4271	9938	293	2006	
477	..	1683	11114	7662	..	1362	6300	..	2003	Bahreïn
521	..	1719	11297	7989	..	1437	6552	..	2004	
563	..	1854	11852	8589	..	1648	6941	..	2005	
577	..	1801	12458	9251	..	1897	7354	..	2006	
234	36	474	105	14207	350	3374	10386	97	2003	Bangladesh
242	36	430	110	14991	350	3364	11171	105	2004	
279	36	479	117	16253	350	3782	12010	111	2005	
274	36	469	120	17067	350	3626	12972	119	2006	
..	..	..	238	146	39	*49	..	57	2003	Bhoutan
..	..	..	237	148	35	*53	..	60	2004	
..	..	..	247	157	40	*53	..	64	2005	
..	..	..	236	152	36	*53	..	63	2006	

Table 2

Production, trade and consumption of commercial energy
Thousand metric tons of oil equivalent and kilograms per capita

Country or area Pays ou zone	Year Année	Primary energy production — Production d'énergie primaire: Total Totale	Solids Solides	Liquids Liquides	Gas Gaz	Electricity Electricité	Changes in stocks Variations des stocks	Imports Importations	Exports Exportations
Brunei Darussalam	2003	22016	..	10492	11524	..	*-96	0	19924
	2004	21739	..	10338	11401	..	55	0	19378
	2005	21309	..	10116	11193	..	*-83	26	19143
	2006	22598	..	10833	11765	..	*-212	0	20537
Cambodia	2003	3	..	..	..	3	..	1079	..
	2004	2	..	..	..	2	..	1202	..
	2005	4	..	..	..	4	..	1278	..
	2006	5	..	..	..	5	..	1404	..
China	2003	1098103	860139	169600	40246	28119	-278	128182	80862
	2004	1242421	995163	175873	36897	34488	-124	179041	72578
	2005	1366651	1101259	181353	45337	38702	-4162	182116	68796
	2006	1460396	1185310	184766	47662	42659	-3286	203060	63566
China, Hong Kong SAR	2003	..	..	..	..	..	-114	22620	1481
	2004	..	..	..	..	..	-2	24563	1635
	2005	..	..	..	..	..	-542	24146	2697
	2006	..	..	..	..	..	630	25378	1597
China, Macao SAR	2003	..	..	..	..	..	-4	625	..
	2004	..	..	..	..	..	18	763	..
	2005	..	..	..	..	..	-2	787	..
	2006	..	..	..	..	..	8	827	..
Cyprus	2003	0	..	..	..	0	-67	2652	..
	2004	0	..	..	..	0	-62	2398	..
	2005	0	..	..	..	0	71	2799	..
	2006	0	..	..	..	0	120	2959	..
Georgia	2003	723	5	140	17	561	-23	1514	124
	2004	634	5	98	11	520	0	1699	106
	2005	618	3	67	12	536	0	2067	90
	2006	549	6	64	16	463	0	2343	77
India	2003	285806	215981	37557	24270	7998	978	110674	12850
	2004	299690	228921	37958	24075	8738	1532	120102	15877
	2005	314387	243028	36651	24490	10217	5996	130539	16996
	2006	330904	257084	38468	24006	11347	6494	146423	24196
Indonesia	2003	200166	73898	57095	67850	1324	6	32844	132882
	2004	214165	89579	52909	70273	1404	578	40533	141777
	2005	229071	108674	50122	68782	1493	570	37727	150854
	2006	261321	142862	48091	68968	1400	524	32935	177604
Iran(Islamic Rep. of)	2003	267945	862	192585	73544	954	-132	10575	131716
	2004	283629	872	200067	81776	914	0	12821	137022
	2005	308277	931	217351	88610	1384	0	12807	153293
	2006	315942	1064	215973	97334	1571	0	16036	151762
Iraq	2003	67456	..	66003	1416	37	0	393	41737
	2004	101419	..	99016	2360	42	459	4473	76100
	2005	94215	..	91766	2405	45	448	5133	68533
	2006	99276	..	96058	3177	42	-1749	5312	74679
Israel	2003	111	96	3	8	4	-103	23863	3092
	2004	1143	97	2	1041	3	-201	23248	3590
	2005	1529	91	2	1433	3	548	22888	3920
	2006	2105	99	2	2002	1	-186	23318	3290
Japan	2003	33517	..	670	2884	29963	-446	430934	4845
	2004	37244	..	692	2994	33558	-1135	437983	5087
	2005	38006	..	734	3215	34057	2445	442087	9000
	2006	38996	..	726	3547	34723	-1174	437804	10365
Jordan	2003	243	..	2	237	*5	-46	5241	..
	2004	247	..	1	241	5	113	6393	..
	2005	205	..	1	199	5	143	7117	..
	2006	191	..	1	185	5	-7	6942	..

Table 2

Production, commerce et consommation d'énergie commerciale
Milliers de tonnes métriques d'équivalent pétrole et kilogrammes par habitant

Bunkers Soutes		Unallocated Quantités	Consumption Consommation						Year Année	Country or area Pays ou zone
Aviation Avion	Marine Maritime	non réparties	Per capita Par habitant	Total Totale	Solids Solides	Liquids Liquides	Gas Gaz	Electricity Electricité		
..	..	-358	7264	2539	..	1131	1409	..	2003	Brunéi Darussalam
..	..	-519	7831	2817	..	1243	1574	..	2004	
..	..	-511	7512	2780	..	1186	1594	..	2005	
..	..	-560	7380	2826	..	1253	1573	..	2006	
23	..	..	81	1060	..	1052	..	8	2003	Cambodge
21	..	..	88	1184	..	1176	..	7	2004	
21	..	..	92	1261	..	1250	..	11	2005	
26	..	..	97	1383	..	1369	..	14	2006	
339	2503	64698	837	1078160	810955	200849	38871	27486	2003	Chine
129	289	80617	978	1267972	957800	241481	34725	33966	2004	
321	927	78315	1077	1404569	1078356	245348	42695	38170	2005	
439	1440	86892	1153	1514405	1173291	253880	45167	42067	2006	
3547	5411	..	1805	12295	5743	4498	1418	635	2003	Chine, Hong-Kong RAS
3243	7722	..	1764	11965	5244	4091	2049	580	2004	
3763	5717	..	1836	12512	5840	4065	2048	559	2005	
3835	7329	..	1747	11986	5733	3542	2164	548	2006	
..	..	..	1402	629	..	613	..	15	2003	Chine, Macao RAS
..	..	..	1601	745	..	732	..	13	2004	
..	..	..	1616	789	..	760	..	29	2005	
..	..	..	1631	819	..	736	..	83	2006	
330	124	36	3092	2228	37	2191	..	0	2003	Chypre
304	55	6	2842	2095	40	2055	..	0	2004	
300	291	0	2819	2137	37	2100	..	0	2005	
310	296	0	2898	2234	38	2196	..	0	2006	
27	..	54	475	2055	30	528	857	640	2003	Géorgie
38	..	21	502	2168	7	527	1004	630	2004	
38	..	15	583	2542	19	676	1195	652	2005	
38	..	15	628	2762	18	682	1533	530	2006	
2470	31	33221	325	346950	230306	84230	24270	8144	2003	Inde
2900	7	31354	341	368142	246275	88909	24075	8884	2004	
3400	5	33907	351	384640	259810	89990	24490	10351	2005	
4101	2	34694	365	407858	277908	94364	24006	11580	2006	
811	490	1592	454	97231	10870	54384	30652	1324	2003	Indonésie
794	358	1364	506	109829	15513	59516	33396	1404	2004	
729	374	2398	509	111880	17781	59492	33115	1493	2005	
717	360	2155	508	112904	22375	54240	34889	1400	2006	
800	585	496	2182	145057	1287	67044	75723	1003	2003	Iran(Rép. islamique)
812	619	88	2340	157905	1117	71864	83982	942	2004	
880	556	-4389	2494	170739	1267	79122	89025	1325	2005	
1032	459	-5052	2607	183771	1351	83032	97838	1550	2006	
418	..	3648	837	22052	..	20599	1416	37	2003	Iraq
1200	..	1382	986	26757	..	24242	2360	156	2004	
774	..	1637	1017	27963	..	25394	2405	164	2005	
812	..	2040	1000	28814	..	25484	3177	154	2006	
*4	272	400	3036	20309	8963	11461	8	-123	2003	Israël
*4	229	-240	3085	21009	9110	10980	1041	-122	2004	
*4	259	-1272	3023	20952	8578	11080	1433	-140	2005	
4	261	-412	3188	22465	9194	11427	2002	-157	2006	
6720	5120	19575	3395	428636	115430	203996	79247	29963	2003	Japon
6952	5360	18757	3487	440206	126224	201990	78435	33558	2004	
7000	6024	19089	3459	436536	123219	200831	78429	34057	2005	
6498	5666	20847	3445	434598	124717	189085	86073	34723	2006	
62	8	65	1032	5395	..	5126	237	32	2003	Jordanie
79	48	188	1217	6212	..	4807	1329	76	2004	
*77	79	342	1220	6680	..	5073	1538	69	2005	
76	41	162	1225	6857	..	4808	2004	46	2006	

Table 2

Production, trade and consumption of commercial energy
Thousand metric tons of oil equivalent and kilograms per capita

Country or area Pays ou zone	Year Année	Primary energy production Production d'énergie primaire					Changes in stocks Variations des stocks	Imports Importations	Exports Exportations
		Total Totale	Solids Solides	Liquids Liquides	Gas Gaz	Electricity Electricité			
Kazakhstan	2003	105442	37297	51933	15470	742	407	12575	69026
	2004	119676	38198	60185	20601	693	400	17216	81703
	2005	124352	38071	62329	23277	675	359	16889	83103
	2006	133974	42271	66444	24591	668	267	19103	89742
Korea, Dem.Ppl's.Rep.	2003	20154	19147	..	..	1008	..	1354	528
	2004	21217	20142	..	..	1075	..	1368	1100
	2005	23187	22058	..	..	1129	..	1202	1963
	2006	23435	22350	..	..	1085	..	989	1737
Korea, Republic of	2003	13232	1484	2	0	11746	2482	191647	22427
	2004	13190	1436	4	0	11750	959	201224	25402
	2005	14908	1274	65	490	13079	-4504	199350	29636
	2006	15137	1271	87	517	13262	2943	211149	32370
Kuwait	2003	124723	..	114453	10269	..	..	589	85707
	2004	135274	..	124221	11053	..	..	113	93408
	2005	150065	..	137670	12394	..	..	0	105226
	2006	155098	..	141990	13108	..	..	0	111831
Kyrgyzstan	2003	1380	123	69	25	1162	-23	1646	303
	2004	1448	135	74	27	1212	-10	1791	464
	2005	1422	99	74	23	1226	0	1715	357
	2006	1463	95	71	18	1280	0	1668	320
Lao People's Dem. Rep.	2003	*529	*267	..	..	263	..	*151	318
	2004	*561	*284	..	..	*277	..	*154	*313
	2005	*585	*296	..	..	*289	..	*161	*319
	2006	*598	*299	..	..	*298	..	*157	*318
Lebanon	2003	59	..	..	..	59	-566	5191	..
	2004	97	..	..	..	97	1	5002	..
	2005	90	..	..	..	90	-417	4812	..
	2006	60	..	..	..	60	0	4443	..
Malaysia	2003	89382	107	39102	49679	494	-587	23747	45829
	2004	90133	268	37275	52089	501	397	29557	49128
	2005	95925	477	37627	57375	446	500	27722	52132
	2006	100550	631	37003	62308	608	114	26597	52605
Maldives	2003	..	..	..	..	..	..	199	..
	2004	..	..	..	..	..	..	250	..
	2005	..	..	..	..	..	..	225	..
	2006	..	..	..	..	..	..	288	..
Mongolia	2003	1742	1742	..	..	..	..	542	101
	2004	2111	2111	..	..	..	..	595	361
	2005	2311	2311	..	..	..	..	582	490
	2006	2482	2482	..	..	..	..	669	569
Myanmar	2003	9109	609	977	7330	193	-88	976	6389
	2004	11906	645	1026	10028	207	0	1154	9128
	2005	12646	794	1114	10480	258	0	1269	9654
	2006	12998	807	1059	10847	286	57	907	9669
Nepal	2003	202	8	..	..	195	..	932	18
	2004	213	6	..	..	207	..	883	10
	2005	231	6	..	..	225	..	1011	11
	2006	236	6	..	..	230	..	1033	12
Occup. Palestinian Terr.	2003	..	..	..	..	..	-1	629	0
	2004	..	..	..	..	..	0	862	15
	2005	..	..	..	..	..	0	1185	18
	2006	..	..	..	..	..	0	*1264	*26
Oman	2003	57595	..	41078	16517	..	-1562	299	47510
	2004	56115	..	39249	16866	..	-1016	422	46370
	2005	56557	..	38879	17678	..	-1485	701	46644
	2006	59443	..	37019	22424	..	2	735	44346

Table 2

Production, commerce et consommation d'énergie commerciale
Milliers de tonnes métriques d'équivalent pétrole et kilogrammes par habitant

Bunkers Soutes		Unallocated Quantités non réparties	Consumption Consommation						Year Année	Country or area Pays ou zone
Aviation Avion	Marine Maritime		Per capita Par habitant	Total Totale	Solids Solides	Liquids Liquides	Gas Gaz	Electricity Electricité		
171	..	544	3211	47868	26683	7255	13314	615	2003	Kazakhstan
223	..	2145	3492	52422	27583	8982	15351	506	2004	
241	..	290	3780	57248	28217	8942	19364	725	2005	
256	..	775	4053	62038	30318	10122	20858	740	2006	
..	..	15	894	20966	18865	1093	..	1008	2003	Corée,Rép.pop.dém.de
..	..	13	909	21473	19296	1102	..	1075	2004	
..	..	10	949	22417	20362	925	..	1129	2005	
..	..	7	957	22681	20887	708	..	1085	2006	
1176	6480	16462	3257	155852	49832	69821	24453	11746	2003	Corée, République de
1286	7135	23234	3253	156398	51969	64582	28097	11750	2004	
2374	10169	19516	3252	157066	52231	61326	30429	13079	2005	
2891	10182	22002	3228	155899	53603	57039	31995	13262	2006	
739	556	9894	11684	27171	..	16902	10269	..	2003	Koweït
552	567	9993	12412	29673	..	18620	11053	..	2004	
594	528	9880	13309	32704	..	20310	12394	..	2005	
572	634	8845	12681	32031	..	18923	13108	..	2006	
..	..	5	544	2741	588	448	681	1024	2003	Kirghizistan
..	..	2	546	2783	555	559	744	926	2004	
..	..	-8	542	2788	516	591	686	995	2005	
..	..	-13	544	2824	480	564	717	1063	2006	
..	..	..	*64	*362	*221	*132	..	9	2003	Rép. dém. pop. lao
..	..	..	*69	*402	*229	*136	..	*38	2004	
..	..	..	*76	*427	*236	*137	..	*55	2005	
..	..	..	*76	*436	*239	*138	..	*59	2006	
129	16	..	1447	5671	140	5472	..	59	2003	Liban
131	17	..	1248	4950	140	4695	..	115	2004	
152	17	..	1284	5151	140	4882	..	129	2005	
106	17	..	1080	4379	140	4100	..	140	2006	
1853	71	10501	2214	55467	5336	19592	30045	494	2003	Malaisie
2074	85	8689	2319	59320	9293	20819	28753	456	2004	
1954	59	8626	2300	60084	7575	21143	31113	254	2005	
2010	50	7471	2424	64587	7800	21062	35334	391	2006	
..	..	..	697	199	..	199	..	..	2003	Maldives
..	..	..	863	250	..	250	..	..	2004	
..	..	..	767	225	..	225	..	..	2005	
..	..	..	965	288	..	288	..	..	2006	
..	..	..	877	2183	1642	527	..	14	2003	Mongolie
..	..	..	931	2345	1751	580	..	14	2004	
..	..	..	943	2403	1822	567	..	13	2005	
..	..	..	1001	2582	1915	655	..	13	2006	
69	3	216	66	3496	97	1722	1484	193	2003	Myanmar
66	3	60	70	3802	102	1797	1696	207	2004	
51	3	56	75	4150	106	1878	1909	258	2005	
77	3	50	72	4047	120	1667	1975	286	2006	
40	..	..	44	1077	204	683	..	190	2003	Népal
54	..	..	42	1032	180	635	..	218	2004	
60	..	..	46	1170	287	653	..	231	2005	
61	..	..	46	1197	294	667	..	236	2006	
..	..	..	179	630	0	431	..	199	2003	Terr. palestiniens occup.
..	..	..	233	847	*1	623	..	223	2004	
..	..	..	310	1166	0	920	..	*246	2005	
..	..	..	*318	*1238	0	*997	..	*241	2006	
369	1	223	4851	11354	..	3310	8044	..	2003	Oman
*200	1	153	4483	10830	..	3356	7474	..	2004	
281	1	415	4545	11404	..	3605	7799	..	2005	
*322	0	777	5717	14732	..	4331	10402	..	2006	

Table 2

Production, trade and consumption of commercial energy

Thousand metric tons of oil equivalent and kilograms per capita

Country or area Pays ou zone	Year Année	Primary energy production Production d'énergie primaire					Changes in stocks Variations des stocks	Imports Importations	Exports Exportations
		Total Totale	Solids Solides	Liquids Liquides	Gas Gaz	Electricity Electricité			
Other Asia	2003	4719	..	41	739	3939	-826	90506	8797
	2004	4776	..	40	773	3963	2545	101841	12059
	2005	4641	..	29	487	4125	364	103757	13953
	2006	4573	..	21	412	4140	1071	106126	13778
Pakistan	2003	31806	1566	3314	24457	2468	-225	13106	503
	2004	34686	2169	3415	26653	2448	-68	16347	301
	2005	36632	2304	3490	27971	2867	*-17	16664	411
	2006	36438	1723	3540	28231	2944	5	19560	440
Philippines	2003	6107	2149	20	2416	1523	116	19242	881
	2004	5227	1273	19	2311	1624	-253	20370	613
	2005	6126	1477	29	3047	1573	-900	19068	1164
	2006	6072	*1518	26	2768	1761	82	18752	1564
Qatar	2003	67754	..	38489	29265		2598	..	51311
	2004	77326	..	40820	36506		-768	..	60852
	2005	84149	..	41463	42686		-1307	..	63588
	2006	99767	..	53633	46134		-41	..	77998
Saudi Arabia	2003	528555	..	481008	47547		40	1275	388105
	2004	547073	..	495418	51655		-46	1524	396053
	2005	575237	..	518469	56768		25	1875	415194
	2006	569645	..	510048	59598		-119	3561	405752
Singapore	2003	..	..	..			-3342	85999	42078
	2004	..	..	..			-2310	97980	47157
	2005	..	..	..			-4405	105496	50712
	2006	..	..	..			-4509	112321	55656
Sri Lanka	2003	285	..			285	-114	3496	0
	2004	255	..			255	-2	4086	38
	2005	297	..			297	41	4013	0
	2006	399	..			399	120	4174	0
Syrian Arab Republic	2003	34409	..	28000	6168	241	11	1100	17010
	2004	30113	..	23355	6393	365	-20	1410	12610
	2005	28030	..	22241	5493	296	18	1718	10202
	2006	26839	..	20823	5673	343	18	1305	8085
Tajikistan	2003	1479	26	18	30	1405	..	2111	400
	2004	1498	41	19	33	1405	..	2236	387
	2005	1565	57	22	27	1459	..	2316	372
	2006	1541	65	22	18	1436	..	2539	371
Thailand	2003	35923	8289	10113	16893	628	-936	52192	7870
	2004	36439	8824	10348	16747	520	-981	58712	8564
	2005	39556	9184	11871	18002	499	-1285	57150	8938
	2006	40128	8359	12880	18191	699	-1969	58056	10311
Timor-Leste	2003	*7317	..	*7317	..	..	..	*92	*7242
	2004	*7367	..	*7367	..	..	..	*97	*7291
	2005	*7394	..	*7394	..	..	..	*98	*7318
	2006	*7407	..	*7407	..	..	..	*99	*7330
Turkey	2003	16544	10630	2351	512	3051	437	62760	3729
	2004	17000	10144	2251	629	3975	-453	65413	4515
	2005	19151	12657	2258	821	3415	-644	70292	4939
	2006	20727	13914	2162	828	3823	203	78121	5998
Turkmenistan	2003	63928	..	10390	53538	0	..	87	45415
	2004	63541	..	10148	53393	0	..	87	46693
	2005	66862	..	9849	57013	0	..	87	49066
	2006	67359	..	10120	57239	0	..	87	48820
United Arab Emirates	2003	169311	..	127590	41722		..	12458	108690
	2004	176233	..	133114	43119		..	13420	113577
	2005	178003	..	134642	43361		..	15078	114860
	2006	188485	..	144378	44106		..	15792	123385

Table 2

Production, commerce et consommation d'énergie commerciale

Milliers de tonnes métriques d'équivalent pétrole et kilogrammes par habitant

Bunkers Soutes		Unallocated Quantités non réparties	Consumption Consommation						Year Année	Country or area Pays ou zone
Aviation Avion	Marine Maritime		Per capita Par habitant	Total Totale	Solids Solides	Liquids Liquides	Gas Gaz	Electricity Electricité		
2126	3036	6388	3349	75704	35776	27972	8017	3939	2003	Autre Asie
2396	2453	8178	3481	78986	37223	27923	9877	3963	2004	
2490	2477	8652	3540	80463	38507	28247	9583	4125	2005	
2537	2374	7020	3682	83919	40310	28670	10799	4140	2006	
142	15	1165	297	43313	2659	13716	24463	2474	2003	Pakistan
168	63	1292	331	49277	4460	15700	26660	2457	2004	
214	80	1727	332	50884	4272	15758	27974	2880	2005	
176	103	1528	343	53748	4667	17887	28235	2959	2006	
588	185	984	279	22595	4304	14353	2416	1523	2003	Philippines
*619	139	867	286	23612	4947	14730	2311	1624	2004	
*722	120	785	273	23302	4767	13915	3047	1573	2005	
828	129	690	248	21532	*4862	12141	2768	1761	2006	
615	..	-127	18216	13357	..	1769	11587	..	2003	Qatar
366	..	1139	20255	15737	..	1862	13875	..	2004	
468	..	1173	24884	20227	..	2244	17983	..	2005	
596	..	798	21805	20416	..	2622	17794	..	2006	
1774	2211	9333	5445	119897	..	72350	47547	..	2003	Arabie saoudite
1695	2249	7265	5907	133284	..	81629	51655	..	2004	
1707	2282	8207	6122	141530	..	84762	56768	..	2005	
1774	2661	6862	6281	148719	..	89121	59598	..	2006	
2420	20662	10803	3196	13378	8	8387	4983	..	2003	Singapour
2980	23395	13254	3186	13504	6	7623	5875	..	2004	
3184	25292	15944	3402	14769	2	8171	6595	..	2005	
3440	27788	15420	3240	14526	4	7829	6692	..	2006	
115	114	131	184	3536	68	3183	..	285	2003	Sri Lanka
132	119	118	202	3937	67	3615	..	255	2004	
134	169	139	195	3828	67	3464	..	297	2005	
123	137	253	198	3940	67	3474	..	399	2006	
100	..	1666	953	16721	3	10309	6168	241	2003	Rép. arabe syrienne
120	..	1151	990	17662	3	10901	6393	365	2004	
108	..	1894	959	17526	3	11735	5493	296	2005	
105	..	1798	969	18139	3	12121	5673	343	2006	
4	..	13	483	3173	31	1226	511	1405	2003	Tadjikistan
4	..	15	496	3327	45	1319	528	1436	2004	
4	..	17	509	3488	60	1411	537	1480	2005	
4	..	16	517	3690	68	1590	543	1488	2006	
..	..	8040	1142	73099	13281	35103	23899	815	2003	Thaïlande
..	..	7612	1245	79904	14859	39977	24289	779	2004	
..	..	8480	1242	80530	14367	39101	26238	823	2005	
..	..	8993	1237	80802	14539	38509	26675	1078	2006	
..	..	0	*92	*92	..	*92	..	..	2003	Timor-Leste
..	..	0	*95	*97	..	*97	..	..	2004	
..	..	0	*94	*98	..	*98	..	..	2005	
..	..	0	*93	*99	..	*99	..	..	2006	
904	626	3063	1004	70545	22127	25629	19690	3100	2003	Turquie
974	1008	3462	1025	72907	22646	25556	20788	3917	2004	
1090	1072	3720	1100	79266	25530	25097	25324	3315	2005	
986	991	4559	1180	86111	28587	24985	28859	3680	2006	
..	..	26	3954	18575	..	4404	14262	-91	2003	Turkménistan
..	..	26	3548	16909	..	4249	12760	-101	2004	
..	..	25	3695	17858	..	4341	13625	-108	2005	
..	..	30	3796	18595	..	5031	13679	-115	2006	
3419	9332	3788	15938	56597	..	21536	35062	..	2003	Emirats arabes unis
3276	10832	3845	15470	58182	..	22031	36151	..	2004	
3609	12050	3571	14380	59052	..	22342	36710	..	2005	
3704	13143	3519	14327	60589	..	23078	37511	..	2006	

Table 2

Production, trade and consumption of commercial energy
Thousand metric tons of oil equivalent and kilograms per capita

Country or area Pays ou zone	Year Année	Primary energy production Production d'énergie primaire					Changes in stocks Variations des stocks	Imports Importations	Exports Exportations
		Total Totale	Solids Solides	Liquids Liquides	Gas Gaz	Electricity Electricité			
Uzbekistan	2003	61512	516	8046	52405	546	12	2296	8059
	2004	62239	727	7533	53415	564	17	2174	10300
	2005	61935	809	6173	54425	527	19	1952	12404
	2006	63778	842	5763	56628	545	20	1984	12645
Viet Nam	2003	33463	11690	17131	3009	1633	0	10437	21571
	2004	45340	17850	20844	5127	1519	700	11526	27018
	2005	50874	22677	19462	6890	1845	633	12347	32271
	2006	53941	26529	18382	7000	2029	800	12258	34045
Yemen	2003	21300	..	21300	..	..	567	2425	17065
	2004	20050	..	20050	..	..	908	2738	15348
	2005	19852	..	19852	..	..	920	2829	14911
	2006	18212	..	18212	..	..	1527	3553	12996
Europe	**2003**	**2139167**	**362297**	**733598**	**872236**	**171036**	**8021**	**1519596**	**1152598**
	2004	**2187268**	**356619**	**761129**	**891998**	**177521**	**10468**	**1577829**	**1230559**
	2005	**2175927**	**358276**	**749647**	**889506**	**178498**	**14063**	**1619516**	**1246811**
	2006	**2170820**	**355719**	**741994**	**894225**	**178881**	**28078**	**1654797**	**1249831**
Albania	2003	853	19	375	15	444	..	935	64
	2004	933	26	420	17	470	..	1029	28
	2005	949	22	447	18	462	..	955	0
	2006	975	22	505	18	430	..	920	0
Austria	2003	6386	300	1033	1985	3067	-68	26858	3265
	2004	6456	61	1099	1865	3431	235	27688	3766
	2005	5951	0	1018	1498	3436	185	29688	4329
	2006	6206	0	1067	1751	3388	727	30369	5106
Belarus	2003	2467	410	1820	234	2	-190	33858	9878
	2004	2498	453	1804	237	3	203	37874	12693
	2005	2524	525	1785	210	3	-102	39380	14746
	2006	2469	483	1780	202	3	16	42362	15894
Belgium	2003	4229	35	0	..	4195	51	77231	23216
	2004	4267	49	0	..	4219	114	79205	25014
	2005	4292	29	13	..	4250	389	78144	25702
	2006	4212	8	22	..	4182	107	77003	24193
Bosnia and Herzegovina	2003	5479	5092	..	..	387	0	1353	448
	2004	5657	5143	..	..	514	3	1776	578
	2005	5938	5423	..	..	516	-15	2012	681
	2006	6300	5796	..	..	504	-15	2184	825
Bulgaria	2003	6343	4513	30	31	1770	-332	11508	2089
	2004	6421	4345	30	311	1735	461	12340	2899
	2005	6523	4040	30	442	2011	-7	13092	3306
	2006	6745	4210	34	429	2072	-178	14276	4394
Croatia	2003	3729	..	1317	1987	424	-142	7171	1842
	2004	3876	..	1274	1995	606	-6	7676	2216
	2005	3833	..	1206	2072	554	4	7859	2326
	2006	4156	..	1165	2463	528	69	7835	2605
Czech Republic	2003	24448	21365	558	146	2379	127	19716	7240
	2004	24590	21259	640	206	2485	-44	19394	6690
	2005	23861	20594	681	197	2388	395	20900	6858
	2006	24053	20897	443	189	2524	407	21626	7573
Denmark	2003	26669	..	18183	8006	480	-130	14442	21755
	2004	29326	..	19319	9438	569	129	13772	24395
	2005	29580	..	18580	10429	571	323	13163	24561
	2006	27820	..	16926	10367	527	-521	13743	22768
Estonia	2003	3441	3439	..	..	2	40	1975	253
	2004	3220	3217	..	..	3	-112	2238	250
	2005	3381	3375	..	..	7	1	2030	210
	2006	3300	3292	..	..	8	130	2161	153

Table 2

Production, commerce et consommation d'énergie commerciale

Milliers de tonnes métriques d'équivalent pétrole et kilogrammes par habitant

Bunkers Soutes		Unallocated Quantités	Consumption Consommation						Year	Country or area
Aviation Avion	Marine Maritime	non réparties	Per capita Par habitant	Total Totale	Solids Solides	Liquids Liquides	Gas Gaz	Electricity Electricité	Année	Pays ou zone
..	..	-2064	2238	57801	503	9793	46967	538	2003	Ouzbékistan
..	..	-1924	2137	56021	710	9159	45597	556	2004	
..	..	-1469	1991	52934	790	7398	44226	520	2005	
..	..	-1432	2021	54529	822	6967	46203	537	2006	
159	..	0	274	22173	7280	10251	3009	1633	2003	Viet Nam
266	..	0	352	28884	10430	11808	5127	1519	2004	
265	..	0	362	30055	10157	12592	5461	1845	2005	
246	..	0	370	31112	11009	12526	5548	2029	2006	
94	126	678	276	5194	..	5194	..	..	2003	Yémen
105	126	869	280	5431	..	5431	..	..	2004	
105	126	865	288	5754	..	5754	..	..	2005	
116	126	783	302	6217	..	6217	..	..	2006	
43497	48293	37375	3256	2368102	476109	761826	959040	171128	2003	Europe
46242	51542	39820	3277	2385350	468729	762095	977052	177473	2004	
49221	53872	40981	3275	2388194	457514	758780	993760	178139	2005	
50307	56689	24718	3308	2414984	471237	779825	985576	178347	2006	
48	..	157	431	1519	21	961	13	523	2003	Albanie
59	..	157	551	1718	28	1187	15	487	2004	
71	..	232	509	1601	25	1066	16	494	2005	
86	..	241	497	1567	25	1044	16	483	2006	
428	..	1093	3536	28526	4170	12412	8394	3550	2003	Autriche
502	..	1110	3505	28530	3984	12383	8467	3696	2004	
566	..	853	3620	29705	4095	12836	9109	3665	2005	
593	..	1109	3507	29041	4044	12728	8292	3977	2006	
..	..	3444	2349	23193	647	4938	17018	590	2003	Bélarus
..	..	3040	2487	24436	553	5130	18469	283	2004	
..	..	2442	2539	24817	547	5095	18825	350	2005	
..	..	3131	2650	25790	522	5722	19168	378	2006	
1478	7098	4369	4369	45249	6216	18285	16002	4746	2003	Belgique
1360	7978	3846	4344	45161	6122	17963	16189	4887	2004	
1287	7895	3689	4162	43473	5501	17430	15750	4792	2005	
1182	8545	2820	4221	44368	4774	17811	16728	5056	2006	
..	..	4	1665	6380	4930	964	179	307	2003	Bosnie y Herzégovine
..	..	21	1778	6830	5070	1131	283	347	2004	
..	..	9	1893	7275	5482	1060	336	397	2005	
..	..	9	1994	7663	5864	1122	355	322	2006	
160	139	1065	1883	14730	7209	3445	2778	1298	2003	Bulgarie
154	117	517	1878	14613	6976	3638	2770	1230	2004	
189	112	810	1965	15206	6840	3891	3116	1359	2005	
181	108	916	2026	15601	6979	3993	3223	1406	2006	
24	22	-144	2086	9264	764	5123	2618	759	2003	Croatie
29	24	239	2030	9013	816	4545	2731	922	2004	
40	25	121	2058	9140	783	4721	2641	994	2005	
40	20	147	2044	9076	733	4719	2612	1012	2006	
203	..	1764	3414	34829	18694	6436	8714	985	2003	République tchèque
291	..	2057	3428	34990	18419	6784	8653	1133	2004	
318	..	2315	3408	34875	18020	6988	8565	1302	2005	
335	..	2235	3415	35128	18322	6954	8415	1438	2006	
720	991	-107	3384	17883	5702	7257	5179	-255	2003	Danemark
821	806	-88	3154	17037	4398	7169	5149	322	2004	
864	833	71	2971	16091	3738	6776	4888	689	2005	
869	1081	-11	3198	17377	5490	6915	5041	-69	2006	
19	114	..	3687	4990	3537	859	756	-161	2003	Estonie
28	153	..	3809	5139	3545	885	861	-152	2004	
42	122	..	3741	5035	3388	891	889	-132	2005	
29	216	..	3672	4933	3209	883	898	-57	2006	

Table 2

Production, trade and consumption of commercial energy

Thousand metric tons of oil equivalent and kilograms per capita

Country or area Pays ou zone	Year Année	Primary energy production Production d'énergie primaire					Changes in stocks Variations des stocks	Imports Importations	Exports Exportations
		Total Totale	Solids Solides	Liquids Liquides	Gas Gaz	Electricity Electricité			
Faeroe Islands	2003	8	..	..	..	8	..	*219	..
	2004	8	..	..	..	8	..	*219	..
	2005	*8	..	..	..	*8	..	*220	..
	2006	*8	..	..	..	*8	..	*220	..
Finland	2003	4637	1850	..	..	2787	498	28305	5682
	2004	4179	920	..	..	3260	-1403	26656	5745
	2005	5462	2261	..	..	3201	701	23675	4685
	2006	6322	3351	..	..	2972	562	26088	5262
France incl. Monaco	2003	48383	1454	1968	1424	43538	-705	167386	26362
	2004	48025	566	1995	1231	44234	-1036	171722	27881
	2005	47066	415	1833	1010	43809	1158	178207	30488
	2006	47435	293	1770	1176	44196	1844	174552	30412
Germany	2003	96089	56034	4412	17699	17944	-1512	240938	28754
	2004	96712	56882	4448	16379	19003	1329	249098	34693
	2005	95507	55309	5613	15816	18769	1596	251332	38721
	2006	94542	52216	7137	15627	19562	1279	255599	41600
Gibraltar	2003	..	..	..	..	..	..	1239	..
	2004	..	..	..	..	..	..	1278	..
	2005	..	..	..	..	..	..	1308	..
	2006	..	..	..	..	..	..	1341	..
Greece	2003	8895	8176	138	34	546	-856	28920	5296
	2004	9255	8545	134	32	544	1016	30704	5043
	2005	9249	8536	101	20	591	-498	29730	5664
	2006	8806	7936	137	29	703	382	32301	6815
Hungary	2003	8225	2743	1959	2561	962	466	20373	2797
	2004	7817	2182	1942	2650	1043	13	19929	2620
	2005	7357	1748	1790	2611	1208	124	22466	3256
	2006	7304	1757	1709	2661	1177	156	22498	3774
Iceland	2003	946	..	..	215	730	-52	921	..
	2004	963	..	..	222	741	31	1047	..
	2005	953	..	..	207	746	20	1032	..
	2006	1083	..	..	230	853	-28	1050	..
Ireland	2003	1945	1220	0	604	121	271	15346	1599
	2004	1880	974	0	765	141	446	15225	1241
	2005	1569	877	1	512	179	53	15256	1394
	2006	1511	819	3	456	233	146	15666	1283
Italy and San Marino	2003	22757	157	5570	12635	4394	-1699	184480	21546
	2004	22474	62	5698	11795	4920	-191	188826	22767
	2005	21685	60	6288	10985	4353	-1621	194455	26805
	2006	20438	13	5966	9991	4468	3159	198832	25400
Latvia	2003	201	2	0	..	199	63	3226	9
	2004	274	3	0	..	272	455	3862	392
	2005	294	3	2	..	290	125	3756	557
	2006	249	3	9	..	236	204	3855	290
Lithuania	2003	1862	10	382	53	1416	129	10566	6248
	2004	1745	11	305	49	1380	156	12277	7749
	2005	1250	16	227	48	960	85	12828	7598
	2006	1071	13	196	48	814	138	12472	6892
Luxembourg	2003	81	..	0	..	81	6	4509	253
	2004	79	..	1	..	78	-13	4936	284
	2005	83	..	1	..	82	-19	5013	284
	2006	87	..	1	..	86	29	5064	289
Malta	2003	..	..	..	..	..	..	909	..
	2004	..	..	..	..	..	..	957	..
	2005	..	..	..	..	..	..	945	..
	2006	..	..	..	..	..	..	918	..

Table 2

Production, commerce et consommation d'énergie commerciale
Milliers de tonnes métriques d'équivalent pétrole et kilogrammes par habitant

Bunkers Soutes		Unallocated Quantités	Consumption Consommation						Year	Country or area
Aviation Avion	Marine Maritime	non réparties	Per capita Par habitant	Total Totale	Solids Solides	Liquids Liquides	Gas Gaz	Electricity Electricité	Année	Pays ou zone
*2	..	..	*4683	*224	..	*217	..	8	2003	Iles Féroé
*2	..	..	*4650	*224	..	*217	..	8	2004	
*2	..	..	*4671	*225	..	*218	..	*8	2005	
*2	..	..	*4671	*225	..	*218	..	*8	2006	
362	650	-1358	5200	27107	8398	10966	4538	3205	2003	Finlande
418	524	-2000	5270	27551	7680	11761	4432	3678	2004	
420	515	-2393	4805	25208	4971	11536	4037	4664	2005	
467	566	-2740	5372	28292	7604	12381	4355	3952	2006	
5079	2693	9855	2866	172486	14805	76167	43687	37827	2003	France y compris Monaco
5427	3051	9666	2886	174758	14267	76971	44609	38911	2004	
5490	2781	10855	2865	174500	14784	75454	45641	38622	2005	
5714	2889	6530	2859	174597	13634	78187	44027	38750	2006	
5737	2641	6453	3574	294954	83442	105926	87923	17663	2003	Allemagne
6201	2704	6292	3571	294592	84125	104211	87479	18778	2004	
6674	2532	6410	3528	290905	80236	102453	89840	18376	2005	
7014	2624	4952	3553	292672	80593	105649	88328	18102	2006	
4	1115	..	4277	120	..	120	..	..	2003	Gibraltar
4	1150	..	4422	124	..	124	..	..	2004	
4	1176	..	4568	128	..	128	..	..	2005	
4	1209	..	4427	128	..	128	..	..	2006	
785	3237	-1263	2777	30616	8904	18734	2251	726	2003	Grèce
809	3263	-699	2760	30527	9126	18138	2476	787	2004	
781	2909	-1317	2831	31439	8970	18937	2615	916	2005	
937	3141	-1982	2854	31814	8208	19490	3052	1064	2006	
204	..	587	2423	24545	3726	6054	13207	1559	2003	Hongrie
233	..	740	2389	24143	3374	6070	13014	1685	2004	
270	..	1127	2483	25049	3054	6813	13438	1743	2005	
273	..	955	2447	24646	2985	7138	12726	1797	2006	
103	68	335	4882	1412	91	591	..	730	2003	Islande
119	71	348	4925	1441	103	597	..	741	2004	
134	65	335	4838	1431	99	586	..	746	2005	
179	35	392	5108	1555	78	624	..	853	2006	
731	172	62	3633	14456	2802	7375	4058	221	2003	Irlande
691	151	6	3603	14569	2501	7741	4050	276	2004	
798	105	136	3472	14340	2917	7213	3855	355	2005	
814	125	-141	3530	14950	2607	7497	4459	386	2006	
2700	3234	-1070	3169	182524	15272	87786	70690	8776	2003	Italie y comp. St. Marin
2704	3381	1611	3112	181027	17190	81638	73354	8844	2004	
2864	3411	1110	3132	183571	16978	79512	78501	8580	2005	
3052	3515	2865	3076	181278	17154	78909	76880	8336	2006	
40	190	8	1340	3117	63	1131	1497	425	2003	Lettonie
48	205	3	1311	3033	51	1050	1480	452	2004	
59	264	4	1323	3043	61	999	1509	475	2005	
66	200	20	1453	3324	55	1254	1563	452	2006	
22	111	140	1673	5779	211	2138	2661	769	2003	Lituanie
11	115	151	1699	5839	206	2221	2651	761	2004	
46	146	120	1782	6083	226	2355	2797	704	2005	
53	141	-105	1893	6424	311	2563	2773	777	2006	
392	..	..	8722	3939	78	2279	1182	400	2003	Luxembourg
427	..	..	9424	4317	94	2522	1333	368	2004	
433	..	..	9453	4397	82	2644	1310	362	2005	
407	..	..	9364	4426	110	2553	1371	391	2006	
79	23	..	2017	806	..	806	..	..	2003	Malte
101	23	..	2069	833	..	833	..	..	2004	
91	23	..	2052	831	..	831	..	..	2005	
77	23	..	2012	818	..	818	..	..	2006	

Table 2

Production, trade and consumption of commercial energy

Thousand metric tons of oil equivalent and kilograms per capita

Country or area Pays ou zone	Year Année	Primary energy production Production d'énergie primaire					Changes in stocks Variations des stocks	Imports Importations	Exports Exportations
		Total Totale	Solids Solides	Liquids Liquides	Gas Gaz	Electricity Electricité			
Netherlands	2003	61676	..	3195	58013	468	-235	129157	98288
	2004	71903	..	2975	68428	500	432	130747	107467
	2005	65701	..	2652	62517	532	1178	144202	112600
	2006	64302	..	2161	61595	545	95	152384	121450
Norway,Svlbd.J.Myn. I	2003	238901	1976	154140	73633	9152	1071	5871	214946
	2004	242795	1949	153183	78243	9419	-396	6087	218699
	2005	239221	987	141691	84756	11787	346	5166	208827
	2006	230036	1608	130942	87127	10359	516	5548	207304
Poland	2003	76233	71132	794	4013	294	260	32287	18156
	2004	75846	70253	900	4364	330	341	34192	18265
	2005	74058	68448	958	4316	336	1954	36595	18307
	2006	72304	66758	953	4312	282	-288	40542	18048
Portugal	2003	1431	..	0		1431	449	23415	1575
	2004	950	..	0		950	-413	23948	1703
	2005	599	..	0		599	415	25992	2145
	2006	1315	..	70		1245	55	24633	3186
Republic of Moldova	2003	6	..	0	..	6	52	3540	12
	2004	13	..	8	..	5	-7	3560	43
	2005	10	..	5	..	5	0	3747	21
	2006	11	..	4	..	7	-20	3546	22
Romania	2003	24783	5724	5909	11587	1562	-249	14001	3833
	2004	24654	5502	5724	11531	1897	1010	16383	4633
	2005	24129	5383	5751	10780	2215	-340	16852	6259
	2006	24408	6044	5676	10625	2063	-837	17360	5737
Russian Federation	2003	1108766	106842	419673	555733	26517	12165	25533	493928
	2004	1160339	108768	457537	566269	27764	6775	22063	544716
	2005	1188192	119007	467819	573466	27899	6859	20337	565719
	2006	1210122	119645	477262	584652	28563	13924	20843	563023
Serbia	2003	10522	8574	773	328	847	0	5433	400
	2004	10661	8767	652	285	956	0	6888	755
	2005	9457	7519	649	254	1035	0	6682	943
	2006	9663	7812	646	262	943	-21	7260	917
Slovakia	2003	3047	907	52	236	1852	-55	16483	4185
	2004	2959	864	53	215	1826	581	17426	4697
	2005	2930	735	65	197	1932	93	17366	4860
	2006	2910	645	69	255	1942	-176	17168	5091
Slovenia	2003	1774	1050	0	5	719	40	4255	588
	2004	1872	1045	0	5	821	40	4402	737
	2005	1794	987	0	4	804	9	4660	862
	2006	1778	983	5	4	786	-93	4787	1011
Spain	2003	17680	6811	515	219	10137	-82	116795	5569
	2004	17235	6632	474	344	9785	-782	125425	7026
	2005	15669	6331	426	160	8752	1777	134433	7229
	2006	16154	6082	313	61	9699	2795	136366	9214
Sweden	2003	10765	233	68	..	10464	1037	32929	10490
	2004	12312	258	144	..	11910	-435	31998	12102
	2005	12982	205	208	..	12570	765	31728	11786
	2006	11605	179	273	..	11152	-731	31320	11652
Switzerland	2003	5562	..	0	27	5535	-160	18126	3463
	2004	5400	..	3	28	5370	15	17976	2963
	2005	4887	..	7	26	4854	138	19241	3230
	2006	5261	..	8	31	5223	73	19011	3215
T.F.Yug.Rep. Macedonia	2003	2108	1989	..	..	118	-37	1376	336
	2004	2080	1953	..	..	127	4	1314	210
	2005	1983	1854	..	..	128	-60	1517	330
	2006	1931	1789	..	..	142	16	1627	360

Table 2

Production, commerce et consommation d'énergie commerciale

Milliers de tonnes métriques d'équivalent pétrole et kilogrammes par habitant

Bunkers Soutes		Unallocated Quantités	Consumption Consommation						Year	Country or area
Aviation Avion	Marine Maritime	non réparties	Per capita Par habitant	Total Totale	Solids Solides	Liquids Liquides	Gas Gaz	Electricity Electricité	Année	Pays ou zone
3288	13774	-16387	5684	92047	8535	41585	39998	1929	2003	Pays-Bas
3518	14965	-14635	5590	90881	8333	39826	40828	1895	2004	
3616	17178	-13689	5451	88965	7992	39338	39531	2105	2005	
3666	17830	-14303	5384	87948	7506	39678	38374	2391	2006	
210	567	391	5848	26782	789	10220	5944	9829	2003	Norvège,Svalbd,J.May
242	520	1798	5844	26936	921	9929	5684	10402	2004	
272	701	4375	5951	27628	776	10319	5782	10751	2005	
378	507	-2484	6086	28364	713	11905	5313	10432	2006	
292	290	1742	2298	87779	57998	17849	12512	-580	2003	Pologne
286	258	1921	2330	88967	57023	19213	13201	-469	2004	
324	328	2123	2296	87617	55376	19273	13594	-625	2005	
431	300	2371	2412	91983	58252	20645	13748	-663	2006	
635	589	1247	1949	20351	3381	12370	2929	1671	2003	Portugal
695	670	1102	2013	21140	3420	12542	3670	1507	2004	
721	589	1227	2037	21490	3408	12729	4167	1186	2005	
772	647	961	1921	20328	3516	11055	4044	1713	2006	
12	..	0	960	3468	89	597	2480	302	2003	Rép. de Moldova
11	..	0	978	3526	84	639	2545	258	2004	
12	..	0	1036	3723	76	646	2726	275	2005	
12	..	0	988	3542	91	630	2513	309	2006	
118	..	401	1596	34681	8111	8821	16366	1383	2003	Roumanie
137	..	1535	1556	33722	8125	8316	15486	1795	2004	
111	..	1089	1566	33862	7915	8491	15491	1966	2005	
137	..	1597	1628	35134	8554	8654	16231	1695	2006	
4876	..	10042	4242	613288	90429	116825	380667	25367	2003	Fédération de Russie
4789	..	7686	4300	618435	87514	118633	385179	27109	2004	
5178	..	9604	4340	621169	86988	118825	388521	26835	2005	
5470	..	9231	4487	639317	89809	123741	398564	27203	2006	
64	..	593	1408	14897	8921	2867	2022	1087	2003	Serbie
47	..	752	1521	15994	9265	3227	2569	933	2004	
50	..	706	1379	14440	8031	3391	2151	867	2005	
54	..	594	1472	15380	8621	3673	2213	873	2006	
34	..	468	2770	14898	4228	2714	6299	1658	2003	Slovaquie
27	..	129	2778	14951	4113	3063	6109	1666	2004	
39	..	162	2810	15141	3826	3126	6537	1652	2005	
40	..	313	2747	14810	4112	2981	5975	1741	2006	
26	0	4	2692	5370	1324	2306	1007	733	2003	Slovénie
20	0	52	2717	5425	1340	2331	999	754	2004	
23	22	56	2740	5483	1293	2382	1032	776	2005	
25	30	54	2758	5539	1300	2449	999	790	2006	
2798	7150	7699	2651	111341	20379	56991	23726	10245	2003	Espagne
3103	7376	7884	2765	118055	21887	58674	27969	9525	2004	
3113	8094	5893	2857	123996	21296	60904	33160	8636	2005	
3245	8451	5257	2804	123557	18904	60770	34466	9417	2006	
513	1645	2291	3094	27718	2633	12530	987	11567	2003	Suède
628	1937	2027	3119	28052	2908	12432	983	11729	2004	
634	1978	2099	3040	27449	2580	11998	936	11934	2005	
663	2126	1914	3006	27300	2624	12025	980	11672	2006	
1210	10	27	2607	19137	142	10808	2920	5268	2003	Suisse
1155	9	7	2580	19227	133	10772	3012	5309	2004	
1180	12	6	2623	19562	149	10920	3092	5400	2005	
1247	9	-17	2638	19744	138	11144	3007	5455	2006	
7	..	6	1565	3172	2088	809	74	200	2003	L'ex-RY Macédoine
6	..	12	1558	3162	2046	823	65	229	2004	
6	..	11	1577	3212	2026	849	71	266	2005	
5	..	24	1545	3153	1888	894	75	296	2006	

Table 2

Production, trade and consumption of commercial energy
Thousand metric tons of oil equivalent and kilograms per capita

Country or area Pays ou zone	Year Année	Primary energy production Production d'énergie primaire					Changes in stocks Variations des stocks	Imports Importations	Exports Exportations
		Total Totale	Solids Solides	Liquids Liquides	Gas Gaz	Electricity Electricité			
Ukraine	2003	62903	33201	4008	17885	7809	0	87422	17094
	2004	62772	30809	4370	19087	8507	308	87354	18159
	2005	63791	31236	4471	19374	8710	-2690	77322	12797
	2006	65053	31902	4615	19655	8882	1720	68533	7832
United Kingdom	2003	234940	17038	106727	102926	8249	-2203	100592	111137
	2004	214822	15121	95998	96006	7697	1209	118337	101443
	2005	193210	12350	85332	87581	7947	720	126231	88720
	2006	178878	11163	80127	80009	7579	2436	140934	86241
Oceania	**2003**	**263241**	**187108**	**32998**	**39209**	**3927**	**344**	**37903**	**170879**
	2004	**268061**	**194640**	**29706**	**39501**	**4214**	**264**	**38591**	**175669**
	2005	**277765**	**204054**	**26591**	**43163**	**3957**	**-1053**	**41266**	**183369**
	2006	**279316**	**204411**	**25997**	**44831**	**4078**	**-1540**	**43728**	**184831**
Australia	2003	250455	184899	29308	34790	1458	493	27344	166100
	2004	255823	192389	26451	35557	1426	146	27428	171451
	2005	265665	201765	23085	39372	1443	-1020	29931	178585
	2006	266467	201883	22130	40928	1526	-1755	32190	179566
Cook Islands	2003	..	..	..	..	..	..	13	..
	2004	..	..	..	..	..	..	18	..
	2005	..	..	..	..	..	..	20	..
	2006	..	..	..	..	..	..	*21	..
Fiji	2003	*57	..	..	..	*57	..	1023	*118
	2004	*58	..	..	..	*58	..	1066	*134
	2005	*58	..	..	..	*58	..	950	*124
	2006	*59	..	..	..	*59	..	984	*119
French Polynesia	2003	10	..	..	..	10	..	312	..
	2004	13	..	..	..	13	..	311	..
	2005	11	..	..	..	11	..	333	..
	2006	14	..	..	..	14	..	326	..
Kiribati	2003	..	..	..	..	..	..	*10	..
	2004	..	..	..	..	..	..	*10	..
	2005	..	..	..	..	..	..	*10	..
	2006	..	..	..	..	..	..	*12	..
Marshall Islands	2003	..	..	..	..	..	..	*28	..
	2004	..	..	..	..	..	..	*29	..
	2005	..	..	..	..	..	..	*29	..
	2006	..	..	..	..	..	..	*30	..
Nauru	2003	..	..	..	..	..	..	*53	..
	2004	..	..	..	..	..	..	*53	..
	2005	..	..	..	..	..	..	*53	..
	2006	..	..	..	..	..	..	*53	..
New Caledonia	2003	28	..	..	..	28	..	868	30
	2004	29	..	..	..	29	..	808	30
	2005	31	..	..	..	31	..	892	*31
	2006	37	..	..	..	37	..	939	*32
New Zealand	2003	10046	2209	1262	4287	2289	-224	6686	2267
	2004	9815	2250	1121	3837	2606	322	7168	1908
	2005	9215	2289	1044	3549	2333	-33	7089	2142
	2006	9534	2528	1000	3643	2363	-78	7161	2389
Niue	2003	..	..	..	..	..	..	*1	..
	2004	..	..	..	..	..	..	*1	..
	2005	..	..	..	..	..	..	*1	..
	2006	..	..	..	..	..	..	*1	..
Palau	2003	*2	..	..	..	*2	..	*78	..
	2004	*2	..	..	..	*2	..	*77	..
	2005	*2	..	..	..	*2	..	*79	..
	2006	*2	..	..	..	*2	..	*83	..

Table 2

Production, commerce et consommation d'énergie commerciale
Milliers de tonnes métriques d'équivalent pétrole et kilogrammes par habitant

Bunkers Soutes		Unallocated Quantités	Consumption Consommation						Year	Country or area
Aviation Avion	Marine Maritime	non réparties	Per capita Par habitant	Total Totale	Solids Solides	Liquids Liquides	Gas Gaz	Electricity Electricité	Année	Pays ou zone
372	..	3002	2716	129856	37115	13016	72340	7385	2003	Ukraine
378	..	3358	2706	127924	33042	13641	73192	8049	2004	
376	..	-153	2778	130783	33823	14008	74960	7992	2005	
335	..	-494	2656	124192	36671	14813	64724	7984	2006	
9720	1770	454	3618	214669	40264	70547	95424	8435	2003	Royaume-Uni
10759	2092	-827	3660	218507	39947	73122	97097	8341	2004	
12122	2056	543	3576	215304	41160	71150	94332	8663	2005	
11451	2352	-1644	3615	218997	45235	75467	90069	8225	2006	
3380	**1136**	**-2129**	**3936**	**127541**	**50729**	**43846**	**29040**	**3927**	**2003**	**Océanie**
3429	**1232**	**-2954**	**3924**	**129019**	**51443**	**44120**	**29242**	**4214**	**2004**	
3831	**1265**	**-2690**	**4026**	**134316**	**54975**	**45969**	**29415**	**3957**	**2005**	
3552	**1429**	**-827**	**4004**	**135609**	**55735**	**45845**	**29951**	**4078**	**2006**	
2246	733	-1960	5537	110192	49338	34775	24621	1458	2003	Australie
2266	842	-2803	5529	111356	50072	34583	25274	1426	2004	
2654	857	-2633	5741	117160	53500	36605	25612	1443	2005	
2387	988	-934	5720	118415	54250	36602	26037	1526	2006	
*2	..	..	616	11	..	11	..	..	2003	Iles Cook
0	..	..	909	18	..	18	..	..	2004	
0	..	..	1014	20	..	20	..	..	2005	
0	..	..	*1009	*21	..	*21	..	..	2006	
*300	*72	..	712	590	*9	523	..	*57	2003	Fidji
*232	*82	..	808	675	*9	608	..	*58	2004	
*227	*72	..	695	585	*8	519	..	*58	2005	
*290	*67	..	665	568	*8	500	..	*59	2006	
*6	*36	..	1131	280	..	269	..	10	2003	Polynésie française
*6	*46	..	1085	272	..	259	..	13	2004	
*6	*47	..	1145	291	..	280	..	11	2005	
*6	*50	..	1108	284	..	270	..	14	2006	
*2	..	..	*88	*8	..	*8	..	..	2003	Kiribati
*2	..	..	*82	*8	..	*8	..	..	2004	
*2	..	..	*80	*8	..	*8	..	..	2005	
*2	..	..	*98	*10	..	*10	..	..	2006	
..	..	..	*502	*28	..	*28	..	..	2003	Îles Marshall
..	..	..	*503	*29	..	*29	..	..	2004	
..	..	..	*488	*29	..	*29	..	..	2005	
..	..	..	*503	*30	..	*30	..	..	2006	
*7	..	..	*3658	*46	..	*46	..	..	2003	Nauru
*7	..	..	*3590	*46	..	*46	..	..	2004	
*7	..	..	*3524	*46	..	*46	..	..	2005	
*7	..	..	*3457	*46	..	*46	..	..	2006	
9	..	..	3759	857	219	610	..	28	2003	Nouvelle-Calédonie
11	..	..	3451	796	197	571	..	29	2004	
10	..	..	3768	882	182	669	..	31	2005	
14	..	..	3905	929	198	695	..	37	2006	
753	262	-162	3451	13837	1162	6099	4287	2289	2003	Nouvelle-Zélande
846	231	-287	3439	13966	1165	6333	3860	2606	2004	
867	258	-370	3279	13442	1284	6263	3562	2333	2005	
786	292	-119	3241	13427	1278	6131	3656	2363	2006	
..	..	..	*574	*1	..	*1	..	..	2003	Nioué
..	..	..	*576	*1	..	*1	..	..	2004	
..	..	..	*602	*1	..	*1	..	..	2005	
..	..	..	*625	*1	..	*1	..	..	2006	
*15	..	..	*3145	*64	..	*62	..	*2	2003	Palaos
*15	..	..	*3075	*63	..	*62	..	*2	2004	
*15	..	..	*3112	*65	..	*64	..	*2	2005	
*15	..	..	*3168	*69	..	*67	..	*2	2006	

Table 2

Production, trade and consumption of commercial energy

Thousand metric tons of oil equivalent and kilograms per capita

Country or area Pays ou zone	Year Année	Primary energy production Production d'énergie primaire					Changes in stocks Variations des stocks	Imports Importations	Exports Exportations
		Total Totale	Solids Solides	Liquids Liquides	Gas Gaz	Electricity Electricité			
Papua New Guinea	2003	2639	..	2427	132	80	*75	1279	2364
	2004	2318	..	2134	107	77	*-204	1410	2147
	2005	2780	..	2462	241	77	0	1666	2487
	2006	3200	..	2867	259	74	294	1713	2726
Samoa	2003	*3	..	..	..	*3	..	*50	..
	2004	*3	..	..	..	*3	..	*52	..
	2005	*3	..	..	..	*3	..	*53	..
	2006	*3	..	..	..	*3	..	*53	..
Solomon Islands	2003	..	..	..	..	..	..	*61	..
	2004	..	..	..	..	..	..	*61	..
	2005	..	..	..	..	..	..	*61	..
	2006	..	..	..	..	..	..	*63	..
Tonga	2003	..	..	..	..	..	..	59	..
	2004	..	..	..	..	..	..	58	..
	2005	..	..	..	..	..	..	*58	..
	2006	..	..	..	..	..	..	*58	..
Vanuatu	2003	..	..	..	..	..	..	*30	..
	2004	..	..	..	..	..	..	*30	..
	2005	..	..	..	..	..	..	*30	..
	2006	..	..	..	..	..	..	*31	..
Wallis and Futuna Is	2003	..	..	..	..	..	..	*9	..
	2004	..	..	..	..	..	..	9	..
	2005	..	..	..	..	..	..	9	..
	2006	..	..	..	..	..	..	9	..

Table 2

Production, commerce et consommation d'énergie commerciale

Milliers de tonnes métriques d'équivalent pétrole et kilogrammes par habitant

Bunkers Soutes		Unallocated Quantités	Consumption Consommation						Year	Country or area
Aviation Avion	Marine Maritime	non réparties	Per capita Par habitant	Total Totale	Solids Solides	Liquids Liquides	Gas Gaz	Electricity Electricité	Année	Pays ou zone
*33	*32	-7	245	1420	..	1208	132	80	2003	Papouasie-Nvl-Guinée
*38	*32	136	266	1579	..	1395	107	77	2004	
*38	*32	312	260	1577	..	1259	241	77	2005	
*39	*32	226	257	1596	..	1263	259	74	2006	
..	..	..	*297	*54	..	*50	..	*3	2003	Samoa
..	..	..	*303	*55	..	*52	..	*3	2004	
..	..	..	*306	*56	..	*53	..	*3	2005	
..	..	..	*303	*56	..	*53	..	*3	2006	
*3	..	..	*130	*58	..	*58	..	..	2003	Iles Salomon
*3	..	..	*127	*58	..	*58	..	..	2004	
*3	..	..	*124	*58	..	*58	..	..	2005	
*3	..	..	*123	*59	..	*59	..	..	2006	
*1	..	..	573	58	..	58	..	..	2003	Tonga
*1	..	..	562	57	..	57	..	..	2004	
*1	..	..	*553	*57	..	*57	..	..	2005	
*1	..	..	*560	*57	..	*57	..	..	2006	
..	..	..	*140	*30	..	*30	..	..	2003	Vanuatu
..	..	..	*139	*30	..	*30	..	..	2004	
..	..	..	*138	*30	..	*30	..	..	2005	
..	..	..	*139	*31	..	*31	..	..	2006	
*1	..	..	*558	*8	..	*8	..	..	2003	Iles Wallis et Futuna
1	..	..	564	9	..	9	..	..	2004	
1	..	..	555	9	..	9	..	..	2005	
1	..	..	537	9	..	9	..	..	2006	

Table 3

Production, trade and consumption of commercial energy
Production, commerce et consommation d'énergie commerciale

Thousand terajoules and gigajoules per capita
Milliers de térajoules et gigajoules par habitant

Table Notes:
Please refer to notes on table 1.

Notes relatives aux tableaux:
Veuillez consulter les notes de bas de page au tableau 1.

- **Please refer to the Definitions Section on pages xv to xxix for the appropriate product description/ classification.**

- **Veuillez consulter la section "définitions" de la page xv à la page xxix pour une description/classification appropriée des produits.**

Figure 7: World commercial primary energy production 1993-2006

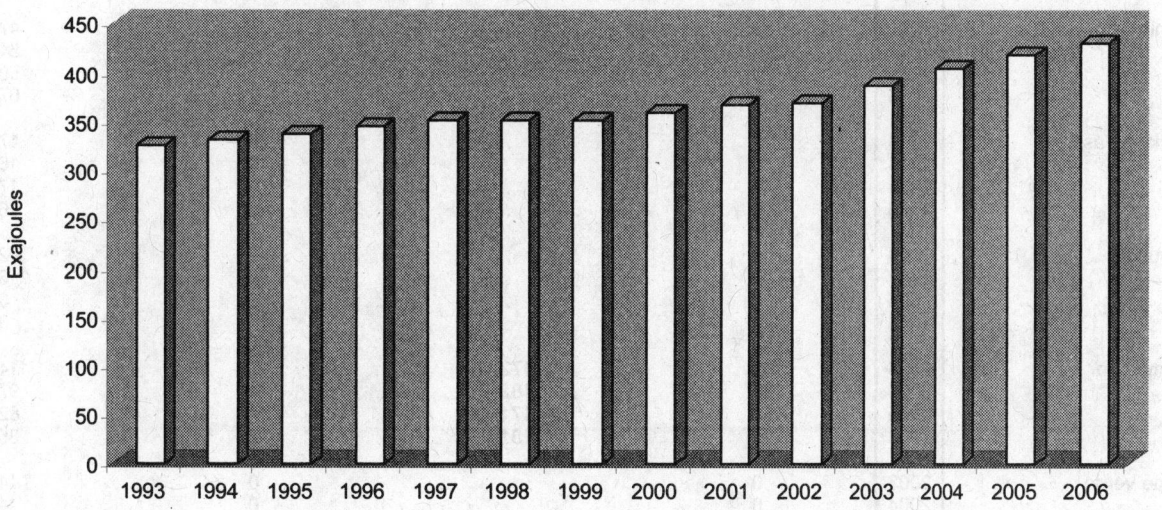

Figure 8: World commercial primary energy production, by type, in 2006

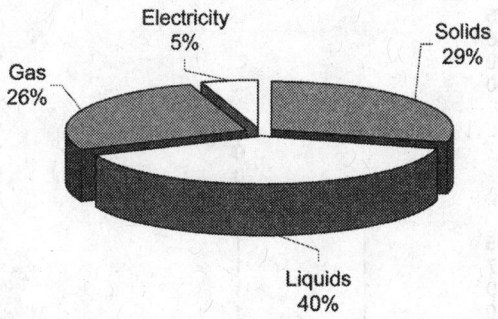

Figure 9: World commercial primary energy production, by region, in 2006

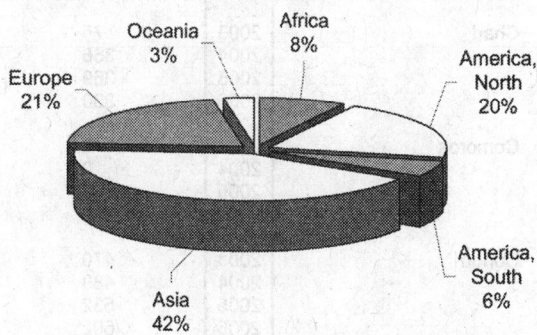

Table 3

Production, trade and consumption of commercial energy

Thousand terajoules and gigajoules per capita

Country or area Pays ou zone	Year Année	Primary energy production Production d'énergie primaire					Changes in stocks Variations des stocks	Imports Importations	Exports Exportations
		Total Totale	Solids Solides	Liquids Liquides	Gas Gaz	Electricity Electricité			
World	**2003**	**385219**	**102449**	**158996**	**104073**	**19702**	**226**	**167674**	**165659**
	2004	**403404**	**110981**	**165010**	**106679**	**20736**	**419**	**179337**	**177119**
	2005	**417010**	**118316**	**167708**	**109629**	**21357**	**84**	**184066**	**183637**
	2006	**429022**	**124679**	**169053**	**113325**	**21965**	**2256**	**188690**	**188904**
Africa	**2003**	**29847**	**5429**	**18384**	**5679**	**355**	**64**	**3477**	**20012**
	2004	**32027**	**5518**	**20090**	**6045**	**375**	**-57**	**3681**	**21765**
	2005	**34369**	**5573**	**21277**	**7142**	**376**	**-28**	**4134**	**23442**
	2006	**35112**	**5566**	**21282**	**7867**	**397**	**39**	**4188**	**24540**
Algeria	2003	7699	..	4450	3248	1	-2	41	5708
	2004	7862	..	4645	3216	1	*6	52	5936
	2005	8364	..	4776	3586	2	3	47	6050
	2006	8538	..	4693	3845	1	30	57	6356
Angola	2003	1833	..	1804	25	4	9	31	1729
	2004	2105	..	2070	28	6	33	33	1972
	2005	2645	..	2609	28	8	5	38	2539
	2006	2981	..	2941	30	10	26	50	2849
Benin	2003	0	..	..	..	0	0	47	14
	2004	0	..	..	..	0	1	54	18
	2005	0	..	..	..	0	-1	50	13
	2006	0	..	..	..	0	-1	67	22
Burkina Faso	2003	0	..	..	..	0	2	17	0
	2004	0	..	..	..	0	-1	16	0
	2005	0	..	..	..	0	0	17	0
	2006	0	..	..	..	0	-4	16	0
Burundi	2003	0	0	..	..	0	0	2	.
	2004	0	0	..	..	0	*1	3	.
	2005	0	0	..	..	0	0	3	.
	2006	0	0	..	..	0	0	3	.
Cameroon	2003	185	..	172	..	13	-7	114	231
	2004	196	..	182	..	14	0	97	229
	2005	185	..	171	..	14	-5	82	210
	2006	195	..	181	..	13	0	95	221
Cape Verde	2003	0	..	..	..	0		*4	
	2004	0	..	..	..	0		*4	
	2005	0	..	..	..	0		*5	
	2006	0	..	..	..	0		*5	
Central African Rep.	2003	0	..	..	..	0		*4	
	2004	0	..	..	..	0		*4	
	2005	0	..	..	..	0		*4	
	2006	0	..	..	..	0		*5	
Chad	2003	75	..	75	..	..		*3	72
	2004	356	..	356	..	..		*3	353
	2005	369	..	369	..	..		*4	366
	2006	330	..	330	..	..		*4	327
Comoros	2003	0	..	..	..	0		*1	
	2004	0	..	..	..	0		*1	
	2005	0	..	..	..	0		*1	
	2006	0	..	..	..	0		*1	
Congo	2003	470	..	468	1	1	..	1	455
	2004	489	..	487	1	1	..	3	466
	2005	532	..	530	1	1	..	5	516
	2006	602	..	600	1	1	..	6	588
Côte d'Ivoire	2003	97	..	43	48	7	*7	125	112
	2004	114	..	47	61	6	-10	151	140
	2005	156	..	83	68	5	*-1	179	189
	2006	200	..	131	64	5	-9	156	239

Table 3

Production, commerce et consommation d'énergie commerciale

Milliers de térajoules et gigajoules par habitant

Bunkers Soutes		Unallocated Quantités non réparties	Consumption Consommation						Year Année	Country or area Pays ou zone
Aviation Avion	Marine Maritime		Per capita Par habitant	Total Totale	Solids Solides	Liquids Liquides	Gas Gaz	Electricity Electricité		
4530	6048	13313	58	362662	104919	133848	104194	19701	2003	**Monde**
4761	6599	13496	60	379898	113706	139196	106259	20738	2004	
5088	7050	13386	61	391321	119336	141123	109509	21353	2005	
5171	7439	12857	61	400648	125106	142305	111282	21955	2006	
190	297	373	15	12374	4038	5124	2851	360	2003	**Afrique**
187	254	328	15	13219	4339	5469	3030	381	2004	
210	268	681	16	13917	4314	5624	3598	381	2005	
213	236	301	15	13961	4327	5687	3545	402	2006	
11	9	215	56	1788	32	860	895	1	2003	Algérie
9	14	114	56	1824	22	964	838	1	2004	
13	14	127	67	2195	27	921	1244	2	2005	
16	13	188	59	1982	31	837	1114	1	2006	
13	0	9	9	104	..	75	25	4	2003	Angola
14	0	11	9	108	..	73	28	6	2004	
12	0	11	10	116	..	80	28	8	2005	
14	0	14	11	129	..	89	30	10	2006	
1	..	..	4	32	..	30	..	2	2003	Bénin
1	..	..	4	34	..	32	..	2	2004	
1	..	..	4	37	..	34	..	2	2005	
1	..	..	5	44	..	42	..	2	2006	
1	..	..	1	15	0	15	..	1	2003	Burkina Faso
1	..	..	1	16	0	15	..	1	2004	
1	..	..	1	16	0	15	..	1	2005	
1	..	..	1	20	0	19	..	1	2006	
0	..	..	0	3	0	2	..	1	2003	Burundi
0	..	..	0	3	0	2	..	1	2004	
0	..	..	0	3	0	2	..	1	2005	
0	..	..	0	3	0	3	..	1	2006	
3	1	18	3	52	..	40	..	13	2003	Cameroun
3	1	7	3	54	..	40	..	14	2004	
3	1	4	3	54	..	40	..	14	2005	
3	2	10	3	55	..	42	..	13	2006	
..	0	..	*8	*4	..	*4	..	0	2003	Cap-Vert
..	0	..	*8	*4	..	*4	..	0	2004	
..	0	..	*9	*4	..	*4	..	0	2005	
..	0	..	*9	*4	..	*4	..	0	2006	
*1	..	..	*1	*4	..	*3	..	0	2003	Rép. centrafricaine
*1	..	..	*1	*4	..	*3	..	0	2004	
*1	..	..	*1	*4	..	*3	..	0	2005	
*1	..	..	*1	*4	..	*3	..	0	2006	
*1	..	3	0	*2	..	*2	..	..	2003	Tchad
*1	..	3	0	*2	..	*2	..	..	2004	
*1	..	3	0	*3	..	*3	..	..	2005	
*1	..	3	0	*3	..	*3	..	..	2006	
..	..	..	*2	*1	..	*1	..	0	2003	Comores
..	..	..	*2	*1	..	*1	..	0	2004	
..	..	..	*2	*1	..	*1	..	0	2005	
..	..	..	*2	*1	..	*1	..	0	2006	
..	..	2	4	14	..	11	1	3	2003	Congo
..	..	11	5	16	..	12	1	3	2004	
..	..	5	5	17	..	13	1	3	2005	
..	..	1	5	19	..	15	1	3	2006	
*5	4	7	5	88	..	39	48	2	2003	Côte d'Ivoire
4	4	18	6	110	..	48	61	1	2004	
4	3	28	6	113	..	45	68	0	2005	
4	3	7	6	112	..	47	64	2	2006	

Table 3

Production, trade and consumption of commercial energy
Thousand terajoules and gigajoules per capita

Country or area Pays ou zone	Year Année	Primary energy production Production d'énergie primaire					Changes in stocks Variations des stocks	Imports Importations	Exports Exportations
		Total Totale	Solids Solides	Liquids Liquides	Gas Gaz	Electricity Electricité			
Dem. Rep. of Congo	2003	71	3	45	..	22	..	21	5
	2004	71	3	43	..	25	..	29	4
	2005	71	4	41	..	27	..	29	4
	2006	69	4	37	..	28	..	29	4
Djibouti	2003	..		..		..	..	12	
	2004	..		..		..	..	13	
	2005	..		..		..	..	13	
	2006	..		..		..	..	14	
Egypt	2003	2936	1	1675	1214	45	*19	110	48
	2004	2948	1	1589	1311	47	*-17	163	45
	2005	3489	1	1560	1880	48	0	291	77
	2006	3384	1	1399	1936	49	-4	296	83
Equatorial Guinea	2003	578	..	559	19	0	..	*2	55
	2004	758	..	739	*19	0	..	*2	73
	2005	771	..	752	*19	0	..	*2	75
	2006	737	..	718	*19	0	..	*2	71
Eritrea	2003	0	..	..	..	0	0	11	
	2004	0	..	..	..	0	-1	10	
	2005	0	..	..	..	0	-2	9	
	2006	0	..	..	..	0	-1	6	
Ethiopia	2003	8	..	..	..	8	-11	53	
	2004	9	..	..	..	9	-17	56	
	2005	10	..	..	..	10	-9	63	
	2006	12	..	..	..	12	-9	70	
Gabon	2003	471	..	463	4	3	-9	5	44
	2004	458	..	449	5	3	-8	4	43
	2005	455	..	448	5	3	-8	6	43
	2006	458	..	449	5	3	-11	8	43
Gambia	2003	..	..	..	..	..	..	*5	
	2004	..	..	..	..	..	..	*5	
	2005	..	..	..	..	..	..	*5	
	2006	..	..	..	..	..	..	*5	
Ghana	2003	14	..	..	..	14	0	111	1
	2004	19	..	..	..	19	0	103	1
	2005	20	..	..	..	20	0	114	1
	2006	20	..	..	..	20	0	133	1
Guinea	2003	*2	..	..	..	*2	..	*17	
	2004	*2	..	..	..	*2	..	*17	
	2005	*2	..	..	..	*2	..	*17	
	2006	*2	..	..	..	*2	..	*17	
Guinea-Bissau	2003	..	..	..	..	..	..	*4	
	2004	..	..	..	..	..	..	*4	
	2005	..	..	..	..	..	..	*4	
	2006	..	..	..	..	..	..	*4	
Kenya	2003	15	..	..	..	15	0	125	1
	2004	14	..	..	..	14	0	154	1
	2005	14	..	..	..	14	2	151	1
	2006	15	..	..	..	15	-8	156	
Liberia	2003	..	..	..	..	..	..	*8	
	2004	..	..	..	..	..	..	9	
	2005	..	..	..	..	..	..	10	
	2006	..	..	..	..	..	..	*11	
Libyan Arab Jamah.	2003	3213	..	2970	243	..	..	0	242
	2004	3555	..	3249	306	..	..	0	272
	2005	3915	..	3485	429	..	..	1	311
	2006	4234	..	3671	562	..	..	0	343

Table 3

Production, commerce et consommation d'énergie commerciale
Milliers de térajoules et gigajoules par habitant

Bunkers Soutes		Unallocated Quantités	Consumption Consommation						Year	Country or area
Aviation Avion	Marine Maritime	non réparties	Per capita Par habitant	Total Totale	Solids Solides	Liquids Liquides	Gas Gaz	Electricity Electricité	Année	Pays ou zone
*4	0	0	1	38	10	10	..	18	2003	Rép. dem. du Congo
5	0	0	1	46	10	16	..	19	2004	
5	0	0	1	47	11	16	..	20	2005	
5	0	0	1	49	12	16	..	22	2006	
4	*3	..	6	5	..	5	..	..	2003	Djibouti
4	*3	..	7	6	..	6	..	..	2004	
4	*3	..	7	6	..	6	..	..	2005	
4	*4	..	7	6	..	6	..	..	2006	
21	115	140	34	2259	16	1017	1183	42	2003	Egypte
30	77	121	34	2444	37	1190	1171	45	2004	
32	83	244	37	2645	37	1271	1292	45	2005	
34	45	83	37	2685	33	1312	1292	47	2006	
..	..	0	46	21	..	*2	19	0	2003	Guinée équatoriale
..	..	0	*44	*21	..	*2	*19	0	2004	
..	..	0	*43	*21	..	*2	*19	0	2005	
..	..	0	*42	*21	..	*2	*19	0	2006	
0	..	..	2	10	..	10	..	0	2003	Erythrée
0	..	..	2	10	..	10	..	0	2004	
0	..	..	2	10	..	10	..	0	2005	
0	..	..	2	7	..	7	..	0	2006	
4	..	..	1	69	..	61	..	8	2003	Ethiopie
4	..	..	1	78	..	69	..	9	2004	
6	..	..	1	76	..	65	..	10	2005	
8	..	..	1	83	..	72	..	12	2006	
3	6	2	19	25	..	17	4	3	2003	Gabon
3	6	1	19	25	..	17	5	3	2004	
3	6	1	21	29	..	21	5	3	2005	
3	6	4	21	29	..	21	5	3	2006	
..	..	..	*3	*4	..	*4	..	..	2003	Gambie
..	..	..	*3	*4	..	*4	..	..	2004	
..	..	..	*3	*4	..	*4	..	..	2005	
..	..	..	*3	*5	..	*5	..	..	2006	
6	..	-2	5	107	..	93	..	14	2003	Ghana
5	..	-3	5	102	..	82	..	20	2004	
5	..	-3	5	113	..	92	..	21	2005	
7	..	1	6	133	..	114	..	20	2006	
*1	..	..	*2	*18	..	*16	..	*2	2003	Guinée
*1	..	..	*2	*18	..	*16	..	*2	2004	
*1	..	..	*2	*18	..	*16	..	*2	2005	
*1	..	..	*2	*18	..	*16	..	*2	2006	
0	..	..	*3	*4	..	*4	..	..	2003	Guinée-Bissau
0	..	..	*3	*4	..	*4	..	..	2004	
0	..	..	*3	*4	..	*4	..	..	2005	
0	..	..	*3	*4	..	*4	..	..	2006	
..	1	2	4	124	3	106	..	15	2003	Kenya
..	2	14	4	134	3	117	..	14	2004	
..	2	5	4	146	3	129	..	14	2005	
..	2	6	4	162	4	144	..	15	2006	
0	*1	..	*2	*7	..	*7	..	..	2003	Libéria
0	*1	..	2	8	..	8	..	..	2004	
0	*1	..	3	9	..	9	..	..	2005	
0	*1	..	*3	*10	..	*10	..	..	2006	
9	4	102	109	677	..	462	215	0	2003	Jamah. arabe libyenne
9	4	103	112	719	..	458	261	0	2004	
8	4	104	104	688	..	463	224	0	2005	
7	4	100	103	693	..	450	243	0	2006	

Table 3

Production, trade and consumption of commercial energy
Thousand terajoules and gigajoules per capita

Country or area Pays ou zone	Year Année	Primary energy production Production d'énergie primaire					Changes in stocks Variations des stocks	Imports Importations	Exports Exportation
		Total Totale	Solids Solides	Liquids Liquides	Gas Gaz	Electricity Electricité			
Madagascar	2003	2	..	..	..	2	..	*36	*
	2004	2	..	..	..	2	..	*39	*
	2005	*2	..	..	..	*2	..	*39	*
	2006	*2	..	..	..	*2	..	*40	*
Malawi	2003	6	2	..	..	4	..	11	
	2004	7	*2	..	..	5	..	*12	
	2005	6	1	..	..	5	..	*12	
	2006	6	*2	..	..	5	..	*11	
Mali	2003	*1	..	..	..	*1	..	8	
	2004	*1	..	..	..	*1	..	*9	
	2005	*1	..	..	..	*1	..	*9	
	2006	*1	..	..	..	*1	..	*9	
Mauritania	2003	..	..	..	..	..	..	19	
	2004	..	..	..	..	..	..	20	
	2005	..	..	..	..	..	..	21	
	2006	..	..	..	..	..	..	21	
Mauritius	2003	0	..	..	..	0	-1	50	
	2004	0	..	..	..	0	1	53	
	2005	0	..	..	..	0	-1	56	
	2006	0	..	..	..	0	-3	59	
Morocco	2003	8	..	0	2	6	4	469	1
	2004	9	..	0	2	7	-8	523	3
	2005	8	..	0	2	6	2	617	2
	2006	9	..	0	3	6	-1	582	1
Mozambique	2003	40	1	..	0	39	2	53	3
	2004	95	0	..	52	42	0	60	9
	2005	136	0	..	88	48	-1	56	12
	2006	160	1	..	105	53	1	59	14
Niger	2003	4	4	..	..	..	..	8	
	2004	5	5	..	..	..	..	8	
	2005	4	4	..	..	..	..	8	
	2006	*4	*4	..	..	..	..	8	
Nigeria	2003	5710	1	4939	742	28	-17	314	520
	2004	6288	0	5390	874	25	9	322	570
	2005	6475	0	5602	851	22	-6	333	568
	2006	6374	0	5235	1112	28	-2	324	574
Réunion	2003	*2	..	..	..	*2	..	*33	
	2004	*2	..	..	..	*2	..	*34	
	2005	*2	..	..	..	*2	..	*34	
	2006	*2	..	..	..	*2	..	*34	
Rwanda	2003	0	..	..	..	0	0	*8	
	2004	0	..	..	..	0	0	8	
	2005	0	..	..	..	0	0	*9	
	2006	0	..	..	..	0	0	*9	
Sao Tome and Principe	2003	0	..	..	..	..	0	*1	
	2004	0	..	..	..	..	0	*1	
	2005	0	..	..	..	..	0	*1	
	2006	0	..	..	..	..	0	*1	
Senegal	2003	2	..	..	0	1	1	74	
	2004	2	..	..	1	1	-2	70	
	2005	2	..	..	1	1	3	82	1
	2006	1	..	..	0	1	-6	48	
Seychelles	2003	..	..	..	..	..	..	12	
	2004	..	..	..	..	..	..	16	
	2005	..	..	..	..	..	..	15	
	2006	..	..	..	..	..	..	16	

Table 3

Production, commerce et consommation d'énergie commerciale
Milliers de térajoules et gigajoules par habitant

Bunkers Soutes		Unallocated Quantités non réparties	Consumption Consommation						Year Année	Country or area Pays ou zone
Aviation Avion	Marine Maritime		Per capita Par habitant	Total Totale	Solids Solides	Liquids Liquides	Gas Gaz	Electricity Electricité		
0	*1	*6	*2	*31	0	*28	..	2	2003	Madagascar
0	*1	*6	*2	*33	0	*31	..	2	2004	
0	*1	*6	*2	*34	0	*32	..	*2	2005	
0	*1	*6	*2	*35	0	*32	..	*2	2006	
..	..	..	1	17	2	11	..	4	2003	Malawi
..	..	..	*2	*18	*2	*12	..	5	2004	
..	..	..	*1	*18	2	*11	..	5	2005	
..	..	..	*1	*18	*1	*11	..	5	2006	
1	..	..	1	8	..	8	..	*1	2003	Mali
1	..	..	*1	*9	..	*8	..	*1	2004	
1	..	..	*1	*9	..	*8	..	*1	2005	
*1	..	..	*1	*9	..	*8	..	*1	2006	
0	0	..	7	19	0	19	..	0	2003	Mauritanie
0	0	..	7	20	0	20	..	0	2004	
0	0	..	7	21	0	21	..	0	2005	
0	0	..	7	21	0	20	..	0	2006	
4	6	..	35	42	9	32	..	0	2003	Maurice
4	6	..	35	43	8	34	..	0	2004	
4	8	..	36	45	11	34	..	0	2005	
4	8	..	40	50	14	36	..	0	2006	
13	1	28	15	420	135	272	2	11	2003	Maroc
14	*1	41	15	452	151	286	2	12	2004	
16	1	48	18	535	187	322	18	9	2005	
18	1	42	17	519	162	321	22	14	2006	
2	2	..	3	53	0	22	0	31	2003	Mozambique
2	2	..	3	61	0	23	0	38	2004	
2	0	..	3	62	0	20	3	39	2005	
2	0	..	3	67	0	21	3	42	2006	
0	..	..	1	12	4	6	..	1	2003	Niger
1	..	..	1	12	5	6	..	1	2004	
1	..	..	1	11	4	6	..	1	2005	
0	..	..	1	11	*4	6	..	1	2006	
17	26	29	6	760	1	449	282	28	2003	Nigéria
8	22	30	6	836	0	434	377	25	2004	
21	20	254	6	838	0	439	376	22	2005	
10	25	22	6	896	0	449	419	28	2006	
..	*1	..	*45	*34	..	*32	..	*2	2003	Réunion
..	*1	..	*45	*35	..	*33	..	*2	2004	
..	*1	..	*45	*35	..	*33	..	*2	2005	
..	*1	..	*44	*35	..	*33	..	*2	2006	
*1	..	..	*1	*8	..	*7	0	1	2003	Rwanda
*1	..	..	1	8	..	7	0	1	2004	
*1	..	..	*1	*9	..	*8	0	*1	2005	
*1	..	..	*1	*9	..	*8	0	1	2006	
..	..	..	*9	*1	..	*1	..	0	2003	Sao Tomé-et-Principe
..	..	..	*9	*1	..	*1	..	0	2004	
..	..	..	*10	*1	..	*1	..	0	2005	
..	..	..	*10	*1	..	*1	..	0	2006	
*10	0	0	6	57	*4	52	0	1	2003	Sénégal
11	0	1	5	54	4	49	1	1	2004	
11	0	0	5	57	4	51	1	1	2005	
10	0	0	4	39	5	33	0	1	2006	
*1	*3	..	92	8	..	8	..	0	2003	Seychelles
*1	*4	..	130	11	..	11	..	0	2004	
*1	*4	..	115	10	..	10	..	0	2005	
*1	*4	..	120	10	..	10	..	0	2006	

Table 3

Production, trade and consumption of commercial energy
Thousand terajoules and gigajoules per capita

Country or area Pays ou zone	Year Année	Primary energy production Production d'énergie primaire					Changes in stocks Variations des stocks	Imports Importations	Exports Exportation
		Total Totale	Solids Solides	Liquids Liquides	Gas Gaz	Electricity Electricité			
Sierra Leone	2003	0	..	..	..	0	..	*15	
	2004	0	..	..	..	0	..	*19	
	2005	0	..	..	..	0	..	*19	*
	2006	0	..	..	..	0	..	*19	*
Somalia	2003	..	..	..	..	..	..	*7	*
	2004	..	..	..	..	..	..	*8	*
	2005	..	..	..	..	..	..	*8	*
	2006	..	..	..	..	..	..	*8	*
South Africa Customs Un.	2003	5449	5305	29	50	64	50	1070	183
	2004	5616	5399	70	77	70	-54	1080	171
	2005	5659	5448	65	83	62	*-1	1241	188
	2006	5652	5445	63	76	69	0	1282	184
St. Helena and Depend.	2003	..	..	..	..	..	..	0	
	2004	..	..	..	..	..	..	0	
	2005	..	..	..	..	..	..	0	
	2006	..	..	..	..	..	..	0	
Sudan	2003	559	..	555	..	4	6	15	43
	2004	632	..	628	..	4	5	16	49
	2005	643	..	638	..	4	-7	13	50
	2006	698	..	693	..	5	38	23	52
Togo	2003	0	..	..	..	0	0	18	
	2004	0	..	..	..	0	0	18	
	2005	0	..	..	..	0	-1	17	
	2006	0	..	..	..	0	-2	13	
Tunisia	2003	219	..	136	82	1	9	234	14
	2004	231	..	144	87	1	2	238	16
	2005	234	..	146	88	1	-5	239	16
	2006	236	..	141	94	0	3	242	15
Uganda	2003	6	..	..	..	6	..	*20	*
	2004	7	..	..	..	7	..	22	*
	2005	7	..	..	..	7	..	28	
	2006	4	..	..	..	4	..	33	
United Rep.Tanzania	2003	11	2	..	0	9	..	47	
	2004	15	2	..	5	8	..	51	
	2005	22	2	..	14	6	..	54	
	2006	22	2	..	15	5	..	57	
Western Sahara	2003	..	..	..	..	..	..	*4	
	2004	..	..	..	..	..	..	*4	
	2005	..	..	..	..	..	..	*4	
	2006	..	..	..	..	..	..	*4	
Zambia	2003	35	5	..	..	30	2	26	
	2004	36	6	..	..	30	2	28	
	2005	38	6	..	..	32	3	29	
	2006	40	6	..	..	34	2	30	
Zimbabwe	2003	123	104	..	..	19	1	46	
	2004	120	100	..	..	20	1	34	
	2005	127	106	..	..	21	0	41	
	2006	121	101	..	..	20	0	39	
America, North	**2003**	**85100**	**20155**	**28743**	**30476**	**5725**	**-291**	**37684**	**1919**
	2004	**85781**	**21208**	**28646**	**30032**	**5895**	**38**	**40113**	**1985**
	2005	**85117**	**21572**	**27827**	**29704**	**6014**	**-162**	**41432**	**1993**
	2006	**86641**	**21946**	**27907**	**30647**	**6141**	**1270**	**41449**	**2055**
Anguilla	2003	..	..	..	..	..	..	1	
	2004	..	..	..	..	..	..	1	
	2005	..	..	..	..	..	..	1	
	2006	..	..	..	..	..	..	1	

Table 3

Production, commerce et consommation d'énergie commerciale
Milliers de térajoules et gigajoules par habitant

Bunkers Soutes		Unallocated Quantités	Consumption Consommation						Year	Country or area
Aviation Avion	Marine Maritime	non réparties	Per capita Par habitant	Total Totale	Solids Solides	Liquids Liquides	Gas Gaz	Electricity Electricité	Année	Pays ou zone
*1	*4	*3	*1	*7	..	*7	..	0	2003	Sierra Leone
1	*4	*4	*2	*9	..	*9	..	0	2004	
*1	*4	*4	*2	*9	..	*9	..	0	2005	
*1	*4	*4	*1	*9	..	*9	..	0	2006	
*2	*1	*-4	*1	*7	..	*7	..	..	2003	Somalie
*2	*1	*-4	*1	*7	..	*7	..	..	2004	
*2	*1	*-4	*1	*7	..	*7	..	..	2005	
*2	*1	*-5	*1	*7	..	*7	..	..	2006	
37	109	-197	92	4688	3718	851	50	68	2003	Un.douan.d'Afr.mérid
33	100	-164	95	5068	3995	871	129	72	2004	
32	111	-172	94	5041	3919	884	169	69	2005	
33	109	-177	95	5121	3956	916	178	71	2006	
..	..	..	*23	0	..	0	..	..	2003	St-Hélène et dépend
..	..	..	17	0	..	0	..	..	2004	
..	..	..	*19	0	..	0	..	..	2005	
..	..	..	*19	0	..	0	..	..	2006	
6	0	4	4	120	..	116	..	4	2003	Soudan
6	0	9	4	133	..	129	..	4	2004	
8	0	8	4	144	..	139	..	4	2005	
9	0	-14	5	164	..	159	..	5	2006	
1	0	..	3	17	..	15	..	2	2003	Togo
2	0	..	3	16	..	14	..	2	2004	
2	0	..	3	15	..	13	..	2	2005	
1	0	..	3	14	..	12	..	2	2006	
..	0	4	30	292	1	163	127	1	2003	Tunisie
..	0	3	30	302	0	169	132	1	2004	
..	0	6	31	307	0	171	136	1	2005	
..	0	7	31	312	0	171	140	0	2006	
..	..	..	*1	*26	..	*20	..	6	2003	Ouganda
..	..	..	1	28	..	22	..	6	2004	
..	..	..	1	34	..	28	..	6	2005	
..	..	..	1	37	..	33	..	4	2006	
3	1	..	1	54	2	43	0	10	2003	Rép. Unie de Tanzanie
3	1	..	2	62	2	46	5	9	2004	
4	1	..	2	72	2	49	14	7	2005	
4	1	..	2	75	2	52	15	6	2006	
0	..	..	*13	*3	..	*3	..	..	2003	Sahara occidental
0	..	..	*12	*3	..	*3	..	..	2004	
0	..	..	*12	*3	..	*3	..	..	2005	
0	..	..	*12	*3	..	*3	..	..	2006	
2	..	2	5	53	4	22	..	28	2003	Zambie
2	..	2	5	56	4	23	..	30	2004	
2	..	2	5	59	4	24	..	31	2005	
2	..	2	5	62	4	25	..	33	2006	
2	..	..	12	161	98	32	..	31	2003	Zimbabwe
0	..	..	11	147	95	26	..	27	2004	
0	..	..	12	162	102	28	..	32	2005	
0	..	..	12	154	97	27	..	30	2006	
862	998	1499	200	100539	20459	43960	30400	5721	2003	**Amérique du Nord**
878	1228	1422	202	102445	21049	45429	30073	5895	2004	
905	1273	957	202	103661	21255	46302	30091	6012	2005	
857	1356	939	200	103126	20946	45973	30072	6136	2006	
..	..	..	44	1	..	1	..	..	2003	Anguilla
..	..	..	46	1	..	1	..	..	2004	
..	..	..	52	1	..	1	..	..	2005	
..	..	..	52	1	..	1	..	..	2006	

Table 3

Production, trade and consumption of commercial energy
Thousand terajoules and gigajoules per capita

| Country or area Pays ou zone | Year Année | Primary energy production Production d'énergie primaire | | | | | Changes in stocks Variations des stocks | Imports Importations | Exports Exportation |
		Total Totale	Solids Solides	Liquids Liquides	Gas Gaz	Electricity Electricité			
Antigua and Barbuda	2003	..	..	..	..	..	..	*8	
	2004	..	..	..	..	..	..	*8	
	2005	..	..	..	..	..	..	*8	
	2006	..	..	..	..	..	..	*9	
Aruba	2003	*5	..	*5	..	..	..	*448	43
	2004	*5	..	*5	..	..	..	*448	43
	2005	*5	..	*5	..	..	..	449	43
	2006	*5	..	*5	..	..	..	*449	*43
Bahamas	2003	..	..	..	..	..	*2	*132	*9
	2004	..	..	..	..	..	0	*134	*9
	2005	..	..	..	..	..	0	*137	*9
	2006	..	..	..	..	..	0	*137	*9
Barbados	2003	4	..	3	1	..	..	14	
	2004	4	..	3	1	..	..	15	
	2005	4	..	3	1	..	..	15	
	2006	3	..	2	1	..	..	16	
Belize	2003	0	..	..	..	0	..	*13	
	2004	0	..	..	..	0	..	*13	
	2005	0	..	..	..	0	..	*13	
	2006	0	..	..	..	0	..	*13	
Bermuda	2003	..	..	..	..	..	..	*8	
	2004	..	..	..	..	..	..	*9	
	2005	..	..	..	..	..	..	*9	
	2006	..	..	..	..	..	..	*9	
British Virgin Islands	2003	..	..	..	..	..	..	*1	
	2004	..	..	..	..	..	..	*1	
	2005	..	..	..	..	..	..	*1	
	2006	..	..	..	..	..	..	*1	
Canada	2003	15763	1272	5971	7032	1488	-182	3188	898
	2004	16124	1366	6183	7017	1558	-306	3278	934
	2005	16256	1336	6106	7169	1646	-248	3275	934
	2006	16628	1370	6410	7206	1642	-64	3108	951
Cayman Islands	2003	..	..	..	..	..	..	*8	
	2004	..	..	..	..	..	..	*8	
	2005	..	..	..	..	..	..	*8	
	2006	..	..	..	..	..	..	*8	
Costa Rica	2003	27	..	..	..	27	-4	84	
	2004	29	..	..	..	29	1	90	
	2005	29	..	..	..	29	-1	88	
	2006	29	..	..	..	29	1	99	
Cuba	2003	182	..	155	26	0	1	185	
	2004	165	..	137	27	0	*1	185	
	2005	151	..	122	29	0	17	222	
	2006	166	..	123	42	0	-1	258	
Dominica	2003	0	..	..	..	0	..	2	
	2004	0	..	..	..	0	..	2	
	2005	0	..	..	..	0	..	*2	
	2006	0	..	..	..	0	..	*2	
Dominican Republic	2003	4	..	..	..	4	0	275	
	2004	6	..	..	..	6	2	260	
	2005	7	..	..	..	7	0	261	
	2006	5	..	..	..	5	-1	265	
El Salvador	2003	9	..	..	..	9	2	94	
	2004	9	..	..	..	9	2	96	
	2005	10	..	..	..	10	3	93	
	2006	11	..	..	..	11	2	90	

Table 3

Production, commerce et consommation d'énergie commerciale
Milliers de térajoules et gigajoules par habitant

Bunkers Soutes — Aviation Avion	Bunkers Soutes — Marine Maritime	Unallocated Quantités non réparties	Consumption Consommation — Per capita Par habitant	Total Totale	Solids Solides	Liquids Liquides	Gas Gaz	Electricity Electricité	Year Année	Country or area Pays ou zone
*2	0	..	*68	*5	..	*5	..	..	2003	Antigua-et-Barbuda
*2	0	..	*70	*6	..	*6	..	..	2004	
*2	0	..	*69	*6	..	*6	..	..	2005	
*2	0	..	*71	*6	..	*6	..	..	2006	
*3	..	0	110	10	..	10	..	..	2003	Aruba
*3	..	0	107	10	..	10	..	..	2004	
*3	..	0	106	11	..	11	..	..	2005	
*3	..	0	*104	*11	..	*11	..	..	2006	
*2	*10	..	*81	*26	0	*26	..	..	2003	Bahamas
*2	*11	..	*93	*28	0	*28	..	..	2004	
*2	*11	..	*90	*29	0	*29	..	..	2005	
*2	*11	..	*90	*30	0	*29	..	..	2006	
..	..	0	54	15	..	14	1	..	2003	Barbade
..	..	0	58	16	..	15	1	..	2004	
..	..	0	60	16	..	15	1	..	2005	
..	..	0	61	17	..	16	1	..	2006	
*1	*1	..	*42	*12	..	*11	..	0	2003	Belize
*1	*1	..	*42	*12	..	*11	..	0	2004	
*1	*1	..	*42	*12	..	*12	..	0	2005	
*1	*1	..	*40	*12	..	*12	..	0	2006	
*1	0	..	*117	*7	..	*7	..	..	2003	Bermudes
*1	0	..	*121	*8	..	*8	..	..	2004	
*1	0	..	*124	*8	..	*8	..	..	2005	
*1	0	..	*124	*8	..	*8	..	..	2006	
..	..	..	*51	*1	..	*1	..	..	2003	Iles Vierges britanniques
..	..	..	*56	*1	..	*1	..	..	2004	
..	..	..	*57	*1	..	*1	..	..	2005	
..	..	..	*61	*1	..	*1	..	..	2006	
29	21	103	315	9991	1100	3718	3709	1464	2003	Canada
37	26	227	315	10071	1076	3845	3630	1521	2004	
35	25	222	314	10156	1053	3791	3752	1560	2005	
35	23	168	308	10062	1033	3759	3698	1573	2006	
*1	..	..	*152	*7	..	*7	..	..	2003	Iles Caïmanes
*1	..	..	*155	*7	..	*7	..	..	2004	
*1	..	..	*144	*7	..	*7	..	..	2005	
*1	..	..	*138	*7	..	*7	..	..	2006	
..	..	6	26	107	4	77	..	26	2003	Costa Rica
..	..	4	27	111	3	80	..	28	2004	
..	..	2	27	115	3	84	..	29	2005	
..	..	1	29	125	3	92	..	29	2006	
9	3	34	28	319	1	292	26	0	2003	Cuba
9	3	15	28	322	1	294	27	0	2004	
9	3	2	30	342	1	312	29	0	2005	
*9	*2	47	33	366	*1	323	42	0	2006	
..	..	..	24	2	..	2	..	0	2003	Dominique
..	..	..	23	2	..	2	..	0	2004	
..	..	..	*25	*2	..	*2	..	0	2005	
..	..	..	*26	*2	..	*2	..	0	2006	
4	..	26	28	249	31	210	4	4	2003	Rép. dominicaine
4	..	8	28	252	23	218	5	6	2004	
4	..	7	28	257	14	225	11	7	2005	
4	..	2	28	264	23	223	13	5	2006	
3	..	1	13	89	0	79	..	10	2003	El Salvador
3	..	-1	13	89	0	79	..	10	2004	
3	..	6	12	85	0	74	..	11	2005	
3	..	2	13	91	0	80	..	11	2006	

Table 3

Production, trade and consumption of commercial energy

Thousand terajoules and gigajoules per capita

Country or area Pays ou zone	Year Année	Primary energy production Production d'énergie primaire					Changes in stocks Variations des stocks	Imports Importations	Exports Exportation
		Total Totale	Solids Solides	Liquids Liquides	Gas Gaz	Electricity Electricité			
Greenland	2003	..	..	..	..	..	..	*8	
	2004	..	..	..	..	..	..	*8	
	2005	..	..	..	..	..	..	*8	
	2006	..	..	..	..	..	..	*9	
Grenada	2003	..				..	..	3	
	2004	..				..	..	3	
	2005	..				..	..	4	
	2006	..				..	..	4	
Guadeloupe	2003	..	..	..	..	..	..	*31	
	2004	..	..	..	..	..	..	*31	
	2005	..	..	..	..	..	..	*32	
	2006	..	..	..	..	..	..	*33	
Guatemala	2003	60	..	51	..	9	0	140	4
	2004	51	..	42	..	9	1	147	4
	2005	51	..	38	..	13	7	156	3
	2006	49	..	34	..	15	-9	146	3
Haiti	2003	1	..	..	..	1	..	23	
	2004	1	..	..	..	1	..	23	
	2005	1	..	..	..	1	..	24	
	2006	1	..	..	..	1	..	24	
Honduras	2003	8	..	..	..	8	10	92	
	2004	8	..	..	..	8	0	95	
	2005	6	..	..	..	6	1	99	
	2006	7	..	..	..	7	0	104	
Jamaica	2003	1	..	..	..	1	1	159	
	2004	1	..	..	..	1	0	156	
	2005	1	..	..	..	1	1	144	
	2006	1	..	..	..	1	0	173	
Martinique	2003	..	..	..	..	..	..	32	*
	2004	..	..	..	..	..	..	33	*
	2005	..	..	..	..	..	..	34	*
	2006	..	..	..	..	..	..	35	*
Mexico	2003	9790	123	7955	1580	132	-44	943	458
	2004	9961	127	8034	1651	148	69	1028	457
	2005	9898	138	7878	1717	165	19	1126	436
	2006	9899	147	7694	1886	173	26	1279	435
Montserrat	2003	..	..	..	..	..	..	*1	
	2004	..	..	..	..	..	..	*1	
	2005	..	..	..	..	..	..	*1	
	2006	..	..	..	..	..	..	*1	
Netherlands Antilles	2003	..	..	..	..	..	..	535	32
	2004	..	..	..	..	..	..	576	34
	2005	..	..	..	..	..	..	617	39
	2006	..	..	..	..	..	..	593	36
Nicaragua	2003	2	..	..	..	2	2	55	
	2004	2	..	..	..	2	-2	54	
	2005	3	..	..	..	3	1	55	
	2006	2	..	..	..	2	1	58	
Panama	2003	10	..	..	..	10	-1	86	
	2004	14	..	..	..	14	-8	74	
	2005	14	..	..	..	14	0	85	
	2006	14	..	..	..	14	0	92	1
Puerto Rico	2003	1	..	..	..	1	..	29	
	2004	1	..	..	..	1	..	27	
	2005	1	..	..	..	1	..	27	
	2006	*1	..	..	..	*1	..	27	

Table 3

Production, commerce et consommation d'énergie commerciale
Milliers de térajoules et gigajoules par habitant

Bunkers Soutes		Unallocated Quantités	Consumption Consommation						Year	Country or area
Aviation Avion	Marine Maritime	non réparties	Per capita Par habitant	Total Totale	Solids Solides	Liquids Liquides	Gas Gaz	Electricity Electricité	Année	Pays ou zone
0	..	..	*134	*8	..	*8	..	..	2003	Groënland
0	..	..	*135	*8	..	*8	..	..	2004	
0	..	..	*137	*8	..	*8	..	..	2005	
0	..	..	*139	*8	..	*8	..	..	2006	
0	..	..	30	3	..	3	..	..	2003	Grenade
0	..	..	30	3	..	3	..	..	2004	
0	..	..	31	3	..	3	..	..	2005	
0	..	..	32	3	..	3	..	..	2006	
*4	..	..	*61	*27	..	*27	..	..	2003	Guadeloupe
*4	..	..	*61	*27	..	*27	..	..	2004	
*5	..	..	*62	*28	..	*28	..	..	2005	
*5	..	..	*61	*28	..	*28	..	..	2006	
2	5	4	12	141	11	123	..	7	2003	Guatemala
2	5	3	12	146	12	127	..	7	2004	
2	5	3	12	155	12	131	..	12	2005	
2	5	4	12	154	13	127	..	14	2006	
1	..	..	3	22	..	21	..	1	2003	Haïti
1	..	..	3	23	..	22	..	1	2004	
1	..	..	3	24	..	23	..	1	2005	
1	..	..	3	24	..	23	..	1	2006	
1	..	..	13	88	5	74	..	9	2003	Honduras
1	..	..	14	101	5	86	..	10	2004	
1	..	..	14	103	5	91	..	6	2005	
1	..	..	15	108	6	96	..	7	2006	
8	1	1	54	142	2	139	..	1	2003	Jamaïque
*8	1	2	52	139	2	137	..	1	2004	
8	1	0	51	134	2	132	..	1	2005	
10	1	1	61	162	1	160	..	1	2006	
0	*2	*-4	*64	*25	..	*25	..	..	2003	Martinique
0	*2	*-4	*65	*26	..	*26	..	..	2004	
0	*2	*-3	*65	*26	..	*26	..	..	2005	
0	*2	*-3	*66	*26	..	*26	..	..	2006	
109	34	293	56	5761	236	3443	1953	129	2003	Mexique
104	32	222	58	5987	212	3597	2034	144	2004	
108	37	294	60	6199	254	3728	2056	161	2005	
116	37	226	61	6415	256	3729	2260	170	2006	
..	0	..	*108	*1	..	*1	..	..	2003	Montserrat
..	0	..	*105	*1	..	*1	..	..	2004	
..	0	..	*104	*1	..	*1	..	..	2005	
..	0	..	*105	*1	..	*1	..	..	2006	
3	71	73	372	66	..	66	..	..	2003	Antilles néerlandaises
3	72	64	525	96	..	96	..	..	2004	
3	72	96	292	54	..	54	..	..	2005	
3	72	104	266	50	..	50	..	..	2006	
..	..	1	10	54	..	52	..	2	2003	Nicaragua
..	..	1	10	56	..	54	..	2	2004	
..	..	1	10	55	..	52	..	3	2005	
..	..	2	10	57	..	54	..	3	2006	
0	..	0	28	88	0	79	..	10	2003	Panama
0	..	0	27	87	0	73	..	14	2004	
0	..	0	28	90	0	76	..	14	2005	
0	..	0	29	96	0	82	..	14	2006	
..	..	..	8	30	..	..	29	1	2003	Porto Rico
..	..	..	7	27	..	..	27	1	2004	
..	..	..	7	27	..	..	27	1	2005	
..	..	..	7	27	..	..	27	*1	2006	

Table 3

Production, trade and consumption of commercial energy
Thousand terajoules and gigajoules per capita

Country or area Pays ou zone	Year Année	Primary energy production Production d'énergie primaire					Changes in stocks Variations des stocks	Imports Importations	Exports Exportations
		Total Totale	Solids Solides	Liquids Liquides	Gas Gaz	Electricity Electricité			
St. Kitts-Nevis	2003	..	..	..	..	..	..	*3	
	2004	..	..	..	..	..	..	*3	
	2005	..	..	..	..	..	..	*3	
	2006	..	..	..	..	..	..	*3	
St. Lucia	2003	..	..	..	..	..	..	*5	
	2004	..	..	..	..	..	..	*5	
	2005	..	..	..	..	..	..	*6	
	2006	..	..	..	..	..	..	*6	
St. Pierre-Miquelon	2003	..	..	..	..	..	..	*1	
	2004	..	..	..	..	..	..	*1	
	2005	..	..	..	..	..	..	*1	
	2006	..	..	..	..	..	..	*1	
St. Vincent-Grenadines	2003	0	..	..	..	0	..	*3	
	2004	0	..	..	..	0	..	*3	
	2005	0	..	..	..	0	..	*3	
	2006	0	..	..	..	0	..	*3	
Trinidad and Tobago	2003	1306	..	334	972	..	14	197	93∎
	2004	1333	..	309	1024	..	13	144	89∎
	2005	1421	..	354	1067	..	3	192	100∎
	2006	1670	..	344	1325	..	-18	198	122∎
United States	2003	57928	18759	14269	20866	4033	-92	30878	374∎
	2004	58068	19715	13932	20312	4110	265	33152	412∎
	2005	57260	20098	13322	19721	4118	35	34234	422∎
	2006	58149	20429	13295	20186	4240	1334	34198	449∎
America, South	**2003**	**21810**	**1666**	**14351**	**3744**	**2048**	**214**	**3343**	**1000∎**
	2004	**22330**	**1767**	**14519**	**3932**	**2112**	**-48**	**3805**	**1103∎**
	2005	**23363**	**1952**	**15111**	**4070**	**2229**	**-6**	**3716**	**1128∎**
	2006	**24113**	**2134**	**15343**	**4274**	**2361**	**-206**	**3822**	**1137∎**
Argentina	2003	3696	2	1881	1664	149	2	76	105∎
	2004	3668	1	1814	1713	138	-5	130	93∎
	2005	3576	1	1742	1685	148	6	192	84
	2006	3703	11	1762	1765	165	-6	148	68
Bolivia	2003	347	..	83	256	8	*-3	14	18∎
	2004	458	..	95	356	8	-21	8	33
	2005	553	..	102	442	9	-20	11	43
	2006	592	..	111	474	8	-39	16	45
Brazil	2003	5272	86	3640	398	1148	27	1866	87∎
	2004	5354	101	3636	420	1197	-32	2161	93∎
	2005	5821	116	4025	429	1250	-9	1933	97∎
	2006	6116	109	4266	435	1305	-18	2006	123∎
Chile	2003	187	16	15	74	81	6	834	6
	2004	165	5	15	68	77	4	917	6
	2005	206	15	14	82	94	17	946	6
	2006	227	11	14	79	123	31	988	8
Colombia	2003	2923	1361	1173	258	130	26	14	190
	2004	2998	1461	1121	271	144	0	13	202
	2005	3137	1607	1101	285	144	15	40	212
	2006	3387	1785	1126	322	154	-55	29	233
Ecuador	2003	942	..	900	16	26	47	89	63
	2004	1202	..	1150	25	27	13	88	85
	2005	1165	..	1114	20	31	4	117	82
	2006	1188	..	1123	33	32	-11	136	86
Falkland Is. (Malvinas)	2003	0	0	..	..	..	..	*1	
	2004	0	0	..	..	..	..	*1	
	2005	0	0	..	..	..	..	*1	
	2006	0	0	..	..	..	..	*1	

Table 3

Production, commerce et consommation d'énergie commerciale
Milliers de térajoules et gigajoules par habitant

Bunkers Soutes		Unallocated Quantités non réparties	Consumption Consommation						Year Année	Country or area Pays ou zone
Aviation Avion	Marine Maritime		Per capita Par habitant	Total Totale	Solids Solides	Liquids Liquides	Gas Gaz	Electricity Electricité		
..	..	..	*69	*3	..	*3	..	..	2003	St-Kitts-Nevis
..	..	..	*72	*3	..	*3	..	..	2004	
..	..	..	*77	*3	..	*3	..	..	2005	
..	..	..	*77	*3	..	*3	..	..	2006	
..	0	..	*30	*5	..	*5	..	..	2003	St-Lucie
..	0	..	*32	*5	..	*5	..	..	2004	
..	0	..	*32	*5	..	*5	..	..	2005	
..	0	..	*32	*5	..	*5	..	..	2006	
..	0	..	*128	*1	..	*1	..	..	2003	St-Pierre-Miquelon
..	0	..	*122	*1	..	*1	..	..	2004	
..	0	..	*128	*1	..	*1	..	..	2005	
..	0	..	*128	*1	..	*1	..	..	2006	
..	..	..	*26	*3	..	*3	..	0	2003	St. Vincent-Grenadines
..	..	..	*27	*3	..	*3	..	0	2004	
..	..	..	*27	*3	..	*3	..	0	2005	
..	..	..	*28	*3	..	*3	..	0	2006	
0	31	23	377	495	..	31	465	..	2003	Trinité-et-Tobago
0	38	12	391	516	..	28	488	..	2004	
3	11	39	416	551	..	41	510	..	2005	
3	*10	19	472	627	..	55	572	..	2006	
678	818	937	284	82736	19069	35397	24213	4056	2003	Etats-Unis
690	1038	868	287	84254	19715	36528	23862	4150	2004	
713	1105	285	287	85145	19911	37320	23706	4207	2005	
655	1191	365	283	84325	19609	36950	23460	4306	2006	
113	**254**	**1265**	**37**	**13300**	**850**	**6668**	**3741**	**2042**	**2003**	**Amérique du Sud**
143	**273**	**714**	**38**	**14014**	**881**	**7085**	**3936**	**2113**	**2004**	
142	**324**	**743**	**39**	**14582**	**912**	**7373**	**4063**	**2235**	**2005**	
162	**306**	**821**	**41**	**15465**	**910**	**7903**	**4283**	**2369**	**2006**	
..	25	204	66	2484	22	890	1404	167	2003	Argentine
..	23	211	69	2639	24	1004	1460	151	2004	
..	29	166	71	2728	38	1034	1494	162	2005	
..	31	211	75	2929	32	1138	1586	174	2006	
..	..	15	19	168	..	72	88	8	2003	Bolivie
..	..	17	15	140	..	68	65	8	2004	
..	..	24	14	130	..	84	37	9	2005	
..	..	43	16	154	..	92	54	8	2006	
46	135	288	32	5769	578	3315	593	1282	2003	Brésil
46	140	271	34	6144	601	3478	733	1331	2004	
46	146	270	34	6321	583	3569	778	1391	2005	
53	142	256	35	6447	577	3603	814	1453	2006	
23	37	35	54	854	102	363	300	88	2003	Chili
25	40	40	57	911	138	391	298	83	2004	
27	52	34	59	955	139	395	319	102	2005	
29	59	-1	62	1017	165	417	303	132	2006	
25	10	77	20	898	115	399	258	126	2003	Colombie
25	17	41	20	904	81	413	271	139	2004	
26	17	57	20	941	113	405	285	137	2005	
28	20	107	21	987	103	414	322	148	2006	
..	11	27	24	308	..	262	16	30	2003	Equateur
..	9	107	24	309	..	252	25	33	2004	
..	28	40	29	389	..	332	20	37	2005	
..	*12	30	32	425	..	354	33	38	2006	
..	..	..	*214	*1	0	*1	..	..	2003	Iles Falkland (Malvinas)
..	..	..	*213	*1	0	*1	..	..	2004	
..	..	..	*224	*1	0	*1	..	..	2005	
..	..	..	*224	*1	0	*1	..	..	2006	

Table 3

Production, trade and consumption of commercial energy
Thousand terajoules and gigajoules per capita

Country or area Pays ou zone	Year Année	Primary energy production Production d'énergie primaire					Changes in stocks Variations des stocks	Imports Importations	Exports Exportations
		Total Totale	Solids Solides	Liquids Liquides	Gas Gaz	Electricity Electricité			
French Guiana	2003	..	..	..	..	..	..	*12	.
	2004	..	..	..	..	..	..	*12	
	2005	..	..	..	..	..	..	*12	
	2006	..	..	..	..	..	..	*12	
Guyana	2003	..	..	..	..	..	..	21	.
	2004	..	..	..	..	..	..	21	
	2005	..	..	..	..	..	..	21	
	2006	..	..	..	..	..	..	21	
Paraguay	2003	186	..	0	..	186	-3	51	163
	2004	187	..	0	..	187	0	54	162
	2005	184	..	0	..	184	-1	49	158
	2006	194	..	0	..	194	-1	52	165
Peru	2003	306	0	213	26	67	37	270	142
	2004	318	1	214	40	63	1	274	122
	2005	366	1	225	68	72	-4	274	145
	2006	447	3	289	78	77	49	278	140
Suriname	2003	27	..	25	..	3	..	11	5
	2004	28	..	26	..	3	..	11	6
	2005	30	..	27	..	3	..	12	6
	2006	31	..	27	..	3	..	12	6
Uruguay	2003	31	..	..	..	31	6	85	11
	2004	17	..	..	..	17	3	116	15
	2005	24	..	..	..	24	-5	108	15
	2006	13	..	..	..	13	2	123	10
Venezuela(Bolivar. Rep.)	2003	7892	199	6421	1054	219	68	..	4970
	2004	7936	198	6448	1039	252	-11	..	5592
	2005	8299	211	6761	1058	270	-9	..	5706
	2006	8215	215	6625	1089	286	-158	..	5407
Asia	**2003**	**147878**	**52197**	**65422**	**26012**	**4247**	**-112**	**57960**	**61044**
	2004	**160467**	**59408**	**68645**	**27669**	**4744**	**38**	**64062**	**65546**
	2005	**171430**	**65675**	**70993**	**29663**	**5099**	**-265**	**65251**	**69090**
	2006	**180574**	**71581**	**72366**	**31222**	**5406**	**41**	**68117**	**72360**
Afghanistan	2003	4	1	..	0	2	..	*7	
	2004	3	1	..	0	2	..	8	
	2005	*3	*1	..	0	*2	..	*9	
	2006	*3	*1	..	0	*2	..	*9	
Armenia	2003	14	..	..	..	14	..	62	
	2004	16	..	..	..	16	..	66	
	2005	16	..	..	..	16	..	81	5
	2006	16	..	..	..	16	..	81	
Azerbaijan	2003	847	..	644	193	9	0	163	459
	2004	856	..	652	195	10	2	204	477
	2005	1158	..	931	216	11	38	198	702
	2006	1616	..	1352	255	9	-6	185	1173
Bahrain	2003	690	..	427	264	..	-25	137	433
	2004	700	..	426	274	..	-13	139	416
	2005	715	..	425	291	..	-10	167	422
	2006	725	..	417	308	..	-21	157	408
Bangladesh	2003	443	..	5	435	4	-6	177	
	2004	476	..	4	468	4	-2	179	
	2005	512	..	4	503	5	-14	188	
	2006	552	..	4	543	5	-5	190	
Bhutan	2003	10	2	..	..	8	..	*3	
	2004	10	1	..	..	9	..	*3	
	2005	11	2	..	..	8	..	*3	
	2006	12	3	..	..	10	..	*3	

Table 3

Production, commerce et consommation d'énergie commerciale

Milliers de térajoules et gigajoules par habitant

Bunkers Soutes		Unallocated Quantités non réparties	Consumption Consommation						Year Année	Country or area Pays ou zone
Aviation Avion	Marine Maritime		Per capita Par habitant	Total Totale	Solids Solides	Liquids Liquides	Gas Gaz	Electricity Electricité		
*1	..	..	*62	*11	..	*11	..	..	2003	Guyane française
*1	..	..	*59	*11	..	*11	..	..	2004	
*1	..	..	*58	*11	..	*11	..	..	2005	
*1	..	..	*59	*12	..	*12	..	..	2006	
1	..	..	28	21	..	21	..	..	2003	Guyana
1	..	..	27	20	..	20	..	..	2004	
1	..	..	27	21	..	21	..	..	2005	
1	..	..	28	21	..	21	..	..	2006	
1	..	0	14	77	..	53	..	24	2003	Paraguay
1	..	0	14	79	..	54	..	25	2004	
1	..	0	13	76	..	50	..	27	2005	
1	..	0	13	81	..	52	..	29	2006	
6	2	-24	15	412	31	289	26	67	2003	Pérou
19	2	-25	17	470	36	331	40	63	2004	
13	10	11	17	465	38	287	68	72	2005	
20	4	-11	19	522	31	335	78	77	2006	
..	..	6	57	27	..	25	..	3	2003	Suriname
..	..	6	56	28	..	25	..	3	2004	
..	..	6	58	29	..	26	..	3	2005	
..	..	6	59	30	..	27	..	3	2006	
1	13	1	25	84	0	54	2	28	2003	Uruguay
2	14	1	30	98	0	68	4	26	2004	
2	15	4	30	99	0	68	4	27	2005	
2	10	4	32	107	0	80	4	23	2006	
10	22	635	85	2187	2	913	1054	219	2003	Venezuela(Rép. bolivar.)
25	27	43	87	2260	0	969	1039	252	2004	
27	26	132	91	2418	2	1091	1058	268	2005	
28	28	176	101	2734	2	1360	1089	284	2006	
1403	2429	8701	35	131960	57514	44364	25834	4248	2003	Asie
1474	2634	9490	38	144948	65659	47458	27088	4743	2004	
1609	2877	9403	40	153548	71399	48131	28919	5100	2005	
1684	3108	9795	41	161308	76860	48172	30864	5411	2006	
0	..	..	0	*10	1	*6	0	3	2003	Afghanistan
0	..	..	0	11	1	8	0	2	2004	
0	..	..	*1	*12	*1	*8	0	*3	2005	
0	..	..	*1	*12	*1	*8	0	*3	2006	
1	..	0	19	73	1	13	45	13	2003	Arménie
2	..	0	24	77	0	13	50	13	2004	
2	..	0	28	89	0	14	62	13	2005	
2	..	0	29	92	0	13	64	15	2006	
8	..	21	63	521	..	160	347	15	2003	Azerbaïdjan
10	..	2	69	570	..	176	379	15	2004	
18	..	8	70	590	..	196	379	15	2005	
21	..	7	72	607	..	179	416	12	2006	
20	..	70	465	321	..	57	264	..	2003	Bahreïn
22	..	72	473	334	..	60	274	..	2004	
24	..	78	496	360	..	69	291	..	2005	
24	..	75	522	387	..	79	308	..	2006	
10	1	20	4	595	15	141	435	4	2003	Bangladesh
10	1	18	5	628	15	141	468	4	2004	
12	1	20	5	680	15	158	503	5	2005	
11	1	20	5	715	15	152	543	5	2006	
..	..	..	10	6	2	*2	..	2	2003	Bhoutan
..	..	..	10	6	1	*2	..	3	2004	
..	..	..	10	7	2	*2	..	3	2005	
..	..	..	10	6	2	*2	..	3	2006	

Table 3

Production, trade and consumption of commercial energy

Thousand terajoules and gigajoules per capita

Country or area Pays ou zone	Year Année	Primary energy production Production d'énergie primaire					Changes in stocks Variations des stocks	Imports Importations	Exports Exportations
		Total Totale	Solids Solides	Liquids Liquides	Gas Gaz	Electricity Electricité			
Brunei Darussalam	2003	922	..	439	482	..	*-4	0	834
	2004	910	..	433	477	..	2	0	811
	2005	892	..	424	469	..	*-3	1	801
	2006	946	..	454	493	..	*-9	0	860
Cambodia	2003	0	..	..	..	0	..	45	..
	2004	0	..	..	..	0	..	50	..
	2005	0	..	..	..	0	..	53	..
	2006	0	..	..	..	0	..	59	..
China	2003	45975	36012	7101	1685	1177	-12	5367	3386
	2004	52018	41665	7363	1545	1444	-5	7496	3039
	2005	57219	46107	7593	1898	1620	-174	7625	2880
	2006	61144	49627	7736	1995	1786	-138	8502	2661
China, Hong Kong SAR	2003	..	..	..	..	..	-5	947	62
	2004	..	..	..	..	..	0	1028	68
	2005	..	..	..	..	..	-23	1011	113
	2006	..	..	..	..	..	26	1063	67
China, Macao SAR	2003	..	..	..	..	..	0	26	..
	2004	..	..	..	..	..	1	32	..
	2005	..	..	..	..	..	0	33	..
	2006	..	..	..	..	..	0	35	..
Cyprus	2003	0	..	..	..	0	-3	111	..
	2004	0	..	..	..	0	-3	100	..
	2005	0	..	..	..	0	3	117	..
	2006	0	..	..	..	0	5	124	..
Georgia	2003	30	0	6	1	23	-1	63	5
	2004	27	0	4	0	22	0	71	4
	2005	26	0	3	1	22	0	87	4
	2006	23	0	3	1	19	0	98	3
India	2003	11966	9043	1572	1016	335	41	4634	538
	2004	12547	9584	1589	1008	366	64	5028	665
	2005	13163	10175	1535	1025	428	251	5465	712
	2006	13854	10764	1611	1005	475	272	6130	1013
Indonesia	2003	8381	3094	2390	2841	55	0	1375	5564
	2004	8967	3751	2215	2942	59	24	1697	5936
	2005	9591	4550	2099	2880	63	24	1580	6316
	2006	10941	5981	2013	2888	59	22	1379	7436
Iran(Islamic Rep. of)	2003	11218	36	8063	3079	40	-6	443	5514
	2004	11875	37	8376	3424	38	0	537	5737
	2005	12907	39	9100	3710	58	0	536	6418
	2006	13228	45	9042	4075	66	0	671	6354
Iraq	2003	2824	..	2763	59	2	0	16	1747
	2004	4246	..	4146	99	2	19	187	3186
	2005	3945	..	3842	101	2	19	215	2869
	2006	4157	..	4022	133	2	-73	222	3127
Israel	2003	5	4	0	0	0	-4	999	129
	2004	48	4	0	44	0	-8	973	150
	2005	64	4	0	60	0	23	958	164
	2006	88	4	0	84	0	-8	976	138
Japan	2003	1403	..	28	121	1254	-19	18042	203
	2004	1559	..	29	125	1405	-48	18337	213
	2005	1591	..	31	135	1426	102	18509	377
	2006	1633	..	30	148	1454	-49	18330	434
Jordan	2003	10	..	0	10	0	-2	219	0
	2004	10	..	0	10	0	5	268	0
	2005	9	..	0	8	0	6	298	0
	2006	8	..	0	8	0	0	291	0

Table 3

Production, commerce et consommation d'énergie commerciale
Milliers de térajoules et gigajoules par habitant

Bunkers Soutes		Unallocated Quantités	Consumption Consommation						Year	Country or area
Aviation Avion	Marine Maritime	non réparties	Per capita Par habitant	Total Totale	Solids Solides	Liquids Liquides	Gas Gaz	Electricity Electricité	Année	Pays ou zone
..	..	-15	304	106	..	47	59	..	2003	Brunéi Darussalam
..	..	-22	328	118	..	52	66	..	2004	
..	..	-21	315	116	..	50	67	..	2005	
..	..	-23	309	118	..	52	66	..	2006	
1	..	..	3	44	..	44	..	0	2003	Cambodge
1	..	..	4	50	..	49	..	0	2004	
1	..	..	4	53	..	52	..	0	2005	
1	..	..	4	58	..	57	..	1	2006	
14	105	2709	35	45140	33953	8409	1627	1151	2003	Chine
5	12	3375	41	53087	40101	10110	1454	1422	2004	
13	39	3279	45	58807	45149	10272	1788	1598	2005	
18	60	3638	48	63405	49123	10629	1891	1761	2006	
149	227	..	76	515	240	188	59	27	2003	Chine, Hong-Kong RAS
136	323	..	74	501	220	171	86	24	2004	
158	239	..	77	524	245	170	86	23	2005	
161	307	..	73	502	240	148	91	23	2006	
..	..	..	59	26	..	26	..	1	2003	Chine, Macao RAS
..	..	..	67	31	..	31	..	1	2004	
..	..	..	68	33	..	32	..	1	2005	
..	..	..	68	34	..	31	..	3	2006	
14	5	2	129	93	2	92	..	0	2003	Chypre
13	2	0	119	88	2	86	..	0	2004	
13	12	0	118	89	2	88	..	0	2005	
13	12	0	121	94	2	92	..	0	2006	
1	..	2	20	86	1	22	36	27	2003	Géorgie
2	..	1	21	91	0	22	42	26	2004	
2	..	1	24	106	1	28	50	27	2005	
2	..	1	26	116	1	29	64	22	2006	
103	1	1391	14	14526	9642	3527	1016	341	2003	Inde
121	0	1313	14	15413	10311	3722	1008	372	2004	
142	0	1420	15	16104	10878	3768	1025	433	2005	
172	0	1453	15	17076	11635	3951	1005	485	2006	
34	21	67	19	4071	455	2277	1283	55	2003	Indonésie
33	15	57	21	4598	650	2492	1398	59	2004	
31	16	100	21	4684	744	2491	1386	63	2005	
30	15	90	21	4727	937	2271	1461	59	2006	
33	24	21	91	6073	54	2807	3170	42	2003	Iran(Rép. islamique)
34	26	4	98	6611	47	3009	3516	39	2004	
37	23	-184	104	7148	53	3313	3727	55	2005	
43	19	-212	109	7694	57	3476	4096	65	2006	
17	..	153	35	923	..	862	59	2	2003	Iraq
50	..	58	41	1120	..	1015	99	7	2004	
32	..	69	43	1171	..	1063	101	7	2005	
34	..	85	42	1206	..	1067	133	6	2006	
0	11	17	127	850	375	480	0	-5	2003	Israël
0	10	-10	129	880	381	460	44	-5	2004	
0	11	-53	127	877	359	464	60	-6	2005	
0	11	-17	133	941	385	478	84	-7	2006	
281	214	820	142	17946	4833	8541	3318	1254	2003	Japon
291	224	785	146	18431	5285	8457	3284	1405	2004	
293	252	799	145	18277	5159	8408	3284	1426	2005	
272	237	873	144	18196	5222	7917	3604	1454	2006	
3	0	3	43	226	..	215	10	1	2003	Jordanie
3	2	8	51	260	..	201	56	3	2004	
*3	3	14	51	280	..	212	64	3	2005	
3	2	7	51	287	..	201	84	2	2006	

Table 3

Production, trade and consumption of commercial energy
Thousand terajoules and gigajoules per capita

| Country or area Pays ou zone | Year Année | Primary energy production Production d'énergie primaire | | | | | Changes in stocks Variations des stocks | Imports Importations | Exports Exportations |
		Total Totale	Solids Solides	Liquids Liquides	Gas Gaz	Electricity Electricité			
Kazakhstan	2003	4415	1562	2174	648	31	17	526	2890
	2004	5011	1599	2520	863	29	17	721	3421
	2005	5206	1594	2610	975	28	15	707	3479
	2006	5609	1770	2782	1030	28	11	800	3757
Korea, Dem.Ppl's.Rep.	2003	844	802	..	..	42	..	57	22
	2004	888	843	..	..	45	..	57	46
	2005	971	924	..	..	47	..	50	82
	2006	981	936	..	..	45	..	41	73
Korea, Republic of	2003	554	62	0	0	492	104	8024	939
	2004	552	60	0	0	492	40	8425	1064
	2005	624	53	3	20	548	-189	8346	1241
	2006	634	53	4	22	555	123	8840	1355
Kuwait	2003	5222	..	4792	430	..	..	25	3588
	2004	5664	..	5201	463	..	..	5	3911
	2005	6283	..	5764	519	..	..	0	4406
	2006	6494	..	5945	549	..	..	0	4682
Kyrgyzstan	2003	58	5	3	1	49	-1	69	13
	2004	61	6	3	1	51	0	75	19
	2005	60	4	3	1	51	0	72	15
	2006	61	4	3	1	54	0	70	13
Lao People's Dem. Rep.	2003	*22	*11	..	..	11	..	*6	13
	2004	*23	*12	..	..	*12	..	*6	*13
	2005	*25	*12	..	..	*12	..	*7	*13
	2006	*25	*13	..	..	*12	..	*7	*13
Lebanon	2003	2	..	..	..	2	-24	217	..
	2004	4	..	..	..	4	0	209	..
	2005	4	..	..	..	4	-17	201	..
	2006	3	..	..	..	3	0	186	..
Malaysia	2003	3742	4	1637	2080	21	-25	994	1919
	2004	3774	11	1561	2181	21	17	1237	2057
	2005	4016	20	1575	2402	19	21	1161	2183
	2006	4210	26	1549	2609	25	5	1114	2202
Maldives	2003	..	..	..	..	..	..	8	..
	2004	..	..	..	..	..	..	10	..
	2005	..	..	..	..	..	..	9	..
	2006	..	..	..	..	..	..	12	..
Mongolia	2003	73	73	..	..	..	..	23	4
	2004	88	88	..	..	..	..	25	15
	2005	97	97	..	..	..	..	24	21
	2006	104	104	..	..	..	..	28	24
Myanmar	2003	381	25	41	307	8	-4	41	267
	2004	498	27	43	420	9	0	48	382
	2005	529	33	47	439	11	0	53	404
	2006	544	34	44	454	12	2	38	405
Nepal	2003	8	0	..	..	8	..	39	1
	2004	9	0	..	..	9	..	37	0
	2005	10	0	..	..	9	..	42	0
	2006	10	0	..	..	10	..	43	0
Occup. Palestinian Terr.	2003	..	..	..	..	..	0	26	0
	2004	..	..	..	..	..	0	36	1
	2005	..	..	..	..	..	0	50	1
	2006	..	..	..	..	..	0	*53	*1
Oman	2003	2411	..	1720	692	..	-65	13	1989
	2004	2349	..	1643	706	..	-43	18	1941
	2005	2368	..	1628	740	..	-62	29	1953
	2006	2489	..	1550	939	..	0	31	1857

Table 3

Production, commerce et consommation d'énergie commerciale

Milliers de térajoules et gigajoules par habitant

Bunkers Soutes		Unallocated Quantités	Consumption Consommation						Year	Country or area
Aviation Avion	Marine Maritime	non réparties	Per capita Par habitant	Total Totale	Solids Solides	Liquids Liquides	Gas Gaz	Electricity Electricité	Année	Pays ou zone
7	..	23	134	2004	1117	304	557	26	2003	Kazakhstan
9	..	90	146	2195	1155	376	643	21	2004	
10	..	12	158	2397	1181	374	811	30	2005	
11	..	32	170	2597	1269	424	873	31	2006	
..	..	1	37	878	790	46	..	42	2003	Corée,Rép.pop.dém.de
..	..	1	38	899	808	46	..	45	2004	
..	..	0	40	939	853	39	..	47	2005	
..	..	0	40	950	875	30	..	45	2006	
49	271	689	136	6525	2086	2923	1024	492	2003	Corée, République de
54	299	973	136	6548	2176	2704	1176	492	2004	
99	426	817	136	6576	2187	2568	1274	548	2005	
121	426	921	135	6527	2244	2388	1340	555	2006	
31	23	414	489	1138	..	708	430	..	2003	Koweït
23	24	418	520	1242	..	780	463	..	2004	
25	22	414	557	1369	..	850	519	..	2005	
24	27	370	531	1341	..	792	549	..	2006	
..	..	0	23	115	25	19	29	43	2003	Kirghizistan
..	..	0	23	117	23	23	31	39	2004	
..	..	0	23	117	22	25	29	42	2005	
..	..	-1	23	118	20	24	30	45	2006	
..	..	..	*3	*15	*9	*6	..	0	2003	Rép. dém. pop. lao
..	..	..	*3	*17	*10	*6	..	*2	2004	
..	..	..	*3	*18	*10	*6	..	*2	2005	
..	..	..	*3	*18	*10	*6	..	*2	2006	
5	1	..	61	237	6	229	..	2	2003	Liban
5	1	..	52	207	6	197	..	5	2004	
6	1	..	54	216	6	204	..	5	2005	
4	1	..	45	183	6	172	..	6	2006	
78	3	440	93	2322	223	820	1258	21	2003	Malaisie
87	4	364	97	2484	389	872	1204	19	2004	
82	2	361	96	2516	317	885	1303	11	2005	
84	2	313	102	2704	327	882	1479	16	2006	
..	..	..	29	8	..	8	..	..	2003	Maldives
..	..	..	36	10	..	10	..	..	2004	
..	..	..	32	9	..	9	..	..	2005	
..	..	..	40	12	..	12	..	..	2006	
..	..	..	37	91	69	22	..	1	2003	Mongolie
..	..	..	39	98	73	24	..	1	2004	
..	..	..	39	101	76	24	..	1	2005	
..	..	..	42	108	80	27	..	1	2006	
3	0	9	3	146	4	72	62	8	2003	Myanmar
3	0	3	3	159	4	75	71	9	2004	
2	0	2	3	174	4	79	80	11	2005	
3	0	2	3	169	5	70	83	12	2006	
2	..	..	2	45	9	29	..	8	2003	Népal
2	..	..	2	43	8	27	..	9	2004	
3	..	..	2	49	12	27	..	10	2005	
3	..	..	2	50	12	28	..	10	2006	
..	..	..	8	26	0	18	..	8	2003	Terr. palestiniens occup.
..	..	..	10	35	0	26	..	9	2004	
..	..	..	13	49	0	39	..	*10	2005	
..	..	..	*13	*52	0	*42	..	*10	2006	
15	0	9	203	475	..	139	337	..	2003	Oman
*8	0	6	188	453	..	140	313	..	2004	
12	0	17	190	477	..	151	327	..	2005	
*13	0	33	239	617	..	181	436	..	2006	

Table 3

Production, trade and consumption of commercial energy
Thousand terajoules and gigajoules per capita

Country or area Pays ou zone	Year Année	Primary energy production Production d'énergie primaire					Changes in stocks Variations des stocks	Imports Importations	Exports Exportations
		Total Totale	Solids Solides	Liquids Liquides	Gas Gaz	Electricity Electricité			
Other Asia	2003	198	..	2	31	165	-35	3789	36
	2004	200	..	2	32	166	107	4264	50
	2005	194	..	1	20	173	15	4344	58
	2006	191	..	1	17	173	45	4443	57
Pakistan	2003	1332	66	139	1024	103	-9	549	2
	2004	1452	91	143	1116	102	-3	684	1
	2005	1534	96	146	1171	120	*-1	698	1
	2006	1526	72	148	1182	123	0	819	1
Philippines	2003	256	90	1	101	64	5	806	3
	2004	219	53	1	97	68	-11	853	2
	2005	256	62	1	128	66	-38	798	4
	2006	254	*64	1	116	74	3	785	6
Qatar	2003	2837	..	1611	1225	..	109	..	214
	2004	3237	..	1709	1528	..	-32	..	254
	2005	3523	..	1736	1787	..	-55	..	266
	2006	4177	..	2246	1932	..	-2	..	326
Saudi Arabia	2003	22130	..	20139	1991	..	2	53	1624
	2004	22905	..	20742	2163	..	-2	64	1658
	2005	24084	..	21707	2377	..	1	79	1738
	2006	23850	..	21355	2495	..	-5	149	1698
Singapore	2003	..	..	..	..	..	-140	3601	176
	2004	..	..	..	..	..	-97	4102	197
	2005	..	..	..	..	..	-184	4417	212
	2006	..	..	..	..	..	-189	4703	233
Sri Lanka	2003	12	..	..	..	12	-5	146	
	2004	11	..	..	..	11	0	171	
	2005	12	..	..	..	12	2	168	
	2006	17	..	..	..	17	5	175	
Syrian Arab Republic	2003	1441	..	1172	258	10	0	46	71
	2004	1261	..	978	268	15	-1	59	52
	2005	1174	..	931	230	12	1	72	42
	2006	1124	..	872	238	14	1	55	33
Tajikistan	2003	62	1	1	1	59	..	88	1
	2004	63	2	1	1	59	..	94	1
	2005	66	2	1	1	61	..	97	1
	2006	65	3	1	1	60	..	106	1
Thailand	2003	1504	347	423	707	26	-39	2185	32
	2004	1526	369	433	701	22	-41	2458	35
	2005	1656	385	497	754	21	-54	2393	37
	2006	1680	350	539	762	29	-82	2431	43
Timor-Leste	2003	*306	..	*306	..	..	..	*4	*303
	2004	*308	..	*308	..	..	..	*4	*305
	2005	*310	..	*310	..	..	..	*4	*306
	2006	.*310	..	*310	..	..	..	*4	*307
Turkey	2003	693	445	98	21	128	18	2628	156
	2004	712	425	94	26	166	-19	2739	189
	2005	802	530	95	34	143	-27	2943	207
	2006	868	583	91	35	160	9	3271	251
Turkmenistan	2003	2677	..	435	2242	0	..	4	1901
	2004	2660	..	425	2235	0	..	4	1955
	2005	2799	..	412	2387	0	..	4	2054
	2006	2820	..	424	2396	0	..	4	2044
United Arab Emirates	2003	7089	..	5342	1747	..	..	522	455
	2004	7379	..	5573	1805	..	..	562	475
	2005	7453	..	5637	1815	..	..	631	480
	2006	7891	..	6045	1847	..	..	661	516

Table 3

Production, commerce et consommation d'énergie commerciale
Milliers de térajoules et gigajoules par habitant

Bunkers Soutes		Unallocated Quantités non réparties	Consumption Consommation						Year Année	Country or area Pays ou zone
Aviation Avion	Marine Maritime		Per capita Par habitant	Total Totale	Solids Solides	Liquids Liquides	Gas Gaz	Electricity Electricité		
89	127	267	140	3170	1498	1171	336	165	2003	Autre Asie
100	103	342	146	3307	1558	1169	414	166	2004	
104	104	362	148	3369	1612	1183	401	173	2005	
106	99	294	154	3514	1688	1200	452	173	2006	
6	1	49	12	1813	111	574	1024	104	2003	Pakistan
7	3	54	14	2063	187	657	1116	103	2004	
9	3	72	14	2130	179	660	1171	121	2005	
7	4	64	14	2250	195	749	1182	124	2006	
25	8	41	12	946	180	601	101	64	2003	Philippines
*26	6	36	12	989	207	617	97	68	2004	
*30	5	33	11	976	200	583	128	66	2005	
35	5	29	10	901	*204	508	116	74	2006	
26	..	-5	763	559	..	74	485	..	2003	Qatar
15	..	48	848	659	..	78	581	..	2004	
20	..	49	1042	847	..	94	753	..	2005	
25	..	33	913	855	..	110	745	..	2006	
74	93	391	228	5020	..	3029	1991	..	2003	Arabie saoudite
71	94	304	247	5580	..	3418	2163	..	2004	
71	96	344	256	5926	..	3549	2377	..	2005	
74	111	287	263	6227	..	3731	2495	..	2006	
101	865	452	134	560	0	351	209	..	2003	Singapour
125	980	555	133	565	0	319	246	..	2004	
133	1059	668	142	618	0	342	276	..	2005	
144	1163	646	136	608	0	328	280	..	2006	
5	5	5	8	148	3	133	..	12	2003	Sri Lanka
6	5	5	8	165	3	151	..	11	2004	
6	7	6	8	160	3	145	..	12	2005	
5	6	11	8	165	3	145	..	17	2006	
4	..	70	40	700	0	432	258	10	2003	Rép. arabe syrienne
5	..	48	41	739	0	456	268	15	2004	
5	..	79	40	734	0	491	230	12	2005	
4	..	75	41	759	0	507	238	14	2006	
0	..	1	20	133	1	51	21	59	2003	Tadjikistan
0	..	1	21	139	2	55	22	60	2004	
0	..	1	21	146	3	59	22	62	2005	
0	..	1	22	154	3	67	23	62	2006	
..	..	337	48	3060	556	1470	1001	34	2003	Thaïlande
..	..	319	52	3345	622	1674	1017	33	2004	
..	..	355	52	3372	602	1637	1099	34	2005	
..	..	377	52	3383	609	1612	1117	45	2006	
..	..	0	*4	*4	..	*4	..	..	2003	Timor-Leste
..	..	0	*4	*4	..	*4	..	..	2004	
..	..	0	*4	*4	..	*4	..	..	2005	
..	..	0	*4	*4	..	*4	..	..	2006	
38	26	128	42	2954	926	1073	824	130	2003	Turquie
41	42	145	43	3052	948	1070	870	164	2004	
46	45	156	46	3319	1069	1051	1060	139	2005	
41	41	191	49	3605	1197	1046	1208	154	2006	
..	..	1	166	778	..	184	597	-4	2003	Turkménistan
..	..	1	149	708	..	178	534	-4	2004	
..	..	1	155	748	..	182	570	-5	2005	
..	..	1	159	779	..	211	573	-5	2006	
143	391	159	667	2370	..	902	1468	..	2003	Emirats arabes unis
137	454	161	648	2436	..	922	1514	..	2004	
151	505	150	602	2472	..	935	1537	..	2005	
155	550	147	600	2537	..	966	1571	..	2006	

Table 3

Production, trade and consumption of commercial energy
Thousand terajoules and gigajoules per capita

Country or area Pays ou zone	Year Année	Primary energy production Production d'énergie primaire					Changes in stocks Variations des stocks	Imports Importations	Exports Exportations
		Total Totale	Solids Solides	Liquids Liquides	Gas Gaz	Electricity Electricité			
Uzbekistan	2003	2575	22	337	2194	23	1	96	337
	2004	2606	30	315	2236	24	1	91	431
	2005	2593	34	258	2279	22	1	82	519
	2006	2670	35	241	2371	23	1	83	529
Viet Nam	2003	1401	489	717	126	68	0	437	903
	2004	1898	747	873	215	64	29	483	1131
	2005	2130	949	815	288	77	27	517	1351
	2006	2258	1111	770	293	85	33	513	1425
Yemen	2003	892	..	892	..	..	24	102	714
	2004	839	..	839	..	..	38	115	643
	2005	831	..	831	..	..	39	118	624
	2006	762	..	762	..	..	64	149	544
Europe	**2003**	**89563**	**15169**	**30714**	**36519**	**7161**	**336**	**63622**	**48257**
	2004	**91577**	**14931**	**31867**	**37346**	**7432**	**438**	**66061**	**51521**
	2005	**91102**	**15000**	**31386**	**37242**	**7473**	**589**	**67806**	**52201**
	2006	**90888**	**14893**	**31066**	**37439**	**7489**	**1176**	**69283**	**52328**
Albania	2003	36	1	16	1	19	..	39	3
	2004	39	1	18	1	20	..	43	1
	2005	40	1	19	1	19	..	40	0
	2006	41	1	21	1	18	..	39	0
Austria	2003	267	13	43	83	128	-3	1124	137
	2004	270	3	46	78	144	10	1159	158
	2005	249	0	43	63	144	8	1243	181
	2006	260	0	45	73	142	30	1271	214
Belarus	2003	103	17	76	10	0	-8	1418	414
	2004	105	19	76	10	0	9	1586	531
	2005	106	22	75	9	0	-4	1649	617
	2006	103	20	75	8	0	1	1774	665
Belgium	2003	177	1	0	..	176	2	3234	972
	2004	179	2	0	..	177	5	3316	1047
	2005	180	1	1	..	178	16	3272	1076
	2006	176	0	1	..	175	4	3224	1013
Bosnia and Herzegovina	2003	229	213	..	..	16	0	57	19
	2004	237	215	..	..	22	0	74	24
	2005	249	227	..	..	22	-1	84	29
	2006	264	243	..	..	21	-1	91	35
Bulgaria	2003	266	189	1	1	74	-14	482	87
	2004	269	182	1	13	73	19	517	121
	2005	273	169	1	18	84	0	548	138
	2006	282	176	1	18	87	-7	598	184
Croatia	2003	156	..	55	83	18	-6	300	77
	2004	162	..	53	84	25	0	321	93
	2005	160	..	50	87	23	0	329	97
	2006	174	..	49	103	22	3	328	109
Czech Republic	2003	1024	895	23	6	100	5	825	303
	2004	1030	890	27	9	104	-2	812	280
	2005	999	862	29	8	100	17	875	287
	2006	1007	875	19	8	106	17	905	317
Denmark	2003	1117	..	761	335	20	-5	605	911
	2004	1228	..	809	395	24	5	577	1021
	2005	1238	..	778	437	24	14	551	1028
	2006	1165	..	709	434	22	-22	575	953
Estonia	2003	144	144	..	..	0	2	83	11
	2004	135	135	..	..	0	-5	94	10
	2005	142	141	..	..	0	0	85	9
	2006	138	138	..	..	0	5	90	6

Table 3

Production, commerce et consommation d'énergie commerciale
Milliers de térajoules et gigajoules par habitant

Bunkers Soutes		Unallocated Quantités non réparties	Consumption Consommation						Year Année	Country or area Pays ou zone
Aviation Avion	Marine Maritime		Per capita Par habitant	Total Totale	Solids Solides	Liquids Liquides	Gas Gaz	Electricity Electricité		
..	..	-86	94	2420	21	410	1966	23	2003	Ouzbékistan
..	..	-81	89	2345	30	383	1909	23	2004	
..	..	-62	83	2216	33	310	1852	22	2005	
..	..	-60	85	2283	34	292	1934	22	2006	
7	..	0	11	928	305	429	126	68	2003	Viet Nam
11	..	0	15	1209	437	494	215	64	2004	
11	..	0	15	1258	425	527	229	77	2005	
10	..	0	15	1303	461	524	232	85	2006	
4	5	28	12	217	..	217	..	..	2003	Yémen
4	5	36	12	227	..	227	..	..	2004	
4	5	36	12	241	..	241	..	..	2005	
5	5	33	13	260	..	260	..	..	2006	
1821	**2022**	**1565**	**136**	**99148**	**19934**	**31896**	**40153**	**7165**	**2003**	**Europe**
1936	**2158**	**1667**	**137**	**99870**	**19625**	**31907**	**40907**	**7430**	**2004**	
2061	**2256**	**1716**	**137**	**99989**	**19155**	**31769**	**41607**	**7458**	**2005**	
2106	**2373**	**1035**	**138**	**101111**	**19730**	**32650**	**41264**	**7467**	**2006**	
2	..	7	18	64	1	40	1	22	2003	Albanie
2	..	7	23	72	1	50	1	20	2004	
3	..	10	21	67	1	45	1	21	2005	
4	..	10	21	66	1	44	1	20	2006	
18	..	46	148	1194	175	520	351	149	2003	Autriche
21	..	46	147	1194	167	518	354	155	2004	
24	..	36	152	1244	171	537	381	153	2005	
25	..	46	147	1216	169	533	347	167	2006	
..	..	144	98	971	27	207	712	25	2003	Bélarus
..	..	127	104	1023	23	215	773	12	2004	
..	..	102	106	1039	23	213	788	15	2005	
..	..	131	111	1080	22	240	803	16	2006	
62	297	183	183	1894	260	766	670	199	2003	Belgique
57	334	161	182	1891	256	752	678	205	2004	
54	331	154	174	1820	230	730	659	201	2005	
50	358	118	177	1858	200	746	700	212	2006	
..	..	0	70	267	206	40	8	13	2003	Bosnie y Herzégovine
..	..	1	74	286	212	47	12	15	2004	
..	..	0	79	305	230	44	14	17	2005	
..	..	0	83	321	246	47	15	13	2006	
7	6	45	79	617	302	144	116	54	2003	Bulgarie
6	5	22	79	612	292	152	116	51	2004	
8	5	34	82	637	286	163	130	57	2005	
8	5	38	85	653	292	167	135	59	2006	
1	1	-6	87	388	32	214	110	32	2003	Croatie
1	1	10	85	377	34	190	114	39	2004	
2	1	5	86	383	33	198	111	42	2005	
2	1	6	86	380	31	198	109	42	2006	
9	..	74	143	1458	783	269	365	41	2003	République tchèque
12	..	86	144	1465	771	284	362	47	2004	
13	..	97	143	1460	754	293	359	55	2005	
14	..	94	143	1471	767	291	352	60	2006	
30	41	-4	142	749	239	304	217	-11	2003	Danemark
34	34	-4	132	713	184	300	216	13	2004	
36	35	3	124	674	157	284	205	29	2005	
36	45	0	134	728	230	290	211	-3	2006	
1	5	..	154	209	148	36	32	-7	2003	Estonie
1	6	..	159	215	148	37	36	-6	2004	
2	5	..	157	211	142	37	37	-6	2005	
1	9	..	154	207	134	37	38	-2	2006	

Table 3

Production, trade and consumption of commercial energy
Thousand terajoules and gigajoules per capita

Country or area Pays ou zone	Year Année	Primary energy production Production d'énergie primaire					Changes in stocks Variations des stocks	Imports Importations	Exports Exportations
		Total Totale	Solids Solides	Liquids Liquides	Gas Gaz	Electricity Electricité			
Faeroe Islands	2003	0	..	..	..	0	..	*9	..
	2004	0	..	..	..	0	..	*9	..
	2005	0	..	..	..	0	..	*9	..
	2006	0	..	..	..	0	..	*9	..
Finland	2003	194	77	..	..	117	21	1185	238
	2004	175	39	..	..	136	-59	1116	241
	2005	229	95	..	..	134	29	991	196
	2006	265	140	..	..	124	24	1092	220
France incl. Monaco	2003	2026	61	82	60	1823	-30	7008	1104
	2004	2011	24	84	52	1852	-43	7190	1167
	2005	1971	17	77	42	1834	48	7461	1276
	2006	1986	12	74	49	1850	77	7308	1273
Germany	2003	4023	2346	185	741	751	-63	10088	1204
	2004	4049	2382	186	686	796	56	10429	1453
	2005	3999	2316	235	662	786	67	10523	1621
	2006	3958	2186	299	654	819	54	10701	1742
Gibraltar	2003	..	..	..	..	..	..	52	..
	2004	..	..	..	..	..	..	54	..
	2005	..	..	..	..	..	..	55	..
	2006	..	..	..	..	..	..	56	..
Greece	2003	372	342	6	1	23	-36	1211	222
	2004	388	358	6	1	23	43	1286	211
	2005	387	357	4	1	25	-21	1245	237
	2006	369	332	6	1	29	16	1352	285
Hungary	2003	344	115	82	107	40	20	853	117
	2004	327	91	81	111	44	1	834	110
	2005	308	73	75	109	51	5	941	136
	2006	306	74	72	111	49	7	942	158
Iceland	2003	40	..	..	9	31	-2	39	..
	2004	40	..	..	9	31	1	44	..
	2005	40	..	..	9	31	1	43	..
	2006	45	..	..	10	36	-1	44	..
Ireland	2003	81	51	0	25	5	11	642	67
	2004	79	41	0	32	6	19	637	52
	2005	66	37	0	21	8	2	639	58
	2006	63	34	0	19	10	6	656	54
Italy and San Marino	2003	953	7	233	529	184	-71	7724	902
	2004	941	3	239	494	206	-8	7906	953
	2005	908	3	263	460	182	-68	8141	1122
	2006	856	1	250	418	187	132	8325	1063
Latvia	2003	8	0	0	..	8	3	135	0
	2004	11	0	0	..	11	19	162	16
	2005	12	0	0	..	12	5	157	23
	2006	10	0	0	..	10	9	161	12
Lithuania	2003	78	0	16	2	59	5	442	262
	2004	73	0	13	2	58	7	514	324
	2005	52	1	9	2	40	4	537	318
	2006	45	1	8	2	34	6	522	289
Luxembourg	2003	3	..	0	..	3	0	189	11
	2004	3	..	0	..	3	-1	207	12
	2005	3	..	0	..	3	-1	210	12
	2006	4	..	0	..	4	1	212	12
Malta	2003	..	..	..	..	..	..	38	..
	2004	..	..	..	..	..	..	40	..
	2005	..	..	..	..	..	..	40	..
	2006	..	..	..	..	..	..	38	..

Table 3

Production, commerce et consommation d'énergie commerciale

Milliers de térajoules et gigajoules par habitant

Bunkers Soutes		Unallocated Quantités	Consumption Consommation						Year	Country or area
Aviation Avion	Marine Maritime	non réparties	Per capita Par habitant	Total Totale	Solids Solides	Liquids Liquides	Gas Gaz	Electricity Electricité	Année	Pays ou zone
0	..	..	*196	*9	..	*9	..	0	2003	Iles Féroé
0	..	..	*195	*9	..	*9	..	0	2004	
0	..	..	*196	*9	..	*9	..	0	2005	
0	..	..	*196	*9	..	*9	..	0	2006	
15	27	-57	218	1135	352	459	190	134	2003	Finlande
17	22	-84	221	1154	322	492	186	154	2004	
18	22	-100	201	1055	208	483	169	195	2005	
20	24	-115	225	1185	318	518	182	165	2006	
213	113	413	120	7222	620	3189	1829	1584	2003	France y compris Monaco
227	128	405	121	7317	597	3223	1868	1629	2004	
230	116	454	120	7306	619	3159	1911	1617	2005	
239	121	273	120	7310	571	3274	1843	1622	2006	
240	111	270	150	12349	3494	4435	3681	740	2003	Allemagne
260	113	263	150	12334	3522	4363	3663	786	2004	
279	106	268	148	12180	3359	4289	3761	769	2005	
294	110	207	149	12254	3374	4423	3698	758	2006	
0	47	..	179	5	..	5	..	..	2003	Gibraltar
0	48	..	185	5	..	5	..	..	2004	
0	49	..	191	5	..	5	..	..	2005	
0	51	..	185	5	..	5	..	..	2006	
33	136	-53	116	1282	373	784	94	30	2003	Grèce
34	137	-29	116	1278	382	759	104	33	2004	
33	122	-55	119	1316	376	793	109	38	2005	
39	131	-83	119	1332	344	816	128	45	2006	
9	..	25	101	1028	156	253	553	65	2003	Hongrie
10	..	31	100	1011	141	254	545	71	2004	
11	..	47	104	1049	128	285	563	73	2005	
11	..	40	102	1032	125	299	533	75	2006	
4	3	14	204	59	4	25	..	31	2003	Islande
5	3	15	206	60	4	25	..	31	2004	
6	3	14	203	60	4	25	..	31	2005	
7	1	16	214	65	3	26	..	36	2006	
31	7	3	152	605	117	309	170	9	2003	Irlande
29	6	0	151	610	105	324	170	12	2004	
33	4	6	145	600	122	302	161	15	2005	
34	5	-6	148	626	109	314	187	16	2006	
113	135	-45	133	7642	639	3675	2960	367	2003	Italie y comp. St. Marin
113	142	67	130	7579	720	3418	3071	370	2004	
120	143	46	131	7686	711	3329	3287	359	2005	
128	147	120	129	7590	718	3304	3219	349	2006	
2	8	0	56	130	3	47	63	18	2003	Lettonie
2	9	0	55	127	2	44	62	19	2004	
2	11	0	55	127	3	42	63	20	2005	
3	8	1	61	139	2	53	65	19	2006	
1	5	6	70	242	9	90	111	32	2003	Lituanie
0	5	6	71	244	9	93	111	32	2004	
2	6	5	75	255	9	99	117	29	2005	
2	6	-4	79	269	13	107	116	33	2006	
16	..	..	365	165	3	95	49	17	2003	Luxembourg
18	..	..	395	181	4	106	56	15	2004	
18	..	..	396	184	3	111	55	15	2005	
17	..	..	392	185	5	107	57	16	2006	
3	1	..	84	34	..	34	..	..	2003	Malte
4	1	..	87	35	..	35	..	..	2004	
4	1	..	86	35	..	35	..	..	2005	
3	1	..	84	34	..	34	..	..	2006	

Table 3

Production, trade and consumption of commercial energy
Thousand terajoules and gigajoules per capita

| Country or area
Pays ou zone | Year
Année | Primary energy production
Production d'énergie primaire | | | | | Changes in
stocks
Variations
des stocks | Imports
Importations | Exports
Exportations |
		Total Totale	Solids Solides	Liquids Liquides	Gas Gaz	Electricity Electricité			
Netherlands	2003	2582	..	134	2429	20	-10	5408	4115
	2004	3010	..	125	2865	21	18	5474	4499
	2005	2751	..	111	2617	22	49	6037	4714
	2006	2692	..	90	2579	23	4	6380	5085
Norway,Svlbd.J.Myn. I	2003	10002	83	6454	3083	383	45	246	8999
	2004	10165	82	6413	3276	394	-17	255	9156
	2005	10016	41	5932	3549	493	14	216	8743
	2006	9631	67	5482	3648	434	22	232	8679
Poland	2003	3192	2978	33	168	12	11	1352	760
	2004	3176	2941	38	183	14	14	1432	765
	2005	3101	2866	40	181	14	82	1532	766
	2006	3027	2795	40	181	12	-12	1697	756
Portugal	2003	60	..	0		60	19	980	66
	2004	40	..	0	..	40	-17	1003	71
	2005	25	..	0		25	17	1088	90
	2006	55	..	3	..	52	2	1031	133
Republic of Moldova	2003	0	..	0	..	0	2	148	1
	2004	1	..	0	..	0	0	149	2
	2005	0	..	0	..	0	0	157	1
	2006	0	..	0	..	0	-1	148	1
Romania	2003	1038	240	247	485	65	-10	586	160
	2004	1032	230	240	483	79	42	686	194
	2005	1010	225	241	451	93	-14	706	262
	2006	1022	253	238	445	86	-35	727	240
Russian Federation	2003	46422	4473	17571	23267	1110	509	1069	20680
	2004	48581	4554	19156	23709	1162	284	924	22806
	2005	49747	4983	19587	24010	1168	287	851	23686
	2006	50665	5009	19982	24478	1196	583	873	23573
Serbia	2003	441	359	32	14	35	0	227	17
	2004	446	367	27	12	40	0	288	32
	2005	396	315	27	11	43	0	280	39
	2006	405	327	27	11	39	-1	304	38
Slovakia	2003	128	38	2	10	78	-2	690	175
	2004	124	36	2	9	76	24	730	197
	2005	123	31	3	8	81	4	727	203
	2006	122	27	3	11	81	-7	719	213
Slovenia	2003	74	44	0	0	30	2	178	25
	2004	78	44	0	0	34	2	184	31
	2005	75	41	0	0	34	0	195	36
	2006	74	41	0	0	33	-4	200	42
Spain	2003	740	285	22	9	424	-3	4890	233
	2004	722	278	20	14	410	-33	5251	294
	2005	656	265	18	7	366	74	5628	303
	2006	676	255	13	3	406	117	5709	386
Sweden	2003	451	10	3	..	438	43	1379	439
	2004	515	11	6	..	499	-18	1340	507
	2005	544	9	9	..	526	32	1328	493
	2006	486	8	11	..	467	-31	1311	488
Switzerland	2003	233	..	0	1	232	-7	759	145
	2004	226	..	0	1	225	1	753	124
	2005	205	..	0	1	203	6	806	135
	2006	220	..	0	1	219	3	796	135
T.F.Yug.Rep. Macedonia	2003	88	83	..	..	5	-2	58	14
	2004	87	82	..	..	5	0	55	9
	2005	83	78	..	..	5	-3	64	14
	2006	81	75	..	..	6	1	68	15

Table 3

Production, commerce et consommation d'énergie commerciale
Milliers de térajoules et gigajoules par habitant

Bunkers Soutes		Unallocated Quantités non réparties	Per capita Par habitant	Consumption Consommation					Year Année	Country or area Pays ou zone
Aviation Avion	Marine Maritime			Total Totale	Solids Solides	Liquids Liquides	Gas Gaz	Electricity Electricité		
138	577	-686	238	3854	357	1741	1675	81	2003	Pays-Bas
147	627	-613	234	3805	349	1667	1709	79	2004	
151	719	-573	228	3725	335	1647	1655	88	2005	
153	747	-599	225	3682	314	1661	1607	100	2006	
9	24	16	245	1121	33	428	249	412	2003	Norvège,Svalbd,J.May
10	22	75	245	1128	39	416	238	436	2004	
11	29	183	249	1157	32	432	242	450	2005	
16	21	-104	255	1188	30	498	222	437	2006	
12	12	73	96	3675	2428	747	524	-24	2003	Pologne
12	11	80	98	3725	2387	804	553	-20	2004	
14	14	89	96	3668	2318	807	569	-26	2005	
18	13	99	101	3851	2439	864	576	-28	2006	
27	25	52	82	852	142	518	123	70	2003	Portugal
29	28	46	84	885	143	525	154	63	2004	
30	25	51	85	900	143	533	174	50	2005	
32	27	40	80	851	147	463	169	72	2006	
1	..	0	40	145	4	25	104	13	2003	Rép. de Moldova
0	..	0	41	148	4	27	107	11	2004	
1	..	0	43	156	3	27	114	12	2005	
1	..	0	41	148	4	26	105	13	2006	
5	..	17	67	1452	340	369	685	58	2003	Roumanie
6	..	64	65	1412	340	348	648	75	2004	
5	..	46	66	1418	331	355	649	82	2005	
6	..	67	68	1471	358	362	680	71	2006	
204	..	420	178	25677	3786	4891	15938	1062	2003	Fédération de Russie
200	..	322	180	25893	3664	4967	16127	1135	2004	
217	..	402	182	26007	3642	4975	16267	1124	2005	
229	..	386	188	26767	3760	5181	16687	1139	2006	
3	..	25	59	624	374	120	85	46	2003	Serbie
2	..	31	64	670	388	135	108	39	2004	
2	..	30	58	605	336	142	90	36	2005	
2	..	25	62	644	361	154	93	37	2006	
1	..	20	116	624	177	114	264	69	2003	Slovaquie
1	..	5	116	626	172	128	256	70	2004	
2	..	7	118	634	160	131	274	69	2005	
2	..	13	115	620	172	125	250	73	2006	
1	0	0	113	225	55	97	42	31	2003	Slovénie
1	0	2	114	227	56	98	42	32	2004	
1	1	2	115	230	54	100	43	32	2005	
1	1	2	115	232	54	103	42	33	2006	
117	299	322	111	4662	853	2386	993	429	2003	Espagne
130	309	330	116	4943	916	2457	1171	399	2004	
130	339	247	120	5191	892	2550	1388	362	2005	
136	354	220	117	5173	791	2544	1443	394	2006	
21	69	96	130	1160	110	525	41	484	2003	Suède
26	81	85	131	1174	122	521	41	491	2004	
27	83	88	127	1149	108	502	39	500	2005	
28	89	80	126	1143	110	503	41	489	2006	
51	0	1	109	801	6	453	122	221	2003	Suisse
48	0	0	108	805	6	451	126	222	2004	
49	1	0	110	819	6	457	129	226	2005	
52	0	-1	110	827	6	467	126	228	2006	
0	..	0	66	133	87	34	3	8	2003	L'ex-RY Macédoine
0	..	1	65	132	86	34	3	10	2004	
0	..	0	66	135	85	36	3	11	2005	
0	..	1	65	132	79	37	3	12	2006	

Table 3

Production, trade and consumption of commercial energy
Thousand terajoules and gigajoules per capita

| Country or area Pays ou zone | Year Année | Primary energy production Production d'énergie primaire | | | | | Changes in stocks Variations des stocks | Imports Importations | Exports Exportations |
		Total Totale	Solids Solides	Liquids Liquides	Gas Gaz	Electricity Electricité			
Ukraine	2003	2634	1390	168	749	327	0	3660	716
	2004	2628	1290	183	799	356	13	3657	760
	2005	2671	1308	187	811	365	-113	3237	536
	2006	2724	1336	193	823	372	72	2869	328
United Kingdom	2003	9836	713	4468	4309	345	-92	4212	4653
	2004	8994	633	4019	4020	322	51	4955	4247
	2005	8089	517	3573	3667	333	30	5285	3715
	2006	7489	467	3355	3350	317	102	5901	3611
Oceania	**2003**	**11021**	**7834**	**1382**	**1642**	**164**	**14**	**1587**	**7154**
	2004	**11223**	**8149**	**1244**	**1654**	**176**	**11**	**1616**	**7355**
	2005	**11629**	**8543**	**1113**	**1807**	**166**	**-44**	**1728**	**7677**
	2006	**11694**	**8558**	**1088**	**1877**	**171**	**-64**	**1831**	**7738**
Australia	2003	10486	7741	1227	1457	61	21	1145	6954
	2004	10711	8055	1107	1489	60	6	1148	7178
	2005	11123	8447	967	1648	60	-43	1253	7477
	2006	11156	8452	927	1714	64	-73	1348	7518
Cook Islands	2003	..	..	..	..	..	..	1	..
	2004	..	..	..	..	..	..	1	..
	2005	..	..	..	..	..	..	1	..
	2006	..	..	..	..	..	..	*1	..
Fiji	2003	*2	..	..	..	*2	..	43	*5
	2004	*2	..	..	..	*2	..	45	*6
	2005	*2	..	..	..	*2	..	40	*5
	2006	*2	..	..	..	*2	..	41	*5
French Polynesia	2003	0	..	..	..	0	..	13	..
	2004	1	..	..	..	1	..	13	..
	2005	0	..	..	..	0	..	14	..
	2006	1	..	..	..	1	..	14	..
Kiribati	2003	..	..	..	..	..	..	0	..
	2004	..	..	..	..	..	..	0	..
	2005	..	..	..	..	..	..	0	..
	2006	..	..	..	..	..	..	*1	..
Marshall Islands	2003	..	..	..	..	..	..	*1	..
	2004	..	..	..	..	..	..	*1	..
	2005	..	..	..	..	..	..	*1	..
	2006	..	..	..	..	..	..	*1	..
Nauru	2003	..	..	..	..	..	..	*2	..
	2004	..	..	..	..	..	..	*2	..
	2005	..	..	..	..	..	..	*2	..
	2006	..	..	..	..	..	..	*2	..
New Caledonia	2003	1	..	..	..	1	..	36	1
	2004	1	..	..	..	1	..	34	1
	2005	1	..	..	..	1	..	37	*1
	2006	2	..	..	..	2	..	39	*1
New Zealand	2003	421	92	53	179	96	-9	280	95
	2004	411	94	47	161	109	13	300	80
	2005	386	96	44	149	98	-1	297	90
	2006	399	106	42	153	99	-3	300	100
Niue	2003	..	..	..	..	..	..	0	..
	2004	..	..	..	..	..	..	0	..
	2005	..	..	..	..	..	..	0	..
	2006	..	..	..	..	..	..	0	..
Palau	2003	0	..	..	..	0	..	*3	..
	2004	0	..	..	..	0	..	*3	..
	2005	0	..	..	..	0	..	*3	..
	2006	0	..	..	..	0	..	*3	..

Table 3

Production, commerce et consommation d'énergie commerciale

Milliers de térajoules et gigajoules par habitant

Bunkers Soutes		Unallocated Quantités	Consumption Consommation						Year	Country or area
Aviation Avion	Marine Maritime	non réparties	Per capita Par habitant	Total Totale	Solids Solides	Liquids Liquides	Gas Gaz	Electricity Electricité	Année	Pays ou zone
16	..	126	114	5437	1554	545	3029	309	2003	Ukraine
16	..	141	113	5356	1383	571	3064	337	2004	
16	..	-6	116	5476	1416	586	3138	335	2005	
14	..	-21	111	5200	1535	620	2710	334	2006	
407	74	19	151	8988	1686	2954	3995	353	2003	Royaume-Uni
450	88	-35	153	9148	1673	3061	4065	349	2004	
508	86	23	150	9014	1723	2979	3949	363	2005	
479	98	-69	151	9169	1894	3160	3771	344	2006	
142	**48**	**-89**	**165**	**5340**	**2124**	**1836**	**1216**	**164**	**2003**	**Océanie**
144	**52**	**-124**	**164**	**5402**	**2154**	**1847**	**1224**	**176**	**2004**	
160	**53**	**-113**	**169**	**5624**	**2302**	**1925**	**1232**	**166**	**2005**	
149	**60**	**-35**	**168**	**5678**	**2333**	**1919**	**1254**	**171**	**2006**	
94	31	-82	232	4614	2066	1456	1031	61	2003	Australie
95	35	-117	231	4662	2096	1448	1058	60	2004	
111	36	-110	240	4905	2240	1533	1072	60	2005	
100	41	-39	239	4958	2271	1532	1090	64	2006	
0	..	..	26	0	..	0	..	..	2003	Iles Cook
0	..	..	38	1	..	1	..	..	2004	
0	..	..	42	1	..	1	..	..	2005	
0	..	..	*42	*1	..	*1	..	..	2006	
*13	*3	..	30	25	0	22	..	*2	2003	Fidji
*10	*3	..	34	28	0	25	..	*2	2004	
*10	*3	..	29	25	0	22	..	*2	2005	
*12	*3	..	28	24	0	21	..	*2	2006	
0	*2	..	47	12	..	11	..	0	2003	Polynésie française
0	*2	..	45	11	..	11	..	1	2004	
0	*2	..	48	12	..	12	..	0	2005	
0	*2	..	46	12	..	11	..	1	2006	
0	..	..	*4	0	..	0	..	..	2003	Kiribati
0	..	..	*3	0	..	0	..	..	2004	
0	..	..	*3	0	..	0	..	..	2005	
0	..	..	*4	0	..	0	..	..	2006	
..	..	..	*21	*1	..	*1	..	..	2003	Îles Marshall
..	..	..	*21	*1	..	*1	..	..	2004	
..	..	..	*20	*1	..	*1	..	..	2005	
..	..	..	*21	*1	..	*1	..	..	2006	
0	..	..	*153	*2	..	*2	..	..	2003	Nauru
0	..	..	*150	*2	..	*2	..	..	2004	
0	..	..	*148	*2	..	*2	..	..	2005	
0	..	..	*145	*2	..	*2	..	..	2006	
0	..	..	157	36	9	26	..	1	2003	Nouvelle-Calédonie
0	..	..	144	33	8	24	..	1	2004	
0	..	..	158	37	8	28	..	1	2005	
1	..	..	164	39	8	29	..	2	2006	
32	11	-7	144	579	49	255	179	96	2003	Nouvelle-Zélande
35	10	-12	144	585	49	265	162	109	2004	
36	11	-15	137	563	54	262	149	98	2005	
33	12	-5	136	562	54	257	153	99	2006	
..	..	..	*24	0	..	0	..	..	2003	Nioué
..	..	..	*24	0	..	0	..	..	2004	
..	..	..	*25	0	..	0	..	..	2005	
..	..	..	*26	0	..	0	..	..	2006	
*1	..	..	*132	*3	..	*3	..	0	2003	Palaos
*1	..	..	*129	*3	..	*3	..	0	2004	
*1	..	..	*130	*3	..	*3	..	0	2005	
*1	..	..	*133	*3	..	*3	..	0	2006	

Table 3

Production, trade and consumption of commercial energy
Thousand terajoules and gigajoules per capita

| Country or area Pays ou zone | Year Année | Primary energy production Production d'énergie primaire | | | | | Changes in stocks Variations des stocks | Imports Importations | Exports Exportations |
		Total Totale	Solids Solides	Liquids Liquides	Gas Gaz	Electricity Electricité			
Papua New Guinea	2003	110	..	102	6	3	*3	54	99
	2004	97	..	89	4	3	*-9	59	90
	2005	116	..	103	10	3	0	70	104
	2006	134	..	120	11	3	12	72	114
Samoa	2003	0	..	..	..	..	0	..	*2	..
	2004	0	..	..	..	..	0	..	*2	..
	2005	0	..	..	..	..	0	..	*2	..
	2006	0	..	..	..	..	0	..	*2	..
Solomon Islands	2003	..	..	..	..	..	..	..	*3	..
	2004	..	..	..	..	..	..	..	*3	..
	2005	..	..	..	..	..	..	..	*3	..
	2006	..	..	..	..	..	..	..	*3	..
Tonga	2003	..	..	..	..	..	..	..	2	..
	2004	..	..	..	..	..	..	..	2	..
	2005	..	..	..	..	..	..	..	*2	..
	2006	..	..	..	..	..	..	..	*2	..
Vanuatu	2003	..	..	..	..	..	..	..	*1	..
	2004	..	..	..	..	..	..	..	*1	..
	2005	..	..	..	..	..	..	..	*1	..
	2006	..	..	..	..	..	..	..	*1	..
Wallis and Futuna Is	2003	..	..	..	..	..	..	..	0	..
	2004	..	..	..	..	..	..	..	0	..
	2005	..	..	..	..	..	..	..	0	..
	2006	..	..	..	..	..	..	..	0	..

Table 3

Production, commerce et consommation d'énergie commerciale
Milliers de térajoules et gigajoules par habitant

Bunkers Soutes		Unallocated Quantités non réparties	Consumption Consommation						Year Année	Country or area Pays ou zone
Aviation Avion	Marine Maritime		Per capita Par habitant	Total Totale	Solids Solides	Liquids Liquides	Gas Gaz	Electricity Electricité		
*1	*1	0	10	59	..	51	6	3	2003	Papouasie-Nvl-Guinée
*2	*1	6	11	66	..	58	4	3	2004	
*2	*1	13	11	66	..	53	10	3	2005	
*2	*1	9	11	67	..	53	11	3	2006	
..	..	..	*12	*2	..	*2	..	0	2003	Samoa
..	..	..	*13	*2	..	*2	..	0	2004	
..	..	..	*13	*2	..	*2	..	0	2005	
..	..	..	*13	*2	..	*2	..	0	2006	
0	..	..	*5	*2	..	*2	..	..	2003	Iles Salomon
0	..	..	*5	*2	..	*2	..	..	2004	
0	..	..	*5	*2	..	*2	..	..	2005	
0	..	..	*5	*2	..	*2	..	..	2006	
0	..	..	24	2	..	2	..	..	2003	Tonga
0	..	..	24	2	..	2	..	..	2004	
0	..	..	*23	*2	..	*2	..	..	2005	
0	..	..	*23	*2	..	*2	..	..	2006	
..	..	..	*6	*1	..	*1	..	..	2003	Vanuatu
..	..	..	*6	*1	..	*1	..	..	2004	
..	..	..	*6	*1	..	*1	..	..	2005	
..	..	..	*6	*1	..	*1	..	..	2006	
0	..	..	*23	0	..	0	..	..	2003	Iles Wallis et Futuna
0	..	..	24	0	..	0	..	..	2004	
0	..	..	23	0	..	0	..	..	2005	
0	..	..	22	0	..	0	..	..	2006	

Table 4

Total energy requirement
Besoins énergétiques totals

Thousand terajoules and gigajoules per capita
Milliers de térajoules et gigajoules par habitant

Table Notes:

Total energy requirement is defined as consumption of commercial energy (see Tables 1-3) plus biogas and traditional fuels which include fuelwood, charcoal, bagasse, animal, vegetal and other wastes. Please refer to notes on table 1.

- **Please refer to the Definitions Section on pages xv to xxix for the appropriate product description/ classification.**

Notes relatives aux tableaux:

La demande énergétique totale est définie par la consommation d'énergie commerciale (voir les Tableaux 1 à 3) à laquelle s'ajoute le biogaz et les combustibles traditionnels, y compris le bois de chauffage, le charbon de bois, la bagasse et les déchets animaux, végétaux et autres. Veuillez consulter les notes de bas de page au tableau 1.

- **Veuillez consulter la section "définitions" de la page xv à la page xxix pour une description/classification appropriée des produits.**

Figure 10: World energy requirement 1993-2006

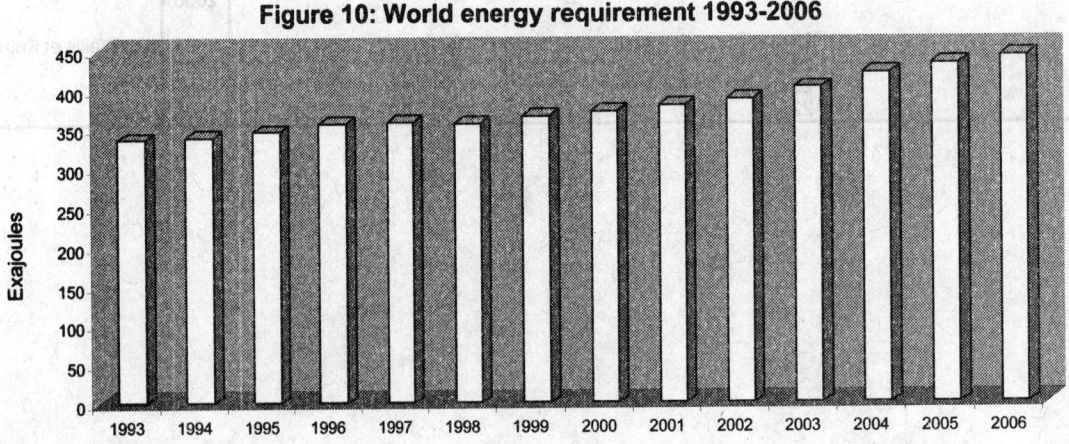

Figure 11: World energy requirement, by region, in 2006

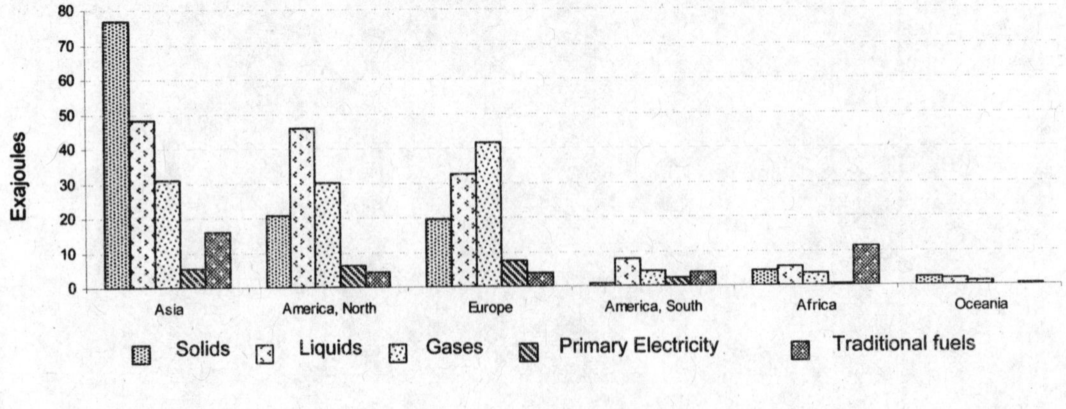

Table 4

Total energy requirement
Besoins énergétiques totales
Thousand terajoules and gigajoules per capita
Milliers de térajoules et gigajoules par habitant

Country or area Pays ou zone	Year Année	Solids Solides	Liquids Liquides	Gases Gaz	Primary electricity Électricité primaire	Traditional fuels Combustibles traditionnels	Requirement Besoins	
							Total Totale	Per capita Par habitant
World **Monde**	**2003**	**104919**	**133848**	**104548**	**19701**	**38299**	**401315**	**64**
	2004	**113706**	**139196**	**106638**	**20738**	**38910**	**419187**	**66**
	2005	**119336**	**141123**	**109895**	**21353**	**39523**	**431230**	**67**
	2006	**125106**	**142305**	**111694**	**21955**	**40512**	**441572**	**68**
Africa **Afrique**	**2003**	**4038**	**5124**	**2851**	**360**	**10470**	**22844**	**27**
	2004	**4339**	**5469**	**3030**	**381**	**10705**	**23924**	**28**
	2005	**4314**	**5624**	**3598**	**381**	**11025**	**24942**	**28**
	2006	**4327**	**5687**	**3545**	**402**	**11332**	**25293**	**28**
Algeria Algérie	2003	32	860	895	1	88	1876	59
	2004	22	964	838	1	90	1914	59
	2005	27	921	1244	2	91	2286	69
	2006	31	837	1114	1	93	2075	62
Angola Angola	2003	..	75	25	4	279	383	34
	2004	..	73	28	6	287	395	35
	2005	..	80	28	8	295	412	35
	2006	..	89	30	10	304	433	36
Benin Bénin	2003	..	30	..	2	72	104	13
	2004	..	32	..	2	74	108	13
	2005	..	34	..	2	76	113	13
	2006	..	42	..	2	78	123	14
Burkina Faso Burkina Faso	2003	0	15	..	1	71	87	7
	2004	0	15	..	1	89	105	8
	2005	0	15	..	1	112	128	10
	2006	0	19	..	1	126	146	11
Burundi Burundi	2003	0	2	..	1	84	86	12
	2004	0	2	..	1	85	88	12
	2005	0	2	..	1	87	89	11
	2006	0	3	..	1	88	91	11
Cameroon Cameroun	2003	..	40	..	13	136	188	11
	2004	..	40	..	14	138	191	11
	2005	..	40	..	14	138	193	11
	2006	..	42	..	13	141	196	11
Cape Verde Cap-Vert	2003	..	*4	..	0	0	*4	*8
	2004	..	*4	..	0	0	*4	*8
	2005	..	*4	..	0	0	*4	*9
	2006	..	*4	..	0	0	*4	*9
Central African Rep. Rép. centrafricaine	2003	..	*3	..	0	19	22	6
	2004	..	*3	..	0	19	22	5
	2005	..	*3	..	0	19	22	5
	2006	..	*3	..	0	19	23	5
Chad Tchad	2003	..	*2	..	..	68	70	8
	2004	..	*2	..	..	69	71	7
	2005	..	*3	..	..	70	73	7
	2006	..	*3	..	..	72	74	7
Comoros Comores	2003	..	*1	..	0	..	*1	*2
	2004	..	*1	..	0	..	*1	*2
	2005	..	*1	..	0	..	*1	*2
	2006	..	*1	..	0	..	*1	*2
Congo Congo	2003	..	11	1	3	16	30	9
	2004	..	12	1	3	16	32	9
	2005	..	13	1	3	18	35	10
	2006	..	15	1	3	17	36	10

Table 4

Total energy requirement
Besoins énergétiques totales
Thousand terajoules and gigajoules per capita
Milliers de térajoules et gigajoules par habitant

Country or area Pays ou zone	Year Année	Solids Solides	Liquids Liquides	Gases Gaz	Primary electricity Électricité primaire	Traditional fuels Combustibles traditionnels	Requirement Besoins	
							Total Totale	Per capita Par habitant
Côte d'Ivoire	2003	..	39	48	2	109	197	11
Côte d'Ivoire	2004	..	48	61	1	110	220	12
	2005	..	45	68	0	112	225	12
	2006	..	47	64	2	113	225	11
Dem. Rep. of Congo	2003	10	10	..	18	681	719	13
Rép. dem. du Congo	2004	10	16	..	19	694	740	13
	2005	11	16	..	20	708	755	13
	2006	12	16	..	22	720	769	13
Djibouti	2003	..	5	..	..	..	5	6
Djibouti	2004	..	6	..	..	..	6	7
	2005	..	6	..	..	..	6	7
	2006	..	6	..	..	..	6	7
Egypt	2003	16	1017	1183	42	213	2472	37
Egypte	2004	37	1190	1171	45	217	2661	37
	2005	37	1271	1292	45	222	2867	40
	2006	33	1312	1292	47	223	2907	40
Equatorial Guinea	2003	..	*2	19	0	4	25	55
Guinée équatoriale	2004	..	*2	*19	0	4	*25	*53
	2005	..	*2	*19	0	4	*25	*51
	2006	..	*2	*19	0	4	*25	*50
Eritrea	2003	..	10	..	0	26	36	9
Erythrée	2004	..	10	..	0	24	34	8
	2005	..	10	..	0	25	35	8
	2006	..	7	..	0	25	33	7
Ethiopia	2003	..	61	..	8	1076	1145	16
Ethiopie	2004	..	69	..	9	1096	1174	17
	2005	..	65	..	10	1115	1191	17
	2006	..	72	..	12	1132	1216	16
Gabon	2003	..	17	4	3	42	67	52
Gabon	2004	..	17	5	3	43	68	50
	2005	..	21	5	3	43	73	52
	2006	..	21	5	3	44	74	52
Gambia	2003	..	*4	..	..	7	12	8
Gambie	2004	..	*4	..	..	7	12	8
	2005	..	*4	..	..	7	12	7
	2006	..	*5	..	..	8	12	7
Ghana	2003	..	93	..	14	259	366	17
Ghana	2004	..	82	..	20	263	365	17
	2005	..	92	..	21	266	379	17
	2006	..	114	..	20	271	404	18
Guinea	2003	..	*16	..	*2	115	133	15
Guinée	2004	..	*16	..	*2	116	133	15
	2005	..	*16	..	*2	116	134	15
	2006	..	*16	..	*2	117	135	15
Guinea-Bissau	2003	..	*4	..	..	4	8	6
Guinée-Bissau	2004	..	*4	..	..	4	8	6
	2005	..	*4	..	..	4	8	6
	2006	..	*4	..	..	4	*8	*6
Kenya	2003	3	106	..	15	239	362	11
Kenya	2004	3	117	..	14	244	378	11
	2005	3	129	..	14	246	392	11
	2006	4	144	..	15	248	410	11

Table 4

Total energy requirement
Besoins énergétiques totales
Thousand terajoules and gigajoules per capita
Milliers de térajoules et gigajoules par habitant

Country or area Pays ou zone	Year Année	Solids Solides	Liquids Liquides	Gases Gaz	Primary electricity Électricité primaire	Traditional fuels Combustibles traditionnels	Requirement Besoins	
							Total Totale	Per capita Par habitant
Liberia	2003	..	*7	..	..	54	61	18
Libéria	2004	..	8	..	..	56	64	18
	2005	..	9	..	..	59	68	19
	2006	..	*10	..	..	62	72	20
Libyan Arab Jamah.	2003	..	462	215	0	6	683	110
Jamah. arabe libyenne	2004	..	458	261	0	6	725	113
	2005	..	463	224	0	6	694	105
	2006	..	450	243	0	7	700	104
Madagascar	2003	0	*28	..	2	120	150	9
Madagascar	2004	0	*31	..	2	123	157	9
	2005	0	*32	..	*2	127	161	9
	2006	0	*32	..	*2	131	165	9
Malawi	2003	2	11	..	4	85	102	9
Malawi	2004	*2	*12	..	5	86	104	9
	2005	2	*11	..	5	87	104	8
	2006	*1	*11	..	5	87	104	8
Mali	2003	..	8	..	*1	49	57	5
Mali	2004	..	*8	..	*1	49	58	5
	2005	..	*8	..	*1	50	59	5
	2006	..	*8	..	*1	51	60	5
Mauritania	2003	0	19	..	0	18	37	13
Mauritanie	2004	0	20	..	0	19	39	13
	2005	0	21	..	0	19	40	14
	2006	0	20	..	0	20	41	14
Mauritius	2003	9	32	..	0	12	54	45
Maurice	2004	8	34	..	0	13	55	45
	2005	11	34	..	0	12	57	46
	2006	14	36	..	0	12	62	49
Morocco	2003	135	272	2	11	19	439	15
Maroc	2004	151	286	2	12	20	471	16
	2005	187	322	18	9	21	556	18
	2006	162	321	22	14	17	536	18
Mozambique	2003	0	22	0	31	301	354	19
Mozambique	2004	0	23	0	38	306	367	19
	2005	0	20	3	39	314	375	19
	2006	0	21	3	42	319	386	19
Niger	2003	4	6	..	1	88	100	8
Niger	2004	5	6	..	1	91	102	8
	2005	4	6	..	1	93	104	8
	2006	*4	6	..	1	95	107	8
Nigeria	2003	1	449	282	28	3279	4039	32
Nigéria	2004	0	434	377	25	3351	4187	32
	2005	0	439	376	22	3425	4263	32
	2006	0	449	419	28	3532	4428	32
Réunion	2003	..	*32	..	*2	*5	*39	*52
Réunion	2004	..	*33	..	*2	*5	*39	*51
	2005	..	*33	..	*2	*5	*39	*51
	2006	..	*33	..	*2	*5	*39	*50
Rwanda	2003	..	*7	0	1	*62	*70	*8
Rwanda	2004	..	7	0	1	*73	*81	*9
	2005	..	*8	0	*1	*83	*92	*10
	2006	..	*8	0	1	93	102	11

Table 4

Total energy requirement
Besoins énergétiques totales
Thousand terajoules and gigajoules per capita
Milliers de térajoules et gigajoules par habitant

Country or area Pays ou zone	Year Année	Solids Solides	Liquids Liquides	Gases Gaz	Primary electricity Électricité primaire	Traditional fuels Combustibles traditionnels	Requirement Besoins Total Totale	Requirement Besoins Per capita Par habitant
Sao Tome and Principe	2003	..	*1	..	0	..	*1	*9
Sao Tomé-et-Principe	2004	..	*1	..	0	..	*1	*9
	2005	..	*1	..	0	..	*1	*10
	2006	..	*1	..	0	..	*1	*10
Senegal	2003	*4	52	0	1	55	112	11
Sénégal	2004	4	49	1	1	55	109	10
	2005	4	51	1	1	57	114	10
	2006	5	33	0	1	58	97	9
Seychelles	2003	..	8	..	0	..	8	92
Seychelles	2004	..	11	..	0	..	11	130
	2005	..	10	..	0	..	10	115
	2006	..	10	..	0	..	10	120
Sierra Leone	2003	..	*7	..	0	59	66	12
Sierra Leone	2004	..	*9	..	0	59	68	12
	2005	..	*9	..	0	59	68	12
	2006	..	*9	..	0	60	69	11
Somalia	2003	..	*7	..	..	113	120	16
Somalie	2004	..	*7	..	..	116	124	16
	2005	..	*7	..	..	120	128	16
	2006	..	*7	..	..	124	131	16
South Africa Customs Un.	2003	3718	851	50	68	686	5373	105
Un.douan.d'Afr.mérid	2004	3995	871	129	72	675	5744	108
	2005	3919	884	169	69	702	5744	107
	2006	3956	916	178	71	703	5823	107
St. Helena and Depend.	2003	..	0	..	..	0	0	*25
St-Hélène et dépend	2004	..	0	..	..	0	0	19
	2005	..	0	..	..	0	0	*20
	2006	..	0	..	..	0	0	*20
Sudan	2003	..	116	..	4	259	380	11
Soudan	2004	..	129	..	4	266	400	12
	2005	..	139	..	4	270	413	12
	2006	..	159	..	5	275	439	12
Togo	2003	..	15	..	2	66	83	17
Togo	2004	..	14	..	2	55	71	14
	2005	..	13	..	2	68	83	16
	2006	..	12	..	2	69	83	15
Tunisia	2003	1	163	127	1	49	341	35
Tunisie	2004	0	169	132	1	51	353	36
	2005	0	171	136	1	53	360	36
	2006	0	171	140	0	55	367	36
Uganda	2003	..	*20	..	6	353	379	15
Ouganda	2004	..	22	..	6	359	387	14
	2005	..	28	..	6	365	399	14
	2006	..	33	..	4	371	408	14
United Rep.Tanzania	2003	2	43	0	10	683	737	20
Rép. Unie de Tanzanie	2004	2	46	5	9	740	802	22
	2005	2	49	14	7	808	880	24
	2006	2	52	15	6	888	962	25
Western Sahara	2003	..	*3	..	..	..	*3	*13
Sahara occidental	2004	..	*3	..	..	..	*3	*12
	2005	..	*3	..	..	..	*3	*12
	2006	..	*3	..	..	..	*3	*12

Table 4

Total energy requirement
Besoins énergétiques totales
Thousand terajoules and gigajoules per capita
Milliers de térajoules et gigajoules par habitant

Country or area Pays ou zone	Year Année	Solids Solides	Liquids Liquides	Gases Gaz	Primary electricity Électricité primaire	Traditional fuels Combustibles traditionnels	Requirement Besoins	
							Total Totale	Per capita Par habitant
Zambia	2003	4	22	..	28	262	315	29
Zambie	2004	4	23	..	30	261	317	29
	2005	4	24	..	31	266	325	28
	2006	4	25	..	33	271	333	28
Zimbabwe	2003	98	32		31	179	340	26
Zimbabwe	2004	95	26		27	180	328	25
	2005	102	28		32	181	343	26
	2006	97	27		30	184	339	26
America, North	**2003**	**20459**	**43960**	**30560**	**5721**	**4326**	**105026**	**209**
Amérique du Nord	**2004**	**21049**	**45429**	**30238**	**5895**	**4412**	**107022**	**211**
	2005	**21255**	**46302**	**30260**	**6012**	**4453**	**108282**	**211**
	2006	**20946**	**45973**	**30242**	**6136**	**4478**	**107775**	**209**
Anguilla	2003	..	1			0	1	48
Anguilla	2004	..	1			0	1	49
	2005	..	1			0	1	56
	2006	..	1			0	1	55
Antigua and Barbuda	2003	..	*5	..	..	..	*5	*68
Antigua-et-Barbuda	2004	..	*6	..	..	..	*6	*70
	2005	..	*6	..	..	..	*6	*69
	2006	..	*6	..	..	..	*6	*71
Aruba	2003	..	10			0	10	110
Aruba	2004	..	10			0	10	107
	2005	..	11			0	11	106
	2006	..	*11			0	*11	*104
Bahamas	2003	0	*26	..	..	0	*26	*81
Bahamas	2004	0	*28	..	..	0	*28	*93
	2005	0	*29	..	..	0	*29	*90
	2006	0	*29	..	..	0	*30	*90
Barbados	2003	..	14	1	..	1	16	57
Barbade	2004	..	15	1	..	1	17	62
	2005	..	15	1	..	1	18	65
	2006	..	16	1	..	1	18	66
Belize	2003	..	*11		0	4	*15	*57
Belize	2004	..	*11		0	4	*16	*57
	2005	..	*12		0	4	*16	*55
	2006	..	*12		0	4	*16	*53
Bermuda	2003	..	*7	..	..	..	*7	*117
Bermudes	2004	..	*8	..	..	..	*8	*121
	2005	..	*8	..	..	..	*8	*124
	2006	..	*8	..	..	..	*8	*124
British Virgin Islands	2003	..	*1	..	..	..	*1	*51
Iles Vierges britanniques	2004	..	*1	..	..	..	*1	*56
	2005	..	*1	..	..	..	*1	*57
	2006	..	*1	..	..	..	*1	*61
Canada	2003	1100	3718	3717	1464	426	10426	329
Canada	2004	1076	3845	3638	1521	437	10517	329
	2005	1053	3791	3760	1560	433	10597	328
	2006	1033	3759	3706	1573	459	10530	323
Cayman Islands	2003	..	*7	..	..	..	*7	*152
Iles Caïmanes	2004	..	*7	..	..	..	*7	*155
	2005	..	*7	..	..	..	*7	*144
	2006	..	*7	..	..	..	*7	*138

Table 4

Total energy requirement
Besoins énergétiques totales
Thousand terajoules and gigajoules per capita
Milliers de térajoules et gigajoules par habitant

Country or area Pays ou zone	Year Année	Solids Solides	Liquids Liquides	Gases Gaz	Primary electricity Électricité primaire	Traditional fuels Combustibles traditionnels	Requirement Besoins	
							Total Totale	Per capita Par habitant
Costa Rica	2003	4	77	..	26	19	126	31
Costa Rica	2004	3	80	..	28	23	134	32
	2005	3	84	..	29	26	141	33
	2006	3	92	..	29	30	155	36
Cuba	2003	1	292	26	0	146	465	41
Cuba	2004	1	294	27	0	139	461	41
	2005	1	312	29	0	101	443	39
	2006	*1	323	42	0	80	446	40
Dominica	2003	..	2	..	0	0	2	25
Dominique	2004	..	2	..	0	0	2	24
	2005	..	*2	..	0	0	*2	*25
	2006	..	*2	..	0	0	*2	*26
Dominican Republic	2003	31	210	4	4	43	292	33
Rép. dominicaine	2004	23	218	5	6	44	296	33
	2005	14	225	11	7	42	299	32
	2006	23	223	13	5	41	305	33
El Salvador	2003	0	79	..	10	70	159	24
El Salvador	2004	0	79	..	10	71	161	24
	2005	0	74	..	11	73	159	23
	2006	0	80	..	11	74	165	24
Greenland	2003	..	*8	..	..	..	*8	*134
Groënland	2004	..	*8	..	..	..	*8	*135
	2005	..	*8	..	..	..	*8	*137
	2006	..	*8	..	..	..	*8	*139
Grenada	2003	..	3	..	..	0	3	32
Grenade	2004	..	3	..	..	0	3	32
	2005	..	3	..	..	0	4	35
	2006	..	3	..	..	0	4	35
Guadeloupe	2003	..	*27	..	..	0	*27	*61
Guadeloupe	2004	..	*27	..	..	0	*27	*61
	2005	..	*28	..	..	0	*28	*63
	2006	..	*28	..	..	0	*28	*62
Guatemala	2003	11	123	..	7	209	350	29
Guatemala	2004	12	127	..	7	221	367	30
	2005	12	131	..	12	224	379	30
	2006	13	127	..	14	227	380	29
Haiti	2003	..	21	..	1	22	44	5
Haïti	2004	..	22	..	1	22	45	5
	2005	..	23	..	1	22	45	5
	2006	..	23	..	1	22	46	5
Honduras	2003	5	74	..	9	87	175	26
Honduras	2004	5	86	..	10	89	190	27
	2005	5	91	..	6	89	192	27
	2006	6	96	..	7	90	198	27
Jamaica	2003	2	139	..	1	16	158	59
Jamaïque	2004	2	137	..	1	17	156	58
	2005	2	132	..	1	15	149	56
	2006	1	160	..	1	15	177	67
Martinique	2003	..	*25	..	..	0	*25	*65
Martinique	2004	..	*26	..	..	0	*26	*66
	2005	..	*26	..	..	0	*26	*66
	2006	..	*26	..	..	0	*27	*67

Table 4

Total energy requirement
Besoins énergétiques totales
Thousand terajoules and gigajoules per capita
Milliers de térajoules et gigajoules par habitant

Country or area Pays ou zone	Year Année	Solids Solides	Liquids Liquides	Gases Gaz	Primary electricity Électricité primaire	Traditional fuels Combustibles traditionnels	Requirement Besoins	
							Total Totale	Per capita Par habitant
Mexico	2003	236	3443	1953	129	574	6336	62
Mexique	2004	212	3597	2034	144	584	6571	64
	2005	254	3728	2057	161	603	6803	65
	2006	256	3729	2260	170	583	6998	67
Montserrat	2003	..	*1	..	..	..	*1	*108
Montserrat	2004	..	*1	..	..	..	*1	*105
	2005	..	*1	..	..	..	*1	*104
	2006	..	*1	..	..	..	*1	*105
Netherlands Antilles	2003	..	66	..	..	0	66	372
Antilles néerlandaises	2004	..	96	..	..	0	96	525
	2005	..	54	..	..	0	54	292
	2006	..	50	..	..	0	50	266
Nicaragua	2003	..	52	..	2	32	86	16
Nicaragua	2004	..	54	..	2	37	93	17
	2005	..	52	..	3	37	92	17
	2006	..	54	..	3	*36	93	17
Panama	2003	0	79	..	10	17	106	34
Panama	2004	0	73	..	14	16	103	33
	2005	0	76	..	14	17	107	33
	2006	0	82	..	14	19	115	35
Puerto Rico	2003	..	..	29	1	..	30	8
Porto Rico	2004	..	..	27	1	..	27	7
	2005	..	..	27	1	..	27	7
	2006	..	..	27	*1	..	27	7
St. Kitts-Nevis	2003	..	*3	..	0	1	*4	*82
St-Kitts-Nevis	2004	..	*3	..	0	1	*4	*83
	2005	..	*3	..	..	1	*4	*88
	2006	..	*3	..	..	0	*3	*77
St. Lucia	2003	..	*5	..	..	0	*5	*30
St-Lucie	2004	..	*5	..	..	0	*5	*32
	2005	..	*5	..	..	0	*5	*32
	2006	..	*5	..	..	0	*5	*32
St. Pierre-Miquelon	2003	..	*1	..	..	..	*1	*128
St-Pierre-Miquelon	2004	..	*1	..	..	..	*1	*122
	2005	..	*1	..	..	..	*1	*128
	2006	..	*1	..	..	..	*1	*128
St. Vincent-Grenadines	2003	..	*3	..	0	0	*3	*26
St. Vincent-Grenadines	2004	..	*3	..	0	0	*3	*27
	2005	..	*3	..	0	0	*3	*27
	2006	..	*3	..	0	0	*3	*28
Trinidad and Tobago	2003	..	31	465	..	3	498	379
Trinité-et-Tobago	2004	..	28	488	..	2	518	393
	2005	..	41	510	..	2	553	418
	2006	..	55	572	..	2	629	474
United States	2003	19069	35397	24366	4056	2655	85543	294
Etats-Unis	2004	19715	36528	24018	4150	2702	87113	297
	2005	19911	37320	23866	4207	2762	88066	297
	2006	19609	36950	23622	4306	2793	87280	292
America, South	**2003**	**850**	**6668**	**3741**	**2042**	**3457**	**16757**	**46**
Amérique du Sud	**2004**	**881**	**7085**	**3936**	**2113**	**3627**	**17641**	**48**
	2005	**912**	**7373**	**4063**	**2235**	**3749**	**18331**	**49**
	2006	**910**	**7903**	**4283**	**2369**	**3939**	**19404**	**51**

Table 4

Total energy requirement
Besoins énergétiques totales
Thousand terajoules and gigajoules per capita
Milliers de térajoules et gigajoules par habitant

Country or area Pays ou zone	Year Année	Solids Solides	Liquids Liquides	Gases Gaz	Primary electricity Électricité primaire	Traditional fuels Combustibles traditionnels	Requirement Besoins	
							Total Totale	Per capita Par habitant
Argentina	2003	22	890	1404	167	126	2610	69
Argentine	2004	24	1004	1460	151	119	2758	72
	2005	38	1034	1494	162	139	2867	74
	2006	32	1138	1586	174	151	3080	79
Bolivia	2003	..	72	88	8	31	199	22
Bolivie	2004	..	68	65	8	33	173	19
	2005	..	84	37	9	31	161	17
	2006	..	92	54	8	31	184	19
Brazil	2003	578	3315	593	1282	2637	8405	47
Brésil	2004	601	3478	733	1331	2805	8949	49
	2005	583	3569	778	1391	2896	9217	50
	2006	577	3603	814	1453	3061	9509	51
Chile	2003	102	363	300	88	114	967	61
Chili	2004	138	391	298	83	120	1031	64
	2005	139	395	319	102	127	1082	66
	2006	165	417	303	132	134	1151	70
Colombia	2003	115	399	258	126	173	1071	24
Colombie	2004	81	413	271	139	172	1076	24
	2005	113	405	285	137	179	1119	24
	2006	103	414	322	148	183	1170	25
Ecuador	2003	..	262	16	30	65	372	29
Equateur	2004	..	252	25	33	65	374	29
	2005	..	332	20	37	66	455	34
	2006	..	354	33	38	67	492	37
Falkland Is. (Malvinas)	2003	0	*1	..	..	..	*1	*214
Iles Falkland (Malvinas)	2004	0	*1	..	..	..	*1	*213
	2005	0	*1	..	..	..	*1	*224
	2006	0	*1	..	..	..	*1	*224
French Guiana	2003	..	*11	..	..	1	*12	*68
Guyane française	2004	..	*11	..	..	1	*12	*64
	2005	..	*11	..	..	1	*12	*63
	2006	..	*12	..	..	1	*13	*65
Guyana	2003	..	21	..	..	17	38	50
Guyana	2004	..	20	..	..	18	38	50
	2005	..	21	..	..	19	39	52
	2006	..	21	..	..	19	40	52
Paraguay	2003	..	53	..	24	87	164	29
Paraguay	2004	..	54	..	25	87	166	29
	2005	..	50	..	27	86	162	28
	2006	..	52	..	29	79	160	27
Peru	2003	31	289	26	67	115	527	20
Pérou	2004	36	331	40	63	108	579	21
	2005	38	287	68	72	105	570	21
	2006	31	335	78	77	110	631	23
Suriname	2003	..	25	..	3	1	28	58
Suriname	2004	..	25	..	3	1	29	58
	2005	..	26	..	3	1	30	60
	2006	..	27	..	3	1	31	61
Uruguay	2003	0	54	2	28	21	105	31
Uruguay	2004	0	68	4	26	21	119	36
	2005	0	68	4	27	21	120	36
	2006	0	80	4	23	23	130	39

Table 4

Total energy requirement
Besoins énergétiques totales
Thousand terajoules and gigajoules per capita
Milliers de térajoules et gigajoules par habitant

Country or area Pays ou zone	Year Année	Solids Solides	Liquids Liquides	Gases Gaz	Primary electricity Électricité primaire	Traditional fuels Combustibles traditionnels	Requirement Besoins	
							Total Totale	Per capita Par habitant
Venezuela(Bolivar. Rep.)	2003	2	913	1054	219	72	2259	88
Venezuela(Rép. bolivar.)	2004	0	969	1039	252	77	2337	89
	2005	2	1091	1058	268	78	2496	94
	2006	2	1360	1089	284	79	2813	104
Asia	**2003**	**57514**	**44364**	**25845**	**4248**	**15923**	**147895**	**39**
Asie	**2004**	**65659**	**47458**	**27101**	**4743**	**15823**	**160784**	**42**
	2005	**71399**	**48131**	**28930**	**5100**	**15946**	**169506**	**44**
	2006	**76860**	**48172**	**30877**	**5411**	**16246**	**177566**	**45**
Afghanistan	2003	1	*6	0	3	15	25	1
Afghanistan	2004	1	8	0	2	16	27	1
	2005	*1	*8	0	*3	16	28	1
	2006	*1	*8	0	*3	16	28	1
Armenia	2003	1	13	45	13	1	73	19
Arménie	2004	0	13	50	13	1	77	24
	2005	0	14	62	13	0	90	28
	2006	0	13	64	15	1	92	29
Azerbaijan	2003	..	160	347	15	0	521	63
Azerbaïdjan	2004	..	176	379	15	0	570	69
	2005	..	196	379	15	0	590	70
	2006	..	179	416	12	0	607	72
Bahrain	2003	..	57	264	..	0	321	465
Bahreïn	2004	..	60	274	..	0	334	473
	2005	..	69	291	..	0	360	496
	2006	..	79	308	..	0	387	522
Bangladesh	2003	15	141	435	4	583	1177	9
Bangladesh	2004	15	141	468	4	587	1214	9
	2005	15	158	503	5	593	1273	9
	2006	15	152	543	5	598	1313	9
Bhutan	2003	2	*2	..	2	40	47	76
Bhoutan	2004	1	*2	..	3	41	47	76
	2005	2	*2	..	3	42	48	76
	2006	2	*2	..	3	42	48	74
Brunei Darussalam	2003	..	47	59	..	1	107	306
Brunéi Darussalam	2004	..	52	66	..	1	119	330
	2005	..	50	67	..	1	117	317
	2006	..	52	66	..	1	119	311
Cambodia	2003	..	44	..	0	90	134	10
Cambodge	2004	..	49	..	0	88	138	10
	2005	..	52	..	0	87	140	10
	2006	..	57	..	1	87	145	10
China	2003	33953	8409	1627	1151	2280	47420	37
Chine	2004	40101	10110	1454	1422	2238	55326	43
	2005	45149	10272	1788	1598	2177	60984	47
	2006	49123	10629	1891	1761	2148	65553	50
China, Hong Kong SAR	2003	240	188	59	27	1	516	76
Chine, Hong-Kong RAS	2004	220	171	86	24	1	502	74
	2005	245	170	86	23	1	525	77
	2006	240	148	91	23	1	503	73
China, Macao SAR	2003	..	26	..	1	0	26	59
Chine, Macao RAS	2004	..	31	..	1	0	31	67
	2005	..	32	..	1	0	33	68
	2006	..	31	..	3	0	34	68

Table 4

Total energy requirement
Besoins énergétiques totales
Thousand terajoules and gigajoules per capita
Milliers de térajoules et gigajoules par habitant

Country or area Pays ou zone	Year Année	Solids Solides	Liquids Liquides	Gases Gaz	Primary electricity Électricité primaire	Traditional fuels Combustibles traditionnels	Requirement Besoins	
							Total Totale	Per capita Par habitant
Cyprus	2003	2	92	0	0	1	94	130
Chypre	2004	2	86	0	0	1	88	120
	2005	2	88	0	0	1	90	119
	2006	2	92	0	0	1	94	122
Georgia	2003	1	22	36	27	27	113	26
Géorgie	2004	0	22	42	26	27	118	27
	2005	1	28	50	27	27	133	31
	2006	1	29	64	22	27	143	32
India	2003	9642	3527	1016	341	7093	21619	20
Inde	2004	10311	3722	1008	372	6953	22367	21
	2005	10878	3768	1025	433	7051	23155	21
	2006	11635	3951	1005	485	7304	24381	22
Indonesia	2003	455	2277	1283	55	2206	6277	29
Indonésie	2004	650	2492	1398	59	2219	6817	31
	2005	744	2491	1386	63	2223	6907	31
	2006	937	2271	1461	59	2275	7002	32
Iran(Islamic Rep. of)	2003	54	2807	3170	42	22	6095	92
Iran(Rép. islamique)	2004	47	3009	3516	39	25	6636	98
	2005	53	3313	3727	55	24	7173	105
	2006	57	3476	4096	65	23	7717	109
Iraq	2003	..	862	59	2	2	925	35
Iraq	2004	..	1015	99	7	2	1122	41
	2005	..	1063	101	7	2	1172	43
	2006	..	1067	133	6	2	1208	42
Israel	2003	375	480	0	-5	0	851	127
Israël	2004	381	460	44	-5	0	880	129
	2005	359	464	60	-6	0	877	127
	2006	385	478	84	-7	0	941	133
Japan	2003	4833	8541	3323	1254	254	18206	144
Japon	2004	5285	8457	3290	1405	253	18690	148
	2005	5159	8408	3290	1426	272	18555	147
	2006	5222	7917	3608	1454	297	18498	147
Jordan	2003	..	215	10	1	3	229	44
Jordanie	2004	..	201	56	3	3	263	52
	2005	..	212	64	3	3	283	52
	2006	..	201	84	2	3	290	52
Kazakhstan	2003	1117	304	557	26	3	2007	135
Kazakhstan	2004	1155	376	643	21	3	2198	146
	2005	1181	374	811	30	3	2400	158
	2006	1269	424	873	31	3	2600	170
Korea, Dem.Ppl's.Rep.	2003	790	46	..	42	47	925	39
Corée,Rép.pop.dém.de	2004	808	46	..	45	47	946	40
	2005	853	39	..	47	48	986	42
	2006	875	30	..	45	48	997	42
Korea, Republic of	2003	2086	2923	1027	492	74	6603	138
Corée, République de	2004	2176	2704	1180	492	82	6634	138
	2005	2187	2568	1277	548	89	6667	138
	2006	2244	2388	1345	555	97	6629	137
Kuwait	2003	..	708	430	..	0	1138	489
Koweït	2004	..	780	463	..	0	1242	520
	2005	..	850	519	..	0	1369	557
	2006	..	792	549	..	0	1341	531

Table 4

Total energy requirement
Besoins énergétiques totales
Thousand terajoules and gigajoules per capita
Milliers de térajoules et gigajoules par habitant

Country or area Pays ou zone	Year Année	Solids Solides	Liquids Liquides	Gases Gaz	Primary electricity Électricité primaire	Traditional fuels Combustibles traditionnels	Requirement Besoins	
							Total Totale	Per capita Par habitant
Kyrgyzstan	2003	25	19	29	43	0	115	23
Kirghizistan	2004	23	23	31	39	0	117	23
	2005	22	25	29	42	0	117	23
	2006	20	24	30	45	0	118	23
Lao People's Dem. Rep.	2003	*9	*6	..	0	55	70	12
Rép. dém. pop. lao	2004	*10	*6	..	*2	55	72	12
	2005	*10	*6	..	*2	55	73	13
	2006	*10	*6	..	*2	55	73	13
Lebanon	2003	6	229	..	2	1	239	61
Liban	2004	6	197	..	5	2	209	53
	2005	6	204	..	5	1	217	54
	2006	6	172	..	6	1	185	46
Malaysia	2003	223	820	1258	21	35	2357	94
Malaisie	2004	389	872	1204	19	34	2518	98
	2005	317	885	1303	11	34	2550	98
	2006	327	882	1479	16	33	2737	103
Maldives	2003	..	8	..	..	4	12	43
Maldives	2004	..	10	..	..	5	16	54
	2005	..	9	..	..	5	14	48
	2006	..	12	..	..	7	19	65
Mongolia	2003	69	22	..	1	4	96	38
Mongolie	2004	73	24	..	1	4	103	41
	2005	76	24	..	1	4	105	41
	2006	80	27	..	1	4	113	44
Myanmar	2003	4	72	62	8	431	578	11
Myanmar	2004	4	75	71	9	436	595	11
	2005	4	79	80	11	440	614	11
	2006	5	70	83	12	442	612	11
Nepal	2003	9	29	2	8	156	203	8
Népal	2004	8	27	2	9	157	202	8
	2005	12	27	2	10	157	208	8
	2006	12	28	2	10	158	210	8
Occup. Palestinian Terr.	2003	0	18	..	8	4	30	9
Terr. palestiniens occup.	2004	0	26	..	9	5	40	11
	2005	0	39	..	*10	4	53	14
	2006	0	*42	..	*10	*4	*56	*14
Oman	2003	..	139	337	..	0	475	203
Oman	2004	..	140	313	..	0	454	188
	2005	..	151	327	..	0	478	190
	2006	..	181	436	..	0	617	239
Other Asia	2003	1498	1171	336	165	19	3189	141
Autre Asie	2004	1558	1169	414	166	22	3329	147
	2005	1612	1183	401	173	38	3407	150
	2006	1688	1200	452	173	38	3551	156
Pakistan	2003	111	574	1024	104	490	2303	16
Pakistan	2004	187	657	1116	103	507	2570	17
	2005	179	660	1171	121	471	2601	17
	2006	195	749	1182	124	478	2728	17
Philippines	2003	180	601	101	64	425	1371	17
Philippines	2004	207	617	97	68	445	1433	17
	2005	200	583	128	66	439	1414	17
	2006	*204	508	116	74	446	1348	15

Table 4

Total energy requirement
Besoins énergétiques totales
Thousand terajoules and gigajoules per capita
Milliers de térajoules et gigajoules par habitant

Country or area Pays ou zone	Year Année	Solids Solides	Liquids Liquides	Gases Gaz	Primary electricity Électricité primaire	Traditional fuels Combustibles traditionnels	Requirement Besoins	
							Total Totale	Per capita Par habitant
Qatar	2003	..	74	485	..	0	559	763
Qatar	2004	..	78	581	..	0	659	848
	2005	..	94	753	..	0	847	1042
	2006	..	110	745	..	0	855	913
Saudi Arabia	2003	..	3029	1991	..	1	5021	228
Arabie saoudite	2004	..	3418	2163	..	1	5582	247
	2005	..	3549	2377	..	1	5927	256
	2006	..	3731	2495	..	1	6228	263
Singapore	2003	0	351	209	..	1	561	134
Singapour	2004	0	319	246	..	1	567	134
	2005	0	342	276	..	1	620	143
	2006	0	328	280	..	1	609	136
Sri Lanka	2003	3	133	..	12	53	201	10
Sri Lanka	2004	3	151	..	11	52	217	11
	2005	3	145	..	12	53	213	11
	2006	3	145	..	17	53	218	11
Syrian Arab Republic	2003	0	432	258	10	0	700	40
Rép. arabe syrienne	2004	0	456	268	15	0	740	41
	2005	0	491	230	12	0	734	40
	2006	0	507	238	14	0	760	41
Tajikistan	2003	1	51	21	59	..	133	20
Tadjikistan	2004	2	55	22	60	..	139	21
	2005	3	59	22	62	..	146	21
	2006	3	67	23	62	..	154	22
Thailand	2003	556	1470	1001	34	700	3761	59
Thaïlande	2004	622	1674	1017	33	707	4053	63
	2005	602	1637	1099	34	788	4160	64
	2006	609	1612	1117	45	756	4139	63
Timor-Leste	2003	..	*4	..	..	..	*4	*4
Timor-Leste	2004	..	*4	..	..	..	*4	*4
	2005	..	*4	..	..	..	*4	*4
	2006	..	*4	..	..	..	*4	*4
Turkey	2003	926	1073	825	130	245	3199	46
Turquie	2004	948	1070	871	164	235	3288	46
	2005	1069	1051	1061	139	227	3546	49
	2006	1197	1046	1209	154	219	3824	52
Turkmenistan	2003	..	184	597	-4	0	778	166
Turkménistan	2004	..	178	534	-4	0	708	149
	2005	..	182	570	-5	0	748	155
	2006	..	211	573	-5	0	779	159
United Arab Emirates	2003	..	902	1468	..	1	2370	667
Emirats arabes unis	2004	..	922	1514	..	1	2437	648
	2005	..	935	1537	..	1	2473	602
	2006	..	966	1571	..	1	2537	600
Uzbekistan	2003	21	410	1966	23	0	2420	94
Ouzbékistan	2004	30	383	1909	23	0	2346	89
	2005	33	310	1852	22	0	2216	83
	2006	34	292	1934	22	0	2283	85
Viet Nam	2003	305	429	126	68	547	1476	18
Viet Nam	2004	437	494	215	64	557	1766	22
	2005	425	527	229	77	559	1817	22
	2006	461	524	232	85	566	1869	22

Table 4

Total energy requirement
Besoins énergétiques totales
Thousand terajoules and gigajoules per capita
Milliers de térajoules et gigajoules par habitant

Country or area Pays ou zone	Year Année	Solids Solides	Liquids Liquides	Gases Gaz	Primary electricity Électricité primaire	Traditional fuels Combustibles traditionnels	Requirement Besoins	
							Total Totale	Per capita Par habitant
Yemen	2003	..	217	..	..	7	225	12
Yémen	2004	..	227	..	..	8	235	12
	2005	..	241	..	..	8	249	12
	2006	..	260	..	..	8	268	13
Europe	**2003**	**19934**	**31896**	**40324**	**7165**	**3674**	**102993**	**142**
Europe	**2004**	**19625**	**31907**	**41097**	**7430**	**3883**	**103942**	**143**
	2005	**19155**	**31769**	**41799**	**7458**	**3896**	**104077**	**143**
	2006	**19730**	**32650**	**41480**	**7467**	**4090**	**105417**	**144**
Albania	2003	1	40	1	22	2	65	18
Albanie	2004	1	50	1	20	2	74	24
	2005	1	45	1	21	2	69	22
	2006	1	44	1	20	2	67	21
Austria	2003	175	520	354	149	118	1314	163
Autriche	2004	167	518	357	155	122	1319	162
	2005	171	537	383	153	122	1368	167
	2006	169	533	349	167	130	1347	163
Belarus	2003	27	207	712	25	15	986	100
Bélarus	2004	23	215	773	12	15	1038	106
	2005	23	213	788	15	15	1054	108
	2006	22	240	803	16	17	1096	113
Belgium	2003	260	766	672	199	128	2024	195
Belgique	2004	256	752	681	205	129	2023	195
	2005	230	730	660	201	129	1949	187
	2006	200	746	701	212	132	1990	189
Bosnia and Herzegovina	2003	206	40	8	13	6	273	71
Bosnie y Herzégovine	2004	212	47	12	15	7	292	76
	2005	230	44	14	17	7	311	81
	2006	246	47	15	13	7	328	85
Bulgaria	2003	302	144	117	54	22	639	82
Bulgarie	2004	292	152	117	51	29	641	82
	2005	286	163	131	57	28	665	86
	2006	292	167	136	59	30	684	89
Croatia	2003	32	214	110	32	16	404	91
Croatie	2004	34	190	114	39	16	394	89
	2005	33	198	111	42	15	398	90
	2006	31	198	109	42	18	398	90
Czech Republic	2003	783	269	366	41	58	1517	149
République tchèque	2004	771	284	365	47	70	1538	151
	2005	754	293	362	55	72	1535	150
	2006	767	291	356	60	79	1553	151
Denmark	2003	239	304	221	-11	87	840	159
Danemark	2004	184	300	220	13	91	808	150
	2005	157	284	209	29	96	774	143
	2006	230	290	215	-3	96	828	152
Estonia	2003	148	36	32	-7	20	229	170
Estonie	2004	148	37	36	-6	23	239	177
	2005	142	37	37	-6	23	234	174
	2006	134	37	38	-2	21	228	170
Faeroe Islands	2003	..	*9	..	0	..	*9	*196
Iles Féroé	2004	..	*9	..	0	..	*9	*195
	2005	..	*9	..	0	..	*9	*196
	2006	..	*9	..	0	..	*9	*196

Table 4

Total energy requirement
Besoins énergétiques totales
Thousand terajoules and gigajoules per capita
Milliers de térajoules et gigajoules par habitant

Country or area Pays ou zone	Year Année	Solids Solides	Liquids Liquides	Gases Gaz	Primary electricity Électricité primaire	Traditional fuels Combustibles traditionnels	Requirement Besoins	
							Total Totale	Per capita Par habitant
Finland	2003	352	459	191	134	305	1441	276
Finlande	2004	322	492	185	154	311	1464	280
	2005	208	483	169	195	290	1346	256
	2006	318	518	182	165	323	1507	286
France incl. Monaco	2003	620	3189	1838	1584	476	7706	128
France y compris Monaco	2004	597	3223	1876	1629	478	7803	129
	2005	619	3159	1920	1617	477	7792	128
	2006	571	3274	1853	1622	466	7786	127
Germany	2003	3494	4435	3720	740	439	12826	155
Allemagne	2004	3522	4363	3704	786	486	12862	156
	2005	3359	4289	3817	769	457	12693	154
	2006	3374	4423	3768	758	530	12854	156
Gibraltar	2003	..	5	..	..	..	5	179
Gibraltar	2004	..	5	..	..	..	5	185
	2005	..	5	..	..	..	5	191
	2006	..	5	..	..	..	5	185
Greece	2003	373	784	96	30	22	1306	118
Grèce	2004	382	759	105	33	25	1305	118
	2005	376	793	111	38	25	1343	121
	2006	344	816	129	45	21	1355	122
Hungary	2003	156	253	554	65	38	1067	105
Hongrie	2004	141	254	546	71	42	1054	104
	2005	128	285	564	73	45	1095	109
	2006	125	299	534	75	49	1082	107
Iceland	2003	4	25	9	31	0	68	236
Islande	2004	4	25	9	31	0	70	238
	2005	4	25	9	31	0	69	232
	2006	3	26	10	36	0	75	246
Ireland	2003	117	309	171	9	5	611	154
Irlande	2004	105	324	171	12	5	617	153
	2005	122	302	163	15	7	609	147
	2006	109	314	188	16	7	634	150
Italy and San Marino	2003	639	3675	2970	367	101	7753	135
Italie y comp. St. Marin	2004	720	3418	3085	370	129	7722	133
	2005	711	3329	3300	359	138	7838	134
	2006	718	3304	3234	349	155	7760	132
Latvia	2003	3	47	63	18	25	156	67
Lettonie	2004	2	44	62	19	30	157	68
	2005	3	42	64	20	31	159	69
	2006	2	53	66	19	37	177	77
Lithuania	2003	9	90	112	32	23	265	77
Lituanie	2004	9	93	111	32	23	268	78
	2005	9	99	117	29	22	277	81
	2006	13	107	116	33	23	292	86
Luxembourg	2003	3	95	50	17	2	167	370
Luxembourg	2004	4	106	56	15	2	183	399
	2005	3	111	55	15	2	186	400
	2006	5	107	58	16	2	188	397
Malta	2003	..	34	..	..	0	34	84
Malte	2004	..	35	..	..	0	35	87
	2005	..	35	..	..	0	35	86
	2006	..	34	..	..	0	34	84

Table 4

Total energy requirement
Besoins énergétiques totales
Thousand terajoules and gigajoules per capita
Milliers de térajoules et gigajoules par habitant

Country or area Pays ou zone	Year Année	Solids Solides	Liquids Liquides	Gases Gaz	Primary electricity Électricité primaire	Traditional fuels Combustibles traditionnels	Requirement Besoins	
							Total Totale	Per capita Par habitant
Netherlands	2003	357	1741	1680	81	57	3916	242
Pays-Bas	2004	349	1667	1715	79	59	3869	238
	2005	335	1647	1648	88	60	3779	232
	2006	314	1661	1602	100	60	3737	229
Norway,Svlbd.J.Myn. I	2003	33	428	249	412	24	1145	250
Norvège,Svalbd,J.May	2004	39	416	237	436	24	1151	250
	2005	32	432	241	450	22	1178	254
	2006	30	498	222	437	22	1208	259
Poland	2003	2428	747	525	-24	186	3863	101
Pologne	2004	2387	804	555	-20	191	3918	103
	2005	2318	807	571	-26	196	3866	101
	2006	2439	864	578	-28	220	4074	107
Portugal	2003	142	518	123	70	116	968	93
Portugal	2004	143	525	154	63	118	1003	96
	2005	143	533	175	50	124	1024	97
	2006	147	463	170	72	124	976	92
Republic of Moldova	2003	4	25	104	13	3	148	41
Rép. de Moldova	2004	4	27	107	11	3	150	42
	2005	3	27	114	12	3	159	44
	2006	4	26	105	13	3	152	42
Romania	2003	340	369	685	58	46	1498	69
Roumanie	2004	340	348	648	75	49	1461	67
	2005	331	355	649	82	40	1458	67
	2006	358	362	680	71	37	1508	70
Russian Federation	2003	3786	4891	15953	1062	541	26233	181
Fédération de Russie	2004	3664	4967	16142	1135	587	26495	184
	2005	3642	4975	16280	1124	572	26592	186
	2006	3760	5181	16702	1139	585	27367	192
Serbia	2003	374	120	85	46	38	662	63
Serbie	2004	388	135	108	39	38	707	67
	2005	336	142	90	36	38	642	61
	2006	361	154	93	37	38	682	65
Slovakia	2003	177	114	266	69	16	642	119
Slovaquie	2004	172	128	258	70	18	647	120
	2005	160	131	276	69	20	656	122
	2006	172	125	253	73	20	643	119
Slovenia	2003	55	97	42	31	5	230	115
Slovénie	2004	56	98	42	32	8	236	118
	2005	54	100	43	32	10	240	120
	2006	54	103	42	33	11	244	121
Spain	2003	853	2386	1004	429	179	4851	115
Espagne	2004	916	2457	1183	399	186	5141	120
	2005	892	2550	1402	362	190	5395	124
	2006	791	2544	1457	394	194	5381	122
Sweden	2003	110	525	43	484	343	1505	168
Suède	2004	122	521	43	491	343	1519	169
	2005	108	502	40	500	367	1517	168
	2006	110	503	42	489	386	1530	168
Switzerland	2003	6	453	126	221	69	874	119
Suisse	2004	6	451	130	222	80	889	119
	2005	6	457	133	226	90	913	122
	2006	6	467	130	228	96	926	124

Table 4

Total energy requirement
Besoins énergétiques totales
Thousand terajoules and gigajoules per capita
Milliers de térajoules et gigajoules par habitant

Country or area Pays ou zone	Year Année	Solids Solides	Liquids Liquides	Gases Gaz	Primary electricity Électricité primaire	Traditional fuels Combustibles traditionnels	Requirement Besoins	
							Total Totale	Per capita Par habitant
T.F.Yug.Rep. Macedonia	2003	87	34	3	8	6	139	69
L'ex-RY Macédoine	2004	86	34	3	10	6	139	68
	2005	85	36	3	11	6	141	69
	2006	79	37	3	12	7	139	68
Ukraine	2003	1554	545	3029	309	72	5509	115
Ukraine	2004	1383	571	3064	337	74	5430	115
	2005	1416	586	3138	335	73	5548	118
	2006	1535	620	2710	334	74	5273	113
United Kingdom	2003	1686	2954	4042	353	68	9103	153
Royaume-Uni	2004	1673	3061	4122	349	66	9271	155
	2005	1723	2979	4010	363	83	9157	152
	2006	1894	3160	3834	344	68	9300	153
Oceania	**2003**	**2124**	**1836**	**1228**	**164**	**448**	**5800**	**179**
Océanie	**2004**	**2154**	**1847**	**1236**	**176**	**461**	**5875**	**179**
	2005	**2302**	**1925**	**1246**	**166**	**454**	**6092**	**183**
	2006	**2333**	**1919**	**1267**	**171**	**427**	**6117**	**181**
Australia	2003	2066	1456	1041	61	340	4963	249
Australie	2004	2096	1448	1070	60	350	5024	249
	2005	2240	1533	1085	60	342	5260	258
	2006	2271	1532	1101	64	315	5284	255
Cook Islands	2003	..	0	..	..	..	0	26
Iles Cook	2004	..	1	..	..	..	1	38
	2005	..	1	..	..	..	1	42
	2006	..	*1	..	..	..	*1	*42
Fiji	2003	0	22	..	*2	9	33	40
Fidji	2004	0	25	..	*2	9	37	44
	2005	0	22	..	*2	8	33	39
	2006	0	21	..	*2	9	32	38
French Polynesia	2003	..	11	..	0	0	12	47
Polynésie française	2004	..	11	..	1	0	11	45
	2005	..	12	..	0	0	12	48
	2006	..	11	..	1	0	12	46
Kiribati	2003	..	0	..	..	..	0	*4
Kiribati	2004	..	0	..	..	..	0	*3
	2005	..	0	..	..	..	0	*3
	2006	..	0	..	..	..	0	*4
Marshall Islands	2003	..	*1	..	..	..	*1	*21
Îles Marshall	2004	..	*1	..	..	..	*1	*21
	2005	..	*1	..	..	..	*1	*20
	2006	..	*1	..	..	..	*1	*21
Nauru	2003	..	*2	..	..	..	*2	*153
Nauru	2004	..	*2	..	..	..	*2	*150
	2005	..	*2	..	..	..	*2	*148
	2006	..	*2	..	..	..	*2	*145
New Caledonia	2003	9	26	..	1	0	36	157
Nouvelle-Calédonie	2004	8	24	..	1	0	33	144
	2005	8	28	..	1	0	37	158
	2006	8	29	..	2	0	39	164
New Zealand	2003	49	255	181	96	38	619	154
Nouvelle-Zélande	2004	49	265	162	109	40	626	154
	2005	54	262	151	98	42	607	148
	2006	54	257	155	99	41	605	146

Table 4

Total energy requirement
Besoins énergétiques totales
Thousand terajoules and gigajoules per capita
Milliers de térajoules et gigajoules par habitant

Country or area Pays ou zone	Year Année	Solids Solides	Liquids Liquides	Gases Gaz	Primary electricity Électricité primaire	Traditional fuels Combustibles traditionnels	Requirement Besoins	
							Total Totale	Per capita Par habitant
Niue	2003	..	0	..	..	..	0	*24
Nioué	2004	..	0	..	..	..	0	*24
	2005	..	0	..	..	..	0	*25
	2006	..	0	..	..	..	0	*26
Palau	2003	..	*3	..	0	..	*3	*132
Palaos	2004	..	*3	..	0	..	*3	*129
	2005	..	*3	..	0	..	*3	*130
	2006	..	*3	..	0	..	*3	*133
Papua New Guinea	2003	..	51	6	3	57	116	20
Papouasie-Nvl-Guinée	2004	..	58	4	3	57	123	21
	2005	..	53	10	3	57	123	20
	2006	..	53	11	3	57	124	20
Samoa	2003	..	*2	..	0	1	*3	*16
Samoa	2004	..	*2	..	0	1	*3	*16
	2005	..	*2	..	0	1	*3	*17
	2006	..	*2	..	0	1	*3	*16
Solomon Islands	2003	..	*2	..	..	*3	*6	*13
Iles Salomon	2004	..	*2	..	..	*3	*6	*12
	2005	..	*2	..	..	*3	*6	*12
	2006	..	*2	..	..	*3	*6	*12
Tonga	2003	..	2	..	..	0	2	24
Tonga	2004	..	2	..	..	0	2	24
	2005	..	*2	..	..	0	*2	*23
	2006	..	*2	..	..	0	*2	*24
Vanuatu	2003	..	*1	..	..	1	*2	*10
Vanuatu	2004	..	*1	..	..	1	*2	*10
	2005	..	*1	..	..	1	*2	*10
	2006	..	*1	..	..	1	*2	*10
Wallis and Futuna Is	2003	..	0	..	..	..	0	*23
Iles Wallis et Futuna	2004	..	0	..	..	..	0	24
	2005	..	0	..	..	..	0	23
	2006	..	0	..	..	..	0	22

Table 5

Production, trade and consumption of solid fuels
Production, commerce et consommation de combustibles solides
Thousand metric tons of coal equivalent and kilograms per capita
Milliers de tonnes métriques d'équivalent houille et kilogrammes par habitant

Table Notes:
Production
Production of Coal, lignite, oil shale and peat.

Imports
Import of Coal, lignite, peat, coke oven coke, gas coke, brown coal coke, hard coal briquettes, lignite-brown coal briquettes and peat briquettes.

Exports
Export of Coal, lignite, peat coke oven coke, gas coke, brown coal coke, hard coal briquettes, lignite-brown coal briquettes and peat briquettes.

Stock change
Coal, lignite, peat, coke oven coke, gas coke, brown coal coke, hard coal briquettes, lignite-brown coal briquettes and peat briquettes.

- **Please refer to the Definitions Section on pages xv to xxix for the appropriate product description/ classification.**

Notes relatives aux tableaux:
Production
Production de houille, lignite, schiste bitumineux et tourbe.

Importations
Importation de houille, lignite, tourbe, coke de four, coke de gaz, coke de lignite, briquettes de houille, briquettes de lignite et briquettes de tourbe.

Exportations
Exportation de houille, lignite, tourbe, coke de four, coke de gaz, coke de lignite, briquettes de houille, briquettes de lignite et briquettes de tourbe.

Variations de stocks
Houille, lignite, tourbe, coke de four, coke de gaz, coke de lignite, briquettes de houille, briquettes de lignite et briquettes de tourbe.

- **Veuillez consulter la section "définitions" de la page xv à la page xxix pour une description/classification appropriée des produits.**

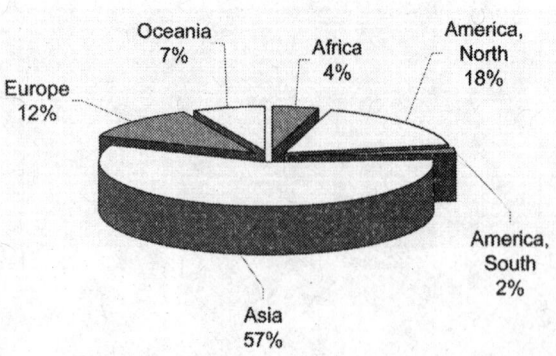

Figure 12: World solid fuel production, by region, in 2006

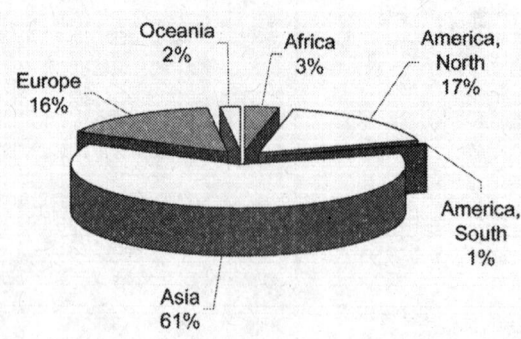

Figure 13: World solid fuel consumption, by region, in 2006

Table 5

Production, trade and consumption of solid fuels
Production, commerce et consommation de combustibles solides

Thousand metric tons of coal equivalent and kilograms per capita
Milliers de tonnes métriques d'équivalent houille et kilogrammes par habitant

Country or area Pays ou zone	Year Année	Production Production	Imports Importations	Exports Exportations	Changes in stocks Variations des stocks	Consumption Consommation	
						Total Totale	Per capita Par habitant
World	**2003**	**3495641**	**699991**	**637583**	**-21880**	**3579930**	**571**
Monde	**2004**	**3786749**	**768112**	**683341**	**-8218**	**3879739**	**612**
	2005	**4037026**	**768478**	**726351**	**7305**	**4071848**	**634**
	2006	**4254146**	**825131**	**785924**	**24645**	**4268709**	**655**
Africa	**2003**	**185229**	**8780**	**54926**	**1300**	**137783**	**163**
Afrique	**2004**	**188273**	**10546**	**52286**	**-1518**	**148051**	**170**
	2005	**190156**	**11801**	**54880**	**-123**	**147199**	**166**
	2006	**189914**	**11126**	**53327**	**87**	**147627**	**161**
Algeria	2003	..	617	..	*-471	1087	34
Algérie	2004	..	956	..	*208	748	23
	2005	..	743	..	-177	920	28
	2006	..	1058	..	10	1048	31
Burundi	2003	2	..	..	..	2	0
Burundi	2004	2	..	..	..	2	0
	2005	2	..	..	..	2	0
	2006	*2	..	..	..	*2	0
Dem. Rep. of Congo	2003	105	226	..	..	331	6
Rép. dem. du Congo	2004	108	250	..	..	358	6
	2005	120	256	..	..	376	7
	2006	124	273	..	..	397	7
Egypt	2003	32	937	408	..	561	8
Egypte	2004	29	1663	416	..	1276	18
	2005	29	1663	416	..	1276	18
	2006	22	1589	496	..	1115	15
Kenya	2003	..	93	..	..	93	3
Kenya	2004	..	108	..	..	108	3
	2005	..	108	..	..	108	3
	2006	..	120	..	..	120	3
Madagascar	2003	..	*10	..	..	*10	*1
Madagascar	2004	..	*10	..	..	*10	*1
	2005	..	*10	..	..	*10	*1
	2006	..	*10	..	..	*10	*1
Malawi	2003	66	2	15	..	53	5
Malawi	2004	*70	*2	*15	..	*57	*5
	2005	45	*30	*15	..	60	5
	2006	*55	*5	*10	..	*50	*4
Mauritius	2003	..	289	..	-27	316	261
Maurice	2004	..	332	..	43	289	237
	2005	..	379	..	15	364	293
	2006	..	490	..	6	484	386
Morocco	2003	..	4611	..	..	4611	160
Maroc	2004	..	5159	..	..	5159	173
	2005	..	6364	..	..	6364	211
	2006	..	5541	..	..	5541	182
Mozambique	2003	37	..	15	22	0	0
Mozambique	2004	17	..	30	-13	0	0
	2005	3	..	10	-7	0	0
	2006	41	..	21	20	0	0
Niger	2003	148	..	..	..	148	13
Niger	2004	157	..	..	..	157	13
	2005	143	..	..	..	143	11
	2006	*144	..	..	..	*144	*11

Table 5

Production, trade and consumption of solid fuels
Production, commerce et consommation de combustibles solides
Thousand metric tons of coal equivalent and kilograms per capita
Milliers de tonnes métriques d'équivalent houille et kilogrammes par habitant

Country or area Pays ou zone	Year Année	Production Production	Imports Importations	Exports Exportations	Changes in stocks Variations des stocks	Consumption Consommation Total Totale	Consumption Consommation Per capita Par habitant
Nigeria	2003	23	*3	..	..	26	0
Nigéria	2004	3	*3	..	..	6	0
	2005	8	*3	..	..	11	0
	2006	8	*3	..	..	11	0
Senegal	2003	..	*120	..	..	*120	*12
Sénégal	2004	..	127	..	..	127	12
	2005	..	152	..	..	152	14
	2006	..	167	..	..	167	15
South Africa Customs Un.	2003	181024	1811	54277	1690	126869	2485
Un.douan.d'Afr.mérid	2004	184210	1898	51610	-1831	136329	2562
	2005	185904	2041	54250	*-19	133714	2497
	2006	185785	1822	52609	*5	134993	2492
Tunisia	2003	..	23	..	..	23	2
Tunisie	2004	..	0	..	..	0	0
	2005	..	0	..	..	0	0
	2006	..	0	..	..	0	0
United Rep.Tanzania	2003	55	..	..	..	55	2
Rép. Unie de Tanzanie	2004	65	..	..	..	65	2
	2005	75	..	..	..	75	2
	2006	80	..	..	..	80	2
Zambia	2003	186	..	5	60	121	11
Zambie	2004	196	..	9	58	129	12
	2005	206	..	10	60	136	12
	2006	206	..	10	51	144	12
Zimbabwe	2003	3550	39	206	26	3357	259
Zimbabwe	2004	3415	39	206	17	3231	248
	2005	3621	52	179	6	3488	266
	2006	3447	49	180	-5	3321	251
America, North	**2003**	**687690**	**45400**	**54744**	**-19746**	**698092**	**1391**
Amérique du Nord	**2004**	**723632**	**47276**	**60424**	**-7725**	**718209**	**1416**
	2005	**736056**	**48977**	**64206**	**-4395**	**725222**	**1416**
	2006	**748817**	**53029**	**63498**	**23662**	**714687**	**1383**
Bahamas	2003	..	*3	..	..	*3	*9
Bahamas	2004	..	*3	..	..	*3	*10
	2005	..	*3	..	..	*3	*9
	2006	..	*4	..	..	*4	*12
Canada	2003	43414	16441	24665	-2360	37549	1185
Canada	2004	46603	14596	25461	-961	36699	1147
	2005	45582	15610	27532	-2256	35916	1112
	2006	46749	14325	26797	-969	35247	1080
Costa Rica	2003	..	143	..	..	143	35
Costa Rica	2004	..	118	..	..	118	28
	2005	..	86	..	..	86	20
	2006	..	117	..	..	117	27
Cuba	2003	..	38	..	*12	26	2
Cuba	2004	..	38	..	*12	26	2
	2005	..	43	..	*10	33	3
	2006	..	40	..	*11	29	3
Dominican Republic	2003	..	1057	..	..	1057	118
Rép. dominicaine	2004	..	777	..	..	777	86
	2005	..	476	..	..	476	52
	2006	..	799	..	..	799	85

Table 5

Production, trade and consumption of solid fuels
Production, commerce et consommation de combustibles solides
Thousand metric tons of coal equivalent and kilograms per capita
Milliers de tonnes métriques d'équivalent houille et kilogrammes par habitant

Country or area Pays ou zone	Year Année	Production Production	Imports Importations	Exports Exportations	Changes in stocks Variations des stocks	Consumption Consommation Total Totale	Consumption Consommation Per capita Par habitant
El Salvador	2003	..	1	..	..	1	0
El Salvador	2004	..	1	..	..	1	0
	2005	..	2	..	..	2	0
	2006	..	1	..	..	1	0
Guatemala	2003	..	369	..	0	369	31
Guatemala	2004	..	416	..	0	416	34
	2005	..	408	..	0	408	32
	2006	..	268	..	-160	428	33
Honduras	2003	..	169	..	0	169	25
Honduras	2004	..	174	..	0	174	25
	2005	..	183	..	0	183	25
	2006	..	192	..	2	190	26
Jamaica	2003	..	85	..	..	85	32
Jamaïque	2004	..	66	..	..	66	25
	2005	..	60	..	..	60	23
	2006	..	32	..	..	32	12
Mexico	2003	4205	4028	2	177	8054	79
Mexique	2004	4348	2913	2	16	7243	70
	2005	4702	4170	2	203	8668	83
	2006	5022	4304	3	573	8750	83
Panama	2003	..	0	..	..	0	0
Panama	2004	..	2	..	..	2	1
	2005	..	2	..	..	2	1
	2006	..	2	..	..	2	1
United States	2003	640071	23067	30077	-17575	650636	2237
Etats-Unis	2004	672681	28172	34960	-6792	672684	2291
	2005	685772	27934	36672	-2351	679386	2292
	2006	697046	32945	36698	24205	669088	2242
America, South	**2003**	**56857**	**21644**	**49327**	**175**	**28999**	**80**
Amérique du Sud	**2004**	**60283**	**23434**	**54338**	**-666**	**30045**	**82**
	2005	**66600**	**23094**	**57169**	**1416**	**31109**	**84**
	2006	**72829**	**22557**	**65077**	**-739**	**31048**	**82**
Argentina	2003	75	848	194	-21	750	20
Argentine	2004	43	911	148	-22	828	22
	2005	21	1482	200	22	1282	33
	2006	360	940	227	-3	1075	28
Brazil	2003	2949	16810	..	32	19727	110
Brésil	2004	3431	16805	..	-282	20518	113
	2005	3970	16090	..	169	19891	108
	2006	3732	15527	..	-426	19685	105
Chile	2003	559	3090	63	92	3493	219
Chili	2004	182	4631	33	84	4696	292
	2005	528	4434	35	193	4733	290
	2006	384	5127	8	-137	5640	343
Colombia	2003	46452	0	42325	204	3923	88
Colombie	2004	49857	3	47413	-325	2772	61
	2005	54845	2	49795	1195	3857	84
	2006	60911	0	57560	-174	3525	75
Falkland Is. (Malvinas)	2003	*4	..	..	..	*4	*1331
Iles Falkland (Malvinas)	2004	*4	..	..	..	*4	*1327
	2005	*4	..	..	..	*4	*1212
	2006	*4	..	..	..	*4	*1210

Table 5

Production, trade and consumption of solid fuels
Production, commerce et consommation de combustibles solides

Thousand metric tons of coal equivalent and kilograms per capita
Milliers de tonnes métriques d'équivalent houille et kilogrammes par habitant

Country or area Pays ou zone	Year Année	Production Production	Imports Importations	Exports Exportations	Changes in stocks Variations des stocks	Consumption Consommation Total Totale	Consumption Consommation Per capita Par habitant
Peru	2003	16	894		-132	1042	39
Pérou	2004	22	1082		-121	1224	45
	2005	42	1084		-163	1289	47
	2006	105	961		1	1064	39
Uruguay	2003	..	2	..	..	2	1
Uruguay	2004	..	2	..	..	2	1
	2005	..	2	..	..	2	1
	2006	..	3	..	..	3	1
Venezuela(Bolivar. Rep.)	2003	6803	..	6744	..	59	2
Venezuela(Rép. bolivar.)	2004	6744	..	6744	..	0	0
	2005	7191	..	7139	..	52	2
	2006	7334	..	7282	..	52	2
Asia	**2003**	**1781001**	**383011**	**199185**	**2396**	**1962431**	**516**
Asie	**2004**	**2027049**	**430755**	**214784**	**2689**	**2240331**	**583**
	2005	**2240887**	**434323**	**234027**	**4992**	**2436191**	**627**
	2006	**2442400**	**464863**	**279328**	**5406**	**2622530**	**665**
Afghanistan	2003	35	..	..	..	35	2
Afghanistan	2004	34	..	..	..	34	1
	2005	*33	..	..	..	*33	*1
	2006	*33	..	..	..	*33	*1
Armenia	2003	..	27	..	..	27	7
Arménie	2004	..	0	..	..	0	0
	2005	..	0	..	..	0	0
	2006	..	1	..	..	1	0
Bangladesh	2003	..	500	..	..	500	4
Bangladesh	2004	..	500	..	..	500	4
	2005	..	500	..	..	500	4
	2006	..	500	..	..	500	4
Bhutan	2003	66	*25	*35	..	56	91
Bhoutan	2004	30	*40	20	..	50	80
	2005	85	*20	48.	..	57	90
	2006	98	*20	66	..	52	80
China	2003	1228770	11098	81376	-14	1158507	899
Chine	2004	1421661	18618	76402	-4409	1368286	1056
	2005	1573227	26175	63558	-4664	1540508	1182
	2006	1693300	38105	59183	-3909	1676130	1276
China, Hong Kong SAR	2003	..	8170	13	-47	8204	1205
Chine, Hong-Kong RAS	2004	..	8172	0	680	7492	1104
	2005	..	8273	0	-69	8343	1224
	2006	..	8716	0	526	8190	1194
Cyprus	2003	..	51	..	-2	53	74
Chypre	2004	..	39	..	-18	57	78
	2005	..	63	..	11	52	69
	2006	..	63	..	9	54	71
Georgia	2003	7	38	2	..	43	10
Géorgie	2004	7	5	2	..	10	2
	2005	4	23	0	..	27	6
	2006	9	19	3	..	26	6
India	2003	308544	23388	1525	1397	329009	308
Inde	2004	327029	28391	1278	2321	351822	326
	2005	347183	34328	1789	8565	371157	339
	2006	367263	40706	1680	9278	397011	355

Production, trade and consumption of solid fuels
Production, commerce et consommation de combustibles solides
Thousand metric tons of coal equivalent and kilograms per capita
Milliers de tonnes métriques d'équivalent houille et kilogrammes par habitant

Table 5

Country or area Pays ou zone	Year Année	Production Production	Imports Importations	Exports Exportations	Changes in stocks Variations des stocks	Consumption Consommation Total Totale	Consumption Consommation Per capita Par habitant
Indonesia	2003	105568	92	90131	0	15529	72
Indonésie	2004	127970	155	105527	437	22162	102
	2005	155248	161	129196	812	25401	116
	2006	204089	176	171551	749	31965	144
Iran(Islamic Rep. of)	2003	1232	627	21	..	1838	28
Iran(Rép. islamique)	2004	1246	470	120	..	1596	24
	2005	1330	520	40	..	1810	26
	2006	1520	460	50	..	1930	27
Israel	2003	137	12296	..	-371	12804	1914
Israël	2004	138	12802	..	-74	13014	1911
	2005	130	12686	..	561	12255	1768
	2006	142	12757	..	-235	13134	1864
Japan	2003	..	167295	2340	55	164900	1306
Japon	2004	..	182146	1833	-6	180319	1428
	2005	..	178032	1509	497	176027	1395
	2006	..	179448	1771	-490	178167	1412
Kazakhstan	2003	53281	1102	15659	606	38119	2557
Kazakhstan	2004	54568	1216	15884	496	39404	2625
	2005	54387	1166	15235	7	40310	2661
	2006	60387	967	18042	0	43312	2829
Korea, Dem.Ppl's.Rep.	2003	27352	353	755	..	26950	1149
Corée,Rép.pop.dém.de	2004	28775	361	1571	..	27565	1167
	2005	31512	381	2804	..	29089	1232
	2006	31929	391	2481	..	29839	1259
Korea, Republic of	2003	2120	68802	..	-267	71189	1488
Corée, République de	2004	2051	73604	..	1414	74241	1544
	2005	1820	71072	..	-1724	74616	1545
	2006	1815	73360	..	-1400	76575	1586
Kyrgyzstan	2003	176	684	20	..	840	167
Kirghizistan	2004	193	627	28	..	792	156
	2005	141	602	6	..	737	143
	2006	135	570	19	..	686	132
Lao People's Dem. Rep.	2003	*381	..	66	..	*315	*56
Rép. dém. pop. lao	2004	*405	..	*79	..	*327	*56
	2005	*423	..	*87	..	*337	*60
	2006	*428	..	*86	..	*342	*59
Lebanon	2003	..	200	..	..	200	51
Liban	2004	..	200	..	..	200	50
	2005	..	200	..	..	200	50
	2006	..	200	..	..	200	49
Malaysia	2003	153	7521	51	0	7623	304
Malaisie	2004	382	12720	135	-308	13275	519
	2005	682	10488	70	279	10821	414
	2006	902	10339	98	0	11143	418
Mongolia	2003	2489	0	144	..	2345	942
Mongolie	2004	3016	1	515	..	2502	993
	2005	3301	0	698	..	2603	1022
	2006	3546	0	811	..	2735	1061
Myanmar	2003	870	..	731	..	138	3
Myanmar	2004	921	..	775	..	146	3
	2005	1134	..	983	..	152	3
	2006	1152	..	982	..	171	3

Table 5

Production, trade and consumption of solid fuels
Production, commerce et consommation de combustibles solides

Thousand metric tons of coal equivalent and kilograms per capita
Milliers de tonnes métriques d'équivalent houille et kilogrammes par habitant

Country or area Pays ou zone	Year Année	Production Production	Imports Importations	Exports Exportations	Changes in stocks Variations des stocks	Consumption Consommation	
						Total Totale	Per capita Par habitant
Nepal	2003	11	280	..	..	291	12
Népal	2004	9	248	..	..	257	10
	2005	9	401	..	..	410	16
	2006	9	411	..	..	420	16
Other Asia	2003	..	51018	0	-90	51108	2261
Autre Asie	2004	..	56326	0	3150	53176	2344
	2005	..	56071	0	1061	55010	2420
	2006	..	58159	20	553	57586	2527
Pakistan	2003	2237	1562	..	..	3799	26
Pakistan	2004	3099	3273	..	..	6371	43
	2005	3291	2812	..	..	6103	40
	2006	2461	4206	..	..	6668	43
Philippines	2003	3070	3079	..	..	6149	76
Philippines	2004	1818	5249	..	..	7068	85
	2005	2110	4700	..	..	6811	80
	2006	*2169	*4777	..	..	*6946	*80
Singapore	2003	..	12	..	..	12	3
Singapour	2004	..	8	..	..	8	2
	2005	..	3	..	..	3	1
	2006	..	6	..	..	6	1
Sri Lanka	2003	..	97	..	..	97	5
Sri Lanka	2004	..	96	..	..	96	5
	2005	..	96	..	..	96	5
	2006	..	96	..	..	96	5
Syrian Arab Republic	2003	..	8	4	..	4	0
Rép. arabe syrienne	2004	..	8	4	..	4	0
	2005	..	8	4	..	4	0
	2006	..	8	4	..	4	0
Tajikistan	2003	38	6	0	..	44	7
Tadjikistan	2004	59	5	0	..	64	10
	2005	82	5	1	..	86	13
	2006	93	6	1	..	98	14
Thailand	2003	11841	7684	..	552	18973	296
Thaïlande	2004	12606	8315	..	-306	21227	331
	2005	13120	7299	..	-106	20525	317
	2006	11941	8924	..	94	20771	318
Turkey	2003	15185	16989	4	560	31610	450
Turquie	2004	14491	17149	0	-711	32351	455
	2005	18082	18124	0	-265	36472	506
	2006	19878	21164	0	203	40839	560
Uzbekistan	2003	737	7	8	17	718	28
Ouzbékistan	2004	1039	10	11	24	1014	39
	2005	1156	11	12	27	1128	42
	2006	1204	11	12	28	1174	44
Viet Nam	2003	16700	0	6300	..	10400	129
Viet Nam	2004	25500	0	10600	..	14900	182
	2005	32396	101	17987	..	14510	175
	2006	37899	296	22468	..	15727	187
Europe	2003	517567	240830	84850	-6608	680155	935
Europe	2004	509456	255436	98026	-2746	669613	920
	2005	511822	249555	100850	6936	653592	896
	2006	508170	272705	108504	-825	673196	922

Table 5

Production, trade and consumption of solid fuels
Production, commerce et consommation de combustibles solides
Thousand metric tons of coal equivalent and kilograms per capita
Milliers de tonnes métriques d'équivalent houille et kilogrammes par habitant

Country or area Pays ou zone	Year Année	Production Production	Imports Importations	Exports Exportations	Changes in stocks Variations des stocks	Consumption Consommation	
						Total Totale	Per capita Par habitant
Albania	2003	27	3	..	..	31	9
Albanie	2004	37	3	..	..	40	13
	2005	31	5	..	..	36	11
	2006	31	4	..	..	35	11
Austria	2003	429	5016	3	-515	5957	738
Autriche	2004	88	5438	63	-229	5692	699
	2005	0	5685	24	-189	5850	713
	2006	0	5378	38	-436	5777	698
Belarus	2003	586	279	104	-164	924	94
Bélarus	2004	648	294	173	-21	791	80
	2005	750	193	165	-3	781	80
	2006	691	166	142	-31	746	77
Belgium	2003	50	9670	926	-86	8880	858
Belgique	2004	70	10130	1196	259	8745	841
	2005	42	9043	1079	147	7859	752
	2006	11	7697	1108	-219	6820	649
Bosnia and Herzegovina	2003	7274	0	225	7	7042	1838
Bosnie y Herzégovine	2004	7347	299	384	20	7242	1885
	2005	7746	592	527	-21	7832	2038
	2006	8280	626	550	-21	8377	2180
Bulgaria	2003	6447	3697	4	-158	10299	1316
Bulgarie	2004	6208	4273	48	467	9966	1281
	2005	5771	3714	19	-305	9772	1263
	2006	6014	3601	3	-358	9971	1295
Croatia	2003	..	1098	8	-2	1092	246
Croatie	2004	..	1277	1	111	1165	262
	2005	..	1020	0	-99	1119	252
	2006	..	1144	0	96	1048	236
Czech Republic	2003	30522	1606	5407	15	26706	2618
République tchèque	2004	30370	1869	5171	755	26313	2578
	2005	29420	1432	5028	81	25743	2515
	2006	29853	2138	6211	-394	26174	2544
Denmark	2003	..	8132	129	-142	8146	1542
Danemark	2004	..	6505	136	87	6283	1163
	2005	..	5119	82	-303	5340	986
	2006	..	7435	94	-502	7843	1443
Estonia	2003	4913	395	117	138	5053	3733
Estonie	2004	4596	413	94	-150	5065	3754
	2005	4821	92	61	13	4840	3595
	2006	4703	60	96	82	4585	3413
Finland	2003	2642	9720	5	361	11997	2301
Finlande	2004	1314	8036	4	-1625	10971	2098
	2005	3229	4773	14	886	7101	1354
	2006	4787	6577	9	491	10863	2063
France incl. Monaco	2003	2076	17760	485	-1799	21150	351
France y compris Monaco	2004	808	20127	920	-367	20382	337
	2005	593	20787	913	-654	21120	347
	2006	419	21248	816	1374	19476	319
Germany	2003	80048	36692	753	-3214	119203	1445
Allemagne	2004	81260	40034	764	352	120178	1457
	2005	79013	37231	846	775	114623	1390
	2006	74595	41717	923	257	115133	1398

Table 5

Production, trade and consumption of solid fuels
Production, commerce et consommation de combustibles solides

Thousand metric tons of coal equivalent and kilograms per capita
Milliers de tonnes métriques d'équivalent houille et kilogrammes par habitant

Country or area Pays ou zone	Year Année	Production Production	Imports Importations	Exports Exportations	Changes in stocks Variations des stocks	Consumption Consommation	
						Total Totale	Per capita Par habitant
Greece	2003	11680	697	95	-438	12720	1154
Grèce	2004	12207	760	57	-128	13038	1179
	2005	12195	604	40	-57	12815	1154
	2006	11338	359	22	-51	11725	1052
Hungary	2003	3918	1447	71	-29	5323	525
Hongrie	2004	3117	1680	141	-163	4820	477
	2005	2498	2039	198	-24	4363	433
	2006	2509	2137	409	-27	4264	423
Iceland	2003	..	130	..	..	130	448
Islande	2004	..	147	..	..	147	502
	2005	..	142	..	..	142	480
	2006	..	111	..	..	111	364
Ireland	2003	1742	2576	26	289	4003	1006
Irlande	2004	1391	2808	27	599	3574	884
	2005	1252	3054	28	112	4167	1009
	2006	1169	2657	22	80	3725	880
Italy and San Marino	2003	225	21564	165	-193	21817	379
Italie y comp. St. Marin	2004	88	25065	244	351	24557	422
	2005	85	24325	229	-74	24255	414
	2006	19	24660	220	-46	24505	416
Latvia	2003	3	85	0	-3	91	39
Lettonie	2004	4	66	0	-3	72	31
	2005	4	81	1	-3	86	38
	2006	5	107	0	32	79	35
Lithuania	2003	15	310	3	20	302	87
Lituanie	2004	16	278	3	-3	294	86
	2005	23	315	2	13	323	95
	2006	18	430	4	-1	444	131
Luxembourg	2003	..	111	..	..	111	247
Luxembourg	2004	..	134	..	..	134	293
	2005	..	116	..	..	116	250
	2006	..	158	..	..	158	334
Netherlands	2003	..	20697	7853	651	12192	753
Pays-Bas	2004	..	21345	9638	-197	11904	732
	2005	..	19326	7732	178	11417	700
	2006	..	21803	10799	281	10722	656
Norway,Svlbd.J.Myn. I	2003	2823	1014	2586	124	1127	246
Norvège,Svalbd,J.May	2004	2785	1179	2628	20	1315	285
	2005	1410	1011	1599	-286	1108	239
	2006	2296	886	2173	-9	1019	219
Poland	2003	101618	2569	21469	-137	82855	2169
Pologne	2004	100361	2554	21488	-35	81462	2134
	2005	97782	3550	20545	1679	79109	2073
	2006	95368	5467	20064	-2447	83218	2182
Portugal	2003	..	4822	0	-8	4830	463
Portugal	2004	..	4732	0	-154	4886	465
	2005	..	4751	0	-118	4869	462
	2006	..	5204	3	178	5023	475
Republic of Moldova	2003	..	175	..	47	128	35
Rép. de Moldova	2004	..	117	..	-3	120	33
	2005	..	105	..	-3	108	30
	2006	..	112	..	-18	130	36

Table 5

Production, trade and consumption of solid fuels
Production, commerce et consommation de combustibles solides
Thousand metric tons of coal equivalent and kilograms per capita
Milliers de tonnes métriques d'équivalent houille et kilogrammes par habitant

Country or area Pays ou zone	Year Année	Production Production	Imports Importations	Exports Exportations	Changes in stocks Variations des stocks	Consumption Consommation	
						Total Totale	Per capita Par habitant
Romania Roumanie	2003	8178	3225	0	-185	11587	533
	2004	7860	3891	41	102	11608	536
	2005	7690	3540	31	-108	11307	523
	2006	8634	3202	17	-401	12220	566
Russian Federation Fédération de Russie	2003	152632	16038	38297	1189	129184	894
	2004	155383	14361	47144	-2420	125020	869
	2005	170011	14459	57397	2805	124268	868
	2006	170922	16538	59857	-696	128299	900
Serbia Serbie	2003	12249	519	24	0	12744	1204
	2004	12524	747	35	0	13236	1259
	2005	10742	864	133	0	11472	1096
	2006	11160	1188	62	-30	12316	1178
Slovakia Slovaquie	2003	1295	4655	96	-185	6040	1123
	2004	1235	4771	50	81	5875	1092
	2005	1050	4849	193	241	5466	1015
	2006	921	4670	191	-475	5875	1090
Slovenia Slovénie	2003	1500	405	3	10	1892	948
	2004	1494	439	15	3	1915	959
	2005	1410	416	6	-28	1847	923
	2006	1404	415	12	-49	1858	925
Spain Espagne	2003	9729	19718	775	-441	29113	693
	2004	9474	22310	1018	-501	31267	732
	2005	9045	22277	630	269	30422	701
	2006	8689	21359	1082	1961	27005	613
Sweden Suède	2003	333	3722	62	231	3762	420
	2004	369	3739	43	-89	4154	462
	2005	292	3623	38	190	3686	408
	2006	256	3292	31	-230	3748	413
Switzerland Suisse	2003	..	107	0	-96	203	28
	2004	..	190	0	0	190	26
	2005	..	130	0	-83	213	29
	2006	..	205	8	0	197	26
T.F.Yug.Rep. Macedonia L'ex-RY Macédoine	2003	2842	209	7	60	2984	1472
	2004	2789	116	12	-28	2922	1440
	2005	2649	129	0	-117	2895	1421
	2006	2556	159	1	17	2697	1322
Ukraine Ukraine	2003	47430	10062	4471	0	53021	1109
	2004	44012	9128	5741	197	47202	999
	2005	44623	6457	2705	55	48319	1026
	2006	45574	9689	2993	-118	52388	1120
United Kingdom Royaume-Uni	2003	24340	31908	682	-1954	57520	970
	2004	21601	36183	749	-33	57068	956
	2005	17643	43707	583	1966	58800	977
	2006	15947	50106	545	887	64621	1067
Oceania Océanie	**2003**	**267297**	**326**	**194551**	**602**	**72469**	**2236**
	2004	**278056**	**664**	**203483**	**1748**	**73490**	**2235**
	2005	**291505**	**727**	**215220**	**-1522**	**78535**	**2354**
	2006	**292016**	**850**	**216190**	**-2946**	**79621**	**2351**
Australia Australie	2003	264141	0	192720	938	70483	3541
	2004	274842	0	201902	1408	71531	3552
	2005	288236	0	213289	-1482	76429	3745
	2006	288405	46	213937	-2986	77500	3744

Table 5

Production, trade and consumption of solid fuels
Production, commerce et consommation de combustibles solides

Thousand metric tons of coal equivalent and kilograms per capita
Milliers de tonnes métriques d'équivalent houille et kilogrammes par habitant

Country or area Pays ou zone	Year Année	Production Production	Imports Importations	Exports Exportations	Changes in stocks Variations des stocks	Consumption Consommation	
						Total Totale	Per capita Par habitant
Fiji	2003	..	*13	..	..	*13	*16
Fidji	2004	..	*13	..	..	*13	*16
	2005	..	*12	..	..	*12	*14
	2006	..	*12	..	..	*12	*14
New Caledonia	2003	..	313	..	..	313	1373
Nouvelle-Calédonie	2004	..	281	..	..	281	1218
	2005	..	260	..	..	260	1111
	2006	..	283	..	..	283	1189
New Zealand	2003	3155	0	1831	-336	1660	414
Nouvelle-Zélande	2004	3214	370	1581	339	1665	410
	2005	3269	455	1931	-40	1834	447
	2006	3611	509	2254	40	1826	441

Table 6

Production, trade and consumption of hard coal
Production, commerce et consommation de houille
Thousand metric tons and kilograms per capita
Milliers de tones métriques et kilogrammes par habitant

Table Notes:

Recovered slurries are included in the production of hard coal for the Czech Republic, Hungary, Spain, and the United Kingdom.

- Data for Austria include hard coal briquettes.

- Data for China include lignite.

- **Please refer to the Definitions Section on pages xv to xxix for the appropriate product description/ classification.**

Notes relatives aux tableaux:

Les schlamms récupérés sont compris dans la production de houille pour la République tchèque, la Hongrie, l'Espagne, et le Royaume-Uni.

- Les données pour l'Autriche comprennent également des briquettes de houille.

- Les données pour la Chine comprennent le lignite.

- **Veuillez consulter la section "définitions" de la page xv à la page xxix pour une description/classification appropriée des produits.**

Figure 14: World coal production 1993-2006

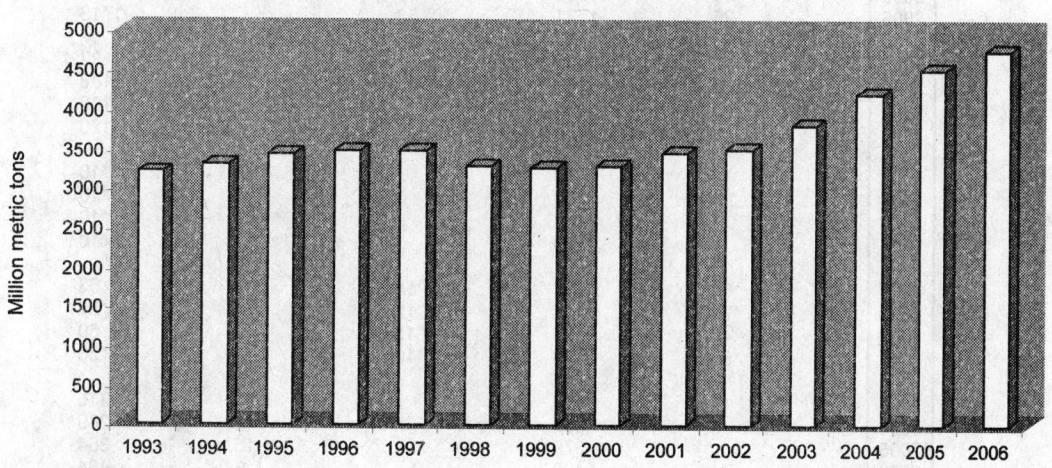

Figure 15: Major hard coal producing countries in 2006

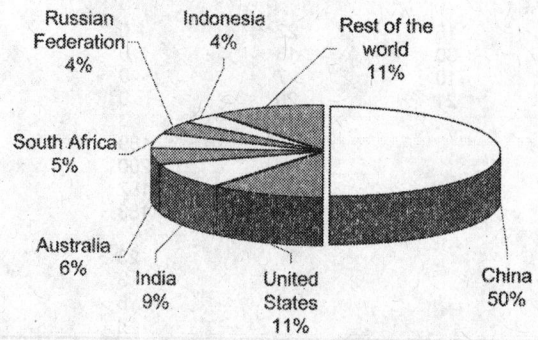

Figure 16: Major hard coal consuming countries in 2006

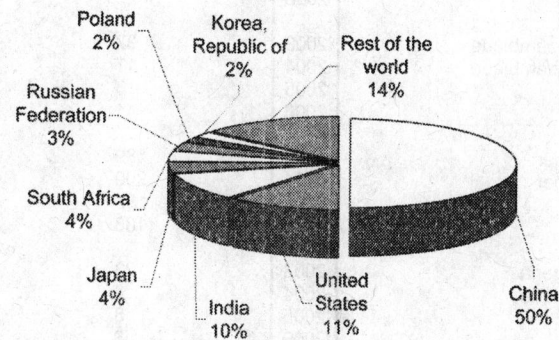

Table 6

Production, trade and consumption of hard coal
Production, commerce et consommation de houille

Thousand metric tons and kilograms per capita
Milliers de tonnes métriques et kilogrammes par habitant

Country or area Pays ou zone	Year Année	Production Production	Imports Importations	Exports Exportations	Changes in stocks Variations des stocks	Consumption Consommation Total Totale	Consumption Consommation Per capita Par habitant
World	**2003**	**3808323**	**698963**	**702370**	**-14927**	**3819844**	**609**
Monde	**2004**	**4189193**	**765289**	**750025**	**2082**	**4202375**	**662**
	2005	**4506029**	**775122**	**804965**	**37754**	**4438433**	**691**
	2006	**4753617**	**831680**	**860832**	**11107**	**4713359**	**723**
Africa	**2003**	**244268**	**8906**	**72013**	**1913**	**179248**	**213**
Afrique	**2004**	**248320**	**10793**	**68505**	**-2064**	**192671**	**222**
	2005	**250735**	**12104**	**71963**	**-55**	**190931**	**215**
	2006	**250443**	**11352**	**69843**	**111**	**191841**	**209**
Algeria	2003	..	604	..	*-370	974	31
Algérie	2004	..	910	..	*295	615	19
	2005	..	689	..	-90	779	24
	2006	..	992	..	44	948	28
Dem. Rep. of Congo	2003	105	34	..	..	139	3
Rép. dem. du Congo	2004	108	45	..	..	153	3
	2005	120	43	..	..	163	3
	2006	124	49	..	..	173	3
Egypt	2003	37	1015	8	..	1044	16
Egypte	2004	33	1850	33	..	1850	26
	2005	33	1850	33	..	1850	26
	2006	25	1771	83	..	1713	24
Kenya	2003	..	92	..	..	92	3
Kenya	2004	..	108	..	..	108	3
	2005	..	108	..	..	108	3
	2006	..	120	..	..	120	3
Madagascar	2003	..	*10	..	..	*10	*1
Madagascar	2004	..	*10	..	..	*10	*1
	2005	..	*10	..	..	*10	*1
	2006	..	*10	..	..	*10	*1
Malawi	2003	66	2	15	..	53	5
Malawi	2004	*70	*2	*15	..	*57	*5
	2005	45	*30	*15	..	60	5
	2006	*55	*5	*10	..	*50	*4
Mauritius	2003	..	289	..	-27	316	261
Maurice	2004	..	332	..	43	289	237
	2005	..	379	..	15	364	293
	2006	..	490	..	6	484	386
Morocco	2003	..	4890	..	..	4890	170
Maroc	2004	..	5472	..	..	5472	183
	2005	..	6750	..	..	6750	224
	2006	..	5877	..	..	5877	193
Mozambique	2003	37	..	15	22	0	0
Mozambique	2004	17	..	30	-13	0	0
	2005	3	..	10	-7	0	0
	2006	41	..	21	20	0	0
Niger	2003	189	..	..	..	189	16
Niger	2004	200	..	..	..	200	16
	2005	182	..	..	..	182	14
	2006	*183	..	..	..	*183	*14
Nigeria	2003	23	..	..	..	23	0
Nigéria	2004	3	..	..	..	3	0
	2005	8	..	..	..	8	0
	2006	8	..	..	..	8	0

Table 6

Production, trade and consumption of hard coal
Production, commerce et consommation de houille
Thousand metric tons and kilograms per capita
Milliers de tonnes métriques et kilogrammes par habitant

Country or area Pays ou zone	Year Année	Production Production	Imports Importations	Exports Exportations	Changes in stocks Variations des stocks	Consumption Consommation	
						Total Totale	Per capita Par habitant
Senegal	2003	..	*120	..	..	*120	*12
Sénégal	2004	..	127	..	..	127	12
	2005	..	152	..	..	152	14
	2006	..	167	..	..	167	15
South Africa Customs Un.	2003	239985	1811	71942	2242	167612	3284
Un.douan.d'Afr.mérid	2004	244175	1898	68389	-2433	180117	3385
	2005	246404	2041	71893	*-19	176571	3298
	2006	246236	1822	69717	*5	178336	3292
United Rep.Tanzania	2003	55	..	..	..	55	2
Rép. Unie de Tanzanie	2004	65	..	..	..	65	2
	2005	75	..	..	..	75	2
	2006	80	..	..	..	80	2
Zambia	2003	221	..	6	71	144	13
Zambie	2004	233	..	11	69	153	14
	2005	244	..	12	71	161	14
	2006	244	..	12	61	171	14
Zimbabwe	2003	3550	39	27	-25	3587	277
Zimbabwe	2004	3415	39	27	-25	3452	265
	2005	3621	52	0	-25	3698	282
	2006	3447	49	0	-25	3521	266
America, North	**2003**	**520607**	**38348**	**55554**	**-17352**	**520753**	**1037**
Amérique du Nord	**2004**	**552163**	**38765**	**62584**	**-5645**	**533989**	**1053**
	2005	**562200**	**41435**	**66454**	**4231**	**532950**	**1041**
	2006	**555785**	**44855**	**66472**	**14869**	**519299**	**1005**
Canada	2003	26590	13577	24996	-1458	16629	525
Canada	2004	29261	12629	25743	-1910	18057	564
	2005	28586	12639	28188	-2070	15107	468
	2006	29900	11296	27427	-2461	16230	497
Costa Rica	2003	..	73	..	..	73	18
Costa Rica	2004	..	63	..	..	63	15
	2005	..	60	..	..	60	14
	2006	..	60	..	..	60	14
Cuba	2003	..	25	..	*12	13	1
Cuba	2004	..	24	..	*12	12	1
	2005	..	22	..	*10	12	1
	2006	..	22	..	*11	11	1
Dominican Republic	2003	..	1057	..	..	1057	118
Rép. dominicaine	2004	..	777	..	..	777	86
	2005	..	476	..	..	476	52
	2006	..	704	..	..	704	75
Guatemala	2003	..	369	..	0	369	31
Guatemala	2004	..	416	..	0	416	34
	2005	..	408	..	0	408	32
	2006	..	268	..	-160	428	33
Honduras	2003	..	169	..	0	169	25
Honduras	2004	..	174	..	0	174	25
	2005	..	183	..	0	183	25
	2006	..	192	..	2	190	26
Jamaica	2003	..	85	..	..	85	32
Jamaïque	2004	..	66	..	..	66	25
	2005	..	60	..	..	60	23
	2006	..	32	..	..	32	12

Table 6

Production, trade and consumption of hard coal
Production, commerce et consommation de houille

Thousand metric tons and kilograms per capita
Milliers de tonnes métriques et kilogrammes par habitant

Country or area Pays ou zone	Year Année	Production Production	Imports Importations	Exports Exportations	Changes in stocks Variations des stocks	Consumption Consommation	
						Total Totale	Per capita Par habitant
Mexico	2003	1626	1204	..	985	1845	18
Mexique	2004	1735	1328	..	1298	1765	17
	2005	1792	1578	..	1544	1826	18
	2006	1914	1663	..	1657	1920	18
United States	2003	492391	21789	30558	-16891	500513	1721
Etats-Unis	2004	521167	23288	36841	-5045	512659	1746
	2005	531822	26009	38266	4747	514818	1737
	2006	523971	30618	39045	15820	499724	1674
America, South	**2003**	**62159**	**17995**	**52242**	**-24**	**27936**	**77**
Amérique du Sud	**2004**	**66108**	**20136**	**57650**	**-818**	**29412**	**80**
	2005	**73126**	**20088**	**60833**	**1267**	**31113**	**84**
	2006	**79745**	**20048**	**69370**	**-968**	**31391**	**83**
Argentina	2003	89	825	0	-13	927	24
Argentine	2004	51	886	0	0	937	25
	2005	25	1441	83	0	1383	36
	2006	427	914	116	-29	1254	32
Brazil	2003	4646	13493	..	-103	18242	102
Brésil	2004	5406	14081	..	-343	19830	109
	2005	6255	13699	..	-50	20004	109
	2006	5881	13398	..	-737	20016	107
Chile	2003	576	2904	..	10	3470	218
Chili	2004	188	4256	..	9	4435	276
	2005	544	4004	..	122	4426	272
	2006	396	5009	..	3	5402	329
Colombia	2003	50025	0	45494	220	4311	97
Colombie	2004	53693	3	50902	-350	3144	69
	2005	59064	3	53607	1287	4172	91
	2006	65596	0	61968	-187	3815	82
Peru	2003	16	772	..	-138	926	34
Pérou	2004	22	909	..	-134	1065	39
	2005	43	940	..	-92	1075	40
	2006	107	725	..	-18	850	31
Uruguay	2003	..	1	..	..	1	0
Uruguay	2004	..	1	..	..	1	0
	2005	..	1	..	..	1	0
	2006	..	2	..	..	2	1
Venezuela(Bolivar. Rep.)	2003	6807	..	6748	..	59	2
Venezuela(Rép. bolivar.)	2004	6748	..	6748	..	0	0
	2005	7195	..	7143	..	52	2
	2006	7338	..	7286	..	52	2
Asia	**2003**	**2312962**	**387209**	**218270**	**7608**	**2474293**	**651**
Asie	**2004**	**2640978**	**433944**	**231067**	**10994**	**2832861**	**738**
	2005	**2914009**	**443973**	**248360**	**24918**	**3084705**	**794**
	2006	**3168172**	**472846**	**291014**	**131**	**3349873**	**850**
Afghanistan	2003	35	..	..	..	35	2
Afghanistan	2004	34	..	..	..	34	1
	2005	*33	..	..	..	*33	*1
	2006	*33	..	..	..	*33	*1
Armenia	2003	..	27	..	..	27	7
Arménie	2004	..	0	..	..	0	0
	2005	..	0	..	..	0	0
	2006	..	1	..	..	1	0

Table 6

Production, trade and consumption of hard coal
Production, commerce et consommation de houille
Thousand metric tons and kilograms per capita
Milliers de tonnes métriques et kilogrammes par habitant

Country or area Pays ou zone	Year Année	Production Production	Imports Importations	Exports Exportations	Changes in stocks Variations des stocks	Consumption Consommation	
						Total Totale	Per capita Par habitant
Bangladesh	2003	..	700	..	..	700	5
Bangladesh	2004	..	700	..	..	700	5
	2005	..	700	..	..	700	5
	2006	..	700	..	..	700	5
Bhutan	2003	66	*25	*35	..	56	91
Bhoutan	2004	30	*40	20	..	50	80
	2005	85	*20	48	..	57	90
	2006	98	*20	66	..	52	80
China	2003	1722000	11098	94029	5049	1634020	1268
Chine	2004	1992324	18614	86664	1620	1922654	1483
	2005	2204729	26171	71724	14554	2144622	1645
	2006	2373000	38105	63273	-9979	2357811	1794
China, Hong Kong SAR	2003	..	10690	13	-47	10724	1575
Chine, Hong-Kong RAS	2004	..	10692	0	680	10012	1476
	2005	..	10825	0	-69	10894	1599
	2006	..	11404	0	526	10878	1586
Cyprus	2003	..	51	..	-2	53	74
Chypre	2004	..	39	..	-18	57	77
	2005	..	63	..	11	52	69
	2006	..	63	..	9	54	70
Georgia	2003	8	6	2	..	12	3
Géorgie	2004	8	6	2	..	12	3
	2005	5	13	0	..	18	4
	2006	11	15	3	..	23	5
India	2003	361246	21683	1627	1893	379409	355
Inde	2004	382615	26128	1374	2678	404691	375
	2005	407039	38586	1989	10344	433292	396
	2006	430850	45000	2010	11001	462839	414
Indonesia	2003	96705	38	90129	0	6614	31
Indonésie	2004	119154	97	105527	437	13287	61
	2005	145355	98	129196	812	15445	70
	2006	193388	113	171551	749	21201	95
Iran(Islamic Rep. of)	2003	1232	627	21	..	1838	28
Iran(Rép. islamique)	2004	1246	470	120	..	1596	24
	2005	1330	520	40	..	1810	26
	2006	1520	460	50	..	1930	27
Israel	2003	..	12295	..	-371	12666	1893
Israël	2004	..	12801	..	-74	12875	1891
	2005	..	12685	..	561	12124	1749
	2006	..	12756	..	-235	12991	1843
Japan	2003	..	166418	1	..	166417	1318
Japon	2004	..	180804	2	..	180802	1432
	2005	..	176985	3	..	176982	1402
	2006	..	179097	2	..	179095	1420
Kazakhstan	2003	80807	356	24587	956	55620	3731
Kazakhstan	2004	83065	485	24288	812	58450	3893
	2005	82788	438	23620	0	59606	3935
	2006	91576	292	28103	0	63765	4165
Korea, Dem.Ppl's.Rep.	2003	23045	162	755	..	22452	957
Corée,Rép.pop.dém.de	2004	24371	166	1571	..	22966	973
	2005	26864	175	2804	..	24235	1026
	2006	27161	180	2481	..	24860	1049

Table 6

Production, trade and consumption of hard coal
Production, commerce et consommation de houille

Thousand metric tons and kilograms per capita
Milliers de tonnes métriques et kilogrammes par habitant

Country or area Pays ou zone	Year Année	Production Production	Imports Importations	Exports Exportations	Changes in stocks Variations des stocks	Consumption Consommation	
						Total Totale	Per capita Par habitant
Korea, Republic of	2003	3298	71866	..	-416	75580	1580
Corée, République de	2004	3191	76353	..	2200	77344	1609
	2005	2832	73896	..	-2682	79410	1644
	2006	2824	76001	..	-2178	81003	1677
Kyrgyzstan	2003	64	1079	31	..	1112	221
Kirghizistan	2004	64	941	44	..	961	189
	2005	49	847	9	..	887	172
	2006	46	802	30	..	818	157
Lao People's Dem. Rep.	2003	*285	..	..	..	*285	*50
Rép. dém. pop. lao	2004	*290	..	..	..	*290	*50
	2005	*300	..	..	..	*300	*53
	2006	*305	..	..	..	*305	*53
Lebanon	2003	..	200	..	..	200	51
Liban	2004	..	200	..	..	200	50
	2005	..	200	..	..	200	50
	2006	..	200	..	..	200	49
Malaysia	2003	153	7521	51	0	7623	304
Malaisie	2004	382	12720	135	-308	13275	519
	2005	682	10488	70	279	10821	414
	2006	902	10340	98	0	11143	418
Mongolia	2003	924	..	..	..	924	371
Mongolie	2004	1120	..	..	..	1120	445
	2005	1225	..	..	..	1225	481
	2006	1316	..	..	..	1316	510
Myanmar	2003	802	..	689	..	113	2
Myanmar	2004	839	..	720	..	119	2
	2005	993	..	869	..	124	2
	2006	1006	..	878	..	128	2
Nepal	2003	11	280	..	..	291	12
Népal	2004	9	248	..	..	257	10
	2005	9	401	..	..	410	16
	2006	9	411	..	..	420	16
Other Asia	2003	..	54747	..	-144	54891	2428
Autre Asie	2004	..	60633	..	3499	57134	2518
	2005	..	60366	..	999	59367	2612
	2006	..	62278	..	431	61847	2714
Pakistan	2003	3312	1578	..	..	4890	34
Pakistan	2004	4587	3307	..	..	7894	53
	2005	4871	2842	..	..	7713	50
	2006	3643	4251	..	..	7894	50
Philippines	2003	178	2450	..	..	2628	32
Philippines	2004	150	4435	..	..	4585	55
	2005	178	3388	..	..	3566	42
	2006	*180	*3420	..	..	*3600	*41
Sri Lanka	2003	..	96	..	..	96	5
Sri Lanka	2004	..	95	..	..	95	5
	2005	..	95	..	..	95	5
	2006	..	95	..	..	95	5
Tajikistan	2003	32	8	0	..	40	6
Tadjikistan	2004	53	7	0	..	60	9
	2005	76	7	1	..	82	12
	2006	87	8	1	..	94	13

Table 6

Production, trade and consumption of hard coal
Production, commerce et consommation de houille
Thousand metric tons and kilograms per capita
Milliers de tonnes métriques et kilogrammes par habitant

Country or area Pays ou zone	Year Année	Production Production	Imports Importations	Exports Exportations	Changes in stocks Variations des stocks	Consumption Consommation Total Totale	Per capita Par habitant
Thailand	2003	..	7042	..	..	7042	110
Thaïlande	2004	..	7536	..	..	7536	117
	2005	..	6703	..	..	6703	103
	2006	..	6252	..	..	6252	96
Turkey	2003	2059	16166	..	690	17535	250
Turquie	2004	1946	16427	..	-531	18904	266
	2005	2170	17360	..	109	19421	269
	2006	2319	20286	..	-193	22798	312
Viet Nam	2003	16700	0	6300	..	10400	129
Viet Nam	2004	25500	0	10600	..	14900	182
	2005	32396	101	17987	..	14510	175
	2006	37899	296	22468	..	15727	187
Europe	**2003**	**427229**	**246179**	**93332**	**-5488**	**585564**	**805**
Europe	**2004**	**427962**	**261304**	**109885**	**-709**	**580090**	**797**
	2005	**437156**	**257189**	**123713**	**8225**	**562407**	**771**
	2006	**431982**	**282230**	**130117**	**-488**	**584583**	**801**
Austria	2003	..	3959	0	-366	4325	536
Autriche	2004	..	4378	21	105	4252	522
	2005	..	4325	3	283	4039	492
	2006	..	4118	0	-111	4229	511
Belarus	2003	..	232	1	-63	294	30
Bélarus	2004	..	247	0	13	234	24
	2005	..	139	0	-29	168	17
	2006	..	102	0	-30	132	14
Belgium	2003	..	9390	926	-94	8558	826
Belgique	2004	..	9790	1267	279	8244	793
	2005	..	8804	1204	126	7474	715
	2006	..	8056	1062	-166	7160	681
Bosnia and Herzegovina	2003	3296	0	..	..	3296	860
Bosnie y Herzégovine	2004	3391	299	..	..	3690	960
	2005	3546	592	..	..	4138	1077
	2006	3616	626	..	..	4242	1104
Bulgaria	2003	87	3930	4	-187	4200	537
Bulgarie	2004	33	4678	8	438	4265	548
	2005	9	4088	0	-264	4361	563
	2006	27	3902	0	-330	4259	553
Croatia	2003	..	1035	7	-2	1030	232
Croatie	2004	..	1218	1	111	1106	249
	2005	..	958	0	-99	1057	238
	2006	..	1083	0	96	987	222
Czech Republic	2003	7865	466	3710	29	4592	450
République tchèque	2004	7316	529	3274	-5	4576	448
	2005	7136	535	3217	84	4370	427
	2006	7748	1037	4427	-29	4387	426
Denmark	2003	..	9515	151	-169	9533	1804
Danemark	2004	..	7592	157	108	7327	1357
	2005	..	5971	96	-358	6233	1151
	2006	..	8688	110	-594	9172	1688
Estonia	2003	..	57	..	13	44	33
Estonie	2004	..	44	..	-14	58	43
	2005	..	54	..	-2	56	42
	2006	..	95	..	25	70	52

Table 6

Production, trade and consumption of hard coal
Production, commerce et consommation de houille
Thousand metric tons and kilograms per capita
Milliers de tonnes métriques et kilogrammes par habitant

Country or area Pays ou zone	Year Année	Production Production	Imports Importations	Exports Exportations	Changes in stocks Variations des stocks	Consumption Consommation	
						Total Totale	Per capita Par habitant
Finland	2003	..	10146	..	1284	8862	1700
Finlande	2004	..	8286	..	204	8082	1546
	2005	..	4723	..	125	4598	876
	2006	..	6684	..	-928	7612	1445
France incl. Monaco	2003	2234	16768	83	-2023	20942	348
France y compris Monaco	2004	872	19460	94	-315	20553	339
	2005	617	19851	295	-969	21142	347
	2006	452	20391	140	1634	19069	312
Germany	2003	28753	34917	195	-2907	66382	804
Allemagne	2004	29151	39536	184	581	67922	823
	2005	28018	37105	255	916	63952	776
	2006	23762	42132	199	157	65538	796
Greece	2003	..	747	60	-146	833	76
Grèce	2004	..	814	22	16	776	70
	2005	..	646	13	70	563	51
	2006	..	383	10	-90	463	42
Hungary	2003	..	1086	1	-55	1140	113
Hongrie	2004	..	1336	6	31	1299	129
	2005	..	1447	1	105	1341	133
	2006	..	1759	3	-95	1851	184
Iceland	2003	..	85	..	..	85	294
Islande	2004	..	104	..	..	104	355
	2005	..	117	..	..	117	395
	2006	..	91	..	..	91	299
Ireland	2003	..	2485	2	-117	2600	653
Irlande	2004	..	2718	5	75	2638	652
	2005	..	2947	7	70	2870	695
	2006	..	2587	3	-4	2588	611
Italy and San Marino	2003	250	20562	..	-334	21146	367
Italie y comp. St. Marin	2004	98	24666	..	484	24280	417
	2005	95	24150	..	5	24240	414
	2006	21	24632	..	-145	24798	421
Latvia	2003	..	124	..	23	101	43
Lettonie	2004	..	95	..	-3	98	42
	2005	..	116	..	-4	120	52
	2006	..	160	..	30	130	57
Lithuania	2003	..	295	0	24	271	78
Lituanie	2004	..	261	1	-3	263	77
	2005	..	293	2	7	284	83
	2006	..	394	3	-5	396	117
Luxembourg	2003	..	106	..	..	106	235
Luxembourg	2004	..	129	..	..	129	282
	2005	..	111	..	..	111	239
	2006	..	153	..	..	153	324
Netherlands	2003	..	21620	7295	658	13667	844
Pays-Bas	2004	..	22603	9292	-240	13551	833
	2005	..	20415	7374	32	13009	797
	2006	..	22844	9858	338	12648	774
Norway,Svlbd.J.Myn. I	2003	2944	671	2697	106	812	177
Norvège,Svalbd,J.May	2004	2904	766	2741	25	904	196
	2005	1471	667	1666	-323	795	171
	2006	2395	528	2266	20	637	137

Table 6

Production, trade and consumption of hard coal
Production, commerce et consommation de houille
Thousand metric tons and kilograms per capita
Milliers de tonnes métriques et kilogrammes par habitant

Country or area Pays ou zone	Year Année	Production Production	Imports Importations	Exports Exportations	Changes in stocks Variations des stocks	Consumption Consommation	
						Total Totale	Per capita Par habitant
Poland	2003	102874	2517	20119	-96	85368	2235
Pologne	2004	101230	2328	19684	-41	83915	2198
	2005	97904	3372	19369	1469	80438	2108
	2006	95223	5271	16735	-2371	86130	2259
Portugal	2003	..	5344	0	-18	5362	514
Portugal	2004	..	5247	0	-267	5514	525
	2005	..	5272	0	-204	5476	519
	2006	..	5782	5	310	5467	517
Republic of Moldova	2003	..	267	..	47	220	61
Rép. de Moldova	2004	..	185	..	-1	186	52
	2005	..	166	..	-1	167	46
	2006	..	176	..	-18	194	54
Romania	2003	10	2462	..	-138	2610	120
Roumanie	2004	0	3043	..	18	3025	140
	2005	0	3134	..	93	3041	141
	2006	0	2786	..	-10	2796	130
Russian Federation	2003	177435	25217	54625	1953	146074	1010
Fédération de Russie	2004	189758	22259	68616	-1577	144978	1008
	2005	209212	22390	86006	4159	141437	988
	2006	210418	25742	91391	-1002	145771	1023
Serbia	2003	54	140	..	..	194	18
Serbie	2004	72	88	..	..	160	15
	2005	95	64	..	..	159	15
	2006	0	60	..	..	60	6
Slovakia	2003	..	4945	..	-145	5090	946
Slovaquie	2004	..	5183	..	32	5151	957
	2005	..	5263	..	280	4983	925
	2006	..	4665	..	-483	5148	955
Slovenia	2003	..	54	0	..	54	27
Slovénie	2004	..	45	0	..	45	23
	2005	..	49	0	..	49	24
	2006	..	47	1	..	46	23
Spain	2003	9406	21552	..	-518	31476	749
Espagne	2004	8911	24473	..	-597	33981	796
	2005	8548	24756	..	356	32948	759
	2006	8353	23704	..	2662	29395	667
Sweden	2003	..	3195	2	270	2923	326
Suède	2004	..	3186	8	-151	3329	370
	2005	..	3203	3	130	3070	340
	2006	..	3052	2	-185	3235	356
Switzerland	2003	..	85	0	-96	181	25
Suisse	2004	..	177	0	0	177	24
	2005	..	100	0	-83	183	25
	2006	..	152	2	-2	152	20
T.F.Yug.Rep. Macedonia	2003	..	75	..	..	75	37
L'ex-RY Macédoine	2004	..	9	..	..	9	4
	2005	..	3	..	..	3	1
	2006	..	57	..	..	57	28
Ukraine	2003	63742	10297	2912	0	71127	1488
Ukraine	2004	59129	9379	3883	161	64464	1364
	2005	60007	7395	3666	122	63614	1351
	2006	61439	9835	3457	-420	68237	1459

Table 6

Production, trade and consumption of hard coal
Production, commerce et consommation de houille
Thousand metric tons and kilograms per capita
Milliers de tonnes métriques et kilogrammes par habitant

Country or area Pays ou zone	Year Année	Production Production	Imports Importations	Exports Exportations	Changes in stocks Variations des stocks	Consumption Consommation Total Totale	Consumption Consommation Per capita Par habitant
United Kingdom	2003	28279	31833	542	-2421	61991	1045
Royaume-Uni	2004	25097	36153	621	-176	60805	1019
	2005	20498	43968	536	2129	61801	1026
	2006	18528	50456	443	1258	67283	1111
Oceania	2003	241098	326	210959	-1584	32049	989
Océanie	2004	253662	348	220334	324	33352	1014
	2005	268803	334	233642	-832	36327	1089
	2006	267490	349	234016	-2548	36371	1074
Australia	2003	238746	..	208749	-1367	31364	1576
Australie	2004	251136	..	218426	-150	32860	1632
	2005	266259	..	231311	-934	35882	1758
	2006	264627	..	231296	-2549	35880	1733
Fiji	2003	..	*13	..	..	*13	*16
Fidji	2004	..	*13	..	..	*13	*16
	2005	..	*12	..	..	*12	*14
	2006	..	*12	..	..	*12	*14
New Caledonia	2003		313	..	..	313	1373
Nouvelle-Calédonie	2004		281	..	..	281	1218
	2005		260	..	..	260	1111
	2006		283	..	..	283	1189
New Zealand	2003	2352	0	2210	-217	359	90
Nouvelle-Zélande	2004	2526	54	1908	474	198	49
	2005	2544	62	2331	102	173	42
	2006	2863	54	2720	1	196	47

Table 7

International trade of hard coal
(Principal importers/exporters)
Thousand metric tons

2005

Importers	Exporters					
	World Monde	Australia Australie	Canada Canada	China Chine	Colombia Colombie	Indonesia Indonésie
Austria	4325	..	..	..	..	
Belgium	8804	2950	270	58	5	
Brazil	15750	6023	1737	384	447	22
Bulgaria	4287	267	267	..	..	
Canada	12767	..	..	51	1316	
Chile	4024	858	546	..	524	131
China	26171	5885	1229	..	..	244
China, Hong Kong SAR	10823	..	..	939	..	982
Denmark	6031	129	..	..	1254	
Finland	4723	487	519	..	..	
France incl. Monaco	19851	5337	491	15	2506	24
Germany	37105	4171	1657	..	3069	
India	38586	14365	..	3081	..	1605
Israel	10918	..	..	2923	..	
Italy and San Marino	24150	2791	1143	..	2997	680
Japan	176985	102460	7572	22057	..	2979
Korea, Republic of	76758	30871	4319	20838	..	1538
Malaysia	10295	3260	..	47	..	674
Morocco	4801	..	..	98	59	
Netherlands	20415	1785	902	83	5703	99
Pakistan	2842	589	104	582	..	109
Philippines	4615	427	..	434	..	343
Poland	3372	35	..	5	56	
Portugal	5272	..	..	..	2314	14
Russian Federation	22391	..	..	7	29	
Slovakia	5263	..	..	..	..	
Spain	24756	3115	301	225	1938	378
Thailand	8497	0	..	21	..	674
Turkey	17360	906	1175	1618	2456	
Ukraine	7721	..	..	..	..	
United Kingdom	43968	4465	1084	134	3297	161
United States	27506	210	1702	18	19247	22

Table 7

Commerce international de houille
(Principaux importateurs/exportateurs)
Milliers de tonnes métriques

2005

Exportateurs						Importtateurs
Kazakhstan Kazakhstan	Poland Pologne	Russian Federation Fédération de Russie	South Africa Customs Un. Un.douan.d'Afr.mérid	United States Etats-Unis	Viet Nam Viet Nam	
..	1835	31	10	501	..	Autriche
..	436	944	2081	1714	98	Belgique
..	..	471	527	4530	131	Brésil
..	..	1309	..	356	75	Bulgarie
..	..	114	..	10478	..	Canada
..	..	..	..	533	..	Chili
..	..	897	0	0	10200	Chine
..	..	59	..	0	0	Chine, Hong-Kong RAS
..	830	1531	1852	66	..	Danemark
..	564	2736	..	382	..	Finlande
..	1451	905	4225	1906	100	France y compris Monaco
..	8756	7546	8305	1267	..	Allemagne
..	..	45	3244	1022	120	Inde
..	..	..	..	30	..	Israël
..	465	1096	4600	2635	..	Italie y comp. St. Marin
..	..	10471	76	1352	2043	Japon
..	..	3507	..	1266	358	Corée, République de
..	..	..	..	..	119	Malaisie
..	436	218	3354	62	..	Maroc
..	97	1609	6084	1654	..	Pays-Bas
..	..	24	94	0	..	Pakistan
..	..	..	..	..	308	Philippines
87	..	2390	..	..	..	Pologne
..	222	..	1985	378	..	Portugal
22112	..	..	..	..	..	Fédération de Russie
..	806	2148	..	290	..	Slovaquie
..	127	4235	8736	1500	15	Espagne
..	..	..	..	0	490	Thaïlande
9	187	6772	1448	1810	..	Turquie
49	27	7431	..	214	..	Ukraine
..	647	17526	13034	1509	..	Royaume-Uni
..	70	357	70	..	85	Etats-Unis

Table 7

International trade of hard coal
(Principal importers/exporters)
Thousand metric tons

2006

Importers	Exporters					
	World Monde	Australia Australie	Canada Canada	China Chine	Colombia Colombie	Indonesia Indonésie
Austria	4118	..	..	..	..	
Belgium	8056	2137	351	27	4	
Brazil	14563	5767	1628	224	310	7
Bulgaria	4392	157	88	..	..	
Canada	11296	..	..	16	285	
Chile	4891	1579	725	..	385	160
China	38105	6898	146	..	..	507
China, Hong Kong SAR	11402	240	..	817	..	1021
Denmark	8688	290	..	..	1537	63
Finland	6684	249	434	..	323	27
France incl. Monaco	20391	5727	474	17	2234	58
Germany	42132	4748	1666	..	4184	
India	43081	15887	43	4093	..	1874
Israel	12532	..	..	2707	..	
Italy and San Marino	24632	3097	1071	..	2034	873
Japan	179097	105762	8772	19465	27	3191
Korea, Republic of	79707	29021	4855	18742	..	2069
Malaysia	11101	3607	..	27	..	721
Morocco	4738	..	..	46	128	2
Netherlands	22844	1827	609	62	5923	315
Pakistan	4251	146	54	107	..	190
Philippines	5956	627	..	459	..	458
Poland	5271	..	..	10	80	
Portugal	5782	..	..	..	3239	47
Russian Federation	25743	..	..	8	28	
Slovakia	4665	..	..	..	..	
Spain	23704	3548	234	294	1535	402
Thailand	11113	1489	..	4	..	800
Turkey	20286	1569	1125	1829	..	
Ukraine	9835	..	..	..	..	
United Kingdom	50456	4018	1282	55	3798	189
United States	32691	222	1749	39	22990	289

2006 Energy Statistics Yearbook United Nations / 2006 Annuaire des statistiques de l'énergie des Nations Unies

Table 7

Commerce international de houille
(Principaux importateurs/exportateurs)
Milliers de tonnes métriques

2006

	Exportateurs					Importtateurs
Kazakhstan Kazakhstan	Poland Pologne	Russian Federation Fédération de Russie	South Africa Customs Un. Un.douan.d'Afr.mérid	United States Etats-Unis	Viet Nam Viet Nam	
..	1918	53	..	306	..	Autriche
..	322	786	2260	1835	19	Belgique
..	70	385	621	4227	143	Brésil
..	35	1469	34	561	106	Bulgarie
..	..	264	..	10174	..	Canada
..	..	..	..	124	..	Chili
1	..	991	..	..	20029	Chine
..	..	126	..	..	..	Chine, Hong-Kong RAS
..	529	2040	3062	274	..	Danemark
23	530	3622	379	791	..	Finlande
..	928	1124	4236	2010	150	France y compris Monaco
..	9186	8712	8570	2058	..	Allemagne
..	..	50	2388	877	304	Inde
..	..	..	..	..	..	Israël
..	286	833	4779	2672	..	Italie y comp. St. Marin
..	..	9435	76	240	2251	Japon
..	..	5032	..	658	635	Corée, République de
..	..	..	15	..	171	Malaisie
..	..	394	3048	316	..	Maroc
..	237	1803	6430	1437	132	Pays-Bas
..	..	5	282	0	..	Pakistan
..	..	..	..	..	267	Philippines
160	..	3330	..	..	..	Pologne
..	..	22	1681	202	..	Portugal
25610	..	..	..	..	..	Fédération de Russie
..	1026	1355	16	207	..	Slovaquie
..	196	3609	8213	1422	110	Espagne
..	..	..	..	..	550	Thaïlande
..	164	8476	2215	1045	..	Turquie
963	36	8793	..	..	..	Ukraine
..	1188	22318	12953	1993	19	Royaume-Uni
..	..	853	56	..	..	Etats-Unis

Table 8

Production, trade and consumption of brown coal/lignite
Production, commerce et consommation de charbon brun/lignite

Thousand metric tons and kilograms per capita
Milliers de tonnes métriques et kilogrammes par habitant

Table Notes

Production and consumption of lignite, sub-bituminous coal and oil shale. Imports, exports and stock change for sub-bituminous coal and lignite.

Data on lignite for the Netherlands and the Russian Federation also include lignite briquettes.

• **Please refer to the Definitions Section on pages xv to xxix for the appropriate product description/ classification.**

Notes relatives aux tableaux

Production et consommation de lignite, charbon sous-bitumineux et schiste bitumineux. Commerce et variations des stocks de charbon sous-bitumineux et lignite.

Les données pour les Pays Bas et la Fédération de Russie comprennent les briquettes de lignite.

• **Veuillez consulter la section "définitions" de la page xv à la page xxix pour une description/classification appropriée des produits.**

Figure 17: World brown coal/lignite production 1993-2006

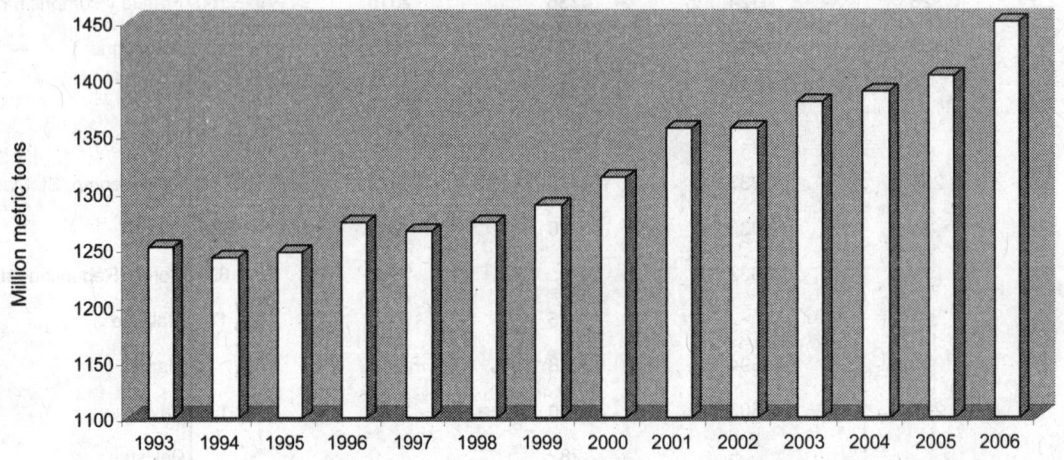

Figure 18: Major brown coal/lignite producing countries in 2006

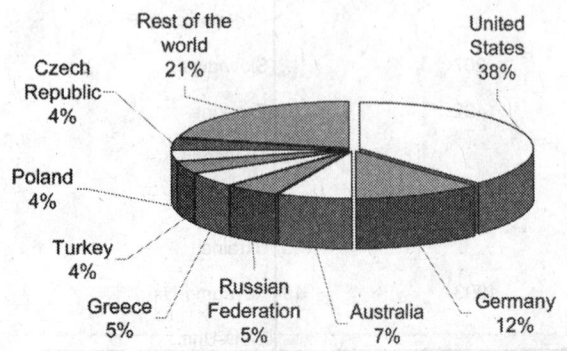

Figure 19: Major brown coal/lignite consuming countries in 2006

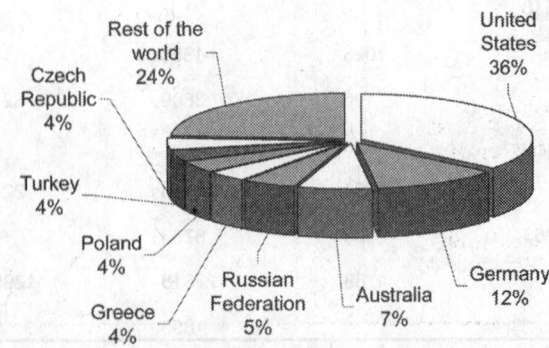

Table 8

Production, trade and consumption of lignite and sub-bituminous coal
Production, commerce et consommation de lignite et charbon sous-bitumineux

Thousand metric tons and kilograms per capita
Milliers de tonnes métriques et kilogrammes par habitant

Country or area Pays ou zone	Year Année	Production Production	Imports Importations	Exports Exportations	Changes in stocks Variations des stocks	Consumption Consommation	
						Total Totale	Per capita Par habitant
World	**2003**	**1378960**	**24696**	**14508**	**-6986**	**1396134**	**223**
Monde	**2004**	**1387923**	**21899**	**13453**	**-6902**	**1403271**	**221**
	2005	**1401474**	**28499**	**15076**	**-23197**	**1438094**	**224**
	2006	**1448507**	**32419**	**14553**	**22728**	**1443645**	**222**
America, North	**2003**	**523433**	**16085**	**8567**	**-9290**	**540241**	**1076**
Amérique du Nord	**2004**	**542845**	**10664**	**6819**	**-3869**	**550559**	**1086**
	2005	**552491**	**15825**	**7180**	**-14294**	**575430**	**1123**
	2006	**590044**	**17701**	**6245**	**26463**	**575037**	**1113**
Canada	2003	35573	9117	109	-1821	46402	1465
Canada	2004	36736	6435	117	2250	40804	1275
	2005	36759	8514	140	-280	45413	1405
	2006	36540	9475	251	3000	42764	1310
Mexico	2003	7973	6036	..	-175	14184	139
Mexique	2004	8147	2768	..	-766	11681	113
	2005	8963	5686	..	-465	15114	145
	2006	9573	5962	..	599	14936	142
United States	2003	479887	932	8458	-7294	479655	1649
Etats-Unis	2004	497962	1461	6702	-5353	498074	1696
	2005	506769	1625	7040	-13549	514903	1737
	2006	543931	2264	5994	22864	517337	1733
Asia	**2003**	**139914**	**3219**	**891**	**507**	**141735**	**37**
Asie	**2004**	**141262**	**4690**	**2186**	**-1229**	**144995**	**38**
	2005	**158037**	**6327**	**3185**	**-1260**	**162439**	**42**
	2006	**166860**	**7255**	**3430**	**1894**	**168791**	**43**
Cyprus	2003	..	0	..	..	0	0
Chypre	2004	..	1	..	..	1	1
	2005	..	1	..	..	1	1
	2006	..	1	..	..	1	1
India	2003	27958	..	..	-519	28477	27
Inde	2004	30337	..	..	309	30028	28
	2005	30066	..	..	-17	30083	27
	2006	31130	..	..	493	30637	27
Indonesia	2003	23021	..	..	..	23021	107
Indonésie	2004	22900	..	..	..	22900	105
	2005	25697	..	..	..	25697	117
	2006	27794	..	..	..	27794	125
Israel	2003	437	..	..	..	437	65
Israël	2004	439	..	..	..	439	64
	2005	413	..	..	..	413	60
	2006	452	..	..	..	452	64
Kazakhstan	2003	4099	0	139	..	3960	266
Kazakhstan	2004	3810	0	249	..	3561	237
	2005	3798	1	518	..	3281	217
	2006	4655	1	449	..	4207	275
Korea, Dem.Ppl's.Rep.	2003	7179	..	..	..	7179	306
Corée,Rép.pop.dém.de	2004	7340	..	..	..	7340	311
	2005	7746	..	..	..	7746	328
	2006	7946	..	..	..	7946	335
Korea, Republic of	2003	..	1741	..	..	1741	36
Corée, République de	2004	..	2610	..	..	2610	54
	2005	..	2862	..	..	2862	59
	2006	..	3706	..	..	3706	77

Table 8

Production, trade and consumption of lignite and sub-bituminous coal
Production, commerce et consommation de lignite et charbon sous-bitumineux

Thousand metric tons and kilograms per capita
Milliers de tonnes métriques et kilogrammes par habitant

Country or area Pays ou zone	Year Année	Production Production	Imports Importations	Exports Exportations	Changes in stocks Variations des stocks	Consumption Consommation	
						Total Totale	Per capita Par habitant
Kyrgyzstan	2003	352	0	1	..	351	70
Kirghizistan	2004	397	78	0	..	475	93
	2005	286	166	0	..	452	88
	2006	276	160	0	..	436	84
Lao People's Dem. Rep.	2003	250	..	171	..	79	14
Rép. dém. pop. lao	2004	300	..	*205	..	95	16
	2005	320	..	*225	..	95	17
	2006	319	..	*223	..	96	17
Mongolia	2003	4742	..	435	..	4307	1730
Mongolie	2004	5745	..	1560	..	4185	1662
	2005	6292	..	2116	..	4176	1639
	2006	6758	..	2457	..	4301	1668
Myanmar	2003	176	..	110	..	66	1
Myanmar	2004	213	..	144	..	69	1
	2005	367	..	295	..	72	1
	2006	380	..	269	..	111	2
Philippines	2003	4425	1459	..	..	5884	73
Philippines	2004	2576	1975	..	..	4551	55
	2005	2986	3268	..	..	6254	73
	2006	*3072	*3329	..	..	*6401	*74
Singapore	2003	..	1	..	..	1	0
Singapour	2004	..	1	..	..	1	0
	2005	..	1	..	..	1	0
	2006	..	0	..	..	0	0
Tajikistan	2003	15	..	..	..	15	2
Tadjikistan	2004	15	..	..	..	15	2
	2005	15	..	..	..	15	2
	2006	15	..	..	..	15	2
Thailand	2003	18843	..	..	879	17964	281
Thaïlande	2004	20060	..	..	-487	20547	320
	2005	20878	..	..	-168	21046	325
	2006	19001	..	..	149	18852	289
Turkey	2003	46504	0	15	102	46387	660
Turquie	2004	44431	0	0	-1114	45545	640
	2005	56170	0	0	-1145	57315	795
	2006	61936	29	0	1179	60786	833
Uzbekistan	2003	1913	18	20	45	1866	72
Ouzbékistan	2004	2699	25	28	63	2633	100
	2005	3003	28	31	70	2930	110
	2006	3126	29	32	73	3050	113
Europe	**2003**	**609868**	**5392**	**5050**	**-2870**	**613080**	**843**
Europe	**2004**	**600126**	**5723**	**4448**	**-4348**	**605749**	**832**
	2005	**587140**	**5325**	**4711**	**-4246**	**592000**	**812**
	2006	**585874**	**6281**	**4878**	**-2999**	**590276**	**809**
Albania	2003	81	9	..	..	90	26
Albanie	2004	109	9	..	..	118	38
	2005	92	13	..	..	105	33
	2006	92	13	..	..	105	33
Austria	2003	1152	5	..	-490	1647	204
Autriche	2004	235	23	..	-970	1228	151
	2005	0	113	..	-1157	1270	155
	2006	0	140	..	-613	753	91

Table 8

Production, trade and consumption of lignite and sub-bituminous coal
Production, commerce et consommation de lignite et charbon sous-bitumineux

Thousand metric tons and kilograms per capita
Milliers de tonnes métriques et kilogrammes par habitant

Country or area Pays ou zone	Year Année	Production Production	Imports Importations	Exports Exportations	Changes in stocks Variations des stocks	Consumption Consommation	
						Total Totale	Per capita Par habitant
Belgium	2003	129	188	35	-11	293	28
Belgique	2004	181	190	47	-4	328	32
	2005	109	206	25	7	283	27
	2006	29	289	16	-11	313	30
Bosnia and Herzegovina	2003	8934	..	505	16	8413	2195
Bosnie y Herzégovine	2004	8884	..	437	45	8402	2187
	2005	9119	..	299	-45	8865	2307
	2006	10125	..	299	-45	9871	2569
Bulgaria	2003	27248	..	0	-237	27485	3513
Bulgarie	2004	26452	..	0	160	26292	3379
	2005	24686	..	0	-184	24870	3213
	2006	25651	..	1	-125	25775	3348
Croatia	2003	..	93	..	..	93	21
Croatie	2004	..	83	..	..	83	19
	2005	..	83	..	..	83	19
	2006	..	84	..	..	84	19
Czech Republic	2003	56041	830	3042	-45	53874	5281
République tchèque	2004	56760	1092	3376	1762	52714	5165
	2005	54890	729	3251	-105	52473	5127
	2006	54705	984	3477	-829	53041	5156
Estonia	2003	14892	1111	9	517	15477	11434
Estonie	2004	13993	1195	9	-324	15503	11490
	2005	14591	180	4	-37	14804	10998
	2006	14095	0	9	58	14028	10441
France incl. Monaco	2003	9	42	..	..	51	1
France y compris Monaco	2004	0	40	..	..	40	1
	2005	0	36	..	..	36	1
	2006	0	36	..	..	36	1
Germany	2003	179085	35	1	-639	179758	2178
Allemagne	2004	181926	17	1	-6	181948	2205
	2005	177907	9	1	23	177892	2157
	2006	176321	53	1	-5	176378	2141
Greece	2003	68299	..	..	-1770	70069	6356
Grèce	2004	70041	..	..	-814	70855	6405
	2005	69398	..	..	-698	70096	6313
	2006	64521	..	..	189	64332	5770
Hungary	2003	13301	317	14	57	13547	1337
Hongrie	2004	11242	385	66	-612	12173	1204
	2005	9570	706	373	-345	10248	1016
	2006	9952	674	488	-46	10184	1011
Ireland	2003	..	50	..	9	41	10
Irlande	2004	..	41	..	8	33	8
	2005	..	52	..	-1	53	13
	2006	..	13	..	4	9	2
Italy and San Marino	2003	..	8	..	..	8	0
Italie y comp. St. Marin	2004	..	9	..	..	9	0
	2005	..	8	..	..	8	0
	2006	..	8	..	..	8	0
Lithuania	2003	..	0	..	..	0	0
Lituanie	2004	..	1	..	..	1	0
	2005	..	3	..	..	3	1
	2006	..	3	..	..	3	1

Table 8

Production, trade and consumption of lignite and sub-bituminous coal
Production, commerce et consommation de lignite et charbon sous-bitumineux

Thousand metric tons and kilograms per capita
Milliers de tonnes métriques et kilogrammes par habitant

Country or area Pays ou zone	Year Année	Production Production	Imports Importations	Exports Exportations	Changes in stocks Variations des stocks	Consumption Consommation	
						Total Totale	Per capita Par habitant
Netherlands	2003	..	39	..	0	39	2
Pays-Bas	2004	..	46	..	2	44	3
	2005	..	50	..	0	50	3
	2006	..	39	..	4	35	2
Poland	2003	60920	0	36	13	60871	1594
Pologne	2004	61198	0	27	-4	61175	1602
	2005	61636	0	8	39	61589	1614
	2006	60844	5	0	49	60800	1594
Romania	2003	33053	827	0	-441	34321	1579
Roumanie	2004	31792	464	0	-318	32574	1503
	2005	31106	988	0	-867	32961	1524
	2006	34923	1293	8	-1419	37627	1743
Russian Federation	2003	79544	127	1317	251	78103	540
Fédération de Russie	2004	69186	170	315	-3019	72060	501
	2005	73668	253	552	213	73156	511
	2006	74148	341	539	21	73929	519
Serbia	2003	40225	126	78	0	40273	3805
Serbie	2004	41085	270	116	0	41239	3921
	2005	35149	265	177	0	35237	3365
	2006	36780	496	6	-97	37367	3575
Slovakia	2003	3097	806	..	-57	3960	736
Slovaquie	2004	2952	663	..	26	3589	667
	2005	2511	737	..	-59	3307	614
	2006	2201	932	..	-35	3168	588
Slovenia	2003	4830	515	11	44	5290	2652
Slovénie	2004	4809	586	49	17	5329	2669
	2005	4540	544	20	-79	5143	2570
	2006	4522	558	34	-139	5185	2582
Spain	2003	11156	..	..	-243	11399	271
Espagne	2004	11576	..	..	-247	11823	277
	2005	10933	..	..	-617	11550	266
	2006	10094	..	..	-9	10103	229
Switzerland	2003	..	4	..	0	4	1
Suisse	2004	..	4	..	0	4	1
	2005	..	39	..	0	39	5
	2006	..	91	..	5	86	11
T.F.Yug.Rep. Macedonia	2003	7382	260	0	156	7486	3693
L'ex-RY Macédoine	2004	7245	235	3	-74	7551	3720
	2005	6881	286	1	-304	7470	3667
	2006	6639	229	0	45	6823	3344
Ukraine	2003	490	0	2	0	488	10
Ukraine	2004	460	200	2	24	634	13
	2005	354	25	0	-30	409	9
	2006	232	0	0	-1	233	5
Oceania	**2003**	**105745**	**0**	**..**	**4667**	**101078**	**3119**
Océanie	**2004**	**103690**	**822**	**..**	**2544**	**101968**	**3101**
	2005	**103806**	**1022**	**..**	**-3397**	**108225**	**3244**
	2006	**105729**	**1182**	**..**	**-2630**	**109541**	**3234**
Australia	2003	102917	..	..	5034	97883	4918
Australie	2004	101061	..	..	2669	98392	4885
	2005	101083	..	..	-3104	104187	5105
	2006	102825	..	..	-2723	105548	5099

Table 8

Production, trade and consumption of lignite and sub-bituminous coal
Production, commerce et consommation de lignite et charbon sous-bitumineux

Thousand metric tons and kilograms per capita
Milliers de tonnes métriques et kilogrammes par habitant

Country or area Pays ou zone	Year Année	Production Production	Imports Importations	Exports Exportations	Changes in stocks Variations des stocks	Consumption Consommation	
						Total Totale	Per capita Par habitant
New Zealand	2003	2828	0	..	-367	3195	797
Nouvelle-Zélande	2004	2629	822	..	-125	3576	880
	2005	2723	1022	..	-293	4038	985
	2006	2904	1182	..	93	3993	964

Table 9

Production, trade and consumption of coke
Production, commerce et consommation de coke
Thousand metric tons and kilograms per capita
Milliers de tonnes métriques et kilogrammes par habitant

Table Notes

Production, trade, stock change and consumption for coke oven coke, brown coal coke, petroleum coke and gas coke.

- **Please refer to the Definitions Section on pages xv to xxix for the appropriate product description/ classification.**

Notes relatives aux tableaux

Production, commerce, variations des stocks et consommation de coke de four, coke de lignite, coke de pétrole et coke de gaz.

- **Veuillez consulter la section "définitions" de la page xv à la page xxix pour une description/classification appropriée des produits.**

Figure 20: World production of coke 1993-2006

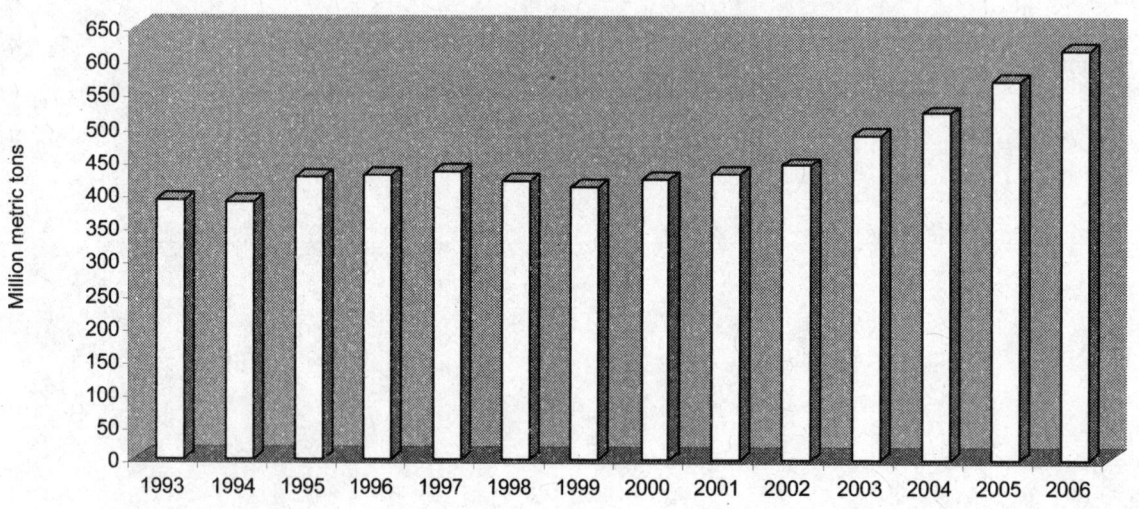

Figure 21: Major coke producing countries in 2006

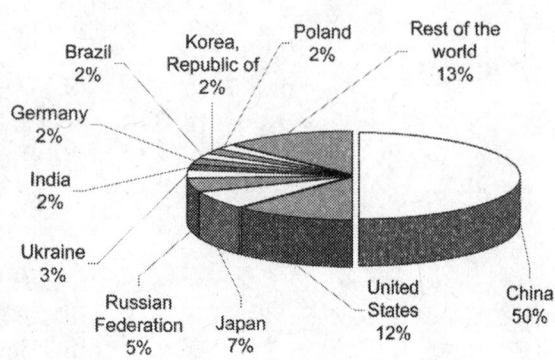

Figure 22: Major coke consuming countries in 2006

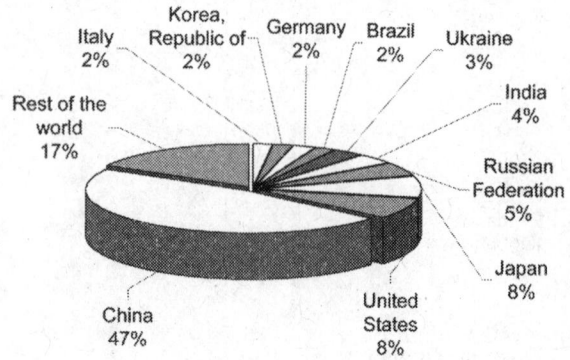

Table 9

Production, trade and consumption of coke
Production, commerce et consommation de coke

Thousand metric tons and kilograms per capita
Milliers de tonnes métriques et kilogrammes par habitant

Country or area Pays ou zone	Year Année	Production Production	Imports Importations	Exports Exportations	Changes in stocks Variations des stocks	Consumption Consommation	
						Total Totale	Per capita Par habitant
World	**2003**	**487357**	**60029**	**62674**	**-4030**	**488742**	**78**
Monde	**2004**	**521183**	**67080**	**66461**	**-6557**	**528360**	**83**
	2005	**568332**	**62757**	**57740**	**-13143**	**586492**	**91**
	2006	**616770**	**64102**	**63071**	**1770**	**616031**	**95**
Africa	**2003**	**4960**	**212**	**645**	**-55**	**4582**	**5**
Afrique	**2004**	**5060**	**235**	**629**	**-50**	**4716**	**5**
	2005	**5058**	**431**	**629**	**-63**	**4923**	**6**
	2006	**4925**	**447**	**671**	**-16**	**4717**	**5**
Algeria	2003	662	14	..	-112	788	25
Algérie	2004	585	51	..	-97	733	23
	2005	531	60	..	-97	688	21
	2006	651	73	..	-38	762	23
Dem. Rep. of Congo	2003	..	107	..	..	107	2
Rép. dem. du Congo	2004	..	118	..	..	118	2
	2005	..	125	..	..	125	2
	2006	..	133	..	..	133	2
Egypt	2003	2155	58	446	..	1767	26
Egypte	2004	2119	56	430	..	1745	25
	2005	2133	56	430	..	1759	25
	2006	1966	51	471	..	1546	21
Kenya	2003	..	*1	..	..	*1	0
Kenya	2004	..	0	..	..	0	0
	2005	..	0	..	..	0	0
	2006	..	0	..	..	0	0
Malawi	2003	..	*3	..	..	*3	0
Malawi	2004	..	*3	..	..	*3	0
	2005	..	*2	..	..	*2	0
	2006	..	*2	..	..	*2	0
Nigeria	2003	..	*3	..	..	*3	0
Nigéria	2004	..	*3	..	..	*3	0
	2005	..	*3	..	..	*3	0
	2006	..	*3	..	..	*3	0
South Africa Customs Un.	2003	1607	..	..	..	1607	31
Un.douan.d'Afr.mérid	2004	1840	..	..	..	1840	35
	2005	1905	..	..	..	1905	36
	2006	1842	..	..	..	1842	34
Tunisia	2003	..	26	..	..	26	3
Tunisie	2004	..	4	..	..	4	0
	2005	..	185	..	..	185	18
	2006	..	*185	..	..	*185	*18
Zambia	2003	*10	..	..	..	*10	*1
Zambie	2004	*10	..	..	..	*10	*1
	2005	*10	..	..	..	*10	*1
	2006	*10	..	..	..	*10	*1
Zimbabwe	2003	526	..	199	57	270	21
Zimbabwe	2004	506	..	199	47	260	20
	2005	479	..	199	34	246	19
	2006	456	..	200	22	234	18
America, North	**2003**	**80072**	**6294**	**25369**	**-565**	**61562**	**123**
Amérique du Nord	**2004**	**84185**	**10738**	**25289**	**-1753**	**71387**	**141**
	2005	**82299**	**7126**	**25438**	**-616**	**64603**	**126**
	2006	**82586**	**8243**	**26064**	**-798**	**65563**	**127**

Table 9

Production, trade and consumption of coke
Production, commerce et consommation de coke
Thousand metric tons and kilograms per capita
Milliers de tonnes métriques et kilogrammes par habitant

Country or area Pays ou zone	Year Année	Production Production	Imports Importations	Exports Exportations	Changes in stocks Variations des stocks	Consumption Consommation Total Totale	Per capita Par habitant
Canada	2003	7279	1659	275	-31	8694	274
Canada	2004	7846	2146	294	-206	9904	310
	2005	7295	1782	318	-126	8885	275
	2006	6835	1875	212	-47	8545	262
Costa Rica	2003	..	78	..	..	78	19
Costa Rica	2004	..	62	..	..	62	15
	2005	..	29	..	..	29	7
	2006	..	63	..	..	63	14
Cuba	2003	18	14	..	..	32	3
Cuba	2004	13	16	..	..	29	3
	2005	17	23	..	..	40	4
	2006	14	*20	..	..	*34	*3
Dominican Republic	2003	..	0	..	..	0	0
Rép. dominicaine	2004	..	0	..	..	0	0
	2005	..	0	..	..	0	0
	2006	..	106	..	..	106	11
El Salvador	2003	..	1	..	..	1	0
El Salvador	2004	..	1	..	..	1	0
	2005	..	2	..	..	2	0
	2006	..	1	..	..	1	0
Honduras	2003	..	0	..	0	0	0
Honduras	2004	..	0	..	0	0	0
	2005	..	77	..	-10	87	12
	2006	..	11	..	1	10	1
Mexico	2003	3208	511	2	-466	4183	41
Mexique	2004	4279	528	2	-625	5430	53
	2005	3487	390	2	-731	4606	44
	2006	3709	323	3	-855	4884	47
Nicaragua	2003	..	58	..	10	48	9
Nicaragua	2004	..	51	..	-1	52	10
	2005	..	51	..	1	50	9
	2006	..	*42	..	0	*42	*8
Panama	2003	..	0	..	..	0	0
Panama	2004	..	2	..	..	2	1
	2005	..	2	..	..	2	1
	2006	..	2	..	..	2	1
United States	2003	69567	3973	25092	-78	48526	167
Etats-Unis	2004	72047	7932	24993	-921	55907	190
	2005	71500	4770	25118	250	50902	172
	2006	72028	5800	25849	103	51876	174
America, South	**2003**	**15944**	**5991**	**1594**	**107**	**20234**	**56**
Amérique du Sud	**2004**	**16624**	**5868**	**2521**	**9**	**19962**	**54**
	2005	**17440**	**5343**	**1382**	**214**	**21187**	**57**
	2006	**16386**	**5275**	**1078**	**-266**	**20849**	**55**
Argentina	2003	2809	0	369	-26	2466	65
Argentine	2004	2783	138	500	-5	2426	63
	2005	2760	153	144	-1	2770	72
	2006	2771	154	144	-1	2782	71
Brazil	2003	9236	5476	309	63	14340	80
Brésil	2004	9802	4857	310	-93	14442	80
	2005	10502	4346	291	201	14356	78
	2006	10198	4440	197	57	14384	77

Table 9

Production, trade and consumption of coke
Production, commerce et consommation de coke
Thousand metric tons and kilograms per capita
Milliers de tonnes métriques et kilogrammes par habitant

Country or area Pays ou zone	Year Année	Production Production	Imports Importations	Exports Exportations	Changes in stocks Variations des stocks	Consumption Consommation	
						Total Totale	Per capita Par habitant
Chile	2003	1012	303	70	92	1153	72
Chili	2004	964	559	37	84	1402	87
	2005	948	611	39	83	1437	88
	2006	993	298	9	-156	1438	88
Colombia	2003	448	..	118	..	330	7
Colombie	2004	470	..	215	..	255	6
	2005	459	..	25	..	434	9
	2006	473	..	26	..	447	10
Peru	2003	25	194	..	3	216	8
Pérou	2004	18	260	..	11	267	10
	2005	0	231	..	-81	312	11
	2006	0	315	..	21	294	11
Uruguay	2003	19	18	..	3	34	10
Uruguay	2004	32	54	..	29	57	17
	2005	32	2	..	-29	63	19
	2006	26	68	..	32	62	19
Venezuela(Bolivar. Rep.)	2003	2395	..	728	-28	1695	66
Venezuela(Rép. bolivar.)	2004	2555	..	1459	-17	1113	43
	2005	2739	..	883	41	1815	68
	2006	1925	..	702	-219	1442	53
Asia	**2003**	**267044**	**15035**	**18176**	**-3750**	**267653**	**70**
Asie	**2004**	**292536**	**17975**	**18739**	**-5695**	**297468**	**77**
	2005	**346653**	**18586**	**15768**	**-14804**	**364275**	**94**
	2006	**393225**	**18756**	**18862**	**2965**	**390154**	**99**
Azerbaijan	2003	21	..	19	..	2	0
Azerbaïdjan	2004	26	..	23	..	3	0
	2005	12	..	10	..	2	0
	2006	67	..	61	..	6	1
China	2003	183492	0	14721	-3729	172500	134
Chine	2004	208231	5	15407	-5737	198566	153
	2005	263027	62	12965	-15515	265639	204
	2006	307582	672	15885	3311	289058	220
Cyprus	2003	..	113	..	-24	137	190
Chypre	2004	..	135	..	-11	146	198
	2005	..	143	..	-11	154	203
	2006	..	153	..	7	146	189
Georgia	2003	..	37	..	..	37	9
Géorgie	2004	..	0	..	..	0	0
	2005	..	13	..	..	13	3
	2006	..	7	..	..	7	2
India	2003	15864	1894	201	..	17557	16
Inde	2004	15835	2515	211	..	18139	17
	2005	16529	4407	199	..	20737	19
	2006	16345	4885	16	..	21214	19
Indonesia	2003	507	88	438	..	157	1
Indonésie	2004	685	136	325	..	496	2
	2005	*650	*120	*350	..	*420	*2
	2006	*640	*115	*340	..	*415	*2
Iran(Islamic Rep. of)	2003	1226	..	..	..	1226	18
Iran(Rép. islamique)	2004	1016	..	..	..	1016	15
	2005	1160	..	..	..	1160	17
	2006	1184	..	..	..	1184	17

Table 9

Production, trade and consumption of coke
Production, commerce et consommation de coke

Thousand metric tons and kilograms per capita
Milliers de tonnes métriques et kilogrammes par habitant

Country or area Pays ou zone	Year Année	Production Production	Imports Importations	Exports Exportations	Changes in stocks Variations des stocks	Consumption Consommation	
						Total Totale	Per capita Par habitant
Israel	2003	..	332	..	..	332	50
Israël	2004	..	784	..	..	784	115
	2005	..	626	..	..	626	90
	2006	..	447	..	..	447	63
Japan	2003	44396	6435	2692	60	48079	381
Japon	2004	43961	7426	2115	-7	49279	390
	2005	44730	7292	1760	557	49705	394
	2006	45852	6425	2057	-547	50767	402
Kazakhstan	2003	2535	974	1	0	3508	235
Kazakhstan	2004	2741	1009	401	-21	3370	224
	2005	2558	986	1	8	3535	233
	2006	2694	868	0	0	3562	233
Korea, Dem.Ppl's.Rep.	2003	..	212	..	..	212	9
Corée,Rép.pop.dém.de	2004	..	217	..	..	217	9
	2005	..	229	..	..	229	10
	2006	..	235	..	..	235	10
Korea, Republic of	2003	10637	425	48	3	11011	230
Corée, République de	2004	10909	689	57	-4	11545	240
	2005	9191	341	52	2	9478	196
	2006	10153	314	63	-5	10409	216
Kyrgyzstan	2003	..	0	..	..	0	0
Kirghizistan	2004	..	0	..	..	0	0
	2005	..	1	..	..	1	0
	2006	..	0	..	..	0	0
Malaysia	2003	..	*3500	0	..	*3500	*140
Malaisie	2004	..	4330	0	..	4330	169
	2005	..	3602	182	..	3420	131
	2006	..	*3500	*200	..	*3300	*124
Mongolia	2003	..	0	..	..	0	0
Mongolie	2004	..	1	..	..	1	0
	2005	..	0	..	..	0	0
	2006	..	0	..	..	0	0
Myanmar	2003	25	..	..	0	25	0
Myanmar	2004	22	..	..	0	22	0
	2005	21	..	..	0	21	0
	2006	22	..	..	5	17	0
Other Asia	2003	4748	203	51	-25	4925	218
Autre Asie	2004	5085	48	195	38	4900	216
	2005	5275	55	244	177	4909	216
	2006	5148	379	235	175	5117	225
Pakistan	2003	547	..	..	..	547	4
Pakistan	2004	890	..	..	..	890	6
	2005	396	..	..	..	396	3
	2006	218	..	..	..	218	1
Philippines	2003	..	75	..	..	75	1
Philippines	2004	..	60	..	..	60	1
	2005	..	60	..	..	60	1
	2006	..	84	..	..	84	1
Singapore	2003	..	28	..	..	28	7
Singapour	2004	..	21	..	..	21	5
	2005	..	19	..	..	19	4
	2006	..	18	..	..	18	4

Table 9

Production, trade and consumption of coke
Production, commerce et consommation de coke

Thousand metric tons and kilograms per capita
Milliers de tonnes métriques et kilogrammes par habitant

Country or area Pays ou zone	Year Année	Production Production	Imports Importations	Exports Exportations	Changes in stocks Variations des stocks	Consumption Consommation	
						Total Totale	Per capita Par habitant
Sri Lanka	2003	..	1	..	..	1	0
Sri Lanka	2004	..	1	..	..	1	0
	2005	..	1	..	..	1	0
	2006	..	1	..	..	1	0
Syrian Arab Republic	2003	*120	11	5	..	*126	*7
Rép. arabe syrienne	2004	*100	9	5	..	*104	*6
	2005	*75	9	5	..	*79	*4
	2006	*72	9	5	..	*76	*4
Tajikistan	2003	..	133	..	..	133	20
Tadjikistan	2004	..	135	..	..	135	20
	2005	..	137	..	..	137	20
	2006	..	137	..	..	137	19
Thailand	2003	..	65	..	..	65	1
Thaïlande	2004	..	64	..	..	64	1
	2005	..	69	..	..	69	1
	2006	..	53	..	..	53	1
Turkey	2003	2878	509	..	-35	3422	49
Turquie	2004	2990	390	..	47	3333	47
	2005	2992	414	..	-22	3428	48
	2006	3213	454	..	19	3648	50
Uzbekistan	2003	48	..	..	..	48	2
Ouzbékistan	2004	45	..	..	..	45	2
	2005	37	..	..	..	37	1
	2006	35	..	..	..	35	1
Europe	**2003**	**115345**	**31570**	**16628**	**93**	**130194**	**179**
Europe	**2004**	**118226**	**31355**	**19023**	**312**	**130246**	**179**
	2005	**112353**	**30235**	**14522**	**1151**	**126915**	**174**
	2006	**115579**	**30386**	**16396**	**-926**	**130495**	**179**
Albania	2003	67	85	34	..	118	33
Albanie	2004	63	89	5	..	147	47
	2005	48	0	0	..	48	15
	2006	65	41	0	..	106	34
Austria	2003	1454	1240	3	36	2655	329
Autriche	2004	1459	1242	42	40	2619	322
	2005	1503	1506	20	-44	3033	370
	2006	1512	1358	42	-102	2930	354
Belarus	2003	..	85	0	2	83	8
Bélarus	2004	..	88	0	-2	90	9
	2005	..	80	1	1	78	8
	2006	..	86	1	3	82	8
Belgium	2003	3217	593	117	51	3642	352
Belgique	2004	3273	420	87	13	3593	346
	2005	3091	328	22	20	3377	323
	2006	3194	261	180	-52	3327	317
Bosnia and Herzegovina	2003	0	..	0	..	0	0
Bosnie y Herzégovine	2004	221	..	210	..	11	3
	2005	456	..	433	..	23	6
	2006	482	..	458	..	24	6
Bulgaria	2003	846	522	0	41	1327	170
Bulgarie	2004	867	399	44	-36	1258	162
	2005	771	538	21	48	1240	160
	2006	696	529	2	-32	1255	163

Table 9

Production, trade and consumption of coke
Production, commerce et consommation de coke
Thousand metric tons and kilograms per capita
Milliers de tonnes métriques et kilogrammes par habitant

Country or area Pays ou zone	Year Année	Production Production	Imports Importations	Exports Exportations	Changes in stocks Variations des stocks	Consumption Consommation	
						Total Totale	Per capita Par habitant
Croatia	2003	105	24	56	-16	89	20
Croatie	2004	112	88	40	2	158	36
	2005	104	196	35	-1	266	60
	2006	114	235	37	14	298	67
Czech Republic	2003	3807	1004	969	12	3830	375
République tchèque	2004	3789	1122	976	7	3928	385
	2005	3643	788	937	60	3434	336
	2006	3662	996	991	-16	3683	358
Denmark	2003	..	319	9	28	282	53
Danemark	2004	..	272	16	-49	305	56
	2005	..	333	20	29	284	52
	2006	..	280	16	-40	304	56
Estonia	2003	30	1	29	1	1	1
Estonie	2004	35	0	35	0	0	0
	2005	37	0	37	0	0	0
	2006	33	0	33	0	0	0
Finland	2003	1022	523	..	-40	1585	304
Finlande	2004	1041	514	..	3	1552	297
	2005	1022	592	..	-17	1631	311
	2006	990	580	..	-22	1592	302
France incl. Monaco	2003	5434	2965	472	84	7843	130
France y compris Monaco	2004	5427	2960	949	-73	7511	124
	2005	5314	3296	755	284	7571	124
	2006	5625	3267	749	-145	8288	136
Germany	2003	9626	6085	821	-298	15188	184
Allemagne	2004	10273	5268	781	-249	15009	182
	2005	10309	4555	735	-70	14199	172
	2006	10290	4675	742	128	14095	171
Greece	2003	154	510	..	34	630	57
Grèce	2004	152	558	..	-38	748	68
	2005	150	627	..	-2	779	70
	2006	171	566	..	-38	775	70
Hungary	2003	887	222	208	-1	902	89
Hongrie	2004	1003	189	231	6	955	94
	2005	949	222	184	9	978	97
	2006	1309	51	366	25	969	96
Iceland	2003	..	191	..	..	191	660
Islande	2004	..	197	..	..	197	673
	2005	..	180	..	..	180	608
	2006	..	213	..	..	213	700
Ireland	2003	..	543	16	..	527	132
Irlande	2004	..	352	0	..	352	87
	2005	..	374	0	..	374	91
	2006	..	378	0	..	378	89
Italy and San Marino	2003	4908	4812	226	232	9262	161
Italie y comp. St. Marin	2004	5457	4341	356	36	9406	162
	2005	6258	3871	422	-411	10118	173
	2006	6214	4083	445	165	9687	164
Latvia	2003	..	41	..	6	35	15
Lettonie	2004	..	36	..	-4	40	17
	2005	..	28	..	8	20	9
	2006	..	18	..	-7	25	11

Table 9

Production, trade and consumption of coke
Production, commerce et consommation de coke

Thousand metric tons and kilograms per capita
Milliers de tonnes métriques et kilogrammes par habitant

Country or area Pays ou zone	Year Année	Production Production	Imports Importations	Exports Exportations	Changes in stocks Variations des stocks	Consumption Consommation	
						Total Totale	Per capita Par habitant
Lithuania	2003	96	14	..	0	110	32
Lituanie	2004	117	16	..	2	131	38
	2005	129	51	..	31	149	44
	2006	109	27	..	-8	144	42
Netherlands	2003	2249	700	574	-7	2382	147
Pays-Bas	2004	2314	427	356	43	2342	144
	2005	2567	1834	1196	151	3054	187
	2006	2265	604	900	-60	2029	124
Norway,Svlbd.J.Myn. I	2003	224	746	90	19	861	188
Norvège,Svalbd,J.May	2004	173	806	17	-4	966	210
	2005	226	742	8	35	925	199
	2006	211	766	9	-36	1004	215
Poland	2003	10112	164	5267	-64	5073	133
Pologne	2004	10559	306	5657	0	5208	136
	2005	8791	392	4950	515	3718	97
	2006	10043	244	6671	-553	4169	109
Portugal	2003	..	573	..	-46	619	59
Portugal	2004	..	752	..	24	728	69
	2005	..	899	..	61	838	79
	2006	..	715	..	-89	804	76
Republic of Moldova	2003	..	6	..	0	6	2
Rép. de Moldova	2004	..	0	..	-2	2	1
	2005	..	0	..	-2	2	1
	2006	..	0	..	0	0	0
Romania	2003	2201	1126	44	-73	3356	154
Roumanie	2004	2395	1575	105	189	3676	170
	2005	2781	853	146	69	3419	158
	2006	2703	738	137	-66	3370	156
Russian Federation	2003	32650	2	3337	9	29306	203
Fédération de Russie	2004	33214	204	3871	79	29468	205
	2005	31014	153	2881	46	28240	197
	2006	31955	52	1828	-31	30210	212
Serbia	2003	..	360	0	0	360	34
Serbie	2004	..	612	0	0	612	58
	2005	..	771	0	0	771	74
	2006	..	1034	1	-3	1036	99
Slovakia	2003	1933	399	106	-23	2249	418
Slovaquie	2004	1935	412	55	50	2242	417
	2005	1973	363	209	-25	2152	399
	2006	1975	622	210	27	2360	438
Slovenia	2003	..	91	..	-4	95	48
Slovénie	2004	..	165	..	1	164	82
	2005	..	170	..	-6	176	88
	2006	..	181	..	-2	183	91
Spain	2003	3293	3906	839	10	6350	151
Espagne	2004	3843	4119	1122	35	6805	159
	2005	3711	3882	760	151	6682	154
	2006	3875	4120	1358	0	6637	151
Sweden	2003	1335	486	58	-38	1801	201
Suède	2004	1429	508	35	63	1839	204
	2005	1467	443	35	81	1794	199
	2006	1234	269	26	-49	1526	168

Table 9

Production, trade and consumption of coke
Production, commerce et consommation de coke

Thousand metric tons and kilograms per capita
Milliers de tonnes métriques et kilogrammes par habitant

Country or area Pays ou zone	Year Année	Production Production	Imports Importations	Exports Exportations	Changes in stocks Variations des stocks	Consumption Consommation	
						Total Totale	Per capita Par habitant
Switzerland	2003	0	70	0	..	70	10
Suisse	2004	32	86	0	..	118	16
	2005	57	94	0	..	151	20
	2006	72	96	7	..	161	22
T.F.Yug.Rep. Macedonia	2003	..	125	14	12	99	49
L'ex-RY Macédoine	2004	..	110	27	-1	84	41
	2005	..	130	21	6	103	51
	2006	..	136	21	13	102	50
Ukraine	2003	23464	1225	2591	0	22098	462
Ukraine	2004	23062	995	3211	57	20789	440
	2005	19751	76	5	-55	19877	422
	2006	20134	1302	441	248	20747	444
United Kingdom	2003	6231	1812	748	126	7169	121
Royaume-Uni	2004	5981	2127	795	120	7193	120
	2005	6231	1868	689	179	7231	120
	2006	6646	1863	725	-198	7982	132
Oceania	**2003**	**3992**	**927**	**262**	**140**	**4517**	**139**
Océanie	**2004**	**4552**	**909**	**260**	**620**	**4581**	**139**
	2005	**4529**	**1036**	**1**	**975**	**4589**	**138**
	2006	**4069**	**995**	**0**	**811**	**4253**	**126**
Australia	2003	3992	808	262	140	4398	221
Australie	2004	4552	779	260	620	4451	221
	2005	4529	914	1	975	4467	219
	2006	4069	872	0	811	4130	200
New Zealand	2003	..	119	..	..	119	30
Nouvelle-Zélande	2004	..	130	..	..	130	32
	2005	..	122	..	..	122	30
	2006	..	123	..	..	123	30

Table 10

Production, trade and consumption of hard coal briquettes
Production, commerce et consommation d'agglomérés (briquettes de houille)
Thousand metric tons and kilograms per capita
Milliers de tonnes métriques et kilogrammes par habitant

Table Notes:
- Please refer to the Definitions Section on pages xv to xxix for the appropriate product description/classification.

Notes relatives aux tableaux:
- Veuillez consulter la section "définitions" de la page xv à la page xxix pour une description/classification appropriée des produits.

Figure 23: Major hard coal briquette producing countries in 2006

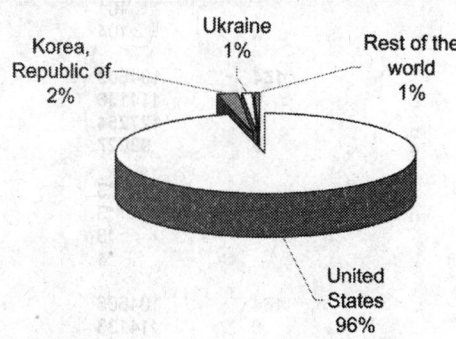

Korea, Republic of 2%
Ukraine 1%
Rest of the world 1%
United States 96%

Figure 24: Major hard coal briquette consuming countries in 2006

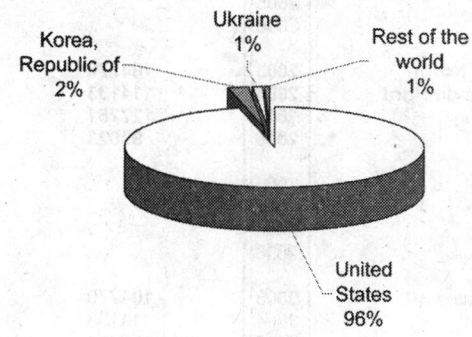

Korea, Republic of 2%
Ukraine 1%
Rest of the world 1%
United States 96%

Table 10

Production, trade and consumption of hard coal briquettes
Production, commerce et consommation d'agglomérés (briquettes de houille)

Thousand metric tons and kilograms per capita
Milliers de tonnes métriques et kilogrammes par habitant

Country or area Pays ou zone	Year Année	Production Production	Imports Importations	Exports. Exportations	Changes in stocks Variations des stocks	Consumption Consommation Total Totale	Per capita Par habitant
World	**2003**	**108390**	**206**	**129**	**162**	**108305**	**17**
Monde	**2004**	**117346**	**210**	**111**	**-24**	**117469**	**19**
	2005	**130865**	**274**	**77**	**-7**	**131069**	**20**
	2006	**103028**	**345**	**213**	**-4**	**103164**	**16**
Africa	**2003**	..	**96**	..	..	**96**	**0**
Afrique	**2004**	..	**99**	..	..	**99**	**0**
	2005	..	**101**	..	..	**101**	**0**
	2006	..	**104**	..	..	**104**	**0**
Dem. Rep. of Congo	2003	..	96	..	..	96	2
Rép. dem. du Congo	2004	..	99	..	..	99	2
	2005	..	101	..	..	101	2
	2006	..	104	..	..	104	2
America, North	**2003**	**104770**	**3**	..	**164**	**104609**	**208**
Amérique du Nord	**2004**	**114133**	**3**	..	**0**	**114136**	**225**
	2005	**127251**	**3**	..	**0**	**127254**	**248**
	2006	**99023**	**4**	..	**0**	**99027**	**192**
Bahamas	2003	..	*3	..	..	*3	*9
Bahamas	2004	..	*3	..	..	*3	*10
	2005	..	*3	..	..	*3	*9
	2006	..	*4	..	..	*4	*12
United States	2003	104770	..	..	164	104606	360
Etats-Unis	2004	114133	..	..	0	114133	389
	2005	127251	..	..	0	127251	429
	2006	99023	..	..	0	99023	332
Asia	**2003**	**1201**	..	..	..	**1201**	**0**
Asie	**2004**	**1408**	..	..	..	**1408**	**0**
	2005	**2039**	..	..	..	**2039**	**1**
	2006	**2435**	..	..	..	**2435**	**1**
Indonesia	2003	20	..	..	..	20	0
Indonésie	2004	22	..	..	..	22	0
	2005	28	..	..	..	28	0
	2006	36	..	..	..	36	0
Kazakhstan	2003	7	..	..	..	7	0
Kazakhstan	2004	1	..	..	..	1	0
	2005	1	..	..	..	1	0
	2006	72	..	..	..	72	5
Korea, Republic of	2003	1174	..	..	..	1174	25
Corée, République de	2004	1385	..	..	..	1385	29
	2005	2010	..	..	..	2010	42
	2006	2327	..	..	..	2327	48
Europe	**2003**	**2419**	**107**	**129**	**-2**	**2399**	**3**
Europe	**2004**	**1805**	**108**	**111**	**-24**	**1826**	**3**
	2005	**1575**	**170**	**77**	**-7**	**1675**	**2**
	2006	**1570**	**237**	**213**	**-4**	**1598**	**2**
Austria	2003	..	2	..	..	2	0
Autriche	2004	..	1	..	..	1	0
	2005	..	1	..	..	1	0
	2006	..	1	..	..	1	0
Belgium	2003	11	9	15	1	4	0
Belgique	2004	10	7	10	-1	8	1
	2005	7	17	13	1	10	1
	2006	5	19	17	0	7	1

Table 10

Production, trade and consumption of hard coal briquettes
Production, commerce et consommation d'agglomérés (briquettes de houille)
Thousand metric tons and kilograms per capita
Milliers de tonnes métriques et kilogrammes par habitant

Country or area Pays ou zone	Year Année	Production Production	Imports Importations	Exports Exportations	Changes in stocks Variations des stocks	Consumption Consommation	
						Total Totale	Per capita Par habitant
France incl. Monaco	2003	41	68	..	-6	115	2
France y compris Monaco	2004	35	76		-3	114	2
	2005	31	118		-1	150	2
	2006	25	121		1	145	2
Germany	2003	114	22	52	4	80	1
Allemagne	2004	102	16	55	3	60	1
	2005	92	9	41	1	59	1
	2006	96	6	44	3	55	1
Ireland	2003	51	0	7	0	44	11
Irlande	2004	55	0	7	-1	49	12
	2005	55	5	6	0	54	13
	2006	56	2	5	0	53	13
Netherlands	2003	..	0	0	0	0	0
Pays-Bas	2004	..	0	0	0	0	0
	2005	..	0	1	-1	0	0
	2006	..	68	66	0	2	0
Slovakia	2003	..	0	..	..	0	0
Slovaquie	2004	..	0	..	..	0	0
	2005	..	12	..	..	12	2
	2006	..	10	..	..	10	2
Ukraine	2003	1810	0	0	..	1810	38
Ukraine	2004	1285	2	0	..	1287	27
	2005	1132	2	0	..	1134	24
	2006	1128	0	63	..	1065	23
United Kingdom	2003	392	6	55	0	343	6
Royaume-Uni	2004	318	6	39	-21	306	5
	2005	258	6	15	-6	255	4
	2006	260	10	12	-2	260	4

Table 11

Production, trade and consumption of briquettes of lignite and peat
Production, commerce et consommation de briquettes de lignite et de tourbe

Thousand metric tons and kilograms per capita
Milliers de tonnes métriques et kilogrammes par habitant

Table Notes:

Production, trade, stock change and consumption for brown coal coke, lignite-brown coal briquettes and peat briquettes.

- **Please refer to the Definitions Section on pages xv to xxix for the appropriate product description/classification.**

Notes relatives aux tableaux:

Production, commerce, variations des stocks et consommation de coke de lignite, briquettes de lignite, et briquettes de tourbe.

- **Veuillez consulter la section "définitions" de la page xv à la page xxix pour une description/classification appropriée des produits.**

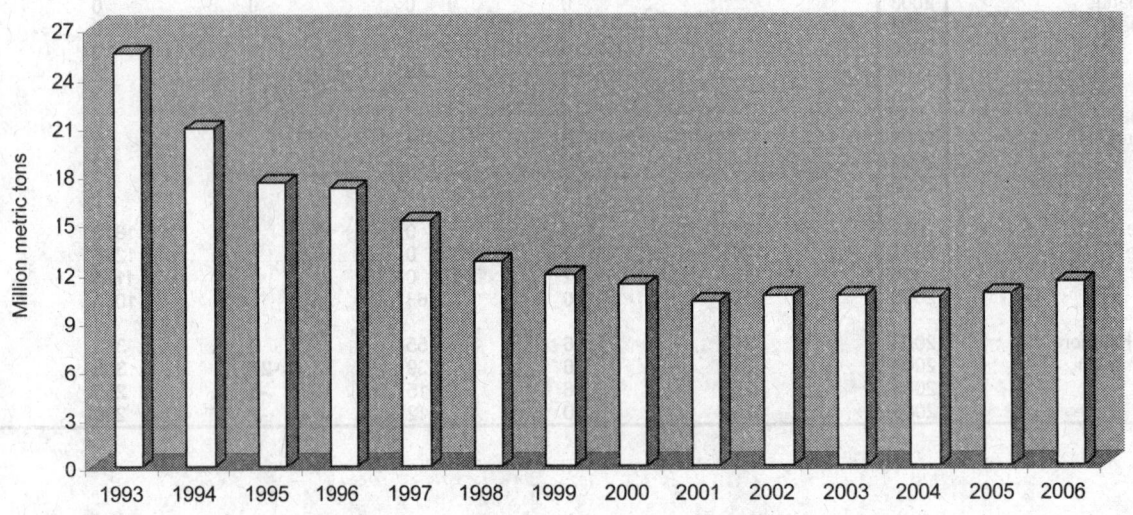

Figure 25: World production of briquettes of lignite and peat 1993-2006

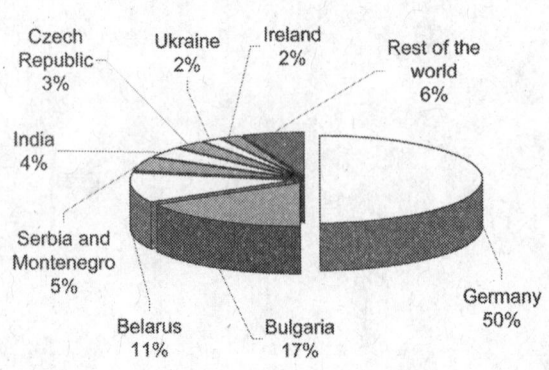

Figure 26: Major briquettes of lignite and peat producing countries in 2006

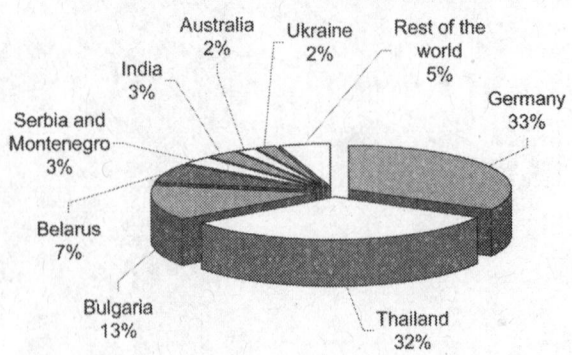

Figure 27: Major briquettes of lignite and peat consuming countries in 2006

Table 11

Production, trade and consumption of briquettes of lignite and peat
Production, commerce et consommation de briquettes de lignite et de tourbe

Thousand metric tons and kilograms per capita
Milliers de tonnes métriques et kilogrammes par habitant

Country or area Pays ou zone	Year Année	Production Production	Imports Importations	Exports Exportations	Changes in stocks Variations des stocks	Consumption Consommation	
						Total Totale	Per capita Par habitant
World	**2003**	**10400**	**2188**	**1126**	**-67**	**11529**	2
Monde	**2004**	**10288**	**2410**	**1180**	**-193**	**11711**	2
	2005	**10539**	**2006**	**1305**	**-212**	**11452**	2
	2006	**11267**	**5146**	**1473**	**-176**	**15116**	2
Asia	**2003**	**722**	**1925**	..	..	**2647**	1
Asie	**2004**	**615**	**2204**	..	..	**2819**	1
	2005	**715**	**1800**	..	..	**2515**	1
	2006	**617**	**4852**	..	..	**5469**	1
India	2003	675	..	..	..	675	1
Inde	2004	456	..	..	..	456	0
	2005	595	..	..	..	595	1
	2006	462	..	..	..	462	0
Thailand	2003	..	1925	..	..	1925	30
Thaïlande	2004	..	2204	..	..	2204	34
	2005	..	1800	..	..	1800	28
	2006	..	4852	..	..	4852	74
Turkey	2003	47	..	..	..	47	1
Turquie	2004	159	..	..	..	159	2
	2005	120	..	..	..	120	2
	2006	155	..	..	..	155	2
Europe	**2003**	**9435**	**263**	**1126**	**38**	**8534**	12
Europe	**2004**	**9503**	**206**	**1180**	**-11**	**8540**	12
	2005	**9651**	**206**	**1305**	**14**	**8538**	12
	2006	**10531**	**294**	**1473**	**79**	**9273**	13
Austria	2003	..	72	0	..	72	9
Autriche	2004	..	59	1	..	58	7
	2005	..	53	5	..	48	6
	2006	..	57	0	..	57	7
Belarus	2003	1100	..	154	-1	947	96
Bélarus	2004	1149	..	258	14	877	89
	2005	1207	..	245	-13	975	100
	2006	1246	..	211	27	1008	104
Belgium	2003	..	6	2	0	4	0
Belgique	2004	..	12	0	0	12	1
	2005	..	11	2	0	9	1
	2006	..	21	3	4	14	1
Bulgaria	2003	1303	..	0	61	1242	159
Bulgarie	2004	1078	..	0	15	1063	137
	2005	1491	..	0	16	1475	191
	2006	1905	..	2	-11	1914	249
Czech Republic	2003	314	0	191	-2	125	12
République tchèque	2004	317	3	161	0	159	16
	2005	301	0	152	2	147	14
	2006	345	1	192	-2	156	15
Estonia	2003	120	..	101	-1	20	15
Estonie	2004	68	..	78	-24	14	10
	2005	52	..	37	1	14	10
	2006	101	..	84	5	12	9
Germany	2003	4843	146	563	-38	4464	54
Allemagne	2004	5256	91	586	11	4750	58
	2005	5252	96	665	18	4665	57
	2006	5624	159	840	30	4913	60

Table 11

Production, trade and consumption of briquettes of lignite and peat
Production, commerce et consommation de briquettes de lignite et de tourbe
Thousand metric tons and kilograms per capita
Milliers de tonnes métriques et kilogrammes par habitant

Country or area Pays ou zone	Year Année	Production Production	Imports Importations	Exports Exportations	Changes in stocks Variations des stocks	Consumption Consommation	
						Total Totale	Per capita Par habitant
Greece	2003	209	..	76	0	133	12
Grèce	2004	189	..	71	-2	120	11
	2005	183	..	54	2	127	11
	2006	129	..	24	-1	106	10
Hungary	2003	29	15	..	-25	69	7
Hongrie	2004	35	13	..	2	46	5
	2005	30	14	..	1	43	4
	2006	24	15	..	0	39	4
Ireland	2003	279	..	27	39	213	54
Irlande	2004	206	..	23	-20	203	50
	2005	215	..	23	-12	204	49
	2006	222	..	22	23	177	42
Lithuania	2003	15	3	..	0	18	5
Lituanie	2004	15	4	..	0	19	6
	2005	11	11	..	3	19	6
	2006	14	15	..	0	29	9
Luxembourg	2003	..	8	..	..	8	18
Luxembourg	2004	..	8	..	..	8	17
	2005	..	8	..	..	8	17
	2006	..	7	..	..	7	15
Poland	2003	..	3	1	..	2	0
Pologne	2004	..	2	0	..	2	0
	2005	..	2	0	..	2	0
	2006	..	4	0	..	4	0
Russian Federation	2003	91	..	4	5	82	1
Fédération de Russie	2004	76	..	0	-12	88	1
	2005	49	..	0	-4	53	0
	2006	57	..	0	-2	59	0
Serbia	2003	770	0	0	0	770	73
Serbie	2004	788	0	0	0	788	75
	2005	595	2	119	0	478	46
	2006	604	5	89	3	517	49
Slovakia	2003	..	1	..	..	1	0
Slovaquie	2004	..	10	..	..	10	2
	2005	..	1	..	..	1	0
	2006	..	1	..	..	1	0
Sweden	2003	..	9	7	..	2	0
Suède	2004	..	4	2	..	2	0
	2005	..	8	3	..	5	1
	2006	..	9	6	..	3	0
Ukraine	2003	362	..	..	0	362	8
Ukraine	2004	326	..	..	5	321	7
	2005	265	..	..	0	265	6
	2006	260	..	..	3	257	5
Oceania	**2003**	**243**	**..**	**..**	**-105**	**348**	**11**
Océanie	**2004**	**170**	**..**	**..**	**-182**	**352**	**11**
	2005	**173**	**..**	**..**	**-226**	**399**	**12**
	2006	**119**	**..**	**..**	**-255**	**374**	**11**
Australia	2003	243	..	..	-105	348	17
Australie	2004	170	..	..	-182	352	17
	2005	173	..	..	-226	399	20
	2006	119	..	..	-255	374	18

Table 12

Production, trade and consumption of peat
Production, commerce et consommation de tourbe
Thousand metric tons and kilograms per capita
Milliers de tonnes métriques et kilogrammes par habitant

Table Notes:
- Please refer to the Definitions Section on pages xv to xxix for the appropriate product description/classification.

Notes relatives aux tableaux:
- Veuillez consulter la section "définitions" de la page xv à la page xxix pour une description/classification appropriée des produits.

Figure 28: World production of peat 1993-2006

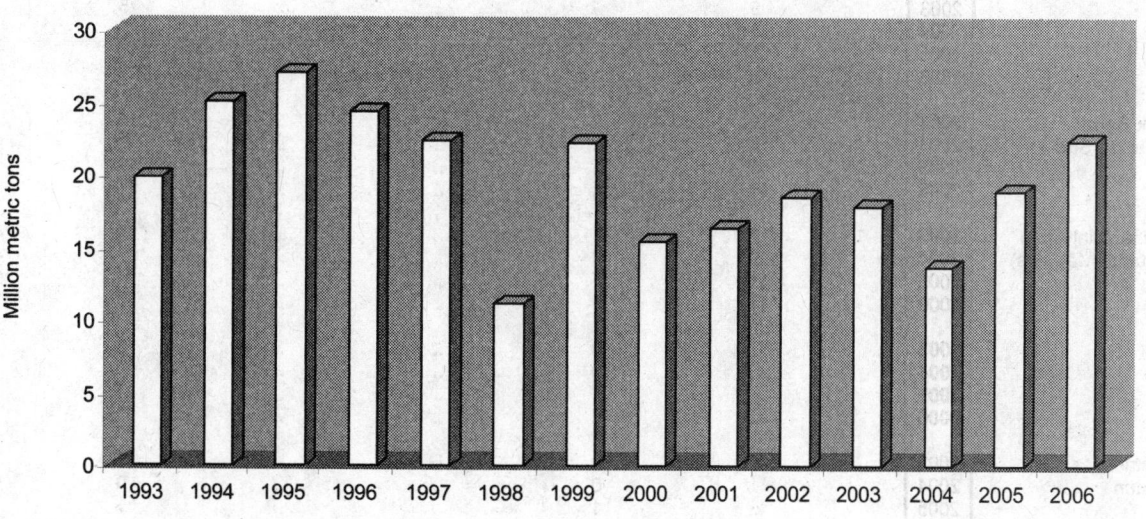

Figure 29: Major peat producing countries in 2006

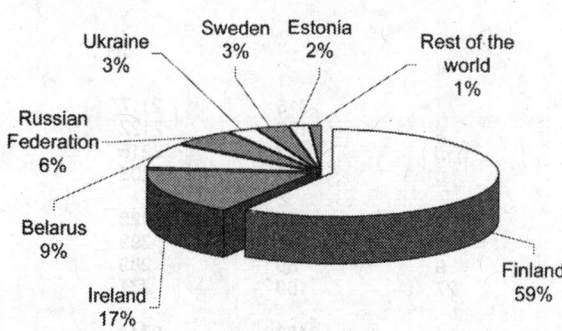

Figure 30: Major peat consuming countries in 2006

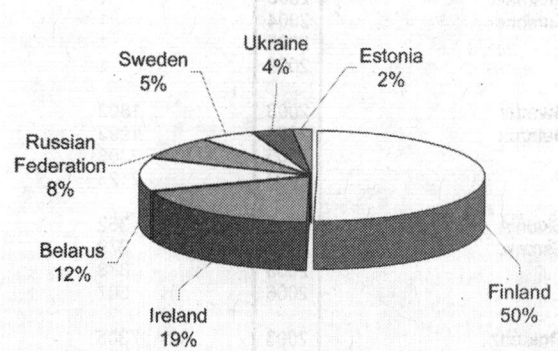

Table 12

Production, trade and consumption of peat
Production, commerce et consommation de tourbe

Thousand metric tons and kilograms per capita
Milliers de tonnes métriques et kilogrammes par habitant

Country or area Pays ou zone	Year Année	Production Production	Imports Importations	Exports Exportations	Changes in stocks Variations des stocks	Consumption Consommation	
						Total Totale	Per capita Par habitant
World	**2003**	**17855**	**352**	**238**	**-2370**	**20339**	**3**
Monde	**2004**	**13609**	**389**	**185**	**-3431**	**17244**	**3**
	2005	**18922**	**312**	**189**	**2661**	**16384**	**3**
	2006	**22367**	**294**	**154**	**4005**	**18502**	**3**
Africa	**2003**	**5**	..	..	..	**5**	**0**
Afrique	**2004**	**5**	..	..	..	**5**	**0**
	2005	**5**	..	..	..	**5**	**0**
	2006	**5**	..	..	..	**5**	**0**
Burundi	2003	5	..	..	..	5	1
Burundi	2004	5	..	..	..	5	1
	2005	5	..	..	..	5	1
	2006	*5	..	..	..	*5	*1
America, South	**2003**	**12**	..	..	..	**12**	**0**
Amérique du Sud	**2004**	**12**	..	..	..	**12**	**0**
	2005	**11**	..	..	..	**11**	**0**
	2006	**11**	..	..	..	**11**	**0**
Falkland Is. (Malvinas)	2003	*12	..	..	..	*12	*4096
Iles Falkland (Malvinas)	2004	*12	..	..	..	*12	*4082
	2005	*11	..	..	..	*11	*3729
	2006	*11	..	..	..	*11	*3723
Asia	**2003**	..	**0**	..	..	**0**	**0**
Asie	**2004**	..	**0**	..	..	**0**	**0**
	2005	..	**1**	..	..	**1**	**0**
	2006	..	**1**	..	..	**1**	**0**
Kazakhstan	2003	..	0	..	..	0	0
Kazakhstan	2004	..	0	..	..	0	0
	2005	..	1	..	..	1	0
	2006	..	1	..	..	1	0
Europe	**2003**	**17838**	**352**	**238**	**-2370**	**20322**	**28**
Europe	**2004**	**13592**	**389**	**185**	**-3431**	**17227**	**24**
	2005	**18906**	**311**	**189**	**2661**	**16367**	**22**
	2006	**22351**	**293**	**154**	**4005**	**18485**	**25**
Austria	2003	1	..	..	..	1	0
Autriche	2004	1	..	..	..	1	0
	2005	1	..	..	..	1	0
	2006	1	..	..	..	1	0
Belarus	2003	1802	..	..	-315	2117	214
Bélarus	2004	1993	..	..	-129	2122	216
	2005	2308	..	..	93	2215	227
	2006	2125	..	..	-80	2205	227
Estonia	2003	362	..	65	-128	425	314
Estonie	2004	279	..	28	-48	299	222
	2005	378	..	9	80	289	215
	2006	507	..	27	109	371	276
Finland	2003	7305	..	14	-2453	9744	1869
Finlande	2004	3633	..	10	-5063	8686	1661
	2005	8928	..	40	2147	6741	1285
	2006	13235	..	26	3979	9230	1753
Germany	2003	145	..	135	..	10	0
Allemagne	2004	133	..	122	..	11	0
	2005	129	..	120	..	9	0
	2006	101	..	93	..	8	0

Table 12

Production, trade and consumption of peat
Production, commerce et consommation de tourbe
Thousand metric tons and kilograms per capita
Milliers de tonnes métriques et kilogrammes par habitant

Country or area Pays ou zone	Year Année	Production Production	Imports Importations	Exports Exportations	Changes in stocks Variations des stocks	Consumption Consommation	
						Total Totale	Per capita Par habitant
Ireland Irlande	2003	5504	..	..	1194	4310	1083
	2004	4395	..	..	1689	2706	669
	2005	3956	..	..	159	3797	919
	2006	3694	..	..	213	3481	822
Latvia Lettonie	2003	8	..	0	-83	91	39
	2004	13	..	0	4	9	4
	2005	12	..	4	0	8	3
	2006	14	..	0	7	7	3
Lithuania Lituanie	2003	46	..	10	-13	49	14
	2004	50	..	5	-2	47	14
	2005	70	..	0	20	50	15
	2006	55	..	3	5	47	14
Romania Roumanie	2003	*10	*3	..	..	*13	*1
	2004	8	*2	..	..	10	0
	2005	*8	*2	..	..	*10	0
	2006	9	19	..	..	28	1
Russian Federation Fédération de Russie	2003	1127	..	..	-572	1699	12
	2004	1487	..	..	82	1405	10
	2005	1650	..	..	71	1579	11
	2006	1362	..	..	-130	1492	10
Sweden Suède	2003	806	346	..	..	1152	129
	2004	893	383	..	..	1276	142
	2005	708	304	..	..	1012	112
	2006	621	266	..	..	887	98
T.F.Yug.Rep. Macedonia L'ex-RY Macédoine	2003	..	1	..	..	1	0
	2004	..	2	..	..	2	1
	2005	..	2	..	..	2	1
	2006	..	2	..	..	2	1
Ukraine Ukraine	2003	722	2	14	0	710	15
	2004	707	2	20	36	653	14
	2005	758	3	16	91	654	14
	2006	627	6	5	-98	726	16

Table 13

Selected series of statistics on renewables and wastes
Séries de statistiques des renouvelables et des déchets
Thousand cubic metres, Thousand metric tons, Gigawatt-hours and Terajoules
Milliers de mètres cubes, Milliers de tonnes métriques, Gigawatt-heures et Térajoules

Table Notes:

Data on fuelwood and charcoal production were primarily taken from information provided by the Food and Agriculture Organization of the United Nations (FAO).

The conversion of fuelwood (solid volume, .33 tce/m3) is based on an average 20-30% moisture content.

The methodology used for estimating fuel bagasse production is derived from the work done by the Economic Commission for Latin America and the Caribbean (ECLAC). Although several different methodologies have been devised, the one selected assumes a yield of 3.26 tons of fuel bagasse at 50% humidity per ton of cane sugar produced. In most cases, bagasse production data were extracted from the Sugar Yearbook of the International Sugar Organization (London).

Liquids and gases include biodiesel, alcohol, biogas and steam/heat from geothermal sources.

Electricity refers to production from geothermal, hydro, solar, wind and wave sources.

Wastes refer to animal, vegetal, municipal and pulp and paper wastes.

Total primary includes all the commodities listed before but charcoal.

The share of total primary indicates the percentage of primary energy produced coming from renewable energy and energy from wastes.

In various cases data were supplied through questionnaires and/or official publications.

- **Please refer to the Definitions Section on pages xv to xxix for the appropriate product description/classification.**

Notes relatives aux tableaux:

Les données relatives à la production du bois de chauffage et du charbon de bois proviennent premièrement des renseignements de l'Organisation des Nations Unies pour l'alimentation et l'agriculture (FAO).

La conversion du bois de chauffage (volume solide, 0,33 tec/m3) est fondée sur une teneur moyenne en humidité de 20 à 30%.

Les méthodes de calcul de la production de bagasse combustible s'inspirent des travaux effectués par la Commission économique pour l'Amérique latine et les Caraïbes (CEPALC). Des diverses formules élaborées, on a retenu celle qui suppose un rendement de 3,26 tonnes de bagasse combustible (d'une teneur en humidité de 50%) par tonne de sucre de canne produite. Les données relatives à la production de bagasse proviennent pour la plupart du Sugar Yearbook publié par l'Organisation internationale du sucre (Londres).

Les liquides et gaz comprennent le biodiesel, l'alcool, le biogaz et la vapeur/chaleur de sources géothermiques.

La colonne Electricité fait référence à la production à partir de sources géothermique, hydraulique, solaire, éolienne et marémotrice.

Les déchets peuvent être d'origine animale, végétale, municipale et de la fabrication de papier.

Le total primaire inclut tous les produits énergétiques listés ci-dessus, à l'exception du charbon de bois.

La part du total primaire indique le pourcentage de l'énergie primaire produite provenant de sources renouvelables et de déchets.

Dans certains cas les données proviennent des questionnaires et/ou des publications officiels.

- **Veuillez consulter la section "définitions" de la page xv à la page xxix pour une description/classification appropriée des produits.**

Figure 31: World fuelwood production 1993-2006

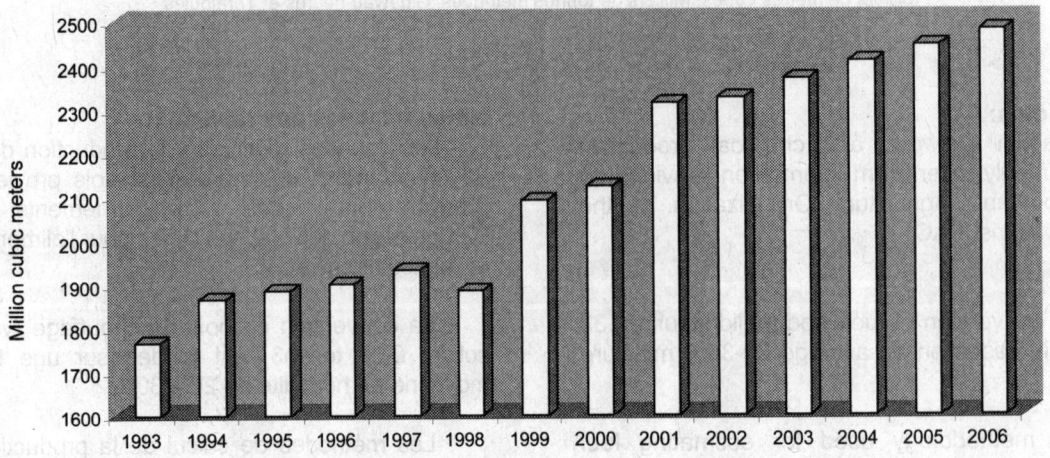

Figure 32: World charcoal production 1993-2006

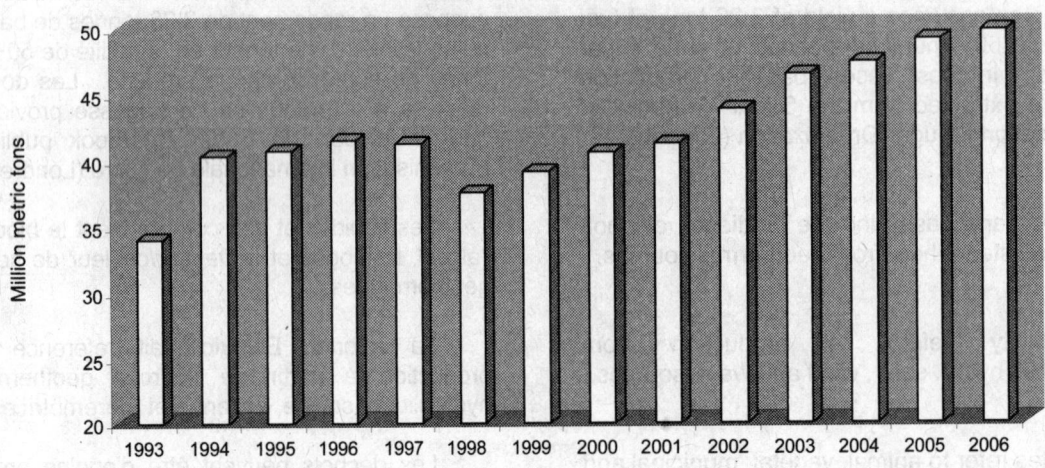

Figure 33: Fuelwood production, by region, in 2006

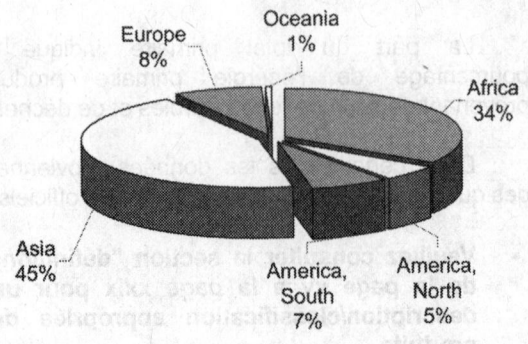

Figure 34: Charcoal production, by region, in 2006

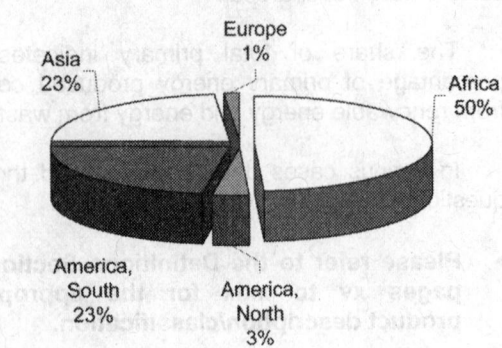

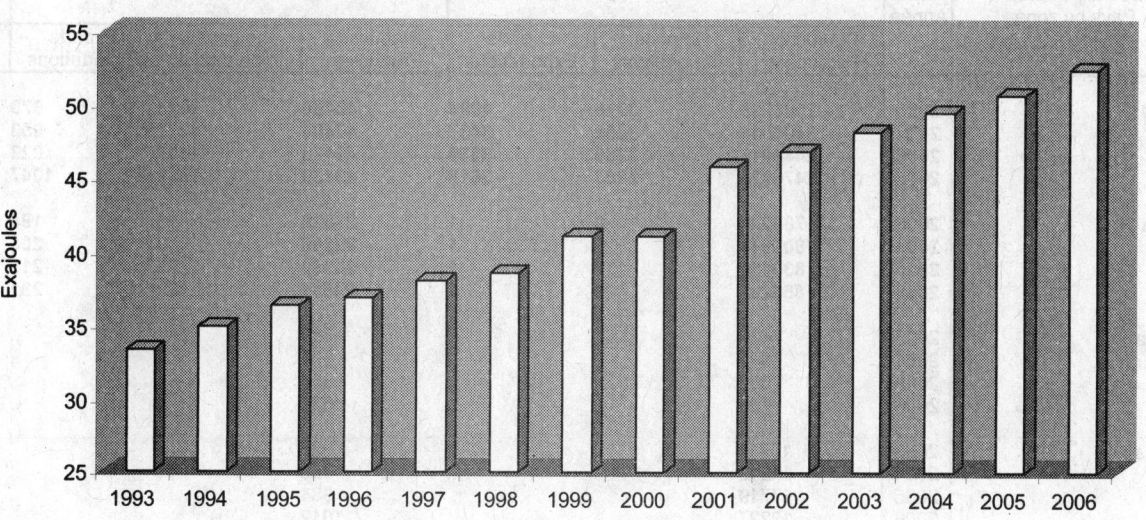

Figure 35: World total primary energy production from renewable sources 1993-2006

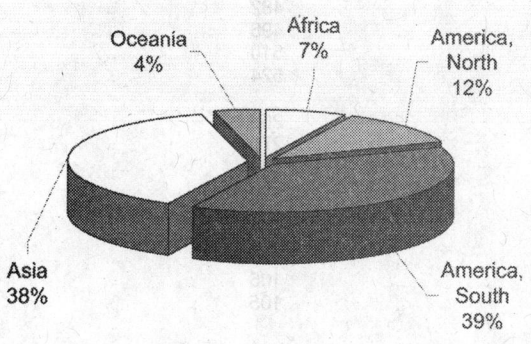

Figure 36: Bagasse production, by region, in 2006

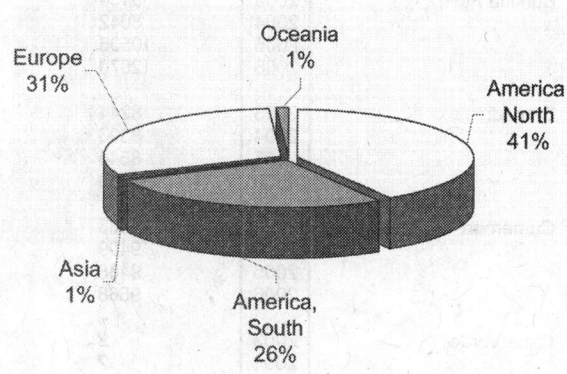

Figure 37: Liquids and gases production from renewable sources, by region, in 2006

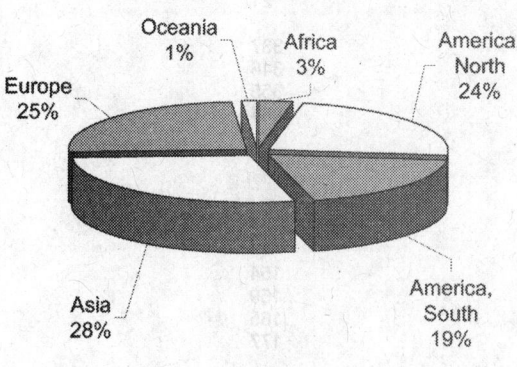

Figure 38: Electricity production from renewable sources, by region, in 2006

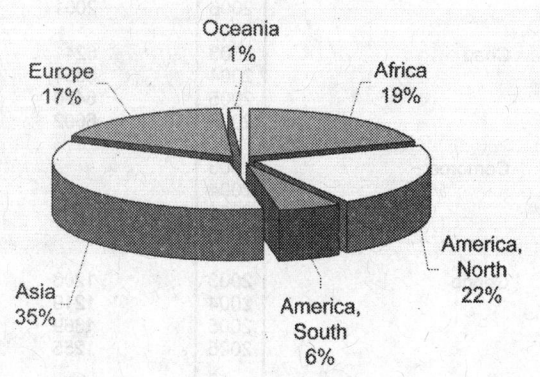

Figure 39: Energy production from wastes, by region, in 2006

Table 13

Selected series of statistics on renewables and wastes
Thousand cubic metres (1000 c.m.) / Thousand metric tons (1000 m.t.) / GWh / Terajoules (TJ)

Country or area Pays ou zone	Year Année	Fuelwood (1000 c.m.) Bois de chauffage (1000 m.c.)			Charcoal (1000 m.t) Charbon de bois (1000 t.m.)			Bagasse (10 m.t.) Bagasse (10 t.m.)
		Production Production	Imports Importations	Exports Exportations	Production Production	Imports Importations	Exports Exportations	Production Production
World	2003	2366283	3326	4084	46460	1123	979	3707
	2004	2406048	3256	3437	47404	1277	953	3575
	2005	2442015	3288	3636	49178	1437	923	3532
	2006	2476823	3903	3618	49739	1588	1047	3884
Africa	2003	788226	0	1	21628	18	194	278
	2004	805844	0	1	22306	19	206	282
	2005	830134	0	1	23330	25	219	297
	2006	853294	0	1	24511	23	231	283
Algeria	2003	7426	..	..	589	..	..	
	2004	7547	..	..	604	..	..	
	2005	7557	..	..	645	..	..	
	2006	7769	..	..	631	..	..	
Angola	2003	16711	..	..	928	..	..	
	2004	17212	..	..	956	..	..	
	2005	17719	..	..	984	..	..	
	2006	18227	..	..	1012	..	..	
Benin	2003	7205	..	..	191	0	..	
	2004	7421	..	..	197	0	..	
	2005	7643	..	..	204	0	..	
	2006	7864	..	..	212	0	..	
Burkina Faso	2003	6154	..	..	482	..	..	1
	2004	8042	..	..	496	..	..	1
	2005	10536	..	..	510	..	..	1
	2006	12070	..	..	524	..	..	1
Burundi	2003	8244	0	..	269	..	..	
	2004	8393	0	..	275	..	..	
	2005	8544	0	..	281	..	..	
	2006	8683	0	..	286	..	..	
Cameroon	2003	9333	..	..	105	..	..	3
	2004	9409	..	..	105	..	..	3
	2005	9488	..	..	105	..	..	3
	2006	9568	..	..	105	..	..	4
Cape Verde	2003	2	0	..	1	..	..	
	2004	2	0	..	1	..	..	
	2005	2	0	..	1	..	..	
	2006	2	0	..	1	..	..	
Central African Rep.	2003	2001	..	..	21	..	..	
	2004	2001	..	..	21	..	..	
	2005	2001	..	..	21	..	..	
	2006	2001	..	..	21	..	..	
Chad	2003	6241	..	..	337	..	..	1
	2004	6364	..	..	346	..	..	
	2005	6490	..	..	355	..	..	
	2006	6602	..	..	364	..	..	
Comoros	2003	..	..	..	..	..	..	
	2004	..	..	..	..	..	..	
	2005	..	..	..	..	..	..	
	2006	..	..	..	..	..	..	
Congo	2003	1203	..	..	154	..	..	
	2004	1219	..	..	159	..	..	
	2005	1369	..	..	165	..	..	
	2006	1255	..	..	177	..	..	
Côte d'Ivoire	2003	8620	..	..	923	..	1	4
	2004	8702	..	..	958	..	1	3
	2005	8702	..	..	995	..	1	
	2006	8742	..	..	1011	..	1	

Table 13

Séries de statistiques des renouvelables et des déchets
Milliers de mètres cubes (1000 m.c.) / Milliers de tonnes métriques (1000 t.m.) / GWh / Tèrajoules (TJ)

Liquids and gases (TJ) / Liquides et gazes (TJ) Production / Production	Electricity (GWh) / Électricité (GWh) Production / Production	Wastes (TJ) / Déchets (TJ) Production / Production	Total primary (TJ) / Totale primaire(TJ) Production / Production	Renewables and wastes (%) / Renouvelables et déchets (%) Share of total primary / Part du total primaire	Year Année	Country or area / Pays ou zone
968273	2837555	12488185	48143534	12	2003	Monde
1083628	3021912	12799845	49495427	12	2004	
1255737	3164703	13062035	50739326	12	2005	
1519329	3308575	13437928	52486277	12	2006	
..	86048	2436987	10159859	27	2003	Afrique
..	90797	2488336	10392678	26	2004	
..	93206	2545805	10692034	25	2005	
..	98594	2618307	10985151	25	2006	
..	265	*3420	72189	1	2003	Algérie
..	251	*3510	73337	1	2004	
..	555	3425	74438	1	2005	
..	218	*3400	75136	1	2006	
..	1241	99200	256280	13	2003	Angola
..	1750	102176	265667	12	2004	
..	2219	105180	274981	10	2005	
..	2665	108198	284248	10	2006	
..	2	198	66105	100	2003	Bénin
..	1	206	68080	100	2004	
..	1	215	70143	100	2005	
..	1	225	72299	100	2006	
..	96	..	57548	100	2003	Burkina Faso
..	102	..	74815	100	2004	
..	101	..	97585	100	2005	
..	80	..	111524	100	2006	
..	102	..	76161	100	2003	Burundi
..	92	..	77484	100	2004	
..	100	..	78869	100	2005	
..	93	..	80089	100	2006	
..	3528	44820	145772	46	2003	Cameroun
..	3920	45647	148702	45	2004	
..	3913	46447	149542	47	2005	
..	3719	47474	151405	46	2006	
..	5	..	33	100	2003	Cap-Vert
..	6	..	37	100	2004	
..	6	..	37	100	2005	
..	7	..	41	100	2006	
..	*84	..	18572	100	2003	Rép. centrafricaine
..	*84	..	18572	100	2004	
..	*85	..	18576	100	2005	
..	*85	..	18576	100	2006	
..	..	..	57828	47	2003	Tchad
..	..	..	58874	16	2004	
..	..	..	60148	16	2005	
..	..	..	61171	18	2006	
..	*2	..	*7	100	2003	Comores
..	*2	..	*7	100	2004	
..	*2	..	*7	100	2005	
..	*2	..	*7	100	2006	
..	342	..	12563	4	2003	Congo
..	398	..	12993	3	2004	
..	355	..	14270	3	2005	
..	372	..	13306	3	2006	
..	1832	..	88965	56	2003	Côte d'Ivoire
..	1748	..	88787	52	2004	
..	1433	..	88278	44	2005	
..	1510	..	88921	38	2006	

Table 13

Selected series of statistics on renewables and wastes
Thousand cubic metres (1000 c.m.) / Thousand metric tons (1000 m.t.) / GWh / Terajoules (TJ)

Country or area Pays ou zone	Year Année	Fuelwood (1000 c.m.) Bois de chauffage (1000 m.c.)			Charcoal (1000 m.t) Charbon de bois (1000 t.m.)			Bagasse (100 m.t.) Bagasse (100 t.m.)
		Production Production	Imports Importations	Exports Exportations	Production Production	Imports Importations	Exports Exportations	Production Production
Dem. Rep. of Congo	2003	68536	..	..	1590	..	..	
	2004	69797	..	..	1646	..	..	
	2005	71086	..	..	1704	..	..	
	2006	72146	..	..	1764	..	..	
Egypt	2003	16642	..	..	1248	..	6	327
	2004	16797	..	..	1264	..	10	355
	2005	16953	..	..	1281	..	10	391
	2006	17064	..	..	1297	..	10	383
Equatorial Guinea	2003	447	..	..	..	..	..	
	2004	447	..	..	..	..	..	
	2005	447	..	..	..	..	..	
	2006	447	..	..	..	..	..	
Eritrea	2003	1961	..	..	85	..	..	*4
	2004	1855	..	..	111	..	..	*5
	2005	1927	..	..	114	..	..	*6
	2006	1985	..	..	117	..	..	*6
Ethiopia	2003	91629	..	..	3140	..	..	96
	2004	93055	..	..	3221	..	..	105
	2005	94508	..	..	3304	..	..	112
	2006	95730	..	..	3386	..	..	117
Gabon	2003	4237	..	..	17	..	..	8
	2004	4304	..	..	17	..	..	6
	2005	4372	..	..	18	..	..	6
	2006	4442	..	..	18	..	..	7
Gambia	2003	629	..	..	50	..	..	
	2004	638	..	..	51	..	..	
	2005	647	..	..	53	..	..	
	2006	656	..	..	54	..	..	
Ghana	2003	25941	..	..	752	..	4	
	2004	26485	..	..	752	..	4	
	2005	27041	..	..	647	..	2	
	2006	27609	..	..	659	..	5	
Guinea	2003	11589	..	..	297	..	..	8
	2004	11639	..	..	304	..	..	8
	2005	11691	..	..	311	..	..	8
	2006	11742	..	..	318	..	..	8
Guinea-Bissau	2003	422	..	..	*1	..	0	
	2004	422	..	..	*1	..	0	
	2005	422	..	..	*1	..	0	
	2006	422	..	..	*1	..	0	
Kenya	2003	20188	..	..	17	..	..	146
	2004	20376	..	..	18	..	..	183
	2005	20570	..	..	18	..	..	173
	2006	20754	..	..	17	..	..	168
Liberia	2003	5351	..	..	175	..	..	
	2004	5577	..	..	183	..	..	
	2005	5813	..	..	192	..	..	
	2006	6035	..	..	243	..	..	
Libyan Arab Jamah.	2003	681	..	..	..	..	..	
	2004	694	..	..	..	..	..	
	2005	708	..	..	..	..	..	
	2006	721	..	..	..	..	..	
Madagascar	2003	10489	..	..	834	..	29	8
	2004	10773	..	..	872	..	29	8
	2005	11058	..	..	910	..	29	6
	2006	11342	..	..	950	..	29	6

Table 13

Séries de statistiques des renouvelables et des déchets

Milliers de mètres cubes (1000 m.c.) / Milliers de tonnes métriques (1000 t.m.) / GWh / Tèrajoules (TJ)

Liquids and gases (TJ) Liquides et gazes (TJ)	Electricity (GWh) Électricité (GWh)	Wastes (TJ) Déchets (TJ)	Total primary (TJ) Totale primaire (TJ)	Renewables and wastes (%) Renouvelables et déchets (%)	Year Année	Country or area Pays ou zone
Production Production	Production Production	Production Production	Production Production	Share of total primary Part du total primaire		
..	6237	9063	657419	94	2003	Rép. dem. du Congo
..	6831	9318	671319	94	2004	
..	7397	9580	685394	94	2005	
..	7863	9849	697023	95	2006	
..	12590	..	222597	8	2003	Egypte
..	13168	..	228217	8	2004	
..	13197	..	232534	7	2005	
..	13542	..	234165	8	2006	
..	*3	..	4094	1	2003	Guinée équatoriale
..	*3	..	4094	1	2004	
..	*3	..	4094	1	2005	
..	*3	..	4094	1	2006	
..	0	5689	23979	100	2003	Erythrée
..	1	3231	20573	100	2004	
..	1	3323	21431	100	2005	
..	2	3417	22053	100	2006	
..	2281	141246	993674	100	2003	Ethiopie
..	2522	144516	1011593	100	2004	
..	2853	147862	1029896	100	2005	
..	3260	151285	1046326	100	2006	
..	900	2344	44899	9	2003	Gabon
..	893	2381	45380	9	2004	
..	814	2419	45801	9	2005	
..	945	2458	46966	9	2006	
..	..	..	5745	100	2003	Gambie
..	..	..	5828	100	2004	
..	..	..	5910	100	2005	
..	..	..	5993	100	2006	
..	3885	..	250886	100	2003	Ghana
..	5281	..	260887	100	2004	
..	5629	..	267218	100	2005	
..	5619	..	272368	100	2006	
..	*420	..	108000	100	2003	Guinée
..	*435	..	108512	100	2004	
..	*435	..	108963	100	2005	
..	*435	..	109430	100	2006	
..	..	..	3855	100	2003	Guinée-Bissau
..	..	..	3855	100	2004	
..	..	..	3855	100	2005	
..	..	..	3855	100	2006	
..	4047	42366	252587	100	2003	Kenya
..	3904	43056	257330	100	2004	
..	3912	43765	259083	100	2005	
..	4178	44493	262086	100	2006	
..	..	..	48870	100	2003	Libéria
..	..	..	50935	100	2004	
..	..	..	53087	100	2005	
..	..	..	55113	100	2006	
..	..	..	6218	0	2003	Jamah. arabe libyenne
..	..	..	6341	0	2004	
..	..	..	6466	0	2005	
..	..	..	6589	0	2006	
..	610	..	98658	100	2003	Madagascar
..	640	..	101353	100	2004	
..	*660	..	104051	100	2005	
..	*675	..	106514	100	2006	

Table 13

Selected series of statistics on renewables and wastes

Thousand cubic metres (1000 c.m.) / Thousand metric tons (1000 m.t.) / GWh / Terajoules (TJ)

Country or area Pays ou zone	Year Année	Fuelwood (1000 c.m.) Bois de chauffage (1000 m.c.)			Charcoal (1000 m.t) Charbon de bois (1000 t.m.)			Bagasse (1000 m.t.) Bagasse (1000 t.m.)
		Production Production	Imports Importations	Exports Exportations	Production Production	Imports Importations	Exports Exportations	Production Production
Malawi	2003	5066	..	..	418	..	..	83
	2004	5103	..	..	427	..	..	83
	2005	5142	..	..	436	..	..	86
	2006	5191	..	..	446	..	..	75
Mali	2003	4906	..	..	106	..	..	11
	2004	4967	..	..	110	..	..	11
	2005	5028	..	..	113	..	..	11
	2006	5085	..	..	117	..	..	11
Mauritania	2003	1541	..	..	146	..	..	
	2004	1581	..	..	152	..	..	
	2005	1623	..	..	158	..	..	
	2006	1663	..	..	163	..	..	
Mauritius	2003	19	..	..	..	1	..	155
	2004	19	..	..	..	0	..	161
	2005	20	..	..	..	0	..	153
	2006	21	..	..	..	1	..	150
Morocco	2003	377	..	..	95	..	..	135
	2004	298	..	..	97	..	..	146
	2005	383	..	..	99	..	..	148
	2006	345	..	..	100	..	..	107
Mozambique	2003	30307	..	..	398	..	..	73
	2004	30634	..	..	406	..	..	66
	2005	30970	..	..	414	..	..	86
	2006	31308	..	..	423	..	..	79
Niger	2003	8393	..	..	468	9	76	
	2004	8598	..	..	483	9	76	
	2005	8808	..	..	500	9	76	
	2006	9013	..	..	516	9	76	
Nigeria	2003	172147	..	1	936	..	..	
	2004	175934	..	1	959	..	..	
	2005	179805	..	1	982	..	..	
	2006	185409	..	1	1006	..	..	9
Réunion	2003	31	..	..	..	1	..	*57
	2004	31	..	..	..	1	..	*57
	2005	31	..	..	..	1	..	*57
	2006	31	..	..	..	1	..	*57
Rwanda	2003	*6502	..	..	*100	..	..	
	2004	*7502	..	..	*150	..	..	
	2005	*8502	..	..	*200	..	..	
	2006	9419	..	..	251	..	..	
Sao Tome and Principe	2003	..	..	..	..	..	..	
	2004	..	..	..	..	..	..	
	2005	..	..	..	..	..	..	
	2006	..	..	..	..	..	..	
Senegal	2003	4402	..	..	336	..	1	29
	2004	4407	..	..	334	..	1	29
	2005	4569	..	..	342	..	1	29
	2006	4573	..	..	383	..	1	31
Sierra Leone	2003	5388	..	..	320	..	..	1
	2004	5405	..	..	328	..	..	2
	2005	5425	..	..	336	..	..	2
	2006	5450	..	..	345	..	..	2
Somalia	2003	10144	..	..	735	..	52	2
	2004	10469	..	..	766	..	50	2
	2005	10806	..	..	797	..	50	1
	2006	11130	..	..	829	..	73	2

Table 13

Séries de statistiques des renouvelables et des déchets

Milliers de mètres cubes (1000 m.c.) / Milliers de tonnes métriques (1000 t.m.) / GWh / Tèrajoules (TJ)

Liquids and gases (TJ) Liquides et gazes (TJ)	Electricity (GWh) Électricité (GWh)	Wastes (TJ) Déchets (TJ)	Total primary (TJ) Totale primaire(TJ)	Renewables and wastes (%) Renouvelables et déchets (%)	Year Année	Country or area Pays ou zone
Production Production	Production Production	Production Production	Production Production	Share of total primary Part du total primaire		
..	1151	20356	77234	97	2003	Malawi
..	1272	*20500	78102	97	2004	
..	1329	*20500	78916	98	2005	
..	1339	*20500	78515	98	2006	
..	*236	..	46512	100	2003	Mali
..	*250	..	47137	100	2004	
..	*258	..	47731	100	2005	
..	*266	..	48257	100	2006	
..	..	..	14076	100	2003	Mauritanie
..	..	..	14443	100	2004	
..	..	..	14826	100	2005	
..	..	..	15192	100	2006	
..	118	..	12622	100	2003	Maurice
..	122	..	13053	100	2004	
..	114	..	12423	100	2005	
..	77	..	12052	100	2006	
..	1659	2850	22714	93	2003	Maroc
..	1815	2850	23435	91	2004	
..	1632	2851	23661	93	2005	
..	1784	2851	20734	89	2006	
..	10871	6799	328377	100	2003	Mozambique
..	11669	9481	336416	87	2004	
..	13265	12206	349467	80	2005	
..	14718	15014	360023	78	2006	
..	..	..	76647	95	2003	Niger
..	..	..	78523	95	2004	
..	..	..	80443	96	2005	
..	..	..	82306	96	2006	
..	7837	1680124	3280450	37	2003	Nigéria
..	6914	1717087	3348677	35	2004	
..	6118	1754863	3418939	35	2005	
..	7715	1808620	3530381	36	2006	
..	*578	..	*6781	100	2003	Réunion
..	*580	..	*6788	100	2004	
..	*580	..	*6788	100	2005	
..	*580	..	*6788	100	2006	
..	119	..	*59804	100	2003	Rwanda
..	*125	..	*68963	100	2004	
..	*130	..	*78116	100	2005	
..	113	..	86421	100	2006	
..	*10	..	*36	100	2003	Sao Tomé-et-Principe
..	*10	..	*36	100	2004	
..	*11	..	*40	100	2005	
..	*11	..	*40	100	2006	
..	339	2387	46071	99	2003	Sénégal
..	296	2557	46135	99	2004	
..	271	2682	47651	99	2005	
..	241	2682	47702	99	2006	
..	16	..	49391	100	2003	Sierra Leone
..	17	..	49570	100	2004	
..	19	..	49758	100	2005	
..	*22	..	49998	100	2006	
..	..	..	92794	100	2003	Somalie
..	..	..	95765	100	2004	
..	..	..	98801	100	2005	
..	..	..	101800	100	2006	

Table 13

Selected series of statistics on renewables and wastes

Thousand cubic metres (1000 c.m.) / Thousand metric tons (1000 m.t.) / GWh / Terajoules (TJ)

Country or area Pays ou zone	Year Année	Fuelwood (1000 c.m.) Bois de chauffage (1000 m.c.)			Charcoal (1000 m.t) Charbon de bois (1000 t.m.)			Bagasse (1000 m.t.) Bagasse (1000 t.m.)
		Production Production	Imports Importations	Exports Exportations	Production Production	Imports Importations	Exports Exportations	Production Production
South Africa Customs Un.	2003	57169	..	..	348	7	25	9193
	2004	56913	..	..	278	9	35	8548
	2005	58636	..	..	343	15	50	9563
	2006	59334	..	..	346	13	36	8611
St. Helena and Depend.	2003	1	..	..	..	..	..	..
	2004	1	..	..	..	..	..	..
	2005	*1	..	..	..	..	..	..
	2006	*1	..	..	..	..	..	..
Sudan	2003	17277	..	..	822	..	1	2236
	2004	17487	..	..	850	..	1	2572
	2005	17703	..	..	879	..	1	2373
	2006	17906	..	..	907	..	1	2501
Togo	2003	5655	..	..	482	..	..	..
	2004	4425	..	..	494	..	..	..
	2005	5763	..	..	509	..	..	..
	2006	5817	..	..	518	..	..	..
Tunisia	2003	3882	..	..	189	..	..	..
	2004	4023	..	..	197	..	..	..
	2005	4169	..	..	206	..	..	..
	2006	4319	..	..	215	..	..	..
Uganda	2003	35693	..	0	772	..	0	626
	2004	36245	..	0	793	..	0	695
	2005	36807	..	0	814	..	0	686
	2006	37354	..	0	836	..	0	678
United Rep.Tanzania	2003	58157	..	..	1700	..	..	709
	2004	62991	..	..	2064	..	..	687
	2005	68577	..	..	2506	..	..	908
	2006	75272	..	..	3042	..	..	839
Zambia	2003	21172	..	..	1041	..	..	749
	2004	21521	..	..	851	..	..	800
	2005	21952	..	..	868	..	..	808
	2006	22391	..	..	886	..	..	815
Zimbabwe	2003	8117	..	..	9	..	..	1572
	2004	8117	..	..	9	..	..	1487
	2005	8117	..	..	9	..	..	1401
	2006	8383	..	..	11	..	..	1453
America, North	**2003**	**123356**	**214**	**401**	**1683**	**66**	**63**	**50197**
	2004	**124648**	**220**	**283**	**1664**	**75**	**63**	**51803**
	2005	**125917**	**260**	**469**	**1915**	**71**	**63**	**47072**
	2006	**127844**	**280**	**366**	**1576**	**72**	**75**	**44974**
Anguilla	2003	*2	..	..	*1	..	..	..
	2004	*2	..	..	*1	..	..	..
	2005	*2	..	..	*1	..	..	..
	2006	*2	..	..	*1	..	..	..
Bahamas	2003	..	3	..	..	0	..	..
	2004	..	0	..	..	0	..	..
	2005	..	0	..	..	0	..	..
	2006	..	1	..	..	0	..	..
Barbados	2003	..	3	..	..	..	..	117
	2004	..	3	..	..	..	..	166
	2005	..	3	..	..	..	..	172
	2006	..	3	..	..	..	..	176
Belize	2003	126	..	..	..	..	..	362
	2004	126	..	..	..	..	..	409
	2005	126	..	..	..	..	..	331
	2006	126	..	..	..	..	..	331

Table 13

Séries de statistiques des renouvelables et des déchets

Milliers de mètres cubes (1000 m.c.) / Milliers de tonnes métriques (1000 t.m.) / GWh / Tèrajoules (TJ)

Liquids and gases (TJ) Liquides et gazes (TJ)	Electricity (GWh) Électricité (GWh)	Wastes (TJ) Déchets (TJ)	Total primary (TJ) Totale primaire(TJ)	Renewables and wastes (%) Renouvelables et déchets (%)	Year Année	Country or area Pays ou zone
Production Production	Production Production	Production Production	Production Production	Share of total primary Part du total primaire		
..	5196	83023	694810	12	2003	Un.douan.d'Afr.mérid
..	6080	82160	689810	11	2004	
..	5975	84024	714872	11	2005	
..	7303	84874	719515	12	2006	
..	..	..	9	100	2003	St-Hélène et dépend
..	..	..	9	100	2004	
..	..	..	*9	100	2005	
..	..	..	*9	100	2006	
..	1163	60651	239882	32	2003	Soudan
..	1057	62409	245771	30	2004	
..	1239	64167	248624	30	2005	
..	1370	65926	253701	29	2006	
..	122	687	52766	100	2003	Togo
..	81	717	41422	100	2004	
..	74	757	53658	100	2005	
..	91	840	54293	100	2006	
..	198	8263	44429	19	2003	Tunisie
..	198	8571	46025	18	2004	
..	187	8892	47640	19	2005	
..	130	9225	49138	19	2006	
..	1796	..	337264	100	2003	Ouganda
..	1940	..	343354	100	2004	
..	1834	..	348040	100	2005	
..	1239	..	350824	100	2006	
..	2548	97548	643306	100	2003	Rép. Unie de Tanzanie
..	2356	100071	689115	99	2004	
..	1778	102669	742353	98	2005	
..	1436	105748	804812	98	2006	
..	8258	33012	261874	98	2003	Zambie
..	8461	33557	266734	98	2004	
..	8884	34228	272920	98	2005	
..	9330	34913	279274	98	2006	
..	5359	92941	198505	66	2003	Zimbabwe
..	5521	94335	199825	67	2004	
..	5834	95750	201701	66	2005	
..	5552	96315	204077	67	2006	
409183	**717221**	**2765035**	**7270169**	**8**	**2003**	**Amérique du Nord**
470555	**724659**	**2825610**	**7443096**	**8**	**2004**	
525844	**756916**	**2885830**	**7649769**	**9**	**2005**	
624779	**780790**	**2918291**	**7868502**	**9**	**2006**	
..	..	..	*18	100	2003	Anguilla
..	..	..	*18	100	2004	
..	..	..	*18	100	2005	
..	..	..	*18	100	2006	
..	..	..	..	..	2003	Bahamas
..	..	..	..	..	2004	
..	..	..	..	..	2005	
..	..	..	..	..	2006	
..	..	..	903	18	2003	Barbade
..	..	..	1280	26	2004	
..	..	..	1330	26	2005	
..	..	..	1356	30	2006	
..	*105	..	4324	100	2003	Belize
..	*105	..	4687	100	2004	
..	*108	..	4096	100	2005	
..	*105	..	4085	100	2006	

Table 13

Selected series of statistics on renewables and wastes

Thousand cubic metres (1000 c.m.) / Thousand metric tons (1000 m.t.) / GWh / Terajoules (TJ)

Country or area Pays ou zone	Year Année	Fuelwood (1000 c.m.) Bois de chauffage (1000 m.c.)			Charcoal (1000 m.t) Charbon de bois (1000 t.m.)			Bagasse (1000 m.t.) Bagasse (1000 t.m.)
		Production Production	Imports Importations	Exports Exportations	Production Production	Imports Importations	Exports Exportations	Production Production
Canada	2003	2844	38	240	..	..	..	..
	2004	2790	66	162	..	..	..	..
	2005	2790	72	340	..	..	..	..
	2006	2790	90	218	..	..	..	..
Costa Rica	2003	1318	..	..	10	..	..	530
	2004	1318	..	..	10	..	..	1097
	2005	1472	..	..	10	..	..	1299
	2006	1960	..	..	11	..	..	1168
Cuba	2003	1829	..	..	60	..	..	7101
	2004	1799	..	..	61	..	..	6951
	2005	1820	..	..	62	..	..	4787
	2006	1584	..	..	59	..	..	3606
Dominica	2003	*1	..	0	..	0	0	..
	2004	*1	..	0	..	0	0	..
	2005	*1	..	0	..	0	0	..
	2006	*1	..	0	..	0	0	..
Dominican Republic	2003	656	..	..	380	..	..	1711
	2004	756	..	..	387	..	..	1726
	2005	820	..	..	389	..	..	1548
	2006	878	..	..	393	..	..	1392
El Salvador	2003	5321	..	..	17	8	..	1222
	2004	5358	..	..	18	9	..	1267
	2005	5508	..	..	19	10	..	1302
	2006	5601	..	..	20	10	..	1407
Grenada	2003	15	..	..	2	..	..	3
	2004	24	..	..	2	..	..	3
	2005	29	..	..	2	..	..	3
	2006	30	..	..	2	..	..	3
Guadeloupe	2003	21	..	..	..	..	..	..
	2004	26	..	..	..	..	..	..
	2005	29	..	..	..	..	..	..
	2006	31	..	..	..	..	..	..
Guatemala	2003	14826	..	..	29	..	..	5870
	2004	15226	..	..	30	..	..	6820
	2005	15683	..	..	31	..	..	6570
	2006	16153	..	..	32	..	..	6391
Haiti	2003	1986	..	..	27	..	..	..
	2004	1993	..	..	28	..	..	..
	2005	2001	..	..	29	..	..	..
	2006	2009	..	..	29	..	..	..
Honduras	2003	8706	..	..	3	..	..	978
	2004	8702	..	..	24	..	..	1163
	2005	8700	..	..	18	..	..	1174
	2006	8670	..	..	25	..	..	1255
Jamaica	2003	577	..	..	9	..	..	501
	2004	570	..	..	9	..	..	591
	2005	563	..	..	9	..	..	410
	2006	559	..	..	9	..	..	469
Martinique	2003	13	..	..	..	..	..	*22
	2004	18	..	..	..	..	..	*22
	2005	21	..	..	..	..	..	*22
	2006	25	..	..	..	..	..	*22
Mexico	2003	38101	..	7	138	2	48	17740
	2004	38280	..	7	139	2	48	18490
	2005	38458	..	7	384	1	42	18318
	2006	38531	..	7	77	1	56	17642

Table 13

Séries de statistiques des renouvelables et des déchets
Milliers de mètres cubes (1000 m.c.) / Milliers de tonnes métriques (1000 t.m.) / GWh / Tèrajoules (TJ)

Liquids and gases (TJ) Liquides et gazes (TJ)	Electricity (GWh) Électricité (GWh)	Wastes (TJ) Déchets (TJ)	Total primary (TJ) Totale primaire (TJ)	Renewables and wastes (%) Renouvelables et déchets (%)	Year Année	Country or area Pays ou zone
Production Production	Production Production	Production Production	Production Production	Share of total primary Part du total primaire		
11984	338465	402351	1658682	10	2003	Canada
12017	342521	412854	1683327	10	2004	
13592	365174	410110	1763701	11	2005	
13122	358092	435103	1762729	11	2006	
..	7397	2849	45608	100	2003	Costa Rica
..	7958	1893	51049	100	2004	
..	8084	*2500	55074	100	2005	
..	8091	3138	59176	100	2006	
1299	128	72861	146154	45	2003	Cuba
1299	88	66920	138636	46	2004	
1658	68	46004	101489	41	2005	
1603	94	35560	79817	33	2006	
..	29	..	114	100	2003	Dominique
..	34	..	132	100	2004	
..	28	..	110	100	2005	
..	*30	..	*117	100	2006	
..	1200	12372	35897	100	2003	Rép. dominicaine
..	1582	12753	38683	100	2004	
..	1896	10954	37224	100	2005	
..	1408	10972	34810	100	2006	
..	2425	11433	78191	100	2003	El Salvador
..	2399	11856	79210	100	2004	
..	2720	12188	82342	100	2005	
..	3102	10871	84057	100	2006	
..	..	..	158	100	2003	Grenade
..	..	..	239	100	2004	
..	..	..	282	100	2005	
..	..	..	292	100	2006	
..	..	..	192	100	2003	Guadeloupe
..	..	..	238	100	2004	
..	..	..	265	100	2005	
..	..	..	283	100	2006	
..	2477	27523	217163	81	2003	Guatemala
..	2434	28266	228743	85	2004	
..	3661	29115	236250	86	2005	
..	4056	29125	240597	88	2006	
..	255	2751	21803	100	2003	Haïti
..	260	2751	21889	100	2004	
..	265	2801	22025	100	2005	
..	271	2871	22190	100	2006	
..	2174	..	94884	100	2003	Honduras
..	2348	..	96901	100	2004	
..	1716	..	94698	100	2005	
..	1938	..	95851	100	2006	
..	146	6125	15791	100	2003	Jamaïque
..	168	6963	17339	100	2004	
..	152	6216	15072	100	2005	
..	166	6378	15704	100	2006	
..	..	..	*289	100	2003	Martinique
..	..	..	*334	100	2004	
..	..	..	362	100	2005	
..	..	..	394	100	2006	
420	26211	86879	666598	6	2003	Mexique
441	31836	89000	696406	7	2004	
432	35083	100351	719738	7	2005	
400	37151	94237	716483	7	2006	

Table 13

Selected series of statistics on renewables and wastes
Thousand cubic metres (1000 c.m.) / Thousand metric tons (1000 m.t.) / GWh / Terajoules (TJ)

Country or area Pays ou zone	Year Année	Fuelwood (1000 c.m.) Bois de chauffage (1000 m.c.)			Charcoal (1000 m.t) Charbon de bois (1000 t.m.)			Bagasse (1000 m.t.) Bagasse (1000 t.m.)
		Production Production	Imports Importations	Exports Exportations	Production Production	Imports Importations	Exports Exportations	Production Production
Nicaragua	2003	2833	..	..	19	..	..	73
	2004	2930	..	..	19	..	..	123
	2005	2902	..	..	14	..	..	131
	2006	*2918	..	..	9	..	..	115
Panama	2003	1234	..	..	5	..	..	47
	2004	1074	..	..	5	..	..	54
	2005	1055	..	..	5	..	..	62
	2006	1160	..	..	5	..	..	54
Puerto Rico	2003	..	..	..	..	..	..	
	2004	..	..	..	..	..	..	
	2005	..	..	..	..	..	..	
	2006	..	..	..	..	..	..	
St. Kitts-Nevis	2003	..	..	..	..	..	..	7
	2004	..	..	..	..	..	..	6
	2005	..	..	..	..	..	..	6
	2006	..	..	..	..	..	..	
St. Vincent-Grenadines	2003	..	..	..	*1	..	0	
	2004	..	..	..	*1	..	0	
	2005	..	..	..	*1	..	0	
	2006	..	..	..	*1	..	0	
Trinidad and Tobago	2003	35	..	..	2	..	..	21
	2004	35	..	..	2	..	..	14
	2005	34	..	..	2	..	..	10
	2006	34	..	..	2	..	..	8
United States	2003	42912	169	154	982	56	15	1253
	2004	43620	151	114	930	64	15	1110
	2005	43903	185	122	940	60	21	902
	2006	44782	186	141	902	61	19	933
America, South	**2003**	**170599**	**..**	**..**	**10726**	**26**	**33**	**12150**
	2004	**180519**	**..**	**..**	**11966**	**53**	**28**	**12680**
	2005	**183803**	**..**	**..**	**11994**	**91**	**23**	**13212**
	2006	**184241**	**..**	**..**	**11518**	**159**	**38**	**14921**
Argentina	2003	3973	..	..	317	..	..	636
	2004	3865	..	..	335	..	..	605
	2005	4373	..	..	526	..	..	705
	2006	4373	..	..	360	..	..	805
Bolivia	2003	2206	..	..	21	..	..	126
	2004	2229	..	..	22	..	..	151
	2005	2252	..	..	23	..	..	130
	2006	2271	..	..	23	..	..	120
Brazil	2003	116593	..	..	8658	25	13	9732
	2004	125827	..	..	10086	52	28	10179
	2005	127020	..	..	9894	90	15	10647
	2006	127384	..	..	9560	158	13	12115
Chile	2003	11647	..	..	252	..	..	
	2004	12321	..	..	252	..	..	
	2005	13117	..	..	251	..	..	
	2006	13903	..	..	251	..	..	
Colombia	2003	7893	..	..	722	..	..	862
	2004	7958	..	..	462	..	..	941
	2005	8540	..	..	477	..	..	959
	2006	8202	..	..	475	..	..	1056
Ecuador	2003	5351	..	..	101	..	..	164
	2004	5429	..	..	99	..	..	162
	2005	5509	..	..	96	..	..	163
	2006	5576	..	..	93	..	..	177

Table 13

Séries de statistiques des renouvelables et des déchets

Milliers de mètres cubes (1000 m.c.) / Milliers de tonnes métriques (1000 t.m.) / GWh / Tèrajoules (TJ)

Liquids and gases (TJ) Liquides et gazes (TJ)	Electricity (GWh) Électricité (GWh)	Wastes (TJ) Déchets (TJ)	Total primary (TJ) Totale primaire (TJ)	Renewables and wastes (%) Renouvelables et déchets (%)	Year Année	Country or area Pays ou zone
Production Production	Production Production	Production Production	Production Production	Share of total primary Part du total primaire		
..	569	..	33618	100	2003	Nicaragua
..	576	..	38390	100	2004	
..	705	..	39170	100	2005	
..	682	..	*38008	100	2006	
..	2890	2218	27581	100	2003	Panama
..	3897	2287	30349	100	2004	
..	3875	2177	30559	100	2005	
..	3903	3998	32867	100	2006	
..	260	..	936	100	2003	Porto Rico
..	140	..	504	100	2004	
..	145	..	522	100	2005	
..	*150	..	*540	100	2006	
..	..	..	556	100	2003	St-Kitts-Nevis
..	..	..	502	100	2004	
..	..	..	502	100	2005	
..	..	..	0	..	2006	
..	21	..	75	100	2003	St. Vincent-Grenadines
..	27	..	98	100	2004	
..	*28	..	*101	100	2005	
..	*29	..	*104	100	2006	
..	..	975	2980	0	2003	Trinité-et-Tobago
..	..	1007	2407	0	2004	
..	..	1039	2184	0	2005	
..	..	1326	2270	0	2006	
395481	332469	2136698	4217653	7	2003	Etats-Unis
456798	328285	2189060	4311736	7	2004	
510163	333208	2262375	4442657	8	2005	
609655	361522	2284712	4676753	8	2006	
319064	**548105**	**650974**	**5439328**	**23**	**2003**	**Amérique du Sud**
323522	**567300**	**652651**	**5646078**	**23**	**2004**	
355260	**602599**	**702269**	**5925559**	**23**	**2005**	
398770	**634461**	**768209**	**6285676**	**24**	**2006**	
..	33922	31375	238896	7	2003	Argentine
..	30599	27200	219395	6	2004	
..	34341	29726	247784	7	2005	
..	38230	38560	278286	8	2006	
..	2243	..	37970	10	2003	Bolivie
..	2149	..	39765	8	2004	
..	2456	..	39474	7	2005	
..	2159	..	37822	6	2006	
319044	305640	569924	3805483	52	2003	Brésil
323520	320823	578053	3991614	53	2004	
354465	337484	626366	4177847	51	2005	
393147	348833	682382	4430084	52	2006	
..	22605	..	187739	65	2003	Chili
..	21268	..	189083	69	2004	
..	26146	..	213906	66	2005	
..	34250	..	250257	71	2006	
0	36219	13054	282115	9	2003	Colombie
0	40111	12992	302786	10	2004	
606	39899	12971	309322	9	2005	
5422	42859	12950	329153	9	2006	
..	7182	..	87430	9	2003	Equateur
..	7413	..	88775	7	2004	
..	8605	..	93930	8	2005	
..	8914	..	96735	8	2006	

Table 13

Selected series of statistics on renewables and wastes

Thousand cubic metres (1000 c.m.) / Thousand metric tons (1000 m.t.) / GWh / Terajoules (TJ)

Country or area Pays ou zone	Year Année	Fuelwood (1000 c.m.) Bois de chauffage (1000 m.c.)			Charcoal (1000 m.t) Charbon de bois (1000 t.m.)			Bagasse (1000 m.t.) Bagasse (1000 t.m.)
		Production Production	Imports Importations	Exports Exportations	Production Production	Imports Importations	Exports Exportations	Production Production
French Guiana	2003	89	..	..	5	..	..	
	2004	95	..	..	5	..	..	
	2005	100	..	..	5	..	..	
	2006	106	..	..	6	..	..	
Guyana	2003	997	..	..	2	..	..	103
	2004	1016	..	..	2	..	..	105
	2005	1121	..	..	2	..	..	109
	2006	1128	..	..	2	..	..	109
Paraguay	2003	8695	..	..	182	0	20	37
	2004	8535	..	..	226	0	0	*37
	2005	8390	..	..	234	0	8	*38
	2006	7630	..	..	257	0	25	*39
Peru	2003	7302	..	..	85	..	..	316
	2004	7302	..	..	84	..	..	264
	2005	7366	..	..	84	..	..	226
	2006	7456	..	..	83	..	..	262
Suriname	2003	44	..	..	2	..	..	1
	2004	44	..	..	7	..	..	1
	2005	45	..	..	7	..	..	1
	2006	45	..	..	7	..	..	2
Uruguay	2003	2063	..	..	..	1	..	3
	2004	2106	..	..	..	1	..	4
	2005	2126	..	..	..	1	..	5
	2006	2283	..	..	..	1	..	4
Venezuela(Bolivar. Rep.)	2003	3746	..	..	379	..	..	166
	2004	3794	..	..	386	..	..	226
	2005	3844	..	..	394	..	..	224
	2006	3885	..	..	400	..	..	228
Asia	**2003**	**1083984**	**345**	**8**	**11888**	**505**	**369**	**15264**
	2004	**1087262**	**325**	**8**	**10925**	**559**	**350**	**13140**
	2005	**1095262**	**361**	**9**	**11360**	**556**	**307**	**12562**
	2006	**1099962**	**279**	**12**	**11449**	**674**	**311**	**14927**
Afghanistan	2003	1389	..	..	90	..	..	
	2004	1427	..	..	93	..	..	
	2005	1467	..	..	97	..	..	
	2006	1467	..	..	97	..	..	
Armenia	2003	56	..	..	..	0	..	
	2004	59	..	..	..	0	..	
	2005	37	..	..	..	0	..	
	2006	60	..	..	..	1	..	
Azerbaijan	2003	7	..	..	..	..	..	
	2004	7	..	..	..	..	..	
	2005	7	..	..	..	..	..	
	2006	7	..	..	..	..	..	
Bahrain	2003	..	..	..	..	3	..	
	2004	..	..	..	..	0	..	
	2005	..	..	..	..	0	..	
	2006	..	..	..	..	2	..	
Bangladesh	2003	27736	..	..	300	..	..	54
	2004	27702	..	..	304	..	..	40
	2005	27670	..	..	308	..	..	39
	2006	27592	..	..	311	..	..	47
Bhutan	2003	4414	..	..	6	..	..	
	2004	4480	..	..	6	..	..	
	2005	4548	..	..	6	..	..	
	2006	4548	..	..	7	..	..	

Table 13

Séries de statistiques des renouvelables et des déchets
Milliers de mètres cubes (1000 m.c.) / Milliers de tonnes métriques (1000 t.m.) / GWh / Tèrajoules (TJ)

Liquids and gases (TJ) Liquides et gazes (TJ)	Electricity (GWh) Électricité (GWh)	Wastes (TJ) Déchets (TJ)	Total primary (TJ) Totale primaire(TJ)	Renewables and wastes (%) Renouvelables et déchets (%)	Year Année	Country or area Pays ou zone
Production Production	Production Production	Production Production	Production Production	Share of total primary Part du total primaire		
..	..	..	815	100	2003	Guyane française
..	..	..	864	100	2004	
..	..	..	917	100	2005	
..	..	..	965	100	2006	
..	..	..	17115	100	2003	Guyana
..	..	..	17440	100	2004	
..	..	..	18666	100	2005	
..	..	..	18788	100	2006	
21	51765	..	268689	100	2003	Paraguay
3	51925	..	267757	100	2004	
189	51160	..	263919	100	2005	
200	53778	..	266484	100	2006	
..	18536	21205	179034	43	2003	Pérou
..	17527	18913	169148	40	2004	
..	19965	17847	174467	38	2005	
..	21486	18839	184552	34	2006	
..	760	..	3264	12	2003	Suriname
..	772	..	3311	12	2004	
..	829	..	3521	12	2005	
..	871	..	3723	13	2006	
..	8530	1570	51373	100	2003	Uruguay
..	4780	1647	38447	100	2004	
..	6685	1514	45397	100	2005	
..	3595	1632	35752	100	2006	
..	60703	13846	279407	4	2003	Venezuela(Rép. bolivar.)
..	69933	13846	317692	4	2004	
..	75031	13846	336409	4	2005	
..	79486	13846	353076	4	2006	
11174	**706394**	**4494683**	**18126812**	**11**	**2003**	**Asie**
12468	**792624**	**4553660**	**18363399**	**11**	**2004**	
12176	**849196**	**4634744**	**18676239**	**10**	**2005**	
14997	**931203**	**4703991**	**19269083**	**10**	**2006**	
..	647	..	15010	93	2003	Afghanistan
..	579	..	15118	94	2004	
..	*595	..	15543	94	2005	
..	*595	..	15543	94	2006	
..	1982	..	7647	100	2003	Arménie
..	2014	..	7789	100	2004	
..	1773	..	6721	100	2005	
..	1825	..	7118	100	2006	
..	2469	..	8956	1	2003	Azerbaïdjan
..	2755	..	9986	1	2004	
..	3009	..	10900	1	2005	
..	2518	..	9133	1	2006	
..	..	..	..	..	2003	Bahreïn
..	..	..	..	..	2004	
..	..	..	..	..	2005	
..	..	..	..	..	2006	
..	1126	316426	577952	57	2003	Bangladesh
..	1226	321805	582357	56	2004	
..	1293	327919	588285	54	2005	
..	1389	333821	594453	52	2006	
..	2199	..	48227	96	2003	Bhoutan
..	2527	..	50013	98	2004	
..	2353	..	50001	95	2005	
..	2646	..	51056	95	2006	

Table 13

Selected series of statistics on renewables and wastes
Thousand cubic metres (1000 c.m.) / Thousand metric tons (1000 m.t.) / GWh / Terajoules (TJ)

Country or area Pays ou zone	Year Année	Fuelwood (1000 c.m.) Bois de chauffage (1000 m.c.)			Charcoal (1000 m.t) Charbon de bois (1000 t.m.)			Bagasse (100 m.t.) Bagasse (100 t.m.)
		Production Production	Imports Importations	Exports Exportations	Production Production	Imports Importations	Exports Exportations	Production Production
Brunei Darussalam	2003	12	..	..	..	..	..	
	2004	12	..	..	..	..	..	
	2005	12	..	..	..	..	..	
	2006	12	..	..	..	..	..	
Cambodia	2003	9561	..	..	89	..	..	
	2004	9389	..	..	91	..	..	
	2005	9224	..	..	92	..	..	
	2006	9224	..	..	94	..	..	
China	2003	215296	7	6	1777	67	108	341
	2004	211315	7	6	1771	71	69	333
	2005	207418	7	6	1764	91	39	298
	2006	203562	18	9	1764	89	49	306
China, Hong Kong SAR	2003	99	..	..	..	10	2	
	2004	97	..	..	..	9	1	
	2005	95	..	..	..	8	1	
	2006	93	..	..	..	9	2	
China, Macao SAR	2003	..	1	..	..	1	..	
	2004	..	1	..	..	2	..	
	2005	..	1	..	..	1	..	
	2006	..	1	..	..	1	..	
Cyprus	2003	30	0	..	3	4		
	2004	26	0	..	2	6		
	2005	25	0	..	2	8		
	2006	23	0	..	2	8		
Georgia	2003	2958	..	..	..	..	..	
	2004	2958	..	..	..	..	..	
	2005	2958	..	..	..	..	..	
	2006	2958	..	..	..	..	..	
India	2003	379336	..	..	2880	0	7	707
	2004	383869	..	..	1715	1	4	470
	2005	388456	..	..	1728	2	5	4960
	2006	392722	..	..	1740	0	3	728
Indonesia	2003	189507	..	1	713	..	144	580
	2004	189115	..	1	699	..	144	725
	2005	188390	..	1	681	..	144	793
	2006	193384	..	1	681	..	144	818
Iran(Islamic Rep. of)	2003	93	1	..	4	..	..	153
	2004	77	1	..	3	..	..	194
	2005	72	1	..	2	..	..	189
	2006	65	1	..	1	..	..	169
Iraq	2003	54	..	..	39	..	..	
	2004	55	..	..	40	..	..	
	2005	56	..	..	41	..	..	
	2006	57	..	..	42	..	..	
Israel	2003	2	..	..	..	7	..	
	2004	2	..	..	..	7	..	
	2005	2	..	..	..	7	..	
	2006	2	..	..	..	7	..	
Japan	2003	1153	1	..	21	..	..	47
	2004	1698	1	..	20	..	..	54
	2005	2007	0	..	20	..	..	42
	2006	2506	0	..	15	..	..	46
Jordan	2003	245	..	..	32	1	..	
	2004	253	..	..	33	1	..	
	2005	262	..	..	34	1	..	
	2006	271	..	..	26	2	..	

Table 13

Séries de statistiques des renouvelables et des déchets
Milliers de mètres cubes (1000 m.c.) / Milliers de tonnes métriques (1000 t.m.) / GWh / Tèrajoules (TJ)

Liquids and gases (TJ) Liquides et gazes (TJ)	Electricity (GWh) Électricité (GWh)	Wastes (TJ) Déchets (TJ)	Total primary (TJ) Totale primaire(TJ)	Renewables and wastes (%) Renouvelables et déchets (%)	Year Année	Country or area Pays ou zone
Production Production	Production Production	Production Production	Production Production	Share of total primary Part du total primaire		
..	..	666	772	0	2003	Brunéi Darussalam
..	..	666	772	0	2004	
..	..	666	772	0	2005	
..	..	666	772	0	2006	
..	41	..	87459	100	2003	Cambodge
..	27	..	85840	100	2004	
..	44	..	84392	100	2005	
..	53	..	84425	100	2006	
..	283703	..	3250790	7	2003	Chine
..	350655	..	3449326	6	2004	
..	397049	..	3553905	6	2005	
..	441315	..	3684440	6	2006	
..	..	..	904	100	2003	Chine, Hong-Kong RAS
..	..	..	886	100	2004	
..	..	..	868	100	2005	
..	..	..	850	100	2006	
..	..	..	..	..	2003	Chine, Macao RAS
..	..	..	..	..	2004	
..	..	..	..	..	2005	
..	..	..	..	..	2006	
0	1	226	508	100	2003	Chypre
0	0	198	439	100	2004	
0	1	176	412	100	2005	
1	1	134	352	100	2006	
3	6527	..	50511	88	2003	Géorgie
3	6049	..	48793	91	2004	
3	6236	..	49467	93	2005	
3	5390	..	46421	93	2006	
..	75248	2999758	7281210	39	2003	Inde
..	84617	3034934	7208493	37	2004	
..	101502	3070527	7366469	37	2005	
..	113368	3105121	7662251	37	2006	
..	15397	414009	2244902	21	2003	Indonésie
..	16325	419628	2261493	20	2004	
..	17364	425357	2269622	19	2005	
..	16282	430147	2318016	18	2006	
..	11099	8714	61347	1	2003	Iran(Rép. islamique)
..	10628	8846	62787	1	2004	
..	16101	8977	82197	1	2005	
..	18267	9107	88547	1	2006	
..	433	..	2052	0	2003	Iraq
..	493	..	2277	0	2004	
..	519	..	2380	0	2005	
..	486	..	2270	0	2006	
..	43	..	173	4	2003	Israël
..	39	..	159	0	2004	
..	39	..	159	0	2005	
..	17	..	79	0	2006	
5443	108465	239390	649476	81	2003	Japon
6206	107842	233041	647121	81	2004	
5950	91338	249755	606094	78	2005	
4793	100415	270322	663021	78	2006	
..	*56	..	2440	25	2003	Jordanie
..	56	..	2513	26	2004	
..	60	..	2609	30	2005	
..	54	..	2670	30	2006	

Table 13

Selected series of statistics on renewables and wastes
Thousand cubic metres (1000 c.m.) / Thousand metric tons (1000 m.t.) / GWh / Terajoules (TJ)

Country or area Pays ou zone	Year Année	Fuelwood (1000 c.m.) Bois de chauffage (1000 m.c.)			Charcoal (1000 m.t) Charbon de bois (1000 t.m.)			Bagasse (1000 m.t.) Bagasse (1000 t.m.)
		Production Production	Imports Importations	Exports Exportations	Production Production	Imports Importations	Exports Exportations	Production Production
Kazakhstan	2003	336	0	..	..	..	..	..
	2004	336	0	..	..	..	..	..
	2005	336	0	..	..	..	..	..
	2006	336	0	..	..	..	..	..
Korea, Dem.Ppl's.Rep.	2003	4685	..	..	146	1	..	..
	2004	4709	..	..	148	1	..	..
	2005	4731	..	..	150	1	..	..
	2006	4748	..	..	151	1	..	..
Korea, Republic of	2003	297	..	..	6	109	1	..
	2004	202	..	..	6	111	1	..
	2005	225	..	..	10	119	1	..
	2006	230	..	..	10	124	1	..
Kuwait	2003	..	..	..	..	8	..	..
	2004	..	..	..	..	0	..	..
	2005	..	..	..	..	0	..	..
	2006	..	..	..	..	0	..	..
Kyrgyzstan	2003	25	..	..	..	..	..	..
	2004	18	..	..	..	..	..	..
	2005	18	..	..	..	..	..	..
	2006	18	..	..	..	..	..	..
Lao People's Dem. Rep.	2003	5915	..	..	18	..	..	..
	2004	5930	..	..	18	..	..	..
	2005	5946	..	..	19	..	..	..
	2006	5946	..	..	19	..	..	..
Lebanon	2003	82	..	..	11	12	..	..
	2004	82	..	..	15	12	..	..
	2005	81	..	..	15	2	..	..
	2006	81	..	..	15	2	..	..
Malaysia	2003	3173	2	..	27	1	33	261
	2004	3120	2	..	27	2	60	261
	2005	3069	2	..	28	3	50	261
	2006	3014	12	..	28	12	53	179
Maldives	2003	..	0	..	..	137	..	..
	2004	..	0	..	..	180	..	..
	2005	..	1	..	..	163	..	..
	2006	..	1	..	..	251	..	..
Mongolia	2003	474	..	..	..	..	..	..
	2004	474	..	..	..	..	..	..
	2005	474	..	..	..	..	..	..
	2006	490	..	..	..	..	..	..
Myanmar	2003	43547	..	..	248	..	..	440
	2004	44023	..	..	250	..	..	489
	2005	44477	..	..	252	..	..	489
	2006	44651	..	..	254	..	..	489
Nepal	2003	12717	..	..	68	..	..	408
	2004	12705	..	..	69	..	..	456
	2005	12696	..	..	70	..	..	424
	2006	12658	..	..	72	..	..	440
Occup. Palestinian Terr.	2003	381	0	0	..	..	..	..
	2004	412	8	0	..	..	..	..
	2005	405	4	1	..	..	..	..
	2006	*400	*4	*1	..	..	..	..
Oman	2003	..	2	1	..	1	..	..
	2004	..	3	1	..	2	..	..
	2005	..	3	1	..	2	..	..
	2006	..	3	1	..	2	..	..

Table 13

Séries de statistiques des renouvelables et des déchets

Milliers de mètres cubes (1000 m.c.) / Milliers de tonnes métriques (1000 t.m.) / GWh / Tèrajoules (TJ)

Liquids and gases (TJ) Liquides et gazes (TJ)	Electricity (GWh) Électricité (GWh)	Wastes (TJ) Déchets (TJ)	Total primary (TJ) Totale primaire(TJ)	Renewables and wastes (%) Renouvelables et déchets (%)	Year Année	Country or area Pays ou zone
Production Production	Production Production	Production Production	Production Production	Share of total primary Part du total primaire		
..	8626	..	34120	1	2003	Kazakhstan
..	8058	..	32075	1	2004	
..	7857	..	31351	1	2005	
..	7769	..	31034	1	2006	
..	11721	..	84978	10	2003	Corée,Rép.pop.dém.de
..	12501	..	88003	10	2004	
..	13133	..	90476	9	2005	
..	12621	..	88789	9	2006	
3543	6937	68178	99399	47	2003	Corée, République de
4045	5937	77129	104389	46	2004	
3850	5334	82750	107860	43	2005	
7632	5489	91120	120615	45	2006	
..	..	..	..	..	2003	Koweït
..	..	..	..	..	2004	
..	..	..	..	..	2005	
..	..	..	..	..	2006	
..	13517	..	48886	84	2003	Kirghizistan
..	14095	..	50903	84	2004	
..	14260	..	51497	86	2005	
..	14888	..	53758	88	2006	
..	3055	..	65012	85	2003	Rép. dém. pop. lao
..	*3222	..	65751	85	2004	
..	*3361	..	66396	84	2005	
..	*3468	..	66781	84	2006	
..	689	..	3229	100	2003	Liban
..	1123	..	4790	100	2004	
..	1048	..	4511	100	2005	
..	695	..	3242	100	2006	
..	5750	3795	55489	1	2003	Malaisie
..	5827	3866	55350	1	2004	
..	5184	3936	52639	1	2005	
..	7072	4001	58362	1	2006	
..	..	..	..	..	2003	Maldives
..	..	..	..	..	2004	
..	..	..	..	..	2005	
..	..	..	..	..	2006	
..	..	..	4325	6	2003	Mongolie
..	..	..	4325	5	2004	
..	..	..	4325	4	2005	
..	..	..	4479	4	2006	
..	2250	23102	432291	54	2003	Myanmar
..	2408	23102	437585	48	2004	
..	2997	23102	443851	47	2005	
..	3324	23300	446815	46	2006	
1873	2263	34381	163692	100	2003	Népal
1903	2402	35145	165247	100	2004	
2078	2612	35926	166621	100	2005	
2126	2674	36752	167496	100	2006	
..	..	313	3795	100	2003	Terr. palestiniens occup.
..	..	674	4433	100	2004	
..	..	192	3888	100	2005	
..	..	*176	*3830	100	2006	
..	..	..	..	..	2003	Oman
..	..	..	..	..	2004	
..	..	..	..	..	2005	
..	..	..	..	..	2006	

Table 13

Selected series of statistics on renewables and wastes
Thousand cubic metres (1000 c.m.) / Thousand metric tons (1000 m.t.) / GWh / Terajoules (TJ)

Country or area Pays ou zone	Year Année	Fuelwood (1000 c.m.) Bois de chauffage (1000 m.c.)			Charcoal (1000 m.t) Charbon de bois (1000 t.m.)			Bagasse (1000 m.t.) Bagasse (1000 t.m.)
		Production Production	Imports Importations	Exports Exportations	Production Production	Imports Importations	Exports Exportations	Production Production
Other Asia	2003	..	..	..	..	..	..	
	2004	..	..	..	..	..	..	
	2005	..	..	..	..	..	..	
	2006	..	..	..	..	..	..	
Pakistan	2003	25311	..	..	60	..	..	13165
	2004	26007	..	..	62	..	..	14526
	2005	26507	..	..	64	..	..	9215
	2006	26131	..	..	65	..	..	10605
Philippines	2003	28481	..	..	1222	..	29	3486
	2004	29313	..	..	1343	..	34	4189
	2005	30168	..	..	1339	..	37	3390
	2006	31041	..	..	1338	..	32	3746
Qatar	2003	..	..	..	..	0	..	
	2004	..	..	..	..	0	..	
	2005	..	..	..	..	0	..	
	2006	..	..	..	..	1	..	
Saudi Arabia	2003	..	4	..	..	48	..	
	2004	..	4	..	..	48	..	
	2005	..	4	..	..	48	..	
	2006	..	4	:.	..	48	..	
Singapore	2003	..	1	..	35	41	35	
	2004	..	1	..	35	39	30	
	2005	..	1	..	35	33	26	
	2006	..	1	..	35	32	23	
Sri Lanka	2003	5711	..	..	1	2	2	*90
	2004	5648	..	..	1	0	0	94
	2005	5586	..	..	1	0	0	220
	2006	5586	..	..	2	0	0	195
Syrian Arab Republic	2003	25	0	..	3	0	3	
	2004	26	0	..	3	0	3	
	2005	27	0	..	3	0	3	
	2006	28	0	..	3	0	2	
Tajikistan	2003	..	..	..	..	..	..	
	2004	..	..	..	..	..	..	
	2005	..	..	..	..	..	..	
	2006	..	..	..	..	..	..	
Thailand	2003	44555	..	..	3428	25	5	1841
	2004	45438	..	..	3493	34	5	1739
	2005	51637	..	..	3917	33	2	1868
	2006	49919	..	..	4069	40	2	16052
Turkey	2003	20674	325	1	..	3	..	
	2004	19844	295	0	..	10	..	
	2005	19008	336	0	..	12	..	
	2006	18280	233	0	..	20	..	
Turkmenistan	2003	3	..	..	..	..	..	
	2004	3	..	..	..	..	..	
	2005	3	..	..	..	..	..	
	2006	3	..	..	..	..	..	
United Arab Emirates	2003	..	..	..	..	23	..	
	2004	..	..	..	..	23	..	
	2005	..	..	..	..	23	..	
	2006	..	..	..	..	23	..	
Uzbekistan	2003	20	..	..	..	..	..	
	2004	18	..	..	..	..	..	
	2005	18	..	..	..	..	..	
	2006	18	..	..	..	..	..	

Table 13

Séries de statistiques des renouvelables et des déchets
Milliers de mètres cubes (1000 m.c.) / Milliers de tonnes métriques (1000 t.m.) / GWh / Tèrajoules (TJ)

Liquids and gases (TJ) Liquides et gazes (TJ)	Electricity (GWh) Électricité (GWh)	Wastes (TJ) Déchets (TJ)	Total primary (TJ) Totale primaire(TJ)	Renewables and wastes (%) Renouvelables et déchets (%)	Year Année	Country or area Pays ou zone
Production Production	Production Production	Production Production	Production Production	Share of total primary Part du total primaire		
..	6920	18997	43905	57	2003	Autre Asie
..	6595	21647	45385	57	2004	
..	8003	37994	66801	76	2005	
..	8278	37988	67785	79	2006	
..	26946	*155338	585149	32	2003	Pakistan
..	25673	*155338	597434	31	2004	
..	30864	*155750	580090	29	2005	
..	31956	*155750	591316	30	2006	
0	17709	103816	454583	72	2003	Philippines
0	18894	106900	474953	77	2004	
0	18290	99610	467139	73	2005	
37	20478	*96159	482313	74	2006	
..	..	..	..	..	2003	Qatar
..	..	..	..	..	2004	
..	..	..	..	..	2005	
..	..	..	..	..	2006	
..	..	..	..	..	2003	Arabie saoudite
..	..	..	..	..	2004	
..	..	..	..	..	2005	
..	..	..	..	..	2006	
..	..	..	..	100	2003	Singapour
..	..	..	..	100	2004	
..	..	..	..	100	2005	
..	..	..	..	100	2006	
..	3313	..	64781	100	2003	Sri Lanka
..	2963	..	62972	100	2004	
..	3455	..	65193	100	2005	
..	4638	..	69212	100	2006	
..	2804	..	10319	1	2003	Rép. arabe syrienne
..	4247	..	15530	1	2004	
..	3445	..	12649	1	2005	
..	3994	..	14631	1	2006	
..	16337	..	58810	95	2003	Tadjikistan
..	16340	..	58820	94	2004	
..	16968	..	61081	93	2005	
..	16702	..	60124	93	2006	
..	7301	51525	626871	33	2003	Thaïlande
..	6042	56350	627407	33	2004	
..	5801	58450	695178	33	2005	
..	8128	57050	666147	32	2006	
312	35483	52810	369657	40	2003	Turquie
311	46239	51152	399134	42	2004	
295	39717	50418	367268	36	2005	
405	44469	49137	376555	35	2006	
..	3	..	42	0	2003	Turkménistan
..	3	..	42	0	2004	
..	3	..	42	0	2005	
..	3	..	42	0	2006	
..	..	..	..	..	2003	Emirats arabes unis
..	..	..	..	..	2004	
..	..	..	..	..	2005	
..	..	..	..	..	2006	
..	6346	..	23025	1	2003	Ouzbékistan
..	6555	..	23762	1	2004	
..	6128	..	22228	1	2005	
..	6334	..	22966	1	2006	

Table 13

Selected series of statistics on renewables and wastes
Thousand cubic metres (1000 c.m.) / Thousand metric tons (1000 m.t.) / GWh / Terajoules (TJ)

Country or area Pays ou zone	Year Année	Fuelwood (1000 c.m.) Bois de chauffage (1000 m.c.)			Charcoal (1000 m.t) Charbon de bois (1000 t.m.)			Bagasse (1000 m.t.) Bagasse (1000 t.m.)
		Production Production	Imports Importations	Exports Exportations	Production Production	Imports Importations	Exports Exportations	Production Production
Viet Nam	2003	55285	..		618	..	..	317
	2004	56056	..		624	..	..	348
	2005	56790	..		631	..	..	285
	2006	57475	..		558	..	..	324
Yemen	2003	339	..		40	..	..	
	2004	355	..		51	..	..	
	2005	355	..		51	..	..	
	2006	355	..		51	..	..	
Europe	**2003**	**183175**	**2766**	**3673**	**507**	**507**	**316**	
	2004	**190279**	**2709**	**3144**	**518**	**570**	**300**	
	2005	**189936**	**2665**	**3156**	**554**	**691**	**305**	
	2006	**195740**	**3341**	**3238**	**661**	**657**	**386**	
Albania	2003	221	..	56	55	..	55	
	2004	221	..	56	55	..	55	
	2005	221	..	56	55	..	55	
	2006	221	..	56	55	..	55	
Andorra	2003	..	2	..	..		..	
	2004	..	2	..	..		..	
	2005	..	2	..	..		..	
	2006	..	*3	..	..		..	
Austria	2003	3337	196	72	..	12	2	
	2004	3541	257	102	..	13	1	
	2005	3686	272	65	..	11	1	
	2006	4706	326	54	..	12	0	
Belarus	2003	1097	1	75	1	0	..	
	2004	1097	1	75	1	0	..	
	2005	1097	1	75	1	0	..	
	2006	1170	1	75	1	0	..	
Belgium	2003	550	..	..	..	64	40	
	2004	600	..	..	..	64	40	
	2005	650	..	..	..	60	43	
	2006	670	..	..	..	64	59	
Bosnia and Herzegovina	2003	669	..	..	6	0	5	
	2004	708	..	..	6	0	*5	
	2005	722	..	..	6	0	*5	
	2006	762	..	..	6	0	*5	
Bulgaria	2003	2188		29	25	..	25	
	2004	2910		9	24	..	24	
	2005	2679		12	24	..	24	
	2006	2886		12	24	..	24	
Croatia	2003	1474	..		3	13	2	
	2004	1439	..		3	12	3	
	2005	1370	..		3	12	3	
	2006	1644	..		3	15	3	
Czech Republic	2003	2751	0	219	..	..	..	
	2004	4080	6	238	..	..	..	
	2005	4273	15	274	..	..	..	
	2006	5230	48	280	..	..	..	
Denmark	2003	1629	288	1	..	20	0	
	2004	1716	292	0	..	17	1	
	2005	1935	305	37	..	24	1	
	2006	1935	305	37	..	24	1	
Estonia	2003	1751	..	323	4	..	4	
	2004	1776	..	137	4	..	3	
	2005	1737	..	117	5	..	5	
	2006	1674	..	51	7	..	4	

Table 13

Séries de statistiques des renouvelables et des déchets

Milliers de mètres cubes (1000 m.c.) / Milliers de tonnes métriques (1000 t.m.) / GWh / Tèrajoules (TJ)

Liquids and gases (TJ) Liquides et gazes (TJ)	Electricity (GWh) Électricité (GWh)	Wastes (TJ) Déchets (TJ)	Total primary (TJ) Totale primaire(TJ)	Renewables and wastes (%) Renouvelables et déchets (%)	Year Année	Country or area Pays ou zone
Production Production	Production Production	Production Production	Production Production	Share of total primary Part du total primaire		
..	18988	..	597780	32	2003	Viet Nam
..	17667	..	602462	25	2004	
..	21456	..	617877	24	2005	
..	23601	..	634895	23	2006	
..	..	*3240	*6339	1	2003	Yémen
..	..	*3240	6481	1	2004	
..	..	*3240	6481	1	2005	
..	..	*3240	6480	1	2006	
216916	**734114**	**1990943**	**6523286**	**7**	**2003**	**Europe**
264011	**797514**	**2127887**	**7000422**	**7**	**2004**	
346843	**816760**	**2139585**	**7161104**	**8**	**2005**	
465599	**816099**	**2274920**	**7465825**	**8**	**2006**	
84	5169	..	20711	57	2003	Albanie
80	5466	..	21776	55	2004	
84	5373	..	21446	53	2005	
84	5001	..	20106	49	2006	
..	..	..	..	..	2003	Andorre
..	..	..	..	..	2004	
..	..	..	..	..	2005	
..	..	..	..	..	2006	
2746	35675	85878	247518	63	2003	Autriche
3687	39906	87630	267306	67	2004	
3761	39959	86406	267671	71	2005	
5153	39406	83713	273697	69	2006	
..	28	5774	15895	9	2003	Bélarus
..	34	5188	15331	9	2004	
..	37	5695	15848	9	2005	
..	36	6523	17341	10	2006	
2157	1404	121956	134191	97	2003	Belgique
3025	1750	122679	137485	96	2004	
3920	1832	122371	138824	98	2005	
4253	1996	125718	143277	99	2006	
..	4501	..	22315	10	2003	Bosnie y Herzégovine
..	5979	..	27992	12	2004	
..	5998	..	28188	11	2005	
..	5857	..	28046	10	2006	
0	3301	1997	33859	15	2003	Bulgarie
0	3364	2110	40794	17	2004	
0	4735	3566	45076	19	2005	
249	4599	3872	47032	19	2006	
0	4936	2503	33731	20	2003	Croatie
0	7054	2723	41254	23	2004	
106	6449	2257	38086	22	2005	
57	6143	2163	39347	21	2006	
5947	1798	34432	71978	7	2003	République tchèque
5248	2572	34658	86421	8	2004	
7034	3048	34879	91908	9	2005	
6782	3307	32942	99394	10	2006	
5376	5584	69390	109741	9	2003	Danemark
6275	6613	72351	118100	9	2004	
6576	6640	75099	123242	9	2005	
7858	6133	75549	123153	10	2006	
113	19	8201	24371	15	2003	Estonie
94	30	8474	24897	16	2004	
149	76	8175	24463	15	2005	
174	89	6107	21892	14	2006	

Table 13

Selected series of statistics on renewables and wastes

Thousand cubic metres (1000 c.m.) / Thousand metric tons (1000 m.t.) / GWh / Terajoules (TJ)

Country or area Pays ou zone	Year Année	Fuelwood (1000 c.m.) Bois de chauffage (1000 m.c.)			Charcoal (1000 m.t) Charbon de bois (1000 t.m.)			Bagasse (1000 m.t.) Bagasse (1000 t.m.)
		Production Production	Imports Importations	Exports Exportations	Production Production	Imports Importations	Exports Exportations	Production Production
Faeroe Islands	2003	..	..	..	..	..	..	
	2004	..	..	..	..	..	..	
	2005	..	..	..	..	..	..	
	2006	..	..	..	..	..	..	
Finland	2003	6686	175	10	..	2	..	
	2004	7071	175	6	..	2	..	
	2005	7317	178	5	..	2	..	
	2006	7764	226	9	..	2	..	
France incl. Monaco	2003	39216	31	408	50	42	15	
	2004	39805	39	418	52	49	18	
	2005	39923	50	464	51	53	18	
	2006	38998	40	556	51	43	14	
Germany	2003	5769	89	15	..	114	3	
	2004	5849	120	32	..	138	3	
	2005	6043	416	70	..	149	3	
	2006	8292	477	52	..	142	3	
Greece	2003	1074	145	15	3	45	..	
	2004	1057	371	15	3	51	..	
	2005	1225	46	16	3	54	..	
	2006	1004	69	7	3	62	..	
Hungary	2003	2782	41	387	2	1	1	
	2004	2673	40	342	2	1	1	
	2005	2483	113	246	0	3	1	
	2006	2337	168	214	2	2	2	
Iceland	2003	..	0	..	..	0	..	
	2004	..	0	..	..	0	..	
	2005	..	0	..	..	0	..	
	2006	..	0	..	..	0	..	
Ireland	2003	30	..	..	..	0	..	
	2004	20	..	..	..	1	..	
	2005	19	..	..	..	1	..	
	2006	16	..	..	..	1	..	
Italy and San Marino	2003	4652	636	0	73	41	0	
	2004	7663	803	0	84	46	1	
	2005	8207	865	1	100	45	0	
	2006	8796	1099	3	129	63	0	
Latvia	2003	991	6	539	10	..	10	
	2004	970	5	390	10	..	9	
	2005	950	4	347	8	..	6	
	2006	979	2	405	7	..	6	
Lithuania	2003	1320	1	75	1	0	1	
	2004	1260	2	42	1	1	1	
	2005	1130	30	43	1	1	1	
	2006	1230	12	80	1	1	1	
Luxembourg	2003	71	51	65	..	0	..	
	2004	70	22	65	..	1	..	
	2005	71	7	58	..	1	..	
	2006	71	20	35	..	1	..	
Netherlands	2003	290	..	..	10	20	10	
	2004	290	..	..	10	24	14	
	2005	290	..	..	9	57	29	
	2006	290	..	..	10	51	6	
Norway,Svlbd.J.Myn. I	2003	1309	294	2	..	41	3	
	2004	1429	164	2	..	34	2	
	2005	1177	111	1	..	77	1	
	2006	1177	175	5	..	28	5	

Table 13

Séries de statistiques des renouvelables et des déchets
Milliers de mètres cubes (1000 m.c.) / Milliers de tonnes métriques (1000 t.m.) / GWh / Tèrajoules (TJ)

Liquids and gases (TJ) quides et gazes (TJ)	Electricity (GWh) Électricité (GWh)	Wastes (TJ) Déchets (TJ)	Total primary (TJ) Totale primaire(TJ)	Renewables and wastes (%) Renouvelables et déchets (%)	Year Année	Country or area Pays ou zone
Production Production	Production Production	Production Production	Production Production	Share of total primary Part du total primaire		
..	90	..	324	100	2003	Iles Féroé
..	90	..	324	100	2004	
..	*90	..	*324	100	2005	
..	*90	..	*324	100	2006	
834	9687	242200	338964	81	2003	Finlande
1109	15193	245075	365453	90	2004	
1746	13958	221586	340396	78	2005	
1526	11654	250221	364601	72	2006	
24498	65278	118681	736299	80	2003	France y compris Monaco
25458	66201	115368	742647	84	2004	
28336	57974	113947	715565	86	2005	
36529	63808	112460	734826	87	2006	
69064	43635	382102	660923	16	2003	Allemagne
83192	53944	427862	758650	18	2004	
145887	55232	394406	794298	20	2005	
227462	60239	446841	966875	24	2006	
1507	6354	10081	44266	11	2003	Grèce
1574	6328	10433	44440	11	2004	
1381	6878	11711	49040	12	2005	
3157	8176	9830	51589	13	2006	
454	175	15895	42383	12	2003	Hongrie
509	211	20054	45731	14	2004	
753	212	23196	47388	15	2005	
1206	229	27785	51159	16	2006	
9015	8495	70	39663	100	2003	Islande
9319	8618	70	40410	100	2004	
8712	8678	70	40019	100	2005	
9631	9925	84	45441	100	2006	
1062	1410	4336	10748	12	2003	Irlande
1250	1639	5286	12619	15	2004	
1471	2087	6778	15936	22	2005	
1473	2710	6903	18278	26	2006	
10691	51104	49171	286306	26	2003	Italie y comp. St. Marin
23935	57226	48112	348025	32	2004	
20959	50630	51426	329588	31	2005	
23276	51962	58896	349547	35	2006	
159	2314	21109	38649	100	2003	Lettonie
295	3158	24340	44865	100	2004	
415	3372	25718	46950	100	2005	
733	2744	32132	51687	100	2006	
140	985	11305	27049	59	2003	Lituanie
258	944	11737	26904	64	2004	
590	822	12091	25963	69	2005	
764	816	12705	27643	73	2006	
173	944	1314	5534	100	2003	Luxembourg
246	907	1596	5747	100	2004	
348	953	1499	5926	100	2005	
410	996	1598	6242	100	2006	
5392	1421	53318	66475	3	2003	Pays-Bas
5340	1995	55459	70630	2	2004	
6753	2189	56722	74004	3	2005	
9504	2874	55450	77949	3	2006	
1079	106443	8717	404916	4	2003	Norvège,Svalbd,J.May
1023	109556	8263	416709	4	2004	
1054	137089	8471	513758	5	2005	
1104	120482	8748	454303	5	2006	

Table 13

Selected series of statistics on renewables and wastes
Thousand cubic metres (1000 c.m.) / Thousand metric tons (1000 m.t.) / GWh / Terajoules (TJ)

Country or area Pays ou zone	Year Année	Fuelwood (1000 c.m.) Bois de chauffage (1000 m.c.) Production Production	Imports Importations	Exports Exportations	Charcoal (1000 m.t) Charbon de bois (1000 t.m.) Production Production	Imports Importations	Exports Exportations	Bagasse (100 m.t.) Bagasse (100 t.m.) Production Production
Poland	2003	14253	..	..	85	13	59	
	2004	14396	..	..	85	16	60	
	2005	14396	..	..	90	22	59	
	2006	14917	..	..	130	31	85	
Portugal	2003	5272	1	1	18	18	..	
	2004	5311	0	2	20	27	..	
	2005	5338	0	5	19	18	..	
	2006	5322	2	8	19	20	..	
Republic of Moldova	2003	308	..	..	..	..	..	
	2004	270	..	..	..	..	..	
	2005	323	..	..	..	..	..	
	2006	328	..	..	..	..	..	
Romania	2003	2904	..	89	26	..	16	
	2004	3016	..	72	26	..	16	
	2005	2960	..	68	26	..	17	
	2006	2625	..	79	26	..	12	
Russian Federation	2003	47413	..	286	60	0	2	
	2004	47814	..	289	60	0	2	
	2005	47013	..	280	70	0	0	
	2006	46013	..	280	70	1	1	
Serbia	2003	4139	..	..	3	..	..	
	2004	4139	..	..	2	..	..	
	2005	4139	..	..	3	..	..	
	2006	4139	..	..	3	..	..	
Slovakia	2003	1492	96	155	45	0	23	
	2004	507	96	68	46	1	6	
	2005	569	5	124	48	1	4	
	2006	672	10	15	83	3	65	
Slovenia	2003	359	1	78	..	1	..	
	2004	725	10	76	..	1	..	
	2005	943	25	124	..	2	..	
	2006	984	74	15	..	3	..	
Spain	2003	12953	24	87	..	32	38	
	2004	13109	18	101	..	42	36	
	2005	13149	44	119	..	45	28	
	2006	13578	42	188	..	37	34	
Sweden	2003	4079	676	14	1	18	0	
	2004	4266	272	37	1	18	1	
	2005	3519	164	32	1	20	1	
	2006	4338	230	42	1	19	1	
Switzerland	2003	1107	8	36	5	10	..	
	2004	1148	6	44	5	10	..	
	2005	1251	7	39	5	32	..	
	2006	1417	8	37	5	32	..	
T.F.Yug.Rep. Macedonia	2003	688	..	..	..	..	..	
	2004	705	..	..	..	..	..	
	2005	664	..	..	..	..	..	
	2006	740	..	..	..	..	..	
Ukraine	2003	8120	..	299	21	..	..	
	2004	8398	..	376	18	..	..	
	2005	8148	..	281	26	..	..	
	2006	8496	..	498	25	..	..	
United Kingdom	2003	229	3	336	..	..	..	
	2004	229	7	151	..	..	..	
	2005	317	4	195	..	..	..	
	2006	317	4	145	..	..	..	

Table 13

Séries de statistiques des renouvelables et des déchets

Milliers de mètres cubes (1000 m.c.) / Milliers de tonnes métriques (1000 t.m.) / GWh / Tèrajoules (TJ)

Liquids and gases (TJ) Liquides et gazes (TJ)	Electricity (GWh) Électricité (GWh)	Wastes (TJ) Déchets (TJ)	Total primary (TJ) Totale primaire (TJ)	Renewables and wastes (%) Renouvelables et déchets (%)	Year Année	Country or area Pays ou zone
Production Production	Production Production	Production Production	Production Production	Share of total primary Part du total primaire		
2840	3417	54866	200175	5	2003	Pologne
2521	3833	58723	206513	6	2004	
6849	3913	62634	215044	6	2005	
9194	3276	81792	239004	7	2006	
35	16644	67030	175129	100	2003	Portugal
187	11051	68101	156568	100	2004	
424	6966	73734	147982	100	2005	
3308	14483	74398	178441	100	2006	
..	64	0	3044	100	2003	Rép. de Moldova
..	59	315	2994	90	2004	
..	63	315	3492	94	2005	
..	77	214	3487	95	2006	
8	13260	19766	94025	9	2003	Roumanie
29	16514	21626	108644	10	2004	
32	20209	13143	112951	11	2005	
184	18357	13429	103665	10	2006	
..	158066	109059	1111049	2	2003	Fédération de Russie
..	178207	152751	1230899	2	2004	
..	175035	144310	1203731	2	2005	
..	175764	165705	1218615	2	2006	
..	9852	0	73264	15	2003	Serbie
..	11122	0	77836	16	2004	
..	12033	0	81115	19	2005	
..	10966	190	77464	17	2006	
425	3673	1899	29171	37	2003	Slovaquie
835	4213	12328	32956	42	2004	
1641	4747	14330	38252	49	2005	
2075	4572	13462	38133	51	2006	
240	3156	2059	16941	27	2003	Slovénie
278	4094	2273	23913	35	2004	
284	3461	2358	23716	36	2005	
575	3591	1693	24184	36	2006	
18809	56017	61285	400034	57	2003	Espagne
21508	50199	66490	388416	56	2004	
24154	44246	70539	374042	57	2005	
21279	52672	71377	406259	61	2006	
4345	54281	298936	535928	98	2003	Suède
7521	61033	301208	567385	98	2004	
9943	73816	332671	640470	99	2005	
12557	62730	343767	621751	99	2006	
2469	36890	58930	204305	99	2003	Suisse
2542	35494	69344	210141	99	2004	
2736	33116	77843	211213	99	2005	
2831	32924	81981	216272	99	2006	
..	1374	..	11231	12	2003	L'ex-RY Macédoine
..	1482	..	11775	13	2004	
..	1492	..	11437	13	2005	
..	1650	..	12700	14	2006	
..	9416	..	108052	4	2003	Ukraine
..	11914	..	119585	5	2004	
..	12544	..	119565	5	2005	
..	13070	..	124638	5	2006	
47253	7251	68685	144130	1	2003	Royaume-Uni
56672	9519	65260	158289	2	2004	
60746	10808	81639	184186	2	2005	
72212	12691	66672	187464	2	2006	

Table 13

Selected series of statistics on renewables and wastes
Thousand cubic metres (1000 c.m.) / Thousand metric tons (1000 m.t.) / GWh / Terajoules (TJ)

Country or area Pays ou zone	Year Année	Fuelwood (1000 c.m.) Bois de chauffage (1000 m.c.)			Charcoal (1000 m.t) Charbon de bois (1000 t.m.)			Bagasse (1000 m.t.) Bagasse (1000 t.m.)
		Production Production	Imports Importations	Exports Exportations	Production Production	Imports Importations	Exports Exportations	Production Production
Oceania	**2003**	**16943**	**2**	**1**	**28**	**1**	**4**	**18575**
	2004	**17496**	**2**	**1**	**25**	**1**	**6**	**19263**
	2005	**16963**	**2**	**1**	**25**	**2**	**6**	**18728**
	2006	**15742**	**2**	**1**	**25**	**2**	**6**	**16596**
Australia	2003	10385	..	..	27	1	4	17328
	2004	10758	..	..	24	1	6	18029
	2005	10227	..	..	24	2	6	17581
	2006	9012	..	..	24	2	6	15417
Fiji	2003	37	..	..	..	..	..	1077
	2004	37	..	..	..	..	..	1077
	2005	37	..	..	..	..	..	997
	2006	37	..	..	..	..	..	105
French Polynesia	2003	..	..	..	..	0	..	
	2004	..	..	..	..	0	..	
	2005	..	..	..	..	0	..	
	2006	..	..	..	..	0	..	
New Caledonia	2003	..	0	..	..	0	..	
	2004	..	0	..	..	0	..	
	2005	..	0	..	..	0	..	
	2006	..	0	..	..	0	..	
New Zealand	2003	688	..	..	1	..	..	
	2004	867	..	..	1	..	..	
	2005	865	..	..	1	..	..	
	2006	860	..	..	1	..	..	
Palau	2003	..	..	..	..	..	..	
	2004	..	..	..	..	..	..	
	2005	..	..	..	..	..	..	
	2006	..	..	..	..	..	..	
Papua New Guinea	2003	5535	..	..	..	..	..	16
	2004	5535	..	..	..	..	..	15
	2005	5535	..	..	..	..	..	14
	2006	5535	..	..	..	..	..	11
Samoa	2003	70	..	..	..	..	..	
	2004	70	..	..	..	..	..	
	2005	70	..	..	..	..	..	
	2006	70	..	..	..	..	..	
Solomon Islands	2003	138	..	..	..	..	..	
	2004	138	..	..	..	..	..	
	2005	138	..	..	..	..	..	
	2006	138	..	..	..	..	..	
Tonga	2003	..	2	..	..	0	..	
	2004	..	2	..	..	0	..	
	2005	..	2	..	..	0	..	
	2006	..	2	..	..	0	..	
Vanuatu	2003	91	..	1	..	..	..	
	2004	91	..	1	..	..	..	
	2005	91	..	1	..	..	..	
	2006	91	..	1	..	..	..	

Table 13

Séries de statistiques des renouvelables et des déchets

Milliers de mètres cubes (1000 m.c.) / Milliers de tonnes métriques (1000 t.m.) / GWh / Tèrajoules (TJ)

Liquids and gases (TJ) Iquides et gazes (TJ)	Electricity (GWh) Électricité (GWh)	Wastes (TJ) Déchets (TJ)	Total primary (TJ) Totale primaire(TJ)	Renewables and wastes (%) Renouvelables et déchets (%)	Year Année	Country or area Pays ou zone
Production Production	Production Production	Production Production	Production Production	Share of total primary Part du total primaire		
11936	45673	149563	624080	5	2003	Océanie
13072	49018	151702	649754	6	2004	
15613	46026	153801	634621	5	2005	
15184	47427	154211	612039	5	2006	
10197	16955	110365	410243	4	2003	Australie
11460	16590	112112	420764	4	2004	
13200	16779	112640	415403	4	2005	
12862	17751	113354	391467	3	2006	
..	*667	..	11056	100	2003	Fidji
..	*669	..	11063	100	2004	
..	*674	..	10463	100	2005	
..	*688	..	10977	100	2006	
..	122	..	439	100	2003	Polynésie française
..	153	..	551	100	2004	
..	131	..	472	100	2005	
..	158	..	569	100	2006	
..	328	..	1181	100	2003	Nouvelle-Calédonie
..	337	..	1213	100	2004	
..	357	..	1285	100	2005	
..	427	..	1537	100	2006	
1739	26618	31948	135788	29	2003	Nouvelle-Zélande
1612	30315	32327	150982	33	2004	
2413	27135	33898	141886	33	2005	
2322	27481	33594	142693	32	2006	
..	*18	..	*65	100	2003	Palaos
..	*18	..	*65	100	2004	
..	*18	..	*65	100	2005	
..	*18	..	*65	100	2006	
..	929	*5250	60397	36	2003	Papouasie-Nvl-Guinée
..	895	*5263	60187	39	2004	
..	891	*5263	60118	35	2005	
..	863	*5263	59794	31	2006	
..	*35	..	820	100	2003	Samoa
..	*40	..	838	100	2004	
..	*40	..	838	100	2005	
..	*40	..	845	100	2006	
..	..	*2000	*3261	100	2003	Iles Salomon
..	..	*2000	*3261	100	2004	
..	..	*2000	*3261	100	2005	
..	..	*2000	*3261	100	2006	
..	..	..	..	..	2003	Tonga
..	..	..	..	..	2004	
..	..	..	..	..	2005	
..	..	..	..	..	2006	
..	..	..	831	100	2003	Vanuatu
..	..	..	831	100	2004	
..	..	..	831	100	2005	
..	..	..	831	100	2006	

Table 14

Production, trade and consumption of crude petroleum
Production, commerce et consommation de pétrole brut
Thousand metric tons; kilograms per capita; reserves production ratio (R/P) in years
Milliers de tonnes métriques; kilogrammes par habitant; le rapport entre réserves et production (R/P) en années

Table Notes:

For Bolivia and Venezuela, data on crude petroleum include condensate.

For Canada, Germany and Greece, data include inputs other than crude petroleum and natural gas liquids.

For South Africa, crude oil production data refer to synthetic oil from coal.

The reserves to production ratio refers to crude petroleum and natural gas liquids

Data on reserves were taken from the Survey of Energy Resources, World Energy Council.

- **Please refer to the Definitions Section on pages xv to xxix for the appropriate product description/classification.**

Notes relatives aux tableaux:

Pour la Bolivie et le Venezuela, les données relatives au pétrole brut comprennent le condensat.

Pour le Canada, l'Allemagne et la Grèce, les données comprennent des charges d'alimentation dans les raffineries autres que le pétrole brut et les liquides de gaz naturel.

Pour l'Afrique du Sud, les données relatives à la production de pétrole brut se rapportent à la production de pétrole synthétique du charbon.

Le rapport entre réserves et production comprend le pétrole brut et les liquides de gaz naturel.

Les données en réserves proviennent de l'enquête des ressources de l'énergie du Conseil Mondial de l'Energie.

- **Veuillez consulter la section "définitions" de la page xv à la page xxix pour une description/classification appropriée des produits.**

Figure 40: World crude petroleum production 1993-2006

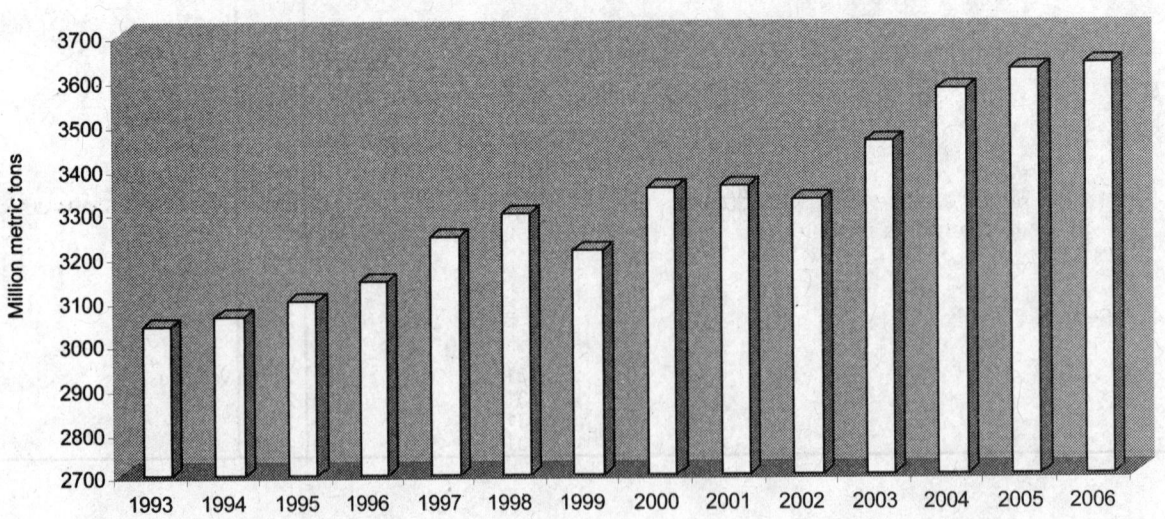

Figure 41: World crude petroleum export 1993-2006

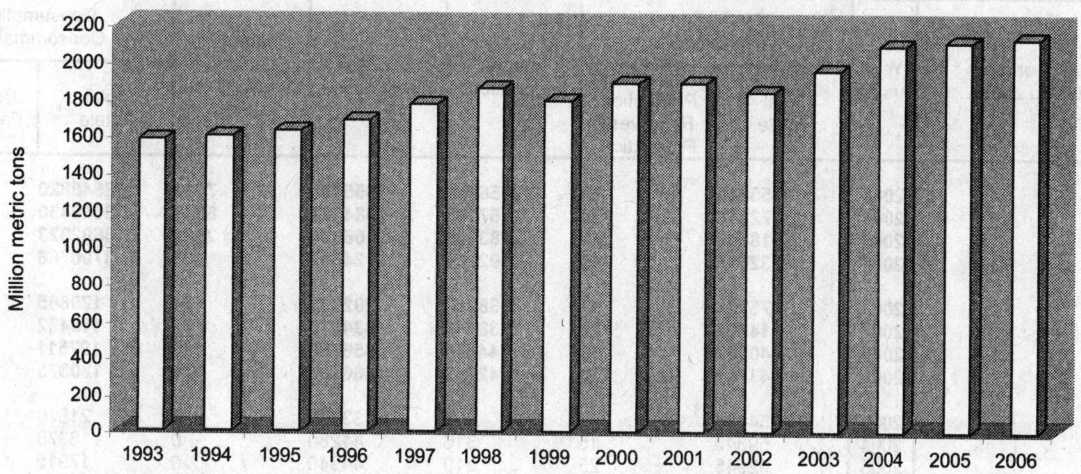

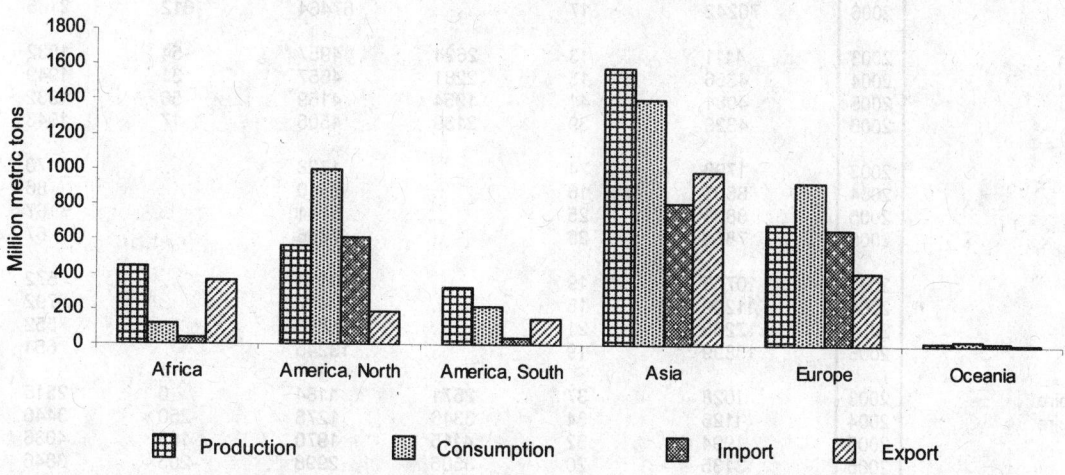

Figure 42: Production, trade, and consumption of crude petroleum, by region, in 2006

Figure 43: Major crude petroleum producing countries in 2006

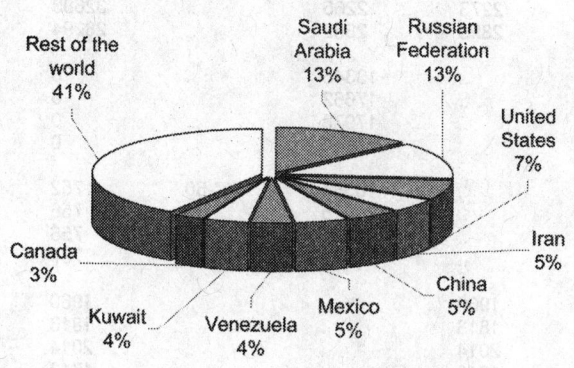

Figure 44: Major crude petroleum consuming countries in 2006

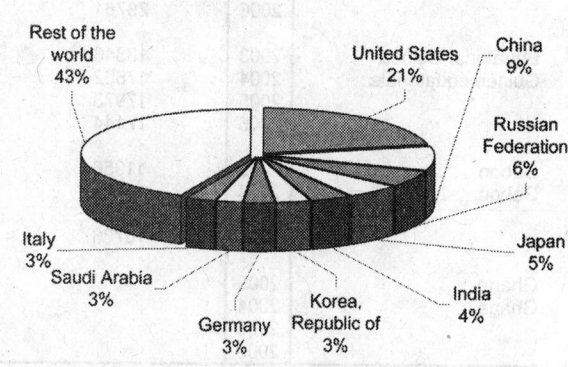

Table 14

Production, trade and consumption of crude petroleum
Production, commerce et consommation de pétrole brut

Thousand metric tons; kilograms per capita; reserves/production ratio (R/P) in years
Milliers de tonnes métriques; kilogrammes par habitant; le rapport entre réserves et production (R/P) en années

Country or area Pays ou zone	Year Année	Production Production		Imports Importations	Exports Exportations	Changes in stocks Variations des stocks	Consumption Consommation	
		Total Totale	Reserves/ Production Réserves/ Production				Total Totale	Per Capita Par habitant
World	**2003**	**3455446**	**39**	**2056031**	**1955594**	**7062**	**3548820**	**566**
Monde	**2004**	**3572516**	**38**	**2167190**	**2084278**	**8998**	**3646430**	**575**
	2005	**3618607**	**40**	**2183149**	**2106305**	**2528**	**3692923**	**575**
	2006	**3632615**	**40**	**2192934**	**2124347**	**435**	**3700766**	**568**
Africa	**2003**	**375721**	**31**	**38210**	**292932**	**134**	**120865**	**143**
Afrique	**2004**	**414762**	**28**	**38486**	**334070**	**745**	**118432**	**136**
	2005	**440157**	**33**	**44278**	**356786**	**139**	**127511**	**144**
	2006	**443739**	**33**	**42749**	**366191**	**-76**	**120373**	**131**
Algeria	2003	54869	15	366	33725	0	21510	675
Algérie	2004	59340	15	316	41280	0	18376	568
	2005	62545	25	310	44940	0	17915	544
	2006	63865	25	331	43954	-24	20266	605
Angola	2003	43083	28	..	40758	217	2108	188
Angola	2004	49443	24	..	46598	780	2065	181
	2005	62314	20	..	60102	129	2083	178
	2006	70242	17	..	67464	612	2166	181
Cameroon	2003	4111	13	2624	4957	-54	1832	108
Cameroun	2004	4356	13	2281	4657	31	1949	112
	2005	4081	41	1954	4159	-56	1932	109
	2006	4326	39	2139	4505	17	1943	107
Chad	2003	1798	74	..	1728	..	70	8
Tchad	2004	8505	16	..	8440	..	66	7
	2005	8808	25	..	8741	..	67	7
	2006	7874	28	..	7806	..	67	6
Congo	2003	10705	19	..	10133	..	572	166
Congo	2004	11209	18	..	10417	..	792	224
	2005	12268	21	..	11716	..	552	153
	2006	13899	19	..	13245	..	654	177
Côte d'Ivoire	2003	1028	37	2671	1184	0	2515	143
Côte d'Ivoire	2004	1126	34	3348	1278	-250	3446	186
	2005	1994	32	4115	1970	103	4036	211
	2006	3135	20	3506	2998	-203	3846	196
Dem. Rep. of Congo	2003	1083	24	..	1083	..	0	0
Rép. dem. du Congo	2004	1033	25	..	1033	..	0	0
	2005	984	26	..	984	..	0	0
	2006	886	29	..	886	..	0	0
Egypt	2003	34992	12	0	2609	..	32383	481
Egypte	2004	33282	13	0	2156	..	31126	437
	2005	32675	13	2273	2265	..	32683	457
	2006	28761	15	2395	2862	..	28294	389
Equatorial Guinea	2003	13346	11	..	13346	..	0	0
Guinée équatoriale	2004	17662	8	..	17662	..	0	0
	2005	17973	14	..	17973	..	0	0
	2006	17144	14	..	17144	..	0	0
Gabon	2003	11056	31	..	10364	*-60	752	578
Gabon	2004	10736	32	..	10015	*-35	756	554
	2005	10690	28	..	9957	*-25	758	543
	2006	10736	27	..	10044	*-95	787	552
Ghana	2003	..	..	1960	..	..	1960	93
Ghana	2004	..	..	1813	..	..	1813	84
	2005	..	..	2014	..	..	2014	91
	2006	..	..	1713	..	..	1713	74

Table 14

Production, trade and consumption of crude petroleum
Production, commerce et consommation de pétrole brut
Thousand metric tons; kilograms per capita; reserves/production ratio (R/P) in years
Milliers de tonnes métriques; kilogrammes par habitant; le rapport entre réserves et production (R/P) en années

Country or area Pays ou zone	Year Année	Production Production		Imports Importations	Exports Exportations	Changes in stocks Variations des stocks	Consumption Consommation	
		Total Totale	Reserves/ Production Réserves/ Production				Total Totale	Per Capita Par habitant
Kenya	2003	..	..	1649	..	0	1649	50
Kenya	2004	..	..	2044	..	0	2044	60
	2005	..	..	1774	..	48	1726	49
	2006	..	..	1543	..	-201	1744	48
Libyan Arab Jamah.	2003	68736	66	..	52642	..	16094	2587
Jamah. arabe libyenne	2004	75287	61	..	59069	..	16218	2526
	2005	80252	64	..	64564	..	15688	2366
	2006	83310	61	..	68173	..	15137	2259
Madagascar	2003	..	..	*472	..	..	*472	*29
Madagascar	2004	..	..	*475	..	..	*475	*28
	2005	..	..	*478	..	..	*478	*27
	2006	..	..	*480	..	..	*480	*26
Morocco	2003	10	22	4467	..	57	4420	153
Maroc	2004	11	20	6133	..	-67	6211	208
	2005	7	20	6975	..	-42	7024	233
	2006	11	12	6261	..	2	6270	206
Nigeria	2003	113914	36	..	108096	-278	6096	48
Nigéria	2004	122948	33	..	117583	233	5132	40
	2005	125542	36	..	115236	0	10306	77
	2006	118419	39	..	112633	-133	5919	42
Senegal	2003	..	..	1179	..	39	1140	112
Sénégal	2004	..	..	1113	..	-58	1171	111
	2005	..	..	990	..	84	906	84
	2006	..	..	208	..	-122	330	30
Sierra Leone	2003	..	..	*262	..	..	*262	*47
Sierra Leone	2004	..	..	*265	..	..	*265	*46
	2005	..	..	*268	..	..	*268	*46
	2006	..	..	*270	..	..	*270	*45
Somalia	2003	..	..	*42	..	..	*42	*5
Somalie	2004	..	..	*53	..	..	*53	*7
	2005	..	..	*53	..	..	*53	*6
	2006	..	..	*58	..	..	*58	*7
South Africa Customs Un.	2003	570	7	20790	0	..	21360	418
Un.douan.d'Afr.mérid	2004	1482	3	19014	1	..	20495	385
	2005	1370	2	21373	5	..	22738	425
	2006	1321	2	22083	5	..	23399	432
Sudan	2003	13250	6	..	9849	..	3401	102
Soudan	2004	15000	5	..	11150	..	3850	112
	2005	15250	57	..	11336	..	3914	111
	2006	16550	52	..	11786	..	4764	131
Tunisia	2003	3170	12	1220	2458	213	1719	175
Tunisie	2004	3342	12	1087	2732	111	1586	160
	2005	3404	20	1119	2838	-102	1787	178
	2006	3260	21	1180	2686	71	1683	166
Zambia	2003	..	..	508	..	..	508	47
Zambie	2004	..	..	544	..	..	544	49
	2005	..	..	582	..	..	582	51
	2006	..	..	582	..	..	582	49
America, North	**2003**	**591110**	**11**	**594411**	**182223**	**5391**	**997907**	**1988**
Amérique du Nord	**2004**	**584277**	**13**	**617758**	**186624**	**6269**	**1009143**	**1990**
	2005	**566876**	**12**	**618983**	**179369**	**7103**	**999386**	**1951**
	2006	**564703**	**12**	**616126**	**187625**	**-1712**	**994917**	**1926**

Table 14

Production, trade and consumption of crude petroleum
Production, commerce et consommation de pétrole brut

Thousand metric tons; kilograms per capita; reserves/production ratio (R/P) in years
Milliers de tonnes métriques; kilogrammes par habitant; le rapport entre réserves et production (R/P) en années

| Country or area Pays ou zone | Year Année | Production Production | | Imports Importations | Exports Exportations | Changes in stocks Variations des stocks | Consumption Consommation | |
		Total Totale	Reserves/ Production Réserves/ Production				Total Totale	Per Capita Par habitant
Aruba	2003	*120	..	*10380	..	..	*10500	*110438
Aruba	2004	*120	..	*10380	..	..	*10500	*107518
	2005	*120	..	10380	..	..	10500	104344
	2006	*120	..	*10380	..	..	*10500	*102121
Barbados	2003	74	13	..	74	..	0	0
Barbade	2004	64	15	..	64	..	0	0
	2005	64	15	..	64	..	0	0
	2006	51	19	..	51	..	0	0
Canada	2003	121027	6	44522	72012	917	92620	2924
Canada	2004	125793	14	45841	76215	-388	95807	2994
	2005	123712	15	45336	73276	2331	93441	2892
	2006	129827	14	41468	82441	-505	89359	2737
Costa Rica	2003	..	..	517	..	-17	534	131
Costa Rica	2004	..	..	517	..	0	517	124
	2005	..	..	534	..	4	530	124
	2006	..	..	659	..	-11	670	154
Cuba	2003	3680	32	2295	..	..	5975	528
Cuba	2004	3253	36	1600	..	..	4853	428
	2005	2876	40	1604	..	..	4480	398
	2006	2900	40	3213	..	..	6113	544
Dominican Republic	2003	..	..	2088	..	0	2088	233
Rép. dominicaine	2004	..	..	2200	..	0	2200	242
	2005	..	..	2159	..	0	2159	234
	2006	..	..	2079	..	56	2023	216
El Salvador	2003	..	..	974	..	27	947	143
El Salvador	2004	..	..	994	..	28	966	143
	2005	..	..	1018	..	28	990	144
	2006	..	..	864	..	-2	866	124
Guatemala	2003	1221	66	..	1116	0	106	9
Guatemala	2004	999	80	..	915	0	84	7
	2005	910	88	..	808	0	102	8
	2006	818	98	..	780	-91	129	10
Jamaica	2003	..	..	883	..	0	883	332
Jamaïque	2004	..	..	731	..	0	731	273
	2005	..	..	470	..	0	470	177
	2006	..	..	1025	..	10	1015	381
Martinique	2003	..	..	713	..	..	713	1826
Martinique	2004	..	..	738	..	..	738	1874
	2005	..	..	758	..	..	758	1907
	2006	..	..	778	..	..	778	1945
Mexico	2003	176612	12	..	104702	-463	72373	710
Mexique	2004	178280	12	..	105180	507	72593	705
	2005	175082	10	..	100111	73	74898	721
	2006	170602	10	..	99134	298	71170	679
Netherlands Antilles	2003	..	..	10531	..	..	10531	58937
Antilles néerlandaises	2004	..	..	10797	..	..	10797	58963
	2005	..	..	12762	..	..	12762	68843
	2006	..	..	12310	..	..	12310	64960
Nicaragua	2003	..	..	856	..	36	820	154
Nicaragua	2004	..	..	809	..	-34	843	157
	2005	..	..	771	..	19	752	138
	2006	..	..	836	..	19	817	148

Table 14

Production, trade and consumption of crude petroleum
Production, commerce et consommation de pétrole brut

Thousand metric tons; kilograms per capita; reserves/production ratio (R/P) in years
Milliers de tonnes métriques; kilogrammes par habitant; le rapport entre réserves et production (R/P) en années

Country or area Pays ou zone	Year Année	Production Production		Imports Importations	Exports Exportations	Changes in stocks Variations des stocks	Consumption Consommation	
		Total Totale	Reserves/ Production Réserves/ Production				Total Totale	Per Capita Par habitant
Trinidad and Tobago	2003	6943	13	4436	3688	69	7622	5796
Trinité-et-Tobago	2004	6336	14	3220	2891	-86	6751	5118
	2005	7474	10	4436	3450	-39	8499	6419
	2006	7122	10	4669	3968	-158	7981	6010
United States	2003	281433	11	516216	631	4822	792196	2724
Etats-Unis	2004	269432	12	539931	1358	6242	801763	2731
	2005	256637	12	538755	1659	4687	789046	2662
	2006	253263	12	537845	1251	-1328	791185	2651
America, South	**2003**	**319311**	**42**	**33601**	**137503**	**434**	**214975**	**593**
Amérique du Sud	**2004**	**320377**	**41**	**40384**	**146567**	**-1226**	**215420**	**587**
	2005	**331445**	**41**	**35084**	**149765**	**-435**	**217199**	**584**
	2006	**326864**	**40**	**35029**	**145116**	**-1606**	**218382**	**579**
Argentina	2003	38125	9	252	11802	0	26575	702
Argentine	2004	35551	9	520	9013	-133	27191	711
	2005	33934	7	215	7653	179	26317	682
	2006	33854	7	79	5519	0	28414	729
Bolivia	2003	1670	30	..	126	*-75	1619	179
Bolivie	2004	1939	26	..	579	-510	1870	203
	2005	2107	24	..	606	-510	2011	213
	2006	2303	22	..	689	-979	2593	269
Brazil	2003	76059	17	17379	12262	-312	81488	455
Brésil	2004	75336	17	22866	12262	91	85849	473
	2005	83027	18	17407	13923	169	86342	469
	2006	87611	17	16974	18666	-695	86614	464
Chile	2003	173	56	10009	..	-123	10305	647
Chili	2004	169	57	10410	..	-533	11112	690
	2005	158	61	10219	..	-217	10594	650
	2006	139	51	10664	..	42	10761	655
Colombia	2003	27908	9	59	11589	144	16234	364
Colombie	2004	26714	9	176	11025	0	15865	350
	2005	26231	7	363	11403	0	15191	330
	2006	26717	7	392	11035	0	16073	344
Ecuador	2003	21422	30	..	12937	585	7900	615
Equateur	2004	27386	24	..	18483	-306	9209	707
	2005	26507	27	..	17977	98	8432	638
	2006	26746	27	..	18680	-124	8190	611
Paraguay	2003	..	..	84	..	-2	86	15
Paraguay	2004	..	..	50	..	-16	67	12
	2005	..	..	36	..	2	34	6
	2006	..	..	0	..	0	0	0
Peru	2003	4708	9	4180	1429	152	7307	272
Pérou	2004	4130	9	4163	824	78	7391	273
	2005	3892	22	4809	638	-83	8146	300
	2006	4001	17	5078	1180	177	7722	282
Suriname	2003	588	44	..	76	..	512	1064
Suriname	2004	612	42	..	88	..	524	1063
	2005	637	27	..	92	..	545	1092
	2006	656	26	..	95	..	561	1113
Uruguay	2003	..	..	1638	..	65	1573	462
Uruguay	2004	..	..	2199	..	78	2121	642
	2005	..	..	2035	..	-99	2134	646
	2006	..	..	1842	..	-53	1895	572

Table 14

Production, trade and consumption of crude petroleum
Production, commerce et consommation de pétrole brut

Thousand metric tons; kilograms per capita; reserves/production ratio (R/P) in years
Milliers de tonnes métriques; kilogrammes par habitant; le rapport entre réserves et production (R/P) en années

Country or area Pays ou zone	Year Année	Production Production — Total Totale	Production Production — Reserves/ Production Réserves/ Production	Imports Importations	Exports Exportations	Changes in stocks Variations des stocks	Consumption Consommation — Total Totale	Consumption Consommation — Per Capita Par habitant
Venezuela(Bolivar. Rep.)	2003	148658	73	..	87282	0	61376	2391
Venezuela(Rép. bolivar.)	2004	148540	73	..	94293	26	54221	2075
	2005	154952	70	..	97473	26	57453	2162
	2006	144837	72	..	89252	26	55559	2055
Asia	**2003**	**1442019**	**66**	**711818**	**874625**	**752**	**1278460**	**336**
Asie	**2004**	**1505803**	**63**	**768721**	**929593**	**444**	**1344487**	**350**
	2005	**1550402**	**63**	**790946**	**970628**	**-4870**	**1375590**	**354**
	2006	**1581213**	**62**	**814588**	**993549**	**-1666**	**1403918**	**356**
Azerbaijan	2003	15251	62	..	8997	-53	6307	766
Azerbaïdjan	2004	15348	62	..	9048	40	6260	754
	2005	21993	43	..	14296	255	7442	887
	2006	31986	29	..	24820	-258	7424	875
Bahrain	2003	9408	2	3283	..	1	12690	18407
Bahreïn	2004	9393	2	3326	..	64	12655	17896
	2005	9303	2	3980	..	0	13283	18330
	2006	9140	2	3760	..	0	12900	17372
Bangladesh	2003	..	80	1335	..	-93	1428	11
Bangladesh	2004	..	89	1252	..	-39	1291	9
	2005	..	31	1063	..	-317	1380	10
	2006	..	32	1253	..	-82	1335	9
Brunei Darussalam	2003	9952	18	..	9809	*-97	240	686
Brunéi Darussalam	2004	9695	18	..	9552	53	90	250
	2005	9557	15	..	9544	*-87	100	270
	2006	10221	14	..	10345	*-219	95	248
China	2003	169600	19	91020	8133	616	251871	195
Chine	2004	175873	19	122720	5492	2978	290123	224
	2005	181353	12	126817	8067	-788	300891	231
	2006	184766	12	145175	6337	1111	322493	245
Cyprus	2003	..	..	969	..	-2	971	1347
Chypre	2004	..	..	243	..	-35	278	377
	2005	..	..	0	..	0	0	0
	2006	..	..	0	..	0	0	0
Georgia	2003	140	36	1	72	..	69	16
Géorgie	2004	98	51	0	61	..	37	9
	2005	67	75	17	64	..	20	5
	2006	64	78	8	53	..	19	4
India	2003	33373	20	90434	..	..	123807	116
Inde	2004	33981	20	95861	..	..	129842	120
	2005	32190	22	99409	..	..	131599	120
	2006	33988	21	110858	..	..	144846	130
Indonesia	2003	53773	12	17550	22626	..	48697	227
Indonésie	2004	49492	13	20175	20250	..	49417	228
	2005	46217	11	16074	16056	..	46235	210
	2006	44040	12	15344	15027	..	44357	200
Iran(Islamic Rep. of)	2003	185544	66	..	111497	..	74047	1114
Iran(Rép. islamique)	2004	191450	63	..	117762	..	73688	1092
	2005	203183	80	..	133453	..	69730	1018
	2006	201196	81	..	130223	..	70973	1007
Iraq	2003	65270	235	..	39973	0	25297	960
Iraq	2004	98127	157	..	74766	0	23361	861
	2005	90859	169	..	67783	0	23076	839
	2006	95066	161	..	73128	-2204	24142	838

Table 14

Production, trade and consumption of crude petroleum
Production, commerce et consommation de pétrole brut

Thousand metric tons; kilograms per capita; reserves/production ratio (R/P) in years
Milliers de tonnes métriques; kilogrammes par habitant; le rapport entre réserves et production (R/P) en années

Country or area Pays ou zone	Year Année	Production Production — Total Totale	Production Production — Reserves/ Production Réserves/ Production	Imports Importations	Exports Exportations	Changes in stocks Variations des stocks	Consumption Consommation — Total Totale	Consumption Consommation — Per Capita Par habitant
Israel	2003	3	333	10552	..	..	10555	1578
Israël	2004	2	500	9320	..	..	9322	1369
	2005	2	330	9372	..	..	9374	1353
	2006	2	330	10114	..	..	10116	1435
Japan	2003	294	14	205106	..	-649	206049	1632
Japon	2004	293	14	200942	..	-496	201731	1598
	2005	317	13	208020	..	276	208061	1648
	2006	281	13	197809	..	-1295	199385	1580
Jordan	2003	2	75	3824	..	*-35	3861	738
Jordanie	2004	1	150	4248	..	67	4182	819
	2005	1	150	4607	..	27	4581	837
	2006	1	150	4263	..	-35	4299	768
Kazakhstan	2003	45376	24	2332	38638	..	9070	608
Kazakhstan	2004	50672	21	3250	41738	..	12184	812
	2005	50870	49	3728	41959	..	12639	834
	2006	54339	46	6439	48232	..	12546	820
Korea, Dem.Ppl's.Rep.	2003	..	..	566	..	..	566	24
Corée,Rép.pop.dém.de	2004	..	..	571	..	..	571	24
	2005	..	..	480	..	..	480	20
	2006	..	..	367	..	..	367	15
Korea, Republic of	2003	0	..	107040	..	1634	105406	2203
Corée, République de	2004	0	..	113582	..	-1055	114637	2384
	2005	54	10	113924	..	-917	114895	2379
	2006	45	12	119890	..	1497	118438	2452
Kuwait	2003	105093	117	..	62100	..	42993	18488
Koweït	2004	114434	108	..	71027	..	43406	18157
	2005	128316	100	..	82762	..	45554	18539
	2006	131865	97	..	86179	..	45686	18087
Kyrgyzstan	2003	69	72	2	..	-23	94	19
Kirghizistan	2004	74	68	7	..	-10	91	18
	2005	74	68	5	..	0	79	15
	2006	71	71	..	..	0	71	14
Malaysia	2003	38318	10	8197	19401	-250	27364	1092
Malaisie	2004	36758	11	7685	18596	427	25420	994
	2005	35471	10	7885	18354	107	24896	953
	2006	34847	10	7861	18288	129	24291	912
Myanmar	2003	967	7	..	31	-56	992	19
Myanmar	2004	1011	7	..	254	0	757	14
	2005	1098	6	..	395	0	703	13
	2006	1049	7	..	111	86	852	15
Oman	2003	40808	19	..	37997	-1495	4306	1840
Oman	2004	38934	20	..	35967	-1021	3988	1651
	2005	38609	19	..	35810	-1568	4367	1741
	2006	36732	20	..	31812	0	4920	1909
Other Asia	2003	41	24	46103	..	218	45926	2032
Autre Asie	2004	40	25	52080	..	356	51764	2281
	2005	29	34	54035	..	172	53892	2371
	2006	21	48	51682	..	-23	51726	2270
Pakistan	2003	3147	12	7143	240	0	10050	69
Pakistan	2004	3232	11	8277	41	134	11334	76
	2005	3272	12	8601	0	0	11873	77
	2006	3298	11	8226	0	281	11243	72

Table 14

Production, trade and consumption of crude petroleum
Production, commerce et consommation de pétrole brut
Thousand metric tons; kilograms per capita; reserves/production ratio (R/P) in years
Milliers de tonnes métriques; kilogrammes par habitant; le rapport entre réserves et production (R/P) en années

Country or area Pays ou zone	Year Année	Production Production		Imports Importations	Exports Exportations	Changes in stocks Variations des stocks	Consumption Consommation	
		Total Totale	Reserves/ Production Réserves/ Production				Total Totale	Per Capita Par habitant
Philippines	2003	20	300	12525	..	114	12431	153
Philippines	2004	19	316	9988	..	-343	10350	125
	2005	29	172	10652	..	-171	10852	127
	2006	25	200	10735	..	83	10677	123
Qatar	2003	33594	52	..	26651	2598	4345	5926
Qatar	2004	35902	49	..	30929	-768	5741	7389
	2005	36225	45	..	32092	-1302	5435	6686
	2006	48685	35	..	43064	-41	5662	6047
Saudi Arabia	2003	437294	76	..	342872	..	94422	4288
Arabie saoudite	2004	444667	73	..	347225	..	97442	4318
	2005	466197	67	..	364323	..	101874	4407
	2006	458951	68	..	358368	..	100583	4248
Singapore	2003	..	..	38804	0	..	38804	9270
Singapour	2004	..	..	45085	0	..	45085	10638
	2005	..	..	54786	165	..	54621	12580
	2006	..	..	52792	190	..	52602	11731
Sri Lanka	2003	..	..	1996	..	-33	2029	105
Sri Lanka	2004	..	..	2206	..	-20	2226	114
	2005	..	..	2008	..	26	1982	101
	2006	..	..	2157	..	6	2151	108
Syrian Arab Republic	2003	28000	15	200	15700	..	12500	712
Rép. arabe syrienne	2004	23355	18	450	11383	..	12422	697
	2005	22241	15	765	10199	..	12807	701
	2006	20823	16	383	8072	..	13134	702
Tajikistan	2003	18	111	..	5	..	13	2
Tadjikistan	2004	19	105	..	4	..	15	2
	2005	22	91	..	5	..	17	2
	2006	22	91	..	6	..	16	2
Thailand	2003	4785	8	38741	3028	-2159	42657	666
Thaïlande	2004	4297	8	43535	2827	-1680	46685	727
	2005	5707	4	41329	3275	-1925	45686	705
	2006	6436	4	41409	3320	-2773	47298	724
Timor-Leste	2003	*130	..	..	*130	..	0	0
Timor-Leste	2004	*135	..	..	*135	..	0	0
	2005	*135	..	..	*135	..	0	0
	2006	*137	..	..	*137	..	0	0
Turkey	2003	2351	17	24095	..	-40	26486	377
Turquie	2004	2251	17	23918	..	184	25985	365
	2005	2258	73	23389	..	-211	25858	359
	2006	2160	76	24063	..	-256	26479	363
Turkmenistan	2003	9600	7	..	2970	..	6630	1411
Turkménistan	2004	9376	7	..	3000	..	6376	1338
	2005	9100	8	..	2510	..	6590	1363
	2006	9350	7	..	1500	..	7850	1602
United Arab Emirates	2003	108020	103	..	90881	..	17139	4827
Emirats arabes unis	2004	112922	99	..	95251	..	17671	4698
	2005	114267	94	..	97235	..	17032	4148
	2006	123397	88	..	105587	..	17810	4211
Uzbekistan	2003	4541	10	..	..	..	4541	176
Ouzbékistan	2004	4298	11	..	..	..	4298	164
	2005	3613	12	..	..	..	3613	136
	2006	3312	13	..	..	..	3312	123

Table 14

Production, trade and consumption of crude petroleum
Production, commerce et consommation de pétrole brut
Thousand metric tons; kilograms per capita; reserves/production ratio (R/P) in years
Milliers de tonnes métriques; kilogrammes par habitant; le rapport entre réserves et production (R/P) en années

Country or area Pays ou zone	Year Année	Production Production – Total Totale	Production Production – Reserves/ Production Réserves/ Production	Imports Importations	Exports Exportations	Changes in stocks Variations des stocks	Consumption Consommation – Total Totale	Consumption Consommation – Per Capita Par habitant
Viet Nam	2003	16598	20	..	16598	0	0	0
Viet Nam	2004	20298	16	..	19598	700	0	0
	2005	18600	21	..	17967	633	0	0
	2006	17400	23	..	16600	800	0	0
Yemen	2003	20639	25	..	16276	556	3807	202
Yémen	2004	19356	26	..	14686	908	3762	194
	2005	19172	19	..	14179	920	4073	204
	2006	17497	21	..	12150	1527	3820	186
Europe	**2003**	**697177**	**15**	**652916**	**449498**	**59**	**900536**	**1238**
Europe	**2004**	**720960**	**15**	**677033**	**470625**	**3523**	**923845**	**1269**
	2005	**705774**	**17**	**668382**	**435416**	**297**	**938443**	**1287**
	2006	**693062**	**17**	**660021**	**419239**	**4715**	**929129**	**1273**
Albania	2003	375	80	..	..	..	375	106
Albanie	2004	420	71	..	..	..	420	135
	2005	447	67	..	..	..	447	142
	2006	505	59	..	..	..	505	160
Austria	2003	919	12	7819	..	-81	8819	1093
Autriche	2004	971	11	7562	..	91	8442	1037
	2005	855	8	7833	..	-55	8743	1065
	2006	856	8	7699	..	83	8472	1023
Belarus	2003	1820	15	14885	801	0	15904	1611
Bélarus	2004	1804	15	17814	1051	103	18464	1879
	2005	1785	15	19318	1346	-78	19835	2029
	2006	1780	15	20906	1138	259	21289	2187
Belgium	2003	..	..	36245	..	10	36235	3499
Belgique	2004	..	..	34407	..	-1	34408	3310
	2005	..	..	31965	..	-154	32119	3075
	2006	..	..	31552	..	103	31449	2992
Bosnia and Herzegovina	2003	..	..	70	..	..	70	18
Bosnie y Herzégovine	2004	..	..	172	..	..	172	45
	2005	..	..	135	..	..	135	35
	2006	..	..	135	..	..	135	35
Bulgaria	2003	30	67	5049	..	32	5047	645
Bulgarie	2004	30	67	5289	..	33	5286	679
	2005	30	67	6043	..	-115	6188	799
	2006	28	71	7096	..	15	7109	923
Croatia	2003	959	7	3766	..	-142	4867	1096
Croatie	2004	890	7	4198	..	9	5079	1144
	2005	830	8	3999	..	-46	4875	1098
	2006	807	8	3799	..	-24	4630	1043
Czech Republic	2003	457	26	6413	133	34	6703	657
République tchèque	2004	565	21	6454	64	-8	6963	682
	2005	569	16	7746	58	258	7999	782
	2006	344	26	7767	42	129	7940	772
Denmark	2003	18143	9	3492	13352	71	8212	1554
Danemark	2004	19262	9	3735	14940	35	8022	1485
	2005	18517	9	2720	13627	-110	7720	1425
	2006	16839	10	2708	11568	-9	7988	1470
Finland	2003	..	..	10931	..	-96	11027	2115
Finlande	2004	..	..	11035	..	221	10814	2068
	2005	..	..	9570	..	-270	9840	1876
	2006	..	..	10662	..	176	10486	1991

Table 14

Production, trade and consumption of crude petroleum
Production, commerce et consommation de pétrole brut

Thousand metric tons; kilograms per capita; reserves/production ratio (R/P) in years
Milliers de tonnes métriques; kilogrammes par habitant; le rapport entre réserves et production (R/P) en années

Country or area Pays ou zone	Year Année	Production Production		Imports Importations	Exports Exportations	Changes in stocks Variations des stocks	Consumption Consommation	
		Total Totale	Reserves/ Production Réserves/ Production				Total Totale	Per Capita Par habitant
France incl. Monaco	2003	1219	13	85366	..	1132	85453	1420
France y compris Monaco	2004	1138	13	85103	..	92	86149	1423
	2005	1079	13	84161	..	-333	85573	1405
	2006	1055	15	81704	..	22	82737	1355
Germany	2003	3690	16	106464	647	242	109265	1324
Allemagne	2004	3463	17	110126	1108	629	111852	1356
	2005	3471	8	112314	703	388	114694	1391
	2006	3383	8	109649	548	917	111567	1355
Greece	2003	120	7	19782	1105	-352	19149	1737
Grèce	2004	118	8	20297	812	953	18650	1686
	2005	89	10	18747	918	-801	18719	1686
	2006	83	11	19836	1054	-61	18926	1698
Hungary	2003	1134	12	5273	0	25	6382	630
Hongrie	2004	1077	12	5483	136	51	6373	631
	2005	948	12	6452	344	-14	7070	701
	2006	886	12	6915	811	73	6917	687
Ireland	2003	..	..	3250	85	-49	3214	808
Irlande	2004	..	..	2894	0	-32	2926	724
	2005	..	..	3268	0	-38	3306	800
	2006	..	..	3183	0	50	3133	740
Italy and San Marino	2003	5570	16	84337	675	433	88799	1542
Italie y comp. St. Marin	2004	5445	16	86867	530	-235	92017	1582
	2005	6111	17	89315	801	493	94132	1606
	2006	5769	18	89315	913	-127	94298	1600
Latvia	2003	..	..	7	..	-1	8	3
Lettonie	2004	..	..	3	..	0	3	1
	2005	..	..	4	..	0	4	2
	2006	..	..	22	..	2	20	9
Lithuania	2003	382	168	7036	288	27	7103	2056
Lituanie	2004	302	212	8728	193	175	8662	2521
	2005	216	296	8913	148	-215	9196	2693
	2006	181	354	8197	115	236	8027	2365
Netherlands	2003	2304	5	48526	1340	-1009	50499	3119
Pays-Bas	2004	2106	5	52074	1178	189	52813	3248
	2005	1492	4	52308	1062	196	52542	3220
	2006	1348	5	47716	651	-377	48790	2987
Norway,Svlbd.J.Myn. I	2003	147011	8	548	132777	886	13896	3034
Norvège,Svalbd,J.May	2004	145463	9	534	131587	-289	14699	3189
	2005	132620	9	791	114604	356	18451	3974
	2006	121383	9	353	108568	510	12658	2716
Poland	2003	765	21	17448	161	528	17524	459
Pologne	2004	886	18	17316	138	-4	18068	473
	2005	848	19	17912	216	353	18191	477
	2006	796	20	19813	282	277	20050	526
Portugal	2003	..	..	12733	..	82	12651	1212
Portugal	2004	..	..	12769	..	69	12700	1209
	2005	..	..	13164	..	23	13141	1246
	2006	..	..	13366	..	118	13248	1252
Republic of Moldova	2003	0	..	..	0	0	0	0
Rép. de Moldova	2004	8	..	..	5	3	0	0
	2005	5	..	..	0	1	4	1
	2006	4	..	..	0	0	4	1

Table 14

Production, trade and consumption of crude petroleum
Production, commerce et consommation de pétrole brut
Thousand metric tons; kilograms per capita; reserves/production ratio (R/P) in years
Milliers de tonnes métriques; kilogrammes par habitant; le rapport entre réserves et production (R/P) en années

Country or area Pays ou zone	Year Année	Production Production		Imports Importations	Exports Exportations	Changes in stocks Variations des stocks	Consumption Consommation	
		Total Totale	Reserves/ Production Réserves/ Production				Total Totale	Per Capita Par habitant
Romania	2003	5651	17	5217	..	-93	10961	504
Roumanie	2004	5462	18	7314	..	238	12538	578
	2005	5511	9	8689	..	-3	14203	657
	2006	5440	9	8678	..	-82	14200	658
Russian Federation	2003	404842	20	5737	227856	-1207	183930	1272
Fédération de Russie	2004	440086	18	4209	257624	1381	185290	1288
	2005	449177	21	2426	252587	456	198560	1387
	2006	457756	21	2320	248445	2138	209493	1470
Serbia	2003	773	28	2910	..	..	3683	348
Serbie	2004	652	34	3314	..	..	3966	377
	2005	649	17	3073	..	..	3722	355
	2006	646	17	2486	..	..	3132	300
Slovakia	2003	42	21	5605	17	-37	5667	1054
Slovaquie	2004	38	24	5970	108	182	5718	1062
	2005	31	29	5353	33	-90	5441	1010
	2006	28	32	5722	28	80	5642	1047
Spain	2003	322	6	57298	..	389	57231	1362
Espagne	2004	255	8	59167	..	-460	59882	1403
	2005	166	127	59544	..	200	59510	1371
	2006	139	151	60468	..	326	60281	1368
Sweden	2003	..	..	20332	..	410	19922	2224
Suède	2004	..	..	20743	..	-23	20766	2309
	2005	..	..	20098	..	89	20009	2216
	2006	..	..	19341	..	-552	19893	2191
Switzerland	2003	..	..	4523	..	23	4500	613
Suisse	2004	..	..	5078	..	-11	5089	683
	2005	..	..	4771	..	-8	4779	641
	2006	..	..	5459	..	25	5434	726
T.F.Yug.Rep. Macedonia	2003	..	..	812	..	-16	828	408
L'ex-RY Macédoine	2004	..	..	827	..	-4	831	409
	2005	..	..	961	..	14	947	465
	2006	..	..	1057	..	-10	1067	523
Ukraine	2003	2814	50	22453	1438	0	23829	498
Ukraine	2004	3003	46	21693	427	0	24269	513
	2005	3149	35	14579	90	-477	18115	385
	2006	3341	33	10650	153	65	13773	295
United Kingdom	2003	97835	6	48589	68823	-1182	78783	1328
Royaume-Uni	2004	87516	6	55858	60724	136	82514	1382
	2005	77179	6	52210	48879	277	80233	1333
	2006	69665	7	51447	44923	353	75836	1252
Oceania	**2003**	**30108**	**10**	**25075**	**18814**	**292**	**36077**	**1113**
Océanie	**2004**	**26337**	**11**	**24808**	**16799**	**-757**	**35103**	**1068**
	2005	**23954**	**10**	**25475**	**14342**	**293**	**34794**	**1043**
	2006	**23034**	**10**	**24421**	**12627**	**780**	**34048**	**1005**
Australia	2003	26628	10	20282	15556	81	31273	1571
Australie	2004	23289	11	20257	14043	-498	30001	1490
	2005	20644	10	20070	11389	242	29083	1425
	2006	19348	10	18837	9409	595	28181	1361
New Zealand	2003	1053	7	4793	896	139	4811	1200
Nouvelle-Zélande	2004	914	8	4421	721	-44	4658	1147
	2005	848	7	4488	609	51	4676	1141
	2006	819	7	4591	736	-109	4783	1154

Table 14

Production, trade and consumption of crude petroleum
Production, commerce et consommation de pétrole brut

Thousand metric tons; kilograms per capita; reserves/production ratio (R/P) in years
Milliers de tonnes métriques; kilogrammes par habitant; le rapport entre réserves et production (R/P) en années

Country or area Pays ou zone	Year Année	Production Production		Imports Importations	Exports Exportations	Changes in stocks Variations des stocks	Consumption Consommation	
		Total Totale	Reserves/ Production Réserves/ Production				Total Totale	Per Capita Par habitant
Papua New Guinea	2003	2427	13	0	2362	*72	-7	-1
Papouasie-Nvl-Guinée	2004	2134	15	130	2035	*-215	444	75
	2005	2462	13	917	2344	0	1035	171
	2006	2867	11	993	2482	294	1084	175

Table 15

International trade of crude petroleum
(Principal importers/exporters)
Thousand metric tons

2005

Importers	Exporters							
	World Monde	Algeria Algérie	Angola Angola	Canada Canada	Iran(Islamic Rep. of) Iran(Rép. islamique)	Iraq Iraq	Kazakhstan Kazakhstan	Kuwait Koweït
Australia	20070	..	..	..	..	18	..	8
Belarus	19318	..	..	..	..	..	..	
Belgium	31965	..	418	..	4513	240	..	7
Brazil	17407	5257	..	..	..	1443	..	
Canada	45336	6308	..	..	..	3544	..	
Chile	10219	..	3014	..	..	..	..	
China	126817	822	17462	0	14273	1170	1291	164
Finland	9570	..	..	..	..	..	102	
France incl. Monaco	84161	5360	4248	..	6857	1441	8550	241
Germany	112314	4572	211	..	475	..	7410	
Greece	18747	..	..	..	5348	113	48	
India	99409	..	..	..	15000		..	1700
Indonesia	16074	129	..	..	..	..	..	
Italy and San Marino	89315	2967	163	..	9559	5855	3023	27
Japan	208020	..	566	..	25905	1490	..	1739
Korea, Republic of	113924	269	..	..	8767	2094	..	1081
Netherlands	52308	443	162	..	1382	764	..	486
Philippines	10652	..	..	..	2688	..	..	
Poland	17912	..	..	..	..	..	148	
Portugal	13164	2983	142	..	352	965	834	
Singapore	54786	..	151	..	1329	..	..	752
South Africa	21373	..	676	..	6747	..	..	
Spain	59544	2959	1681	..	4929	2912	..	
Sweden	20098	..	..	..	574	..	..	
Thailand	41329	542	1	..	..	706	..	41
Turkey	23389	..	..	..	6887	976	..	
United Kingdom	52210	1619	40	..				
United States	538755	10541	22885	82983	..	26821	..	1149

Table 15

Commerce international de pétrole brut
(Principaux importateurs/exportateurs)
Milliers de tonnes métriques

2005

				Exportateurs					
Libyan Arab Jamah. Jamah. arabe libyenne	Mexico Mexique	Nigeria Nigéria	Norway,Svlb d.J.Myn. l Norvège,Sva lbd,J.May	Russian Federation Fédération de Russie	Saudi Arabia Arabie saoudite	United Arab Emirates Emirats arabes unis	United Kingdom Royaume-Uni	Venezuela(B olivar. Rep.) Venezuela(R ép. bolivar.)	Importtateurs
80	..	..	..	..	2480	1533	..	..	Australie
..	..	..	..	19318	..	..	..	..	Bélarus
67	..	320	2749	13433	5267	..	2381	810	Belgique
..	..	6463	..	..	3352	..	..	..	Brésil
132	1529	1301	12168	..	3765	..	9329	2536	Canada
..	..	612	..	..	..	..	..	..	Chili
2259	..	1310	518	12777	22179	2568	0	1927	Chine
..	..	..	110	7999	..	..	401	..	Finlande
4498	..	2848	16095	9594	10312	121	4432	122	France y compris Monaco
12915	36	2124	17289	38170	4137	..	14670	1332	Allemagne
1283	..	57	..	6084	5814	..	..	..	Grèce
..	2000	5000	..	..	30000	18000	..	..	Inde
135	..	2113	..	..	5366	0	..	..	Indonésie
23344	86	1551	3314	18440	12586	..	..	36	Italie y comp. St. Marin
..	..	1710	..	1484	63979	51781	..	..	Japon
..	..	882	..	1128	33807	20310	288	..	Corée, République de
278	..	1635	6312	15848	12709	..	4386	1007	Pays-Bas
..	..	..	..	..	5886	415	..	..	Philippines
..	..	..	130	17466	..	..	87	..	Pologne
700	1077	1288	247	..	1150	852	251	..	Portugal
..	..	..	..	..	19634	3469	..	121	Singapour
..	..	1476	..	..	7393	458	0	..	Afrique du Sud
6176	9006	7127	2954	8548	6331	..	513	1092	Espagne
..	..	126	5022	7139	..	..	821	1124	Suède
..	..	..	..	..	9890	15850	..	..	Thaïlande
4540	..	..	..	6997	3494	..	..	..	Turquie
529	442	324	37373	5051	1313	87	..	1466	Royaume-Uni
3144	79390	54868	7495	10123	72789	387	11587	82603	Etats-Unis

Table 15

International trade of crude petroleum
(Principal importers/exporters)
Thousand metric tons

2006

Importers	Exporters							
	World Monde	Algeria Algérie	Angola Angola	Canada Canada	Iran(Islamic Rep. of) Iran(Rép. islamique)	Iraq Iraq	Kazakhstan Kazakhstan	Kuwait Koweït
Australia	18837	..	..	..	..	..	..	
Belarus	20906	..	..	..	..	..	..	
Belgium	31552	..	34	..	4934	132		5
Brazil	16974	2970	927	..	..	1327	..	
Canada	41468	8177	1121		..	3353		
Chile	10664	..	2676	..	..	..	..	
China	145175	257	23452	44	16772	1046	2683	280
Finland	10662	..	..		..	..	132	
France incl. Monaco	81704	3492	3233	..	6729	3488	8060	157
Germany	109649	2337	150		162	60	7613	
Greece	19836	..	..	..	5944	0	1353	
India	110858	520	539	..	16501	12832	..	1149
Indonesia	15344	263	..	..	..	..	..	
Italy and San Marino	89315	2694	90	..	9648	6801	2131	6
Japan	197809	68	1261		21184	1931	..	1666
Korea, Republic of	119890	910	392	..	10147	2446	..	1257
Netherlands	47716	98	39	..	410	1870	..	494
Philippines	10735	..	..	..	3363	..	..	
Poland	19813	..	..	..	..	..	49	26
Portugal	13366	1906	143	..	781	823	701	
Singapore	52792	..	34	41	1521	..	..	951
South Africa	22083	..	759	..	6349	429		
Spain	60468	1512	561	..	5189	3292		
Sweden	19341	..	..	..	289	..		
Thailand	41409	652	276	..	..	686	..	24
Turkey	24063	..		..	8971	551	..	
United Kingdom	51447	1827	..	..	..	..	..	
United States	537845	16783	25700	91511	..	28056	..	906

Table 15

Commerce international de pétrole brut
(Principaux importateurs/exportateurs)
Milliers de tonnes métriques

2006

				Exportateurs					Importtateurs
ibyan Arab Jamah. Jamah. arabe libyenne	Mexico Mexique	Nigeria Nigéria	Norway,Svlb d.J.Myn. l Norvège,Sva lbd,J.May	Russian Federation Fédération de Russie	Saudi Arabia Arabie saoudite	United Arab Emirates Emirats arabes unis	United Kingdom Royaume-U ni	Venezuela(B olivar. Rep.) Venezuela(R ép. bolivar.)	
..			..	1282	690				Australie
				20906	..			..	Bélarus
..		518	2815	12602	5649	..	2373	955	Belgique
357		7153			3114		..	..	Brésil
..	1867	1627	9021	1059	3403	..	6345	1601	Canada
		879		..	..		..	..	Chili
3386		452	327	15965	23872	3044	0	4201	Chine
..		..	822	7203	..		1149	..	Finlande
4193		4047	13095	9764	8681	1373	6483	576	France y compris Monaco
12370	34	3118	18520	36915	3561	..	13451	1434	Allemagne
2222		40	..	5379	4818	..	..	..	Grèce
130	2048	13694	..	320	24795	7398	..	2020	Inde
780				..	5348	..	0	..	Indonésie
23790	..	1915	3817	13956	10173	..	191	71	Italie y comp. St. Marin
		973		3371	52876	57876	..	..	Japon
..	..	1126	..	1897	34761	21195	..	..	Corée, République de
67	47	1808	3908	17955	9304	..	4907	1034	Pays-Bas
..		..	..	..	6356	554		..	Philippines
..		..	137	19156	..		159	..	Pologne
974	670	1172	380	136	1386	..	774	540	Portugal
..		..	..	247	17298	5566	0	142	Singapour
656	..	2770	..	140	7610	405	..	105	Afrique du Sud
5534	7561	6016	1806	11772	6489	..	232	3267	Espagne
..	..	..		7033	..	..	642	1100	Suède
..	..	56		166	7268	13903	..	..	Thaïlande
4166	..	..	..	6787	3503	..	..	..	Turquie
1250	340	422	31798	8933	197	216	..	1521	Royaume-Uni
4573	80445	54264	5121	5387	71678	208	11587	76783	Etats-Unis

Table 16

Refinery distillation capacity, throughput and output
Capacité de traitement des raffineries, quantités traitées et production totale
Thousand metric tons
Milliers de tonnes métriques

Table Notes:

Output is equal to the sum of "production from refineries" for aviation gasolene, motor gasolene, jet fuel, kerosene, gas-diesel oils, residual fuel oil, liquefied petroleum gas, feedstocks, naphtha, white spirit, lubricants, bitumen asphalt, petroleum waxes, petroleum coke, other petroleum products and refinery gas.

Throughput is equal to the sum of "conversion in refineries" for crude petroleum, feedstocks, natural gas and natural gas liquids n.e.s.

- **Please refer to the Definitions Section on pages xv to xxix for the appropriate product description/ classification.**

Notes relatives aux tableaux:

Production est égal à la production de raffinerie pour essence d'aviation, essence d'auto, carburateurs, pétrole lampant, carburant diesel, mazout résiduel, gaz de pétrole liquéfies, produits d'alimentation de raffinerie, naphta, essences spéciales, lubrifiants, gaz de bitumen, cires de pétrole (paraffines), coke de pétrole, autres produits pétroliers et gaz de raffinerie.

Quantités traitées est égal a la somme de « conversion en raffineries » pour pétrole brut, produits d'alimentation de raffinerie, gaz naturel et liquides de gaz naturel n.d.a.

- **Veuillez consulter la section "définitions" de la page xv à la page xxix pour une description/classification appropriée des produits.**

Figure 45: Refinery distillation capacity, throughput and output, by region, in 2006

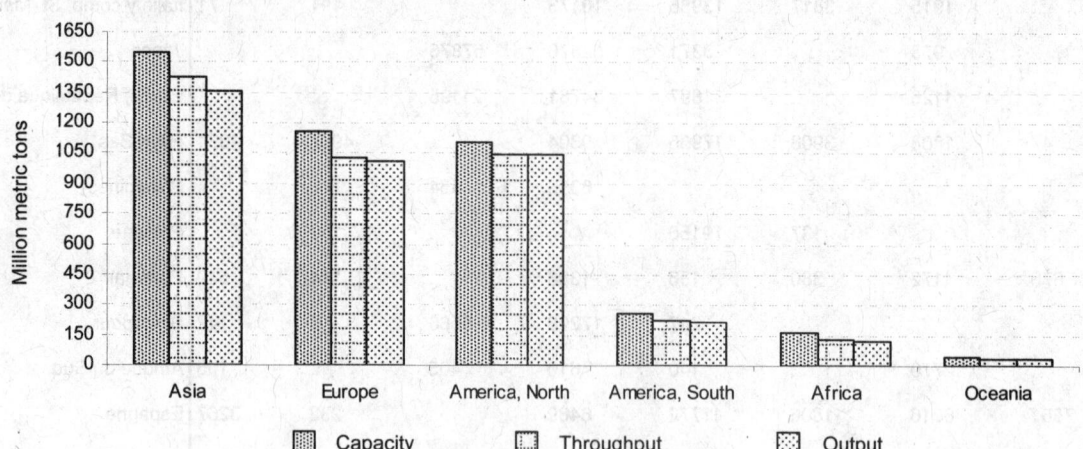

Figure 46: Refinery utilization (expressed as throughput to capacity), 1993-2006, selected regions

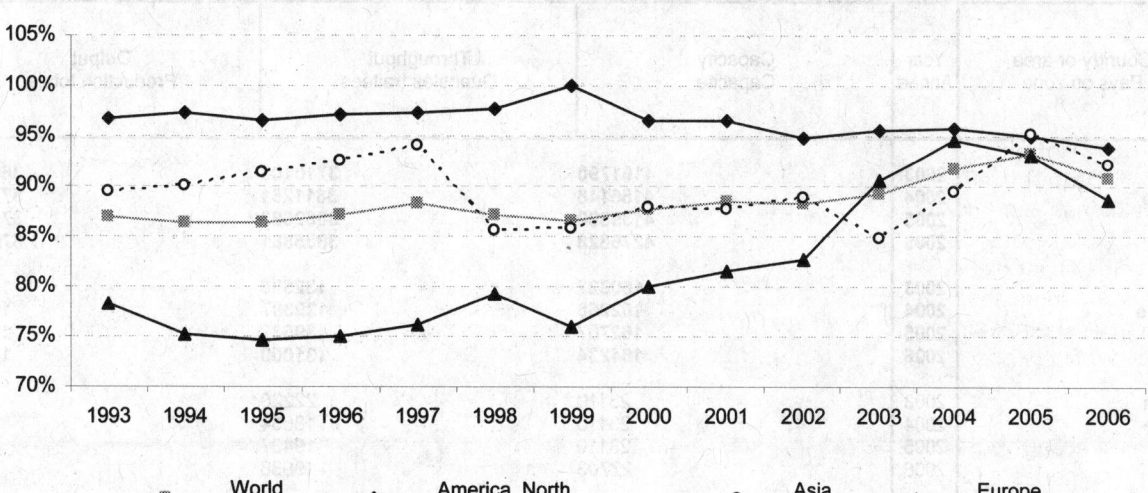

Figure 47: World total refinery distillation capacity 1993-2006

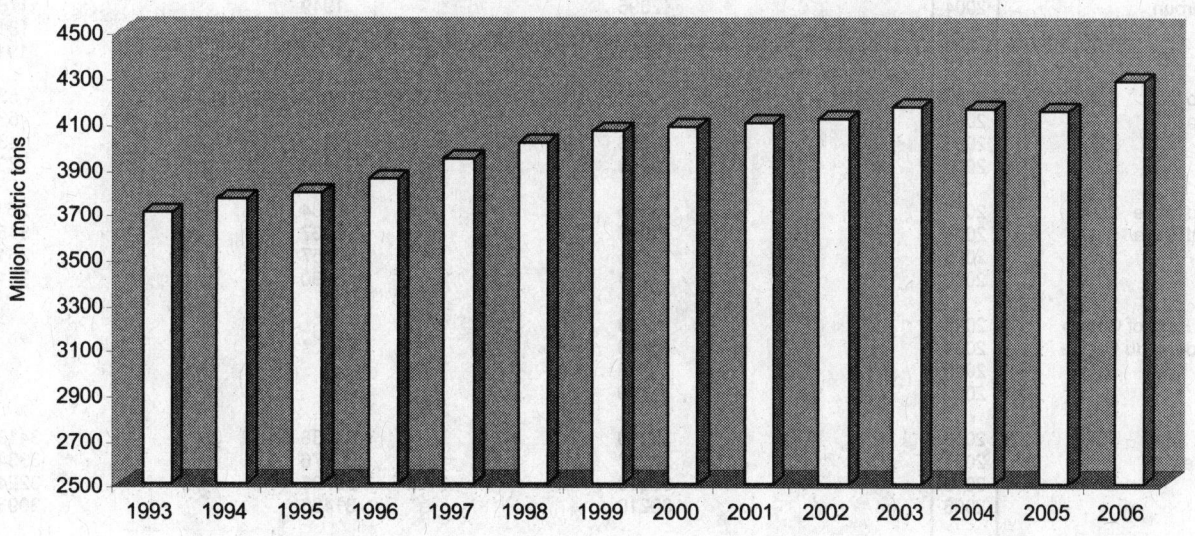

Table 16

Refinery distillation capacity, throughput and output
Capacité de traitement des raffineries, quantités traitées et production totale

Thousand metric tons
Milliers de tonnes métriques

Country or area Pays ou zone	Year Année	Capacity Capacité	Throughput Quantités traitées	Output Production totale
World	**2003**	**4161790**	**3710108**	**3601890**
Monde	**2004**	**4156148**	**3811261**	**3716091**
	2005	**4139890**	**3862683**	**3758040**
	2006	**4276828**	**3885881**	**3790835**
Africa	**2003**	**160322**	**132536**	**123779**
Afrique	**2004**	**162266**	**129397**	**122086**
	2005	**162767**	**139582**	**123809**
	2006	**164234**	**131000**	**124350**
Algeria	2003	23110	22220	20765
Algérie	2004	23110	18634	18959
	2005	23110	19437	18299
	2006	22703	19938	19248
Angola	2003	2263	2042	1952
Angola	2004	2263	2000	1878
	2005	2750	2017	1893
	2006	2750	2097	1993
Cameroon	2003	*1847	1832	1401
Cameroun	2004	*2096	1949	1783
	2005	2096	1932	1815
	2006	2096	1943	1911
Congo	2003	1050	572	532
Congo	2004	1050	533	537
	2005	1050	552	430
	2006	1048	654	633
Côte d'Ivoire	2003	3995	2604	2511
Côte d'Ivoire	2004	*3995	3467	3154
	2005	*3995	4057	3619
	2006	3254	3990	3816
Dem. Rep. of Congo	2003	749	..	..
Rép. dem. du Congo	2004	749	..	..
	2005	749	..	..
	2006	749	..	..
Egypt	2003	36210	35938	34135
Egypte	2004	36210	34276	33343
	2005	36210	35796	32242
	2006	36210	31436	30933
Gabon	2003	1198	*845	839
Gabon	2004	1198	*815	808
	2005	1198	*830	819
	2006	1198	*810	778
Ghana	2003	1527	1391	1396
Ghana	2004	1335	1770	1683
	2005	1335	1567	1592
	2006	1335	962	920
Kenya	2003	4492	*1569	1600
Kenya	2004	4492	*1963	1712
	2005	4492	1645	1610
	2006	4267	1651	1612
Liberia	2003	749	..	..
Libéria	2004	749	..	..
	2005	749	..	..
	2006	749	..	..

Table 16

Refinery distillation capacity, throughput and output
Capacité de traitement des raffineries, quantités traitées et production totale

Thousand metric tons
Milliers de tonnes métriques

Country or area Pays ou zone	Year Année	Capacity Capacité	Throughput Quantités traitées	Output Production totale
Libyan Arab Jamah.	2003	19000	16094	14971
Jamah. arabe libyenne	2004	19000	16218	15087
	2005	19000	15688	14593
	2006	19000	15137	14081
Madagascar	2003	*814	*472	*331
Madagascar	2004	*814	*475	*331
	2005	*814	*478	*335
	2006	*814	*480	*335
Mauritania	2003	1000	..	..
Mauritanie	2004	1000	..	..
	2005	1000	..	..
	2006	1000	..	..
Morocco	2003	4420	4420	4337
Maroc	2004	6211	6211	6015
	2005	7024	7024	6769
	2006	7024	6270	6062
Mozambique	2003	*800	..	..
Mozambique	2004	0	..	..
	2005	0	..	..
	2006	0	..	..
Nigeria	2003	22204	6395	5595
Nigéria	2004	22204	5482	4882
	2005	22204	10706	4818
	2006	22204	6319	5586
Senegal	2003	*1200	1140	1126
Sénégal	2004	1446	1171	1138
	2005	1446	906	892
	2006	1348	*330	339
Sierra Leone	2003	499	*262	*230
Sierra Leone	2004	499	*265	*208
	2005	499	*268	*199
	2006	499	*270	*210
Somalia	2003	498	*42	*140
Somalie	2004	498	*53	*145
	2005	498	*53	*145
	2006	498	*58	176
South Africa Customs Un.	2003	22909	29070	26479
Un.douan.d'Afr.mérid	2004	23558	28136	24787
	2005	22759	30343	27771
	2006	24371	31227	28487
Sudan	2003	6089	3401	3231
Soudan	2004	6089	3850	3553
	2005	6089	3914	3639
	2006	7332	5149	4988
Tunisia	2003	1856	1719	1727
Tunisie	2004	1856	1586	1567
	2005	1856	1787	1777
	2006	1856	1697	1690
United Rep.Tanzania	2003	744	..	..
Rép. Unie de Tanzanie	2004	744	..	..
	2005	744	..	..
	2006	744	..	..

Table 16

Refinery distillation capacity, throughput and output
Capacité de traitement des raffineries, quantités traitées et production totale

Thousand metric tons
Milliers de tonnes métriques

Country or area Pays ou zone	Year Année	Capacity Capacité	Throughput Quantités traitées	Output Production totale
Zambia	2003	1100	508	482
Zambie	2004	1100	544	516
	2005	1100	582	552
	2006	1185	582	552
America, North	**2003**	**1078524**	**1031068**	**1030158**
Amérique du Nord	**2004**	**1092723**	**1047508**	**1051618**
	2005	**1098516**	**1042549**	**1047045**
	2006	**1109919**	**1041020**	**1046245**
Aruba	2003	12750	*10500	10000
Aruba	2004	12750	*10500	10000
	2005	12750	*10500	10000
	2006	13513	*10500	*10000
Canada	2003	103014	101512	103168
Canada	2004	103613	104103	105339
	2005	100669	100022	102266
	2006	101877	98856	100678
Costa Rica	2003	1247	520	469
Costa Rica	2004	1247	517	475
	2005	1247	486	498
	2006	1247	672	671
Cuba	2003	7487	2624	2563
Cuba	2004	7487	2523	2221
	2005	7487	2323	2310
	2006	7487	2624	2181
Dominican Republic	2003	2594	2088	1430
Rép. dominicaine	2004	2594	2200	1976
	2005	2594	2159	1970
	2006	2594	2023	1936
El Salvador	2003	2198	947	931
El Salvador	2004	2198	966	1008
	2005	2198	990	857
	2006	2198	866	832
Guatemala	2003	1123	0	0
Guatemala	2004	1123	81	64
	2005	1123	65	66
	2006	1123	68	67
Jamaica	2003	1745	883	866
Jamaïque	2004	1745	731	731
	2005	1745	470	469
	2006	1745	1015	1014
Martinique	2003	848	708	*804
Martinique	2004	848	733	*820
	2005	848	753	*823
	2006	848	773	*825
Mexico	2003	83990	72373	67302
Mexique	2004	83990	72593	69230
	2005	83990	74898	69812
	2006	83990	71170	67745
Netherlands Antilles	2003	15971	11054	10891
Antilles néerlandaises	2004	15971	11970	11793
	2005	15971	12976	12788
	2006	15971	12387	12204

Table 16

Refinery distillation capacity, throughput and output
Capacité de traitement des raffineries, quantités traitées et production totale
Thousand metric tons
Milliers de tonnes métriques

Country or area Pays ou zone	Year Année	Capacity Capacité	Throughput Quantités traitées	Output Production totale
Nicaragua	2003	997	820	821
Nicaragua	2004	997	843	849
	2005	997	752	760
	2006	997	826	812
Trinidad and Tobago	2003	8734	7666	7170
Trinité-et-Tobago	2004	8734	7785	6553
	2005	8713	8560	7655
	2006	8713	8041	7619
United States	2003	835826	819373	823743
Etats-Unis	2004	849426	831963	840558
	2005	858184	827595	836772
	2006	867616	831199	839661
America, South	**2003**	**253710**	**219062**	**200892**
Amérique du Sud	**2004**	**255591**	**219401**	**214286**
	2005	**257259**	**221258**	**216055**
	2006	**255126**	**223723**	**217349**
Argentina	2003	31191	29865	24222
Argentine	2004	33282	30956	24860
	2005	33282	30141	24971
	2006	33282	32355	26182
Bolivia	2003	2695	*1670	1726
Bolivie	2004	2695	*1890	1930
	2005	2695	1994	2193
	2006	2695	2593	2396
Brazil	2003	103551	82314	83764
Brésil	2004	103551	86937	88595
	2005	103551	87570	88879
	2006	102291	88592	89913
Chile	2003	11330	10305	10245
Chili	2004	11330	11112	10959
	2005	11867	10594	10415
	2006	11867	10761	11351
Colombia	2003	19969	15898	16085
Colombie	2004	19969	15500	16523
	2005	15966	14918	15343
	2006	15966	15894	15195
Ecuador	2003	9228	7743	7442
Equateur	2004	9228	8225	6767
	2005	9228	7973	7614
	2006	8374	7513	7642
Paraguay	2003	370	86	84
Paraguay	2004	370	67	64
	2005	370	34	33
	2006	370	0	0
Peru	2003	7951	7878	7856
Pérou	2004	7951	8030	7984
	2005	9732	8071	7942
	2006	9732	8175	8081
Suriname	2003	375	356	372
Suriname	2004	375	342	374
	2005	375	376	390
	2006	375	387	401

Table 16

Refinery distillation capacity, throughput and output
Capacité de traitement des raffineries, quantités traitées et production totale

Thousand metric tons
Milliers de tonnes métriques

Country or area Pays ou zone	Year Année	Capacity Capacité	Throughput Quantités traitées	Output Production totale
Uruguay	2003	2492	1572	1543
Uruguay	2004	2501	2121	2065
	2005	2512	2134	2021
	2006	2493	1894	1789
Venezuela(Bolivar. Rep.)	2003	64558	61376	47554
Venezuela(Rép. bolivar.)	2004	64339	54221	54165
	2005	67681	57453	56254
	2006	67681	55559	54399
Asia	**2003**	**1523200**	**1291060**	**1228762**
Asie	**2004**	**1522737**	**1361951**	**1288826**
	2005	**1468282**	**1397185**	**1322094**
	2006	**1545730**	**1423553**	**1353131**
Azerbaijan	2003	22060	6281	6164
Azerbaïdjan	2004	22060	6300	6630
	2005	22060	7392	7692
	2006	19914	7486	7724
Bahrain	2003	14000	12690	12521
Bahreïn	2004	14000	12655	12575
	2005	14000	13283	13143
	2006	14000	12900	12764
Bangladesh	2003	1647	1528	1457
Bangladesh	2004	1647	1381	1315
	2005	1647	1476	1384
	2006	1647	1428	1347
Brunei Darussalam	2003	1000	726	707
Brunéi Darussalam	2004	1000	671	594
	2005	1000	603	597
	2006	1000	647	640
China	2003	280445	238440	223602
Chine	2004	274056	277373	248272
	2005	308245	290405	261630
	2006	311739	310460	278518
Cyprus	2003	1200	971	968
Chypre	2004	1200	278	279
	2005	0	0	0
	2006	0	0	0
Georgia	2003	299	25	23
Géorgie	2004	1248	26	24
	2005	5440	14	13
	2006	*5440	13	12
India	2003	116968	123807	114505
Inde	2004	127368	129842	123493
	2005	127368	131599	122761
	2006	132468	144846	138864
Indonesia	2003	52744	50327	50581
Indonésie	2004	52669	50915	51785
	2005	52744	48427	47719
	2006	52718	47011	46751
Iran(Islamic Rep. of)	2003	73567	79920	79313
Iran(Rép. islamique)	2004	73567	80971	79976
	2005	73567	82206	81239
	2006	78159	84013	82961

Table 16

Refinery distillation capacity, throughput and output
Capacité de traitement des raffineries, quantités traitées et production totale
Thousand metric tons
Milliers de tonnes métriques

Country or area Pays ou zone	Year Année	Capacity Capacité	Throughput Quantités traitées	Output Production totale
Iraq	2003	25966	23297	20704
Iraq	2004	25966	20405	20180
	2005	25966	20120	19607
	2006	27495	21049	20152
Israel	2003	13476	11131	11071
Israël	2004	12977	10793	10761
	2005	14224	11939	11821
	2006	10980	11738	11463
Japan	2003	304102	208689	201836
Japon	2004	285486	205864	198842
	2005	188960	211663	204241
	2006	233415	202403	195768
Jordan	2003	5977	*3860	3948
Jordanie	2004	5977	4182	4167
	2005	5977	4581	4306
	2006	5977	4299	4252
Kazakhstan	2003	21312	9518	8630
Kazakhstan	2004	21312	12834	10131
	2005	21312	13154	12432
	2006	17224	12160	11898
Korea, Dem.Ppl's.Rep.	2003	3544	566	539
Corée,Rép.pop.dém.de	2004	3544	571	545
	2005	3544	480	459
	2006	3544	367	352
Korea, Republic of	2003	121567	112315	110633
Corée, République de	2004	121567	116983	115773
	2005	125025	121276	119778
	2006	128593	124057	122425
Kuwait	2003	41446	41504	41488
Koweït	2004	46683	41693	41412
	2005	46683	42914	42208
	2006	46484	44282	43699
Kyrgyzstan	2003	499	94	88
Kirghizistan	2004	499	91	88
	2005	499	79	86
	2006	499	71	83
Malaysia	2003	25736	26335	23051
Malaisie	2004	25736	24799	23796
	2005	25736	23992	23286
	2006	27191	24349	24154
Myanmar	2003	2845	992	769
Myanmar	2004	2845	757	690
	2005	2845	703	641
	2006	2845	852	791
Oman	2003	3990	4457	4072
Oman	2004	3990	3900	3826
	2005	3990	3990	3942
	2006	3990	4494	4130
Other Asia	2003	47365	57620	50744
Autre Asie	2004	50051	64210	55873
	2005	51956	61169	58340
	2006	64384	58546	56623

Table 16

Refinery distillation capacity, throughput and output
Capacité de traitement des raffineries, quantités traitées et production totale

Thousand metric tons
Milliers de tonnes métriques

Country or area Pays ou zone	Year Année	Capacity Capacité	Throughput Quantités traitées	Output Production totale
Pakistan	2003	11330	9757	9679
Pakistan	2004	12730	11334	11232
	2005	12880	11351	11379
	2006	13426	11243	11036
Philippines	2003	20658	12104	11954
Philippines	2004	20658	*10180	9748
	2005	20658	10297	10157
	2006	16620	10262	10238
Qatar	2003	5000	4345	5017
Qatar	2004	6500	5741	5201
	2005	6500	5435	4908
	2006	6500	5662	5549
Saudi Arabia	2003	103014	93590	90267
Arabie saoudite	2004	103663	100907	97649
	2005	104362	104560	100593
	2006	106583	102992	100660
Singapore	2003	61689	37502	34591
Singapour	2004	61938	44194	40034
	2005	61240	54620	47895
	2006	66710	52601	46681
Sri Lanka	2003	2350	*2102	2075
Sri Lanka	2004	2350	*2320	2308
	2005	2350	*2110	2070
	2006	2350	2048	2116
Syrian Arab Republic	2003	12910	12500	12337
Rép. arabe syrienne	2004	12910	12450	12868
	2005	12910	12807	12468
	2006	12910	13134	12871
Tajikistan	2003	*100	13	11
Tadjikistan	2004	*100	15	13
	2005	*100	17	14
	2006	*100	16	12
Thailand	2003	38936	42488	34795
Thaïlande	2004	38936	46498	39208
	2005	38936	45539	37501
	2006	38963	47114	38724
Turkey	2003	29247	26717	26461
Turquie	2004	31293	26281	26002
	2005	29347	25886	25638
	2006	35651	26532	26235
Turkmenistan	2003	11829	6630	6505
Turkménistan	2004	11829	6376	6255
	2005	11829	6590	6466
	2006	11829	7850	7702
United Arab Emirates	2003	23315	17139	16803
Emirats arabes unis	2004	23315	17671	17325
	2005	23315	17032	16698
	2006	23315	17810	17461
Uzbekistan	2003	11095	7540	7318
Ouzbékistan	2004	11095	7062	6887
	2005	11095	5767	5620
	2006	11095	5382	5245

Table 16

Refinery distillation capacity, throughput and output
Capacité de traitement des raffineries, quantités traitées et production totale

Thousand metric tons
Milliers de tonnes métriques

Country or area Pays ou zone	Year Année	Capacity Capacité	Throughput Quantités traitées	Output Production totale
Yemen	2003	9972	3540	3535
Yémen	2004	9972	3428	3068
	2005	9972	3708	3362
	2006	9972	3436	3230
Europe	**2003**	**1097207**	**994725**	**978133**
Europe	**2004**	**1071150**	**1013052**	**999458**
	2005	**1100137**	**1023146**	**1010198**
	2006	**1159854**	**1029072**	**1013167**
Albania	2003	1313	375	356
Albanie	2004	1313	420	399
	2005	1313	447	443
	2006	1313	505	499
Austria	2003	10500	9159	9897
Autriche	2004	10500	8882	9691
	2005	13026	9227	9807
	2006	10411	9058	8989
Belarus	2003	25404	13425	13024
Bélarus	2004	25255	16717	15846
	2005	25504	18105	17732
	2006	24620	19304	18592
Belgium	2003	28698	45917	45489
Belgique	2004	32392	43582	43233
	2005	28898	37534	37046
	2006	39459	37433	36386
Bosnia and Herzegovina	2003	*200	81	76
Bosnie y Herzégovine	2004	*200	184	170
	2005	*200	146	143
	2006	*200	146	143
Bulgaria	2003	5750	5336	5174
Bulgarie	2004	5750	5847	5779
	2005	5750	6598	6297
	2006	5750	7303	7136
Croatia	2003	18666	5385	5358
Croatie	2004	18367	5346	5321
	2005	20114	5157	5141
	2006	12493	4837	4823
Czech Republic	2003	9882	6715	6732
République tchèque	2004	10131	6978	6999
	2005	10082	8074	8132
	2006	9882	8033	8179
Denmark	2003	8784	8251	8154
Danemark	2004	9633	8055	7954
	2005	9433	7725	7499
	2006	8804	7931	7853
Finland	2003	13190	13011	13105
Finlande	2004	11579	13442	13506
	2005	11529	12648	12839
	2006	12567	13757	13826
France incl. Monaco	2003	105111	88132	87523
France y compris Monaco	2004	102216	89010	88406
	2005	106009	86967	86293
	2006	97764	87453	86839

Table 16

Refinery distillation capacity, throughput and output
Capacité de traitement des raffineries, quantités traitées et production totale

Thousand metric tons
Milliers de tonnes métriques

Country or area Pays ou zone	Year Année	Capacity Capacité	Throughput Quantités traitées	Output Production totale
Germany Allemagne	2003 2004 2005 2006	127720 124576 129816 120653	117221 120784 123653 121418	116165 119954 122675 120571
Greece Grèce	2003 2004 2005 2006	23957 23707 24855 20613	22153 20999 21246 22289	22113 20991 21240 22245
Hungary Hongrie	2003 2004 2005 2006	8036 6287 5191 8036	7308 7166 8311 8566	7287 7149 8234 8512
Ireland Irlande	2003 2004 2005 2006	3544 3544 3544 3544	3225 2942 3311 3141	3130 2895 3120 3231
Italy and San Marino Italie y comp. St. Marin	2003 2004 2005 2006	114843 94829 *115000 116650	98234 99092 100988 99787	97840 98140 100598 99199
Lithuania Lituanie	2003 2004 2005 2006	13126 13126 13126 9483	7168 8678 9226 8254	7106 8629 9206 8248
Netherlands Pays-Bas	2003 2004 2005 2006	45967 49211 44320 60486	83351 84561 85341 81817	82275 83486 84900 80881
Norway,Svlbd.J.Myn. I Norvège,Svalbd,J.May	2003 2004 2005 2006	15472 15472 15472 15472	14936 14324 15728 16716	14645 14093 15424 16402
Poland Pologne	2003 2004 2005 2006	21461 20164 20862 24780	18335 19181 19304 22154	17992 18535 18465 20947
Portugal Portugal	2003 2004 2005 2006	15183 15183 15183 15183	13267 13353 13618 13704	13223 13293 13563 13664
Romania Roumanie	2003 2004 2005 2006	25155 25205 25155 25784	12736 13418 14565 14382	12040 13077 14867 14407
Russian Federation Fédération de Russie	2003 2004 2005 2006	212817 199790 199790 266470	197294 196417 212137 223928	190284 193930 205702 216548
Serbia Serbie	2003 2004 2005 2006	7886 7686 7736 10721	3683 3966 3722 3132	3438 3518 3302 2779

Table 16

Refinery distillation capacity, throughput and output
Capacité de traitement des raffineries, quantités traitées et production totale
Thousand metric tons
Milliers de tonnes métriques

Country or area Pays ou zone	Year Année	Capacity Capacité	Throughput Quantités traitées	Output Production totale
Slovakia	2003	5740	6064	6154
Slovaquie	2004	5740	6463	6575
	2005	5740	6015	6191
	2006	5740	6103	6276
Slovenia	2003	*674	..	..
Slovénie	2004	674	..	..
	2005	674	..	..
	2006	674	..	..
Spain	2003	65935	58187	57640
Espagne	2004	76562	60057	59483
	2005	81803	60893	60310
	2006	63461	61944	61350
Sweden	2003	21147	20308	19384
Suède	2004	21661	21374	20308
	2005	21661	20698	19800
	2006	21661	20894	19861
Switzerland	2003	6588	4588	4614
Suisse	2004	6588	5167	5214
	2005	6588	4788	4855
	2006	6588	5433	5500
T.F.Yug.Rep. Macedonia	2003	2496	1005	972
L'ex-RY Macédoine	2004	2496	1033	990
	2005	2496	1189	1147
	2006	2496	1087	1026
Ukraine	2003	48263	25289	22414
Ukraine	2004	46366	25793	22068
	2005	45867	19649	19224
	2006	43911	15350	15175
United Kingdom	2003	83699	84586	84529
Royaume-Uni	2004	84947	89821	89826
	2005	83400	86136	86003
	2006	94185	83213	83080
Oceania	**2003**	**48827**	**41657**	**40166**
Océanie	**2004**	**51681**	**39952**	**39818**
	2005	**52929**	**38963**	**38839**
	2006	**41965**	**37512**	**36593**
Australia	2003	43472	36364	34985
Australie	2004	44769	34386	34286
	2005	46017	32826	32684
	2006	35172	31293	30509
New Zealand	2003	5290	5293	5181
Nouvelle-Zélande	2004	5290	5102	5082
	2005	5290	5144	5209
	2006	5171	5159	5074
Papua New Guinea	2003	*65	0	0
Papouasie-Nvl-Guinée	2004	1622	464	450
	2005	1622	993	946
	2006	1622	1060	1010

Table 17

Production, trade and consumption of liquefied petroleum gas
Production, commerce et consommation de gaz de pétrole liquéfiés
Thousand metric tons and kilograms per capita
Milliers de tonnes métriques et kilogrammes par habitant

Table Notes:
Production from refineries and plants.

- **Please refer to the Definitions Section on pages xv to xxix for the appropriate product description/ classification.**

Notes relatives aux tableaux:
Production à partir des raffineries et des usines.

- **Veuillez consulter la section "définitions" de la page xv à la page xxix pour une description/classification appropriée des produits.**

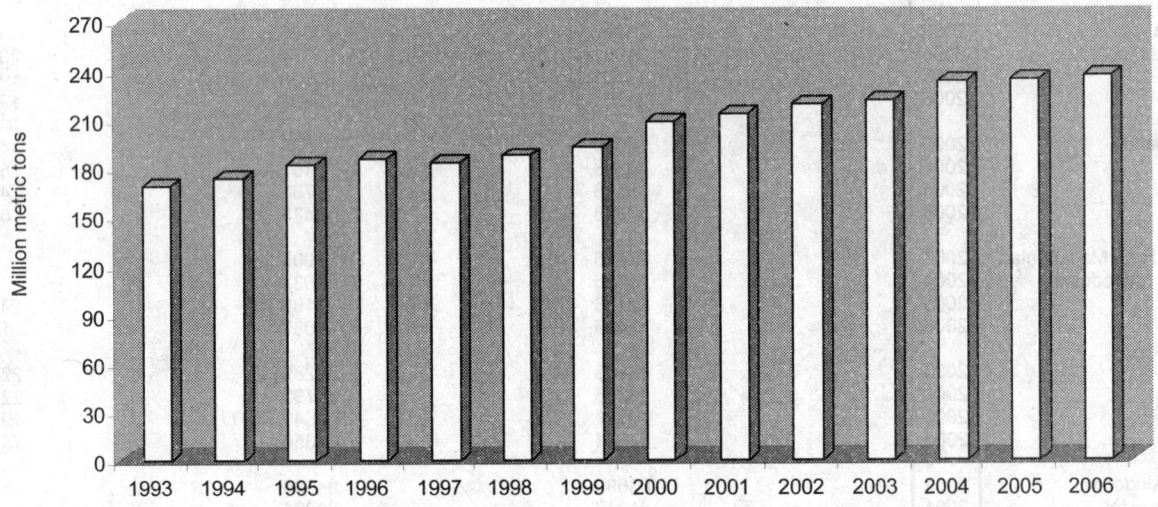

Figure 48: World liquefied petroleum gas production 1993-2006

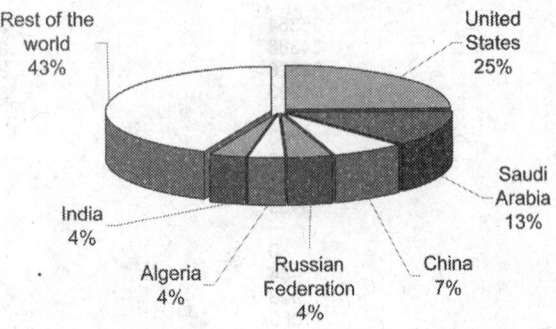

Figure 49: Major LPG producing countries in 2006

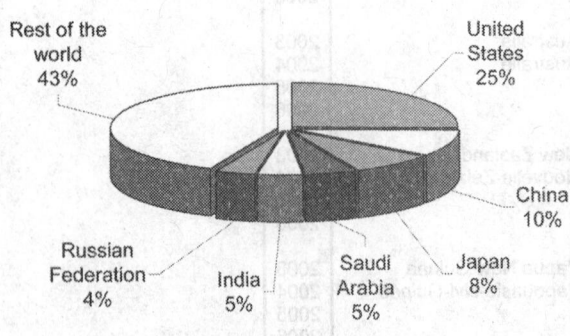

Figure 50: Major LPG consuming countries in 2006

Table 17

Production, trade and consumption of liquefied petroleum gas (LPG)
Production, commerce et consommation de gaz de pétrole liquéfiés (GPL)
Thousand metric tons and kilograms per capita
Milliers de tonnes métriques et kilogrammes par habitant

Country or area Pays ou zone	Year Année	Production Production	Imports Importations	Exports Exportations	Changes in stocks Variations des stocks	Consumption Consommation	
						Total Totale	Per Capita Par habitant
World **Monde**	**2003**	**220197**	**57872**	**62908**	**-459**	**215620**	**34**
	2004	**231966**	**60498**	**65286**	**763**	**226416**	**36**
	2005	**233905**	**62726**	**68436**	**360**	**227834**	**35**
	2006	**236492**	**63397**	**66443**	**754**	**232690**	**36**
Africa **Afrique**	**2003**	**12827**	**3374**	**8325**	**63**	**7813**	**9**
	2004	**12369**	**3646**	**7718**	**-49**	**8346**	**10**
	2005	**12600**	**4387**	**7908**	**-13**	**9092**	**10**
	2006	**12191**	**4346**	**7514**	**-64**	**9087**	**10**
Algeria Algérie	2003	9756	..	7947	..	1809	57
	2004	9223	..	7296	..	1927	60
	2005	9337	..	7482	..	1855	56
	2006	8750	..	7010	..	1740	52
Angola Angola	2003	40	44	..	..	84	8
	2004	28	52	..	..	80	7
	2005	24	71	..	..	95	8
	2006	24	74	..	..	98	8
Benin Bénin	2003	..	10	0	-1	11	1
	2004	..	10	0	-1	11	1
	2005	..	14	6	-1	9	1
	2006	..	14	7	1	6	1
Burkina Faso Burkina Faso	2003	..	10	..	0	10	1
	2004	..	14	..	2	12	1
	2005	..	16	..	3	13	1
	2006	..	9	..	-7	17	1
Burundi Burundi	2003	..	*2	..	..	*2	0
	2004	..	*2	..	..	*2	0
	2005	..	*2	..	..	*2	0
	2006	..	*2	..	..	*2	0
Cameroon Cameroun	2003	21	..	..	-19	40	2
	2004	28	..	..	-12	40	2
	2005	26	..	..	-17	43	2
	2006	22	..	..	-21	43	2
Cape Verde Cap-Vert	2003	..	*8	..	..	*8	*17
	2004	..	*8	..	..	*8	*17
	2005	..	*9	..	..	*9	*19
	2006	..	*8	..	..	*8	*16
Chad Tchad	2003	..	*1	..	..	*1	0
	2004	..	*1	..	..	*1	0
	2005	..	*1	..	..	*1	0
	2006	..	*1	..	..	*1	0
Congo Congo	2003	4	..	..	..	4	1
	2004	5	..	..	..	5	1
	2005	5	..	..	..	5	1
	2006	7	..	..	..	7	2
Côte d'Ivoire Côte d'Ivoire	2003	72	27	0	..	99	6
	2004	96	23	30	..	89	5
	2005	87	0	0	..	87	5
	2006	101	0	0	..	101	5
Djibouti Djibouti	2003	..	25	..	..	25	32
	2004	..	30	..	..	30	38
	2005	..	30	..	..	30	37
	2006	..	30	..	..	30	37

Table 17

Production, trade and consumption of liquefied petroleum gas (LPG)
Production, commerce et consommation de gaz de pétrole liquéfiés (GPL)
Thousand metric tons and kilograms per capita
Milliers de tonnes métriques et kilogrammes par habitant

Country or area Pays ou zone	Year Année	Production Production	Imports Importations	Exports Exportations	Changes in stocks Variations des stocks	Consumption Consommation	
						Total Totale	Per Capita Par habitant
Egypt	2003	1739	1354	..	17	3076	46
Egypte	2004	1724	1518	..	-125	3367	47
	2005	1713	1889	..	0	3602	50
	2006	1711	1961	..	-82	3754	52
Eritrea	2003	..	4	..	0	4	1
Erythrée	2004	..	5	..	0	5	1
	2005	..	5	..	0	5	1
	2006	..	2	..	-1	3	1
Ethiopia	2003	..	1	..	-1	2	0
Ethiopie	2004	..	0	..	0	0	0
	2005	..	0	..	0	0	0
	2006	..	0	..	0	0	0
Gabon	2003	9	11	..	0	20	15
Gabon	2004	9	11	..	0	20	15
	2005	10	12	..	1	21	15
	2006	7	15	..	0	22	15
Gambia	2003	..	*2	..	..	*2	*1
Gambie	2004	..	*2	..	..	*2	*1
	2005	..	*2	..	..	*2	*1
	2006	..	*2	..	..	*2	*1
Ghana	2003	53	17	0	..	70	3
Ghana	2004	66	11	6	..	71	3
	2005	78	10	0	..	88	4
	2006	36	68	10	..	94	4
Guinea-Bissau	2003	..	*1	..	..	*1	*1
Guinée-Bissau	2004	..	*1	..	..	*1	*1
	2005	..	*1	..	..	*1	*1
	2006	..	*2	..	..	*2	*1
Kenya	2003	24	19	2	..	41	1
Kenya	2004	27	19	4	..	42	1
	2005	26	26	4	..	48	1
	2006	30	29	4	..	55	2
Liberia	2003	..	*3	..	..	*3	*1
Libéria	2004	..	*3	..	..	*3	*1
	2005	..	*3	..	..	*3	*1
	2006	..	*3	..	..	*3	*1
Libyan Arab Jamah.	2003	310	..	270	..	40	6
Jamah. arabe libyenne	2004	310	..	270	..	40	6
	2005	350	..	305	..	45	7
	2006	395	..	344	..	51	8
Madagascar	2003	*6	*3	..	..	*9	*1
Madagascar	2004	*6	*3	..	..	*9	*1
	2005	*6	*3	..	..	*9	*1
	2006	*6	*3	..	..	*9	0
Malawi	2003	..	1	..	..	1	0
Malawi	2004	..	*1	..	..	*1	0
	2005	..	*1	..	..	*1	0
	2006	..	*2	..	..	*2	0
Mauritania	2003	..	23	..	..	23	8
Mauritanie	2004	..	24	..	..	24	8
	2005	..	29	..	..	29	10
	2006	..	30	..	..	30	10

Table 17

Production, trade and consumption of liquefied petroleum gas (LPG)
Production, commerce et consommation de gaz de pétrole liquéfiés (GPL)

Thousand metric tons and kilograms per capita
Milliers de tonnes métriques et kilogrammes par habitant

Country or area Pays ou zone	Year Année	Production Production	Imports Importations	Exports Exportations	Changes in stocks Variations des stocks	Consumption Consommation	
						Total Totale	Per Capita Par habitant
Mauritius	2003	..	52		0	52	43
Maurice	2004	..	54		-1	55	45
	2005	..	63		2	61	49
	2006	..	59		-4	63	50
Morocco	2003	67	1219		-2	1288	45
Maroc	2004	104	1288		1	1391	47
	2005	204	1599		0	1803	60
	2006	192	1387		0	1579	52
Mozambique	2003	..	11	..	..	11	1
Mozambique	2004	..	12	..	..	12	1
	2005	..	14	..	..	14	1
	2006	..	14	..	..	14	1
Nigeria	2003	17	..	2	-9	24	0
Nigéria	2004	17	..	0	0	17	0
	2005	17	..	0	0	17	0
	2006	20	..	0	0	20	0
Réunion	2003	..	*38	..	..	*38	*50
Réunion	2004	..	*38	..	..	*38	*50
	2005	..	*38	..	..	*38	*49
	2006	..	*38	..	..	*38	*48
Senegal	2003	12	106	1	0	117	12
Sénégal	2004	10	122	3	2	127	12
	2005	3	133	3	-1	134	12
	2006	0	132	0	-1	133	12
Seychelles	2003	..	2	..	..	2	23
Seychelles	2004	..	3	..	..	3	40
	2005	..	2	..	..	2	24
	2006	..	3	..	..	3	34
Somalia	2003	0	*5	0	..	*5	*1
Somalie	2004	0	*5	0	..	*5	*1
	2005	0	*5	0	..	*5	*1
	2006	31	0	*26	..	5	1
South Africa Customs Un.	2003	307	41	..	..	348	7
Un.douan.d'Afr.mérid	2004	305	43	..	..	348	7
	2005	297	46	..	..	343	6
	2006	327	46	..	..	373	7
Sudan	2003	284	..	103	78	103	3
Soudan	2004	300	..	109	85	106	3
	2005	305	..	108	0	197	6
	2006	419	..	113	0	306	8
Togo	2003	..	2	..	..	2	0
Togo	2004	..	2	..	..	2	0
	2005	..	2	..	..	2	0
	2006	..	3	..	..	3	1
Tunisia	2003	103	322	..	0	425	43
Tunisie	2004	108	329	..	0	437	44
	2005	109	351	..	0	460	46
	2006	110	398	..	51	457	45
Uganda	2003	..	1	..	..	1	0
Ouganda	2004	..	*1	..	..	*1	0
	2005	..	0	..	..	0	0
	2006	..	0	..	..	0	0

Table 17

Production, trade and consumption of liquefied petroleum gas (LPG)
Production, commerce et consommation de gaz de pétrole liquéfiés (GPL)
Thousand metric tons and kilograms per capita
Milliers de tonnes métriques et kilogrammes par habitant

Country or area Pays ou zone	Year Année	Production Production	Imports Importations	Exports Exportations	Changes in stocks Variations des stocks	Consumption Consommation	
						Total Totale	Per Capita Par habitant
United Rep.Tanzania	2003	..	5	..	..	5	0
Rép. Unie de Tanzanie	2004	..	6	..	..	6	0
	2005	..	6	..	..	6	0
	2006	..	6	..	..	6	0
Zambia	2003	3	..	..	..	3	0
Zambie	2004	3	..	..	..	3	0
	2005	3	..	..	..	3	0
	2006	3	..	..	..	3	0
Zimbabwe	2003	..	4	..	..	4	0
Zimbabwe	2004	..	4	..	..	4	0
	2005	..	4	..	..	4	0
	2006	..	4	..	..	4	0
America, North	**2003**	**64804**	**4883**	**1061**	**-612**	**69238**	**138**
Amérique du Nord	**2004**	**67431**	**5137**	**950**	**414**	**71205**	**140**
	2005	**64382**	**5054**	**1105**	**485**	**67846**	**132**
	2006	**62159**	**5781**	**1171**	**270**	**66500**	**129**
Antigua and Barbuda	2003	..	*2	..	..	*2	*25
Antigua-et-Barbuda	2004	..	*2	..	..	*2	*25
	2005	..	*2	..	..	*2	*24
	2006	..	*3	..	..	*3	*36
Aruba	2003	..	*20	..	..	*20	*210
Aruba	2004	..	*20	..	..	*20	*205
	2005	..	*21	..	..	*21	*209
	2006	..	*21	..	..	*21	*204
Bahamas	2003	..	*18	..	..	*18	*56
Bahamas	2004	..	*19	..	..	*19	*63
	2005	..	*20	..	..	*20	*62
	2006	..	*21	..	..	*21	*64
Barbados	2003	1	11	..	..	12	44
Barbade	2004	1	11	..	..	12	45
	2005	1	12	..	..	13	47
	2006	1	12	..	..	13	47
Belize	2003	..	*17	..	..	*17	*62
Belize	2004	..	*18	..	..	*18	*64
	2005	..	*19	..	..	*19	*65
	2006	..	*19	..	..	*19	*62
Bermuda	2003	..	*12	..	..	*12	*190
Bermudes	2004	..	*12	..	..	*12	*190
	2005	..	*13	..	..	*13	*204
	2006	..	*13	..	..	*13	*204
Canada	2003	1991	..	321	0	1670	53
Canada	2004	1955	..	258	6	1691	53
	2005	1779	..	288	37	1454	45
	2006	1730	..	292	-37	1475	45
Cayman Islands	2003	..	*4	..	..	*4	*92
Iles Caïmanes	2004	..	*4	..	..	*4	*90
	2005	..	*4	..	..	*4	*83
	2006	..	*4	..	..	*4	*77
Costa Rica	2003	2	89	..	1	90	22
Costa Rica	2004	2	99	..	2	99	24
	2005	2	93	..	0	95	22
	2006	4	101	..	1	104	24

Table 17

Production, trade and consumption of liquefied petroleum gas (LPG)
Production, commerce et consommation de gaz de pétrole liquéfiés (GPL)
Thousand metric tons and kilograms per capita
Milliers de tonnes métriques et kilogrammes par habitant

Country or area Pays ou zone	Year Année	Production Production	Imports Importations	Exports Exportations	Changes in stocks Variations des stocks	Consumption Consommation	
						Total Totale	Per Capita Par habitant
Cuba	2003	93	71	..	..	164	15
Cuba	2004	63	112	..	..	175	15
	2005	82	105	..	..	187	17
	2006	62	103	..	..	165	15
Dominica	2003	..	2	..	..	2	29
Dominique	2004	..	2	..	..	2	29
	2005	..	*2	..	..	*2	*29
	2006	..	*2	..	..	*2	*29
Dominican Republic	2003	42	468	..	0	510	57
Rép. dominicaine	2004	33	554	..	0	587	65
	2005	35	638	..	0	673	73
	2006	33	687	..	-1	721	77
El Salvador	2003	12	172	3	-3	184	28
El Salvador	2004	14	170	12	2	170	25
	2005	16	221	56	-5	186	27
	2006	17	217	39	-14	209	30
Grenada	2003	..	9	..	..	9	86
Grenade	2004	..	6	..	..	6	57
	2005	..	6	..	..	6	57
	2006	..	7	..	..	7	62
Guadeloupe	2003	..	*24	..	..	*24	*55
Guadeloupe	2004	..	*25	..	..	*25	*56
	2005	..	*26	..	..	*26	*58
	2006	..	*27	..	..	*27	*59
Guatemala	2003	..	221	0	0	221	18
Guatemala	2004	..	242	0	-3	245	20
	2005	..	297	3	54	240	19
	2006	..	304	58	7	238	18
Haiti	2003	..	13	..	..	13	2
Haïti	2004	..	13	..	..	13	2
	2005	..	13	..	..	13	2
	2006	..	13	..	..	13	2
Honduras	2003	..	71	17	1	53	8
Honduras	2004	..	75	23	0	52	7
	2005	..	86	21	-4	69	10
	2006	..	105	35	0	70	10
Jamaica	2003	7	69	..	1	75	28
Jamaïque	2004	7	66	..	0	73	27
	2005	0	75	..	-1	76	29
	2006	9	73	..	1	81	30
Martinique	2003	*26	*2	*10	..	*18	*46
Martinique	2004	*27	*2	*10	..	*19	*48
	2005	*27	*2	*10	..	*19	*48
	2006	*27	*2	*10	..	*19	*48
Mexico	2003	1059	2793	9	-2	3845	38
Mexique	2004	1056	2812	8	-54	3914	38
	2005	1039	2426	56	37	3372	32
	2006	1014	2685	69	-47	3677	35
Netherlands Antilles	2003	85	22	49	..	58	325
Antilles néerlandaises	2004	78	22	42	..	58	317
	2005	119	22	83	..	58	313
	2006	90	22	54	..	58	306

Table 17

Production, trade and consumption of liquefied petroleum gas (LPG)
Production, commerce et consommation de gaz de pétrole liquéfiés (GPL)
Thousand metric tons and kilograms per capita
Milliers de tonnes métriques et kilogrammes par habitant

Country or area Pays ou zone	Year Année	Production Production	Imports Importations	Exports Exportations	Changes in stocks Variations des stocks	Consumption Consommation	
						Total Totale	Per Capita Par habitant
Nicaragua	2003	21	34	..	..	55	10
Nicaragua	2004	17	39	..	..	56	10
	2005	15	42	..	..	57	10
	2006	15	43	..	..	58	10
Panama	2003	..	128	..	0	128	41
Panama	2004	..	156	..	50	106	33
	2005	..	116	..	0	116	36
	2006	..	159	..	0	159	48
St. Lucia	2003	..	*9	..	..	*9	*54
St-Lucie	2004	..	*9	..	..	*9	*56
	2005	..	*9	..	..	*9	*55
	2006	..	*10	..	..	*10	*60
St. Vincent-Grenadines	2003	..	*6	..	..	*6	*57
St. Vincent-Grenadines	2004	..	*6	..	..	*6	*57
	2005	..	*6	..	..	*6	*58
	2006	..	*7	..	..	*7	*68
Trinidad and Tobago	2003	726	..	652	..	74	56
Trinité-et-Tobago	2004	710	..	597	..	113	86
	2005	686	..	589	..	97	73
	2006	771	..	613	..	158	119
United States	2003	60739	597	..	-610	61946	213
Etats-Unis	2004	63468	641	..	411	63698	217
	2005	60581	779	..	367	60993	206
	2006	58386	1122	..	360	59148	198
America, South	**2003**	**14979**	**2676**	**4227**	**-50**	**13478**	**37**
Amérique du Sud	**2004**	**16477**	**2622**	**4074**	**35**	**14990**	**41**
	2005	**18234**	**1992**	**4703**	**173**	**15351**	**41**
	2006	**18287**	**2449**	**4050**	**109**	**16577**	**44**
Argentina	2003	4143	..	1896	-23	2270	60
Argentine	2004	4431	..	1806	-12	2637	69
	2005	4290	..	2032	7	2251	58
	2006	4643	..	1382	0	3261	84
Bolivia	2003	301	..	18	0	283	31
Bolivie	2004	322	..	3	0	319	35
	2005	333	..	4	0	329	35
	2006	353	..	0	-8	361	37
Brazil	2003	4934	1101	71	-79	6043	34
Brésil	2004	5144	1101	71	-79	6253	34
	2005	5780	511	82	-6	6215	34
	2006	5405	856	18	-7	6250	33
Chile	2003	533	592	119	15	991	62
Chili	2004	681	537	164	100	954	59
	2005	621	611	116	130	986	61
	2006	530	725	125	140	990	60
Colombia	2003	868	0	78	33	758	17
Colombie	2004	688	1	12	31	646	14
	2005	689	2	10	14	667	14
	2006	694	0	13	14	668	14
Ecuador	2003	231	556	..	0	787	61
Equateur	2004	215	637	..	-30	883	68
	2005	228	688	..	0	916	69
	2006	242	724	..	0	966	72

Table 17

Production, trade and consumption of liquefied petroleum gas (LPG)
Production, commerce et consommation de gaz de pétrole liquéfiés (GPL)

Thousand metric tons and kilograms per capita
Milliers de tonnes métriques et kilogrammes par habitant

Country or area Pays ou zone	Year Année	Production Production	Imports Importations	Exports Exportations	Changes in stocks Variations des stocks	Consumption Consommation	
						Total Totale	Per Capita Par habitant
French Guiana	2003	..	*2	..	..	*2	*11
Guyane française	2004	..	*2	..	..	*2	*10
	2005	..	*2	..	..	*2	*10
	2006	..	*2	..	..	*2	*10
Guyana	2003	..	9	..	..	9	12
Guyana	2004	..	9	..	..	9	12
	2005	..	10	..	..	10	13
	2006	..	10	..	..	10	13
Paraguay	2003	..	72	..	..	72	13
Paraguay	2004	..	79	..	..	79	14
	2005	..	82	..	..	82	14
	2006	..	82	..	..	82	14
Peru	2003	319	293	0	13	599	22
Pérou	2004	355	231	42	25	519	19
	2005	738	62	100	43	657	24
	2006	777	8	25	35	725	26
Suriname	2003	..	22	..	..	22	45
Suriname	2004	..	22	..	..	22	45
	2005	..	23	..	..	23	46
	2006	..	24	..	..	24	48
Uruguay	2003	66	29	0	0	95	28
Uruguay	2004	86	2	2	0	86	26
	2005	91	2	6	-2	89	27
	2006	77	18	5	-1	91	27
Venezuela(Bolivar. Rep.)	2003	3585	..	2045	-8	1548	60
Venezuela(Rép. bolivar.)	2004	4555	..	1974	0	2581	99
	2005	5464	..	2353	-13	3124	118
	2006	5566	..	2482	-64	3148	116
Asia	**2003**	**85938**	**34204**	**36108**	**4**	**84030**	**22**
Asie	**2004**	**92658**	**35067**	**37622**	**399**	**89704**	**23**
	2005	**94930**	**36282**	**39166**	**-353**	**92398**	**24**
	2006	**98022**	**34934**	**37690**	**326**	**94940**	**24**
Armenia	2003	..	1	..	..	1	0
Arménie	2004	..	1	..	..	1	0
	2005	..	20	..	..	20	6
	2006	..	15	..	..	15	5
Azerbaijan	2003	148	3	10	-2	143	17
Azerbaïdjan	2004	182	0	15	0	167	20
	2005	185	0	24	3	158	19
	2006	195	0	46	1	148	17
Bahrain	2003	201	..	165	2	34	49
Bahreïn	2004	204	..	163	5	36	51
	2005	218	..	169	11	38	52
	2006	215	..	164	12	39	53
Bangladesh	2003	20	..	..	..	20	0
Bangladesh	2004	16	..	..	..	16	0
	2005	12	..	..	..	12	0
	2006	8	..	..	..	8	0
Bhutan	2003	..	*4	..	..	*4	*7
Bhoutan	2004	..	*4	..	..	*4	*6
	2005	..	*4	..	..	*4	*6
	2006	..	*4	..	..	*4	*6

Table 17

Production, trade and consumption of liquefied petroleum gas (LPG)
Production, commerce et consommation de gaz de pétrole liquéfiés (GPL)

Thousand metric tons and kilograms per capita
Milliers de tonnes métriques et kilogrammes par habitant

Country or area Pays ou zone	Year Année	Production Production	Imports Importations	Exports Exportations	Changes in stocks Variations des stocks	Consumption Consommation Total Totale	Consumption Consommation Per Capita Par habitant
Brunei Darussalam	2003	14	..	..	..	14	40
Brunéi Darussalam	2004	15	..	..	..	15	42
	2005	15	..	..	..	15	41
	2006	15	..	..	..	15	39
Cambodia	2003	..	197	..	..	197	15
Cambodge	2004	..	228	..	..	228	17
	2005	..	233	..	..	233	17
	2006	..	295	..	..	295	21
China	2003	12117	6367	24	99	18361	14
Chine	2004	14170	6410	32	37	20511	16
	2005	14327	6170	27	-52	20522	16
	2006	17453	5356	151	13	22645	17
China, Hong Kong SAR	2003	..	331	2	*2	327	48
Chine, Hong-Kong RAS	2004	..	336	2	0	334	49
	2005	..	394	0	-1	395	58
	2006	..	431	0	9	422	62
China, Macao SAR	2003	..	27	..	-1	28	62
Chine, Macao RAS	2004	..	30	..	1	29	62
	2005	..	30	..	0	30	61
	2006	..	33	..	1	32	64
Cyprus	2003	28	28	..	1	55	76
Chypre	2004	9	45	..	1	53	72
	2005	0	49	..	-2	51	67
	2006	0	54	..	1	53	69
Georgia	2003	..	31	15	..	16	4
Géorgie	2004	..	29	14	..	15	3
	2005	..	39	14	..	25	6
	2006	..	42	14	..	28	6
India	2003	7551	1673	0	..	9224	9
Inde	2004	7825	2240	145	..	9920	9
	2005	7710	2719	53	..	10376	9
	2006	8408	2288	86	..	10610	9
Indonesia	2003	2007	0	1170	0	837	4
Indonésie	2004	2514	2	1101	*250	1165	5
	2005	1819	22	1076	0	765	3
	2006	1279	69	364	0	984	4
Iran(Islamic Rep. of)	2003	3750	323	1561	-121	2633	40
Iran(Rép. islamique)	2004	4146	346	1672	0	2820	42
	2005	3689	274	1270	0	2693	39
	2006	4086	228	1768	0	2546	36
Iraq	2003	848	361	..	0	1209	46
Iraq	2004	938	658	..	129	1467	54
	2005	951	671	..	126	1496	54
	2006	1032	559	..	128	1463	51
Israel	2003	474	108	91	..	491	73
Israël	2004	532	73	112	..	493	72
	2005	566	78	119	..	525	76
	2006	471	158	121	..	508	72
Japan	2003	4527	14003	54	-47	18523	147
Japon	2004	4448	13905	61	-246	18538	147
	2005	4895	14107	5	310	18687	148
	2006	4647	14102	3	-73	18819	149

Table 17

Production, trade and consumption of liquefied petroleum gas (LPG)
Production, commerce et consommation de gaz de pétrole liquéfiés (GPL)

Thousand metric tons and kilograms per capita
Milliers de tonnes métriques et kilogrammes par habitant

Country or area Pays ou zone	Year Année	Production Production	Imports Importations	Exports Exportations	Changes in stocks Variations des stocks	Consumption Consommation	
						Total Totale	Per Capita Par habitant
Jordan	2003	134	174	..	-3	311	59
Jordanie	2004	116	179	..	3	292	57
	2005	118	178	..	-2	298	54
	2006	139	202	..	-6	347	62
Kazakhstan	2003	1179	7	653	0	533	36
Kazakhstan	2004	1507	5	881	0	631	42
	2005	1478	7	1047	-2	440	29
	2006	1106	4	802	12	296	19
Korea, Republic of	2003	3613	4338	249	1	7701	161
Corée, République de	2004	3326	4110	83	62	7291	152
	2005	3213	4275	62	-109	7535	156
	2006	3098	4670	66	28	7674	159
Kuwait	2003	3250	..	3039	..	211	91
Koweït	2004	3515	..	3375	..	140	59
	2005	3368	..	3179	..	189	77
	2006	3671	..	3560	..	111	44
Kyrgyzstan	2003	..	8	..	..	8	2
Kirghizistan	2004	..	0	..	..	0	0
	2005	..	0	..	..	0	0
	2006	..	0	..	..	0	0
Lao People's Dem. Rep.	2003	..	*18	..	..	*18	*3
Rép. dém. pop. lao	2004	..	*18	..	..	*18	*3
	2005	..	*18	..	..	*18	*3
	2006	..	*18	..	..	*18	*3
Lebanon	2003	..	205	..	..	205	52
Liban	2004	..	220	..	..	220	55
	2005	..	166	..	..	166	41
	2006	..	161	..	..	161	40
Malaysia	2003	1582	610	700	-11	1503	60
Malaisie	2004	1303	257	236	51	1273	50
	2005	2470	440	1641	-13	1282	49
	2006	2503	314	1039	0	1778	67
Myanmar	2003	16	..	..	2	14	0
Myanmar	2004	20	..	..	0	20	0
	2005	19	..	..	0	19	0
	2006	10	..	..	-5	15	0
Nepal	2003	..	64	..	..	64	3
Népal	2004	..	78	..	..	78	3
	2005	..	89	..	..	89	4
	2006	..	91	..	..	91	4
Occup. Palestinian Terr.	2003	..	89	..	..	89	25
Terr. palestiniens occup.	2004	..	104	..	..	104	29
	2005	..	*121	..	..	*121	*32
	2006	..	*125	..	..	*125	*32
Oman	2003	117	0	4	0	113	48
Oman	2004	116	1	1	0	116	48
	2005	*95	0	0	1	*94	*37
	2006	*118	0	14	2	*102	*40
Other Asia	2003	1379	805	363	47	1774	78
Autre Asie	2004	1466	876	368	20	1954	86
	2005	1632	911	366	-26	2203	97
	2006	1593	1067	313	36	2311	101

Table 17

Production, trade and consumption of liquefied petroleum gas (LPG)
Production, commerce et consommation de gaz de pétrole liquéfiés (GPL)

Thousand metric tons and kilograms per capita
Milliers de tonnes métriques et kilogrammes par habitant

Country or area Pays ou zone	Year Année	Production Production	Imports Importations	Exports Exportations	Changes in stocks Variations des stocks	Consumption Consommation	
						Total Totale	Per Capita Par habitant
Pakistan	2003	380	35	..	..	415	3
Pakistan	2004	412	40	..	..	452	3
	2005	557	25	..	..	582	4
	2006	436	66	..	..	502	3
Philippines	2003	397	560	8	4	945	12
Philippines	2004	263	743	0	4	1002	12
	2005	322	639	0	-590	1551	18
	2006	333	622	0	-5	960	11
Qatar	2003	122	..	..	..	122	166
Qatar	2004	128	..	..	..	128	165
	2005	131	..	..	..	131	161
	2006	151	..	..	..	151	161
Saudi Arabia	2003	27093	..	17798	..	9295	422
Arabie saoudite	2004	29719	..	18724	..	10995	487
	2005	30979	..	19412	..	11567	500
	2006	30641	..	19074	..	11567	488
Singapore	2003	870	4	682	..	192	46
Singapour	2004	872	5	706	..	171	40
	2005	848	5	559	..	294	68
	2006	634	2	317	..	319	71
Sri Lanka	2003	15	141	..	..	156	8
Sri Lanka	2004	15	145	..	..	160	8
	2005	13	150	..	..	163	8
	2006	15	158	..	..	173	9
Syrian Arab Republic	2003	286	217	..	..	503	29
Rép. arabe syrienne	2004	286	217	..	..	503	28
	2005	328	204	..	..	532	29
	2006	321	173	..	..	494	26
Tajikistan	2003	..	5	..	..	5	1
Tadjikistan	2004	..	6	..	..	6	1
	2005	..	7	..	..	7	1
	2006	..	7	..	..	7	1
Thailand	2003	3446	0	795	17	2634	41
Thaïlande	2004	3917	4	1039	86	2796	44
	2005	4011	0	979	14	3018	47
	2006	4032	0	595	120	3317	51
Timor-Leste	2003	*2193	..	*2193	..	0	0
Timor-Leste	2004	*2200	..	*2200	..	0	0
	2005	*2210	..	*2210	..	0	0
	2006	*2215	..	*2215	..	0	0
Turkey	2003	758	3088	297	14	3535	50
Turquie	2004	762	3378	224	-4	3920	55
	2005	766	3631	261	-21	4157	58
	2006	808	2800	66	52	3490	48
Turkmenistan	2003	..	80	..	..	80	17
Turkménistan	2004	..	80	..	..	80	17
	2005	..	80	..	..	80	17
	2006	..	80	..	..	80	16
United Arab Emirates	2003	6985	..	6161	..	824	232
Emirats arabes unis	2004	7252	..	6395	..	857	228
	2005	7526	..	6638	..	888	216
	2006	7807	..	6890	..	917	217

Table 17

Production, trade and consumption of liquefied petroleum gas (LPG)
Production, commerce et consommation de gaz de pétrole liquéfiés (GPL)

Thousand metric tons and kilograms per capita
Milliers de tonnes métriques et kilogrammes par habitant

Country or area Pays ou zone	Year Année	Production Production	Imports Importations	Exports Exportations	Changes in stocks Variations des stocks	Consumption Consommation	
						Total Totale	Per Capita Par habitant
Uzbekistan	2003	44	..	..	..	44	2
Ouzbékistan	2004	40	..	..	..	40	2
	2005	32	..	..	..	32	1
	2006	30	..	..	..	30	1
Viet Nam	2003	307	299	..	..	606	7
Viet Nam	2004	335	294	..	..	629	8
	2005	343	526	..	..	869	10
	2006	483	740	..	..	1223	15
Yemen	2003	87	..	74	..	13	1
Yémen	2004	89	..	73	..	16	1
	2005	84	..	55	..	29	1
	2006	69	..	22	..	47	2
Europe	**2003**	**39799**	**12528**	**13162**	**104**	**39061**	**54**
Europe	**2004**	**41552**	**13569**	**14907**	**-17**	**40231**	**55**
	2005	**42314**	**14679**	**15541**	**34**	**41418**	**57**
	2006	**43996**	**15501**	**16013**	**94**	**43390**	**59**
Albania	2003	0	40	..	..	40	11
Albanie	2004	1	45	..	..	46	15
	2005	0	57	..	..	57	18
	2006	0	70	..	..	70	22
Austria	2003	50	137	9	1	177	22
Autriche	2004	57	132	17	-5	177	22
	2005	107	133	20	0	220	27
	2006	50	155	21	2	182	22
Belarus	2003	216	85	70	0	231	23
Bélarus	2004	418	30	179	40	229	23
	2005	459	4	265	-30	228	23
	2006	483	32	329	-52	238	24
Belgium	2003	627	131	350	-2	410	40
Belgique	2004	511	188	369	-2	332	32
	2005	462	205	373	2	292	28
	2006	403	254	373	-3	287	27
Bosnia and Herzegovina	2003	1	21	1	..	21	5
Bosnie y Herzégovine	2004	3	18	0	..	21	5
	2005	2	28	0	..	30	8
	2006	2	26	0	..	28	7
Bulgaria	2003	85	268	0	-1	354	45
Bulgarie	2004	103	233	1	4	331	43
	2005	105	286	0	3	388	50
	2006	127	280	5	2	400	52
Croatia	2003	437	7	264	0	180	41
Croatie	2004	443	8	249	0	202	46
	2005	431	3	227	3	204	46
	2006	399	2	172	1	228	51
Czech Republic	2003	168	115	47	1	235	23
République tchèque	2004	181	140	68	1	252	25
	2005	184	127	95	-3	219	21
	2006	204	124	124	3	201	20
Denmark	2003	168	3	104	-1	68	13
Danemark	2004	164	4	94	-2	76	14
	2005	145	3	87	1	60	11
	2006	166	4	102	1	67	12

Table 17

Production, trade and consumption of liquefied petroleum gas (LPG)
Production, commerce et consommation de gaz de pétrole liquéfiés (GPL)

Thousand metric tons and kilograms per capita
Milliers de tonnes métriques et kilogrammes par habitant

Country or area Pays ou zone	Year Année	Production Production	Imports Importations	Exports Exportations	Changes in stocks Variations des stocks	Consumption Consommation	
						Total Totale	Per Capita Par habitant
Estonia	2003	..	6	..	..	6	4
Estonie	2004	..	7	..	..	7	5
	2005	..	6	..	..	6	4
	2006	..	7	..	..	7	5
Finland	2003	273	233	4	24	478	92
Finlande	2004	267	196	2	-28	489	94
	2005	315	219	0	56	478	91
	2006	402	162	0	-14	578	110
France incl. Monaco	2003	3071	1674	1647	-3	3101	52
France y compris Monaco	2004	2979	2089	1508	-19	3579	59
	2005	2868	2237	1668	10	3427	56
	2006	2774	2523	1647	-23	3673	60
Germany	2003	3056	649	579	4	3122	38
Allemagne	2004	2918	628	599	-15	2962	36
	2005	2951	704	613	-4	3046	37
	2006	2925	784	574	5	3130	38
Greece	2003	672	8	274	-4	410	37
Grèce	2004	598	14	207	-2	407	37
	2005	655	11	259	-1	408	37
	2006	653	22	236	2	437	39
Hungary	2003	392	54	140	1	305	30
Hongrie	2004	408	94	191	-3	314	31
	2005	393	116	43	4	462	46
	2006	373	92	112	1	352	35
Iceland	2003	..	2	..	0	2	7
Islande	2004	..	2	..	0	2	7
	2005	..	2	..	0	2	7
	2006	..	1	..	-1	2	7
Ireland	2003	59	102	21	0	140	35
Irlande	2004	53	112	20	0	145	36
	2005	57	119	20	3	153	37
	2006	51	118	17	2	150	35
Italy and San Marino	2003	2610	1690	471	-100	3929	68
Italie y comp. St. Marin	2004	2613	1600	575	22	3616	62
	2005	2517	1720	597	45	3595	61
	2006	2275	1644	537	8	3374	57
Latvia	2003	..	57	5	0	52	22
Lettonie	2004	..	65	8	2	55	24
	2005	..	71	15	0	56	24
	2006	..	69	16	-6	59	26
Lithuania	2003	435	74	219	3	287	83
Lituanie	2004	526	71	268	0	329	96
	2005	555	67	250	-4	376	110
	2006	474	90	220	2	342	101
Luxembourg	2003	..	22	7	..	15	33
Luxembourg	2004	..	20	7	..	13	28
	2005	..	17	5	..	12	26
	2006	..	14	4	..	10	21
Malta	2003	..	17	..	..	17	43
Malte	2004	..	17	..	..	17	42
	2005	..	18	..	..	18	44
	2006	..	20	..	..	20	49

Table 17

Production, trade and consumption of liquefied petroleum gas (LPG)
Production, commerce et consommation de gaz de pétrole liquéfiés (GPL)
Thousand metric tons and kilograms per capita
Milliers de tonnes métriques et kilogrammes par habitant

Country or area Pays ou zone	Year Année	Production Production	Imports Importations	Exports Exportations	Changes in stocks Variations des stocks	Consumption Consommation	
						Total Totale	Per Capita Par habitant
Netherlands	2003	4780	1667	2097	-20	4370	270
Pays-Bas	2004	5070	2079	2391	19	4739	291
	2005	4579	2160	2181	-37	4595	282
	2006	4069	2409	2556	-18	3940	241
Norway,Svlbd.J.Myn. I	2003	6167	284	4492	79	1880	410
Norvège,Svalbd,J.May	2004	6423	143	5025	-7	1548	336
	2005	6628	247	5264	8	1603	345
	2006	8255	238	5563	22	2908	624
Poland	2003	269	1779	12	21	2015	53
Pologne	2004	259	1989	14	2	2232	58
	2005	284	2140	25	10	2389	63
	2006	282	2168	35	8	2407	63
Portugal	2003	379	615	60	7	927	89
Portugal	2004	365	625	69	-11	932	89
	2005	391	564	94	-6	867	82
	2006	406	545	84	9	858	81
Republic of Moldova	2003	..	56	1	3	52	14
Rép. de Moldova	2004	..	57	1	2	54	15
	2005	..	58	1	2	55	15
	2006	..	50	0	-1	51	14
Romania	2003	327	65	43	5	344	16
Roumanie	2004	366	70	47	0	389	18
	2005	658	58	75	-9	650	30
	2006	677	62	111	1	627	29
Russian Federation	2003	8571	1	1087	44	7441	51
Fédération de Russie	2004	8760	9	997	-28	7800	54
	2005	9428	3	1113	2	8316	58
	2006	10368	9	1187	43	9147	64
Serbia	2003	79	0	3	..	76	7
Serbie	2004	95	63	1	..	157	15
	2005	89	74	1	..	162	15
	2006	75	93	1	..	167	16
Slovakia	2003	152	60	3	2	207	38
Slovaquie	2004	206	57	0	-4	267	50
	2005	181	72	4	0	249	46
	2006	137	69	3	0	203	38
Slovenia	2003	..	88	0	0	88	44
Slovénie	2004	..	86	0	3	83	42
	2005	..	87	0	-2	89	44
	2006	..	97	5	9	83	41
Spain	2003	1211	995	143	-2	2065	49
Espagne	2004	1058	1095	242	14	1897	44
	2005	1050	1026	228	9	1839	42
	2006	1522	906	282	-17	2163	49
Sweden	2003	360	1093	405	68	980	109
Suède	2004	423	1018	424	-40	1057	118
	2005	433	1160	399	1	1193	132
	2006	302	1402	326	66	1312	144
Switzerland	2003	178	41	22	1	196	27
Suisse	2004	196	45	25	1	215	29
	2005	197	51	49	-1	200	27
	2006	223	48	56	1	214	29

Table 17

Production, trade and consumption of liquefied petroleum gas (LPG)
Production, commerce et consommation de gaz de pétrole liquéfiés (GPL)

Thousand metric tons and kilograms per capita
Milliers de tonnes métriques et kilogrammes par habitant

Country or area Pays ou zone	Year Année	Production Production	Imports Importations	Exports Exportations	Changes in stocks Variations des stocks	Consumption Consommation	
						Total Totale	Per Capita Par habitant
T.F.Yug.Rep. Macedonia	2003	21	21	5	0	37	18
L'ex-RY Macédoine	2004	20	23	3	-1	41	20
	2005	24	26	4	1	45	22
	2006	29	30	6	-1	54	26
Ukraine	2003	978	2	233	0	747	16
Ukraine	2004	988	8	274	6	716	15
	2005	948	16	268	-8	704	15
	2006	938	49	151	0	836	18
United Kingdom	2003	4007	366	344	-27	4056	68
Royaume-Uni	2004	5080	489	1032	34	4503	75
	2005	5218	784	1298	-21	4725	78
	2006	4952	833	1158	42	4585	76
Oceania	**2003**	**1850**	**207**	**25**	**32**	**2000**	**62**
Océanie	**2004**	**1479**	**458**	**15**	**-18**	**1940**	**59**
	2005	**1445**	**332**	**13**	**35**	**1728**	**52**
	2006	**1836**	**386**	**6**	**20**	**2196**	**65**
Australia	2003	1694	153	..	31	1816	91
Australie	2004	1312	401	..	-20	1733	86
	2005	1271	276	..	35	1512	74
	2006	1679	306	..	22	1963	95
Fiji	2003	..	13	..	..	13	16
Fidji	2004	..	14	..	..	14	17
	2005	..	12	..	..	12	14
	2006	..	14	..	..	14	16
French Polynesia	2003	..	9	..	..	9	36
Polynésie française	2004	..	8	..	..	8	32
	2005	..	8	..	..	8	31
	2006	..	8	..	..	8	31
New Caledonia	2003	..	8	..	..	8	35
Nouvelle-Calédonie	2004	..	8	..	..	8	35
	2005	..	9	..	..	9	38
	2006	..	9	..	..	9	38
New Zealand	2003	156	11	25	1	141	35
Nouvelle-Zélande	2004	167	8	15	2	158	39
	2005	156	12	13	0	155	38
	2006	135	39	6	-2	170	41
Papua New Guinea	2003	0	12	..	..	12	2
Papouasie-Nvl-Guinée	2004	0	18	..	..	18	3
	2005	18	13	..	..	31	5
	2006	22	9	..	..	31	5
Solomon Islands	2003	..	*1	..	..	*1	*2
Iles Salomon	2004	..	*1	..	..	*1	*2
	2005	..	*1	..	..	*1	*2
	2006	..	*1	..	..	*1	*2
Wallis and Futuna Is	2003	..	0	..	..	0	*9
Iles Wallis et Futuna	2004	..	0	..	..	0	8
	2005	..	0	..	..	0	8
	2006	..	0	..	..	0	8

Table 18

Production, trade and consumption of aviation gasolene
Production, commerce et consommation d'essence aviation
Thousand metric tons
Milliers de tonnes métriques

Table Notes:
Production from refineries and plants.

- **Please refer to the Definitions Section on pages xv to xxix for the appropriate product description/ classification.**

Notes relatives aux tableaux:
Production à partir des raffineries et des usines.

- **Veuillez consulter la section "définitions" de la page xv à la page xxix pour une description/classification appropriée des produits.**

Figure 51: World production of aviation gasolene 1993-2006

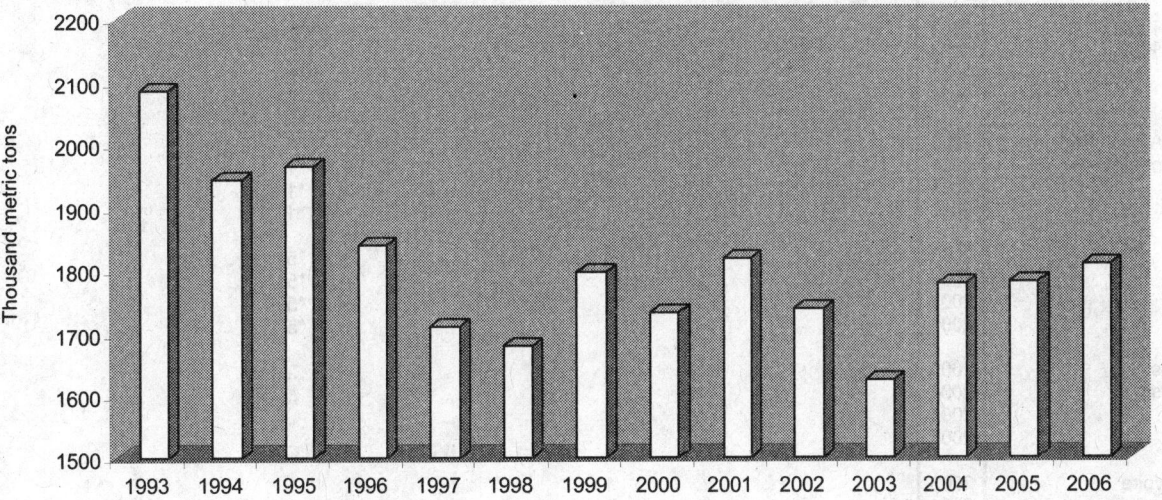

Figure 52: Major aviation gasolene producing countries in 2006

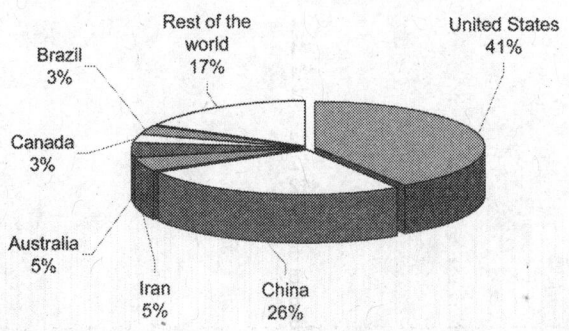

Figure 53: Major aviation gasolene consuming countries in 2006

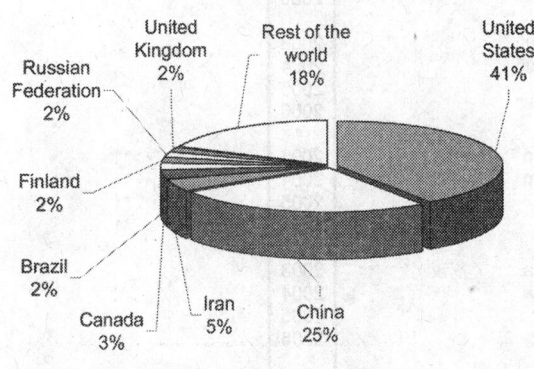

Table 18

Production, trade and consumption of aviation gasolene
Productiom, commerce et consommation d'essence aviation

Thousand metric tons
Milliers de tonnes métriques

Country or area Pays ou zone	Year Année	Production Production	Imports Importations	Exports Exportations	Bunkers Soutes	Changes in stocks Variations des stocks	Consumption Consommation
World	2003	1621	387	231	160	5	1612
Monde	2004	1775	531	200	155	-10	1961
	2005	1778	494	182	152	23	1915
	2006	1808	440	196	164	6	1882
Africa	2003	104	136	69	90	..	81
Afrique	2004	67	138	36	88	..	81
	2005	59	135	35	86	..	73
	2006	81	123	37	95	..	72
Algeria	2003	*32	..	32	..	..	0
Algérie	2004	25	..	25	..	..	0
	2005	*25	..	*25	..	..	0
	2006	*27	..	*27	..	..	0
Burkina Faso	2003	..	*5	..	..	..	*5
Burkina Faso	2004	..	*5	..	..	..	*5
	2005	..	*5	..	..	..	*5
	2006	..	*5	..	..	..	*5
Central African Rep.	2003	..	*1	..	*1	..	0
Rép. centrafricaine	2004	..	*1	..	*1	..	0
	2005	..	*1	..	*1	..	0
	2006	..	*1	..	*1	..	0
Chad	2003	..	*5	..	*5	..	0
Tchad	2004	..	*5	..	*5	..	0
	2005	..	*5	..	*5	..	0
	2006	..	*5	..	*5	..	0
Comoros	2003	..	*1	..	..	..	*1
Comores	2004	..	*1	..	..	..	*1
	2005	..	*1	..	..	..	*1
	2006	..	*1	..	..	..	*1
Côte d'Ivoire	2003	..	1	..	1	..	0
Côte d'Ivoire	2004	..	1	..	1	..	0
	2005	..	1	..	1	..	0
	2006	..	1	..	1	..	0
Dem. Rep. of Congo	2003	..	22	..	16	..	6
Rép. dem. du Congo	2004	..	22	..	16	..	6
	2005	..	22	..	16	..	6
	2006	..	22	..	16	..	6
Djibouti	2003	..	*1	..	*1	..	0
Djibouti	2004	..	*1	..	*1	..	0
	2005	..	*1	..	*1	..	0
	2006	..	*1	..	*1	..	0
Gabon	2003	*1	13	*1	12	..	1
Gabon	2004	*1	13	*1	12	..	1
	2005	*1	13	*1	12	..	1
	2006	*1	13	*1	12	..	1
Ghana	2003	..	5	..	5	..	0
Ghana	2004	..	*5	..	5	..	0
	2005	..	5	..	5	..	0
	2006	..	5	..	5	..	0
Guinea	2003	..	*16	..	*12	..	*4
Guinée	2004	..	*16	..	*12	..	*4
	2005	..	*16	..	*12	..	*4
	2006	..	*16	..	*12	..	*4

Table 18

Production, trade and consumption of aviation gasolene
Productiom, commerce et consommation d'essence aviation

Thousand metric tons
Milliers de tonnes métriques

Country or area Pays ou zone	Year Année	Production Production	Imports Importations	Exports Exportations	Bunkers Soutes	Changes in stocks Variations des stocks	Consumption Consommation
Kenya	2003	..	2	..	..	..	2
Kenya	2004	..	2	..	..	..	2
	2005	..	2	..	..	..	2
	2006	..	2	..	..	..	2
Liberia	2003	..	*6	..	*1	..	*5
Libéria	2004	..	*6	..	*1	..	*5
	2005	..	*6	..	*1	..	*5
	2006	..	*6	..	*1	..	*5
Libyan Arab Jamah.	2003	3	..	..	..	..	3
Jamah. arabe libyenne	2004	3	..	..	..	..	3
	2005	3	..	..	..	..	3
	2006	3	..	..	..	..	3
Madagascar	2003	..	*1	..	*1	..	0
Madagascar	2004	..	*1	..	*1	..	0
	2005	..	*1	..	*1	..	0
	2006	..	*1	..	*1	..	0
Mali	2003	..	*1	..	*1	..	0
Mali	2004	..	*1	..	*1	..	0
	2005	..	*1	..	*1	..	0
	2006	..	*1	..	*1	..	0
Mauritania	2003	..	24	..	..	..	24
Mauritanie	2004	..	26	..	..	..	26
	2005	..	26	..	..	..	26
	2006	..	17	..	..	..	17
Nigeria	2003	..	*2	..	*2	..	0
Nigéria	2004	..	*2	..	*2	..	0
	2005	..	2	..	2	..	0
	2006	..	*2	..	*2	..	0
Sao Tome and Principe	2003	..	*1	..	..	..	*1
Sao Tomé-et-Principe	2004	..	*1	..	..	..	*1
	2005	..	*1	..	..	..	*1
	2006	..	*2	..	..	..	*2
Senegal	2003	*15	*10	..	*20	..	*5
Sénégal	2004	*12	*12	..	*19	..	*5
	2005	*12	*10	..	*17	..	*5
	2006	31	*5	..	*25	..	11
Sierra Leone	2003	..	*6	..	*6	..	0
Sierra Leone	2004	..	5	..	5	..	0
	2005	..	*5	..	*5	..	0
	2006	..	*6	..	*6	..	0
South Africa Customs Un.	2003	53	6	36	..	..	23
Un.douan.d'Afr.mérid	2004	26	6	10	..	..	22
	2005	18	5	9	..	..	14
	2006	19	5	9	..	..	15
Western Sahara	2003	..	*2	..	*2	..	0
Sahara occidental	2004	..	*2	..	*2	..	0
	2005	..	*2	..	*2	..	0
	2006	..	*2	..	*2	..	0
Zambia	2003	..	3	..	*3	..	0
Zambie	2004	..	3	..	3	..	0
	2005	..	3	..	3	..	0
	2006	..	3	..	3	..	0

Table 18

Production, trade and consumption of aviation gasolene
Productiom, commerce et consommation d'essence aviation

Thousand metric tons
Milliers de tonnes métriques

Country or area Pays ou zone	Year Année	Production Production	Imports Importations	Exports Exportations	Bunkers Soutes	Changes in stocks Variations des stocks	Consumption Consommation
Zimbabwe	2003	..	1	..	1	..	0
Zimbabwe	2004	..	1	..	1	..	0
	2005	..	1	..	1	..	0
	2006	..	1	..	1	..	0
America, North	**2003**	**759**	**47**	**25**	**24**	**-15**	**772**
Amérique du Nord	**2004**	**797**	**65**	**26**	**25**	**6**	**805**
	2005	**793**	**140**	**23**	**28**	**2**	**880**
	2006	**831**	**86**	**23**	**28**	**-4**	**870**
Antigua and Barbuda	2003	..	*2	..	..	..	*2
Antigua-et-Barbuda	2004	..	*2	..	..	..	*2
	2005	..	*2	..	..	..	*2
	2006	..	*2	..	..	..	*2
Bahamas	2003	..	*4	..	*2	..	*2
Bahamas	2004	..	*4	..	*2	..	*2
	2005	..	*4	..	*2	..	*2
	2006	..	*4	..	*2	..	*2
Belize	2003	..	*3	..	*1	..	*2
Belize	2004	..	*4	..	*1	..	*3
	2005	..	*4	..	*1	..	*3
	2006	..	*4	..	*1	..	*3
Canada	2003	83	..	14	..	-1	70
Canada	2004	73	..	13	..	0	60
	2005	76	..	9	..	5	62
	2006	64	..	5	..	-5	64
Cayman Islands	2003	..	*3	..	..	..	*3
Iles Caïmanes	2004	..	*3	..	..	..	*3
	2005	..	*3	..	..	..	*3
	2006	..	*3	..	..	..	*3
Costa Rica	2003	..	3	1	..	0	2
Costa Rica	2004	..	2	0	..	-1	3
	2005	..	3	0	..	0	3
	2006	..	3	0	..	1	2
Cuba	2003	..	6	..	5	..	1
Cuba	2004	..	*7	..	*5	..	*2
	2005	..	6	..	6	..	0
	2006	..	5	..	5	..	0
Grenada	2003	..	*3	..	*3	..	0
Grenade	2004	..	*3	..	*3	..	0
	2005	..	*3	..	*3	..	0
	2006	..	*3	..	*3	..	0
Guadeloupe	2003	..	*10	..	*10	..	0
Guadeloupe	2004	..	*10	..	*10	..	0
	2005	..	*12	..	*12	..	0
	2006	..	*13	..	*13	..	0
Jamaica	2003	..	1	..	..	..	1
Jamaïque	2004	..	0	..	..	..	0
	2005	..	1	..	..	..	1
	2006	..	1	..	..	..	1
Martinique	2003	..	*3	..	*3	..	0
Martinique	2004	..	*4	..	*4	..	0
	2005	..	*4	..	*4	..	0
	2006	..	*4	..	*4	..	0

Table 18

Production, trade and consumption of aviation gasolene
Productiom, commerce et consommation d'essence aviation

Thousand metric tons
Milliers de tonnes métriques

Country or area Pays ou zone	Year Année	Production Production	Imports Importations	Exports Exportations	Bunkers Soutes	Changes in stocks Variations des stocks	Consumption Consommation
Mexico	2003	13	4	..	..	..	17
Mexique	2004	5	13	..	..	..	18
	2005	2	18	..	..	..	20
	2006	2	19	..	..	..	21
Netherlands Antilles	2003	16	..	10	..	..	6
Antilles néerlandaises	2004	21	..	13	..	..	8
	2005	22	..	14	..	..	8
	2006	26	..	18	..	..	8
United States	2003	647	5	..	..	-14	666
Etats-Unis	2004	698	13	..	..	7	704
	2005	693	80	..	..	-3	776
	2006	739	25	..	..	0	764
America, South	**2003**	**105**	**22**	**11**	**11**	**13**	**93**
Amérique du Sud	**2004**	**85**	**20**	**10**	**9**	**1**	**85**
	2005	**78**	**18**	**14**	**9**	**2**	**72**
	2006	**74**	**12**	**4**	**9**	**-1**	**75**
Argentina	2003	0	8	1	..	..	7
Argentine	2004	0	12	1	..	..	11
	2005	2	11	1	..	..	12
	2006	0	5	1	..	..	4
Bolivia	2003	2	..	..	..	..	2
Bolivie	2004	3	..	..	..	..	3
	2005	4	..	..	..	..	4
	2006	4	..	..	..	..	4
Brazil	2003	51	3	10	..	0	44
Brésil	2004	56	1	9	..	1	47
	2005	49	0	13	..	1	35
	2006	46	0	3	..	-4	47
Chile	2003	11	..	..	4	7	0
Chili	2004	6	..	..	4	1	1
	2005	5	..	..	4	1	0
	2006	7	..	..	4	3	0
Colombia	2003	17	..	..	..	..	17
Colombie	2004	16	..	..	..	..	16
	2005	14	..	..	..	..	14
	2006	13	..	..	..	..	13
Ecuador	2003	..	4	..	..	..	4
Equateur	2004	..	0	..	..	..	0
	2005	..	0	..	..	..	0
	2006	..	0	..	..	..	0
French Guiana	2003	..	*3	..	*1	..	*2
Guyane française	2004	..	*3	..	*1	..	*2
	2005	..	*3	..	*1	..,	*2
	2006	..	*3	..	*1	..,	*2
Paraguay	2003	..	0	..	..	..	0
Paraguay	2004	..	1	..	..	..	1
	2005	..	1	..	..	..	1
	2006	..	1	..	..	..	1
Peru	2003	..	1	..	..	..	1
Pérou	2004	..	1	..	..	..	1
	2005	..	1	..	..	..	1
	2006	..	1	..	..	..	1

Table 18

Production, trade and consumption of aviation gasolene
Productiom, commerce et consommation d'essence aviation
Thousand metric tons
Milliers de tonnes métriques

Country or area Pays ou zone	Year Année	Production Production	Imports Importations	Exports Exportations	Bunkers Soutes	Changes in stocks Variations des stocks	Consumption Consommation
Uruguay	2003	..	3	..	..	1	2
Uruguay	2004	..	2	..	..	-1	3
	2005	..	2	..	..	0	2
	2006	..	2	..	..	0	2
Venezuela(Bolivar. Rep.)	2003	24	..	..	6	5	13
Venezuela(Rép. bolivar.)	2004	4	..	..	4	0	0
	2005	4	..	..	4	0	0
	2006	4	..	..	4	0	0
Asia	**2003**	**328**	**30**	**..**	**19**	**5**	**334**
Asie	**2004**	**538**	**31**	**..**	**19**	**0**	**550**
	2005	**564**	**31**	**..**	**18**	**2**	**575**
	2006	**584**	**36**	**..**	**18**	**0**	**602**
China	2003	201	..	..	..	..	201
Chine	2004	417	..	..	..	..	417
	2005	446	..	..	..	..	446
	2006	477	..	..	..	..	477
Indonesia	2003	8	1	..	..	6	3
Indonésie	2004	4	0	..	..	0	4
	2005	4	0	..	..	2	2
	2006	3	0	..	..	0	3
Iran(Islamic Rep. of)	2003	*98	..	..	*5	..	*93
Iran(Rép. islamique)	2004	*100	..	..	*5	..	*95
	2005	*100	..	..	*5	..	*95
	2006	*90	..	..	*5	..	*85
Israel	2003	..	*10	..	*4	..	*6
Israël	2004	..	*10	..	*4	..	*6
	2005	..	*10	..	*4	..	*6
	2006	..	*10	..	4	..	*6
Japan	2003	12	..	..	..	..	12
Japon	2004	8	..	..	..	..	8
	2005	6	..	..	..	..	6
	2006	6	..	..	..	..	6
Jordan	2003	6	..	..	6	..	0
Jordanie	2004	6	..	..	6	..	0
	2005	6	..	..	6	..	0
	2006	6	..	..	6	..	0
Kazakhstan	2003	..	1	..	..	..	1
Kazakhstan	2004	..	1	..	..	..	1
	2005	..	1	..	..	..	1
	2006	..	1	..	..	..	1
Kuwait	2003	..	1	..	1	..	0
Koweït	2004	..	1	..	1	..	0
	2005	..	0	..	0	..	0
	2006	..	0	..	0	..	0
Lao People's Dem. Rep.	2003	..	*10	..	..	..	*10
Rép. dém. pop. lao	2004	..	*11	..	..	..	*11
	2005	..	*11	..	..	..	*11
	2006	..	*11	..	..	..	*11
Lebanon	2003	..	*3	..	..	..	*3
Liban	2004	..	*2	..	..	..	*2
	2005	..	*3	..	..	..	*3
	2006	..	*3	..	..	..	*3

Table 18

Production, trade and consumption of aviation gasolene
Productiom, commerce et consommation d'essence aviation
Thousand metric tons
Milliers de tonnes métriques

Country or area Pays ou zone	Year Année	Production Production	Imports Importations	Exports Exportations	Bunkers Soutes	Changes in stocks Variations des stocks	Consumption Consommation
Malaysia	2003	..	2	..	2	..	0
Malaisie	2004	..	2	..	2	..	0
	2005	..	2	..	2	..	0
	2006	..	2	..	2	..	0
Philippines	2003	..	1	..	..	..	1
Philippines	2004	..	3	..	..	..	3
	2005	..	3	..	..	..	3
	2006	..	3	..	..	..	3
Singapore	2003	..	0	..	..	..	0
Singapour	2004	..	0	..	..	..	0
	2005	..	0	..	..	..	0
	2006	..	5	..	..	..	5
Uzbekistan	2003	3	..	..	..	..	3
Ouzbékistan	2004	3	..	..	..	..	3
	2005	2	..	..	..	..	2
	2006	2	..	..	..	..	2
Yemen	2003	..	1	..	1	..	0
Yémen	2004	..	1	..	1	..	0
	2005	..	1	..	1	..	0
	2006	..	1	..	1	..	0
Europe	**2003**	**221**	**80**	**91**	**9**	**7**	**194**
Europe	**2004**	**207**	**90**	**102**	**5**	**-13**	**203**
	2005	**179**	**107**	**82**	**5**	**-2**	**201**
	2006	**155**	**142**	**72**	**4**	**11**	**210**
Belgium	2003	..	2	..	..	..	2
Belgique	2004	..	2	..	..	..	2
	2005	..	2	..	..	..	2
	2006	..	2	..	..	..	2
Bulgaria	2003	..	1	..	..	..	1
Bulgarie	2004	..	1	..	..	..	1
	2005	..	1	..	..	..	1
	2006	..	0	..	..	..	0
Croatia	2003	..	1	..	..	..	1
Croatie	2004	..	1	..	..	..	1
	2005	..	1	..	..	..	1
	2006	..	1	..	..	..	1
Czech Republic	2003	2	2	..	..	0	4
République tchèque	2004	0	2	..	..	-1	3
	2005	0	2	..	..	0	2
	2006	0	2	..	..	0	2
Denmark	2003	..	3	..	..	0	3
Danemark	2004	..	2	..	..	-1	3
	2005	..	2	..	..	0	2
	2006	..	3	..	..	1	2
Estonia	2003	..	0	..	..	..	0
Estonie	2004	..	0	..	..	..	0
	2005	..	6	..	..	..	6
	2006	..	3	..	..	..	3
Finland	2003	..	5	0	..	..	5
Finlande	2004	..	6	2	..	..	4
	2005	..	9	1	..	..	8
	2006	..	41	4	..	..	37

Table 18

Production, trade and consumption of aviation gasolene
Productiom, commerce et consommation d'essence aviation
Thousand metric tons
Milliers de tonnes métriques

Country or area Pays ou zone	Year Année	Production Production	Imports Importations	Exports Exportations	Bunkers Soutes	Changes in stocks Variations des stocks	Consumption Consommation
France incl. Monaco	2003	68	6	30	..	6	38
France y compris Monaco	2004	58	5	32	..	-7	38
	2005	44	9	32	..	-1	22
	2006	30	18	29	..	-1	20
Germany	2003	..	21	2	..	0	19
Allemagne	2004	..	17	1	..	-1	17
	2005	..	18	2	..	0	16
	2006	..	17	2	..	0	15
Hungary	2003	..	2	..	2	..	0
Hongrie	2004	..	3	..	1	..	2
	2005	..	3	..	*1	..	2
	2006	..	2	..	*1	..	1
Iceland	2003	..	1	..	..	..	1
Islande	2004	..	1	..	..	..	1
	2005	..	1	..	..	..	1
	2006	..	1	..	..	..	1
Ireland	2003	..	1	..	..	..	1
Irlande	2004	..	1	..	..	..	1
	2005	..	1	..	..	..	1
	2006	..	1	..	..	..	1
Italy and San Marino	2003	6	..	..	..	..	6
Italie y comp. St. Marin	2004	12	..	..	..	..	12
	2005	6	..	..	..	..	6
	2006	16	..	..	..	..	16
Lithuania	2003	..	1	..	..	..	1
Lituanie	2004	..	1	..	..	..	1
	2005	..	1	..	..	..	1
	2006	..	1	..	..	..	1
Netherlands	2003	57	0	51	..	2	4
Pays-Bas	2004	57	2	58	..	-2	3
	2005	52	0	39	..	-2	15
	2006	37	0	30	..	2	5
Norway,Svlbd.J.Myn. l	2003	..	2	0	..	..	2
Norvège,Svalbd,J.May	2004	..	3	0	..	..	3
	2005	..	3	3	..	..	0
	2006	..	2	0	..	..	2
Poland	2003	5	1	2	4	0	0
Pologne	2004	3	1	1	3	0	0
	2005	4	1	2	3	0	0
	2006	7	1	4	3	1	0
Portugal	2003	..	2	..	..	-1	3
Portugal	2004	..	3	..	..	1	2
	2005	..	3	..	..	0	3
	2006	..	2	..	..	-1	3
Romania	2003	2	0	1	..	-1	2
Roumanie	2004	3	0	0	..	0	3
	2005	1	2	0	..	0	3
	2006	1	1	0	..	0	2
Russian Federation	2003	37	..	..	..	..	37
Fédération de Russie	2004	37	..	..	..	..	37
	2005	37	..	..	..	..	37
	2006	37	..	..	..	..	37

Table 18

Production, trade and consumption of aviation gasolene
Productiom, commerce et consommation d'essence aviation
Thousand metric tons
Milliers de tonnes métriques

Country or area Pays ou zone	Year Année	Production Production	Imports Importations	Exports Exportations	Bunkers Soutes	Changes in stocks Variations des stocks	Consumption Consommation
Slovakia	2003	..	0	..	..	..	0
Slovaquie	2004	..	1	..	..	..	1
	2005	..	12	..	..	..	12
	2006	..	3	..	..	..	3
Slovenia	2003	..	1	..	..	..	1
Slovénie	2004	..	1	..	..	..	1
	2005	..	1	..	..	..	1
	2006	..	1	..	..	..	1
Spain	2003	12	8	..	..	1	19
Espagne	2004	0	11	..	..	0	11
	2005	0	10	..	..	1	9
	2006	0	11	..	..	0	11
Sweden	2003	..	3	..	..	-1	4
Suède	2004	..	3	..	..	-1	4
	2005	..	3	..	..	-1	4
	2006	..	5	..	..	2	3
Switzerland	2003	..	5	..	..	0	5
Suisse	2004	..	4	..	..	0	4
	2005	..	4	..	..	-1	5
	2006	..	8	..	..	1	7
Ukraine	2003	6	..	..	..	..	6
Ukraine	2004	6	..	..	..	..	6
	2005	3	..	..	..	..	3
	2006	2	..	..	..	..	2
United Kingdom	2003	26	12	5	3	1	29
Royaume-Uni	2004	31	19	8	1	-1	42
	2005	32	12	3	1	2	38
	2006	25	16	3	0	6	32
Oceania	**2003**	**104**	**72**	**35**	**7**	**-5**	**139**
Océanie	**2004**	**81**	**186**	**26**	**9**	**-4**	**236**
	2005	**105**	**62**	**28**	**6**	**19**	**114**
	2006	**83**	**40**	**60**	**10**	**0**	**53**
Australia	2003	104	44	35	..	-2	115
Australie	2004	81	155	26	..	-6	216
	2005	105	33	28	..	19	91
	2006	83	6	60	..	0	29
Fiji	2003	..	3	..	*3	..	0
Fidji	2004	..	5	..	*5	..	0
	2005	..	2	..	*2	..	0
	2006	..	6	..	*6	..	0
French Polynesia	2003	..	*1	..	*1	..	0
Polynésie française	2004	..	*1	..	*1	..	0
	2005	..	*1	..	*1	..	0
	2006	..	*1	..	*1	..	0
Kiribati	2003	..	*1	..	*1	..	0
Kiribati	2004	..	*1	..	*1	..	0
	2005	..	*1	..	*1	..	0
	2006	..	*1	..	*1	..	0
New Zealand	2003	..	13	..	..	-3	16
Nouvelle-Zélande	2004	..	14	..	..	2	12
	2005	..	14	..	..	0	14
	2006	..	15	..	..	0	15

Table 18

Production, trade and consumption of aviation gasolene
Productiom, commerce et consommation d'essence aviation
Thousand metric tons
Milliers de tonnes métriques

Country or area Pays ou zone	Year Année	Production Production	Imports Importations	Exports Exportations	Bunkers Soutes	Changes in stocks Variations des stocks	Consumption Consommation
Palau	2003	..	*1	..	*1	..	0
Palaos	2004	..	*1	..	*1	..	0
	2005	..	*1	..	*1	..	0
	2006	..	*1	..	*1	..	0
Papua New Guinea	2003	..	*8	..	..	..	*8
Papouasie-Nvl-Guinée	2004	..	*8	..	..	..	*8
	2005	..	*9	..	..	..	*9
	2006	..	*9	..	..	..	*9
Solomon Islands	2003	..	*1	..	*1	..	0
Iles Salomon	2004	..	*1	..	*1	..	0
	2005	..	*1	..	*1	..	0
	2006	..	*1	..	*1	..	0

Table 19

Production, trade and consumption of motor gasolene
Production, commerce et consommation d'essence auto
Thousand metric tons and kilograms per capita
Milliers de tonnes métriques et kilogrammes par habitant

Table Notes:
Production from refineries and plants.

- **Please refer to the Definitions Section on pages xv to xxix for the appropriate product description/ classification.**

Notes relatives aux tableaux:
Production à partir des raffineries et des usines.

- **Veuillez consulter la section "définitions" de la page xv à la page xxix pour une description/classification appropriée des produits.**

Figure 54: World production of motor gasolene 1993-2006

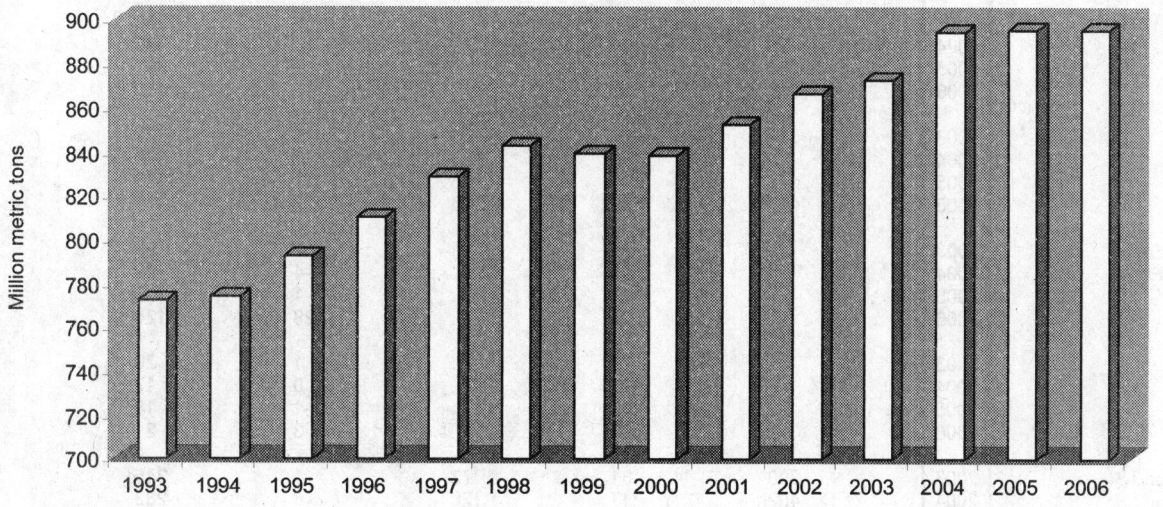

Figure 55: Major motor gasolene producing countries in 2006

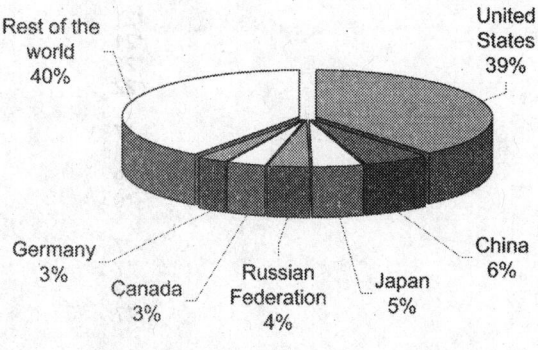

Figure 56: Major motor gasolene consuming countries in 2006

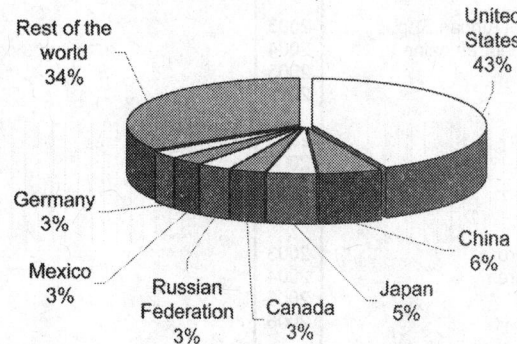

Table 19

Production, trade and consumption of motor gasolene
Production, commerce et consommation d'essence auto

Thousand metric tons and kilograms per capita
Milliers de tonnes métriques et kilogrammes par habitant

Country or area / Pays ou zone	Year / Année	Production / Production	Imports / Importations	Exports / Exportations	Changes in stocks / Variations des stocks	Consumption / Consommation Total / Totale	Per Capita / Par habitant
World	**2003**	**872360**	**121110**	**130699**	**-44**	**862815**	**138**
Monde	**2004**	**893725**	**137250**	**146164**	**2443**	**882368**	**139**
	2005	**895220**	**154244**	**155083**	**-2461**	**896842**	**140**
	2006	**895350**	**161808**	**155441**	**-1764**	**903480**	**139**
Africa	**2003**	**22575**	**9800**	**5489**	**659**	**26227**	**31**
Afrique	**2004**	**21343**	**10577**	**4812**	**-35**	**27143**	**31**
	2005	**18611**	**11250**	**2286**	**439**	**27136**	**31**
	2006	**20361**	**10857**	**2939**	**570**	**27709**	**30**
Algeria	2003	1893	..	12	-3	1884	59
Algérie	2004	1925	..	0	49	1876	58
	2005	2059	..	77	203	1779	54
	2006	2320	..	357	254	1709	51
Angola	2003	108	158	..	..	266	24
Angola	2004	96	254	..	..	350	31
	2005	134	247	..	..	381	33
	2006	98	352	..	..	450	38
Benin	2003	..	381	65	-5	321	40
Bénin	2004	..	450	123	2	325	40
	2005	..	401	45	21	335	39
	2006	..	570	176	23	371	42
Burkina Faso	2003	..	97	..	5	92	7
Burkina Faso	2004	..	94	..	-4	99	8
	2005	..	100	..	-1	100	8
	2006	..	96	..	-28	124	9
Burundi	2003	..	20	..	1	20	3
Burundi	2004	..	17	..	0	17	2
	2005	..	18	..	-1	18	2
	2006	..	25	..	3	21	3
Cameroon	2003	290	31	72	4	245	14
Cameroun	2004	402	17	128	8	283	16
	2005	393	0	115	-6	284	16
	2006	354	0	82	-16	288	16
Cape Verde	2003	..	*7	..	..	*7	*15
Cap-Vert	2004	..	*8	..	..	*8	*17
	2005	..	*9	..	..	*9	*19
	2006	..	*10	..	..	*10	*20
Central African Rep.	2003	..	*21	..	..	*21	*5
Rép. centrafricaine	2004	..	*21	..	..	*21	*5
	2005	..	*21	..	..	*21	*5
	2006	..	*22	..	..	*22	*5
Chad	2003	..	*7	..	..	*7	*1
Tchad	2004	..	*8	..	..	*8	*1
	2005	..	*9	..	..	*9	*1
	2006	..	*9	..	..	*9	*1
Comoros	2003	..	*7	..	..	*7	*11
Comores	2004	..	*7	..	..	*7	*11
	2005	..	*7	..	..	*7	*10
	2006	..	*7	..	..	*7	*10
Congo	2003	53	0	0	..	53	15
Congo	2004	49	14	5	..	58	17
	2005	47	20	0	..	67	19
	2006	53	31	0	..	84	23

Table 19

Production, trade and consumption of motor gasolene
Production, commerce et consommation d'essence auto

Thousand metric tons and kilograms per capita
Milliers de tonnes métriques et kilogrammes par habitant

Country or area Pays ou zone	Year Année	Production Production	Imports Importations	Exports Exportations	Changes in stocks Variations des stocks	Consumption Consommation	
						Total Totale	Per Capita Par habitant
Côte d'Ivoire	2003	359	27	268	*46	72	4
Côte d'Ivoire	2004	436	0	356	*5	75	4
	2005	494	59	438	*42	73	4
	2006	605	0	530	-64	139	7
Dem. Rep. of Congo	2003	..	103	..	..	103	2
Rép. dem. du Congo	2004	..	104	..	..	104	2
	2005	..	103	..	..	103	2
	2006	..	103	..	..	103	2
Djibouti	2003	..	20	..	..	20	26
Djibouti	2004	..	25	..	..	25	32
	2005	..	25	..	..	25	31
	2006	..	28	..	..	28	34
Egypt	2003	6306	26	3343	*415	2574	38
Egypte	2004	*5000	0	*2545	*-250	*2705	*38
	2005	2972	0	*76	0	2896	40
	2006	3659	0	373	0	3286	45
Equatorial Guinea	2003	..	*8	..	..	*8	*17
Guinée équatoriale	2004	..	*8	..	..	*8	*17
	2005	..	*8	..	..	*8	*17
	2006	..	*9	..	..	*9	*18
Eritrea	2003	..	18	..	1	17	4
Erythrée	2004	..	11	..	0	11	3
	2005	..	5	..	-2	7	2
	2006	..	4	..	-1	5	1
Ethiopia	2003	..	117	..	-63	180	3
Ethiopie	2004	..	129	..	-75	204	3
	2005	..	137	..	-11	148	2
	2006	..	148	..	3	145	2
Gabon	2003	69	3	24	5	43	33
Gabon	2004	68	0	26	-2	44	32
	2005	79	0	34	12	33	24
	2006	44	2	27	-17	36	25
Gambia	2003	..	*36	..	..	*36	*24
Gambie	2004	..	*37	..	..	*37	*24
	2005	..	*37	..	..	*37	*23
	2006	..	*38	..	..	*38	*23
Ghana	2003	434	232	104	..	562	27
Ghana	2004	580	185	151	..	614	28
	2005	567	168	204	..	531	24
	2006	294	360	100	..	554	24
Guinea	2003	..	*79	..	..	*79	*9
Guinée	2004	..	*79	..	..	*79	*9
	2005	..	*81	..	..	*81	*9
	2006	..	*82	..	..	*82	*9
Guinea-Bissau	2003	..	*19	..	..	*19	*15
Guinée-Bissau	2004	..	*19	..	..	*19	*15
	2005	..	*19	..	..	*19	*14
	2006	..	*20	..	..	*20	*15
Kenya	2003	263	118	43	..	338	10
Kenya	2004	275	136	69	..	342	10
	2005	266	192	67	..	391	11
	2006	179	313	45	..	447	12

Table 19

Production, trade and consumption of motor gasolene
Production, commerce et consommation d'essence auto

Thousand metric tons and kilograms per capita
Milliers de tonnes métriques et kilogrammes par habitant

Country or area Pays ou zone	Year Année	Production Production	Imports Importations	Exports Exportations	Changes in stocks Variations des stocks	Consumption Consommation	
						Total Totale	Per Capita Par habitant
Liberia	2003	..	*38	*1	..	*37	*11
Libéria	2004	..	44	*1	..	43	12
	2005	..	50	*1	..	49	14
	2006	..	*59	*1	..	*58	*16
Libyan Arab Jamah.	2003	1517	..	89	..	1428	230
Jamah. arabe libyenne	2004	1507	..	88	..	1419	221
	2005	1237	..	72	..	1165	176
	2006	1237	..	72	..	1165	174
Madagascar	2003	*113	*40	..	..	*153	*9
Madagascar	2004	*113	*40	..	..	*153	*9
	2005	*114	*41	..	..	*155	*9
	2006	*114	*41	..	..	*155	*8
Malawi	2003	..	89	..	..	89	8
Malawi	2004	..	*95	..	..	*95	*8
	2005	..	*90	..	..	*90	*7
	2006	..	*92	..	..	*92	*7
Mali	2003	..	66	..	..	66	6
Mali	2004	..	*66	..	..	*66	*6
	2005	..	*67	..	..	*67	*6
	2006	..	*67	..	..	*67	*6
Mauritania	2003	..	27	..	..	27	9
Mauritanie	2004	..	28	..	..	28	10
	2005	..	25	..	..	25	9
	2006	..	21	..	..	21	7
Mauritius	2003	..	87	..	-2	89	74
Maurice	2004	..	88	..	-2	90	74
	2005	..	87	..	-6	93	75
	2006	..	89	..	0	89	71
Morocco	2003	132	242	..	-1	375	13
Maroc	2004	257	111	..	-13	381	13
	2005	372	4	..	13	363	12
	2006	373	17	..	-12	402	13
Mozambique	2003	..	91	..	21	70	4
Mozambique	2004	..	91	..	24	67	3
	2005	..	77	..	-3	80	4
	2006	..	84	..	12	72	4
Niger	2003	..	58	..	..	58	5
Niger	2004	..	53	..	..	53	4
	2005	..	52	..	..	52	4
	2006	..	50	..	..	50	4
Nigeria	2003	1036	5404	10	..	6430	51
Nigéria	2004	534	5874	0	..	6408	50
	2005	275	6385	0	..	6660	50
	2006	993	5408	5	..	6396	46
Réunion	2003	..	*137	..	..	*137	*181
Réunion	2004	..	*140	..	..	*140	*183
	2005	..	*140	..	..	*140	*180
	2006	..	*140	..	..	*140	*176
Rwanda	2003	..	*34	..	..	*34	*4
Rwanda	2004	..	35	..	..	35	4
	2005	..	*37	..	..	*37	*4
	2006	..	*37	..	..	*37	*4

Table 19

Production, trade and consumption of motor gasolene
Production, commerce et consommation d'essence auto
Thousand metric tons and kilograms per capita
Milliers de tonnes métriques et kilogrammes par habitant

Country or area Pays ou zone	Year Année	Production Production	Imports Importations	Exports Exportations	Changes in stocks Variations des stocks	Consumption Consommation	
						Total Totale	Per Capita Par habitant
Sao Tome and Principe	2003	..	*6	..	..	*6	*42
Sao Tomé-et-Principe	2004	..	*6	..	..	*6	*41
	2005	..	*7	..	..	*7	*47
	2006	..	*7	..	..	*7	*46
Senegal	2003	151	8	48	6	105	10
Sénégal	2004	148	8	48	2	106	10
	2005	118	38	55	-5	106	10
	2006	46	63	49	0	60	5
Seychelles	2003	..	12	..	..	12	144
Seychelles	2004	..	30	..	..	30	369
	2005	..	13	..	..	13	160
	2006	..	10	..	..	10	118
Sierra Leone	2003	*31	*5	12	..	*24	*4
Sierra Leone	2004	*32	55	15	..	72	13
	2005	*32	*55	*17	..	*70	*12
	2006	*33	*50	*18	..	*65	*11
Somalia	2003	5	*30	..	..	*35	*5
Somalie	2004	5	*30	..	..	*35	*4
	2005	5	*30	..	..	*35	*4
	2006	5	*30	..	..	*35	*4
South Africa Customs Un.	2003	8360	962	923	..	8399	165
Un.douan.d'Afr.mérid	2004	8343	1238	732	..	8849	166
	2005	7858	1467	552	..	8773	164
	2006	7938	1504	558	..	8884	164
St. Helena and Depend.	2003	..	*1	..	..	*1	*136
St-Hélène et dépend	2004	..	1	..	..	1	135
	2005	..	*1	..	..	*1	*134
	2006	..	*1	..	..	*1	*133
Sudan	2003	1111	..	475	201	435	13
Soudan	2004	1228	..	525	218	485	14
	2005	1247	..	533	173	541	15
	2006	1712	..	546	489	677	19
Togo	2003	..	103	..	-2	105	21
Togo	2004	..	104	..	-5	109	21
	2005	..	110	..	-4	114	21
	2006	..	79	..	-8	87	16
Tunisia	2003	234	215	..	31	418	42
Tunisie	2004	226	199	..	8	417	42
	2005	216	217	..	13	420	42
	2006	178	160	..	-68	406	40
Uganda	2003	..	*155	..	..	*155	*6
Ouganda	2004	..	167	..	..	167	6
	2005	..	173	..	..	173	6
	2006	..	191	..	..	191	7
United Rep.Tanzania	2003	..	176	..	..	176	5
Rép. Unie de Tanzanie	2004	..	189	..	..	189	5
	2005	..	202	..	..	202	5
	2006	..	214	..	..	214	6
Western Sahara	2003	..	*6	..	..	*6	*23
Sahara occidental	2004	..	*6	..	..	*6	*22
	2005	..	*6	..	..	*6	*22
	2006	..	*6	..	..	*6	*22

Table 19

Production, trade and consumption of motor gasolene
Production, commerce et consommation d'essence auto

Thousand metric tons and kilograms per capita
Milliers de tonnes métriques et kilogrammes par habitant

Country or area Pays ou zone	Year Année	Production Production	Imports Importations	Exports Exportations	Changes in stocks Variations des stocks	Consumption Consommation	
						Total Totale	Per Capita Par habitant
Zambia	2003	110	40	..	..	150	14
Zambie	2004	118	39	..	..	157	14
	2005	126	38	..	..	164	14
	2006	126	46	..	..	172	15
Zimbabwe	2003	..	234	..	..	234	18
Zimbabwe	2004	..	216	..	..	216	17
	2005	..	172	..	..	172	13
	2006	..	164	..	..	164	12
America, North	**2003**	**406361**	**44995**	**19218**	**-572**	**432710**	**862**
Amérique du Nord	**2004**	**409008**	**50712**	**19328**	**1379**	**439013**	**866**
	2005	**407872**	**61954**	**20005**	**-932**	**450753**	**880**
	2006	**404041**	**65171**	**18630**	**364**	**450218**	**872**
Antigua and Barbuda	2003	..	*37	*5	..	*32	*400
Antigua-et-Barbuda	2004	..	*38	*5	..	*33	*407
	2005	..	*38	*5	..	*33	*399
	2006	..	*39	*5	..	*34	*404
Aruba	2003	..	*55	..	..	*55	*578
Aruba	2004	..	*55	..	..	*55	*563
	2005	..	*56	..	..	*56	*556
	2006	..	*56	..	..	*56	*545
Bahamas	2003	..	*79	..	..	*79	*248
Bahamas	2004	..	*81	..	..	*81	*270
	2005	..	*83	..	..	*83	*257
	2006	..	*84	..	..	*84	*257
Barbados	2003	..	96	..	..	96	353
Barbade	2004	..	92	..	..	92	338
	2005	..	96	..	..	96	351
	2006	..	98	..	..	98	357
Belize	2003	..	*144	..	..	*144	*526
Belize	2004	..	*145	..	..	*145	*513
	2005	..	*149	..	..	*149	*511
	2006	..	*149	..	..	*149	*490
Bermuda	2003	..	*25	..	..	*25	*397
Bermudes	2004	..	*26	..	..	*26	*411
	2005	..	*25	..	..	*25	*393
	2006	..	*25	..	..	*25	*392
British Virgin Islands	2003	..	*10	..	..	*10	*469
Iles Vierges britanniques	2004	..	*11	..	..	*11	*507
	2005	..	*11	..	..	*11	*500
	2006	..	*12	..	..	*12	*533
Canada	2003	33689	1985	6852	-36	28858	911
Canada	2004	33024	2810	6680	-5	29159	911
	2005	32270	3654	6865	-16	29075	900
	2006	30889	4624	5921	3	29589	906
Cayman Islands	2003	..	*24	..	..	*24	*551
Iles Caïmanes	2004	..	*24	..	..	*24	*542
	2005	..	*24	..	..	*24	*496
	2006	..	*25	..	..	*25	*481
Costa Rica	2003	0	515	..	-32	547	134
Costa Rica	2004	14	621	..	21	614	147
	2005	85	483	..	-18	586	137
	2006	105	516	..	14	607	139

Table 19

Production, trade and consumption of motor gasolene
Production, commerce et consommation d'essence auto

Thousand metric tons and kilograms per capita
Milliers de tonnes métriques et kilogrammes par habitant

Country or area Pays ou zone	Year Année	Production Production	Imports Importations	Exports Exportations	Changes in stocks Variations des stocks	Consumption Consommation	
						Total Totale	Per Capita Par habitant
Cuba	2003	412	0	..	..	412	36
Cuba	2004	331	51	..	..	382	34
	2005	407	25	..	..	432	38
	2006	317	134	..	..	451	40
Dominica	2003	..	15	..	..	15	214
Dominique	2004	..	12	..	..	12	171
	2005	..	*13	..	..	*13	*189
	2006	..	*13	..	..	*13	*191
Dominican Republic	2003	284	715	..	0	999	112
Rép. dominicaine	2004	445	640	..	0	1085	119
	2005	447	592	..	0	1039	113
	2006	440	543	..	-12	995	106
El Salvador	2003	135	280	2	-3	416	63
El Salvador	2004	143	297	2	-3	441	65
	2005	112	292	6	-9	407	59
	2006	112	308	2	1	416	60
Greenland	2003	..	*15	..	..	*15	*266
Groënland	2004	..	*15	..	..	*15	*266
	2005	..	*15	..	..	*15	*266
	2006	..	*16	..	..	*16	*284
Grenada	2003	..	27	..	..	27	258
Grenade	2004	..	26	..	..	26	252
	2005	..	28	..	..	28	267
	2006	..	29	..	..	29	272
Guadeloupe	2003	..	*148	..	..	*148	*337
Guadeloupe	2004	..	*150	..	..	*150	*337
	2005	..	*154	..	..	*154	*346
	2006	..	*157	..	..	*157	*343
Guatemala	2003	0	791	0	0	791	65
Guatemala	2004	0	817	0	24	793	64
	2005	1	829	2	3	825	65
	2006	1	882	11	8	863	66
Haiti	2003	..	108	..	..	108	13
Haïti	2004	..	111	..	..	111	13
	2005	..	114	..	..	114	13
	2006	..	119	..	..	119	14
Honduras	2003	..	315	..	-4	319	46
Honduras	2004	..	305	..	0	305	43
	2005	..	333	..	9	324	45
	2006	..	340	..	0	340	46
Jamaica	2003	111	376	..	-31	518	195
Jamaïque	2004	95	467	..	11	551	206
	2005	52	435	..	-10	497	187
	2006	124	388	..	-8	520	195
Martinique	2003	*161	*8	*46	..	*123	*315
Martinique	2004	*163	*9	*46	..	*126	*320
	2005	*164	*10	*46	..	*128	*322
	2006	*164	*14	*46	..	*132	*330
Mexico	2003	18587	5135	2745	-439	21416	210
Mexique	2004	19855	6951	2962	9	23835	231
	2005	20399	9348	3061	88	26598	256
	2006	20658	10493	3356	-77	27872	266

Table 19

Production, trade and consumption of motor gasolene
Production, commerce et consommation d'essence auto

Thousand metric tons and kilograms per capita
Milliers de tonnes métriques et kilogrammes par habitant

Country or area Pays ou zone	Year Année	Production Production	Imports Importations	Exports Exportations	Changes in stocks Variations des stocks	Consumption Consommation	
						Total Totale	Per Capita Par habitant
Montserrat	2003	..	*10	..	..	*10	*1112
Montserrat	2004	..	*10	..	..	*10	*1082
	2005	..	*10	..	..	*10	*1071
	2006	..	*10	..	..	*10	*1059
Netherlands Antilles	2003	1412	395	1687	..	120	672
Antilles néerlandaises	2004	1788	399	2066	..	121	661
	2005	1925	405	2207	..	123	664
	2006	1524	412	1811	..	125	660
Nicaragua	2003	96	73	..	-7	176	33
Nicaragua	2004	99	86	..	4	181	34
	2005	87	92	..	-5	184	34
	2006	91	104	..	0	195	35
Panama	2003	..	381	4	-26	403	129
Panama	2004	..	319	0	-106	425	134
	2005	..	400	0	0	400	124
	2006	..	430	0	0	430	131
St. Kitts-Nevis	2003	..	*10	..	..	*10	*225
St-Kitts-Nevis	2004	..	*10	..	..	*10	*227
	2005	..	*11	..	..	*11	*256
	2006	..	*11	..	..	*11	*256
St. Lucia	2003	..	*39	..	..	*39	*240
St-Lucie	2004	..	*41	..	..	*41	*253
	2005	..	*42	..	..	*42	*255
	2006	..	*43	..	..	*43	*258
St. Pierre-Miquelon	2003	..	*4	..	..	*4	*571
St-Pierre-Miquelon	2004	..	*4	..	..	*4	*571
	2005	..	*4	..	..	*4	*570
	2006	..	*4	..	..	*4	*569
St. Vincent-Grenadines	2003	..	*18	..	..	*18	*171
St. Vincent-Grenadines	2004	..	*17	..	..	*17	*163
	2005	..	*16	..	..	*16	*154
	2006	..	*16	..	..	*16	*155
Trinidad and Tobago	2003	1216	253	1117	239	113	86
Trinité-et-Tobago	2004	1096	181	824	286	167	127
	2005	1350	103	1108	88	257	194
	2006	1388	65	1045	0	408	307
United States	2003	350258	32909	6760	-233	376640	1295
Etats-Unis	2004	351954	35890	6743	1137	379964	1294
	2005	350574	44064	6705	-1061	388994	1312
	2006	348229	45013	6433	435	386374	1295
America, South	**2003**	**41760**	**1859**	**9596**	**535**	**33488**	**92**
Amérique du Sud	**2004**	**45264**	**1513**	**13709**	**541**	**32526**	**89**
	2005	**48020**	**1986**	**14205**	**483**	**35318**	**95**
	2006	**46702**	**1857**	**11352**	**452**	**36755**	**97**
Argentina	2003	4636	6	2265	66	2311	61
Argentine	2004	4018	18	2015	18	2003	52
	2005	4348	11	2169	-3	2193	57
	2006	4305	13	1472	-37	2883	74
Bolivia	2003	406	42	113	0	335	37
Bolivie	2004	455	0	327	0	128	14
	2005	430	0	0	0	430	46
	2006	500	0	46	13	441	46

Table 19

Production, trade and consumption of motor gasolene
Production, commerce et consommation d'essence auto

Thousand metric tons and kilograms per capita
Milliers de tonnes métriques et kilogrammes par habitant

Country or area Pays ou zone	Year Année	Production Production	Imports Importations	Exports Exportations	Changes in stocks Variations des stocks	Consumption Consommation	
						Total Totale	Per Capita Par habitant
Brazil	2003	13477	134	1983	-10	11638	65
Brésil	2004	13738	41	1492	1	12286	68
	2005	14337	53	1985	107	12298	67
	2006	14981	21	1997	-72	13077	70
Chile	2003	2265	455	679	-41	2082	131
Chili	2004	2384	441	701	-8	2132	132
	2005	2257	560	647	89	2081	128
	2006	2482	541	734	210	2079	127
Colombia	2003	4756	215	846	158	3967	89
Colombie	2004	4963	49	498	92	4422	98
	2005	4252	103	713	-81	3722	81
	2006	3618	1	377	-216	3458	74
Ecuador	2003	1516	559	303	0	1772	138
Equateur	2004	895	538	159	152	1122	86
	2005	1615	710	0	0	2325	176
	2006	1226	726	0	0	1952	146
Falkland Is. (Malvinas)	2003	..	*1	..	..	*1	*341
Iles Falkland (Malvinas)	2004	..	*1	..	..	*1	*340
	2005	..	*1	..	..	*1	*339
	2006	..	*1	..	..	*1	*338
French Guiana	2003	..	*35	..	..	*35	*193
Guyane française	2004	..	*35	..	..	*35	*183
	2005	..	*35	..	..	*35	*179
	2006	..	*36	..	..	*36	*183
Guyana	2003	..	85	..	..	85	112
Guyana	2004	..	97	..	..	97	129
	2005	..	100	..	..	100	133
	2006	..	100	..	..	100	132
Paraguay	2003	10	171	..	-7	188	33
Paraguay	2004	8	150	..	-5	163	28
	2005	4	162	..	0	166	28
	2006	0	187	..	4	183	30
Peru	2003	1470	37	253	326	928	35
Pérou	2004	1744	41	551	309	925	34
	2005	2220	96	1037	362	917	34
	2006	2208	85	858	540	895	33
Suriname	2003	..	78	..	..	78	161
Suriname	2004	..	80	..	..	80	162
	2005	..	83	..	..	83	166
	2006	..	84	..	..	84	167
Uruguay	2003	321	42	114	47	202	59
Uruguay	2004	503	22	330	-18	213	65
	2005	447	72	296	9	214	65
	2006	396	62	221	10	227	68
Venezuela(Bolivar. Rep.)	2003	12903	..	3040	-4	9867	384
Venezuela(Rép. bolivar.)	2004	16555	..	7636	0	8919	341
	2005	18110	..	7358	0	10752	405
	2006	16986	..	5647	0	11339	419
Asia	**2003**	**193697**	**29397**	**31378**	**-1180**	**192896**	**51**
Asie	**2004**	**203143**	**39762**	**34446**	**611**	**207848**	**54**
	2005	**206205**	**41424**	**37871**	**-2944**	**212703**	**55**
	2006	**209617**	**44375**	**37053**	**-2888**	**219827**	**56**

Table 19

Production, trade and consumption of motor gasolene
Production, commerce et consommation d'essence auto

Thousand metric tons and kilograms per capita
Milliers de tonnes métriques et kilogrammes par habitant

Country or area Pays ou zone	Year Année	Production Production	Imports Importations	Exports Exportations	Changes in stocks Variations des stocks	Consumption Consommation	
						Total Totale	Per Capita Par habitant
Afghanistan	2003	..	75	..	..	75	3
Afghanistan	2004	..	36	..	..	36	2
	2005	..	*38	..	..	*38	*2
	2006	..	*38	..	..	*38	*2
Armenia	2003	..	192	..	..	192	51
Arménie	2004	..	190	..	..	190	59
	2005	..	184	..	..	184	57
	2006	..	172	..	..	172	53
Azerbaijan	2003	720	..	259	10	451	55
Azerbaïdjan	2004	852	..	389	-6	469	56
	2005	906	..	323	7	576	69
	2006	1043	..	337	-14	720	85
Bahrain	2003	810	..	418	-37	429	622
Bahreïn	2004	755	..	280	7	468	662
	2005	789	..	422	-169	536	740
	2006	766	..	409	-192	549	739
Bangladesh	2003	150	140	..	-9	299	2
Bangladesh	2004	136	148	..	13	271	2
	2005	145	167	..	23	289	2
	2006	140	166	..	-2	308	2
Bhutan	2003	..	*7	..	..	*7	*11
Bhoutan	2004	..	*8	..	..	*8	*13
	2005	..	*8	..	..	*8	*13
	2006	..	*8	..	..	*8	*12
Brunei Darussalam	2003	202	0	..	4	198	566
Brunéi Darussalam	2004	201	0	..	-1	202	562
	2005	196	9	..	0	205	554
	2006	209	0	..	2	207	540
Cambodia	2003	..	139	..	..	139	11
Cambodge	2004	..	143	..	..	143	11
	2005	..	160	..	..	160	12
	2006	..	152	..	..	152	11
China	2003	47909	..	7542	-357	40724	32
Chine	2004	52236	..	5407	274	46555	36
	2005	53884	..	5597	186	48101	37
	2006	55473	..	3505	75	51893	39
China, Hong Kong SAR	2003	..	501	42	-9	468	69
Chine, Hong-Kong RAS	2004	..	509	50	-7	466	69
	2005	..	493	38	3	452	66
	2006	..	468	42	-7	433	63
China, Macao SAR	2003	..	36	..	..	36	80
Chine, Macao RAS	2004	..	39	..	..	39	84
	2005	..	40	..	..	40	82
	2006	..	41	..	..	41	82
Cyprus	2003	146	110	..	-5	261	362
Chypre	2004	40	239	..	-6	285	387
	2005	0	331	..	4	327	431
	2006	0	335	..	29	306	397
Georgia	2003	..	328	0	..	328	76
Géorgie	2004	..	294	4	..	290	67
	2005	..	334	0	..	334	77
	2006	..	324	0	..	324	74

Table 19

Production, trade and consumption of motor gasolene
Production, commerce et consommation d'essence auto

Thousand metric tons and kilograms per capita
Milliers de tonnes métriques et kilogrammes par habitant

Country or area Pays ou zone	Year Année	Production Production	Imports Importations	Exports Exportations	Changes in stocks Variations des stocks	Consumption Consommation	
						Total Totale	Per Capita Par habitant
India	2003	10999	..	2906	..	8093	8
Inde	2004	11057	..	2897	..	8160	8
	2005	10502	..	2273	..	8229	8
	2006	12539	..	3696	..	8843	8
Indonesia	2003	8584	3211	101	..	11694	55
Indonésie	2004	8825	4849	30	..	13644	63
	2005	8325	5358	0	..	13683	62
	2006	8411	5516	0	..	13927	63
Iran(Islamic Rep. of)	2003	10730	4066	..	..	14796	223
Iran(Rép. islamique)	2004	10836	6118	..	..	16954	251
	2005	11394	6677	..	..	18071	264
	2006	12047	7400	..	..	19447	276
Iraq	2003	3097	0	301	0	2796	106
Iraq	2004	3278	1656	0	153	4781	176
	2005	3185	2631	0	149	5667	206
	2006	3233	2835	0	151	5917	205
Israel	2003	2231	651	741	..	2141	320
Israël	2004	2467	444	718	..	2193	322
	2005	2729	257	794	..	2192	316
	2006	2592	600	771	..	2421	344
Japan	2003	43140	1370	197	-15	44328	351
Japon	2004	42715	2140	82	52	44721	354
	2005	43259	1642	383	59	44459	352
	2006	42437	1666	234	-17	43886	348
Jordan	2003	667	39	..	91	615	118
Jordanie	2004	579	135	..	46	668	131
	2005	613	93	..	-1	707	129
	2006	675	68	..	-19	762	136
Kazakhstan	2003	1841	500	192	1	2148	144
Kazakhstan	2004	1928	802	321	38	2371	158
	2005	2359	746	667	24	2414	159
	2006	2345	707	201	94	2757	180
Korea, Dem.Ppl's.Rep.	2003	185	24	..	..	209	9
Corée,Rép.pop.dém.de	2004	188	23	..	..	211	9
	2005	159	19	..	..	178	8
	2006	122	14	..	..	136	6
Korea, Republic of	2003	8564	240	1587	35	7182	150
Corée, République de	2004	8850	133	2154	-21	6850	142
	2005	8654	6	1702	-53	7011	145
	2006	8707	0	2327	77	6303	131
Kuwait	2003	1355	560	28	..	1887	811
Koweït	2004	1931	107	28	..	2010	841
	2005	2812	0	701	..	2111	859
	2006	3023	0	797	..	2226	881
Kyrgyzstan	2003	27	196	0	..	223	44
Kirghizistan	2004	19	275	0	..	294	58
	2005	13	274	5	..	282	55
	2006	10	220	0	..	230	44
Lao People's Dem. Rep.	2003	..	*22	..	..	*22	*4
Rép. dém. pop. lao	2004	..	*24	..	..	*24	*4
	2005	..	*24	..	..	*24	*4
	2006	..	*24	..	..	*24	*4

Table 19

Production, trade and consumption of motor gasolene
Production, commerce et consommation d'essence auto

Thousand metric tons and kilograms per capita
Milliers de tonnes métriques et kilogrammes par habitant

Country or area Pays ou zone	Year Année	Production Production	Imports Importations	Exports Exportations	Changes in stocks Variations des stocks	Consumption Consommation Total Totale	Per Capita Par habitant
Lebanon	2003	..	1490	..	..	1490	380
Liban	2004	..	1263	..	..	1263	319
	2005	..	1273	..	..	1273	317
	2006	..	1225	..	..	1225	302
Malaysia	2003	4363	2399	42	-63	6783	271
Malaisie	2004	4496	3347	505	-31	7370	288
	2005	4040	3596	79	-12	7569	290
	2006	4270	3264	234	0	7300	274
Maldives	2003	..	12	..	..	12	42
Maldives	2004	..	18	..	..	18	62
	2005	..	19	..	..	19	65
	2006	..	23	..	..	23	77
Mongolia	2003	..	259	..	..	259	104
Mongolie	2004	..	270	..	..	270	107
	2005	..	255	..	..	255	100
	2006	..	280	..	..	280	109
Myanmar	2003	307	6	..	-16	329	6
Myanmar	2004	309	20	..	0	329	6
	2005	302	35	..	0	337	6
	2006	357	18	..	-2	377	7
Nepal	2003	..	51	..	..	51	2
Népal	2004	..	54	..	..	54	2
	2005	..	56	..	..	56	2
	2006	..	57	..	..	57	2
Occup. Palestinian Terr.	2003	..	76	..	..	76	22
Terr. palestiniens occup.	2004	..	98	..	..	98	27
	2005	..	110	..	..	110	29
	2006	..	*115	..	..	*115	*30
Oman	2003	642	185	..	-16	843	360
Oman	2004	593	380	..	0	973	403
	2005	618	405	..	0	1023	408
	2006	597	575	..	0	1172	455
Other Asia	2003	9317	169	2200	-282	7568	335
Autre Asie	2004	11179	95	3464	60	7750	342
	2005	11249	38	3594	-213	7906	348
	2006	11138	19	3430	20	7707	338
Pakistan	2003	1075	..	21	0	1054	7
Pakistan	2004	1326	..	1	5	1320	9
	2005	1195	..	5	0	1190	8
	2006	1218	..	89	-9	1138	7
Philippines	2003	1844	975	0	2	2817	35
Philippines	2004	1501	1401	40	40	2822	34
	2005	1629	1155	84	42	2658	31
	2006	1582	1114	44	-73	2725	31
Qatar	2003	1815	..	1184	..	631	861
Qatar	2004	1709	..	1094	..	615	792
	2005	1722	..	1006	..	716	881
	2006	1729	..	937	..	792	846
Saudi Arabia	2003	12600	1191	2357	67	11367	516
Arabie saoudite	2004	13605	1423	2916	73	12039	534
	2005	13400	1758	2327	78	12753	552
	2006	12025	3391	2160	-261	13517	571

Table 19

Production, trade and consumption of motor gasolene
Production, commerce et consommation d'essence auto

Thousand metric tons and kilograms per capita
Milliers de tonnes métriques et kilogrammes par habitant

Country or area Pays ou zone	Year Année	Production Production	Imports Importations	Exports Exportations	Changes in stocks Variations des stocks	Consumption Consommation	
						Total Totale	Per Capita Par habitant
Singapore	2003	3350	4674	7791	-504	737	176
Singapour	2004	3948	6941	10313	-131	707	167
	2005	4879	7129	14205	-2924	727	167
	2006	4699	7378	14129	-2822	770	172
Sri Lanka	2003	196	117	..	-15	328	17
Sri Lanka	2004	203	179	..	-2	384	20
	2005	161	259	..	-5	425	22
	2006	194	263	..	1	456	23
Syrian Arab Republic	2003	1262	..	394	..	868	49
Rép. arabe syrienne	2004	1338	..	300	..	1038	58
	2005	1257	..	0	..	1257	69
	2006	1345	..	9	..	1336	71
Tajikistan	2003	..	957	..	..	957	146
Tadjikistan	2004	..	1037	..	..	1037	155
	2005	..	1117	..	..	1117	163
	2006	..	1277	..	..	1277	179
Thailand	2003	6012	97	772	23	5314	83
Thaïlande	2004	6674	143	1012	97	5708	89
	2005	6428	0	1408	-26	5046	78
	2006	6331	0	1338	-32	5025	77
Timor-Leste	2003	..	*11	..	..	*11	*11
Timor-Leste	2004	..	*12	..	..	*12	*12
	2005	..	*12	..	..	*12	*12
	2006	..	*12	..	..	*12	*11
Turkey	2003	3837	447	1654	-85	2715	39
Turquie	2004	3479	759	1865	-42	2415	34
	2005	3609	619	1671	-116	2673	37
	2006	3659	850	1673	113	2723	37
Turkmenistan	2003	1321	..	559	..	762	162
Turkménistan	2004	1270	..	537	..	733	154
	2005	1313	..	555	..	758	157
	2006	1564	..	661	..	903	184
United Arab Emirates	2003	1498	1604	..	..	3102	874
Emirats arabes unis	2004	1746	1343	..	..	3089	821
	2005	1866	1355	..	..	3221	784
	2006	2626	754	..	..	3380	799
Uzbekistan	2003	1842	..	41	..	1801	70
Ouzbékistan	2004	1736	..	39	..	1697	65
	2005	1418	..	32	..	1386	52
	2006	1323	..	30	..	1293	48
Viet Nam	2003	..	2175	49	..	2126	26
Viet Nam	2004	..	2604	0	..	2604	32
	2005	..	2631	0	..	2631	32
	2006	..	2780	0	..	2780	33
Yemen	2003	1059	96	..	..	1155	61
Yémen	2004	1138	63	..	..	1201	62
	2005	1195	111	..	..	1306	65
	2006	1188	226	..	..	1414	69
Europe	**2003**	**193339**	**32661**	**64211**	**601**	**161188**	**222**
Europe	**2004**	**199860**	**32044**	**73279**	**-219**	**158844**	**218**
	2005	**199595**	**34144**	**80116**	**501**	**153122**	**210**
	2006	**200915**	**35619**	**84898**	**-274**	**151910**	**208**

Table 19

Production, trade and consumption of motor gasolene
Production, commerce et consommation d'essence auto
Thousand metric tons and kilograms per capita
Milliers de tonnes métriques et kilogrammes par habitant

Country or area Pays ou zone	Year Année	Production Production	Imports Importations	Exports Exportations	Changes in stocks Variations des stocks	Consumption Consommation	
						Total Totale	Per Capita Par habitant
Albania	2003	6	145	6	..	145	41
Albanie	2004	35	140	0	..	175	56
	2005	14	167	0	..	181	58
	2006	35	173	0	..	208	66
Austria	2003	1811	879	474	12	2204	273
Autriche	2004	1738	1043	614	11	2156	265
	2005	1798	1090	767	50	2071	252
	2006	1615	959	562	8	2004	242
Belarus	2003	1895	78	1035	0	938	95
Bélarus	2004	2842	32	1886	23	965	98
	2005	3330	1	2265	33	1033	106
	2006	3498	34	2477	-66	1121	115
Belgium	2003	5865	1121	4859	-54	2181	211
Belgique	2004	5789	1078	4991	-13	1889	182
	2005	5056	1623	4814	118	1747	167
	2006	5357	1188	5148	-69	1466	139
Bosnia and Herzegovina	2003	9	250	5	..	254	66
Bosnie y Herzégovine	2004	26	259	0	..	285	74
	2005	18	239	0	..	257	67
	2006	18	261	0	..	279	73
Bulgaria	2003	967	62	443	-3	589	75
Bulgarie	2004	1401	71	907	-2	567	73
	2005	1381	139	933	43	544	70
	2006	1560	263	1187	29	607	79
Croatia	2003	1261	88	631	-38	756	170
Croatie	2004	1226	136	609	30	723	163
	2005	1168	256	706	9	709	160
	2006	1083	306	680	-1	710	160
Czech Republic	2003	1344	984	184	49	2095	205
République tchèque	2004	1289	940	184	-26	2071	203
	2005	1467	802	162	72	2035	199
	2006	1594	621	293	-94	2016	196
Denmark	2003	2082	868	1012	-25	1963	371
Danemark	2004	1986	876	958	-26	1930	357
	2005	1919	1034	1054	32	1867	345
	2006	1987	915	1086	0	1816	334
Estonia	2003	..	296	..	-10	306	226
Estonie	2004	..	290	..	3	287	213
	2005	..	295	..	5	290	215
	2006	..	320	..	12	308	229
Faeroe Islands	2003	..	*14	..	..	*14	*292
Iles Féroé	2004	..	*14	..	..	*14	*290
	2005	..	*14	..	..	*14	*290
	2006	..	*14	..	..	*14	*290
Finland	2003	4304	422	2561	-10	2175	417
Finlande	2004	4321	361	2774	-16	1924	368
	2005	4061	335	2383	5	2008	383
	2006	4298	56	2414	24	1916	364
France incl. Monaco	2003	16804	957	6394	-82	11449	190
France y compris Monaco	2004	16926	195	7142	-497	10476	173
	2005	16305	1255	7711	329	9520	156
	2006	17214	1954	8308	-163	11023	180

Table 19

Production, trade and consumption of motor gasolene
Production, commerce et consommation d'essence auto

Thousand metric tons and kilograms per capita
Milliers de tonnes métriques et kilogrammes par habitant

Country or area Pays ou zone	Year Année	Production Production	Imports Importations	Exports Exportations	Changes in stocks Variations des stocks	Consumption Consommation	
						Total Totale	Per Capita Par habitant
Germany	2003	26449	5183	4153	611	26868	326
Allemagne	2004	26467	4106	5263	-598	25908	314
	2005	27240	3240	5706	280	24494	297
	2006	26576	2124	5597	-461	23564	286
Gibraltar	2003	..	22	..	..	22	786
Gibraltar	2004	..	23	..	..	23	821
	2005	..	24	..	..	24	857
	2006	..	23	..	..	23	797
Greece	2003	3653	749	942	-53	3513	319
Grèce	2004	3629	1059	1216	-11	3483	315
	2005	4058	1023	1261	-1	3821	344
	2006	4327	1002	1351	259	3719	334
Hungary	2003	1477	286	343	-7	1427	141
Hongrie	2004	1465	369	342	24	1468	145
	2005	1321	515	340	11	1485	147
	2006	1302	424	253	-42	1515	150
Iceland	2003	..	139	..	-6	145	501
Islande	2004	..	152	..	3	149	509
	2005	..	163	..	14	149	504
	2006	..	165	..	-4	169	555
Ireland	2003	639	1113	191	-29	1590	400
Irlande	2004	552	1190	122	82	1538	380
	2005	683	1010	176	-82	1599	387
	2006	634	1143	103	12	1662	392
Italy and San Marino	2003	20699	430	5197	-48	15980	277
Italie y comp. St. Marin	2004	20662	339	5751	118	15132	260
	2005	21189	322	7507	-119	14123	241
	2006	20967	193	7756	168	13236	225
Latvia	2003	..	322	0	-7	329	141
Lettonie	2004	..	418	76	5	337	146
	2005	..	413	67	8	338	147
	2006	..	561	126	42	393	172
Lithuania	2003	1882	1	1563	12	308	89
Lituanie	2004	2331	3	2062	-3	275	80
	2005	2462	25	2177	73	237	69
	2006	2163	87	2033	-63	280	82
Luxembourg	2003	..	573	1	5	567	1255
Luxembourg	2004	..	529	1	-2	530	1157
	2005	..	479	1	-8	486	1045
	2006	..	454	0	3	451	954
Malta	2003	..	70	..	..	70	175
Malte	2004	..	58	..	..	58	144
	2005	..	68	..	..	68	168
	2006	..	76	..	..	76	187
Netherlands	2003	15730	7821	13800	321	9430	582
Pays-Bas	2004	15539	7904	14743	211	8489	522
	2005	14234	9177	16253	17	7141	438
	2006	13794	10513	17308	80	6919	424
Norway,Svlbd.J.Myn. I	2003	3546	308	2411	-18	1461	319
Norvège,Svalbd,J.May	2004	3261	422	2168	-59	1574	342
	2005	3829	310	2509	33	1597	344
	2006	4134	193	2967	-2	1362	292

Table 19

Production, trade and consumption of motor gasolene
Production, commerce et consommation d'essence auto

Thousand metric tons and kilograms per capita
Milliers de tonnes métriques et kilogrammes par habitant

Country or area Pays ou zone	Year Année	Production Production	Imports Importations	Exports Exportations	Changes in stocks Variations des stocks	Consumption Consommation	
						Total Totale	Per Capita Par habitant
Poland	2003	3871	536	416	-54	4045	106
Pologne	2004	3978	601	444	40	4095	107
	2005	4117	606	696	47	3980	104
	2006	4155	602	636	63	4058	106
Portugal	2003	2732	55	782	8	1997	191
Portugal	2004	2551	130	805	-32	1908	182
	2005	2466	128	792	36	1766	167
	2006	2750	104	1270	-74	1658	157
Republic of Moldova	2003	..	203	..	9	194	54
Rép. de Moldova	2004	..	210	..	-2	212	59
	2005	..	216	..	2	214	60
	2006	..	193	..	-6	199	56
Romania	2003	3295	74	1725	75	1569	72
Roumanie	2004	3419	86	1963	21	1521	70
	2005	4237	61	2715	16	1567	72
	2006	4145	65	2791	-39	1458	68
Russian Federation	2003	29315	0	3922	-269	25662	178
Fédération de Russie	2004	30505	517	4219	352	26451	184
	2005	32011	8	5923	-164	26260	183
	2006	34368	7	6307	175	27893	196
Serbia	2003	617	0	147	..	470	44
Serbie	2004	821	151	0	..	972	92
	2005	770	252	0	..	1022	98
	2006	648	462	0	..	1110	106
Slovakia	2003	1597	246	1130	39	674	125
Slovaquie	2004	1670	215	1275	-20	630	117
	2005	1584	295	1187	42	650	121
	2006	1449	255	1090	1	613	114
Slovenia	2003	..	782	27	6	749	375
Slovénie	2004	..	718	30	22	666	334
	2005	..	729	62	12	655	327
	2006	..	700	75	-15	640	319
Spain	2003	9047	974	1888	-70	8203	195
Espagne	2004	10434	737	2588	18	8565	201
	2005	10152	743	2866	-10	8039	185
	2006	10038	575	3520	-1	7094	161
Sweden	2003	4309	1750	1963	6	4090	457
Suède	2004	4506	1801	2360	6	3941	438
	2005	4045	1789	1916	24	3894	431
	2006	4182	1734	2198	-84	3802	419
Switzerland	2003	1072	2689	0	-42	3803	518
Suisse	2004	1362	2389	1	32	3718	499
	2005	1268	2326	0	7	3587	481
	2006	1465	2003	0	-6	3474	464
T.F.Yug.Rep. Macedonia	2003	126	38	53	-15	126	62
L'ex-RY Macédoine	2004	146	32	58	-2	122	60
	2005	183	20	85	1	117	57
	2006	190	10	90	3	107	52
Ukraine	2003	4308	111	350	0	4069	85
Ukraine	2004	4394	275	393	92	4184	89
	2005	4609	575	496	-68	4756	101
	2006	3926	1098	274	8	4742	101

Table 19

Production, trade and consumption of motor gasolene
Production, commerce et consommation d'essence auto
Thousand metric tons and kilograms per capita
Milliers de tonnes métriques et kilogrammes par habitant

Country or area Pays ou zone	Year Année	Production Production	Imports Importations	Exports Exportations	Changes in stocks Variations des stocks	Consumption Consommation	
						Total Totale	Per Capita Par habitant
United Kingdom	2003	22627	2022	5603	288	18758	316
Royaume-Uni	2004	24589	2175	7334	-3	19433	326
	2005	22620	2377	6586	-366	18777	312
	2006	21443	3789	6998	29	18205	300
Oceania	**2003**	**14628**	**2398**	**807**	**-87**	**16306**	**503**
Océanie	**2004**	**15107**	**2642**	**590**	**166**	**16993**	**517**
	2005	**14917**	**3486**	**599**	**-8**	**17812**	**534**
	2006	**13714**	**3929**	**569**	**12**	**17061**	**504**
Australia	2003	13108	1223	771	-13	13573	682
Australie	2004	13453	1388	569	84	14188	704
	2005	13218	2288	566	0	14940	732
	2006	12153	2695	522	40	14286	690
Cook Islands	2003	..	5	..	..	5	272
Iles Cook	2004	..	5	..	..	5	246
	2005	..	5	..	..	5	248
	2006	..	*5	..	..	*5	*235
Fiji	2003	..	108	*17	..	91	110
Fidji	2004	..	94	*16	..	78	93
	2005	..	74	*16	..	58	69
	2006	..	83	*16	..	67	79
French Polynesia	2003	..	47	..	..	47	190
Polynésie française	2004	..	47	..	..	47	187
	2005	..	49	..	..	49	192
	2006	..	48	..	..	48	187
Kiribati	2003	..	*2	..	..	*2	*22
Kiribati	2004	..	*2	..	..	*2	*20
	2005	..	*2	..	..	*2	*19
	2006	..	*3	..	..	*3	*28
Nauru	2003	..	*5	..	..	*5	*398
Nauru	2004	..	*5	..	..	*5	*390
	2005	..	*5	..	..	*5	*383
	2006	..	*5	..	..	*5	*376
New Caledonia	2003	..	68	6	..	62	272
Nouvelle-Calédonie	2004	..	63	5	..	58	251
	2005	..	57	*5	..	52	222
	2006	..	49	*4	..	45	189
New Zealand	2003	1520	776	13	-74	2357	588
Nouvelle-Zélande	2004	1627	873	0	82	2418	595
	2005	1645	839	12	-8	2480	605
	2006	1482	872	0	-28	2382	575
Palau	2003	..	*24	..	..	*24	*1182
Palaos	2004	..	*24	..	..	*24	*1164
	2005	..	*24	..	..	*24	*1148
	2006	..	*24	..	..	*24	*1108
Papua New Guinea	2003	0	89	0	..	89	15
Papouasie-Nvl-Guinée	2004	27	89	0	..	116	20
	2005	54	90	0	..	144	24
	2006	79	90	27	..	142	23
Samoa	2003	..	*18	..	..	*18	*100
Samoa	2004	..	*19	..	..	*19	*105
	2005	..	*19	..	..	*19	*104
	2006	..	*19	..	..	*19	*103

Table 19

Production, trade and consumption of motor gasolene
Production, commerce et consommation d'essence auto
Thousand metric tons and kilograms per capita
Milliers de tonnes métriques et kilogrammes par habitant

Country or area Pays ou zone	Year Année	Production Production	Imports Importations	Exports Exportations	Changes in stocks Variations des stocks	Consumption Consommation	
						Total Totale	Per Capita Par habitant
Solomon Islands	2003	..	*11	..	..	*11	*25
Iles Salomon	2004	..	*12	..	..	*12	*26
	2005	..	*12	..	..	*12	*25
	2006	..	*13	..	..	*13	*27
Tonga	2003	..	14	..	..	14	139
Tonga	2004	..	13	..	..	13	127
	2005	..	*14	..	..	*14	*137
	2006	..	*14	..	..	*14	*138
Vanuatu	2003	..	*6	..	..	*6	*28
Vanuatu	2004	..	*6	..	..	*6	*28
	2005	..	*6	..	..	*6	*28
	2006	..	*7	..	..	*7	*32
Wallis and Futuna Is	2003	..	*2	..	..	*2	*138
Iles Wallis et Futuna	2004	..	2	..	..	2	131
	2005	..	2	..	..	2	120
	2006	..	2	..	..	2	111

Table 20

Production, trade and consumption of kerosene
Production, commerce et consommation de pétrole lampant

Thousand metric tons and kilograms per capita
Milliers de tonnes métriques et kilogrammes par habitant

Table Notes:
Production from refineries and plants.

- **Please refer to the Definitions Section on pages xv to xxix for the appropriate product description/ classification.**

Notes relatives aux tableaux:
Production à partir des raffineries et des usines.

- **Veuillez consulter la section "définitions" de la page xv à la page xxix pour une description/classification appropriée des produits.**

Figure 57: World production of kerosene 1993-2006

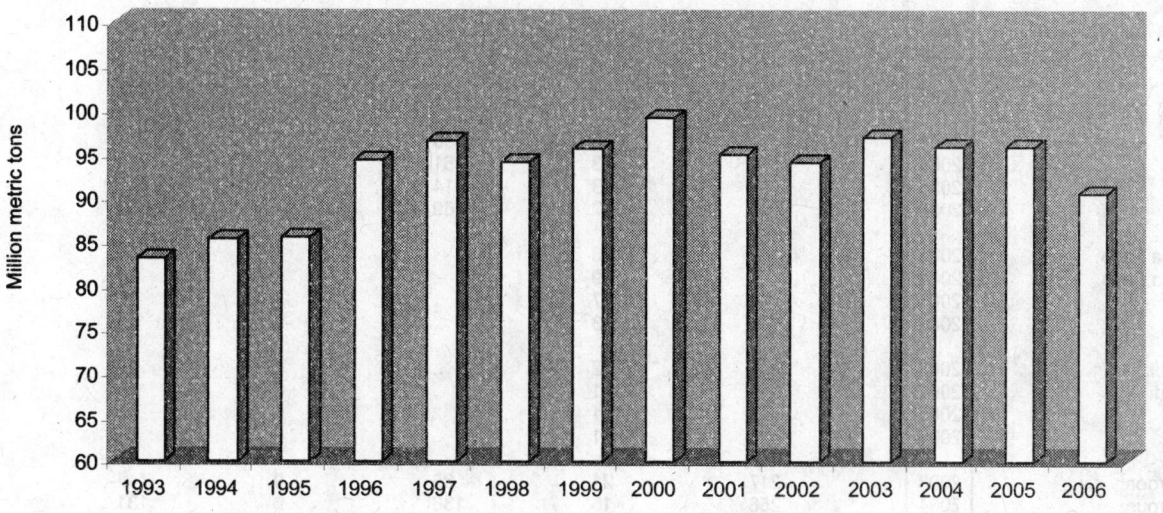

Figure 58: Major kerosene producing countries in 2006

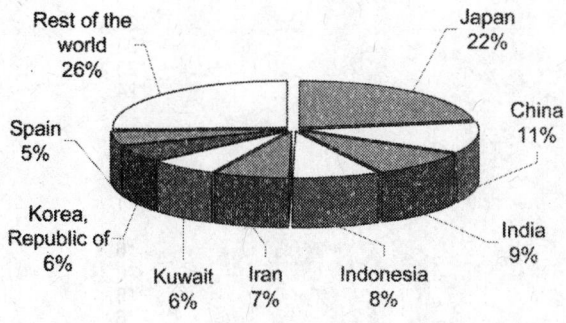

Figure 59: Major kerosene consuming countries in 2006

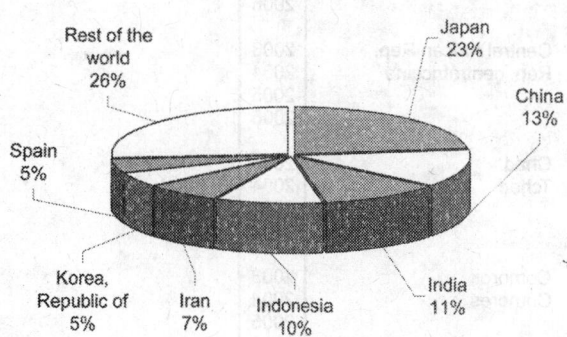

Table 20

Production, trade and consumption of kerosene
Production, commerce et consommation de pétrole lampant

Thousand metric tons and kilograms per capita
Milliers de tonnes métriques et kilogrammes par habitant

Country or area Pays ou zone	Year Année	Production Production	Imports Importations	Exports Exportations	Changes in stocks Variations des stocks	Consumption Consommation	
						Total Totale	Per Capita Per habitant
World	2003	96940	16289	19713	241	93275	15
Monde	2004	95433	14323	16362	260	93134	15
	2005	95666	15276	18637	556	91748	14
	2006	90571	17952	19176	785	88562	14
Africa	2003	3838	2366	667	28	5509	7
Afrique	2004	3423	2193	809	-150	4957	6
	2005	3525	2029	935	35	4583	5
	2006	3467	2913	1143	-47	5284	6
Algeria	2003	12	..	..	..	12	0
Algérie	2004	14	..	..	..	14	0
	2005	11	..	..	..	11	0
	2006	10	..	..	..	10	0
Angola	2003	32	217	..	..	249	22
Angola	2004	41	111	..	..	152	13
	2005	31	50	..	..	81	7
	2006	5	91	..	..	96	8
Benin	2003	..	256	38	7	211	27
Bénin	2004	..	303	51	2	250	30
	2005	..	273	14	-12	271	32
	2006	..	357	69	-14	302	34
Burkina Faso	2003	..	36	..	0	36	3
Burkina Faso	2004	..	29	..	1	28	2
	2005	..	17	..	-4	21	2
	2006	..	13	..	-9	23	2
Burundi	2003	..	2	..	0	1	0
Burundi	2004	..	1	..	0	0	0
	2005	..	1	..	0	1	0
	2006	..	1	..	0	1	0
Cameroon	2003	217	21	85	9	144	8
Cameroun	2004	258	15	136	6	131	8
	2005	352	0	245	-6	113	6
	2006	300	0	189	-8	119	7
Cape Verde	2003	..	*5	..	..	*5	*11
Cap-Vert	2004	..	*5	..	..	*5	*11
	2005	..	*5	..	..	*5	*10
	2006	..	*5	..	..	*5	*10
Central African Rep.	2003	..	*23	..	..	*23	*6
Rép. centrafricaine	2004	..	*23	..	..	*23	*6
	2005	..	*23	..	..	*23	*5
	2006	..	*24	..	..	*24	*6
Chad	2003	..	*1	..	..	*1	0
Tchad	2004	..	*1	..	..	*1	0
	2005	..	*1	..	..	*1	0
	2006	..	*1	..	..	*1	0
Comoros	2003	..	*6	..	..	*6	*9
Comores	2004	..	*6	..	..	*6	*9
	2005	..	*6	..	..	*6	*9
	2006	..	*6	..	..	*6	*9
Congo	2003	21	..	..	..	21	6
Congo	2004	19	..	..	..	19	5
	2005	13	..	..	..	13	4
	2006	12	..	..	..	12	3

Table 20

Production, trade and consumption of kerosene
Production, commerce et consommation de pétrole lampant

Thousand metric tons and kilograms per capita
Milliers de tonnes métriques et kilogrammes par habitant

Country or area Pays ou zone	Year Année	Production Production	Imports Importations	Exports Exportations	Changes in stocks Variations des stocks	Consumption Consommation	
						Total Totale	Per Capita Per habitant
Côte d'Ivoire	2003	638	10	415	*143	90	5
Côte d'Ivoire	2004	681	10	577	*20	94	5
	2005	714	12	627	*30	69	4
	2006	976	0	829	0	147	7
Dem. Rep. of Congo	2003	..	7	..	..	7	0
Rép. dem. du Congo	2004	..	7	..	..	7	0
	2005	..	7	..	..	7	0
	2006	..	7	..	..	7	0
Djibouti	2003	..	*14	..	..	*14	*18
Djibouti	2004	..	*14	..	..	*14	*18
	2005	..	*14	..	..	*14	*17
	2006	..	*15	..	..	*15	*18
Egypt	2003	918	..	56	..	862	13
Egypte	2004	507	..	0	..	507	7
	2005	523	..	0	..	523	7
	2006	167	..	0	..	167	2
Equatorial Guinea	2003	..	*9	..	..	*9	*19
Guinée équatoriale	2004	..	*9	..	..	*9	*19
	2005	..	*9	..	..	*9	*19
	2006	..	*10	..	..	*10	*20
Eritrea	2003	..	23	..	2	21	5
Erythrée	2004	..	18	..	-3	21	5
	2005	..	17	..	-5	22	5
	2006	..	11	..	-2	13	3
Ethiopia	2003	..	215	..	-114	329	5
Ethiopie	2004	..	221	..	-151	372	5
	2005	..	223	..	-7	230	3
	2006	..	234	..	-9	243	3
Gabon	2003	21	8	..	4	25	19
Gabon	2004	19	6	..	2	23	17
	2005	26	5	..	7	24	17
	2006	20	3	..	5	18	13
Gambia	2003	..	*10	*1	..	*9	*6
Gambie	2004	..	*10	*1	..	*9	*6
	2005	..	*10	*1	..	*9	*6
	2006	..	*11	*1	..	*10	*6
Ghana	2003	67	49	..	..	116	6
Ghana	2004	24	49	..	..	73	3
	2005	25	49	..	..	74	3
	2006	65	49	..	..	114	5
Guinea	2003	..	*38	..	..	*38	*4
Guinée	2004	..	*38	..	..	*38	*4
	2005	..	*39	..	..	*39	*4
	2006	..	*39	..	..	*39	*4
Guinea-Bissau	2003	..	*7	..	..	*7	*6
Guinée-Bissau	2004	..	*7	..	..	*7	*5
	2005	..	*7	..	..	*7	*5
	2006	..	*7	..	..	*7	*5
Kenya	2003	88	215	27	..	276	8
Kenya	2004	95	254	0	..	349	10
	2005	92	307	0	..	399	11
	2006	118	328	0	..	446	12

Table 20

Production, trade and consumption of kerosene
Production, commerce et consommation de pétrole lampant
Thousand metric tons and kilograms per capita
Milliers de tonnes métriques et kilogrammes par habitant

Country or area Pays ou zone	Year Année	Production Production	Imports Importations	Exports Exportations	Changes in stocks Variations des stocks	Consumption Consommation	
						Total Totale	Per Capita Per habitant
Liberia	2003	..	*2	..	..	*2	0
Libéria	2004	..	2	..	..	2	1
	2005	..	2	..	..	2	1
	2006	..	*3	..	..	*3	*1
Libyan Arab Jamah.	2003	319	..	26	..	293	47
Jamah. arabe libyenne	2004	322	..	27	..	295	46
	2005	287	..	24	..	263	40
	2006	269	..	23	..	246	37
Madagascar	2003	*67	*15	..	..	*82	*5
Madagascar	2004	*67	*15	..	..	*82	*5
	2005	*68	*15	..	..	*83	*5
	2006	*68	*15	..	..	*83	*5
Malawi	2003	..	22	..	..	22	2
Malawi	2004	..	*23	..	..	*23	*2
	2005	..	*20	..	..	*20	*2
	2006	..	*20	..	..	*20	*2
Mali	2003	..	18	..	..	18	2
Mali	2004	..	*19	..	..	*19	*2
	2005	..	*19	..	..	*19	*2
	2006	..	*19	..	..	*19	*2
Mauritania	2003	..	1	..	..	1	0
Mauritanie	2004	..	1	..	..	1	0
	2005	..	1	..	..	1	0
	2006	..	*1	..	..	*1	0
Mauritius	2003	..	20	..	2	18	15
Maurice	2004	..	30	..	5	25	20
	2005	..	28	..	0	28	23
	2006	..	6	..	0	6	5
Morocco	2003	52	..	..	-3	55	2
Maroc	2004	12	..	..	-5	17	1
	2005	2	..	..	-3	5	0
	2006	3	..	..	1	2	0
Mozambique	2003	..	36	..	..	36	2
Mozambique	2004	..	37	..	..	37	2
	2005	..	34	..	..	34	2
	2006	..	28	..	..	28	1
Niger	2003	..	11	..	..	11	1
Niger	2004	..	11	..	..	11	1
	2005	..	7	..	..	7	1
	2006	..	3	..	..	3	0
Nigeria	2003	480	638	2	..	1116	9
Nigéria	2004	441	503	0	..	944	7
	2005	405	397	0	..	802	6
	2006	561	1172	8	..	1725	12
Réunion	2003	..	*70	..	..	*70	*93
Réunion	2004	..	*70	..	..	*70	*91
	2005	..	*70	..	..	*70	*90
	2006	..	*70	..	..	*70	*88
Rwanda	2003	..	*11	..	..	*11	*1
Rwanda	2004	..	12	..	..	12	1
	2005	..	*13	..	..	*13	*1
	2006	..	*14	..	..	*14	*2

Table 20

Production, trade and consumption of kerosene
Production, commerce et consommation de pétrole lampant
Thousand metric tons and kilograms per capita
Milliers de tonnes métriques et kilogrammes par habitant

Country or area Pays ou zone	Year Année	Production Production	Imports Importations	Exports Exportations	Changes in stocks Variations des stocks	Consumption Consommation	
						Total Totale	Per Capita Per habitant
Sao Tome and Principe	2003	..	*2	..	..	*2	*14
Sao Tomé-et-Principe	2004	..	*2	..	..	*2	*14
	2005	..	*3	..	..	*3	*20
	2006	..	*3	..	..	*3	*20
Senegal	2003	26	..	4	..	22	2
Sénégal	2004	19	..	3	..	16	2
	2005	19	..	6	..	13	1
	2006	5	..	2	..	3	0
Seychelles	2003	..	*5	..	..	*5	*60
Seychelles	2004	..	*5	..	..	*5	*61
	2005	..	*5	..	..	*5	*60
	2006	..	*5	..	..	*5	*59
Sierra Leone	2003	*10	*4	..	..	*14	*3
Sierra Leone	2004	*10	22	..	..	32	5
	2005	*10	*22	..	..	*32	*5
	2006	*11	*24	..	..	*35	*6
Somalia	2003	25	*3	..	..	28	4
Somalie	2004	25	*3	..	..	28	3
	2005	30	0	..	..	30	4
	2006	30	0	..	..	30	4
South Africa Customs Un.	2003	620	33	6	..	647	13
Un.douan.d'Afr.mérid	2004	633	24	6	..	651	12
	2005	618	24	9	..	633	12
	2006	624	24	9	..	639	12
St. Helena and Depend.	2003	..	*1	..	..	*1	*136
St-Hélène et dépend	2004	..	0	..	..	0	0
	2005	..	0	..	..	0	0
	2006	..	0	..	..	0	0
Sudan	2003	36	..	..	..	36	1
Soudan	2004	41	..	..	..	41	1
	2005	42	..	..	..	42	1
	2006	59	..	..	..	59	2
Togo	2003	..	61	..	..	61	12
Togo	2004	..	40	..	..	40	8
	2005	..	58	..	..	58	11
	2006	..	39	..	..	39	7
Tunisia	2003	165	..	..	-22	187	19
Tunisie	2004	169	..	..	-27	196	20
	2005	229	..	..	36	193	19
	2006	136	..	..	-11	147	15
Uganda	2003	..	*50	..	..	*50	*2
Ouganda	2004	..	40	..	..	40	1
	2005	..	47	..	..	47	2
	2006	..	55	..	..	55	2
United Rep.Tanzania	2003	..	132	..	..	132	4
Rép. Unie de Tanzanie	2004	..	141	..	..	141	4
	2005	..	151	..	..	151	4
	2006	..	160	..	..	160	4
Western Sahara	2003	..	*4	..	..	*4	*15
Sahara occidental	2004	..	*4	..	..	*4	*15
	2005	..	*4	..	..	*4	*15
	2006	..	*4	..	..	*4	*14

Table 20

Production, trade and consumption of kerosene
Production, commerce et consommation de pétrole lampant

Thousand metric tons and kilograms per capita
Milliers de tonnes métriques et kilogrammes par habitant

Country or area Pays ou zone	Year Année	Production Production	Imports Importations	Exports Exportations	Changes in stocks Variations des stocks	Consumption Consommation	
						Total Totale	Per Capita Per habitant
Zambia	2003	24	..	7	..	17	2
Zambie	2004	26	..	8	..	18	2
	2005	28	..	9	..	19	2
	2006	28	..	13	..	15	1
Zimbabwe	2003	..	56	..	..	56	4
Zimbabwe	2004	..	54	..	..	54	4
	2005	..	34	..	..	34	3
	2006	..	34	..	..	34	3
America, North	**2003**	**5162**	**987**	**719**	**32**	**5398**	**11**
Amérique du Nord	**2004**	**5651**	**803**	**522**	**-98**	**6030**	**12**
	2005	**5793**	**1070**	**483**	**103**	**6277**	**12**
	2006	**4839**	**1085**	**527**	**-247**	**5644**	**11**
Bahamas	2003	..	*58	..	..	*58	*182
Bahamas	2004	..	*59	..	..	*59	*197
	2005	..	*60	..	..	*60	*186
	2006	..	*61	..	..	*61	*187
Barbados	2003	..	3	..	..	3	11
Barbade	2004	..	3	..	..	3	10
	2005	..	3	..	..	3	10
	2006	..	3	..	..	3	10
Bermuda	2003	..	*17	..	..	*17	*270
Bermudes	2004	..	*18	..	..	*18	*280
	2005	..	*18	..	..	*18	*283
	2006	..	*18	..	..	*18	*282
British Virgin Islands	2003	..	*2	..	..	*2	*94
Iles Vierges britanniques	2004	..	*2	..	..	*2	*92
	2005	..	*2	..	..	*2	*91
	2006	..	*3	..	..	*3	*133
Canada	2003	1575	38	132	4	1477	47
Canada	2004	1519	14	88	-10	1455	45
	2005	1625	28	108	72	1473	46
	2006	1578	127	101	-59	1663	51
Costa Rica	2003	5	..	..	0	5	1
Costa Rica	2004	1	..	..	1	0	0
	2005	2	..	..	0	2	0
	2006	3	..	..	0	3	1
Cuba	2003	191	..	..	0	191	17
Cuba	2004	219	..	..	0	219	19
	2005	228	..	..	12	216	19
	2006	126	..	..	0	126	11
Dominica	2003	..	1	..	..	1	14
Dominique	2004	..	1	..	..	1	14
	2005	..	*1	..	..	*1	*15
	2006	..	*1	..	..	*1	*15
Dominican Republic	2003	190	123	..	0	313	35
Rép. dominicaine	2004	188	156	..	0	344	38
	2005	197	143	..	0	340	37
	2006	207	127	..	-2	336	36
El Salvador	2003	19	11	1	0	29	4
El Salvador	2004	21	11	1	0	31	5
	2005	22	11	1	0	32	5
	2006	16	14	0	-2	32	5

Table 20

Production, trade and consumption of kerosene
Production, commerce et consommation de pétrole lampant
Thousand metric tons and kilograms per capita
Milliers de tonnes métriques et kilogrammes par habitant

Country or area Pays ou zone	Year Année	Production Production	Imports Importations	Exports Exportations	Changes in stocks Variations des stocks	Consumption Consommation	
						Total Totale	Per Capita Per habitant
Grenada	2003	..	5	..	..	5	48
Grenade	2004	..	5	..	..	5	50
	2005	..	6	..	..	6	57
	2006	..	6	..	..	6	54
Guadeloupe	2003	..	*57	..	..	*57	*130
Guadeloupe	2004	..	*57	..	..	*57	*128
	2005	..	*59	..	..	*59	*132
	2006	..	*60	..	..	*60	*131
Guatemala	2003	..	44	..	0	44	4
Guatemala	2004	..	49	..	2	47	4
	2005	..	40	..	-1	41	3
	2006	..	42	..	1	41	3
Haiti	2003	..	61	..	..	61	7
Haïti	2004	..	75	..	..	75	9
	2005	..	75	..	..	75	9
	2006	..	77	..	..	77	9
Honduras	2003	..	44	..	14	30	4
Honduras	2004	..	44	..	0	44	6
	2005	..	46	..	0	46	6
	2006	..	70	..	0	70	10
Jamaica	2003	19	26	..	..	45	17
Jamaïque	2004	2	*6	..	..	*8	*3
	2005	12	22	..	..	34	13
	2006	12	22	..	..	34	13
Martinique	2003	*140	*1	*63	..	*78	*200
Martinique	2004	*142	*1	*63	..	*80	*203
	2005	*143	*1	*63	..	*81	*204
	2006	*143	*1	*63	..	*81	*203
Mexico	2003	67	..	..	2	65	1
Mexique	2004	306	..	..	-2	308	3
	2005	330	..	..	2	328	3
	2006	331	..	..	-2	333	3
Montserrat	2003	..	*1	..	..	*1	*111
Montserrat	2004	..	*1	..	..	*1	*108
	2005	..	*1	..	..	*1	*107
	2006	..	*1	..	..	*1	*106
Netherlands Antilles	2003	45	..	..	..	45	252
Antilles néerlandaises	2004	45	..	..	..	45	246
	2005	46	..	..	..	46	248
	2006	47	..	..	..	47	248
Nicaragua	2003	32	..	1	1	30	6
Nicaragua	2004	31	..	2	-2	31	6
	2005	28	..	0	2	26	5
	2006	36	..	2	8	26	5
Panama	2003	..	187	182	-8	13	4
Panama	2004	..	201	196	-6	11	3
	2005	..	215	210	0	5	2
	2006	..	221	215	0	6	2
St. Kitts-Nevis	2003	..	*9	..	..	*9	*202
St-Kitts-Nevis	2004	..	*9	..	..	*9	*205
	2005	..	*10	..	..	*10	*233
	2006	..	*10	..	..	*10	*233

Table 20

Production, trade and consumption of kerosene
Production, commerce et consommation de pétrole lampant

Thousand metric tons and kilograms per capita
Milliers de tonnes métriques et kilogrammes par habitant

Country or area Pays ou zone	Year Année	Production Production	Imports Importations	Exports Exportations	Changes in stocks Variations des stocks	Consumption Consommation	
						Total Totale	Per Capita Per habitant
St. Lucia	2003	..	*1	..	..	*1	*6
St-Lucie	2004	..	*1	..	..	*1	*6
	2005	..	*1	..	..	*1	*6
	2006	..	*1	..	..	*1	*6
Trinidad and Tobago	2003	6	..	..	..	6	5
Trinité-et-Tobago	2004	10	..	..	..	10	8
	2005	10	..	..	..	10	8
	2006	*10	..	..	..	*10	*8
United States	2003	2873	298	340	19	2812	10
Etats-Unis	2004	3167	90	172	-81	3166	11
	2005	3150	328	101	16	3361	11
	2006	2330	220	146	-191	2595	9
America, South	**2003**	**957**	**43**	**..**	**-94**	**1094**	**3**
Amérique du Sud	**2004**	**722**	**43**	**..**	**-6**	**771**	**2**
	2005	**614**	**45**	**..**	**59**	**599**	**2**
	2006	**373**	**53**	**..**	**-17**	**443**	**1**
Argentina	2003	28	..	..	..	28	1
Argentine	2004	29	..	..	..	29	1
	2005	24	..	..	..	24	1
	2006	23	..	..	..	23	1
Bolivia	2003	26	..	..	..	26	3
Bolivie	2004	19	..	..	..	19	2
	2005	22	..	..	..	22	2
	2006	21	..	..	..	21	2
Brazil	2003	157	..	..	0	157	1
Brésil	2004	92	..	..	0	92	1
	2005	41	..	..	-6	47	0
	2006	31	..	..	-4	35	0
Chile	2003	87	0	..	-33	120	8
Chili	2004	96	1	..	-11	108	7
	2005	89	0	..	-5	94	6
	2006	58	0	..	-14	72	4
Colombia	2003	116	..	..	..	116	3
Colombie	2004	122	..	..	..	122	3
	2005	122	..	..	..	122	3
	2006	128	..	..	..	128	3
Falkland Is. (Malvinas)	2003	..	*2	..	..	*2	*683
Iles Falkland (Malvinas)	2004	..	*2	..	..	*2	*680
	2005	..	*3	..	..	*3	*1017
	2006	..	*3	..	..	*3	*1015
French Guiana	2003	..	*21	..	..	*21	*116
Guyane française	2004	..	*21	..	..	*21	*110
	2005	..	*21	..	..	*21	*107
	2006	..	*22	..	..	*22	*112
Guyana	2003	..	15	..	..	15	20
Guyana	2004	..	15	..	..	15	20
	2005	..	16	..	..	16	21
	2006	..	21	..	..	21	28
Paraguay	2003	2	0	..	..	2	0
Paraguay	2004	3	0	..	..	3	0
	2005	2	0	..	..	2	0
	2006	0	2	..	..	2	0

Table 20

Production, trade and consumption of kerosene
Production, commerce et consommation de pétrole lampant

Thousand metric tons and kilograms per capita
Milliers de tonnes métriques et kilogrammes par habitant

Country or area Pays ou zone	Year Année	Production Production	Imports Importations	Exports Exportations	Changes in stocks Variations des stocks	Consumption Consommation	
						Total Totale	Per Capita Per habitant
Peru	2003	510	..	..	-62	572	21
Pérou	2004	329	..	..	5	324	12
	2005	282	..	..	70	212	8
	2006	83	..	..	0	83	3
Suriname	2003	..	5	..	..	5	10
Suriname	2004	..	4	..	..	4	8
	2005	..	5	..	..	5	10
	2006	..	5	..	..	5	10
Uruguay	2003	11	..	..	1	10	3
Uruguay	2004	9	..	..	0	9	3
	2005	9	..	..	0	9	3
	2006	8	..	..	1	7	2
Venezuela(Bolivar. Rep.)	2003	21	..	..	..	21	1
Venezuela(Rép. bolivar.)	2004	23	..	..	..	23	1
	2005	23	..	..	..	23	1
	2006	21	..	..	..	21	1
Asia	**2003**	**79703**	**11090**	**16956**	**309**	**73528**	**19**
Asie	**2004**	**76239**	**9186**	**13829**	**327**	**71268**	**19**
	2005	**76812**	**9732**	**15914**	**409**	**70221**	**18**
	2006	**72551**	**11256**	**16011**	**867**	**66930**	**17**
Afghanistan	2003	..	0	..	..	0	0
Afghanistan	2004	..	2	..	..	2	0
	2005	..	*2	..	..	*2	0
	2006	..	*2	..	..	*2	0
Armenia	2003	..	3	..	..	3	1
Arménie	2004	..	0	..	..	0	0
	2005	..	0	..	..	0	0
	2006	..	0	..	..	0	0
Azerbaijan	2003	133	..	..	..	133	16
Azerbaïdjan	2004	111	..	..	..	111	13
	2005	117	..	..	..	117	14
	2006	44	..	..	..	44	5
Bahrain	2003	581	..	535	12	34	49
Bahreïn	2004	315	..	339	-60	36	51
	2005	329	..	337	-46	38	52
	2006	320	..	313	-32	39	53
Bangladesh	2003	358	303	..	-17	678	5
Bangladesh	2004	324	348	..	-17	689	5
	2005	346	341	..	-17	704	5
	2006	335	275	..	-17	627	4
Bhutan	2003	..	*12	..	..	*12	*20
Bhoutan	2004	..	*13	..	..	*13	*21
	2005	..	*13	..	..	*13	*20
	2006	..	*13	..	..	*13	*20
Brunei Darussalam	2003	3	..	..	..	3	9
Brunéi Darussalam	2004	3	..	..	..	3	8
	2005	3	..	..	..	3	8
	2006	4	..	..	..	4	10
Cambodia	2003	..	42	..	..	42	3
Cambodge	2004	..	47	..	..	47	4
	2005	..	54	..	..	54	4
	2006	..	69	..	..	69	5

Table 20

Production, trade and consumption of kerosene
Production, commerce et consommation de pétrole lampant

Thousand metric tons and kilograms per capita
Milliers de tonnes métriques et kilogrammes par habitant

Country or area Pays ou zone	Year Année	Production Production	Imports Importations	Exports Exportations	Changes in stocks Variations des stocks	Consumption Consommation	
						Total Totale	Per Capita Per habitant
China	2003	8553	3174	2759	177	8791	7
Chine	2004	9622	2820	2050	-27	10419	8
	2005	10065	3283	2687	-35	10696	8
	2006	9755	5609	3711	49	11604	9
China, Hong Kong SAR	2003	..	60	8	0	52	8
Chine, Hong-Kong RAS	2004	..	58	5	1	52	8
	2005	..	37	5	0	32	5
	2006	..	28	4	0	24	3
China, Macao SAR	2003	..	6	..	1	5	11
Chine, Macao RAS	2004	..	6	..	0	6	13
	2005	..	6	..	0	6	12
	2006	..	6	..	-1	7	14
Cyprus	2003	38	0	..	5	33	46
Chypre	2004	11	0	..	-3	14	19
	2005	0	15	..	1	14	18
	2006	0	10	..	0	10	13
Georgia	2003	..	26	..	..	26	6
Géorgie	2004	..	26	..	..	26	6
	2005	..	26	..	..	26	6
	2006	..	43	..	..	43	10
India	2003	10187	926	..	..	11113	10
Inde	2004	9298	211	..	..	9509	9
	2005	9078	881	..	..	9959	9
	2006	8491	1424	..	..	9915	9
Indonesia	2003	7565	1997	..	..	9562	45
Indonésie	2004	7341	2362	..	..	9703	45
	2005	7131	2174	..	..	9305	42
	2006	7165	1491	..	..	8656	39
Iran(Islamic Rep. of)	2003	7339	..	448	..	6891	104
Iran(Rép. islamique)	2004	6830	..	178	..	6652	99
	2005	6214	..	95	..	6119	89
	2006	6308	..	80	..	6228	88
Iraq	2003	1064	0	114	..	950	36
Iraq	2004	1127	124	0	..	1251	46
	2005	1095	181	0	..	1276	46
	2006	1112	227	0	..	1339	46
Israel	2003	1118	404	404	..	1118	167
Israël	2004	1107	339	419	..	1027	151
	2005	1112	341	421	..	1032	149
	2006	1170	328	420	..	1078	153
Japan	2003	22031	1893	148	-80	23856	189
Japon	2004	22014	1052	126	-63	23003	182
	2005	22790	914	313	437	22954	182
	2006	20120	455	406	0	20169	160
Jordan	2003	191	..	..	-24	215	41
Jordanie	2004	162	..	..	-53	215	42
	2005	231	..	..	75	156	29
	2006	136	..	..	-19	155	28
Kazakhstan	2003	51	15	24	0	42	3
Kazakhstan	2004	50	38	27	0	61	4
	2005	41	33	9	0	65	4
	2006	53	19	6	-2	68	4

Table 20

Production, trade and consumption of kerosene
Production, commerce et consommation de pétrole lampant

Thousand metric tons and kilograms per capita
Milliers de tonnes métriques et kilogrammes par habitant

Country or area Pays ou zone	Year Année	Production Production	Imports Importations	Exports Exportations	Changes in stocks Variations des stocks	Consumption Consommation	
						Total Totale	Per Capita Per habitant
Korea, Dem.Ppl's.Rep.	2003	37	2	..	..	39	2
Corée,Rép.pop.dém.de	2004	37	2	..	..	39	2
	2005	31	1	..	..	32	1
	2006	24	1	..	..	25	1
Korea, Republic of	2003	8397	844	1698	119	7424	155
Corée, République de	2004	6599	178	994	-258	6041	126
	2005	5791	54	575	-240	5510	114
	2006	5410	43	609	316	4528	94
Kuwait	2003	4912	..	4867	..	45	19
Koweït	2004	4636	..	4590	..	46	19
	2005	6058	..	6030	..	28	11
	2006	5748	..	5719	..	29	11
Lao People's Dem. Rep.	2003	..	*20	..	..	*20	*4
Rép. dém. pop. lao	2004	..	*21	..	..	*21	*4
	2005	..	*21	..	..	*21	*4
	2006	..	*21	..	..	*21	*4
Lebanon	2003	..	1	..	..	1	0
Liban	2004	..	1	..	..	1	0
	2005	..	1	..	..	1	0
	2006	..	1	..	..	1	0
Malaysia	2003	952	35	953	-21	55	2
Malaisie	2004	572	3	453	17	105	4
	2005	513	114	665	*-50	13	0
	2006	536	99	320	0	315	12
Maldives	2003	..	5	..	..	5	18
Maldives	2004	..	8	..	..	8	28
	2005	..	1	..	..	1	3
	2006	..	4	..	..	4	13
Mongolia	2003	..	24	..	..	24	10
Mongolie	2004	..	23	..	..	23	9
	2005	..	19	..	..	19	7
	2006	..	41	..	..	41	16
Myanmar	2003	1	..	..	..	1	0
Myanmar	2004	1	..	..	..	1	0
	2005	1	..	..	..	1	0
	2006	1	..	..	..	1	0
Nepal	2003	..	299	..	..	299	12
Népal	2004	..	225	..	..	225	9
	2005	..	225	..	..	225	9
	2006	..	230	..	..	230	9
Occup. Palestinian Terr.	2003	..	4	0	..	4	1
Terr. palestiniens occup.	2004	..	8	0	..	8	2
	2005	..	5	1	..	4	1
	2006	..	*5	*1	..	*5	*1
Oman	2003	4	..	..	..	4	2
Oman	2004	5	..	..	..	5	2
	2005	11	..	..	..	11	4
	2006	16	..	..	..	16	6
Other Asia	2003	320	..	274	-15	61	3
Autre Asie	2004	216	..	0	164	52	2
	2005	26	..	0	-30	56	2
	2006	39	..	0	-15	54	2

Table 20

Production, trade and consumption of kerosene
Production, commerce et consommation de pétrole lampant
Thousand metric tons and kilograms per capita
Milliers de tonnes métriques et kilogrammes par habitant

Country or area Pays ou zone	Year Année	Production Production	Imports Importations	Exports Exportations	Changes in stocks Variations des stocks	Consumption Consommation	
						Total Totale	Per Capita Per habitant
Pakistan	2003	284	..	0	0	284	2
Pakistan	2004	203	..	1	-30	232	2
	2005	209	..	0	*-25	234	2
	2006	207	..	0	-4	211	1
Philippines	2003	362	34	..	4	392	5
Philippines	2004	229	150	..	2	377	5
	2005	210	93	..	-10	313	4
	2006	170	80	..	41	209	2
Qatar	2003	4	..	..	..	4	5
Qatar	2004	0	..	..	..	0	0
	2005	0	..	..	..	0	0
	2006	0	..	..	..	0	0
Saudi Arabia	2003	3747	..	3526	..	221	10
Arabie saoudite	2004	3524	..	3316	..	208	9
	2005	3576	..	3365	..	211	9
	2006	3559	..	3349	..	210	9
Singapore	2003	426	259	908	*-281	58	14
Singapour	2004	501	445	1095	*-208	59	14
	2005	619	417	1410	-433	59	14
	2006	596	263	1046	-254	67	15
Sri Lanka	2003	152	21	..	-25	198	10
Sri Lanka	2004	140	54	..	11	183	9
	2005	139	24	..	5	158	8
	2006	144	38	..	19	163	8
Syrian Arab Republic	2003	39	122	1	..	160	9
Rép. arabe syrienne	2004	58	103	0	..	161	9
	2005	54	123	0	..	177	10
	2006	54	123	0	..	177	9
Thailand	2003	550	..	86	436	28	0
Thaïlande	2004	920	..	48	853	19	0
	2005	799	..	2	781	16	0
	2006	820	..	27	778	15	0
Turkey	2003	80	144	135	18	71	1
Turquie	2004	64	159	188	-2	37	1
	2005	24	0	0	-4	28	0
	2006	32	0	0	8	24	0
Uzbekistan	2003	117	..	..	..	117	5
Ouzbékistan	2004	110	..	..	..	110	4
	2005	90	..	..	..	90	3
	2006	84	..	..	..	84	3
Viet Nam	2003	..	415	68	..	347	4
Viet Nam	2004	..	360	0	..	360	4
	2005	..	333	0	..	333	4
	2006	..	308	0	..	308	4
Yemen	2003	107	..	..	..	107	6
Yémen	2004	109	..	..	..	109	6
	2005	109	..	..	..	109	5
	2006	98	..	..	..	98	5
Europe	**2003**	**7089**	**1712**	**1353**	**-68**	**7516**	**10**
Europe	**2004**	**9223**	**2031**	**1187**	**177**	**9890**	**14**
	2005	**8815**	**2317**	**1290**	**-45**	**9887**	**14**
	2006	**9247**	**2562**	**1480**	**229**	**10100**	**14**

Table 20

Production, trade and consumption of kerosene
Production, commerce et consommation de pétrole lampant

Thousand metric tons and kilograms per capita
Milliers de tonnes métriques et kilogrammes par habitant

Country or area Pays ou zone	Year Année	Production Production	Imports Importations	Exports Exportations	Changes in stocks Variations des stocks	Consumption Consommation	
						Total Totale	Per Capita Per habitant
Albania	2003	5	..	..	..	5	1
Albanie	2004	7	..	..	..	7	2
	2005	9	..	..	..	9	3
	2006	10	..	..	..	10	3
Austria	2003	1	4	..	..	5	1
Autriche	2004	1	3	..	..	4	0
	2005	1	3	..	..	4	0
	2006	13	2	..	..	15	2
Belarus	2003	130	2	120	0	12	1
Bélarus	2004	169	1	169	-3	4	0
	2005	192	1	170	17	6	1
	2006	462	0	465	-9	6	1
Belgium	2003	62	66	23	0	105	10
Belgique	2004	78	62	26	-9	123	12
	2005	65	68	43	8	82	8
	2006	42	61	36	4	63	6
Croatia	2003	1	1	1	0	1	0
Croatie	2004	1	1	1	0	1	0
	2005	1	1	1	0	1	0
	2006	2	1	1	1	1	0
Czech Republic	2003	..	5	..	..	5	0
République tchèque	2004	..	3	..	..	3	0
	2005	..	4	..	..	4	0
	2006	..	5	..	..	5	0
Finland	2003	..	15	36	..	-21	-4
Finlande	2004	..	17	67	..	-50	-10
	2005	..	40	110	..	-70	-13
	2006	..	63	103	..	-40	-8
France incl. Monaco	2003	76	183	30	0	229	4
France y compris Monaco	2004	76	214	27	-4	267	4
	2005	75	246	34	4	283	5
	2006	121	165	27	22	237	4
Germany	2003	10	11	3	-1	19	0
Allemagne	2004	7	14	3	1	17	0
	2005	14	13	3	1	23	0
	2006	5	16	3	1	17	0
Greece	2003	19	..	2	1	16	1
Grèce	2004	29	..	5	-3	27	2
	2005	41	..	15	5	21	2
	2006	34	..	14	-3	23	2
Ireland	2003	315	363	54	-3	627	158
Irlande	2004	252	383	13	-5	627	155
	2005	239	310	7	-8	550	133
	2006	228	310	4	5	529	125
Italy and San Marino	2003	330	167	238	-64	323	6
Italie y comp. St. Marin	2004	254	352	152	120	334	6
	2005	33	636	316	37	316	5
	2006	30	492	143	82	297	5
Latvia	2003	..	0	0	..	0	0
Lettonie	2004	..	3	0	..	3	1
	2005	..	2	0	..	2	1
	2006	..	6	1	..	5	2

Table 20

Production, trade and consumption of kerosene
Production, commerce et consommation de pétrole lampant

Thousand metric tons and kilograms per capita
Milliers de tonnes métriques et kilogrammes par habitant

Country or area Pays ou zone	Year Année	Production Production	Imports Importations	Exports Exportations	Changes in stocks Variations des stocks	Consumption Consommation	
						Total Totale	Per Capita Per habitant
Luxembourg	2003	..	1	..	..	1	2
Luxembourg	2004	..	1	..	..	1	2
	2005	..	1	..	..	1	2
	2006	..	1	..	..	1	2
Malta	2003	..	10	..	..	10	25
Malte	2004	..	10	..	..	10	25
	2005	..	15	..	..	15	37
	2006	..	2	..	..	2	5
Netherlands	2003	498	493	171	41	779	48
Pays-Bas	2004	379	491	216	-20	674	41
	2005	469	507	256	-17	737	45
	2006	368	727	230	28	837	51
Norway,Svlbd.J.Myn. I	2003	196	23	72	-2	149	33
Norvège,Svalbd,J.May	2004	228	0	46	55	127	28
	2005	143	1	28	-10	126	27
	2006	232	3	133	2	100	21
Poland	2003	9	..	0	2	7	0
Pologne	2004	36	..	37	-2	1	0
	2005	17	..	17	0	0	0
	2006	1	..	0	0	1	0
Portugal	2003	1	3	..	-1	5	0
Portugal	2004	2	3	..	0	5	0
	2005	3	2	..	1	4	0
	2006	2	1	..	0	3	0
Republic of Moldova	2003	..	15	..	2	13	4
Rép. de Moldova	2004	..	1	..	-1	2	1
	2005	..	0	..	-1	1	0
	2006	..	0	..	0	0	0
Romania	2003	33	0	0	-1	34	2
Roumanie	2004	45	1	11	0	35	2
	2005	56	1	5	0	52	2
	2006	22	0	4	0	18	1
Russian Federation	2003	66	..	..	..	66	0
Fédération de Russie	2004	66	..	..	..	66	0
	2005	70	..	..	..	70	0
	2006	74	..	..	..	74	1
Serbia	2003	82	0	47	..	35	3
Serbie	2004	10	12	0	..	22	2
	2005	9	14	0	..	23	2
	2006	8	17	0	..	25	2
Slovakia	2003	1	13	0	1	13	2
Slovaquie	2004	1	90	1	0	90	17
	2005	2	34	3	-1	34	6
	2006	1	11	1	0	11	2
Slovenia	2003	..	2	..	..	2	1
Slovénie	2004	..	1	..	..	1	1
	2005	..	1	..	..	1	0
	2006	..	1	..	..	1	0
Spain	2003	1732	..	..	-1	1733	41
Espagne	2004	3969	..	..	-10	3979	93
	2005	4027	..	..	-55	4082	94
	2006	4199	..	..	-11	4210	96

Table 20

Production, trade and consumption of kerosene
Production, commerce et consommation de pétrole lampant

Thousand metric tons and kilograms per capita
Milliers de tonnes métriques et kilogrammes par habitant

Country or area Pays ou zone	Year Année	Production Production	Imports Importations	Exports Exportations	Changes in stocks Variations des stocks	Consumption Consommation	
						Total Totale	Per Capita Per habitant
Sweden	2003	..	4	0	0	4	0
Suède	2004	..	4	0	0	4	0
	2005	..	3	0	-1	4	0
	2006	..	3	1	1	1	0
Switzerland	2003	..	4	..	..	4	1
Suisse	2004	..	4	..	..	4	1
	2005	..	4	..	..	4	1
	2006	..	4	..	..	4	1
Ukraine	2003	1	0	..	0	1	0
Ukraine	2004	0	0	..	0	0	0
	2005	24	2	..	-1	27	1
	2006	19	1	..	0	20	0
United Kingdom	2003	3521	327	556	-42	3334	56
Royaume-Uni	2004	3613	360	413	58	3502	59
	2005	3325	408	282	-24	3475	58
	2006	3374	670	314	107	3623	60
Oceania	**2003**	**191**	**91**	**18**	**33**	**230**	**7**
Océanie	**2004**	**175**	**68**	**15**	**10**	**218**	**7**
	2005	**107**	**83**	**15**	**-5**	**180**	**5**
	2006	**94**	**83**	**15**	**0**	**162**	**5**
Australia	2003	188	3	..	30	161	8
Australie	2004	145	0	..	4	141	7
	2005	105	0	..	-4	109	5
	2006	92	0	..	0	92	4
Fiji	2003	..	*33	*18	..	*15	*18
Fidji	2004	..	*30	*15	..	*15	*18
	2005	..	*30	*15	..	*15	*18
	2006	..	*30	*15	..	*15	*18
French Polynesia	2003	..	*1	..	..	*1	*4
Polynésie française	2004	..	*1	..	..	*1	*4
	2005	..	*1	..	..	*1	*4
	2006	..	*1	..	..	*1	*4
Kiribati	2003	..	*2	..	..	*2	*22
Kiribati	2004	..	*2	..	..	*2	*20
	2005	..	*2	..	..	*2	*19
	2006	..	*2	..	..	*2	*19
New Caledonia	2003	..	0	..	..	0	0
Nouvelle-Calédonie	2004	..	5	..	..	5	22
	2005	..	0	..	..	0	0
	2006	..	0	..	..	0	0
New Zealand	2003	3	..	..	0	3	1
Nouvelle-Zélande	2004	3	..	..	0	3	1
	2005	2	..	..	-1	3	1
	2006	2	..	..	0	2	0
Palau	2003	..	*2	..	..	*2	*99
Palaos	2004	..	*2	..	..	*2	*97
	2005	..	*2	..	..	*2	*96
	2006	..	*2	..	..	*2	*92
Papua New Guinea	2003	0	36	..	*3	32	6
Papouasie-Nvl-Guinée	2004	27	*12	..	*6	33	6
	2005	0	*32	..	0	*32	*5
	2006	0	*32	..	0	*32	*5

Table 20

Production, trade and consumption of kerosene
Production, commerce et consommation de pétrole lampant

Thousand metric tons and kilograms per capita
Milliers de tonnes métriques et kilogrammes par habitant

Country or area Pays ou zone	Year Année	Production Production	Imports Importations	Exports Exportations	Changes in stocks Variations des stocks	Consumption Consommation	
						Total Totale	Per Capita Per habitant
Samoa	2003	..	*8	..	..	*8	*44
Samoa	2004	..	*8	..	..	*8	*44
	2005	..	*9	..	..	*9	*49
	2006	..	*9	..	..	*9	*49
Solomon Islands	2003	..	*2	..	..	*2	*4
Iles Salomon	2004	..	*2	..	..	*2	*4
	2005	..	*2	..	..	*2	*4
	2006	..	*2	..	..	*2	*4
Tonga	2003	..	3	..	..	3	30
Tonga	2004	..	5	..	..	5	49
	2005	..	*4	..	..	*4	*39
	2006	..	4	..	..	4	40
Vanuatu	2003	..	*1	..	..	*1	*5
Vanuatu	2004	..	*1	..	..	*1	*5
	2005	..	*1	..	..	*1	*5
	2006	..	*1	..	..	*1	*5

Table 21

Production, trade and consumption of jet fuels
Production, commerce et consommation de carburéacteurs
Thousand metric tons and kilograms per capita
Milliers de tonnes métriques et kilogrammes par habitant

Table Notes:
Production from refineries and plants.

- **Please refer to the Definitions Section on pages xv to xxix for the appropriate product description/ classification.**

Notes relatives aux tableaux:
Production à partir des raffineries et des usines.

- **Veuillez consulter la section "définitions" de la page xv à la page xxix pour une description/classification appropriée des produits.**

Figure 60: World production of jet fuels 1993-2006

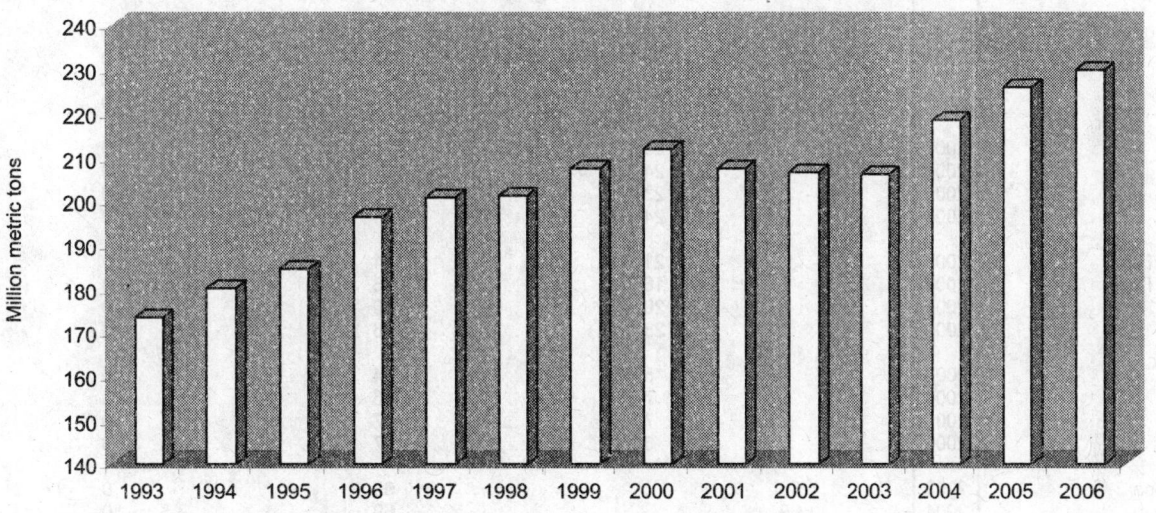

Figure 61: Major jet fuel producing countries in 2006

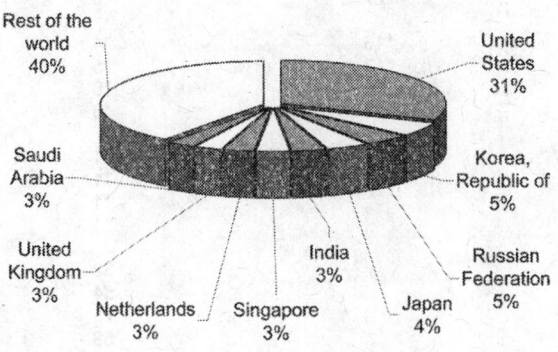

Figure 62: Major jet fuel consuming countries in 2006

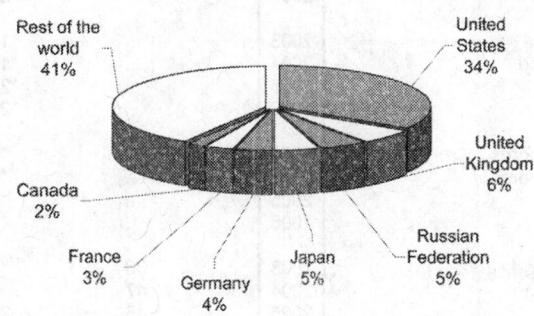

Table 21

Production, trade and consumption of jet fuels
Production, commerce et consommation de carburéacteurs
Thousand metric tons and kilograms per capita
Milliers de tonnes métriques et kilogrammes par habitant

Country or area Pays ou zone	Year Année	Production Production	Imports Importations	Exports Exportations	Bunkers Soutes	Changes in stocks Variations des stocks	Consumption Consommation	
							Total Totale	Per capita Par habitant
World	**2003**	**205889**	**41633**	**43100**	**104323**	**-496**	**100596**	**16**
Monde	**2004**	**218075**	**46382**	**50405**	**109921**	**-1116**	**105247**	**17**
	2005	**225774**	**54031**	**55870**	**117288**	**-494**	**107142**	**17**
	2006	**229540**	**53346**	**57824**	**119080**	**-30**	**106013**	**16**
Africa	**2003**	**7977**	**1980**	**3112**	**4293**	**56**	**2497**	**3**
Afrique	**2004**	**8034**	**2102**	**3173**	**4239**	**-12**	**2735**	**3**
	2005	**8429**	**2232**	**3056**	**4778**	**-3**	**2831**	**3**
	2006	**7941**	**2559**	**2601**	**4818**	**80**	**3001**	**3**
Algeria	2003	1315	..	916	265	5	129	4
Algérie	2004	986	..	632	212	0	142	4
	2005	1069	..	709	308	0	52	2
	2006	965	..	494	360	0	111	3
Angola	2003	352	0	60	292	..	0	0
Angola	2004	302	30	0	332	..	0	0
	2005	290	0	13	277	..	0	0
	2006	323	7	0	330	..	0	0
Benin	2003	..	25	..	25	..	0	0
Bénin	2004	..	24	..	24	..	0	0
	2005	..	23	..	23	..	0	0
	2006	..	24	..	24	..	0	0
Burkina Faso	2003	..	21	..	14	6	0	0
Burkina Faso	2004	..	16	..	16	0	0	0
	2005	..	20	..	20	0	0	0
	2006	..	28	..	16	12	0	0
Burundi	2003	..	5	..	4	0	0	0
Burundi	2004	..	7	..	6	1	0	0
	2005	..	7	..	7	0	0	0
	2006	..	6	..	7	0	0	0
Cameroon	2003	69	..	..	69	..	0	0
Cameroun	2004	69	..	..	69	..	0	0
	2005	62	..	..	62	..	0	0
	2006	71	..	..	71	..	0	0
Central African Rep.	2003	..	*25	..	*25	..	0	0
Rép. centrafricaine	2004	..	*25	..	*25	..	0	0
	2005	..	*25	..	*25	..	0	0
	2006	..	*27	..	*27	..	0	0
Chad	2003	..	*17	..	*13	..	*4	0
Tchad	2004	..	*18	..	*13	..	*5	*1
	2005	..	*20	..	*14	..	*6	*1
	2006	..	*20	..	*14	..	*6	*1
Comoros	2003	..	*1	..	..	..	*1	*2
Comores	2004	..	*1	..	..	..	*1	*2
	2005	..	*1	..	..	..	*1	*1
	2006	..	*1	..	..	..	*1	*1
Congo	2003	38	0	..	..	..	38	11
Congo	2004	47	7	..	..	..	54	15
	2005	45	30	..	..	..	75	21
	2006	53	16	..	..	..	69	19
Côte d'Ivoire	2003	104	..	..	*104	..	0	0
Côte d'Ivoire	2004	88	..	..	88	..	0	0
	2005	88	..	..	88	..	0	0
	2006	88	..	..	88	..	0	0

Table 21

Production, trade and consumption of jet fuels
Production, commerce et consommation de carburéacteurs
Thousand metric tons and kilograms per capita
Milliers de tonnes métriques et kilogrammes par habitant

Country or area Pays ou zone	Year Année	Production Production	Imports Importations	Exports Exportations	Bunkers Soutes	Changes in stocks Variations des stocks	Consumption Consommation	
							Total Totale	Per capita Par habitant
Dem. Rep. of Congo	2003	..	78	..	*78	..	0	0
Rép. dem. du Congo	2004	..	101	..	101	..	0	0
	2005	..	100	..	100	..	0	0
	2006	..	100	..	100	..	0	0
Djibouti	2003	..	95	..	95	..	0	0
Djibouti	2004	..	95	..	95	..	0	0
	2005	..	100	..	100	..	0	0
	2006	..	100	..	100	..	0	0
Egypt	2003	1469	..	518	475	..	476	7
Egypte	2004	2080	..	884	690	..	506	7
	2005	2146	..	867	738	..	541	8
	2006	2033	..	716	776	..	541	7
Eritrea	2003	..	14	..	11	..	3	1
Erythrée	2004	..	14	..	11	..	3	1
	2005	..	15	..	9	..	6	1
	2006	..	9	..	7	..	2	0
Ethiopia	2003	..	85	..	85	..	0	0
Ethiopie	2004	..	96	..	96	..	0	0
	2005	..	146	..	146	..	0	0
	2006	..	177	..	177	..	0	0
Gabon	2003	54	20	19	66	-11	0	0
Gabon	2004	45	13	18	53	-13	0	0
	2005	59	10	18	54	-3	0	0
	2006	55	7	17	50	-5	0	0
Ghana	2003	91	35	..	132	-6	0	0
Ghana	2004	107	0	..	107	0	0	0
	2005	113	0	..	119	-6	0	0
	2006	46	100	..	152	-6	0	0
Guinea	2003	..	*9	..	*9	..	0	0
Guinée	2004	..	*9	..	*9	..	0	0
	2005	..	*10	..	*10	..	0	0
	2006	..	*10	..	*10	..	0	0
Guinea-Bissau	2003	..	*10	..	*10	..	0	0
Guinée-Bissau	2004	..	*10	..	*10	..	0	0
	2005	..	*10	..	*10	..	0	0
	2006	..	*10	..	*10	..	0	0
Kenya	2003	204	319	31	..	..	492	15
Kenya	2004	212	356	31	..	..	537	16
	2005	205	439	30	..	..	614	17
	2006	226	509	33	..	..	702	19
Liberia	2003	..	*18	..	*2	..	*16	*5
Libéria	2004	..	23	..	*2	..	21	6
	2005	..	20	..	*2	..	18	5
	2006	..	*24	..	*2	..	*22	*6
Libyan Arab Jamah.	2003	1491	..	1285	206	..	0	0
Jamah. arabe libyenne	2004	1504	..	1296	208	..	0	0
	2005	1339	..	1154	185	..	0	0
	2006	1255	..	1082	173	..	0	0
Madagascar	2003	*1	..	..	*1	..	0	0
Madagascar	2004	*1	..	..	*1	..	0	0
	2005	*1	..	..	*1	..	0	0
	2006	*1	..	..	*1	..	0	0

Table 21

Production, trade and consumption of jet fuels
Production, commerce et consommation de carburéacteurs
Thousand metric tons and kilograms per capita
Milliers de tonnes métriques et kilogrammes par habitant

Country or area Pays ou zone	Year Année	Production Production	Imports Importations	Exports Exportations	Bunkers Soutes	Changes in stocks Variations des stocks	Consumption Consommation	
							Total Totale	Per capita Par habitant
Malawi	2003	..	11	..	..	..	11	1
Malawi	2004	..	*12	..	..	..	*12	*1
	2005	..	*12	..	..	..	*12	*1
	2006	..	*11	..	..	..	*11	*1
Mali	2003	..	18	..	18	..	0	0
Mali	2004	..	*19	..	19	..	0	0
	2005	..	*19	..	19	..	0	0
	2006	..	*19	..	*19	..	0	0
Mauritius	2003	..	208	..	89	-5	124	102
Maurice	2004	..	227	..	88	2	137	112
	2005	..	220	..	97	-15	138	111
	2006	..	236	..	100	-5	141	113
Morocco	2003	108	190	..	292	6	0	0
Maroc	2004	174	100	..	321	-47	0	0
	2005	264	108	..	368	4	0	0
	2006	236	179	..	417	-2	0	0
Mozambique	2003	..	33	..	38	-5	0	0
Mozambique	2004	..	37	..	40	-3	0	0
	2005	..	38	..	44	-6	0	0
	2006	..	49	..	54	-5	0	0
Niger	2003	..	10	..	10	..	0	0
Niger	2004	..	12	..	12	..	0	0
	2005	..	13	..	13	..	0	0
	2006	..	11	..	11	..	0	0
Nigeria	2003	386	..	..	386	..	0	0
Nigéria	2004	189	..	..	189	..	0	0
	2005	480	..	..	480	..	0	0
	2006	226	..	..	226	..	0	0
Réunion	2003	..	*159	..	..	..	*159	*211
Réunion	2004	..	*160	..	..	..	*160	*209
	2005	..	*160	..	..	..	*160	*206
	2006	..	*160	..	..	..	*160	*201
Rwanda	2003	..	*19	..	*12	..	*7	*1
Rwanda	2004	..	19	..	*12	..	7	1
	2005	..	*20	..	*12	..	*8	*1
	2006	..	*23	..	*12	..	*11	*1
Senegal	2003	126	54	13	*205	-2	*-36	*-4
Sénégal	2004	132	24	8	226	-3	-75	-7
	2005	89	76	21	227	5	-88	-8
	2006	31	85	7	217	-1	-107	-10
Seychelles	2003	..	31	..	*26	..	5	63
Seychelles	2004	..	46	..	*30	..	16	196
	2005	..	32	..	*26	..	6	68
	2006	..	35	..	*29	..	6	73
Sierra Leone	2003	*20	..	..	*20	..	0	0
Sierra Leone	2004	*21	..	..	21	..	0	0
	2005	*21	..	..	*21	..	0	0
	2006	*22	..	..	*22	..	0	0
Somalia	2003	*80	..	*35	*45	..	0	0
Somalie	2004	*80	..	*35	*45	..	0	0
	2005	*75	..	*30	*45	..	0	0
	2006	*75	..	*30	*45	..	0	0

Table 21

Production, trade and consumption of jet fuels
Production, commerce et consommation de carburéacteurs
Thousand metric tons and kilograms per capita
Milliers de tonnes métriques et kilogrammes par habitant

Country or area Pays ou zone	Year Année	Production Production	Imports Importations	Exports Exportations	Bunkers Soutes	Changes in stocks Variations des stocks	Consumption Consommation Total Totale	Per capita Par habitant
South Africa Customs Un.	2003	1874	48	235	859	..	828	16
Un.douan.d'Afr.mérid	2004	1778	175	269	757	..	927	17
	2005	1840	141	214	743	..	1024	19
	2006	1908	146	222	770	..	1062	20
Sudan	2003	170	..	..	132	38	0	0
Soudan	2004	192	..	..	138	54	0	0
	2005	214	..	..	195	19	0	0
	2006	294	..	..	219	75	0	0
Togo	2003	..	30	..	26	1	3	1
Togo	2004	..	57	..	39	3	15	3
	2005	..	45	..	48	-11	8	1
	2006	..	45	..	34	-2	13	2
Tunisia	2003	0	228	..	..	28	200	20
Tunisie	2004	0	225	..	..	-5	230	23
	2005	0	223	..	..	10	213	21
	2006	4	227	..	..	19	212	21
Uganda	2003	..	*36	..	..	..	*36	*1
Ouganda	2004	..	*37	..	..	..	*37	*1
	2005	..	*37	..	..	..	*37	*1
	2006	..	*38	..	..	..	*38	*1
United Rep.Tanzania	2003	..	72	..	72	..	0	0
Rép. Unie de Tanzanie	2004	..	77	..	77	..	0	0
	2005	..	83	..	83	..	0	0
	2006	..	88	..	88	..	0	0
Western Sahara	2003	..	*4	..	*4	..	0	0
Sahara occidental	2004	..	*4	..	*4	..	0	0
	2005	..	*4	..	*4	..	0	0
	2006	..	*4	..	*4	..	0	0
Zambia	2003	25	19	..	44	..	0	0
Zambie	2004	27	19	..	46	..	0	0
	2005	29	19	..	48	..	0	0
	2006	29	22	..	51	..	0	0
Zimbabwe	2003	..	34	..	34	..	0	0
Zimbabwe	2004	..	7	..	7	..	0	0
	2005	..	7	..	7	..	0	0
	2006	..	7	..	7	..	0	0
America, North	**2003**	**78650**	**6704**	**3153**	**19878**	**-235**	**62558**	**125**
Amérique du Nord	**2004**	**82407**	**7545**	**4279**	**20288**	**370**	**65015**	**128**
	2005	**82969**	**11031**	**5177**	**20894**	**-1**	**67930**	**133**
	2006	**79673**	**10678**	**4342**	**19797**	**-77**	**66289**	**128**
Antigua and Barbuda	2003	..	*72	..	*47	..	*25	*313
Antigua-et-Barbuda	2004	..	*74	..	*48	..	*26	*321
	2005	..	*75	..	*48	..	*27	*326
	2006	..	*77	..	*48	..	*29	*345
Aruba	2003	..	*73	..	*73	..	0	0
Aruba	2004	..	*73	..	*73	..	0	0
	2005	..	*75	..	*75	..	0	0
	2006	..	*75	..	*75	..	0	0
Bahamas	2003	..	*40	..	*40	..	0	0
Bahamas	2004	..	*41	..	*41	..	0	0
	2005	..	*43	..	*43	..	0	0
	2006	..	*44	..	*44	..	0	0

Table 21

Production, trade and consumption of jet fuels
Production, commerce et consommation de carburéacteurs

Thousand metric tons and kilograms per capita
Milliers de tonnes métriques et kilogrammes par habitant

Country or area Pays ou zone	Year Année	Production Production	Imports Importations	Exports Exportations	Bunkers Soutes	Changes in stocks Variations des stocks	Consumption Consommation	
							Total Totale	Per capita Par habitant
Belize	2003	..	*20	..	*20	..	0	0
Belize	2004	..	*21	..	*21	..	0	0
	2005	..	*22	..	*22	..	0	0
	2006	..	*22	..	*22	..	0	0
Bermuda	2003	..	*16	..	*16	..	0	0
Bermudes	2004	..	*17	..	*17	..	0	0
	2005	..	*17	..	*17	..	0	0
	2006	..	*19	..	*19	..	0	0
Canada	2003	4200	1293	388	677	90	4338	137
Canada	2004	4597	1641	678	858	55	4647	145
	2005	4363	2186	659	809	0	5081	157
	2006	3869	2413	540	800	-54	4996	153
Cayman Islands	2003	..	*21	..	*21	..	0	0
Iles Caïmanes	2004	..	*22	..	*22	..	0	0
	2005	..	*22	..	*22	..	0	0
	2006	..	*23	..	*23	..	0	0
Costa Rica	2003	..	122	22	..	2	98	24
Costa Rica	2004	..	160	49	..	1	110	26
	2005	..	188	3	..	0	185	43
	2006	..	190	1	..	0	189	43
Cuba	2003	..	330	..	209	..	121	11
Cuba	2004	..	*320	..	211	..	*109	*10
	2005	..	336	..	212	..	124	11
	2006	..	337	..	*200	..	137	12
Dominican Republic	2003	54	35	..	89	0	0	0
Rép. dominicaine	2004	54	44	..	98	0	0	0
	2005	56	41	..	97	0	0	0
	2006	59	36	..	96	-1	0	0
El Salvador	2003	45	23	0	68	0	0	0
El Salvador	2004	49	24	0	73	0	0	0
	2005	51	25	0	76	0	0	0
	2006	39	32	1	73	-3	0	0
Greenland	2003	..	*13	*5	*8	..	0	0
Groënland	2004	..	*13	*5	*8	..	0	0
	2005	..	*13	*5	*8	..	0	0
	2006	..	*14	*5	*9	..	0	0
Grenada	2003	..	*5	..	*5	..	0	0
Grenade	2004	..	*5	..	*5	..	0	0
	2005	..	*4	..	*4	..	0	0
	2006	..	*4	..	*4	..	0	0
Guadeloupe	2003	..	*90	..	*90	..	0	0
Guadeloupe	2004	..	*90	..	*90	..	0	0
	2005	..	*92	..	*92	..	0	0
	2006	..	*93	..	*93	..	0	0
Guatemala	2003	..	40	..	40	0	0	0
Guatemala	2004	..	44	..	43	*1	0	0
	2005	..	36	..	37	-1	0	0
	2006	..	38	..	37	1	0	0
Haiti	2003	..	26	..	26	..	0	0
Haïti	2004	..	24	..	24	..	0	0
	2005	..	23	..	23	..	0	0
	2006	..	24	..	24	..	0	0

Table 21

Production, trade and consumption of jet fuels
Production, commerce et consommation de carburéacteurs
Thousand metric tons and kilograms per capita
Milliers de tonnes métriques et kilogrammes par habitant

Country or area Pays ou zone	Year Année	Production Production	Imports Importations	Exports Exportations	Bunkers Soutes	Changes in stocks Variations des stocks	Consumption Consommation Total Totale	Consumption Consommation Per capita Par habitant
Honduras	2003	..	25	..	25	0	0	0
Honduras	2004	..	28	..	28	0	0	0
	2005	..	24	..	27	-3	0	0
	2006	..	29	..	29	0	0	0
Jamaica	2003	62	152	..	189	10	15	6
Jamaïque	2004	63	*120	..	*180	0	*3	*1
	2005	41	149	..	177	2	11	4
	2006	63	184	..	229	0	18	7
Mexico	2003	2717	..	347	2473	*-105	2	0
Mexique	2004	2770	..	310	2410	-22	72	1
	2005	3125	..	317	2480	-35	363	3
	2006	3172	..	287	2655	66	164	2
Netherlands Antilles	2003	768	60	758	70	..	0	0
Antilles néerlandaises	2004	786	61	776	71	..	0	0
	2005	872	62	862	72	..	0	0
	2006	825	63	815	73	..	0	0
Trinidad and Tobago	2003	685	0	683	8	*-12	6	5
Trinité-et-Tobago	2004	615	38	591	6	56	0	0
	2005	827	0	753	58	16	0	0
	2006	773	0	800	73	-102	2	2
United States	2003	70119	4248	950	15684	-220	57953	199
Etats-Unis	2004	73473	4685	1870	15961	279	60048	205
	2005	73634	7598	2578	16495	20	62139	210
	2006	70873	6961	1893	15171	16	60754	204
America, South	**2003**	**10007**	**536**	**3694**	**2608**	**401**	**3841**	**11**
Amérique du Sud	**2004**	**10659**	**194**	**3723**	**3306**	**-122**	**3946**	**11**
	2005	**10844**	**422**	**4143**	**3288**	**-316**	**4151**	**11**
	2006	**10448**	**749**	**4292**	**3742**	**-798**	**3960**	**10**
Argentina	2003	1135	0	43	..	0	1092	29
Argentine	2004	1209	0	30	..	4	1175	31
	2005	1264	0	98	..	-20	1186	31
	2006	1191	2	60	..	-7	1140	29
Bolivia	2003	121	..	25	..	..	96	11
Bolivie	2004	122	..	24	..	..	98	11
	2005	125	..	0	..	..	125	13
	2006	131	..	0	..	..	131	14
Brazil	2003	3073	285	39	1066	29	2224	12
Brésil	2004	3357	88	46	1056	-3	2346	13
	2005	3337	263	35	1066	-18	2517	14
	2006	3037	568	38	1232	19	2316	12
Chile	2003	574	16	6	523	61	0	0
Chili	2004	650	33	0	579	104	0	0
	2005	574	83	0	616	41	0	0
	2006	660	93	0	658	95	0	0
Colombia	2003	1254	6	316	571	120	253	6
Colombie	2004	861	5	265	569	7	25	1
	2005	858	5	251	597	12	2	0
	2006	718	4	221	642	-141	0	0
Ecuador	2003	239	4	89	..	..	154	12
Equateur	2004	279	0	0	..	..	279	21
	2005	297	0	0	..	..	297	22
	2006	348	0	0	..	..	348	26

Table 21

Production, trade and consumption of jet fuels
Production, commerce et consommation de carburéacteurs

Thousand metric tons and kilograms per capita
Milliers de tonnes métriques et kilogrammes par habitant

Country or area Pays ou zone	Year Année	Production Production	Imports Importations	Exports Exportations	Bunkers Soutes	Changes in stocks Variations des stocks	Consumption Consommation	
							Total Totale	Per capita Par habitant
French Guiana	2003	..	*16	..	*16	..	0	0
Guyane française	2004	..	*16	..	*16	..	0	0
	2005	..	*16	..	*16	..	0	0
	2006	..	*18	..	*18	..	0	0
Guyana	2003	..	12	..	12	..	0	0
Guyana	2004	..	12	..	12	..	0	0
	2005	..	12	..	12	..	0	0
	2006	..	12	..	12	..	0	0
Paraguay	2003	..	25	..	25	0	0	0
Paraguay	2004	..	17	..	18	-1	0	0
	2005	..	19	..	19	0	0	0
	2006	..	22	..	24	-1	0	0
Peru	2003	382	144	199	135	192	0	0
Pérou	2004	418	0	199	429	-210	0	0
	2005	270	0	297	303	-330	0	0
	2006	504	1	321	452	-268	0	0
Suriname	2003	..	22	..	..	..	22	46
Suriname	2004	..	23	..	..	..	23	47
	2005	..	24	..	..	..	24	48
	2006	..	24	..	..	..	24	48
Uruguay	2003	24	6	..	32	-1	-1	0
Uruguay	2004	44	0	..	44	0	0	0
	2005	41	0	..	42	-1	0	0
	2006	53	4	..	55	1	1	0
Venezuela(Bolivar. Rep.)	2003	3205	..	2977	228	0	0	0
Venezuela(Rép. bolivar.)	2004	3719	..	3159	583	-23	0	0
	2005	4078	..	3462	616	0	0	0
	2006	3806	..	3652	649	-495	0	0
Asia	**2003**	**56842**	**11106**	**22322**	**32128**	**-934**	**14432**	**4**
Asie	**2004**	**63406**	**12642**	**27282**	**33963**	**-1458**	**16262**	**4**
	2005	**70031**	**12143**	**30419**	**36922**	**-471**	**15303**	**4**
	2006	**75899**	**11496**	**33705**	**38538**	**258**	**14894**	**4**
Afghanistan	2003	..	*48	..	*8	..	*40	*2
Afghanistan	2004	..	62	..	0	..	62	3
	2005	..	*65	..	*10	..	*55	*2
	2006	..	*65	..	*10	..	*55	*2
Armenia	2003	..	26	..	26	..	0	0
Arménie	2004	..	38	..	38	..	0	0
	2005	..	44	..	44	..	0	0
	2006	..	39	..	39	..	0	0
Azerbaijan	2003	521	..	329	195	-3	0	0
Azerbaïdjan	2004	536	..	323	221	-8	0	0
	2005	630	..	202	415	13	0	0
	2006	693	..	212	485	-4	0	0
Bahrain	2003	1866	..	1932	462	-528	0	0
Bahreïn	2004	2178	..	2142	505	-469	0	0
	2005	2276	..	1858	546	-128	0	0
	2006	2210	..	1798	559	-147	0	0
Bangladesh	2003	2	212	..	227	-13	0	0
Bangladesh	2004	2	220	..	235	-13	0	0
	2005	1	254	..	270	-15	0	0
	2006	1	250	..	266	-15	0	0

Table 21

Production, trade and consumption of jet fuels
Production, commerce et consommation de carburéacteurs

Thousand metric tons and kilograms per capita
Milliers de tonnes métriques et kilogrammes par habitant

Country or area Pays ou zone	Year Année	Production Production	Imports Importations	Exports Exportations	Bunkers Soutes	Changes in stocks Variations des stocks	Consumption Consommation	
							Total Totale	Per capita Par habitant
Bhutan	2003	..	*1	..	..	..	*1	*2
Bhoutan	2004	..	*1	..	..	..	*1	*2
	2005	..	*1	..	..	..	*1	*2
	2006	..	*1	..	..	..	*1	*2
Brunei Darussalam	2003	82	..	..	..	-2	84	240
Brunéi Darussalam	2004	80	..	..	..	2	78	217
	2005	78	..	..	..	0	78	211
	2006	79	..	..	..	0	79	206
Cambodia	2003	..	22	..	22	..	0	0
Cambodge	2004	..	20	..	20	..	0	0
	2005	..	20	..	20	..	0	0
	2006	..	25	..	25	..	0	0
China, Hong Kong SAR	2003	..	4115	128	3438	-20	569	84
Chine, Hong-Kong RAS	2004	..	4119	121	3143	-381	1237	182
	2005	..	4534	141	3647	-398	1144	168
	2006	..	4713	224	3717	-104	875	128
China, Macao SAR	2003	..	107	..	..	..	107	239
Chine, Macao RAS	2004	..	160	..	..	..	160	344
	2005	..	165	..	..	..	165	338
	2006	..	200	..	..	..	200	398
Cyprus	2003	..	323	..	320	3	0	0
Chypre	2004	..	297	..	295	0	2	3
	2005	..	306	..	291	4	11	15
	2006	..	321	..	300	18	3	4
Georgia	2003	..	26	..	26	..	0	0
Géorgie	2004	..	37	..	37	..	0	0
	2005	..	37	..	37	..	0	0
	2006	..	37	..	37	..	0	0
India	2003	4180	2	1678	2394	0	110	0
Inde	2004	5201	3	2480	2811	*-90	3	0
	2005	6196	2	2781	3295	0	122	0
	2006	7805	2	3662	3975	0	170	0
Indonesia	2003	1349	56	..	786	..	619	3
Indonésie	2004	1414	312	..	770	..	956	4
	2005	1418	0	..	707	..	711	3
	2006	1256	0	..	695	..	561	3
Iran(Islamic Rep. of)	2003	868	..	..	770	..	98	1
Iran(Rép. islamique)	2004	795	..	..	782	..	13	0
	2005	848	..	..	848	..	0	0
	2006	1042	..	..	995	..	47	1
Iraq	2003	573	0	168	405	0	0	0
Iraq	2004	607	601	0	1163	45	0	0
	2005	590	204	0	750	44	0	0
	2006	599	233	0	787	45	0	0
Japan	2003	7671	2635	225	6513	60	3508	28
Japon	2004	7902	2877	404	6738	9	3628	29
	2005	8896	2577	667	6784	76	3946	31
	2006	10433	1348	1153	6298	124	4206	33
Jordan	2003	268	..	..	54	1	213	41
Jordanie	2004	291	..	..	70	-4	225	44
	2005	*300	..	..	*69	*-7	*238	*43
	2006	312	..	..	68	1	243	43

Table 21

Production, trade and consumption of jet fuels
Production, commerce et consommation de carburéacteurs

Thousand metric tons and kilograms per capita
Milliers de tonnes métriques et kilogrammes par habitant

Country or area Pays ou zone	Year Année	Production Production	Imports Importations	Exports Exportations	Bunkers Soutes	Changes in stocks Variations des stocks	Consumption Consommation	
							Total Totale	Per capita Par habitant
Kazakhstan	2003	257	71	144	170	-18	32	2
Kazakhstan	2004	244	185	159	213	13	44	3
	2005	207	164	45	230	19	77	5
	2006	260	97	31	248	-11	89	6
Korea, Republic of	2003	6944	436	3489	1140	33	2718	57
Corée, République de	2004	9665	26	5740	1246	106	2599	54
	2005	10755	0	6877	2300	-212	1790	37
	2006	12021	0	7869	2802	70	1280	27
Kuwait	2003	2227	..	1512	715	..	0	0
Koweït	2004	2258	..	1724	534	..	0	0
	2005	1586	..	1010	576	..	0	0
	2006	2619	..	2065	554	..	0	0
Kyrgyzstan	2003	..	170	137	..	..	33	7
Kirghizistan	2004	..	193	143	..	..	50	10
	2005	..	210	85	..	..	125	24
	2006	..	216	87	..	..	129	25
Lao People's Dem. Rep.	2003	..	*11	..	..	..	*11	*2
Rép. dém. pop. lao	2004	..	*10	..	..	..	*10	*2
	2005	..	*10	..	..	..	*10	*2
	2006	..	*11	..	..	..	*11	*2
Lebanon	2003	..	125	..	125	..	0	0
Liban	2004	..	127	..	127	..	0	0
	2005	..	147	..	147	..	0	0
	2006	..	103	..	103	..	0	0
Malaysia	2003	2293	57	552	1794	-18	22	1
Malaisie	2004	2608	45	644	2008	-13	13	1
	2005	2472	112	692	1892	-6	6	0
	2006	2523	121	713	1946	*-15	0	0
Maldives	2003	..	13	..	..	..	13	46
Maldives	2004	..	16	..	..	..	16	55
	2005	..	13	..	..	..	13	44
	2006	..	17	..	..	..	17	57
Myanmar	2003	65	3	..	67	1	0	0
Myanmar	2004	61	3	..	64	0	0	0
	2005	46	3	..	49	0	0	0
	2006	52	23	..	75	0	0	0
Nepal	2003	..	39	..	39	..	0	0
Népal	2004	..	53	..	52	..	1	0
	2005	..	60	..	58	..	2	0
	2006	..	61	..	59	..	2	0
Oman	2003	217	102	10	358	*-49	0	0
Oman	2004	178	20	0	*193	*5	0	0
	2005	183	168	0	272	*79	0	0
	2006	292	20	0	*312	0	0	0
Other Asia	2003	2366	..	466	2060	-249	89	4
Autre Asie	2004	3029	..	909	2322	-231	29	1
	2005	4108	..	1646	2413	33	16	1
	2006	4432	..	1805	2459	157	11	0
Pakistan	2003	997	..	160	138	58	641	4
Pakistan	2004	1185	..	217	163	88	717	5
	2005	1258	..	333	207	0	718	5
	2006	1165	..	303	171	-25	716	5

Table 21

Production, trade and consumption of jet fuels
Production, commerce et consommation de carburéacteurs

Thousand metric tons and kilograms per capita
Milliers de tonnes métriques et kilogrammes par habitant

Country or area Pays ou zone	Year Année	Production Production	Imports Importations	Exports Exportations	Bunkers Soutes	Changes in stocks Variations des stocks	Consumption Consommation	
							Total Totale	Per capita Par habitant
Philippines	2003	634	202	..	570	1	265	3
Philippines	2004	590	373	..	*600	6	357	4
	2005	665	243	..	*700	-12	220	3
	2006	740	289	..	802	5	222	3
Qatar	2003	921	..	325	596	..	0	0
Qatar	2004	956	..	601	355	..	0	0
	2005	916	..	462	454	..	0	0
	2006	1035	..	457	578	..	0	0
Saudi Arabia	2003	4519	..	2227	1719	..	573	26
Arabie saoudite	2004	4923	..	2732	1643	..	548	24
	2005	6627	..	4422	1654	..	551	24
	2006	6193	..	3901	1719	..	573	24
Singapore	2003	6322	1781	5917	2345	*-159	0	0
Singapour	2004	6481	2084	6190	2888	*-513	0	0
	2005	7610	2048	6532	3086	*40	0	0
	2006	7458	2282	6459	3334	*-53	0	0
Sri Lanka	2003	96	129	..	111	-10	124	6
Sri Lanka	2004	126	174	..	128	-7	179	9
	2005	114	208	..	130	-1	193	10
	2006	131	223	..	119	13	222	11
Syrian Arab Republic	2003	204	38	..	97	11	134	8
Rép. arabe syrienne	2004	245	90	..	116	-19	238	13
	2005	221	100	..	105	17	199	11
	2006	215	103	..	102	17	199	11
Tajikistan	2003	..	4	..	4	..	0	0
Tadjikistan	2004	..	4	..	4	..	0	0
	2005	..	4	..	4	..	0	0
	2006	..	4	..	4	..	0	0
Thailand	2003	3253	33	428	..	-29	2887	45
Thaïlande	2004	3774	41	300	..	48	3467	54
	2005	3711	2	459	..	-41	3295	51
	2006	4299	26	781	..	75	3469	53
Turkey	2003	1682	8	11	876	-15	818	12
Turquie	2004	1767	25	12	944	-32	868	12
	2005	1997	18	33	1056	25	901	13
	2006	1644	274	88	956	107	767	11
Turkmenistan	2003	309	..	..	..	..	309	66
Turkménistan	2004	297	..	..	..	..	297	62
	2005	307	..	..	..	..	307	64
	2006	366	..	..	..	..	366	75
United Arab Emirates	2003	5454	..	2140	3314	..	0	0
Emirats arabes unis	2004	5400	..	2225	3175	..	0	0
	2005	5404	..	1906	3498	..	0	0
	2006	5385	..	1795	3590	..	0	0
Uzbekistan	2003	314	..	..	..	..	314	12
Ouzbékistan	2004	296	..	..	..	..	296	11
	2005	242	..	..	..	..	242	9
	2006	226	..	..	..	..	226	8
Viet Nam	2003	..	311	57	154	..	100	1
Viet Nam	2004	..	426	0	258	..	168	2
	2005	..	424	0	257	..	167	2
	2006	..	392	0	238	..	154	2

Table 21

Production, trade and consumption of jet fuels
Production, commerce et consommation de carburéacteurs
Thousand metric tons and kilograms per capita
Milliers de tonnes métriques et kilogrammes par habitant

Country or area Pays ou zone	Year Année	Production Production	Imports Importations	Exports Exportations	Bunkers Soutes	Changes in stocks Variations des stocks	Consumption Consommation Total Totale	Consumption Consommation Per capita Par habitant
Yemen	2003	388	..	287	90	11	0	0
Yémen	2004	317	..	216	101	0	0	0
	2005	369	..	268	101	0	0	0
	2006	413	..	302	111	0	0	0
Europe	**2003**	**47501**	**20335**	**10288**	**42147**	**305**	**15096**	**21**
Europe	**2004**	**48702**	**22722**	**11508**	**44811**	**73**	**15032**	**21**
	2005	**48304**	**26909**	**12874**	**47699**	**288**	**14352**	**20**
	2006	**50436**	**26662**	**12740**	**48752**	**567**	**15039**	**21**
Albania	2003	1	46	..	47	..	0	0
Albanie	2004	16	41	..	57	..	0	0
	2005	0	69	..	69	..	0	0
	2006	0	83	..	83	..	0	0
Austria	2003	446	52	7	415	-3	79	10
Autriche	2004	455	139	7	487	5	95	12
	2005	592	91	5	549	21	108	13
	2006	526	197	4	575	33	111	13
Belgium	2003	2048	1044	1613	1432	-3	50	5
Belgique	2004	2143	1230	1948	1318	56	51	5
	2005	1678	1119	1574	1247	*-30	6	1
	2006	1744	823	1398	1146	-8	31	3
Bosnia and Herzegovina	2003	..	7	..	..	..	7	2
Bosnie y Herzégovine	2004	..	5	..	..	..	5	1
	2005	..	5	..	..	..	5	1
	2006	..	5	..	..	..	5	1
Bulgaria	2003	144	50	20	155	-3	22	3
Bulgarie	2004	142	50	25	149	0	18	2
	2005	144	52	6	183	-5	12	2
	2006	151	41	0	175	-7	24	3
Croatia	2003	75	2	12	23	-3	45	10
Croatie	2004	91	0	9	28	4	50	11
	2005	99	3	2	39	7	54	12
	2006	67	28	2	39	-3	57	13
Czech Republic	2003	140	99	..	197	-11	53	5
République tchèque	2004	147	189	..	282	28	26	3
	2005	132	206	..	308	1	29	3
	2006	121	228	..	325	10	14	1
Denmark	2003	611	528	494	698	-93	40	8
Danemark	2004	606	709	420	796	35	64	12
	2005	507	970	379	837	218	43	8
	2006	608	575	444	842	-138	35	6
Estonia	2003	..	20	..	18	2	0	0
Estonie	2004	..	27	..	27	-2	2	1
	2005	..	41	..	41	0	0	0
	2006	..	31	..	28	3	0	0
Faeroe Islands	2003	..	*2	..	*2	..	0	0
Iles Féroé	2004	..	*2	..	*2	..	0	0
	2005	..	*2	..	*2	..	0	0
	2006	..	*2	..	*2	..	0	0
Finland	2003	614	0	43	351	7	213	41
Finlande	2004	714	0	118	405	1	190	36
	2005	592	63	44	407	-6	210	40
	2006	715	17	43	453	6	230	44

Table 21

Production, trade and consumption of jet fuels
Production, commerce et consommation de carburéacteurs
Thousand metric tons and kilograms per capita
Milliers de tonnes métriques et kilogrammes par habitant

Country or area Pays ou zone	Year Année	Production Production	Imports Importations	Exports Exportations	Bunkers Soutes	Changes in stocks Variations des stocks	Consumption Consommation	
							Total Totale	Per capita Par habitant
France incl. Monaco	2003	5169	2460	864	4922	-25	1868	31
France y compris Monaco	2004	5616	2480	875	5260	43	1918	32
	2005	5478	2952	1253	5321	-15	1871	31
	2006	5633	3087	1439	5538	118	1625	27
Germany	2003	4194	3310	289	5560	11	1644	20
Allemagne	2004	4424	3888	534	6010	-46	1814	22
	2005	4252	4510	455	6468	99	1740	21
	2006	4412	4570	503	6798	103	1578	19
Gibraltar	2003	..	4	..	4	..	0	0
Gibraltar	2004	..	4	..	4	..	0	0
	2005	..	4	..	4	..	0	0
	2006	..	4	..	4	..	0	0
Greece	2003	1630	295	867	761	11	286	26
Grèce	2004	1720	240	568	784	87	521	47
	2005	1737	292	812	757	6	454	41
	2006	1423	447	694	908	-42	310	28
Hungary	2003	202	0	5	196	1	0	0
Hongrie	2004	239	0	17	225	-3	0	0
	2005	266	2	11	261	-4	0	0
	2006	280	1	10	264	7	0	0
Iceland	2003	..	110	..	100	4	6	21
Islande	2004	..	124	..	115	3	6	21
	2005	..	139	..	130	3	6	20
	2006	..	167	..	173	-14	8	26
Ireland	2003	..	990	11	708	205	66	17
Irlande	2004	..	965	0	670	-68	363	90
	2005	..	1118	0	773	-20	365	88
	2006	..	1154	0	789	160	205	48
Italy and San Marino	2003	4187	37	523	2617	78	1006	17
Italie y comp. St. Marin	2004	3787	141	384	2621	-67	990	17
	2005	3910	159	386	2776	-98	1005	17
	2006	4081	116	227	2958	-44	1056	18
Latvia	2003	..	36	..	39	-3	0	0
Lettonie	2004	..	110	..	47	1	62	27
	2005	..	165	..	57	1	107	47
	2006	..	65	..	64	-2	3	1
Lithuania	2003	695	16	415	21	-1	276	80
Lituanie	2004	850	0	544	11	-7	302	88
	2005	832	0	495	45	27	265	78
	2006	764	13	511	51	-9	224	66
Luxembourg	2003	..	377	..	380	-3	0	0
Luxembourg	2004	..	411	..	414	-3	0	0
	2005	..	420	..	420	0	0	0
	2006	..	399	..	394	5	0	0
Malta	2003	..	77	..	77	..	0	0
Malte	2004	..	98	..	98	..	0	0
	2005	..	88	..	88	..	0	0
	2006	..	75	..	75	..	0	0
Netherlands	2003	6669	589	3612	3187	14	445	27
Pays-Bas	2004	6935	1268	4345	3410	36	412	25
	2005	6990	1905	5124	3505	50	216	13
	2006	6914	2336	5547	3553	44	106	6

Table 21

Production, trade and consumption of jet fuels
Production, commerce et consommation de carburéacteurs

Thousand metric tons and kilograms per capita
Milliers de tonnes métriques et kilogrammes par habitant

Country or area Pays ou zone	Year Année	Production Production	Imports Importations	Exports Exportations	Bunkers Soutes	Changes in stocks Variations des stocks	Consumption Consommation Total Totale	Consumption Consommation Per capita Par habitant
Norway,Svlbd.J.Myn. I	2003	415	262	29	204	-2	446	97
Norvège,Svalbd,J.May	2004	423	265	44	235	-27	436	95
	2005	644	162	123	264	-3	422	91
	2006	644	241	107	366	-10	422	91
Poland	2003	647	1	361	279	7	1	0
Pologne	2004	679	2	418	274	-12	1	0
	2005	644	0	338	311	-7	2	0
	2006	853	0	439	415	-3	2	0
Portugal	2003	703	106	20	615	24	150	14
Portugal	2004	779	56	54	674	-41	148	14
	2005	854	69	0	699	16	208	20
	2006	856	46	0	748	0	154	15
Republic of Moldova	2003	..	15	..	12	2	1	0
Rép. de Moldova	2004	..	13	..	11	-1	3	1
	2005	..	14	..	12	-1	3	1
	2006	..	18	..	12	1	5	1
Romania	2003	158	40	84	114	0	0	0
Roumanie	2004	177	40	80	133	-1	5	0
	2005	191	19	101	108	-1	2	0
	2006	238	1	91	133	3	12	1
Russian Federation	2003	9453	..	..	4726	..	4727	33
Fédération de Russie	2004	9283	..	..	4641	..	4642	32
	2005	10036	..	..	5018	..	5018	35
	2006	10602	..	..	5301	..	5301	37
Serbia	2003	85	0	23	62	..	0	0
Serbie	2004	56	1	11	46	..	0	0
	2005	53	1	6	48	..	0	0
	2006	45	7	0	52	..	0	0
Slovakia	2003	63	9	32	33	0	7	1
Slovaquie	2004	61	3	19	26	11	8	1
	2005	36	42	27	38	2	11	2
	2006	46	1	7	39	1	0	0
Slovenia	2003	..	28	2	25	1	0	0
Slovénie	2004	..	22	1	19	2	0	0
	2005	..	21	0	22	-1	0	0
	2006	..	25	1	24	0	0	0
Spain	2003	3061	860	349	2712	-37	897	21
Espagne	2004	2713	943	166	3007	-29	512	12
	2005	2653	1328	120	3017	134	710	16
	2006	2612	2025	162	3145	57	1273	29
Sweden	2003	109	592	15	497	-50	239	27
Suède	2004	208	780	69	609	-53	363	40
	2005	70	818	13	614	20	241	27
	2006	179	837	15	643	35	323	36
Switzerland	2003	344	907	..	1173	12	66	9
Suisse	2004	350	807	..	1119	-10	48	6
	2005	212	967	..	1144	-2	37	5
	2006	228	1012	..	1209	1	30	4
T.F.Yug.Rep. Macedonia	2003	0	12	5	7	0	0	0
L'ex-RY Macédoine	2004	0	11	6	5	0	0	0
	2005	23	5	21	6	1	0	0
	2006	33	0	27	5	1	0	0

Table 21

Production, trade and consumption of jet fuels
Production, commerce et consommation de carburéacteurs
Thousand metric tons and kilograms per capita
Milliers de tonnes métriques et kilogrammes par habitant

Country or area Pays ou zone	Year Année	Production Production	Imports Importations	Exports Exportations	Bunkers Soutes	Changes in stocks Variations des stocks	Consumption Consommation	
							Total Totale	Per capita Par habitant
Ukraine	2003	361	6	6	361	0	0	0
Ukraine	2004	473	0	88	366	19	0	0
	2005	512	6	183	364	-29	0	0
	2006	400	2	74	325	3	0	0
United Kingdom	2003	5277	7346	587	9417	163	2456	41
Royaume-Uni	2004	5615	7658	758	10426	112	1977	33
	2005	5167	9082	1396	11747	-96	1202	20
	2006	6261	7983	995	11098	256	1895	31
Oceania	**2003**	**4912**	**971**	**531**	**3269**	**-89**	**2172**	**67**
Océanie	**2004**	**4867**	**1177**	**440**	**3314**	**33**	**2257**	**69**
	2005	**5198**	**1294**	**200**	**3707**	**9**	**2575**	**77**
	2006	**5143**	**1203**	**143**	**3433**	**-60**	**2830**	**84**
Australia	2003	4080	341	511	2177	-67	1800	90
Australie	2004	3937	499	420	2196	-5	1825	91
	2005	4221	779	180	2572	17	2231	109
	2006	4128	647	100	2313	-45	2407	116
Cook Islands	2003	..	2	..	*2	..	0	0
Iles Cook	2004	..	0		0	..	0	0
	2005	..	0		0	..	0	0
	2006	..	0		0	..	0	0
Fiji	2003	..	316	*20	*288	..	8	10
Fidji	2004	..	248	*20	*220	..	8	10
	2005	..	246	*20	*218	..	8	9
	2006	..	303	*20	*275	..	8	9
French Polynesia	2003	..	18	..	*5	..	13	53
Polynésie française	2004	..	*18	..	*5	..	*13	*52
	2005	..	*18	..	*5	..	*13	*51
	2006	..	*17	..	*5	..	*12	*47
Kiribati	2003	..	*1	..	*1	..	0	0
Kiribati	2004	..	*1	..	*1	..	0	0
	2005	..	*1	..	*1	..	0	0
	2006	..	*1	..	*1	..	0	0
Nauru	2003	..	*7	..	*7	..	0	0
Nauru	2004	..	*7	..	*7	..	0	0
	2005	..	*7	..	*7	..	0	0
	2006	..	*7	..	*7	..	0	0
New Caledonia	2003	..	9	..	9	..	0	0
Nouvelle-Calédonie	2004	..	11	..	11	..	0	0
	2005	..	10	..	10	..	0	0
	2006	..	14	..	14	..	0	0
New Zealand	2003	832	179	..	730	-22	303	76
Nouvelle-Zélande	2004	930	283	..	820	34	359	88
	2005	887	215	..	840	-8	270	66
	2006	909	196	..	762	-15	358	86
Palau	2003	..	*14	..	*14	..	0	0
Palaos	2004	..	*14	..	*14	..	0	0
	2005	..	*14	..	*14	..	0	0
	2006	..	*14	..	*14	..	0	0
Papua New Guinea	2003	0	81	0	*32	0	48	8
Papouasie-Nvl-Guinée	2004	0	93	0	*36	*4	52	9
	2005	90	0	0	*36	0	53	9
	2006	106	0	23	*38	0	45	7

Table 21

Production, trade and consumption of jet fuels
Production, commerce et consommation de carburéacteurs

Thousand metric tons and kilograms per capita
Milliers de tonnes métriques et kilogrammes par habitant

Country or area Pays ou zone	Year Année	Production Production	Imports Importations	Exports Exportations	Bunkers Soutes	Changes in stocks Variations des stocks	Consumption Consommation	
							Total Totale	Per capita Par habitant
Solomon Islands	2003	..	*2	..	*2	..	0	0
Iles Salomon	2004	..	*2	..	*2	..	0	0
	2005	..	*2	..	*2	..	0	0
	2006	..	*2	..	*2	..	0	0
Tonga	2003	..	*1	..	*1	..	0	0
Tonga	2004	..	*1	..	*1	..	0	0
	2005	..	*1	..	*1	..	0	0
	2006	..	*1	..	*1	..	0	0
Wallis and Futuna Is	2003	..	*1	..	*1	..	0	0
Iles Wallis et Futuna	2004	..	1	..	1	..	0	0
	2005	..	1	..	1	..	0	0
	2006	..	1	..	1	..	0	0

Table 22

Production, trade and consumption of gas-diesel oils
Production, commerce et consommation de gazole/carburant diesel
Thousand metric tons and kilograms per capita
Milliers de tonnes métriques et kilogrammes par habitant

Table Notes:
Production from refineries and plants.

- **Please refer to the Definitions Section on pages xv to xxix for the appropriate product description/ classification.**

Notes relatives aux tableaux:
Production à partir des raffineries et des usines.

- **Veuillez consulter la section "définitions" de la page xv à la page xxix pour une description/classification appropriée des produits.**

Figure 63: World production of gas-diesel oils 1993-2006

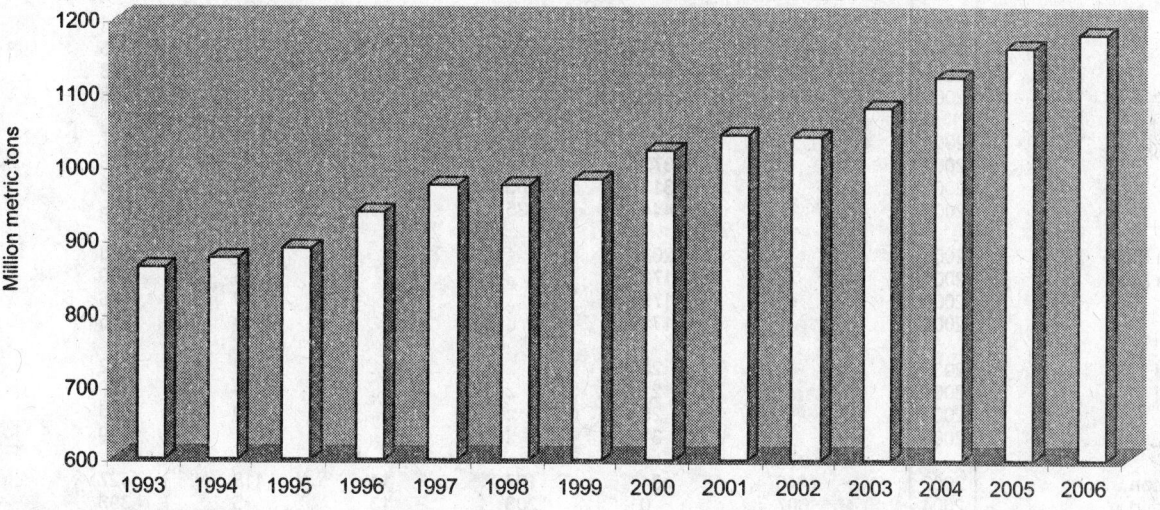

Figure 64: Major gas-diesel oils producing countries in 2006

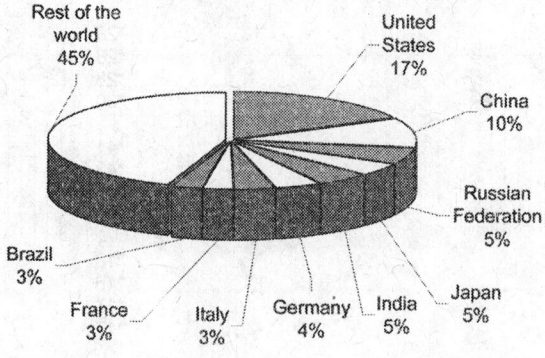

Figure 65: Major gas-diesel oils consuming countries in 2006

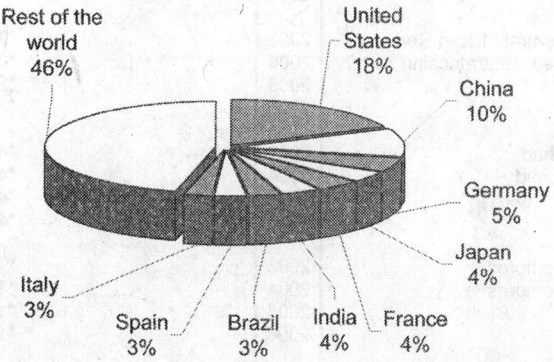

Table 22

Production, trade and consumption of gas-diesel oils
Production, commerce et consommation de gazole/carburant diesel

Thousand metric tons and kilograms per capita
Milliers de tonnes métriques et kilogrammes par habitant

Country or area Pays ou zone	Year Année	Production Production	Imports Importations	Exports Exportations	Bunkers Soutes	Changes in stocks Variations des stocks	Consumption Consommation Total Totale	Per capita Par habitant
World	2003	1078043	194427	211269	25391	-1076	1036887	165
Monde	2004	1123160	208945	218190	27608	-3919	1090227	172
	2005	1162425	220324	237194	25424	5834	1114297	174
	2006	1180533	237217	256042	26448	2156	1133104	174
Africa	2003	35441	12830	4098	1586	-320	42907	51
Afrique	2004	36087	13306	3330	1509	-445	45000	52
	2005	37797	14619	4962	1483	-954	46925	53
	2006	38959	16263	5057	1578	188	48399	53
Algeria	2003	6186	..	1156	66	204	4760	149
Algérie	2004	6340	..	486	66	0	5788	179
	2005	5946	..	179	66	0	5701	173
	2006	6385	..	159	55	381	5790	173
Angola	2003	683	291	..	..	..	974	87
Angola	2004	669	326	..	..	..	995	87
	2005	675	508	..	..	..	1183	101
	2006	681	645	..	..	..	1326	111
Benin	2003	..	344	186	..	11	147	18
Bénin	2004	..	372	215	..	19	138	17
	2005	..	313	205	..	-30	138	16
	2006	..	444	225	..	-20	239	27
Burkina Faso	2003	..	202	..	..	24	178	14
Burkina Faso	2004	..	172	..	..	-8	180	14
	2005	..	179	..	..	-9	188	15
	2006	..	171	..	..	-44	215	16
Burundi	2003	..	20	..	..	-2	22	3
Burundi	2004	..	21	..	..	0	20	3
	2005	..	25	..	..	0	25	3
	2006	..	31	..	..	1	29	4
Cameroon	2003	446	34	157	14	-118	427	25
Cameroun	2004	607	0	203	13	-5	396	23
	2005	610	0	202	10	-4	402	23
	2006	577	124	250	34	8	409	23
Cape Verde	2003	..	*32	..	*6	..	*26	*56
Cap-Vert	2004	..	*34	..	*7	..	*27	*58
	2005	..	*44	..	*10	..	*34	*71
	2006	..	*46	..	*10	..	*36	*74
Central African Rep.	2003	..	*28	..	..	..	*28	*7
Rép. centrafricaine	2004	..	*28	..	..	..	*28	*7
	2005	..	*28	..	..	..	*28	*7
	2006	..	*30	..	..	..	*30	*7
Chad	2003	..	*41	..	..	..	*41	*4
Tchad	2004	..	*43	..	..	..	*43	*4
	2005	..	*46	..	..	..	*46	*5
	2006	..	*48	..	..	..	*48	*5
Comoros	2003	..	*16	..	..	..	*16	*25
Comores	2004	..	*16	..	..	..	*16	*25
	2005	..	*17	..	..	..	*17	*25
	2006	..	*17	..	..	..	*17	*24
Congo	2003	119	0	..	..	..	119	35
Congo	2004	120	24	..	..	..	144	41
	2005	110	28	..	..	..	138	38
	2006	123	48	..	..	..	171	46

Table 22

Production, trade and consumption of gas-diesel oils
Production, commerce et consommation de gazole/carburant diesel
Thousand metric tons and kilograms per capita
Milliers de tonnes métriques et kilogrammes par habitant

Country or area Pays ou zone	Year Année	Production Production	Imports Importations	Exports Exportations	Bunkers Soutes	Changes in stocks Variations des stocks	Consumption Consommation Total Totale	Per capita Par habitant
Côte d'Ivoire	2003	788	92	430	15	*-30	464	26
Côte d'Ivoire	2004	1180	0	682	15	*-13	496	27
	2005	1205	52	901	0	*-206	562	29
	2006	1269	0	755	15	0	499	25
Dem. Rep. of Congo	2003	..	120	..	..	..	120	2
Rép. dem. du Congo	2004	..	253	..	..	..	253	5
	2005	..	251	..	..	..	251	4
	2006	..	251	..	..	..	251	4
Djibouti	2003	..	45	..	*30	..	15	19
Djibouti	2004	..	50	..	*32	..	18	23
	2005	..	50	..	*31	..	19	24
	2006	..	50	..	*31	..	19	23
Egypt	2003	8235	447	424	201	..	8057	120
Egypte	2004	7922	1055	227	185		8565	120
	2005	8179	1431	0	198		9412	132
	2006	8440	1396	0	124		9712	133
Equatorial Guinea	2003	..	*37	..	..	..	*37	*80
Guinée équatoriale	2004	..	*30	..	..	..	*30	*63
	2005	..	*30	..	..	..	*30	*62
	2006	..	*32	..	..	..	*32	*65
Eritrea	2003	..	130	..	..	13	117	28
Erythrée	2004	..	114	..	..	-19	133	31
	2005	..	101	..	..	-25	126	28
	2006	..	72	..	..	-22	94	20
Ethiopia	2003	..	698	..	..	-111	809	12
Ethiopie	2004	..	721	..	..	-194	915	13
	2005	..	811	..	..	-224	1035	15
	2006	..	925	..	..	-246	1171	16
Gabon	2003	210	57	27	45	..	195	150
Gabon	2004	228	42	22	46	..	202	148
	2005	225	105	6	45	..	279	200
	2006	213	139	2	47	..	303	212
Gambia	2003	..	*56	*1	..	..	*55	*37
Gambie	2004	..	*56	*1	..	..	*55	*36
	2005	..	*56	*1	..	..	*55	*34
	2006	..	*58	*1	..	..	*57	*35
Ghana	2003	493	254	0	..	..	747	36
Ghana	2004	625	314	42	..	..	897	41
	2005	520	393	0	..	..	913	41
	2006	294	780	66	..	..	1008	44
Guinea	2003	..	*78	..	..	..	*78	*9
Guinée	2004	..	*78	..	..	..	*78	*9
	2005	..	*79	..	..	..	*79	*9
	2006	..	*79	..	..	..	*79	*9
Guinea-Bissau	2003	..	*34	..	..	..	*34	*27
Guinée-Bissau	2004	..	*34	..	..	..	*34	*26
	2005	..	*34	..	..	..	*34	*26
	2006	..	*35	..	..	..	*35	*26
Kenya	2003	411	427	98	2	..	738	23
Kenya	2004	387	685	106	16	..	950	28
	2005	374	692	102	18	..	946	27
	2006	368	811	101	20	..	1058	29

Table 22

Production, trade and consumption of gas-diesel oils
Production, commerce et consommation de gazole/carburant diesel

Thousand metric tons and kilograms per capita
Milliers de tonnes métriques et kilogrammes par habitant

Country or area Pays ou zone	Year Année	Production Production	Imports Importations	Exports Exportations	Bunkers Soutes	Changes in stocks Variations des stocks	Consumption Consommation Total Totale	Consumption Consommation Per capita Par habitant
Liberia	2003	..	*69	..	*2	..	*67	*19
Libéria	2004	..	73	..	*2	..	71	20
	2005	..	101	..	*2	..	99	28
	2006	..	*101	..	*2	..	*99	*27
Libyan Arab Jamah.	2003	4737	..	207	..	..	4530	728
Jamah. arabe libyenne	2004	4782	..	257	..	..	4525	705
	2005	4849	..	317	..	..	4532	684
	2006	4503	..	349	..	..	4154	620
Madagascar	2003	*57	*300	..	*4	..	*353	*21
Madagascar	2004	*57	*360	..	*4	..	*413	*24
	2005	*58	*375	..	*4	..	*429	*24
	2006	*58	*385	..	*4	..	*439	*24
Malawi	2003	..	135	..	..	..	135	12
Malawi	2004	..	*140	..	..	..	*140	*12
	2005	..	*135	..	..	..	*135	*11
	2006	..	*135	..	..	..	*135	*11
Mali	2003	..	*82	..	..	..	*82	*8
Mali	2004	..	*88	..	..	..	*88	*8
	2005	..	*87	..	..	..	*87	*7
	2006	..	*87	..	..	..	*87	*7
Mauritania	2003	..	289	..	*5	..	284	99
Mauritanie	2004	..	318	..	*5	..	313	108
	2005	..	308	..	*5	..	303	104
	2006	..	304	..	*5	..	299	100
Mauritius	2003	..	309	..	99	1	209	173
Maurice	2004	..	320	..	105	1	214	175
	2005	..	330	..	135	-17	212	171
	2006	..	327	..	122	-23	228	182
Morocco	2003	1535	1592	..	13	28	3086	107
Maroc	2004	2254	978	..	*13	-11	3230	108
	2005	2295	997	..	13	14	3265	108
	2006	2033	1387	..	13	21	3386	111
Mozambique	2003	..	431	..	44	6	381	20
Mozambique	2004	..	413	..	42	-20	391	20
	2005	..	331	..	3	0	328	17
	2006	..	377	..	3	0	374	19
Niger	2003	..	62	..	..	..	62	5
Niger	2004	..	68	..	..	..	68	6
	2005	..	75	..	..	..	75	6
	2006	..	76	..	..	..	76	6
Nigeria	2003	1418	1147	20	619	-107	2033	16
Nigéria	2004	1179	975	0	515	-9	1648	13
	2005	980	829	0	469	-1	1341	10
	2006	1260	845	0	600	90	1415	10
Réunion	2003	..	*247	..	*9	..	*238	*315
Réunion	2004	..	*250	..	*10	..	*240	*313
	2005	..	*250	..	*10	..	*240	*309
	2006	..	*250	..	*10	..	*240	*302
Rwanda	2003	..	*96	..	..	..	*96	*11
Rwanda	2004	..	98	..	..	..	98	11
	2005	..	*102	..	..	..	*102	*11
	2006	..	*105	..	..	..	*105	*11

Table 22

Production, trade and consumption of gas-diesel oils
Production, commerce et consommation de gazole/carburant diesel
Thousand metric tons and kilograms per capita
Milliers de tonnes métriques et kilogrammes par habitant

Country or area Pays ou zone	Year Année	Production Production	Imports Importations	Exports Exportations	Bunkers Soutes	Changes in stocks Variations des stocks	Consumption Consommation Total Totale	Consumption Consommation Per capita Par habitant
Sao Tome and Principe	2003	..	*21	..	..	..	*21	*147
Sao Tomé-et-Principe	2004	..	*21	..	..	..	*21	*144
	2005	..	*22	..	..	..	*22	*148
	2006	..	*22	..	..	..	*22	*145
Senegal	2003	463	209	115	11	-14	560	55
Sénégal	2004	471	187	108	0	8	542	51
	2005	356	401	174	0	3	580	53
	2006	115	295	64	0	-26	372	34
Seychelles	2003	..	172	..	*69	..	103	1249
Seychelles	2004	..	251	..	*101	..	151	1829
	2005	..	241	..	*97	..	145	1748
	2006	..	255	..	*102	..	153	1811
Sierra Leone	2003	*74	*61	*4	*68	..	*63	*11
Sierra Leone	2004	*60	69	*4	*70	..	*55	*10
	2005	*60	*70	*4	*71	..	*55	*9
	2006	*60	*60	*4	*66	..	*50	*8
Somalia	2003	10	85	..	*10	..	85	11
Somalie	2004	10	85	..	*10	..	85	11
	2005	10	90	..	*11	..	89	11
	2006	10	90	..	*11	..	89	11
South Africa Customs Un.	2003	7593	1228	1273	238	..	7310	143
Un.douan.d'Afr.mérid	2004	7141	1275	977	238	..	7201	135
	2005	9201	1563	2871	273	..	7620	142
	2006	9873	1644	3081	293	..	8143	150
St. Helena and Depend.	2003	..	*2	..	..	..	*2	*271
St-Hélène et dépend	2004	..	2	..	..	..	2	270
	2005	..	*2	..	..	..	*2	*308
	2006	..	*2	..	..	..	*2	*307
Sudan	2003	1273	141	..	8	-193	1599	48
Soudan	2004	1400	155	..	8	-176	1723	50
	2005	1423	193	..	8	-346	1954	55
	2006	1952	216	..	8	68	2092	58
Togo	2003	..	138	..	7	5	126	25
Togo	2004	..	115	..	5	4	106	21
	2005	..	100	..	3	1	96	18
	2006	..	87	..	2	-19	104	19
Tunisia	2003	502	1216	..	..	-37	1755	178
Tunisie	2004	432	1345	..	..	-23	1800	181
	2005	482	1207	..	..	-110	1799	179
	2006	506	1305	..	..	18	1793	177
Uganda	2003	..	*190	..	..	..	*190	*7
Ouganda	2004	..	215	..	..	..	215	8
	2005	..	340	..	..	..	340	12
	2006	..	439	..	..	..	439	15
United Rep.Tanzania	2003	..	580	..	1	..	579	16
Rép. Unie de Tanzanie	2004	..	623	..	1	..	622	17
	2005	..	667	..	1	..	666	18
	2006	..	706	..	1	..	705	18
Western Sahara	2003	..	*46	..	..	..	*46	*176
Sahara occidental	2004	..	*46	..	..	..	*46	*172
	2005	..	*46	..	..	..	*46	*169
	2006	..	*46	..	..	..	*46	*167

Table 22

Production, trade and consumption of gas-diesel oils
Production, commerce et consommation de gazole/carburant diesel

Thousand metric tons and kilograms per capita
Milliers de tonnes métriques et kilogrammes par habitant

Country or area Pays ou zone	Year Année	Production Production	Imports Importations	Exports Exportations	Bunkers Soutes	Changes in stocks Variations des stocks	Consumption Consommation	
							Total Totale	Per capita Par habitant
Zambia	2003	208	53	..	..	..	261	24
Zambie	2004	223	49	..	..	..	272	25
	2005	239	46	..	..	..	285	25
	2006	239	63	..	..	..	302	26
Zimbabwe	2003	..	445	..	..	..	445	34
Zimbabwe	2004	..	319	..	..	..	319	24
	2005	..	437	..	..	..	437	33
	2006	..	422	..	..	..	422	32
America, North	**2003**	**239843**	**22464**	**15664**	**7589**	**708**	**238345**	**475**
Amérique du Nord	**2004**	**247074**	**21823**	**15954**	**9076**	**-1585**	**245452**	**484**
	2005	**254143**	**23772**	**17508**	**8142**	**1722**	**250543**	**489**
	2006	**259052**	**26551**	**22669**	**8452**	**1704**	**252777**	**489**
Anguilla	2003	..	13	..	..	..	13	1036
Anguilla	2004	..	14	..	..	..	14	1076
	2005	..	17	..	..	..	17	1232
	2006	..	17	..	..	..	17	1224
Antigua and Barbuda	2003	..	*52	*3	..	..	*49	*613
Antigua-et-Barbuda	2004	..	*53	*3	..	..	*50	*617
	2005	..	*54	*4	..	..	*50	*604
	2006	..	*55	*5	..	..	*50	*595
Aruba	2003	..	*26	..	..	..	*26	*273
Aruba	2004	..	*26	..	..	..	*26	*266
	2005	..	*27	..	..	..	*27	*268
	2006	..	*27	..	..	..	*27	*263
Bahamas	2003	..	*370	*25	*45	*30	*270	*846
Bahamas	2004	..	*362	*26	*47	0	*289	*964
	2005	..	*362	*26	*47	0	*289	*895
	2006	..	*365	*25	*45	0	*295	*902
Barbados	2003	..	69	..	..	..	69	254
Barbade	2004	..	76	..	..	..	76	281
	2005	..	79	..	..	..	79	291
	2006	..	81	..	..	..	81	296
Belize	2003	..	*99	..	*12	..	*87	*318
Belize	2004	..	*102	..	*12	..	*90	*318
	2005	..	*106	..	*13	..	*93	*319
	2006	..	*109	..	*13	..	*96	*315
Bermuda	2003	..	*101	..	..	..	*101	*1602
Bermudes	2004	..	*106	..	..	..	*106	*1666
	2005	..	*110	..	..	..	*110	*1730
	2006	..	*110	..	..	..	*110	*1724
British Virgin Islands	2003	..	*13	..	..	..	*13	*609
Iles Vierges britanniques	2004	..	*15	..	..	..	*15	*692
	2005	..	*16	..	..	..	*16	*727
	2006	..	*17	..	..	..	*17	*756
Canada	2003	31136	611	7244	86	-106	24523	774
Canada	2004	31590	928	7047	88	-140	25523	798
	2005	30745	1020	6589	77	101	24998	774
	2006	30704	958	6833	77	83	24669	756
Cayman Islands	2003	..	*124	..	..	..	*124	*2846
Iles Caïmanes	2004	..	*129	..	..	..	*129	*2916
	2005	..	*132	..	..	..	*132	*2730
	2006	..	*135	..	..	..	*135	*2597

Table 22

Production, trade and consumption of gas-diesel oils
Production, commerce et consommation de gazole/carburant diesel

Thousand metric tons and kilograms per capita
Milliers de tonnes métriques et kilogrammes par habitant

Country or area Pays ou zone	Year Année	Production Production	Imports Importations	Exports Exportations	Bunkers Soutes	Changes in stocks Variations des stocks	Consumption Consommation	
							Total Totale	Per capita Par habitant
Costa Rica	2003	168	575	1	..	-37	779	191
Costa Rica	2004	163	597	0	..	-14	774	185
	2005	153	635	0	..	-2	790	185
	2006	230	734	0	..	22	942	216
Cuba	2003	444	844	..	*15	0	1273	113
Cuba	2004	385	1260	..	*15	0	1630	144
	2005	395	1251	..	*15	377	1254	112
	2006	420	980	..	*15	0	1385	123
Dominica	2003	..	19	..	..	..	19	271
Dominique	2004	..	20	..	..	..	20	286
	2005	..	*21	..	..	..	*21	*305
	2006	..	*22	..	..	..	*22	*324
Dominican Republic	2003	411	1054	..	..	0	1465	164
Rép. dominicaine	2004	417	1051	..	..	17	1451	160
	2005	423	1056	..	..	4	1475	160
	2006	424	1054	..	..	-18	1496	160
El Salvador	2003	195	470	22	..	4	638	96
El Salvador	2004	199	480	23	..	4	652	96
	2005	198	411	15	..	-39	633	92
	2006	176	483	16	..	-33	676	97
Greenland	2003	..	*164	*2	..	..	*162	*2873
Groënland	2004	..	*165	*2	..	..	*163	*2891
	2005	..	*168	*2	..	..	*166	*2945
	2006	..	*170	*2	..	..	*168	*2981
Grenada	2003	..	31	..	..	..	31	296
Grenade	2004	..	34	..	..	..	34	323
	2005	..	36	..	..	..	36	343
	2006	..	37	..	..	..	37	350
Guadeloupe	2003	..	*110	..	..	..	*110	*251
Guadeloupe	2004	..	*110	..	..	..	*110	*247
	2005	..	*118	..	..	..	*118	*265
	2006	..	*120	..	..	..	*120	*262
Guatemala	2003	0	1094	0	120	0	974	81
Guatemala	2004	0	1085	0	120	0	965	78
	2005	25	1217	3	120	94	1025	81
	2006	22	1197	55	120	-4	1048	80
Haiti	2003	..	299	..	..	..	299	36
Haïti	2004	..	313	..	..	..	313	37
	2005	..	313	..	..	..	313	37
	2006	..	320	..	..	..	320	37
Honduras	2003	..	977	0	..	198	779	114
Honduras	2004	..	822	0	..	5	817	116
	2005	..	814	2	..	-19	831	115
	2006	..	638	0	..	-71	709	96
Jamaica	2003	158	391	24	16	-1	510	192
Jamaïque	2004	129	*470	67	11	0	*521	*195
	2005	87	496	0	16	35	532	201
	2006	226	541	0	16	2	749	281
Martinique	2003	*177	*35	*28	*27	..	*157	*402
Martinique	2004	*178	*36	*28	*28	..	*158	*401
	2005	*179	*36	*28	*28	..	*159	*400
	2006	*179	*36	*28	*28	..	*159	*398

Table 22

Production, trade and consumption of gas-diesel oils
Production, commerce et consommation de gazole/carburant diesel

Thousand metric tons and kilograms per capita
Milliers de tonnes métriques et kilogrammes par habitant

Country or area Pays ou zone	Year Année	Production Production	Imports Importations	Exports Exportations	Bunkers Soutes	Changes in stocks Variations des stocks	Consumption Consommation	
							Total Totale	Per capita Par habitant
Mexico	2003	15182	1150	144	718	-11	15481	152
Mexique	2004	16057	729	380	665	-54	15795	153
	2005	17157	2098	194	760	205	18096	174
	2006	17692	3492	597	761	154	19672	188
Montserrat	2003	..	*13	..	*1	..	*12	*1278
Montserrat	2004	..	*13	..	*1	..	*12	*1244
	2005	..	*13	..	*1	..	*12	*1231
	2006	..	*13	..	*1	..	*12	*1271
Netherlands Antilles	2003	2102	391	1914	227	..	352	1970
Antilles néerlandaises	2004	2182	395	2006	229	..	342	1868
	2005	2631	401	2462	232	..	338	1823
	2006	2652	408	2459	236	..	365	1926
Nicaragua	2003	211	173	2	..	-3	385	72
Nicaragua	2004	210	195	1	..	0	404	75
	2005	183	214	0	..	-1	398	73
	2006	199	210	0	..	-1	410	74
Panama	2003	..	787	..	..	0	787	253
Panama	2004	..	605	..	..	-121	726	229
	2005	..	612	..	..	0	612	190
	2006	..	692	..	..	0	692	211
St. Kitts-Nevis	2003	..	*53	..	..	..	*53	*1191
St-Kitts-Nevis	2004	..	*55	..	..	..	*55	*1250
	2005	..	*56	..	..	..	*56	*1302
	2006	..	*56	..	..	..	*56	*1302
St. Lucia	2003	..	*64	..	..	..	*64	*395
St-Lucie	2004	..	*67	..	..	..	*67	*413
	2005	..	*70	..	..	..	*70	*423
	2006	..	*70	..	..	..	*70	*423
St. Pierre-Miquelon	2003	..	*23	..	*6	..	*17	*2429
St-Pierre-Miquelon	2004	..	*22	..	*6	..	*16	*2286
	2005	..	*23	..	*6	..	*17	*2424
	2006	..	*23	..	*6	..	*17	*2420
St. Vincent-Grenadines	2003	..	*38	..	..	..	*38	*361
St. Vincent-Grenadines	2004	..	*39	..	..	..	*39	*373
	2005	..	*40	..	..	..	*40	*386
	2006	..	*41	..	..	..	*41	*396
Trinidad and Tobago	2003	1522	0	887	383	-24	276	210
Trinité-et-Tobago	2004	1421	0	875	452	-24	118	89
	2005	1764	32	1364	92	51	289	218
	2006	1861	0	1530	100	-54	285	215
United States	2003	188137	12231	5368	5933	658	188409	648
Etats-Unis	2004	194143	11450	5496	7402	-1258	193953	661
	2005	200203	11719	6819	6735	916	197452	666
	2006	204267	13338	11119	7034	1624	197828	663
America, South	**2003**	**66813**	**7834**	**10177**	**1193**	**926**	**62351**	**172**
Amérique du Sud	**2004**	**71887**	**7696**	**9095**	**1554**	**498**	**68436**	**186**
	2005	**71026**	**8801**	**8716**	**1574**	**-210**	**69747**	**187**
	2006	**71939**	**10196**	**11304**	**1474**	**-911**	**70267**	**186**
Argentina	2003	9957	197	1337	184	39	8594	227
Argentine	2004	10590	376	907	191	-2	9870	258
	2005	10143	585	270	164	-23	10317	267
	2006	10733	378	433	163	-79	10594	272

Table 22

Production, trade and consumption of gas-diesel oils
Production, commerce et consommation de gazole/carburant diesel

Thousand metric tons and kilograms per capita
Milliers de tonnes métriques et kilogrammes par habitant

Country or area Pays ou zone	Year Année	Production Production	Imports Importations	Exports Exportations	Bunkers Soutes	Changes in stocks Variations des stocks	Consumption Consommation	
							Total Totale	Per capita Par habitant
Bolivia	2003	482	280	..	..	11	751	83
Bolivie	2004	622	190	..	..	0	812	88
	2005	601	251	..	..	37	815	86
	2006	620	370	..	..	48	942	98
Brazil	2003	30608	3320	118	596	158	33056	185
Brésil	2004	34079	2342	72	767	256	35326	195
	2005	33368	2582	274	639	-137	35174	191
	2006	33597	3081	557	605	266	35250	189
Chile	2003	3865	668	328	..	-21	4226	265
Chili	2004	3693	1238	58	..	64	4809	299
	2005	3534	1737	200	..	84	4987	306
	2006	3717	2275	356	..	465	5171	315
Colombia	2003	3308	34	116	218	0	3008	67
Colombie	2004	3689	74	140	374	28	3221	71
	2005	3660	316	0	390	-180	3766	82
	2006	4457	200	71	442	-51	4194	90
Ecuador	2003	1600	808	29	..	0	2379	185
Equateur	2004	1621	698	0	..	297	2022	155
	2005	1787	1124	17	..	0	2894	219
	2006	1715	1532	0	..	0	3247	242
Falkland Is. (Malvinas)	2003	..	*9	..	..	..	*9	*3072
Iles Falkland (Malvinas)	2004	..	*9	..	..	..	*9	*3061
	2005	..	*9	..	..	..	*9	*3051
	2006	..	*9	..	..	..	*9	*3046
French Guiana	2003	..	*62	..	..	..	*62	*343
Guyane française	2004	..	*62	..	..	..	*62	*324
	2005	..	*62	..	..	..	*62	*317
	2006	..	*64	..	..	..	*64	*325
Guyana	2003	..	250	..	..	..	250	332
Guyana	2004	..	255	..	..	..	255	337
	2005	..	263	..	..	..	263	347
	2006	..	265	..	..	..	265	348
Paraguay	2003	42	799	..	..	-88	930	164
Paraguay	2004	33	929	..	..	14	948	164
	2005	16	794	..	..	-28	838	142
	2006	0	864	..	..	-17	880	147
Peru	2003	1883	1108	..	43	167	2781	103
Pérou	2004	1999	1307	..	56	-152	3402	126
	2005	2415	801	..	225	31	2960	109
	2006	2638	769	..	99	208	3100	113
Suriname	2003	39	133	..	..	..	172	357
Suriname	2004	39	134	..	..	..	173	351
	2005	41	140	..	..	..	181	363
	2006	41	144	..	..	..	185	367
Uruguay	2003	618	167	24	98	-4	667	196
Uruguay	2004	807	82	3	107	-7	786	238
	2005	810	137	40	97	5	805	244
	2006	760	246	0	97	44	865	261
Venezuela(Bolivar. Rep.)	2003	14411	..	8226	54	665	5467	213
Venezuela(Rép. bolivar.)	2004	14715	..	7915	59	0	6741	258
	2005	14651	..	7915	59	0	6677	251
	2006	13661	..	9887	68	-1795	5501	204

Table 22

Production, trade and consumption of gas-diesel oils
Production, commerce et consommation de gazole/carburant diesel

Thousand metric tons and kilograms per capita
Milliers de tonnes métriques et kilogrammes par habitant

Country or area Pays ou zone	Year Année	Production Production	Imports Importations	Exports Exportations	Bunkers Soutes	Changes in stocks Variations des stocks	Consumption Consommation Total Totale	Per capita Par habitant
Asia	**2003**	**386074**	**51850**	**73313**	**6551**	**-2750**	**360810**	**95**
Asie	**2004**	**413993**	**60238**	**77118**	**7394**	**-1881**	**391599**	**102**
	2005	**434225**	**55976**	**83790**	**6211**	**283**	**399917**	**103**
	2006	**444683**	**57452**	**87882**	**6616**	**-484**	**408121**	**104**
Afghanistan	2003	..	*25	..	..	..	*25	*1
Afghanistan	2004	..	83	..	..	..	83	4
	2005	..	*90	..	..	..	*90	*4
	2006	..	*90	..	..	..	*90	*4
Armenia	2003	..	109	..	..	..	109	29
Arménie	2004	..	108	..	..	..	108	34
	2005	..	116	..	..	..	116	36
	2006	..	113	..	..	..	113	35
Azerbaijan	2003	1641	0	1101	..	27	513	62
Azerbaïdjan	2004	1789	40	1140	..	-40	729	88
	2005	2101	82	1407	..	-7	783	93
	2006	2095	27	1415	..	-24	731	86
Bahrain	2003	4295	..	4104	..	-2	193	280
Bahreïn	2004	4500	..	4149	..	126	225	318
	2005	4702	..	4355	..	33	314	433
	2006	4566	..	4215	..	30	321	432
Bangladesh	2003	303	1505	..	..	..	1808	13
Bangladesh	2004	274	1547	..	..	..	1821	13
	2005	293	1890	..	..	..	2183	16
	2006	284	1790	..	..	..	2074	15
Bhutan	2003	..	*24	..	..	..	*24	*39
Bhoutan	2004	..	*25	..	..	..	*25	*40
	2005	..	*25	..	..	..	*25	*39
	2006	..	*25	..	..	..	*25	*39
Brunei Darussalam	2003	165	0	..	..	-1	166	475
Brunéi Darussalam	2004	173	0	..	..	1	172	478
	2005	178	16	..	..	4	190	513
	2006	190	0	..	..	5	185	483
Cambodia	2003	..	531	..	..	..	531	40
Cambodge	2004	..	580	..	..	..	580	43
	2005	..	610	..	..	..	610	45
	2006	..	568	..	..	..	568	40
China	2003	85328	848	2240	268	-675	84343	65
Chine	2004	98436	2749	637	60	-1124	101612	78
	2005	110902	532	1476	155	-77	109880	84
	2006	117624	705	776	149	-956	118360	90
China, Hong Kong SAR	2003	..	5391	135	2365	-29	2920	429
Chine, Hong-Kong RAS	2004	..	5269	156	3227	56	1830	270
	2005	..	3512	71	1578	-2	1865	274
	2006	..	3762	99	2247	-127	1543	225
China, Macao SAR	2003	..	130	..	..	-6	136	303
Chine, Macao RAS	2004	..	201	..	..	13	188	404
	2005	..	167	..	..	-2	169	346
	2006	..	146	..	..	0	146	291
Cyprus	2003	327	252	..	36	2	541	751
Chypre	2004	88	480	..	28	-16	556	754
	2005	0	603	..	67	17	519	685
	2006	0	629	..	106	46	477	619

Table 22

Production, trade and consumption of gas-diesel oils
Production, commerce et consommation de gazole/carburant diesel

Thousand metric tons and kilograms per capita
Milliers de tonnes métriques et kilogrammes par habitant

Country or area Pays ou zone	Year Année	Production Production	Imports Importations	Exports Exportations	Bunkers Soutes	Changes in stocks Variations des stocks	Consumption Consommation	
							Total Totale	Per capita Par habitant
Georgia	2003	2	110	7	..	-23	128	30
Géorgie	2004	2	166	7	..	0	161	37
	2005	1	251	0	..	0	252	58
	2006	0	246	0	..	0	246	56
India	2003	41966	72	5790	31	..	36217	34
Inde	2004	47426	814	7286	7	..	40947	38
	2005	48495	732	8464	5	..	40758	37
	2006	54268	918	11345	2	..	43839	39
Indonesia	2003	13786	8200	..	262	..	21724	101
Indonésie	2004	14661	10403	..	278	..	24786	114
	2005	13889	12174	..	294	..	25769	117
	2006	13216	8616	..	280	..	21552	97
Iran(Islamic Rep. of)	2003	22958	0	188	..	..	22770	343
Iran(Rép. islamique)	2004	23771	0	578	..	..	23193	344
	2005	24375	89	446	..	..	24018	351
	2006	24762	1566	0	..	..	26328	373
Iraq	2003	6610	0	867	..	0	5743	218
Iraq	2004	4906	1140	0	..	110	5936	219
	2005	4766	1107	0	..	107	5766	210
	2006	4838	1124	0	..	109	5853	203
Israel	2003	2977	895	715	64	..	3093	462
Israël	2004	2750	886	857	40	..	2739	402
	2005	3042	526	948	60	..	2560	369
	2006	3231	510	860	33	..	2848	404
Japan	2003	57402	1277	1091	150	24	57414	455
Japon	2004	57059	753	1275	144	-319	56712	449
	2005	57700	699	3408	184	402	54405	431
	2006	54711	276	4150	166	-34	50705	402
Jordan	2003	1160	292	..	0	9	1443	276
Jordanie	2004	1223	543	..	12	-16	1770	347
	2005	1395	785	..	35	76	2069	378
	2006	1412	518	..	13	45	1872	334
Kazakhstan	2003	2128	361	634	..	0	1855	124
Kazakhstan	2004	2888	525	912	..	0	2501	167
	2005	3705	237	1499	..	235	2208	146
	2006	4065	389	1488	..	76	2890	189
Korea, Dem.Ppl's.Rep.	2003	201	75	..	..	..	276	12
Corée,Rép.pop.dém.de	2004	203	75	..	..	..	278	12
	2005	171	63	..	..	..	234	10
	2006	131	48	..	..	..	179	8
Korea, Republic of	2003	27801	1548	8152	865	167	20165	421
Corée, République de	2004	29048	622	9139	884	213	19434	404
	2005	31508	297	11515	1069	-468	19689	408
	2006	32392	257	12198	1014	370	19067	395
Kuwait	2003	12426	..	11111	132	..	1183	509
Koweït	2004	12204	..	11054	132	..	1018	426
	2005	12397	..	10822	132	..	1443	587
	2006	11079	..	9076	118	..	1885	746
Kyrgyzstan	2003	22	74	0	..	..	96	19
Kirghizistan	2004	27	116	6	..	..	137	27
	2005	31	102	19	..	..	114	22
	2006	31	98	0	..	..	129	25

Table 22

Production, trade and consumption of gas-diesel oils
Production, commerce et consommation de gazole/carburant diesel

Thousand metric tons and kilograms per capita
Milliers de tonnes métriques et kilogrammes par habitant

Country or area Pays ou zone	Year Année	Production Production	Imports Importations	Exports Exportations	Bunkers Soutes	Changes in stocks Variations des stocks	Consumption Consommation	
							Total Totale	Per capita Par habitant
Lao People's Dem. Rep.	2003	..	*25		..	..	*25	*4
Rép. dém. pop. lao	2004	..	*26	..	..	..	*26	*4
	2005	..	*26		..	..	*26	*5
	2006	..	*26		..	..	*26	*5
Lebanon	2003	..	1829		..	-374	2203	562
Liban	2004	..	1747	..	..	1	1746	440
	2005	..	1588		..	-47	1635	408
	2006	..	1596		..	0	1596	394
Malaysia	2003	8922	1506	1925	46	-230	8687	347
Malaisie	2004	9463	1839	1821	64	122	9294	363
	2005	9020	1276	1276	36	239	8744	335
	2006	8734	1202	1491	33	0	8412	316
Maldives	2003	..	165	..			165	579
Maldives	2004	..	203	..		..	203	701
	2005	..	188	..		..	188	640
	2006	..	239	..		..	239	799
Mongolia	2003	..	215	..			215	86
Mongolie	2004	..	258	..		..	258	102
	2005	..	271	..		..	271	106
	2006	..	310	..		..	310	120
Myanmar	2003	249	899		3	-12	1157	22
Myanmar	2004	196	1032	..	3	0	1225	23
	2005	173	1116		3	0	1286	23
	2006	274	816		3	-11	1098	19
Nepal	2003	..	240	..			240	10
Népal	2004	..	254	..		..	254	10
	2005	..	256	..		..	256	10
	2006	..	262	..		..	262	10
Occup. Palestinian Terr.	2003	..	246	0		-1	247	70
Terr. palestiniens occup.	2004	..	409	15		0	394	108
	2005	..	676	17		0	659	175
	2006	..	*750	*25		0	*725	*186
Oman	2003	878	0	194	0	..	684	292
Oman	2004	864	1	118	1	..	746	309
	2005	894	101	28	0	..	967	385
	2006	905	109	31	0	..	983	381
Other Asia	2003	9671	21	4437	168	-166	5253	232
Autre Asie	2004	11229	0	5756	187	33	5253	232
	2005	12719	0	7301	258	-18	5178	228
	2006	12920	68	7337	181	288	5182	227
Pakistan	2003	2937	4104	75	3	0	6963	48
Pakistan	2004	3603	4220	34	23	-72	7838	53
	2005	3419	4104	61	24	11	7427	48
	2006	3383	3972	33	18	-79	7383	47
Philippines	2003	3851	2251	131	78	42	5851	72
Philippines	2004	3004	2828	105	35	12	5680	69
	2005	3399	2223	168	21	-90	5523	65
	2006	3612	1721	309	43	9	4972	57
Qatar	2003	965	..	447	..	..	518	706
Qatar	2004	979	..	450	..	..	529	681
	2005	924	..	104	..	..	820	1009
	2006	994	..	0	..	..	994	1062

Table 22

Production, trade and consumption of gas-diesel oils
Production, commerce et consommation de gazole/carburant diesel
Thousand metric tons and kilograms per capita
Milliers de tonnes métriques et kilogrammes par habitant

Country or area Pays ou zone	Year Année	Production Production	Imports Importations	Exports Exportations	Bunkers Soutes	Changes in stocks Variations des stocks	Consumption Consommation	
							Total Totale	Per capita Par habitant
Saudi Arabia	2003	28899	24	8454	..	-82	20551	933
Arabie saoudite	2004	31486	29	10323	..	-67	21259	942
	2005	31685	29	9048	..	64	22602	978
	2006	32412	0	7871	..	-116	24657	1041
Singapore	2003	9938	6179	14404	1501	-1132	1344	321
Singapour	2004	11711	5628	14424	1507	24	1384	327
	2005	14474	3860	14679	1546	786	1323	305
	2006	13939	6124	16698	1592	372	1401	312
Sri Lanka	2003	622	912	..	35	-35	1534	80
Sri Lanka	2004	693	1166	..	37	30	1792	92
	2005	591	856	..	44	6	1397	71
	2006	628	966	..	41	55	1498	75
Syrian Arab Republic	2003	3906	484	..	..	..	4390	250
Rép. arabe syrienne	2004	4123	511	..	..	..	4634	260
	2005	3934	488	..	..	..	4422	242
	2006	3934	488	..	..	..	4422	236
Tajikistan	2003	..	72	..	..	..	72	11
Tadjikistan	2004	..	78	..	..	..	78	12
	2005	..	84	..	..	..	84	12
	2006	..	95	..	..	..	95	13
Thailand	2003	15608	504	1789	..	-303	14626	228
Thaïlande	2004	17511	614	2053	..	-860	16932	264
	2005	16378	599	1506	..	-849	16320	252
	2006	16737	304	2448	..	-708	15301	234
Timor-Leste	2003	..	*80	..	..	..	*80	*80
Timor-Leste	2004	..	*83	..	..	..	*83	*81
	2005	..	*84	..	..	..	*84	*81
	2006	..	*85	..	..	..	*85	*80
Turkey	2003	8087	2715	931	384	50	9437	134
Turquie	2004	7665	3818	903	564	-108	10124	142
	2005	7601	4146	1278	538	-138	10069	140
	2006	7549	6436	1773	409	166	11637	159
Turkmenistan	2003	2622	..	1654	..	..	968	206
Turkménistan	2004	2522	..	1591	..	..	931	195
	2005	2607	..	1645	..	..	962	199
	2006	3105	..	1959	..	..	1146	234
United Arab Emirates	2003	4609	1607	2206	96	..	3914	1102
Emirats arabes unis	2004	4754	1417	2075	97	..	3999	1063
	2005	4262	1853	1760	98	..	4257	1037
	2006	4428	1977	1829	104	..	4472	1057
Uzbekistan	2003	1993	..	270	..	..	1723	67
Ouzbékistan	2004	1879	..	254	..	..	1625	62
	2005	1535	..	208	..	..	1327	50
	2006	1433	..	194	..	..	1239	46
Viet Nam	2003	..	4654	247	..	..	4407	54
Viet Nam	2004	..	5477	0	..	..	5477	67
	2005	..	5892	280	..	..	5612	68
	2006	..	5520	262	..	..	5258	62
Yemen	2003	819	1399	14	64	..	2140	114
Yémen	2004	883	1475	0	64	..	2294	118
	2005	959	1555	1	64	..	2449	123
	2006	801	1965	0	64	..	2702	131

Table 22

Production, trade and consumption of gas-diesel oils
Production, commerce et consommation de gazole/carburant diesel
Thousand metric tons and kilograms per capita
Milliers de tonnes métriques et kilogrammes par habitant

Country or area Pays ou zone	Year Année	Production Production	Imports Importations	Exports Exportations	Bunkers Soutes	Changes in stocks Variations des stocks	Consumption Consommation Total Totale	Per capita Par habitant
Europe	2003	336425	96163	107048	8201	463	316876	436
Europe	2004	340617	101804	111706	7805	-487	323397	444
	2005	352249	111784	121821	7778	5058	329376	452
	2006	354085	119476	128589	7954	1606	335412	459
Albania	2003	95	501	..	..	..	596	169
Albanie	2004	73	654	..	..	..	727	233
	2005	72	602	..	..	..	674	215
	2006	99	478	..	..	..	577	183
Austria	2003	3849	4351	539	..	-29	7690	953
Autriche	2004	3529	4883	580	..	205	7627	937
	2005	3894	5055	909	..	-50	8090	986
	2006	3685	4830	615	..	146	7754	936
Belarus	2003	4913	248	3493	..	0	1668	169
Bélarus	2004	5845	202	4250	..	-12	1809	184
	2005	6426	317	4691	..	5	2047	209
	2006	6616	929	5366	..	-149	2328	239
Belgium	2003	13013	6657	7419	665	132	11454	1106
Belgique	2004	12327	8080	8193	496	-158	11876	1142
	2005	11938	9693	8919	518	269	11925	1142
	2006	12660	8165	7932	644	80	12169	1158
Bosnia and Herzegovina	2003	19	423	12	..	..	430	112
Bosnie y Herzégovine	2004	42	473	0	..	..	515	134
	2005	31	466	0	..	..	497	129
	2006	31	501	0	..	..	532	138
Bulgaria	2003	1878	183	512	137	-44	1456	186
Bulgarie	2004	1915	180	467	115	-22	1535	197
	2005	2270	362	665	110	120	1737	224
	2006	2521	582	1085	106	2	1910	248
Croatia	2003	1873	234	454	6	-25	1672	376
Croatie	2004	1741	471	495	8	-10	1719	387
	2005	1603	543	349	9	10	1778	400
	2006	1565	686	394	7	28	1822	410
Czech Republic	2003	2590	1280	640	..	59	3171	311
République tchèque	2004	2673	1260	365	..	28	3540	347
	2005	3067	1311	524	..	11	3843	376
	2006	3128	1262	360	..	69	3961	385
Denmark	2003	3451	1927	1137	485	34	3722	704
Danemark	2004	3329	1829	1141	378	-168	3807	705
	2005	3224	2105	967	326	296	3740	691
	2006	3298	2392	1672	307	-113	3824	704
Estonia	2003	..	504	..	44	-24	484	358
Estonie	2004	..	599	..	50	2	547	405
	2005	..	586	..	45	-15	556	413
	2006	..	632	..	45	35	552	411
Faeroe Islands	2003	..	*199	..	..	..	*199	*4152
Iles Féroé	2004	..	*199	..	..	..	*199	*4124
	2005	..	*200	..	..	..	*200	*4144
	2006	..	*200	..	..	..	*200	*4144
Finland	2003	5038	2082	2243	94	142	4641	890
Finlande	2004	5078	1990	1882	49	-174	5311	1016
	2005	4964	2492	1839	49	101	5467	1042
	2006	5502	2482	2222	61	30	5671	1077

Table 22

Production, trade and consumption of gas-diesel oils
Production, commerce et consommation de gazole/carburant diesel

Thousand metric tons and kilograms per capita
Milliers de tonnes métriques et kilogrammes par habitant

Country or area Pays ou zone	Year Année	Production Production	Imports Importations	Exports Exportations	Bunkers Soutes	Changes in stocks Variations des stocks	Consumption Consommation	
							Total Totale	Per capita Par habitant
France incl. Monaco	2003	34979	16778	2106	317	431	48903	813
France y compris Monaco	2004	34421	16865	1746	291	124	49125	811
	2005	33590	19830	3642	258	787	48733	800
	2006	33733	16873	3437	222	-47	46994	770
Germany	2003	48638	14633	6328	501	596	55846	677
Allemagne	2004	49551	13121	8150	442	-677	54757	664
	2005	52137	13612	10003	434	1256	54056	656
	2006	50854	16290	10876	521	-509	56256	683
Gibraltar	2003	..	195	..	132	..	63	2250
Gibraltar	2004	..	201	..	136	..	65	2321
	2005	..	206	..	139	..	67	2393
	2006	..	211	..	144	..	67	2320
Greece	2003	6053	3003	1102	497	-129	7586	688
Grèce	2004	5369	3672	1164	472	204	7201	651
	2005	5653	3757	1480	384	271	7275	655
	2006	6452	3594	2311	398	204	7133	640
Hungary	2003	3124	923	1376	..	86	2585	255
Hongrie	2004	2989	1173	1298	..	40	2824	279
	2005	3515	1339	1377	..	43	3434	340
	2006	3498	1319	1257	..	-63	3623	360
Iceland	2003	..	384	..	63	-31	352	1217
Islande	2004	..	466	..	69	16	381	1302
	2005	..	418	..	62	-11	367	1240
	2006	..	386	..	32	-7	361	1186
Ireland	2003	988	2351	118	107	-86	3200	804
Irlande	2004	964	2510	124	101	-10	3259	806
	2005	1097	2168	154	80	136	2895	701
	2006	1121	2177	82	75	-140	3281	775
Italy and San Marino	2003	38389	724	9611	677	-617	29442	511
Italie y comp. St. Marin	2004	39536	1011	9545	684	-222	30540	525
	2005	39844	1524	9572	636	-131	31291	534
	2006	39805	1602	8952	607	389	31459	534
Latvia	2003	..	669	0	73	4	592	255
Lettonie	2004	..	776	50	75	6	645	279
	2005	..	900	116	90	36	658	286
	2006	..	896	106	65	17	708	309
Lithuania	2003	2064	39	1651	18	33	401	116
Lituanie	2004	2523	123	2180	20	-24	470	137
	2005	2781	87	2194	18	63	593	174
	2006	2246	92	1660	15	-15	678	200
Luxembourg	2003	..	1646	5	..	4	1637	3625
Luxembourg	2004	..	1915	6	..	-8	1917	4185
	2005	..	2083	8	..	-10	2085	4482
	2006	..	2058	4	..	20	2034	4304
Malta	2003	..	181	..	..	..	181	453
Malte	2004	..	160	..	..	..	160	397
	2005	..	164	..	..	..	164	405
	2006	..	148	..	..	..	148	364
Netherlands	2003	20787	9342	20552	1879	-540	8238	509
Pays-Bas	2004	20234	10013	20177	1825	325	7920	487
	2005	21346	9650	21061	1934	546	7455	457
	2006	19685	13642	24299	1929	-14	7113	435

Table 22

Production, trade and consumption of gas-diesel oils
Production, commerce et consommation de gazole/carburant diesel

Thousand metric tons and kilograms per capita
Milliers de tonnes métriques et kilogrammes par habitant

Country or area Pays ou zone	Year Année	Production Production	Imports Importations	Exports Exportations	Bunkers Soutes	Changes in stocks Variations des stocks	Consumption Consommation	
							Total Totale	Per capita Par habitant
Norway,Svlbd.J.Myn. I	2003	6635	777	2727	300	60	4325	944
Norvège,Svalbd,J.May	2004	6241	819	2725	262	-65	4138	898
	2005	6835	576	2458	404	107	4442	957
	2006	7101	916	2960	320	54	4683	1005
Poland	2003	6722	1376	161	46	-27	7918	207
Pologne	2004	7371	2238	240	39	148	9182	240
	2005	7459	2749	596	116	149	9347	245
	2006	8336	2541	313	87	543	9934	261
Portugal	2003	4955	949	51	149	352	5352	513
Portugal	2004	4703	841	71	145	-155	5483	522
	2005	4906	877	211	136	59	5377	510
	2006	5102	638	314	135	23	5268	498
Republic of Moldova	2003	..	301	..	..	10	291	81
Rép. de Moldova	2004	..	324	..	..	-3	327	91
	2005	..	334	..	..	3	331	92
	2006	..	326	..	..	-9	335	93
Romania	2003	3988	500	1350	..	6	3132	144
Roumanie	2004	4170	433	1591	..	-52	3064	141
	2005	4709	191	1900	..	-74	3074	142
	2006	4593	252	1603	..	-53	3295	153
Russian Federation	2003	53930	1	30029	..	-224	24126	167
Fédération de Russie	2004	55389	2	30140	..	-174	25425	177
	2005	60003	1	33983	..	164	25857	181
	2006	64166	0	36825	..	310	27031	190
Serbia	2003	1254	70	0	..	..	1324	125
Serbie	2004	1315	3	59	..	..	1259	120
	2005	1234	152	62	..	..	1324	126
	2006	1038	465	65	..	..	1438	138
Slovakia	2003	2349	233	1587	..	77	918	171
Slovaquie	2004	2598	445	2013	..	-6	1036	192
	2005	2455	515	1825	..	41	1104	205
	2006	2587	499	1899	..	18	1169	217
Slovenia	2003	..	1393	55	..	23	1315	659
Slovénie	2004	..	1520	81	..	8	1431	717
	2005	..	1641	141	..	24	1476	738
	2006	..	1798	304	..	-58	1552	773
Spain	2003	21631	10800	747	936	23	30725	731
Espagne	2004	21563	11830	656	923	-12	31826	745
	2005	23457	13217	822	980	875	33997	783
	2006	23844	13605	950	1047	461	34991	794
Sweden	2003	6942	2311	3810	168	144	5131	573
Suède	2004	7238	1895	4290	143	26	4674	520
	2005	6951	1867	3807	150	199	4662	516
	2006	7204	1835	4154	143	-29	4771	525
Switzerland	2003	1893	4028	9	10	-68	5970	813
Suisse	2004	2148	3831	4	9	28	5938	797
	2005	2170	4347	2	12	149	6354	852
	2006	2573	4160	3	9	89	6632	886
T.F.Yug.Rep. Macedonia	2003	322	84	82	..	-9	333	164
L'ex-RY Macédoine	2004	359	70	85	..	4	340	167
	2005	394	90	140	..	2	342	168
	2006	443	80	172	..	10	341	167

Table 22

Production, trade and consumption of gas-diesel oils
Production, commerce et consommation de gazole/carburant diesel
Thousand metric tons and kilograms per capita
Milliers de tonnes métriques et kilogrammes par habitant

Country or area Pays ou zone	Year Année	Production Production	Imports Importations	Exports Exportations	Bunkers Soutes	Changes in stocks Variations des stocks	Consumption Consommation	
							Total Totale	Per capita Par habitant
Ukraine Ukraine	2003	6484	380	1614	..	0	5250	110
	2004	6544	511	1315	..	47	5693	120
	2005	5533	835	1089	..	-89	5368	114
	2006	4519	1871	578	..	0	5812	124
United Kingdom Royaume-Uni	2003	27579	3503	5528	897	100	24557	414
	2004	28839	4216	6623	1073	254	25105	421
	2005	28691	4922	6315	888	-284	26694	443
	2006	26080	8063	5819	1035	284	27005	446
Oceania Océanie	**2003**	**13448**	**3286**	**968**	**271**	**-103**	**15598**	**481**
	2004	**13503**	**4078**	**987**	**270**	**-19**	**16343**	**497**
	2005	**12985**	**5371**	**397**	**235**	**-64**	**17788**	**533**
	2006	**11815**	**7279**	**540**	**374**	**53**	**18127**	**535**
Australia Australie	2003	11430	1372	878	80	-73	11917	599
	2004	11590	1571	838	85	-26	12264	609
	2005	10790	3328	299	51	-36	13804	676
	2006	9466	5168	354	195	26	14059	679
Cook Islands Iles Cook	2003	..	6	..	..	..	6	326
	2004	..	13	..	..	..	13	640
	2005	..	15	..	..	..	15	743
	2006	..	*16	..	..	..	*16	*751
Fiji Fidji	2003	..	514	*60	*70	..	384	463
	2004	..	640	*80	*80	..	480	575
	2005	..	554	*70	*70	..	414	492
	2006	..	512	*65	*65	..	382	448
French Polynesia Polynésie française	2003	..	133	..	*33	..	100	404
	2004	..	139	..	*42	..	97	386
	2005	..	145	..	*43	..	102	401
	2006	..	151	..	*45	..	106	414
Kiribati Kiribati	2003	..	*4	..	..	..	*4	*43
	2004	..	*4	..	..	..	*4	*40
	2005	..	*4	..	..	..	*4	*39
	2006	..	*5	..	..	..	*5	*47
Marshall Islands Îles Marshall	2003	..	*27	..	..	..	*27	*495
	2004	..	*29	..	..	..	*29	*496
	2005	..	*28	..	..	..	*28	*481
	2006	..	*30	..	..	..	*30	*496
Nauru Nauru	2003	..	*4	..	..	..	*4	*318
	2004	..	*4	..	..	..	*4	*312
	2005	..	*4	..	..	..	*4	*307
	2006	..	*4	..	..	..	*4	*301
New Caledonia Nouvelle-Calédonie	2003	..	135	23	..	..	112	491
	2004	..	125	24	..	..	101	438
	2005	..	147	*25	..	..	122	521
	2006	..	204	*27	..	..	177	744
New Zealand Nouvelle-Zélande	2003	2018	355	7	62	-30	2334	582
	2004	1763	787	5	37	7	2501	616
	2005	1785	709	3	45	-28	2474	604
	2006	1819	753	0	43	27	2502	604
Niue Nioué	2003	..	*1	..	..	..	*1	*565
	2004	..	*1	..	..	..	*1	*568
	2005	..	*1	..	..	..	*1	*593
	2006	..	*1	..	..	..	*1	*615

Table 22

Production, trade and consumption of gas-diesel oils
Production, commerce et consommation de gazole/carburant diesel

Thousand metric tons and kilograms per capita
Milliers de tonnes métriques et kilogrammes par habitant

Country or area Pays ou zone	Year Année	Production Production	Imports Importations	Exports Exportations	Bunkers Soutes	Changes in stocks Variations des stocks	Consumption Consommation	
							Total Totale	Per capita Par habitant
Palau	2003	..	*11	..	..	..	*11	*542
Palaos	2004	..	*11	..	..	..	*11	*534
	2005	..	*11	..	..	..	*11	*526
	2006	..	*11	..	..	..	*11	*508
Papua New Guinea	2003	0	602	0	*26	..	576	99
Papouasie-Nvl-Guinée	2004	150	635	40	*26	..	719	121
	2005	410	306	0	*26	..	690	114
	2006	530	306	94	*26	..	716	115
Samoa	2003	..	*23	..	..	..	*23	*128
Samoa	2004	..	*23	..	..	..	*23	*127
	2005	..	*23	..	..	..	*23	*125
	2006	..	*23	..	..	..	*23	*124
Solomon Islands	2003	..	*43	..	..	..	*43	*96
Iles Salomon	2004	..	*42	..	..	..	*42	*91
	2005	..	*42	..	..	..	*42	*89
	2006	..	*42	..	..	..	*42	*87
Tonga	2003	..	28	..	..	..	28	277
Tonga	2004	..	26	..	..	..	26	255
	2005	..	*25	..	..	..	*25	*244
	2006	..	*25	..	..	..	*25	*247
Vanuatu	2003	..	*22	..	..	..	*22	*104
Vanuatu	2004	..	*22	..	..	..	*22	*103
	2005	..	*22	..	..	..	*22	*102
	2006	..	*22	..	..	..	*22	*100
Wallis and Futuna Is	2003	..	*6	..	..	..	*6	*397
Iles Wallis et Futuna	2004	..	6	..	..	..	6	411
	2005	..	7	..	..	..	7	414
	2006	..	7	..	..	..	7	406

Table 23

Production, trade and consumption of residual fuel oil
Production, commerce et consommation de mazout résiduel
Thousand metric tons and kilograms per capita
Milliers de tonnes métriques et kilogrammes par habitant

Table Notes:
Production from refineries and plants.

- **Please refer to the Definitions Section on pages xv to xxix for the appropriate product description /classification.**

Notes relatives aux tableaux:
Production à partir des raffineries et des usines.

- **Veuillez consulter la section "définitions" de la page xv à la page xxix pour une description/classification appropriée des produits.**

Figure 66: World production of residual fuel oil 1993-2006

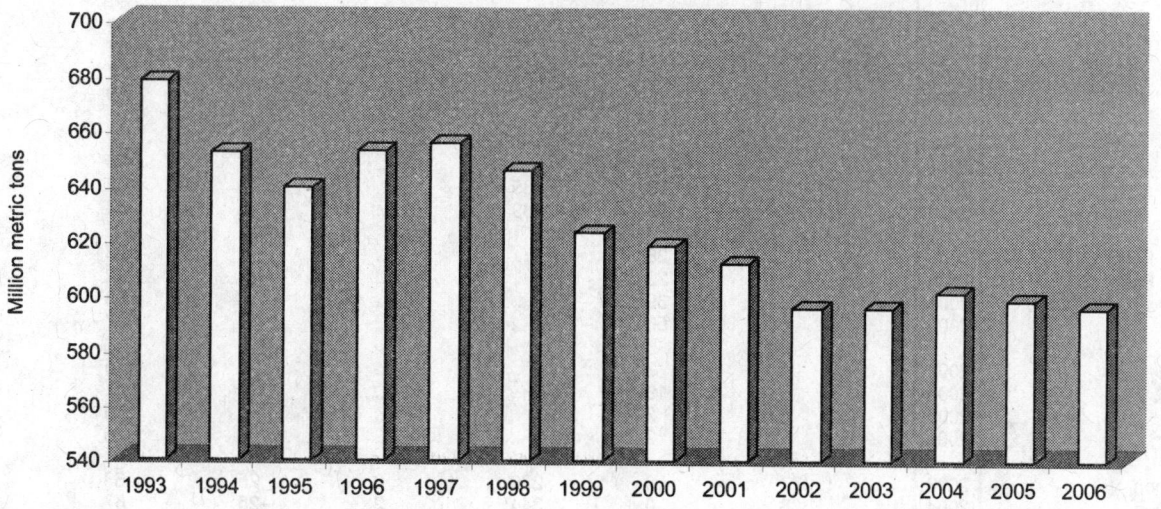

Figure 67: Major residual fuel oil producing countries in 2006

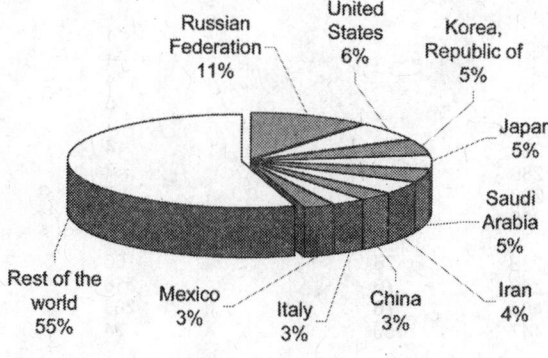

Figure 68: Major residual fuel oil consuming countries in 2006

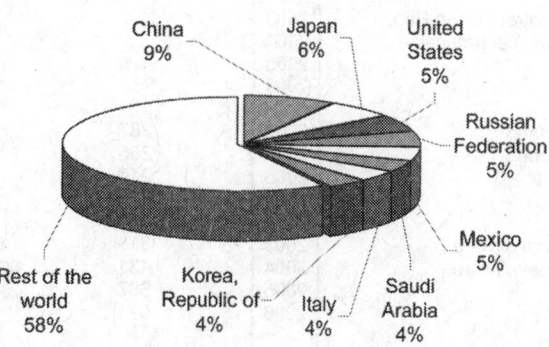

Table 23

Production, trade and consumption of residual fuel oil
Production, commerce et consommation de mazout résiduel
Thousand metric tons and kilograms per capita
Milliers de tonnes métriques et kilogrammes par habitant

Country or area Pays ou zone	Year Année	Production Production	Imports Importations	Exports Exportations	Bunkers Soutes	Changes in stocks Variations des stocks	Consumption Consommation	
							Total Totale	Per capita Par habitant
World	**2003**	**594417**	**170234**	**221946**	**119732**	**1503**	**421471**	**67**
Monde	**2004**	**601312**	**195325**	**243245**	**130723**	**-888**	**423558**	**67**
	2005	**598400**	**205651**	**255362**	**143845**	**-5572**	**410416**	**64**
	2006	**595209**	**201915**	**267878**	**152155**	**1028**	**376063**	**58**
Africa	**2003**	**33990**	**3137**	**17570**	**5540**	**-28**	**14045**	**17**
Afrique	**2004**	**34162**	**3382**	**14809**	**4582**	**-339**	**18493**	**21**
	2005	**35051**	**3165**	**13377**	**4947**	**-228**	**20120**	**23**
	2006	**34147**	**3414**	**13219**	**4064**	**124**	**20154**	**22**
Algeria	2003	6093	157	6012	151	79	8	0
Algérie	2004	5560	234	5563	267	-44	8	0
	2005	5055	269	4971	266	-24	111	3
	2006	5337	253	5242	263	81	4	0
Angola	2003	609	..	477	0	..	132	12
Angola	2004	604	..	517	0	..	87	8
	2005	609	..	531	1	..	77	7
	2006	644	..	584	1	..	59	5
Benin	2003	..	39	28	..	-1	12	2
Bénin	2004	..	48	36	..	-1	13	2
	2005	..	85	35	..	7	43	5
	2006	..	88	39	..	-5	54	6
Burkina Faso	2003	..	28	..	..	4	23	2
Burkina Faso	2004	..	22	..	..	-10	32	2
	2005	..	39	..	..	5	33	3
	2006	..	50	..	..	-6	57	4
Burundi	2003	..	2	..	..	*-3	*5	*1
Burundi	2004	..	19	..	..	*12	7	1
	2005	..	2	..	..	*-3	*5	*1
	2006	..	2	..	..	*-3	*5	*1
Cameroon	2003	327	0	239	0	25	63	4
Cameroun	2004	388	0	344	2	-25	67	4
	2005	341	9	277	2	-19	90	5
	2006	354	11	235	8	13	109	6
Cape Verde	2003	..	*36	..	..	..	*36	*79
Cap-Vert	2004	..	*39	..	..	..	*39	*84
	2005	..	*40	..	..	..	*40	*84
	2006	..	*41	..	..	..	*41	*84
Central African Rep.	2003	..	*4	..	..	..	*4	*1
Rép. centrafricaine	2004	..	*4	..	..	..	*4	*1
	2005	..	*4	..	..	..	*4	*1
	2006	..	*5	..	..	..	*5	*1
Congo	2003	287	..	273	..	..	14	4
Congo	2004	295	..	288	..	..	7	2
	2005	210	..	203	..	..	7	2
	2006	377	..	365	..	..	12	3
Côte d'Ivoire	2003	318	62	238	76	..	66	4
Côte d'Ivoire	2004	431	212	249	76	..	318	17
	2005	687	0	408	76	..	203	11
	2006	521	0	447	50	..	24	1
Dem. Rep. of Congo	2003	..	13	5	2	..	6	0
Rép. dem. du Congo	2004	..	13	5	2	..	6	0
	2005	..	13	5	2	..	6	0
	2006	..	13	5	2	..	6	0

Table 23

Production, trade and consumption of residual fuel oil
Production, commerce et consommation de mazout résiduel
Thousand metric tons and kilograms per capita
Milliers de tonnes métriques et kilogrammes par habitant

Country or area Pays ou zone	Year Année	Production Production	Imports Importations	Exports Exportations	Bunkers Soutes	Changes in stocks Variations des stocks	Consumption Consommation	
							Total Totale	Per capita Par habitant
Djibouti	2003	..	80	..	*42	..	38	49
Djibouti	2004	..	85	..	*43	..	42	53
	2005	..	90	..	*43	..	47	58
	2006	..	100	..	*53	..	47	57
Egypt	2003	10532	..	3466	2555	..	4511	67
Egypte	2004	11273	..	1174	1670	..	8429	118
	2005	11643	..	830	1788	..	9025	126
	2006	10653	..	208	965	..	9480	130
Eritrea	2003	..	64	0	..	-5	69	17
Erythrée	2004	..	68	3	..	-3	68	16
	2005	..	65	0	..	-7	72	16
	2006	..	53	0	..	-3	56	12
Ethiopia	2003	..	133	..	..	26	107	2
Ethiopie	2004	..	156	..	..	35	121	2
	2005	..	158	..	..	37	121	2
	2006	..	159	..	..	38	121	2
Gabon	2003	302	..	268	100	-163	97	75
Gabon	2004	324	..	269	103	-143	95	70
	2005	305	..	254	108	-184	127	91
	2006	324	..	272	108	-153	97	68
Gambia	2003	..	*1	..	..	..	*1	*1
Gambie	2004	..	*1	..	..	..	*1	*1
	2005	..	*1	..	..	..	*1	*1
	2006	..	*2	..	..	..	*2	*1
Ghana	2003	216	..	152	..	..	64	3
Ghana	2004	239	..	191	..	..	48	2
	2005	242	..	191	..	..	51	2
	2006	156	..	46	..	..	110	5
Guinea	2003	..	*179	..	..	..	*179	*21
Guinée	2004	..	*179	..	..	..	*179	*20
	2005	..	*181	..	..	..	*181	*20
	2006	..	*181	..	..	..	*181	*20
Guinea-Bissau	2003	..	*27	..	..	..	*27	*21
Guinée-Bissau	2004	..	*27	..	..	..	*27	*21
	2005	..	*27	..	..	..	*27	*20
	2006	..	*27	..	..	..	*27	*20
Kenya	2003	524	133	116	11	..	530	16
Kenya	2004	620	50	209	21	..	440	13
	2005	549	44	30	24	..	539	15
	2006	596	46	29	27	..	586	16
Liberia	2003	..	*50	..	*11	..	*39	*11
Libéria	2004	..	*50	..	*11	..	*39	*11
	2005	..	*50	..	*11	..	*39	*11
	2006	..	*50	..	*11	..	*39	*11
Libyan Arab Jamah.	2003	4556	..	1768	90	..	2698	434
Jamah. arabe libyenne	2004	4597	..	1930	90	..	2577	401
	2005	4443	..	1309	90	..	3044	459
	2006	4419	..	1156	90	..	3173	474
Madagascar	2003	*77	*15	*20	*13	..	*59	*4
Madagascar	2004	*77	*15	*20	*13	..	*59	*3
	2005	*78	*15	*20	*13	..	*60	*3
	2006	*78	*15	*20	*13	..	*60	*3

Table 23

Production, trade and consumption of residual fuel oil
Production, commerce et consommation de mazout résiduel
Thousand metric tons and kilograms per capita
Milliers de tonnes métriques et kilogrammes par habitant

Country or area Pays ou zone	Year Année	Production Production	Imports Importations	Exports Exportations	Bunkers Soutes	Changes in stocks Variations des stocks	Consumption Consommation Total Totale	Per capita Par habitant
Malawi	2003	..	*1	..	..	..	*1	0
Malawi	2004	..	*1	..	..	..	*1	0
	2005	..	*1	..	..	..	*1	0
	2006	..	*1	..	..	..	*1	0
Mali	2003	..	*10	..	..	..	*10	*1
Mali	2004	..	*11	..	..	..	*11	*1
	2005	..	*12	..	..	..	*12	*1
	2006	..	*12	..	..	..	*12	*1
Mauritania	2003	..	76	..	..	..	76	27
Mauritanie	2004	..	77	..	..	..	77	27
	2005	..	99	..	..	..	99	34
	2006	..	108	..	..	..	108	36
Mauritius	2003	..	288	..	35	-7	260	215
Maurice	2004	..	289	..	40	-21	270	221
	2005	..	330	..	55	11	264	212
	2006	..	327	..	59	-40	308	246
Morocco	2003	1747	..	299	..	8	1440	50
Maroc	2004	2264	..	785	..	-50	1529	51
	2005	2545	..	581	..	52	1912	63
	2006	2265	..	327	..	-41	1979	65
Mozambique	2003	..	27	..	..	4	23	1
Mozambique	2004	..	22	..	..	-1	23	1
	2005	..	7	..	..	-1	8	0
	2006	..	0	..	..	-2	2	0
Niger	2003	..	19	..	..	..	19	2
Niger	2004	..	11	..	..	..	11	1
	2005	..	3	..	..	..	3	0
	2006	..	9	..	..	..	9	1
Nigeria	2003	1838	..	1247	..	0	591	5
Nigéria	2004	1866	..	1035	..	0	831	6
	2005	1894	..	859	..	-133	1168	9
	2006	2159	..	1471	..	0	688	5
Réunion	2003	..	*129	..	*22	..	*107	*142
Réunion	2004	..	*133	..	*23	..	*110	*144
	2005	..	*134	..	*23	..	*111	*143
	2006	..	*136	..	*24	..	*112	*141
Rwanda	2003	..	*19	..	..	..	*19	*2
Rwanda	2004	..	20	..	..	..	20	2
	2005	..	*21	..	..	..	*21	*2
	2006	..	*23	..	..	..	*23	*2
Senegal	2003	316	115	4	..	-11	438	43
Sénégal	2004	327	104	12	..	7	412	39
	2005	279	176	8	..	-3	450	41
	2006	100	233	19	..	19	295	27
Seychelles	2003	..	55	..	*1	..	54	651
Seychelles	2004	..	49	..	*1	..	48	577
	2005	..	59	..	*2	..	57	683
	2006	..	67	..	*2	..	65	774
Sierra Leone	2003	*55	*29	..	*19	..	*65	*12
Sierra Leone	2004	*45	34	..	*20	..	*59	*10
	2005	*35	*35	..	*20	..	*50	*9
	2006	*40	*30	..	*20	..	*50	*8

Table 23

Production, trade and consumption of residual fuel oil
Production, commerce et consommation de mazout résiduel
Thousand metric tons and kilograms per capita
Milliers de tonnes métriques et kilogrammes par habitant

Country or area Pays ou zone	Year Année	Production Production	Imports Importations	Exports Exportations	Bunkers Soutes	Changes in stocks Variations des stocks	Consumption Consommation Total Totale	Per capita Par habitant
Somalia	2003	20	*10	..	*10	..	20	3
Somalie	2004	25	*5	..	*10	..	20	3
	2005	25	*5	..	*10	..	20	2
	2006	25	*5	..	*10	..	20	2
South Africa Customs Un.	2003	5162	135	2373	2380	..	544	11
Un.douan.d'Afr.mérid	2004	4192	150	1594	2168	..	580	11
	2005	5040	124	2265	2391	..	508	9
	2006	4906	122	2205	2327	..	496	9
Sudan	2003	328	209	..	..	-4	541	16
Soudan	2004	361	230	..	..	-83	674	20
	2005	377	119	..	..	-21	517	15
	2006	504	322	..	..	249	577	16
Togo	2003	..	47	..	..	-2	49	10
Togo	2004	..	50	..	..	-3	53	10
	2005	..	25	..	..	-3	28	5
	2006	..	6	..	..	-16	22	4
Tunisia	2003	609	750	585	0	8	766	78
Tunisie	2004	595	770	585	0	-24	804	81
	2005	609	706	600	0	40	675	67
	2006	604	698	549	9	-22	766	76
Uganda	2003	..	*43	..	..	..	*43	*2
Ouganda	2004	..	*44	..	..	..	*44	*2
	2005	..	50	..	..	..	50	2
	2006	..	43	..	..	..	43	1
United Rep.Tanzania	2003	..	130	..	22	..	108	3
Rép. Unie de Tanzanie	2004	..	138	..	22	..	116	3
	2005	..	146	..	22	..	124	3
	2006	..	153	..	22	..	131	3
Western Sahara	2003	..	*22	..	..	..	*22	*84
Sahara occidental	2004	..	*22	..	..	..	*22	*82
	2005	..	*22	..	..	..	*22	*81
	2006	..	*22	..	..	..	*22	*80
Zambia	2003	74	..	..	..	14	60	6
Zambie	2004	79	..	..	..	15	64	6
	2005	85	..	..	..	18	67	6
	2006	85	..	..	..	15	70	6
America, North	**2003**	**80680**	**33940**	**23941**	**16278**	**1032**	**73369**	**146**
Amérique du Nord	**2004**	**79551**	**40162**	**23802**	**20297**	**749**	**74865**	**148**
	2005	**76647**	**46463**	**26779**	**22340**	**-1605**	**75595**	**148**
	2006	**73497**	**35980**	**28456**	**24021**	**2054**	**54946**	**106**
Antigua and Barbuda	2003	..	*20	..	*3	..	*17	*213
Antigua-et-Barbuda	2004	..	*22	..	*3	..	*19	*235
	2005	..	*23	..	*3	..	*20	*242
	2006	..	*24	..	*3	..	*21	*250
Aruba	2003	..	*146	..	..	..	*146	*1536
Aruba	2004	..	*146	..	..	..	*146	*1495
	2005	..	*148	..	..	..	*148	*1471
	2006	..	*148	..	..	..	*148	*1439
Bahamas	2003	..	*2600	*2200	*200	*20	*180	*564
Bahamas	2004	..	*2650	*2240	*208	0	*202	*674
	2005	..	*2700	*2250	*220	0	*230	*712
	2006	..	*2700	*2250	*220	0	*230	*703

Table 23

Production, trade and consumption of residual fuel oil
Production, commerce et consommation de mazout résiduel

Thousand metric tons and kilograms per capita
Milliers de tonnes métriques et kilogrammes par habitant

Country or area Pays ou zone	Year Année	Production Production	Imports Importations	Exports Exportations	Bunkers Soutes	Changes in stocks Variations des stocks	Consumption Consommation	
							Total Totale	Per capita Par habitant
Barbados	2003	..	139	..	..	..	139	512
Barbade	2004	..	163	..	..	..	163	597
	2005	..	169	..	..	..	169	619
	2006	..	172	..	..	..	172	629
Belize	2003	..	*4	..	..	..	*4	*15
Belize	2004	..	*4	..	..	..	*4	*14
	2005	..	*5	..	..	..	*5	*17
	2006	..	*5	..	..	..	*5	*16
Bermuda	2003	..	*20	..	*3	..	*17	*270
Bermudes	2004	..	*20	..	*3	..	*17	*268
	2005	..	*21	..	*3	..	*18	*283
	2006	..	*21	..	*3	..	*18	*282
Canada	2003	7989	3502	2776	423	24	8268	261
Canada	2004	8724	2782	3505	532	37	7432	232
	2005	8263	2611	3496	531	-84	6931	215
	2006	7763	1490	3539	475	58	5181	159
Costa Rica	2003	222	26	0	..	-13	261	64
Costa Rica	2004	247	11	0	..	4	254	61
	2005	227	55	0	..	1	281	66
	2006	295	7	28	..	-11	285	65
Cuba	2003	1024	816	..	52	22	1766	156
Cuba	2004	858	1014	..	57	*15	1800	159
	2005	879	1934	..	58	0	2755	245
	2006	892	1342	..	*40	-25	2219	197
Dominican Republic	2003	449	1164	..	..	0	1613	180
Rép. dominicaine	2004	839	807	..	..	19	1627	179
	2005	812	909	..	..	-9	1730	188
	2006	762	829	..	..	-40	1631	174
El Salvador	2003	485	237	152	..	18	553	83
El Salvador	2004	543	231	229	..	7	538	80
	2005	419	169	36	..	93	460	67
	2006	437	196	15	..	109	508	73
Guadeloupe	2003	..	*289	..	..	..	*289	*659
Guadeloupe	2004	..	*292	..	..	..	*292	*656
	2005	..	*296	..	..	..	*296	*665
	2006	..	*296	..	..	..	*296	*647
Guatemala	2003	..	831	0	..	0	831	69
Guatemala	2004	..	914	0	..	0	914	74
	2005	..	932	0	..	15	917	72
	2006	..	741	1	..	-22	762	59
Haiti	2003	..	16	..	..	..	16	2
Haïti	2004	..	11	..	..	..	11	1
	2005	..	12	..	..	..	12	1
	2006	..	12	..	..	..	12	1
Honduras	2003	..	592	0	..	31	561	82
Honduras	2004	..	822	2	..	0	820	117
	2005	..	839	0	..	43	795	110
	2006	..	1133	0	..	76	1057	143
Jamaica	2003	495	1824	106	14	58	2141	806
Jamaïque	2004	370	1787	56	14	0	2087	780
	2005	268	1715	0	14	0	1969	743
	2006	561	1840	0	14	-16	2403	902

Table 23

Production, trade and consumption of residual fuel oil
Production, commerce et consommation de mazout résiduel

Thousand metric tons and kilograms per capita
Milliers de tonnes métriques et kilogrammes par habitant

Country or area Pays ou zone	Year Année	Production Production	Imports Importations	Exports Exportations	Bunkers Soutes	Changes in stocks Variations des stocks	Consumption Consommation Total Totale	Consumption Consommation Per capita Par habitant
Martinique Martinique	2003	*300	*2	*73	*17	..	*212	*543
	2004	*310	*2	*73	*17	..	*222	*564
	2005	*310	*2	*73	*17	..	*222	*558
	2006	*312	*3	*73	*17	..	*225	*563
Mexico Mexique	2003	22581	1147	1219	87	-180	22602	222
	2004	21089	1012	150	99	-4	21856	212
	2005	20019	1057	47	106	-54	20977	202
	2006	16914	778	44	108	-129	17669	168
Netherlands Antilles Antilles néerlandaises	2003	4269	814	3151	1490	..	442	2474
	2004	4257	823	3113	1490	..	477	2605
	2005	4712	835	3576	1490	..	481	2595
	2006	4540	850	3394	1490	..	506	2670
Nicaragua Nicaragua	2003	400	125	0	..	6	519	98
	2004	427	101	0	..	-9	537	100
	2005	378	141	5	..	15	499	91
	2006	404	137	16	..	-12	537	97
Panama Panama	2003	..	527	1	..	16	510	164
	2004	..	440	0	..	0	440	139
	2005	..	649	0	..	0	649	201
	2006	..	635	0	..	0	635	193
St. Lucia St-Lucie	2003	..	*5	..	*5	..	0	*1
	2004	..	*5	..	*5	..	0	*2
	2005	..	*6	..	*6	..	0	0
	2006	..	*6	..	*6	..	0	0
Trinidad and Tobago Trinité-et-Tobago	2003	3247	..	2871	358	15	3	2
	2004	2971	..	2482	443	43	3	2
	2005	3180	..	3022	172	-17	3	2
	2006	2951	..	*2900	*150	-106	7	5
United States Etats-Unis	2003	39219	19093	11392	13626	1015	32279	111
	2004	38916	26103	11952	17426	637	35004	119
	2005	37180	31235	14274	19720	-1607	36028	122
	2006	37666	22614	16196	21495	2171	20418	68
America, South Amérique du Sud	**2003**	**42985**	**524**	**22234**	**4904**	**1685**	**14685**	**41**
	2004	**46406**	**514**	**26101**	**4983**	**-127**	**15963**	**43**
	2005	**44668**	**1123**	**24407**	**6184**	**-783**	**15983**	**43**
	2006	**46554**	**1109**	**26065**	**5865**	**-1790**	**17523**	**46**
Argentina Argentine	2003	1946	7	851	405	1	696	18
	2004	2368	0	625	351	9	1383	36
	2005	2795	401	1011	533	14	1638	42
	2006	3422	113	970	581	-5	1989	51
Bolivia Bolivie	2003	0	..	..	..	..	0	0
	2004	0	..	..	..	..	0	0
	2005	0	..	..	..	..	0	0
	2006	1	..	..	..	..	1	0
Brazil Brésil	2003	15779	88	5566	2637	10	7654	43
	2004	16074	124	6969	2592	-248	6885	38
	2005	15461	50	5334	2874	-117	7420	40
	2006	15661	239	6084	2804	34	6978	37
Chile Chili	2003	1814	75	375	889	-75	700	44
	2004	2294	0	483	970	63	778	48
	2005	2306	121	591	1257	-73	652	40
	2006	2646	16	674	1416	-145	717	44

Table 23

Production, trade and consumption of residual fuel oil
Production, commerce et consommation de mazout résiduel

Thousand metric tons and kilograms per capita
Milliers de tonnes métriques et kilogrammes par habitant

Country or area Pays ou zone	Year Année	Production Production	Imports Importations	Exports Exportations	Bunkers Soutes	Changes in stocks Variations des stocks	Consumption Consommation	
							Total Totale	Per capita Par habitant
Colombia	2003	2932	3	2682	28	4	220	5
Colombie	2004	3330	4	3064	15	70	185	4
	2005	3056	147	3261	19	-242	165	4
	2006	2792	87	3505	19	-801	156	3
Ecuador	2003	3646	..	1869	260	553	964	75
Equateur	2004	3657	..	1700	228	184	1545	119
	2005	3492	..	1615	678	0	1199	91
	2006	3922	..	2047	*300	-130	1705	127
French Guiana	2003	..	*145	..	..	..	*145	*801
Guyane française	2004	..	*145	..	..	..	*145	*758
	2005	..	*145	..	..	..	*145	*742
	2006	..	*150	..	..	..	*150	*761
Guyana	2003	..	129	..	..	..	129	171
Guyana	2004	..	94	..	..	..	94	124
	2005	..	97	..	..	..	97	128
	2006	..	95	..	..	..	95	125
Paraguay	2003	30	47	..	..	29	48	8
Paraguay	2004	20	36	..	..	-3	60	10
	2005	11	57	..	..	0	68	11
	2006	0	53	..	..	1	52	9
Peru	2003	3245	..	1506	..	165	1574	59
Pérou	2004	3324	..	1282	..	57	1985	73
	2005	2958	..	1322	..	-88	1724	63
	2006	2878	..	908	..	467	1503	55
Suriname	2003	333	..	53	..	..	280	581
Suriname	2004	335	..	54	..	..	281	570
	2005	349	..	56	..	..	293	587
	2006	360	..	58	..	..	302	599
Uruguay	2003	448	30	16	219	18	225	66
Uruguay	2004	518	111	0	233	2	394	119
	2005	505	105	14	260	-16	352	106
	2006	381	356	0	151	8	578	174
Venezuela(Bolivar. Rep.)	2003	12812	..	9315	466	980	2050	80
Venezuela(Rép. bolivar.)	2004	14486	..	11924	594	-261	2229	85
	2005	13735	..	11203	563	-261	2230	84
	2006	14491	..	11819	594	-1220	3298	122
Asia	**2003**	**249050**	**80337**	**66208**	**51822**	**-1694**	**213051**	**56**
Asie	**2004**	**247470**	**99913**	**71657**	**55900**	**-260**	**220085**	**57**
	2005	**246917**	**97128**	**71725**	**62964**	**-2342**	**211697**	**54**
	2006	**246599**	**99383**	**81397**	**68111**	**-1031**	**197505**	**50**
Afghanistan	2003	..	*1	..	..	..	*1	0
Afghanistan	2004	..	0	..	..	..	0	0
	2005	..	*1	..	..	..	*1	0
	2006	..	*1	..	..	..	*1	0
Armenia	2003	..	0	..	..	..	0	0
Arménie	2004	..	1	..	..	..	1	0
	2005	..	0	..	..	..	0	0
	2006	..	0	..	..	..	0	0
Azerbaijan	2003	2470	0	146	..	7	2317	281
Azerbaïdjan	2004	2521	146	338	..	-28	2357	284
	2005	3061	209	392	..	253	2625	313
	2006	2899	104	925	..	-57	2135	252

Table 23

Production, trade and consumption of residual fuel oil
Production, commerce et consommation de mazout résiduel

Thousand metric tons and kilograms per capita
Milliers de tonnes métriques et kilogrammes par habitant

Country or area Pays ou zone	Year Année	Production Production	Imports Importations	Exports Exportations	Bunkers Soutes	Changes in stocks Variations des stocks	Consumption Consommation	
							Total Totale	Per capita Par habitant
Bahrain	2003	3008	..	3041	..	-33	0	0
Bahreïn	2004	2734	..	2708	..	26	0	0
	2005	2857	..	2795	..	62	0	0
	2006	2775	..	2706	..	-172	241	325
Bangladesh	2003	58	339	..	36	..	361	3
Bangladesh	2004	53	358	..	36	..	375	3
	2005	57	378	..	36	..	399	3
	2006	55	405	..	36	..	424	3
Brunei Darussalam	2003	77	..	..	..	..	77	220
Brunéi Darussalam	2004	89	..	..	..	..	89	247
	2005	92	..	..	..	..	92	249
	2006	103	..	..	..	..	103	269
Cambodia	2003	..	110	..	..	..	110	8
Cambodge	2004	..	142	..	..	..	142	11
	2005	..	155	..	..	..	155	11
	2006	..	243	..	..	..	243	17
China	2003	20048	18236	441	2251	-115	35707	28
Chine	2004	20293	30592	1817	230	832	48006	37
	2005	17674	26086	2300	777	-135	40818	31
	2006	17847	17993	2581	1300	-841	32800	25
China, Hong Kong SAR	2003	..	4001	898	3037	19	47	7
Chine, Hong-Kong RAS	2004	..	5500	1036	4486	-74	52	8
	2005	..	6245	2065	4152	-27	55	8
	2006	..	6542	835	5093	479	135	20
China, Macao SAR	2003	..	296	..	..	2	294	656
Chine, Macao RAS	2004	..	304	..	..	4	300	645
	2005	..	340	..	..	0	340	697
	2006	..	307	..	..	8	299	595
Cyprus	2003	362	821	..	88	-49	1144	1588
Chypre	2004	112	925	..	27	20	990	1343
	2005	0	1298	..	225	49	1024	1351
	2006	0	1404	..	190	11	1203	1561
Georgia	2003	13	11	14	..	..	10	2
Géorgie	2004	14	19	17	..	..	16	4
	2005	4	12	0	..	..	16	4
	2006	4	13	0	..	..	17	4
India	2003	13372	876	1124	..	..	13124	12
Inde	2004	14970	741	1792	..	..	13919	13
	2005	14305	789	1800	..	..	13294	12
	2006	15697	986	3759	..	..	12924	12
Indonesia	2003	11755	1404	5131	226	..	7802	36
Indonésie	2004	10995	1791	6349	76	..	6361	29
	2005	10105	1258	4763	76	..	6524	30
	2006	9686	1290	4919	76	..	5981	27
Iran(Islamic Rep. of)	2003	26566	..	14094	590	..	11882	179
Iran(Rép. islamique)	2004	25840	..	12651	624	..	12565	186
	2005	26241	..	12708	561	..	12972	189
	2006	26351	..	13394	463	..	12494	177
Iraq	2003	7404	..	279	..	..	7125	271
Iraq	2004	8257	..	1346	..	..	6911	255
	2005	8022	..	757	..	..	7265	264
	2006	8392	..	1565	..	..	6827	237

Table 23

Production, trade and consumption of residual fuel oil
Production, commerce et consommation de mazout résiduel
Thousand metric tons and kilograms per capita
Milliers de tonnes métriques et kilogrammes par habitant

Country or area Pays ou zone	Year Année	Production Production	Imports Importations	Exports Exportations	Bunkers Soutes	Changes in stocks Variations des stocks	Consumption Consommation Total Totale	Consumption Consommation Per capita Par habitant
Israel	2003	3440	1479	954	209	158	3598	538
Israël	2004	3168	1215	1298	190	-151	3046	447
	2005	3504	1136	1436	200	157	2847	411
	2006	3223	509	892	230	-22	2632	373
Japan	2003	34028	1893	1381	5012	-91	29619	235
Japon	2004	30985	2223	1756	5260	-27	26219	208
	2005	31419	3730	3018	5889	-72	26314	208
	2006	28315	2933	3003	5546	61	22638	179
Jordan	2003	1251	870	..	8	-89	2202	421
Jordanie	2004	1516	99	..	36	70	1509	296
	2005	1466	19	..	44	-28	1469	268
	2006	1345	0	..	28	28	1289	230
Kazakhstan	2003	2584	76	944	..	0	1716	115
Kazakhstan	2004	2708	196	883	..	0	2021	135
	2005	3874	256	1745	..	73	2312	153
	2006	3333	55	711	..	92	2585	169
Korea, Dem.Ppl's.Rep.	2003	116	442	..	..	..	558	24
Corée,Rép.pop.dém.de	2004	117	446	..	..	..	563	24
	2005	98	374	..	..	..	472	20
	2006	75	286	..	..	..	361	15
Korea, Republic of	2003	30095	2290	6882	5652	-198	20049	419
Corée, République de	2004	29912	1236	6836	6293	216	17803	370
	2005	31305	621	8434	9165	-357	14684	304
	2006	30793	1320	8748	9234	212	13919	288
Kuwait	2003	9800	..	2434	426	..	6940	2984
Koweït	2004	9760	..	954	437	..	8369	3501
	2005	9166	..	22	398	..	8746	3559
	2006	11951	..	3732	519	..	7700	3048
Kyrgyzstan	2003	39	35	0	..	..	74	15
Kirghizistan	2004	42	18	0	..	..	60	12
	2005	42	18	10	..	..	50	10
	2006	42	17	0	..	..	59	11
Lao People's Dem. Rep.	2003	..	*22	..	..	..	*22	*4
Rép. dém. pop. lao	2004	..	*21	..	..	..	*21	*4
	2005	..	*22	..	..	..	*22	*4
	2006	..	*22	..	..	..	*22	*4
Lebanon	2003	..	1285	..	16	-188	1457	372
Liban	2004	..	1383	..	17	0	1366	345
	2005	..	1360	..	17	-373	1716	428
	2006	..	1040	..	17	0	1023	252
Malaysia	2003	1777	1617	1742	25	15	1612	64
Malaisie	2004	1828	2419	2552	20	34	1640	64
	2005	1792	1756	1226	22	40	2259	86
	2006	1992	1548	1364	17	0	2159	81
Mongolia	2003	..	12	..	..	..	12	5
Mongolie	2004	..	11	..	..	..	11	4
	2005	..	5	..	..	..	5	2
	2006	..	4	..	..	..	4	2
Myanmar	2003	67	55	..	..	-6	128	2
Myanmar	2004	49	83	..	..	0	132	2
	2005	48	97	..	..	0	145	3
	2006	41	36	..	..	-15	92	2

Table 23

Production, trade and consumption of residual fuel oil
Production, commerce et consommation de mazout résiduel
Thousand metric tons and kilograms per capita
Milliers de tonnes métriques et kilogrammes par habitant

Country or area Pays ou zone	Year Année	Production Production	Imports Importations	Exports Exportations	Bunkers Soutes	Changes in stocks Variations des stocks	Consumption Consommation	
							Total Totale	Per capita Par habitant
Nepal	2003	..	8	..	..	..	8	0
Népal	2004	..	2	..	..	..	2	0
	2005	..	3	..	..	..	3	0
	2006	..	3	..	..	..	3	0
Oman	2003	2259	..	640	1	..	1618	691
Oman	2004	2121	..	663	0	..	1458	604
	2005	2167	..	718	1	..	1448	577
	2006	2244	..	252	0	..	1992	773
Other Asia	2003	14402	373	788	2891	-192	11288	499
Autre Asie	2004	13810	355	1081	2283	144	10657	470
	2005	12549	130	464	2235	-472	10452	460
	2006	11714	2406	329	2210	533	11048	485
Pakistan	2003	3058	666	..	12	-281	3993	27
Pakistan	2004	3132	1456	..	40	-188	4736	32
	2005	3358	1906	..	56	0	5208	34
	2006	3193	4309	..	85	-154	7571	48
Philippines	2003	3899	403	746	107	-53	3502	43
Philippines	2004	3537	1024	469	104	23	3965	48
	2005	3463	617	913	100	-17	3084	36
	2006	3150	701	1215	86	25	2525	29
Qatar	2003	429	..	429	..	0	0	0
Qatar	2004	618	..	609	..	0	9	12
	2005	356	..	361	..	-5	0	0
	2006	724	..	692	..	0	32	34
Saudi Arabia	2003	25432	..	8960	2231	53	14188	644
Arabie saoudite	2004	25944	..	8757	2269	-55	14973	664
	2005	26722	..	10183	2302	-123	14360	621
	2006	27177	..	8977	2685	275	15240	644
Singapore	2003	6084	29158	11596	19308	-1221	5559	1328
Singapour	2004	7170	31667	13522	22060	-1466	4721	1114
	2005	8862	30414	12036	23933	-1742	5049	1163
	2006	8534	36548	15732	26404	-1621	4567	1019
Sri Lanka	2003	745	76	0	79	6	736	38
Sri Lanka	2004	855	49	38	82	-15	799	41
	2005	762	398	0	125	10	1025	52
	2006	716	254	0	96	24	850	43
Syrian Arab Republic	2003	4921	..	900	..	..	4021	229
Rép. arabe syrienne	2004	5015	..	917	..	..	4098	230
	2005	4938	..	0	..	..	4938	270
	2006	5288	..	0	..	..	5288	283
Tajikistan	2003	..	28	..	..	..	28	4
Tadjikistan	2004	..	28	..	..	..	28	4
	2005	..	27	..	..	..	27	4
	2006	..	27	..	..	..	27	4
Thailand	2003	5947	207	765	..	472	4917	77
Thaïlande	2004	6335	709	1015	..	299	5730	89
	2005	6409	1499	939	..	500	6469	100
	2006	6578	1148	1475	..	144	6107	94
Turkey	2003	8038	736	525	238	90	7921	113
Turquie	2004	7845	785	1102	439	76	7013	99
	2005	7208	748	1427	531	-135	6133	85
	2006	7271	468	2105	581	-41	5094	70

Table 23

Production, trade and consumption of residual fuel oil
Production, commerce et consommation de mazout résiduel

Thousand metric tons and kilograms per capita
Milliers de tonnes métriques et kilogrammes par habitant

Country or area Pays ou zone	Year Année	Production Production	Imports Importations	Exports Exportations	Bunkers Soutes	Changes in stocks Variations des stocks	Consumption Consommation Total Totale	Per capita Par habitant
Turkmenistan	2003	1822	..	819	..	..	1003	213
Turkménistan	2004	1752	..	788	..	..	964	202
	2005	1811	..	815	..	..	996	206
	2006	2157	..	971	..	..	1186	242
United Arab Emirates	2003	1173	9224	..	9317	..	1080	304
Emirats arabes unis	2004	1291	10665	..	10829	..	1127	300
	2005	1299	11879	..	12057	..	1121	273
	2006	1173	13109	..	13153	..	1129	267
Uzbekistan	2003	1925	..	..	..	..	1925	75
Ouzbékistan	2004	1814	..	..	..	..	1814	69
	2005	1482	..	..	..	..	1482	56
	2006	1383	..	..	..	..	1383	51
Viet Nam	2003	..	2376	133	..	..	2243	28
Viet Nam	2004	..	2120	0	..	..	2120	26
	2005	..	2199	0	..	..	2199	26
	2006	..	2020	0	..	..	2020	24
Yemen	2003	586	911	402	62	..	1033	55
Yémen	2004	268	1184	363	62	..	1027	53
	2005	399	1143	398	62	..	1082	54
	2006	378	1332	515	62	..	1133	55
Europe	**2003**	**186043**	**50680**	**91860**	**40319**	**591**	**103953**	**143**
Europe	**2004**	**192201**	**49068**	**106671**	**43994**	**-1012**	**91616**	**126**
	2005	**193453**	**55600**	**118587**	**46375**	**-590**	**84681**	**116**
	2006	**192875**	**59782**	**118113**	**49035**	**1682**	**83827**	**115**
Albania	2003	45	0	..	..	..	45	13
Albanie	2004	67	6	..	..	..	73	23
	2005	68	0	..	..	..	68	22
	2006	48	0	..	..	..	48	15
Austria	2003	1062	328	55	..	-8	1343	166
Autriche	2004	1032	306	55	..	130	1153	142
	2005	1009	182	72	..	-6	1125	137
	2006	915	199	58	..	-24	1080	130
Belarus	2003	4790	717	3863	..	0	1644	167
Bélarus	2004	5501	783	4491	..	176	1617	165
	2005	6313	259	5293	..	8	1271	130
	2006	6329	280	5320	..	-146	1435	147
Belgium	2003	8689	4457	4024	6480	141	2501	242
Belgique	2004	8380	5364	4430	7541	86	1687	162
	2005	8042	5982	4723	7435	-10	1876	180
	2006	7128	7097	4461	7961	148	1655	157
Bosnia and Herzegovina	2003	36	193	13	..	-5	221	58
Bosnie y Herzégovine	2004	78	182	0	..	-11	271	71
	2005	74	164	0	..	0	238	62
	2006	74	170	0	..	0	244	63
Bulgaria	2003	718	131	503	..	-49	395	50
Bulgarie	2004	965	136	851	..	-47	297	38
	2005	1230	93	919	..	64	340	44
	2006	1512	77	1286	..	-25	328	43
Croatia	2003	1036	326	4	16	-13	1355	305
Croatie	2004	1012	213	304	16	-14	919	207
	2005	1160	85	234	16	30	965	217
	2006	1097	118	226	13	-1	977	220

Table 23

Production, trade and consumption of residual fuel oil
Production, commerce et consommation de mazout résiduel
Thousand metric tons and kilograms per capita
Milliers de tonnes métriques et kilogrammes par habitant

Country or area Pays ou zone	Year Année	Production Production	Imports Importations	Exports Exportations	Bunkers Soutes	Changes in stocks Variations des stocks	Consumption Consommation	
							Total Totale	Per capita Par habitant
Czech Republic	2003	445	140	80	..	-5	510	50
République tchèque	2004	394	205	48	..	-4	555	54
	2005	581	100	131	..	13	537	52
	2006	381	144	89	..	27	409	40
Denmark	2003	1519	921	1161	503	47	729	138
Danemark	2004	1557	900	1393	426	26	612	113
	2005	1405	1200	1544	507	90	464	86
	2006	1471	1042	1152	776	31	554	102
Estonia	2003	..	86	..	70	*-24	40	30
Estonie	2004	..	112	..	103	-10	19	14
	2005	..	88	..	77	2	9	7
	2006	..	181	..	172	21	-12	-9
Finland	2003	1267	983	23	560	-7	1674	321
Finlande	2004	1445	654	141	478	-100	1580	302
	2005	1318	803	67	469	82	1503	286
	2006	1272	737	78	509	-13	1435	272
France incl. Monaco	2003	10919	2364	7084	2392	-373	4180	69
France y compris Monaco	2004	11887	3767	7998	2780	42	4834	80
	2005	11823	3860	7914	2541	42	5186	85
	2006	11955	5480	7384	2687	160	7204	118
Germany	2003	12232	3249	4004	2151	75	9251	112
Allemagne	2004	14013	2762	5377	2275	-233	9356	113
	2005	13340	3060	5668	2110	-26	8648	105
	2006	13684	3321	5892	2114	-63	9062	110
Gibraltar	2003	..	1023	..	990	..	33	1179
Gibraltar	2004	..	1055	..	1021	..	34	1214
	2005	..	1079	..	1044	..	35	1250
	2006	..	1108	..	1072	..	36	1247
Greece	2003	7456	184	649	2757	36	4198	381
Grèce	2004	7095	171	748	2809	-159	3868	350
	2005	6956	264	604	2542	47	4027	363
	2006	6953	389	835	2761	-16	3762	337
Hungary	2003	367	404	83	..	22	666	66
Hongrie	2004	313	205	109	..	-75	484	48
	2005	218	123	56	..	-5	290	29
	2006	232	94	60	..	19	247	25
Iceland	2003	..	58	..	4	-19	73	252
Islande	2004	..	55	..	1	9	45	154
	2005	..	63	..	2	13	48	162
	2006	..	71	..	3	-1	69	227
Ireland	2003	1005	1177	1080	64	3	1035	260
Irlande	2004	966	1318	942	49	54	1239	306
	2005	948	1145	1013	24	-16	1072	260
	2006	1101	1085	1062	49	-13	1088	257
Italy and San Marino	2003	18018	9873	3372	2569	-110	22060	383
Italie y comp. St. Marin	2004	17543	5625	3740	2711	-527	17244	296
	2005	19032	3625	5452	2790	-55	14470	247
	2006	17621	4029	4676	2925	-400	14449	245
Latvia	2003	..	224	0	117	3	104	45
Lettonie	2004	..	208	200	130	-7	-115	-50
	2005	..	244	293	174	-10	-213	-93
	2006	..	161	0	135	-6	32	14

Table 23

Production, trade and consumption of residual fuel oil
Production, commerce et consommation de mazout résiduel

Thousand metric tons and kilograms per capita
Milliers de tonnes métriques et kilogrammes par habitant

Country or area Pays ou zone	Year Année	Production Production	Imports Importations	Exports Exportations	Bunkers Soutes	Changes in stocks Variations des stocks	Consumption Consommation	
							Total Totale	Per capita Par habitant
Lithuania	2003	1381	124	979	94	30	402	116
Lituanie	2004	1673	159	1347	96	20	369	107
	2005	1799	158	1417	129	48	363	106
	2006	1938	152	1664	127	-56	355	105
Luxembourg	2003	..	5	..	..	..	5	11
Luxembourg	2004	..	4	..	..	..	4	9
	2005	..	2	..	..	..	2	4
	2006	..	2	..	..	..	2	4
Malta	2003	..	548	..	23	..	525	1313
Malte	2004	..	609	..	23	..	586	1455
	2005	..	586	..	23	..	563	1390
	2006	..	592	..	23	..	569	1400
Netherlands	2003	12333	14086	11344	11972	365	2738	169
Pays-Bas	2004	13073	15453	13230	13229	17	2050	126
	2005	12394	22395	17069	15350	248	2122	130
	2006	12151	23914	17733	16013	248	2071	127
Norway,Svlbd.J.Myn. I	2003	1702	1437	1809	265	-22	1087	237
Norvège,Svalbd,J.May	2004	1845	1419	1739	256	-15	1284	279
	2005	1610	1705	1727	294	43	1251	269
	2006	1957	1770	2177	184	-50	1416	304
Poland	2003	3253	32	640	245	48	2352	62
Pologne	2004	2754	84	597	220	5	2016	53
	2005	2537	13	488	212	0	1850	48
	2006	2824	83	782	214	79	1832	48
Portugal	2003	2388	1010	352	442	21	2583	247
Portugal	2004	2969	645	476	527	-178	2789	266
	2005	3062	1548	766	455	131	3258	309
	2006	2920	571	1177	514	-57	1857	175
Republic of Moldova	2003	..	23	0	..	-4	27	7
Rép. de Moldova	2004	..	19	0	..	-2	21	6
	2005	..	16	1	..	-3	18	5
	2006	..	19	2	..	0	17	5
Romania	2003	1562	947	219	..	22	2268	104
Roumanie	2004	1559	671	411	..	123	1696	78
	2005	1707	335	727	..	-146	1461	68
	2006	1303	473	395	..	-86	1467	68
Russian Federation	2003	56377	1	31925	..	429	24024	166
Fédération de Russie	2004	58330	16	36755	..	-135	21726	151
	2005	62365	15	43452	..	-1067	19995	140
	2006	65189	28	43875	..	1639	19703	138
Serbia	2003	919	0	0	..	..	919	87
Serbie	2004	853	11	122	..	..	742	71
	2005	801	12	32	..	..	781	75
	2006	674	174	0	..	..	848	81
Slovakia	2003	635	64	274	..	-7	432	80
Slovaquie	2004	585	41	157	..	0	469	87
	2005	543	31	113	..	-44	505	94
	2006	654	104	212	..	64	482	89
Slovenia	2003	..	63	0	0	2	61	31
Slovénie	2004	..	52	2	0	-2	52	26
	2005	..	71	0	22	-3	52	26
	2006	..	84	0	30	2	52	26

Table 23

Production, trade and consumption of residual fuel oil
Production, commerce et consommation de mazout résiduel
Thousand metric tons and kilograms per capita
Milliers de tonnes métriques et kilogrammes par habitant

Country or area Pays ou zone	Year Année	Production Production	Imports Importations	Exports Exportations	Bunkers Soutes	Changes in stocks Variations des stocks	Consumption Consommation	
							Total Totale	Per capita Par habitant
Spain	2003	10130	3499	992	6250	-330	6717	160
Espagne	2004	9125	3940	1431	6483	-13	5164	121
	2005	9019	4162	1461	7152	-71	4639	107
	2006	9245	3558	2029	7442	137	3195	73
Sweden	2003	5170	759	2860	1488	286	1295	145
Suède	2004	5450	329	2937	1808	-291	1325	147
	2005	5576	539	3015	1842	193	1065	118
	2006	5226	637	3206	1998	-25	684	75
Switzerland	2003	759	2	581	..	-16	196	27
Suisse	2004	701	0	549	..	-27	179	24
	2005	611	0	427	..	50	134	18
	2006	583	0	475	..	-39	147	20
T.F.Yug.Rep. Macedonia	2003	343	26	178	..	-49	240	118
L'ex-RY Macédoine	2004	282	19	32	..	28	241	119
	2005	295	14	55	..	-2	256	126
	2006	327	0	39	..	-11	299	147
Ukraine	2003	7970	8	7324	..	0	654	14
Ukraine	2004	7766	18	7123	..	0	661	14
	2005	5889	52	5402	..	-94	633	13
	2006	3834	506	3397	..	0	943	20
United Kingdom	2003	11517	1208	6385	867	102	5371	91
Royaume-Uni	2004	12988	1552	8936	1012	122	4470	75
	2005	11728	1527	8452	1165	-136	3774	63
	2006	12277	1332	8371	1313	139	3786	62
Oceania	**2003**	**1669**	**1617**	**134**	**869**	**-84**	**2367**	**73**
Océanie	**2004**	**1521**	**2286**	**205**	**967**	**100**	**2535**	**77**
	2005	**1664**	**2172**	**487**	**1036**	**-26**	**2340**	**70**
	2006	**1537**	**2248**	**628**	**1059**	**-10**	**2107**	**62**
Australia	2003	1310	579	90	658	-101	1242	62
Australie	2004	1071	1314	74	762	92	1457	72
	2005	1085	1215	189	812	-5	1304	64
	2006	1051	1343	463	797	-44	1178	57
Fiji	2003	..	1	..	*1	..	0	0
Fidji	2004	..	1	..	*1	..	0	0
	2005	..	2	..	*1	..	1	1
	2006	..	4	..	*1	..	3	4
French Polynesia	2003	..	98	..	*3	..	95	384
Polynésie française	2004	..	92	..	*3	..	89	355
	2005	..	106	..	*3	..	103	405
	2006	..	95	..	*4	..	91	355
Nauru	2003	..	*37	..	..	..	*37	*2944
Nauru	2004	..	*37	..	..	..	*37	*2889
	2005	..	*37	..	..	..	*37	*2836
	2006	..	*37	..	..	..	*37	*2782
New Caledonia	2003	..	426	..	..	..	426	1868
Nouvelle-Calédonie	2004	..	397	..	..	..	397	1720
	2005	..	485	..	..	..	485	2073
	2006	..	462	..	..	..	462	1941
New Zealand	2003	359	3	42	201	17	102	25
Nouvelle-Zélande	2004	350	0	59	195	8	88	22
	2005	439	0	153	214	-21	93	23
	2006	381	0	69	251	34	27	7

Table 23

Production, trade and consumption of residual fuel oil
Production, commerce et consommation de mazout résiduel

Thousand metric tons and kilograms per capita
Milliers de tonnes métriques et kilogrammes par habitant

Country or area Pays ou zone	Year Année	Production Production	Imports Importations	Exports Exportations	Bunkers Soutes	Changes in stocks Variations des stocks	Consumption Consommation	
							Total Totale	Per capita Par habitant
Palau	2003	..	*24	..	..	..	*24	*1187
Palaos	2004	..	*24	..	..	..	*24	*1146
	2005	..	*25	..	..	..	*25	*1210
	2006	..	*29	..	..	..	*29	*1334
Papua New Guinea	2003	0	437	*2	6	..	429	74
Papouasie-Nvl-Guinée	2004	100	410	72	*6	..	432	73
	2005	140	289	145	*6	..	279	46
	2006	105	265	96	*6	..	268	43
Tonga	2003	..	*12	..	..	..	*12	*116
Tonga	2004	..	*12	..	..	..	*12	*120
	2005	..	*13	..	..	..	*13	*122
	2006	..	*13	..	..	..	*13	*124

Table 24

Production, trade and consumption of energy petroleum products
Production, commerce et consommation de produits pétroliers énergétiques

Thousand metric tons and kilograms per capita
Milliers de tonnes métriques et kilogrammes par habitant

Table Notes:
Production

Production refers to aviation gasoline, motor gasoline, jet fuels, kerosene, gas diesel oil, residual fuel oil, natural gasoline, condensate, feedstocks, petroleum coke, liquefied petroleum gas and refinery gas. Production from refineries and plants.

Imports and Exports

Refer to the same products listed above except refinery gas.

Bunkers

Aviation gasoline, jet fuel, kerosene, gas-diesel oils and residual fuel oil.

- **Please refer to the Definitions Section on pages xv to xxix for the appropriate product description /classification.**

Notes relatives aux tableaux:
Production

Production d'essence d'aviation, d'essence d'automobile, de carburéacteurs, de pétrole lampant, de carburant diesel, de mazout résiduel, d'essence naturelle, de condensat d'usine, de produits d'alimentation de raffinerie, de coke de pétrole, de gaz de pétrole liquéfiés et de gaz de raffinerie. Production à partir des raffineries et des usines.

Importations et importations

Se reporter aux mêmes produits mentionnés dans la production à l'exception des gaz de raffinerie.

Soutages

Essence d'aviation, carburateurs, pétrole lampant, produits d'alimentation de raffinerie et mazout résiduel.

- **Veuillez consulter la section "définitions" de la page xv à la page xxix pour une description/classification appropriée des produits.**

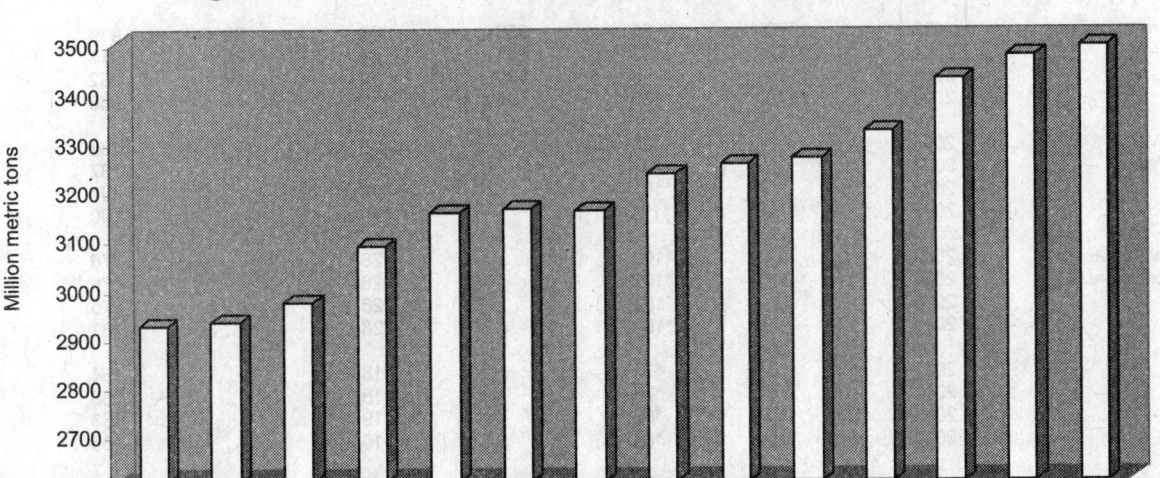

Figure 69: World production of energy petroleum products 1993-2006

Table 24

Production, trade and consumption of energy petroleum products
Production, commerce et consommation de produits pétroliers énergétiques

Thousand metric tons and kilograms per capita
Milliers de tonnes métriques et kilogrammes par habitant

Country or area Pays ou zone	Year Année	Production Production	Imports Importations	Exports Exportations	Bunkers Soutes	Changes in stocks Variations des stocks	Consumption Consommation	
							Total Totale	Per capita Par habitant
World	**2003**	**3316487**	**675086**	**754615**	**249976**	**1277**	**2985705**	**476**
Monde	**2004**	**3423709**	**746343**	**804217**	**268545**	**-2186**	**3099476**	**489**
	2005	**3471693**	**802865**	**856624**	**287051**	**-649**	**3131532**	**488**
	2006	**3493543**	**834048**	**889565**	**298299**	**2390**	**3137338**	**482**
Africa	**2003**	**138719**	**33715**	**53182**	**11514**	**458**	**107280**	**127**
Afrique	**2004**	**137032**	**35372**	**48270**	**10423**	**-1031**	**114743**	**132**
	2005	**137114**	**38025**	**46370**	**11298**	**-724**	**118195**	**133**
	2006	**138107**	**40869**	**46010**	**10560**	**912**	**121494**	**133**
Algeria	2003	40274	157	29927	482	285	9737	306
Algérie	2004	39061	234	27585	545	5	11160	345
	2005	37994	269	27254	640	179	10190	310
	2006	38294	253	*26789	678	716	10364	310
Angola	2003	1869	710	537	292	..	1750	156
Angola	2004	1784	773	517	332	..	1708	150
	2005	1807	876	544	278	..	1861	159
	2006	1821	1169	584	331	..	2075	173
Benin	2003	..	1055	317	25	11	702	88
Bénin	2004	..	1207	425	24	21	737	90
	2005	..	1109	305	23	-15	796	94
	2006	..	1497	516	24	-15	972	111
Burkina Faso	2003	..	398	..	14	39	345	27
Burkina Faso	2004	..	352	..	16	-20	355	27
	2005	..	375	..	20	-6	361	28
	2006	..	373	..	16	-83	440	32
Burundi	2003	..	50	..	4	-4	50	7
Burundi	2004	..	66	..	6	*13	47	6
	2005	..	54	..	7	*-4	51	7
	2006	..	66	..	7	2	58	7
Cameroon	2003	1370	86	553	83	-99	919	54
Cameroun	2004	1752	32	811	84	-28	917	53
	2005	1784	9	839	74	-52	932	52
	2006	1678	135	756	113	-24	968	53
Cape Verde	2003	..	*88	..	*6	..	*82	*179
Cap-Vert	2004	..	*94	..	*7	..	*87	*186
	2005	..	*107	..	*10	..	*97	*203
	2006	..	*110	..	*10	..	*100	*204
Central African Rep.	2003	..	*102	..	*26	..	*76	*19
Rép. centrafricaine	2004	..	*102	..	*26	..	*76	*18
	2005	..	*102	..	*26	..	*76	*18
	2006	..	*109	..	*28	..	*81	*19
Chad	2003	..	*72	..	*18	..	*54	*6
Tchad	2004	..	*76	..	*18	..	*58	*6
	2005	..	*82	..	*19	..	*63	*6
	2006	..	*84	..	*19	..	*65	*6
Comoros	2003	..	*31	..	..	..	*31	*49
Comores	2004	..	*31	..	..	..	*31	*48
	2005	..	*32	..	..	..	*32	*47
	2006	..	*32	..	..	..	*32	*46
Congo	2003	522	0	273	..	..	249	72
Congo	2004	535	45	293	..	..	288	81
	2005	430	78	203	..	..	305	84
	2006	625	95	365	..	..	355	96

Table 24

Production, trade and consumption of energy petroleum products
Production, commerce et consommation de produits pétroliers énergétiques
Thousand metric tons and kilograms per capita
Milliers de tonnes métriques et kilogrammes par habitant

Country or area Pays ou zone	Year Année	Production Production	Imports Importations	Exports Exportations	Bunkers Soutes	Changes in stocks Variations des stocks	Consumption Consommation	
							Total Totale	Per capita Par habitant
Côte d'Ivoire	2003	2299	308	1351	*196	*159	901	51
Côte d'Ivoire	2004	2942	267	1894	180	*12	1123	61
	2005	3308	145	2374	165	*-134	1048	55
	2006	3591	208	2561	154	-1	1085	55
Dem. Rep. of Congo	2003	..	343	5	*96	..	242	4
Rép. dem. du Congo	2004	..	500	5	119	..	376	7
	2005	..	496	5	118	..	373	6
	2006	..	496	5	118	..	373	6
Djibouti	2003	..	280	..	168	..	112	144
Djibouti	2004	..	300	..	171	..	129	163
	2005	..	310	..	175	..	135	168
	2006	..	324	..	185	..	139	169
Egypt	2003	33641	1827	7807	3231	*432	23998	357
Egypte	2004	32581	2573	*4830	2545	*-375	28154	395
	2005	31247	3320	1773	2724	0	30070	420
	2006	30700	3357	1297	1865	-82	30977	426
Equatorial Guinea	2003	..	*54	..	..	..	*54	*117
Guinée équatoriale	2004	..	*47	..	..	..	*47	*99
	2005	..	*47	..	..	..	*47	*97
	2006	..	*51	..	..	..	*51	*103
Eritrea	2003	..	253	0	11	11	231	55
Erythrée	2004	..	230	3	11	-25	241	55
	2005	..	208	0	9	-39	238	53
	2006	..	151	0	7	-29	173	37
Ethiopia	2003	..	1249	..	85	-263	1427	20
Ethiopie	2004	..	1323	..	96	-385	1612	23
	2005	..	1475	..	146	-205	1534	22
	2006	..	1643	..	177	-214	1680	22
Gabon	2003	696	112	339	223	-165	411	316
Gabon	2004	714	85	336	214	-156	405	297
	2005	725	145	313	219	-167	505	362
	2006	684	179	319	217	-170	497	348
Gambia	2003	..	*105	*2	..	..	*103	*69
Gambie	2004	..	*106	*2	..	..	*104	*67
	2005	..	*106	*2	..	..	*104	*65
	2006	..	*111	*2	..	..	*109	*66
Ghana	2003	1396	592	256	137	-6	1601	76
Ghana	2004	1683	564	390	112	0	1745	81
	2005	1592	625	395	124	-6	1704	77
	2006	920	1362	222	157	-6	1909	83
Guinea	2003	..	*399	..	*21	..	*378	*44
Guinée	2004	..	*399	..	*21	..	*378	*43
	2005	..	*406	..	*22	..	*384	*43
	2006	..	*407	..	*22	..	*385	*42
Guinea-Bissau	2003	..	*98	..	*10	..	*88	*69
Guinée-Bissau	2004	..	*98	..	*10	..	*88	*68
	2005	..	*98	..	*10	..	*88	*66
	2006	..	*101	..	*10	..	*91	*67
Kenya	2003	1578	1233	317	13	..	2481	76
Kenya	2004	1687	1502	419	37	..	2733	80
	2005	1586	1702	233	42	..	3013	85
	2006	1586	2038	212	47	..	3365	92

Table 24

Production, trade and consumption of energy petroleum products
Production, commerce et consommation de produits pétroliers énergétiques
Thousand metric tons and kilograms per capita
Milliers de tonnes métriques et kilogrammes par habitant

Country or area Pays ou zone	Year Année	Production Production	Imports Importations	Exports Exportations	Bunkers Soutes	Changes in stocks Variations des stocks	Consumption Consommation	
							Total Totale	Per capita Par habitant
Liberia	2003	..	*186	*1	*16	..	*169	*48
Libéria	2004	..	201	*1	*16	..	184	52
	2005	..	232	*1	*16	..	215	60
	2006	..	*247	*1	*16	..	*230	*62
Libyan Arab Jamah.	2003	13463	..	3645	296	..	9522	1531
Jamah. arabe libyenne	2004	13559	..	3868	298	..	9393	1463
	2005	13024	..	3181	275	..	9568	1443
	2006	12579	..	3026	263	..	9290	1387
Madagascar	2003	*321	*374	*20	*19	..	*656	*40
Madagascar	2004	*321	*434	*20	*19	..	*716	*42
	2005	*325	*450	*20	*19	..	*736	*42
	2006	*325	*460	*20	*19	..	*746	*41
Malawi	2003	..	262	..	..	..	262	23
Malawi	2004	..	*275	..	..	..	*275	*23
	2005	..	*261	..	..	..	*261	*21
	2006	..	*263	..	..	..	*263	*21
Mali	2003	..	195	..	19	..	176	16
Mali	2004	..	*204	..	20	..	*184	*16
	2005	..	*205	..	20	..	*185	*16
	2006	..	*205	..	*20	..	*185	*15
Mauritania	2003	..	440	..	*5	..	435	152
Mauritanie	2004	..	474	..	*5	..	469	162
	2005	..	488	..	*5	..	483	166
	2006	..	481	..	*5	..	476	159
Mauritius	2003	..	964	..	223	-11	752	621
Maurice	2004	..	1008	..	233	-16	791	648
	2005	..	1058	..	287	-25	796	640
	2006	..	1044	..	281	-72	835	667
Morocco	2003	3726	3243	299	305	36	6329	220
Maroc	2004	5182	2477	785	334	-125	6665	223
	2005	5815	2708	581	381	80	7481	248
	2006	5221	2970	327	430	-33	7467	245
Mozambique	2003	..	629	..	82	26	521	28
Mozambique	2004	..	612	..	82	0	530	27
	2005	..	501	..	47	-10	464	24
	2006	..	552	..	57	5	490	25
Niger	2003	..	160	..	10	..	150	13
Niger	2004	..	156	..	12	..	144	12
	2005	..	151	..	13	..	138	11
	2006	..	149	..	11	..	138	11
Nigeria	2003	5310	7191	1281	1007	-116	10329	82
Nigéria	2004	4363	7354	1035	706	-9	9985	77
	2005	4190	7613	859	951	-134	10127	76
	2006	5319	7427	1484	828	90	10344	74
Réunion	2003	..	*780	..	*31	..	*749	*992
Réunion	2004	..	*791	..	*33	..	*758	*989
	2005	..	*792	..	*33	..	*759	*977
	2006	..	*794	..	*34	..	*760	*955
Rwanda	2003	..	*179	..	*12	..	*167	*19
Rwanda	2004	..	185	..	*12	..	173	19
	2005	..	*193	..	*12	..	*181	*20
	2006	..	*202	..	*12	..	*190	*20

Table 24

Production, trade and consumption of energy petroleum products
Production, commerce et consommation de produits pétroliers énergétiques
Thousand metric tons and kilograms per capita
Milliers de tonnes métriques et kilogrammes par habitant

Country or area Pays ou zone	Year Année	Production Production	Imports Importations	Exports Exportations	Bunkers Soutes	Changes in stocks Variations des stocks	Consumption Consommation	
							Total Totale	Per capita Par habitant
Sao Tome and Principe	2003	..	*30	..	..	..	*30	*210
Sao Tomé-et-Principe	2004	..	*30	..	..	..	*30	*205
	2005	..	*33	..	..	..	*33	*222
	2006	..	*34	..	..	..	*34	*224
Senegal	2003	1117	502	185	*236	-21	1219	120
Sénégal	2004	1127	457	182	245	16	1141	108
	2005	884	834	267	244	-1	1208	111
	2006	336	813	141	242	-9	775	70
Seychelles	2003	..	277	..	*96	..	181	2191
Seychelles	2004	..	385	..	*132	..	253	3072
	2005	..	352	..	*125	..	227	2743
	2006	..	375	..	*133	..	243	2869
Sierra Leone	2003	*190	*105	16	*113	..	*166	*30
Sierra Leone	2004	*168	184	19	*116	..	*217	*38
	2005	*158	*187	*21	*117	..	*207	*35
	2006	*166	*170	*22	*114	..	*200	*33
Somalia	2003	*140	133	*35	*70	..	*168	*22
Somalie	2004	*145	128	*35	*70	..	*168	*21
	2005	*145	130	*30	*71	..	*174	*21
	2006	176	125	*56	*71	..	174	21
South Africa Customs Un.	2003	25473	2453	4846	3477	..	19603	384
Un.douan.d'Afr.mérid	2004	23825	2911	3588	3163	..	19985	376
	2005	26263	3370	5920	3407	..	20307	379
	2006	27024	3491	6084	3390	..	21042	388
St. Helena and Depend.	2003	..	*4	..	..	..	*4	*543
St-Hélène et dépend	2004	..	3	..	..	..	3	405
	2005	..	*3	..	..	..	*3	*442
	2006	..	*3	..	..	..	*3	*440
Sudan	2003	3205	350	578	140	120	2717	82
Soudan	2004	3525	385	634	146	98	3032	88
	2005	3611	312	641	203	-175	3254	92
	2006	4943	538	659	227	881	3714	102
Togo	2003	..	381	..	33	2	346	70
Togo	2004	..	368	..	44	-1	325	64
	2005	..	340	..	51	-17	306	57
	2006	..	259	..	36	-45	268	50
Tunisia	2003	1672	2731	585	0	8	3810	387
Tunisie	2004	1588	2872	585	0	-71	3946	397
	2005	1701	2889	600	0	-11	4001	399
	2006	1594	2973	549	9	-13	4022	397
Uganda	2003	..	*475	..	..	..	*475	*19
Ouganda	2004	..	504	..	..	..	504	19
	2005	..	647	..	..	..	647	23
	2006	..	766	..	..	..	766	26
United Rep.Tanzania	2003	..	1095	..	95	..	1000	28
Rép. Unie de Tanzanie	2004	..	1174	..	100	..	1074	30
	2005	..	1255	..	106	..	1149	31
	2006	..	1327	..	111	..	1216	32
Western Sahara	2003	..	*84	..	*6	..	*78	*298
Sahara occidental	2004	..	*84	..	*6	..	*78	*291
	2005	..	*84	..	*6	..	*78	*287
	2006	..	*84	..	*6	..	*78	*283

Table 24

Production, trade and consumption of energy petroleum products
Production, commerce et consommation de produits pétroliers énergétiques

Thousand metric tons and kilograms per capita
Milliers de tonnes métriques et kilogrammes par habitant

Country or area Pays ou zone	Year Année	Production Production	Imports Importations	Exports Exportations	Bunkers Soutes	Changes in stocks Variations des stocks	Consumption Consommation	
							Total Totale	Per capita Par habitant
Zambia	2003	457	115	7	47	14	504	47
Zambie	2004	490	110	8	49	15	528	48
	2005	525	106	9	51	18	553	48
	2006	525	134	13	54	15	577	49
Zimbabwe	2003	..	774	..	35	..	739	57
Zimbabwe	2004	..	601	..	8	..	593	46
	2005	..	655	..	8	..	647	49
	2006	..	632	..	8	..	624	47
America, North	**2003**	**989769**	**136078**	**98426**	**43810**	**863**	**982748**	**1958**
Amérique du Nord	**2004**	**1009087**	**156651**	**98822**	**49690**	**1001**	**1016226**	**2004**
	2005	**1007914**	**183185**	**104778**	**51425**	**432**	**1034465**	**2020**
	2006	**1001595**	**185798**	**110314**	**52320**	**3913**	**1020846**	**1976**
Anguilla	2003	..	13	..	..	..	13	1036
Anguilla	2004	..	14	..	..	..	14	1076
	2005	..	17	..	..	..	17	1232
	2006	..	17	..	..	..	17	1224
Antigua and Barbuda	2003	..	*185	*8	*50	..	*127	*1588
Antigua-et-Barbuda	2004	..	*191	*8	*51	..	*132	*1630
	2005	..	*194	*9	*51	..	*134	*1619
	2006	..	*200	*10	*51	..	*139	*1653
Aruba	2003	10000	*320	10000	*73	..	247	2598
Aruba	2004	10000	*320	10000	*73	..	247	2529
	2005	10000	*327	10000	*75	..	252	2504
	2006	*10000	*327	*10000	*75	..	*252	*2451
Bahamas	2003	..	*3169	*2225	*287	*50	*607	*1903
Bahamas	2004	..	*3216	*2266	*298	0	*652	*2176
	2005	..	*3272	*2276	*312	0	*684	*2118
	2006	..	*3279	*2275	*311	0	*693	*2119
Barbados	2003	1	318	..	..	..	319	1174
Barbade	2004	1	345	..	..	..	346	1270
	2005	1	359	..	..	..	360	1318
	2006	1	366	..	..	..	367	1339
Belize	2003	..	*287	..	*33	..	*254	*928
Belize	2004	..	*294	..	*34	..	*260	*920
	2005	..	*305	..	*36	..	*269	*922
	2006	..	*308	..	*36	..	*272	*894
Bermuda	2003	..	*191	..	*19	..	*172	*2728
Bermudes	2004	..	*198	..	*20	..	*178	*2814
	2005	..	*204	..	*20	..	*184	*2894
	2006	..	*206	..	*22	..	*184	*2884
British Virgin Islands	2003	..	*25	..	..	..	*25	*1172
Iles Vierges britanniques	2004	..	*28	..	..	..	*28	*1291
	2005	..	*29	..	..	..	*29	*1318
	2006	..	*32	..	..	..	*32	*1422
Canada	2003	90176	8908	17935	1186	-11	79974	2525
Canada	2004	90635	10056	18433	1478	-71	80851	2527
	2005	88583	11193	18178	1417	111	80070	2478
	2006	85832	11387	17345	1352	-12	78534	2405
Cayman Islands	2003	..	*176	..	*21	..	*155	*3557
Iles Caïmanes	2004	..	*182	..	*22	..	*160	*3617
	2005	..	*185	..	*22	..	*163	*3371
	2006	..	*190	..	*23	..	*167	*3212

Table 24

Production, trade and consumption of energy petroleum products
Production, commerce et consommation de produits pétroliers énergétiques

Thousand metric tons and kilograms per capita
Milliers de tonnes métriques et kilogrammes par habitant

Country or area Pays ou zone	Year Année	Production Production	Imports Importations	Exports Exportations	Bunkers Soutes	Changes in stocks Variations des stocks	Consumption Consommation Total Totale	Consumption Consommation Per capita Par habitant
Costa Rica	2003	397	1330	24	..	-79	1782	436
Costa Rica	2004	427	1490	49	..	14	1854	444
	2005	469	1457	3	..	-19	1942	455
	2006	637	1551	29	..	27	2132	490
Cuba	2003	2218	2067	..	281	22	3982	352
Cuba	2004	1896	2764	..	288	*15	4357	384
	2005	2041	3657	..	291	389	5018	446
	2006	1861	2901	..	*260	-25	4527	403
Dominica	2003	..	37	..	..	..	37	529
Dominique	2004	..	35	..	..	..	35	500
	2005	..	*37	..	..	..	*37	*537
	2006	..	*38	..	..	..	*38	*559
Dominican Republic	2003	1430	3559	..	89	0	4900	548
Rép. dominicaine	2004	1976	3252	..	98	36	5094	561
	2005	1970	3379	..	97	-5	5257	570
	2006	1936	3276	..	96	-74	5190	555
El Salvador	2003	907	1194	180	68	17	1835	276
El Salvador	2004	986	1213	267	73	11	1848	274
	2005	832	1128	113	76	39	1732	252
	2006	811	1250	73	73	58	1857	266
Greenland	2003	..	*192	*7	*8	..	*177	*3139
Groënland	2004	..	*193	*7	*8	..	*178	*3157
	2005	..	*196	*7	*8	..	*181	*3211
	2006	..	*200	*7	*9	..	*184	*3265
Grenada	2003	..	80	..	*8	..	72	688
Grenade	2004	..	80	..	*8	..	72	682
	2005	..	83	..	*7	..	76	724
	2006	..	85	..	*7	..	78	739
Guadeloupe	2003	..	*728	..	*100	..	*628	*1431
Guadeloupe	2004	..	*734	..	*100	..	*634	*1425
	2005	..	*757	..	*104	..	*653	*1467
	2006	..	*766	..	*106	..	*660	*1442
Guatemala	2003	0	3021	0	160	0	2861	237
Guatemala	2004	0	3151	0	163	24	2964	239
	2005	26	3351	8	157	163	3048	240
	2006	23	3203	125	157	-9	2952	227
Haiti	2003	..	524	..	26	..	498	59
Haïti	2004	..	547	..	24	..	523	62
	2005	..	550	..	23	..	527	62
	2006	..	565	..	24	..	541	63
Honduras	2003	..	2024	17	25	240	1742	254
Honduras	2004	..	2096	25	28	5	2038	290
	2005	..	2219	23	27	17	2152	299
	2006	..	2326	35	29	6	2256	306
Jamaica	2003	852	2839	130	219	37	3305	1243
Jamaïque	2004	666	2916	123	*205	11	3243	1212
	2005	460	2893	0	207	26	3120	1177
	2006	995	3049	0	259	-21	3806	1429
Martinique	2003	*804	*51	*220	*47	..	*588	*1506
Martinique	2004	*820	*54	*220	*49	..	*605	*1537
	2005	*823	*55	*220	*49	..	*609	*1532
	2006	*825	*60	*220	*49	..	*616	*1540

Table 24

Production, trade and consumption of energy petroleum products
Production, commerce et consommation de produits pétroliers énergétiques

Thousand metric tons and kilograms per capita
Milliers de tonnes métriques et kilogrammes par habitant

Country or area Pays ou zone	Year Année	Production Production	Imports Importations	Exports Exportations	Bunkers Soutes	Changes in stocks Variations des stocks	Consumption Consommation	
							Total Totale	Per capita Par habitant
Mexico	2003	64589	10229	4464	3317	-735	67772	664
Mexique	2004	66539	11517	3810	3178	-127	71195	691
	2005	66952	14947	3675	3367	243	74614	718
	2006	64836	17467	4353	3546	-35	74439	710
Montserrat	2003	..	*24	..	*1	..	*23	*2501
Montserrat	2004	..	*24	..	*1	..	*23	*2434
	2005	..	*24	..	*1	..	*23	*2409
	2006	..	*24	..	*1	..	*23	*2437
Netherlands Antilles	2003	8697	2205	7569	1787	..	1546	8652
Antilles néerlandaises	2004	9157	2873	8016	1790	..	2224	12145
	2005	10327	1939	9204	1794	..	1268	6840
	2006	9704	1832	8551	1799	..	1186	6259
Nicaragua	2003	778	463	3	..	7	1231	232
Nicaragua	2004	806	472	3	..	-8	1283	238
	2005	711	540	5	..	12	1234	226
	2006	763	536	18	..	-5	1286	233
Panama	2003	..	2010	187	2	-18	1839	590
Panama	2004	..	1721	196	0	-183	1708	538
	2005	..	1992	210	0	0	1782	552
	2006	..	2137	215	0	0	1922	585
St. Kitts-Nevis	2003	..	*72	..	..	..	*72	*1618
St-Kitts-Nevis	2004	..	*74	..	..	..	*74	*1682
	2005	..	*77	..	..	..	*77	*1791
	2006	..	*77	..	..	..	*77	*1791
St. Lucia	2003	..	*117	..	*5	..	*112	*697
St-Lucie	2004	..	*123	..	*5	..	*118	*729
	2005	..	*128	..	*6	..	*122	*738
	2006	..	*130	..	*6	..	*124	*746
St. Pierre-Miquelon	2003	..	*27	..	*6	..	*21	*3000
St-Pierre-Miquelon	2004	..	*26	..	*6	..	*20	*2857
	2005	..	*27	..	*6	..	*21	*2995
	2006	..	*27	..	*6	..	*21	*2989
St. Vincent-Grenadines	2003	..	*62	..	..	..	*62	*590
St. Vincent-Grenadines	2004	..	*62	..	..	..	*62	*593
	2005	..	*62	..	..	..	*62	*598
	2006	..	*64	..	..	..	*64	*618
Trinidad and Tobago	2003	7612	253	6210	749	218	688	523
Trinité-et-Tobago	2004	7024	219	5369	901	361	612	464
	2005	8043	135	6836	322	138	882	666
	2006	8093	65	6888	323	-262	1209	910
United States	2003	801308	89379	49247	35243	1115	805082	2768
Etats-Unis	2004	818154	106172	50030	40789	913	832594	2836
	2005	816677	127468	54010	42950	-682	847867	2860
	2006	815278	127855	60170	43700	4264	834999	2798
America, South	**2003**	**191301**	**16349**	**51129**	**8715**	**3347**	**144459**	**399**
Amérique du Sud	**2004**	**205846**	**15604**	**58817**	**9853**	**820**	**151961**	**414**
	2005	**209131**	**17145**	**57363**	**11055**	**-597**	**158456**	**426**
	2006	**209595**	**19584**	**57967**	**11091**	**-3150**	**163272**	**433**
Argentina	2003	24413	218	6546	589	68	17428	460
Argentine	2004	25224	544	5720	542	36	19470	509
	2005	25370	1161	5581	697	-50	20303	526
	2006	26785	665	4318	744	-153	22541	578

Table 24

Production, trade and consumption of energy petroleum products
Production, commerce et consommation de produits pétroliers énergétiques

Thousand metric tons and kilograms per capita
Milliers de tonnes métriques et kilogrammes par habitant

Country or area Pays ou zone	Year Année	Production Production	Imports Importations	Exports Exportations	Bunkers Soutes	Changes in stocks Variations des stocks	Consumption Consommation	
							Total Totale	Per capita Par habitant
Bolivia	2003	1512	322	156	..	11	1667	185
Bolivie	2004	1729	190	354		0	1565	170
	2005	1716	251	4	..	37	1926	204
	2006	1847	370	46	..	53	2118	220
Brazil	2003	74203	7768	8096	4299	78	69498	388
Brésil	2004	78984	6508	8969	4415	-103	72211	398
	2005	79814	6063	8014	4579	-168	73452	399
	2006	80179	7703	8894	4641	249	74098	397
Chile	2003	9404	1806	1507	1416	-87	8374	526
Chili	2004	10060	2250	1406	1553	313	9038	561
	2005	9694	3112	1554	1877	267	9108	559
	2006	10701	3650	1889	2078	754	9630	586
Colombia	2003	14111	258	4038	817	315	9199	206
Colombie	2004	14552	133	3979	958	228	9520	210
	2005	13546	572	4236	1006	-476	9353	203
	2006	13247	292	4188	1104	-1195	9442	202
Ecuador	2003	7232	1931	2290	260	553	6060	472
Equateur	2004	6668	1873	1859	228	603	5851	449
	2005	7465	2522	1632	678	0	7677	581
	2006	7453	2982	2047	*300	-130	8218	613
Falkland Is. (Malvinas)	2003	..	*12	..	..		*12	*4096
Iles Falkland (Malvinas)	2004	..	*12	..	..		*12	*4082
	2005	..	*13	..	..		*13	*4407
	2006	..	*13	..	..		*13	*4399
French Guiana	2003	..	*284	..	*17		*267	*1475
Guyane française	2004	..	*284	..	*17		*267	*1396
	2005	..	*284	..	*17		*267	*1366
	2006	..	*295	..	*19		*276	*1401
Guyana	2003	..	499	..	12		488	648
Guyana	2004	..	482	..	12		470	623
	2005	..	498	..	12		485	641
	2006	..	503	..	12		491	645
Paraguay	2003	84	1115	..	25	-67	1240	218
Paraguay	2004	64	1213	..	18	5	1254	217
	2005	33	1115	..	19	-28	1157	196
	2006	0	1211	..	24	-13	1201	200
Peru	2003	7917	1583	1958	178	801	6563	244
Pérou	2004	8275	1580	2074	485	34	7262	268
	2005	9010	960	2756	528	88	6598	243
	2006	9193	864	2112	551	982	6412	234
Suriname	2003	372	260	53	..	..	578	1201
Suriname	2004	374	263	54	..	..	583	1183
	2005	390	275	56	..	..	609	1220
	2006	401	281	58	..	..	624	1237
Uruguay	2003	1530	294	154	349	65	1256	369
Uruguay	2004	2058	272	335	384	5	1606	486
	2005	2008	319	356	399	-34	1606	486
	2006	1758	755	226	303	95	1889	570
Venezuela(Bolivar. Rep.)	2003	50523	..	26331	753	1609	21829	850
Venezuela(Rép. bolivar.)	2004	57857	..	34067	1240	-301	22851	875
	2005	60084	..	33174	1242	-233	25901	975
	2006	58031	..	34189	1315	-3793	26320	974

Table 24

Production, trade and consumption of energy petroleum products
Production, commerce et consommation de produits pétroliers énergétiques

Thousand metric tons and kilograms per capita
Milliers de tonnes métriques et kilogrammes par habitant

Country or area Pays ou zone	Year Année	Production Production	Imports Importations	Exports Exportations	Bunkers Soutes	Changes in stocks Variations des stocks	Consumption Consommation Total Totale	Per capita Par habitant
Asia	**2003**	**1099771**	**228045**	**251986**	**90845**	**-5712**	**990697**	**261**
Asie	**2004**	**1152415**	**268829**	**268194**	**97404**	**-2134**	**1057779**	**275**
	2005	**1185689**	**266849**	**285247**	**106432**	**-4634**	**1065494**	**274**
	2006	**1207284**	**271607**	**301293**	**113708**	**-2250**	**1066140**	**271**
Afghanistan	2003	..	149		*8	..	141	6
Afghanistan	2004	..	183		0	..	183	8
	2005	..	*196		*10	..	*186	*8
	2006	..	*196		*10	..	*186	*8
Armenia	2003	..	331		26	..	305	80
Arménie	2004	..	338		38	..	300	93
	2005	..	364		44	..	320	100
	2006	..	339		39	..	300	93
Azerbaijan	2003	5749	3	1864	195	39	3654	444
Azerbaïdjan	2004	6144	186	2228	221	-82	3963	477
	2005	7157	291	2358	415	269	4406	525
	2006	7183	131	2996	485	-98	3931	463
Bahrain	2003	11015	..	10195	462	-586	944	1369
Bahreïn	2004	10939	..	9781	505	-365	1018	1440
	2005	11437	..	9936	546	-237	1192	1645
	2006	11110	..	9605	559	-501	1447	1949
Bangladesh	2003	929	2499		263	-39	3204	24
Bangladesh	2004	839	2621		271	-17	3206	23
	2005	878	3030		306	-9	3611	26
	2006	844	2886		302	-34	3462	24
Bhutan	2003	..	*48		..	..	*48	*78
Bhoutan	2004	..	*51		..	..	*51	*82
	2005	..	*51		..	..	*51	*80
	2006	..	*51		..	..	*51	*79
Brunei Darussalam	2003	1083	0	..	..	1	1082	3095
Brunéi Darussalam	2004	1190	0	..	..	2	1188	3303
	2005	1115	25	..	..	4	1136	3069
	2006	1207	0	..	..	7	1200	3133
Cambodia	2003	..	1041		22	..	1019	77
Cambodge	2004	..	1160		20	..	1140	85
	2005	..	1232		20	..	1212	89
	2006	..	1352		25	..	1327	93
China	2003	187012	28625	13006	2848	-871	200654	156
Chine	2004	212352	42571	10338	415	-8	244178	188
	2005	225341	36128	12291	1243	-113	248048	190
	2006	238365	30335	12141	1874	-1660	256345	195
China, Hong Kong SAR	2003	..	14399	1213	8840	-37	4383	644
Chine, Hong-Kong RAS	2004	..	15791	1370	10856	-405	3971	585
	2005	..	15215	2320	9377	-425	3943	579
	2006	..	15944	1204	11057	250	3432	500
China, Macao SAR	2003	..	602		..	-4	606	1351
Chine, Macao RAS	2004	..	740		..	18	722	1552
	2005	..	748		..	-2	750	1536
	2006	..	733		..	8	725	1444
Cyprus	2003	922	1647		444	-67	2192	3042
Chypre	2004	269	2121		350	-15	2055	2788
	2005	0	2745		583	62	2100	2770
	2006	0	2906		596	112	2198	2851

Table 24

Production, trade and consumption of energy petroleum products
Production, commerce et consommation de produits pétroliers énergétiques

Thousand metric tons and kilograms per capita
Milliers de tonnes métriques et kilogrammes par habitant

Country or area Pays ou zone	Year Année	Production Production	Imports Importations	Exports Exportations	Bunkers Soutes	Changes in stocks Variations des stocks	Consumption Consommation	
							Total Totale	Per capita Par habitant
Georgia	2003	15	532	36	26	-23	508	117
Géorgie	2004	16	571	42	37	0	508	118
	2005	5	699	14	37	0	653	150
	2006	4	705	14	37	0	658	150
India	2003	93717	3549	11502	2425	0	83339	78
Inde	2004	101771	4009	14656	2818	*-90	88396	82
	2005	102479	6911	15413	3300	0	90677	83
	2006	114591	6703	22548	3977	0	94769	85
Indonesia	2003	46368	14897	6838	1274	6	53147	248
Indonésie	2004	47294	19790	7805	1124	*250	57905	267
	2005	44027	21036	6189	1077	2	57795	263
	2006	42347	17027	5623	1051	0	52700	237
Iran(Islamic Rep. of)	2003	72959	4389	16841	1365	-121	59263	892
Iran(Rép. islamique)	2004	72968	6464	15629	1411	0	62392	925
	2005	73511	7040	15074	1414	0	64063	936
	2006	75336	9194	15802	1463	0	67265	954
Iraq	2003	20072	361	1729	405	0	18299	695
Iraq	2004	19617	4179	1346	1163	437	20850	768
	2005	19099	4794	757	750	426	21960	799
	2006	19703	4978	1565	787	433	21896	760
Israel	2003	10240	4653	2905	277	158	11553	1727
Israël	2004	10024	4966	3404	234	-151	11503	1689
	2005	10953	4608	3718	264	157	11422	1648
	2006	10687	4194	3064	267	-22	11572	1642
Japan	2003	177382	27079	3189	11675	219	189378	1500
Japon	2004	173798	27304	3784	12142	-790	185966	1473
	2005	177980	28252	7880	12857	1633	183862	1457
	2006	169502	25249	9040	12010	519	173182	1373
Jordan	2003	3730	1375	..	68	-15	5052	966
Jordanie	2004	3935	956	..	124	46	4721	925
	2005	4173	1075	..	154	113	4981	910
	2006	4067	788	..	115	30	4710	841
Kazakhstan	2003	8319	1031	2591	166	-17	6610	443
Kazakhstan	2004	9792	1752	3183	216	51	8094	539
	2005	12080	1444	5012	234	349	7929	523
	2006	11524	1272	3239	248	261	9048	591
Korea, Dem.Ppl's.Rep.	2003	539	543	..	..	..	1082	46
Corée,Rép.pop.dém.de	2004	545	546	..	..	..	1091	46
	2005	459	457	..	..	..	916	39
	2006	352	349	..	..	..	701	30
Korea, Republic of	2003	87616	10695	22105	7657	210	68339	1428
Corée, République de	2004	89574	6917	25003	8423	321	62744	1305
	2005	93298	6238	29217	12535	-1435	59219	1226
	2006	94555	6653	31880	13050	1030	55248	1144
Kuwait	2003	34358	561	22991	1274	..	10654	4581
Koweït	2004	34696	108	21725	1104	..	11975	5009
	2005	35788	0	21764	1106	..	12918	5257
	2006	38505	0	24949	1191	..	12365	4895
Kyrgyzstan	2003	88	483	137	..	..	434	86
Kirghizistan	2004	88	602	149	..	..	541	106
	2005	86	604	119	..	..	571	111
	2006	83	551	87	..	..	547	105

Table 24

Production, trade and consumption of energy petroleum products
Production, commerce et consommation de produits pétroliers énergétiques

Thousand metric tons and kilograms per capita
Milliers de tonnes métriques et kilogrammes par habitant

Country or area Pays ou zone	Year Année	Production Production	Imports Importations	Exports Exportations	Bunkers Soutes	Changes in stocks Variations des stocks	Consumption Consommation Total Totale	Consumption Consommation Per capita Par habitant
Lao People's Dem. Rep.	2003	..	*128	..	..	..	*128	*23
Rép. dém. pop. lao	2004	..	*131	..	..	..	*131	*22
	2005	..	*132	..	..	..	*132	*23
	2006	..	*133	..	..	..	*133	*23
Lebanon	2003	..	4938	..	141	-562	5359	1368
Liban	2004	..	4743	..	144	1	4598	1160
	2005	..	4538	..	164	-420	4794	1195
	2006	..	4129	..	120	0	4009	989
Malaysia	2003	20117	9833	5914	1867	-328	22497	898
Malaisie	2004	20450	12561	6212	2095	180	24525	959
	2005	20475	11373	5760	1953	198	23937	916
	2006	20891	10171	5361	1998	*-15	23718	890
Maldives	2003	..	195	..	..	..	195	684
Maldives	2004	..	245	..	..	..	245	846
	2005	..	221	..	..	..	221	752
	2006	..	283	..	..	..	283	947
Mongolia	2003	..	510	..	..	..	510	205
Mongolie	2004	..	562	..	..	..	562	223
	2005	..	550	..	..	..	550	216
	2006	..	635	..	..	..	635	246
Myanmar	2003	767	963	..	70	-31	1691	32
Myanmar	2004	693	1138	..	67	0	1764	32
	2005	645	1251	..	52	0	1844	33
	2006	790	893	..	78	-28	1633	29
Nepal	2003	..	701	..	39	..	662	27
Népal	2004	..	666	..	52	..	614	25
	2005	..	689	..	58	..	631	25
	2006	..	704	..	59	..	645	25
Occup. Palestinian Terr.	2003	..	414	0	..	-1	415	118
Terr. palestiniens occup.	2004	..	618	15	..	0	603	166
	2005	..	912	18	..	0	894	238
	2006	..	*995	*26	..	0	*970	*249
Oman	2003	4117	287	848	359	*-65	3262	1393
Oman	2004	3877	402	782	*194	*5	3298	1365
	2005	3968	674	746	273	*80	3543	1412
	2006	4172	704	297	*312	2	4265	1655
Other Asia	2003	38925	1389	8579	5119	-920	27536	1218
Autre Asie	2004	42862	1350	11773	4792	177	27470	1211
	2005	44467	1117	13615	4906	-725	27788	1223
	2006	43919	3601	13429	4850	1023	28218	1238
Pakistan	2003	8909	4805	256	153	-223	13528	93
Pakistan	2004	10054	5716	253	226	-197	15488	104
	2005	10189	6035	399	287	*-14	15552	101
	2006	9793	8347	425	274	-271	17712	113
Philippines	2003	11265	4426	885	755	0	14051	173
Philippines	2004	9345	6522	614	*739	87	14427	175
	2005	9909	4973	1165	*821	-677	13573	159
	2006	9823	4530	1568	931	2	11852	136
Qatar	2003	4330	..	2385	596	0	1349	1840
Qatar	2004	4466	..	2754	355	0	1357	1747
	2005	4125	..	1933	454	-5	1743	2144
	2006	4723	..	2086	578	0	2059	2199

Table 24

Production, trade and consumption of energy petroleum products
Production, commerce et consommation de produits pétroliers énergétiques
Thousand metric tons and kilograms per capita
Milliers de tonnes métriques et kilogrammes par habitant

Country or area Pays ou zone	Year Année	Production Production	Imports Importations	Exports Exportations	Bunkers Soutes	Changes in stocks Variations des stocks	Consumption Consommation	
							Total Totale	Per capita Par habitant
Saudi Arabia	2003	104368	1215	43322	3950	38	58273	2646
Arabie saoudite	2004	111492	1452	46768	3912	-49	62313	2762
	2005	115372	1787	48757	3956	19	64427	2787
	2006	114437	3391	45332	4404	-102	68194	2880
Singapore	2003	27447	42070	41298	23154	-3297	8362	1998
Singapour	2004	31222	46782	46250	26455	-2294	7593	1792
	2005	37958	43889	49421	28565	-4273	8134	1873
	2006	36501	52613	54381	31330	-4378	7781	1735
Sri Lanka	2003	1876	1396	0	225	-79	3126	162
Sri Lanka	2004	2085	1767	38	247	17	3550	182
	2005	1824	1895	0	299	15	3405	173
	2006	1875	1902	0	256	112	3409	171
Syrian Arab Republic	2003	10738	863	1295	97	11	10198	581
Rép. arabe syrienne	2004	11165	921	1217	116	-19	10772	604
	2005	10807	915	0	105	17	11600	635
	2006	11229	887	9	102	17	11988	640
Tajikistan	2003	..	1198	..	4	..	1194	182
Tadjikistan	2004	..	1287	..	4	..	1283	191
	2005	..	1375	..	4	..	1371	200
	2006	..	1546	..	4	..	1542	216
Thailand	2003	38815	841	4669	..	818	34169	534
Thaïlande	2004	43820	1511	5526	..	867	38938	607
	2005	42119	2100	5414	..	689	38116	588
	2006	43459	1478	6752	..	696	37489	574
Timor-Leste	2003	*6659	*91	*6659	..	..	*91	*91
Timor-Leste	2004	*6700	*95	*6700	..	..	*95	*93
	2005	*6725	*96	*6725	..	..	*96	*92
	2006	*6735	*97	*6735	..	..	*97	*91
Turkey	2003	23058	7138	3553	1498	63	25082	357
Turquie	2004	22178	8924	4294	1947	-111	24972	351
	2005	21775	9162	4670	2125	-332	24474	340
	2006	21563	10828	5705	1946	357	24383	334
Turkmenistan	2003	6505	80	3032	..	..	3553	756
Turkménistan	2004	6255	80	2916	..	..	3419	717
	2005	6466	80	3015	..	..	3531	731
	2006	7702	80	3591	..	..	4191	855
United Arab Emirates	2003	19885	12435	10507	12727	..	9086	2559
Emirats arabes unis	2004	20615	13425	10695	14101	..	9244	2458
	2005	20522	15087	10304	15653	..	9652	2350
	2006	21592	15840	10514	16847	..	10071	2381
Uzbekistan	2003	6524	..	311	..	..	6213	241
Ouzbékistan	2004	6145	..	293	..	..	5852	223
	2005	5019	..	240	..	..	4779	180
	2006	4685	..	224	..	..	4461	165
Viet Nam	2003	307	10230	554	154	..	9829	121
Viet Nam	2004	335	11281	0	258	..	11358	138
	2005	343	12005	280	257	..	11811	142
	2006	483	11760	262	238	..	11743	140
Yemen	2003	3046	2407	777	217	11	4448	236
Yémen	2004	2804	2723	652	228	0	4647	240
	2005	3115	2810	722	228	0	4975	249
	2006	2947	3524	839	238	0	5394	262

Table 24

Production, trade and consumption of energy petroleum products
Production, commerce et consommation de produits pétroliers énergétiques

Thousand metric tons and kilograms per capita
Milliers de tonnes métriques et kilogrammes par habitant

Country or area Pays ou zone	Year Année	Production Production	Imports Importations	Exports Exportations	Bunkers Soutes	Changes in stocks Variations des stocks	Consumption Consommation	
							Total Totale	Per capita Par habitant
Europe	**2003**	**858091**	**248527**	**296184**	**90676**	**2683**	**717075**	**986**
Europe	**2004**	**880656**	**256777**	**326788**	**96616**	**-997**	**715026**	**982**
	2005	**893665**	**282614**	**359945**	**101857**	**5194**	**709283**	**973**
	2006	**901136**	**299112**	**371010**	**105745**	**3211**	**720282**	**987**
Albania	2003	227	817	40	47	..	957	271
Albanie	2004	270	975	5	57	..	1183	379
	2005	222	895	0	69	..	1048	334
	2006	271	845	0	83	..	1033	328
Austria	2003	7588	6186	1109	415	175	12075	1497
Autriche	2004	7202	6840	1278	487	248	12029	1478
	2005	7776	6923	1804	549	-104	12450	1517
	2006	7259	6919	1279	575	218	12106	1462
Belarus	2003	12311	1130	8581	..	0	4860	492
Bélarus	2004	15200	1048	10975	..	224	5049	514
	2005	17139	582	12684	..	33	5004	512
	2006	17882	1275	13957	..	-422	5622	578
Belgium	2003	31378	16867	21309	8577	286	18073	1745
Belgique	2004	30086	19924	23014	9355	-53	17694	1702
	2005	27934	22464	23680	9200	342	17176	1644
	2006	28114	21396	22117	9751	128	17514	1666
Bosnia and Herzegovina	2003	65	905	31	..	-5	944	246
Bosnie y Herzégovine	2004	149	949	0	..	-11	1109	289
	2005	125	913	0	..	0	1038	270
	2006	125	974	0	..	0	1099	286
Bulgaria	2003	3916	1140	1478	292	-107	3393	434
Bulgarie	2004	4679	1326	2251	264	-83	3573	459
	2005	5286	1652	2523	293	283	3839	496
	2006	6088	1660	3563	281	-40	3944	512
Croatia	2003	5047	1187	1421	45	-91	4859	1094
Croatie	2004	4890	1155	1707	52	2	4284	965
	2005	4807	1352	1554	64	63	4478	1008
	2006	4537	1494	1512	59	-30	4490	1011
Czech Republic	2003	4814	2633	951	197	94	6205	608
République tchèque	2004	4806	2745	665	282	26	6578	644
	2005	5567	2558	913	308	93	6811	666
	2006	5578	2392	868	325	16	6761	657
Denmark	2003	8149	4603	3968	1686	-35	7133	1350
Danemark	2004	7948	4672	4130	1600	-156	7046	1305
	2005	7495	5675	4175	1670	665	6660	1230
	2006	7840	5181	4566	1925	-270	6800	1251
Estonia	2003	..	912	..	132	-56	836	618
Estonie	2004	..	1035	..	180	-7	862	639
	2005	..	1022	..	163	-8	867	644
	2006	..	1174	..	245	71	858	639
Faeroe Islands	2003	..	*215	..	*2	..	*213	*4445
Iles Féroé	2004	..	*215	..	*2	..	*213	*4414
	2005	..	*216	..	*2	..	*214	*4434
	2006	..	*216	..	*2	..	*214	*4434
Finland	2003	12078	3770	4910	1005	329	9604	1842
Finlande	2004	12463	3227	4986	932	-474	10246	1960
	2005	11898	4048	4444	925	340	10237	1951
	2006	12849	3620	4864	1023	41	10541	2002

Table 24

Production, trade and consumption of energy petroleum products
Production, commerce et consommation de produits pétroliers énergétiques

Thousand metric tons and kilograms per capita
Milliers de tonnes métriques et kilogrammes par habitant

Country or area Pays ou zone	Year Année	Production Production	Imports Importations	Exports Exportations	Bunkers Soutes	Changes in stocks Variations des stocks	Consumption Consommation	
							Total Totale	Per capita Par habitant
France incl. Monaco	2003	74165	25903	18210	7631	-28	74255	1234
France y compris Monaco	2004	75107	27295	19427	8331	-428	75072	1240
	2005	73322	32160	22366	8120	1302	73694	1210
	2006	74659	31906	22319	8447	-122	75921	1243
Germany	2003	100830	27941	16087	8212	1319	103153	1250
Allemagne	2004	103599	25394	20610	8727	-1619	101275	1228
	2005	106211	25919	23110	9012	1630	98378	1193
	2006	104605	28110	24101	9433	-887	100068	1215
Gibraltar	2003	..	1244	..	1126	..	118	4214
Gibraltar	2004	..	1283	..	1161	..	122	4357
	2005	..	1313	..	1187	..	126	4500
	2006	..	1346	..	1220	..	126	4364
Greece	2003	20167	5981	3836	4015	-191	18488	1677
Grèce	2004	19115	6939	3908	4065	166	17915	1620
	2005	19768	7382	4431	3683	341	18695	1684
	2006	20627	8493	5441	4067	454	19158	1718
Hungary	2003	6024	1711	2089	198	84	5364	530
Hongrie	2004	5880	1909	2069	226	140	5354	530
	2005	6182	2188	1918	262	101	6089	604
	2006	6184	2012	1793	265	-270	6408	636
Iceland	2003	..	832	..	167	-52	717	2479
Islande	2004	..	945	..	185	31	729	2492
	2005	..	933	..	194	19	720	2434
	2006	..	978	..	208	-27	797	2619
Ireland	2003	3099	6648	1491	879	87	7290	1832
Irlande	2004	2874	6848	1221	820	54	7627	1886
	2005	3115	6250	1370	877	14	7104	1720
	2006	3223	6378	1268	913	36	7384	1744
Italy and San Marino	2003	88184	23440	19911	5863	-704	86554	1503
Italie y comp. St. Marin	2004	88757	18601	21144	6016	-91	80289	1380
	2005	91405	16864	24828	6202	-1053	78292	1336
	2006	89810	17779	23309	6490	109	77681	1318
Latvia	2003	..	1342	5	229	2	1106	476
Lettonie	2004	..	1610	334	252	4	1020	441
	2005	..	1815	491	321	42	961	418
	2006	..	1770	249	264	38	1219	533
Lithuania	2003	6811	274	4827	133	87	2038	590
Lituanie	2004	8319	375	6401	127	-12	2178	634
	2005	8870	435	6533	192	272	2308	676
	2006	7957	683	6088	193	-127	2486	732
Luxembourg	2003	..	2624	13	380	6	2225	4927
Luxembourg	2004	..	2880	14	414	-13	2465	5381
	2005	..	3002	14	420	-18	2586	5559
	2006	..	2928	8	394	28	2498	5285
Malta	2003	..	903	..	100	..	803	2008
Malte	2004	..	952	..	121	..	831	2064
	2005	..	939	..	111	..	828	2045
	2006	..	913	..	98	..	815	2005
Netherlands	2003	65245	33998	51627	17038	183	30395	1877
Pays-Bas	2004	65801	37210	55160	18464	586	28801	1771
	2005	64640	47199	62812	20789	805	27433	1681
	2006	61361	53541	67703	21495	370	25334	1551

Table 24

Production, trade and consumption of energy petroleum products
Production, commerce et consommation de produits pétroliers énergétiques

Thousand metric tons and kilograms per capita
Milliers de tonnes métriques et kilogrammes par habitant

Country or area Pays ou zone	Year Année	Production Production	Imports Importations	Exports Exportations	Bunkers Soutes	Changes in stocks Variations des stocks	Consumption Consommation	
							Total Totale	Per capita Par habitant
Norway,Svlbd.J.Myn. I	2003	19325	3458	11630	769	91	10293	2247
Norvège,Svalbd,J.May	2004	19001	3420	11764	753	-118	10022	2175
	2005	20340	3364	12118	962	189	10435	2248
	2006	22993	3738	13916	870	9	11936	2561
Poland	2003	15471	4043	1592	574	-3	17351	454
Pologne	2004	15816	5328	1751	536	181	18676	489
	2005	15726	6009	2162	642	224	18707	490
	2006	17319	6276	2209	719	684	19983	524
Portugal	2003	11158	3843	1265	1206	352	12178	1166
Portugal	2004	11369	3460	1475	1346	-369	12377	1179
	2005	11682	4393	1863	1290	322	12600	1194
	2006	12036	2838	2845.	1397	-219	10851	1025
Republic of Moldova	2003	..	613	1	12	22	578	160
Rép. de Moldova	2004	..	624	1	11	-7	619	172
	2005	..	638	2	12	2	622	173
	2006	..	606	2	12	-15	607	169
Romania	2003	10837	1742	3466	114	32	8967	413
Roumanie	2004	11512	1579	4162	133	91	8705	402
	2005	13531	844	5634	108	-205	8838	409
	2006	12913	1049	5115	133	-190	8904	413
Russian Federation	2003	171555	3	66963	4726	-20	99889	691
Fédération de Russie	2004	175177	544	72111	4641	15	98954	688
	2005	186292	27	84471	5018	-1065	97895	684
	2006	197412	44	88194	5301	2167	101794	714
Serbia	2003	3036	70	220	62	..	2824	267
Serbie	2004	3150	241	193	46	..	3152	300
	2005	2956	505	101	48	..	3312	316
	2006	2488	1218	66	52	..	3588	343
Slovakia	2003	5179	750	3080	33	109	2707	503
Slovaquie	2004	5569	1044	3536	26	-12	3063	569
	2005	5269	1185	3263	38	31	3122	580
	2006	5330	1087	3339	39	86	2953	548
Slovenia	2003	..	2391	84	25	32	2250	1128
Slovénie	2004	..	2505	114	19	37	2335	1170
	2005	..	2665	203	44	28	2390	1194
	2006	..	2838	385	54	-57	2456	1223
Spain	2003	49299	21508	4208	9898	-184	56885	1354
Espagne	2004	51683	22789	5220	10413	292	58547	1371
	2005	53260	24931	5647	11149	767	60628	1397
	2006	54371	25402	7254	11634	577	60308	1369
Sweden	2003	17328	6678	9284	2153	460	12109	1352
Suède	2004	18417	6070	10337	2560	-347	11937	1327
	2005	17620	6649	9682	2606	537	11444	1267
	2006	17682	6914	10442	2784	-20	11390	1254
Switzerland	2003	4427	7796	612	1183	-113	10541	1436
Suisse	2004	5034	7224	579	1128	24	10527	1413
	2005	4756	7782	478	1156	202	10702	1435
	2006	5418	7305	534	1218	47	10924	1460
T.F.Yug.Rep. Macedonia	2003	812	269	329	7	-61	806	398
L'ex-RY Macédoine	2004	807	247	199	6	28	821	404
	2005	921	268	326	6	9	848	416
	2006	1026	241	354	5	15	893	438

Table 24

Production, trade and consumption of energy petroleum products
Production, commerce et consommation de produits pétroliers énergétiques

Thousand metric tons and kilograms per capita
Milliers de tonnes métriques et kilogrammes par habitant

Country or area Pays ou zone	Year Année	Production Production	Imports Importations	Exports Exportations	Bunkers Soutes	Changes in stocks Variations des stocks	Consumption Consommation	
							Total Totale	Per capita Par habitant
Ukraine	2003	20491	951	9610	361	0	11471	240
Ukraine	2004	20564	1141	9254	366	164	11921	252
	2005	17906	1924	7450	364	-289	12305	261
	2006	13941	4020	4490	325	13	13133	281
United Kingdom	2003	79075	21206	21946	11184	583	66568	1122
Royaume-Uni	2004	85412	24209	26793	12512	490	69826	1170
	2005	81644	26731	26895	13801	-720	68399	1136
	2006	79238	31553	26860	13446	800	69685	1150
Oceania	**2003**	**38837**	**12372**	**3708**	**4416**	**-362**	**43447**	**1341**
Océanie	**2004**	**38673**	**13110**	**3326**	**4560**	**155**	**43742**	**1330**
	2005	**38179**	**15046**	**2922**	**4984**	**-320**	**45639**	**1368**
	2006	**35826**	**17079**	**2971**	**4875**	**-246**	**45304**	**1337**
Australia	2003	33734	6944	3475	2915	-243	34531	1735
Australie	2004	33302	7084	2975	3043	22	34346	1705
	2005	32306	9732	2445	3435	*-265	36423	1785
	2006	29979	11794	2508	3305	*-251	36211	1749
Cook Islands	2003	..	13	..	*2	..	11	598
Iles Cook	2004	..	18	..	0	..	18	887
	2005	..	20	..	0	..	20	990
	2006	..	*21	..	0	..	*21	*986
Fiji	2003	..	988	*115	*362	..	511	617
Fidji	2004	..	1032	*131	*306	..	595	713
	2005	..	920	*121	*291	..	508	603
	2006	..	952	*116	*347	..	489	573
French Polynesia	2003	..	307	..	*42	..	265	1072
Polynésie française	2004	..	306	..	*51	..	255	1016
	2005	..	328	..	*52	..	276	1084
	2006	..	321	..	*55	..	266	1038
Kiribati	2003	..	*10	..	*2	..	*8	*86
Kiribati	2004	..	*10	..	*2	..	*8	*79
	2005	..	*10	..	*2	..	*8	*78
	2006	..	*12	..	*2	..	*10	*95
Marshall Islands	2003	..	*27	..	..	..	*27	*495
Îles Marshall	2004	..	*29	..	..	..	*29	*496
	2005	..	*28	..	..	..	*28	*481
	2006	..	*30	..	..	..	*30	*496
Nauru	2003	..	*53	..	*7	..	*46	*3660
Nauru	2004	..	*53	..	*7	..	*46	*3591
	2005	..	*53	..	*7	..	*46	*3525
	2006	..	*53	..	*7	..	*46	*3459
New Caledonia	2003	..	646	29	9	..	608	2667
Nouvelle-Calédonie	2004	..	609	29	11	..	569	2465
	2005	..	708	*30	10	..	668	2855
	2006	..	738	*31	14	..	693	2912
New Zealand	2003	5103	1838	87	993	-122	5983	1492
Nouvelle-Zélande	2004	5067	2423	79	1052	123	6236	1535
	2005	5162	2222	181	1099	-55	6159	1503
	2006	5005	2157	75	1056	5	6026	1454
Niue	2003	..	*1	..	..	..	*1	*565
Nioué	2004	..	*1	..	..	..	*1	*568
	2005	..	*1	..	..	..	*1	*593
	2006	..	*1	..	..	..	*1	*615

Table 24

Production, trade and consumption of energy petroleum products
Production, commerce et consommation de produits pétroliers énergétiques

Thousand metric tons and kilograms per capita
Milliers de tonnes métriques et kilogrammes par habitant

Country or area Pays ou zone	Year Année	Production Production	Imports Importations	Exports Exportations	Bunkers Soutes	Changes in stocks Variations des stocks	Consumption Consommation	
							Total Totale	Per capita Par habitant
Palau	2003	..	*76	..	*15	..	*61	*3009
Palaos	2004	..	*76	..	*15	..	*61	*2941
	2005	..	*77	..	*15	..	*62	*2980
	2006	..	*81	..	*15	..	*66	*3042
Papua New Guinea	2003	0	1264	*2	*64	*3	1195	206
Papouasie-Nvl-Guinée	2004	304	1264	112	*68	*10	1378	232
	2005	711	740	145	*68	0	1238	204
	2006	842	711	241	*70	0	1242	200
Samoa	2003	..	*49	..	..	..	*49	*272
Samoa	2004	..	*50	..	..	..	*50	*275
	2005	..	*51	..	..	..	*51	*278
	2006	..	*51	..	..	..	*51	*276
Solomon Islands	2003	..	*60	..	*3	..	*57	*127
Iles Salomon	2004	..	*60	..	*3	..	*57	*124
	2005	..	*60	..	*3	..	*57	*121
	2006	..	*61	..	*3	..	*58	*120
Tonga	2003	..	58	..	*1	..	57	561
Tonga	2004	..	57	..	*1	..	56	551
	2005	..	*57	..	*1	..	*56	*543
	2006	..	*57	..	*1	..	*56	*549
Vanuatu	2003	..	*29	..	..	..	*29	*137
Vanuatu	2004	..	*29	..	..	..	*29	*136
	2005	..	*29	..	..	..	*29	*135
	2006	..	*30	..	..	..	*30	*136
Wallis and Futuna Is	2003	..	*9	..	*1	..	*8	*545
Iles Wallis et Futuna	2004	..	9	..	1	..	9	550
	2005	..	9	..	1	..	9	542
	2006	..	9	..	1	..	8	524

Table 25

Production of non-energy products from refineries - by type
Production des raffineries - produits non-énergétiques - par catégorie
Thousand metric tons
Milliers de tonnes métriques

Table Notes:
Total

Naphtha, white spirit, lubricants, bitumen asphalt, petroleum waxes, petroleum coke and other petroleum products.

- **Please refer to the Definitions Section on pages xv to xxix for the appropriate product description /classification.**

Notes relatives aux tableaux:
Total

Naphtas, essences spéciales, lubrifiants, asphalte de bitume, cires de pétrole, coke de pétrole, et autres produits pétroliers.

- **Veuillez consulter la section "définitions" de la page xv à la page xxix pour une description/classification appropriée des produits.**

Figure 70: Production of non-energy products from refineries, by type and region, in 2006

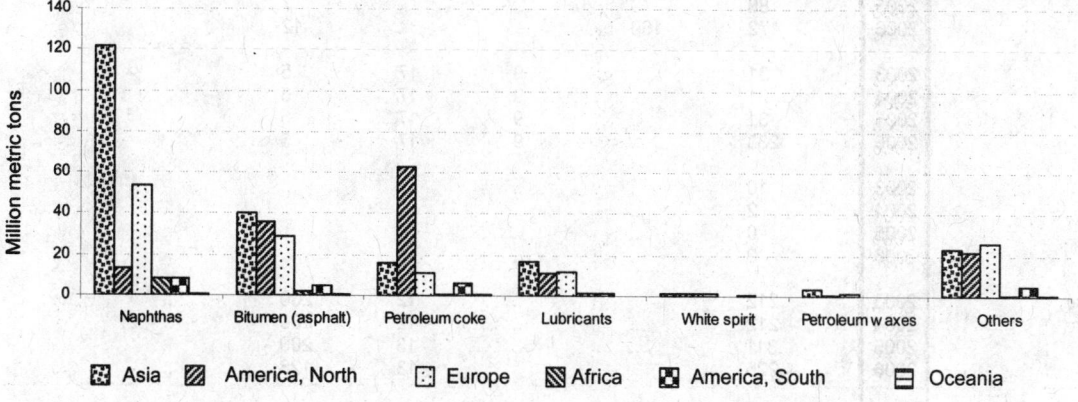

Figure 71: World non-energy products production from refineries, by type, in 2006

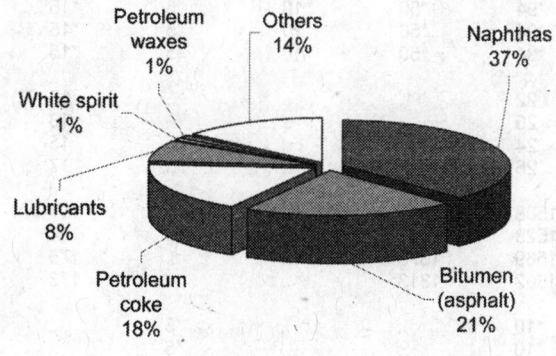

Table 25

Production of non-energy products from refineries - by type
Production des raffineries - produits non-énergétiques - par catégorie
Thousand metric tons
Milliers de tonnes métriques

Country or area Pays ou zone	Year Année	Total Totale	Naphthas Naphtas	White spirit Essences spéciales	Lubricants Lubrifiants	Bitumen (asphalt) Bitumen (brai)	Petroleum waxes Cires de pétrole	Petroleum coke Coke de pétrole	Others Autres
World	2003	514528	203210	5964	36102	98446	4338	86992	79476
Monde	2004	539356	204182	5772	41223	108080	4994	96024	79080
	2005	537211	206188	5604	40988	109777	5062	96353	73240
	2006	548303	206687	5247	42646	112787	5150	97789	77997
Africa	2003	14361	9965	105	1098	2084	75	432	603
Afrique	2004	13534	8688	113	1149	2117	89	432	946
	2005	14802	9038	114	1381	2600	63	446	1160
	2006	13812	8447	111	1342	2455	58	404	995
Algeria	2003	4626	4164	17	140	305	..	..	..
Algérie	2004	3536	3096	16	162	262	..	..	..
	2005	3636	3216	13	153	254	..	..	..
	2006	3709	3279	*13	148	269	..	..	..
Angola	2003	83	77	..	..	6	..	..	..
Angola	2004	94	85	..	..	9	..	..	..
	2005	86	79	..	..	7	..	..	..
	2006	172	160	..	..	12	..	..	..
Cameroon	2003	31	..	9	17	5	..	..	0
Cameroun	2004	31	..	9	17	5	..	..	0
	2005	31	..	9	17	5	..	..	0
	2006	233	..	9	17	5	..	..	202
Congo	2003	10	..	..	2	..	..	..	8
Congo	2004	2	..	..	2	..	..	..	0
	2005	0	..	..	0	..	..	..	0
	2006	8	..	..	0	..	..	..	8
Côte d'Ivoire	2003	212	..	..	12	200	..	..	0
Côte d'Ivoire	2004	212	..	..	12	200	..	..	0
	2005	311	..	..	13	200	..	..	98
	2006	225	..	..	13	128	..	..	84
Egypt	2003	5578	3598	..	355	890	..	432	303
Egypte	2004	5517	3389	..	395	876	..	432	425
	2005	5697	3499	..	408	905	..	446	439
	2006	4952	2926	..	368	815	..	404	439
Gabon	2003	*143	*82	*13	*9	*21	..	..	*18
Gabon	2004	*94	*50	*10	*5	*15	..	..	*14
	2005	*94	*50	*10	*5	*15	..	..	*14
	2006	*94	*50	*10	*5	*15	..	..	*14
Kenya	2003	22	..	..	..	13	..	..	9
Kenya	2004	25	..	..	..	16	..	..	9
	2005	24	..	..	..	15	..	..	9
	2006	26	..	..	..	17	..	..	9
Libyan Arab Jamah.	2003	1508	1345	..	..	147	..	..	16
Jamah. arabe libyenne	2004	1528	1358	..	..	154	..	..	16
	2005	1569	1378	..	..	175	..	..	16
	2006	1502	1313	..	..	173	..	..	16
Madagascar	2003	*10	..	..	*5	..	..	..	*5
Madagascar	2004	*10	..	..	*5	..	..	..	*5
	2005	*10	..	..	*5	..	..	..	*5
	2006	*10	..	..	*5	..	..	..	*5
Morocco	2003	611	553	..	0	58	0	..	..
Maroc	2004	833	625	..	64	141	3	..	..
	2005	954	650	..	101	198	5	..	..
	2006	841	530	..	96	213	2	..	..

Table 25

Production of non-energy products from refineries - by type
Production des raffineries - produits non-énergétiques - par catégorie
Thousand metric tons
Milliers de tonnes métriques

Country or area Pays ou zone	Year Année	Total Totale	Naphthas Naphtas	White spirit Essences spéciales	Lubricants Lubrifiants	Bitumen (asphalt) Bitumen (brai)	Petroleum waxes Cires de pétrole	Petroleum coke Coke de pétrole	Others Autres
Nigeria	2003	285	..	..	72	26	..	..	187
Nigéria	2004	519	..	..	76	22	..	..	421
	2005	628	..	..	80	19	..	..	529
	2006	267	..	..	113	25	..	..	129
Senegal	2003	9	0	..	5	..	..	..	*4
Sénégal	2004	11	3	..	5	..	..	..	*3
	2005	8	0	..	5	..	..	..	*3
	2006	*3	0	..	0	..	..	..	*3
Sierra Leone	2003	*40	*8	..	*18	..	..	..	*14
Sierra Leone	2004	*40	*8	..	*18	..	..	..	*14
	2005	*41	*8	..	*19	..	..	..	*14
	2006	*44	*9	..	*20	..	..	..	*15
South Africa Customs Un.	2003	1006	..	58	446	408	75	..	19
Un.douan.d'Afr.mérid	2004	962	..	70	376	412	86	..	18
	2005	1508	..	73	564	802	58	..	11
	2006	1463	..	71	547	778	56	..	11
Sudan	2003	26	26	..	..	..	..	..	..
Soudan	2004	28	28	..	..	..	..	..	..
	2005	28	28	..	..	..	..	..	..
	2006	45	45	..	..	..	..	..	..
Tunisia	2003	137	112	8	17	..	..	..	0
Tunisie	2004	66	46	8	12	..	..	..	0
	2005	150	130	9	11	..	..	..	0
	2006	191	135	8	*10	..	..	..	38
Zambia	2003	25	..	..	..	5	..	..	20
Zambie	2004	26	..	..	..	5	..	..	21
	2005	27	..	..	..	5	..	..	22
	2006	27	..	..	..	5	..	..	22
America, North	**2003**	**141923**	**15104**	**2369**	**10040**	**35097**	**729**	**59856**	**18728**
Amérique du Nord	**2004**	**151440**	**16596**	**1990**	**10755**	**36743**	**703**	**64060**	**20593**
	2005	**144613**	**13876**	**1703**	**10254**	**36322**	**738**	**62334**	**19386**
	2006	**147740**	**13753**	**1594**	**11013**	**36011**	**684**	**62936**	**21749**
Canada	2003	17096	3741	114	1136	4389	..	4104	3612
Canada	2004	19210	4131	70	1242	4898	..	4506	4363
	2005	17673	3182	61	1128	4620	..	3990	4692
	2006	18482	3692	43	1129	4567	..	3636	5415
Costa Rica	2003	72	40	..	..	32	..	..	..
Costa Rica	2004	48	23	..	..	25	..	..	..
	2005	29	16	..	..	13	..	..	..
	2006	34	8	..	..	26	..	..	..
Cuba	2003	363	238	..	48	45	..	18	14
Cuba	2004	338	214	..	50	47	..	13	14
	2005	286	169	..	43	43	..	17	14
	2006	334	210	..	45	50	..	14	*15
El Salvador	2003	24	..	..	..	..	..	..	24
El Salvador	2004	23	..	..	..	..	..	..	23
	2005	25	..	..	..	..	..	..	25
	2006	21	..	..	..	..	..	..	21
Guatemala	2003	0	..	..	..	..	..	..	0
Guatemala	2004	64	..	..	..	..	..	..	64
	2005	40	..	..	..	..	..	..	40
	2006	44	..	..	..	..	..	..	44

Table 25

Production of non-energy products from refineries - by type
Production des raffineries - produits non-énergétiques - par catégorie

Thousand metric tons
Milliers de tonnes métriques

Country or area Pays ou zone	Year Année	Total Totale	Naphthas Naphtas	White spirit Essences spéciales	Lubricants Lubrifiants	Bitumen (asphalt) Bitumen (brai)	Petroleum waxes Cires de pétrole	Petroleum coke Coke de pétrole	Others Autres
Jamaica	2003	14	..	..	..	14	..	..	..
Jamaïque	2004	65	..	..	..	65	..	..	..
	2005	9	..	..	..	9	..	..	..
	2006	19	..	..	..	19	..	..	..
Mexico	2003	4459	875	..	..	..	..	1746	1838
Mexique	2004	5525	897	..	..	..	..	2834	1794
	2005	4855	967	..	..	..	..	1995	1893
	2006	5048	1135	..	..	..	..	2139	1774
Netherlands Antilles	2003	2194	..	..	254	693	..	..	1247
Antilles néerlandaises	2004	2636	..	..	382	994	..	..	1260
	2005	2461	..	..	409	774	..	..	1278
	2006	2500	..	..	377	822	..	..	1301
Nicaragua	2003	43	..	..	..	12	..	..	31
Nicaragua	2004	43	..	..	..	13	..	..	30
	2005	49	..	..	..	21	..	..	28
	2006	*49	..	..	..	*21	..	..	*28
Trinidad and Tobago	2003	182	133	..	..	24	..	..	25
Trinité-et-Tobago	2004	164	118	..	..	21	..	..	25
	2005	199	147	..	..	27	..	..	25
	2006	194	143	..	..	26	..	..	25
United States	2003	117476	10077	2255	8602	29888	729	53988	11937
Etats-Unis	2004	123324	11213	1920	9081	30680	703	56707	13020
	2005	118987	9395	1642	8674	30815	738	56332	11391
	2006	121015	8565	1551	9462	30480	684	57147	13126
America, South	**2003**	**24576**	**8785**	**705**	**1393**	**3121**	**40**	**6065**	**4466**
Amérique du Sud	**2004**	**24922**	**8645**	**751**	**1230**	**3564**	**60**	**6201**	**4471**
	2005	**26317**	**8425**	**672**	**1260**	**4292**	**124**	**7080**	**4464**
	2006	**26698**	**8659**	**591**	**1385**	**4633**	**31**	**6235**	**5164**
Argentina	2003	4433	1803	108	420	479	2	1621	..
Argentine	2004	4609	1831	124	375	645	2	1632	..
	2005	4469	1746	132	345	666	1	1579	..
	2006	4659	1929	146	344	659	2	1579	..
Bolivia	2003	499	..	..	12	3	..	..	484
Bolivie	2004	505	..	..	13	4	..	..	488
	2005	786	..	..	14	4	..	..	768
	2006	874	..	..	15	5	..	..	854
Brazil	2003	12395	6479	551	727	1135	..	2030	1473
Brésil	2004	12497	6325	588	629	1415	..	1982	1558
	2005	12958	6144	507	648	1420	..	2730	1509
	2006	13366	6211	413	633	1865	..	2705	1539
Chile	2003	976	185	43	80	652	16	..	..
Chili	2004	*1034	174	37	*86	*711	*26	..	..
	2005	844	230	33	81	500	0	..	..
	2006	*777	217	*30	*80	*450	0	..	..
Colombia	2003	2084	316	..	..	..	..	..	1768
Colombie	2004	2022	315	..	..	..	..	..	1707
	2005	1848	305	..	..	..	..	..	1543
	2006	1999	302	..	..	..	..	..	1697
Ecuador	2003	281	..	..	..	..	..	..	281
Equateur	2004	173	..	..	..	..	..	..	173
	2005	241	..	..	..	..	..	..	241
	2006	*250	..	..	..	..	..	..	*250

Table 25

Production of non-energy products from refineries - by type
Production des raffineries - produits non-énergétiques - par catégorie

Thousand metric tons
Milliers de tonnes métriques

Country or area Pays ou zone	Year Année	Total Totale	Naphthas Naphtas	White spirit Essences spéciales	Lubricants Lubrifiants	Bitumen (asphalt) Bitumen (brai)	Petroleum waxes Cires de pétrole	Petroleum coke Coke de pétrole	Others Autres
Peru	2003	102	..	..	..	..	..	..	102
Pérou	2004	124	..	..	..	..	..	..	124
	2005	176	..	..	..	..	..	..	176
	2006	216	..	..	..	..	..	..	216
Uruguay	2003	32	2	3	..	8	..	19	..
Uruguay	2004	39	0	2	..	5	..	32	..
	2005	45	0	0	..	13	..	32	..
	2006	57	0	2	..	29	..	26	..
Venezuela(Bolivar. Rep.)	2003	3774	..	..	154	844	22	2395	358
Venezuela(Rép. bolivar.)	2004	3919	..	..	127	784	32	2555	421
	2005	4950	..	..	172	1689	123	2739	227
	2006	4500	..	..	313	1625	29	1925	608
Asia	**2003**	**193240**	**112239**	**1276**	**11857**	**31784**	**2078**	**10589**	**23417**
Asie	**2004**	**208263**	**114286**	**1555**	**14788**	**37296**	**3003**	**14651**	**22684**
	2005	**211965**	**117329**	**1662**	**15595**	**37685**	**3026**	**14892**	**21776**
	2006	**223487**	**121872**	**1651**	**16831**	**40038**	**3302**	**16530**	**23263**
Azerbaijan	2003	436	309	..	26	79	..	21	1
Azerbaïdjan	2004	512	334	..	49	103	..	26	0
	2005	547	368	..	39	128	..	12	0
	2006	608	302	..	77	162	..	67	0
Bahrain	2003	1673	1437	..	..	206	..	..	30
Bahreïn	2004	1803	1376	..	..	392	..	..	35
	2005	1885	1438	..	..	410	..	..	37
	2006	1831	1397	..	..	398	..	..	36
Bangladesh	2003	528	38	2	14	..	..	..	474
Bangladesh	2004	476	34	2	13	..	..	..	427
	2005	506	36	2	14	..	..	..	454
	2006	503	35	2	14	..	..	..	452
Brunei Darussalam	2003	124	124	..	..	..	..	..	..
Brunéi Darussalam	2004	0	0	..	..	..	..	..	..
	2005	0	0	..	..	..	..	..	..
	2006	0	0	..	..	..	..	..	..
China	2003	42325	26571	..	3509	4787	1723	5735	..
Chine	2004	44775	18949	..	5326	9026	2619	8855	..
	2005	45199	19066	..	5358	9229	2636	8910	..
	2006	50052	21182	..	5953	10090	2928	9899	..
Cyprus	2003	46	..	..	..	30	..	..	16
Chypre	2004	10	..	..	..	9	..	..	1
	2005	0	..	..	..	0	..	..	0
	2006	0	..	..	..	0	..	..	0
Georgia	2003	8	..	..	..	8	..	..	..
Géorgie	2004	8	..	..	..	8	..	..	..
	2005	8	..	..	..	8	..	..	..
	2006	8	..	..	..	8	..	..	..
India	2003	25897	11317	..	666	3397	53	2743	7721
Inde	2004	27140	14100	..	646	3349	74	3162	5809
	2005	25649	14509	..	677	3576	66	3182	3639
	2006	30145	16660	..	825	3891	61	3779	4929
Indonesia	2003	4894	2221	205	404	537	26	507	994
Indonésie	2004	5374	2276	358	398	541	28	685	1088
	2005	5328	2554	*350	339	430	*30	*650	975
	2006	5941	3061	*300	386	531	*30	*640	993

Table 25

Production of non-energy products from refineries - by type
Production des raffineries - produits non-énergétiques - par catégorie

Thousand metric tons
Milliers de tonnes métriques

Country or area Pays ou zone	Year Année	Total Totale	Naphthas Naphtas	White spirit Essences spéciales	Lubricants Lubrifiants	Bitumen (asphalt) Bitumen (brai)	Petroleum waxes Cires de pétrole	Petroleum coke Coke de pétrole	Others Autres
Iran(Islamic Rep. of)	2003	7004	2390	*300	832	2695	..	..	787
Iran(Rép. islamique)	2004	7658	2560	*300	892	3063	..	..	843
	2005	8378	2099	*300	1437	3679	..	..	863
	2006	8275	1949	*250	1568	4299	..	..	209
Iraq	2003	1311	511	..	232	477	91	..	..
Iraq	2004	1387	540	..	246	505	96	..	..
	2005	1348	525	..	239	491	93	..	..
	2006	1368	533	..	243	498	94	..	..
Israel	2003	831	532	..	*40	134	..	..	125
Israël	2004	737	453	..	*40	126	..	..	118
	2005	868	501	..	*40	198	..	..	129
	2006	776	417	..	*40	184	..	..	135
Japan	2003	25205	14071	67	2312	5529	118	751	2357
Japon	2004	25840	14552	64	2326	5671	115	796	2316
	2005	27076	15969	68	2346	5395	111	815	2372
	2006	27100	15938	66	2378	5435	102	834	2347
Jordan	2003	218	..	..	*16	198	..	..	4
Jordanie	2004	232	..	..	16	212	..	..	4
	2005	133	..	..	*15	114	..	..	4
	2006	185	..	..	14	167	..	..	4
Kazakhstan	2003	372	..	2	1	102	..	61	206
Kazakhstan	2004	420	..	3	1	102	..	82	232
	2005	417	..	3	1	109	..	66	238
	2006	440	..	3	1	88	..	66	282
Korea, Republic of	2003	23237	17520	315	1380	2848	13	220	941
Corée, République de	2004	26441	19746	449	1861	3156	16	242	971
	2005	26736	20751	533	1770	2482	13	256	931
	2006	28135	21537	633	1987	2657	14	265	1042
Kuwait	2003	10282	8213	..	..	96	..	..	1973
Koweït	2004	10133	7906	..	..	91	..	..	2136
	2005	9673	7481	..	..	214	..	..	1978
	2006	8750	7639	..	..	179	..	..	932
Malaysia	2003	3660	*940	..	*94	2626	..	..	0
Malaisie	2004	3825	*1314	..	*94	2417	..	..	0
	2005	4526	184	..	*94	2124	..	..	2124
	2006	*4960	*200	..	*90	2470	..	..	*2200
Myanmar	2003	36	..	..	..	..	2	25	9
Myanmar	2004	33	..	..	..	..	2	22	9
	2005	32	..	..	..	..	2	21	9
	2006	32	..	..	..	..	1	22	9
Oman	2003	25	..	..	25	..	..	..	..
Oman	2004	25	..	..	25	..	..	..	..
	2005	25	..	..	25	..	..	..	..
	2006	25	..	..	25	..	..	..	..
Other Asia	2003	12177	7824	137	19	1286	..	358	2553
Autre Asie	2004	13647	8908	131	178	1274	..	636	2520
	2005	14741	9790	103	279	1375	..	868	2326
	2006	13555	8999	104	250	1038	..	851	2313
Pakistan	2003	925	467	..	177	228	4	..	49
Pakistan	2004	1348	796	..	194	307	6	..	45
	2005	1392	846	..	199	296	5	..	46
	2006	1467	925	..	210	276	*5	..	51

Table 25

Production of non-energy products from refineries - by type
Production des raffineries - produits non-énergétiques - par catégorie
Thousand metric tons
Milliers de tonnes métriques

Country or area Pays ou zone	Year Année	Total Totale	Naphthas Naphtas	White spirit Essences spéciales	Lubricants Lubrifiants	Bitumen (asphalt) Bitumen (brai)	Petroleum waxes Cires de pétrole	Petroleum coke Coke de pétrole	Others Autres
Philippines	2003	689	529	28	..	33	..	..	99
Philippines	2004	403	246	28	..	0	..	..	129
	2005	248	121	28	..	0	..	..	99
	2006	415	213	28	..	0	..	..	174
Qatar	2003	687	687	..	..	..	..	..	..
Qatar	2004	735	735	..	..	..	..	..	..
	2005	783	783	..	..	..	..	..	..
	2006	826	826	..	..	..	..	..	..
Saudi Arabia	2003	12117	7558	..	..	1683	..	..	2876
Arabie saoudite	2004	14721	9708	..	..	*1803	..	..	3210
	2005	15102	9949	..	..	*1930	..	..	3223
	2006	15594	9865	..	..	*1800	..	..	3929
Singapore	2003	7144	3284	196	1575	1644	..	..	445
Singapour	2004	8812	3870	197	1951	1974	..	..	820
	2005	9937	4783	255	2183	1975	..	..	741
	2006	10180	4606	240	2487	1745	..	..	1102
Sri Lanka	2003	199	99	3	*15	41	..	..	41
Sri Lanka	2004	223	103	4	16	50	..	..	50
	2005	246	118	4	*16	52	..	..	56
	2006	241	109	6	*16	55	..	..	55
Syrian Arab Republic	2003	1719	707	3	..	554	*2	*120	333
Rép. arabe syrienne	2004	1803	855	2	..	*500	2	*100	344
	2005	1736	907	2	..	*400	*2	*75	350
	2006	1714	907	2	..	*390	*2	*72	341
Tajikistan	2003	11	11	..	..	..	..	..	..
Tadjikistan	2004	13	13	..	..	..	..	..	..
	2005	14	14	..	..	..	..	..	..
	2006	12	12	..	..	..	..	..	..
Thailand	2003	916	..	..	..	916	..	..	..
Thaïlande	2004	994	..	..	..	994	..	..	..
	2005	1093	..	..	..	1093	..	..	..
	2006	1235	..	..	..	1235	..	..	..
Turkey	2003	3403	1354	3	280	1410	45	..	311
Turquie	2004	3824	1573	3	292	1391	44	..	521
	2005	3863	1488	3	341	1761	67	..	203
	2006	4672	1488	7	96	2220	64	..	797
United Arab Emirates	2003	3777	3143	..	..	..	..	..	634
Emirats arabes unis	2004	3830	3182	..	..	..	..	..	648
	2005	3567	2916	..	..	..	..	..	651
	2006	3541	2916	..	..	..	..	..	625
Uzbekistan	2003	875	..	15	240	135	1	48	436
Ouzbékistan	2004	817	..	14	224	126	1	45	407
	2005	662	..	11	183	103	1	37	327
	2006	618	..	10	171	96	1	35	305
Yemen	2003	489	382	..	..	105	..	..	2
Yémen	2004	264	157	..	..	106	..	..	1
	2005	247	133	..	..	113	..	..	1
	2006	283	156	..	..	126	..	..	*1
Europe	**2003**	**137515**	**56786**	**1385**	**11188**	**25511**	**1389**	**9374**	**31882**
Europe	**2004**	**138435**	**55665**	**1248**	**12707**	**27564**	**1131**	**9980**	**30140**
	2005	**137430**	**57052**	**1339**	**12317**	**28331**	**1103**	**11062**	**26226**
	2006	**134114**	**53479**	**1201**	**11877**	**29075**	**1069**	**11200**	**26213**

Table 25

Production of non-energy products from refineries - by type
Production des raffineries - produits non-énergétiques - par catégorie
Thousand metric tons
Milliers de tonnes métriques

Country or area Pays ou zone	Year Année	Total Totale	Naphthas Naphtas	White spirit Essences spéciales	Lubricants Lubrifiants	Bitumen (asphalt) Bitumen (brai)	Petroleum waxes Cires de pétrole	Petroleum coke Coke de pétrole	Others Autres
Albania	2003	196	..	..	27	44	..	67	58
Albanie	2004	192	..	..	29	53	..	63	47
	2005	269	..	..	31	87	..	48	103
	2006	293	..	..	33	83	..	65	112
Austria	2003	2368	740	..	123	398	..	59	1048
Autriche	2004	2548	863	..	108	433	..	59	1085
	2005	2097	637	..	111	466	..	66	817
	2006	1795	913	..	120	392	..	65	305
Belarus	2003	713	..	..	270	443	..	..	..
Bélarus	2004	646	..	..	*200	446	..	..	..
	2005	593	..	..	*150	443	..	..	..
	2006	710	..	..	*100	610	..	..	..
Belgium	2003	14467	2460	116	0	333	..	356	11202
Belgique	2004	13455	2318	98	0	880	..	308	9851
	2005	9347	1624	86	0	1076	..	235	6326
	2006	8571	1229	84	2	1406	..	299	5551
Bosnia and Herzegovina	2003	11	..	..	11	0	..	..	..
Bosnie y Herzégovine	2004	21	..	..	12	9	..	..	..
	2005	18	..	..	11	7	..	..	..
	2006	18	..	..	11	7	..	..	..
Bulgaria	2003	1258	663	7	..	113	..	..	475
Bulgarie	2004	1100	546	5	..	133	..	..	416
	2005	1011	521	5	..	181	..	..	304
	2006	1048	583	3	..	232	..	..	230
Croatia	2003	549	165	..	12	213	8	105	46
Croatie	2004	686	212	..	62	217	9	112	74
	2005	578	177	..	61	181	7	104	48
	2006	533	128	..	53	216	7	114	15
Czech Republic	2003	1918	479	2	94	389	4	..	950
République tchèque	2004	2193	561	0	125	468	4	..	1035
	2005	2565	706	0	139	536	6	..	1178
	2006	2601	708	0	112	496	11	..	1274
Denmark	2003	5	0	..	..	5	..	..	..
Danemark	2004	6	6	..	..	0	..	..	..
	2005	4	4	..	..	0	..	..	..
	2006	13	13	..	..	0	..	..	..
Finland	2003	1154	188	114	250	425	..	127	50
Finlande	2004	1180	258	109	250	351	..	137	75
	2005	1069	205	147	211	311	..	128	67
	2006	1097	254	112	263	276	..	120	72
France incl. Monaco	2003	14345	6000	99	1843	3478	191	833	1901
France y compris Monaco	2004	14381	5682	153	1870	3544	164	885	2083
	2005	13967	5384	156	1855	3598	142	869	1963
	2006	13135	5036	161	1610	3599	107	936	1686
Germany	2003	17134	8693	36	1594	3520	216	1799	1276
Allemagne	2004	18149	9389	11	2084	3342	263	1794	1266
	2005	18376	9063	0	2045	3601	252	1912	1503
	2006	17884	8510	0	2264	3520	279	1918	1393
Greece	2003	2100	1037	..	200	495	..	154	214
Grèce	2004	2028	960	..	188	548	..	152	180
	2005	1622	678	..	190	410	..	150	194
	2006	1789	726	..	215	461	..	171	216

Table 25

Production of non-energy products from refineries - by type
Production des raffineries - produits non-énergétiques - par catégorie
Thousand metric tons
Milliers de tonnes métriques

Country or area Pays ou zone	Year Année	Total Totale	Naphthas Naphtas	White spirit Essences spéciales	Lubricants Lubrifiants	Bitumen (asphalt) Bitumen (brai)	Petroleum waxes Cires de pétrole	Petroleum coke Coke de pétrole	Others Autres
Hungary	2003	1858	895	201	116	312	40	294	0
Hongrie	2004	1887	842	28	189	323	43	300	162
	2005	2659	1155	34	209	477	47	296	441
	2006	2951	1175	25	182	482	50	331	706
Ireland	2003	31	31	..	..	..	..	..	..
Irlande	2004	21	21	..	..	..	..	..	..
	2005	5	5	..	..	..	..	..	..
	2006	8	8	..	..	..	..	..	..
Italy and San Marino	2003	10737	3615	17	1296	3265	40	1081	1423
Italie y comp. St. Marin	2004	10778	3048	12	1294	3502	54	1395	1473
	2005	10877	3117	44	1286	3423	64	1684	1259
	2006	10915	2982	12	1196	3766	86	1526	1347
Lithuania	2003	391	..	122	20	104	..	96	49
Lituanie	2004	427	..	90	20	133	..	117	67
	2005	465	..	79	20	163	..	129	74
	2006	400	..	55	22	153	..	109	61
Netherlands	2003	17030	10222	294	578	297	120	0	5519
Pays-Bas	2004	17685	11084	314	619	521	134	0	5013
	2005	20708	13906	300	552	408	126	224	5192
	2006	19520	11643	256	581	398	125	0	6517
Norway,Svlbd.J.Myn. I	2003	1359	1135	..	..	..	..	224	..
Norvège,Svalbd,J.May	2004	1365	1192	..	..	..	..	173	..
	2005	1592	1366	..	..	..	..	226	..
	2006	1489	1278	..	..	..	..	211	..
Poland	2003	2521	836	23	161	873	60	..	568
Pologne	2004	2719	889	21	210	997	48	..	554
	2005	2739	949	51	191	1139	36	..	373
	2006	3628	1415	52	229	1549	45	..	338
Portugal	2003	2065	1130	34	125	376	14	..	386
Portugal	2004	1924	1175	35	154	419	19	..	122
	2005	1881	1188	35	134	386	16	..	122
	2006	1628	1037	34	148	340	20	..	49
Romania	2003	1766	460	13	107	204	6	563	413
Roumanie	2004	2285	639	32	161	203	5	720	525
	2005	2226	507	46	98	157	6	890	522
	2006	2407	582	50	74	242	6	913	540
Russian Federation	2003	19790	11124	..	2896	4526	183	1061	..
Fédération de Russie	2004	19693	11081	..	2877	4612	183	940	..
	2005	20426	11116	..	3110	4986	198	1016	..
	2006	20390	11150	..	3037	4725	224	1254	..
Serbia	2003	402	126	..	42	152	..	..	82
Serbie	2004	368	151	..	46	89	..	..	82
	2005	346	142	..	43	84	..	..	77
	2006	291	119	..	36	71	..	..	65
Slovakia	2003	1022	515	35	50	85	1	47	289
Slovaquie	2004	1058	573	38	14	68	0	52	313
	2005	978	560	34	2	49	0	56	277
	2006	996	543	30	1	49	0	50	323
Spain	2003	9140	1917	152	280	2303	46	799	3643
Espagne	2004	8804	521	178	427	2747	111	1004	3816
	2005	8099	530	172	404	2900	105	1049	2939
	2006	8015	417	207	418	2840	93	1036	3004

Table 25

Production of non-energy products from refineries - by type
Production des raffineries - produits non-énergétiques - par catégorie

Thousand metric tons
Milliers de tonnes métriques

Country or area Pays ou zone	Year Année	Total Totale	Naphthas Naphtas	White spirit Essences spéciales	Lubricants Lubrifiants	Bitumen (asphalt) Bitumen (brai)	Petroleum waxes Cires de pétrole	Petroleum coke Coke de pétrole	Others Autres
Sweden	2003	2103	664	..	337	708	..	47	347
Suède	2004	1948	295	..	418	795	..	57	383
	2005	2236	263	..	356	837	..	56	724
	2006	2225	239	..	343	856	..	46	741
Switzerland	2003	187	15	..	..	139	..	0	33
Suisse	2004	212	0	..	..	137	..	32	43
	2005	156	0	..	..	62	..	57	37
	2006	154	1	..	..	42	..	72	39
T.F.Yug.Rep. Macedonia	2003	160	160	..	..	..	..	..	..
L'ex-RY Macédoine	2004	183	183	..	..	..	..	..	..
	2005	226	226	..	..	..	..	..	..
	2006	0	0	..	..	..	..	..	..
Ukraine	2003	1955	0	16	180	386	..	32	1341
Ukraine	2004	1539	0	24	214	398	..	35	868
	2005	1318	0	14	172	451	..	0	681
	2006	1234	56	13	210	515	..	0	440
United Kingdom	2003	8780	3516	104	576	1925	460	1630	569
Royaume-Uni	2004	8954	3176	100	1136	2196	94	1645	607
	2005	8977	3023	136	936	1912	98	1867	1005
	2006	8376	2734	107	617	1749	16	1964	1189
Oceania	**2003**	**2913**	**331**	**124**	**526**	**849**	**27**	**676**	**380**
Océanie	**2004**	**2761**	**302**	**115**	**594**	**796**	**8**	**700**	**246**
	2005	**2084**	**468**	**114**	**181**	**547**	**8**	**539**	**227**
	2006	**2452**	**477**	**99**	**198**	**575**	**6**	**484**	**613**
Australia	2003	2679	331	124	526	702	27	676	293
Australie	2004	2434	157	115	594	691	8	700	169
	2005	1646	233	114	181	430	8	539	141
	2006	2080	309	99	198	445	6	484	539
New Zealand	2003	234	..	..	..	147	..	..	87
Nouvelle-Zélande	2004	182	..	..	..	105	..	..	77
	2005	203	..	..	..	117	..	..	86
	2006	204	..	..	..	130	..	..	74
Papua New Guinea	2003	0	0	..	..	..	..	..	..
Papouasie-Nvl-Guinée	2004	145	145	..	..	..	..	..	..
	2005	235	235	..	..	..	..	..	..
	2006	168	168	..	..	..	..	..	..

Table 26

Production of energy products from refineries - by type
Production des raffineries - produits énergétiques - par catégorie

Thousand metric tons
Milliers de tonnes métriques

Table Notes:
Total

Aviation gasolene, motor gasolene, jet fuels, kerosene, gas-diesel oils, residual fuel oil, liquefied petroleum gas, refinery gas and feedstocks.

Aruba produces only feedstocks to be further refined abroad.

- **Please refer to the Definitions Section on pages xv to xxix for the appropriate product description /classification.**

Notes relatives aux tableaux:
Total

Essence aviation, essence auto, carburéacteurs, pétrole lampant, gazole carburant diesel, mazout résiduel, G.P.L., gaz de raffinerie et charges d'alimentation de raffineries.

Aruba produit seulement des matières de base à raffiner encore à l'étranger.

- **Veuillez consulter la section "définitions" de la page xv à la page xxix pour une description/classification appropriée des produits.**

Figure 72: Production of energy products from refineries, by type and region, in 2006

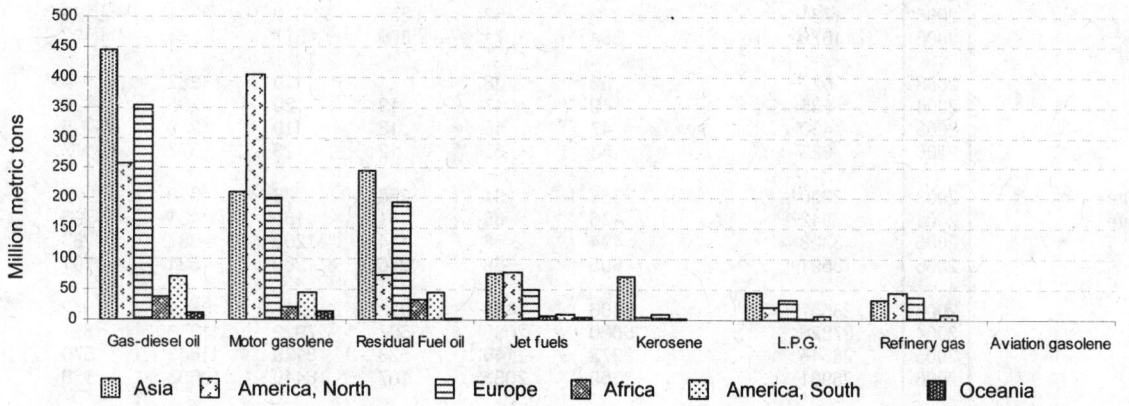

Figure 73: World production of energy products from refineries, by type, in 2006

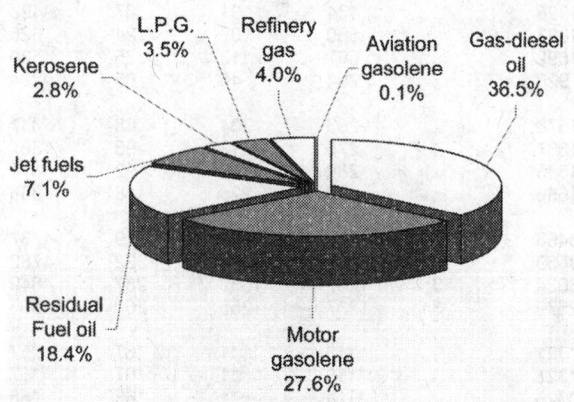

Table 26

Production of energy products from refineries - by type
Production des rafinneries - produits énergétiques - par catégorie
Thousand metric tons
Milliers de tonnes métriques

Country or area Pays ou zone	Year Année	Total Totale	Aviation gasolene Essence aviation	Motor gasolene Essence auto	Jet fuels Carbu-réacteurs	Kerosene Pétrole lampant	Gas-diesel oil Gazole carburant diesel	Residual Fuel oil Mazout résiduel	L.P.G. G.P.L.	Refinery gas Gaz de rafinnerie
World	**2003**	**3087362**	**1621**	**870904**	**205889**	**96940**	**1078043**	**594417**	**106759**	**122788**
Monde	**2004**	**3176736**	**1775**	**892178**	**218075**	**95433**	**1123160**	**601312**	**110127**	**124676**
	2005	**3220829**	**1778**	**893024**	**225774**	**95666**	**1162201**	**598400**	**108539**	**125447**
	2006	**3242532**	**1808**	**893345**	**229540**	**90571**	**1180533**	**595209**	**112288**	**129238**
Africa	**2003**	**109418**	**104**	**22575**	**7977**	**3838**	**35441**	**33990**	**2528**	**2965**
Afrique	**2004**	**108552**	**67**	**21343**	**8034**	**3423**	**36087**	**34162**	**2488**	**2948**
	2005	**109007**	**59**	**18611**	**8429**	**3525**	**37797**	**35051**	**2567**	**2968**
	2006	**110538**	**81**	**20361**	**7941**	**3467**	**38959**	**34147**	**2693**	**2889**
Algeria	2003	16139	*32	1893	1315	12	6186	6093	608	..
Algérie	2004	15423	25	1925	986	14	6340	5560	573	..
	2005	14663	*25	2059	1069	11	5946	5055	498	..
	2006	15539	*27	2320	965	10	6385	5337	495	..
Angola	2003	1869	..	108	352	32	683	609	40	45
Angola	2004	1784	..	96	302	41	669	604	28	44
	2005	1807	..	134	290	31	675	609	24	44
	2006	1821	..	98	323	5	681	644	24	46
Cameroon	2003	1370	..	290	69	217	446	327	21	..
Cameroun	2004	1752	..	402	69	258	607	388	28	..
	2005	1784	..	393	62	352	610	341	26	..
	2006	1678	..	354	71	300	577	354	22	..
Congo	2003	522	..	53	38	21	119	287	4	..
Congo	2004	535	..	49	47	19	120	295	5	..
	2005	430	..	47	45	13	110	210	5	..
	2006	625	..	53	53	12	123	377	7	..
Côte d'Ivoire	2003	2299	..	359	104	638	788	318	72	20
Côte d'Ivoire	2004	2942	..	436	88	681	1180	431	96	29
	2005	3308	..	494	88	714	1205	687	87	33
	2006	3591	..	605	88	976	1269	521	101	31
Egypt	2003	28557	..	6306	1469	918	8235	10532	642	455
Egypte	2004	27826	..	*5000	2080	507	7922	11273	551	493
	2005	26545	..	2972	2146	523	8179	11643	570	512
	2006	25981	..	3659	2033	167	8440	10653	538	491
Gabon	2003	696	*1	69	54	21	210	302	9	*30
Gabon	2004	714	*1	68	45	19	228	324	9	*20
	2005	725	*1	79	59	26	225	305	10	*20
	2006	684	*1	44	55	20	213	324	7	*20
Ghana	2003	1396	..	434	91	67	493	216	53	42
Ghana	2004	1683	..	580	107	24	625	239	66	42
	2005	1592	..	567	113	25	520	242	78	47
	2006	920	..	294	46	65	294	156	36	29
Kenya	2003	1578	..	263	204	88	411	524	24	64
Kenya	2004	1687	..	275	212	95	387	620	27	71
	2005	1586	..	266	205	92	374	549	26	74
	2006	1586	..	179	226	118	368	596	30	69
Libyan Arab Jamah.	2003	13463	3	1517	1491	319	4737	4556	310	530
Jamah. arabe libyenne	2004	13559	3	1507	1504	322	4782	4597	310	534
	2005	13024	3	1237	1339	287	4849	4443	350	516
	2006	12579	3	1237	1255	269	4503	4419	395	498
Madagascar	2003	*321	..	*113	*1	*67	*57	*77	*6	..
Madagascar	2004	*321	..	*113	*1	*67	*57	*77	*6	..
	2005	*325	..	*114	*1	*68	*58	*78	*6	..
	2006	*325	..	*114	*1	*68	*58	*78	*6	..

Table 26

Production of energy products from refineries - by type
Production des rafinneries - produits énergétiques - par catégorie
Thousand metric tons
Milliers de tonnes métriques

Country or area Pays ou zone	Year Année	Total Totale	Aviation gasolene Essence aviation	Motor gasolene Essence auto	Jet fuels Carbu-réacteurs	Kerosene Pétrole lampant	Gas-diesel oil Gazole carburant diesel	Residual Fuel oil Mazout résiduel	L.P.G. G.P.L.	Refinery gas Gaz de rafinnerie
Morocco	2003	3726	..	132	108	52	1535	1747	67	85
Maroc	2004	5182	..	257	174	12	2254	2264	104	117
	2005	5815	..	372	264	2	2295	2545	204	133
	2006	5221	..	373	236	3	2033	2265	192	119
Nigeria	2003	5310	..	1036	386	480	1418	1838	17	135
Nigéria	2004	4363	..	534	189	441	1179	1866	17	137
	2005	4190	..	275	480	405	980	1894	17	139
	2006	5319	..	993	226	561	1260	2159	20	100
Senegal	2003	1117	*15	151	126	26	463	316	12	8
Sénégal	2004	1127	*12	148	132	19	471	327	10	8
	2005	884	*12	118	89	19	356	279	3	8
	2006	336	31	46	31	5	115	100	0	8
Sierra Leone	2003	*190	..	*31	*20	*10	*74	*55	..	..
Sierra Leone	2004	*168	..	*32	*21	*10	*60	*45	..	..
	2005	*158	..	*32	*21	*10	*60	*35	..	..
	2006	*166	..	*33	*22	*11	*60	*40	..	..
Somalia	2003	*140	..	5	*80	25	10	20	0	..
Somalie	2004	*145	..	5	*80	25	10	25	0	..
	2005	*145	..	5	*75	30	10	25	0	..
	2006	176	..	5	*75	30	10	25	31	..
South Africa Customs Un.	2003	25473	53	8360	1874	620	7593	5162	307	1504
Un.douan.d'Afr.mérid	2004	23825	26	8343	1778	633	7141	4192	305	1407
	2005	26263	18	7858	1840	618	9201	5040	297	1391
	2006	27024	19	7938	1908	624	9873	4906	327	1429
Sudan	2003	3205	..	1111	170	36	1273	328	284	3
Soudan	2004	3525	..	1228	192	41	1400	361	300	3
	2005	3611	..	1247	214	42	1423	377	305	3
	2006	4943	..	1712	294	59	1952	504	419	3
Tunisia	2003	1590	..	234	0	165	502	609	49	31
Tunisie	2004	1501	..	226	0	169	432	595	50	29
	2005	1627	..	216	0	229	482	609	58	33
	2006	1499	..	178	4	136	506	604	40	31
Zambia	2003	457	..	110	25	24	208	74	3	13
Zambie	2004	490	..	118	27	26	223	79	3	14
	2005	525	..	126	29	28	239	85	3	15
	2006	525	..	126	29	28	239	85	3	15
America, North	**2003**	**888235**	**759**	**406361**	**78650**	**5162**	**239843**	**80680**	**23126**	**43653**
Amérique du Nord	**2004**	**900178**	**797**	**409008**	**82407**	**5651**	**247074**	**79551**	**22583**	**43108**
	2005	**902432**	**793**	**407872**	**82969**	**5793**	**254143**	**76647**	**21234**	**42981**
	2006	**898505**	**831**	**404041**	**79673**	**4839**	**259052**	**73497**	**22005**	**44567**
Aruba	2003	10000	..	..	..	..	..	..	..	..
Aruba	2004	10000	..	..	..	..	..	..	..	..
	2005	10000	..	..	..	..	..	..	..	..
	2006	*10000	..	..	..	..	..	..	..	..
Canada	2003	86072	83	33689	4200	1575	31136	7989	1991	5409
Canada	2004	86129	73	33024	4597	1519	31590	8724	1955	4647
	2005	84593	76	32270	4363	1625	30745	8263	1779	5472
	2006	82196	64	30889	3869	1578	30704	7763	1730	5599
Costa Rica	2003	397	..	0	..	5	168	222	2	..
Costa Rica	2004	427	..	14	..	1	163	247	2	..
	2005	469	..	85	..	2	153	227	2	..
	2006	637	..	105	..	3	230	295	4	..

Table 26

Production of energy products from refineries - by type
Production des rafinneries - produits énergétiques - par catégorie

Thousand metric tons
Milliers de tonnes métriques

Country or area Pays ou zone	Year Année	Total Totale	Aviation gasolene Essence aviation	Motor gasolene Essence auto	Jet fuels Carbu- réacteurs	Kerosene Pétrole lampant	Gas-diesel oil Gazole carburant diesel	Residual Fuel oil Mazout résiduel	L.P.G. G.P.L.	Refinery gas Gaz de rafinnerie
Cuba	2003	2200	..	412	..	191	444	1024	93	36
Cuba	2004	1883	..	331	..	219	385	858	63	27
	2005	2024	..	407	..	228	395	879	82	33
	2006	1847	..	317	..	126	420	892	62	30
Dominican Republic	2003	1430	..	284	54	190	411	449	42	0
Rép. dominicaine	2004	1976	..	445	54	188	417	839	33	0
	2005	1970	..	447	56	197	423	812	35	0
	2006	1936	..	440	59	207	424	762	33	11
El Salvador	2003	907	..	135	45	19	195	485	12	15
El Salvador	2004	986	..	143	49	21	199	543	14	16
	2005	832	..	112	51	22	198	419	16	14
	2006	811	..	112	39	16	176	437	17	15
Guatemala	2003	0	..	0	..	..	0	..	..	..
Guatemala	2004	0	..	0	..	..	0	..	..	..
	2005	26	..	1	..	..	25	..	..	..
	2006	23	..	1	..	..	22	..	..	..
Jamaica	2003	852	..	111	62	19	158	495	7	..
Jamaïque	2004	666	..	95	63	2	129	370	7	..
	2005	460	..	52	41	12	87	268	0	..
	2006	995	..	124	63	12	226	561	9	..
Martinique	2003	*804	..	*161	..	*140	*177	*300	*26	..
Martinique	2004	*820	..	*163	..	*142	*178	*310	*27	..
	2005	*823	..	*164	..	*143	*179	*310	*27	..
	2006	*825	..	*164	..	*143	*179	*312	*27	..
Mexico	2003	62843	13	18587	2717	67	15182	22581	1059	2637
Mexique	2004	63705	5	19855	2770	306	16057	21089	1056	2567
	2005	64957	2	20399	3125	330	17157	20019	1039	2886
	2006	62697	2	20658	3172	331	17692	16914	1014	2914
Netherlands Antilles	2003	8697	16	1412	768	45	2102	4269	85	..
Antilles néerlandaises	2004	9157	21	1788	786	45	2182	4257	78	..
	2005	10327	22	1925	872	46	2631	4712	119	..
	2006	9704	26	1524	825	47	2652	4540	90	..
Nicaragua	2003	778	..	96	..	32	211	400	21	18
Nicaragua	2004	806	..	99	..	31	210	427	17	22
	2005	711	..	87	..	28	183	378	15	20
	2006	763	..	91	..	36	199	404	15	*18
Trinidad and Tobago	2003	6988	..	1216	685	6	1522	3247	102	210
Trinité-et-Tobago	2004	6389	..	1096	615	10	1421	2971	75	201
	2005	7456	..	1350	827	10	1764	3180	99	226
	2006	7425	..	1388	773	*10	1861	2951	103	339
United States	2003	706267	647	350258	70119	2873	188137	39219	19686	35328
Etats-Unis	2004	717234	698	351954	73473	3167	194143	38916	19255	35628
	2005	717785	693	350574	73634	3150	200203	37180	18021	34330
	2006	718646	739	348229	70873	2330	204267	37666	18901	35641
America, South	**2003**	**176316**	**105**	**40307**	**10007**	**957**	**66813**	**42985**	**7563**	**7580**
Amérique du Sud	**2004**	**189364**	**85**	**43769**	**10659**	**722**	**71887**	**46406**	**7741**	**8096**
	2005	**189738**	**78**	**45862**	**10844**	**614**	**71026**	**44668**	**8176**	**8470**
	2006	**190651**	**74**	**44720**	**10448**	**373**	**71939**	**46554**	**7610**	**8932**
Argentina	2003	19789	0	4636	1135	28	9957	1946	1140	947
Argentine	2004	20251	0	4018	1209	29	10590	2368	1090	947
	2005	20502	2	4348	1264	24	10143	2795	1001	925
	2006	21523	0	4305	1191	23	10733	3422	960	889

Table 26

Production of energy products from refineries - by type
Production des rafinneries - produits énergétiques - par catégorie
Thousand metric tons
Milliers de tonnes métriques

Country or area Pays ou zone	Year Année	Total Totale	Aviation gasolene Essence aviation	Motor gasolene Essence auto	Jet fuels Carbu- réacteurs	Kerosene Pétrole lampant	Gas-diesel oil Gazole carburant diesel	Residual Fuel oil Mazout résiduel	L.P.G. G.P.L.	Refinery gas Gaz de rafinnerie
Bolivia	2003	1227	2	406	121	26	482	0	65	124
Bolivie	2004	1425	3	455	122	19	622	0	68	137
	2005	1407	4	430	125	22	601	0	74	151
	2006	1522	4	500	131	21	620	1	78	167
Brazil	2003	71369	51	13329	3073	157	30608	15779	4278	4094
Brésil	2004	76098	56	13575	3357	92	34079	16074	4403	4462
	2005	75921	49	14141	3337	41	33368	15461	4813	4711
	2006	76547	46	14981	3037	31	33597	15661	4478	4716
Chile	2003	9269	11	2265	574	87	3865	1814	398	255
Chili	2004	9925	6	2384	650	96	3693	2294	546	256
	2005	9571	5	2257	574	89	3534	2306	498	308
	2006	10574	7	2482	660	58	3717	2646	403	601
Colombia	2003	14001	17	4756	1254	116	3308	2932	758	861
Colombie	2004	14501	16	4963	861	122	3689	3330	636	883
	2005	13495	14	4252	858	122	3660	3056	638	895
	2006	13196	13	3618	718	128	4457	2792	643	826
Ecuador	2003	7161	..	1516	239	..	1600	3646	160	..
Equateur	2004	6594	..	895	279	..	1621	3657	141	..
	2005	7373	..	1615	297	..	1787	3492	182	..
	2006	7392	..	1226	348	..	1715	3922	181	..
Paraguay	2003	84	..	10	..	2	42	30	..	..
Paraguay	2004	64	..	8	..	3	33	20	..	..
	2005	33	..	4	..	2	16	11	..	..
	2006	0	..	0	..	0	0	0	..	..
Peru	2003	7754	..	1359	382	510	1883	3245	267	108
Pérou	2004	7860	..	1458	418	329	1999	3324	226	106
	2005	7766	..	1489	270	282	2415	2958	225	127
	2006	7865	..	1464	504	83	2638	2878	193	105
Suriname	2003	372	..	..	..	..	39	333	..	..
Suriname	2004	374	..	..	..	..	39	335	..	..
	2005	390	..	..	..	..	41	349	..	..
	2006	401	..	..	..	..	41	360	..	..
Uruguay	2003	1511	..	321	24	11	618	448	66	23
Uruguay	2004	2026	..	503	44	9	807	518	86	59
	2005	1976	..	447	41	9	810	505	91	73
	2006	1732	..	396	53	8	760	381	77	57
Venezuela(Bolivar. Rep.)	2003	43780	24	11709	3205	21	14411	12812	431	1168
Venezuela(Rép. bolivar.)	2004	50246	4	15509	3719	23	14715	14486	545	1245
	2005	51304	4	16879	4078	23	14651	13735	654	1280
	2006	49899	4	15748	3806	21	13661	14491	597	1571
Asia	**2003**	**1035522**	**328**	**193694**	**56842**	**79703**	**386074**	**249050**	**40900**	**28931**
Asie	**2004**	**1080562**	**538**	**203139**	**63406**	**76239**	**413993**	**247470**	**44806**	**30971**
	2005	**1110129**	**564**	**206201**	**70031**	**76812**	**434225**	**246917**	**43266**	**32114**
	2006	**1129644**	**584**	**209613**	**75899**	**72551**	**444683**	**246599**	**46212**	**33503**
Azerbaijan	2003	5728	..	720	521	133	1641	2470	148	95
Azerbaïdjan	2004	6118	..	852	536	111	1789	2521	182	127
	2005	7145	..	906	630	117	2101	3061	185	145
	2006	7116	..	1043	693	44	2095	2899	195	147
Bahrain	2003	10848	..	810	1866	581	4295	3008	34	254
Bahreïn	2004	10772	..	755	2178	315	4500	2734	37	253
	2005	11258	..	789	2276	329	4702	2857	39	266
	2006	10933	..	766	2210	320	4566	2775	38	258

Table 26

Production of energy products from refineries - by type
Production des rafinneries - produits énergétiques - par catégorie

Thousand metric tons
Milliers de tonnes métriques

Country or area Pays ou zone	Year Année	Total Totale	Aviation gasolene Essence aviation	Motor gasolene Essence auto	Jet fuels Carbu- réacteurs	Kerosene Pétrole lampant	Gas-diesel oil Gazole carburant diesel	Residual Fuel oil Mazout résiduel	L.P.G. G.P.L.	Refinery gas Gaz de rafinnerie
Bangladesh	2003	929	..	150	2	358	303	58	20	38
Bangladesh	2004	839	..	136	2	324	274	53	16	34
	2005	878	..	145	1	346	293	57	12	24
	2006	844	..	140	1	335	284	55	8	21
Brunei Darussalam	2003	583		202	82	3	165	77	..	54
Brunéi Darussalam	2004	594		201	80	3	173	89	..	48
	2005	597		196	78	3	178	92	..	50
	2006	640		209	79	4	190	103	..	55
China	2003	181277	201	47909	..	8553	85328	20048	12117	7121
Chine	2004	203497	417	52236	..	9622	98436	20293	14170	8323
	2005	216431	446	53884	..	10065	110902	17674	14327	9133
	2006	228466	477	55473	..	9755	117624	17847	17453	9837
Cyprus	2003	922	..	146	..	38	327	362	28	21
Chypre	2004	269	..	40	..	11	88	112	9	9
	2005	0	..	0	..	0	0	0	0	0
	2006	0	..	0	..	0	0	0	0	0
Georgia	2003	15	..	..	..	..	2	13	..	..
Géorgie	2004	16	..	..	..	..	2	14	..	..
	2005	5	..	..	..	..	1	4	..	..
	2006	4	..	..	..	..	0	4	..	..
India	2003	88608	..	10999	4180	10187	41966	13372	5185	2719
Inde	2004	96353	..	11057	5201	9298	47426	14970	5569	2832
	2005	97112	..	10502	6196	9078	48495	14305	5525	3011
	2006	108719	..	12539	7805	8491	54268	15697	6315	3604
Indonesia	2003	45687	8	8584	1349	7565	13786	11755	1833	807
Indonésie	2004	46411	4	8825	1414	7341	14661	10995	2316	855
	2005	42391	4	8325	1418	7131	13889	10105	833	686
	2006	40810	3	8411	1256	7165	13216	9686	382	691
Iran(Islamic Rep. of)	2003	72309	*98	10730	868	7339	22958	26566	3750	..
Iran(Rép. islamique)	2004	72318	*100	10836	795	6830	23771	25840	4146	..
	2005	72861	*100	11394	848	6214	24375	26241	3689	..
	2006	74686	*90	12047	1042	6308	24762	26351	4086	..
Iraq	2003	19393	..	3097	573	1064	6610	7404	169	476
Iraq	2004	18793	..	3278	607	1127	4906	8257	114	504
	2005	18259	..	3185	590	1095	4766	8022	111	490
	2006	18784	..	3233	599	1112	4838	8392	113	497
Israel	2003	10240	..	2231	..	1118	2977	3440	474	..
Israël	2004	10024	..	2467	..	1107	2750	3168	532	..
	2005	10953	..	2729	..	1112	3042	3504	566	..
	2006	10687	..	2592	..	1170	3231	3223	471	..
Japan	2003	176631	12	43140	7671	22031	57402	34028	4527	7820
Japon	2004	173002	8	42715	7902	22014	57059	30985	4448	7871
	2005	177165	6	43259	8896	22790	57700	31419	4895	8200
	2006	168668	6	42437	10433	20120	54711	28315	4647	7999
Jordan	2003	3730	6	667	268	191	1160	1251	134	*53
Jordanie	2004	3935	6	579	291	162	1223	1516	116	42
	2005	4173	6	613	*300	231	1395	1466	118	44
	2006	4067	6	675	312	136	1412	1345	139	42
Kazakhstan	2003	8258	..	1841	257	51	2128	2584	1179	218
Kazakhstan	2004	9710	..	1928	244	50	2888	2708	1507	386
	2005	12014	..	2359	207	41	3705	3874	1478	350
	2006	11458	..	2345	260	53	4065	3333	1106	296

Table 26

Production of energy products from refineries - by type
Production des rafinneries - produits énergétiques - par catégorie
Thousand metric tons
Milliers de tonnes métriques

Country or area Pays ou zone	Year Année	Total Totale	Aviation gasolene Essence aviation	Motor gasolene Essence auto	Jet fuels Carbu- réacteurs	Kerosene Pétrole lampant	Gas-diesel oil Gazole carburant diesel	Residual Fuel oil Mazout résiduel	L.P.G. G.P.L.	Refinery gas Gaz de rafinnerie
Korea, Dem.Ppl's.Rep.	2003	539	..	185	..	37	201	116	..	..
Corée,Rép.pop.dém.de	2004	545	..	188	..	37	203	117	..	..
	2005	459	..	159	..	31	171	98	..	..
	2006	352	..	122	..	24	131	75	..	..
Korea, Republic of	2003	87396	..	8564	6944	8397	27801	30095	3613	1982
Corée, République de	2004	89332	..	8850	9665	6599	29048	29912	3326	1932
	2005	93042	..	8654	10755	5791	31508	31305	3213	1816
	2006	94290	..	8707	12021	5410	32392	30793	3098	1869
Kuwait	2003	31206	..	1355	2227	4912	12426	9800	98	388
Koweït	2004	31279	..	1931	2258	4636	12204	9760	98	392
	2005	32535	..	2812	1586	6058	12397	9166	115	401
	2006	34949	..	3023	2619	5748	11079	11951	115	414
Kyrgyzstan	2003	88	..	27	..	..	22	39	..	..
Kirghizistan	2004	88	..	19	..	..	27	42	..	..
	2005	86	..	13	..	..	31	42	..	..
	2006	83	..	10	..	..	31	42	..	..
Malaysia	2003	19391	..	4363	2293	952	8922	1777	856	228
Malaisie	2004	19971	..	4496	2608	572	9463	1828	824	180
	2005	18760	..	4040	2472	513	9020	1792	755	169
	2006	19194	..	4270	2523	536	8734	1992	806	333
Myanmar	2003	733	..	304	65	1	249	67	10	37
Myanmar	2004	657	..	305	61	1	196	49	10	35
	2005	609	..	298	46	1	173	48	8	35
	2006	759	..	353	52	1	274	41	5	33
Oman	2003	4047	..	642	217	4	878	2259	47	..
Oman	2004	3801	..	593	178	5	864	2121	40	..
	2005	3917	..	618	183	11	894	2167	44	..
	2006	4105	..	597	292	16	905	2244	51	..
Other Asia	2003	38567	..	9317	2366	320	9671	14402	1379	1112
Autre Asie	2004	42226	..	11179	3029	216	11229	13810	1466	1297
	2005	43599	..	11249	4108	26	12719	12549	1632	1316
	2006	43068	..	11138	4432	39	12920	11714	1593	1232
Pakistan	2003	8754	..	1075	997	284	2937	3058	225	178
Pakistan	2004	9884	..	1326	1185	203	3603	3132	242	193
	2005	9987	..	1195	1258	209	3419	3358	355	193
	2006	9569	..	1218	1165	207	3383	3193	212	191
Philippines	2003	11265	..	1844	634	362	3851	3899	397	278
Philippines	2004	9345	..	1501	590	229	3004	3537	263	221
	2005	9909	..	1629	665	210	3399	3463	322	221
	2006	9823	..	1582	740	170	3612	3150	333	236
Qatar	2003	4330	..	1815	921	4	965	429	122	74
Qatar	2004	4466	..	1709	956	0	979	618	128	76
	2005	4125	..	1722	916	0	924	356	131	*76
	2006	4723	..	1729	1035	0	994	724	151	90
Saudi Arabia	2003	78150	..	12600	4519	3747	28899	25432	875	2078
Arabie saoudite	2004	82928	..	13605	4923	3524	31486	25944	1155	2291
	2005	85491	..	13400	6627	3576	31685	26722	1098	2383
	2006	85066	..	12025	6193	3559	32412	27177	1270	2430
Singapore	2003	27447	..	3350	6322	426	9938	6084	870	457
Singapour	2004	31222	..	3948	6481	501	11711	7170	872	539
	2005	37958	..	4879	7610	619	14474	8862	848	666
	2006	36501	..	4699	7458	596	13939	8534	634	641

Table 26

Production of energy products from refineries - by type
Production des rafinneries - produits énergétiques - par catégorie
Thousand metric tons
Milliers de tonnes métriques

Country or area Pays ou zone	Year Année	Total Totale	Aviation gasolene Essence aviation	Motor gasolene Essence auto	Jet fuels Carbu-réacteurs	Kerosene Pétrole lampant	Gas-diesel oil Gazole carburant diesel	Residual Fuel oil Mazout résiduel	L.P.G. G.P.L.	Refinery gas Gaz de rafinnerie
Sri Lanka	2003	1876	..	196	96	152	622	745	15	50
Sri Lanka	2004	2085	..	203	126	140	693	855	15	53
	2005	1824	..	161	114	139	591	762	13	44
	2006	1875	..	194	131	144	628	716	15	47
Syrian Arab Republic	2003	10618	..	1262	204	39	3906	4921	286	..
Rép. arabe syrienne	2004	11065	..	1338	245	58	4123	5015	286	..
	2005	10732	..	1257	221	54	3934	4938	328	..
	2006	11157	..	1345	215	54	3934	5288	321	..
Thailand	2003	33879	..	6012	3253	550	15608	5947	1527	982
Thaïlande	2004	38214	..	6674	3774	920	17511	6335	1926	1074
	2005	36408	..	6428	3711	799	16378	6409	1632	1051
	2006	37489	..	6331	4299	820	16737	6578	1636	1088
Turkey	2003	23058	..	3837	1682	80	8087	8038	758	576
Turquie	2004	22178	..	3479	1767	64	7665	7845	762	596
	2005	21775	..	3609	1997	24	7601	7208	766	570
	2006	21563	..	3659	1644	32	7549	7271	808	600
Turkmenistan	2003	6505	..	1321	309	..	2622	1822	..	431
Turkménistan	2004	6255	..	1270	297	..	2522	1752	..	414
	2005	6466	..	1313	307	..	2607	1811	..	428
	2006	7702	..	1564	366	..	3105	2157	..	510
United Arab Emirates	2003	13026	..	1498	5454	..	4609	1173	126	166
Emirats arabes unis	2004	13495	..	1746	5400	..	4754	1291	132	172
	2005	13131	..	1866	5404	..	4262	1299	135	165
	2006	13920	..	2626	5385	..	4428	1173	135	173
Uzbekistan	2003	6443	3	1842	314	117	1993	1925	11	238
Ouzbékistan	2004	6070	3	1736	296	110	1879	1814	10	222
	2005	4958	2	1418	242	90	1535	1482	8	181
	2006	4627	2	1323	226	84	1433	1383	7	169
Yemen	2003	3046	..	1059	388	107	819	586	87	..
Yémen	2004	2804	..	1138	317	109	883	268	89	..
	2005	3115	..	1195	369	109	959	399	84	..
	2006	2947	..	1188	413	98	801	378	69	..
Europe	**2003**	**840618**	**221**	**193339**	**47501**	**7089**	**336425**	**186043**	**31700**	**38300**
Europe	**2004**	**861023**	**207**	**199812**	**48702**	**9223**	**340617**	**192201**	**31947**	**38314**
	2005	**872768**	**179**	**199561**	**48304**	**8815**	**352025**	**193453**	**32737**	**37694**
	2006	**879053**	**155**	**200896**	**50436**	**9247**	**354085**	**192875**	**33132**	**38227**
Albania	2003	160	..	6	1	5	95	45	0	8
Albanie	2004	207	..	35	16	7	73	67	1	8
	2005	174	..	14	0	9	72	68	0	11
	2006	206	..	35	0	10	99	48	0	14
Austria	2003	7529	..	1811	446	1	3849	1062	50	310
Autriche	2004	7143	..	1738	455	1	3529	1032	57	331
	2005	7710	..	1798	592	1	3894	1009	107	309
	2006	7194	..	1615	526	13	3685	915	50	390
Belarus	2003	12311	..	1895	..	130	4913	4790	216	367
Bélarus	2004	15200	..	2842	..	169	5845	5501	418	425
	2005	17139	..	3330	..	192	6426	6313	459	419
	2006	17882	..	3498	..	462	6616	6329	483	494
Belgium	2003	31022	..	5865	2048	62	13013	8689	627	718
Belgique	2004	29778	..	5789	2143	78	12327	8380	511	550
	2005	27699	..	5056	1678	65	11938	8042	462	458
	2006	27815	..	5357	1744	42	12660	7128	403	481

Table 26

Production of energy products from refineries - by type
Production des rafinneries - produits énergétiques - par catégorie
Thousand metric tons
Milliers de tonnes métriques

Country or area Pays ou zone	Year Année	Total Totale	Aviation gasolene Essence aviation	Motor gasolene Essence auto	Jet fuels Carbu-réacteurs	Kerosene Pétrole lampant	Gas-diesel oil Gazole carburant diesel	Residual Fuel oil Mazout résiduel	L.P.G. G.P.L.	Refinery gas Gaz de rafinnerie
Bosnia and Herzegovina	2003	65	..	9	..	..	19	36	1	..
Bosnie y Herzégovine	2004	149	..	26	..	..	42	78	3	..
	2005	125	..	18	..	..	31	74	2	..
	2006	125	..	18	..	..	31	74	2	..
Bulgaria	2003	3916	..	967	144	..	1878	718	85	124
Bulgarie	2004	4679	..	1401	142	..	1915	965	103	153
	2005	5286	..	1381	144	..	2270	1230	105	156
	2006	6088	..	1560	151	..	2521	1512	127	217
Croatia	2003	4809	..	1261	75	1	1873	1036	304	259
Croatie	2004	4635	..	1226	91	1	1741	1012	300	264
	2005	4563	..	1168	99	1	1603	1160	291	241
	2006	4290	..	1083	67	2	1565	1097	266	210
Czech Republic	2003	4814	2	1344	140	..	2590	445	168	125
République tchèque	2004	4806	0	1289	147	..	2673	394	181	122
	2005	5567	0	1467	132	..	3067	581	184	136
	2006	5578	0	1594	121	..	3128	381	204	150
Denmark	2003	8149	..	2082	611	..	3451	1519	168	318
Danemark	2004	7948	..	1986	606	..	3329	1557	164	306
	2005	7495	..	1919	507	..	3224	1405	145	295
	2006	7840	..	1987	608	..	3298	1471	166	310
Finland	2003	11951	..	4304	614	..	5038	1267	273	455
Finlande	2004	12326	..	4321	714	..	5078	1445	267	501
	2005	11770	..	4061	592	..	4964	1318	315	520
	2006	12729	..	4298	715	..	5502	1272	402	540
France incl. Monaco	2003	73178	68	16804	5169	76	34979	10919	2917	2246
France y compris Monaco	2004	74025	58	16878	5616	76	34421	11887	2830	2259
	2005	72326	44	16271	5478	75	33590	11823	2775	2270
	2006	73704	30	17195	5633	121	33733	11955	2774	2263
Germany	2003	99031	..	26449	4194	10	48638	12232	3056	4452
Allemagne	2004	101805	..	26467	4424	7	49551	14013	2918	4425
	2005	104299	..	27240	4252	14	52137	13340	2951	4365
	2006	102687	..	26576	4412	5	50854	13684	2925	4231
Greece	2003	20013	..	3653	1630	19	6053	7456	672	530
Grèce	2004	18963	..	3629	1720	29	5369	7095	598	523
	2005	19618	..	4058	1737	41	5653	6956	655	518
	2006	20456	..	4327	1423	34	6452	6953	653	614
Hungary	2003	5429	..	1477	202	..	3124	367	91	168
Hongrie	2004	5262	..	1465	239	..	2989	313	90	166
	2005	5575	..	1321	266	..	3515	218	82	173
	2006	5561	..	1302	280	..	3498	232	81	168
Ireland	2003	3099	..	639	..	315	988	1005	59	93
Irlande	2004	2874	..	552	..	252	964	966	53	87
	2005	3115	..	683	..	239	1097	948	57	91
	2006	3223	..	634	..	228	1121	1101	51	88
Italy and San Marino	2003	87103	6	20699	4187	330	38389	18018	2610	2864
Italie y comp. St. Marin	2004	87362	12	20662	3787	254	39536	17543	2613	2955
	2005	89721	6	21189	3910	33	39844	19032	2517	3190
	2006	88284	16	20967	4081	30	39805	17621	2275	3489
Lithuania	2003	6715	..	1882	695	..	2064	1381	435	258
Lituanie	2004	8202	..	2331	850	..	2523	1673	526	299
	2005	8741	..	2462	832	..	2781	1799	555	312
	2006	7848	..	2163	764	..	2246	1938	474	263

Table 26

Production of energy products from refineries - by type
Production des rafinneries - produits énergétiques - par catégorie

Thousand metric tons
Milliers de tonnes métriques

Country or area Pays ou zone	Year Année	Total Totale	Aviation gasolene Essence aviation	Motor gasolene Essence auto	Jet fuels Carbu-réacteurs	Kerosene Pétrole lampant	Gas-diesel oil Gazole carburant diesel	Residual Fuel oil Mazout résiduel	L.P.G. G.P.L.	Refinery gas Gaz de rafinnerie
Netherlands	2003	65245	57	15730	6669	498	20787	12333	4780	4391
Pays-Bas	2004	65801	57	15539	6935	379	20234	13073	5070	4514
	2005	64192	52	14234	6990	469	21122	12394	4579	4352
	2006	61361	37	13794	6914	368	19685	12151	4069	4343
Norway,Svlbd.J.Myn. I	2003	13286	..	3546	415	196	6635	1702	352	440
Norvège,Svalbd,J.May	2004	12728	..	3261	423	228	6241	1845	323	407
	2005	13832	..	3829	644	143	6835	1610	346	425
	2006	14913	..	4134	644	232	7101	1957	386	459
Poland	2003	15471	5	3871	647	9	6722	3253	269	695
Pologne	2004	15816	3	3978	679	36	7371	2754	259	736
	2005	15726	4	4117	644	17	7459	2537	284	664
	2006	17319	7	4155	853	1	8336	2824	282	861
Portugal	2003	11158	..	2732	703	1	4955	2388	379	..
Portugal	2004	11369	..	2551	779	2	4703	2969	365	..
	2005	11682	..	2466	854	3	4906	3062	391	..
	2006	12036	..	2750	856	2	5102	2920	406	..
Romania	2003	10274	2	3295	158	33	3988	1562	327	909
Roumanie	2004	10792	3	3419	177	45	4170	1559	366	1053
	2005	12641	1	4237	191	56	4709	1707	658	1082
	2006	12000	1	4145	238	22	4593	1303	677	1021
Russian Federation	2003	170494	37	29315	9453	66	53930	56377	8571	12745
Fédération de Russie	2004	174237	37	30505	9283	66	55389	58330	8760	11867
	2005	185276	37	32011	10036	70	60003	62365	9428	11326
	2006	196158	37	34368	10602	74	64166	65189	10368	11354
Serbia	2003	3036	..	617	85	82	1254	919	79	..
Serbie	2004	3150	..	821	56	10	1315	853	95	..
	2005	2956	..	770	53	9	1234	801	89	..
	2006	2488	..	648	45	8	1038	674	75	..
Slovakia	2003	5132	..	1597	63	1	2349	635	152	335
Slovaquie	2004	5517	..	1670	61	1	2598	585	206	396
	2005	5213	..	1584	36	2	2455	543	181	412
	2006	5280	..	1449	46	1	2587	654	137	406
Spain	2003	48500	12	9047	3061	1732	21631	10130	1211	1676
Espagne	2004	50679	0	10434	2713	3969	21563	9125	1058	1817
	2005	52211	0	10152	2653	4027	23457	9019	1050	1853
	2006	53335	0	10038	2612	4199	23844	9245	1522	1875
Sweden	2003	17281	..	4309	109	..	6942	5170	360	391
Suède	2004	18360	..	4506	208	..	7238	5450	423	535
	2005	17564	..	4045	70	..	6951	5576	433	489
	2006	17636	..	4182	179	..	7204	5226	302	543
Switzerland	2003	4427	..	1072	344	..	1893	759	178	181
Suisse	2004	5002	..	1362	350	..	2148	701	196	245
	2005	4699	..	1268	212	..	2170	611	197	241
	2006	5346	..	1465	228	..	2573	583	223	274
T.F.Yug.Rep. Macedonia	2003	812	..	126	0	..	322	343	21	0
L'ex-RY Macédoine	2004	807	..	146	0	..	359	282	20	0
	2005	921	..	183	23	..	394	295	24	2
	2006	1026	..	190	33	..	443	327	29	4
Ukraine	2003	20459	6	4308	361	1	6484	7970	978	351
Ukraine	2004	20529	6	4394	473	0	6544	7766	988	358
	2005	17906	3	4609	512	24	5533	5889	948	388
	2006	13941	2	3926	400	19	4519	3834	938	303

Table 26

Production of energy products from refineries - by type
Production des rafinneries - produits énergétiques - par catégorie

Thousand metric tons
Milliers de tonnes métriques

Country or area Pays ou zone	Year Année	Total Totale	Aviation gasolene Essence aviation	Motor gasolene Essence auto	Jet fuels Carbu- réacteurs	Kerosene Pétrole lampant	Gas-diesel oil Gazole carburant diesel	Residual Fuel oil Mazout résiduel	L.P.G. G.P.L.	Refinery gas Gaz de rafinnerie
United Kingdom	2003	75749	26	22627	5277	3521	27579	11517	2311	2891
Royaume-Uni	2004	80872	31	24589	5615	3613	28839	12988	2185	3012
	2005	77026	32	22620	5167	3325	28691	11728	2467	2996
	2006	74704	25	21443	6261	3374	26080	12277	2382	2862
Oceania	**2003**	**37253**	**104**	**14628**	**4912**	**191**	**13448**	**1669**	**942**	**1359**
Océanie	**2004**	**37056**	**81**	**15107**	**4867**	**175**	**13503**	**1521**	**562**	**1240**
	2005	**36755**	**105**	**14917**	**5198**	**107**	**12985**	**1664**	**560**	**1220**
	2006	**34141**	**83**	**13714**	**5143**	**94**	**11815**	**1537**	**635**	**1120**
Australia	2003	32306	104	13108	4080	188	11430	1310	942	1144
Australie	2004	31852	81	13453	3937	145	11590	1071	562	1013
	2005	31038	105	13218	4221	105	10790	1085	542	972
	2006	28429	83	12153	4128	92	9466	1051	613	843
New Zealand	2003	4947	..	1520	832	3	2018	359	..	215
Nouvelle-Zélande	2004	4900	..	1627	930	3	1763	350	..	227
	2005	5006	..	1645	887	2	1785	439	..	248
	2006	4870	..	1482	909	2	1819	381	..	277
Papua New Guinea	2003	0	..	0	0	0	0	0	0	..
Papouasie-Nvl-Guinée	2004	304	..	27	0	27	150	100	0	..
	2005	711	..	54	90	0	410	140	18	..
	2006	842	..	79	106	0	530	105	22	..

Table 27

Capacity and production of natural gas liquid plants - by type
Capacité et production des usines d'extraction de liquides de gaz naturel - par catégorie

Capacities in million cubic metres and production in thousand metric tons
Capacités en million de mètres cubes et production en milliers de tonnes métriques

Table Notes:
Total production

Aviation gasolene, motor gasolene, natural gasolene, jet fuel, kerosene, gas-diesel oils, residual fuel oil, liquefied petroleum gas, plant condensate, naphtha, white spirit, petroleum coke, lubricants, bitumen asphalt, petroleum waxes, natural gas liquids n.e.s. and other petroleum products.

Other natural gas liquids

Total production excluding natural gasolene, plant condensate and liquefied petroleum gas.

- **Please refer to the Definitions Section on pages xv to xxix for the appropriate product description /classification.**

Notes relatives aux tableaux:
Production totale

Essence d'aviation, essence d'auto, essence naturelle, carburéacteurs, carburant diesel, mazout résiduel, gaz de pétrole liquéfiés, condensats d'usine, naphtas, essences spéciales, coke de pétrole, lubrifiants, asphalte de bitume, cires de pétrole, liquides de gaz naturel n.d.a. et autres produits pétroliers.

Autres produits pétroliers

Production totale non compris l'essence naturelle, les condensats d'usine et les gaz de pétrole liquéfies.

- **Veuillez consulter la section "définitions" de la page xv à la page xxix pour une description/classification appropriée des produits.**

Figure 74: World natural gas liquids plant capacity, by region, in 2006

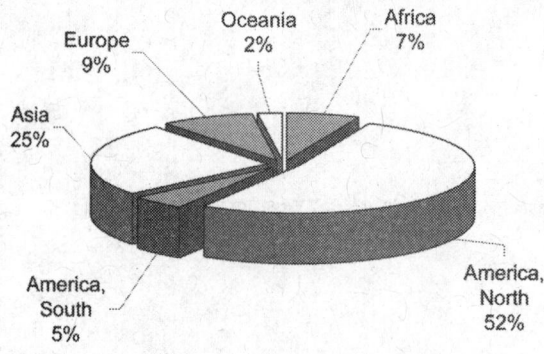

Figure 75: World natural gas liquids production from plants, by type, in 2006

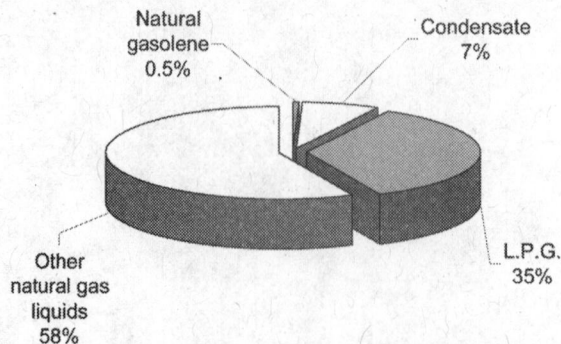

Table 27

Capacity and production of natural gas liquid plants - by type
Capacité et production des usines d'extraction de liquides de gaz naturel - par catégorie

Capacities in million cubic metres and production in thousand metric tons
Capacités en millions de mètres cubes et production en milliers de tonnes métriques

Country or area Pays ou zone	Year Année	Capacity Capacité	Total production Production totale	Natural gasolene Essence naturelle	Condensate Condensats d'usine	L.P.G. G.P.L.	Other natural gas liquids Autres condensats de gaz naturel
World	**2003**	**2395016**	**302938**	**1503**	**25736**	**113438**	**162260**
Monde	**2004**	**2434810**	**325593**	**1576**	**25987**	**121840**	**176190**
	2005	**2470605**	**339355**	**1602**	**25122**	**125366**	**187265**
	2006	**2556854**	**350830**	**1591**	**25422**	**124204**	**199613**
Africa	**2003**	**165219**	**58714**	**28**	**18542**	**10299**	**29845**
Afrique	**2004**	**168865**	**60283**	**29**	**18138**	**9881**	**32235**
	2005	**168406**	**63035**	**23**	**17605**	**10033**	**35374**
	2006	**168406**	**59828**	**25**	**17642**	**9498**	**32663**
Algeria	2003	51956	47632	..	14987	9148	23497
Algérie	2004	55294	47804	..	14988	8650	24166
	2005	55143	47740	..	14492	8839	24409
	2006	55143	44669	..	*14500	8255	21914
Congo	2003	*660	437	..	..	..	437
Congo	2004	*660	386	..	..	..	386
	2005	*660	368	..	..	..	368
	2006	*660	397	..	..	..	397
Egypt	2003	46614	4652	..	3555	1097	..
Egypte	2004	46742	4323	..	3150	1173	..
	2005	46614	4256	..	3113	1143	..
	2006	46614	4315	..	3142	1173	..
Libyan Arab Jamah.	2003	50614	2045	..	..	..	2045
Jamah. arabe libyenne	2004	50753	2140	..	..	..	2140
	2005	50614	2769	..	..	..	2769
	2006	50614	4059	..	..	..	4059
Nigeria	2003	13106	3752	..	..	..	3752
Nigéria	2004	13142	5360	..	..	..	5360
	2005	13106	7657	..	..	..	7657
	2006	13106	6122	..	..	..	6122
South Africa Customs Un.	2003	*471	114	..	..	..	114
Un.douan.d'Afr.mérid	2004	*471	183	..	..	..	183
	2005	*471	171	..	..	..	171
	2006	*471	171	..	..	..	171
Tunisia	2003	1798	82	28	..	54	..
Tunisie	2004	1803	87	29	..	58	..
	2005	1798	74	23	..	51	..
	2006	1798	95	*25	..	70	..
America, North	**2003**	**1301895**	**82895**	**..**	**..**	**41678**	**41217**
Amérique du Nord	**2004**	**1339678**	**85800**	**..**	**..**	**44849**	**40951**
	2005	**1369654**	**82662**	**..**	**..**	**43148**	**39514**
	2006	**1337457**	**84308**	**..**	**..**	**40154**	**44154**
Barbados	2003	*100	1	..	..	1	..
Barbade	2004	*100	1	..	..	1	..
	2005	*100	1	..	..	1	..
	2006	*100	1	..	..	1	..
Canada	2003	510761	19901	..	..	..	19901
Canada	2004	544140	20190	..	..	..	20190
	2005	581058	20368	..	..	..	20368
	2006	546767	21438	..	..	..	21438
Mexico	2003	52495	12404	..	..	..	12404
Mexique	2004	52639	12617	..	..	..	12617
	2005	52497	12123	..	..	..	12123
	2006	50428	12192	..	..	..	12192

Table 27

Capacity and production of natural gas liquid plants - by type
Capacité et production des usines d'extraction de liquides de gaz naturel - par catégorie

Capacities in million cubic metres and production in thousand metric tons
Capacités en millions de mètres cubes et production en milliers de tonnes métriques

Country or area Pays ou zone	Year Année	Capacity Capacité	Total production Production totale	Natural gasolene Essence naturelle	Condensate Condensats d'usine	L.P.G. G.P.L.	Other natural gas liquids Autres condensats de gaz naturel
Trinidad and Tobago	2003	14408	955	..	..	624	331
Trinité-et-Tobago	2004	14447	972		..	635	337
	2005	14408	899			587	312
	2006	14408	1023			668	355
United States	2003	724131	49634	..	..	41053	8581
Etats-Unis	2004	728352	52020		..	44213	7807
	2005	721591	49271	..	..	42560	6711
	2006	725754	49654			39485	10169
America, South	**2003**	**121188**	**14662**	**50**	**..**	**7417**	**7195**
Amérique du Sud	**2004**	**126183**	**17295**	**50**	**..**	**8736**	**8509**
	2005	**125839**	**19451**	**96**	**..**	**10059**	**9296**
	2006	**125839**	**27871**	**50**	**..**	**10677**	**17144**
Argentina	2003	50493	6293	..	..	3003	3290
Argentine	2004	50631	7214	..	..	3341	3873
	2005	50493	7113	..	..	3289	3824
	2006	50493	7624	..	..	3683	3941
Bolivia	2003	9124	286	50	..	236	..
Bolivie	2004	9149	304	*50	..	254	..
	2005	9124	309	*50	..	259	..
	2006	9124	325	*50	..	275	..
Brazil	2003	11198	3022	..	..	656	2366
Brésil	2004	11228	3510	..	..	741	2769
	2005	11198	4298	..	..	967	3331
	2006	11198	4533	..	..	927	3606
Chile	2003	4930	182	..	..	135	47
Chili	2004	4944	184	..	..	135	49
	2005	4930	171	..	..	123	48
	2006	4930	177	..	..	127	*50
Colombia	2003	3442	110	..	..	110	..
Colombie	2004	3451	52	..	..	52	..
	2005	3442	52	..	..	52	..
	2006	3442	51	..	..	51	..
Ecuador	2003	424	71	0	..	71	..
Equateur	2004	425	74	0	..	74	..
	2005	424	92	46	..	46	..
	2006	424	61	0	..	61	..
Peru	2003	989	350	..	..	52	298
Pérou	2004	5656	901	..	..	129	772
	2005	5640	1375	..	..	513	862
	2006	5640	2686	..	..	584	2102
Venezuela(Bolivar. Rep.)	2003	40588	4348	..	..	3154	1194
Venezuela(Rép. bolivar.)	2004	40699	5056	..	..	4010	1046
	2005	40588	6041	..	..	4810	1231
	2006	40588	12414	..	..	4969	7445
Asia	**2003**	**518563**	**111686**	**1425**	**7194**	**45038**	**58029**
Asie	**2004**	**523884**	**123915**	**1497**	**7849**	**47852**	**66717**
	2005	**531247**	**134549**	**1483**	**7517**	**51664**	**73885**
	2006	**649528**	**136346**	**1516**	**7780**	**51810**	**75240**
Azerbaijan	2003	*2000	130	..	..	..	130
Azerbaïdjan	2004	*2000	201	..	..	..	201
	2005	*2000	221	..	..	..	221
	2006	*2000	281	..	..	..	281

Table 27

Capacity and production of natural gas liquid plants - by type
Capacité et production des usines d'extraction de liquides de gaz naturel - par catégorie

Capacities in million cubic metres and production in thousand metric tons
Capacités en millions de mètres cubes et production en milliers de tonnes métriques

Country or area Pays ou zone	Year Année	Capacity Capacité	Total production Production totale	Natural gasolene Essence naturelle	Condensate Condensats d'usine	L.P.G. G.P.L.	Other natural gas liquids Autres condensats de gaz naturel
Bahrain Bahreïn	2003 2004 2005 2006	2894 2902 2894 2894	722 718 778 769	.. ..	.. ..	167 167 179 177	555 551 599 592
Bangladesh Bangladesh	2003 2004 2005 2006	1447 1451 1447 1447	100 90 96 93	.. ..	.. ..	.. ..	100 90 96 93
Brunei Darussalam Brunéi Darussalam	2003 2004 2005 2006	12217 12250 12217 12217	500 596 518 567	334 347 321 346	152 234 182 206	14 15 15 15	.. ..
India Inde	2003 2004 2005 2006	38158 38263 38158 38158	3876 3684 4133 4150	.. ..	.. ..	2366 2256 2185 2093	1510 1428 1948 2057
Indonesia Indonésie	2003 2004 2005 2006	76715 76925 82399 82399	3078 3166 3618 3753	.. ..	.. ..	174 198 986 897	2904 2968 2632 2856
Iran(Islamic Rep. of) Iran(Rép. islamique)	2003 2004 2005 2006	60640 60806 60640 177175	6523 7983 13126 13690	*650 *650 *650 *650	.. ..	.. ..	5873 7333 12476 13040
Iraq Iraq	2003 2004 2005 2006	21509 21567 21509 21509	679 824 840 919	.. ..	.. ..	679 824 840 919	.. ..
Japan Japon	2003 2004 2005 2006	.. ..	348 370 386 412	.. ..	.. ..	.. ..	348 370 386 412
Kazakhstan Kazakhstan	2003 2004 2005 2006	*17000 *21000 *24000 *25000	6075 8813 10616 11215	.. ..	.. ..	.. ..	6075 8813 10616 11215
Kuwait Koweït	2003 2004 2005 2006	17364 17412 17364 18110	8672 9067 8666 9380	.. ..	.. ..	3152 3417 3253 3556	5520 5650 5413 5824
Malaysia Malaisie	2003 2004 2005 2006	43927 44047 43927 43927	726 479 1997 1997	.. ..	.. ..	726 479 1714 1697	0 0 283 *300
Myanmar Myanmar	2003 2004 2005 2006	248 249 248 248	9 14 15 9	.. ..	.. ..	6 10 11 5	3 4 4 4
Oman Oman	2003 2004 2005 2006	8537 8561 8537 8537	250 292 250 266	.. ..	.. ..	70 76 *51 *67	180 216 199 199

Table 27

Capacity and production of natural gas liquid plants - by type
Capacité et production des usines d'extraction de liquides de gaz naturel - par catégorie

Capacities in million cubic metres and production in thousand metric tons
Capacités en millions de mètres cubes et production en milliers de tonnes métriques

Country or area Pays ou zone	Year Année	Capacity Capacité	Total production Production totale	Natural gasolene Essence naturelle	Condensate Condensats d'usine	L.P.G. G.P.L.	Other natural gas liquids Autres condensats de gaz naturel
Pakistan	2003	12351	155	..	..	155	..
Pakistan	2004	12385	170	..	..	170	..
	2005	12351	202	..	..	202	..
	2006	12351	224	..	..	224	..
Qatar	2003	10439	4535		..	..	4535
Qatar	2004	10468	4556		..	..	4556
	2005	10439	4853		..	..	4853
	2006	10439	4584		..	..	4584
Saudi Arabia	2003	103770	40498		..	26218	14280
Arabie saoudite	2004	104055	47018		..	28564	18454
	2005	103770	48427	..	..	29881	18546
	2006	103770	47338	..	..	29371	17967
Thailand	2003	11059	4936	441	2576	1919	
Thaïlande	2004	11089	5606	500	3115	1991	
	2005	11059	5711	512	2820	2379	..
	2006	11059	5970	520	3054	2396	..
Timor-Leste	2003	*10000	*6659	..	*4466	*2193	
Timor-Leste	2004	*10000	*6700	..	*4500	*2200	
	2005	*10000	*6725	..	*4515	*2210	
	2006	*10000	*6735	..	*4520	*2215	..
Turkmenistan	2003	*2000	732	..	..	..	732
Turkménistan	2004	*2000	715	..	..	..	715
	2005	*2000	694	..	..	..	694
	2006	*2000	713	..	..	..	713
United Arab Emirates	2003	40547	18130		..	6859	11271
Emirats arabes unis	2004	40658	18707		..	7120	11587
	2005	40547	18876	..	..	7391	11485
	2006	40547	19438	..	..	7672	11766
Uzbekistan	2003	*6000	3247	..	..	33	3214
Ouzbékistan	2004	*6000	2997	..	..	30	2967
	2005	*6000	2372	..	..	24	2348
	2006	*6000	2271	..	..	23	2248
Viet Nam	2003	1550	494	..	..	307	187
Viet Nam	2004	1555	506	..	..	335	171
	2005	1550	799	..	..	343	456
	2006	1550	910	..	..	483	427
Yemen	2003	18191	612	..	..	..	612
Yémen	2004	18241	643	..	..	..	643
	2005	18191	630	..	..	..	630
	2006	18191	662	..	..	..	662
Europe	**2003**	**220380**	**32304**	..	..	**8099**	**24205**
Europe	**2004**	**220970**	**35179**	..	..	**9605**	**25574**
	2005	**220380**	**37225**	..	..	**9577**	**27648**
	2006	**221000**	**39771**	..	..	**10864**	**28907**
Austria	2003	889	92	..	..	..	92
Autriche	2004	891	90	..	..	..	90
	2005	889	110	..	..	..	110
	2006	889	127	..	..	..	127
Croatia	2003	*700	332	..	..	133	199
Croatie	2004	*700	356	..	..	143	213
	2005	*700	348	..	..	140	208
	2006	*700	332	..	..	133	199

Table 27

Capacity and production of natural gas liquid plants - by type
Capacité et production des usines d'extraction de liquides de gaz naturel - par catégorie

Capacities in million cubic metres and production in thousand metric tons
Capacités en millions de mètres cubes et production en milliers de tonnes métriques

Country or area Pays ou zone	Year Année	Capacity Capacité	Total production Production totale	Natural gasolene Essence naturelle	Condensate Condensats d'usine	L.P.G. G.P.L.	Other natural gas liquids Autres condensats de gaz naturel
France incl. Monaco	2003	5891	340	..	..	154	186
France y compris Monaco	2004	5907	423	..	..	149	274
	2005	5891	275	..	..	93	182
	2006	5891	64	..	..	0	64
Greece	2003	295	17	..	..	..	17
Grèce	2004	*295	15	..	..	..	15
	2005	*295	11	..	..	..	11
	2006	*295	11	..	..	..	11
Hungary	2003	11756	764	..	..	301	463
Hongrie	2004	11788	801	..	..	318	483
	2005	11756	775	..	..	311	464
	2006	11756	751	..	..	292	459
Netherlands	2003	7493	825	..	..	..	825
Pays-Bas	2004	7514	804	..	..	..	804
	2005	7493	1038	..	..	..	1038
	2006	7493	674	..	..	..	674
Norway,Svlbd.J.Myn. I	2003	32557	6605	..	..	5815	790
Norvège,Svalbd,J.May	2004	32647	7152	..	..	6100	1052
	2005	32557	8404	..	..	6282	2122
	2006	32557	8856	..	..	7869	987
Romania	2003	*700	239	..	..	..	239
Roumanie	2004	*700	243	..	..	..	243
	2005	*700	222	..	..	..	222
	2006	*700	219	..	..	..	219
Russian Federation	2003	14528	13740	..	..	..	13740
Fédération de Russie	2004	14568	16167	..	..	..	16167
	2005	14528	17271	..	..	..	17271
	2006	14528	18071	..	..	..	18071
Slovakia	2003	*600	6	..	..	..	6
Slovaquie	2004	*600	4	..	..	..	4
	2005	*600	3	..	..	..	3
	2006	*600	3	..	..	..	3
Ukraine	2003	*3000	1106	..	..	..	1106
Ukraine	2004	*3000	1266	..	..	..	1266
	2005	*3000	1225	..	..	..	1225
	2006	*3000	1180	..	..	..	1180
United Kingdom	2003	141971	8238	..	..	1696	6542
Royaume-Uni	2004	142360	7858	..	..	2895	4963
	2005	141971	7543	..	..	2751	4792
	2006	142591	9483	..	..	2570	6913
Oceania	**2003**	**67771**	**2677**	**..**	**..**	**908**	**1769**
Océanie	**2004**	**55230**	**3121**	**..**	**..**	**917**	**2204**
	2005	**55079**	**2433**	**..**	**..**	**885**	**1548**
	2006	**54624**	**2706**	**..**	**..**	**1201**	**1505**
Australia	2003	58009	2483	..	..	752	1731
Australie	2004	45441	2929	..	..	750	2179
	2005	45317	2251	..	..	729	1522
	2006	44862	2538	..	..	1066	1472
New Zealand	2003	9762	194	..	..	156	38
Nouvelle-Zélande	2004	9789	192	..	..	167	25
	2005	9762	182	..	..	156	26
	2006	9762	168	..	..	135	33

Table 28

Production, trade and consumption of natural gas
Production, commerce et consommation de gaz naturel

Terajoules and megajoules per capita
Térajoules et mégajoules par habitant

Table Notes:
Production

Refers to net production: gross production minus re-injected, minus flared and vented, minus extraction loss shrinkage.

- Please refer to the Definitions Section on pages xv to xxix for the appropriate product description /classification.

Notes relatives aux tableaux :
Production

Production en gros moins réinjectées, moins brûlées à la torchère ou éventées, moins perte par extraction et réduction.

- Veuillez consulter la section "définitions" de la page xv à la page xxix pour une description/classification appropriée des produits.

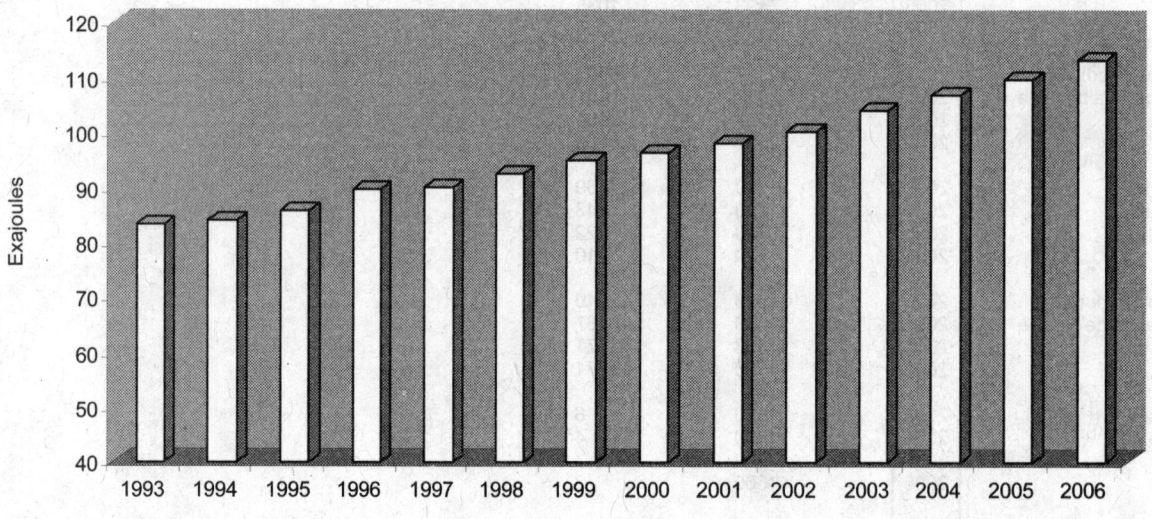

Figure 76: World production of natural gas 1993-2006

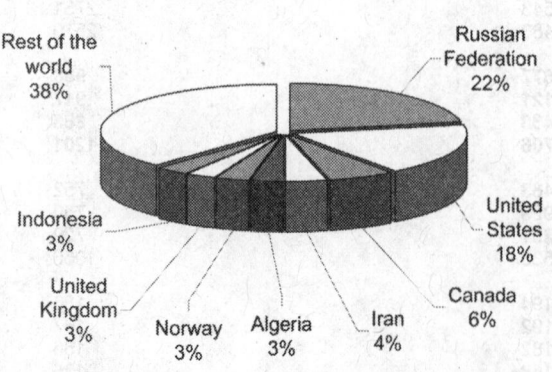

Figure 77: Major natural gas producing countries in 2006

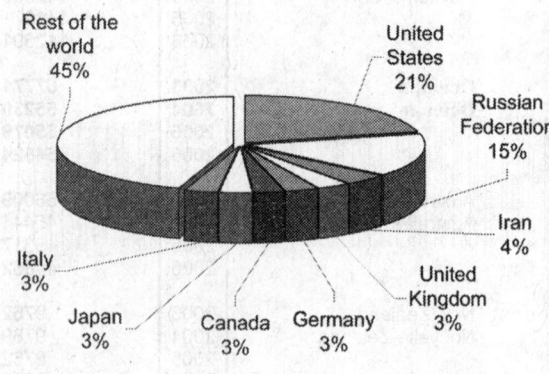

Figure 78: Major natural gas consuming countries in 2006

Table 28

Production, trade and consumption of natural gas
Production, commerce et consommation de gaz naturel

Terajoules and megajoules per capita
Térajoules et mégajoules par habitant

Country or area Pays ou zone	Year Année	Production Production	Imports Importations	Exports Exportations	Changes in stocks Variations des stocks	Consumption Consommation	
						Total Totale	Per capita Par habitant
World	**2003**	**104039984**	**29253201**	**28644641**	**456522**	**104192022**	**16621**
Monde	**2004**	**106644763**	**31148474**	**31100653**	**438862**	**106253722**	**16749**
	2005	**109598318**	**32443112**	**32757573**	**-204133**	**109487990**	**17054**
	2006	**113290917**	**33467688**	**34140757**	**1357334**	**111260514**	**17077**
Africa	**2003**	**5678973**	**65227**	**2893026**	**..**	**2851175**	**3382**
Afrique	**2004**	**6044955**	**121635**	**3136584**	**..**	**3030006**	**3488**
	2005	**7142386**	**172037**	**3716901**	**..**	**3597522**	**4049**
	2006	**7866551**	**187519**	**4509217**	**..**	**3544853**	**3868**
Algeria	2003	3248416	..	2353418	..	894998	28102
Algérie	2004	3216262	..	2378557	..	837705	25884
	2005	3586296	..	2341995	..	1244301	37814
	2006	3844884	..	2731032	..	1113852	33268
Angola	2003	24700	..	..	..	24700	2208
Angola	2004	28500	..	..	..	28500	2502
	2005	28500	..	..	..	28500	2434
	2006	30400	..	..	..	30400	2535
Congo	2003	650	..	..	..	650	188
Congo	2004	769	..	..	..	769	218
	2005	890	..	..	..	890	247
	2006	923	..	..	..	923	250
Côte d'Ivoire	2003	47770	..	..	..	47770	2714
Côte d'Ivoire	2004	60709	..	..	..	60709	3273
	2005	67803	..	..	..	67803	3550
	2006	63681	..	..	..	63681	3239
Egypt	2003	1214024	..	30666	..	1183358	17580
Egypte	2004	1311413	..	140030	..	1171383	16447
	2005	1880223	..	588222	..	1292001	18057
	2006	1935875	..	643468	..	1292407	17753
Equatorial Guinea	2003	18773	..	..	..	18773	40634
Guinée équatoriale	2004	*18730	..	..	..	*18730	*39598
	2005	*18730	..	..	..	*18730	*38698
	2006	*18730	..	..	..	*18730	*37762
Gabon	2003	4421	..	..	..	4421	3401
Gabon	2004	4912	..	..	..	4912	3600
	2005	4912	..	..	..	4912	3519
	2006	4912	..	..	..	4912	3444
Libyan Arab Jamah.	2003	243200	..	28500	..	214700	34512
Jamah. arabe libyenne	2004	306280	..	45600	..	260680	40604
	2005	429400	..	205200	..	224200	33816
	2006	562400	..	319580	..	242820	36242
Morocco	2003	1633	0	..	..	1633	57
Maroc	2004	1977	0	..	..	1977	66
	2005	1782	15849	..	..	17631	584
	2006	2600	19683	..	..	22283	731
Mozambique	2003	106	..	0	..	106	6
Mozambique	2004	52312	..	52189	..	123	6
	2005	88029	..	85173	..	2856	147
	2006	105358	..	102061	..	3297	167
Nigeria	2003	742296	..	459810	..	282486	2239
Nigéria	2004	873602	..	496350	..	377252	2920
	2005	850658	..	474667	..	375991	2811
	2006	1111761	..	693076	..	418685	2991

Table 28

Production, trade and consumption of natural gas
Production, commerce et consommation de gaz naturel

Terajoules and megajoules per capita
Térajoules et mégajoules par habitant

Country or area Pays ou zone	Year Année	Production Production	Imports Importations	Exports Exportations	Changes in stocks Variations des stocks	Consumption Consommation	
						Total Totale	Per capita Par habitant
Rwanda	2003	12	..	..	..	12	1
Rwanda	2004	*20	..	..	..	*20	*2
	2005	*23	..	..	..	*23	*3
	2006	*24	..	..	..	*24	*3
Senegal	2003	423	..	..	..	423	42
Sénégal	2004	506	..	..	..	506	48
	2005	533	..	..	..	533	49
	2006	483	..	..	..	483	44
South Africa Customs Un.	2003	50218	0	..	..	50218	984
Un.douan.d'Afr.mérid	2004	77172	52189	..	..	129361	2431
	2005	82976	86026	..	..	169002	3156
	2006	75529	102061	..	..	177590	3278
Tunisia	2003	82331	65227	20632	..	126926	12899
Tunisie	2004	86816	69446	23858	..	132404	13331
	2005	87857	70162	21644	..	136375	13598
	2006	94391	65775	*20000	..	140166	13842
United Rep.Tanzania	2003	0	..	..	..	0	0
Rép. Unie de Tanzanie	2004	4975	..	..	..	4975	137
	2005	13774	..	..	..	13774	368
	2006	14600	..	..	..	14600	382
America, North	**2003**	**30476452**	**5041597**	**5106955**	**11593**	**30399501**	**60558**
Amérique du Nord	**2004**	**30032263**	**5491674**	**5468190**	**-17184**	**30072931**	**59296**
	2005	**29704467**	**5442743**	**5410064**	**-354168**	**30091314**	**58750**
	2006	**30646765**	**5310771**	**5444729**	**441130**	**30071677**	**58211**
Barbados	2003	1020	..	..	..	1020	3755
Barbade	2004	973	..	..	..	973	3570
	2005	1028	..	..	..	1028	3764
	2006	1048	..	..	..	1048	3824
Canada	2003	7032164	369794	3876239	-183243	3708962	117090
Canada	2004	7016682	414979	4022042	-220123	3629742	113446
	2005	7169112	364396	4065937	-284510	3752081	116120
	2006	7206362	369342	3906417	-28558	3697845	113259
Cuba	2003	25675	..	..	..	25675	2271
Cuba	2004	27470	..	..	..	27470	2423
	2005	28992	..	..	..	28992	2579
	2006	42337	..	..	..	42337	3766
Dominican Republic	2003	..	4308	..	..	4308	481
Rép. dominicaine	2004	..	5237	..	..	5237	577
	2005	..	10613	..	..	10613	1150
	2006	..	12932	..	..	12932	1383
Mexico	2003	1579524	375146	0	1811	1952859	19146
Mexique	2004	1651290	434882	0	52638	2033534	19743
	2005	1716773	348548	9832	-958	2056447	19784
	2006	1885615	385705	13466	-1695	2259549	21545
Puerto Rico	2003	..	28728	..	..	28728	7407
Porto Rico	2004	..	26518	..	..	26518	6808
	2005	..	26518	..	..	26518	6779
	2006	..	26518	..	..	26518	6751
Trinidad and Tobago	2003	971764	..	507206	..	464558	353276
Trinité-et-Tobago	2004	1024185	..	536381	..	487804	369829
	2005	1067201	..	557680	..	509521	384835
	2006	1325454	..	753520	..	571934	430673

Table 28

Production, trade and consumption of natural gas
Production, commerce et consommation de gaz naturel
Terajoules and megajoules per capita
Térajoules et mégajoules par habitant

Country or area Pays ou zone	Year Année	Production Production	Imports Importations	Exports Exportations	Changes in stocks Variations des stocks	Consumption Consommation	
						Total Totale	Per capita Par habitant
United States	2003	20866305	4263621	723510	193025	24213391	83250
Etats-Unis	2004	20311663	4610058	909767	150301	23861653	81266
	2005	19721361	4692668	776615	-68700	23706114	79977
	2006	20185949	4516274	771326	471383	23459514	78606
America, South	**2003**	**3744351**	**439939**	**431358**	**11224**	**3741709**	**10328**
Amérique du Sud	**2004**	**3932148**	**589475**	**575272**	**8995**	**3937356**	**10723**
	2005	**4070096**	**660545**	**659340**	**7470**	**4063830**	**10919**
	2006	**4273621**	**671603**	**662195**	**0**	**4283029**	**11355**
Argentina	2003	1664109	3539	263577	..	1404071	37076
Argentine	2004	1713297	31309	284171	..	1460435	38205
	2005	1685308	62704	254027	..	1493985	38712
	2006	1764945	63575	242488	..	1586032	40698
Bolivia	2003	255726	..	167781	..	87945	9745
Bolivie	2004	355620	..	291101	..	64519	6992
	2005	442468	..	405313	..	37155	3941
	2006	473592	..	419707	..	53885	5597
Brazil	2003	397527	195770	..	..	593297	3315
Brésil	2004	420030	313155	..	..	733185	4038
	2005	429095	348458	..	..	777553	4222
	2006	434855	379109	..	..	813964	4358
Chile	2003	73681	238369	..	11224	300826	18885
Chili	2004	67617	241084	..	8995	299706	18618
	2005	82254	245644	..	7470	320428	19664
	2006	78786	224632	..	0	303418	18464
Colombia	2003	257762	..	..	..	257762	5784
Colombie	2004	271346	..	..	..	271346	5990
	2005	284720	..	..	..	284720	6183
	2006	321698	..	..	..	321698	6878
Ecuador	2003	16234	..	..	..	16234	1264
Equateur	2004	25108	..	..	..	25108	1927
	2005	20411	..	..	..	20411	1545
	2006	33281	..	..	..	33281	2482
Peru	2003	25802	..	..	..	25802	960
Pérou	2004	40321	..	..	..	40321	1489
	2005	68008	..	..	..	68008	2502
	2006	77826	..	..	..	77826	2843
Uruguay	2003	..	2261	..	..	2261	663
Uruguay	2004	..	3927	..	..	3927	1189
	2005	..	3739	..	..	3739	1131
	2006	..	4287	..	..	4287	1293
Venezuela(Bolivar. Rep.)	2003	1053511	..	..	..	1053511	41035
Venezuela(Rép. bolivar.)	2004	1038809	..	..	..	1038809	39759
	2005	1057831	..	..	..	1057831	39802
	2006	1088638	..	..	..	1088638	40274
Asia	**2003**	**26012452**	**6849719**	**6999721**	**28509**	**25833941**	**6796**
Asie	**2004**	**27669272**	**7373789**	**7925879**	**28814**	**27088368**	**7054**
	2005	**29663356**	**7627332**	**8381125**	**-8618**	**28918181**	**7444**
	2006	**31221693**	**8360531**	**8670130**	**48560**	**30863534**	**7831**
Afghanistan	2003	242	..	..	..	242	11
Afghanistan	2004	119	..	..	..	119	5
	2005	*100	..	..	..	*100	*4
	2006	*100	..	..	..	*100	*4

Table 28

Production, trade and consumption of natural gas
Production, commerce et consommation de gaz naturel

Terajoules and megajoules per capita
Térajoules et mégajoules par habitant

Country or area Pays ou zone	Year Année	Production Production	Imports Importations	Exports Exportations	Changes in stocks Variations des stocks	Consumption Consommation	
						Total Totale	Per capita Par habitant
Armenia	2003	..	45278	0	..	45278	11918
Arménie	2004	..	50782	490	..	50292	15648
	2005	..	63525	1244	..	62281	19367
	2006	..	64693	829	..	63864	19827
Azerbaijan	2003	193326	153778	0	452	346652	42100
Azerbaïdjan	2004	194905	187218	0	3551	378572	45575
	2005	216096	178549	0	15947	378698	45127
	2006	255073	172898	2536	9365	416070	49039
Bahrain	2003	263779	..	..	..	263779	382611
Bahreïn	2004	274330	..	..	..	274330	387932
	2005	290590	..	..	..	290590	401010
	2006	307881	..	..	..	307881	414620
Bangladesh	2003	434849	..	..	..	434849	3226
Bangladesh	2004	467723	..	..	..	467723	3422
	2005	502829	..	..	..	502829	3628
	2006	543096	..	..	..	543096	3830
Brunei Darussalam	2003	482490	..	423510	..	58980	168707
Brunéi Darussalam	2004	477318	..	411413	..	65905	183222
	2005	468618	..	401876	..	66742	180335
	2006	492586	..	426723	..	65863	171966
China	2003	1685000	..	57553	..	1627447	1263
Chine	2004	1544800	..	90914	..	1453886	1122
	2005	1898173	..	110625	..	1787548	1371
	2006	1995497	..	104440	..	1891057	1439
China, Hong Kong SAR	2003	..	57590	..	-1789	59379	8719
Chine, Hong-Kong RAS	2004	..	83197	..	-2598	85795	12648
	2005	..	83389	..	-2362	85751	12586
	2006	..	91483	..	870	90613	13209
Georgia	2003	712	35169	..	..	35881	8289
Géorgie	2004	461	41575	..	..	42036	9734
	2005	516	49532	..	..	50048	11475
	2006	649	63514	..	..	64163	14589
India	2003	1016146	..	..	..	1016146	951
Inde	2004	1007951	..	..	..	1007951	934
	2005	1025355	..	..	..	1025355	937
	2006	1005064	..	..	..	1005064	899
Indonesia	2003	2840729	..	1557375	..	1283354	5990
Indonésie	2004	2942183	..	1543980	..	1398203	6441
	2005	2879750	..	1493301	..	1386449	6305
	2006	2887554	..	1426833	..	1460721	6578
Iran(Islamic Rep. of)	2003	3079135	225549	134322	..	3170362	47700
Iran(Rép. islamique)	2004	3423814	230469	138140	..	3516143	52108
	2005	3709933	203707	186351	..	3727289	54439
	2006	4075188	246502	225388	..	4096302	58107
Iraq	2003	59280	..	..	..	59280	2251
Iraq	2004	98799	..	..	..	98799	3641
	2005	100700	..	..	..	100700	3662
	2006	132998	..	..	..	132998	4616
Israel	2003	321	..	..	..	321	48
Israël	2004	43585	..	..	..	43585	6401
	2005	59988	..	..	..	59988	8656
	2006	83815	..	..	..	83815	11893

Table 28

Production, trade and consumption of natural gas
Production, commerce et consommation de gaz naturel
Terajoules and megajoules per capita
Térajoules et mégajoules par habitant

Country or area Pays ou zone	Year Année	Production Production	Imports Importations	Exports Exportations	Changes in stocks Variations des stocks	Consumption Consommation	
						Total Totale	Per capita Par habitant
Japan	2003	120758	3194295	..	-2873	3317926	26281
Japon	2004	125356	3166545	..	7971	3283930	26011
	2005	134612	3153883	..	4816	3283679	26015
	2006	148485	3452108	..	-3099	3603692	28564
Jordan	2003	9902	0	..	..	9902	1893
Jordanie	2004	10098	45551	..	..	55649	10904
	2005	8315	56082	..	..	64397	11766
	2006	7754	76129	..	..	83883	14979
Kazakhstan	2003	647698	339361	429626	..	557433	37389
Kazakhstan	2004	862531	454665	674496	..	642700	42810
	2005	974571	438122	601971	..	810722	53523
	2006	1029558	431762	588043	..	873277	57047
Korea, Republic of	2003	0	1057773	..	33994	1023779	21396
Corée, République de	2004	0	1205771	..	29389	1176382	24466
	2005	20495	1214706	..	-38317	1273518	26370
	2006	21631	1374628	..	57417	1338842	27721
Kuwait	2003	429950	..	..	..	429950	184890
Koweït	2004	462773	..	..	..	462773	193581
	2005	518914	..	..	..	518914	211176
	2006	548804	..	..	..	548804	217267
Kyrgyzstan	2003	1054	27470	..	..	28524	5661
Kirghizistan	2004	1132	30017	..	..	31149	6116
	2005	975	27747	..	..	28722	5584
	2006	741	29265	..	..	30006	5779
Malaysia	2003	2079956	30111	852155	..	1257912	50219
Malaisie	2004	2180862	31428	1008475	..	1203815	47059
	2005	2402160	56066	1155603	..	1302623	49856
	2006	2608702	65976	1195331	..	1479347	55531
Myanmar	2003	306893	..	244747	..	62146	1168
Myanmar	2004	419860	..	348831	..	71029	1308
	2005	438767	..	358856	..	79911	1445
	2006	454124	..	371416	..	82708	1469
Oman	2003	691553	..	354757	..	336796	143880
Oman	2004	706149	..	393211	..	312938	129550
	2005	740145	..	413612	..	326533	130153
	2006	938861	..	503358	..	435503	168996
Other Asia	2003	30961	302611	..	-2090	335662	14850
Autre Asie	2004	32374	372921	..	-8242	413537	18226
	2005	20400	388504	..	7664	401240	17653
	2006	17251	421309	..	-13563	452123	19839
Pakistan	2003	1023969	..	..	-258	1024227	7018
Pakistan	2004	1115913	..	..	-308	1116221	7506
	2005	1171106	..	..	-101	1171207	7632
	2006	1181984	..	..	-147	1182131	7541
Philippines	2003	101146	..	..	..	101146	1247
Philippines	2004	96743	..	..	..	96743	1170
	2005	127566	..	..	..	127566	1497
	2006	115873	..	..	..	115873	1332
Qatar	2003	1225260	..	740121	..	485139	661640
Qatar	2004	1528453	..	947540	..	580913	747697
	2005	1787162	..	1034260	..	752902	926258
	2006	1931540	..	1186537	..	745002	795699

Table 28

Production, trade and consumption of natural gas
Production, commerce et consommation de gaz naturel

Terajoules and megajoules per capita
Térajoules et mégajoules par habitant

Country or area Pays ou zone	Year Année	Production Production	Imports Importations	Exports Exportations	Changes in stocks Variations des stocks	Consumption Consommation Total Totale	Per capita Par habitant
Saudi Arabia	2003	1990700	..	..	..	1990700	90408
Arabie saoudite	2004	2162680	..	..	..	2162680	95847
	2005	2376770	..	..	..	2376770	102806
	2006	2495244	..	..	..	2495244	105379
Singapore	2003	..	208631	..	..	208631	49839
Singapour	2004	..	245965	..	..	245965	58034
	2005	..	276122	..	..	276122	63596
	2006	..	280197	..	..	280197	62490
Syrian Arab Republic	2003	258245	..	..	..	258245	14715
Rép. arabe syrienne	2004	267670	..	..	..	267670	15011
	2005	229970	..	..	..	229970	12588
	2006	237510	..	..	..	237510	12690
Tajikistan	2003	1254	20140	..	..	21394	3255
Tadjikistan	2004	1368	20737	..	..	22105	3294
	2005	1113	21351	..	..	22464	3279
	2006	760	21984	..	..	22744	3189
Thailand	2003	707276	293327	..	..	1000603	15630
Thaïlande	2004	701157	315779	..	..	1016936	15846
	2005	753708	344825	..	..	1098533	16943
	2006	761621	355208	..	..	1116829	17102
Turkey	2003	21448	803993	..	1073	824368	11738
Turquie	2004	26350	843063	..	-949	870362	12232
	2005	34355	1029654	..	3735	1060274	14713
	2006	34662	1171307	..	-2283	1208252	16557
Turkmenistan	2003	2241513	..	1644383	..	597130	127103
Turkménistan	2004	2235451	..	1701216	..	534235	112093
	2005	2387007	..	1816553	..	570454	118027
	2006	2396479	..	1823761	..	572718	116905
United Arab Emirates	2003	1746810	..	278850	..	1467960	413393
Emirats arabes unis	2004	1805310	..	291720	..	1513590	402443
	2005	1815450	..	278460	..	1536990	374289
	2006	1846650	..	276120	..	1570530	371371
Uzbekistan	2003	2194105	54643	282322	..	1966426	76135
Ouzbékistan	2004	2236391	48106	375453	..	1909044	72839
	2005	2278677	41568	468584	..	1851661	69630
	2006	2370882	41568	478031	..	1934419	71696
Viet Nam	2003	125993	..	0	..	125993	1557
Viet Nam	2004	214663	..	0	..	214663	2617
	2005	288471	..	59829	..	228642	2751
	2006	293076	..	60784	..	232292	2760
Europe	**2003**	**36486165**	**16856719**	**12787842**	**405190**	**40149852**	**55209**
Europe	**2004**	**37312306**	**17571901**	**13564206**	**418220**	**40901781**	**56191**
	2005	**37210883**	**18540455**	**14014046**	**151194**	**41586098**	**57026**
	2006	**37405317**	**18881022**	**14174758**	**867648**	**41243933**	**56492**
Albania	2003	544	..	..	..	544	154
Albanie	2004	636	..	..	..	636	204
	2005	670	..	..	..	670	213
	2006	670	..	..	..	670	213
Austria	2003	82603	317283	40567	7889	351430	43564
Autriche	2004	77550	331352	51847	2568	354487	43548
	2005	62081	377950	38916	19898	381217	46453
	2006	72756	409720	105443	30104	346929	41890

Table 28

Production, trade and consumption of natural gas
Production, commerce et consommation de gaz naturel

Terajoules and megajoules per capita
Térajoules et mégajoules par habitant

Country or area Pays ou zone	Year Année	Production Production	Imports Importations	Exports Exportations	Changes in stocks Variations des stocks	Consumption Consommation	
						Total Totale	Per capita Par habitant
Belarus Bélarus	2003 2004 2005 2006	9810 9942 8806 8458	699560 758652 777075 802874	.. ..	-3128 -4673 -2278 8805	712498 773267 788159 802527	72160 78707 80628 82458
Belgium Belgique	2003 2004 2005 2006	.. ..	662591 677290 660160 699213	.. ..	-7390 -506 3624 1649	669981 677796 656536 697564	64696 65195 62851 66363
Bosnia and Herzegovina Bosnie y Herzégovine	2003 2004 2005 2006	.. ..	7511 11837 14058 14871	.. ..	.. ..	7511 11837 14058 14871	1960 3081 3659 3870
Bulgaria Bulgarie	2003 2004 2005 2006	597 12432 17884 17391	109593 111129 114340 121355	.. ..	-6136 7602 1778 3810	116326 115959 130446 134936	14869 14903 16854 17526
Croatia Croatie	2003 2004 2005 2006	83205 83528 86769 103113	43274 40037 43096 42807	12996 13209 16971 34033	3876 -3997 2318 2531	109607 114353 110576 109356	24675 25759 24894 24630
Czech Republic République tchèque	2003 2004 2005 2006	6098 7555 7170 6853	360045 333350 353726 372534	1928 3329 3220 4721	-604 -24717 -688 22556	364819 362293 358364 352110	35761 35495 35017 34228
Denmark Danemark	2003 2004 2005 2006	335062 395033 436520 433718	.. ..	120692 171722 233085 218084	-2445 7748 -1226 4593	216815 215563 204661 211041	41032 39910 37788 38833
Estonia Estonie	2003 2004 2005 2006	.. ..	31635 36032 37201 37595	.. ..	.. ..	31635 36032 37201 37595	23372 26704 27636 27982
Finland Finlande	2003 2004 2005 2006	.. ..	190004 183779 167381 180308	.. ..	.. ..	190004 183779 167381 180308	36448 35152 31906 34238
France incl. Monaco France y compris Monaco	2003 2004 2005 2006	59621 51530 42275 49242	1788025 1857438 1936328 1867698	41904 58546 42020 31598	-23331 -17279 25692 42032	1829073 1867701 1910891 1843310	30390 30844 31375 30184
Germany Allemagne	2003 2004 2005 2006	740615 685342 661721 653696	3187328 3389857 3420663 3519141	282769 324436 362714 428634	-36000 88200 -41760 46080	3681174 3662563 3761430 3698123	44609 44394 45613 44899
Greece Grèce	2003 2004 2005 2006	1442 1337 851 1209	93138 101125 108495 126604	.. ..	319 -1220 -141 11	94261 103682 109487 127802	8551 9373 9860 11464
Hungary Hongrie	2003 2004 2005 2006	106329 110100 108422 110660	462396 431618 456244 443423	0 0 0 5347	15786 -3135 2056 15922	552939 544853 562610 532814	54587 53908 55775 52904

Table 28

Production, trade and consumption of natural gas
Production, commerce et consommation de gaz naturel
Terajoules and megajoules per capita
Térajoules et mégajoules par habitant

Country or area Pays ou zone	Year Année	Production Production	Imports Importations	Exports Exportations	Changes in stocks Variations des stocks	Consumption Consommation	
						Total Totale	Per capita Par habitant
Ireland	2003	25293	145769	..	1145	169917	42705
Irlande	2004	32025	137683	..	143	169565	41932
	2005	21437	140007	..	37	161407	39075
	2006	19107	167581	..	-4	186692	44084
Italy and San Marino	2003	529017	2392454	14516	-52692	2959647	51379
Italie y comp. St. Marin	2004	493813	2587295	15050	-5145	3071203	52792
	2005	459905	2798826	15088	-43053	3286696	56080
	2006	418301	2948903	14058	134343	3218803	54610
Latvia	2003	..	65403	..	2728	62675	26953
Lettonie	2004	..	80880	..	18897	61983	26800
	2005	..	66710	..	3541	63169	27459
	2006	..	71174	..	5738	65436	28600
Lithuania	2003	..	109549	..	37	109512	31704
Lituanie	2004	..	108991	..	-223	109214	31789
	2005	..	115949	..	744	115205	33742
	2006	..	115354	..	1191	114163	33636
Luxembourg	2003	..	49499	..	..	49499	109601
Luxembourg	2004	..	55794	..	..	55794	121796
	2005	..	54829	..	..	54829	117872
	2006	..	57404	..	..	57404	121454
Netherlands	2003	2428905	849263	1603074	447	1674647	103418
Pays-Bas	2004	2864924	628124	1784604	-925	1709369	105140
	2005	2617469	764779	1738959	24	1643265	100691
	2006	2578865	839298	1822321	202	1595640	97677
Norway,Svlbd.J.Myn. I	2003	3082859	..	2835323	..	247536	54049
Norvège,Svalbd,J.May	2004	3275892	..	3039744	..	236148	51239
	2005	3548571	..	3308519	..	240052	51708
	2006	3647849	..	3427370	..	220479	47309
Poland	2003	167997	350607	1767	-7010	523847	13715
Pologne	2004	182698	379467	1753	7728	552684	14476
	2005	180700	398547	1667	8431	569149	14914
	2006	180514	415736	1745	18892	575613	15095
Portugal	2003	..	122968	..	328	122640	11746
Portugal	2004	..	153733	..	57	153676	14633
	2005	..	181102	..	6620	174482	16539
	2006	..	170340	..	1026	169314	15997
Republic of Moldova	2003	..	103659	..	-159	103818	28736
Rép. de Moldova	2004	..	106513	..	-40	106553	29566
	2005	..	114075	..	-40	114115	31741
	2006	..	105553	..	356	105197	29342
Romania	2003	485135	197100	..	-2974	685209	31528
Roumanie	2004	482759	191269	..	25664	648364	29915
	2005	451305	194935	..	-2346	648586	29994
	2006	444656	222880	..	-12013	679549	31483
Russian Federation	2003	23252111	329000	7116778	526556	15937777	110246
Fédération de Russie	2004	23693333	258889	7530000	295556	16126666	112130
	2005	23996973	288486	7788529	230316	16266614	113662
	2006	24463654	270562	7624125	423016	16687075	117113
Serbia	2003	13723	70955	..	..	84678	8001
Serbie	2004	11951	95592	..	..	107543	10226
	2005	10631	79420	..	..	90051	8600
	2006	10970	81682	..	..	92652	8865

Table 28

Production, trade and consumption of natural gas
Production, commerce et consommation de gaz naturel

Terajoules and megajoules per capita
Térajoules et mégajoules par habitant

Country or area Pays ou zone	Year Année	Production Production	Imports Importations	Exports Exportations	Changes in stocks Variations des stocks	Consumption Consommation	
						Total Totale	Per capita Par habitant
Slovakia	2003	7745	256076	151	-38	263708	49026
Slovaquie	2004	6603	264166	39	14944	255786	47521
	2005	5876	281273	14461	-1019	273707	50806
	2006	8187	264567	22994	-419	250179	46405
Slovenia	2003	199	41982	..	..	42181	21143
Slovénie	2004	201	41608	..	..	41809	20942
	2005	160	43050	..	..	43210	21593
	2006	160	41673	..	..	41833	20828
Spain	2003	9149	984756	..	565	993340	23648
Espagne	2004	14398	1145112	..	-11478	1170988	27429
	2005	6694	1407156	..	25505	1388345	31991
	2006	2545	1462006	..	21510	1443041	32746
Sweden	2003	..	41322	..	..	41322	4613
Suède	2004	..	41142	..	..	41142	4575
	2005	..	39199	..	..	39199	4341
	2006	..	41024	..	..	41024	4518
Switzerland	2003	..	122238	..	..	122238	16651
Suisse	2004	..	126105	..	..	126105	16925
	2005	..	129460	..	..	129460	17356
	2006	..	125878	..	..	125878	16820
T.F.Yug.Rep. Macedonia	2003	..	3082	..	-8	3090	1524
L'ex-RY Macédoine	2004	..	2725	..	5	2720	1340
	2005	..	2952	..	-14	2966	1456
	2006	..	3136	..	13	3123	1531
Ukraine	2003	748794	2357979	78040	0	3028733	63345
Ukraine	2004	799130	2424391	159124	0	3064397	64826
	2005	811148	2348848	103637	-82069	3138428	66668
	2006	822932	1959623	156	72538	2709861	57957
United Kingdom	2003	4309312	310675	637337	-12571	3995221	67340
Royaume-Uni	2004	4019594	478926	410803	22446	4065271	68095
	2005	3666845	624135	346260	-4756	3949476	65596
	2006	3349811	878505	434129	23166	3771021	62241
Oceania	**2003**	**1641590**	**0**	**425739**	**6**	**1215845**	**37518**
Océanie	**2004**	**1653819**	**0**	**430522**	**17**	**1223280**	**37203**
	2005	**1807130**	**0**	**576096**	**-11**	**1231045**	**36902**
	2006	**1876971**	**56242**	**679728**	**-4**	**1253489**	**37006**
Australia	2003	1456588	0	425739	..	1030849	51794
Australie	2004	1488699	0	430522	..	1058177	52542
	2005	1648435	0	576096	..	1072339	52542
	2006	1713590	56242	679728	..	1090104	52658
New Zealand	2003	179476	..	..	6	179470	44765
Nouvelle-Zélande	2004	160640	..	..	17	160623	39549
	2005	148597	..	..	-11	148608	36256
	2006	152529	..	..	-4	152533	36815
Papua New Guinea	2003	5526	..	..	..	5526	953
Papouasie-Nvl-Guinée	2004	4480	..	..	..	4480	755
	2005	10098	..	..	..	10098	1664
	2006	10852	..	..	..	10852	1750

Table 29

International trade of natural gas
(Principal importers/exporters)
Terajoules

2005

Importers	Exporters							
	World Monde	Algeria Algérie	Australia Australie	Canada Canada	Egypt Egypte	Indonesia Indonésie	Kazakhstan Kazakhstan	Malaysia Malaisie
Austria	364456	..	..	..	..	..	..	
Belarus	785103	..	..	..	..	..	..	
Belgium	660160	128211	..	..	..	..	..	
Brazil	348458	..	..	..	..	..	..	
Canada	364396	..	..	..	..	..	..	
Czech Republic	353726	..	..	..	..	..	..	
Finland	167381	..	..	..	..	..	..	
France incl. Monaco	1936328	309486	..	..	60030	..	..	
Germany	3420663	..	..	..	..	..	..	
Hungary	456244	..	..	..	..	..	8481	
Italy and San Marino	2798826	1046378	..	..	..	..	..	
Japan	3154120	3031	569379	..	6446	752206	..	7153
Kazakhstan	438122	..	..	..	..	..	..	
Korea, Republic of	1214706	..	40729	..	14687	299450	..	2551
Mexico	348548	..	..	..	0	..	..	
Netherlands	764779	..	..	..	..	..	..	
Poland	398547	..	..	..	..	..	36107	
Portugal	181102	112022	..	..	..	..	..	
Russian Federation	288486	..	..	..	..	..	..	
Singapore	276122	..	..	..	..	94006	..	23
Slovakia	281273	..	..	..	..	..	..	
Spain	1407156	609182	..	..	142389	..	..	109
Thailand	344825	..	..	..	..	..	..	
Turkey	1029654	158992	..	..	..	..	..	
Ukraine	2348848	..	..	..	..	..	..	
United Kingdom	624135	16570	..	..	0	..	..	
United States	4692668	111736	..	3978532	79598	..	..	100

Table 29

Commerce international du gaz naturel
(Principaux importateurs/exportateurs)
Térajoules

2005

Exportateurs								Importtateurs
Netherlands Pays-Bas	Nigeria Nigéria	Norway,Svlbd. J.Myn. I Norvège,Svalb d,J.May	Qatar Qatar	Russian Federation Fédération de Russie	Trinidad and Tobago Trinité-et-Toba go	Turkmenistan Turkménistan	United States Etats-Unis	
..	..	42650	..	258085	..	..	..	Autriche
..	..	..	..	785103	..	..	..	Bélarus
221957	..	211617	..	33776	..	..	..	Belgique
..	..	..	..	.,	..	..	..	Brésil
..	..	..	..	..	..	..	364396	Canada
..	..	84661	..	269065	..	..	..	République tchèque
..	..	..	..	167381	..	..	..	Finlande
314150	146596	447040	..	378093	..	..	..	France y compris Monaco
735193	..	1097831	..	1425938	..	..	..	Allemagne
..	..	..	..	335020	..	64160	..	Hongrie
306324	..	218046	..	888721	10135	..	..	Italie y comp. St. Marin
..	..	..	348274	..	3035	..	68048	Japon
..	..	..	..	265854	..	46564	0	Kazakhstan
..	..	..	338037	..	..	..	..	Corée, République de
..	..	..	..	..	..	..	348548	Mexique
..	..	..	..	..	..	..	..	Pays-Bas
..	..	19436	..	262629	..	8609	..	Pologne
..	69080	..	..	..	..	..	..	Portugal
..	..	..	..	..	..	*288486	..	Fédération de Russie
171	..	..	..	..	..	..	48541	Singapour
..	..	..	..	281273	..	..	..	Slovaquie
..	220643	89018	195713	..	16318	..	..	Espagne
..	..	..	..	..	..	..	0	Thaïlande
..	42832	..	..	660621	..	..	..	Turquie
..	..	..	..	1371042	..	903921	..	Ukraine
..	..	460416	..	..	3220	..	..	Royaume-Uni
..	9544	..	3544	487084	..	..	..	Etats-Unis

Table 29

International trade of natural gas
(Principal importers/exporters)
Terajoules

2006

Importers	World Monde	Algeria Algérie	Australia Australie	Canada Canada	Egypt Egypte	Indonesia Indonésie	Kazakhstan Kazakhstan	Malaysia Malaisie
Austria	399731	..	..	..	..	..	..	
Belarus	811169	..	..	..	..	..	..	
Belgium	699213	118639	..	..	..	..	..	30(
Brazil	379109	..	..	..	..	..	..	
Canada	369342	..	..	..	..	..	..	
Czech Republic	372534	..	..	..	..	..	..	
Finland	180308	..	..	..	..	..	..	
France incl. Monaco	1867698	293945	..	..	90828	..	..	
Germany	3519141	..	..	..	..	..	..	
Hungary	443423	..	..	..	..	..	..	
Italy and San Marino	2948903	1049617	..	..	..	..	..	
Japan	3452108	10033	687390	..	30291	760709	..	6663(
Kazakhstan	431762	..	..	..	..	..	..	
Korea, Republic of	1374628	13111	38165	..	51974	275407	..	3018!
Mexico	385705	..	..	..	10866	..	..	
Netherlands	839298	..	..	..	..	..	..	
Poland	415736	..	..	..	..	..	..	
Portugal	170340	85964	..	..	..	..	..	
Russian Federation	270562	..	..	..	..	..	..	
Singapore	280197	..	..	..	..	*96000	..	*24!
Slovakia	264567	..	..	..	..	..	..	
Spain	1462006	474579	..	..	181718	..	..	
Thailand	355208	..	..	..	..	..	..	
Turkey	1171307	173481	..	..	..	..	..	
Ukraine	1959623	..	..	..	..	..	248681	
United Kingdom	878505	74584	..	..	44874	..	..	
United States	4516274	19920	..	3859772	130654	..	..	

Table 29

Commerce international du gaz naturel
(Principaux importateurs/exportateurs)
Térajoules

2006

				Exportateurs				Importtateurs
etherlands Pays-Bas	Nigeria Nigéria	Norway,Svlbd. J.Myn. I Norvège,Svalb d,J.May	Qatar Qatar	Russian Federation Fédération de Russie	Trinidad and Tobago Trinité-et-Toba go	Turkmenistan Turkménistan	United States Etats-Unis	
..	..	49635	..	228312	..	..	..	Autriche
..	..	..	..	811169	..	..	..	Bélarus
254183	6388	214725	16946	28194	6138	..	..	Belgique
..	..	..	..	..	..	..	..	Brésil
..	..	..	..	..	..	..	369342	Canada
..	..	95888	..	276646	..	..	..	République tchèque
..	..	..	..	180308	..	..	..	Finlande
346253	170787	529322	..	292239	..	..	..	France y compris Monaco
824318	..	1069246	..	1477669	..	..	..	Allemagne
..	..	..	..	351905	..	34986	..	Hongrie
357073	..	218885	..	858012	953	..	..	Italie y comp. St. Marin
..	..	..	420228	..	15036	..	61455	Japon
..	..	..	..	274412	..	70538	..	Kazakhstan
..	6334	..	354573	..	2812	..	..	Corée, République de
..	2662	..	5577	..	12137	..	354463	Mexique
..	..	..	..	..	..	..	..	Pays-Bas
..	..	14453	..	286175	..	1549	..	Pologne
..	84376	..	..	..	..	..	..	Portugal
..	..	..	..	..	..	*270562	..	Fédération de Russie
*175	..	..	..	..	..	..	*48650	Singapour
..	..	..	..	264567	..	..	..	Slovaquie
..	299435	85579	225408	..	134143	..	..	Espagne
..	..	..	..	..	..	..	0	Thaïlande
..	46531	..	..	728211	..	..	..	Turquie
..	..	..	..	163888	..	1428871	..	Ukraine
32886	..	565333	2804	..	13010	..	..	Royaume-Uni
..	62867	..	0	429610	..	..	..	Etats-Unis

Table 30

Production of other gases - by type
Production d'autres gaz - par catégorie
Terajoules
Térajoules

Table Notes:
Total

Liquefied petroleum gas production by refinery and plant, refinery gas production from refinery, production of gasworks gas, coke oven gas, blast furnace gas and biogas.

- **Please refer to the Definitions Section on pages xv to xxix for the appropriate product description /classification.**

Notes relatives aux tableaux:
Total

Production de gaz de pétrole liquéfiés par raffinement, production de gaz raffiné naturellement, production de gaz d'usine à gaz, gaz de cokerie, gaz de haut-fourneau et biogaz.

- **Veuillez consulter la section "définitions" de la page xv à la page xxix pour une description/classification appropriée des produits.**

Figure 79: Production of other gases by type, by region, in 2006

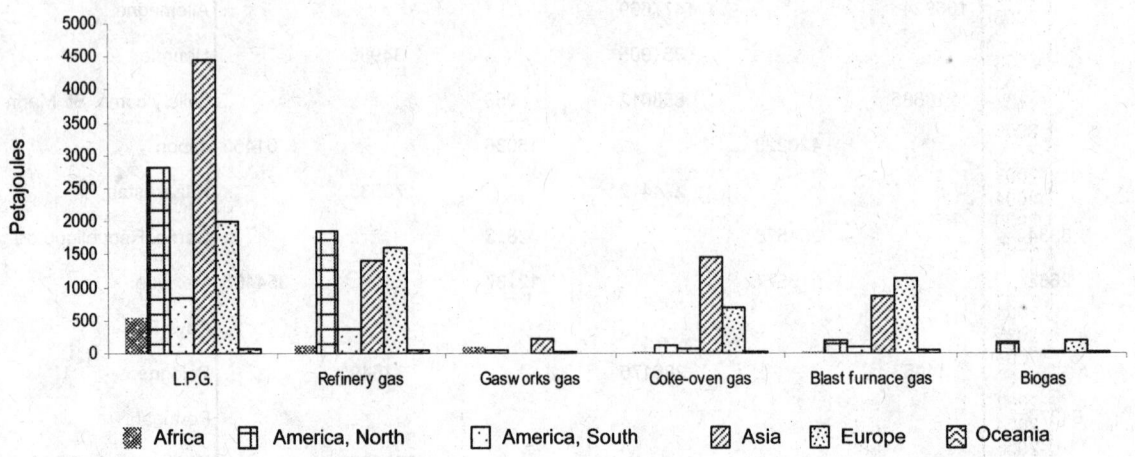

Figure 80: World production of other gases, by type, in 2006

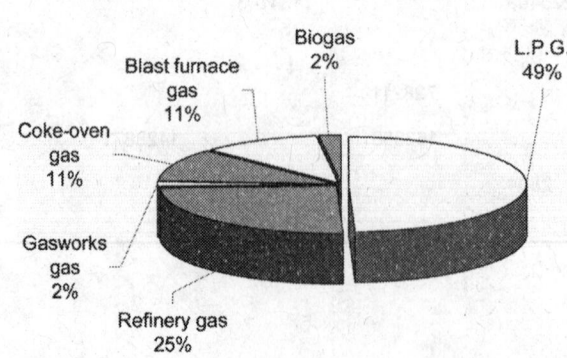

Table 30

Production of other gases - by type
Production d'autres gaz - par catégorie
Terajoules
Térajoules

Country or area Pays ou zone	Year Année	Total Totale	L.P.G. G.P.L.	Refinery gas Gaz de raffinerie	Gasworks gas Gaz d'usines à gaz	Coke-oven gas Gaz de cokerie	Blast furnace gas Gaz de haut-fourneau	Biogas Biogaz
rld nde	2003	20236120	10028656	5141871	376282	2006725	2357633	324953
	2004	20851922	10564674	5220935	343320	1995195	2376239	351558
	2005	21222733	10652969	5253228	398798	2261932	2278780	377026
	2006	21773568	10770783	5411984	401858	2403350	2385903	399690
ca que	2003	806763	584199	124162	49224	16198	32979	..
	2004	795191	563331	123450	51051	17854	39504	..
	2005	843005	573849	124288	87292	18165	39411	..
	2006	817911	555241	120980	87292	17512	36886	..
eria érie	2003	452868	444327	..	..	1047	7494	..
	2004	428781	420052	..	..	960	7769	..
	2005	433194	425244	..	..	886	7064	..
	2006	405974	398510	..	..	842	6622	..
ola ola	2003	3706	1822	1884	..	..	..	..
	2004	3118	1275	1843	..	..	..	..
	2005	2936	1093	1843	..	..	..	..
	2006	3019	1093	1926	..	..	..	..
neroon neroun	2003	956	956	..	..	..	..	..
	2004	1275	1275	..	..	..	..	..
	2005	1184	1184	..	..	..	..	..
	2006	1002	1002	..	..	..	..	..
go go	2003	182	182	..	..	..	..	..
	2004	228	228	..	..	..	..	..
	2005	228	228	..	..	..	..	..
	2006	319	319	..	..	..	..	..
e d'Ivoire e d'Ivoire	2003	4123	3285	838	..	..	..	..
	2004	5584	4370	1214	..	..	..	..
	2005	5339	3957	1382	..	..	..	..
	2006	5898	4600	1298	..	..	..	..
n. Rep. of Congo . dem. du Congo	2003	932	..	..	..	..	932	..
	2004	1022	..	..	..	..	1022	..
	2005	1086	..	..	..	..	1086	..
	2006	1154	..	..	..	..	1154	..
pt pte	2003	105364	79201	19054	380	..	6729	..
	2004	110442	78518	20645	380	..	10899	..
	2005	110736	78017	21441	380	..	10899	..
	2006	108307	77926	20561	380	..	9440	..
on on	2003	*1666	410	*1256	..	..	..	..
	2004	*1247	410	*838	..	..	..	..
	2005	*1293	455	*838	..	..	..	..
	2006	*1156	319	*838	..	..	..	..
na na	2003	4173	2414	1759	..	..	..	..
	2004	4765	3006	1759	..	..	..	..
	2005	5521	3552	1968	..	..	..	..
	2006	2854	1640	1214	..	..	..	..
ya ya	2003	3773	1093	2680	..	..	..	..
	2004	4203	1230	2973	..	..	..	..
	2005	4283	1184	3099	..	..	..	..
	2006	4256	1366	2889	..	..	..	..
an Arab Jamah. ah. arabe libyenne	2003	36313	14119	22194	..	..	..	..
	2004	36480	14119	22362	..	..	..	..
	2005	37548	15940	21608	..	..	..	..
	2006	38844	17990	20854	..	..	..	..

Table 30

Production of other gases - by type
Production d'autres gaz - par catégorie

Terajoules
Térajoules

Country or area Pays ou zone	Year Année	Total Totale	L.P.G. G.P.L.	Refinery gas Gaz de raffinerie	Gasworks gas Gaz d'usines à gaz	Coke-oven gas Gaz de cokerie	Blast furnace gas Gaz de haut-fourneau	Biogas Biogaz
Madagascar	2003	*273	*273	..		..	..	
Madagascar	2004	*273	*273				..	
	2005	*273	*273				..	
	2006	*273	*273				..	
Morocco	2003	6611	3051	3559			..	
Maroc	2004	9636	4737	4899				
	2005	14860	9291	5570				
	2006	13728	8744	4983				
Nigeria	2003	6428	774	5653			..	
Nigéria	2004	6511	774	5737				
	2005	6595	774	5821				
	2006	5098	911	4188				
Senegal	2003	882	547	335			..	
Sénégal	2004	790	455	335				
	2005	472	137	335				
	2006	335	0	335				
Somalia	2003	0	0	..		..	..	
Somalie	2004	0	0	..		..		
	2005	0	0	..				
	2006	1426	1426	..				
South Africa Customs Un.	2003	154280	13982	62982	48844	12668	15804	
Un.douan.d'Afr.mérid	2004	156076	13891	58920	50671	14505	18090	
	2005	192434	13527	58250	86912	15017	18729	
	2006	194278	14893	59841	86912	14517	18115	
Sudan	2003	13060	12934	126	..	..	..	
Soudan	2004	13789	13663	126	..	..	..	
	2005	14017	13891	126	..	..	..	
	2006	19209	19083	126	..	..	..	
Tunisia	2003	6217	4691	1298	..	..	228	
Tunisie	2004	6133	4919	1214	..	..	0	
	2005	6346	4964	1382	..	..	0	
	2006	6308	5010	1298	..	..	0	
Zambia	2003	681	137	544	..	..	..	
Zambie	2004	723	137	586	..	..	..	
	2005	765	137	628	..	..	..	
	2006	765	137	628	..	..	..	
Zimbabwe	2003	4275	..	..	..	2483	1792	
Zimbabwe	2004	4113	..	..	..	2389	1724	
	2005	3895	..	..	..	2262	1633	
	2006	3708	..	..	..	2153	1555	
America, North	**2003**	**5327399**	**2951430**	**1828021**	**57832**	**125044**	**204460**	**160**
Amérique du Nord	**2004**	**5447083**	**3071100**	**1805170**	**51968**	**129226**	**224550**	**165**
	2005	**5285453**	**2932232**	**1799872**	**55962**	**123321**	**205746**	**168**
	2006	**5251401**	**2830981**	**1866288**	**58732**	**123423**	**201357**	**170**
Barbados	2003	43	43			..		
Barbade	2004	44	44			..		
	2005	46	46			..		
	2006	46	46			..		
Canada	2003	381465	90678	226507	..	28859	27416	8
Canada	2004	350322	89039	194598	..	30076	28572	8
	2005	375739	81023	229145	..	29504	28029	8
	2006	379378	78791	234464	..	29787	28298	8

Table 30

Production of other gases - by type
Production d'autres gaz - par catégorie
Terajoules
Térajoules

Country or area Pays ou zone	Year Année	Total Totale	L.P.G. G.P.L.	Refinery gas Gaz de raffinerie	Gasworks gas Gaz d'usines à gaz	Coke-oven gas Gaz de cokerie	Blast furnace gas Gaz de haut-fourneau	Biogas Biogaz
sta Rica	2003	755	91	..	..	..	664	..
sta Rica	2004	616	91	..	..	..	525	..
	2005	337	91	..	..	..	246	..
	2006	718	182	..	..	..	536	..
ba	2003	9174	4236	1508	3395	..	36	
ba	2004	7616	2869	1131	3448	..	168	
	2005	8669	3735	1382	3324	..	228	
	2006	7724	2824	1256	3500	..	144	
minican Republic	2003	1913	1913	0	..	..	..	..
. dominicaine	2004	1503	1503	0	..	..	..	..
	2005	1594	1594	0	..	..	..	..
	2006	1964	1503	461	..	..	..	..
Salvador	2003	1194	546	636	..	..	11	..
Salvador	2004	1314	654	650	..	..	11	..
	2005	1344	747	586	..	..	11	..
	2006	1425	785	628	..	..	11	..
naica	2003	319	319	..	..	..	..	..
naïque	2004	327	327	..	..	..	..	..
	2005	0	0	..	..	..	..	..
	2006	410	410	..	..	..	..	..
rtinique	2003	*1184	*1184	..	..	..	..	..
rtinique	2004	*1230	*1230	..	..	..	..	..
	2005	*1230	*1230	..	..	..	..	..
	2006	*1230	*1230	..	..	..	..	..
xico	2003	171628	48231	110427	..	2087	10463	420
xique	2004	164633	48094	107496	..	1430	7172	441
	2005	175112	47320	120854	..	984	5522	432
	2006	173174	46182	122027	..	965	3601	400
herlands Antilles	2003	3871	3871	..	..	..	..	..
lles néerlandaises	2004	3552	3552	..	..	..	..	..
	2005	5420	5420	..	..	..	..	..
	2006	4099	4099	..	..	..	..	..
aragua	2003	1710	956	754	..	..	..	..
aragua	2004	1696	774	921	..	..	..	..
	2005	1521	683	838	..	..	..	..
	2006	*1437	683	*754	..	..	..	..
idad and Tobago	2003	41859	33065	8794	..	..	..	..
iité-et-Tobago	2004	40753	32336	8417	..	..	..	..
	2005	40707	31243	9464	..	..	..	..
	2006	49310	35114	14196	..	..	..	..
ted States	2003	4712283	2766297	1479395	54437	94098	165870	152186
ts-Unis	2004	4873477	2890587	1491958	48520	97720	188102	156590
	2005	4673734	2759101	1437603	52638	92833	171710	159849
	2006	4630487	2659132	1492503	55232	92671	168767	162182
erica, South	**2003**	**1180981**	**682204**	**317408**	**6280**	**77794**	**97295**	**..**
érique du Sud	**2004**	**1274563**	**750432**	**339018**	**5213**	**83615**	**96285**	**..**
	2005	**1370789**	**830460**	**354698**	**5527**	**81781**	**98323**	**..**
	2006	**1386825**	**832876**	**374050**	**5500**	**79079**	**95320**	**..**
entina	2003	247539	188689	39657	..	8097	11097	..
entine	2004	262744	201805	39657	..	9009	12273	..
	2005	256044	195384	38735	..	9446	12479	..
	2006	270614	211461	37228	..	9446	12479	..

Table 30

Production of other gases - by type
Production d'autres gaz - par catégorie

Terajoules
Térajoules

Country or area Pays ou zone	Year Année	Total Totale	L.P.G. G.P.L.	Refinery gas Gaz de raffinerie	Gasworks gas Gaz d'usines à gaz	Coke-oven gas Gaz de cokerie	Blast furnace gas Gaz de haut-fourneau	Biogas Biogaz
Bolivia	2003	18879	13686	5193	..	..	..	
Bolivie	2004	20402	14665	5737	..	..	..	
	2005	21489	15166	6323	..	..	..	
	2006	23070	16077	6993	..	..	..	
Brazil	2003	540089	224714	171435	..	61550	82390	
Brésil	2004	566508	234278	186864	..	65335	80031	
	2005	606199	263244	197298	..	64249	81408	
	2006	584000	246165	197493	..	62190	78152	
Chile	2003	46674	24275	10678	5828	5893	..	
Chili	2004	53790	31015	10720	4974	7080	..	
	2005	52616	28283	12898	5527	5908	..	
	2006	60298	24138	25167	*5500	5492	..	
Colombia	2003	80261	39532	36049	..	2254	2426	
Colombie	2004	73072	31320	36995	..	2191	2566	
	2005	73587	31391	37467	..	2178	2551	
	2006	70741	31620	34597	..	1951	2572	
Ecuador	2003	10521	10521		..	..	..	
Equateur	2004	9809	9809		..	..	..	
	2005	10384	10384		..	..	..	
	2006	11022	11022		..	..	..	
Peru	2003	20433	14529	4523	..	..	1382	
Pérou	2004	22022	16168	4439	..	..	1415	
	2005	40815	33611	5318	..	..	1885	
	2006	41902	35388	4397	..	..	2117	
Uruguay	2003	4421	3006	963	452	..	..	
Uruguay	2004	6626	3917	2471	239	..	..	
	2005	7201	4145	3057	0	..	..	
	2006	5894	3507	2387	0	..	..	
Venezuela(Bolivar. Rep.)	2003	212164	163252	48911	..	..	..	
Venezuela(Rép. bolivar.)	2004	259589	207453	52136	..	..	..	
	2005	302454	248852	53601	..	..	..	
	2006	319285	253498	65787	..	..	..	
Asia	**2003**	**7393462**	**3913961**	**1211519**	**232872**	**1160514**	**863496**	**11**
Asie	**2004**	**7719356**	**4220008**	**1296933**	**205492**	**1125669**	**858971**	**12:**
	2005	**8104788**	**4323487**	**1344807**	**218582**	**1384802**	**821378**	**11**
	2006	**8423494**	**4464314**	**1402972**	**217773**	**1471214**	**854111**	**13**
Azerbaijan	2003	10719	6741	3978	..	..	..	
Azerbaïdjan	2004	13607	8289	5318	..	..	..	
	2005	14498	8426	6072	..	..	..	
	2006	15037	8881	6156	..	..	..	
Bahrain	2003	19791	9154	10637	..	..	..	
Bahreïn	2004	19886	9291	10595	..	..	..	
	2005	21068	9929	11139	..	..	..	
	2006	20596	9792	10804	..	..	..	
Bangladesh	2003	2502	911	1591	..	..	..	
Bangladesh	2004	2152	729	1424	..	..	..	
	2005	1552	547	1005	..	..	..	
	2006	1244	364	879	..	..	..	
Brunei Darussalam	2003	2899	638	2261	..	..	..	
Brunéi Darussalam	2004	2693	683	2010	..	..	..	
	2005	2777	683	2094	..	..	..	
	2006	2986	683	2303	..	..	..	

Table 30

Production of other gases - by type
Production d'autres gaz - par catégorie
Terajoules
Térajoules

Country or area Pays ou zone	Year Année	Total Totale	L.P.G. G.P.L.	Refinery gas Gaz de raffinerie	Gasworks gas Gaz d'usines à gaz	Coke-oven gas Gaz de cokerie	Blast furnace gas Gaz de haut-fourneau	Biogas Biogaz
nina hine	2003 2004 2005 2006	1679193 1765082 2078328 2334710	551857 645358 652509 794879	298199 348534 382454 411934	196931 169509 182354 181706	632206 601681 861012 946190	.. ..	.. ..
hina, Hong Kong SAR nine, Hong-Kong RAS	2003 2004 2005 2006	27002 27137 27261 27034	.. ..	.. ..	27002 27137 27261 27034	.. ..	.. ..	.. ..
yprus hypre	2003 2004 2005 2006	2155 787 0 1	1275 410 0 0	879 377 0 0	.. ..	.. ..	.. ..	0 0 0 1
eorgia éorgie	2003 2004 2005 2006	3 3 3 3	.. ..	.. ..	.. ..	.. ..	.. ..	3 3 3 3
dia de	2003 2004 2005 2006	598968 608925 619712 697817	343903 356382 351144 382934	113861 118593 126089 150921	630 593 621 649	.. ..	140574 133357 141858 163313	.. ..
donesia donésie	2003 2004 2005 2006	128574 153702 114971 90537	91407 114498 82845 58251	33794 35804 28727 28936	3373 *3400 *3400 *3350	.. ..	.. ..	.. ..
an(Islamic Rep. of) an(Rép. islamique)	2003 2004 2005 2006	181469 197675 178114 196402	170790 188825 168012 186093	.. ..	.. ..	.. ..	10679 8850 10102 10309	.. ..
aq aq	2003 2004 2005 2006	58554 63826 63832 67814	38621 42720 43312 47001	19933 21106 20519 20812	.. ..	.. ..	.. ..	.. ..
rael raël	2003 2004 2005 2006	21588 24229 25778 21451	21588 24229 25778 21451	.. ..	.. ..	.. ..	.. ..	.. ..
apan apon	2003 2004 2005 2006	1400726 1393950 1390434 1380749	206178 202580 222938 211643	327470 329606 343383 334966	.. ..	378564 372542 376806 380012	483071 483016 441357 449335	5443 6206 5950 4793
ordan ordanie	2003 2004 2005 2006	8322 7042 7217 8089	6103 5283 5374 6331	*2219 1759 1843 1759	.. ..	.. ..	.. ..	.. ..
azakhstan azakhstan	2003 2004 2005 2006	62839 84768 81984 62767	53705 68612 67328 50372	9133 16156 14657 12395	.. ..	.. ..	.. ..	.. ..
orea, Dem.Ppl's.Rep. orée,Rép.pop.dém.de	2003 2004 2005 2006	1956 2000 2111 2165	.. ..	.. ..	.. ..	.. ..	1956 2000 2111 2165	.. ..

Table 30

Production of other gases - by type
Production d'autres gaz - par catégorie
Terajoules
Térajoules

Country or area Pays ou zone	Year Année	Total Totale	L.P.G. G.P.L.	Refinery gas Gaz de raffinerie	Gasworks gas Gaz d'usines à gaz	Coke-oven gas Gaz de cokerie	Blast furnace gas Gaz de haut-fourneau	Biogas Biogaz
Korea, Republic of	2003	475530	164550	82998	..	84688	139824	34
Corée, République de	2004	461550	151479	80904	..	83860	141446	38
	2005	447219	146333	76047	..	80666	140767	34
	2006	447554	141095	78266	..	79759	142577	58
Kuwait	2003	164266	148018	16248	..	..		
Koweït	2004	176503	160087	16415	..	..		
	2005	170184	153392	16792	..	..		
	2006	184529	167192	17337	..	..		
Malaysia	2003	81598	72051	9548	..	..	..	
Malaisie	2004	66873	59336	7538	..	..	..	
	2005	119554	112475	7078	..	..	..	
	2006	127941	113997	13945	..	..	..	
Myanmar	2003	2278	729	1549	..	..	..	
Myanmar	2004	2377	911	1466	..	..	..	
	2005	2331	865	1466	..	..	..	
	2006	1837	455	1382	..	..	..	
Nepal	2003	1873	..	..	..	..	..	18
Népal	2004	1903	..	..	..	..	..	19
	2005	2078	..	..	..	..	..	20
	2006	2126	..	..	..	..	..	21
Oman	2003	5320	5320	..	..	..	..	
Oman	2004	5306	5306	..	..	..	..	
	2005	*4327	*4327	..	..	..	..	
	2006	*5374	*5374	..	..	..	..	
Other Asia	2003	198100	62805	46566	..	44135	44594	
Autre Asie	2004	211721	66768	54313	..	45779	44861	
	2005	215830	74328	55109	..	44489	41904	
	2006	212432	72552	51591	..	43088	45201	
Pakistan	2003	29587	17307	7454	..	..	4826	
Pakistan	2004	34691	18764	8082	..	..	7845	
	2005	36943	25368	8082	..	..	3493	
	2006	29773	19857	7998	..	..	1917	
Philippines	2003	30463	18081	11642	..	..	741	
Philippines	2004	21821	11978	9255	..	..	588	
	2005	24617	14665	9255	..	..	697	
	2006	25877	15166	9883	..	..	828	
Qatar	2003	8655	5556	3099	..	..	..	
Qatar	2004	9012	5830	3183	..	..	..	
	2005	9149	5966	*3183	..	..	..	
	2006	10646	6877	3769	..	..	..	
Saudi Arabia	2003	1320942	1233924	87018	..	..		
Arabie saoudite	2004	1449460	1353522	95938	..	..		
	2005	1510698	1410908	99791	..	..		
	2006	1497272	1395514	101759	..	..		
Singapore	2003	63697	39623	19137	4936	..	..	
Singapour	2004	67139	39714	22571	4853	..	..	
	2005	71457	38621	27889	4946	..	..	
	2006	60751	28875	26843	5034	..	..	
Sri Lanka	2003	2777	683	2094	..	..	..	
Sri Lanka	2004	2903	683	2219	..	..	..	
	2005	2435	592	1843	..	..	..	
	2006	2651	683	1968	..	..	..	

Table 30

Production of other gases - by type
Production d'autres gaz - par catégorie
Terajoules
Térajoules

Country or area Pays ou zone	Year Année	Total Totale	L.P.G. G.P.L.	Refinery gas Gaz de raffinerie	Gasworks gas Gaz d'usines à gaz	Coke-oven gas Gaz de cokerie	Blast furnace gas Gaz de haut-fourneau	Biogas Biogaz
rian Arab Republic p. arabe syrienne	2003	13048	13026	..	..	..	*22	..
	2004	13048	13026	..	..	..	22	..
	2005	14960	14938	..	..	..	22	..
	2006	14642	14620	..	..	..	22	..
ailand aïlande	2003	198654	156945	41122	..	..	587	..
	2004	223946	178396	44975	..	..	575	..
	2005	227309	182677	44012	..	..	620	..
	2006	229668	183633	45561	..	..	474	..
nor-Leste nor-Leste	2003	*99878	*99878	..	..	..	..	..
	2004	*100197	*100197	..	..	..	..	..
	2005	*100652	*100652	..	..	..	..	..
	2006	*100880	*100880	..	..	..	..	..
rkey rquie	2003	116498	34522	24121	..	20921	36622	312
	2004	118192	34705	24958	..	21807	36411	311
	2005	119327	34887	23869	..	21829	38447	295
	2006	122391	36800	25126	..	22165	37970	331
rkmenistan rkménistan	2003	18049	..	18049	..	..	..	..
	2004	17337	..	17337	..	..	..	..
	2005	17923	..	17923	..	..	..	..
	2006	21357	..	21357	..	..	..	..
ited Arab Emirates nirats arabes unis	2003	325076	318125	6951	..	..	..	..
	2004	337488	330285	7203	..	..	..	..
	2005	349674	342764	6910	..	..	..	..
	2006	362807	355562	7245	..	..	..	..
bekistan uzbékistan	2003	11970	2004	9966	..	..	..	..
	2004	11118	1822	9296	..	..	..	..
	2005	9037	1457	7580	..	..	..	..
	2006	8443	1366	7077	..	..	..	..
et Nam et Nam	2003	13982	13982	..	..	..	..	..
	2004	15257	15257	..	..	..	..	..
	2005	15622	15622	..	..	..	..	..
	2006	21998	21998	..	..	..	..	..
men men	2003	3962	3962	..	..	..	..	..
	2004	4053	4053	..	..	..	..	..
	2005	3826	3826	..	..	..	..	..
	2006	3143	3143	..	..	..	..	..
rope urope	**2003**	**5292261**	**1812606**	**1603851**	**26744**	**599744**	**1108011**	**141306**
	2004	**5398450**	**1892444**	**1604437**	**24497**	**609817**	**1106121**	**161134**
	2005	**5398063**	**1927149**	**1578474**	**25376**	**624578**	**1060654**	**181832**
	2006	**5661436**	**2003754**	**1600794**	**25993**	**682665**	**1145692**	**202538**
bania banie	2003	335	0	335	..	..	..	..
	2004	381	46	335	..	..	..	..
	2005	461	0	461	..	..	..	..
	2006	586	0	586	..	..	..	..
stria utriche	2003	56248	2277	12982	..	10932	28463	1594
	2004	58904	2596	13861	..	10971	29577	1899
	2005	57876	4873	12940	..	9871	28902	1290
	2006	58951	2277	16332	..	9871	28970	1501
elarus élarus	2003	25206	9838	15368	..	..	..	..
	2004	36835	19037	17797	..	..	..	..
	2005	38451	20905	17546	..	..	..	..
	2006	42684	21998	20687	..	..	..	..

Table 30

Production of other gases - by type
Production d'autres gaz - par catégorie
Terajoules
Térajoules

Country or area Pays ou zone	Year Année	Total Totale	L.P.G. G.P.L.	Refinery gas Gaz de raffinerie	Gasworks gas Gaz d'usines à gaz	Coke-oven gas Gaz de cokerie	Blast furnace gas Gaz de haut-fourneau	Biogas Biogaz
Belgium	2003	118255	28556	30067	..	21094	36381	2
Belgique	2004	110021	23273	23032	..	22393	38298	3
	2005	99260	21041	19179	..	21868	33776	3
	2006	98095	18354	20142	..	21259	34998	3
Bosnia and Herzegovina	2003	46	46	..	..	0	..	
Bosnie y Herzégovine	2004	1916	137	..	..	1779	..	
	2005	3614	91	..	..	3523	..	
	2006	3815	91	..	..	3724	..	
Bulgaria	2003	25277	3871	5193	..	6577	9636	
Bulgarie	2004	25615	4691	6407	..	6222	8295	
	2005	24394	4782	6533	..	5501	7578	
	2006	27177	5784	9087	..	4760	7546	
Croatia	2003	31340	19903	10846	591	..	..	
Croatie	2004	31704	20176	11055	473	..	..	
	2005	30384	19629	10092	556	..	..	1
	2006	27620	18172	8794	597	..	..	
Czech Republic	2003	82645	7651	5235	14555	25235	28240	17
République tchèque	2004	83884	8243	5109	14007	24997	29425	21
	2005	80913	8380	5695	14765	24502	25236	23
	2006	86675	9291	6281	15022	24842	28582	26
Denmark	2003	25231	7651	13317	685	..	..	35
Danemark	2004	24699	7469	12814	678	..	..	37
	2005	23406	6604	12353	619	..	..	38
	2006	25016	7560	12982	555	..	..	39
Estonia	2003	6011	..	..	5898	..	..	1
Estonie	2004	4565	..	..	4471	..	..	
	2005	4605	..	..	4456	..	..	1
	2006	5227	..	..	5053	..	..	1
Finland	2003	57909	12434	19054	..	8047	17541	8
Finlande	2004	59837	12160	20980	..	7704	17884	11
	2005	63356	14346	21776	..	7425	18063	17
	2006	68385	18309	22613	..	7289	18648	15
France incl. Monaco	2003	340945	139866	94053	..	35169	63350	85
France y compris Monaco	2004	335524	135676	94598	..	32831	63734	86
	2005	330531	130620	95059	..	32288	63350	92
	2006	329055	126339	94765	..	32932	65521	94
Germany	2003	586572	139182	186432	757	60878	160877	384
Allemagne	2004	595069	132897	185301	803	65035	169505	415
	2005	605495	134400	182789	787	64406	167360	557
	2006	621612	133216	177177	780	67729	172988	697
Greece	2003	54307	30606	22194	..	..	..	15
Grèce	2004	50710	27235	21901	..	..	..	15
	2005	52904	29831	21692	..	..	..	13
	2006	56833	29740	25712	..	..	..	13
Hungary	2003	36003	17853	7035	..	4416	6502	1
Hongrie	2004	35598	18582	6951	..	4337	5448	2
	2005	37787	17899	7245	..	4563	7784	2
	2006	40483	16988	7035	..	8200	7748	5
Iceland	2003	0	..	..	..	..	..	
Islande	2004	28	..	..	..	..	..	
	2005	42	..	..	..	..	..	
	2006	12	..	..	..	..	..	

Table 30

Production of other gases - by type
Production d'autres gaz - par catégorie

Terajoules
Térajoules

Country or area Pays ou zone	Year Année	Total Totale	L.P.G. G.P.L.	Refinery gas Gaz de raffinerie	Gasworks gas Gaz d'usines à gaz	Coke-oven gas Gaz de cokerie	Blast furnace gas Gaz de haut-fourneau	Biogas Biogaz
land ande	2003 2004 2005 2006	7644 7307 7841 7361	2687 2414 2596 2323	3894 3643 3811 3685	.. ..	.. ..	.. ..	1062 1250 1434 1353
ly and San Marino lie y comp. St. Marin	2003 2004 2005 2006	297647 303328 314532 321475	118870 119006 114634 103613	119933 123744 133584 146105	.. ..	15263 14347 14147 15752	32890 32878 38607 40980	10691 13353 13559 15025
tvia ttonie	2003 2004 2005 2006	159 295 341 336	.. ..	.. ..	.. ..	.. ..	.. ..	159 295 341 336
huania uanie	2003 2004 2005 2006	30694 36545 38419 32684	19812 23956 25277 21588	10804 12521 13065 11013	.. ..	.. ..	.. ..	78 68 77 83
xembourg xembourg	2003 2004 2005 2006	173 209 311 373	.. ..	.. ..	.. ..	.. ..	.. ..	173 209 311 373
etherlands ays-Bas	2003 2004 2005 2006	465409 482057 452740 425173	217700 230908 208546 185319	183878 189028 182244 181867	.. ..	19054 19379 19141 18515	39385 37457 37714 33563	5392 5285 5095 5909
orway,Svlbd.J.Myn. l orvège,Svalbd,J.May	2003 2004 2005 2006	301904 312664 322563 398501	280870 292529 301866 375966	18425 17044 17797 19221	.. ..	.. ..	1530 2068 1846 2210	1079 1023 1054 1104
land ologne	2003 2004 2005 2006	157597 159582 135373 160258	12251 11796 12934 12843	29104 30821 27806 36055	153 136 114 118	83434 81052 68830 79680	31031 33836 23446 28948	1624 1941 2243 2613
ortugal ortugal	2003 2004 2005 2006	17296 16811 18232 18876	17261 16624 17808 18491	.. ..	.. ..	.. ..	.. ..	35 187 424 385
omania oumanie	2003 2004 2005 2006	88091 98602 112682 109073	14893 16669 29968 30833	38065 44095 45310 42755	.. ..	10161 11323 12589 12503	24972 26514 24815 22981	.. ..
ussian Federation édération de Russie	2003 2004 2005 2006	1360384 1311421 1352976 1470538	390358 398965 429389 472200	533710 496942 474288 475460	.. ..	79065 82316 104753 135971	357252 333197 344547 386907	.. ..
erbia erbie	2003 2004 2005 2006	3598 4327 7168 8340	3598 4327 4053 3416	.. ..	.. ..	.. ..	0 0 3115 4924	.. ..
ovakia lovaquie	2003 2004 2005 2006	59144 63405 63341 65099	6923 9382 8243 6240	14028 16583 17253 17002	.. ..	15025 14883 14717 14842	23011 22310 22923 26698	157 247 205 318

Table 30

Production of other gases - by type
Production d'autres gaz - par catégorie

Terajoules
Térajoules

Country or area Pays ou zone	Year Année	Total Totale	L.P.G. G.P.L.	Refinery gas Gaz de raffinerie	Gasworks gas Gaz d'usines à gaz	Coke-oven gas Gaz de cokerie	Blast furnace gas Gaz de haut-fourneau	Biogas Biogaz
Slovenia	2003	240	..	..	..	..	..	
Slovénie	2004	278	..	..	..	..	..	
	2005	284	..	..	..	..	..	
	2006	353	..	..	..	..	..	
Spain	2003	177610	55154	70184	1599	22368	17562	107
Espagne	2004	178109	48186	76089	1779	21857	17845	12
	2005	179899	47821	77596	1931	21110	18172	13
	2006	201769	69318	78518	1797	21675	16460	14
Sweden	2003	61028	16396	16374	2406	8414	15950	1
Suède	2004	71656	19265	22404	2030	9745	16734	1
	2005	69586	19721	20477	2028	9340	16773	1
	2006	64752	13754	22739	1935	10079	15107	1
Switzerland	2003	18255	8107	7580	100	..	..	2
Suisse	2004	21737	8927	10260	120	..	..	24
	2005	21633	8972	10092	120	..	..	2
	2006	24273	10156	11474	136	..	..	2
T.F.Yug.Rep. Macedonia	2003	956	956	0	..	..	..	
L'ex-RY Macédoine	2004	911	911	0	..	..	..	
	2005	1177	1093	84	..	..	..	
	2006	1488	1321	168	..	..	..	
Ukraine	2003	356017	44542	14698	..	140182	156594	
Ukraine	2004	370305	44997	14992	..	145972	164344	
	2005	330126	43176	16248	..	152371	118331	
	2006	355592	42720	12688	..	157466	142717	
United Kingdom	2003	442085	182495	121064	..	34430	56844	47
Royaume-Uni	2004	503612	231364	126131	..	32674	56772	56
	2005	515360	237649	125460	..	33633	58316	60
	2006	502895	225534	119849	..	35576	59196	627
Oceania	**2003**	**235255**	**84256**	**56909**	**3330**	**27431**	**51392**	**119**
Océanie	**2004**	**217279**	**67360**	**51926**	**5099**	**29014**	**50808**	**130**
	2005	**220635**	**65791**	**51089**	**6059**	**29285**	**53268**	**151**
	2006	**232502**	**83617**	**46901**	**6568**	**29457**	**52537**	**134**
Australia	2003	198016	77152	47906	3330	27431	32000	101
Australie	2004	179793	59754	42420	5099	29014	32046	114
	2005	181730	57886	40703	6059	29285	35066	127
	2006	193272	76468	35301	6568	29457	34377	111
New Zealand	2003	37239	7105	9003	..	..	19392	17
Nouvelle-Zélande	2004	37486	7606	9506	..	..	18762	16
	2005	38105	7105	10385	..	..	18202	24
	2006	38230	6148	11600	..	..	18160	23
Papua New Guinea	2003	0	0	..	..	..	..	
Papouasie-Nvl-Guinée	2004	0	0	..	..	..	..	
	2005	800	800	..	..	..	..	
	2006	1000	1000	..	..	..	..	

Table 31

Production, trade and consumption of gases
Production, commerce et consommation de gaz

Terajoules and megajoules per capita
Térajoules et mégajoules par habitant

Table Notes
Production

Gross natural gas production minus re-injected minus flared and vented minus extraction loss shrinkage plus gasworks gas plus coke oven gas plus blast furnace gas plus biogas plus liquefied petroleum gas production by refinery and plant plus refinery gas production from refinery.

Imports

Imports of natural gas, gasworks gas and liquefied petroleum gas.

Exports

Exports of natural gas, gasworks gas and liquefied petroleum gas.

Stock change

Change in stocks of natural gas, gasworks gas, coke oven gas, liquefied petroleum gas and refinery gas.

- **Please refer to the Definitions Section on pages xv to xxix for the appropriate product description /classification.**

Notes relatives aux tableaux:
Production

Production en gros de gaz naturel moins réinjectées moins brûlées à la torchère ou éventées moins perte par extraction et réduction plus gaz d'usine à gaz plus gaz de cokerie plus gaz de haut-fourneau plus biogaz plus production de gaz de pétrole liquéfiés par raffinement, production de gaz raffiné naturellement.

Importations

Importation de gaz naturel, gaz d'usine à gaz et gaz de pétrole liquéfiés.

Exportations

Exportation de gaz naturel, gaz d'usine à gaz et gaz de pétrole liquéfiés.

Variations de stocks

Variations de stocks de gaz naturel, gaz d'usine à gaz, gaz de cokerie, gaz de pétrole liquéfies et gaz de raffinerie.

- **Veuillez consulter la section "définitions" de la page xv à la page xxix pour une description/classification appropriée des produits.**

Figure 81: World production of gases 1993-2006

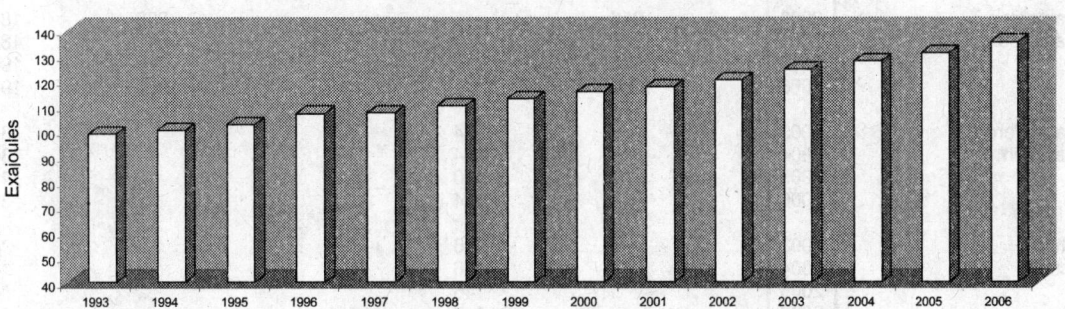

Figure 82: World gases consumption, by region, in 2006

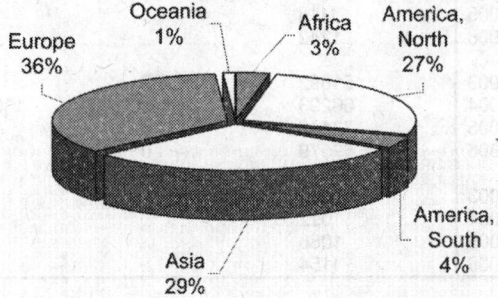

Table 31

Production, trade and consumption of gases
Production, commerce et consommation de gaz

Terajoules and megajoules per capita
Térajoules et mégajoules par habitant

Country or area Pays ou zone	Year Année	Production Production	Imports Importations	Exports Exportations	Changes in stocks Variations des stocks	Consumption Consommation	
						Total Totale	Per Capita Par habitant
World	**2003**	**124276104**	**31888926**	**31509714**	**436676**	**124218641**	**198**
Monde	**2004**	**127496685**	**33903810**	**34074044**	**475063**	**126851387**	**199**
	2005	**130821050**	**35299911**	**35874432**	**-186792**	**130433320**	**203**
	2006	**135064485**	**36355019**	**37166855**	**1392071**	**132860578**	**203**
Africa	**2003**	**6485736**	**218878**	**3272179**	**2855**	**3429580**	**40**
Afrique	**2004**	**6840146**	**287693**	**3488093**	**-2234**	**3641981**	**41**
	2005	**7985391**	**371844**	**4077063**	**-608**	**4280780**	**48**
	2006	**8684462**	**385433**	**4851431**	**-2935**	**4221399**	**46**
Algeria	2003	3701284	..	2715356	..	985928	309
Algérie	2004	3645043	..	2710846	..	934197	288
	2005	4019490	..	2682755	..	1336735	406
	2006	4250858	..	3050295	..	1200563	358
Angola	2003	28406	2004	..	..	30410	27
Angola	2004	31618	2368	..	..	33986	29
	2005	31436	3234	..	..	34669	29
	2006	33419	3370	..	..	36790	30
Benin	2003	..	455	0	-46	501	
Bénin	2004	..	455	0	-46	501	
	2005	..	638	273	-46	410	
	2006	..	638	319	46	273	
Burkina Faso	2003	..	442	..	-15	457	
Burkina Faso	2004	..	638	..	89	549	
	2005	..	706	..	120	585	
	2006	..	414	..	-339	754	
Burundi	2003	..	*91	..	..	*91	*
Burundi	2004	..	*91	..	..	*91	*
	2005	..	*91	..	..	*91	*
	2006	..	*91	..	..	*91	*
Cameroon	2003	956	..	..	-865	1822	1
Cameroun	2004	1275	..	..	-547	1822	1
	2005	1184	..	..	-774	1958	1
	2006	1002	..	..	-956	1958	1
Cape Verde	2003	..	*364	..	..	*364	*7
Cap-Vert	2004	..	*364	..	..	*364	*7
	2005	..	*410	..	..	*410	*8
	2006	..	*364	..	..	*364	*7
Chad	2003	..	*46	..	..	*46	
Tchad	2004	..	*46	..	..	*46	
	2005	..	*46	..	..	*46	
	2006	..	*46	..	..	*46	
Congo	2003	832	..	..	..	832	2
Congo	2004	997	..	..	..	997	2
	2005	1118	..	..	..	1118	3
	2006	1242	..	..	..	1242	3
Côte d'Ivoire	2003	51892	1239	0	..	53131	301
Côte d'Ivoire	2004	66293	1048	1366	..	65974	355
	2005	73142	0	0	..	73142	383
	2006	69579	0	0	..	69579	354
Dem. Rep. of Congo	2003	932	..	..	..	932	1
Rép. dem. du Congo	2004	1022	..	..	..	1022	1
	2005	1086	..	..	..	1086	1
	2006	1154	..	..	..	1154	1

Table 31

Production, trade and consumption of gases
Production, commerce et consommation de gaz
Terajoules and megajoules per capita
Térajoules et mégajoules par habitant

Country or area Pays ou zone	Year Année	Production Production	Imports Importations	Exports Exportations	Changes in stocks Variations des stocks	Consumption Consommation	
						Total Totale	Per Capita Par habitant
bouti	2003	..	1139	..	..	1139	1465
bouti	2004	..	1366	..	..	1366	1730
	2005	..	1366	..	..	1366	1699
	2006	..	1366	..	..	1366	1668
ypt	2003	1319388	61667	30666	774	1349614	20050
ypte	2004	1421855	69136	140030	-5693	1356654	19048
	2005	1990959	86033	588222	0	1488770	20807
	2006	2044182	89312	643468	-3735	1493760	20519
quatorial Guinea	2003	18773	..	..	..	18773	40634
inée équatoriale	2004	*18730	..	..	..	*18730	*39598
	2005	*18730	..	..	..	*18730	*38698
	2006	*18730	..	..	..	*18730	*37762
itrea	2003	..	182	..	0	182	44
ythrée	2004	..	228	..	0	228	52
	2005	..	228	..	0	228	50
	2006	..	91	..	-46	137	29
hiopia	2003	..	46	..	-46	91	1
hiopie	2004	..	0	..	0	0	0
	2005	..	0	..	0	0	0
	2006	..	0	..	0	0	0
abon	2003	6087	501	..	0	6588	5068
abon	2004	6159	501	..	0	6660	4882
	2005	6205	547	..	46	6706	4805
	2006	6068	683	..	0	6751	4733
ambia	2003	..	*91	..	..	*91	*61
ambie	2004	..	*91	..	..	*91	*59
	2005	..	*91	..	..	*91	*57
	2006	..	*91	..	..	*91	*55
hana	2003	4173	774	0	..	4947	235
hana	2004	4765	501	273	..	4992	230
	2005	5521	455	0	..	5976	270
	2006	2854	3097	455	..	5496	239
uinea-Bissau	2003	..	*46	..	..	*46	*36
uinée-Bissau	2004	..	*46	..	..	*46	*35
	2005	..	*46	..	..	*46	*34
	2006	..	*91	..	..	*91	*67
enya	2003	3773	865	91	..	4547	139
enya	2004	4203	865	182	..	4886	143
	2005	4283	1184	182	..	5285	150
	2006	4256	1321	182	..	5394	148
beria	2003	..	*137	..	..	*137	*39
béria	2004	..	*137	..	..	*137	*39
	2005	..	*137	..	..	*137	*38
	2006	..	*137	..	..	*137	*37
byan Arab Jamah.	2003	279513	..	40797	..	238716	38373
amah. arabe libyenne	2004	342761	..	57897	..	284864	44371
	2005	466948	..	219091	..	247857	37384
	2006	601244	..	335247	..	265997	39701
adagascar	2003	*273	*137	..	..	*410	*25
adagascar	2004	*273	*137	..	..	*410	*24
	2005	*273	*137	..	..	*410	*23
	2006	*273	*137	..	..	*410	*22

Table 31

Production, trade and consumption of gases
Production, commerce et consommation de gaz

Terajoules and megajoules per capita
Térajoules et mégajoules par habitant

Country or area Pays ou zone	Year Année	Production Production	Imports Importations	Exports Exportations	Changes in stocks Variations des stocks	Consumption Consommation	
						Total Totale	Per Capita Par habitant
Malawi	2003	..	39	..	..	39	
Malawi	2004	..	*46	..	..	*46	
	2005	..	*46	..	..	*46	
	2006	..	*91	..	..	*91	
Mauritania	2003	..	1048	..	..	1048	3
Mauritanie	2004	..	1093	..	..	1093	3
	2005	..	1321	..	..	1321	4
	2006	..	1366	..	..	1366	4
Mauritius	2003	..	2368	..	0	2368	19
Maurice	2004	..	2459	..	-46	2505	20
	2005	..	2869	..	91	2778	22
	2006	..	2687	..	-182	2869	22
Morocco	2003	8244	55518	..	-91	63853	22
Maroc	2004	11613	58661	..	46	70228	23
	2005	16642	88674	..	0	105316	34
	2006	16328	82853	..	0	99180	32
Mozambique	2003	106	501	0	..	607	
Mozambique	2004	52312	547	52189	..	670	
	2005	88029	629	85173	..	3485	1
	2006	105358	638	102061	..	3935	1
Nigeria	2003	748724	..	459901	-410	289233	22
Nigéria	2004	880113	..	496350	0	383763	29
	2005	857253	..	474667	0	382586	28
	2006	1116859	..	693076	0	423783	30
Réunion	2003	..	*1731	..	..	*1731	*22
Réunion	2004	..	*1731	..	..	*1731	*22
	2005	..	*1731	..	..	*1731	*22
	2006	..	*1731	..	..	*1731	*21
Rwanda	2003	12	..	..	..	12	
Rwanda	2004	*20	..	..	..	*20	
	2005	*23	..	..	..	*23	
	2006	*24	..	..	..	*24	
Senegal	2003	1305	4828	46	0	6087	5
Sénégal	2004	1296	5556	137	91	6625	6
	2005	1005	6057	137	-46	6971	6
	2006	818	6012	0	-46	6875	6
Seychelles	2003	..	87	..	..	87	10
Seychelles	2004	..	150	..	..	150	18
	2005	..	91	..	..	91	10
	2006	..	132	..	..	132	15
Somalia	2003	0	*246	0	..	*246	*
Somalie	2004	0	*246	0	..	*246	*
	2005	0	*246	0	..	*246	*
	2006	1426	0	*1180	..	246	
South Africa Customs Un.	2003	204498	1851	..	..	206348	40
Un.douan.d'Afr.mérid	2004	233248	54166	..	..	287414	54
	2005	275410	88134	..	..	363544	67
	2006	269807	104167	..	..	373974	69
Sudan	2003	13060	..	4691	3552	4817	1
Soudan	2004	13789	..	4964	3871	4953	1
	2005	14017	..	4919	0	9098	2
	2006	19209	..	5146	0	14062	3

Table 31

Production, trade and consumption of gases
Production, commerce et consommation de gaz
Terajoules and megajoules per capita
Térajoules et mégajoules par habitant

Country or area Pays ou zone	Year Année	Production Production	Imports Importations	Exports Exportations	Changes in stocks Variations des stocks	Consumption Consommation	
						Total Totale	Per Capita Par habitant
Togo	2003	..	91	..	..	91	18
Togo	2004	..	91	..	..	91	18
	2005	..	91	..	..	91	17
	2006	..	137	..	..	137	26
Tunisia	2003	88548	79892	20632	0	147809	15021
Tunisie	2004	92949	84430	23858	0	153521	15457
	2005	94203	86148	21644	0	158707	15825
	2006	100699	83902	*20000	2323	162278	16025
Uganda	2003	..	46	..	..	46	2
Ouganda	2004	..	*46	..	..	*46	*2
	2005	..	5	..	..	5	0
	2006	..	14	..	..	14	0
United Rep.Tanzania	2003	0	228	..	..	228	6
Rép. Unie de Tanzanie	2004	4975	273	..	..	5248	145
	2005	13774	273	..	..	14047	376
	2006	14600	273	..	..	14873	389
Zambia	2003	681	..	..	..	681	63
Zambie	2004	723	..	..	..	723	65
	2005	765	..	..	..	765	67
	2006	765	..	..	..	765	65
Zimbabwe	2003	4275	182	..	..	4457	344
Zimbabwe	2004	4113	182	..	..	4295	330
	2005	3895	182	..	..	4077	311
	2006	3708	182	..	..	3890	294
America, North	**2003**	**35803851**	**5264002**	**5155273**	**-16271**	**35928850**	**71573**
Amérique du Nord	**2004**	**35479346**	**5725629**	**5511462**	**1649**	**35691864**	**70375**
	2005	**34989919**	**5672936**	**5460410**	**-332082**	**35534527**	**69377**
	2006	**35898166**	**5574072**	**5498039**	**453435**	**35520764**	**68759**
Antigua and Barbuda	2003	..	*91	..	..	*91	*1139
Antigua-et-Barbuda	2004	..	*91	..	..	*91	*1125
	2005	..	*91	..	..	*91	*1100
	2006	..	*137	..	..	*137	*1625
Aruba	2003	..	*911	..	..	*911	*9581
Aruba	2004	..	*911	..	..	*911	*9327
	2005	..	*956	..	..	*956	*9504
	2006	..	*956	..	..	*956	*9302
Bahamas	2003	..	*820	..	..	*820	*2570
Bahamas	2004	..	*865	..	..	*865	*2887
	2005	..	*911	..	..	*911	*2820
	2006	..	*956	..	..	*956	*2925
Barbados	2003	1063	499	..	..	1562	5751
Barbade	2004	1017	513	..	..	1530	5616
	2005	1073	533	..	..	1607	5885
	2006	1094	544	..	..	1638	5978
Belize	2003	..	*774	..	..	*774	*2829
Belize	2004	..	*820	..	..	*820	*2901
	2005	..	*865	..	..	*865	*2966
	2006	..	*865	..	..	*865	*2843
Bermuda	2003	..	*547	..	..	*547	*8669
Bermudes	2004	..	*547	..	..	*547	*8631
	2005	..	*592	..	..	*592	*9314
	2006	..	*592	..	..	*592	*9281

Table 31

Production, trade and consumption of gases
Production, commerce et consommation de gaz

Terajoules and megajoules per capita
Térajoules et mégajoules par habitant

Country or area Pays ou zone	Year Année	Production Production	Imports Importations	Exports Exportations	Changes in stocks Variations des stocks	Consumption Consommation	
						Total Totale	Per Capita Par habitant
Canada	2003	7413629	369794	3890859	-183243	4075808	1286
Canada	2004	7367004	414979	4033792	-219850	3968041	1240
	2005	7544851	364396	4079054	-282825	4113018	1272
	2006	7585740	369342	3919716	-30243	4065609	1245
Cayman Islands	2003	..	*182	..	..	*182	*41
Iles Caïmanes	2004	..	*182	..	..	*182	*41
	2005	..	*182	..	..	*182	*37
	2006	..	*182	..	..	*182	*35
Costa Rica	2003	755	4053	..	46	4763	11
Costa Rica	2004	616	4509	..	91	5034	12
	2005	337	4236	..	0	4573	10
	2006	718	4600	..	46	5273	12
Cuba	2003	34849	3234	..	..	38083	33
Cuba	2004	35086	5101	..	..	40187	35
	2005	37661	4782	..	..	42443	37
	2006	50061	4691	..	..	54752	48
Dominica	2003	..	91	..	..	91	13
Dominique	2004	..	91	..	..	91	13
	2005	..	*91	..	..	*91	*13
	2006	..	*91	..	..	*91	*13
Dominican Republic	2003	1913	25623	..	0	27535	307
Rép. dominicaine	2004	1503	30468	..	0	31971	35
	2005	1594	39670	..	0	41264	44
	2006	1964	44221	..	-46	46230	49
El Salvador	2003	1194	7823	133	-127	9011	13
El Salvador	2004	1314	7728	552	69	8422	12
	2005	1344	10050	2533	-226	9087	13
	2006	1425	9888	1784	-650	10178	14
Grenada	2003	..	410	..	..	410	39
Grenade	2004	..	274	..	..	274	26
	2005	..	273	..	..	273	26
	2006	..	298	..	..	298	28
Guadeloupe	2003	..	*1093	..	..	*1093	*249
Guadeloupe	2004	..	*1139	..	..	*1139	*25
	2005	..	*1184	..	..	*1184	*265
	2006	..	*1230	..	..	*1230	*26
Guatemala	2003	..	10065	0	0	10065	8
Guatemala	2004	..	11015	0	-137	11152	90
	2005	..	13525	130	2442	10953	8
	2006	..	13829	2657	339	10832	8
Haiti	2003	..	586	..	..	586	
Haïti	2004	..	601	..	..	601	
	2005	..	592	..	..	592	
	2006	..	592	..	..	592	
Honduras	2003	..	3234	774	46	2414	3
Honduras	2004	..	3416	1048	0	2368	33
	2005	..	3915	955	-169	3129	4
	2006	..	4782	1594	0	3188	4
Jamaica	2003	319	3143	..	46	3416	128
Jamaïque	2004	327	2995	..	0	3322	124
	2005	0	3416	..	-46	3461	130
	2006	410	3325	..	46	3689	13

Table 31

Production, trade and consumption of gases
Production, commerce et consommation de gaz

Terajoules and megajoules per capita
Térajoules et mégajoules par habitant

Country or area Pays ou zone	Year Année	Production Production	Imports Importations	Exports Exportations	Changes in stocks Variations des stocks	Consumption Consommation	
						Total Totale	Per Capita Par habitant
Martinique	2003	*1184	*91	*455	..	*820	*2099
Martinique	2004	*1230	*91	*455	..	*865	*2198
	2005	*1230	*91	*455	..	*865	*2177
	2006	*1230	*91	*455	..	*865	*2163
Mexico	2003	1751152	502350	410	1720	2251373	22072
Mexique	2004	1815923	562952	364	50179	2328332	22605
	2005	1891885	459038	12382	727	2337814	22490
	2006	2058789	507991	16609	-3836	2554007	24353
Netherlands Antilles	2003	3871	1002	2232	..	2642	14784
Antilles néerlandaises	2004	3552	1002	1913	..	2642	14426
	2005	5420	1002	3780	..	2642	14250
	2006	4099	1002	2459	..	2642	13940
Nicaragua	2003	1710	1548	..	..	3259	613
Nicaragua	2004	1696	1776	..	..	3472	645
	2005	1521	1913	..	..	3434	629
	2006	*1437	1958	..	..	3395	614
Panama	2003	..	5830	..	0	5830	1871
Panama	2004	..	7105	..	2277	4828	1522
	2005	..	5283	..	0	5283	1637
	2006	..	7241	..	0	7241	2205
Puerto Rico	2003	..	28728	..	..	28728	7407
Porto Rico	2004	..	26518	..	..	26518	6808
	2005	..	26518	..	..	26518	6779
	2006	..	26518	..	..	26518	6751
St. Lucia	2003	..	*396	..	..	*396	*2466
St-Lucie	2004	..	*414	..	..	*414	*2552
	2005	..	*410	..	..	*410	*2487
	2006	..	*455	..	..	*455	*2730
St. Vincent-Grenadines	2003	..	*273	..	..	*273	*2599
St. Vincent-Grenadines	2004	..	*273	..	..	*273	*2614
	2005	..	*273	..	..	*273	*2634
	2006	..	*319	..	..	*319	*3080
Trinidad and Tobago	2003	1013623	..	536901	..	476722	362526
Trinité-et-Tobago	2004	1064938	..	563571	..	501368	380112
	2005	1107908	..	584505	..	523403	395319
	2006	1374764	..	781438	..	593326	446782
United States	2003	25578588	4290811	723510	165243	28980646	99641
États-Unis	2004	25185140	4639252	909767	169020	28745605	97900
	2005	24395095	4728147	776615	-51985	28398612	95808
	2006	24816436	4567374	771326	487779	28124705	94238
America, South	**2003**	**4925333**	**561821**	**623868**	**10053**	**4853234**	**13396**
Amérique du Sud	**2004**	**5206710**	**708881**	**760818**	**12040**	**5142734**	**14005**
	2005	**5440885**	**751291**	**873529**	**16303**	**5302344**	**14247**
	2006	**5660445**	**783132**	**846646**	**4951**	**5591980**	**14826**
Argentina	2003	1911648	3539	349928	-1048	1566306	41360
Argentine	2004	1976041	31309	366423	-547	1641473	42941
	2005	1941352	62704	346572	319	1657165	42940
	2006	2035559	63575	305430	0	1793704	46027
Bolivia	2003	274604	..	168601	0	106004	11746
Bolivie	2004	376022	..	291237	0	84785	9189
	2005	463958	..	405496	0	58462	6201
	2006	496662	..	419707	-364	77320	8031

Table 31

Production, trade and consumption of gases
Production, commerce et consommation de gaz

Terajoules and megajoules per capita
Térajoules et mégajoules par habitant

Country or area Pays ou zone	Year Année	Production Production	Imports Importations	Exports Exportations	Changes in stocks Variations des stocks	Consumption Consommation	
						Total Totale	Per Capita Par habitant
Brazil	2003	937616	245914	3234	-3598	1183894	6614
Brésil	2004	986538	363299	3234	-3598	1350202	7436
	2005	1035294	371731	3735	-273	1403564	7620
	2006	1018855	418095	820	-319	1436449	7691
Chile	2003	120355	265331	5420	12990	367276	23057
Chili	2004	121407	265541	7469	15006	364472	22641
	2005	134870	273471	5283	14357	388701	23851
	2006	139084	257651	5693	6376	384666	23409
Colombia	2003	338023	0	3552	1480	332991	7473
Colombie	2004	344418	46	547	1412	342505	7560
	2005	358307	80	451	626	357310	7760
	2006	392439	0	590	625	391224	8364
Ecuador	2003	26755	25322	..	0	52077	4055
Equateur	2004	34918	29028	..	-1372	65318	5015
	2005	30795	31334	..	0	62130	470
	2006	44302	32974	..	0	77276	5763
French Guiana	2003	..	*91	..	..	*91	*503
Guyane française	2004	..	*91	..	..	*91	*479
	2005	..	*91	..	..	*91	*466
	2006	..	*91	..	..	*91	*462
Guyana	2003	..	420	..	..	420	551
Guyana	2004	..	428	..	..	428	56
	2005	..	442	..	..	442	58
	2006	..	444	..	..	444	58
Paraguay	2003	..	3294	..	..	3294	58
Paraguay	2004	..	3599	..	..	3599	62
	2005	..	3737	..	..	3737	63
	2006	..	3737	..	..	3737	62
Peru	2003	46235	13344	0	592	58987	219
Pérou	2004	62343	10521	1913	1139	69812	257
	2005	108823	2824	4554	1958	105134	386
	2006	119728	364	1139	1594	117359	428
Suriname	2003	..	984	..	..	984	204
Suriname	2004	..	1002	..	..	1002	203
	2005	..	1048	..	..	1048	209
	2006	..	1093	..	..	1093	216
Uruguay	2003	4421	3582	0	0	8003	234
Uruguay	2004	6626	4018	91	0	10553	319
	2005	7201	3830	273	-91	10849	328
	2006	5894	5107	228	-46	10818	326
Venezuela(Bolivar. Rep.)	2003	1265674	..	93133	-364	1172906	4568
Venezuela(Rép. bolivar.)	2004	1298397	..	89904	0	1208494	4625
	2005	1360285	..	107165	-592	1253712	4717
	2006	1407923	..	113040	-2915	1297798	4801
Asia	**2003**	**33405914**	**8407506**	**8644224**	**28691**	**33140505**	**871**
Asie	**2004**	**35388628**	**8970874**	**9639336**	**46965**	**34673201**	**902**
	2005	**37768145**	**9279740**	**10164896**	**-24689**	**36907678**	**950**
	2006	**39645186**	**9951565**	**10386683**	**63407**	**39146661**	**993**
Afghanistan	2003	242	..	..	..	242	1
Afghanistan	2004	119	..	..	..	119	*
	2005	*100	..	..	..	*100	*
	2006	*100	..	..	..	*100	*

Table 31

Production, trade and consumption of gases
Production, commerce et consommation de gaz

Terajoules and megajoules per capita
Térajoules et mégajoules par habitant

Country or area Pays ou zone	Year Année	Production Production	Imports Importations	Exports Exportations	Changes in stocks Variations des stocks	Consumption Consommation	
						Total Totale	Per Capita Par habitant
rmenia	2003	..	45324	0	..	45324	11930
rménie	2004	..	50828	490	..	50338	15662
	2005	..	64436	1244	..	63192	19650
	2006	..	65376	829	..	64547	20039
zerbaijan	2003	204045	153915	455	361	357143	43374
zerbaïdjan	2004	208512	187218	683	3551	391496	47131
	2005	230594	178549	1093	16084	391966	46708
	2006	270110	172898	4631	9411	428966	50559
ahrain	2003	283570	..	7515	91	275964	400285
ahreïn	2004	294216	..	7424	228	286564	405232
	2005	311658	..	7697	501	303460	418770
	2006	328477	..	7469	547	320461	431562
angladesh	2003	437351	..	..	..	437351	3244
angladesh	2004	469875	..	..	..	469875	3437
	2005	504381	..	..	..	504381	3639
	2006	544340	..	..	..	544340	3839
hutan	2003	..	*182	..	..	*182	*297
houtan	2004	..	*182	..	..	*182	*292
	2005	..	*182	..	..	*182	*287
	2006	..	*182	..	..	*182	*282
runei Darussalam	2003	485389	..	423510	..	61879	176999
runéi Darussalam	2004	480011	..	411413	..	68598	190710
	2005	471395	..	401876	..	69519	187838
	2006	495572	..	426723	..	68849	179763
ambodia	2003	..	8972	..	..	8972	682
ambodge	2004	..	10384	..	..	10384	775
	2005	..	10612	..	..	10612	777
	2006	..	13435	..	..	13435	946
hina	2003	3364193	289979	58646	4509	3591016	2787
hine	2004	3309882	291937	92371	1685	3507763	2706
	2005	3976501	281006	111855	-2368	4148021	3182
	2006	4330207	243934	111317	592	4462231	3396
hina, Hong Kong SAR	2003	27002	72665	91	-1698	101274	14871
hine, Hong-Kong RAS	2004	27137	98500	91	-2598	128144	18890
	2005	27261	101333	0	-2408	131002	19228
	2006	27034	111112	0	1280	136867	19951
hina, Macao SAR	2003	..	1230	..	-46	1275	2843
hine, Macao RAS	2004	..	1366	..	46	1321	2838
	2005	..	1366	..	0	1366	2799
	2006	..	1503	..	46	1457	2903
yprus	2003	2155	1275	..	46	3384	4697
hypre	2004	787	2049	..	46	2791	3786
	2005	0	2232	..	-91	2323	3064
	2006	1	2459	..	46	2415	3132
eorgia	2003	715	36581	683	..	36613	8458
éorgie	2004	464	42896	638	..	42722	9893
	2005	519	51308	638	..	51190	11737
	2006	652	65427	638	..	65441	14880
dia	2003	1615113	76195	0	..	1691309	1583
de	2004	1616876	102019	6604	..	1712291	1586
	2005	1645067	123834	2414	..	1766487	1614
	2006	1702881	104205	3917	..	1803169	1613

Table 31

Production, trade and consumption of gases
Production, commerce et consommation de gaz

Terajoules and megajoules per capita
Térajoules et mégajoules par habitant

Country or area Pays ou zone	Year Année	Production Production	Imports Importations	Exports Exportations	Changes in stocks Variations des stocks	Consumption Consommation	
						Total Totale	Per Capita Par habitant
Indonesia	2003	2969303	0	1610661	0	1358641	634
Indonésie	2004	3095885	91	1594124	*11386	1490466	686
	2005	2994721	1002	1542306	0	1453417	660
	2006	2978091	3143	1443411	0	1537823	692
Iran(Islamic Rep. of)	2003	3260604	240260	205416	-5511	3300958	4966
Iran(Rép. islamique)	2004	3621490	246227	214290	0	3653428	5414
	2005	3888047	216186	244192	0	3860041	5637
	2006	4271590	256886	305910	0	4222566	5989
Iraq	2003	117834	16441	..	0	134275	509
Iraq	2004	162625	29968	..	5875	186718	688
	2005	164531	30560	..	5739	189353	688
	2006	200812	25459	..	5830	220442	765
Israel	2003	21909	4919	4145	..	22683	339
Israël	2004	67814	3325	5101	..	66038	969
	2005	85766	3552	5420	..	83899	1210
	2006	105266	7196	5511	..	106951	1517
Japan	2003	1521484	3832048	2459	-5014	5356086	4242
Japon	2004	1519306	3799834	2778	-3233	5319595	4213
	2005	1525046	3796372	228	18935	5302256	4200
	2006	1529234	4094369	137	-6424	5629891	4462
Jordan	2003	18224	7925	..	-137	26286	502
Jordanie	2004	17140	53703	..	137	70707	1385
	2005	15532	64189	..	-91	79812	1458
	2006	15843	85329	..	-273	101446	1811
Kazakhstan	2003	710537	339680	459366	0	590850	3963
Kazakhstan	2004	947299	454893	714620	0	687571	4579
	2005	1056555	438441	649656	-91	845432	5581
	2006	1092325	431944	624569	547	899153	5873
Korea, Dem.Ppl's.Rep.	2003	1956	..	..	..	1956	8
Corée,Rép.pop.dém.de	2004	2000	..	..	..	2000	8
	2005	2111	..	..	..	2111	8
	2006	2165	..	..	..	2165	9
Korea, Republic of	2003	475530	1255343	11340	34040	1685493	3522
Corée, République de	2004	461550	1392957	3780	32213	1818514	3782
	2005	467714	1409407	2824	-43281	1917578	3970
	2006	469185	1587318	3006	58692	1994805	4130
Kuwait	2003	594216	..	138408	..	455808	19600
Koweït	2004	639276	..	153711	..	485565	20311
	2005	689098	..	144784	..	544314	22151
	2006	733333	..	162137	..	571196	22613
Kyrgyzstan	2003	1054	27834	..	..	28888	573
Kirghizistan	2004	1132	30017	..	..	31149	611
	2005	975	27747	..	..	28722	558
	2006	741	29265	..	..	30006	577
Lao People's Dem. Rep.	2003	..	*820	..	..	*820	*14
Rép. dém. pop. lao	2004	..	*820	..	..	*820	*14
	2005	..	*820	..	..	*820	*14
	2006	..	*820	..	..	*820	*14
Lebanon	2003	..	9337	..	..	9337	238
Liban	2004	..	10020	..	..	10020	252
	2005	..	7560	..	..	7560	188
	2006	..	7333	..	..	7333	180

Table 31

Production, trade and consumption of gases
Production, commerce et consommation de gaz

Terajoules and megajoules per capita
Térajoules et mégajoules par habitant

Country or area Pays ou zone	Year Année	Production Production	Imports Importations	Exports Exportations	Changes in stocks Variations des stocks	Consumption Consommation	
						Total Totale	Per Capita Par habitant
Malaysia	2003	2161554	57893	884036	-501	1335912	53333
Malaisie	2004	2247735	43144	1019229	2301	1269349	49621
	2005	2521714	76109	1230336	-586	1368073	52361
	2006	2736643	80277	1242651	0	1574269	59094
Myanmar	2003	309171	..	244747	91	64333	1209
Myanmar	2004	422237	..	348831	0	73406	1352
	2005	441098	..	358856	0	82242	1487
	2006	455961	..	371416	-228	84773	1505
Nepal	2003	1873	2915	..	..	4788	197
Népal	2004	1903	3552	..	..	5455	220
	2005	2078	4053	..	..	6131	242
	2006	2126	4145	..	..	6271	242
Occup. Palestinian Terr.	2003	..	4053	..	..	4053	1153
Terr. palestiniens occup.	2004	..	4737	..	..	4737	1302
	2005	..	*5488	..	..	*5488	*1459
	2006	..	*5693	..	..	*5693	*1464
Oman	2003	696873	0	354939	0	341934	146075
Oman	2004	711455	27	393252	0	318230	131741
	2005	744472	0	413612	46	330814	131860
	2006	944235	0	503996	91	440148	170799
Other Asia	2003	229061	339274	16532	51	551752	24411
Autre Asie	2004	244095	412818	16760	-7331	647483	28537
	2005	236230	429995	16669	6480	643075	28292
	2006	229683	469904	14255	-11923	697255	30595
Pakistan	2003	1053556	1594	..	-258	1055408	7231
Pakistan	2004	1150604	1822	..	-308	1152734	7751
	2005	1208049	1139	..	-101	1209289	7880
	2006	1211757	3006	..	-147	1214909	7750
Philippines	2003	131609	25505	364	182	156568	1931
Philippines	2004	118564	33839	0	182	152221	1841
	2005	152183	29103	0	-26871	208156	2442
	2006	141750	28328	0	-228	170306	1958
Qatar	2003	1233915	..	740121	..	493794	673444
Qatar	2004	1537465	..	947540	..	589925	759296
	2005	1796311	..	1034260	..	762051	937514
	2006	1942185	..	1186537	..	755648	807069
Saudi Arabia	2003	3311642	..	810592	..	2501050	113586
Arabie saoudite	2004	3612140	..	852766	..	2759374	122292
	2005	3887468	..	884100	..	3003368	129909
	2006	3992516	..	868706	..	3123810	131924
Singapore	2003	63697	208813	31061	..	241449	57679
Singapour	2004	67139	246193	32154	..	281177	66342
	2005	71457	276350	25459	..	322347	74243
	2006	60751	280288	14437	..	326602	72839
Sri Lanka	2003	2777	6422	..	..	9199	478
Sri Lanka	2004	2903	6604	..	..	9506	488
	2005	2435	6832	..	..	9266	471
	2006	2651	7196	..	..	9847	495
Syrian Arab Republic	2003	271293	9883	..	..	281176	16021
Rép. arabe syrienne	2004	280718	9883	..	..	290601	16297
	2005	244930	9291	..	..	254221	13915
	2006	252152	7879	..	..	260031	13893

Table 31

Production, trade and consumption of gases
Production, commerce et consommation de gaz

Terajoules and megajoules per capita
Térajoules et mégajoules par habitant

Country or area Pays ou zone	Year Année	Production Production	Imports Importations	Exports Exportations	Changes in stocks Variations des stocks	Consumption Consommation	
						Total Totale	Per Capita Par habitant
Tajikistan	2003	1254	20368	..	..	21622	328
Tadjikistan	2004	1368	21010	..	..	22378	333
	2005	1113	21670	..	..	22783	332
	2006	760	22303	..	..	23063	323
Thailand	2003	905930	293327	36207	774	1162275	1815
Thaïlande	2004	925103	315961	47320	3917	1189827	1854
	2005	981017	344825	44588	638	1280616	1975
	2006	991289	355208	27099	5465	1313934	2012
Timor-Leste	2003	*99878	..	*99878	..	0	
Timor-Leste	2004	*100197	..	*100197	..	0	
	2005	*100652	..	*100652	..	0	
	2006	*100880	..	*100880	..	0	
Turkey	2003	137946	944633	13527	1711	1067342	1519
Turquie	2004	144542	996911	10202	-1131	1132382	1591
	2005	153682	1195024	11887	2779	1334041	1851
	2006	157053	1298830	3006	85	1452792	1990
Turkmenistan	2003	2259562	3644	1644383	..	618822	13172
Turkménistan	2004	2252788	3644	1701216	..	555215	11649
	2005	2404930	3644	1816553	..	592020	12248
	2006	2417836	3644	1823761	..	597718	12200
United Arab Emirates	2003	2071886	..	559447	..	1512440	42591
Emirats arabes unis	2004	2142798	..	582974	..	1559824	41473
	2005	2165124	..	580781	..	1584343	38582
	2006	2209457	..	589918	..	1619538	38296
Uzbekistan	2003	2206075	54643	282322	..	1978396	7659
Ouzbékistan	2004	2247509	48106	375453	..	1920162	7326
	2005	2287714	41568	468584	..	1860698	6996
	2006	2379325	41568	478031	..	1942862	7200
Viet Nam	2003	139975	13618	0	..	153593	189
Viet Nam	2004	229920	13390	0	..	243310	296
	2005	304093	23956	59829	..	268220	322
	2006	315074	33703	60784	..	287992	342
Yemen	2003	3962	..	3370	..	592	3
Yémen	2004	4053	..	3325	..	729	3
	2005	3826	..	2505	..	1321	6
	2006	3143	..	1002	..	2141	10
Europe	**2003**	**41778426**	**17427294**	**13387292**	**409885**	**45408544**	**6244**
Europe	**2004**	**42710756**	**18189888**	**14243130**	**417446**	**46240068**	**6352**
	2005	**42608946**	**19208995**	**14721845**	**152701**	**46943395**	**6437**
	2006	**43066753**	**19587000**	**14904054**	**872306**	**46877392**	**6420**
Albania	2003	879	1822	..	..	2701	76
Albanie	2004	1017	2049	..	..	3066	98
	2005	1131	2596	..	..	3727	118
	2006	1256	3188	..	..	4444	141
Austria	2003	138851	323523	40977	7935	413462	5125
Autriche	2004	136454	337364	52621	2340	418856	5145
	2005	119957	384007	39827	19898	444239	5413
	2006	131707	416779	106399	30195	411892	4973
Belarus	2003	35016	703431	3188	-3128	738387	7478
Bélarus	2004	46777	760018	8152	-2851	801494	8158
	2005	47257	777257	12069	-3644	816089	8348
	2006	51142	804331	14984	6437	834053	8569

Table 31

Production, trade and consumption of gases
Production, commerce et consommation de gaz

Terajoules and megajoules per capita
Térajoules et mégajoules par habitant

Country or area Pays ou zone	Year Année	Production Production	Imports Importations	Exports Exportations	Changes in stocks Variations des stocks	Consumption Consommation	
						Total Totale	Per Capita Par habitant
Belgium	2003	118255	668557	15940	-7481	778353	75161
Belgique	2004	110021	685852	16806	-597	779664	74994
	2005	99260	669497	16988	3715	748053	71612
	2006	98095	710781	16988	1512	790375	75192
Bosnia and Herzegovina	2003	46	8467	46	..	8467	2209
Bosnie y Herzégovine	2004	1916	12657	0	..	14572	3792
	2005	3614	15333	0	..	18947	4931
	2006	3815	16055	0	..	19870	5171
Bulgaria	2003	25874	121799	0	-6182	153854	19666
Bulgarie	2004	38047	121741	46	7784	151958	19529
	2005	42278	127366	0	1915	167729	21671
	2006	44568	134107	228	3901	174547	22671
Croatia	2003	114545	43593	25020	3876	129242	29095
Croatie	2004	115232	40401	24549	-3997	135081	30428
	2005	117153	43233	27309	2455	130621	29407
	2006	130733	42898	41867	2577	129188	29096
Czech Republic	2003	88743	365283	4069	-558	450515	44161
République tchèque	2004	91439	339726	6426	-24671	449411	44030
	2005	88083	359510	7547	-825	440871	43079
	2006	93528	378181	10368	22693	438649	42640
Denmark	2003	360293	137	125429	-2491	237492	44945
Danemark	2004	419732	182	176003	7657	236254	43741
	2005	459926	137	237047	-1180	224196	41395
	2006	458734	182	222729	4639	231548	42607
Estonia	2003	6011	31908	..	..	37919	28015
Estonie	2004	4565	36351	..	..	40916	30324
	2005	4605	37474	..	..	42079	31260
	2006	5227	37914	..	..	43141	32110
Finland	2003	57909	200616	182	1093	257250	49348
Finlande	2004	59837	192706	91	-1275	253727	48531
	2005	63356	177355	0	2550	238161	45398
	2006	68385	187686	0	-638	256708	48746
France incl. Monaco	2003	400566	1864266	116915	-23468	2171384	36077
France y compris Monaco	2004	387054	1952579	127226	-18144	2230552	36836
	2005	372806	2038210	117987	26147	2266881	37220
	2006	378297	1982606	106609	40984	2213310	36242
Germany	2003	1327187	3216886	309139	-35818	4270752	51754
Allemagne	2004	1280411	3418459	351717	87517	4259636	51631
	2005	1267216	3452726	390632	-41942	4371252	53008
	2006	1275308	3554847	454776	46308	4329071	52559
Greece	2003	55749	93502	12479	137	136635	12395
Grèce	2004	52047	101763	9428	-1311	145694	13171
	2005	53755	108996	11796	-187	151142	13612
	2006	58042	127606	10748	102	174798	15679
Hungary	2003	142332	464855	6376	15832	584980	57750
Hongrie	2004	145698	435899	8699	-3272	576170	57006
	2005	146209	461527	1958	2238	603540	59833
	2006	151143	447613	10448	15968	572341	56828
Iceland	2003	0	91	..	0	91	315
Islande	2004	28	91	..	0	119	407
	2005	42	91	..	0	133	450
	2006	12	46	..	-46	103	339

Table 31

Production, trade and consumption of gases
Production, commerce et consommation de gaz

Terajoules and megajoules per capita
Térajoules et mégajoules par habitant

Country or area Pays ou zone	Year Année	Production Production	Imports Importations	Exports Exportations	Changes in stocks Variations des stocks	Consumption Consommation	
						Total Totale	Per Capita Par habitant
Ireland	2003	32937	150414	956	1145	181250	4555
Irlande	2004	39332	142784	911	143	181062	4477
	2005	29278	145427	911	174	173620	4203
	2006	26468	172955	774	464	198185	4679
Italy and San Marino	2003	826664	2469423	35967	-57246	3317366	5758
Italie y comp. St. Marin	2004	797141	2660165	41238	-4143	3420212	5879
	2005	774437	2877162	42278	-41004	3650324	6228
	2006	739776	3023777	38515	134707	3590331	6091
Latvia	2003	159	67999	228	2728	65202	2804
Lettonie	2004	295	83840	364	18988	64783	2801
	2005	341	69944	683	3541	66060	2871
	2006	336	74317	729	5465	68459	2992
Lithuania	2003	30694	112919	9974	174	133465	3863
Lituanie	2004	36545	112225	12206	-223	136787	3981
	2005	38419	119000	11386	562	145472	4260
	2006	32684	119453	10020	1282	140835	4149
Luxembourg	2003	173	50501	319	..	50355	11149
Luxembourg	2004	209	56705	319	..	56595	12354
	2005	311	55603	228	..	55687	11971
	2006	373	58042	182	..	58232	12320
Malta	2003	..	774	..	..	774	193
Malte	2004	..	774	..	..	774	192
	2005	..	820	..	..	820	202
	2006	..	911	..	..	911	224
Netherlands	2003	2894314	925185	1698580	-464	2121383	13100
Pays-Bas	2004	3346981	722810	1893500	-60	2176351	13386
	2005	3070209	863154	1838290	-1661	2096734	12847
	2006	3004038	949013	1938731	-618	2014938	12330
Norway,Svlbd.J.Myn. l	2003	3384763	12934	3039907	3598	354193	7733
Norvège,Svalbd,J.May	2004	3588556	6513	3268603	-319	326785	7090
	2005	3871134	11249	3548263	364	333756	7189
	2006	4046350	10839	3680731	1002	375456	8056
Poland	2003	325594	431630	2314	-6054	760964	1992
Pologne	2004	342280	470054	2391	7819	802124	2100
	2005	316073	496011	2806	8886	800392	2097
	2006	340772	514475	3339	19256	832652	2183
Portugal	2003	17296	150978	2733	647	164894	1579
Portugal	2004	16811	182198	3143	-444	196310	1869
	2005	18232	206789	4281	6347	214393	2032
	2006	18876	195161	3826	1436	208776	1972
Republic of Moldova	2003	..	106209	46	-22	106186	2939
Rép. de Moldova	2004	..	109109	46	51	109012	3024
	2005	..	116717	46	51	116620	3240
	2006	..	107830	0	310	107520	2999
Romania	2003	573226	200060	1958	-2746	774074	3560
Roumanie	2004	581361	194457	2141	25664	748013	3453
	2005	563987	197577	3416	-2756	760903	3518
	2006	553729	225704	5055	-11967	786344	3640
Russian Federation	2003	24612495	329046	7166284	528560	17246697	11934
Fédération de Russie	2004	25004754	259299	7575407	294281	17394365	12091
	2005	25349949	288623	7839219	230407	17568945	12271
	2006	25934192	270972	7678186	424974	18102004	12701

Table 31

Production, trade and consumption of gases
Production, commerce et consommation de gaz
Terajoules and megajoules per capita
Térajoules et mégajoules par habitant

Country or area Pays ou zone	Year Année	Production Production	Imports Importations	Exports Exportations	Changes in stocks Variations des stocks	Consumption Consommation	
						Total Totale	Per Capita Par habitant
rbia rbie	2003	17321	70955	137	..	88139	8328
	2004	16278	98461	46	..	114693	10906
	2005	17799	82790	46	..	100544	9602
	2006	19310	85918	46	..	105182	10063
ovakia ovaquie	2003	66889	258809	288	53	325357	60487
	2004	70008	266762	39	14762	321969	59817
	2005	69217	284552	14643	-1019	340145	63139
	2006	73286	267710	23131	-419	318284	59038
ovenia ovénie	2003	439	45990	0	0	46429	23273
	2004	479	45525	0	137	45867	22975
	2005	444	47012	0	-91	47547	23760
	2006	513	46091	228	410	45966	22886
ain pagne	2003	186759	1030072	6513	474	1209845	28803
	2004	192507	1194983	11022	-10840	1387309	32496
	2005	186593	1453884	10384	25915	1604179	36964
	2006	204314	1503269	12843	20736	1674004	37987
veden ède	2003	61028	91102	18445	3097	130588	14577
	2004	71656	87506	19311	-1822	141673	15753
	2005	69586	92030	18172	46	143398	15881
	2006	64752	104877	14847	3006	151775	16714
vitzerland isse	2003	18255	124105	1002	46	141313	19250
	2004	21737	128154	1139	46	148708	19958
	2005	21633	131783	2232	-46	151230	20274
	2006	24273	128064	2550	46	149741	20008
.Yug.Rep. Macedonia x-RY Macédoine	2003	956	4038	228	-8	4775	2356
	2004	911	3773	137	-41	4587	2260
	2005	1177	4136	182	32	5099	2503
	2006	1488	4502	273	-33	5750	2818
raine raine	2003	1104811	2358070	88652	0	3374229	70571
	2004	1169435	2424755	171603	273	3422314	72397
	2005	1141274	2349577	115843	-82433	3457441	73445
	2006	1178524	1961855	7033	72538	3060807	65463
ited Kingdom yaume-Uni	2003	4751397	327344	653004	-13843	4439580	74830
	2004	4523206	501197	457804	23994	4542604	76091
	2005	4182205	659841	405376	-5754	4442425	73783
	2006	3852706	916443	486869	25079	4257201	70266
ceania **éanie**	**2003**	**1876845**	**9425**	**426878**	**1463**	**1457928**	**44988**
	2004	**1871098**	**20845**	**431205**	**-803**	**1461541**	**44450**
	2005	**2027765**	**15104**	**576688**	**1583**	**1464598**	**43904**
	2006	**2109473**	**73818**	**680001**	**907**	**1502383**	**44354**
stralia stralie	2003	1654604	6968	425739	1412	1234421	62023
	2004	1668492	18263	430522	-911	1257144	62421
	2005	1830165	12570	576096	1594	1265045	61984
	2006	1906862	70178	679728	1002	1296310	62619
ji	2003	..	592	..	..	592	715
	2004	..	638	..	..	638	764
	2005	..	547	..	..	547	649
	2006	..	638	..	..	638	747
ench Polynesia lynésie française	2003	..	410	..	..	410	1657
	2004	..	364	..	..	364	1452
	2005	..	364	..	..	364	1431
	2006	..	364	..	..	364	1422

Table 31

Production, trade and consumption of gases
Production, commerce et consommation de gaz

Terajoules and megajoules per capita
Térajoules et mégajoules par habitant

Country or area Pays ou zone	Year Année	Production Production	Imports Importations	Exports Exportations	Changes in stocks Variations des stocks	Consumption Consommation	
						Total Totale	Per Capita Par habitant
New Caledonia	2003	..	364	..	..	364	159
Nouvelle-Calédonie	2004	..	364	..	..	364	15?
	2005	..	410	..	..	410	175
	2006	..	410	..	..	410	172
New Zealand	2003	216715	501	1139	52	216026	5388
Nouvelle-Zélande	2004	198126	364	683	108	197699	4867
	2005	186702	547	592	-11	186668	4554
	2006	190759	1776	273	-95	192357	4642
Papua New Guinea	2003	5526	537	..	..	6063	10?
Papouasie-Nvl-Guinée	2004	4480	800	..	..	5280	8?
	2005	10898	615	..	..	11513	18?
	2006	11852	400	..	..	12252	19?
Solomon Islands	2003	..	*46	..	..	*46	*1?
Iles Salomon	2004	..	*46	..	..	*46	*?
	2005	..	*46	..	..	*46	*?
	2006	..	*46	..	..	*46	*?
Wallis and Futuna Is	2003	..	*6	..	..	*6	*4?
Iles Wallis et Futuna	2004	..	6	..	..	6	3?
	2005	..	6	..	..	6	3?
	2006	..	6	..	..	6	3?

Table 32

Net installed capacity of electric generating plants - by type
Puissance nette installée des centrales électriques - par catégorie

Thousand kilowatts
Milliers de kilowatts

Table Notes:

For this specific table, Geothermal Net Installed Capacity refers to geothermal, wind, solar, tide and wave installed capacities, whenever they are available in the country.

For Japan, geothermal capacity includes fuel cell capacity.

For Austria data are given in gross maximum capacity.

- **Please refer to the Definitions Section on pages xv to xxix for the appropriate product description /classification.**

Notes relatives aux tableaux :

Pour ce tableau spécifique, les données relatives à la capacité géothermique des centrales électriques se rapportent à la capacité géothermique, éolienne, solaire, marémotrice et énergie des vagues quand elles sont disponibles dans le pays.

Pour le Japon, la capacité géothermique se rapporte à la capacité de piles à combustible.

Pour l'Autriche les données représentent la capacité maximale brute.

- **Veuillez consulter la section "définitions" de la page xv à la page xxix pour une description/classification appropriée des produits.**

Figure 83: Net installed capacity of electricity generating plants in 2006

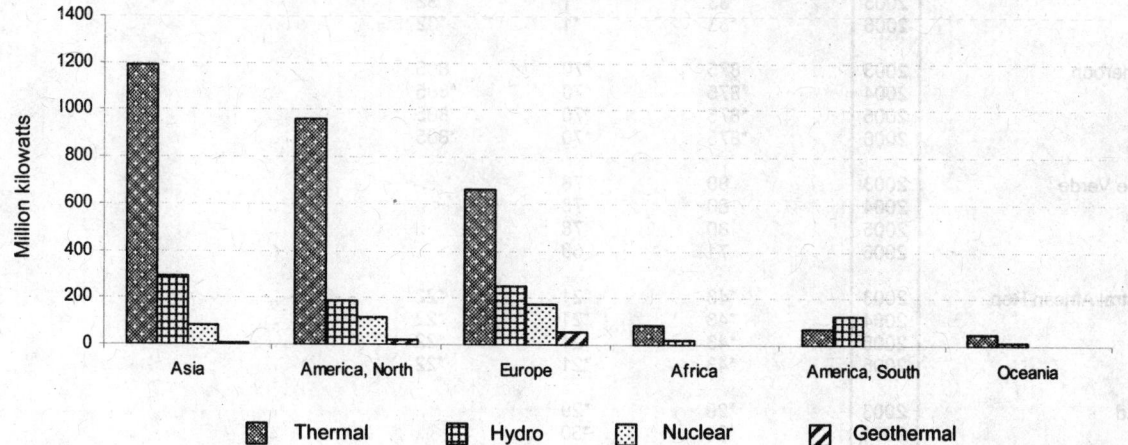

Table 32

Net installed capacity of electric generating plants by type

Thousand kilowatts

Country or area Pays ou zone	Year Année	Self-producers and public utilities Autoproducteurs et services publics					Self- Auto-	
		Total Totale	Thermal Thermique	Hydro Hydraulique	Nuclear Nucléaire	Geothermal Géother- -mique	Total Totale	Therm Thermi
World	**2003**	**3925276**	**2682768**	**822762**	**372771**	**46976**	**261925**	**2**
	2004	**4066130**	**2778887**	**853872**	**378469**	**54902**	**276481**	**2**
	2005	**4212605**	**2894058**	**870657**	**381744**	**66146**	**267815**	**2**
	2006	**4368673**	**3014976**	**889211**	**384510**	**79977**	**275126**	**2**
Africa	**2003**	**103843**	**79488**	**22247**	**1842**	**265**	**5567**	
	2004	**107179**	**82414**	**22629**	**1842**	**293**	**5684**	
	2005	**110355**	**84776**	**23366**	**1842**	**370**	**5619**	
	2006	**112550**	**86815**	**23479**	**1842**	**413**	**6008**	
Algeria	2003	6840	6565	275	..	..	379	
	2004	7246	6971	275	..	..	492	
	2005	7492	7217	275	..	..	390	
	2006	7892	7617	275	..	..	*492	
Angola	2003	*500	*110	*390	..	..	*30	
	2004	*705	*110	*595	..	..	*30	
	2005	*915	*135	*780	..	..	*30	
	2006	*915	*135	*780	..	..	*30	
Benin	2003	58	57	*1	..	..	*2	
	2004	58	57	*1	..	..	*2	
	2005	*60	*59	*1	..	..	*4	
	2006	*60	*59	*1	..	..	*4	
Burkina Faso	2003	*105	*75	*30	..	..	..	
	2004	*105	*75	*30	..	..	..	
	2005	*120	*90	*30	..	..	..	
	2006	*120	*90	*30	..	..	..	
Burundi	2003	*33	*1	*32	..	..	..	
	2004	*33	*1	*32	..	..	..	
	2005	*33	*1	*32	..	..	..	
	2006	*33	*1	*32	..	..	..	
Cameroon	2003	875	*70	805	..	..	..	
	2004	*875	*70	*805	..	..	..	
	2005	*875	*70	*805	..	..	..	
	2006	*875	*70	*805	..	..	..	
Cape Verde	2003	80	78	..	..	..	2	*1
	2004	80	78	..	..	..	2	*1
	2005	80	78	..	..	..	2	*1
	2006	71	69	..	..	..	2	*1
Central African Rep.	2003	*43	*21	*22	..	..	..	
	2004	*43	*21	*22	..	..	..	
	2005	*43	*21	*22	..	..	..	
	2006	*43	*21	*22	..	..	..	
Chad	2003	*29	*29	..	..	..	..	
	2004	*30	*30	..	..	..	..	
	2005	*30	*30	..	..	..	..	
	2006	*30	*30	..	..	..	..	
Comoros	2003	*5	*4	*1	..	..	..	
	2004	*5	*4	*1	..	..	..	
	2005	*5	*4	*1	..	..	..	
	2006	*5	*4	*1	..	..	..	
Congo	2003	*112	*20	*92	..	..	..	
	2004	*112	*20	*92	..	..	..	
	2005	*112	*20	*92	..	..	..	
	2006	*112	*20	*92	..	..	..	
Côte d'Ivoire	2003	*1368	*470	*898	..	..	10	
	2004	*1378	*480	*898	..	..	*10	
	2005	*1378	*480	*898	..	..	*10	
	2006	*1378	*480	*898	..	..	*10	

Table 32

Puissance nette installée des centrales électriques - par catégorie
Milliers de kilowatts

| producers producteurs | | | Public utilities Services publics | | | | | Year Année | Country or area Pays ou zone |
Hydro draulique	Nuclear Nucléaire	Geothermal Géothermique	Total Totale	Thermal Thermique	Hydro Hydraulique	Nuclear Nucléaire	Geothermal Géothermique		
18700	..	2769	3663352	2442312	804062	372771	44207	2003	**Monde**
17548	..	3534	3789649	2523488	836324	378469	51369	2004	
17956	..	4927	3944789	2649126	852701	381744	61219	2005	
18539	..	6411	4093547	2764799	870672	384510	73566	2006	
697	..	10	98276	74628	21550	1842	255	2003	**Afrique**
703	..	12	101495	77445	21926	1842	281	2004	
703	..	12	104736	79872	22663	1842	358	2005	
703	..	12	106542	81522	22776	1842	401	2006	
..	..	..	6461	6186	275	..	..	2003	Algérie
..	..	..	6754	6479	275	..	..	2004	
..	..	..	7102	6827	275	..	..	2005	
..	..	..	7400	7125	275	..	..	2006	
..	..	..	*470	*80	*390	..	..	2003	Angola
..	..	..	*675	*80	*595	..	..	2004	
..	..	..	*885	*105	*780	..	..	2005	
..	..	..	*885	*105	*780	..	..	2006	
..	..	..	56	55	*1	..	..	2003	Bénin
..	..	..	56	55	*1	..	..	2004	
..	..	..	*56	*55	*1	..	..	2005	
..	..	..	*56	*55	*1	..	..	2006	
..	..	..	*105	*75	*30	..	..	2003	Burkina Faso
..	..	..	*105	*75	*30	..	..	2004	
..	..	..	*120	*90	*30	..	..	2005	
..	..	..	*120	*90	*30	..	..	2006	
..	..	..	*33	*1	*32	..	..	2003	Burundi
..	..	..	*33	*1	*32	..	..	2004	
..	..	..	*33	*1	*32	..	..	2005	
..	..	..	*33	*1	*32	..	..	2006	
..	..	..	875	*70	805	..	..	2003	Cameroun
..	..	..	*875	*70	*805	..	..	2004	
..	..	..	*875	*70	*805	..	..	2005	
..	..	..	*875	*70	*805	..	..	2006	
..	..	..	79	77	..	..	2	2003	Cap-Vert
..	..	..	79	77	..	..	2	2004	
..	..	..	79	77	..	..	2	2005	
..	..	..	70	68	..	..	2	2006	
..	..	..	*43	*21	*22	..	..	2003	Rép. centrafricaine
..	..	..	*43	*21	*22	..	..	2004	
..	..	..	*43	*21	*22	..	..	2005	
..	..	..	*43	*21	*22	..	..	2006	
..	..	..	*29	*29	..	..	..	2003	Tchad
..	..	..	*30	*30	..	..	..	2004	
..	..	..	*30	*30	..	..	..	2005	
..	..	..	*30	*30	..	..	..	2006	
..	..	..	*5	*4	*1	..	..	2003	Comores
..	..	..	*5	*4	*1	..	..	2004	
..	..	..	*5	*4	*1	..	..	2005	
..	..	..	*5	*4	*1	..	..	2006	
..	..	..	*112	*20	*92	..	..	2003	Congo
..	..	..	*112	*20	*92	..	..	2004	
..	..	..	*112	*20	*92	..	..	2005	
..	..	..	*112	*20	*92	..	..	2006	
..	..	..	*1358	*460	*898	..	..	2003	Côte d'Ivoire
..	..	..	*1368	*470	*898	..	..	2004	
..	..	..	*1368	*470	*898	..	..	2005	
..	..	..	*1368	*470	*898	..	..	2006	

Table 32

Net installed capacity of electric generating plants by type
Thousand kilowatts

Country or area Pays ou zone	Year Année	Self-producers and public utilities Autoproducteurs et services publics					Self- Auto-	
		Total Totale	Thermal Thermique	Hydro Hydraulique	Nuclear Nucléaire	Geothermal Géother- -mique	Total Totale	Thermal Thermique
Dem. Rep. of Congo	2003	*2568	*33	*2535	..	..	*565	
	2004	*2573	*33	*2540	..	..	*568	
	2005	*2573	*33	*2540	..	..	*568	
	2006	*2573	*33	*2540	..	..	*568	
Djibouti	2003	112	112	..	..	..	..	
	2004	118	118	..	..	..	..	
	2005	118	118	..	..	..	..	
	2006	118	118	..	..	..	..	
Egypt	2003	16966	14250	2653	..	63	*683	*6
	2004	19255	16452	2740	..	63	*683	*6
	2005	20409	17529	2740	..	140	*683	*6
	2006	20949	18026	2740	..	183	*683	*6
Equatorial Guinea	2003	*13	*10	*3	..	..	..	
	2004	*13	*10	*3	..	..	..	
	2005	*13	*10	*3	..	..	..	
	2006	*13	*10	*3	..	..	..	
Eritrea	2003	*166	*166	..	..	0	*6	
	2004	*167	*166	..	..	*1	*6	
	2005	*167	*166	..	..	*1	*6	
	2006	*167	*166	..	..	*1	*6	
Ethiopia	2003	*536	*75	*451	..	*10	*48	*
	2004	*537	*75	*451	..	*11	*49	*
	2005	*586	*75	*500	..	*11	*49	*
	2006	*686	*75	*600	..	*11	*49	*
Gabon	2003	*419	*244	*175	..	..	*97	*
	2004	*419	*244	*175	..	..	*97	*
	2005	*420	*245	*175	..	..	*97	*
	2006	*420	*245	*175	..	..	*97	*
Gambia	2003	*30	*30	..	..	..	*3	
	2004	*30	*30	..	..	..	*3	
	2005	*30	*30	..	..	..	*3	
	2006	*31	*31	..	..	..	*3	
Ghana	2003	*1431	*292	*1139	..	..	*2	
	2004	1472	*292	1180	..	..	*2	
	2005	*1472	*292	*1180	..	..	*2	
	2006	*1622	*442	*1180	..	..	*2	
Guinea	2003	*197	*145	52	..	..	*105	*1
	2004	*197	*145	52	..	..	*105	*1
	2005	*200	*145	*55	..	..	*105	*1
	2006	*200	*145	*55	..	..	*105	*1
Guinea-Bissau	2003	*21	*21	..	..	..	*1	
	2004	*21	*21	..	..	..	*1	
	2005	*21	*21	..	..	..	*1	
	2006	*21	*21	..	..	..	*1	
Kenya	2003	*1186	*409	*677	..	*100	*176	*1
	2004	*1278	*476	*677	..	*125	*176	*1
	2005	*1311	*506	*680	..	*125	*176	*1
	2006	*1311	*506	*680	..	*125	*176	*1
Liberia	2003	*188	*188	..	..	..	..	
	2004	*188	*188	..	..	..	..	
	2005	*188	*188	..	..	..	..	
	2006	*188	*188	..	..	..	..	
Libyan Arab Jamah.	2003	4556	4556	..	..	..	..	
	2004	4556	4556	..	..	..	..	
	2005	5125	5125	..	..	..	..	
	2006	5330	5330	..	..	..	..	

Table 32

Puissance nette installée des centrales électriques - par catégorie
Milliers de kilowatts

producers producteurs			Public utilities Services publics					Year Année	Country or area Pays ou zone
Hydro draulique	Nuclear Nucléaire	Geothermal Géother-mique	Total Totale	Thermal Thermique	Hydro Hydraulique	Nuclear Nucléaire	Geothermal Géother-mique		
*562	..	..	*2003	*30	*1973	..	..	2003	Rép. dem. du Congo
*565	..	..	*2005	*30	*1975	..	..	2004	
*565	..	..	*2005	*30	*1975	..	..	2005	
*565	..	..	*2005	*30	*1975	..	..	2006	
..	..	..	112	112	..	..	..	2003	Djibouti
..	..	..	118	118	..	..	..	2004	
..	..	..	118	118	..	..	..	2005	
..	..	..	118	118	..	..	..	2006	
..	..	..	16283	13567	2653	..	63	2003	Egypte
..	..	..	18572	15769	2740	..	63	2004	
..	..	..	19726	16846	2740	..	140	2005	
..	..	..	20266	17343	2740	..	183	2006	
..	..	..	*13	*10	*3	..	..	2003	Guinée équatoriale
..	..	..	*13	*10	*3	..	..	2004	
..	..	..	*13	*10	*3	..	..	2005	
..	..	..	*13	*10	*3	..	..	2006	
..	..	..	*160	*160	..	..	0	2003	Erythrée
..	..	..	*161	*160	..	..	*1	2004	
..	..	..	*161	*160	..	..	*1	2005	
..	..	..	*161	*160	..	..	*1	2006	
..	..	*9	*488	*36	*451	..	*1	2003	Ethiopie
..	..	*10	*488	*36	*451	..	*1	2004	
..	..	*10	*537	*36	*500	..	*1	2005	
..	..	*10	*637	*36	*600	..	*1	2006	
..	..	..	*322	*147	*175	..	..	2003	Gabon
..	..	..	*322	*147	*175	..	..	2004	
..	..	..	*323	*148	*175	..	..	2005	
..	..	..	*323	*148	*175	..	..	2006	
..	..	..	*27	*27	..	..	..	2003	Gambie
..	..	..	*27	*27	..	..	..	2004	
..	..	..	*27	*27	..	..	..	2005	
..	..	..	*28	*28	..	..	..	2006	
..	..	..	*1429	*290	*1139	..	..	2003	Ghana
..	..	..	1470	*290	1180	..	..	2004	
..	..	..	*1470	*290	*1180	..	..	2005	
..	..	..	*1620	*440	*1180	..	..	2006	
..	..	..	92	40	52	..	..	2003	Guinée
..	..	..	92	40	52	..	..	2004	
..	..	..	*95	*40	*55	..	..	2005	
..	..	..	*95	*40	*55	..	..	2006	
..	..	..	*20	*20	..	..	..	2003	Guinée-Bissau
..	..	..	*20	*20	..	..	..	2004	
..	..	..	*20	*20	..	..	..	2005	
..	..	..	*20	*20	..	..	..	2006	
..	..	..	*1010	*233	*677	..	*100	2003	Kenya
..	..	..	*1102	*300	*677	..	*125	2004	
..	..	..	*1135	*330	*680	..	*125	2005	
..	..	..	*1135	*330	*680	..	*125	2006	
..	..	..	*188	*188	..	..	..	2003	Libéria
..	..	..	*188	*188	..	..	..	2004	
..	..	..	*188	*188	..	..	..	2005	
..	..	..	*188	*188	..	..	..	2006	
..	..	..	4556	4556	..	..	..	2003	Jamah. arabe libyenne
..	..	..	4556	4556	..	..	..	2004	
..	..	..	5125	5125	..	..	..	2005	
..	..	..	5330	5330	..	..	..	2006	

Table 32

Net installed capacity of electric generating plants by type
Thousand kilowatts

Country or area Pays ou zone	Year Année	Self-producers and public utilities Autoproducteurs et services publics					Self- Auto-	
		Total Totale	Thermal Thermique	Hydro Hydraulique	Nuclear Nucléaire	Geothermal Géother- -mique	Total Totale	Thermal Thermique
Madagascar	2003	*228	*122	*106	..	..	*32	*:
	2004	*228	*122	*106	..	..	*32	*:
	2005	*228	*122	*106	..	..	*32	*:
	2006	*228	*122	*106	..	..	*32	*:
Malawi	2003	473	*183	290	..	..	*172	*1
	2004	476	*186	290	..	..	*174	*1
	2005	476	*186	290	..	..	*174	*1
	2006	*476	*186	*290	..	..	*174	*1
Mali	2003	*114	*64	*50	..	..	*18	*
	2004	*114	*64	*50	..	..	*18	*
	2005	*114	*64	*50	..	..	*18	*
	2006	*114	*64	*50	..	..	*18	*
Mauritania	2003	75	75	..	..	..	..	
	2004	75	75	..	..	..	..	
	2005	75	75	..	..	..	..	
	2006	94	94	..	..	..	..	
Mauritius	2003	651	592	59	..	..	237	2
	2004	654	595	59	..	..	236	2
	2005	688	629	59	..	..	271	2
	2006	711	652	59	..	..	269	2
Morocco	2003	4838	3524	1260	..	54	424	4
	2004	4851	3524	1273	..	54	*420	*4
	2005	5252	3469	1729	..	54	*420	*4
	2006	5816	4033	1729	..	54	*420	*4
Mozambique	2003	2369	204	2165	..	..	..	
	2004	2369	204	2165	..	..	..	
	2005	2369	204	2165	..	..	..	
	2006	2369	204	2165	..	..	..	
Niger	2003	*145	*145	..	..	..	*40	*
	2004	*145	*145	..	..	..	*40	*
	2005	*145	*145	..	..	..	*40	*
	2006	*145	*145	..	..	..	*40	*
Nigeria	2003	5881	3500	2381	..	..	40	
	2004	5881	3500	2381	..	..	40	
	2005	5881	3500	2381	..	..	40	
	2006	*5881	*3500	*2381	..	..	*40	
Réunion	2003	*439	*315	*124	..	..	*45	*
	2004	*439	*315	*124	..	..	*45	*
	2005	*439	*315	*124	..	..	*45	*
	2006	*439	*315	*124	..	..	*45	*
Rwanda	2003	*38	*3	*35	..	..	*1	
	2004	*31	*4	*27	..	..	*1	
	2005	*39	*4	*35	..	..	*1	
	2006	*42	*5	*37	..	..	*1	
Sao Tome and Principe	2003	*5	*3	*2	..	..	..	
	2004	*5	*3	*2	..	..	..	
	2005	*5	*3	*2	..	..	..	
	2006	*5	*3	*2	..	..	..	
Senegal	2003	452	391	*60	..	*1	*127	*1
	2004	488	426	*60	..	*2	*128	*1
	2005	569	507	*60	..	*2	128	1
	2006	524	462	*60	..	*2	*128	*1
Seychelles	2003	*95	*95	..	..	..	..	
	2004	*95	*95	..	..	..	..	
	2005	*95	*95	..	..	..	..	
	2006	*95	*95	..	..	..	..	

Table 32

Puissance nette installée des centrales électriques - par catégorie
Milliers de kilowatts

producers producteurs			Public utilities Services publics					Year Année	Country or area Pays ou zone
Hydro Hydraulique	Nuclear Nucléaire	Geothermal Géother-mique	Total Totale	Thermal Thermique	Hydro Hydraulique	Nuclear Nucléaire	Geothermal Géother-mique		
..	..	..	*196	*90	*106	..	..	2003	Madagascar
..	..	..	*196	*90	*106	..	..	2004	
..	..	..	*196	*90	*106	..	..	2005	
..	..	..	*196	*90	*106	..	..	2006	
*4	..	..	301	*15	286	..	..	2003	Malawi
*4	..	..	302	16	286	..	..	2004	
*4	..	..	302	16	286	..	..	2005	
*4	..	..	*302	*16	*286	..	..	2006	
..	..	..	*96	*46	*50	..	..	2003	Mali
..	..	..	*96	*46	*50	..	..	2004	
..	..	..	*96	*46	*50	..	..	2005	
..	..	..	*96	*46	*50	..	..	2006	
..	..	..	75	75	..	..	..	2003	Mauritanie
..	..	..	75	75	..	..	..	2004	
..	..	..	75	75	..	..	..	2005	
..	..	..	94	94	..	..	..	2006	
..	..	..	414	355	59	..	..	2003	Maurice
..	..	..	418	359	59	..	..	2004	
..	..	..	417	358	59	..	..	2005	
..	..	..	442	383	59	..	..	2006	
..	..	..	4414	3100	1260	..	54	2003	Maroc
..	..	..	4431	3104	1273	..	54	2004	
..	..	..	4832	3049	1729	..	54	2005	
..	..	..	5396	3613	1729	..	54	2006	
..	..	..	2369	204	2165	..	..	2003	Mozambique
..	..	..	2369	204	2165	..	..	2004	
..	..	..	2369	204	2165	..	..	2005	
..	..	..	2369	204	2165	..	..	2006	
..	..	..	*105	*105	..	..	..	2003	Niger
..	..	..	*105	*105	..	..	..	2004	
..	..	..	*105	*105	..	..	..	2005	
..	..	..	*105	*105	..	..	..	2006	
40	..	..	5841	3500	2341	..	..	2003	Nigéria
40	..	..	5841	3500	2341	..	..	2004	
40	..	..	5841	3500	2341	..	..	2005	
*40	..	..	*5841	*3500	*2341	..	..	2006	
..	..	..	*394	*270	*124	..	..	2003	Réunion
..	..	..	*394	*270	*124	..	..	2004	
..	..	..	*394	*270	*124	..	..	2005	
..	..	..	*394	*270	*124	..	..	2006	
..	..	..	*37	*2	*35	..	..	2003	Rwanda
..	..	..	*30	*3	*27	..	..	2004	
..	..	..	*38	*3	*35	..	..	2005	
..	..	..	*41	*4	*37	..	..	2006	
..	..	..	*5	*3	*2	..	..	2003	Sao Tomé-et-Principe
..	..	..	*5	*3	*2	..	..	2004	
..	..	..	*5	*3	*2	..	..	2005	
..	..	..	*5	*3	*2	..	..	2006	
..	..	*1	325	265	*60	..	..	2003	Sénégal
..	..	*2	360	300	*60	..	..	2004	
..	..	*2	441	381	*60	..	..	2005	
..	..	*2	396	336	*60	..	..	2006	
..	..	..	*95	*95	..	..	..	2003	Seychelles
..	..	..	*95	*95	..	..	..	2004	
..	..	..	*95	*95	..	..	..	2005	
..	..	..	*95	*95	..	..	..	2006	

Table 32

Net installed capacity of electric generating plants by type

Thousand kilowatts

Country or area Pays ou zone	Year Année	Self-producers and public utilities Autoproducteurs et services publics					Self- Auto-	
		Total Totale	Thermal Thermique	Hydro Hydraulique	Nuclear Nucléaire	Geothermal Géother- -mique	Total Totale	Thermal Thermique
Sierra Leone	2003	*50	*46	*4	..	..	*8	
	2004	*49	*45	*4	..	..	*7	
	2005	*49	*45	*4	..	..	*7	
	2006	*50	*46	*4	..	..	*7	
Somalia	2003	66	66	..	..	..	..	
	2004	66	66	..	..	..	..	
	2005	60	60	..	..	..	..	
	2006	60	60	..	..	..	..	
South Africa Customs Un.	2003	*40475	*37163	*1454	1842	*16	*1636	*15
	2004	*40475	*37163	*1454	1842	*16	*1636	*15
	2005	*40475	*37163	*1454	1842	*16	*1636	*15
	2006	*40477	*37165	*1454	1842	*16	*1638	*15
St. Helena and Depend.	2003	*4	*4	..	..	..	..	
	2004	4	4	..	..	..	..	
	2005	*4	*4	..	..	..	..	
	2006	*4	*4	..	..	..	..	
Sudan	2003	888	580	308	..	..	..	
	2004	938	630	308	..	..	..	
	2005	961	624	337	..	..	..	
	2006	1060	718	342	..	..	..	
Togo	2003	*48	*18	*30	..	..	*3	
	2004	*48	*18	*30	..	..	*3	
	2005	*48	*18	*30	..	..	*3	
	2006	*48	*18	*30	..	..	*3	
Tunisia	2003	2942	2861	62	..	19	548	5
	2004	3060	2979	62	..	19	548	5
	2005	3299	3218	62	..	19	548	5
	2006	3334	3252	63	..	19	835	8
Uganda	2003	*268	1	*267	..	..	*8	
	2004	*307	*1	*306	..	..	*11	
	2005	311	1	310	..	..	*11	
	2006	418	103	315	..	..	11	
United Rep.Tanzania	2003	*445	*85	*360	..	..	*20	*..
	2004	*470	*110	*360	..	..	*20	*..
	2005	*580	*220	*360	..	..	*20	*..
	2006	*580	*220	*360	..	..	*20	*..
Western Sahara	2003	*58	*58	..	..	..	..	
	2004	*58	*58	..	..	..	..	
	2005	*58	*58	..	..	..	..	
	2006	*58	*58	..	..	..	..	
Zambia	2003	*2260	*15	*2245	..	..	*50	
	2004	*2260	*15	*2245	..	..	*50	
	2005	*2260	*15	*2245	..	..	*50	
	2006	*2260	*15	*2245	..	..	*50	
Zimbabwe	2003	*2099	*1345	754	..	..	*50	*..
	2004	*2099	*1345	754	..	..	*50	*..
	2005	*2099	*1345	*754	..	..	*50	*..
	2006	*2099	*1345	*754	..	..	*50	*..
America, North	**2003**	**1229818**	**918002**	**183812**	**117395**	**10609**	**52553**	**464**
	2004	**1251348**	**935911**	**184465**	**119730**	**11241**	**50188**	**447**
	2005	**1272364**	**951914**	**186148**	**120295**	**14008**	**50179**	**445**
	2006	**1288163**	**962702**	**187480**	**120295**	**17686**	**51021**	**452**
Anguilla	2003	17	17	..	..	..	..	
	2004	17	17	..	..	..	..	
	2005	17	17	..	..	..	..	
	2006	24	24	..	..	..	..	

Table 32

Puissance nette installée des centrales électriques - par catégorie
Milliers de kilowatts

producers producteurs			Public utilities Services publics					Year Année	Country or area Pays ou zone
Hydro draulique	Nuclear Nucléaire	Geothermal Géother-mique	Total Totale	Thermal Thermique	Hydro Hydraulique	Nuclear Nucléaire	Geothermal Géother-mique		
..	..	..	*42	*38	*4	..	..	2003	Sierra Leone
..	..	..	*42	*38	*4	..	..	2004	
..	..	..	*42	*38	*4	..	..	2005	
..	..	..	*43	*39	*4	..	..	2006	
..	..	..	66	66	..	..	..	2003	Somalie
..	..	..	66	66	..	..	..	2004	
..	..	..	60	60	..	..	..	2005	
..	..	..	60	60	..	..	..	2006	
*39	..	..	*38839	*35566	*1415	1842	*16	2003	Un.douan.d'Afr.mérid
*39	..	..	*38839	*35566	*1415	1842	*16	2004	
*39	..	..	*38839	*35566	*1415	1842	*16	2005	
*39	..	..	*38839	*35566	*1415	1842	*16	2006	
..	..	..	*4	*4	..	..	..	2003	St-Hélène et dépend
..	..	..	4	4	..	..	..	2004	
..	..	..	*4	*4	..	..	..	2005	
..	..	..	*4	*4	..	..	..	2006	
..	..	..	888	580	308	..	..	2003	Soudan
..	..	..	938	630	308	..	..	2004	
..	..	..	961	624	337	..	..	2005	
..	..	..	1060	718	342	..	..	2006	
..	..	..	*45	*15	*30	..	..	2003	Togo
..	..	..	*45	*15	*30	..	..	2004	
..	..	..	*45	*15	*30	..	..	2005	
..	..	..	*45	*15	*30	..	..	2006	
..	..	..	2394	2313	62	..	19	2003	Tunisie
..	..	..	2512	2431	62	..	19	2004	
..	..	..	2751	2670	62	..	19	2005	
..	..	..	2499	2417	63	..	19	2006	
*7	..	..	*260	0	*260	..	..	2003	Ouganda
*10	..	..	*296	0	*296	..	..	2004	
*10	..	..	300	0	300	..	..	2005	
10	..	..	407	102	305	..	..	2006	
..	..	..	*425	*65	*360	..	..	2003	Rép. Unie de Tanzanie
..	..	..	*450	*90	*360	..	..	2004	
..	..	..	*560	*200	*360	..	..	2005	
..	..	..	*560	*200	*360	..	..	2006	
..	..	..	*58	*58	..	..	..	2003	Sahara occidental
..	..	..	*58	*58	..	..	..	2004	
..	..	..	*58	*58	..	..	..	2005	
..	..	..	*58	*58	..	..	..	2006	
*45	..	..	*2210	*10	*2200	..	..	2003	Zambie
*45	..	..	*2210	*10	*2200	..	..	2004	
*45	..	..	*2210	*10	*2200	..	..	2005	
*45	..	..	*2210	*10	*2200	..	..	2006	
..	..	..	*2049	*1295	754	..	..	2003	Zimbabwe
..	..	..	*2049	*1295	754	..	..	2004	
..	..	..	*2049	*1295	*754	..	..	2005	
..	..	..	*2049	*1295	*754	..	..	2006	
6026	..	77	1177265	871553	177786	117395	10532	2003	**Amérique du Nord**
5352	..	77	1201159	891151	179114	119730	11164	2004	
5568	..	77	1222185	907379	180580	120295	13931	2005	
5710	..	77	1237142	917467	181771	120295	17609	2006	
..	..	..	17	17	..	..	..	2003	Anguilla
..	..	..	17	17	..	..	..	2004	
..	..	..	17	17	..	..	..	2005	
..	..	..	24	24	..	..	..	2006	

Table 32

Net installed capacity of electric generating plants by type
Thousand kilowatts

Country or area Pays ou zone	Year Année	Self-producers and public utilities Autoproducteurs et services publics					Self- Auto-	
		Total Totale	Thermal Thermique	Hydro Hydraulique	Nuclear Nucléaire	Geothermal Géother- -mique	Total Totale	Thermal Thermique
Antigua and Barbuda	2003	27	27	..	..	..	1	
	2004	27	27	..	..	..	1	
	2005	27	27	..	..	..	1	
	2006	27	27	..	..	..	1	
Aruba	2003	149	149	..	..	..	..	
	2004	149	149	..	..	..	..	
	2005	149	149	..	..	..	..	
	2006	149	149	..	..	..	..	
Bahamas	2003	455	455	..	..	..	*55	*5
	2004	455	455	..	..	..	*55	*5
	2005	493	493	..	..	..	*55	*5
	2006	493	493	..	..	..	*55	*5
Barbados	2003	216	216	..	..	..	*6	
	2004	216	216	..	..	..	*6	
	2005	216	216	..	..	..	*6	
	2006	216	216	..	..	..	*6	
Belize	2003	*50	*33	*17	..	..	..	
	2004	*50	*33	*17	..	..	..	
	2005	*51	*33	*18	..	..	..	
	2006	*51	*33	*18	..	..	..	
Bermuda	2003	175	175	..	..	..	..	
	2004	*175	*175	..	..	..	..	
	2005	175	175	..	..	..	..	
	2006	*175	*175	..	..	..	..	
British Virgin Islands	2003	10	10	..	..	..	..	
	2004	10	10	..	..	..	..	
	2005	10	10	..	..	..	..	
	2006	10	10	..	..	..	..	
Canada	2003	118271	36923	70374	10615	359	10261	529
	2004	120459	36319	70857	12805	478	8545	411
	2005	122838	36794	71978	13345	721	7982	337
	2006	125814	38308	72661	13345	1500	7959	328
Cayman Islands	2003	123	123	..	..	..	..	
	2004	123	123	..	..	..	..	
	2005	107	107	..	..	..	..	
	2006	121	121	..	..	..	..	
Costa Rica	2003	1964	446	1296	..	223	271	*5
	2004	1945	446	1304	..	196	293	*5
	2005	1949	449	1304	..	196	271	*5
	2006	2083	476	1411	..	196	335	*5
Cuba	2003	3874	3817	57	..	..	572	57
	2004	3764	3705	59	..	..	460	46
	2005	4275	4227	48	..	..	677	67
	2006	5176	5128	48	..	..	446	44
Dominica	2003	22	14	8	..	..	..	
	2004	22	14	8	..	..	..	
	2005	24	16	8	..	..	..	
	2006	*24	*16	*8	..	..	..	
Dominican Republic	2003	5530	4988	542	..	..	2106	210
	2004	5396	4853	543	..	..	2106	210
	2005	5519	5048	471	..	..	2352	235
	2006	5548	5079	469	..	..	2352	235
El Salvador	2003	1106	515	430	..	161	53	5
	2004	1096	515	430	..	151	53	5
	2005	1236	624	461	..	151	62	6
	2006	1230	619	460	..	151	62	6

Table 32

Puissance nette installée des centrales électriques - par catégorie
Milliers de kilowatts

producers producteurs			Public utilities Services publics					Year Année	Country or area Pays ou zone
Hydro hydraulique	Nuclear Nucléaire	Geothermal Géothermique	Total Totale	Thermal Thermique	Hydro Hydraulique	Nuclear Nucléaire	Geothermal Géothermique		
..	..	..	26	26	..	..	..	2003	Antigua-et-Barbuda
..	..	..	26	26	..	..	..	2004	
..	..	..	26	26	..	..	..	2005	
..	..	..	26	26	..	..	..	2006	
..	..	..	149	149	..	..	..	2003	Aruba
..	..	..	149	149	..	..	..	2004	
..	..	..	149	149	..	..	..	2005	
..	..	..	149	149	..	..	..	2006	
..	..	..	400	400	..	..	..	2003	Bahamas
..	..	..	400	400	..	..	..	2004	
..	..	..	438	438	..	..	..	2005	
..	..	..	438	438	..	..	..	2006	
..	..	..	210	210	..	..	..	2003	Barbade
..	..	..	210	210	..	..	..	2004	
..	..	..	210	210	..	..	..	2005	
..	..	..	210	210	..	..	..	2006	
..	..	..	*50	*33	*17	..	..	2003	Belize
..	..	..	*50	*33	*17	..	..	2004	
..	..	..	*51	*33	*18	..	..	2005	
..	..	..	*51	*33	*18	..	..	2006	
..	..	..	175	175	..	..	..	2003	Bermudes
..	..	..	*175	*175	..	..	..	2004	
..	..	..	175	175	..	..	..	2005	
..	..	..	*175	*175	..	..	..	2006	
..	..	..	10	10	..	..	..	2003	Iles Vierges britanniques
..	..	..	10	10	..	..	..	2004	
..	..	..	10	10	..	..	..	2005	
..	..	..	10	10	..	..	..	2006	
4966	..	..	108010	31628	65408	10615	359	2003	Canada
4432	..	..	111914	32206	66425	12805	478	2004	
4609	..	..	114856	33421	67369	13345	721	2005	
4672	..	..	117855	35021	67989	13345	1500	2006	
..	..	..	123	123	..	..	..	2003	Iles Caïmanes
..	..	..	123	123	..	..	..	2004	
..	..	..	107	107	..	..	..	2005	
..	..	..	121	121	..	..	..	2006	
161	..	*60	1693	396	1135	..	163	2003	Costa Rica
183	..	*60	1652	396	1120	..	136	2004	
161	..	*60	1678	399	1143	..	136	2005	
225	..	*60	1748	426	1186	..	136	2006	
..	..	..	3302	3245	57	..	..	2003	Cuba
..	..	..	3304	3245	59	..	..	2004	
..	..	..	3598	3550	48	..	..	2005	
..	..	..	4730	4682	48	..	..	2006	
..	..	..	22	14	8	..	..	2003	Dominique
..	..	..	22	14	8	..	..	2004	
..	..	..	24	16	8	..	..	2005	
..	..	..	*24	*16	*8	..	..	2006	
..	..	..	3424	2882	542	..	..	2003	Rép. dominicaine
..	..	..	3290	2747	543	..	..	2004	
..	..	..	3167	2696	471	..	..	2005	
..	..	..	3196	2727	469	..	..	2006	
..	..	..	1053	462	430	..	161	2003	El Salvador
..	..	..	1043	462	430	..	151	2004	
..	..	..	1174	562	461	..	151	2005	
..	..	..	1169	557	460	..	151	2006	

Table 32

Net installed capacity of electric generating plants by type
Thousand kilowatts

Country or area Pays ou zone	Year Année	Self-producers and public utilities Autoproducteurs et services publics					Self-Auto-	
		Total Totale	Thermal Thermique	Hydro Hydraulique	Nuclear Nucléaire	Geothermal Géother--mique	Total Totale	Thermal Thermique
Greenland	2003	*137	*137	..	..	..	*27	*
	2004	*137	*137	..	..	..	*27	*
	2005	*137	*137	..	..	..	*27	*
	2006	*137	*137	..	..	..	*27	*
Grenada	2003	32	32	..	..	..	..	
	2004	32	32	..	..	..	..	
	2005	32	32	..	..	..	..	
	2006	32	32	..	..	..	..	
Guadeloupe	2003	411	411	..	..	..	..	
	2004	411	411	..	..	..	..	
	2005	411	411	..	..	..	..	
	2006	411	411	..	..	..	..	
Guatemala	2003	1980	1353	627	..	..	188	1
	2004	1954	1272	682	..	..	*150	*1
	2005	2062	1345	717	..	..	136	1
	2006	2084	1345	739	..	..	136	1
Haiti	2003	221	158	63	..	..	..	
	2004	221	158	63	..	..	..	
	2005	221	158	63	..	..	..	
	2006	221	158	63	..	..	..	
Honduras	2003	1088	623	466	..	0	48	
	2004	1088	623	466	..	0	48	
	2005	1502	1022	480	..	0	52	
	2006	1579	1074	505	..	0	52	5
Jamaica	2003	811	787	24	..	..	148	1
	2004	811	787	24	..	..	148	1
	2005	838	816	22	..	..	197	19
	2006	818	796	22	..	..	197	19
Martinique	2003	*396	*396	..	..	..	..	
	2004	*396	*396	..	..	..	..	
	2005	*396	*396	..	..	..	..	
	2006	*396	*396	..	..	..	..	
Mexico	2003	49553	37559	9650	1365	979	4567	45
	2004	51863	38954	10565	1365	979	4567	45
	2005	51071	38156	10571	1365	979	4537	448
	2006	53795	40634	10734	1365	1062	4682	463
Montserrat	2003	10	10	..	..	..	..	
	2004	10	10	..	..	..	..	
	2005	*10	*10	..	..	..	..	
	2006	*10	*10	..	..	..	..	
Netherlands Antilles	2003	*210	*210	..	..	..	*100	*10
	2004	*210	*210	..	..	..	*100	*10
	2005	*210	*210	..	..	..	*100	*10
	2006	*210	*210	..	..	..	*100	*10
Nicaragua	2003	692	510	104	..	78	65	6
	2004	749	566	105	..	78	122	12
	2005	768	575	105	..	88	127	12
	2006	761	568	105	..	88	127	12
Panama	2003	1565	732	833	..	..	*10	*1
	2004	1603	771	833	..	..	*20	*2
	2005	1684	777	907	..	..	176	11
	2006	1468	621	847	..	..	176	11
Puerto Rico	2003	4979	4879	100	..	..	*61	*6
	2004	5358	5258	100	..	..	*61	*6
	2005	*5411	*5311	*100	..	..	*61	*6
	2006	*5451	*5351	*100	..	..	*61	*6

Table 32

Puissance nette installée des centrales électriques - par catégorie
Milliers de kilowatts

producers producteurs			Public utilities Services publics					Year Année	Country or area Pays ou zone
Hydro Hydraulique	Nuclear Nucléaire	Geothermal Géother-mique	Total Totale	Thermal Thermique	Hydro Hydraulique	Nuclear Nucléaire	Geothermal Géother-mique		
..	..	..	*110	*110	..	..	..	2003	Groënland
..	..	..	*110	*110	..	..	..	2004	
..	..	..	*110	*110	..	..	..	2005	
..	..	..	*110	*110	..	..	..	2006	
..	..	..	32	32	..	..	..	2003	Grenade
..	..	..	32	32	..	..	..	2004	
..	..	..	32	32	..	..	..	2005	
..	..	..	32	32	..	..	..	2006	
..	..	..	411	411	..	..	..	2003	Guadeloupe
..	..	..	411	411	..	..	..	2004	
..	..	..	411	411	..	..	..	2005	
..	..	..	411	411	..	..	..	2006	
..	..	..	1792	1165	627	..	..	2003	Guatemala
..	..	..	1804	1122	682	..	..	2004	
..	..	..	1926	1209	717	..	..	2005	
..	..	..	1948	1209	739	..	..	2006	
..	..	..	221	158	63	..	..	2003	Haïti
..	..	..	221	158	63	..	..	2004	
..	..	..	221	158	63	..	..	2005	
..	..	..	221	158	63	..	..	2006	
2	..	..	1041	577	464	..	0	2003	Honduras
2	..	..	1041	577	464	..	0	2004	
2	..	..	1450	972	478	..	0	2005	
2	..	..	1527	1024	503	..	0	2006	
..	..	..	663	639	24	..	..	2003	Jamaïque
..	..	..	663	639	24	..	..	2004	
..	..	..	641	619	22	..	..	2005	
..	..	..	621	599	22	..	..	2006	
..	..	..	*396	*396	..	..	..	2003	Martinique
..	..	..	*396	*396	..	..	..	2004	
..	..	..	*396	*396	..	..	..	2005	
..	..	..	*396	*396	..	..	..	2006	
35	..	17	44986	33044	9615	1365	962	2003	Mexique
35	..	17	47296	34439	10530	1365	962	2004	
35	..	17	46534	33671	10536	1365	962	2005	
35	..	17	49113	36004	10699	1365	1045	2006	
..	..	..	10	10	..	..	..	2003	Montserrat
..	..	..	10	10	..	..	..	2004	
..	..	..	*10	*10	..	..	..	2005	
..	..	..	*10	*10	..	..	..	2006	
..	..	..	*110	*110	..	..	..	2003	Antilles néerlandaises
..	..	..	*110	*110	..	..	..	2004	
..	..	..	*110	*110	..	..	..	2005	
..	..	..	*110	*110	..	..	..	2006	
..	..	..	627	445	104	..	78	2003	Nicaragua
..	..	..	627	444	105	..	78	2004	
..	..	..	641	448	105	..	88	2005	
..	..	..	634	441	105	..	88	2006	
0	..	..	1555	722	833	..	..	2003	Panama
0	..	..	1583	751	833	..	..	2004	
61	..	..	1508	662	846	..	..	2005	
61	..	..	1292	506	786	..	..	2006	
..	..	..	4918	4818	100	..	..	2003	Porto Rico
..	..	..	5297	5197	100	..	..	2004	
..	..	..	*5350	*5250	*100	..	..	2005	
..	..	..	*5390	*5290	*100	..	..	2006	

Table 32

Net installed capacity of electric generating plants by type
Thousand kilowatts

Country or area Pays ou zone	Year Année	Self-producers and public utilities Autoproducteurs et services publics					Self-Auto-	
		Total Totale	Thermal Thermique	Hydro Hydraulique	Nuclear Nucléaire	Geothermal Géother--mique	Total Totale	Therma Thermiqu
St. Kitts-Nevis	2003	20	20	..	..	..	4	
	2004	*21	*21	..	..	..	*4	
	2005	*21	*21	..	..	..	*4	
	2006	*21	*21	..	..	..	*4	
St. Lucia	2003	57	57	..	..	..	..	
	2004	57	57	..	..	..	..	
	2005	66	66	..	..	..	..	
	2006	66	66	..	..	..	..	
St. Pierre-Miquelon	2003	*27	*27	..	..	..	..	
	2004	*27	*27	..	..	..	..	
	2005	*27	*27	..	..	..	..	
	2006	*27	*27	..	..	..	..	
St. Vincent-Grenadines	2003	31	24	7	..	..	..	
	2004	33	26	7	..	..	..	
	2005	*35	*27	*8	..	..	..	
	2006	*36	*28	*8	..	..	..	
Trinidad and Tobago	2003	1480	1480	..	..	..	*64	
	2004	1480	1480	..	..	..	*64	
	2005	1480	1480	..	..	..	*64	
	2006	1480	1480	..	..	..	*64	
Turks and Caicos Islands	2003	*4	*4	..	..	..	..	
	2004	*4	*4	..	..	..	..	
	2005	*4	*4	..	..	..	..	
	2006	*4	*4	..	..	..	..	
United States	2003	1033803	820364	99215	105415	8809	33804	32
	2004	1050656	837333	98404	105560	9359	33216	32
	2005	1068570	852226	98887	105585	11872	33150	32
	2006	1077692	858137	99282	105585	14688	34037	33
United States Virgin Is.	2003	323	323	..	..	..	143	
	2004	*323	*323	..	..	..	*143	*
	2005	*323	*323	..	..	..	*143	*
	2006	*323	*323	..	..	..	*143	*
America, South	**2003**	**181680**	**60639**	**117989**	**3025**	**27**	**12796**	**10**
	2004	**188191**	**64255**	**120864**	**3025**	**47**	**12911**	**11**
	2005	**191720**	**64975**	**123673**	**3025**	**47**	**13534**	**11**
	2006	**196544**	**67390**	**126084**	**3025**	**45**	**15643**	**13.**
Argentina	2003	28064	17218	9801	1018	27	2385	2.
	2004	28185	17288	9852	1018	27	2499	2
	2005	28185	17288	9852	1018	27	2499	2
	2006	28185	17288	9852	1018	27	2499	2
Bolivia	2003	1314	874	440	..	..	108	
	2004	1420	959	461	..	..	108	
	2005	1379	918	461	..	..	112	
	2006	1403	918	485	..	..	112	
Brazil	2003	87005	16705	68293	2007	..	6718	5
	2004	90733	19727	68999	2007	..	6625	5
	2005	93157	20293	70857	2007	..	6857	5
	2006	96634	21194	73433	2007	..	8340	6
Chile	2003	11454	7287	4167		..	719	
	2004	12294	7488	4806		..	732	
	2005	13007	8193	4814		..	1024	
	2006	13651	8638	5013		..	1282	1
Colombia	2003	13560	4667	8893	..	0	383	
	2004	13734	4758	8956	..	20	383	
	2005	13699	4695	8984	..	20	383	
	2006	13278	4707	8552	..	18	486	

Table 32

Puissance nette installée des centrales électriques - par catégorie
Milliers de kilowatts

producers producteurs			Public utilities Services publics					Year Année	Country or area Pays ou zone
Hydro ydraulique	Nuclear Nucléaire	Geothermal Géother- mique	Total Totale	Thermal Thermique	Hydro Hydraulique	Nuclear Nucléaire	Geothermal Géother- mique		
..	..	..	16	16	..	..	..	2003	St-Kitts-Nevis
..	..	..	*17	*17	..	..	..	2004	
..	..	..	*17	*17	..	..	..	2005	
..	..	..	*17	*17	..	..	..	2006	
..	..	..	57	57	..	..	..	2003	St-Lucie
..	..	..	57	57	..	..	..	2004	
..	..	..	66	66	..	..	..	2005	
..	..	..	66	66	..	..	..	2006	
..	..	..	*27	*27	..	..	..	2003	St-Pierre-Miquelon
..	..	..	*27	*27	..	..	..	2004	
..	..	..	*27	*27	..	..	..	2005	
..	..	..	*27	*27	..	..	..	2006	
..	..	..	31	24	7	..	..	2003	St. Vincent-Grenadines
..	..	..	33	26	7	..	..	2004	
..	..	..	*35	*27	*8	..	..	2005	
..	..	..	*36	*28	*8	..	..	2006	
..	..	..	1416	1416	..	..	..	2003	Trinité-et-Tobago
..	..	..	1416	1416	..	..	..	2004	
..	..	..	1416	1416	..	..	..	2005	
..	..	..	1416	1416	..	..	..	2006	
..	..	..	*4	*4	..	..	..	2003	Iles Turques et Caiques
..	..	..	*4	*4	..	..	..	2004	
..	..	..	*4	*4	..	..	..	2005	
..	..	..	*4	*4	..	..	..	2006	
863	..	..	999999	787423	98352	105415	8809	2003	Etats-Unis
700	..	..	1017440	804817	97704	105560	9359	2004	
700	..	..	1035420	819776	98187	105585	11872	2005	
715	..	..	1043655	824815	98567	105585	14688	2006	
..	..	..	180	180	..	..	..	2003	Iles Vierges américaines
..	..	..	*180	*180	..	..	..	2004	
..	..	..	*180	*180	..	..	..	2005	
..	..	..	*180	*180	..	..	..	2006	
2176	**..**	**..**	**168883**	**50018**	**115813**	**3025**	**27**	**2003**	**Amérique du Sud**
1897	**..**	**..**	**175280**	**53242**	**118967**	**3025**	**47**	**2004**	
2076	**..**	**..**	**178186**	**53518**	**121597**	**3025**	**47**	**2005**	
2299	**..**	**..**	**180901**	**54046**	**123785**	**3025**	**45**	**2006**	
21	..	..	25679	14854	9780	1018	27	2003	Argentine
21	..	..	25686	14810	9831	1018	27	2004	
21	..	..	25686	14810	9831	1018	27	2005	
21	..	..	25686	14810	9831	1018	27	2006	
24	..	..	1206	790	416	..	..	2003	Bolivie
24	..	..	1312	875	437	..	..	2004	
24	..	..	1267	830	437	..	..	2005	
24	..	..	1291	830	461	..	..	2006	
*1706	..	..	80287	11693	66587	2007	..	2003	Brésil
1427	..	..	84108	14529	67572	2007	..	2004	
1583	..	..	86300	15019	69274	2007	..	2005	
1666	..	..	88294	14520	71767	2007	..	2006	
78	..	..	10735	6646	4089	..	..	2003	Chili
78	..	..	11562	6834	4728	..	..	2004	
86	..	..	11983	7255	4728	..	..	2005	
*200	..	..	12369	7556	4813	..	..	2006	
41	..	..	13177	4325	8852	..	0	2003	Colombie
41	..	..	13351	4416	8915	..	20	2004	
41	..	..	13316	4353	8943	..	20	2005	
41	..	..	12791	4262	8511	..	18	2006	

Table 32

Net installed capacity of electric generating plants by type
Thousand kilowatts

Country or area / Pays ou zone	Year / Année	Self-producers and public utilities / Autoproducteurs et services publics					Self- Auto-	
		Total Totale	Thermal Thermique	Hydro Hydraulique	Nuclear Nucléaire	Geothermal Géother- -mique	Total Totale	Thermal Thermique
Ecuador	2003	3303	1569	1734	..	..	134	
	2004	3331	1598	1733	..	..	169	
	2005	3567	1803	1764	..	..	230	
	2006	3998	2197	1801	..	..	472	
Falkland Is. (Malvinas)	2003	*9	*9	..	..	..	*2	
	2004	*9	*9	..	..	..	*2	
	2005	*9	*9	..	..	..	*2	
	2006	*9	*9	..	..	..	*2	
French Guiana	2003	140	140	..	..	..	..	
	2004	140	140	..	..	..	..	
	2005	140	140	..	..	..	..	
	2006	140	140	..	..	..	..	
Guyana	2003	308	308	..	..	..	170	
	2004	308	308	..	..	..	170	
	2005	308	308	..	..	..	170	
	2006	308	308	..	..	..	170	
Paraguay	2003	7416	6	7410	..	..	..	
	2004	7416	6	7410	..	..	..	
	2005	7416	6	7410	..	..	..	
	2006	7416	6	7410	..	..	..	
Peru	2003	5969	2937	3032	..	..	875	
	2004	6015	2960	3056	..	..	920	9
	2005	6238	3031	3207	..	..	1019	9
	2006	6628	3414	3214	..	..	1003	9
Suriname	2003	389	200	189	..	..	329	1
	2004	389	200	189	..	..	329	1
	2005	389	200	189	..	..	329	1
	2006	389	200	189	..	..	329	1
Uruguay	2003	2171	633	1538	..	..	63	
	2004	2093	555	1538	..	..	63	
	2005	2092	554	1538	..	..	63	
	2006	2291	753	1538	..	..	63	
Venezuela(Bolivar. Rep.)	2003	20577	8086	12491	..	..	910	9
	2004	22124	8260	13864	..	..	910	9
	2005	22135	7538	14597	..	..	846	8
	2006	22215	7618	14597	..	..	885	8
Asia	**2003**	**1241726**	**923107**	**238330**	**75190**	**5099**	**106478**	**1012**
	2004	**1345876**	**996875**	**264754**	**78620**	**5627**	**122497**	**1165**
	2005	**1453866**	**1087591**	**277050**	**82702**	**6523**	**110964**	**1043**
	2006	**1574674**	**1192959**	**289447**	**84667**	**7601**	**114404**	**1068**
Afghanistan	2003	*489	*115	*374	..	..	*62	*
	2004	*489	*115	*374	..	..	*62	*
	2005	*489	*115	*374	..	..	*62	*
	2006	*489	*115	*374	..	..	*62	*
Armenia	2003	3377	1799	1170	408	..	43	
	2004	3206	1774	1024	408	..	43	
	2005	3209	1774	1027	408	..	43	
	2006	3210	1775	1027	408	..	44	
Azerbaijan	2003	5673	4703	970	..	..	*200	*2
	2004	5665	4695	970	..	..	*200	*2
	2005	5157	4187	970	..	..	*200	*2
	2006	5624	4599	1025	..	..	*200	*2
Bahrain	2003	2629	2629	..	..	..	*210	*2
	2004	2659	2659	..	..	..	*240	*2
	2005	1889	1889	..	..	..	*250	*2
	2006	2500	2500	..	..	..	*300	*3

Table 32

Puissance nette installée des centrales électriques - par catégorie

Milliers de kilowatts

producers producteurs			Public utilities Services publics					Year Année	Country or area Pays ou zone
Hydro Hydraulique	Nuclear Nucléaire	Geothermal Géothermique	Total Totale	Thermal Thermique	Hydro Hydraulique	Nuclear Nucléaire	Geothermal Géothermique		
31	..	..	3169	1466	1703	..	..	2003	Equateur
30	..	..	3162	1459	1703	..	..	2004	
44	..	..	3337	1617	1720	..	..	2005	
70	..	..	3526	1795	1731	..	..	2006	
..	..	..	*7	*7	..	..	..	2003	Iles Falkland (Malvinas)
..	..	..	*7	*7	..	..	..	2004	
..	..	..	*7	*7	..	..	..	2005	
..	..	..	*7	*7	..	..	..	2006	
..	..	..	140	140	..	..	..	2003	Guyane française
..	..	..	140	140	..	..	..	2004	
..	..	..	140	140	..	..	..	2005	
..	..	..	140	140	..	..	..	2006	
..	..	..	138	138	..	..	..	2003	Guyana
..	..	..	138	138	..	..	..	2004	
..	..	..	138	138	..	..	..	2005	
..	..	..	138	138	..	..	..	2006	
..	..	..	7416	6	7410	..	..	2003	Paraguay
..	..	..	7416	6	7410	..	..	2004	
..	..	..	7416	6	7410	..	..	2005	
..	..	..	7416	6	7410	..	..	2006	
85	..	..	5094	2148	2947	..	..	2003	Pérou
87	..	..	5095	2126	2969	..	..	2004	
88	..	..	5219	2100	3119	..	..	2005	
88	..	..	5625	2499	3126	..	..	2006	
189	..	..	60	60	..	..	..	2003	Suriname
189	..	..	60	60	..	..	..	2004	
189	..	..	60	60	..	..	..	2005	
189	..	..	60	60	..	..	..	2006	
..	..	..	2108	570	1538	..	..	2003	Uruguay
..	..	..	2030	492	1538	..	..	2004	
..	..	..	2029	491	1538	..	..	2005	
..	..	..	2228	690	1538	..	..	2006	
..	..	..	19667	7176	12491	..	..	2003	Venezuela(Rép. bolivar.)
..	..	..	21214	7350	13864	..	..	2004	
..	..	..	21289	6692	14597	..	..	2005	
..	..	..	21330	6733	14597	..	..	2006	
3662	..	1609	1135248	821901	234668	75190	3490	2003	Asie
3784	..	2128	1223379	880290	260970	78620	3499	2004	
3694	..	2882	1342903	983203	273356	82702	3641	2005	
3695	..	3828	1460270	1086078	285752	84667	3773	2006	
*7	..	..	*427	*60	*367	..	..	2003	Afghanistan
*7	..	..	*427	*60	*367	..	..	2004	
*7	..	..	*427	*60	*367	..	..	2005	
*7	..	..	*427	*60	*367	..	..	2006	
..	..	..	3334	1756	1170	408	..	2003	Arménie
..	..	..	3163	1731	1024	408	..	2004	
..	..	..	3166	1731	1027	408	..	2005	
..	..	..	3166	1731	1027	408	..	2006	
..	..	..	5473	4503	970	..	..	2003	Azerbaïdjan
..	..	..	5465	4495	970	..	..	2004	
..	..	..	4957	3987	970	..	..	2005	
..	..	..	5424	4399	1025	..	..	2006	
..	..	..	2419	2419	..	..	..	2003	Bahreïn
..	..	..	2419	2419	..	..	..	2004	
..	..	..	1639	1639	..	..	..	2005	
..	..	..	2200	2200	..	..	..	2006	

Table 32

Net installed capacity of electric generating plants by type
Thousand kilowatts

Country or area Pays ou zone	Year Année	Self-producers and public utilities Autoproducteurs et services publics					Self- Auto-	
		Total Totale	Thermal Thermique	Hydro Hydraulique	Nuclear Nucléaire	Geothermal Géother--mique	Total Totale	Thermal Thermique
Bangladesh	2003	4058	3828	230	..	..	1258	12
	2004	4263	4033	230	..	..	1258	12
	2005	*4263	*4033	*230	..	..	*1258	*12
	2006	5245	5015	230	..	..	*1258	*12
Bhutan	2003	438	9	429	..	..	..	
	2004	438	9	429	..	..	..	
	2005	478	9	469	..	..	..	
	2006	478	9	469	..	..	..	
Brunei Darussalam	2003	873	873	..	..	..	63	
	2004	874	874	..	..	..	64	
	2005	759	759	..	..	..	68	
	2006	759	759	..	..	..	68	
Cambodia	2003	187	175	12	..	0	78	
	2004	190	177	13	..	0	76	
	2005	232	219	13	..	0	116	1
	2006	341	327	13	..	*1	204	2
China	2003	356620	265547	86075	4998	..	..	
	2004	419158	304900	108260	5998	..	..	
	2005	508000	383540	117888	6572	..	..	
	2006	*602570	*469000	*126000	7570	..	..	
China, Hong Kong SAR	2003	11683	11683	..	..	..	..	
	2004	11683	11683	..	..	..	..	
	2005	11804	11804	..	..	..	..	
	2006	12380	12380	..	..	..	..	
China, Macao SAR	2003	489	489		..	..	..	
	2004	488	488		..	..	..	
	2005	488	488		..	..	..	
	2006	472	472		..	..	..	
Cyprus	2003	995	994	..	..	*1	6	
	2004	995	994	..	..	*1	6	
	2005	1125	1124	..	..	1	6	
	2006	1136	1135	..	..	*1	16	
Georgia	2003	*4374	*1642	*2732	..	..	..	
	2004	*4374	*1642	*2732	..	..	..	
	2005	*4374	*1642	*2732	..	..	..	
	2006	*4374	*1642	*2732	..	..	..	
India	2003	131424	99197	29507	2720	..	18740	187
	2004	137529	103817	30942	2770	..	19103	191
	2005	145695	110009	32326	3360	..	21408	214
	2006	157070	118456	34714	3900	..	24681	246
Indonesia	2003	26431	20898	4533	..	*1000	*4605	*32
	2004	26669	21099	4570	..	*1000	*4605	*32
	2005	27725	22137	4588	..	*1000	*4605	*32
	2006	27791	22203	4588	..	*1000	*4655	*32
Iran(Islamic Rep. of)	2003	39613	35183	4430	..	..	6201	62
	2004	*42749	*37916	*4833	..	..	6298	62
	2005	*44390	*39325	*5065	..	..	*6325	*63
	2006	*44390	*39325	*5065	..	..	*6325	*63
Iraq	2003	8400	5780	2620	..	..	*400	*4
	2004	8400	5780	2620	..	..	*400	*4
	2005	8400	5780	2620	..	..	*400	*4
	2006	8400	5780	2620	..	..	*400	*4
Israel	2003	10317	10307	*5	..	*5	*200	*1
	2004	10309	10299	*5	..	*5	*200	*1
	2005	*10318	*10308	*5	..	*5	*203	*1
	2006	11106	11096	*5	..	*5	*203	*1

Table 32

Puissance nette installée des centrales électriques - par catégorie
Milliers de kilowatts

| producers producteurs | | | Public utilities Services publics | | | | | Year Année | Country or area Pays ou zone |
Hydro Hydraulique	Nuclear Nucléaire	Geothermal Géother-mique	Total Totale	Thermal Thermique	Hydro Hydraulique	Nuclear Nucléaire	Geothermal Géother-mique		
..	..	..	2800	2570	230	..	..	2003	Bangladesh
..	..	..	3005	2775	230	..	..	2004	
..	..	..	*3005	*2775	*230	..	..	2005	
..	..	..	3987	3757	230	..	..	2006	
..	..	..	438	9	429		..	2003	Bhoutan
..	..	..	438	9	429		..	2004	
..	..	..	478	9	469		..	2005	
..	..	..	478	9	469		..	2006	
..	..	..	810	810	..	..	..	2003	Brunéi Darussalam
..	..	..	810	810	..	..	..	2004	
..	..	..	691	691	..	..	..	2005	
..	..	..	691	691	..	..	..	2006	
..	..	..	110	98	12	..	0	2003	Cambodge
..	..	..	113	100	13	..	0	2004	
..	..	..	116	103	13	..	0	2005	
..	..	..	137	123	13	..	*1	2006	
..	..	..	356620	265547	86075	4998	..	2003	Chine
..	..	..	419158	304900	108260	5998	..	2004	
..	..	..	508000	383540	117888	6572	..	2005	
..	..	..	*602570	*469000	*126000	7570	..	2006	
..	..	..	11683	11683	..	..	..	2003	Chine, Hong-Kong RAS
..	..	..	11683	11683	..	..	..	2004	
..	..	..	11804	11804	..	..	..	2005	
..	..	..	12380	12380	..	..	..	2006	
..	..	..	489	489	..	..	..	2003	Chine, Macao RAS
..	..	..	488	488	..	..	..	2004	
..	..	..	488	488	..	..	..	2005	
..	..	..	472	472	..	..	..	2006	
..	..	..	989	988	..	..	*1	2003	Chypre
..	..	..	989	988	..	..	*1	2004	
..	..	..	1119	1118	..	..	1	2005	
..	..	..	1120	1119	..	..	*1	2006	
..	..	..	*4374	*1642	*2732	..	..	2003	Géorgie
..	..	..	*4374	*1642	*2732	..	..	2004	
..	..	..	*4374	*1642	*2732	..	..	2005	
..	..	..	*4374	*1642	*2732	..	..	2006	
..	..	..	112684	80457	29507	2720	..	2003	Inde
..	..	..	118426	84714	30942	2770	..	2004	
..	..	..	124287	88601	32326	3360	..	2005	
..	..	..	132389	93775	34714	3900	..	2006	
*1367	..	..	21826	17660	3166	..	*1000	2003	Indonésie
*1367	..	..	22064	17861	3203	..	*1000	2004	
*1367	..	..	23120	18899	3221	..	*1000	2005	
*1367	..	..	23136	18915	3221	..	*1000	2006	
..	..	..	33412	28982	4430	..	..	2003	Iran(Rép. islamique)
..	..	..	*36451	*31618	*4833	..	..	2004	
..	..	..	*38065	*33000	*5065	..	..	2005	
..	..	..	*38065	*33000	*5065	..	..	2006	
..	..	..	8000	5380	2620	..	..	2003	Iraq
..	..	..	8000	5380	2620	..	..	2004	
..	..	..	8000	5380	2620	..	..	2005	
..	..	..	8000	5380	2620	..	..	2006	
*5	..	*5	10117	10117	..	..	..	2003	Israël
*5	..	*5	10109	10109	..	..	..	2004	
*5	..	*5	*10115	*10115	..	..	..	2005	
*5	..	*5	10903	10903	..	..	..	2006	

Table 32

Net installed capacity of electric generating plants by type

Thousand kilowatts

Country or area Pays ou zone	Year Année	Self-producers and public utilities Autoproducteurs et services publics					Self- Auto-	
		Total Totale	Thermal Thermique	Hydro Hydraulique	Nuclear Nucléaire	Geothermal Géother- -mique	Total Totale	Thermal Thermique
Japan	2003	270579	176222	46712	45742	1903	38628	35836
	2004	275268	178973	46737	47122	2436	41561	38231
	2005	277323	177268	47292	49580	3183	42129	38052
	2006	278777	177839	47358	49467	4113	43957	38949
Jordan	2003	1789	1776	12	..	*1	97	97
	2004	2077	2060	16	..	*1	139	139
	2005	2077	2060	16	..	1	139	139
	2006	2076	2063	12	..	1	193	193
Kazakhstan	2003	18650	16387	2263	..	..	..	
	2004	18763	16500	2263	..	..	..	
	2005	18734	16517	2217	..	..	..	
	2006	*18734	*16517	*2217	..	..	..	
Korea, Dem.Ppl's.Rep.	2003	9500	4500	5000	..	..	..	
	2004	9500	4500	5000	..	..	..	
	2005	9500	4500	5000	..	..	..	
	2006	*9500	*4500	*5000	..	..	..	
Korea, Republic of	2003	60697	41061	3877	15716	43	6005	5980
	2004	64532	43899	3879	16716	38	5613	5602
	2005	66537	45365	3883	17176	113	5821	5805
	2006	70081	46666	5485	17716	214	5600	5560
Kuwait	2003	9855	9855	..	..	..	*92	*92
	2004	9855	9855	..	..	..	*92	*92
	2005	10855	10855	..	..	..	*92	*92
	2006	10855	10855	..	..	..	*92	*92
Kyrgyzstan	2003	3697	*728	2969	..	..	1	
	2004	*3697	*728	*2969	..	..	1	
	2005	*3697	*728	*2969	..	..	1	
	2006	*3697	*728	*2969	..	..	*1	
Lao People's Dem. Rep.	2003	682	*50	456	..	*176	*176	
	2004	682	*50	456	..	176	176	
	2005	742	*50	516	..	*176	*176	
	2006	742	*50	516	..	*176	*176	
Lebanon	2003	2661	2383	278	..	..	*388	*300
	2004	2659	2383	276	..	..	*490	*300
	2005	2312	2040	272	..	..	*390	*200
	2006	2312	2040	272	..	..	*390	*200
Malaysia	2003	16631	14565	2066	..	..	5953	5953
	2004	22923	20835	2089	..	..	12223	12223
	2005	21278	19208	2070	..	..	2243	2243
	2006	*22061	*19998	2063	..	..	*2335	*2333
Maldives	2003	49	49	..	..	..	..	
	2004	49	49	..	..	..	..	
	2005	*49	*49	..	..	..	..	
	2006	58	58	..	..	..	..	
Mongolia	2003	832	832	..	..	..	*60	*6
	2004	832	832	..	..	..	*60	*6
	2005	832	832	..	..	..	60	6
	2006	832	832	..	..	..	60	6
Myanmar	2003	*1213	*813	*400	..	..	..	
	2004	*1263	*813	*450	..	..	..	
	2005	*1363	*813	*550	..	..	..	
	2006	*1413	*813	*600	..	..	..	
Nepal	2003	606	55	551	..	..	148	
	2004	610	57	553	..	..	149	
	2005	*611	*57	*554	..	..	*150	
	2006	*611	*57	*554	..	..	*150	

Table 32

Puissance nette installée des centrales électriques - par catégorie
Milliers de kilowatts

producers producteurs			Public utilities Services publics					Year Année	Country or area Pays ou zone
Hydro Hydraulique	Nuclear Nucléaire	Geothermal Géother-mique	Total Totale	Thermal Thermique	Hydro Hydraulique	Nuclear Nucléaire	Geothermal Géother-mique		
1390	..	1402	231951	140386	45322	45742	501	2003	Japon
1395	..	1935	233707	140742	45342	47122	501	2004	
1395	..	2682	235194	139216	45897	49580	501	2005	
1396	..	3612	234820	138890	45962	49467	501	2006	
..	..	..	1692	1679	12	..	*1	2003	Jordanie
..	..	..	1938	1921	16	..	*1	2004	
..	..	..	1938	1921	16	..	1	2005	
..	..	..	1883	1870	12	..	1	2006	
..	..	..	18650	16387	2263	..	..	2003	Kazakhstan
..	..	..	18763	16500	2263	..	..	2004	
..	..	..	18734	16517	2217	..	..	2005	
..	..	..	*18734	*16517	*2217	..	..	2006	
..	..	..	9500	4500	5000	..	..	2003	Corée,Rép.pop.dém.de
..	..	..	9500	4500	5000	..	..	2004	
..	..	..	9500	4500	5000	..	..	2005	
..	..	..	*9500	*4500	*5000	..	..	2006	
..	..	25	54692	35081	3877	15716	*18	2003	Corée, République de
..	..	11	58919	38297	3879	16716	27	2004	
..	..	16	60716	39560	3883	17176	97	2005	
..	..	34	64481	41100	5485	17716	180	2006	
..	..	..	9763	9763	..	..	..	2003	Koweït
..	..	..	9763	9763	..	..	..	2004	
..	..	..	10763	10763	..	..	..	2005	
..	..	..	10763	10763	..	..	..	2006	
1	..	..	3696	*728	2968	..	..	2003	Kirghizistan
1	..	..	*3696	*728	*2968	..	..	2004	
1	..	..	*3696	*728	*2968	..	..	2005	
*1	..	..	*3696	*728	*2968	..	..	2006	
..	..	*176	506	*50	456	..	..	2003	Rép. dém. pop. lao
..	..	176	506	*50	456	..	..	2004	
..	..	*176	566	*50	516	..	..	2005	
..	..	*176	566	*50	516	..	..	2006	
88	..	..	2273	2083	190	..	..	2003	Liban
190	..	..	2169	2083	86	..	..	2004	
190	..	..	1922	1840	82	..	..	2005	
190	..	..	1922	1840	82	..	..	2006	
..	..	..	10678	8612	2066	..	..	2003	Malaisie
..	..	..	10701	8612	2089	..	..	2004	
..	..	..	19035	16965	2070	..	..	2005	
..	..	..	*19726	*17663	2063	..	..	2006	
..	..	..	49	49	..	..	..	2003	Maldives
..	..	..	49	49	..	..	..	2004	
..	..	..	*49	*49	..	..	..	2005	
..	..	..	58	58	..	..	..	2006	
..	..	..	772	772	..	..	..	2003	Mongolie
..	..	..	772	772	..	..	..	2004	
..	..	..	772	772	..	..	..	2005	
..	..	..	772	772	..	..	..	2006	
..	..	..	*1213	*813	*400	..	..	2003	Myanmar
..	..	..	*1263	*813	*450	..	..	2004	
..	..	..	*1363	*813	*550	..	..	2005	
..	..	..	*1413	*813	*600	..	..	2006	
148	..	..	458	55	403	..	..	2003	Népal
149	..	..	461	57	404	..	..	2004	
*150	..	..	*461	*57	*404	..	..	2005	
*150	..	..	*461	*57	*404	..	..	2006	

Table 32

Net installed capacity of electric generating plants by type

Thousand kilowatts

Country or area Pays ou zone	Year Année	Self-producers and public utilities Autoproducteurs et services publics					Self-Auto-	
		Total Totale	Thermal Thermique	Hydro Hydraulique	Nuclear Nucléaire	Geothermal Géother- -mique	Total Totale	Thermal Thermique
Occup. Palestinian Terr.	2003	140	140	..	..	..	..	
	2004	140	140	..	..	..	..	
	2005	140	140	..	..	..	..	
	2006	*140	*140	..	..	..	..	
Oman	2003	2788	2788	..	..	..	..	
	2004	3024	3024	..	..	..	..	
	2005	2983	2983	..	..	..	..	
	2006	3323	3323	..	..	..	..	
Other Asia	2003	39786	30132	4510	5144	..	*6500	*650
	2004	41292	31639	4509	5144	..	*6700	*670
	2005	42863	33148	4571	5144	..	*6700	*670
	2006	44070	34415	4511	5144	..	*6700	*670
Pakistan	2003	17798	12290	5046	462	..	*5	*
	2004	19399	12438	6499	462	..	*15	*1
	2005	19480	12519	6499	462	..	*30	*3
	2006	19449	12508	6479	462	..	*30	*3
Philippines	2003	15150	10335	2883	..	1932	*26	*1
	2004	15574	10409	3233	..	1932	*26	*1
	2005	15645	10403	3238	..	2004	*26	*1
	2006	15829	10552	3273	..	2004	*26	*1
Qatar	2003	*2676	*2676	..	..	..	*1869	*186
	2004	*2900	*2900	..	..	..	*2006	*200
	2005	*2829	*2829	..	..	..	*1935	*193
	2006	3028	3028	..	..	..	2272	227
Saudi Arabia	2003	30219	30219	..	..		*3200	*320
	2004	30673	30673	..	..		*3250	*325
	2005	33535	33535	..	..		*3300	*330
	2006	35885	35885	..	..		*3300	*330
Singapore	2003	8848	8848	..	..	..	..	
	2004	8848	8848	..	..	..	..	
	2005	10159	10159	..	..	..	..	
	2006	10785	10785	..	..	..	..	
Sri Lanka	2003	2710	1460	1247	..	3	*227	*22
	2004	2726	1442	1281	..	3	*227	*22
	2005	2638	1342	1293	..	3	*227	*22
	2006	2661	1342	1316	..	3	*227	*22
Syrian Arab Republic	2003	7679	6151	1528	..	..	*600	*60
	2004	7679	6151	1528	..	..	*600	*60
	2005	7525	5997	1528	..	..	*600	*60
	2006	7625	6097	1528	..	..	*600	*60
Tajikistan	2003	*4443	*389	*4054	..	..	..	
	2004	*4443	*389	*4054	..	..	..	
	2005	*4443	*389	*4054	..	..	..	
	2006	*4443	*389	*4054	..	..	..	
Thailand	2003	30155	27181	2973	..	1	*5350	*535
	2004	37586	34109	3476	..	1	11679	1167
	2005	33348	29871	3476	..	1	7079	707
	2006	32051	28574	3476	..	1	5236	523
Timor-Leste	2003	*45	*45	..	..	..	..	
	2004	*50	*50	..	..	..	..	
	2005	*52	*52	..	..	..	..	
	2006	*52	*52	..	..	..	..	
Turkey	2003	35587	22974	12579	..	34	4542	390
	2004	36824	24145	12645	..	34	4380	372
	2005	38843	25901	12906	..	36	4062	349
	2006	40565	27420	13063	..	82	3778	321

Table 32

Puissance nette installée des centrales électriques - par catégorie
Milliers de kilowatts

producers producteurs			Public utilities Services publics					Year Année	Country or area Pays ou zone
Hydro Hydraulique	Nuclear Nucléaire	Geothermal Géother-mique	Total Totale	Thermal Thermique	Hydro Hydraulique	Nuclear Nucléaire	Geothermal Géother-mique		
..	..	..	140	140	..	..	..	2003	Terr. palestiniens occup.
..	..	..	140	140	..	..	..	2004	
..	..	..	140	140	..	..	..	2005	
..	..	..	*140	*140	..	..	..	2006	
..	..	..	2788	2788	..	..	..	2003	Oman
..	..	..	3024	3024	..	..	..	2004	
..	..	..	2983	2983	..	..	..	2005	
..	..	..	3323	3323	..	..	..	2006	
..	..	..	33286	23632	4510	5144	..	2003	Autre Asie
..	..	..	34592	24939	4509	5144	..	2004	
..	..	..	36163	26448	4571	5144	..	2005	
..	..	..	37370	27715	4511	5144	..	2006	
..	..	..	17793	12285	5046	462	..	2003	Pakistan
..	..	..	19384	12423	6499	462	..	2004	
..	..	..	19450	12489	6499	462	..	2005	
..	..	..	19419	12478	6479	462	..	2006	
*16	..	..	15124	10325	2867	..	1932	2003	Philippines
*16	..	..	15548	10399	3217	..	1932	2004	
*16	..	..	15619	10393	3222	..	2004	2005	
*16	..	..	15803	10542	3257	..	2004	2006	
..	..	..	807	807	..	..	..	2003	Qatar
..	..	..	894	894	..	..	..	2004	
..	..	..	894	894	..	..	..	2005	
..	..	..	756	756	..	..	..	2006	
..	..	..	27019	27019	..	..	..	2003	Arabie saoudite
..	..	..	27423	27423	..	..	..	2004	
..	..	..	30235	30235	..	..	..	2005	
..	..	..	32585	32585	..	..	..	2006	
..	..	..	8848	8848	..	..	..	2003	Singapour
..	..	..	8848	8848	..	..	..	2004	
..	..	..	10159	10159	..	..	..	2005	
..	..	..	10785	10785	..	..	..	2006	
..	..	..	2483	1233	1247	..	3	2003	Sri Lanka
..	..	..	2499	1215	1281	..	3	2004	
..	..	..	2411	1115	1293	..	3	2005	
..	..	..	2434	1115	1316	..	3	2006	
..	..	..	7079	5551	1528	..	..	2003	Rép. arabe syrienne
..	..	..	7079	5551	1528	..	..	2004	
..	..	..	6925	5397	1528	..	..	2005	
..	..	..	7025	5497	1528	..	..	2006	
..	..	..	*4443	*389	*4054	..	..	2003	Tadjikistan
..	..	..	*4443	*389	*4054	..	..	2004	
..	..	..	*4443	*389	*4054	..	..	2005	
..	..	..	*4443	*389	*4054	..	..	2006	
..	..	..	24805	21831	2973	..	1	2003	Thaïlande
..	..	..	25907	22430	3476	..	1	2004	
..	..	..	26269	22792	3476	..	1	2005	
..	..	..	26815	23338	3476	..	1	2006	
..	..	..	*45	*45	..	..	..	2003	Timor-Leste
..	..	..	*50	*50	..	..	..	2004	
..	..	..	*52	*52	..	..	..	2005	
..	..	..	*52	*52	..	..	..	2006	
640	..	1	31045	19073	11939	..	33	2003	Turquie
654	..	1	32444	20420	11991	..	33	2004	
563	..	3	34781	22405	12343	..	33	2005	
563	..	1	36787	24206	12500	..	81	2006	

Table 32

Net installed capacity of electric generating plants by type
Thousand kilowatts

Country or area Pays ou zone	Year Année	Self-producers and public utilities Autoproducteurs et services publics					Self- Auto-	
		Total Totale	Thermal Thermique	Hydro Hydraulique	Nuclear Nucléaire	Geothermal Géother- -mique	Total Totale	Thermal Thermique
Turkmenistan	2003	*3921	*3920	*1	..	..	..	
	2004	*3921	*3920	*1	..	..	..	
	2005	*3921	*3920	*1	..	..	..	
	2006	*3921	*3920	*1	..	..	..	
United Arab Emirates	2003	12172	12172	..	..	..	..	
	2004	13550	13550	..	..	..	..	
	2005	15710	15710	..	..	..	..	
	2006	*15710	*15710	..	..	..	..	
Uzbekistan	2003	*11709	*9999	*1710	..	..	*155	*15
	2004	*11709	*9999	*1710	..	..	*155	*15
	2005	*11709	*9999	*1710	..	..	*155	*15
	2006	*11709	*9999	*1710	..	..	*155	*15
Viet Nam	2003	9302	5174	4128	..	..	*300	*30
	2004	11573	7445	4128	..	..	*300	*30
	2005	*12228	*8100	*4128	..	..	*600	*60
	2006	*12228	*8100	*4128	..	..	*600	*60
Yemen	2003	1087	1087	..	..	..	*90	*9
	2004	1117	1117	..	..	..	*100	*10
	2005	1110	1110	..	..	..	*105	*10
	2006	*1115	*1115	..	..	..	*110	*11
Europe	**2003**	**1107563**	**656697**	**245312**	**175319**	**30235**	**80700**	**7389**
	2004	**1111414**	**653469**	**246094**	**175252**	**36599**	**81021**	**7429**
	2005	**1122361**	**659368**	**245341**	**173880**	**43772**	**82895**	**7543**
	2006	**1134356**	**659334**	**247641**	**174681**	**52700**	**83078**	**7486**
Albania	2003	1669	224	1445	..	..	224	22
	2004	1669	224	1445	..	..	224	22
	2005	*1669	224	*1445	..	..	224	22
	2006	*1669	*224	*1445	..	..	*224	*22
Austria	2003	20279	6177	13750	..	352	1664	110
	2004	20981	6326	14086	..	569	1406	105
	2005	18914	6254	11811	..	849	1651	120
	2006	19201	6344	11853	..	1004	1676	122
Belarus	2003	7956	7944	11	..	1	296	29
	2004	7956	7944	11	..	1	296	29
	2005	8024	8011	12	..	1	296	29
	2006	*8024	*8011	*12	..	1	*296	*29
Belgium	2003	15616	8366	*1421	5761	68	408	40
	2004	15660	8364	1415	5802	79	487	48
	2005	16094	8682	1432	5891	89	564	56
	2006	16258	8807	1414	5825	212	496	49
Bosnia and Herzegovina	2003	4337	*1957	2380	..	..	*20	*2
	2004	4368	*1957	2411	..	..	*20	*2
	2005	4341	*1930	2411	..	..	*30	*3
	2006	*4341	*1930	*2411	..	..	*30	*3
Bulgaria	2003	11997	6759	2515	2723	0	340	34
	2004	11979	6689	2567	2722	1	270	27
	2005	11973	6682	2567	2722	*2	263	26
	2006	*11975	*6682	*2567	*2722	*4	*263	*26
Croatia	2003	3918	1843	2075	..	0	228	22
	2004	*3911	*1843	*2066	..	*2	*228	*22
	2005	3866	1800	2060	..	6	213	20
	2006	3879	1802	2060	..	17	215	21
Czech Republic	2003	17343	11423	2149	3760	11	2173	205
	2004	17434	11498	2160	3760	16	2237	208
	2005	17412	11456	2167	3760	29	2290	213
	2006	17508	11528	2175	3760	45	2353	219

Table 32

Puissance nette installée des centrales électriques - par catégorie

Milliers de kilowatts

producers producteurs			Public utilities Services publics					Year Année	Country or area Pays ou zone
Hydro Hydraulique	Nuclear Nucléaire	Geothermal Géother-mique	Total Totale	Thermal Thermique	Hydro Hydraulique	Nuclear Nucléaire	Geothermal Géother-mique		
..	..	..	*3921	*3920	*1	..	..	2003	Turkménistan
..	..	..	*3921	*3920	*1	..	..	2004	
..	..	..	*3921	*3920	*1	..	..	2005	
..	..	..	*3921	*3920	*1	..	..	2006	
..	..	..	12172	12172	..	..	..	2003	Emirats arabes unis
..	..	..	13550	13550	..	..	..	2004	
..	..	..	15710	15710	..	..	..	2005	
..	..	..	*15710	*15710	..	..	..	2006	
..	..	..	*11554	*9844	*1710	..	..	2003	Ouzbékistan
..	..	..	*11554	*9844	*1710	..	..	2004	
..	..	..	*11554	*9844	*1710	..	..	2005	
..	..	..	*11554	*9844	*1710	..	..	2006	
..	..	..	9002	4874	4128	..	..	2003	Viet Nam
..	..	..	11273	7145	4128	..	..	2004	
..	..	..	*11628	*7500	*4128	..	..	2005	
..	..	..	*11628	*7500	*4128	..	..	2006	
..	..	..	997	997	..	..	..	2003	Yémen
..	..	..	1017	1017	..	..	..	2004	
..	..	..	1005	1005	..	..	..	2005	
..	..	..	*1005	*1005	..	..	..	2006	
5741	..	1065	1026863	582803	239571	175319	29170	2003	Europe
5412	..	1312	1030393	579172	240682	175252	35287	2004	
5510	..	1948	1039466	583931	239831	173880	41824	2005	
5727	..	2486	1051278	584469	241914	174681	50214	2006	
..	..	..	1445	..	1445	..	..	2003	Albanie
..	..	..	1445	..	1445	..	..	2004	
..	..	..	*1445	..	*1445	..	..	2005	
..	..	..	*1445	..	*1445	..	..	2006	
564	..	..	18615	5077	13186	..	352	2003	Autriche
347	..	..	19575	5267	13739	..	569	2004	
449	..	..	17263	5052	11362	..	849	2005	
449	..	..	17525	5117	11404	..	1004	2006	
3	..	1	7660	7652	8	..	..	2003	Bélarus
3	..	1	7660	7652	8	..	..	2004	
3	..	1	7728	7719	9	..	..	2005	
*3	..	1	*7728	*7719	*9	..	..	2006	
..	..	2	15208	7960	*1421	5761	66	2003	Belgique
..	..	2	15173	7879	1415	5802	77	2004	
..	..	2	15530	8120	1432	5891	87	2005	
..	..	2	15762	8313	1414	5825	210	2006	
..	..	..	4317	*1937	2380	..	..	2003	Bosnie y Herzégovine
..	..	..	4348	*1937	2411	..	..	2004	
..	..	..	4311	*1900	2411	..	..	2005	
..	..	..	*4311	*1900	*2411	..	..	2006	
..	..	..	11657	6419	2515	2723	0	2003	Bulgarie
..	..	..	11709	6419	2567	2722	1	2004	
..	..	..	11710	6419	2567	2722	*2	2005	
..	..	..	*11712	*6419	*2567	*2722	*4	2006	
*4	..	..	3690	1619	2071	..	0	2003	Croatie
*4	..	..	*3683	*1619	*2062	..	*2	2004	
4	..	..	3653	1591	2056	..	6	2005	
4	..	..	3664	1591	2056	..	17	2006	
123	..	..	15170	9373	2026	3760	11	2003	République tchèque
155	..	..	15197	9416	2005	3760	16	2004	
155	..	..	15122	9321	2012	3760	29	2005	
155	..	..	15155	9330	2020	3760	45	2006	

Table 32

Net installed capacity of electric generating plants by type
Thousand kilowatts

Country or area Pays ou zone	Year Année	Self-producers and public utilities Autoproducteurs et services publics					Self- Auto-	
		Total Totale	Thermal Thermique	Hydro Hydraulique	Nuclear Nucléaire	Geothermal Géother- -mique	Total Totale	Thermal Thermique
Denmark	2003	13593	10462	11	..	3120	573	5;
	2004	13343	10204	11	..	3128	607	6(
	2005	13349	10205	11	..	3133	639	6;
	2006	13016	9868	9	..	3139	624	6;
Estonia	2003	*2550	*2544	*4	..	*2	25	
	2004	2387	2375	4	..	8	27	;
	2005	2289	2254	4	..	31	27	;
	2006	*2289	*2254	*4	..	*31	*27	*;
Faeroe Islands	2003	*87	*55	*32	..	..	..	
	2004	*87	*55	*32	..	..	..	
	2005	*87	*55	*32	..	..	..	
	2006	*87	*55	*32	..	..	..	
Finland	2003	16556	10864	2966	2671	55	2270	22;
	2004	16567	10811	2999	2671	86	2270	22;
	2005	16468	10676	3035	2671	86	2270	22;
	2006	16562	10738	3062	2671	91	2270	22;
France incl. Monaco	2003	116765	27715	25214	63363	473	5902	55;
	2004	116978	27898	25100	63363	617	5673	53;
	2005	116222	26873	25109	63260	980	6724	63;
	2006	116179	26159	25109	63260	1651	6774	63;
Germany	2003	125057	80365	8256	21439	14997	10318	102;
	2004	124574	78413	8271	20552	17338	10313	102;
	2005	125031	76375	8341	20378	19937	10621	105;
	2006	131583	78927	8995	20208	23453	9797	97;
Gibraltar	2003	35	35	..	..	..	..	
	2004	*35	*35	..	..	..	..	
	2005	*35	*35	..	..	..	..	
	2006	*35	*35	..	..	..	..	
Greece	2003	12080	8629	3079	..	372	246	2;
	2004	12431	8861	3099	..	471	259	2;
	2005	13306	9708	3106	..	492	257	2;
	2006	13570	9682	3134	..	754	242	2;
Hungary	2003	8311	6388	54	1866	3	185	1;
	2004	8581	6661	51	1866	3	*135	*1;
	2005	8586	6654	49	1866	17	135	1;
	2006	8620	6672	49	1866	33	135	1;
Iceland	2003	1507	150	1155	..	202	31	
	2004	1508	143	1163	..	202	31	
	2005	1537	142	1163	..	232	31	
	2006	1725	140	1163	..	422	28	
Ireland	2003	5680	4899	532	..	249	136	1;
	2004	5839	4929	532	..	378	142	1;
	2005	6270	5250	526	..	494	145	1;
	2006	6443	5171	526	..	746	262	2;
Italy and San Marino	2003	88168	64056	22505	..	1607	*9855	*80;
	2004	86420	62236	22384	..	1800	*9856	*80;
	2005	90514	65535	22639	..	2340	*9856	*80;
	2006	94492	69159	22715	..	2618	*9856	*80;
Latvia	2003	2155	592	1537	..	26	33	
	2004	2157	594	1536	..	27	33	
	2005	2166	603	1536	..	27	34	
	2006	*2168	*605	*1536	..	*27	*34	*;
Lithuania	2003	5730	2494	869	2367	0	66	
	2004	5733	2495	870	2367	1	64	
	2005	4556	2495	877	1183	1	62	
	2006	*4563	*2495	*877	1190	*1	*62	*;

Table 32

Puissance nette installée des centrales électriques - par catégorie
Milliers de kilowatts

| producers producteurs | | | Public utilities Services publics | | | | | Year Année | Country or area Pays ou zone |
Hydro Hydraulique	Nuclear Nucléaire	Geothermal Géother- mique	Total Totale	Thermal Thermique	Hydro Hydraulique	Nuclear Nucléaire	Geothermal Géother- mique		
..	..	*1	13020	9890	11	..	3119	2003	Danemark
..	..	*1	12736	9598	11	..	3127	2004	
..	..	*1	12710	9567	11	..	3132	2005	
..	..	*1	12392	9245	9	..	3138	2006	
..	..	*1	*2525	*2520	*4	..	*1	2003	Estonie
..	..	1	2360	2349	4	..	7	2004	
..	..	1	2262	2228	4	..	30	2005	
..	..	*1	*2262	*2228	*4	..	*30	2006	
..	..	..	*87	*55	*32	..	..	2003	Iles Féroé
..	..	..	*87	*55	*32	..	..	2004	
..	..	..	*87	*55	*32	..	..	2005	
..	..	..	*87	*55	*32	..	..	2006	
..	..	..	14286	8594	2966	2671	55	2003	Finlande
..	..	..	14297	8541	2999	2671	86	2004	
..	..	..	14198	8406	3035	2671	86	2005	
..	..	..	14292	8468	3062	2671	91	2006	
267	..	52	110863	22132	24947	63363	421	2003	France y compris Monaco
271	..	55	111305	22551	24829	63363	562	2004	
268	..	64	109498	20481	24841	63260	916	2005	
268	..	114	109405	19767	24841	63260	1537	2006	
91	..	..	114739	70138	8165	21439	14997	2003	Allemagne
86	..	..	114261	68186	8185	20552	17338	2004	
64	..	..	114410	65818	8277	20378	19937	2005	
67	..	..	121786	69197	8928	20208	23453	2006	
..	..	..	35	35	..	..	..	2003	Gibraltar
..	..	..	*35	*35	..	..	..	2004	
..	..	..	*35	*35	..	..	..	2005	
..	..	..	*35	*35	..	..	..	2006	
..	..	..	11834	8383	3079	..	372	2003	Grèce
..	..	..	12172	8602	3099	..	471	2004	
..	..	..	13049	9451	3106	..	492	2005	
..	..	..	13328	9440	3134	..	754	2006	
..	..	..	8126	6203	54	1866	3	2003	Hongrie
..	..	..	8446	6526	51	1866	3	2004	
..	..	..	8451	6519	49	1866	17	2005	
..	..	..	8485	6537	49	1866	33	2006	
4	..	..	1476	123	1151	..	202	2003	Islande
4	..	..	1477	116	1159	..	202	2004	
4	..	..	1506	115	1159	..	232	2005	
1	..	..	1697	113	1162	..	422	2006	
..	..	..	5544	4763	532	..	249	2003	Irlande
..	..	..	5697	4787	532	..	378	2004	
..	..	..	6125	5105	526	..	494	2005	
..	..	..	6181	4909	526	..	746	2006	
*1845	..	0	78313	56046	20660	..	1607	2003	Italie y comp. St. Marin
*1845	..	1	76564	54226	20539	..	1799	2004	
*1845	..	1	80658	57525	20794	..	2339	2005	
*1845	..	1	84636	61149	20870	..	2617	2006	
6	..	1	2122	566	1531	..	25	2003	Lettonie
6	..	*1	2124	568	1530	..	26	2004	
6	..	*1	2132	576	1530	..	26	2005	
*6	..	*1	*2134	*578	*1530	..	*26	2006	
..	..	..	5664	2428	869	2367	0	2003	Lituanie
..	..	..	5669	2431	870	2367	1	2004	
..	..	..	4494	2433	877	1183	1	2005	
..	..	..	*4501	*2433	*877	1190	*1	2006	

Table 32

Net installed capacity of electric generating plants by type
Thousand kilowatts

Country or area Pays ou zone	Year Année	Self-producers and public utilities Autoproducteurs et services publics					Self- Auto-	
		Total Totale	Thermal Thermique	Hydro Hydraulique	Nuclear Nucléaire	Geothermal Géother--mique	Total Totale	Thermal Thermique
Luxembourg	2003	1630	452	1140	..	38	115	9
	2004	1659	459	1140	..	60	131	10
	2005	1661	460	1140	..	61	133	10
	2006	1665	463	1140	..	62	133	10
Malta	2003	921	921	..		..	..	
	2004	921	921	..		..	..	
	2005	921	921	..		..	..	
	2006	*921	*921	..		..	..	
Netherlands	2003	20926	19488	37	449	952	2752	255
	2004	21833	20225	37	449	1122	3238	301
	2005	21800	20039	37	449	1275	2996	278
	2006	22977	20820	37	510	1610	3818	350
Norway,Svlbd.J.Myn. I	2003	28466	283	28086	..	97	952	13
	2004	27959	285	27522	..	152	954	14
	2005	28424	304	27850	..	270	968	15
	2006	29513	309	28920	..	284	1004	15
Poland	2003	31642	29334	2273	..	35	2070	206
	2004	31888	29566	2282	..	40	2066	206
	2005	32257	29815	2321	..	121	2054	205
	2006	32360	29857	2331	..	172	2037	203
Portugal	2003	11621	6749	4588		284	1224	121
	2004	12713	7292	4852		569	1283	127
	2005	13391	7277	5034		1080	1312	130
	2006	14459	7685	5065		1709	1320	131
Republic of Moldova	2003	*1022	*966	*56	..	..	*7	*
	2004	*1022	*966	*56	..	..	*7	*
	2005	*1022	*966	*56	..	..	*7	*
	2006	*1025	*969	*56	..	..	*10	*1
Romania	2003	*21188	*14361	*6120	707	..	*887	*86
	2004	*20188	*13361	*6120	707	..	*887	*86
	2005	18950	11954	6289	707	..	627	60
	2006	*18950	*11954	*6289	707	..	*627	*60
Russian Federation	2003	231333	163382	45132	22742	77	*16473	*1616
	2004	232471	164124	45525	22742	80	*16473	*1616
	2005	233120	164485	45835	22742	58	*16473	*1616
	2006	221404	151513	46062	23742	87	16013	1551
Serbia	2003	*11783	*7970	*3813	..	..	0	
	2004	*11783	*7970	*3813	..	..	0	
	2005	*11813	*8000	*3813	..	..	*30	*3
	2006	*11813	*8000	*3813	..	..	*30	*3
Slovakia	2003	8212	3062	2507	2640	3	692	59
	2004	8278	3117	2518	2640	3	600	57
	2005	8257	3100	2512	2640	5	564	53
	2006	8219	3061	2513	2640	5	620	59
Slovenia	2003	2992	1357	979	656	..	182	7
	2004	2992	1357	979	656	..	182	7
	2005	2992	1357	979	656	..	182	7
	2006	2992	1357	979	656	..	182	7
Spain	2003	*68906	*37310	*18043	7581	*5972	6694	648
	2004	*69575	*35477	*18167	7577	*8354	*7213	*700
	2005	*76574	*40799	*18220	7577	*9978	*7214	*700
	2006	*82142	*44471	*18314	7446	*11911	*7214	*700
Sweden	2003	33364	7378	16143	9441	402	1024	97
	2004	33695	7424	16345	9471	455	987	98
	2005	33390	7077	16345	9471	497	987	98
	2006	34127	7882	16270	9454	521	1100	109

Table 32

Puissance nette installée des centrales électriques - par catégorie
Milliers de kilowatts

producers producteurs			Public utilities Services publics					Year Année	Country or area Pays ou zone
Hydro Hydraulique	Nuclear Nucléaire	Geothermal Géother-mique	Total Totale	Thermal Thermique	Hydro Hydraulique	Nuclear Nucléaire	Geothermal Géother-mique		
6	..	16	1515	359	1134	..	22	2003	Luxembourg
6	..	25	1528	359	1134	..	35	2004	
6	..	26	1528	359	1134	..	35	2005	
2	..	27	1532	359	1138	..	35	2006	
..	..	..	921	921	..	..	..	2003	Malte
..	..	..	921	921	..	..	..	2004	
..	..	..	921	921	..	..	..	2005	
..	..	..	*921	*921	..	..	..	2006	
..	..	193	18174	16929	37	449	759	2003	Pays-Bas
..	..	227	18595	17214	37	449	895	2004	
..	..	216	18804	17259	37	449	1059	2005	
..	..	311	19159	17313	37	510	1299	2006	
814	..	..	27514	145	27272	..	97	2003	Norvège,Svalbd,J.May
814	..	..	27005	145	26708	..	152	2004	
814	..	..	27456	150	27036	..	270	2005	
845	..	..	28509	150	28075	..	284	2006	
1	..	..	29572	27265	2272	..	35	2003	Pologne
1	..	..	29822	27501	2281	..	40	2004	
1	..	..	30203	27762	2320	..	121	2005	
1	..	..	30323	27821	2330	..	172	2006	
7	..	..	10397	5532	4581	..	284	2003	Portugal
6	..	..	11430	6015	4846	..	569	2004	
6	..	..	12079	5971	5028	..	1080	2005	
5	..	..	13139	6370	5060	..	1709	2006	
..	..	..	*1015	*959	*56	..	..	2003	Rép. de Moldova
..	..	..	*1015	*959	*56	..	..	2004	
..	..	..	*1015	*959	*56	..	..	2005	
..	..	..	*1015	*959	*56	..	..	2006	
*26	..	..	*20301	*13500	*6094	707	..	2003	Roumanie
*26	..	..	*19301	*12500	*6094	707	..	2004	
23	..	..	18323	11350	6266	707	..	2005	
*23	..	..	*18323	*11350	*6266	707	..	2006	
*304	..	..	214860	147213	44828	22742	77	2003	Fédération de Russie
*304	..	..	215998	147955	45221	22742	80	2004	
*304	..	..	216647	148316	45531	22742	58	2005	
500	..	..	205391	136000	45562	23742	87	2006	
..	..	..	*11783	*7970	*3813	..	..	2003	Serbie
..	..	..	*11783	*7970	*3813	..	..	2004	
..	..	..	*11783	*7970	*3813	..	..	2005	
..	..	..	*11783	*7970	*3813	..	..	2006	
94	..	3	7520	2467	2413	2640	..	2003	Slovaquie
25	..	3	7678	2545	2493	2640	..	2004	
24	..	5	7693	2565	2488	2640	..	2005	
25	..	5	7599	2471	2488	2640	..	2006	
104	..	..	2810	1279	875	656	..	2003	Slovénie
104	..	..	2810	1279	875	656	..	2004	
104	..	..	2810	1279	875	656	..	2005	
104	..	..	2810	1279	875	656	..	2006	
*200	..	*13	*62212	*30829	*17843	7581	*5959	2003	Espagne
*200	..	*13	*62362	*28477	*17967	7577	*8341	2004	
*200	..	*14	*69360	*33799	*18020	7577	*9964	2005	
*200	..	*14	*74928	*37471	*18114	7446	*11897	2006	
45	..	..	32340	6399	16098	9441	402	2003	Suède
3	..	..	32708	6440	16342	9471	455	2004	
3	..	..	32403	6093	16342	9471	497	2005	
2	..	..	33027	6784	16268	9454	521	2006	

Table 32

Net installed capacity of electric generating plants by type
Thousand kilowatts

| Country or area
Pays ou zone | Year
Année | Self-producers and public utilities
Autoproducteurs et services publics | | | | | Self-
Auto- | |
		Total Totale	Thermal Thermique	Hydro Hydraulique	Nuclear Nucléaire	Geothermal Géother- -mique	Total Totale	Thermal Thermique
Switzerland	2003	19044	833	14965	3220	26	1875	791
	2004	19082	860	14970	3220	32	1909	819
	2005	19123	855	15010	3220	38	1915	816
	2006	19115	844	15010	3220	41	1894	792
T.F.Yug.Rep. Macedonia	2003	1460	1012	448	..	..	*2	*2
	2004	1561	1012	549	..	..	*2	*2
	2005	1561	1012	549	..	..	*2	*2
	2006	1561	1012	549	..	..	*2	*2
Ukraine	2003	52690	36026	4766	11835	63	3530	3513
	2004	52863	35184	4781	12835	63	3486	3470
	2005	52538	34920	4717	12835	66	3364	3355
	2006	53783	34968	4897	13835	83	3358	3349
United Kingdom	2003	78974	61872	4256	12098	748	7228	6314
	2004	80333	63314	4225	11852	942	7025	5947
	2005	81858	64128	4301	11852	1577	7735	6000
	2006	83143	65960	4248	10969	1966	8052	5933
Oceania	**2003**	**60648**	**44835**	**15072**	**..**	**741**	**3831**	**3425**
	2004	**62123**	**45963**	**15065**	**..**	**1095**	**4180**	**3775**
	2005	**61938**	**45433**	**15079**	**..**	**1426**	**4624**	**4211**
	2006	**62387**	**45776**	**15079**	**..**	**1532**	**4972**	**4559**
American Samoa	2003	*60	*60	..	..	..	..	..
	2004	*60	*60	..	..	..	..	..
	2005	*60	*60	..	..	..	..	..
	2006	*60	*60	..	..	..	..	..
Australia	2003	50031	40523	9278	..	230	3068	2745
	2004	51116	41396	9271	..	449	3399	3074
	2005	50958	40863	9285	..	810	3838	3508
	2006	51368	41193	9285	..	890	4173	3843
Cook Islands	2003	*8	*8	..	..	..	..	..
	2004	*8	*8	..	..	..	..	..
	2005	*8	*8	..	..	..	..	..
	2006	*8	*8	..	..	..	..	..
Fiji	2003	*165	*74	*91	..	..	*44	*44
	2004	*165	*74	*91	..	..	*44	*44
	2005	*165	*74	*91	..	..	*44	*44
	2006	*165	*74	*91	..	..	*44	*44
French Polynesia	2003	*110	*90	*20	..	..	..	..
	2004	*113	*93	*20	..	..	..	..
	2005	*113	*93	*20	..	..	..	..
	2006	*113	*93	*20	..	..	..	..
Guam	2003	552	552	..	..	..	..	..
	2004	552	552	..	..	..	..	..
	2005	552	552	..	..	..	..	..
	2006	552	552	..	..	..	..	..
Kiribati	2003	*3	*3	..	..	..	..	..
	2004	*3	*3	..	..	..	..	..
	2005	*4	*4	..	..	..	..	..
	2006	*4	*4	..	..	..	..	..
Marshall Islands	2003	17	17	..	..	..	..	..
	2004	17	17	..	..	..	..	..
	2005	17	17	..	..	..	..	..
	2006	17	17	..	..	..	..	..
Nauru	2003	*10	*10	..	..	..	..	..
	2004	*10	*10	..	..	..	..	..
	2005	*10	*10	..	..	..	..	..
	2006	*10	*10	..	..	..	..	..

Table 32

Puissance nette installée des centrales électriques - par catégorie
Milliers de kilowatts

producers producteurs			Public utilities Services publics					Year Année	Country or area Pays ou zone
Hydro ydraulique	Nuclear Nucléaire	Geothermal Géother-mique	Total Totale	Thermal Thermique	Hydro Hydraulique	Nuclear Nucléaire	Geothermal Géother-mique		
1058	..	26	17169	42	13907	3220	..	2003	Suisse
1058	..	32	17173	41	13912	3220	..	2004	
1061	..	38	17208	39	13949	3220	..	2005	
1061	..	41	17221	52	13949	3220	..	2006	
..	..	..	1458	1010	448	..	..	2003	L'ex-RY Macédoine
..	..	..	1559	1010	549	..	..	2004	
..	..	..	1559	1010	549	..	..	2005	
..	..	..	1559	1010	549	..	..	2006	
9	..	8	49160	32513	4757	11835	55	2003	Ukraine
8	..	8	49377	31714	4773	12835	55	2004	
8	..	1	49174	31565	4709	12835	65	2005	
8	..	1	50425	31619	4889	13835	82	2006	
166	..	748	71746	55558	4090	12098	..	2003	Royaume-Uni
136	..	942	73308	57367	4089	11852	..	2004	
158	..	1577	74123	58128	4143	11852	..	2005	
153	..	1966	75091	60027	4095	10969	..	2006	
398	**..**	**8**	**56817**	**41410**	**14674**	**..**	**733**	**2003**	**Océanie**
400	**..**	**5**	**57943**	**42188**	**14665**	**..**	**1090**	**2004**	
405	**..**	**8**	**57314**	**41222**	**14674**	**..**	**1418**	**2005**	
405	**..**	**8**	**57415**	**41217**	**14674**	**..**	**1524**	**2006**	
..	..	..	*60	*60	..	..	..	2003	Samoa américaines
..	..	..	*60	*60	..	..	..	2004	
..	..	..	*60	*60	..	..	..	2005	
..	..	..	*60	*60	..	..	..	2006	
323	..	..	46963	37778	8955	..	230	2003	Australie
325	..	..	47717	38322	8946	..	449	2004	
330	..	..	47120	37355	8955	..	810	2005	
330	..	..	47195	37350	8955	..	890	2006	
..	..	..	*8	*8	..	..	..	2003	Iles Cook
..	..	..	*8	*8	..	..	..	2004	
..	..	..	*8	*8	..	..	..	2005	
..	..	..	*8	*8	..	..	..	2006	
..	..	..	*121	*30	*91	..	..	2003	Fidji
..	..	..	*121	*30	*91	..	..	2004	
..	..	..	*121	*30	*91	..	..	2005	
..	..	..	*121	*30	*91	..	..	2006	
..	..	..	*110	*90	*20	..	..	2003	Polynésie française
..	..	..	*113	*93	*20	..	..	2004	
..	..	..	*113	*93	*20	..	..	2005	
..	..	..	*113	*93	*20	..	..	2006	
..	..	..	552	552	..	..	..	2003	Guam
..	..	..	552	552	..	..	..	2004	
..	..	..	552	552	..	..	..	2005	
..	..	..	552	552	..	..	..	2006	
..	..	..	*3	*3	..	..	..	2003	Kiribati
..	..	..	*3	*3	..	..	..	2004	
..	..	..	*4	*4	..	..	..	2005	
..	..	..	*4	*4	..	..	..	2006	
..	..	..	17	17	..	..	..	2003	Îles Marshall
..	..	..	17	17	..	..	..	2004	
..	..	..	17	17	..	..	..	2005	
..	..	..	17	17	..	..	..	2006	
..	..	..	*10	*10	..	..	..	2003	Nauru
..	..	..	*10	*10	..	..	..	2004	
..	..	..	*10	*10	..	..	..	2005	
..	..	..	*10	*10	..	..	..	2006	

Table 32

Net installed capacity of electric generating plants by type
Thousand kilowatts

| Country or area Pays ou zone | Year Année | Self-producers and public utilities Autoproducteurs et services publics | | | | | Self- Auto- | |
		Total Totale	Thermal Thermique	Hydro Hydraulique	Nuclear Nucléaire	Geothermal Géother- -mique	Total Totale	Thermal Thermique
New Caledonia	2003	328	247	78	..	3	..	
	2004	372	283	78	..	11	..	
	2005	375	283	78	..	14	..	
	2006	386	283	78	..	25	..	
New Zealand	2003	8572	2719	5345	..	508	314	30
	2004	8915	2935	5345	..	635	332	32
	2005	8884	2937	5345	..	602	337	32
	2006	8912	2950	5345	..	617	350	34
Niue	2003	*1	*1	..	..	..	..	
	2004	*1	*1	..	..	..	..	
	2005	*1	*1	..	..	..	..	
	2006	*1	*1	..	..	..	..	
Palau	2003	*52	*42	*10	..	..	*2	*
	2004	*52	*42	*10	..	..	*2	*
	2005	*52	*42	*10	..	..	*2	*
	2006	*52	*42	*10	..	..	*2	*
Papua New Guinea	2003	666	428	238	..	..	394	31
	2004	*666	*428	*238	..	..	*394	*31
	2005	*666	*428	*238	..	..	*394	*31
	2006	*666	*428	*238	..	..	*394	*31
Samoa	2003	*29	*17	12	..	..	*2	*
	2004	*29	*17	12	..	..	*2	*
	2005	*29	*17	*12	..	..	*2	*
	2006	*29	*17	*12	..	..	*2	*
Solomon Islands	2003	*14	*14	..	..	..	*5	*
	2004	*14	*14	..	..	..	*5	*
	2005	*14	*14	..	..	..	*5	*
	2006	*14	*14	..	..	..	*5	*
Tonga	2003	*12	*12	..	..	..	..	
	2004	*12	*12	..	..	..	..	
	2005	*12	*12	..	..	..	..	
	2006	*12	*12	..	..	..	..	
Vanuatu	2003	*12	*12	..	..	..	*2	*
	2004	*12	*12	..	..	..	*2	*
	2005	*12	*12	..	..	..	*2	*
	2006	*12	*12	..	..	..	*2	*
Wallis and Futuna Is	2003	*5	*5	..	..	..	..	
	2004	*6	*6	..	..	..	..	
	2005	*6	*6	..	..	..	..	
	2006	*6	*6	..	..	..	..	

Table 32

Puissance nette installée des centrales électriques - par catégorie
Milliers de kilowatts

producers producteurs			Public utilities Services publics					Year Année	Country or area Pays ou zone
Hydro Hydraulique	Nuclear Nucléaire	Geothermal Géother-mique	Total Totale	Thermal Thermique	Hydro Hydraulique	Nuclear Nucléaire	Geothermal Géother-mique		
..	..	..	328	247	78	..	3	2003	Nouvelle-Calédonie
..	..	..	372	283	78	..	11	2004	
..	..	..	375	283	78	..	14	2005	
..	..	..	386	283	78	..	25	2006	
..	..	8	8258	2413	5345	..	500	2003	Nouvelle-Zélande
..	..	5	8583	2608	5345	..	630	2004	
..	..	8	8547	2608	5345	..	594	2005	
..	..	8	8562	2608	5345	..	609	2006	
..	..	..	*1	*1	..	..	..	2003	Nioué
..	..	..	*1	*1	..	..	..	2004	
..	..	..	*1	*1	..	..	..	2005	
..	..	..	*1	*1	..	..	..	2006	
..	..	..	*50	*40	*10	..	..	2003	Palaos
..	..	..	*50	*40	*10	..	..	2004	
..	..	..	*50	*40	*10	..	..	2005	
..	..	..	*50	*40	*10	..	..	2006	
75	..	..	272	109	163	..	..	2003	Papouasie-Nvl-Guinée
*75	..	..	*272	*109	*163	..	..	2004	
*75	..	..	*272	*109	*163	..	..	2005	
*75	..	..	*272	*109	*163	..	..	2006	
..	..	..	*27	*15	12	..	..	2003	Samoa
..	..	..	*27	*15	12	..	..	2004	
..	..	..	*27	*15	*12	..	..	2005	
..	..	..	*27	*15	*12	..	..	2006	
..	..	..	*9	*9	..	..	..	2003	Iles Salomon
..	..	..	*9	*9	..	..	..	2004	
..	..	..	*9	*9	..	..	..	2005	
..	..	..	*9	*9	..	..	..	2006	
..	..	..	*12	*12	..	..	..	2003	Tonga
..	..	..	*12	*12	..	..	..	2004	
..	..	..	*12	*12	..	..	..	2005	
..	..	..	*12	*12	..	..	..	2006	
..	..	..	*10	*10	..	..	..	2003	Vanuatu
..	..	..	*10	*10	..	..	..	2004	
..	..	..	*10	*10	..	..	..	2005	
..	..	..	*10	*10	..	..	..	2006	
..	..	..	*5	*5	..	..	..	2003	Iles Wallis et Futuna
..	..	..	*6	*6	..	..	..	2004	
..	..	..	*6	*6	..	..	..	2005	
..	..	..	*6	*6	..	..	..	2006	

Table 33

Utilization of installed electric generating capacity - by type
Utilisation de la capacité des centrales électriques - par catégorie
Kilowatt-hours per kilowatt
Kilowattheures par kilowatt

Table Notes:

Data on utilization are derived by dividing the data on electricity production shown in Table 34 by the net installed capacity shown in Table 32.

For this specific table, Geothermal refers to geothermal, wind, solar, tide and wave, whenever they are available in the country.

For Japan, geothermal capacity includes fuel cell capacity.

For Austria data are given in gross maximum capacity.

● **Please refer to the Definitions Section on pages xv to xxix for the appropriate product description /classification.**

Notes relatives aux tableaux:

Les données sur l'utilisation sont obtenues en divisant la production (Tableau 34) par la puissance nette installée (Tableau 32).

Pour ce tableau spécifique, les données relatives à la géothermique se rapportent à géothermique, éolienne, solaire, marémotrice et énergie des vagues quand elles sont disponibles dans le pays.

Pour le Japon, la capacité géothermique se rapporte aussi à la capacité des piles à combustible.

Pour l'Autriche les données représentent la capacité maximale brute.

● **Veuillez consulter la section "définitions" de la page xv à la page xxix pour une description/classification appropriée des produits.**

Figure 84: Utilization of installed electric generating capacity, by region, by type, in 2006

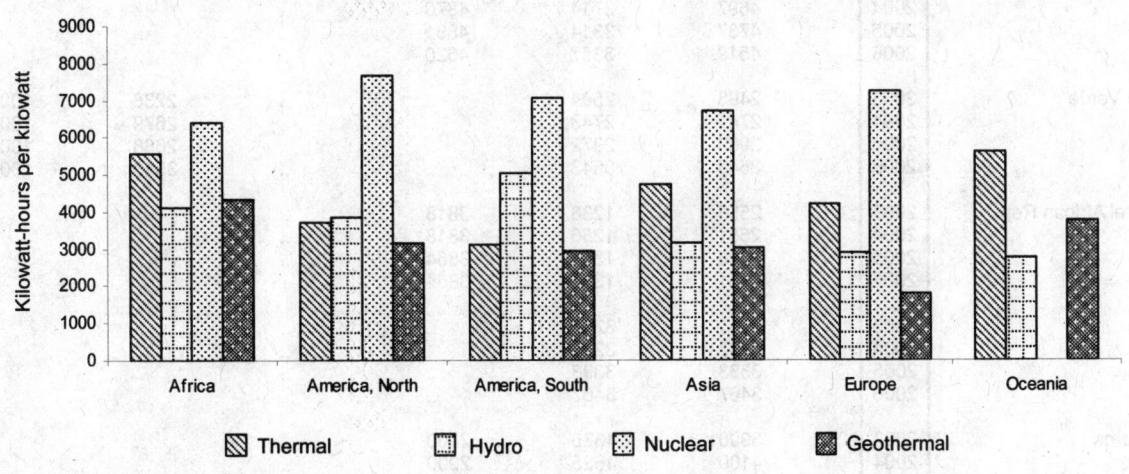

Table 33

Utilization of installed electric generating capacity - by type
Kilowatt-hours per kilowatt

Country or area Pays ou zone	Year Année	Self-producers and public utilities Autoproducteurs et services publics					Self-Auto-	
		Total Totale	Thermal Thermique	Hydro Hydraulique	Nuclear Nucléaire	Geothermal Géother-mique	Total Totale	Thermal Thermiqu
World	**2003**	**4276**	**4217**	**3308**	**7070**	**2454**	**3759**	3
	2004	**4316**	**4243**	**3378**	**7235**	**2494**	**3729**	3
	2005	**4354**	**4288**	**3455**	**7251**	**2360**	**3833**	3
	2006	**4360**	**4294**	**3517**	**7264**	**2266**	**3822**	3
Africa	**2003**	**4903**	**5163**	**3806**	**6875**	**5163**	**4405**	4
	2004	**5033**	**5282**	**3930**	**7256**	**6369**	**4388**	4
	2005	**5111**	**5420**	**3914**	**6131**	**4729**	**4568**	5
	2006	**5265**	**5554**	**4122**	**6395**	**4368**	**3651**	3
Algeria	2003	4323	4464	964	..	..	1000	1
	2004	4313	4447	913	..	..	742	
	2005	4388	4478	2018	..	..	1000	1
	2006	4464	4596	793	..	..	919	
Angola	2003	3990	6855	3182	..	..	4967	4
	2004	3177	4455	2941	..	..	3233	3
	2005	2877	3059	2845	..	..	2733	2
	2006	3234	2178	3417	..	..	1933	1
Benin	2003	1379	1368	2000	..	..	5500	5
	2004	1397	1404	1000	..	..	5000	5
	2005	1783	1797	1000	..	..	6250	6
	2006	2133	2153	1000	..	..	6750	6
Burkina Faso	2003	4234	4649	3197	..	..		
	2004	4508	4957	3383	..	..		
	2005	4302	4620	3350	..	..		
	2006	4565	5197	2670	..	..		
Burundi	2003	3136	2000	3172	..	..	..	
	2004	2836	2000	2863			..	
	2005	3100	2000	3134			..	
	2006	2888	2000	2916			..	
Cameroon	2003	4210	2229	4383	..	..	..	
	2004	4697	2714	4870	..	..	..	
	2005	4737	3314	4861	..	..	..	
	2006	4519	3357	4620	..	..	..	
Cape Verde	2003	2496	2504	..	..	2238	1000	1
	2004	2741	2743	..	..	2679	1000	1
	2005	2963	2972	..	..	2688	1000	1
	2006	3543	3543	..	..	3543	1000	1
Central African Rep.	2003	2558	1238	3818	..	..	..	
	2004	2581	1286	3818	..	..	..	
	2005	2628	1333	3864	..	..	..	
	2006	2651	1381	3864	..	..	..	
Chad	2003	3241	3241	..	..			
	2004	3233	3233	..				
	2005	3333	3333	..				
	2006	3467	3467	..				
Comoros	2003	3900	4375	2000			..	
	2004	4100	4625	2000			..	
	2005	4260	4825	2000			..	
	2006	4400	5000	2000			..	
Congo	2003	3643	3300	3717			..	
	2004	4152	3350	4326			..	
	2005	3875	3950	3859			..	
	2006	4045	4050	4043			..	
Côte d'Ivoire	2003	3723	6938	2040	..	..	580	5
	2004	3921	7615	1947	..	..	500	
	2005	4039	8610	1596	..	..	260	2
	2006	4017	8385	1682	..	..	500	5

Table 33

Utilisation de la capacité des centrales électriques - par catégorie
Kilowatt-heures par kilowatt

producers producteurs			Public utilities Services publics					Year Année	Country or area Pays ou zone
Hydro Hydraulique	Nuclear Nucléaire	Geothermal Géother-mique	Total Totale	Thermal Thermique	Hydro Hydraulique	Nuclear Nucléaire	Geothermal Géother-mique		
3961	..	1236	4313	4260	3293	7070	2531	2003	Monde
4389	..	1340	4359	4296	3357	7235	2573	2004	
4179	..	1235	4389	4327	3440	7251	2451	2005	
4209	..	1206	4396	4333	3502	7264	2358	2006	
1043	..	200	4931	5181	3895	6875	5358	2003	Afrique
1134	..	261	5069	5309	4019	7256	6618	2004	
1255	..	333	5140	5442	3996	6131	4876	2005	
1257	..	333	5356	5656	4210	6395	4489	2006	
..	..	..	4518	4676	964	..	..	2003	Algérie
..	..	..	4573	4728	913	..	..	2004	
..	..	..	4574	4677	2018	..	..	2005	
..	..	..	4699	4850	793	..	..	2006	
..	..	..	3928	7563	3182	..	..	2003	Angola
..	..	..	3175	4913	2941	..	..	2004	
..	..	..	2881	3152	2845	..	..	2005	
..	..	..	3278	2248	3417	..	..	2006	
..	..	..	1232	1218	2000	..	..	2003	Bénin
..	..	..	1268	1273	1000	..	..	2004	
..	..	..	1464	1473	1000	..	..	2005	
..	..	..	1804	1818	1000	..	..	2006	
..	..	..	4234	4649	3197	..	..	2003	Burkina Faso
..	..	..	4508	4957	3383	..	..	2004	
..	..	..	4302	4620	3350	..	..	2005	
..	..	..	4565	5197	2670	..	..	2006	
..	..	..	3136	2000	3172	..	..	2003	Burundi
..	..	..	2836	2000	2863	..	..	2004	
..	..	..	3100	2000	3134	..	..	2005	
..	..	..	2888	2000	2916	..	..	2006	
..	..	..	4210	2229	4383	..	..	2003	Cameroun
..	..	..	4697	2714	4870	..	..	2004	
..	..	..	4737	3314	4861	..	..	2005	
..	..	..	4519	3357	4620	..	..	2006	
..	..	..	2515	2523	..	..	2238	2003	Cap-Vert
..	..	..	2763	2765	..	..	2679	2004	
..	..	..	2988	2998	..	..	2688	2005	
..	..	..	3580	3581	..	..	3543	2006	
..	..	..	2558	1238	3818	..	..	2003	Rép. centrafricaine
..	..	..	2581	1286	3818	..	..	2004	
..	..	..	2628	1333	3864	..	..	2005	
..	..	..	2651	1381	3864	..	..	2006	
..	..	..	3241	3241	..	..	..	2003	Tchad
..	..	..	3233	3233	..	..	..	2004	
..	..	..	3333	3333	..	..	..	2005	
..	..	..	3467	3467	..	..	..	2006	
..	..	..	3900	4375	2000	..	..	2003	Comores
..	..	..	4100	4625	2000	..	..	2004	
..	..	..	4260	4825	2000	..	..	2005	
..	..	..	4400	5000	2000	..	..	2006	
..	..	..	3643	3300	3717	..	..	2003	Congo
..	..	..	4152	3350	4326	..	..	2004	
..	..	..	3875	3950	3859	..	..	2005	
..	..	..	4045	4050	4043	..	..	2006	
..	..	..	3746	7076	2040	..	..	2003	Côte d'Ivoire
..	..	..	3946	7766	1947	..	..	2004	
..	..	..	4067	8788	1596	..	..	2005	
..	..	..	4042	8553	1682	..	..	2006	

Table 33

Utilization of installed electric generating capacity - by type
Kilowatt-hours per kilowatt

| Country or area Pays ou zone | Year Année | Self-producers and public utilities Autoproducteurs et services publics | | | | | Self- Auto- | |
		Total Totale	Thermal Thermique	Hydro Hydraulique	Nuclear Nucléaire	Geothermal Géother- -mique	Total Totale	Thermal Thermique
Dem. Rep. of Congo	2003	2437	636	2460	..	..	342	
	2004	2663	667	2689	..	..	373	
	2005	2883	697	2912	..	..	396	
	2006	3065	727	3095	..	..	421	
Djibouti	2003	1786	1786		..	..	..	
	2004	1822	1822		..	..	..	
	2005	2161	2161		..	..	..	
	2006	2373	2373		..	..	..	
Egypt	2003	5419	5568	4637	..	4540	4319	43
	2004	5261	5357	4615	..	8302	4319	43
	2005	5473	5619	4615	..	3943	4392	43
	2006	5652	5817	4717	..	3366	4392	43
Equatorial Guinea	2003	2000	2300	1000	..	..		
	2004	2077	2400	1000	..	..		
	2005	2115	2450	1000	..	..		
	2006	2192	2550	1000	..	..		
Eritrea	2003	1663	1663	..	..	..	2000	20
	2004	1695	1699	..	..	1000	1500	15
	2005	1731	1735	..	..	1000	1500	15
	2006	1611	1608	..	..	2000	1500	15
Ethiopia	2003	4295	280	5055	..	100	..	
	2004	4730	240	5590	..	91	..	
	2005	4901	253	5704	..	91	..	
	2006	4767	133	5432	..	91	..	
Gabon	2003	3589	2475	5143	..	..	1948	19
	2004	3668	2639	5103	..	..	2062	20
	2005	3836	3253	4651	..	..	2557	25
	2006	4110	3188	5400	..	..	2711	27
Gambia	2003	5040	5040	..	..	..	5400	54
	2004	5207	5207	..	..	..	5400	54
	2005	5367	5367	..	..	..	5333	53
	2006	5355	5355	..	..	..	5333	53
Ghana	2003	4126	6918	3411	..	..	2500	25
	2004	4106	2613	4475	..	..	2500	25
	2005	4615	3986	4770	..	..	2500	25
	2006	5200	6371	4762	..	..	3000	30
Guinea	2003	3970	2497	8077	..	..	3010	30
	2004	4066	2524	8365	..	..	3048	30
	2005	4080	2628	7909	..	..	3143	31
	2006	4180	2766	7909	..	..	3143	31
Guinea-Bissau	2003	2905	2905	..	..	..	5000	50
	2004	3000	3000	..	..	..	5000	50
	2005	3048	3048	..	..	..	5000	50
	2006	3143	3143	..	..	..	6000	60
Kenya	2003	4642	3567	4815	..	7870	1824	18
	2004	4608	4170	4238	..	8280	1824	18
	2005	4579	4132	4450	..	7088	1824	18
	2006	4941	4543	4821	..	7200	1824	18
Liberia	2003	1702	1702	..	..	..	..	
	2004	1755	1755	..	..	..	..	
	2005	1798	1798	..	..	..	..	
	2006	1867	1867	..	..	..	..	
Libyan Arab Jamah.	2003	4158	4158	..	..	..	..	
	2004	4434	4434	..	..	..	..	
	2005	4355	4355	..	..	..	..	
	2006	4501	4501	..	..	..	..	

Table 33

Utilisation de la capacité des centrales électriques - par catégorie
Kilowatt-heures par kilowatt

producers producteurs			Public utilities Services publics					Year Année	Country or area Pays ou zone
Hydro Hydraulique	Nuclear Nucléaire	Geothermal Géother-mique	Total Totale	Thermal Thermique	Hydro Hydraulique	Nuclear Nucléaire	Geothermal Géother-mique		
343	..	..	3028	700	3063	..	..	2003	Rép. dem. du Congo
375	..	..	3312	733	3351	..	..	2004	
398	..	..	3588	767	3631	..	..	2005	
423	..	..	3814	800	3860	..	..	2006	
..	..	..	1786	1786	..	..	..	2003	Djibouti
..	..	..	1822	1822	..	..	..	2004	
..	..	..	2161	2161	..	..	..	2005	
..	..	..	2373	2373	..	..	..	2006	
..	..	..	5465	5631	4637	..	4540	2003	Egypte
..	..	..	5296	5402	4615	..	8302	2004	
..	..	..	5510	5669	4615	..	3943	2005	
..	..	..	5695	5874	4717	..	3366	2006	
..	..	..	2000	2300	1000	..	..	2003	Guinée équatoriale
..	..	..	2077	2400	1000	..	..	2004	
..	..	..	2115	2450	1000	..	..	2005	
..	..	..	2192	2550	1000	..	..	2006	
..	..	..	1650	1650	..	..	..	2003	Erythrée
..	..	..	1702	1706	..	..	1000	2004	
..	..	..	1739	1744	..	..	1000	2005	
..	..	..	1615	1613	..	..	2000	2006	
..	..	..	4717	583	5055	..	1000	2003	Ethiopie
..	..	..	5205	500	5590	..	1000	2004	
..	..	..	5348	528	5704	..	1000	2005	
..	..	..	5133	278	5432	..	1000	2006	
..	..	..	4084	2823	5143	..	..	2003	Gabon
..	..	..	4152	3020	5103	..	..	2004	
..	..	..	4220	3709	4651	..	..	2005	
..	..	..	4529	3500	5400	..	..	2006	
..	..	..	5000	5000	..	..	..	2003	Gambie
..	..	..	5185	5185	..	..	..	2004	
..	..	..	5370	5370	..	..	..	2005	
..	..	..	5357	5357	..	..	..	2006	
..	..	..	4129	6948	3411	..	..	2003	Ghana
..	..	..	4108	2614	4475	..	..	2004	
..	..	..	4618	3997	4770	..	..	2005	
..	..	..	5203	6386	4762	..	..	2006	
..	..	..	5065	1150	8077	..	..	2003	Guinée
..	..	..	5228	1150	8365	..	..	2004	
..	..	..	5116	1275	7909	..	..	2005	
..	..	..	5326	1775	7909	..	..	2006	
..	..	..	2800	2800	..	..	..	2003	Guinée-Bissau
..	..	..	2900	2900	..	..	..	2004	
..	..	..	2950	2950	..	..	..	2005	
..	..	..	3000	3000	..	..	..	2006	
..	..	..	5134	4884	4815	..	7870	2003	Kenya
..	..	..	5053	5547	4238	..	8280	2004	
..	..	..	5006	5364	4450	..	7088	2005	
..	..	..	5424	5994	4821	..	7200	2006	
..	..	..	1702	1702	..	..	..	2003	Libéria
..	..	..	1755	1755	..	..	..	2004	
..	..	..	1798	1798	..	..	..	2005	
..	..	..	1867	1867	..	..	..	2006	
..	..	..	4158	4158	..	..	..	2003	Jamah. arabe libyenne
..	..	..	4434	4434	..	..	..	2004	
..	..	..	4355	4355	..	..	..	2005	
..	..	..	4501	4501	..	..	..	2006	

Table 33

Utilization of installed electric generating capacity - by type
Kilowatt-hours per kilowatt

Country or area Pays ou zone	Year Année	Self-producers and public utilities Autoproducteurs et services publics					Self- Auto-	
		Total Totale	Thermal Thermique	Hydro Hydraulique	Nuclear Nucléaire	Geothermal Géother- -mique	Total Totale	Thermal Thermique
Madagascar	2003	3947	2377	5755	..	..	3906	390
	2004	4342	2869	6038	..	..	4688	468
	2005	4539	3074	6226	..	..	5000	500
	2006	4671	3197	6368	..	..	5313	531
Malawi	2003	2827	1016	3969	..	..	779	75
	2004	3103	1102	4386	..	..	851	81
	2005	3244	1156	4583	..	..	885	85
	2006	3269	1167	4617	..	..	897	86
Mali	2003	3939	3328	4720	..	..	2500	250
	2004	4079	3359	5000	..	..	2500	250
	2005	4167	3391	5160	..	..	2500	250
	2006	4289	3484	5320	..	..	2500	250
Mauritania	2003	3231	3231	..	..	..	..	..
	2004	3508	3508	..	..	..	..	..
	2005	3329	3329	..	..	..	..	..
	2006	2948	2948	..	..	..	..	..
Mauritius	2003	3198	3318	2000	..	..	3996	399
	2004	3310	3434	2068	..	..	3983	398
	2005	3301	3429	1932	..	..	3923	392
	2006	3305	3486	1305	..	..	4625	462
Morocco	2003	3743	4667	1156	..	3759	4231	423
	2004	3986	4972	1269	..	3685	4562	456
	2005	4276	6003	825	..	3815	5298	529
	2006	3988	5308	926	..	3389	5471	547
Mozambique	2003	4604	181	5021	..	..	..	..
	2004	4945	225	5389	..	..	..	..
	2005	5608	103	6127	..	..	..	..
	2006	6221	98	6798	..	..	..	..
Niger	2003	1321	1321	..	..	..	3723	372
	2004	1463	1463	..	..	..	4155	415
	2005	1346	1346	..	..	..	3800	380
	2006	1233	1233	..	..	..	3813	381
Nigeria	2003	3432	3528	3291	..	..	3075	..
	2004	3439	3803	2903	..	..	3950	..
	2005	3480	4100	2570	..	..	5050	..
	2006	3930	4399	3240	..	..	4500	..
Réunion	2003	3686	3302	4661	..	..	3733	373
	2004	3763	3403	4677	..	..	3778	377
	2005	3827	3492	4677	..	..	3778	377
	2006	3895	3587	4677	..	..	3778	377
Rwanda	2003	3226	1333	3389	..	..	2000	200
	2004	4194	1250	4630	..	..	2000	200
	2005	3462	1250	3714	..	..	2000	200
	2006	2810	1000	3054	..	..	2000	200
Sao Tome and Principe	2003	3600	2667	5000	..	..	..	..
	2004	3600	2667	5000	..	..	..	..
	2005	3800	2667	5500	..	..	..	..
	2006	3800	2667	5500	..	..	..	..
Senegal	2003	4772	4650	5617	..	2000	5339	536
	2004	4829	4831	4883	..	2000	5875	592
	2005	4561	4584	4450	..	2000	3836	386
	2006	4643	4745	3950	..	2000	5836	589
Seychelles	2003	2356	2356	..	..	..	..	..
	2004	2379	2379	..	..	..	..	..
	2005	2432	2432	..	..	..	..	..
	2006	2653	2653	..	..	..	..	..

Table 33

Utilisation de la capacité des centrales électriques - par catégorie

Kilowatt-heures par kilowatt

producers producteurs			Public utilities Services publics					Year Année	Country or area Pays ou zone
Hydro Hydraulique	Nuclear Nucléaire	Geothermal Géother-mique	Total Totale	Thermal Thermique	Hydro Hydraulique	Nuclear Nucléaire	Geothermal Géother-mique		
..	..	..	3954	1833	5755	..	..	2003	Madagascar
..	..	..	4286	2222	6038	..	..	2004	
..	..	..	4464	2389	6226	..	..	2005	
..	..	..	4566	2444	6368	..	..	2006	
2000	..	..	3997	4000	3997	..	..	2003	Malawi
2250	..	..	4401	4125	4416	..	..	2004	
2250	..	..	4603	4375	4615	..	..	2005	
2250	..	..	4636	4375	4650	..	..	2006	
..	..	..	4208	3652	4720	..	..	2003	Mali
..	..	..	4375	3696	5000	..	..	2004	
..	..	..	4479	3739	5160	..	..	2005	
..	..	..	4625	3870	5320	..	..	2006	
..	..	..	3231	3231	..	..	..	2003	Mauritanie
..	..	..	3508	3508	..	..	..	2004	
..	..	..	3329	3329	..	..	..	2005	
..	..	..	2948	2948	..	..	..	2006	
..	..	..	2742	2865	2000	..	..	2003	Maurice
..	..	..	2931	3072	2068	..	..	2004	
..	..	..	2897	3056	1932	..	..	2005	
..	..	..	2502	2687	1305	..	..	2006	
..	..	..	3696	4727	1156	..	3759	2003	Maroc
..	..	..	3931	5027	1269	..	3685	2004	
..	..	..	4187	6100	825	..	3815	2005	
..	..	..	3872	5289	926	..	3389	2006	
..	..	..	4604	181	5021	..	..	2003	Mozambique
..	..	..	4945	225	5389	..	..	2004	
..	..	..	5608	103	6127	..	..	2005	
..	..	..	6221	98	6798	..	..	2006	
..	..	..	406	406	..	..	..	2003	Niger
..	..	..	437	437	..	..	..	2004	
..	..	..	411	411	..	..	..	2005	
..	..	..	250	250	..	..	..	2006	
3075	..	..	3434	3528	3295	..	..	2003	Nigéria
3950	..	..	3435	3803	2886	..	..	2004	
5050	..	..	3470	4100	2527	..	..	2005	
4500	..	..	3926	4399	3218	..	..	2006	
..	..	..	3680	3230	4661	..	..	2003	Réunion
..	..	..	3761	3341	4677	..	..	2004	
..	..	..	3832	3444	4677	..	..	2005	
..	..	..	3909	3556	4677	..	..	2006	
..	..	..	3259	1000	3389	..	..	2003	Rwanda
..	..	..	4267	1000	4630	..	..	2004	
..	..	..	3500	1000	3714	..	..	2005	
..	..	..	2829	750	3054	..	..	2006	
..	..	..	3600	2667	5000	..	..	2003	Sao Tomé-et-Principe
..	..	..	3600	2667	5000	..	..	2004	
..	..	..	3800	2667	5500	..	..	2005	
..	..	..	3800	2667	5500	..	..	2006	
..	..	2000	4551	4309	5617	..	..	2003	Sénégal
..	..	2000	4458	4373	4883	..	..	2004	
..	..	2000	4771	4822	4450	..	..	2005	
..	..	2000	4258	4313	3950	..	..	2006	
..	..	..	2356	2356	..	..	..	2003	Seychelles
..	..	..	2379	2379	..	..	..	2004	
..	..	..	2432	2432	..	..	..	2005	
..	..	..	2653	2653	..	..	..	2006	

Table 33

Utilization of installed electric generating capacity - by type
Kilowatt-hours per kilowatt

Country or area Pays ou zone	Year Année	Self-producers and public utilities Autoproducteurs et services publics					Self- Auto-	
		Total Totale	Thermal Thermique	Hydro Hydraulique	Nuclear Nucléaire	Geothermal Géother- -mique	Total Totale	Thermal Thermique
Sierra Leone	2003	2872	2774	4000	..	..	3750	37
	2004	2445	2287	4225	..	..	4286	42
	2005	1706	1440	4700	..	..	3857	38
	2006	1980	1674	5500	..	..	3857	38
Somalia	2003	4242	4242	..	..	..	..	
	2004	4242	4242	..	..	..	..	
	2005	4833	4833	..	..	..	..	
	2006	4917	4917	..	..	..	..	
South Africa Customs Un.	2003	5860	5902	3536	6875	3313	7285	73
	2004	6111	6132	4144	7256	3313	7215	72
	2005	6126	6208	4072	6131	3313	7388	74
	2006	6346	6399	4985	6395	3313	6469	65
St. Helena and Depend.	2003	1750	1750	..	..	..		
	2004	2000	2000	..	..	..		
	2005	2000	2000	..	..	..		
	2006	2000	2000	..	..	..		
Sudan	2003	3777	3778	3776	..	..	..	
	2004	4140	4486	3432	..	..	..	
	2005	4291	4623	3677	..	..	..	
	2006	3971	3954	4006	..	..	..	
Togo	2003	3667	3000	4067	..	..	667	6
	2004	3875	5833	2700	..	..	1333	13
	2005	3938	6389	2467	..	..	1667	16
	2006	4604	7222	3033	..	..	3667	36
Tunisia	2003	4021	4065	2661	..	1737	6438	64
	2004	4070	4114	2484	..	2316	6916	69
	2005	3943	3984	2339	..	2211	7015	70
	2006	4236	4303	1460	..	2000	1207	12
Uganda	2003	6725	6200	6727	..	..	5625	50
	2004	6326	2200	6340	..	..	4273	10
	2005	5904	2200	5916	..	..	4273	10
	2006	3864	3650	3933	..	..	4273	10
United Rep.Tanzania	2003	5973	1294	7078	..	..	3650	36
	2004	6155	4882	6544	..	..	4300	43
	2005	5233	5714	4939	..	..	4950	49
	2006	4786	6091	3989	..	..	5300	53
Western Sahara	2003	1552	1552	..	..	..	..	
	2004	1552	1552	..	..	..	..	
	2005	1552	1552	..	..	..	..	
	2006	1552	1552	..	..	..	..	
Zambia	2003	3676	3400	3678	..	..	4180	38
	2004	3766	3467	3768	..	..	4380	40
	2005	3955	3667	3957	..	..	4640	46
	2006	4153	3733	4155	..	..	4860	48
Zimbabwe	2003	4192	2558	7107	..	..	..	
	2004	4630	3120	7322	..	..	..	
	2005	4892	3297	7737	..	..	..	
	2006	4657	3141	7363	..	..	..	
America, North	**2003**	**4064**	**3712**	**3703**	**7438**	**3444**	**4595**	**442**
	2004	**4083**	**3709**	**3705**	**7625**	**3661**	**4896**	**465**
	2005	**4143**	**3783**	**3814**	**7594**	**3353**	**4682**	**446**
	2006	**4100**	**3715**	**3865**	**7690**	**3169**	**4908**	**465**
Anguilla	2003	3476	3476	..	..	..	..	
	2004	3696	3696	..	..	..	..	
	2005	4286	4286	..	..	..	..	
	2006	3313	3313	..	..	..	..	

Table 33

Utilisation de la capacité des centrales électriques - par catégorie
Kilowatt-heures par kilowatt

producers producteurs			Public utilities Services publics					Year Année	Country or area Pays ou zone
Hydro ydraulique	Nuclear Nucléaire	Geothermal Géothermique	Total Totale	Thermal Thermique	Hydro Hydraulique	Nuclear Nucléaire	Geothermal Géothermique		
..	..	..	2705	2568	4000	..	..	2003	Sierra Leone
..	..	..	2138	1918	4225			2004	
..	..	..	1348	995	4700			2005	
..	..	..	1674	1282	5500		..	2006	
..	..	..	4242	4242	..	..	..	2003	Somalie
..	..	..	4242	4242	..	..	..	2004	
..	..	..	4833	4833	..	..	..	2005	
..	..	..	4917	4917	..	..	..	2006	
4436	..	..	5800	5836	3512	6875	3313	2003	Un.douan.d'Afr.mérid
4436	..	..	6064	6080	4136	7256	3313	2004	
4897	..	..	6073	6152	4049	6131	3313	2005	
4897	..	..	6341	6394	4987	6395	3313	2006	
..	..	..	1750	1750	..	..	..	2003	St-Hélène et dépend
..	..	..	2000	2000	..	..	..	2004	
..	..	..	2000	2000	..	..	..	2005	
..	..	..	2000	2000	..	..	..	2006	
..	..	..	3777	3778	3776	..	..	2003	Soudan
..	..	..	4140	4486	3432	..	..	2004	
..	..	..	4291	4623	3677	..	..	2005	
..	..	..	3971	3954	4006	..	..	2006	
..	..	..	3867	3467	4067	..	..	2003	Togo
..	..	..	4044	6733	2700	..	..	2004	
..	..	..	4089	7333	2467	..	..	2005	
..	..	..	4667	7933	3033	..	..	2006	
..	..	..	3467	3503	2661	..	1737	2003	Tunisie
..	..	..	3449	3483	2484	..	2316	2004	
..	..	..	3331	3362	2339	..	2211	2005	
..	..	..	5248	5372	1460	..	2000	2006	
5714	..	..	6758	..	6754	..	..	2003	Ouganda
4600	..	..	6403	..	6399	..	..	2004	
4600	..	..	5964	..	5960	..	..	2005	
4600	..	..	3853	3676	3911	..	..	2006	
..	..	..	6082	569	7078	..	..	2003	Rép. Unie de Tanzanie
..	..	..	6238	5011	6544	..	..	2004	
..	..	..	5243	5790	4939	..	..	2005	
..	..	..	4768	6170	3989	..	..	2006	
..	..	..	1552	1552	..	..	..	2003	Sahara occidental
..	..	..	1552	1552	..	..	..	2004	
..	..	..	1552	1552	..	..	..	2005	
..	..	..	1552	1552	..	..	..	2006	
4222	..	..	3665	3200	3667	..	..	2003	Zambie
4422	..	..	3752	3200	3755	..	..	2004	
4644	..	..	3939	3200	3943	..	..	2005	
4867	..	..	4137	3200	4141	..	..	2006	
..	..	..	4294	2656	7107	..	..	2003	Zimbabwe
..	..	..	4743	3241	7322	..	..	2004	
..	..	..	5012	3425	7737	..	..	2005	
..	..	..	4771	3262	7363	..	..	2006	
5893	..	5377	4040	3674	3629	7438	3430	2003	**Amérique du Nord**
6892	..	5701	4049	3661	3610	7625	3647	2004	
6412	..	5506	4121	3749	3734	7594	3341	2005	
6587	..	5506	4067	3666	3780	7690	3159	2006	
..	..	..	3476	3476	..	..	..	2003	Anguilla
..	..	..	3696	3696	..	..	..	2004	
..	..	..	4286	4286	..	..	..	2005	
..	..	..	3313	3313	..	..	..	2006	

Table 33

Utilization of installed electric generating capacity - by type
Kilowatt-hours per kilowatt

| Country or area Pays ou zone | Year Année | Self-producers and public utilities Autoproducteurs et services publics | | | | | Self- Auto- | |
		Total Totale	Thermal Thermique	Hydro Hydraulique	Nuclear Nucléaire	Geothermal Géother- -mique	Total Totale	Thermal Thermique
Antigua and Barbuda	2003	4037	4037	..	..	..	1000	1000
	2004	4111	4111	..	..	..	1000	1000
	2005	4222	4222	..	..	..	1000	1000
	2006	4296	4296	..	..	..	1000	1000
Aruba	2003	5650	5650	..	..		..	.
	2004	5811	5811	..	..		..	
	2005	6111	6111	..	..		..	
	2006	6104	6104	..	..		..	
Bahamas	2003	4374	4374	..	..	..	1273	1273
	2004	4587	4587	..	..	..	1273	1273
	2005	4239	4239	..	..	..	1273	1273
	2006	4239	4239	..	..	..	1273	1273
Barbados	2003	4032	4032	..	..	..	6500	6500
	2004	4145	4145	..	..	..	6665	6665
	2005	4304	4304	..	..	..	6920	6920
	2006	4388	4388	..	..	..	7055	7055
Belize	2003	3380	1939	6176	..	..	..	..
	2004	3540	2182	6176	..	..	..	..
	2005	3588	2273	6000	..	..	..	..
	2006	3745	2606	5833	..	..	..	..
Bermuda	2003	3794	3794	..	..	..	..	..
	2004	3777	3777	..	..	..	..	..
	2005	3914	3914	..	..	..	..	..
	2006	3977	3977	..	..	..	..	..
British Virgin Islands	2003	4500	4500	..	..	..	..	..
	2004	4500	4500	..	..	..	..	..
	2005	4500	4500	..	..	..	..	..
	2006	4800	4800	..	..	..	..	..
Canada	2003	4988	4784	4797	7055	2457	4663	3320
	2004	4969	4561	4813	7059	2994	5950	4442
	2005	5114	4648	5052	6897	2107	6170	5275
	2006	4869	4087	4893	7341	1701	6538	5664
Cayman Islands	2003	3984	3984	..	..	..	..	..
	2004	3520	3520	..	..	..	..	..
	2005	4243	4243	..	..	..	..	..
	2006	4444	4444	..	..	..	..	..
Costa Rica	2003	3852	379	4648	..	6169	4326	240
	2004	4133	186	4982	..	7453	4096	340
	2005	4234	376	5035	..	7733	4460	840
	2006	4175	1275	4678	..	7597	4612	1480
Cuba	2003	4081	4109	2246	..	..	1918	1918
	2004	4158	4201	1492	..	..	2563	2563
	2005	3588	3613	1411	..	..	1185	1185
	2006	3182	3193	1950	..	..	1740	1740
Dominica	2003	3591	3571	3625	..	..	..	..
	2004	3591	3214	4250	..	..	..	..
	2005	3500	3500	3500	..	..	..	..
	2006	3542	3438	3750	..	..	..	..
Dominican Republic	2003	2439	2464	2214	..	..	1362	1362
	2004	2550	2509	2913	..	..	1390	1390
	2005	2337	2180	4025	..	..	1190	1190
	2006	2550	2509	3002	..	..	1306	1306
El Salvador	2003	3734	3309	3395	..	5993	970	970
	2004	4079	4021	3230	..	6687	970	970
	2005	3874	3316	3621	..	6951	812	812
	2006	4549	4031	4262	..	7540	503	503

Table 33

Utilisation de la capacité des centrales électriques - par catégorie
Kilowatt-heures par kilowatt

producers producteurs			Public utilities Services publics					Year Année	Country or area Pays ou zone
Hydro Hydraulique	Nuclear Nucléaire	Geothermal Géother-mique	Total Totale	Thermal Thermique	Hydro Hydraulique	Nuclear Nucléaire	Geothermal Géother-mique		
..	..	..	4154	4154	..	..	..	2003	Antigua-et-Barbuda
..	..	..	4231	4231	..	..	..	2004	
..	..	..	4346	4346	..	..	..	2005	
..	..	..	4423	4423	..	..	..	2006	
..	..	..	5650	5650	..	..	..	2003	Aruba
..	..	..	5811	5811	..	..	..	2004	
..	..	..	6111	6111	..	..	..	2005	
..	..	..	6104	6104	..	..	..	2006	
..	..	..	4800	4800	..	..	..	2003	Bahamas
..	..	..	5043	5043	..	..	..	2004	
..	..	..	4612	4612	..	..	..	2005	
..	..	..	4612	4612	..	..	..	2006	
..	..	..	3962	3962	..	..	..	2003	Barbade
..	..	..	4073	4073	..	..	..	2004	
..	..	..	4229	4229	..	..	..	2005	
..	..	..	4312	4312	..	..	..	2006	
..	..	..	3380	1939	6176	..	..	2003	Belize
..	..	..	3540	2182	6176	..	..	2004	
..	..	..	3588	2273	6000	..	..	2005	
..	..	..	3745	2606	5833	..	..	2006	
..	..	..	3794	3794	..	..	..	2003	Bermudes
..	..	..	3777	3777	..	..	..	2004	
..	..	..	3914	3914	..	..	..	2005	
..	..	..	3977	3977	..	..	..	2006	
..	..	..	4500	4500	..	..	..	2003	Iles Vierges britanniques
..	..	..	4500	4500	..	..	..	2004	
..	..	..	4500	4500	..	..	..	2005	
..	..	..	4800	4800	..	..	..	2006	
6094	..	..	5019	5029	4698	7055	2457	2003	Canada
7350	..	..	4894	4576	4644	7059	2994	2004	
6826	..	..	5041	4584	4931	6897	2107	2005	
7152	..	..	4756	3939	4737	7341	1701	2006	
..	..	..	3984	3984	..	..	..	2003	Iles Caïmanes
..	..	..	3520	3520	..	..	..	2004	
..	..	..	4243	4243	..	..	..	2005	
..	..	..	4444	4444	..	..	..	2006	
4897	..	6200	3776	397	4613	..	6158	2003	Costa Rica
4306	..	6583	4139	167	5093	..	7836	2004	
4885	..	6333	4197	318	5056	..	8350	2005	
4760	..	6667	4092	1251	4663	..	8007	2006	
..	..	..	4456	4495	2246	..	..	2003	Cuba
..	..	..	4380	4433	1492	..	..	2004	
..	..	..	4041	4076	1411	..	..	2005	
..	..	..	3318	3332	1950	..	..	2006	
..	..	..	3591	3571	3625	..	..	2003	Dominique
..	..	..	3591	3214	4250	..	..	2004	
..	..	..	3500	3500	3500	..	..	2005	
..	..	..	3542	3438	3750	..	..	2006	
..	..	..	3102	3269	2214	..	..	2003	Rép. dominicaine
..	..	..	3292	3367	2913	..	..	2004	
..	..	..	3189	3043	4025	..	..	2005	
..	..	..	3466	3546	3002	..	..	2006	
..	..	..	3872	3576	3395	..	5993	2003	El Salvador
..	..	..	4235	4368	3230	..	6687	2004	
..	..	..	4035	3590	3621	..	6951	2005	
..	..	..	4762	4421	4262	..	7540	2006	

Table 33

Utilization of installed electric generating capacity - by type
Kilowatt-hours per kilowatt

Country or area Pays ou zone	Year Année	Self-producers and public utilities Autoproducteurs et services publics					Self-Auto-	
		Total Totale	Thermal Thermique	Hydro Hydraulique	Nuclear Nucléaire	Geothermal Géother--mique	Total Totale	Thermal Thermique
Greenland	2003	2226	2226	..	..	..	2074	207
	2004	2226	2226	..	..	..	2074	207
	2005	2226	2226	..	..	..	2074	207
	2006	2226	2226	..	..	..	2074	207
Grenada	2003	4781	4781			..	..	
	2004	4921	4921			..	..	
	2005	5188	5188			..	..	
	2006	5355	5355			..	..	
Guadeloupe	2003	2835	2835	..		..	..	
	2004	2871	2871	..		..	..	
	2005	2895	2895	..		..	..	
	2006	2981	2981	..		..	..	
Guatemala	2003	3313	3019	3949		..	4513	451
	2004	3587	3596	3569		..	5800	580
	2005	3662	2893	5106		..	5403	540
	2006	3797	2868	5487		..	3020	302
Haiti	2003	2421	1772	4048		..	..	
	2004	2475	1816	4127		..	..	
	2005	2516	1842	4206		..	..	
	2006	2579	1892	4302		..	..	
Honduras	2003	4162	3783	4670		..	337	34
	2004	4481	4061	5044		..	358	37
	2005	3692	3747	3578		..	1013	104
	2006	3392	3182	3842		..	1249	128
Jamaica	2003	8811	8895	6083		..	23311	2331
	2004	8899	8957	7000		..	23649	2364
	2005	8981	9037	6909		..	17924	1792
	2006	9136	9180	7545		..	17822	1782
Martinique	2003	2992	2992	..		..	..	
	2004	3018	3018	..		..	..	
	2005	3043	3043	..		..	..	
	2006	3068	3068	..		..	..	
Mexico	2003	4397	4823	2060	7694	6465	3267	3267
	2004	4321	4699	2386	6736	6769	3382	338
	2005	4599	4954	2623	7916	7506	3510	351
	2006	4641	4962	2832	7960	6360	5248	528
Montserrat	2003	2100	2100	..	..	..	..	
	2004	2100	2100	..	..	..	..	
	2005	2170	2170	..	..	..	..	
	2006	2190	2190	..	..	..	..	
Netherlands Antilles	2003	5624	5624		..	..	6250	6250
	2004	5762	5762		..	..	6400	6400
	2005	5943	5943		..	..	6600	6600
	2006	6052	6052		..	..	6720	6720
Nicaragua	2003	3913	4194	2865		3474	1815	1815
	2004	3768	3968	3057		3269	1107	1107
	2005	3732	3758	4133		3080	1307	1307
	2006	3887	4007	3533		3534	1118	1118
Panama	2003	3392	3303	3469		..	2700	2700
	2004	3433	2086	4680		..	1500	1500
	2005	3386	2351	4272		..	886	1357
	2006	4061	3316	4608		..	1313	2009
Puerto Rico	2003	4676	4718	2600		..	4098	4098
	2004	4504	4563	1400		..	4098	4098
	2005	4613	4672	1450		..	4098	4098
	2006	4733	4793	1500		..	4098	4098

Table 33

Utilisation de la capacité des centrales électriques - par catégorie
Kilowatt-heures par kilowatt

producers producteurs			Public utilities Services publics					Year Année	Country or area Pays ou zone
Hydro Hydraulique	Nuclear Nucléaire	Geothermal Géother- mique	Total Totale	Thermal Thermique	Hydro Hydraulique	Nuclear Nucléaire	Geothermal Géother- mique		
..	..	..	2264	2264	..	..	..	2003	Groënland
..	..	..	2264	2264	..	..	..	2004	
..	..	..	2264	2264	..	..	..	2005	
..	..	..	2264	2264	..	..	..	2006	
..	..	..	4781	4781	..	..	..	2003	Grenade
..	..	..	4921	4921	..	..	..	2004	
..	..	..	5188	5188	..	..	..	2005	
..	..	..	5355	5355	..	..	..	2006	
..	..	..	2835	2835	..	..	..	2003	Guadeloupe
..	..	..	2871	2871	..	..	..	2004	
..	..	..	2895	2895	..	..	..	2005	
..	..	..	2981	2981	..	..	..	2006	
..	..	..	3188	2778	3949	..	..	2003	Guatemala
..	..	..	3403	3302	3569	..	..	2004	
..	..	..	3540	2610	5106	..	..	2005	
..	..	..	3851	2850	5487	..	..	2006	
..	..	..	2421	1772	4048	..	..	2003	Haïti
..	..	..	2475	1816	4127	..	..	2004	
..	..	..	2516	1842	4206	..	..	2005	
..	..	..	2579	1892	4302	..	..	2006	
..	..	..	4337	4057	4685	..	..	2003	Honduras
..	..	..	4669	4355	5060	..	..	2004	
..	..	..	3787	3886	3589	..	..	2005	
..	..	..	3464	3274	3853	..	..	2006	
..	..	..	5575	5556	6083	..	..	2003	Jamaïque
..	..	..	5606	5554	7000	..	..	2004	
..	..	..	6232	6208	6909	..	..	2005	
..	..	..	6380	6337	7545	..	..	2006	
..	..	..	2992	2992	..	..	..	2003	Martinique
..	..	..	3018	3018	..	..	..	2004	
..	..	..	3043	3043	..	..	..	2005	
..	..	..	3068	3068	..	..	..	2006	
3629	..	2471	4511	5036	2054	7694	6535	2003	Mexique
3714	..	2588	4411	4872	2381	6736	6843	2004	
3457	..	2588	4706	5145	2621	7916	7593	2005	
2543	..	1412	4583	4921	2833	7960	6440	2006	
..	..	..	2100	2100	..	..	..	2003	Montserrat
..	..	..	2100	2100	..	..	..	2004	
..	..	..	2170	2170	..	..	..	2005	
..	..	..	2190	2190	..	..	..	2006	
..	..	..	5055	5055	..	..	..	2003	Antilles néerlandaises
..	..	..	5182	5182	..	..	..	2004	
..	..	..	5345	5345	..	..	..	2005	
..	..	..	5445	5445	..	..	..	2006	
..	..	..	4131	4542	2865	..	3474	2003	Nicaragua
..	..	..	4285	4755	3057	..	3269	2004	
..	..	..	4212	4453	4133	..	3080	2005	
..	..	..	4442	4839	3533	..	3534	2006	
..	..	..	3396	3312	3469	..	..	2003	Panama
..	..	..	3458	2101	4680	..	..	2004	
..	..	..	3678	2524	4580	..	..	2005	
..	..	..	4436	3613	4966	..	..	2006	
..	..	..	4683	4726	2600	..	..	2003	Porto Rico
..	..	..	4508	4568	1400	..	..	2004	
..	..	..	4619	4679	1450	..	..	2005	
..	..	..	4740	4802	1500	..	..	2006	

Table 33

Utilization of installed electric generating capacity - by type
Kilowatt-hours per kilowatt

Country or area Pays ou zone	Year Année	Self-producers and public utilities Autoproducteurs et services publics					Self- Auto-	
		Total Totale	Thermal Thermique	Hydro Hydraulique	Nuclear Nucléaire	Geothermal Géother- -mique	Total Totale	Thermal Thermique
St. Kitts-Nevis	2003	6350	6350	..	..	..	3000	30..
	2004	6190	6190	..	..	..	3000	30..
	2005	6333	6333	..	..	..	3250	32..
	2006	6429	6429	..	..	..	3500	35..
St. Lucia	2003	5264	5264	..	..	..	..	
	2004	5432	5432	..	..	..	..	
	2005	4918	4918	..	..	..	..	
	2006	5027	5027	..	..	..	..	
St. Pierre-Miquelon	2003	1926	1926	..	..	..		
	2004	1926	1926	..	..	..		
	2005	2000	2000	..	..	..		
	2006	2000	2000	..	..	..		
St. Vincent-Grenadines	2003	3536	3676	3044	..	..		
	2004	3714	3671	3871	..	..		
	2005	3543	3556	3500	..	..		
	2006	3528	3500	3625	..	..		
Trinidad and Tobago	2003	4349	4349		..	..	281	28..
	2004	4345	4345		..	..	281	28..
	2005	4769	4769		..	..	563	56..
	2006	4663	4663		..	..	625	62..
Turks and Caicos Islands	2003	2500	2500	..	..	..	..	
	2004	2775	2775	..	..	..	..	
	2005	3075	3075	..	..	..	..	
	2006	3375	3375	..	..	..	..	
United States	2003	3948	3610	3081	7473	3033	4957	495..
	2004	3973	3622	3027	7705	3244	5058	506..
	2005	4018	3696	3013	7678	2970	4786	478..
	2006	3990	3639	3200	7730	2983	4772	478..
United States Virgin Is.	2003	3220	3220	..	..	..	3042	304..
	2004	3251	3251	..	..	..	3077	307..
	2005	3282	3282	..	..	..	3112	311..
	2006	3297	3297	..	..	..	3112	311..
America, South	**2003**	**4104**	**2914**	**4644**	**6917**	**2926**	**4356**	**396..**
	2004	**4201**	**3172**	**4692**	**6440**	**2688**	**4535**	**401..**
	2005	**4291**	**3129**	**4871**	**5530**	**2698**	**4606**	**414..**
	2006	**4411**	**3133**	**5031**	**7089**	**2952**	**4140**	**358..**
Argentina	2003	3300	2969	3453	7432	2889	3517	350..
	2004	3557	3574	3098	7730	2667	3554	355..
	2005	3798	3809	3478	6751	2778	4156	416..
	2006	4087	4007	3873	7555	2593	3845	383..
Bolivia	2003	3249	2318	5098	..	..	2176	279..
	2004	3199	2496	4661	..	..	5381	669..
	2005	3793	3022	5328	..	..	2875	333..
	2006	3773	3414	4452	..	..	2875	318..
Brazil	2003	4188	2716	4475	6656	..	5218	473..
	2004	4270	2790	4649	5785	..	5723	494..
	2005	4325	2741	4763	4910	..	5802	519..
	2006	4339	2679	4750	6853	..	4999	429..
Chile	2003	4259	3592	5424	..	..	4693	434..
	2004	4228	4102	4425	..	..	4116	426..
	2005	4181	3447	5431	..	..	3463	318..
	2006	4216	2698	6832	..	..	2819	182..
Colombia	2003	3516	2457	4072	..	..	6071	603..
	2004	3657	2127	4472	..	2667	4485	425..
	2005	3698	2294	4435	..	2537	3965	365..
	2006	4124	2528	5004	..	3424	4968	482..

Table 33

Utilisation de la capacité des centrales électriques - par catégorie
Kilowatt-heures par kilowatt

producers producteurs			Public utilities Services publics					Year Année	Country or area Pays ou zone
Hydro Hydraulique	Nuclear Nucléaire	Geothermal Géothermique	Total Totale	Thermal Thermique	Hydro Hydraulique	Nuclear Nucléaire	Geothermal Géothermique		
..	..	..	7188	7188	..	..	..	2003	St-Kitts-Nevis
..	..	..	6941	6941	..	..	..	2004	
..	..	..	7059	7059	..	..	..	2005	
..	..	..	7118	7118	..	..	..	2006	
..	..	..	5264	5264	..	..	..	2003	St-Lucie
..	..	..	5432	5432	..	..	..	2004	
..	..	..	4918	4918	..	..	..	2005	
..	..	..	5027	5027	..	..	..	2006	
..	..	..	1926	1926	..	..	..	2003	St-Pierre-Miquelon
..	..	..	1926	1926	..	..	..	2004	
..	..	..	2000	2000	..	..	..	2005	
..	..	..	2000	2000	..	..	..	2006	
..		..	3536	3676	3044		..	2003	St. Vincent-Grenadines
..		..	3714	3671	3871		..	2004	
..		..	3543	3556	3500		..	2005	
..		..	3528	3500	3625		..	2006	
..		..	4533	4533	..	..	..	2003	Trinité-et-Tobago
..		..	4528	4528	..	..	..	2004	
..		..	4959	4959	..	..	..	2005	
..		..	4845	4845	..	..	..	2006	
..	..	..	2500	2500	..	..	..	2003	Iles Turques et Caiques
..	..	..	2775	2775	..	..	..	2004	
..	..	..	3075	3075	..	..	..	2005	
..	..	..	3375	3375	..	..	..	2006	
5027	..	..	3914	3553	3064	7473	3033	2003	Etats-Unis
4841	..	..	3938	3564	3014	7705	3244	2004	
4759	..	..	3994	3653	3000	7678	2970	2005	
4243	..	..	3965	3592	3192	7730	2983	2006	
..	..	..	3361	3361	..	..	..	2003	Iles Vierges américaines
..	..	..	3389	3389	..	..	..	2004	
..	..	..	3417	3417	..	..	..	2005	
..	..	..	3444	3444	..	..	..	2006	
6262	..	..	**4085**	**2691**	**4614**	**6917**	**2926**	**2003**	**Amérique du Sud**
7528	..	..	**4176**	**2997**	**4647**	**6440**	**2688**	**2004**	
7170	..	..	**4267**	**2912**	**4832**	**5530**	**2698**	**2005**	
7345	..	..	**4435**	**3021**	**4988**	**7089**	**2952**	**2006**	
4952	..	..	3280	2884	3450	7432	2889	2003	Argentine
3810	..	..	3558	3578	3097	7730	2667	2004	
3381	..	..	3763	3749	3478	6751	2778	2005	
4810	..	..	4111	4036	3871	7555	2593	2006	
0	..	..	3345	2267	5393	..	..	2003	Bolivie
800	..	..	3019	2093	4873	..	..	2004	
1208	..	..	3874	2989	5554	..	..	2005	
1750	..	..	3851	3439	4592	..	..	2006	
6648	..	..	4101	1852	4419	6656	..	2003	Brésil
8559	..	..	4156	2020	4567	5785	..	2004	
7836	..	..	4208	1881	4692	4910	..	2005	
7830	..	..	4277	1937	4678	6853	..	2006	
7577	..	..	4230	3520	5383	..	..	2003	Chili
2897	..	..	4236	4087	4450	..	..	2004	
6535	..	..	4242	3481	5411	..	..	2005	
8195	..	..	4361	2823	6775	..	..	2006	
6362	..	..	3442	2174	4062	..	..	2003	Colombie
6362	..	..	3633	1962	4464	..	2667	2004	
6531	..	..	3691	2187	4425	..	2537	2005	
6531	..	..	4092	2288	4996	..	3424	2006	

Table 33

Utilization of installed electric generating capacity - by type
Kilowatt-hours per kilowatt

| Country or area
Pays ou zone | Year
Année | Self-producers and public utilities
Autoproducteurs et services publics | | | | | Self-
Auto- | |
		Total Totale	Thermal Thermique	Hydro Hydraulique	Nuclear Nucléaire	Geothermal Géother- -mique	Total Totale	Thermal Thermique
Ecuador	2003	3496	2782	4141	..	..	3067	252
	2004	3778	3237	4277	..	..	6982	731
	2005	3758	2662	4878	..	..	5848	610
	2006	3705	2686	4949	..	..	3898	363
Falkland Is. (Malvinas)	2003	1778	1778	..	..		1000	100
	2004	1789	1789	..	..		1000	100
	2005	1811	1811	..	..		1000	100
	2006	1822	1822	..	..		1000	100
French Guiana	2003	3143	3143	..	..		..	..
	2004	3071	3071	..	..		..	..
	2005	3071	3071	..	..		..	..
	2006	3071	3071	..	..		..	..
Guyana	2003	2666	2666	..	..		1950	195
	2004	2716	2716	..	..		1988	198
	2005	2802	2802	..	..		2050	205
	2006	2821	2821	..	..		2064	206
Paraguay	2003	6980	164	6985	..		..	
	2004	7001	75	7007	..		..	
	2005	6898	107	6904	..		..	
	2006	7251	126	7257	..		..	
Peru	2003	3874	1564	6112	..		2022	171
	2004	4059	2328	5735	..		1962	151
	2005	4114	1880	6225	..		1825	144
	2006	4128	1721	6684	..		1750	132
Suriname	2003	3846	3680	4021	..	..	4134	428
	2004	3879	3685	4085	..	..	4170	428
	2005	4039	3710	4386	..	..	4343	428
	2006	4158	3733	4608	..	..	4471	428
Uruguay	2003	3951	77	5546	..		667	66
	2004	2818	2016	3108	..		667	66
	2005	3673	1803	4346	..		667	66
	2006	2452	2687	2337	..		841	84
Venezuela(Bolivar. Rep.)	2003	4385	3653	4859	..	..	2680	268
	2004	4451	3457	5044	..	..	1867	186
	2005	4587	3518	5140	..	..	2071	207
	2006	4968	4053	5445	..	..	1843	184
Asia	**2003**	**4555**	**4849**	**2876**	**6297**	**4095**	**3333**	**340**
	2004	**4555**	**4828**	**2910**	**6682**	**3921**	**3056**	**310**
	2005	**4555**	**4787**	**2985**	**6857**	**3386**	**3353**	**346**
	2006	**4544**	**4739**	**3138**	**6738**	**3024**	**3253**	**338**
Afghanistan	2003	1996	2861	1730	..	..	2419	245
	2004	1900	3043	1548	..	..	2419	245
	2005	1963	3174	1591	..	..	2419	245
	2006	1963	3174	1591	..	..	2419	245
Armenia	2003	1629	845	1694	4897	..	..	.
	2004	1881	909	1967	5890	..	..	.
	2005	1969	1030	1726	6657	..	..	.
	2006	1882	832	1777	6716	..	..	.
Azerbaijan	2003	3752	4001	2545	..	..	680	680
	2004	3838	4044	2840	..	..	1995	1995
	2005	4435	4744	3102	..	..	2595	2595
	2006	4364	4789	2457	..	..	3085	3085
Bahrain	2003	2955	2955	..	..	..	5452	5452
	2004	3177	3177	..	..	..	6338	6338
	2005	4605	4605	..	..	..	6264	6264
	2006	3929	3929	..	..	..	5893	5893

Table 33

Utilisation de la capacité des centrales électriques - par catégorie
Kilowatt-heures par kilowatt

producers producteurs			Public utilities Services publics					Year Année	Country or area Pays ou zone
Hydro Hydraulique	Nuclear Nucléaire	Geothermal Géother-mique	Total Totale	Thermal Thermique	Hydro Hydraulique	Nuclear Nucléaire	Geothermal Géother-mique		
4871	..	..	3514	2800	4128	..	..	2003	Equateur
5433	..	..	3607	2849	4257	..	..	2004	
4773	..	..	3614	2267	4880	..	..	2005	
5429	..	..	3680	2474	4930	..	..	2006	
..	..	..	2000	2000	..	..	..	2003	Iles Falkland (Malvinas)
..	..	..	2014	2014	..	..	..	2004	
..	..	..	2043	2043	..	..	..	2005	
..	..	..	2057	2057	..	..	..	2006	
..	..	..	3143	3143	..	..	..	2003	Guyane française
..	..	..	3071	3071	..	..	..	2004	
..	..	..	3071	3071	..	..	..	2005	
..	..	..	3071	3071	..	..	..	2006	
..	..	..	3550	3550	..	..	..	2003	Guyana
..	..	..	3618	3618	..	..	..	2004	
..	..	..	3732	3732	..	..	..	2005	
..	..	..	3756	3756	..	..	..	2006	
..	..	..	6980	164	6985	..	..	2003	Paraguay
..	..	..	7001	75	7007	..	..	2004	
..	..	..	6898	107	6904	..	..	2005	
..	..	..	7251	126	7257	..	..	2006	
4855	..	..	4193	1508	6149	..	..	2003	Pérou
6290	..	..	4437	2648	5719	..	..	2004	
5827	..	..	4560	2071	6236	..	..	2005	
6159	..	..	4552	1865	6699	..	..	2006	
4021	..	..	2267	2267	..	..	..	2003	Suriname
4085	..	..	2283	2283	..	..	..	2004	
4386	..	..	2367	2367	..	..	..	2005	
4608	..	..	2444	2444	..	..	..	2006	
..	..	..	4049	12	5546	..	..	2003	Uruguay
..	..	..	2885	2189	3108	..	..	2004	
..	..	..	3766	1949	4346	..	..	2005	
..	..	..	2498	2855	2337	..	..	2006	
..	..	..	4464	3776	4859	..	..	2003	Venezuela(Rép. bolivar.)
..	..	..	4562	3654	5044	..	..	2004	
..	..	..	4687	3701	5140	..	..	2005	
..	..	..	5097	4344	5445	..	..	2006	
2562	..	**798**	**4670**	**5028**	**2881**	**6297**	**5615**	**2003**	**Asie**
2728	..	**834**	**4705**	**5056**	**2913**	**6682**	**5798**	**2004**	
2292	..	**755**	**4655**	**4928**	**2995**	**6857**	**5469**	**2005**	
2293	..	**570**	**4645**	**4872**	**3148**	**6738**	**5514**	**2006**	
2143	..	..	1934	3233	1722	..	..	2003	Afghanistan
2143	..	..	1824	3583	1537	..	..	2004	
2143	..	..	1897	3833	1580	..	..	2005	
2143	..	..	1897	3833	1580	..	..	2006	
..	..	..	1650	866	1694	4897	..	2003	Arménie
..	..	..	1906	932	1967	5890	..	2004	
..	..	..	1995	1056	1726	6657	..	2005	
..	..	..	1908	853	1777	6716	..	2006	
..	..	..	3864	4149	2545	..	..	2003	Azerbaïdjan
..	..	..	3906	4135	2840	..	..	2004	
..	..	..	4509	4852	3102	..	..	2005	
..	..	..	4411	4866	2457	..	..	2006	
..	..	..	2738	2738	..	..	..	2003	Bahreïn
..	..	..	2864	2864	..	..	..	2004	
..	..	..	4351	4351	..	..	..	2005	
..	..	..	3661	3661	..	..	..	2006	

Table 33

Utilization of installed electric generating capacity - by type
Kilowatt-hours per kilowatt

Country or area Pays ou zone	Year Année	Self-producers and public utilities Autoproducteurs et services publics					Self- Auto-	
		Total Totale	Thermal Thermique	Hydro Hydraulique	Nuclear Nucléaire	Geothermal Géother- -mique	Total Totale	Thermal Thermique
Bangladesh	2003	4724	4714	4896	..	..	5006	5006
	2004	4884	4858	5330	..	..	5944	5944
	2005	5162	5136	5622	..	..	6311	6311
	2006	4519	4449	6039	..	..	6587	6587
Bhutan	2003	5023	111	5126	..	..	..	..
	2004	5774	222	5890	..	..	..	..
	2005	4927	222	5017	..	..	..	..
	2006	5540	222	5642	..	..	..	..
Brunei Darussalam	2003	3630	3630	..	..	..	5635	5635
	2004	3703	3703	..	..	..	5156	5156
	2005	4300	4300	..	..	..	5162	5162
	2006	4345	4345	..	..	..	5147	5147
Cambodia	2003	3405	3407	3375	..	..	5364	5364
	2004	3913	4045	2108	..	..	5547	5547
	2005	3786	3809	3385	..	..	5014	5014
	2006	3617	3610	3923	..	2000	4324	4324
China	2003	5348	5951	3296	8671	..	..	..
	2004	5234	5879	3239	8414	..	..	..
	2005	4916	5338	3368	8078	..	..	..
	2006	4756	5052	3502	7245	..	..	..
China, Hong Kong SAR	2003	3039	3039	..	..	..	..	..
	2004	3178	3178	..	..	..	..	..
	2005	3257	3257	..	..	..	..	..
	2006	3119	3119	..	..	..	..	..
China, Macao SAR	2003	3638	3638	..	..	..	..	..
	2004	4008	4008	..	..	..	..	..
	2005	4154	4154	..	..	..	..	..
	2006	3534	3534	..	..	..	..	..
Cyprus	2003	4073	4076	..	..	1000	1333	1333
	2004	4221	4225	..	..	0	4000	4000
	2005	3891	3893	..	..	1000	4667	4667
	2006	4095	4098	..	..	1000	2063	2063
Georgia	2003	1637	386	2389	..	..	..	..
	2004	1583	533	2214	..	..	..	..
	2005	1661	628	2283	..	..	..	..
	2006	1737	1345	1973	..	..	..	..
India	2003	4819	5446	2550	6537	..	3638	3638
	2004	4842	5435	2734	6141	..	3739	3739
	2005	4786	5258	3140	5159	..	3429	3429
	2006	4737	5168	3266	4771	..	3104	3104
Indonesia	2003	4273	4668	2003	..	6315	87	89
	2004	4506	4921	2117	..	6651	162	219
	2005	4594	4969	2345	..	6604	81	103
	2006	4790	5262	2097	..	6658	89	113
Iran(Islamic Rep. of)	2003	3852	4022	2505	..	..	900	900
	2004	3884	4098	2199	..	..	1115	1115
	2005	4064	4178	3179	..	..	1126	1126
	2006	4529	4648	3606	..	..	1320	1320
Iraq	2003	3374	4828	165	..	..	..	..
	2004	3845	5502	188	..	..	..	..
	2005	4048	5793	198	..	..	..	..
	2006	3794	5430	185	..	..	..	..
Israel	2003	4560	4560	6200	..	2400	6230	6332
	2004	4703	4704	5600	..	2200	6250	6374
	2005	4831	4832	5600	..	2200	6458	6591
	2006	4665	4668	3000	..	400	6887	7155

Table 33

Utilisation de la capacité des centrales électriques - par catégorie

Kilowatt-heures par kilowatt

producers producteurs			Public utilities Services publics					Year Année	Country or area Pays ou zone
Hydro Hydraulique	Nuclear Nucléaire	Geothermal Géother-mique	Total Totale	Thermal Thermique	Hydro Hydraulique	Nuclear Nucléaire	Geothermal Géother-mique		
..	..	..	4597	4570	4896	..	..	2003	Bangladesh
..	..	..	4440	4366	5330	..	..	2004	
..	..	..	4681	4603	5622	..	..	2005	
..	..	..	3867	3734	6039	..	..	2006	
..	..	..	5023	111	5126		..	2003	Bhoutan
..	..	..	5774	222	5890	..	..	2004	
..	..	..	4927	222	5017	..	..	2005	
..	..	..	5540	222	5642	..	..	2006	
..	..	..	3474	3474	..	..	..	2003	Brunéi Darussalam
..	..	..	3588	3588	..	..	..	2004	
..	..	..	4216	4216	..	..	..	2005	
..	..	..	4266	4266	..	..	..	2006	
..	..	..	2019	1852	3375	..	..	2003	Cambodge
..	..	..	2811	2902	2108	..	..	2004	
..	..	..	2562	2458	3385	..	..	2005	
..	..	..	2569	2431	3923	..	2000	2006	
..	..	..	5348	5951	3296	8671	..	2003	Chine
..	..	..	5234	5879	3239	8414	..	2004	
..	..	..	4916	5338	3368	8078	..	2005	
..	..	..	4756	5052	3502	7245	..	2006	
..	..	..	3039	3039	..	..	..	2003	Chine, Hong-Kong RAS
..	..	..	3178	3178	..	..	..	2004	
..	..	..	3257	3257	..	..	..	2005	
..	..	..	3119	3119	..	..	..	2006	
..	..	..	3444	3444	..	..	..	2003	Chine, Macao RAS
..	..	..	3820	3820	..	..	..	2004	
..	..	..	3893	3893	..	..	..	2005	
..	..	..	3269	3269	..	..	..	2006	
..	..	..	4090	4093	..	..	1000	2003	Chypre
..	..	..	4222	4227	..	..	0	2004	
..	..	..	3887	3889	..	..	1000	2005	
..	..	..	4124	4127	..	..	1000	2006	
..	..	..	1637	386	2389	..	..	2003	Géorgie
..	..	..	1583	533	2214	..	..	2004	
..	..	..	1661	628	2283	..	..	2005	
..	..	..	1737	1345	1973	..	..	2006	
..	..	..	5015	5867	2550	6537	..	2003	Inde
..	..	..	5020	5818	2734	6141	..	2004	
..	..	..	5019	5700	3140	5159	..	2005	
..	..	..	5042	5711	3266	4771	..	2006	
81	..	..	5156	5507	2833	..	6315	2003	Indonésie
27	..	..	5412	5774	3008	..	6651	2004	
30	..	..	5493	5803	3328	..	6604	2005	
30	..	..	5735	6157	2975	..	6658	2006	
..	..	..	4400	4690	2505	..	..	2003	Iran(Rép. islamique)
..	..	..	4362	4692	2199	..	..	2004	
..	..	..	4552	4763	3179	..	..	2005	
..	..	..	5062	5285	3606	..	..	2006	
..	..	..	3543	5187	165	..	..	2003	Iraq
..	..	..	4037	5911	188	..	..	2004	
..	..	..	4250	6223	198	..	..	2005	
..	..	..	3984	5833	185	..	..	2006	
6200	..	2400	4527	4527	..	..	..	2003	Israël
5600	..	2200	4672	4672	..	..	..	2004	
5600	..	2200	4798	4798	..	..	..	2005	
3000	..	400	4624	4624	..	..	..	2006	

Table 33

Utilization of installed electric generating capacity - by type
Kilowatt-hours per kilowatt

Country or area Pays ou zone	Year Année	Self-producers and public utilities Autoproducteurs et services publics					Self- Auto-	
		Total Totale	Thermal Thermique	Hydro Hydraulique	Nuclear Nucléaire	Geothermal Géother- -mique	Total Totale	Thermal Thermique
Japan	2003	3870	3964	2229	5247	2270	3306	330
	2004	3910	3833	2207	5994	1924	3137	317
	2005	3960	3961	1826	6147	1565	3066	317
	2006	3947	3917	2018	6134	1175	2900	305
Jordan	2003	4496	4498	4417	..	3000	4258	425
	2004	4319	4327	3313	..	3000	3568	356
	2005	4647	4656	3563	..	3000	3712	371
	2006	5356	5364	4250	..	3000	2456	245
Kazakhstan	2003	3424	3371	3811		..	..	
	2004	3568	3569	3560		..	..	
	2005	3625	3636	3544		..	..	
	2006	3825	3868	3504		..	..	
Korea, Dem.Ppl's.Rep.	2003	2210	2062	2344		..	..	
	2004	2313	2105	2500		..	..	
	2005	2412	2174	2626		..	..	
	2006	2362	2181	2524		..	..	
Korea, Republic of	2003	5687	5080	1781	8251	767	4449	446
	2004	5705	5274	1516	7820	1500	5165	517
	2005	5852	5230	1336	8546	1283	4569	457
	2006	5765	5353	952	8396	1262	4396	441
Kuwait	2003	4039	4039	..	..	..	..	
	2004	4186	4186	..	..	..	..	
	2005	4029	4029	..	..	..	..	
	2006	4386	4386	..	..	..	..	
Kyrgyzstan	2003	4213	2830	4552	..	..	4000	
	2004	4412	3047	4747	..	..	0	
	2005	4440	2962	4803	..	..	0	
	2006	4621	3015	5014	..	..	0	
Lao People's Dem. Rep.	2003	4945	6360	6274	..	1098	1098	
	2004	5193	6400	6640	..	1098	1098	
	2005	4967	6500	6138	..	1098	1098	
	2006	5120	6640	6345	..	1098	1098	
Lebanon	2003	4430	4657	2480	..	..	6397	640
	2004	4157	4167	4067	..	..	4037	320
	2005	4812	4940	3851	..	..	4979	499
	2006	4608	4882	2555	..	..	5026	683
Malaysia	2003	4716	4990	2783	..	..	349	34
	2004	3589	3670	2790	..	..	342	34
	2005	4103	4275	2504	..	..	2088	208
	2006	4150	4225	3428	..	..	2510	251
Maldives	2003	2878	2878	..		..	..	
	2004	3265	3265	..		..	..	
	2005	3776	3776	..		..	..	
	2006	3655	3655	..		..	..	
Mongolia	2003	3772	3772		..	..	817	81
	2004	3970	3970	..	..	..	800	80
	2005	4109	4109	..	..	..	633	63
	2006	4260	4260	..	..	..	383	38
Myanmar	2003	4473	3907	5625	..	..	..	
	2004	4440	3936	5351	..	..	..	
	2005	4413	3712	5449	..	..	..	
	2006	4362	3493	5540	..	..	..	
Nepal	2003	3741	73	4107	..	..	88	
	2004	3961	246	4344	..	..	94	
	2005	4291	175	4715	..	..	100	
	2006	4393	175	4827	..	..	100	

Table 33

Utilisation de la capacité des centrales électriques - par catégorie
Kilowatt-heures par kilowatt

producers producteurs			Public utilities Services publics					Year Année	Country or area Pays ou zone
Hydro ydraulique	Nuclear Nucléaire	Geothermal Géother-mique	Total Totale	Thermal Thermique	Hydro Hydraulique	Nuclear Nucléaire	Geothermal Géother-mique		
5815	..	758	3963	4131	2119	5247	6499	2003	Japon
5476	..	799	4047	4013	2106	5994	6265	2004	
4710	..	726	4121	4178	1738	6147	6054	2005	
4707	..	539	4143	4158	1936	6134	5754	2006	
..	..	..	4510	4512	4417	..	3000	2003	Jordanie
..	..	..	4373	4382	3313	..	3000	2004	
..	..	..	4714	4724	3563	..	3000	2005	
..	..	..	5654	5664	4250	..	3000	2006	
..	..	..	3424	3371	3811	..	..	2003	Kazakhstan
..	..	..	3568	3569	3560	..	..	2004	
..	..	..	3625	3636	3544	..	..	2005	
..	..	..	3825	3868	3504	..	..	2006	
..	..	..	2210	2062	2344	..	..	2003	Corée,Rép.pop.dém.de
..	..	..	2313	2105	2500	..	..	2004	
..	..	..	2412	2174	2626	..	..	2005	
..	..	..	2362	2181	2524	..	..	2006	
..	..	400	5823	5184	1781	8251	1278	2003	Corée, République de
..	..	1727	5757	5289	1516	7820	1407	2004	
..	..	1188	5975	5326	1336	8546	1299	2005	
..	..	941	5884	5479	952	8396	1322	2006	
..	..	..	4077	4077	..	..	..	2003	Koweït
..	..	..	4226	4226	..	..	..	2004	
..	..	..	4063	4063	..	..	..	2005	
..	..	..	4423	4423	..	..	..	2006	
4000	..	..	4213	2830	4553	..	..	2003	Kirghizistan
0	..	..	4413	3047	4749	..	..	2004	
0	..	..	4441	2962	4804	..	..	2005	
0	..	..	4622	3015	5016	..	..	2006	
..	..	1098	6283	6360	6274	..	..	2003	Rép. dém. pop. lao
..	..	1098	6617	6400	6640	..	..	2004	
..	..	1098	6170	6500	6138	..	..	2005	
..	..	1098	6371	6640	6345	..	..	2006	
6364	..	..	4094	4405	681	..	..	2003	Liban
5353	..	..	4184	4306	1227	..	..	2004	
4963	..	..	4778	4934	1274	..	..	2005	
3121	..	..	4523	4670	1244	..	..	2006	
..	..	..	7150	8198	2783	..	..	2003	Malaisie
..	..	..	7299	8393	2790	..	..	2004	
..	..	..	4340	4564	2504	..	..	2005	
..	..	..	4345	4452	3428	..	..	2006	
..	..	..	2878	2878	..	..	..	2003	Maldives
..	..	..	3265	3265	..	..	..	2004	
..	..	..	3776	3776	..	..	..	2005	
..	..	..	3655	3655	..	..	..	2006	
..	..	..	4001	4001	..	..	..	2003	Mongolie
..	..	..	4216	4216	..	..	..	2004	
..	..	..	4380	4380	..	..	..	2005	
..	..	..	4561	4561	..	..	..	2006	
..	..	..	4473	3907	5625	..	..	2003	Myanmar
..	..	..	4440	3936	5351	..	..	2004	
..	..	..	4413	3712	5449	..	..	2005	
..	..	..	4362	3493	5540	..	..	2006	
88	..	..	4921	73	5583	..	..	2003	Népal
94	..	..	5210	246	5911	..	..	2004	
100	..	..	5655	175	6428	..	..	2005	
100	..	..	5790	175	6582	..	..	2006	

Table 33

Utilization of installed electric generating capacity - by type
Kilowatt-hours per kilowatt

Country or area / Pays ou zone	Year / Année	Self-producers and public utilities / Autoproducteurs et services publics					Self- / Auto-	
		Total / Totale	Thermal / Thermique	Hydro / Hydraulique	Nuclear / Nucléaire	Geothermal / Géother--mique	Total / Totale	Thermal / Thermique
Occup. Palestinian Terr.	2003	2446	2446	..	..	..	..	
	2004	2825	2825	..	..	..	..	
	2005	3575	3575	..	..	..	..	
	2006	3714	3714	..	..	..	..	
Oman	2003	3843	3843	..	..	..	..	
	2004	3803	3803	..	..	..	..	
	2005	4240	4240	..	..	..	..	
	2006	4088	4088	..	..	..	..	
Other Asia	2003	5255	5418	1529	7560	..	5844	58
	2004	5289	5447	1457	7677	..	6359	63
	2005	5306	5414	1730	7771	..	6337	63
	2006	5341	5440	1773	7751	..	6302	63
Pakistan	2003	4542	4241	5340	3810	..	800	8
	2004	4418	4601	3950	6050	..	4667	46
	2005	4817	4832	4749	5377	..	6767	67
	2006	5057	5125	4932	4952	..	4567	45
Philippines	2003	3492	3405	2735	..	5084	1308	170
	2004	3593	3561	2663	..	5322	1308	170
	2005	3615	3678	2590	..	4941	1308	170
	2006	3589	3444	3042	..	5250	1308	170
Qatar	2003	4489	4489	..	..	..	4501	450
	2004	4563	4563	..	..	..	5094	509
	2005	5089	5089	..	..	..	5722	572
	2006	5061	5061	..	..	..	5193	519
Saudi Arabia	2003	5063	5063	..	..	..	7697	769
	2004	5212	5212	..	..	..	7404	740
	2005	5252	5252	..	..	..	7852	785
	2006	5010	5010	..	..	..	7671	767
Singapore	2003	3993	3993	..	..	..	..	
	2004	4160	4160	..	..	..	..	
	2005	3761	3761	..	..	..	..	
	2006	3657	3657	..	..	..	..	
Sri Lanka	2003	2845	3012	2654	..	1000	441	44
	2004	2993	3603	2311	..	1000	507	50
	2005	3324	3960	2671	..	667	529	52
	2006	3528	3540	3523	..	667	529	52
Syrian Arab Republic	2003	3846	4346	1835	..	..	1937	193
	2004	4177	4524	2779	..	..	2045	204
	2005	4643	5251	2255	..	..	1953	195
	2006	4890	5460	2614	..	..	1953	195
Tajikistan	2003	3716	445	4030	..	..	..	
	2004	3712	391	4030	..	..	..	
	2005	3847	316	4185	..	..	..	
	2006	3812	602	4120	..	..	..	
Thailand	2003	3879	4035	2455	..	3167	2509	250
	2004	3345	3509	1738	..	1462	1157	115
	2005	3964	4231	1668	..	1917	1936	193
	2006	4329	4571	2337	..	2167	2622	262
Timor-Leste	2003	6667	6667	..	..	..	..	
	2004	6140	6140	..	..	..	..	
	2005	6038	6038	..	..	..	..	
	2006	6154	6154	..	..	..	..	
Turkey	2003	3950	4575	2809	..	4412	5092	578
	2004	4092	4326	3644	..	4441	5424	595
	2005	4170	4720	3065	..	4250	4207	464
	2006	4346	4808	3387	..	2695	3821	411

Table 33

Utilisation de la capacité des centrales électriques - par catégorie
Kilowatt-heures par kilowatt

producers producteurs			Public utilities Services publics					Year Année	Country or area Pays ou zone
Hydro Hydraulique	Nuclear Nucléaire	Geothermal Géother-mique	Total Totale	Thermal Thermique	Hydro Hydraulique	Nuclear Nucléaire	Geothermal Géother-mique		
..	..	..	2446	2446	..	..	..	2003	Terr. palestiniens occup.
..	..	..	2825	2825	..	..	..	2004	
..	..	..	3575	3575	..	..	..	2005	
..	..	..	3714	3714	..	..	..	2006	
..	..	..	3843	3843	..	..	..	2003	Oman
..	..	..	3803	3803	..	..	..	2004	
..	..	..	4240	4240	..	..	..	2005	
..	..	..	4088	4088	..	..	..	2006	
..	..	..	5140	5301	1529	7560	..	2003	Autre Asie
..	..	..	5082	5201	1457	7677	..	2004	
..	..	..	5115	5181	1730	7771	..	2005	
..	..	..	5168	5232	1773	7751	..	2006	
..	..	..	4543	4243	5340	3810	..	2003	Pakistan
..	..	..	4417	4601	3950	6050	..	2004	
..	..	..	4814	4827	4749	5377	..	2005	
..	..	..	5058	5127	4932	4952	..	2006	
1063	..	..	3495	3406	2745	..	5084	2003	Philippines
1063	..	..	3597	3563	2671	..	5322	2004	
1063	..	..	3618	3680	2598	..	4941	2005	
1063	..	..	3593	3446	3052	..	5250	2006	
..	..	..	4460	4460	..	..	..	2003	Qatar
..	..	..	3372	3372	..	..	..	2004	
..	..	..	3717	3717	..	..	..	2005	
..	..	..	4664	4664	..	..	..	2006	
..	..	..	4751	4751	..	..	..	2003	Arabie saoudite
..	..	..	4952	4952	..	..	..	2004	
..	..	..	4968	4968	..	..	..	2005	
..	..	..	4740	4740	..	..	..	2006	
..	..	..	3993	3993	..	..	..	2003	Singapour
..	..	..	4160	4160	..	..	..	2004	
..	..	..	3761	3761	..	..	..	2005	
..	..	..	3657	3657	..	..	..	2006	
..	..	..	3065	3486	2654	..	1000	2003	Sri Lanka
..	..	..	3218	4181	2311	..	1000	2004	
..	..	..	3587	4658	2671	..	667	2005	
..	..	..	3808	4153	3523	..	667	2006	
..	..	..	4008	4606	1835	..	..	2003	Rép. arabe syrienne
..	..	..	4358	4792	2779	..	..	2004	
..	..	..	4876	5618	2255	..	..	2005	
..	..	..	5140	5843	2614	..	..	2006	
..	..	..	3716	445	4030	..	..	2003	Tadjikistan
..	..	..	3712	391	4030	..	..	2004	
..	..	..	3847	316	4185	..	..	2005	
..	..	..	3812	602	4120	..	..	2006	
..	..	..	4175	4409	2455	..	3167	2003	Thaïlande
..	..	..	4331	4733	1738	..	1462	2004	
..	..	..	4511	4944	1668	..	1917	2005	
..	..	..	4662	5008	2337	..	2167	2006	
..	..	..	6667	6667	..	..	..	2003	Timor-Leste
..	..	..	6140	6140	..	..	..	2004	
..	..	..	6038	6038	..	..	..	2005	
..	..	..	6154	6154	..	..	..	2006	
855	..	5000	3783	4327	2913	..	4394	2003	Turquie
2381	..	5000	3913	4029	3713	..	4424	2004	
1483	..	2000	4165	4731	3137	..	4455	2005	
2139	..	5000	4400	4900	3443	..	2667	2006	

Table 33

Utilization of installed electric generating capacity - by type

Kilowatt-hours per kilowatt

Country or area Pays ou zone	Year Année	Self-producers and public utilities Autoproducteurs et services publics					Self- Auto-	
		Total Totale	Thermal Thermique	Hydro Hydraulique	Nuclear Nucléaire	Geothermal Géother- -mique	Total Totale	Thermal Thermique
Turkmenistan	2003	2754	2754	3000	..	..	..	
	2004	3040	3040	3000	..	..	..	
	2005	3270	3270	3000	..	..	..	
	2006	3481	3481	3000	..	..	..	
United Arab Emirates	2003	4063	4063	..	..	..	..	
	2004	3868	3868	..	..	..	..	
	2005	3864	3864	..	..	..	..	
	2006	4250	4250	..	..	..	..	
Uzbekistan	2003	4219	4306	3711	..	..	1271	127
	2004	4358	4448	3833	..	..	1316	13
	2005	4074	4158	3584	..	..	1252	12
	2006	4210	4297	3704	..	..	1297	129
Viet Nam	2003	4400	4240	4599	..	..	5213	52
	2004	3977	3810	4280	..	..	2620	262
	2005	4372	3952	5197	..	..	4592	459
	2006	4620	4061	5717	..	..	4525	45
Yemen	2003	3766	3766	..	..	..	6533	653
	2004	3883	3883	..	..	..	6300	630
	2005	4271	4271	..	..	..	6505	650
	2006	4787	4787	..	..	..	6345	634
Europe	**2003**	**4151**	**3972**	**2777**	**7159**	**1746**	**3605**	**372**
	2004	**4223**	**4023**	**2965**	**7230**	**1855**	**3847**	**397**
	2005	**4243**	**4074**	**3001**	**7242**	**1839**	**3802**	**394**
	2006	**4273**	**4196**	**2914**	**7238**	**1793**	**3914**	**409**
Albania	2003	3134	272	3577	..	..	272	27
	2004	3331	415	3783	..	..	415	41
	2005	3261	313	3718	..	..	313	31
	2006	3052	415	3461	..	..	415	41
Austria	2003	2964	3955	2567	..	1080	4325	557
	2004	3056	3829	2766	..	1647	5453	604
	2005	3473	4113	3269	..	1583	4992	583
	2006	3304	3790	3178	..	1732	5088	596
Belarus	2003	3347	3348	2545	..	0	2331	233
	2004	3923	3924	3000	..	1000	2841	283
	2005	3859	3860	3000	..	1000	2865	286
	2006	3964	3966	2917	..	1000	2976	297
Belgium	2003	5419	4285	926	8224	1294	3010	302
	2004	5469	4374	1136	8154	1810	2953	295
	2005	5402	4321	1120	8079	2562	2975	298
	2006	5252	4173	1151	8008	1736	3252	325
Bosnia and Herzegovina	2003	2598	3457	1891	..	..	6850	685
	2004	2915	3452	2480	..	..	6900	690
	2005	2911	3440	2488	..	..	5867	586
	2006	3074	3880	2429	..	..	6533	653
Bulgaria	2003	3551	3258	1313	6346	..	6200	620
	2004	3474	3206	1310	6177	1000	6393	639
	2005	3705	3139	1843	6853	2500	6285	628
	2006	3828	3255	1784	7161	5000	6722	672
Croatia	2003	3221	4169	2379	..	..	2390	237
	2004	3399	3387	3413	..	1000	2307	226
	2005	3223	3341	3125	..	1667	2465	243
	2006	3204	3489	2973	..	1118	2279	225
Czech Republic	2003	4799	4864	835	6881	364	4354	443
	2004	4837	4821	1186	7001	625	4380	448
	2005	4743	4784	1397	6577	724	4419	448
	2006	4818	4772	1497	6927	1111	4340	443

Table 33

Utilisation de la capacité des centrales électriques - par catégorie
Kilowatt-heures par kilowatt

producers producteurs			Public utilities Services publics					Year Année	Country or area Pays ou zone
Hydro Hydraulique	Nuclear Nucléaire	Geothermal Géothermique	Total Totale	Thermal Thermique	Hydro Hydraulique	Nuclear Nucléaire	Geothermal Géothermique		
..	..	..	2754	2754	3000	..	..	2003	Turkménistan
..	..	..	3040	3040	3000	..	..	2004	
..	..	..	3270	3270	3000	..	..	2005	
..	..	..	3481	3481	3000	..	..	2006	
..	..	..	4063	4063	..	..	..	2003	Emirats arabes unis
..	..	..	3868	3868	..	..	..	2004	
..	..	..	3864	3864	..	..	..	2005	
..	..	..	4250	4250	..	..	..	2006	
..	..	..	4259	4354	3711	..	..	2003	Ouzbékistan
..	..	..	4399	4497	3833	..	..	2004	
..	..	..	4112	4204	3584	..	..	2005	
..	..	..	4249	4344	3704	..	..	2006	
..	..	..	4372	4180	4599	..	..	2003	Viet Nam
..	..	..	4013	3860	4280	..	..	2004	
..	..	..	4361	3901	5197	..	..	2005	
..	..	..	4625	4024	5717	..	..	2006	
..	..	..	3517	3517	..	..	..	2003	Yémen
..	..	..	3645	3645	..	..	..	2004	
..	..	..	4038	4038	..	..	..	2005	
..	..	..	4616	4616	..	..	..	2006	
2468	**..**	**1575**	**4194**	**4004**	**2785**	**7159**	**1752**	**2003**	**Europe**
2604	**..**	**1898**	**4253**	**4030**	**2973**	**7230**	**1853**	**2004**	
2627	**..**	**1756**	**4278**	**4091**	**3009**	**7242**	**1843**	**2005**	
2367	**..**	**2034**	**4302**	**4210**	**2927**	**7238**	**1781**	**2006**	
..	..	..	3577	..	3577	..	..	2003	Albanie
..	..	..	3783	..	3783	..	..	2004	
..	..	..	3718	..	3718	..	..	2005	
..	..	..	3461	..	3461	..	..	2006	
1883	..	..	2842	3603	2596	..	1080	2003	Autriche
3648	..	..	2884	3384	2744	..	1647	2004	
2746	..	..	3327	3705	3290	..	1583	2005	
2686	..	..	3134	3268	3197	..	1732	2006	
3000	..	0	3386	3387	2375	..	..	2003	Bélarus
3667	..	1000	3965	3966	2750	..	..	2004	
3667	..	1000	3897	3898	2778	..	..	2005	
3667	..	1000	4002	4004	2667	..	..	2006	
..	..	1000	5484	4349	926	8224	1303	2003	Belgique
..	..	2000	5550	4461	1136	8154	1805	2004	
..	..	1500	5490	4414	1120	8079	2586	2005	
..	..	2500	5315	4227	1151	8008	1729	2006	
..	..	..	2578	3422	1891	..	..	2003	Bosnie y Herzégovine
..	..	..	2897	3416	2480	..	..	2004	
..	..	..	2891	3402	2488	..	..	2005	
..	..	..	3050	3838	2429	..	..	2006	
..	..	..	3474	3102	1313	6346	..	2003	Bulgarie
..	..	..	3407	3072	1310	6177	1000	2004	
..	..	..	3647	3010	1843	6853	2500	2005	
..	..	..	3763	3113	1784	7161	5000	2006	
3250	..	..	3272	4418	2377	..	..	2003	Croatie
4500	..	..	3467	3542	3411	..	1000	2004	
4000	..	..	3268	3460	3124	..	1667	2005	
3500	..	..	3259	3652	2972	..	1118	2006	
3016	..	..	4863	4957	702	6881	364	2003	République tchèque
2987	..	..	4905	4896	1047	7001	625	2004	
3548	..	..	4792	4853	1231	6577	724	2005	
2968	..	..	4893	4850	1385	6927	1111	2006	

Table 33

Utilization of installed electric generating capacity - by type

Kilowatt-hours per kilowatt

| Country or area
Pays ou zone | Year
Année | Self-producers and public utilities
Autoproducteurs et services publics | | | | | Self-
Auto- | |
		Total Totale	Thermal Thermique	Hydro Hydraulique	Nuclear Nucléaire	Geothermal Géother- -mique	Total Totale	Thermal Thermique
Denmark	2003	3397	3880	1909	..	1783	4820	4
	2004	3030	3314	2455	..	2105	4509	4
	2005	2723	2912	2091	..	2112	4495	4
	2006	3512	4011	2556	..	1946	4170	4
Estonia	2003	3984	3986	3250	..	3000	6640	6
	2004	4243	4252	5500	..	1000	5296	5
	2005	4370	4404	5500	..	1742	4630	4
	2006	4154	4179	3250	..	2452	4296	4
Faeroe Islands	2003	3103	3273	2813	..	..	..	
	2004	3333	3636	2813	..	..	..	
	2005	3333	3636	2813	..	..	..	
	2006	3391	3727	2813	..	..	..	
Finland	2003	5088	4769	3234	8510	1727	4978	4
	2004	5182	4434	5025	8505	1419	4660	4
	2005	4284	3121	4542	8712	2012	4222	4
	2006	4969	4446	3754	8576	1747	4671	4
France incl. Monaco	2003	4855	2187	2551	6961	1987	3201	3
	2004	4909	2145	2592	7074	1825	3478	3
	2005	4957	2481	2248	7138	1543	3280	3
	2006	4945	2312	2434	7117	1630	3154	3
Germany	2003	4852	4953	2960	7699	1280	3852	3
	2004	4939	5028	3370	8129	1503	4867	4
	2005	4963	5267	3203	8002	1430	4189	4
	2006	4839	5185	3035	8277	1404	5216	5
Gibraltar	2003	3829	3829	..	..	..	..	
	2004	3886	3886	..	..	..	..	
	2005	4143	4143	..	..	..	..	
	2006	4314	4314	..	..	..	..	
Greece	2003	4840	6040	1732	..	2745	4179	4
	2004	4774	5983	1680	..	2382	3803	3
	2005	4511	5474	1806	..	2575	4226	4
	2006	4480	5434	2066	..	2255	4256	4
Hungary	2003	4108	3594	3167	5902	1333	2032	2
	2004	3928	3240	4020	6385	2000	2993	2
	2005	4164	3263	4122	7414	588	3044	3
	2006	4160	3323	3796	7214	1303	2637	2
Iceland	2003	5640	40	6137	..	6960	161	
	2004	5718	42	6134	..	7342	161	
	2005	5649	42	6035	..	7147	161	
	2006	5757	43	6271	..	6235	179	
Ireland	2003	4457	4880	1797	..	1823	4662	46
	2004	4379	4855	1850	..	1733	4704	47
	2005	4142	4549	1854	..	2251	4345	43
	2006	4353	4900	2068	..	2174	6065	60
Italy and San Marino	2003	3333	3790	1967	..	4246	1981	23
	2004	3510	3955	2230	..	4063	1932	22
	2005	3355	3862	1896	..	3290	2008	23
	2006	3324	3791	1912	..	3259	1863	21
Latvia	2003	1845	2806	1474	..	1846	2424	27
	2004	2174	2577	2024	..	1815	2758	30
	2005	2265	2542	2165	..	1741	2618	29
	2006	2256	3549	1757	..	1704	2382	27
Lithuania	2003	3401	1211	1133	6542	..	3015	30
	2004	3362	1294	1084	6380	1000	5234	52
	2005	3245	1453	935	8738	2000	6016	60
	2006	2735	1208	914	7270	14000	5887	58

Table 33

Utilisation de la capacité des centrales électriques - par catégorie
Kilowatt-heures par kilowatt

producers producteurs			Public utilities Services publics					Year Année	Country or area Pays ou zone
Hydro Hydraulique	Nuclear Nucléaire	Geothermal Géothermique	Total Totale	Thermal Thermique	Hydro Hydraulique	Nuclear Nucléaire	Geothermal Géothermique		
..	..	2000	3335	3826	1909	..	1783	2003	Danemark
..	..	2000	2960	3239	2455	..	2105	2004	
..	..	2000	2634	2806	2091	..	2112	2005	
..	..	2000	3479	4000	2556	..	1946	2006	
..	..	1000	3958	3958	3250	..	5000	2003	Estonie
..	..	1000	4231	4238	5500	..	1000	2004	
..	..	1000	4366	4399	5500	..	1767	2005	
..	..	1000	4152	4176	3250	..	2500	2006	
..	..	..	3103	3273	2813	..	..	2003	Iles Féroé
..	..	..	3333	3636	2813	..	..	2004	
..	..	..	3333	3636	2813	..	..	2005	
..	..	..	3391	3727	2813	..	..	2006	
..	..	..	5105	4714	3234	8510	1727	2003	Finlande
..	..	..	5265	4374	5025	8505	1419	2004	
..	..	..	4294	2824	4542	8712	2012	2005	
..	..	..	5017	4386	3754	8576	1747	2006	
3169	..	1173	4944	1926	2545	6961	2088	2003	France y compris Monaco
3387	..	1745	4982	1824	2584	7074	1833	2004	
3011	..	1625	5061	2223	2240	7138	1537	2005	
3257	..	1956	5056	2034	2425	7117	1606	2006	
5297	..	..	4941	5115	2934	7699	1280	2003	Allemagne
5616	..	..	4946	5053	3346	8129	1503	2004	
5641	..	..	5035	5442	3184	8002	1430	2005	
5373	..	..	4809	5181	3018	8277	1404	2006	
..	..	..	3829	3829	..	..	..	2003	Gibraltar
..	..	..	3886	3886	..	..	..	2004	
..	..	..	4143	4143	..	..	..	2005	
..	..	..	4314	4314	..	..	..	2006	
..	..	..	4854	6094	1732	..	2745	2003	Grèce
..	..	..	4795	6049	1680	..	2382	2004	
..	..	..	4516	5508	1806	..	2575	2005	
..	..	..	4484	5464	2066	..	2255	2006	
..	..	..	4156	3640	3167	5902	1333	2003	Hongrie
..	..	..	3943	3245	4020	6385	2000	2004	
..	..	..	4182	3267	4122	7414	588	2005	
..	..	..	4184	3337	3796	7214	1303	2006	
1000	..	..	5755	41	6155	..	6960	2003	Islande
1000	..	..	5835	43	6152	..	7342	2004	
1000	..	..	5762	43	6053	..	7147	2005	
4000	..	..	5849	44	6273	..	6235	2006	
..	..	..	4452	4886	1797	..	1823	2003	Irlande
..	..	..	4371	4859	1850	..	1733	2004	
..	..	..	4137	4555	1854	..	2251	2005	
..	..	..	4280	4837	2068	..	2174	2006	
591	..	..	3503	4003	2090	..	4246	2003	Italie y comp. St. Marin
538	..	3000	3713	4206	2382	..	4063	2004	
433	..	3000	3520	4069	2026	..	3290	2005	
466	..	3000	3495	4001	2040	..	3259	2006	
1333	..	1000	1836	2809	1475	..	1880	2003	Lettonie
1833	..	0	2165	2555	2025	..	1885	2004	
1667	..	0	2259	2524	2167	..	1808	2005	
1000	..	0	2254	3585	1759	..	1769	2006	
..	..	..	3406	1161	1133	6542	..	2003	Lituanie
..	..	..	3341	1190	1084	6380	1000	2004	
..	..	..	3207	1337	935	8738	2000	2005	
..	..	..	2692	1089	914	7270	14000	2006	

Table 33

Utilization of installed electric generating capacity - by type

Kilowatt-hours per kilowatt

Country or area Pays ou zone	Year Année	Self-producers and public utilities Autoproducteurs et services publics					Self- Auto-	
		Total Totale	Thermal Thermique	Hydro Hydraulique	Nuclear Nucléaire	Geothermal Géother- -mique	Total Totale	Thermal Thermique
Luxembourg	2003	2221	5920	804	..	711	3261	39
	2004	2484	7002	754	..	800	3481	44
	2005	2489	6917	775	..	1148	3519	44
	2006	2602	7207	804	..	1274	3737	45
Malta	2003	2428	2428	..	..	..	..	
	2004	2406	2406	..	..	..	..	
	2005	2432	2432	..	..	..	..	
	2006	2493	2493	..	..	..	..	
Netherlands	2003	4624	4686	1946	8949	1417	4907	51
	2004	4615	4695	2568	8512	1693	4099	42
	2005	4597	4692	2378	8902	1648	5129	54
	2006	4210	4341	2865	6802	1719	4130	43
Norway,Svlbd.J.Myn. I	2003	3773	3431	3782	..	2247	5429	48
	2004	3956	3688	3971	..	1711	5704	56
	2005	4859	3388	4904	..	1874	6430	49
	2006	4122	3854	4142	..	2370	5341	56
Poland	2003	4792	5053	1449	..	3543	3864	38
	2004	4834	5084	1617	..	3550	3958	39
	2005	4865	5132	1628	..	1116	3956	39
	2006	4998	5307	1296	..	1488	4037	40
Portugal	2003	4032	4476	3499	..	2074	4125	41
	2004	3548	4670	2091	..	1587	3976	39
	2005	3478	5443	1017	..	1710	4216	42
	2006	3392	4497	2264	..	1764	4355	43
Republic of Moldova	2003	3379	3508	1143	..	..	5714	57
	2004	3535	3679	1054	..	..	5429	54
	2005	3781	3935	1125	..	..	5857	58
	2006	3736	3872	1375	..	..	6200	62
Romania	2003	2602	2575	2167	6939	..	2050	20
	2004	2799	2578	2698	7847	..	2646	26
	2005	3135	2815	3213	7857	..	3815	38
	2006	3309	3238	2919	7966	..	4356	43
Russian Federation	2003	3961	3721	3495	6611	4325	2852	284
	2004	4009	3710	3905	6363	5125	2906	28
	2005	4088	3822	3809	6571	7190	2867	28
	2006	4498	4380	3805	6589	5379	3168	31
Serbia	2003	3001	3201	2584	..	..	..	
	2004	3198	3333	2917	..	..		
	2005	3088	3055	3156	..	..	6267	62
	2006	3088	3190	2876	..	..	4600	46
Slovakia	2003	3797	3149	1465	6767	333	3603	387
	2004	3693	2993	1671	6449	2000	3827	386
	2005	3809	2897	1887	6715	1200	4316	438
	2006	3823	2886	1817	6823	1200	4513	458
Slovenia	2003	4685	4168	3224	7938	..	3648	423
	2004	5104	4214	4182	8322	..	3346	474
	2005	5052	4254	3535	8970	..	3236	466
	2006	5052	4404	3668	8457	..	3110	406
Spain	2003	3784	3828	2433	8162	2029	5033	508
	2004	4025	4685	1896	8395	1886	5308	539
	2005	3840	4713	1264	7594	2126	5573	569
	2006	3689	4278	1611	8075	1945	5335	543
Sweden	2003	4059	1863	3320	7141	1689	4862	489
	2004	4503	1780	3682	8181	1868	5052	505
	2005	4745	1731	4458	7642	1883	5027	503
	2006	4199	1725	3795	7085	1894	4906	490

Table 33

Utilisation de la capacité des centrales électriques - par catégorie
Kilowatt-heures par kilowatt

producers producteurs			Public utilities Services publics					Year Année	Country or area Pays ou zone
Hydro ydraulique	Nuclear Nucléaire	Geothermal Géother- mique	Total Totale	Thermal Thermique	Hydro Hydraulique	Nuclear Nucléaire	Geothermal Géother- mique		
833	..	63	2142	6426	804	..	1182	2003	Luxembourg
833	..	360	2399	7721	753	..	1114	2004	
833	..	692	2400	7624	774	..	1486	2005	
2500	..	778	2504	7983	801	..	1657	2006	
..	..	..	2428	2428	..	..	..	2003	Malte
..	..	..	2406	2406	..	..	..	2004	
..	..	..	2432	2432	..	..	..	2005	
..	..	..	2493	2493	..	..	..	2006	
..	..	1301	4581	4612	1946	8949	1447	2003	Pays-Bas
..	..	1520	4705	4765	2568	8512	1737	2004	
..	..	1458	4512	4576	2378	8902	1686	2005	
..	..	1585	4226	4339	2865	6802	1751	2006	
5527	..	..	3716	2083	3730	..	2247	2003	Norvège,Svalbd,J.May
5710	..	..	3894	1772	3918	..	1711	2004	
6711	..	..	4803	1793	4849	..	1874	2005	
5283	..	..	4079	1953	4108	..	2370	2006	
2000	..	..	4857	5143	1449	..	3543	2003	Pologne
2000	..	..	4895	5169	1617	..	3550	2004	
2000	..	..	4927	5219	1628	..	1116	2005	
2000	..	..	5063	5400	1295	..	1488	2006	
2429	..	..	4021	4551	3501	..	2074	2003	Portugal
2500	..	..	3500	4816	2091	..	1587	2004	
1333	..	..	3398	5709	1016	..	1710	2005	
2400	..	..	3295	4525	2264	..	1764	2006	
..	..	..	3363	3492	1143	..	..	2003	Rép. de Moldova
..	..	..	3522	3666	1054	..	..	2004	
..	..	..	3767	3921	1125	..	..	2005	
..	..	..	3711	3848	1375	..	..	2006	
1923	..	..	2627	2608	2168	6939	..	2003	Roumanie
2269	..	..	2806	2572	2700	7847	..	2004	
3304	..	..	3112	2761	3213	7857	..	2005	
4130	..	..	3273	3178	2914	7966	..	2006	
3105	..	..	4046	3817	3497	6611	4325	2003	Fédération de Russie
3776	..	..	4093	3800	3906	6363	5125	2004	
3684	..	..	4181	3927	3810	6571	7190	2005	
2380	..	..	4601	4515	3821	6589	5379	2006	
..	..	..	3001	3201	2584	..	..	2003	Serbie
..	..	..	3198	3333	2917	..	..	2004	
..	..	..	3080	3043	3156	..	..	2005	
..	..	..	3084	3184	2876	..	..	2006	
1979	..	333	3814	2973	1445	6767	..	2003	Slovaquie
3120	..	2000	3682	2796	1656	6449	..	2004	
3417	..	1200	3772	2587	1873	6715	..	2005	
3400	..	1200	3766	2480	1801	6823	..	2006	
3212	..	..	4753	4164	3225	7938	..	2003	Slovénie
2298	..	..	5218	4181	4406	8322	..	2004	
2163	..	..	5170	4228	3698	8970	..	2005	
2394	..	..	5178	4425	3819	8457	..	2006	
3500	..	3615	3649	3565	2421	8162	2025	2003	Espagne
2480	..	4692	3876	4512	1889	8395	1882	2004	
1750	..	1786	3660	4511	1258	7594	2127	2005	
2095	..	2286	3531	4062	1606	8075	1944	2006	
4267	..	..	4034	1400	3318	7141	1689	2003	Suède
5333	..	..	4486	1280	3681	8181	1868	2004	
3667	..	..	4736	1197	4459	7642	1883	2005	
6000	..	..	4175	1210	3794	7085	1894	2006	

Table 33

Utilization of installed electric generating capacity - by type
Kilowatt-hours per kilowatt

Country or area Pays ou zone	Year Année	Self-producers and public utilities Autoproducteurs et services publics					Self- Auto-	
		Total Totale	Thermal Thermique	Hydro Hydraulique	Nuclear Nucléaire	Geothermal Géother- -mique	Total Totale	Thermal Thermique
Switzerland	2003	3527	3352	2463	8536	846	2840	334
	2004	3422	3314	2369	8372	719	2693	318
	2005	3117	3694	2204	7249	711	2809	369
	2006	3350	3908	2191	8639	927	2930	402
T.F.Yug.Rep. Macedonia	2003	4614	5299	3067	..	..	2500	250
	2004	4270	5122	2699			1500	150
	2005	4447	5385	2718			1500	150
	2006	4488	5292	3005			500	50
Ukraine	2003	3423	2485	1970	6878	397	1699	169
	2004	3446	2365	2487	6780	397	1851	184
	2005	3541	2427	2651	6915	576	1933	192
	2006	3596	2576	2662	6522	422	1815	181
United Kingdom	2003	5048	4893	1401	7331	1722	5626	613
	2004	4928	4838	1794	6750	2058	6279	697
	2005	4893	4804	1835	6886	1849	5775	679
	2006	4791	4703	1991	6879	2153	5673	683
Oceania	**2003**	**4588**	**5188**	**2789**	..	**4896**	**4419**	**473**
	2004	**4615**	**5171**	**2999**	..	**3500**	**3784**	**401**
	2005	**4806**	**5539**	**2740**	..	**3305**	**3558**	**374**
	2006	**4878**	**5613**	**2761**	..	**3776**	**3460**	**362**
American Samoa	2003	3133	3133	..	..	..	..	..
	2004	3133	3133	..				
	2005	3150	3150	..				
	2006	3217	3217	..				
Australia	2003	4560	5211	1751	..	3070	4231	462
	2004	4588	5265	1713	..	1579	3446	371
	2005	4818	5597	1711	..	1101	3188	341
	2006	4899	5678	1726	..	1935	3090	328
Cook Islands	2003	3638	3638	..	..	..	..	..
	2004	3725	3725	..				
	2005	3738	3738	..				
	2006	4025	4025	..				
Fiji	2003	4921	1959	7330	..	..	2250	225
	2004	4945	1986	7352	..	..	2295	229
	2005	4988	2014	7407	..	..	2318	231
	2006	5091	2054	7560	..	..	2364	236
French Polynesia	2003	5473	5333	6100	..	..	..	
	2004	5690	5269	7650	..	..	..	
	2005	5584	5376	6550	..	..	..	
	2006	5903	5473	7900	..	..	..	
Guam	2003	3220	3220	..	..	..	..	
	2004	3402	3402	..				
	2005	3437	3437	..				
	2006	3426	3426	..				
Kiribati	2003	4500	4500	..	..	..	..	
	2004	4667	4667	..				
	2005	3625	3625	..				
	2006	3750	3750	..				
Marshall Islands	2003	5605	5605	..	..	..	..	
	2004	5890	5890	..				
	2005	5843	5843	..				
	2006	6047	6047	..				
Nauru	2003	3100	3100	..	..	..	..	
	2004	3190	3190	..				
	2005	3260	3260	..				
	2006	3340	3340	..				

Table 33

Utilisation de la capacité des centrales électriques - par catégorie
Kilowatt-heures par kilowatt

producers producteurs			Public utilities Services publics					Year Année	Country or area Pays ou zone
Hydro Hydraulique	Nuclear Nucléaire	Geothermal Géother- mique	Total Totale	Thermal Thermique	Hydro Hydraulique	Nuclear Nucléaire	Geothermal Géother- mique		
2512	..	846	3602	3500	2460	8536	..	2003	Suisse
2371	..	719	3503	5854	2369	8372	..	2004	
2205	..	711	3152	3692	2204	7249	..	2005	
2191	..	927	3396	2135	2191	8639	..	2006	
..	..	..	4617	5305	3067	..	..	2003	L'ex-RY Macédoine
..	..	..	4273	5129	2699	..	..	2004	
..	..	..	4451	5393	2718	..	..	2005	
..	..	..	4493	5302	3005	..	..	2006	
3667	..	..	3547	2570	1967	6878	455	2003	Ukraine
4500	..	..	3558	2422	2483	6780	455	2004	
4125	..	..	3651	2480	2649	6915	585	2005	
3000	..	..	3714	2657	2661	6522	427	2006	
3976	..	1722	4990	4752	1296	7331	..	2003	Royaume-Uni
4978	..	2058	4798	4617	1688	6750	..	2004	
6127	..	1849	4801	4599	1671	6886	..	2005	
5739	..	2153	4696	4492	1851	6879	..	2006	
1668	**..**	**5750**	**4600**	**5225**	**2820**	**..**	**4887**	**2003**	**Océanie**
1575	**..**	**5400**	**4675**	**5275**	**3038**	**..**	**3491**	**2004**	
1543	**..**	**7125**	**4907**	**5722**	**2773**	**..**	**3283**	**2005**	
1558	**..**	**8250**	**5001**	**5833**	**2795**	**..**	**3753**	**2006**	
..	..	..	3133	3133	..	..	..	2003	Samoa américaines
..	..	..	3133	3133	..	..	..	2004	
..	..	..	3150	3150	..	..	..	2005	
..	..	..	3217	3217	..	..	..	2006	
867	..	..	4581	5253	1783	..	3070	2003	Australie
862	..	..	4670	5389	1744	..	1579	2004	
830	..	..	4950	5803	1743	..	1101	2005	
848	..	..	5059	5925	1759	..	1935	2006	
..	..	..	3638	3638	..	..	..	2003	Iles Cook
..	..	..	3725	3725	..	..	..	2004	
..	..	..	3738	3738	..	..	..	2005	
..	..	..	4025	4025	..	..	..	2006	
..	..	..	5893	1533	7330	..	..	2003	Fidji
..	..	..	5909	1533	7352	..	..	2004	
..	..	..	5959	1567	7407	..	..	2005	
..	..	..	6083	1600	7560	..	..	2006	
..	..	..	5473	5333	6100	..	..	2003	Polynésie française
..	..	..	5690	5269	7650	..	..	2004	
..	..	..	5584	5376	6550	..	..	2005	
..	..	..	5903	5473	7900	..	..	2006	
..	..	..	3220	3220	..	..	..	2003	Guam
..	..	..	3402	3402	..	..	..	2004	
..	..	..	3437	3437	..	..	..	2005	
..	..	..	3426	3426	..	..	..	2006	
..	..	..	4500	4500	..	..	..	2003	Kiribati
..	..	..	4667	4667	..	..	..	2004	
..	..	..	3625	3625	..	..	..	2005	
..	..	..	3750	3750	..	..	..	2006	
..	..	..	5605	5605	..	..	..	2003	Îles Marshall
..	..	..	5890	5890	..	..	..	2004	
..	..	..	5843	5843	..	..	..	2005	
..	..	..	6047	6047	..	..	..	2006	
..	..	..	3100	3100	..	..	..	2003	Nauru
..	..	..	3190	3190	..	..	..	2004	
..	..	..	3260	3260	..	..	..	2005	
..	..	..	3340	3340	..	..	..	2006	

Table 33

Utilization of installed electric generating capacity - by type
Kilowatt-hours per kilowatt

Country or area Pays ou zone	Year Année	Self-producers and public utilities Autoproducteurs et services publics					Self- Auto-	
		Total Totale	Thermal Thermique	Hydro Hydraulique	Nuclear Nucléaire	Geothermal Géother- -mique	Total Totale	Thermal Thermique
New Caledonia	2003	5360	5789	4141	..	1667	..	
	2004	4511	4739	4179	..	1000	..	
	2005	5021	5392	4346	..	1286	..	
	2006	4990	5297	5000	..	1480	..	
New Zealand	2003	4812	5382	4434	..	5742	6420	64
	2004	4812	4289	5089	..	4901	5590	55
	2005	4855	5449	4365	..	6317	5623	55
	2006	4883	5437	4388	..	6525	5589	55
Niue	2003	3000	3000	..	..	..	..	
	2004	3000	3000	..	..	..	..	
	2005	3000	3000	..	..	..	..	
	2006	3000	3000	..	..	..	..	
Palau	2003	2462	2619	1800	..	..	3000	30
	2004	2462	2619	1800	..	..	3000	30
	2005	2577	2762	1800	..	..	3000	30
	2006	2904	3167	1800	..	..	3000	30
Papua New Guinea	2003	4772	5255	3903	..	..	4579	44
	2004	5207	6012	3761	..	..	5381	55
	2005	4508	4932	3744	..	..	5566	57
	2006	4523	5021	3626	..	..	5637	58
Samoa	2003	3655	4176	2917	..	..	2500	25
	2004	3793	4118	3333	..	..	2500	25
	2005	3828	4176	3333	..	..	2500	25
	2006	3862	4235	3333	..	..	2500	25
Solomon Islands	2003	4500	4500	..	..	..	1400	14
	2004	4500	4500	..	..	..	1400	14
	2005	5286	5286	..	..	..	1400	14
	2006	5357	5357	..	..	..	1400	14
Tonga	2003	3750	3750	..	..	..	..	
	2004	3917	3917	..	..	..	..	
	2005	4000	4000	..	..	..	..	
	2006	4000	4000	..	..	..	..	
Vanuatu	2003	3667	3667	..	..	..	5000	500
	2004	3667	3667	..	..	..	5000	500
	2005	3750	3750	..	..	..	5000	500
	2006	3750	3750	..	..	..	5000	500
Wallis and Futuna Is	2003	3507	3507	..	..	..	..	
	2004	3529	3529	..	..	..	..	
	2005	3506	3506	..	..	..	..	
	2006	3394	3394	..	..	..	..	

Table 33

Utilisation de la capacité des centrales électriques - par catégorie

Kilowatt-heures par kilowatt

producers producteurs			Public utilities Services publics					Year Année	Country or area Pays ou zone
Hydro Hydraulique	Nuclear Nucléaire	Geothermal Géother-mique	Total Totale	Thermal Thermique	Hydro Hydraulique	Nuclear Nucléaire	Geothermal Géother-mique		
..	..	..	5360	5789	4141	..	1667	2003	Nouvelle-Calédonie
..	..	..	4511	4739	4179	..	1000	2004	
..	..	..	5021	5392	4346	..	1286	2005	
..	..	..	4990	5297	5000	..	1480	2006	
..	..	5750	4751	5248	4434	..	5742	2003	Nouvelle-Zélande
..	..	5400	4782	4125	5089	..	4897	2004	
..	..	7125	4825	5431	4365	..	6306	2005	
..	..	8250	4854	5426	4388	..	6502	2006	
..	..	..	3000	3000	..	..	..	2003	Nioué
..	..	..	3000	3000	..	..	..	2004	
..	..	..	3000	3000	..	..	..	2005	
..	..	..	3000	3000	..	..	..	2006	
..	..	..	2440	2600	1800	..	..	2003	Palaos
..	..	..	2440	2600	1800	..	..	2004	
..	..	..	2560	2750	1800	..	..	2005	
..	..	..	2900	3175	1800	..	..	2006	
5120	..	..	5051	7606	3344	..	..	2003	Papouasie-Nvl-Guinée
4667	..	..	4956	7367	3344	..	..	2004	
4680	..	..	2974	2468	3313	..	..	2005	
4680	..	..	2908	2560	3141	..	..	2006	
..	..	..	3741	4400	2917	..	..	2003	Samoa
..	..	..	3889	4333	3333	..	..	2004	
..	..	..	3926	4400	3333	..	..	2005	
..	..	..	3963	4467	3333	..	..	2006	
..	..	..	6222	6222	..	..	..	2003	Iles Salomon
..	..	..	6222	6222	..	..	..	2004	
..	..	..	7444	7444	..	..	..	2005	
..	..	..	7556	7556	..	..	..	2006	
..	..	..	3750	3750	..	..	..	2003	Tonga
..	..	..	3917	3917	..	..	..	2004	
..	..	..	4000	4000	..	..	..	2005	
..	..	..	4000	4000	..	..	..	2006	
..	..	..	3400	3400	..	..	..	2003	Vanuatu
..	..	..	3400	3400	..	..	..	2004	
..	..	..	3500	3500	..	..	..	2005	
..	..	..	3500	3500	..	..	..	2006	
..	..	..	3507	3507	..	..	..	2003	Iles Wallis et Futuna
..	..	..	3529	3529	..	..	..	2004	
..	..	..	3506	3506	..	..	..	2005	
..	..	..	3394	3394	..	..	..	2006	

Table 34

Production of electricity - by type
Production d'électricité - par catégorie
Million kilowatt-hours
Milliers de kilowattheures

Table Notes:

For this specific table, Geothermal production refers to geothermal, wind, solar, tide and wave electricity production, whenever they are available in the country.

Production data for the Dominican Republic, and Zimbabwe refer to net production.

For Japan, geothermal production includes fuel cell power.

For Brazil and India, thermal production includes also wind electricity.

There are no separate categories for every type of electricity generated, production data from renewable sources in many cases are reported only in total electricity production.

- **Please refer to the Definitions Section on pages xv to xxix for the appropriate product description /classification.**

Notes relatives aux tableaux:

Pour ce tableau spécifique, les données relatives à la production géothermique se rapportent à la production géothermique, éolienne, solaire, marémotrice et énergie des vagues quand elles sont disponibles dans le pays.

Les chiffres relatifs à la production pour la République dominicaine, et le Zimbabwe se rapportent à la production nette.

Pour le Japon, les données relatives à la production géothermique se rapportent aussi à la production d'énergie des piles à combustible.

Pour le Brésil et l'Inde, les données relatives à la production thermique incluent la production d'électricité éolienne.

Il n'y pas de catégorie séparée pour chaque type d'électricité produite, les données de production · des sources renouvelables dans beaucoup de cas sont seulement rapportées dans la production d'électricité totale.

- **Veuillez consulter la section "définitions" de la page xv à la page xxix pour une description/classification appropriée des produits.**

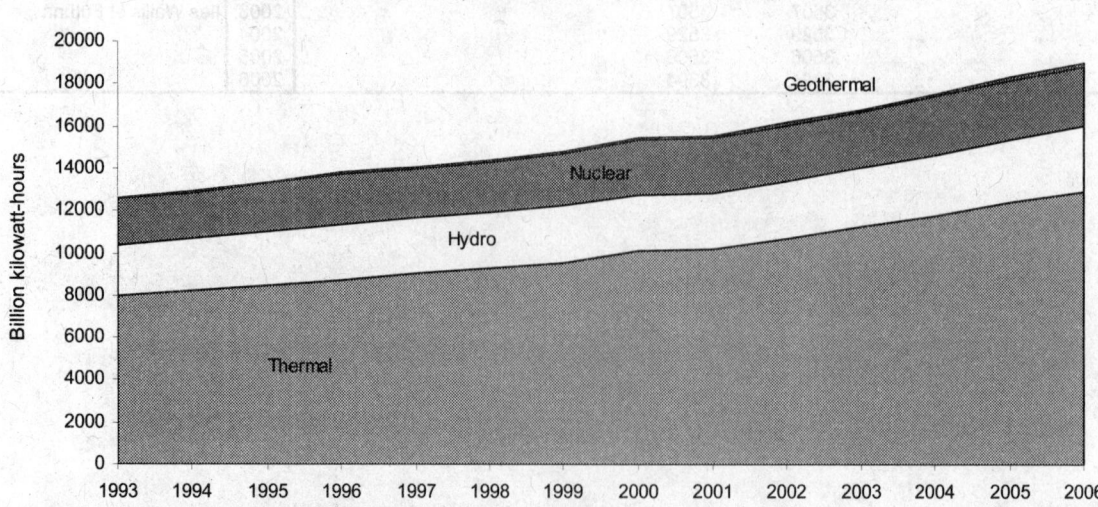

Figure 85: World electricity generation by type 1993-2006

Figure 86: World electricity production, by type and region, in 2006

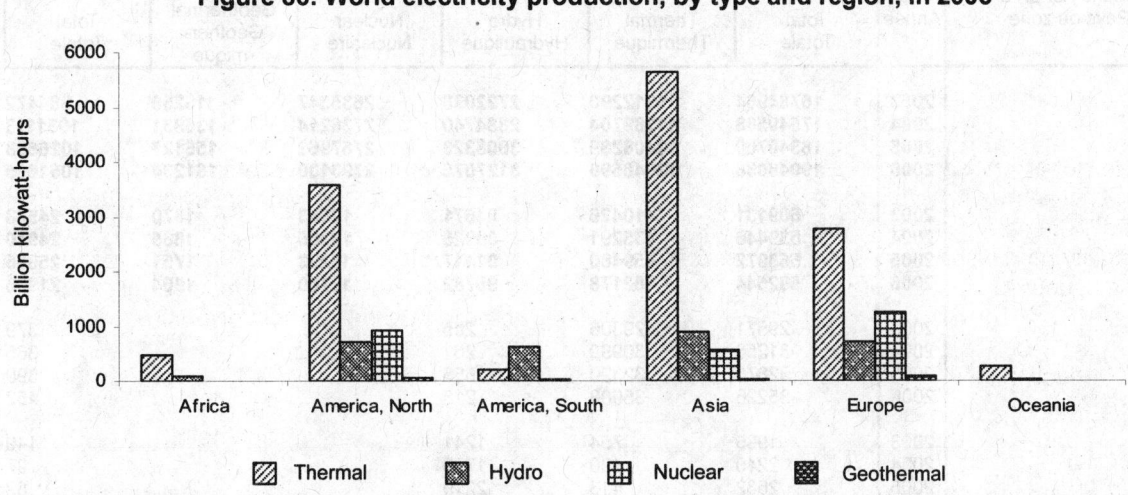

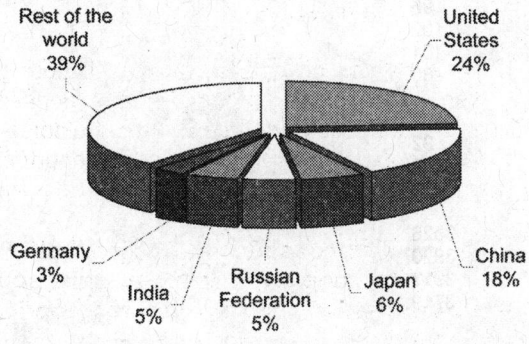

Figure 87: Major thermal producing countries in 2006

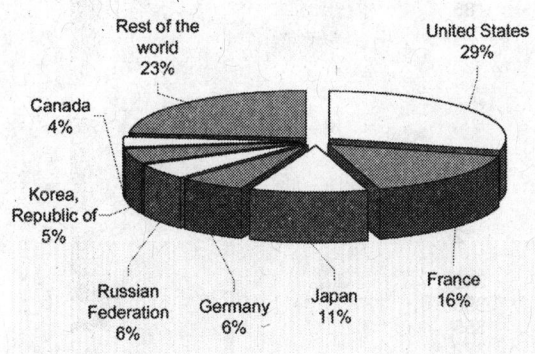

Figure 89: Major nuclear producing countries in 2006

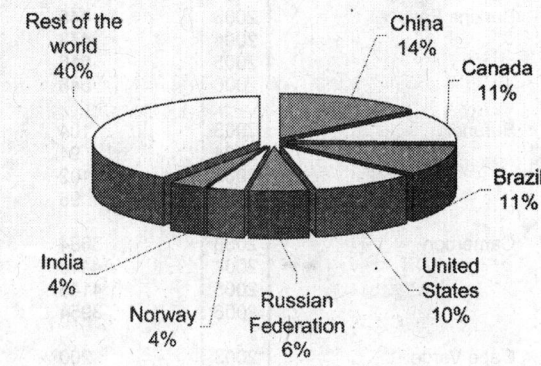

Figure 88: Major hydro producing countries in 2006

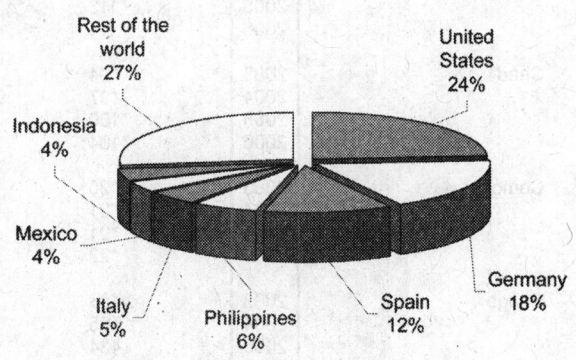

Figure 90: Major geothermal producing countries in 2006

Table 34

Production of electricity - by type

Million kilowatt-hours

Country or area Pays ou zone	Year Année	Self-producers and public utilities Autoproducteurs et services publics					Self-Auto-	
		Total Totale	Thermal Thermique	Hydro Hydraulique	Nuclear Nucléaire	Geothermal Géother--mique	Total Totale	Thermal Thermique
World	**2003**	**16784964**	**11312290**	**2722038**	**2635347**	**115290**	**984472**	**90697**
	2004	**17549588**	**11789704**	**2884740**	**2738214**	**136931**	**1031113**	**94936**
	2005	**18340700**	**12408289**	**3008323**	**2767962**	**156127**	**1026508**	**94539**
	2006	**19048038**	**12946598**	**3127076**	**2793130**	**181234**	**1051665**	**96589**
Africa	**2003**	**509131**	**410426**	**84671**	**12663**	**1370**	**24523**	**2379**
	2004	**539446**	**435291**	**88925**	**13365**	**1865**	**24940**	**2414**
	2005	**563972**	**459480**	**91447**	**11293**	**1751**	**25665**	**2477**
	2006	**592544**	**482178**	**96782**	**11780**	**1804**	**21936**	**2104**
Algeria	2003	29571	29306	265	..	..	379	37
	2004	31250	30999	251	..	..	365	36
	2005	32875	32320	555	..	..	390	39
	2006	35226	35008	218	..	..	452	45
Angola	2003	1995	754	1241	..	..	149	14
	2004	2240	490	1750	..	..	97	9
	2005	2632	413	2219	..	..	82	8
	2006	2959	294	2665	..	..	58	5
Benin	2003	80	78	2	..	..	11	
	2004	81	80	1	..	..	10	1
	2005	107	106	1	..	..	25	2
	2006	128	127	1	..	..	27	2
Burkina Faso	2003	445	349	96	..	..	..	
	2004	473	372	102	..	..	..	
	2005	516	416	101	..	..	..	
	2006	548	468	80	..	..	..	
Burundi	2003	104	*2	102	..	..	..	
	2004	94	*2	92	..	..	..	
	2005	102	*2	100	..	..	..	
	2006	95	*2	93	..	..	..	
Cameroon	2003	3684	156	3528	..	..	..	
	2004	4110	190	3920	..	..	..	
	2005	4145	232	3913	..	..	..	
	2006	3954	235	3719	..	..	..	
Cape Verde	2003	200	194	..	..	5	*1	*
	2004	220	213	..	..	6	*1	*
	2005	237	231	..	..	6	*1	*
	2006	252	245	..	..	7	*1	*
Central African Rep.	2003	*110	*26	*84	..	..	..	
	2004	*111	*27	*84	..	..	..	
	2005	*113	*28	*85	..	..	..	
	2006	*114	*29	*85	..	..	..	
Chad	2003	*94	*94	..	..	..	..	
	2004	*97	*97	..	..	..	..	
	2005	*100	*100	..	..	..	..	
	2006	*104	*104	..	..	..	..	
Comoros	2003	*20	*18	*2	..	..	..	
	2004	*21	*19	*2	..	..	..	
	2005	*21	*19	*2	..	..	..	
	2006	*22	*20	*2	..	..	..	
Congo	2003	408	66	342	..	..	..	
	2004	465	67	398	..	..	..	
	2005	434	79	355	..	..	..	
	2006	453	81	372	..	..	..	
Côte d'Ivoire	2003	5093	3261	1832	..	..	6	
	2004	5403	3655	1748	..	..	5	
	2005	5566	4133	1433	..	..	3	
	2006	5535	4025	1510	..	..	*5	*

Table 34

Production d'électricité - par catégorie
Millions de kilowatt-heures

producers producteurs			Public utilities Services publics					Year Année	Country or area Pays ou zone
Hydro Hydraulique	Nuclear Nucléaire	Geothermal Géother-mique	Total Totale	Thermal Thermique	Hydro Hydraulique	Nuclear Nucléaire	Geothermal Géother-mique		
74079	..	3422	15800492	10405319	2647959	2635347	111867	2003	Monde
77009	..	4734	16518475	10840334	2807730	2738214	132196	2004	
75031	..	6083	17314193	11462896	2933292	2767962	150043	2005	
78038	..	7731	17996373	11980702	3049038	2793130	173503	2006	
727	..	2	484608	386632	83944	12663	1368	2003	Afrique
797	..	3	514506	411151	88128	13365	1862	2004	
882	..	4	538307	434701	90565	11293	1747	2005	
884	..	4	570609	461131	95898	11780	1800	2006	
..	..	..	29192	28927	265	..	..	2003	Algérie
..	..	..	30885	30634	251	..	..	2004	
..	..	..	32485	31930	555	..	..	2005	
..	..	..	34774	34556	218	..	..	2006	
..	..	..	1846	605	1241	..	..	2003	Angola
..	..	..	2143	393	1750	..	..	2004	
..	..	..	2550	331	2219	..	..	2005	
..	..	..	2901	236	2665	..	..	2006	
..	..	..	69	67	2	..	..	2003	Bénin
..	..	..	71	70	1	..	..	2004	
..	..	..	82	81	1	..	..	2005	
..	..	..	101	100	1	..	..	2006	
..	..	..	445	349	96	..	..	2003	Burkina Faso
..	..	..	473	372	102	..	..	2004	
..	..	..	516	416	101	..	..	2005	
..	..	..	548	468	80	..	..	2006	
..	..	..	104	*2	102	..	..	2003	Burundi
..	..	..	94	*2	92	..	..	2004	
..	..	..	102	*2	100	..	..	2005	
..	..	..	95	*2	93	..	..	2006	
..	..	..	3684	156	3528	..	..	2003	Cameroun
..	..	..	4110	190	3920	..	..	2004	
..	..	..	4145	232	3913	..	..	2005	
..	..	..	3954	235	3719	..	..	2006	
..	..	..	199	193	..	..	5	2003	Cap-Vert
..	..	..	219	212	..	..	6	2004	
..	..	..	236	230	..	..	6	2005	
..	..	..	251	244	..	..	7	2006	
..	..	..	*110	*26	*84	..	..	2003	Rép. centrafricaine
..	..	..	*111	*27	*84	..	..	2004	
..	..	..	*113	*28	*85	..	..	2005	
..	..	..	*114	*29	*85	..	..	2006	
..	..	..	*94	*94	..	..	..	2003	Tchad
..	..	..	*97	*97	..	..	..	2004	
..	..	..	*100	*100	..	..	..	2005	
..	..	..	*104	*104	..	..	..	2006	
..	..	..	*20	*18	*2	..	..	2003	Comores
..	..	..	*21	*19	*2	..	..	2004	
..	..	..	*21	*19	*2	..	..	2005	
..	..	..	*22	*20	*2	..	..	2006	
..	..	..	408	66	342	..	..	2003	Congo
..	..	..	465	67	398	..	..	2004	
..	..	..	434	79	355	..	..	2005	
..	..	..	453	81	372	..	..	2006	
..	..	..	5087	3255	1832	..	..	2003	Côte d'Ivoire
..	..	..	5398	3650	1748	..	..	2004	
..	..	..	5563	4130	1433	..	..	2005	
..	..	..	5530	4020	1510	..	..	2006	

Table 34

Production of electricity - by type
Million kilowatt-hours

Country or area Pays ou zone	Year Année	Self-producers and public utilities Autoproducteurs et services publics					Self-Auto-	
		Total Totale	Thermal Thermique	Hydro Hydraulique	Nuclear Nucléaire	Geothermal Géother--mique	Total Totale	Thermal Thermique
Dem. Rep. of Congo	2003	6258	21	6237		..	193	
	2004	6852	22	6830		..	212	
	2005	7419	23	7396		..	225	
	2006	7886	24	7862		..	239	
Djibouti	2003	200	200	..		..	..	
	2004	215	215	..		..	..	
	2005	255	255	..		..	..	
	2006	280	280	..		..	..	
Egypt	2003	91932	79343	12303	..	286	*2950	*29
	2004	101299	88132	12644	..	523	*2950	*29
	2005	111690	98494	12644	..	552	*3000	*30
	2006	118407	104866	12925	..	616	*3000	*30
Equatorial Guinea	2003	*26	*23	*3		..	..	
	2004	*27	*24	*3		..	..	
	2005	*28	*25	*3		..	..	
	2006	*29	*26	*3		..	..	
Eritrea	2003	276	276	..		0	12	
	2004	283	282	..		1	9	
	2005	289	288	..		1	9	
	2006	269	267	..		2	9	
Ethiopia	2003	2302	*21	2280		1	..	
	2004	2540	18	2521		1	..	
	2005	2872	19	2852		1	..	
	2006	3270	10	3259		1	..	
Gabon	2003	1504	604	900	..	..	189	1
	2004	1537	644	893	..	..	200	2
	2005	1611	797	814	..	..	248	2
	2006	1726	781	945	..	..	263	2
Gambia	2003	*151	*151	..		..	*16	*
	2004	*156	*156	..		..	*16	*
	2005	*161	*161	..		..	*16	*
	2006	*166	*166	..		..	*16	*
Ghana	2003	5905	2020	3885		..	*5	
	2004	6044	763	5281		..	*5	
	2005	6793	1164	5629		..	*5	
	2006	8435	2816	5619		..	*6	
Guinea	2003	*782	*362	*420		..	*316	*3
	2004	*801	*366	*435		..	*320	*3
	2005	*816	*381	*435		..	*330	*3
	2006	*836	*401	*435		..	*330	*3
Guinea-Bissau	2003	*61	*61	..		..	*5	
	2004	*63	*63	..		..	*5	
	2005	*64	*64	..		..	*5	
	2006	*66	*66	..		..	*6	
Kenya	2003	5506	1459	3260		787	321	3
	2004	5889	1985	2869		1035	321	3
	2005	6003	2091	3026		886	321	3
	2006	6477	2299	3278		900	321	3
Liberia	2003	320	320	..		..	..	
	2004	330	330	..		..	..	
	2005	*338	*338	..		..	..	
	2006	*351	*351	..		..	..	
Libyan Arab Jamah.	2003	18943	18943	..		..	..	
	2004	20202	20202	..		..	..	
	2005	22317	22317	..		..	..	
	2006	23992	23992	..		..	..	

Table 34

Production d'électricité - par catégorie
Millions de kilowatt-heures

producers producteurs			Public utilities Services publics					Year Année	Country or area Pays ou zone
Hydro Hydraulique	Nuclear Nucléaire	Geothermal Géother-mique	Total Totale	Thermal Thermique	Hydro Hydraulique	Nuclear Nucléaire	Geothermal Géother-mique		
193	..	..	6065	21	6044	..	..	2003	Rép. dem. du Congo
212	..	..	6640	22	6618	..	..	2004	
225	..	..	7194	23	7171	..	..	2005	
239	..	..	7647	24	7623	..	..	2006	
..	..	..	200	200		..	..	2003	Djibouti
..	..	..	215	215		..	..	2004	
..	..	..	255	255		..	..	2005	
..	..	..	280	280		..	..	2006	
..	..	..	88982	76393	12303	..	286	2003	Egypte
..	..	..	98349	85182	12644	..	523	2004	
..	..	..	108690	95494	12644	..	552	2005	
..	..	..	115407	101866	12925	..	616	2006	
..	..	..	*26	*23	*3	..	..	2003	Guinée équatoriale
..	..	..	*27	*24	*3	..	..	2004	
..	..	..	*28	*25	*3	..	..	2005	
..	..	..	*29	*26	*3	..	..	2006	
..	..	..	264	264		..	0	2003	Erythrée
..	..	..	274	273		..	1	2004	
..	..	..	280	279		..	1	2005	
..	..	..	260	258		..	2	2006	
..	..	..	2302	*21	2280	..	1	2003	Ethiopie
..	..	..	2540	18	2521	..	1	2004	
..	..	..	2872	19	2852	..	1	2005	
..	..	..	3270	10	3259	..	1	2006	
..	..	..	1315	415	900	..	..	2003	Gabon
..	..	..	1337	444	893	..	..	2004	
..	..	..	1363	549	814	..	..	2005	
..	..	..	1463	518	945	..	..	2006	
..	..	..	*135	*135	..	..	..	2003	Gambie
..	..	..	*140	*140	..	..	..	2004	
..	..	..	*145	*145	..	..	..	2005	
..	..	..	*150	*150	..	..	..	2006	
..	..	..	5900	2015	3885	..	..	2003	Ghana
..	..	..	6039	758	5281	..	..	2004	
..	..	..	6788	1159	5629	..	..	2005	
..	..	..	8429	2810	5619	..	..	2006	
..	..	..	*466	*46	*420	..	..	2003	Guinée
..	..	..	*481	*46	*435	..	..	2004	
..	..	..	*486	*51	*435	..	..	2005	
..	..	..	*506	*71	*435	..	..	2006	
..	..	..	*56	*56	..	..	..	2003	Guinée-Bissau
..	..	..	*58	*58	..	..	..	2004	
..	..	..	*59	*59	..	..	..	2005	
..	..	..	*60	*60	..	..	..	2006	
..	..	..	5185	1138	3260	..	787	2003	Kenya
..	..	..	5568	1664	2869	..	1035	2004	
..	..	..	5682	1770	3026	..	886	2005	
..	..	..	6156	1978	3278	..	900	2006	
..	..	..	320	320	..	..	..	2003	Libéria
..	..	..	330	330	..	..	..	2004	
..	..	..	*338	*338	..	..	..	2005	
..	..	..	*351	*351	..	..	..	2006	
..	..	..	18943	18943	..	..	..	2003	Jamah. arabe libyenne
..	..	..	20202	20202	..	..	..	2004	
..	..	..	22317	22317	..	..	..	2005	
..	..	..	23992	23992	..	..	..	2006	

Table 34

Production of electricity - by type
Million kilowatt-hours

Country or area Pays ou zone	Year Année	Self-producers and public utilities Autoproducteurs et services publics					Self- Auto-	
		Total Totale	Thermal Thermique	Hydro Hydraulique	Nuclear Nucléaire	Geothermal Géother- -mique	Total Totale	Thermal Thermique
Madagascar	2003	900	*290	610	..	..	*125	*12
	2004	990	*350	640	..	..	*150	*15
	2005	*1035	*375	*660	..	..	*160	*16
	2006	*1065	*390	*675	..	..	*170	*17
Malawi	2003	1337	*186	1151	..	..	*134	*12
	2004	1477	*205	1272	..	..	*148	*13
	2005	1544	*215	1329	..	..	*154	*14
	2006	1556	*217	1339	..	..	*156	*14
Mali	2003	*449	*213	*236	..	..	*45	*4
	2004	*465	*215	*250	..	..	*45	*4
	2005	*475	*217	*258	..	..	*45	*4
	2006	*489	*223	*266	..	..	*45	*4
Mauritania	2003	242	242	..	..	..	..	
	2004	263	263	..	..	..	..	
	2005	250	250	..	..	..	..	
	2006	277	277	..	..	..	..	
Mauritius	2003	2082	1964	118	..	..	947	94
	2004	2165	2043	122	..	..	940	94
	2005	2271	2157	114	..	..	1063	106
	2006	2350	2273	77	..	..	1244	124
Morocco	2003	18107	16448	1456	..	203	1794	179
	2004	19336	17521	1616	..	199	1916	191
	2005	22456	20824	1426	..	206	2225	222
	2006	23192	21408	1601	..	183	2298	229
Mozambique	2003	10907	37	10870	..	..	..	
	2004	11714	46	11668	..	..	..	
	2005	13285	21	13264	..	..	..	
	2006	14737	20	14717	..	..	..	
Niger	2003	*192	*192	..	..	..	*149	*14
	2004	*212	*212	..	..	..	*166	*16
	2005	*195	*195	..	..	..	*152	*15
	2006	*179	*179	..	..	..	*153	*15
Nigeria	2003	20183	12347	7836	..	..	123	
	2004	20224	13311	6913	..	..	158	
	2005	20468	14350	6118	..	..	202	
	2006	23110	15396	7714	..	..	180	
Réunion	2003	*1618	*1040	*578	..	..	*168	*16
	2004	*1652	*1072	*580	..	..	*170	*17
	2005	*1680	*1100	*580	..	..	*170	*17
	2006	*1710	*1130	*580	..	..	*170	*17
Rwanda	2003	123	*4	119	..	..	*2	*
	2004	*130	*5	*125	..	..	*2	*
	2005	*135	*5	*130	..	..	*2	*
	2006	118	5	113	..	..	2	
Sao Tome and Principe	2003	*18	*8	*10	..	..	..	
	2004	*18	*8	*10	..	..	..	
	2005	*19	*8	*11	..	..	..	
	2006	*19	*8	*11	..	..	..	
Senegal	2003	2157	1818	337	..	2	678	67
	2004	2354	2058	293	..	3	749	74
	2005	2595	2324	267	..	4	491	48
	2006	2433	2192	237	..	4	747	74
Seychelles	2003	224	224	..	..	..	..	
	2004	226	226	..	..	..	..	
	2005	231	231	..	..	..	..	
	2006	252	252	..	..	..	..	

Table 34

Production d'électricité - par catégorie
Millions de kilowatt-heures

producers producteurs			Public utilities Services publics					Year Année	Country or area Pays ou zone
Hydro Hydraulique	Nuclear Nucléaire	Geothermal Géothermique	Total Totale	Thermal Thermique	Hydro Hydraulique	Nuclear Nucléaire	Geothermal Géothermique		
..	..	..	775	*165	610	..	..	2003	Madagascar
..	..	..	840	*200	640	..	..	2004	
..	..	..	*875	*215	*660	..	..	2005	
..	..	..	*895	*220	*675	..	..	2006	
*8	..	..	1203	*60	1143	..	..	2003	Malawi
*9	..	..	1329	*66	1263	..	..	2004	
*9	..	..	1390	*70	1320	..	..	2005	
*9	..	..	1400	*70	1330	..	..	2006	
..	..	..	*404	*168	*236	..	..	2003	Mali
..	..	..	*420	*170	*250	..	..	2004	
..	..	..	*430	*172	*258	..	..	2005	
..	..	..	*444	*178	*266	..	..	2006	
..	..	..	242	242	..	..	..	2003	Mauritanie
..	..	..	263	263	..	..	..	2004	
..	..	..	250	250	..	..	..	2005	
..	..	..	277	277	..	..	..	2006	
..	..	..	1135	1017	118	..	..	2003	Maurice
..	..	..	1225	1103	122	..	..	2004	
..	..	..	1208	1094	114	..	..	2005	
..	..	..	1106	1029	77	..	..	2006	
..	..	..	16313	14654	1456	..	203	2003	Maroc
..	..	..	17420	15605	1616	..	199	2004	
..	..	..	20231	18599	1426	..	206	2005	
..	..	..	20894	19110	1601	..	183	2006	
..	..	..	10907	37	10870	..	..	2003	Mozambique
..	..	..	11714	46	11668	..	..	2004	
..	..	..	13285	21	13264	..	..	2005	
..	..	..	14737	20	14717	..	..	2006	
..	..	..	43	43	..	..	..	2003	Niger
..	..	..	46	46	..	..	..	2004	
..	..	..	43	43	..	..	..	2005	
..	..	..	26	26	..	..	..	2006	
123	..	..	20060	12347	7713	..	..	2003	Nigéria
158	..	..	20066	13311	6755	..	..	2004	
202	..	..	20266	14350	5916	..	..	2005	
180	..	..	22930	15396	7534	..	..	2006	
..	..	..	*1450	*872	*578	..	..	2003	Réunion
..	..	..	*1482	*902	*580	..	..	2004	
..	..	..	*1510	*930	*580	..	..	2005	
..	..	..	*1540	*960	*580	..	..	2006	
..	..	..	121	*2	119	..	..	2003	Rwanda
..	..	..	*128	*3	*125	..	..	2004	
..	..	..	*133	*3	*130	..	..	2005	
..	..	..	116	3	113	..	..	2006	
..	..	..	*18	*8	*10	..	..	2003	Sao Tomé-et-Principe
..	..	..	*18	*8	*10	..	..	2004	
..	..	..	*19	*8	*11	..	..	2005	
..	..	..	*19	*8	*11	..	..	2006	
..	..	2	1479	1142	337	..	..	2003	Sénégal
..	..	3	1605	1312	293	..	..	2004	
..	..	4	2104	1837	267	..	..	2005	
..	..	4	1686	1449	237	..	..	2006	
..	..	..	224	224	..	..	..	2003	Seychelles
..	..	..	226	226	..	..	..	2004	
..	..	..	231	231	..	..	..	2005	
..	..	..	252	252	..	..	..	2006	

Table 34

Production of electricity - by type
Million kilowatt-hours

| Country or area
Pays ou zone | Year
Année | Self-producers and public utilities
Autoproducteurs et services publics | | | | | Self-
Auto- | |
		Total Totale	Thermal Thermique	Hydro Hydraulique	Nuclear Nucléaire	Geothermal Géother- -mique	Total Totale	Thermal Thermique
Sierra Leone	2003	144	128	16	..	..	*30	*3
	2004	120	103	17	..	..	*30	*3
	2005	84	65	19	..	..	*27	*2
	2006	*99	*77	*22	..	..	*27	*2
Somalia	2003	280	280	..	..	..	..	
	2004	280	280	..	..	..	..	
	2005	290	290	..	..	..	..	
	2006	295	295	..	..	..	..	
South Africa Customs Un.	2003	237177	219318	5143	12663	53	11918	1174
	2004	247331	227886	6027	13365	53	11804	1163
	2005	247959	230692	5922	11293	53	12088	1189
	2006	256882	237800	7249	11780	53	10596	1040
St. Helena and Depend.	2003	*7	*7	..	..	..	..	
	2004	8	8	..	..	..	..	
	2005	*8	*8	..	..	..	..	
	2006	*8	*8	..	..	..	..	
Sudan	2003	3354	2191	1163	..	..	..	
	2004	3883	2826	1057	..	..	..	
	2005	4124	2885	1239	..	..	..	
	2006	4209	2839	1370	..	..	..	
Togo	2003	176	54	122	..	..	2	
	2004	186	105	81	..	..	4	
	2005	189	115	74	..	..	5	
	2006	221	130	91	..	..	11	1
Tunisia	2003	11829	11631	165	..	33	3528	3528
	2004	12455	12257	154	..	44	3790	3790
	2005	13007	12820	145	..	42	3844	3844
	2006	14122	13992	92	..	38	1008	1008
Uganda	2003	1802	*6	1796	..	..	*45	*
	2004	1942	2	1940	..	..	*47	*1
	2005	1836	2	1834	..	..	47	1
	2006	1615	376	1239	..	..	*47	*1
United Rep.Tanzania	2003	2658	110	2548	..	..	73	73
	2004	2893	537	2356	..	..	86	86
	2005	3035	1257	1778	..	..	99	99
	2006	2776	1340	1436	..	..	106	106
Western Sahara	2003	90	90	..	..	..	..	..
	2004	90	90	..	..	..	..	..
	2005	90	90	..	..	..	..	..
	2006	*90	*90	..	..	..	..	..
Zambia	2003	8308	51	8257	..	..	209	19
	2004	8512	52	8460	..	..	219	20
	2005	8938	55	8883	..	..	232	23
	2006	9385	56	9329	..	..	243	24
Zimbabwe	2003	8799	3440	5359	..	..	..	..
	2004	9718	4197	5521	..	..	..	..
	2005	10269	4435	5834	..	..	..	..
	2006	9776	4224	5552	..	..	..	..
America, North	**2003**	**4997761**	**3407386**	**680624**	**873212**	**36540**	**241496**	**205567**
	2004	**5108687**	**3471166**	**683450**	**912920**	**41151**	**245726**	**208404**
	2005	**5271402**	**3600976**	**709894**	**913571**	**46961**	**234918**	**198795**
	2006	**5281822**	**3576070**	**724675**	**925025**	**56053**	**250414**	**212380**
Anguilla	2003	58	58	..	..	..	..	..
	2004	62	62	..	..	..	..	..
	2005	72	72	..	..	..	..	..
	2006	80	80	..	..	..	..	..

Table 34

Production d'électricité - par catégorie
Millions de kilowatt-heures

producers producteurs			Public utilities Services publics					Year Année	Country or area Pays ou zone
Hydro Hydraulique	Nuclear Nucléaire	Geothermal Géother-mique	Total Totale	Thermal Thermique	Hydro Hydraulique	Nuclear Nucléaire	Geothermal Géother-mique		
..	..	..	114	98	16	..	..	2003	Sierra Leone
..	..	..	90	73	17	..	..	2004	
..	..	..	57	38	19	..	..	2005	
..	..	..	*72	*50	*22	..	..	2006	
..	..	..	280	280	..	..	..	2003	Somalie
..	..	..	280	280	..	..	..	2004	
..	..	..	290	290	..	..	..	2005	
..	..	..	295	295	..	..	..	2006	
173	..	..	225259	207573	4970	12663	53	2003	Un.douan.d'Afr.mérid
173	..	..	235527	216255	5854	13365	53	2004	
191	..	..	235872	218795	5731	11293	53	2005	
191	..	..	246286	227395	7058	11780	53	2006	
..	..	..	*7	*7	..	..	..	2003	St-Hélène et dépend
..	..	..	8	8	..	..	..	2004	
..	..	..	*8	*8	..	..	..	2005	
..	..	..	*8	*8	..	..	..	2006	
..	..	..	3354	2191	1163	..	..	2003	Soudan
..	..	..	3883	2826	1057	..	..	2004	
..	..	..	4124	2885	1239	..	..	2005	
..	..	..	4209	2839	1370	..	..	2006	
..	..	..	174	52	122	..	..	2003	Togo
..	..	..	182	101	81	..	..	2004	
..	..	..	184	110	74	..	..	2005	
..	..	..	210	119	91	..	..	2006	
..	..	..	8301	8103	165	..	33	2003	Tunisie
..	..	..	8665	8467	154	..	44	2004	
..	..	..	9163	8976	145	..	42	2005	
..	..	..	13114	12984	92	..	38	2006	
*40	..	..	1757	1	1756	..	..	2003	Ouganda
*46	..	..	1895	1	1894	..	..	2004	
46	..	..	1789	1	1788	..	..	2005	
*46	..	..	1568	375	1193	..	..	2006	
..	..	..	2585	37	2548	..	..	2003	Rép. Unie de Tanzanie
..	..	..	2807	451	2356	..	..	2004	
..	..	..	2936	1158	1778	..	..	2005	
..	..	..	2670	1234	1436	..	..	2006	
..	..	..	90	90	..	..	..	2003	Sahara occidental
..	..	..	90	90	..	..	..	2004	
..	..	..	90	90	..	..	..	2005	
..	..	..	*90	*90	..	..	..	2006	
190	..	..	8099	32	8067	..	..	2003	Zambie
199	..	..	8293	32	8261	..	..	2004	
209	..	..	8706	32	8674	..	..	2005	
219	..	..	9142	32	9110	..	..	2006	
..	..	..	8799	3440	5359	..	..	2003	Zimbabwe
..	..	..	9718	4197	5521	..	..	2004	
..	..	..	10269	4435	5834	..	..	2005	
..	..	..	9776	4224	5552	..	..	2006	
35515	..	414	4756265	3201819	645109	873212	36126	2003	**Amérique du Nord**
36883	..	439	4862961	3262762	646567	912920	40712	2004	
35699	..	424	5036484	3402181	674195	913571	46537	2005	
37610	..	424	5031408	3363689	687065	925025	55629	2006	
..	..	..	58	58	..	..	..	2003	Anguilla
..	..	..	62	62	..	..	..	2004	
..	..	..	72	72	..	..	..	2005	
..	..	..	80	80	..	..	..	2006	

Table 34

Production of electricity - by type
Million kilowatt-hours

Country or area Pays ou zone	Year Année	Self-producers and public utilities Autoproducteurs et services publics					Self- Auto-	
		Total Totale	Thermal Thermique	Hydro Hydraulique	Nuclear Nucléaire	Geothermal Géother- -mique	Total Totale	Thermal Thermique
Antigua and Barbuda	2003	*109	*109	..	..	..	*1	
	2004	*111	*111	..	..	..	*1	
	2005	*114	*114	..	..	..	*1	
	2006	*116	*116	..	..	..	*1	
Aruba	2003	842	842	..	..	..	..	
	2004	866	866	..	..	..	..	
	2005	911	911	..	..	..	..	
	2006	910	910	..	..	..	..	
Bahamas	2003	1990	1990		..	..	*70	*7
	2004	*2087	*2087		..	..	*70	*7
	2005	*2090	*2090		..	..	*70	*7
	2006	*2090	*2090	..	..	..	*70	*7
Barbados	2003	871	871		..	..	39	3
	2004	895	895		..	..	40	4
	2005	930	930		..	..	42	4
	2006	948	948	..	..	..	42	4
Belize	2003	*169	*64	*105	..	..	..	
	2004	*177	*72	*105	..	..	..	
	2005	*183	*75	*108	..	..	..	
	2006	*191	*86	*105	..	..	..	
Bermuda	2003	664	664		..	..	..	
	2004	*661	*661		..	..	..	
	2005	*685	*685		..	..	..	
	2006	*696	*696		..	..	..	
British Virgin Islands	2003	*45	*45		..	..	..	
	2004	*45	*45		..	..	..	
	2005	*45	*45		..	..	..	
	2006	*48	*48		..	..	..	
Canada	2003	589967	176637	337556	74892	882	47843	1758
	2004	598514	165633	341063	90387	1431	50847	1827
	2005	628194	171009	363626	92040	1519	49251	1779
	2006	612594	156567	355511	97964	2552	52035	1861
Cayman Islands	2003	490	490	..	..	..	..	
	2004	433	433	..	..	..	..	
	2005	454	454	..	..	..	..	
	2006	536	536	..	..	..	..	
Costa Rica	2003	7565	169	6022	..	1374	1172	1
	2004	8040	83	6495	..	1462	1201	1
	2005	8252	169	6566	..	1517	1210	*4
	2006	8697	607	6601	..	1489	1545	7
Cuba	2003	15811	15683	128	..	..	1097	109
	2004	15652	15564	88	..	..	1179	117
	2005	15341	15273	68	..	..	802	80
	2006	16469	16375	94	..	..	776	77
Dominica	2003	79	50	29	..	..	..	
	2004	79	45	34	..	..	..	
	2005	84	56	28	..	..	..	
	2006	*85	*55	*30	..	..	..	
Dominican Republic	2003	13489	12289	1200	..	..	2869	286
	2004	13759	12177	1582	..	..	2927	292
	2005	12899	11003	1896	..	..	2800	280
	2006	14150	12742	1408	..	..	3072	307
El Salvador	2003	4128	1703	1459	..	966	51	5
	2004	4468	2069	1388	..	1011	51	5
	2005	4788	2068	1669	..	1051	50	5
	2006	5597	2495	1962	..	1140	31	3

Table 34

Production d'électricité - par catégorie
Millions de kilowatt-heures

producers producteurs			Public utilities Services publics					Year Année	Country or area Pays ou zone
Hydro Hydraulique	Nuclear Nucléaire	Geothermal Géother-mique	Total Totale	Thermal Thermique	Hydro Hydraulique	Nuclear Nucléaire	Geothermal Géother-mique		
..	..	..	*108	*108	..	..	..	2003	Antigua-et-Barbuda
..	..	..	*110	*110	..	..	..	2004	
..	..	..	*113	*113	..	..	..	2005	
..	..	..	*115	*115	..	..	..	2006	
..	..	..	842	842	..	..	..	2003	Aruba
..	..	..	866	866	..	..	..	2004	
..	..	..	911	911	..	..	..	2005	
..	..	..	910	910	..	..	..	2006	
..	..	..	1920	1920	..	..	..	2003	Bahamas
..	..	..	*2017	*2017	..	..	..	2004	
..	..	..	*2020	*2020	..	..	..	2005	
..	..	..	*2020	*2020	..	..	..	2006	
..	..	..	832	832	..	..	..	2003	Barbade
..	..	..	855	855	..	..	..	2004	
..	..	..	888	888	..	..	..	2005	
..	..	..	905	905	..	..	..	2006	
..	..	..	*169	*64	*105	..	..	2003	Belize
..	..	..	*177	*72	*105	..	..	2004	
..	..	..	*183	*75	*108	..	..	2005	
..	..	..	*191	*86	*105	..	..	2006	
..	..	..	664	664	..	..	..	2003	Bermudes
..	..	..	*661	*661	..	..	..	2004	
..	..	..	*685	*685	..	..	..	2005	
..	..	..	*696	*696	..	..	..	2006	
..	..	..	*45	*45	..	..	..	2003	Iles Vierges britanniques
..	..	..	*45	*45	..	..	..	2004	
..	..	..	*45	*45	..	..	..	2005	
..	..	..	*48	*48	..	..	..	2006	
30262	..	..	542124	159056	307294	74892	882	2003	Canada
32575	..	..	547667	147361	308488	90387	1431	2004	
31459	..	..	578943	153217	332167	92040	1519	2005	
33416	..	..	560559	137948	322095	97964	2552	2006	
..	..	..	490	490	..	..	..	2003	Iles Caïmanes
..	..	..	433	433	..	..	..	2004	
..	..	..	454	454	..	..	..	2005	
..	..	..	536	536	..	..	..	2006	
788	..	372	6393	157	5234	..	1002	2003	Costa Rica
789	..	395	6839	66	5706	..	1067	2004	
788	..	*380	7042	127	5778	..	1137	2005	
1071	..	400	7152	533	5530	..	1089	2006	
..	..	..	14714	14586	128	..	..	2003	Cuba
..	..	..	14473	14385	88	..	..	2004	
..	..	..	14539	14471	68	..	..	2005	
..	..	..	15693	15599	94	..	..	2006	
..	..	..	79	50	29	..	..	2003	Dominique
..	..	..	79	45	34	..	..	2004	
..	..	..	84	56	28	..	..	2005	
..	..	..	*85	*55	*30	..	..	2006	
..	..	..	10620	9420	1200	..	..	2003	Rép. dominicaine
..	..	..	10832	9250	1582	..	..	2004	
..	..	..	10099	8203	1896	..	..	2005	
..	..	..	11078	9670	1408	..	..	2006	
..	..	..	4077	1652	1459	..	966	2003	El Salvador
..	..	..	4417	2018	1388	..	1011	2004	
..	..	..	4738	2018	1669	..	1051	2005	
..	..	..	5566	2464	1962	..	1140	2006	

Table 34

Production of electricity - by type
Million kilowatt-hours

Country or area Pays ou zone	Year Année	Self-producers and public utilities Autoproducteurs et services publics					Self- Auto-	
		Total Totale	Thermal Thermique	Hydro Hydraulique	Nuclear Nucléaire	Geothermal Géother- -mique	Total Totale	Thermal Thermique
Greenland	2003	*305	*305	..	..	..	*56	*5
	2004	*305	*305	..	..	..	*56	*5
	2005	*305	*305	..	..	..	*56	*5
	2006	*305	*305	..	..	..	*56	*5
Grenada	2003	153	153	..			..	
	2004	157	157	..			..	
	2005	166	166	..			..	
	2006	171	171	..			..	
Guadeloupe	2003	1165	1165	..			..	
	2004	*1180	*1180	..			..	
	2005	*1190	*1190	..			..	
	2006	*1225	*1225	..			..	
Guatemala	2003	6561	4084	2477		..	847	84
	2004	7009	4575	2434		..	870	87
	2005	7550	3890	3660		..	735	73
	2006	7911	3856	4055		..	411	41
Haiti	2003	535	280	255		..	..	
	2004	547	287	260		..	..	
	2005	556	291	265		..	..	
	2006	570	299	271		..	..	
Honduras	2003	4530	2356	2174		..	16	1
	2004	4877	2529	2348		..	17	1
	2005	5545	3830	1716		..	52	5
	2006	5356	3417	1938		..	64	6
Jamaica	2003	7146	7000	146		..	3450	345
	2004	7217	7049	168		..	3500	350
	2005	7526	7374	152		..	3531	353
	2006	7473	7307	166		..	3511	351
Martinique	2003	*1185	*1185	..		..	..	
	2004	*1195	*1195	..		..	..	
	2005	*1205	*1205	..		..	..	
	2006	*1215	*1215	..		..	..	
Mexico	2003	217867	181156	19880	10502	6329	14919	1475
	2004	224077	183050	25206	9194	6627	15444	1527
	2005	234895	189010	27732	10805	7348	15924	15759
	2006	249648	201634	30394	10866	6754	24569	24456
Montserrat	2003	21	21	..		..	..	
	2004	21	21	..		..	..	
	2005	*22	*22	..		..	..	
	2006	*22	*22	..		..	..	
Netherlands Antilles	2003	1181	1181	..		..	625	62
	2004	1210	1210	..		..	640	64
	2005	1248	1248	..		..	660	66
	2006	1271	1271	..		..	672	672
Nicaragua	2003	2708	2139	298		271	118	118
	2004	2822	2246	321		255	135	135
	2005	2866	2161	434		271	166	166
	2006	2958	2276	371		311	142	142
Panama	2003	5308	2418	2890		..	27	27
	2004	5504	1607	3897		..	30	30
	2005	5702	1827	3875		..	156	156
	2006	5962	2059	3903		..	231	231
Puerto Rico	2003	23280	23020	260		..	*250	*250
	2004	24130	23990	140		..	*250	*250
	2005	24960	24815	145		..	*250	*250
	2006	*25800	*25650	*150		..	*250	*250

Table 34

Production d'électricité - par catégorie
Millions de kilowatt-heures

producers producteurs			Public utilities Services publics					Year Année	Country or area Pays ou zone
Hydro Hydraulique	Nuclear Nucléaire	Geothermal Géother- mique	Total Totale	Thermal Thermique	Hydro Hydraulique	Nuclear Nucléaire	Geothermal Géother- mique		
..	..	..	*249	*249	..	..	..	2003	Groënland
..	..	..	*249	*249	..	..	..	2004	
..	..	..	*249	*249	..	..	..	2005	
..	..	..	*249	*249	..	..	..	2006	
..	..	..	153	153	..	..	..	2003	Grenade
..	..	..	157	157	..	..	..	2004	
..	..	..	166	166	..	..	..	2005	
..	..	..	171	171	..	..	..	2006	
..	..	..	1165	1165	..	..	..	2003	Guadeloupe
..	..	..	*1180	*1180	..	..	..	2004	
..	..	..	*1190	*1190	..	..	..	2005	
..	..	..	*1225	*1225	..	..	..	2006	
..	..	..	5714	3237	2477	..	..	2003	Guatemala
..	..	..	6139	3705	2434	..	..	2004	
..	..	..	6816	3155	3660	..	..	2005	
..	..	..	7501	3445	4055	..	..	2006	
..	..	..	535	280	255	..	..	2003	Haïti
..	..	..	547	287	260	..	..	2004	
..	..	..	556	291	265	..	..	2005	
..	..	..	570	299	271	..	..	2006	
..	..	..	4514	2340	2174	..	..	2003	Honduras
..	..	..	4860	2512	2348	..	..	2004	
..	..	..	5493	3778	1716	..	..	2005	
..	..	..	5291	3353	1938	..	..	2006	
..	..	..	3696	3550	146	..	..	2003	Jamaïque
..	..	..	3717	3549	168	..	..	2004	
..	..	..	3995	3843	152	..	..	2005	
..	..	..	3962	3796	166	..	..	2006	
..	..	..	*1185	*1185	..	..	..	2003	Martinique
..	..	..	*1195	*1195	..	..	..	2004	
..	..	..	*1205	*1205	..	..	..	2005	
..	..	..	*1215	*1215	..	..	..	2006	
127	..	42	202948	166406	19753	10502	6287	2003	Mexique
130	..	44	208633	167780	25076	9194	6583	2004	
121	..	44	218971	173251	27611	10805	7304	2005	
89	..	24	225079	177178	30305	10866	6730	2006	
..	..	..	21	21	..	..	..	2003	Montserrat
..	..	..	21	21	..	..	..	2004	
..	..	..	*22	*22	..	..	..	2005	
..	..	..	*22	*22	..	..	..	2006	
..	..	..	556	556	..	..	..	2003	Antilles néerlandaises
..	..	..	570	570	..	..	..	2004	
..	..	..	588	588	..	..	..	2005	
..	..	..	599	599	..	..	..	2006	
..	..	..	2590	2021	298	..	271	2003	Nicaragua
..	..	..	2687	2111	321	..	255	2004	
..	..	..	2700	1995	434	..	271	2005	
..	..	..	2816	2134	371	..	311	2006	
..	..	..	5281	2391	2890	..	..	2003	Panama
..	..	..	5474	1577	3897	..	..	2004	
..	..	..	5546	1671	3875	..	..	2005	
..	..	..	5731	1828	3903	..	..	2006	
..	..	..	23030	22770	260	..	..	2003	Porto Rico
..	..	..	23880	23740	140	..	..	2004	
..	..	..	24710	24565	145	..	..	2005	
..	..	..	*25550	*25400	*150	..	..	2006	

Table 34

Production of electricity - by type
Million kilowatt-hours

Country or area Pays ou zone	Year Année	Self-producers and public utilities Autoproducteurs et services publics					Self- Auto-	
		Total Totale	Thermal Thermique	Hydro Hydraulique	Nuclear Nucléaire	Geothermal Géother- -mique	Total Totale	Thermal Thermique
St. Kitts-Nevis	2003	127	127	..	..	..	12	1
	2004	*130	*130	..	..	..	*12	*1
	2005	*133	*133	..	..	..	*13	*1
	2006	*135	*135	..	..	..	*14	*1
St. Lucia	2003	299	299			..	..	
	2004	309	309			..	..	
	2005	324	324			..	..	
	2006	331	331			..	..	
St. Pierre-Miquelon	2003	*52	*52	..	..	..	..	
	2004	*52	*52	..	..	..	..	
	2005	*54	*54	..	..	..	..	
	2006	*54	*54	..	..	..	..	
St. Vincent-Grenadines	2003	108	88	21	..	..	..	
	2004	121	94	27	..	..	..	
	2005	*124	*96	*28	..	..	..	
	2006	*127	*98	*29	..	..	..	
Trinidad and Tobago	2003	6437	6437	..	..	..	18	1
	2004	6430	6430	..	..	..	*18	*1
	2005	7058	7058	..	..	..	36	3
	2006	6901	6901	..	..	..	40	4
Turks and Caicos Islands	2003	*10	*10	..	..	..	..	
	2004	*11	*11	..	..	..	..	
	2005	*12	*12	..	..	..	..	
	2006	*14	*14	..	..	..	..	
United States	2003	4081466	2961206	305724	787818	26718	167581	16324
	2004	4174484	3032886	297894	813339	30365	167998	16460
	2005	4293860	3149953	297926	810726	35255	158669	15533
	2006	4300103	3122415	317686	816195	43807	162437	15940
United States Virgin Is.	2003	*1040	*1040	..	..	..	*435	*43
	2004	*1050	*1050	..	..	..	*440	*44
	2005	*1060	*1060	..	..	..	*445	*44
	2006	*1065	*1065	..	..	..	*445	*44
America, South	**2003**	**745700**	**176715**	**547982**	**20924**	**79**	**55735**	**4210**
	2004	**790558**	**203823**	**567129**	**19480**	**125**	**58546**	**4426**
	2005	**822595**	**203316**	**602426**	**16728**	**125**	**62335**	**4744**
	2006	**866989**	**211133**	**634277**	**21445**	**134**	**64756**	**4786**
Argentina	2003	92609	51124	33841	7566	78	8387	828
	2004	100260	61794	30525	7869	72	8881	880
	2005	107053	65842	34263	6873	75	10387	1031
	2006	115197	69279	38157	7691	70	9609	950
Bolivia	2003	4269	2026	2243	..	..	235	23
	2004	4542	2393	2149	..	..	581	56
	2005	5230	2774	2456	..	..	322	29
	2006	5293	3134	2159	..	..	322	28
Brazil	2003	364339	45365	305616	13358	..	35057	2371
	2004	387451	55043	320797	11611	..	37912	2569
	2005	402938	55626	337457	9855	..	39782	2737
	2006	419336	56777	348805	13754	..	41692	2864
Chile	2003	48780	26177	22603	..		3374	278
	2004	51984	30718	21266	..		3013	278
	2005	54383	28239	26144	..		3546	298
	2006	57555	23308	34247	..		3614	197
Colombia	2003	47682	11466	36216	..	0	2328	206
	2004	50228	10120	40056	..	52	1720	145
	2005	50665	10769	39846	..	49	1520	125
	2006	54755	11899	42793	..	63	2416	214

Table 34

Production d'électricité - par catégorie
Millions de kilowatt-heures

producers producteurs			Public utilities Services publics					Year Année	Country or area Pays ou zone
Hydro Hydraulique	Nuclear Nucléaire	Geothermal Géother-mique	Total Totale	Thermal Thermique	Hydro Hydraulique	Nuclear Nucléaire	Geothermal Géother-mique		
..	..	..	115	115	..	..	..	2003	St-Kitts-Nevis
..	..	..	*118	*118	..	..	..	2004	
..	..	..	*120	*120	..	..	..	2005	
..	..	..	*121	*121	..	..	..	2006	
..	..	..	299	299	..	..	..	2003	St-Lucie
..	..	..	309	309	..	..	..	2004	
..	..	..	324	324	..	..	..	2005	
..	..	..	331	331	..	..	..	2006	
..	..	..	*52	*52	..	..	..	2003	St-Pierre-Miquelon
..	..	..	*52	*52	..	..	..	2004	
..	..	..	*54	*54	..	..	..	2005	
..	..	..	*54	*54	..	..	..	2006	
..	..	..	108	88	21	..	..	2003	St. Vincent-Grenadines
..	..	..	121	94	27	..	..	2004	
..	..	..	*124	*96	*28	..	..	2005	
..	..	..	*127	*98	*29	..	..	2006	
..	..	..	6419	6419	..	..	..	2003	Trinité-et-Tobago
..	..	..	6412	6412	..	..	..	2004	
..	..	..	7022	7022	..	..	..	2005	
..	..	..	6861	6861	..	..	..	2006	
..	..	..	*10	*10	..	..	..	2003	Iles Turques et Caiques
..	..	..	*11	*11	..	..	..	2004	
..	..	..	*12	*12	..	..	..	2005	
..	..	..	*14	*14	..	..	..	2006	
4338	..	..	3913885	2797963	301386	787818	26718	2003	Etats-Unis
3389	..	..	4006486	2868277	294505	813339	30365	2004	
3331	..	..	4135191	2994615	294595	810726	35255	2005	
3034	..	..	4137666	2963012	314652	816195	43807	2006	
..	..	..	*605	*605	..	..	..	2003	Iles Vierges américaines
..	..	..	*610	*610	..	..	..	2004	
..	..	..	*615	*615	..	..	..	2005	
..	..	..	*620	*620	..	..	..	2006	
13626	**..**	**..**	**689966**	**134606**	**534356**	**20924**	**79**	**2003**	**Amérique du Sud**
14282	**..**	**..**	**732011**	**159559**	**552847**	**19480**	**125**	**2004**	
14887	**..**	**..**	**760261**	**155869**	**587539**	**16728**	**125**	**2005**	
16889	**..**	**..**	**802233**	**163266**	**617388**	**21445**	**134**	**2006**	
104	..	..	84222	42841	33737	7566	78	2003	Argentine
80	..	..	91379	52993	30445	7869	72	2004	
71	..	..	96666	55526	34192	6873	75	2005	
101	..	..	105588	59771	38056	7691	70	2006	
0	..	..	4035	1791	2243	..	..	2003	Bolivie
19	..	..	3961	1831	2129	..	..	2004	
29	..	..	4908	2481	2427	..	..	2005	
42	..	..	4971	2854	2117	..	..	2006	
11342	..	..	329282	21650	294274	13358	..	2003	Brésil
12213	..	..	349539	29344	308584	11611	..	2004	
12404	..	..	363156	28248	325053	9855	..	2005	
13044	..	..	377644	28129	335761	13754	..	2006	
591	..	..	45406	23394	22012	..	..	2003	Chili
226	..	..	48971	27931	21040	..	..	2004	
562	..	..	50837	25255	25582	..	..	2005	
1639	..	..	53941	21333	32608	..	..	2006	
263	..	..	45354	9401	35953	..	0	2003	Colombie
263	..	..	48508	8663	39793	..	52	2004	
270	..	..	49145	9519	39576	..	49	2005	
270	..	..	52339	9753	42523	..	63	2006	

Table 34

Production of electricity - by type
Million kilowatt-hours

Country or area Pays ou zone	Year Année	Self-producers and public utilities Autoproducteurs et services publics					Self- Auto-	
		Total Totale	Thermal Thermique	Hydro Hydraulique	Nuclear Nucléaire	Geothermal Géother- -mique	Total Totale	Thermal Thermique
Ecuador	2003	11546	4365	7181	..	..	411	26
	2004	12585	5173	7412	..	..	1180	101
	2005	13404	4800	8604	..	..	1345	113
	2006	14814	5901	8913	..	..	1840	146
Falkland Is. (Malvinas)	2003	*16	*16	..	..	..	*2	*
	2004	*16	*16	..	..	..	*2	*
	2005	*16	*16	..	..	..	*2	*
	2006	*16	*16	..	..	..	*2	*
French Guiana	2003	440	440	..	..	..	..	
	2004	430	430	..	..	..	..	
	2005	430	430	..	..	..	..	
	2006	430	430	..	..	..	..	
Guyana	2003	820	820	..	..	..	332	33
	2004	835	835	..	..	..	338	33
	2005	862	862	..	..	..	349	34
	2006	867	867	..	..	..	351	351
Paraguay	2003	51762	1	51761	..	..	..	
	2004	51921	0	51921	..	..	..	
	2005	51156	1	51156	..	..	..	
	2006	53774	1	53774	..	..	..	
Peru	2003	23128	4593	18534	..	1	1769	1354
	2004	24415	6889	17525	..	1	1806	1260
	2005	25660	5697	19962	..	1	1859	1347
	2006	27358	5874	21483	..	1	1755	1213
Suriname	2003	1496	736	760	..	..	1360	600
	2004	1509	737	772	..	..	1372	600
	2005	1571	742	829	..	..	1429	600
	2006	1618	747	871	..	..	1471	600
Uruguay	2003	8578	49	8529	..	..	42	42
	2004	5899	1119	4780	..	..	42	42
	2005	7683	999	6684	..	..	42	42
	2006	5618	2023	3595	..	..	53	53
Venezuela(Bolivar. Rep.)	2003	90235	29537	60698	..	..	2439	2439
	2004	98482	28555	69927	..	..	1699	1699
	2005	101544	26519	75025	..	..	1752	1752
	2006	110357	30877	79480	..	..	1631	1631
Asia	**2003**	**5656352**	**4476562**	**685460**	**473453**	**20877**	**354899**	**344235**
	2004	**6130540**	**4812654**	**770496**	**525325**	**22065**	**374356**	**362257**
	2005	**6622834**	**5206578**	**827038**	**567128**	**22090**	**372009**	**361366**
	2006	**7155055**	**5653403**	**908145**	**570523**	**22984**	**372179**	**361528**
Afghanistan	2003	976	329	647	..	..	*150	*135
	2004	929	350	579	..	..	*150	*135
	2005	*960	*365	*595	..	..	*150	*135
	2006	*960	*365	*595	..	..	*150	*135
Armenia	2003	5501	1521	1982	1998	..	..	..
	2004	6030	1613	2014	2403	..	..	..
	2005	6317	1828	1773	2716	..	..	..
	2006	6041	1476	1825	2740	..	..	..
Azerbaijan	2003	21286	18817	2469	..	..	136	136
	2004	21743	18988	2755	..	..	399	399
	2005	22872	19863	3009	..	..	519	519
	2006	24542	22024	2518	..	..	617	617
Bahrain	2003	7768	7768	..	..	..	1145	1145
	2004	8448	8448	..	..	..	1521	1521
	2005	8698	8698	..	..	..	1566	1566
	2006	9822	9822	..	..	..	1768	1768

Table 34

Production d'électricité - par catégorie
Millions de kilowatt-heures

Hydro Hydraulique	producers producteurs Nuclear Nucléaire	Geothermal Géother-mique	Total Totale	Thermal Thermique	Public utilities Services publics Hydro Hydraulique	Nuclear Nucléaire	Geothermal Géother-mique	Year Année	Country or area Pays ou zone
151	..	..	11135	4105	7030	..	..	2003	Equateur
163	..	..	11405	4156	7249	..	..	2004	
210	..	..	12059	3665	8394	..	..	2005	
380	..	..	12974	4441	8533	..	..	2006	
..	..	..	*14	*14	..	..	..	2003	Iles Falkland (Malvinas)
..	..	..	*14	*14	..	..	..	2004	
..	..	..	*14	*14	..	..	..	2005	
..	..	..	*14	*14	..	..	..	2006	
..	..	..	440	440	..	..	..	2003	Guyane française
..	..	..	430	430	..	..	..	2004	
..	..	..	430	430	..	..	..	2005	
..	..	..	430	430	..	..	..	2006	
..	..	..	488	488	..	..	..	2003	Guyana
..	..	..	497	497	..	..	..	2004	
..	..	..	513	513	..	..	..	2005	
..	..	..	517	517	..	..	..	2006	
..	..	..	51762	1	51761	..	..	2003	Paraguay
..	..	..	51921	0	51921	..	..	2004	
..	..	..	51156	1	51156	..	..	2005	
..	..	..	53774	1	53774	..	..	2006	
415	..	..	21359	3239	18119	..	1	2003	Pérou
546	..	..	22609	5629	16979	..	1	2004	
512	..	..	23801	4350	19450	..	1	2005	
542	..	..	25603	4661	20941	..	1	2006	
760	..	..	136	136	..	..	..	2003	Suriname
772	..	..	137	137	..	..	..	2004	
829	..	..	142	142	..	..	..	2005	
871	..	..	147	147	..	..	..	2006	
..	..	..	8536	7	8529	..	..	2003	Uruguay
..	..	..	5857	1077	4780	..	..	2004	
..	..	..	7641	957	6684	..	..	2005	
..	..	..	5565	1970	3595	..	..	2006	
..	..	..	87797	27099	60698	..	..	2003	Venezuela(Rép. bolivar.)
..	..	..	96783	26856	69927	..	..	2004	
..	..	..	99792	24767	75025	..	..	2005	
..	..	..	108726	29246	79480	..	..	2006	
9381	..	1283	5301453	4132327	676079	473453	19594	2003	Asie
10324	..	1775	5756184	4450397	760172	525325	20290	2004	
8465	..	2177	6250825	4845212	818573	567128	19912	2005	
8471	..	2180	6782876	5291875	899674	570523	20804	2006	
*15	..	..	826	194	632	..	..	2003	Afghanistan
*15	..	..	779	215	564	..	..	2004	
*15	..	..	*810	*230	*580	..	..	2005	
*15	..	..	*810	*230	*580	..	..	2006	
..	..	..	5501	1521	1982	1998	..	2003	Arménie
..	..	..	6030	1613	2014	2403	..	2004	
..	..	..	6317	1828	1773	2716	..	2005	
..	..	..	6041	1476	1825	2740	..	2006	
..	..	..	21150	18681	2469	..	..	2003	Azerbaïdjan
..	..	..	21344	18589	2755	..	..	2004	
..	..	..	22353	19344	3009	..	..	2005	
..	..	..	23925	21407	2518	..	..	2006	
..	..	..	6623	6623	..	..	..	2003	Bahreïn
..	..	..	6927	6927	..	..	..	2004	
..	..	..	7132	7132	..	..	..	2005	
..	..	..	8054	8054	..	..	..	2006	

Table 34

Production of electricity - by type
Million kilowatt-hours

Country or area Pays ou zone	Year Année	Self-producers and public utilities Autoproducteurs et services publics					Self- Auto-	
		Total Totale	Thermal Thermique	Hydro Hydraulique	Nuclear Nucléaire	Geothermal Géother- -mique	Total Totale	Thermal Thermique
Bangladesh	2003	19170	18044	1126	..	..	6298	629
	2004	20820	19594	1226	..	..	7478	747
	2005	22006	20713	1293	..	..	7939	793
	2006	23703	22314	1389	..	..	8286	828
Bhutan	2003	2200	1	2199	..	..	..	
	2004	2529	2	2527	..	..	..	
	2005	2355	2	2353	..	..	..	
	2006	2648	2	2646	..	..	..	
Brunei Darussalam	2003	3169	3169	..	..	..	355	35
	2004	3236	3236	..	..	..	330	33
	2005	3264	3264	..	..	..	351	35
	2006	3298	3298	..	..	..	350	35
Cambodia	2003	637	596	41	..	0	416	41
	2004	743	715	27	..	0	424	42
	2005	880	836	44	..	0	582	58
	2006	1235	1182	51	..	2	882	88
China	2003	1907380	1580360	283680	43340	..	..	
	2004	2193736	1792640	350627	50469	..	..	
	2005	2497441	2047336	397017	53088	..	..	
	2006	2865726	2369603	441280	54843	..	..	
China, Hong Kong SAR	2003	35506	35506	..	..	..	..	
	2004	37129	37129	..	..	..	..	
	2005	38448	38448	..	..	..	..	
	2006	38613	38613	..	..	..	..	
China, Macao SAR	2003	1779	1779	..	..	..	95	9
	2004	1956	1956	..	..	..	92	9
	2005	2027	2027	..	..	..	127	12
	2006	1668	1668	..	..	..	125	12
Cyprus	2003	4053	4052	..	..	1	8	
	2004	4200	4200	..	..	0	24	2
	2005	4377	4376	..	..	1	28	2
	2006	4652	4651	..	..	1	33	3
Georgia	2003	7160	634	6526	..	..	..	
	2004	6924	875	6049	..	..	..	
	2005	7267	1031	6236	..	..	..	
	2006	7599	2209	5390	..	..	..	
India	2003	633275	540253	75242	17780	..	68173	6817
	2004	665873	564252	84610	17011	..	71417	7141
	2005	697234	578406	101494	17334	..	73404	7340
	2006	744119	612153	113359	18607	..	76606	7660
Indonesia	2003	112944	97548	9081	..	6315	400	28
	2004	120160	103836	9673	..	6651	747	71
	2005	127369	110006	10759	..	6604	374	33
	2006	133108	116827	9623	..	6658	414	37
Iran(Islamic Rep. of)	2003	152599	141501	11098	..	..	5579	5579
	2004	166016	155389	10627	..	..	7024	702
	2005	180390	164290	16100	..	..	7120	712
	2006	201029	182763	18266	..	..	8347	8347
Iraq	2003	28340	27907	433	..	..	..	
	2004	32295	31802	493	..	..	..	
	2005	34000	33481	519	..	..	..	
	2006	31869	31383	486	..	..	..	
Israel	2003	47041	46998	31	..	12	1246	1203
	2004	48481	48442	28	..	11	1250	1211
	2005	49843	49804	28	..	11	1311	1272
	2006	51811	51794	15	..	2	1398	138

Table 34

Production d'électricité - par catégorie
Millions de kilowatt-heures

| producers producteurs | | | Public utilities Services publics | | | | | Year Année | Country or area Pays ou zone |
Hydro Hydraulique	Nuclear Nucléaire	Geothermal Géother- mique	Total Totale	Thermal Thermique	Hydro Hydraulique	Nuclear Nucléaire	Geothermal Géother- mique		
..	..	..	12872	11746	1126	..	..	2003	Bangladesh
..	..	..	13342	12116	1226	..	..	2004	
..	..	..	14067	12774	1293	..	..	2005	
..	..	..	15417	14028	1389	..	..	2006	
..	..	..	2200	1	2199	..	..	2003	Bhoutan
..	..	..	2529	2	2527	..	..	2004	
..	..	..	2355	2	2353	..	..	2005	
..	..	..	2648	2	2646	..	..	2006	
..	..	..	2814	2814		..	..	2003	Brunéi Darussalam
..	..	..	2906	2906	..	..	..	2004	
..	..	..	2913	2913	..	..	..	2005	
..	..	..	2948	2948	..	..	..	2006	
..	..	..	221	181	41	..	0	2003	Cambodge
..	..	..	319	291	27	..	0	2004	
..	..	..	298	254	44	..	0	2005	
..	..	..	*353	*300	51	..	2	2006	
..	..	..	1907380	1580360	283680	43340	..	2003	Chine
..	..	..	2193736	1792640	350627	50469	..	2004	
..	..	..	2497441	2047336	397017	53088	..	2005	
..	..	..	2865726	2369603	441280	54843	..	2006	
..	..	..	35506	35506	..	..	..	2003	Chine, Hong-Kong RAS
..	..	..	37129	37129	..	..	..	2004	
..	..	..	38448	38448	..	..	..	2005	
..	..	..	38613	38613	..	..	..	2006	
..	..	..	1684	1684		..	..	2003	Chine, Macao RAS
..	..	..	1864	1864		..	..	2004	
..	..	..	1900	1900	..	..	..	2005	
..	..	..	1543	1543	..	..	..	2006	
..	..	..	4045	4044	..	..	1	2003	Chypre
..	..	..	4176	4176	..	..	0	2004	
..	..	..	4349	4348	..	..	1	2005	
..	..	..	4619	4618	..	..	1	2006	
..	..	..	7160	634	6526	..	..	2003	Géorgie
..	..	..	6924	875	6049	..	..	2004	
..	..	..	7267	1031	6236	..	..	2005	
..	..	..	7599	2209	5390	..	..	2006	
..	..	..	565102	472080	75242	17780	..	2003	Inde
..	..	..	594456	492835	84610	17011	..	2004	
..	..	..	623830	505002	101494	17334	..	2005	
..	..	..	667513	535547	113359	18607	..	2006	
111	..	..	112544	97259	8970	..	6315	2003	Indonésie
37	..	..	119413	103126	9636	..	6651	2004	
41	..	..	126995	109673	10718	..	6604	2005	
41	..	..	132694	116454	9582	..	6658	2006	
..	..	..	147020	135922	11098	..	..	2003	Iran(Rép. islamique)
..	..	..	158992	148365	10627	..	..	2004	
..	..	..	173270	157170	16100	..	..	2005	
..	..	..	192682	174416	18266	..	..	2006	
..	..	..	28340	27907	433	..	..	2003	Iraq
..	..	..	32295	31802	493	..	..	2004	
..	..	..	34000	33481	519	..	..	2005	
..	..	..	31869	31383	486	..	..	2006	
31	..	12	45795	45795	..	..	..	2003	Israël
28	..	11	47231	47231	..	..	..	2004	
28	..	11	48532	48532	..	..	..	2005	
15	..	2	50413	50413	..	..		2006	

Table 34

Production of electricity - by type

Million kilowatt-hours

| Country or area
Pays ou zone | Year
Année | Self-producers and public utilities
Autoproducteurs et services publics | | | | | Self-
Auto- | |
		Total Totale	Thermal Thermique	Hydro Hydraulique	Nuclear Nucléaire	Geothermal Géother- -mique	Total Totale	Thermal Thermique
Japan	2003	1047041	698572	104137	240013	4319	127716	11857
	2004	1076244	685969	103147	282442	4686	130382	12119
	2005	1098315	702229	86350	304755	4981	129161	12064
	2006	1100364	696531	95576	303426	4831	127480	11896
Jordan	2003	8044	7988	*53	..	3	413	413
	2004	8970	8914	53	..	3	496	496
	2005	9651	9591	57	..	3	516	516
	2006	11120	11066	51	..	3	474	474
Kazakhstan	2003	63866	55241	8625	..	..	..	
	2004	66942	58885	8057	..	..	..	
	2005	67916	60060	7856	..	..	..	
	2006	71653	63885	7768	..	..	..	
Korea, Dem.Ppl's.Rep.	2003	20999	9279	11720	..	..	..	
	2004	21974	9474	12500	..	..	..	
	2005	22913	9781	13132	..	..	..	
	2006	22436	9816	12620	..	..	..	
Korea, Republic of	2003	345192	208584	6903	129672	33	26719	26709
	2004	368162	231510	5880	130715	57	28989	28970
	2005	389390	237277	5189	146779	145	26596	26577
	2006	404021	249783	5219	148749	270	24615	24583
Kuwait	2003	39802	39802	..	..	..	..	
	2004	41256	41256	..	..	..	..	
	2005	43734	43734	..	..	..	..	
	2006	47607	47607	..	..	..	..	
Kyrgyzstan	2003	15576	2060	13516	..	..	4	
	2004	16312	2218	14094	..	..	0	
	2005	16415	2156	14259	..	..	0	
	2006	17082	2195	14887	..	..	0	
Lao People's Dem. Rep.	2003	3372	318	2861	..	*193	*193	
	2004	*3541	*320	*3028	..	*193	*193	
	2005	*3685	*325	*3167	..	*193	*193	
	2006	*3799	*332	*3274	..	*193	*193	
Lebanon	2003	11787	11098	689	..	..	2482	1922
	2004	11054	9931	1123	..	..	1978	961
	2005	11125	10078	1048	..	..	1942	999
	2006	10654	9959	695	..	..	*1960	*1367
Malaysia	2003	78427	72677	5750	..	..	2080	2080
	2004	82282	76456	5827	..	..	4175	4175
	2005	87300	82116	5184	..	..	4684	4684
	2006	91563	84492	7071	..	..	5861	5861
Maldives	2003	141	141	..	..	..	..	
	2004	160	160	..	..	..	..	
	2005	*185	*185	..	..	..	..	
	2006	212	212	..	..	..	..	
Mongolia	2003	3138	3138	..	..	..	49	49
	2004	3303	3303	..	..	..	48	48
	2005	3419	3419	..	..	..	38	38
	2006	3544	3544	..	..	..	23	23
Myanmar	2003	5426	3176	2250	..	..	..	
	2004	5608	3200	2408	..	..	..	
	2005	6015	3018	2997	..	..	..	
	2006	6164	2840	3324	..	..	..	
Nepal	2003	2267	4	2263	..	..	13	
	2004	2416	14	2402	..	..	14	
	2005	2622	10	2612	..	..	15	
	2006	2684	10	2674	..	..	15	

Table 34

Production d'électricité - par catégorie
Millions de kilowatt-heures

producers producteurs			Public utilities Services publics					Year Année	Country or area Pays ou zone
Hydro ydraulique	Nuclear Nucléaire	Geothermal Géother-mique	Total Totale	Thermal Thermique	Hydro Hydraulique	Nuclear Nucléaire	Geothermal Géother-mique		
8083	..	1063	919325	580002	96054	240013	3256	2003	Japon
7639	..	1547	945862	564773	95508	282442	3139	2004	
6571	..	1948	969154	581587	79779	304755	3033	2005	
6571	..	1948	972884	577570	89005	303426	2883	2006	
..	..	..	7631	7575	*53	..	3	2003	Jordanie
..	..	..	8474	8418	53	..	3	2004	
..	..	..	9135	9075	57	..	3	2005	
..	..	..	10646	10592	51	..	3	2006	
..	..	..	63866	55241	8625	..	..	2003	Kazakhstan
..	..	..	66942	58885	8057	..	..	2004	
..	..	..	67916	60060	7856	..	..	2005	
..	..	..	71653	63885	7768	..	..	2006	
..	..	..	20999	9279	11720	..	..	2003	Corée,Rép.pop.dém.de
..	..	..	21974	9474	12500	..	..	2004	
..	..	..	22913	9781	13132	..	..	2005	
..	..	..	22436	9816	12620	..	..	2006	
..	..	10	318473	181875	6903	129672	23	2003	Corée, République de
..	..	19	339173	202540	5880	130715	38	2004	
..	..	19	362794	210700	5189	146779	126	2005	
..	..	32	379406	225200	5219	148749	238	2006	
..	..	..	39802	39802	..	..	..	2003	Koweït
..	..	..	41256	41256	..	..	..	2004	
..	..	..	43734	43734	..	..	..	2005	
..	..	..	47607	47607	..	..	..	2006	
4	..	..	15572	2060	13512	..	..	2003	Kirghizistan
0	..	..	16312	2218	14094	..	..	2004	
0	..	..	16415	2156	14259	..	..	2005	
0	..	..	17082	2195	14887	..	..	2006	
..	..	*193	3179	318	2861	..	..	2003	Rép. dém. pop. lao
..	..	*193	*3348	*320	*3028	..	..	2004	
..	..	*193	*3492	*325	*3167	..	..	2005	
..	..	*193	*3606	*332	*3274	..	..	2006	
560	..	..	9305	9176	129	..	..	2003	Liban
1017	..	..	9076	8970	106	..	..	2004	
943	..	..	9183	9079	105	..	..	2005	
593	..	..	8694	8592	102	..	..	2006	
..	..	..	76347	70597	5750	..	..	2003	Malaisie
..	..	..	78107	72280	5827	..	..	2004	
..	..	..	82616	77432	5184	..	..	2005	
..	..	..	85702	78631	7071	..	..	2006	
..	..	..	141	141	..	..	..	2003	Maldives
..	..	..	160	160	..	..	..	2004	
..	..	..	*185	*185	..	..	..	2005	
..	..	..	212	212	..	..	..	2006	
..	..	..	3089	3089	..	..	..	2003	Mongolie
..	..	..	3255	3255	..	..	..	2004	
..	..	..	3381	3381	..	..	..	2005	
..	..	..	3521	3521	..	..	..	2006	
..	..	..	5426	3176	2250	..	..	2003	Myanmar
..	..	..	5608	3200	2408	..	..	2004	
..	..	..	6015	3018	2997	..	..	2005	
..	..	..	6164	2840	3324	..	..	2006	
13	..	..	2254	4	2250	..	..	2003	Népal
14	..	..	2402	14	2388	..	..	2004	
15	..	..	2607	10	2597	..	..	2005	
15	..	..	2669	10	2659	..	..	2006	

Table 34

Production of electricity - by type
Million kilowatt-hours

| Country or area Pays ou zone | Year Année | Self-producers and public utilities Autoproducteurs et services publics | | | | | Self- Auto- | |
		Total Totale	Thermal Thermique	Hydro Hydraulique	Nuclear Nucléaire	Geothermal Géother--mique	Total Totale	Thermal Thermique
Occup. Palestinian Terr.	2003	342	342	..	..	..	..	
	2004	396	396	..	..	..	..	
	2005	501	501	..	..	..	..	
	2006	*520	*520	..	..	..	..	
Oman	2003	10714	10714		..	..	..	
	2004	11499	11499		..	..	..	
	2005	12648	12648		..	..	..	
	2006	13585	13585		..	..	..	
Other Asia	2003	209076	163267	6895	38890	24	37989	3798
	2004	218410	172326	6568	39490	26	42607	4260
	2005	227449	179475	7910	39972	92	42459	4245
	2006	235371	187224	7999	39870	278	42225	4222
Pakistan	2003	80830	52126	26944	1760	..	4	
	2004	85698	57232	25671	2795	..	70	7
	2005	93832	60486	30862	2484	..	203	20
	2006	98350	64109	31953	2288	..	137	13
Philippines	2003	52897	35189	7886	..	9822	*34	*1
	2004	55957	37065	8610	..	10282	*34	*1
	2005	56549	38260	8387	..	9902	*34	*1
	2006	56818	36342	9956	..	10520	*34	*1
Qatar	2003	12012	12012	..	..	..	8413	841
	2004	13233	13233	..	..	..	10218	1021
	2005	14396	14396	..	..	..	11073	1107
	2006	15325	15325	..	..	..	11799	1179
Saudi Arabia	2003	153000	153000	..	..	..	24629	2462
	2004	159875	159875	..	..	..	24063	2406
	2005	176124	176124	..	..	..	25910	2591
	2006	179782	179782	..	..	..	25315	2531
Singapore	2003	35331	35331	..	..	..	..	
	2004	36810	36810	..	..	..	..	
	2005	38213	38213	..	..	..	..	
	2006	39442	39442	..	..	..	..	
Sri Lanka	2003	7711	4398	3310	..	3	*100	*10
	2004	8158	5195	2960	..	3	115	11
	2005	8769	5314	3453	..	2	*120	*12
	2006	9389	4751	4636	..	2	*120	*12
Syrian Arab Republic	2003	29534	26730	2804	..	..	1162	116
	2004	32077	27830	4247	..	..	1227	122
	2005	34935	31490	3445	..	..	1172	117
	2006	37283	33289	3994	..	..	1172	117
Tajikistan	2003	16509	173	16336	..	..	..	
	2004	16491	152	16339	..	..	..	
	2005	17090	123	16967	..	..	..	
	2006	16935	234	16701	..	..	..	
Thailand	2003	116983	109682	7299	..	2	13422	1342
	2004	125727	119685	6040	..	2	13514	1351
	2005	132197	126397	5798	..	2	13702	1370
	2006	138742	130614	8125	..	3	13731	1373
Timor-Leste	2003	*300	*300	..	..	..	..	
	2004	*307	*307	..	..	..	..	
	2005	*314	*314	..	..	..	..	
	2006	*320	*320	..	..	..	..	
Turkey	2003	140581	105101	35330	..	150	23127	2257
	2004	150698	104463	46084	..	151	23757	2219
	2005	161956	122242	39561	..	153	17088	1624
	2006	176299	131834	44244	..	221	14435	1322

2006 Energy Statistics Yearbook United Nations / 2006 Annuaire des statistiques de l' énergie des Nations Unies

Table 34

Production d'électricité - par catégorie
Millions de kilowatt-heures

Hydro ydraulique	Nuclear Nucléaire	Geothermal Géother-mique	Total Totale	Thermal Thermique	Hydro Hydraulique	Nuclear Nucléaire	Geothermal Géother-mique	Year Année	Country or area Pays ou zone
	producers producteurs				Public utilities Services publics				
..	..	..	342	342	..	..	..	2003	Terr. palestiniens occup.
..	..	..	396	396	..	..	..	2004	
..	..	..	501	501	..	..	..	2005	
..	..	..	*520	*520	..	..	..	2006	
..	..	..	10714	10714	..	..	..	2003	Oman
..	..	..	11499	11499	..	..	..	2004	
..	..	..	12648	12648	..	..	..	2005	
..	..	..	13585	13585	..	..	..	2006	
..	..	..	171087	125278	6895	38890	24	2003	Autre Asie
..	..	..	175803	129719	6568	39490	26	2004	
..	..	..	184990	137016	7910	39972	92	2005	
..	..	..	193146	144999	7999	39870	278	2006	
..	..	..	80826	52122	26944	1760	..	2003	Pakistan
..	..	..	85628	57162	25671	2795	..	2004	
..	..	..	93629	60283	30862	2484	..	2005	
..	..	..	98213	63972	31953	2288	..	2006	
*17	..	..	52863	35172	7869	..	9822	2003	Philippines
*17	..	..	55923	37048	8593	..	10282	2004	
*17	..	..	56515	38243	8370	..	9902	2005	
*17	..	..	56784	36325	9939	..	10520	2006	
..	..	..	3599	3599	..	..	..	2003	Qatar
..	..	..	3015	3015	..	..	..	2004	
..	..	..	3323	3323	..	..	..	2005	
..	..	..	3526	3526	..	..	..	2006	
..	..	..	128371	128371	..	..	..	2003	Arabie saoudite
..	..	..	135812	135812	..	..	..	2004	
..	..	..	150214	150214	..	..	..	2005	
..	..	..	154467	154467	..	..	..	2006	
..	..	..	35331	35331	..	..	..	2003	Singapour
..	..	..	36810	36810	..	..	..	2004	
..	..	..	38213	38213	..	..	..	2005	
..	..	..	39442	39442	..	..	..	2006	
..	..	..	7611	4298	3310	..	3	2003	Sri Lanka
..	..	..	8043	5080	2960	..	3	2004	
..	..	..	8649	5194	3453	..	2	2005	
..	..	..	9269	4631	4636	..	2	2006	
..	..	..	28372	25568	2804	..	..	2003	Rép. arabe syrienne
..	..	..	30850	26603	4247	..	..	2004	
..	..	..	33763	30318	3445	..	..	2005	
..	..	..	36111	32117	3994	..	..	2006	
..	..	..	16509	173	16336	..	..	2003	Tadjikistan
..	..	..	16491	152	16339	..	..	2004	
..	..	..	17090	123	16967	..	..	2005	
..	..	..	16935	234	16701	..	..	2006	
..	..	..	103561	96260	7299	..	2	2003	Thaïlande
..	..	..	112213	106171	6040	..	2	2004	
..	..	..	118495	112695	5798	..	2	2005	
..	..	..	125011	116883	8125	..	3	2006	
..	..	..	*300	*300	..	..	..	2003	Timor-Leste
..	..	..	*307	*307	..	..	..	2004	
..	..	..	*314	*314	..	..	..	2005	
..	..	..	*320	*320	..	..	..	2006	
547	..	5	117454	82526	34783	..	145	2003	Turquie
1557	..	5	126941	82268	44527	..	146	2004	
835	..	6	144868	105995	38726	..	147	2005	
1204	..	5	161864	118608	43040	..	216	2006	

Table 34

Production of electricity - by type
Million kilowatt-hours

Country or area Pays ou zone	Year Année	Self-producers and public utilities Autoproducteurs et services publics					Self- Auto-	
		Total Totale	Thermal Thermique	Hydro Hydraulique	Nuclear Nucléaire	Geothermal Géother- -mique	Total Totale	Thermal Thermique
Turkmenistan	2003	10800	10797	3	..	..	..	
	2004	11920	11917	3	..	..	..	
	2005	12820	12817	3	..	..	..	
	2006	13650	13647	3	..	..	..	
United Arab Emirates	2003	49450	49450		..	..	..	
	2004	52417	52417		..	..	..	
	2005	60698	60698		..	..	..	
	2006	66768	66768		..	..	..	
Uzbekistan	2003	49400	43055	6345	..	..	197	19
	2004	51030	44476	6554	..	..	204	20
	2005	47706	41578	6128	..	..	194	19
	2006	49299	42966	6333	..	..	201	20
Viet Nam	2003	40925	21939	18986	..	..	1564	156
	2004	46029	28363	17666	..	..	786	78
	2005	53463	32009	21454	..	..	2755	275
	2006	56494	32895	23599	..	..	2715	271
Yemen	2003	4094	4094	..	..	..	588	58
	2004	4337	4337	..	..	..	630	63
	2005	4741	4741	..	..	..	683	68
	2006	5337	5337	..	..	..	698	69
Europe	**2003**	**4597760**	**2608610**	**681260**	**1255095**	**52795**	**290891**	**27504**
	2004	**4693652**	**2629078**	**729558**	**1267124**	**67892**	**311727**	**29514**
	2005	**4762228**	**2686291**	**736209**	**1259242**	**80486**	**315127**	**29723**
	2006	**4847282**	**2766891**	**721560**	**1264357**	**94474**	**325175**	**30656**
Albania	2003	5230	61	5169	..	..	61	6
	2004	5559	93	5466	..	..	93	9
	2005	5443	70	5373	..	..	70	7
	2006	5094	93	5001	..	..	93	9
Austria	2003	60100	24428	35292	..	380	7196	613
	2004	64125	24222	38966	..	937	7667	640
	2005	65681	25725	38612	..	1344	8242	700
	2006	63445	24042	37664	..	1739	8528	732
Belarus	2003	26627	26599	28	..	0	690	68
	2004	31210	31176	33	..	1	841	82
	2005	30961	30924	36	..	1	848	83
	2006	31811	31775	35	..	1	881	86
Belgium	2003	84630	35847	1316	47379	88	1228	122
	2004	85643	36581	1607	47312	143	1438	143
	2005	86944	37517	1604	47595	228	1678	167
	2006	85391	36750	1628	46645	368	1613	160
Bosnia and Herzegovina	2003	11266	6765	4501	..	..	137	13
	2004	12734	6755	5979	..	..	138	13
	2005	12637	6639	5998	..	..	176	17
	2006	13346	7489	5857	..	..	196	19
Bulgaria	2003	42600	22019	3301	17280	0	2108	210
	2004	41621	21442	3363	16815	1	1726	172
	2005	44365	20977	4730	18653	5	1653	165
	2006	45843	21751	4579	19493	20	1768	176
Croatia	2003	12620	7684	4936	..	0	545	53
	2004	13295	6242	7051	..	2	526	50
	2005	12462	6014	6438	..	10	525	50
	2006	12430	6287	6124	..	19	490	47
Czech Republic	2003	83227	55557	1794	25872	4	9462	909
	2004	84333	55436	2562	26325	10	9798	933
	2005	82578	54802	3027	24728	21	10120	957
	2006	84361	55008	3257	26046	50	10213	975

Table 34

Production d'électricité - par catégorie
Millions de kilowatt-heures

producers producteurs			Public utilities Services publics					Year Année	Country or area Pays ou zone
Hydro Hydraulique	Nuclear Nucléaire	Geothermal Géother- mique	Total Totale	Thermal Thermique	Hydro Hydraulique	Nuclear Nucléaire	Geothermal Géother- mique		
..	..	..	10800	10797	3	..	..	2003	Turkménistan
..	..	..	11920	11917	3	..	..	2004	
..	..	..	12820	12817	3	..	..	2005	
..	..	..	13650	13647	3	..	..	2006	
..	..	..	49450	49450	..	..	..	2003	Emirats arabes unis
..	..	..	52417	52417	..	..	..	2004	
..	..	..	60698	60698	..	..	..	2005	
..	..	..	66768	66768	..	..	..	2006	
..	..	..	49203	42858	6345	..	..	2003	Ouzbékistan
..	..	..	50826	44272	6554	..	..	2004	
..	..	..	47512	41384	6128	..	..	2005	
..	..	..	49098	42765	6333	..	..	2006	
..	..	..	39361	20375	18986	..	..	2003	Viet Nam
..	..	..	45243	27577	17666	..	..	2004	
..	..	..	50708	29254	21454	..	..	2005	
..	..	..	53779	30180	23599	..	..	2006	
..	..	..	3506	3506	..	..	..	2003	Yémen
..	..	..	3707	3707	..	..	..	2004	
..	..	..	4058	4058	..	..	..	2005	
..	..	..	4639	4639	..	..	..	2006	
14166	..	**1677**	**4306869**	**2333562**	**667094**	**1255095**	**51118**	**2003**	**Europe**
14093	..	**2490**	**4381925**	**2333934**	**715465**	**1267124**	**65402**	**2004**	
14473	..	**3421**	**4447101**	**2389058**	**721736**	**1259242**	**77065**	**2005**	
13553	..	**5057**	**4522107**	**2460326**	**708007**	**1264357**	**89417**	**2006**	
..	..	..	5169	..	5169	..	..	2003	Albanie
..	..	..	5466	..	5466	..	..	2004	
..	..	..	5373	..	5373	..	..	2005	
..	..	..	5001	..	5001	..	..	2006	
1062	..	..	52904	18294	34230	..	380	2003	Autriche
1266	..	..	56458	17821	37700	..	937	2004	
1233	..	..	57439	18716	37379	..	1344	2005	
1206	..	..	54917	16720	36458	..	1739	2006	
9	..	0	25937	25918	19	..	..	2003	Bélarus
11	..	1	30369	30347	22	..	..	2004	
11	..	1	30113	30088	25	..	..	2005	
11	..	1	30930	30906	24	..	..	2006	
..	..	2	83402	34621	1316	47379	86	2003	Belgique
..	..	4	84205	35147	1607	47312	139	2004	
..	..	3	85266	35842	1604	47595	225	2005	
..	..	5	83778	35142	1628	46645	363	2006	
..	..	..	11129	6628	4501	..	..	2003	Bosnie y Herzégovine
..	..	..	12596	6617	5979	..	..	2004	
..	..	..	12461	6463	5998	..	..	2005	
..	..	..	13150	7293	5857	..	..	2006	
..	..	..	40492	19911	3301	17280	0	2003	Bulgarie
..	..	..	39895	19716	3363	16815	1	2004	
..	..	..	42712	19324	4730	18653	5	2005	
..	..	..	44075	19983	4579	19493	20	2006	
13	..	..	12075	7152	4923	..	0	2003	Croatie
18	..	..	12769	5734	7033	..	2	2004	
16	..	..	11937	5505	6422	..	10	2005	
14	..	..	11940	5811	6110	..	19	2006	
371	..	..	73765	46466	1423	25872	4	2003	République tchèque
463	..	..	74535	46101	2099	26325	10	2004	
550	..	..	72458	45232	2477	24728	21	2005	
460	..	..	74148	45255	2797	26046	50	2006	

Table 34

Production of electricity - by type
Million kilowatt-hours

Country or area Pays ou zone	Year Année	Self-producers and public utilities Autoproducteurs et services publics					Self- Auto-	
		Total Totale	Thermal Thermique	Hydro Hydraulique	Nuclear Nucléaire	Geothermal Géother- -mique	Total Totale	Thermal Thermique
Denmark	2003	46181	40597	21	..	5563	2762	276
	2004	40433	33821	27	..	6585	2737	273
	2005	36355	29716	23	..	6616	2872	287
	2006	45716	39583	23	..	6110	2602	260
Estonia	2003	10159	10140	13	..	6	166	16
	2004	10128	10098	22	..	8	143	14
	2005	10002	9926	22	..	54	125	12
	2006	9508	9419	13	..	76	116	11
Faeroe Islands	2003	270	180	90	..	..	..	
	2004	290	200	90	..	..	..	
	2005	*290	*200	*90	..	..	..	
	2006	*295	*205	*90	..	..	..	
Finland	2003	84230	51813	9591	22731	95	11301	1130
	2004	85847	47939	15070	22716	122	10578	1057
	2005	70550	33322	13784	23271	173	9585	958
	2006	82304	47745	11494	22906	159	10603	1060
France incl. Monaco	2003	566948	60605	64333	441070	940	18894	1798
	2004	574278	59841	65070	448241	1126	19732	1871
	2005	576170	66672	56457	451529	1512	22054	2114
	2006	574473	60479	61112	450191	2691	21362	2026
Germany	2003	606719	398027	24440	165060	19192	39741	3925
	2004	615287	394282	27874	167065	26066	50193	4971
	2005	620574	402291	26717	163055	28511	44492	4413
	2006	636761	409258	27304	167269	32930	51097	5073
Gibraltar	2003	134	134	..	..	..	..	
	2004	136	136	..	..	..	..	
	2005	145	145	..	..	..	..	
	2006	151	151	..	..	..	..	
Greece	2003	58471	52118	5332	..	1021	1028	102
	2004	59346	53019	5205	..	1122	985	98
	2005	60020	53143	5610	..	1267	1086	108
	2006	60789	52614	6475	..	1700	1030	103
Hungary	2003	34145	22957	171	11013	4	376	37
	2004	33708	21582	205	11915	6	404	40
	2005	35756	21710	202	13834	10	411	41
	2006	35859	22169	186	13461	43	356	35
Iceland	2003	8500	6	7088	..	1406	5	
	2004	8623	6	7134	..	1483	5	
	2005	8683	6	7019	..	1658	5	
	2006	9930	6	7293	..	2631	5	
Ireland	2003	25317	23907	956	..	454	634	63
	2004	25569	23930	984	..	655	668	66
	2005	25970	23883	975	..	1112	630	63
	2006	28046	25336	1088	..	1622	1589	158
Italy and San Marino	2003	293884	242784	44277	..	6823	19523	1843
	2004	303347	246126	49908	..	7313	19040	1804
	2005	303699	253073	42927	..	7699	19790	1898
	2006	314121	262163	43425	..	8533	18357	1749
Latvia	2003	3975	1661	2266	..		48	80	7
	2004	4689	1531	3109	..	49	91	8
	2005	4905	1533	3325	..	47	89	7
	2006	4891	2147	2698	..	46	81	7
Lithuania	2003	19488	3019	985	15484	0	199	19
	2004	19274	3228	943	15102	1	335	33
	2005	14784	3625	820	10337	2	373	37
	2006	12482	3015	802	8651	14	365	36

Table 34

Production d'électricité - par catégorie
Millions de kilowatt-heures

producers producteurs			Public utilities Services publics					Year Année	Country or area Pays ou zone
Hydro ydraulique	Nuclear Nucléaire	Geothermal Géother- mique	Total Totale	Thermal Thermique	Hydro Hydraulique	Nuclear Nucléaire	Geothermal Géother- mique		
..	..	2	43419	37837	21	..	5561	2003	Danemark
..	..	2	37696	31086	27	..	6583	2004	
..	..	2	33483	26846	23	..	6614	2005	
..	..	2	43114	36983	23	..	6108	2006	
..	..	1	9993	9975	13	..	5	2003	Estonie
..	..	1	9985	9956	22	..	7	2004	
..	..	1	9877	9802	22	..	53	2005	
..	..	1	9392	9304	13	..	75	2006	
..	..	..	270	180	90	..	..	2003	Iles Féroé
..	..	..	290	200	90	..	..	2004	
..	..	..	*290	*200	*90	..	..	2005	
..	..	..	*295	*205	*90	..	..	2006	
..	..	..	72929	40512	9591	22731	95	2003	Finlande
..	..	..	75269	37361	15070	22716	122	2004	
..	..	..	60965	23737	13784	23271	173	2005	
..	..	..	71701	37142	11494	22906	159	2006	
846	..	61	548054	42618	63487	441070	879	2003	France y compris Monaco
918	..	96	554546	41123	64152	448241	1030	2004	
807	..	104	554116	45529	55650	451529	1408	2005	
873	..	223	553111	40213	60239	450191	2468	2006	
482	..	..	566978	358768	23958	165060	19192	2003	Allemagne
483	..	..	565094	344572	27391	167065	26066	2004	
361	..	..	576082	358160	26356	163055	28511	2005	
360	..	..	585664	358521	26944	167269	32930	2006	
..	..	..	134	134	..	..	..	2003	Gibraltar
..	..	..	136	136	..	..	..	2004	
..	..	..	145	145	..	..	..	2005	
..	..	..	151	151	..	..	..	2006	
..	..	..	57443	51090	5332	..	1021	2003	Grèce
..	..	..	58361	52034	5205	..	1122	2004	
..	..	..	58934	52057	5610	..	1267	2005	
..	..	..	59759	51584	6475	..	1700	2006	
..	..	..	33769	22581	171	11013	4	2003	Hongrie
..	..	..	33304	21178	205	11915	6	2004	
..	..	..	35345	21299	202	13834	10	2005	
..	..	..	35503	21813	186	13461	43	2006	
4	..	..	8495	5	7084	..	1406	2003	Islande
4	..	..	8618	5	7130	..	1483	2004	
4	..	..	8678	5	7015	..	1658	2005	
4	..	..	9925	5	7289	..	2631	2006	
..	..	..	24683	23273	956	..	454	2003	Irlande
..	..	..	24901	23262	984	..	655	2004	
..	..	..	25340	23253	975	..	1112	2005	
..	..	..	26457	23747	1088	..	1622	2006	
1091	..	0	274361	224352	43186	..	6823	2003	Italie y comp. St. Marin
992	..	3	284307	228081	48916	..	7310	2004	
799	..	3	283909	234085	42128	..	7696	2005	
859	..	3	295764	244668	42566	..	8530	2006	
8	..	1	3895	1590	2258	..	47	2003	Lettonie
11	..	0	4598	1451	3098	..	49	2004	
10	..	0	4816	1454	3315	..	47	2005	
6	..	0	4810	2072	2692	..	46	2006	
..	..	..	19289	2820	985	15484	0	2003	Lituanie
..	..	..	18939	2893	943	15102	1	2004	
..	..	..	14411	3252	820	10337	2	2005	
..	..	..	12117	2650	802	8651	14	2006	

Table 34

Production of electricity - by type
Million kilowatt-hours

Country or area Pays ou zone	Year Année	Self-producers and public utilities Autoproducteurs et services publics					Self- Auto-	
		Total Totale	Thermal Thermique	Hydro Hydraulique	Nuclear Nucléaire	Geothermal Géother- -mique	Total Totale	Thermal Thermique
Luxembourg	2003	3620	2676	917	..	27	375	3.
	2004	4121	3214	859	..	48	456	4.
	2005	4135	3182	883	..	70	468	4.
	2006	4333	3337	917	..	79	497	4.
Malta	2003	2236	2236	..	..	..	..	
	2004	2216	2216	..	..	..	..	
	2005	2240	2240	..	..	..	..	
	2006	2296	2296	..	..	..	..	
Netherlands	2003	96763	91324	72	4018	1349	13505	132.
	2004	100770	94953	95	3822	1900	13272	129.
	2005	100219	94033	88	3997	2101	15367	150.
	2006	96733	90390	106	3469	2768	15768	152.
Norway,Svlbd.J.Myn. l	2003	107405	971	106216	..	218	5168	6.
	2004	110598	1051	109287	..	260	5442	7.
	2005	138108	1030	136572	..	506	6224	7.
	2006	121663	1191	119799	..	673	5362	8.
Poland	2003	151631	148214	3293	..	124	7998	79.
	2004	154159	150326	3691	..	142	8177	81.
	2005	156936	153023	3778	..	135	8126	81.
	2006	161742	158466	3020	..	256	8223	82.
Portugal	2003	46852	30209	16054	..	589	5049	50.
	2004	45105	34055	10147	..	903	5101	50.
	2005	46575	39610	5118	..	1847	5531	55.
	2006	49041	34559	11467	..	3015	5748	57.
Republic of Moldova	2003	3453	3389	64	..	..	*40	*.
	2004	3613	3554	59	..	..	38	3.
	2005	3864	3801	63	..	..	41	4.
	2006	3829	3752	77	..	..	62	6.
Romania	2003	55140	36975	13259	4906	..	1818	176.
	2004	56499	34438	16513	5548	..	2347	228.
	2005	59413	33651	20207	5555	..	2392	231.
	2006	62697	38709	18356	5632	..	2731	263.
Russian Federation	2003	916286	607891	157720	150342	333	46984	4604.
	2004	931865	608965	177783	144707	410	47868	4672.
	2005	953074	628607	174604	149446	417	47228	4610.
	2006	995785	663599	175282	156436	468	50731	4954.
Serbia	2003	35366	25515	9851	..	..	0	
	2004	37686	26565	11121	..	..	0	
	2005	36474	24442	12032	..	..	188	18.
	2006	36481	25516	10965	..	..	138	13.
Slovakia	2003	31178	9641	3672	17864	1	2493	230.
	2004	30567	9328	4207	17026	6	2296	221.
	2005	31455	8981	4741	17727	6	2434	234.
	2006	31418	8834	4566	18012	6	2798	270.
Slovenia	2003	14019	5656	3156	5207	..	664	33.
	2004	15271	5718	4094	5459	..	609	37.
	2005	15117	5772	3461	5884	..	589	36.
	2006	15115	5976	3591	5548	..	566	31.
Spain	2003	260727	142839	43897	61875	12116	33693	3294.
	2004	280007	166206	34439	63606	15756	38288	3773.
	2005	294077	192296	23025	57539	21217	40202	3982.
	2006	303051	190257	29503	60126	23165	38488	3803.
Sweden	2003	135435	13743	53598	67415	679	4979	478.
	2004	151726	13212	60178	77486	850	4986	497.
	2005	158434	12247	72874	72377	936	4962	495.
	2006	143299	13597	61738	66977	987	5397	53.

Table 34

Production d'électricité - par catégorie
Millions de kilowatt-heures

producers producteurs			Public utilities Services publics					Year Année	Country or area Pays ou zone
Hydro Hydraulique	Nuclear Nucléaire	Geothermal Géother-mique	Total Totale	Thermal Thermique	Hydro Hydraulique	Nuclear Nucléaire	Geothermal Géother-mique		
5	..	1	3245	2307	912	..	26	2003	Luxembourg
5	..	9	3665	2772	854	..	39	2004	
5	..	18	3667	2737	878	..	52	2005	
5	..	21	3836	2866	912	..	58	2006	
..	..	..	2236	2236	..	..	..	2003	Malte
..	..	..	2216	2216	..	..	..	2004	
..	..	..	2240	2240	..	..	..	2005	
..	..	..	2296	2296	..	..	..	2006	
..	..	251	83258	78070	72	4018	1098	2003	Pays-Bas
..	..	345	87498	82026	95	3822	1555	2004	
..	..	315	84852	78981	88	3997	1786	2005	
..	..	493	80965	75115	106	3469	2275	2006	
4499	..	..	102237	302	101717	..	218	2003	Norvège,Svalbd,J.May
4648	..	..	105156	257	104639	..	260	2004	
5463	..	..	131884	269	131109	..	506	2005	
4464	..	..	116301	293	115335	..	673	2006	
2	..	..	143633	140218	3291	..	124	2003	Pologne
2	..	..	145982	142151	3689	..	142	2004	
2	..	..	148810	144899	3776	..	135	2005	
2	..	..	153519	150245	3018	..	256	2006	
17	..	..	41803	25177	16037	..	589	2003	Portugal
15	..	..	40004	28969	10132	..	903	2004	
8	..	..	41044	34087	5110	..	1847	2005	
12	..	..	43293	28823	11455	..	3015	2006	
..	..	..	3413	3349	64	..	..	2003	Rép. de Moldova
..	..	..	3575	3516	59	..	..	2004	
..	..	..	3823	3760	63	..	..	2005	
..	..	..	3767	3690	77	..	..	2006	
50	..	..	53322	35207	13209	4906	..	2003	Roumanie
59	..	..	54152	32150	16454	5548	..	2004	
76	..	..	57021	31335	20131	5555	..	2005	
95	..	..	59966	36073	18261	5632	..	2006	
944	..	..	869302	561851	156776	150342	333	2003	Fédération de Russie
1148	..	..	883997	562245	176635	144707	410	2004	
1120	..	..	905846	582499	173484	149446	417	2005	
1190	..	..	945054	614058	174092	156436	468	2006	
..	..	..	35366	25515	9851	..	..	2003	Serbie
..	..	..	37686	26565	11121	..	..	2004	
..	..	..	36286	24254	12032	..	..	2005	
..	..	..	36343	25378	10965	..	..	2006	
186	..	1	28685	7335	3486	17864	..	2003	Slovaquie
78	..	6	28271	7116	4129	17026	..	2004	
82	..	6	29021	6635	4659	17727	..	2005	
85	..	6	28620	6127	4481	18012	..	2006	
334	..	..	13355	5326	2822	5207	..	2003	Slovénie
239	..	..	14662	5348	3855	5459	..	2004	
225	..	..	14528	5408	3236	5884	..	2005	
249	..	..	14549	5659	3342	5548	..	2006	
700	..	47	227034	109893	43197	61875	12069	2003	Espagne
496	..	61	241719	128475	33943	63606	15695	2004	
350	..	25	253875	152469	22675	57539	21192	2005	
419	..	32	264563	152220	29084	60126	23133	2006	
192	..	..	130456	8956	53406	67415	679	2003	Suède
16	..	..	146740	8242	60162	77486	850	2004	
11	..	..	153472	7296	72863	72377	936	2005	
12	..	..	137902	8212	61726	66977	987	2006	

Table 34

Production of electricity - by type
Million kilowatt-hours

Country or area Pays ou zone	Year Année	Self-producers and public utilities Autoproducteurs et services publics					Self- Auto-	
		Total Totale	Thermal Thermique	Hydro Hydraulique	Nuclear Nucléaire	Geothermal Géother- -mique	Total Totale	Thermal Thermique
Switzerland	2003	67166	2792	36865	27487	22	5325	264
	2004	65299	2850	35468	26958	23	5141	261
	2005	59612	3158	33086	23341	27	5380	301
	2006	64038	3298	32883	27819	38	5550	318
T.F.Yug.Rep. Macedonia	2003	6737	5363	1374	..	..	5	
	2004	6665	5183	1482	..	..	3	
	2005	6942	5450	1492	..	..	3	
	2006	7006	5356	1650	..	..	1	
Ukraine	2003	180354	89533	9390	81406	25	5996	596
	2004	182157	83222	11888	87022	25	6453	641
	2005	186055	84756	12505	88756	38	6501	646
	2006	193381	90087	13034	90225	35	6095	607
United Kingdom	2003	398671	302735	5962	88686	1288	40663	3871
	2004	395853	306336	7579	79999	1939	44112	4149
	2005	400524	308099	7891	81618	2916	44667	4078
	2006	398327	310186	8458	75451	4232	45675	4056
Oceania	**2003**	**278260**	**232591**	**42041**	..	**3628**	**16928**	**1621**
	2004	**286705**	**237691**	**45182**	..	**3832**	**15817**	**1516**
	2005	**297669**	**251647**	**41309**	..	**4713**	**16454**	**1577**
	2006	**304345**	**256922**	**41638**	..	**5785**	**17205**	**1650**
American Samoa	2003	188	188	..	..	..	..	
	2004	188	188	..	..	..	..	
	2005	189	189	..	..	..	..	
	2006	*193	*193	..	..	..	..	
Australia	2003	228118	211164	16248	..	706	12981	1270
	2004	234542	217953	15880	..	709	11712	1143
	2005	245495	228717	15886	..	892	12236	1196
	2006	251659	233909	16028	..	1722	12896	1261
Cook Islands	2003	29	29	..	..	..	..	
	2004	30	30	..	..	..	..	
	2005	30	30	..	..	..	..	
	2006	32	32	..	..	..	..	
Fiji	2003	*812	*145	*667	..	..	*99	*9
	2004	*816	*147	*669	..	..	*101	*10
	2005	*823	*149	*674	..	..	*102	*10
	2006	*840	*152	*688	..	..	*104	*10
French Polynesia	2003	602	480	122	..	..	..	
	2004	643	490	153	..	..	..	
	2005	631	500	131	..	..	..	
	2006	667	509	158	..	..	..	
Guam	2003	1777	1777	..	..	..	..	
	2004	1878	1878	..	..	..	..	
	2005	1897	1897	..	..	..	..	
	2006	1891	1891	..	..	..	..	
Kiribati	2003	*14	*14	..	..	..	..	
	2004	*14	*14	..	..	..	..	
	2005	*15	*15	..	..	..	..	
	2006	*15	*15	..	..	..	..	
Marshall Islands	2003	96	96	..	..	..	..	
	2004	101	101	..	..	..	..	
	2005	101	101	..	..	..	..	
	2006	*104	*104	..	..	..	..	
Nauru	2003	*31	*31	..	..	..	..	
	2004	*32	*32	..	..	..	..	
	2005	*33	*33	..	..	..	..	
	2006	*33	*33	..	..	..	..	

Table 34

Production d'électricité - par catégorie
Millions de kilowatt-heures

producers producteurs			Public utilities Services publics					Year Année	Country or area Pays ou zone
Hydro Hydraulique	Nuclear Nucléaire	Geothermal Géother-mique	Total Totale	Thermal Thermique	Hydro Hydraulique	Nuclear Nucléaire	Geothermal Géother-mique		
2658	..	22	61841	147	34207	27487	..	2003	Suisse
2508	..	23	60158	240	32960	26958	..	2004	
2339	..	27	54232	144	30747	23341	..	2005	
2325	..	38	58488	111	30558	27819	..	2006	
..	..	..	6732	5358	1374	..	..	2003	L'ex-RY Macédoine
..	..	..	6662	5180	1482	..	..	2004	
..	..	..	6939	5447	1492	..	..	2005	
..	..	..	7005	5355	1650	..	..	2006	
33	..	..	174358	83570	9357	81406	25	2003	Ukraine
36	..	..	175704	76805	11852	87022	25	2004	
33	..	..	179554	78288	12472	88756	38	2005	
24	..	..	187286	84016	13010	90225	35	2006	
660	..	1288	358008	264020	5302	88686	..	2003	Royaume-Uni
677	..	1939	351741	264840	6902	79999	..	2004	
968	..	2916	355857	267316	6923	81618	..	2005	
878	..	4232	352652	269621	7580	75451	..	2006	
664	**..**	**46**	**261332**	**216373**	**41377**	**..**	**3582**	**2003**	**Océanie**
630	**..**	**27**	**270888**	**222531**	**44552**	**..**	**3805**	**2004**	
625	**..**	**57**	**281215**	**235875**	**40684**	**..**	**4656**	**2005**	
631	**..**	**66**	**287140**	**240414**	**41007**	**..**	**5719**	**2006**	
..	..	..	188	188	..	..	..	2003	Samoa américaines
..	..	..	188	188	..	..	..	2004	
..	..	..	189	189	..	..	..	2005	
..	..	..	*193	*193	..	..	..	2006	
280	..	..	215137	198463	15968	..	706	2003	Australie
280	..	..	222830	206521	15600	..	709	2004	
274	..	..	233259	216755	15612	..	892	2005	
280	..	..	238763	221293	15748	..	1722	2006	
..	..	..	29	29	..	..	..	2003	Iles Cook
..	..	..	30	30	..	..	..	2004	
..	..	..	30	30	..	..	..	2005	
..	..	..	32	32	..	..	..	2006	
..	..	..	*713	*46	*667	..	..	2003	Fidji
..	..	..	*715	*46	*669	..	..	2004	
..	..	..	*721	*47	*674	..	..	2005	
..	..	..	*736	*48	*688	..	..	2006	
..	..	..	602	480	122	..	..	2003	Polynésie française
..	..	..	643	490	153	..	..	2004	
..	..	..	631	500	131	..	..	2005	
..	..	..	667	509	158	..	..	2006	
..	..	..	1777	1777	..	..	..	2003	Guam
..	..	..	1878	1878	..	..	..	2004	
..	..	..	1897	1897	..	..	..	2005	
..	..	..	1891	1891	..	..	..	2006	
..	..	..	*14	*14	..	..	..	2003	Kiribati
..	..	..	*14	*14	..	..	..	2004	
..	..	..	*15	*15	..	..	..	2005	
..	..	..	*15	*15	..	..	..	2006	
..	..	..	96	96	..	..	..	2003	Îles Marshall
..	..	..	101	101	..	..	..	2004	
..	..	..	101	101	..	..	..	2005	
..	..	..	*104	*104	..	..	..	2006	
..	..	..	*31	*31	..	..	..	2003	Nauru
..	..	..	*32	*32	..	..	..	2004	
..	..	..	*33	*33	..	..	..	2005	
..	..	..	*33	*33	..	..	..	2006	

Table 34

Production of electricity - by type

Million kilowatt-hours

Country or area Pays ou zone	Year Année	Self-producers and public utilities Autoproducteurs et services publics					Self- Auto-	
		Total Totale	Thermal Thermique	Hydro Hydraulique	Nuclear Nucléaire	Geothermal Géother- -mique	Total Totale	Thermal Thermique
New Caledonia	2003	1758	1430	323	..	5	..	
	2004	1678	1341	326	..	11	..	
	2005	1883	1526	339	..	18	..	
	2006	1926	1499	390		37	..	
New Zealand	2003	41249	14633	23699	..	2917	2016	19
	2004	42901	12588	27201	..	3112	1856	18
	2005	43136	16003	23330	..	3803	1895	18
	2006	43519	16040	23453	..	4026	1956	18
Niue	2003	*3	*3	..	..	..	..	
	2004	*3	*3	..	..	..	..	
	2005	*3	*3	..	..	..	..	
	2006	*3	*3	..	..	..	..	
Palau	2003	128	110	*18	..	..	*6	
	2004	*128	*110	*18	..	..	*6	
	2005	*134	*116	*18	..	..	*6	
	2006	*151	*133	*18	..	..	*6	
Papua New Guinea	2003	3178	2249	929	..	..	1804	14
	2004	3468	2573	895	..	..	2120	17
	2005	3002	2111	891	..	..	2193	18
	2006	3012	2149	863	..	..	2221	18
Samoa	2003	*106	*71	*35	..	..	*5	
	2004	*110	*70	*40	..	..	*5	
	2005	*111	*71	*40	..	..	*5	
	2006	*112	*72	*40	..	..	*5	
Solomon Islands	2003	*63	*63	..	..	..	*7	
	2004	63	63	..	..	..	*7	
	2005	74	74	..	..	..	*7	
	2006	75	75	..	..	..	*7	
Tonga	2003	45	45	..	..	..	..	
	2004	47	47	..	..	..	..	
	2005	*48	*48	..	..	..	..	
	2006	*48	*48	..	..	..	..	
Vanuatu	2003	*44	*44	..	..	..	*10	*
	2004	*44	*44	..	..	..	*10	*
	2005	*45	*45	..	..	..	*10	*
	2006	*45	*45	..	..	..	*10	*
Wallis and Futuna Is	2003	19	19	..	..	..	..	
	2004	19	19	..	..	..	..	
	2005	20	20	..	..	..	..	
	2006	20	20	..	..	..	..	

Table 34

Production d'électricité - par catégorie

Millions de kilowatt-heures

producers producteurs			Public utilities Services publics					Year Année	Country or area Pays ou zone
Hydro Hydraulique	Nuclear Nucléaire	Geothermal Géother-mique	Total Totale	Thermal Thermique	Hydro Hydraulique	Nuclear Nucléaire	Geothermal Géother-mique		
..	..	..	1758	1430	323	..	5	2003	Nouvelle-Calédonie
..	..	..	1678	1341	326	..	11	2004	
..	..	..	1883	1526	339	..	18	2005	
..	..	..	1926	1499	390	..	37	2006	
..	..	46	39233	12663	23699	..	2871	2003	Nouvelle-Zélande
..	..	27	41045	10759	27201	..	3085	2004	
..	..	57	41241	14165	23330	..	3746	2005	
..	..	66	41563	14150	23453	..	3960	2006	
..	..	..	*3	*3	..	..	..	2003	Nioué
..	..	..	*3	*3	..	..	..	2004	
..	..	..	*3	*3	..	..	..	2005	
..	..	..	*3	*3	..	..	..	2006	
..	..	..	122	104	*18	..	..	2003	Palaos
..	..	..	*122	*104	*18	..	..	2004	
..	..	..	*128	*110	*18	..	..	2005	
..	..	..	*145	*127	*18	..	..	2006	
384	..	..	1374	829	545	..	..	2003	Papouasie-Nvl-Guinée
350	..	..	1348	803	545	..	..	2004	
351	..	..	809	269	540	..	..	2005	
351	..	..	791	279	512	..	..	2006	
..	..	..	*101	*66	*35	..	..	2003	Samoa
..	..	..	*105	*65	*40	..	..	2004	
..	..	..	*106	*66	*40	..	..	2005	
..	..	..	*107	*67	*40	..	..	2006	
..	..	..	*56	*56	..	..	..	2003	Iles Salomon
..	..	..	56	56	..	..	..	2004	
..	..	..	67	67	..	..	..	2005	
..	..	..	68	68	..	..	..	2006	
..	..	..	45	45	..	..	..	2003	Tonga
..	..	..	47	47	..	..	..	2004	
..	..	..	*48	*48	..	..	..	2005	
..	..	..	*48	*48	..	..	..	2006	
..	..	..	*34	*34	..	..	..	2003	Vanuatu
..	..	..	*34	*34	..	..	..	2004	
..	..	..	*35	*35	..	..	..	2005	
..	..	..	*35	*35	..	..	..	2006	
..	..	..	19	19	..	..	..	2003	Iles Wallis et Futuna
..	..	..	19	19	..	..	..	2004	
..	..	..	20	20	..	..	..	2005	
..	..	..	20	20	..	..	..	2006	

Table 35

Production, trade and consumption of electricity
Production, commerce et consommation d'électricité
Million kilowatt-hours and kilowatt-hours per capita
Milliers de kilowattheures et kilowattheures par habitant

Table Notes:

Production data for the Dominican Republic, Mexico, the United States and Zimbabwe refer to net production.

- **Please refer to the Definitions Section on pages xv to xxix for the appropriate product description /classification.**

Notes relatives aux tableaux:

Les chiffres relatifs à la production pour la République dominicaine, le Mexique, les Etats-Unis, et le Zimbabwe se rapportent à la production nette.

- **Veuillez consulter la section "définitions" de la page xv à la page xxix pour une description/classification appropriée des produits.**

Figure 91: World electricity generation 1993-2006

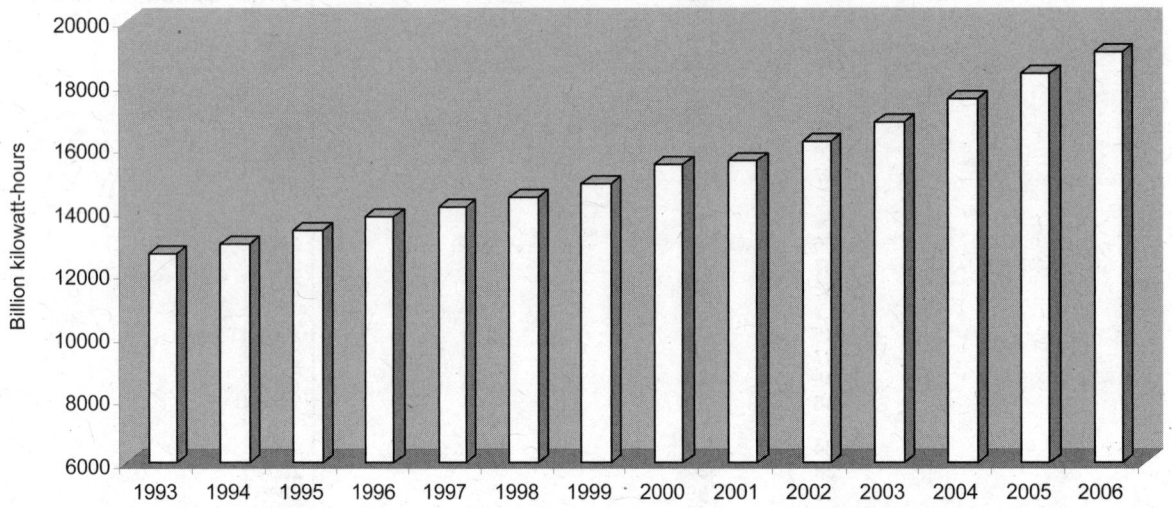

Figure 92: Major electricity producing countries in 2006

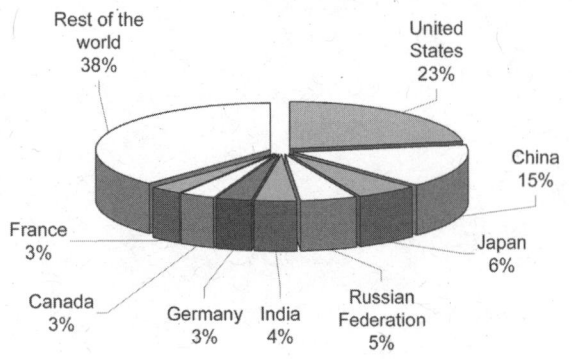

Figure 93: Major electricity consuming countries in 2006

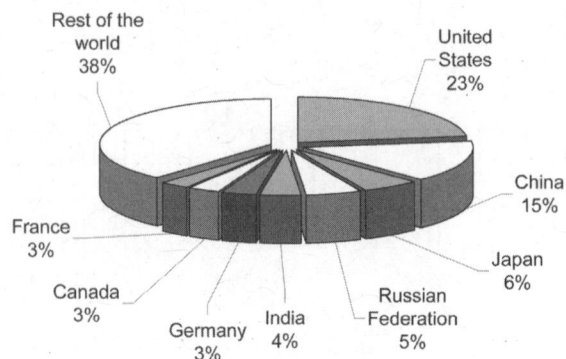

Table 35

Production, trade and consumption of electricity
Production, commerce et consommation d'électricité
Million kilowatt-hours and kilowatt-hours per capita
Millions de kilowatt-heures et kilowatt-heures par habitant

Country or area Pays ou zone	Year Année	Production Production	Imports Importations	Exports Exportations	Consumption Consommation	
					Total Totale	Per Capita Par habitant
World	**2003**	**16784964**	**555730**	**555970**	**16784725**	**2678**
Monde	**2004**	**17549588**	**555644**	**555052**	**17550179**	**2766**
	2005	**18340700**	**616242**	**617322**	**18339621**	**2857**
	2006	**19048038**	**611488**	**614242**	**19045284**	**2923**
Africa	**2003**	**509131**	**26852**	**25434**	**510548**	**606**
Afrique	**2004**	**539446**	**30318**	**28749**	**541015**	**623**
	2005	**563972**	**32612**	**31163**	**565420**	**636**
	2006	**592544**	**33004**	**31789**	**593759**	**648**
Algeria	2003	29571	223	212	29582	929
Algérie	2004	31250	211	197	31264	966
	2005	32875	248	275	32848	998
	2006	35226	382	300	35308	1055
Angola	2003	1995	..	..	1995	178
Angola	2004	2240	..	..	2240	197
	2005	2632	..	..	2632	225
	2006	2959	..	..	2959	247
Benin	2003	80	513	..	593	74
Bénin	2004	81	578	..	659	80
	2005	107	595	..	702	83
	2006	128	590	..	718	82
Burkina Faso	2003	445	69	..	514	40
Burkina Faso	2004	473	96	..	570	43
	2005	516	125	..	642	50
	2006	548	139	..	687	50
Burundi	2003	104	53	..	156	22
Burundi	2004	94	64	..	158	21
	2005	102	72	..	174	22
	2006	95	59	..	154	19
Cameroon	2003	3684	..	..	3684	216
Cameroun	2004	4110	..	..	4110	236
	2005	4145	..	..	4145	233
	2006	3954	..	..	3954	218
Cape Verde	2003	200	..	..	200	433
Cap-Vert	2004	220	..	..	220	469
	2005	237	..	..	237	496
	2006	252	..	..	252	517
Central African Rep.	2003	*110	..	..	*110	*27
Rép. centrafricaine	2004	*111	..	..	*111	*27
	2005	*113	..	..	*113	*27
	2006	*114	..	..	*114	*27
Chad	2003	*94	..	..	*94	*10
Tchad	2004	*97	..	..	*97	*10
	2005	*100	..	..	*100	*10
	2006	*104	..	..	*104	*10
Comoros	2003	*20	..	..	*20	*31
Comores	2004	*21	..	..	*21	*31
	2005	*21	..	..	*21	*32
	2006	*22	..	..	*22	*32
Congo	2003	408	359	..	767	222
Congo	2004	465	404	..	869	246
	2005	434	418	..	852	236
	2006	453	411	..	864	234

Table 35

Production, trade and consumption of electricity
Production, commerce et consommation d'électricité
Million kilowatt-hours and kilowatt-hours per capita
Millions de kilowatt-heures et kilowatt-heures par habitant

Country or area Pays ou zone	Year Année	Production Production	Imports Importations	Exports Exportations	Consumption Consommation	
					Total Totale	Per Capita Par habitant
Côte d'Ivoire	2003	5093	..	1325	3768	214
Côte d'Ivoire	2004	5403	..	1409	3994	215
	2005	5566	..	1396	4170	218
	2006	5535	..	1066	4469	227
Dem. Rep. of Congo	2003	6258	6	1330	4934	91
Rép. dem. du Congo	2004	6852	6	1456	5402	97
	2005	7419	6	1800	5625	98
	2006	7886	6	1799	6093	100
Djibouti	2003	200	..	..	200	257
Djibouti	2004	215	..	..	215	272
	2005	255	..	..	255	317
	2006	280	..	..	280	342
Egypt	2003	91932	153	1025	91060	1353
Egypte	2004	101299	174	873	100600	1412
	2005	111690	168	946	110912	1550
	2006	118407	208	557	118058	1622
Equatorial Guinea	2003	*26	..	..	*26	*56
Guinée équatoriale	2004	*27	..	..	*27	*57
	2005	*28	..	..	*28	*57
	2006	*29	..	..	*29	*57
Eritrea	2003	276	..	..	276	66
Erythrée	2004	283	..	..	283	65
	2005	289	..	..	289	64
	2006	269	..	..	269	57
Ethiopia	2003	2302	..	..	2302	33
Ethiopie	2004	2540	..	..	2540	36
	2005	2872	..	..	2872	40
	2006	3270	..	..	3270	44
Gabon	2003	1504	..	..	1504	1157
Gabon	2004	1537	..	..	1537	1126
	2005	1611	..	..	1611	1154
	2006	1726	..	..	1726	1210
Gambia	2003	*151	..	..	*151	*101
Gambie	2004	*156	..	..	*156	*101
	2005	*161	..	..	*161	*101
	2006	*166	..	..	*166	*101
Ghana	2003	5905	940	854	5991	285
Ghana	2004	6044	878	665	6257	289
	2005	6793	815	639	6969	315
	2006	8435	629	755	8309	361
Guinea	2003	*782	..	..	*782	*90
Guinée	2004	*801	..	..	*801	*91
	2005	*816	..	..	*816	*91
	2006	*836	..	..	*836	*91
Guinea-Bissau	2003	*61	..	..	*61	*48
Guinée-Bissau	2004	*63	..	..	*63	*49
	2005	*64	..	..	*64	*48
	2006	*66	..	..	*66	*49
Kenya	2003	5506	171	0	5677	174
Kenya	2004	5889	84	0	5973	175
	2005	6003	15	24	5994	170
	2006	6477	13	73	6417	176

Table 35

Production, trade and consumption of electricity
Production, commerce et consommation d'électricité

Million kilowatt-hours and kilowatt-hours per capita
Millions de kilowatt-heures et kilowatt-heures par habitant

Country or area Pays ou zone	Year Année	Production Production	Imports Importations	Exports Exportations	Consumption Consommation	
					Total Totale	Per Capita Par habitant
Liberia	2003	320	..	..	320	92
Libéria	2004	330	..	..	330	94
	2005	*338	..	..	*338	*94
	2006	*351	..	..	*351	*95
Libyan Arab Jamah.	2003	18943	0	0	18943	3045
Jamah. arabe libyenne	2004	20202	0	0	20202	3147
	2005	22317	152	105	22364	3373
	2006	23992	126	93	24025	3586
Madagascar	2003	900	..	..	900	55
Madagascar	2004	990	..	..	990	58
	2005	*1035	..	..	*1035	*58
	2006	*1065	..	..	*1065	*58
Malawi	2003	1337	..	7	1330	115
Malawi	2004	1477	..	8	1469	123
	2005	1544	..	10	1534	124
	2006	1556	..	*10	1546	121
Mali	2003	*449	..	..	*449	*41
Mali	2004	*465	..	..	*465	*41
	2005	*475	..	..	*475	*41
	2006	*489	..	..	*489	*41
Mauritania	2003	242	77	..	320	112
Mauritanie	2004	263	69	..	332	115
	2005	250	134	..	383	132
	2006	277	125	..	402	134
Mauritius	2003	2082	..	..	2082	1721
Maurice	2004	2165	..	..	2165	1775
	2005	2271	..	..	2271	1827
	2006	2350	..	..	2350	1876
Morocco	2003	18107	1417	..	19524	678
Maroc	2004	19336	1512	..	20848	699
	2005	22456	802	..	23258	771
	2006	23192	1998	..	25190	826
Mozambique	2003	10907	7363	9643	8627	459
Mozambique	2004	11714	9267	10402	10579	545
	2005	13285	9588	12001	10872	560
	2006	14737	9839	12825	11751	594
Niger	2003	*192	275	..	466	39
Niger	2004	*212	295	..	507	42
	2005	*195	339	..	534	42
	2006	*179	357	..	535	41
Nigeria	2003	20183	..	..	20183	160
Nigéria	2004	20224	..	..	20224	157
	2005	20468	..	..	20468	153
	2006	23110	..	..	23110	165
Réunion	2003	*1618	..	..	*1618	*2143
Réunion	2004	*1652	..	..	*1652	*2156
	2005	*1680	..	..	*1680	*2162
	2006	*1710	..	..	*1710	*2148
Rwanda	2003	123	150	8	265	30
Rwanda	2004	*130	120	10	240	26
	2005	*135	*120	*10	*245	*27
	2006	118	112	*10	220	24

Table 35

Production, trade and consumption of electricity
Production, commerce et consommation d'électricité

Million kilowatt-hours and kilowatt-hours per capita
Millions de kilowatt-heures et kilowatt-heures par habitant

Country or area Pays ou zone	Year Année	Production Production	Imports Importations	Exports Exportations	Consumption Consommation Total Totale	Consumption Consommation Per Capita Par habitant
Sao Tome and Principe	2003	*18	..	..	*18	*126
Sao Tomé-et-Principe	2004	*18	..	..	*18	*123
	2005	*19	..	..	*19	*128
	2006	*19	..	..	*19	*125
Senegal	2003	2157	..	..	2157	212
Sénégal	2004	2354	..	..	2354	223
	2005	2595	..	..	2595	239
	2006	2433	..	..	2433	221
Seychelles	2003	224	..	25	199	2399
Seychelles	2004	226	..	24	203	2455
	2005	231	..	24	207	2495
	2006	252	..	25	227	2682
Sierra Leone	2003	144	..	..	144	26
Sierra Leone	2004	120	..	..	120	21
	2005	84	..	..	84	14
	2006	*99	..	..	*99	*16
Somalia	2003	280	..	..	280	36
Somalie	2004	280	..	..	280	35
	2005	290	..	..	290	35
	2006	295	..	..	295	35
South Africa Customs Un.	2003	237177	11345	10316	238207	4667
Un.douan.d'Afr.mérid	2004	247331	13918	13277	247971	4661
	2005	247959	15355	13453	249861	4666
	2006	256882	14374	13802	257454	4752
St. Helena and Depend.	2003	*7	..	..	*7	*950
St-Hélène et dépend	2004	8	..	..	8	1079
	2005	*8	..	..	*8	*1072
	2006	*8	..	..	*8	*1066
Sudan	2003	3354	..	..	3354	101
Soudan	2004	3883	..	..	3883	113
	2005	4124	..	..	4124	117
	2006	4209	..	..	4209	116
Togo	2003	176	458	..	634	128
Togo	2004	186	489	..	675	133
	2005	189	511	..	700	131
	2006	221	505	..	726	136
Tunisia	2003	11829	0	20	11809	1200
Tunisie	2004	12455	0	27	12428	1251
	2005	13007	0	36	12971	1293
	2006	14122	142	135	14129	1395
Uganda	2003	1802	..	*165	1637	64
Ouganda	2004	1942	..	*170	1772	65
	2005	1836	..	*165	1671	59
	2006	1615	..	50	1565	54
United Rep.Tanzania	2003	2658	95	..	2753	76
Rép. Unie de Tanzanie	2004	2893	113	..	3006	83
	2005	3035	136	..	3171	85
	2006	2776	123	..	2899	76
Western Sahara	2003	90	..	..	90	344
Sahara occidental	2004	90	..	..	90	336
	2005	90	..	..	90	331
	2006	*90	..	..	*90	*326

Table 35

Production, trade and consumption of electricity
Production, commerce et consommation d'électricité
Million kilowatt-hours and kilowatt-hours per capita
Millions de kilowatt-heures et kilowatt-heures par habitant

Country or area Pays ou zone	Year Année	Production Production	Imports Importations	Exports Exportations	Consumption Consommation	
					Total Totale	Per Capita Par habitant
Zambia	2003	8308	..	504	7804	726
Zambie	2004	8512	..	231	8281	747
	2005	8938	..	243	8695	757
	2006	9385	..	255	9130	774
Zimbabwe	2003	8799	3185	0	11984	926
Zimbabwe	2004	9718	2040	0	11758	903
	2005	10269	3013	36	13246	1010
	2006	9776	2867	34	12609	953
America, North	**2003**	**4997761**	**56020**	**57243**	**4996538**	**9954**
Amérique du Nord	**2004**	**5108687**	**58234**	**58370**	**5108551**	**10073**
	2005	**5271402**	**64884**	**65179**	**5271108**	**10291**
	2006	**5281822**	**67142**	**68546**	**5280418**	**10221**
Anguilla	2003	58	..	..	58	4585
Anguilla	2004	62	..	..	62	4774
	2005	72	..	..	72	5279
	2006	80	..	..	80	5577
Antigua and Barbuda	2003	*109	..	..	*109	*1363
Antigua-et-Barbuda	2004	*111	..	..	*111	*1370
	2005	*114	..	..	*114	*1377
	2006	*116	..	..	*116	*1379
Aruba	2003	842	..	..	842	8854
Aruba	2004	866	..	..	866	8866
	2005	911	..	..	911	9048
	2006	910	..	..	910	8846
Bahamas	2003	1990	..	..	1990	6238
Bahamas	2004	*2087	..	..	*2087	*6964
	2005	*2090	..	..	*2090	*6471
	2006	*2090	..	..	*2090	*6391
Barbados	2003	871	..	..	871	3206
Barbade	2004	895	..	..	895	3286
	2005	930	..	..	930	3405
	2006	948	..	..	948	3459
Belize	2003	*169	*25	..	*194	*709
Belize	2004	*177	*25	..	*202	*715
	2005	*183	*29	..	*212	*727
	2006	*191	*29	..	*220	*723
Bermuda	2003	664	..	..	664	10533
Bermudes	2004	*661	..	..	*661	*10439
	2005	*685	..	..	*685	*10775
	2006	*696	..	..	*696	*10910
British Virgin Islands	2003	*45	..	..	*45	*2110
Iles Vierges britanniques	2004	*45	..	..	*45	*2075
	2005	*45	..	..	*45	*2045
	2006	*48	..	..	*48	*2133
Canada	2003	589967	24520	31311	583176	18411
Canada	2004	598514	22785	33249	588050	18379
	2005	628194	19677	43528	604343	18703
	2006	612594	23624	42736	593482	18177
Cayman Islands	2003	490	..	..	490	11245
Iles Caïmanes	2004	433	..	..	433	9788
	2005	454	..	..	454	9389
	2006	536	..	..	536	10309

Table 35

Production, trade and consumption of electricity
Production, commerce et consommation d'électricité

Million kilowatt-hours and kilowatt-hours per capita
Millions de kilowatt-heures et kilowatt-heures par habitant

Country or area Pays ou zone	Year Année	Production Production	Imports Importations	Exports Exportations	Consumption Consommation	
					Total Totale	Per Capita Par habitant
Costa Rica	2003	7565	194	273	7486	1831
Costa Rica	2004	8040	202	440	7802	1867
	2005	8252	81	70	8263	1937
	2006	8697	149	60	8786	2018
Cuba	2003	15811	..	..	15811	1398
Cuba	2004	15652	..	..	15652	1380
	2005	15341	..	..	15341	1365
	2006	16469	..	..	16469	1465
Dominica	2003	79	..	..	79	1129
Dominique	2004	79	..	..	79	1129
	2005	84	..	..	84	1219
	2006	*85	..	..	*85	*1250
Dominican Republic	2003	13489	..	..	13489	1508
Rép. dominicaine	2004	13759	..	..	13759	1515
	2005	12899	..	..	12899	1398
	2006	14150	..	..	14150	1513
El Salvador	2003	4128	428	103	4453	671
El Salvador	2004	4468	466	84	4850	718
	2005	4788	322	38	5072	738
	2006	5597	11	9	5599	801
Greenland	2003	*305	..	..	*305	*5409
Groënland	2004	*305	..	..	*305	*5409
	2005	*305	..	..	*305	*5410
	2006	*305	..	..	*305	*5412
Grenada	2003	153	..	..	153	1463
Grenade	2004	157	..	..	157	1500
	2005	166	..	..	166	1581
	2006	171	..	..	171	1617
Guadeloupe	2003	1165	..	..	1165	2654
Guadeloupe	2004	*1180	..	..	*1180	*2655
	2005	*1190	..	..	*1190	*2671
	2006	*1225	..	..	*1225	*2675
Guatemala	2003	6561	31	428	6164	510
Guatemala	2004	7009	41	464	6586	532
	2005	7550	23	335	7238	570
	2006	7911	8	88	7832	602
Haiti	2003	535	..	..	535	64
Haïti	2004	547	..	..	547	65
	2005	556	..	..	556	65
	2006	570	..	..	570	66
Honduras	2003	4530	331	..	4861	709
Honduras	2004	4877	357	..	5234	745
	2005	5545	58	..	5604	779
	2006	5356	20	..	5376	730
Jamaica	2003	7146	..	..	7146	2689
Jamaïque	2004	7217	..	..	7217	2697
	2005	7526	..	..	7526	2839
	2006	7473	..	..	7473	2806
Martinique	2003	*1185	..	..	*1185	*3034
Martinique	2004	*1195	..	..	*1195	*3035
	2005	*1205	..	..	*1205	*3031
	2006	*1215	..	..	*1215	*3038

Table 35

Production, trade and consumption of electricity
Production, commerce et consommation d'électricité
Million kilowatt-hours and kilowatt-hours per capita
Millions de kilowatt-heures et kilowatt-heures par habitant

Country or area Pays ou zone	Year Année	Production Production	Imports Importations	Exports Exportations	Consumption Consommation	
					Total Totale	Per Capita Par habitant
Mexico	2003	217867	87	953	217001	2127
Mexique	2004	224077	47	1006	223118	2166
	2005	234895	87	1291	233691	2248
	2006	249648	523	1299	248872	2373
Montserrat	2003	21	..	..	21	2335
Montserrat	2004	21	..	..	21	2271
	2005	*22	..	..	*22	*2323
	2006	*22	..	..	*22	*2320
Netherlands Antilles	2003	1181	..	..	1181	6610
Antilles néerlandaises	2004	1210	..	..	1210	6608
	2005	1248	..	..	1248	6732
	2006	1271	..	..	1271	6707
Nicaragua	2003	2708	12	21	2699	508
Nicaragua	2004	2822	23	22	2823	524
	2005	2866	25	8	2883	528
	2006	2958	53	0	3011	545
Panama	2003	5308	2	182	5128	1646
Panama	2004	5504	78	207	5375	1695
	2005	5702	55	106	5651	1751
	2006	5962	34	83	5913	1801
Puerto Rico	2003	23280	..	..	23280	6002
Porto Rico	2004	24130	..	..	24130	6195
	2005	24960	..	..	24960	6380
	2006	*25800	..	..	*25800	*6569
St. Kitts-Nevis	2003	127	..	..	127	2854
St-Kitts-Nevis	2004	*130	..	..	*130	*2955
	2005	*133	..	..	*133	*3093
	2006	*135	..	..	*135	*3140
St. Lucia	2003	299	..	..	299	1861
St-Lucie	2004	309	..	..	309	1899
	2005	324	..	..	324	1964
	2006	331	..	..	331	1983
St. Pierre-Miquelon	2003	*52	..	..	*52	*7429
St-Pierre-Miquelon	2004	*52	..	..	*52	*7429
	2005	*54	..	..	*54	*7701
	2006	*54	..	..	*54	*7687
St. Vincent-Grenadines	2003	108	..	..	108	1029
St. Vincent-Grenadines	2004	121	..	..	121	1154
	2005	*124	..	..	*124	*1195
	2006	*127	..	..	*127	*1227
Trinidad and Tobago	2003	6437	..	..	6437	4895
Trinité-et-Tobago	2004	6430	..	..	6430	4875
	2005	7058	..	..	7058	5331
	2006	6901	..	..	6901	5197
Turks and Caicos Islands	2003	*10	..	..	*10	*398
Iles Turques et Caiques	2004	*11	..	..	*11	*404
	2005	*12	..	..	*12	*402
	2006	*14	..	..	*14	*409
United States	2003	4081466	30390	23972	4087884	14055
Etats-Unis	2004	4174484	34210	22898	4185796	14256
	2005	4293860	44527	19803	4318584	14570
	2006	4300103	42691	24271	4318523	14470

Table 35

Production, trade and consumption of electricity
Production, commerce et consommation d'électricité
Million kilowatt-hours and kilowatt-hours per capita
Millions de kilowatt-heures et kilowatt-heures par habitant

Country or area Pays ou zone	Year Année	Production Production	Imports Importations	Exports Exportations	Consumption Consommation	
					Total Totale	Per Capita Par habitant
United States Virgin Is.	2003	*1040	..	..	*1040	*9528
Iles Vierges américaines	2004	*1050	..	..	*1050	*9602
	2005	*1060	..	..	*1060	*9672
	2006	*1065	..	..	*1065	*9703
America, South	**2003**	**745700**	**48311**	**50042**	**743970**	**2054**
Amérique du Sud	**2004**	**790558**	**50951**	**50848**	**790661**	**2153**
	2005	**822595**	**52702**	**51217**	**824081**	**2214**
	2006	**866989**	**55581**	**53413**	**869156**	**2304**
Argentina	2003	92609	7578	2543	97644	2578
Argentine	2004	100260	7612	4143	103729	2714
	2005	107053	8017	4140	110930	2874
	2006	115197	7417	5059	117555	3017
Bolivia	2003	4269	9	..	4279	474
Bolivie	2004	4542	5	..	4547	493
	2005	5230	*5	..	5235	555
	2006	5293	*5	..	5298	550
Brazil	2003	364339	37151	6	401484	2243
Brésil	2004	387451	37392	7	424836	2340
	2005	402938	39202	160	441980	2400
	2006	419336	41447	283	460500	2466
Chile	2003	48780	1950	..	50730	3185
Chili	2004	51984	1903	..	53887	3347
	2005	54383	2152	..	56535	3469
	2006	57555	2285	..	59840	3642
Colombia	2003	47682	69	1182	46569	1045
Colombie	2004	50228	48	1682	48594	1073
	2005	50665	16	1758	48923	1063
	2006	54755	21	1813	52963	1132
Ecuador	2003	11546	1120	0	12666	986
Equateur	2004	12585	1642	0	14227	1092
	2005	13404	1723	16	15111	1143
	2006	14814	1570	1	16383	1222
Falkland Is. (Malvinas)	2003	*16	..	..	*16	*5461
Iles Falkland (Malvinas)	2004	*16	..	..	*16	*5476
	2005	*16	..	..	*16	*5525
	2006	*16	..	..	*16	*5550
French Guiana	2003	440	..	..	440	2431
Guyane française	2004	430	..	..	430	2248
	2005	430	..	..	430	2199
	2006	430	..	..	430	2183
Guyana	2003	820	..	..	820	1089
Guyana	2004	835	..	..	835	1106
	2005	862	..	..	862	1137
	2006	867	..	..	867	1141
Paraguay	2003	51762	0	45173	6590	1161
Paraguay	2004	51921	0	44997	6925	1196
	2005	51156	2	43784	7375	1250
	2006	53774	1	45699	8076	1344
Peru	2003	23128		..	23128	860
Pérou	2004	24415		..	24415	902
	2005	25660		..	25660	944
	2006	27358		..	27358	999

Table 35

Production, trade and consumption of electricity
Production, commerce et consommation d'électricité

Million kilowatt-hours and kilowatt-hours per capita
Millions de kilowatt-heures et kilowatt-heures par habitant

Country or area Pays ou zone	Year Année	Production Production	Imports Importations	Exports Exportations	Consumption Consommation	
					Total Totale	Per Capita Par habitant
Suriname	2003	1496	..	..	1496	3109
Suriname	2004	1509	..	..	1509	3062
	2005	1571	..	..	1571	3148
	2006	1618	..	..	1618	3208
Uruguay	2003	8578	434	1138	7874	2310
Uruguay	2004	5899	2348	19	8228	2492
	2005	7683	1585	841	8427	2549
	2006	5618	2835	16	8437	2546
Venezuela(Bolivar. Rep.)	2003	90235	..	0	90235	3515
Venezuela(Rép. bolivar.)	2004	98482	..	0	98482	3769
	2005	101544	..	518	101026	3801
	2006	110357	..	542	109815	4063
Asia	**2003**	**5656352**	**47359**	**47131**	**5656580**	**1488**
Asie	**2004**	**6130540**	**52967**	**53354**	**6130153**	**1596**
	2005	**6622834**	**55711**	**55253**	**6623291**	**1705**
	2006	**7155055**	**58508**	**57023**	**7156540**	**1816**
Afghanistan	2003	976	*100	..	1076	48
Afghanistan	2004	929	*100	..	1029	44
	2005	*960	*100	..	*1060	*47
	2006	*960	*100	..	*1060	*47
Armenia	2003	5501	307	583	5225	1375
Arménie	2004	6030	260	1012	5278	1642
	2005	6317	338	1151	5504	1711
	2006	6041	355	755	5641	1751
Azerbaijan	2003	21286	2436	871	22851	2775
Azerbaïdjan	2004	21743	2373	1008	23108	2782
	2005	22872	2082	880	24074	2869
	2006	24542	1766	879	25429	2997
Bahrain	2003	7768	..	..	7768	11267
Bahreïn	2004	8448	..	..	8448	11946
	2005	8698	..	..	8698	12003
	2006	9822	..	..	9822	13227
Bangladesh	2003	19170	..	..	19170	142
Bangladesh	2004	20820	..	..	20820	152
	2005	22006	..	..	22006	159
	2006	23703	..	..	23703	167
Bhutan	2003	2200	24	1560	664	1084
Bhoutan	2004	2529	19	1845	703	1127
	2005	2355	21	1624	752	1184
	2006	2648	34	1943	739	1142
Brunei Darussalam	2003	3169	..	..	3169	9065
Brunéi Darussalam	2004	3236	..	..	3236	8996
	2005	3264	..	..	3264	8819
	2006	3298	..	..	3298	8611
Cambodia	2003	637	58	..	695	53
Cambodge	2004	743	60	..	802	60
	2005	880	82	..	962	70
	2006	1235	110	..	1345	95
China	2003	1907380	2980	10339	1900021	1475
Chine	2004	2193736	3400	9476	2187660	1688
	2005	2497441	5011	11194	2491258	1911
	2006	2865726	5389	12271	2858844	2176

Table 35

Production, trade and consumption of electricity
Production, commerce et consommation d'électricité

Million kilowatt-hours and kilowatt-hours per capita
Millions de kilowatt-heures et kilowatt-heures par habitant

Country or area Pays ou zone	Year Année	Production Production	Imports Importations	Exports Exportations	Consumption Consommation	
					Total Totale	Per Capita Par habitant
China, Hong Kong SAR	2003	35506	10397	3008	42895	6299
Chine, Hong-Kong RAS	2004	37129	9837	3087	43879	6468
	2005	38448	11001	4498	44951	6598
	2006	38613	10897	4528	44982	6557
China, Macao SAR	2003	1779	180	..	1959	4368
Chine, Macao RAS	2004	1956	151	..	2107	4528
	2005	2027	341	..	2368	4851
	2006	1668	965	..	2633	5244
Cyprus	2003	4053	..	..	4053	5624
Chypre	2004	4200	..	..	4200	5698
	2005	4377	..	..	4377	5774
	2006	4652	..	..	4652	6035
Georgia	2003	7160	1071	159	8072	1865
Géorgie	2004	6924	1281	0	8205	1900
	2005	7267	1468	122	8613	1975
	2006	7599	857	83	8373	1904
India	2003	633275	1748	58	634965	594
Inde	2004	665873	1735	40	667568	618
	2005	697234	1763	209	698788	638
	2006	744119	3010	300	746829	668
Indonesia	2003	112944	..	..	112944	527
Indonésie	2004	120160	..	..	120160	554
	2005	127369	..	..	127369	579
	2006	133108	..	..	133108	599
Iran(Islamic Rep. of)	2003	152599	1489	919	153169	2305
Iran(Rép. islamique)	2004	166016	2170	1837	166349	2465
	2005	180390	2074	2761	179703	2625
	2006	201029	2540	2775	200794	2848
Iraq	2003	28340	0	..	28340	1076
Iraq	2004	32295	1318	..	33613	1239
	2005	34000	1388	..	35388	1287
	2006	31869	1301	..	33170	1151
Israel	2003	47041	..	1470	45571	6812
Israël	2004	48481	..	1459	47022	6906
	2005	49843	..	1663	48180	6952
	2006	51811	..	1844	49967	7090
Japan	2003	1047041	..	..	1047041	8294
Japon	2004	1076244	..	..	1076244	8525
	2005	1098315	..	..	1098315	8702
	2006	1100364	..	..	1100364	8722
Jordan	2003	8044	321	1	8364	1599
Jordanie	2004	8970	826	1	9795	1919
	2005	9651	741	4	10388	1898
	2006	11120	514	36	11598	2071
Kazakhstan	2003	63866	3506	4975	62397	4185
Kazakhstan	2004	66942	5234	7403	64773	4314
	2005	67916	4552	3978	68490	4522
	2006	71653	4161	3326	72488	4735
Korea, Dem.Ppl's.Rep.	2003	20999	..	..	20999	895
Corée,Rép.pop.dém.de	2004	21974	..	..	21974	931
	2005	22913	..	..	22913	970
	2006	22436	..	..	22436	946

Table 35

Production, trade and consumption of electricity
Production, commerce et consommation d'électricité
Million kilowatt-hours and kilowatt-hours per capita
Millions de kilowatt-heures et kilowatt-heures par habitant

Country or area Pays ou zone	Year Année	Production Production	Imports Importations	Exports Exportations	Consumption Consommation	
					Total Totale	Per Capita Par habitant
Korea, Republic of	2003	345192	..	..	345192	7214
Corée, République de	2004	368162	..	..	368162	7657
	2005	389390	..	..	389390	8063
	2006	404021	..	..	404021	8365
Kuwait	2003	39802	..	..	39802	17116
Koweït	2004	41256	..	..	41256	17258
	2005	43734	..	..	43734	17798
	2006	47607	..	..	47607	18847
Kyrgyzstan	2003	15576	108	1716	13968	2772
Kirghizistan	2004	16312	54	3382	12984	2549
	2005	16415	0	2684	13731	2670
	2006	17082	0	2521	14561	2805
Lao People's Dem. Rep.	2003	3372	217	3166	423	75
Rép. dém. pop. lao	2004	*3541	217	*3000	*758	*130
	2005	*3685	281	*3000	*966	*172
	2006	*3799	*222	*3000	*1021	*178
Lebanon	2003	11787	0	..	11787	3009
Liban	2004	11054	216	..	11270	2842
	2005	11125	455	..	11580	2887
	2006	10654	929	..	11583	2856
Malaysia	2003	78427	0	0	78427	3131
Malaisie	2004	82282	93	616	81759	3196
	2005	87300	0	2231	85068	3256
	2006	91563	0	2524	89039	3342
Maldives	2003	141	..	..	141	495
Maldives	2004	160	..	..	160	553
	2005	*185	..	..	*185	*630
	2006	212	..	..	212	709
Mongolia	2003	3138	171	7	3302	1326
Mongolie	2004	3303	171	8	3466	1376
	2005	3419	168	12	3575	1403
	2006	3544	168	21	3691	1431
Myanmar	2003	5426	..	..	5426	102
Myanmar	2004	5608	..	..	5608	103
	2005	6015	..	..	6015	109
	2006	6164	..	..	6164	109
Nepal	2003	2267	150	206	2211	91
Népal	2004	2416	241	111	2546	103
	2005	2622	202	133	2691	106
	2006	2684	207	136	2755	106
Occup. Palestinian Terr.	2003	342	2316	..	2658	756
Terr. palestiniens occup.	2004	396	2599	..	2994	823
	2005	501	*2863	..	*3363	*894
	2006	*520	*2800	..	*3320	*854
Oman	2003	10714	..	..	10714	4577
Oman	2004	11499	..	..	11499	4760
	2005	12648	..	..	12648	5041
	2006	13585	..	..	13585	5272
Other Asia	2003	209076	..	..	209076	9250
Autre Asie	2004	218410	..	..	218410	9626
	2005	227449	..	..	227449	10007
	2006	235371	..	..	235371	10328

Table 35

Production, trade and consumption of electricity
Production, commerce et consommation d'électricité

Million kilowatt-hours and kilowatt-hours per capita
Millions de kilowatt-heures et kilowatt-heures par habitant

Country or area Pays ou zone	Year Année	Production Production	Imports Importations	Exports Exportations	Consumption Consommation	
					Total Totale	Per Capita Par habitant
Pakistan	2003	80830	73	..	80903	554
Pakistan	2004	85698	109	..	85807	577
	2005	93832	146	..	93978	612
	2006	98350	171	..	98521	628
Philippines	2003	52897	..	..	52897	652
Philippines	2004	55957	..	..	55957	677
	2005	56549	..	..	56549	663
	2006	56818	..	..	56818	653
Qatar	2003	12012	..	..	12012	16382
Qatar	2004	13233	..	..	13233	17032
	2005	14396	..	..	14396	17711
	2006	15325	..	..	15325	16368
Saudi Arabia	2003	153000	..	..	153000	6949
Arabie saoudite	2004	159875	..	..	159875	7085
	2005	176124	..	..	176124	7618
	2006	179782	..	..	179782	7593
Singapore	2003	35331	..	..	35331	8440
Singapour	2004	36810	..	..	36810	8685
	2005	38213	..	..	38213	8801
	2006	39442	..	..	39442	8796
Sri Lanka	2003	7711	..	..	7711	401
Sri Lanka	2004	8158	..	..	8158	419
	2005	8769	..	..	8769	446
	2006	9389	..	..	9389	472
Syrian Arab Republic	2003	29534	..	..	29534	1683
Rép. arabe syrienne	2004	32077	..	..	32077	1799
	2005	34935	..	..	34935	1912
	2006	37283	..	..	37283	1992
Tajikistan	2003	16509	4605	4596	16518	2513
Tadjikistan	2004	16491	4810	4451	16850	2511
	2005	17090	4508	4257	17341	2531
	2006	16935	4839	4231	17543	2460
Thailand	2003	116983	2479	296	119166	1861
Thaïlande	2004	125727	3388	372	128743	2006
	2005	132197	4419	642	135974	2097
	2006	138742	5159	750	143151	2192
Timor-Leste	2003	*300	..	..	*300	*300
Timor-Leste	2004	*307	..	..	*307	*301
	2005	*314	..	..	*314	*301
	2006	*320	..	..	*320	*301
Turkey	2003	140581	1158	588	141151	2010
Turquie	2004	150698	463	1144	150017	2108
	2005	161956	636	1798	160794	2231
	2006	176299	573	2236	174636	2393
Turkmenistan	2003	10800	..	1065	9735	2072
Turkménistan	2004	11920	..	1173	10747	2255
	2005	12820	..	1260	11560	2392
	2006	13650	..	1340	12310	2513
United Arab Emirates	2003	49450	..	..	49450	13926
Emirats arabes unis	2004	52417	..	..	52417	13937
	2005	60698	..	..	60698	14781
	2006	66768	..	..	66768	15788

Table 35

Production, trade and consumption of electricity
Production, commerce et consommation d'électricité

Million kilowatt-hours and kilowatt-hours per capita
Millions de kilowatt-heures et kilowatt-heures par habitant

Country or area Pays ou zone	Year Année	Production Production	Imports Importations	Exports Exportations	Consumption Consommation	
					Total Totale	Per Capita Par habitant
Uzbekistan	2003	49400	11465	11548	49317	1909
Ouzbékistan	2004	51030	11843	11929	50944	1944
	2005	47706	11071	11152	47625	1791
	2006	49299	11441	11524	49216	1824
Viet Nam	2003	40925	..	..	40925	506
Viet Nam	2004	46029	..	..	46029	561
	2005	53463	..	..	53463	643
	2006	56494	..	..	56494	671
Yemen	2003	4094	..	..	4094	218
Yémen	2004	4337	..	..	4337	224
	2005	4741	..	..	4741	237
	2006	5337	..	..	5337	259
Europe	**2003**	**4597760**	**377188**	**376120**	**4598828**	**6324**
Europe	**2004**	**4693652**	**363174**	**363732**	**4693094**	**6447**
	2005	**4762228**	**410333**	**414509**	**4758052**	**6525**
	2006	**4847282**	**397252**	**403471**	**4841063**	**6631**
Albania	2003	5230	1242	326	6146	1743
Albanie	2004	5559	477	274	5762	1847
	2005	5443	371	0	5814	1850
	2006	5094	611	0	5705	1811
Austria	2003	60100	19002	13389	65713	8146
Autriche	2004	64125	16629	13548	67206	8256
	2005	65681	20397	17732	68346	8328
	2006	63445	21257	14407	70295	8488
Belarus	2003	26627	10818	3987	33458	3389
Bélarus	2004	31210	7975	4723	34462	3508
	2005	30961	9091	5053	34999	3580
	2006	31811	10149	5789	36171	3717
Belgium	2003	84630	14664	8254	91040	8791
Belgique	2004	85643	14567	6790	93420	8986
	2005	86944	14328	8024	93248	8927
	2006	85391	18853	8696	95548	9090
Bosnia and Herzegovina	2003	11266	2082	3015	10333	2696
Bosnie y Herzégovine	2004	12734	1653	3598	10789	2808
	2005	12637	2251	3628	11260	2930
	2006	13346	3015	5123	11238	2924
Bulgaria	2003	42600	1283	6772	37111	4743
Bulgarie	2004	41621	741	6620	35742	4593
	2005	44365	799	8380	36784	4753
	2006	45843	1139	8882	38100	4949
Croatia	2003	12620	4479	586	16513	3717
Croatie	2004	13295	5298	1633	16960	3820
	2005	12462	8746	3634	17574	3956
	2006	12430	8313	2691	18052	4066
Czech Republic	2003	83227	10086	26299	67014	6569
République tchèque	2004	84333	9776	25493	68616	6722
	2005	82578	12351	24985	69944	6834
	2006	84361	11466	24097	71730	6973
Denmark	2003	46181	7023	15568	37636	7123
Danemark	2004	40433	8673	11545	37561	6954
	2005	36355	12943	11574	37724	6965
	2006	45716	6767	13702	38781	7136

Table 35

Production, trade and consumption of electricity
Production, commerce et consommation d'électricité

Million kilowatt-hours and kilowatt-hours per capita
Millions de kilowatt-heures et kilowatt-heures par habitant

Country or area Pays ou zone	Year Année	Production Production	Imports Importations	Exports Exportations	Consumption Consommation	
					Total Totale	Per Capita Par habitant
Estonia	2003	10159	93	1989	8263	6105
Estonie	2004	10128	347	2141	8334	6177
	2005	10002	345	1953	8394	6236
	2006	9508	251	1001	8758	6519
Faeroe Islands	2003	270	..	..	270	5634
Iles Féroé	2004	290	..	..	290	6009
	2005	*290	..	..	*290	*6009
	2006	*295	..	..	*295	*6112
Finland	2003	84230	11882	7030	89082	17088
Finlande	2004	85847	11667	6797	90717	17352
	2005	70550	17948	933	87565	16691
	2006	82304	14118	2717	93705	17793
France incl. Monaco	2003	566948	6959	73373	500534	8316
France y compris Monaco	2004	574278	6571	68477	512372	8461
	2005	576170	8062	68390	515842	8470
	2006	574473	8522	71857	511138	8370
Germany	2003	606719	49107	52379	603447	7313
Allemagne	2004	615287	48187	50808	612666	7426
	2005	620574	56861	61427	616008	7470
	2006	636761	48464	65441	619784	7525
Gibraltar	2003	134	..	..	134	4786
Gibraltar	2004	136	..	..	136	4857
	2005	145	..	..	145	5179
	2006	151	..	..	151	5229
Greece	2003	58471	4169	2076	60564	5494
Grèce	2004	59346	4854	2034	62166	5620
	2005	60020	5616	1836	63800	5746
	2006	60789	6140	1938	64991	5830
Hungary	2003	34145	14077	7138	41084	4056
Hongrie	2004	33708	10524	3056	41176	4074
	2005	35756	15637	9410	41983	4162
	2006	35859	15393	8186	43066	4276
Iceland	2003	8500	..	..	8500	29384
Islande	2004	8623	..	..	8623	29472
	2005	8683	..	..	8683	29348
	2006	9930	..	..	9930	32629
Ireland	2003	25317	1176	10	26483	6656
Irlande	2004	25569	1574	0	27143	6712
	2005	25970	2045	1	28014	6782
	2006	28046	1787	9	29824	7042
Italy and San Marino	2003	293884	51486	518	344852	5987
Italie y comp. St. Marin	2004	303347	46426	791	348982	5999
	2005	303699	50264	1109	352854	6021
	2006	314121	46596	1611	359106	6093
Latvia	2003	3975	2671	38	6608	2842
Lettonie	2004	4689	2733	636	6786	2934
	2005	4905	2855	707	7053	3066
	2006	4891	2810	302	7399	3234
Lithuania	2003	19488	4144	11674	11958	3462
Lituanie	2004	19274	4293	11488	12079	3516
	2005	14784	5641	8607	11818	3461
	2006	12482	5812	6240	12054	3551

Table 35

Production, trade and consumption of electricity
Production, commerce et consommation d'électricité

Million kilowatt-hours and kilowatt-hours per capita
Millions de kilowatt-heures et kilowatt-heures par habitant

Country or area Pays ou zone	Year Année	Production Production	Imports Importations	Exports Exportations	Consumption Consommation	
					Total Totale	Per Capita Par habitant
Luxembourg	2003	3620	6481	2777	7324	16217
Luxembourg	2004	4121	6506	3132	7495	16361
	2005	4135	6392	3131	7396	15900
	2006	4333	6824	3267	7890	16694
Malta	2003	2236	..	..	2236	5592
Malte	2004	2216	..	..	2216	5503
	2005	2240	..	..	2240	5531
	2006	2296	..	..	2296	5649
Netherlands	2003	96763	20801	3809	113755	7025
Pays-Bas	2004	100770	21405	5188	116987	7196
	2005	100219	23691	5398	118512	7262
	2006	96733	27346	5887	118192	7235
Norway,Svlbd.J.Myn. I	2003	107405	13422	5548	115279	25171
Norvège,Svalbd,J.May	2004	110598	15254	3828	122024	26477
	2005	138108	3652	15695	126065	27155
	2006	121663	9802	8947	122518	26289
Poland	2003	151631	4985	15146	141470	3704
Pologne	2004	154159	5312	14605	144866	3794
	2005	156936	5002	16188	145750	3819
	2006	161742	4789	15775	150756	3954
Portugal	2003	46852	5898	3104	49646	4755
Portugal	2004	45105	8612	2131	51586	4912
	2005	46575	9626	2802	53399	5062
	2006	49041	8624	3183	54482	5147
Republic of Moldova	2003	3453	3583	131	6905	1911
Rép. de Moldova	2004	3613	3361	424	6550	1817
	2005	3864	3361	220	7005	1948
	2006	3829	3741	229	7341	2048
Romania	2003	55140	962	3046	53056	2441
Roumanie	2004	56499	2584	3766	55317	2552
	2005	59413	2321	5224	56510	2613
	2006	62697	989	5262	58424	2707
Russian Federation	2003	916286	8240	21619	902907	6246
Fédération de Russie	2004	931865	12179	19800	924244	6426
	2005	953074	10139	22520	940693	6573
	2006	995785	5115	20927	979973	6878
Serbia	2003	35366	4576	1786	38156	3605
Serbie	2004	37686	5975	6248	37413	3557
	2005	36474	6751	8694	34531	3298
	2006	36481	8567	9377	35671	3413
Slovakia	2003	31178	8623	10878	28923	5377
Slovaquie	2004	30567	8731	10593	28705	5333
	2005	31455	8005	11270	28190	5233
	2006	31418	8590	10921	29087	5395
Slovenia	2003	14019	5975	5811	14183	7109
Slovénie	2004	15271	6314	7094	14491	7258
	2005	15117	7234	7558	14793	7392
	2006	15115	7071	7020	15166	7551
Spain	2003	260727	9520	8257	261990	6237
Espagne	2004	280007	8111	11139	276979	6488
	2005	294077	10212	11555	292734	6745
	2006	303051	8832	12106	299777	6803

Table 35

Production, trade and consumption of electricity
Production, commerce et consommation d'électricité

Million kilowatt-hours and kilowatt-hours per capita
Millions de kilowatt-heures et kilowatt-heures par habitant

Country or area Pays ou zone	Year Année	Production Production	Imports Importations	Exports Exportations	Consumption Consommation	
					Total Totale	Per Capita Par habitant
Sweden	2003	135435	24287	11457	148265	16551
Suède	2004	151726	15646	17750	149622	16637
	2005	158434	14576	21968	151042	16727
	2006	143299	17537	11497	149339	16446
Switzerland	2003	67166	30084	33196	64054	8726
Suisse	2004	65299	27056	27759	64596	8669
	2005	59612	38346	31996	65962	8843
	2006	64038	33803	31100	66741	8918
T.F.Yug.Rep. Macedonia	2003	6737	953	..	7690	3794
L'ex-RY Macédoine	2004	6665	1176	..	7841	3863
	2005	6942	1599	..	8541	4193
	2006	7006	1795	..	8801	4314
Ukraine	2003	180354	7236	12175	175415	3669
Ukraine	2004	182157	2203	7529	176831	3741
	2005	186055	1715	10068	177702	3775
	2006	193381	2082	12519	182944	3913
United Kingdom	2003	398671	5119	2959	400831	6756
Royaume-Uni	2004	395853	9784	2294	403343	6756
	2005	400524	11160	2839	408845	6790
	2006	398327	10282	2765	405844	6699
Oceania	**2003**	**278260**	**0**	**..**	**278260**	**8586**
Océanie	**2004**	**286705**	**0**	**..**	**286705**	**8720**
	2005	**297669**	**0**	**..**	**297669**	**8923**
	2006	**304345**	**1**	**..**	**304346**	**8985**
American Samoa	2003	188	..	..	188	3003
Samoa américaines	2004	188	..	..	188	2933
	2005	189	..	..	189	2885
	2006	*193	..	..	*193	*2885
Australia	2003	228118	..	..	228118	11462
Australie	2004	234542	..	..	234542	11646
	2005	245495	..	..	245495	12029
	2006	251659	..	..	251659	12157
Cook Islands	2003	29	..	..	29	1582
Iles Cook	2004	30	..	..	30	1468
	2005	30	..	..	30	1480
	2006	32	..	..	32	1512
Fiji	2003	*812	0	..	*812	*980
Fidji	2004	*816	0	..	*816	*977
	2005	*823	0	..	*823	*977
	2006	*840	1	..	*841	*985
French Polynesia	2003	602	..	..	602	2434
Polynésie française	2004	643	..	..	643	2562
	2005	631	..	..	631	2478
	2006	667	..	..	667	2603
Guam	2003	1777	..	..	1777	10904
Guam	2004	1878	..	..	1878	11306
	2005	1897	..	..	1897	11255
	2006	1891	..	..	1891	11058
Kiribati	2003	*14	..	..	*14	*145
Kiribati	2004	*14	..	..	*14	*139
	2005	*15	..	..	*15	*141
	2006	*15	..	..	*15	*142

Table 35

Production, trade and consumption of electricity
Production, commerce et consommation d'électricité
Million kilowatt-hours and kilowatt-hours per capita
Millions de kilowatt-heures et kilowatt-heures par habitant

Country or area Pays ou zone	Year Année	Production Production	Imports Importations	Exports Exportations	Consumption Consommation	
					Total Totale	Per Capita Par habitant
Marshall Islands	2003	96	..		96	1753
Îles Marshall	2004	101	..	..	101	1754
	2005	101	..	..	101	1703
	2006	*104	..	..	*104	*1719
Nauru	2003	*31	..		*31	*2466
Nauru	2004	*32	..	..	*32	*2490
	2005	*33	..	..	*33	*2498
	2006	*33	..	..	*33	*2511
New Caledonia	2003	1758	..		1758	7711
Nouvelle-Calédonie	2004	1678	..	..	1678	7271
	2005	1883	..	..	1883	8047
	2006	1926	..	..	1926	8092
New Zealand	2003	41249	..		41249	10289
Nouvelle-Zélande	2004	42901	..	..	42901	10563
	2005	43136	..	..	43136	10524
	2006	43519	..	..	43519	10504
Niue	2003	*3	..		*3	*1696
Nioué	2004	*3	..	..	*3	*1704
	2005	*3	..	..	*3	*1780
	2006	*3	..	..	*3	*1846
Palau	2003	128	..		128	6304
Palaos	2004	*128	..	..	*128	*6211
	2005	*134	..	..	*134	*6410
	2006	*151	..	..	*151	*6968
Papua New Guinea	2003	3178	..		3178	548
Papouasie-Nvl-Guinée	2004	3468	..	..	3468	584
	2005	3002	..	..	3002	495
	2006	3012	..	..	3012	486
Samoa	2003	*106	..		*106	*589
Samoa	2004	*110	..	..	*110	*606
	2005	*111	..	..	*111	*606
	2006	*112	..	..	*112	*606
Solomon Islands	2003	*63	..		*63	*141
Iles Salomon	2004	63	..	..	63	137
	2005	74	..	..	74	157
	2006	75	..	..	75	155
Tonga	2003	45	..		45	446
Tonga	2004	47	..	..	47	461
	2005	*48	..	..	*48	*469
	2006	*48	..	..	*48	*475
Vanuatu	2003	*44	..		*44	*208
Vanuatu	2004	*44	..	..	*44	*206
	2005	*45	..	..	*45	*209
	2006	*45	..	..	*45	*204
Wallis and Futuna Is	2003	19	..		19	1244
Iles Wallis et Futuna	2004	19	..	..	19	1252
	2005	20	..	..	20	1269
	2006	20	..	..	20	1218

Table 36

Production of Heat – by type
Production de chaleur – par catégorie
Terajoules
Térajoules

Table Notes:

Heat from geothermal sources includes heat from non-specified sources

Heat from thermal power plants includes heat from nuclear and thermal CHP (combined heat and power) plants.

- **Please refer to the Definitions Section on pages xv to xxix for the appropriate product description /classification.**

Notes relatives aux tableaux:

La chaleur des sources géothermiques inclut la chaleur des sources non-indiquées

La chaleur des centrales thermiques inclut la chaleur des centrales de cogénération chaleur/électricité nucléaires et thermiques.

- **Veuillez consulter la section "définitions" de la page xv à la page xxix pour une description/classification appropriée des produits.**

Figure 94: World heat production, 1993-2006

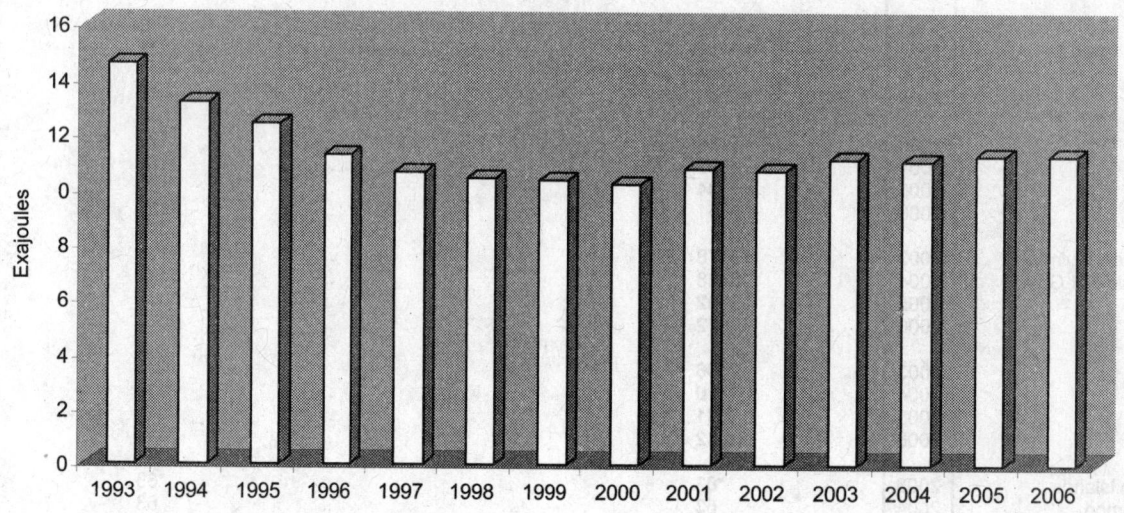

Figure 95: Major heat producing countries in 2006

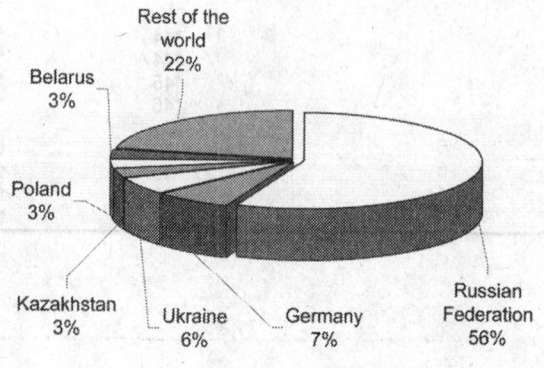

Figure 96: World heat production by type, in 2006

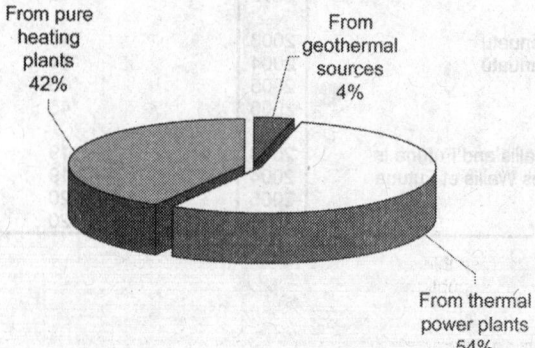

Table 36

Production of heat - by type
Production de chaleur - par catégorie
Terajoules
Térajoules

Country or area Pays ou zone	Year Année	From geothermal sources De sources géothermiques	From thermal power plants Des centrales thermiques	From pure heating plants Des centrales de chaleur	Total production Production totale
World	**2003**	**29994**	**6330167**	**4763242**	**11123403**
Monde	**2004**	**34630**	**6301310**	**4728684**	**11064624**
	2005	**406651**	**6162216**	**4650685**	**11219552**
	2006	**418080**	**6168445**	**4681416**	**11267941**
Africa	**2003**	..	**6000**	**3000**	**9000**
Afrique	**2004**	..	**5500**	**4000**	**9500**
	2005	..	**5480**	**4140**	**9620**
	2006	..	**5500**	**4150**	**9650**
South Africa Customs Un.	2003	..	*6000	*3000	*9000
Un.douan.d'Afr.mérid	2004	..	*5500	*4000	*9500
	2005	..	5480	4140	9620
	2006	..	*5500	*4150	*9650
America, North	**2003**	**4**	**406119**	..	**406123**
Amérique du Nord	**2004**	**1**	**277204**	..	**277205**
	2005	**0**	**284325**	..	**284325**
	2006	**0**	**248633**	..	**248633**
Canada	2003	..	39354	..	39354
Canada	2004	..	41102	..	41102
	2005	..	34552	..	34552
	2006	..	34852	..	34852
United States	2003	4	366765	..	366769
Etats-Unis	2004	1	236102	..	236103
	2005	0	249773	..	249773
	2006	0	213781	..	213781
Asia	**2003**	**8120**	**602992**	**84261**	**695373**
Asie	**2004**	**8248**	**655675**	**89970**	**753893**
	2005	**8784**	**688237**	**96526**	**793547**
	2006	**8617**	**701982**	**95715**	**806314**
Armenia	2003	..	1220	221	1441
Arménie	2004	..	1039	188	1227
	2005	..	1605	233	1838
	2006	..	1759	247	2006
Azerbaijan	2003	..	23509	..	23509
Azerbaïdjan	2004	..	23312	..	23312
	2005	..	23279	..	23279
	2006	..	23660	..	23660
Georgia	2003	..	3390	..	3390
Géorgie	2004	..	3641	..	3641
	2005	..	2506	..	2506
	2006	..	1371	..	1371
Japan	2003	3806	..	19841	23647
Japon	2004	3990	..	21636	25626
	2005	4046	..	21938	25984
	2006	3686	..	21320	25006
Kazakhstan	2003	..	358086	..	358086
Kazakhstan	2004	..	366675	..	366675
	2005	..	382264	..	382264
	2006	..	395386	..	395386
Korea, Republic of	2003	0	130118	11093	141211
Corée, République de	2004	0	170167	15142	185309
	2005	502	170544	21453	192499
	2006	731	166875	21348	188954

Table 36

Production of heat - by type
Production de chaleur - par catégorie

Terajoules
Térajoules

Country or area Pays ou zone	Year Année	From geothermal sources De sources géothermiques	From thermal power plants Des centrales thermiques	From pure heating plants Des centrales de chaleur	Total production Production totale
Kyrgyzstan	2003	..	7100	..	7100
Kirghizistan	2004	..	7375	..	7375
	2005	..	7347	..	7347
	2006	..	7441	..	7441
Mongolia	2003	..	30	..	30
Mongolie	2004	..	33	..	33
	2005	..	33	..	33
	2006	..	33	..	33
Occup. Palestinian Terr.	2003	4314	..	..	4314
Terr. palestiniens occup.	2004	4258	..	..	4258
	2005	4236	..	..	4236
	2006	*4200	..	..	*4200
Tajikistan	2003	..	3667	..	3667
Tadjikistan	2004	..	3663	..	3663
	2005	..	3795	..	3795
	2006	..	3759	..	3759
Turkey	2003	..	15367	..	15367
Turquie	2004	..	18831	..	18831
	2005	..	35597	..	35597
	2006	..	40137	..	40137
Turkmenistan	2003	..	5213	..	5213
Turkménistan	2004	..	5754	..	5754
	2005	..	6189	..	6189
	2006	..	6590	..	6590
Uzbekistan	2003	..	55292	53106	108398
Ouzbékistan	2004	..	55185	53004	108189
	2005	..	55078	52902	107980
	2006	..	54971	52800	107771
Europe	**2003**	**21870**	**5315056**	**4675981**	**10012907**
Europe	**2004**	**25377**	**5362931**	**4634714**	**10023022**
	2005	**397354**	**5184174**	**4550019**	**10131547**
	2006	**408947**	**5212330**	**4581551**	**10202828**
Albania	2003	84	219	50	353
Albanie	2004	80	126	50	256
	2005	84	92	50	226
	2006	84	92	50	226
Austria	2003	520	35827	20034	56381
Autriche	2004	523	37043	18476	56042
	2005	619	38251	18653	57523
	2006	790	44316	20809	65915
Belarus	2003	..	155443	135819	291262
Bélarus	2004	..	132225	157010	289235
	2005	..	135386	153520	288906
	2006	..	137895	153456	291351
Belgium	2003	0	22801	216	23017
Belgique	2004	0	23260	112	23372
	2005	2902	19172	241	22315
	2006	2791	31279	204	34274
Bosnia and Herzegovina	2003	..	0	2196	2196
Bosnie y Herzégovine	2004	..	497	2153	2650
	2005	..	1513	2120	3633
	2006	..	1600	2231	3831

Table 36

Production of heat - by type
Production de chaleur - par catégorie
Terajoules
Térajoules

Country or area Pays ou zone	Year Année	From geothermal sources De sources géothermiques	From thermal power plants Des centrales thermiques	From pure heating plants Des centrales de chaleur	Total production Production totale
Bulgaria	2003	..	41867	12036	53903
Bulgarie	2004	..	39916	10831	50747
	2005	..	39024	13087	52111
	2006	..	38560	11897	50457
Croatia	2003	..	9653	3470	13123
Croatie	2004	..	9561	3281	12842
	2005	..	9847	3478	13325
	2006	..	8888	2984	11872
Czech Republic	2003	0	112122	35159	147281
République tchèque	2004	10	111075	33322	144407
	2005	40	107057	32159	139256
	2006	494	100643	30163	131300
Denmark	2003	133	105700	24550	130383
Danemark	2004	132	105761	23948	129841
	2005	119	107080	22323	129522
	2006	313	105884	23166	129363
Estonia	2003	1	10322	15279	25602
Estonie	2004	0	9844	17123	26967
	2005	0	9522	17255	26777
	2006	0	9277	17712	26989
Finland	2003	84	132465	37835	170384
Finlande	2004	3129	128178	38689	169996
	2005	3117	121170	38800	163087
	2006	2402	152197	44869	199468
France incl. Monaco	2003	..	161997	6832	168829
France y compris Monaco	2004	..	166456	6256	172712
	2005	..	169144	5714	174858
	2006	..	159723	5678	165401
Germany	2003	410	632093	81155	713658
Allemagne	2004	411	647983	80237	728631
	2005	450	648132	166173	814755
	2006	577	646469	161728	808774
Greece	2003	..	1930	..	1930
Grèce	2004	..	1817	..	1817
	2005	..	2049	..	2049
	2006	..	2349	..	2349
Hungary	2003	257	44030	19688	63975
Hongrie	2004	229	40841	21452	62522
	2005	235	41679	21683	63597
	2006	169	41017	20247	61433
Iceland	2003	9631	..	76	9707
Islande	2004	9907	..	56	9963
	2005	9237	..	56	9293
	2006	10177	..	56	10233
Italy and San Marino	2003	..	0	..	0
Italie y comp. St. Marin	2004	..	189576	..	189576
	2005	..	193064	..	193064
	2006	..	208899	..	208899
Latvia	2003	..	15124	18392	33516
Lettonie	2004	..	14817	16276	31093
	2005	..	14677	16467	31144
	2006	..	16657	13399	30056

Table 36

Production of heat - by type
Production de chaleur - par catégorie

Terajoules
Térajoules

Country or area Pays ou zone	Year Année	From geothermal sources De sources géothermiques	From thermal power plants Des centrales thermiques	From pure heating plants Des centrales de chaleur	Total production Production totale
Lithuania	2003	7573	22654	21140	51367
Lituanie	2004	6703	24986	17863	49552
	2005	7099	25074	17727	49900
	2006	7341	26912	18025	52278
Luxembourg	2003	..	1948	..	1948
Luxembourg	2004	..	2151	..	2151
	2005	..	2544	..	2544
	2006	..	2689	..	2689
Netherlands	2003	..	109600	4707	114307
Pays-Bas	2004	..	120813	5107	125920
	2005	..	155106	15757	170863
	2006	..	127288	14295	141583
Norway,Svlbd.J.Myn. I	2003	1189	3529	6986	11704
Norvège,Svalbd,J.May	2004	2794	3820	5662	12276
	2005	3311	3636	5931	12878
	2006	2785	3864	6799	13448
Poland	2003	..	225409	142806	368215
Pologne	2004	..	219274	126614	345888
	2005	..	219975	120741	340716
	2006	..	220861	120345	341206
Portugal	2003	..	9448	..	9448
Portugal	2004	..	10789	..	10789
	2005	..	13712	..	13712
	2006	..	13840	..	13840
Republic of Moldova	2003	..	5122	1723	6845
Rép. de Moldova	2004	..	7401	5689	13090
	2005	..	7769	5937	13706
	2006	..	8891	5987	14878
Romania	2003	8	110658	39370	150036
Roumanie	2004	29	99686	35710	135425
	2005	32	100098	27544	127674
	2006	184	99646	23606	123436
Russian Federation	2003	0	3114065	3191714	6305779
Fédération de Russie	2004	0	2963940	3176342	6140282
	2005	368804	2650959	3114120	6133883
	2006	379730	2691490	3203226	6274446
Serbia	2003	..	0	21284	21284
Serbie	2004	..	0	26306	26306
	2005	..	10761	38038	48799
	2006	..	8569	36430	44999
Slovakia	2003	140	30247	25167	55554
Slovaquie	2004	145	27856	25859	53860
	2005	143	26151	26251	52545
	2006	168	24057	22552	46777
Slovenia	2003	..	6560	3005	9565
Slovénie	2004	..	6753	2965	9718
	2005	..	7104	2980	10084
	2006	..	6992	2623	9615
Sweden	2003	1840	103394	72413	177647
Suède	2004	1285	111809	64490	177584
	2005	1162	111424	68480	181066
	2006	942	110464	69884	181290

Table 36

Production of heat - by type
Production de chaleur - par catégorie
Terajoules
Térajoules

Country or area Pays ou zone	Year Année	From geothermal sources De sources géothermiques	From thermal power plants Des centrales thermiques	From pure heating plants Des centrales de chaleur	Total production Production totale
Switzerland	2003	..	11367	4673	16040
Suisse	2004	..	11559	5181	16740
	2005	..	11956	5344	17300
	2006	..	13017	4493	17510
T.F.Yug.Rep. Macedonia	2003	..	844	5816	6660
L'ex-RY Macédoine	2004	..	670	5188	5858
	2005	..	552	5530	6082
	2006	..	450	5256	5706
Ukraine	2003	..	78618	642565	721183
Ukraine	2004	..	92448	610231	702679
	2005	..	180494	527151	707645
	2006	..	147555	482994	630549
United Kingdom	2003	..	..	79825	79825
Royaume-Uni	2004	..	..	92235	92235
	2005	..	..	56709	56709
	2006	..	..	56387	56387
Oceania	**2003**	**0**	..	..	**0**
Océanie	**2004**	**1004**	..	..	**1004**
	2005	**513**	..	..	**513**
	2006	**516**	..	..	**516**
New Zealand	2003	0	..	..	0
Nouvelle-Zélande	2004	1004	..	..	1004
	2005	513	..	..	513
	2006	516	..	..	516

Table 37

Production of uranium (uranium content)
Production d'uranium (contenu en uranium)

Metric tons
Tonnes métriques

Country or area Pays ou zone	2003	2004	2005	2006
World **Monde**	**35519**	**40381**	**41962**	**39634**
Africa **Afrique**	**5943**	**6970**	**7141**	**7044**
Niger Niger	3143	3185	3322	3443
South Africa Customs Un. Un.douan.d'Afr.mérid	*2800	3785	3819	3601
America, North **Amérique du Nord**	**11224**	**12540**	**12799**	**11667**
Canada Canada	10455	11597	11628	9862
United States Etats-Unis	769	943	1171	1805
America, South **Amérique du Sud**	**271**	**353**	**129**	**231**
Argentina Argentine	0	1	0	0
Brazil Brésil	271	352	129	231
Asia **Asie**	**5930**	**6804**	**7666**	**8566**
China Chine	*730	*730	*750	*750
India Inde	*230	*230	*230	*230
Iran(Islamic Rep. of) Iran(Rép. islamique)	0	0	0	*5
Kazakhstan Kazakhstan	3327	3719	4346	5281
Pakistan Pakistan	*40	*38	*40	*40
Uzbekistan Ouzbékistan	1603	2087	*2300	*2260
Europe **Europe**	**4578**	**4732**	**4715**	**4533**
Czech Republic République tchèque	452	412	409	375
France incl. Monaco France y compris Monaco	9	*6	*4	*3
Germany Allemagne	150	77	94	65
Hungary Hongrie	4	2	3	2
Romania Roumanie	*90	90	*90	*90

Table 37

Production of uranium (uranium content)
Production d'uranium (contenu en uranium)

Metric tons
Tonnes métriques

Country or area Pays ou zone	2003	2004	2005	2006
Russian Federation Fédération de Russie	3073	3290	3285	3190
Ukraine Ukraine	*800	855	830	808
Oceania **Océanie**	**7573**	**8982**	**9512**	**7593**
Australia Australie	7573	8982	9512	7593

Table 38

Selected energy resources and reserves
Million metric tons unless otherwise indicated

Country or area Pays ou zone	Bituminous coal / Anthracite Houille bitumineux / Anthracite			Sub-bituminous coal / Lignite Charbon sous bitumineux / Lignite			Peat Tourbe	
	Proved amount in place Quantités avérées en place	Proved recoverable reserves Réserves récupérables avérées	Estimated additional amount in place Quantités additionnelles estimées en place	Proved amount in place Quantités avérées en place	Proved recoverable reserves Réserves récupérables avérées	Estimated additional amount in place Quantités additionnelles estimées en place	Proved amount in place Quantités avérées en place	Proved recoverable reserves Réserves récupérable avérées
Afghanistan	112	66	400	..	..	..	..	
Albania	..	..	..	794	794	..	..	15
Algeria	64	59	164	..	..	..	..	
Angola	..	..	..				..	
Argentina	4	..	..	8047	424	273	90	*6
Armenia								
Australia	90400	37100	125000	48000	39500	215000	..	
Austria	1	0	3	333	25	61	..	
Azerbaijan	..	..		..			..	
Bahrain	..	..						
Bangladesh	1054	..	..	..	..	..	*138	
Barbados	..	..		..				
Belarus	..	..		..			323	32
Belgium	715	410	1400	..	..	..	..	
Belize	..			..			..	
Benin	..			..			..	
Bhutan	..			..			..	
Bolivia	..	1		..			..	
Bosnia and Herzegovina	..			..			..	
Brazil	..	..	..	17017	7068	15319	0	
Brunei Darussalam	..						..	
Bulgaria	428	5	1200	3988	1991	2618	5	
Burkina Faso	..			..			..	
Burundi	..	..	..	..	..	..	56	5
Cambodia	..			..			..	
Cameroon	..			..			..	
Canada	8625	3471	26045	14355	3107	31990	1092	
Central African Rep.	..	..	..	4	3		..	
Chad	..			..				
Chile	79	31	125	4579	1150	5000	..	
China	114500	62200	363200	108800	52300	304700	4687	32
Colombia	7064	6578	13173	411	381	3176	..	
Congo	..			..				
Costa Rica	..	..		27	..	22	48	
Côte d'Ivoire	..			..			..	
Croatia	4	4	..	41	33	..	..	
Cuba	..	..		..	..		..	
Cyprus	..			..			..	
Czech Republic	5880	1673	..	2928	2828	..	..	
Dem. Rep. of Congo	720	88		..	..		..	
Denmark	..	..		63	..	0	..	
Dominica	..			..			..	
Dominican Republic	..	..		..	..		..	
Ecuador	..	..		30	24	6	..	
Egypt	25	21		27	22	52	..	
El Salvador	..			..			..	
Equatorial Guinea	..			..			..	
Estonia	..			..			2000	200
Ethiopia	..	..	..	23	11	..	..	
Faeroe Islands	..			..			..	
Falkland Is. (Malvinas)	..			..			..	
Fiji	..			..			..	
Finland	..			..			850	42
France incl. Monaco	593	95	200	124	21	165	..	
French Polynesia	..	..		..			..	
Gabon	..			..			..	
Georgia	..			..			..	
Germany	319	152	8065	7136	6556	34100	157	9
Ghana	..	..		..				
Greece	..	..		5312	3900	0	4000	

Table 38

Ressources et réserves énergétiques choisies
Million de tonnes métriques sauf ou indiqué

Peat Tourbe — Estimated additional amount in place / Quantités additionnelles estimées en place	Proved recoverable reserves / Réserves récupérables avérées — Natural gas (billions cubic metres) / Gaz naturel (billions de mètres cubes)	Crude oil and NGL / Pétrole brut et LGN	Oil shale / Schiste bitumineux	Bituminous sands / Sables bitumineux	Uranium (metric tons) / Uranium (tonnes métriques) — Reasonably assured resources / Ressources raisonnablement assurées	Estimated additional resources / Ressources additionnelles estimées	Hydropower (Gross theoretical capability) Energie hydraulique (Capacité brute théorique) (GWH/Year Année)	Country or area Pays ou zone
..	50	..	..	..	..	..	0	Afghanistan
..	2	30	..	6	..	..	40000	Albanie
..	4504	2731	..	..	19500	..	12000	Algérie
..	113	1221	..	74	..	..	150000	Angola
50	439	300	57	..	7100	8600	354000	Argentine
..	176	..	44	..	..	..	22000	Arménie
..	755	225	4531	..	747000	396000	265000	Australie
..	15	8	1	..	0	1700	150000	Autriche
..	1350	950	..	20	..	..	44000	Azerbaïdjan
..	92	16	..	..	..	..	..	Bahreïn
*138	436	3	..	..	..	..	4000	Bangladesh
..	0	1	..	..	..	..	..	Barbade
1479	3	27	1000	..	..	..	8000	Bélarus
..	0	..	..	..	..	..	1000	Belgique
..	..	..	..	..	..	..	1000	Belize
..	1	1	..	..	..	..	2000	Bénin
..	..	..	..	..	..	..	263000	Bhoutan
..	740	57	..	..	..	..	178000	Bolivie
..	..	..	..	..	..	..	70000	Bosnie y Herzégovine
487	306	1591	11734	..	157700	121000	3040000	Brésil
..	340	150	..	..	..	..	..	Brunéi Darussalam
..	1	2	18	..	5900	6300	27000	Bulgarie
..	..	..	..	..	..	..	1000	Burkina Faso
0	..	..	..	..	..	..	6000	Burundi
..	..	..	..	..	..	..	88000	Cambodge
..	150	168	..	..	..	..	294000	Cameroun
336908	1633	2106	2192	27603	345200	98600	2216000	Canada
..	..	..	..	..	12000	..	7000	Rép. centrafricaine
..	..	222	..	..	..	..	150	Tchad
..	98	16	3	..	600	900	227000	Chili
952	2350	2212	2290	119	38000	21700	6083000	Chine
..	140	197	..	5	..	..	1000000	Colombie
..	91	269	..	1	..	..	50000	Congo
22	..	..	..	..	..	..	223000	Costa Rica
..	42	64	..	..	..	..	46000	Côte d'Ivoire
..	27	9	..	..	..	..	20000	Croatie
280	71	116	..	8	..	..	3000	Cuba
..	..	..	..	..	..	..	59000	Chypre
..	4	9	..	..	500	100	13000	République tchèque
..	1	26	14310	5	1400	1300	1397000	Rép. dem. du Congo
..	82	170	..	..	20250	12000	120	Danemark
..	..	..	..	..	..	..	200	Dominique
..	..	..	..	..	..	..	50000	Rép. dominicaine
..	10	719	..	7	..	..	167000	Equateur
..	1894	495	816	8	..	..	125000	Egypte
..	..	..	..	..	..	..	7000	El Salvador
..	73	245	..	..	..	..	..	Guinée équatoriale
..	..	..	2494	..	..	..	2000	Estonie
..	25	*1	..	..	..	..	650000	Ethiopie
..	..	..	..	..	..	..	1000	Iles Féroé
28	..	..	..	..	..	..	..	Iles Falkland (Malvinas)
..	..	..	..	..	..	..	3000	Fidji
2200	..	..	..	..	1100	2900	48000	Finlande
..	10	17	1002	..	15700	11700	270000	France y compris Monaco
..	..	..	..	..	..	..	1000	Polynésie française
..	30	294	..	..	4830	1000	190000	Gabon
..	8	5	..	0	..	..	180000	Géorgie
200	178	28	286	..	3000	4000	120000	Allemagne
..	24	2	..	..	..	..	26000	Ghana
..	1	1	..	..	1000	6000	80000	Grèce

Table 38

Selected energy resources and reserves
Million metric tons unless otherwise indicated

Country or area / Pays ou zone	Bituminous coal / Anthracite Houille bitumineux / Anthracite			Sub-bituminous coal / Lignite Charbon sous bitumineux / Lignite			Peat Tourbe	
	Proved amount in place / Quantités avérées en place	Proved recoverable reserves / Réserves récupérables avérées	Estimated additional amount in place / Quantités additionnelles estimées en place	Proved amount in place / Quantités avérées en place	Proved recoverable reserves / Réserves récupérables avérées	Estimated additional amount in place / Quantités additionnelles estimées en place	Proved amount in place / Quantités avérées en place	Proved recoverable reserves / Réserves récupérables avérées
Greenland	..	..	..	183	183	200	..	..
Grenada	..	..	..	..	..	..	..	..
Guatemala	..	..	..	..	..	..	..	..
Guinea	..	..	..	..	..	..	..	..
Guinea-Bissau	..	..	..	..	..	..	..	..
Guyana								
Haiti	..	..	..	13	..	27	..	..
Honduras	..	..	..	21	..	..	..	..
Hungary	1597	199	298	9006	3103	2630	..	..
Iceland								
India	95866	52240	157435	4258	4258	32893	..	..
Indonesia	3448	1721	6035	9018	2607	38704	49000	0
Iran(Islamic Rep. of)	11143	1386	..	2295	..	..	..	..
Iraq								
Ireland	19	14	26	12	9	29	154	106
Israel	..	..	..	..	..	..	500	386
Italy and San Marino	..	..	..	10	10	600	..	..
Jamaica	..	..	..	..	..	..	200	32
Japan	4768	355	6298	175	17	7122	..	..
Jordan								
Kazakhstan	..	28170	..	..	3130	..	..	..
Kenya								
Korea, Dem.Ppl's.Rep.	2000	300	2700	300	300	2200	..	..
Korea, Republic of	138	82	272	222	135	812	..	..
Kuwait								
Kyrgyzstan	..	..	..	..	812	..	..	..
Lao People's Dem. Rep.								
Latvia	..	..	..	..	..	..	190	94
Lebanon								
Liberia								
Libyan Arab Jamah.								
Lithuania	..	..	..	..	..	..	937	269
Madagascar	1000	..	..	75	..	..	..	..
Malawi	15	2	..	..	2	..	..	..
Malaysia	15	4	78	126	..	575	..	..
Mali	..	..	..	..	..	3	..	..
Mauritius								
Mexico	1211	860	1960	732	351	213	..	..
Mongolia	12000	..	..	12000	..	..	..	..
Morocco	16	5	..	42	..	2	..	..
Mozambique	..	212	155	..	..	..	..	..
Myanmar	5	2	120	..	..	80	..	..
Nepal	..	..	..	1	1	7	..	..
Netherlands	1406	497	2750	..	..	..	120	120
New Caledonia	4	2	8	..	..	..	..	..
New Zealand	45	33	942	2673	538	11902	1640	0
Nicaragua								
Niger	..	70	..	..	..	..	..	..
Nigeria	..	21	21	338	169	1000	..	..
Norway,Svlbd.J.Myn. l	54	1	..	64	5	100	745	350
Oman								
Pakistan	1	1	5	3303	1981	68068	..	..
Panama								
Papua New Guinea								
Paraguay								
Peru	..	140	0	..	100	..	..	..
Philippines	50	41	8	394	275	37	..	..
Poland	15291	6012	27405	1878	1490	11837	890	0
Portugal	8	3	0	38	33	0	..	..
Qatar								

Table 38

Ressources et réserves énergétiques choisies
Million de tonnes métriques sauf ou indiqué

Peat Tourbe — Estimated additional amount in place / Quantités additionnelles estimées en place	Proved recoverable reserves / Réserves récupérables avérées				Uranium (metric tons) / Uranium (tonnes métriques)		Hydropower (Gross theoretical capability) Energie hydraulique (Capacité brute théorique) (GWH/Year Année)	Country or area Pays ou zone
	Natural gas (billions cubic metres) / Gaz naturel (billions de mètres cubes)	Crude oil and NGL / Pétrole brut et LGN	Oil shale / Schiste bitumineux	Bituminous sands / Sables bitumineux	Reasonably assured resources / Ressources raisonnablement assurées	Estimated additional resources / Ressources additionnelles estimées		
..	..	..	..	..	20300	12000	800000	Groënland
							38	Grenade
..	3	80	..	..	..	..	54000	Guatemala
..	..	..	..	..	..	..	26000	Guinée
..	..	..	..	..	..	..	1000	Guinée-Bissau
..	..	..	..	..	..	..	64000	Guyana
..	..	..	..	..	..	..	4000	Haïti
..	..	..	..	..	..	..	16000	Honduras
238	67	20	8	..	..	13800	10000	Hongrie
..	..	..	..	..	..	..	184000	Islande
..	1101	786	..	..	42600	22300	2638000	Inde
0	2754	570	..	67	4600	1200	2147000	Indonésie
..	26740	17340	..	..	400	1100	176000	Iran(Rép. islamique)
..	3170	15478	..	..	..	..	225000	Iraq
140	10	..	..	..	..	..	1000	Irlande
1000	34	1	550	0	..	..	0	Israël
2500	170	106	10446	48	4800	1300	340000	Italie y comp. St. Marin
0	..	..	..	..	..	..	1000	Jamaïque
..	51	9	..	..	6600	..	718000	Japon
..	15	0	5242	5	30400	48600	4000	Jordanie
..	3000	3000	400	6679	513900	302200	170000	Kazakhstan
..	..	..	..	..	..	..	24000	Kenya
..	..	..	..	..	..	..	..	Corée,Rép.pop.dém.de
..	..	*1	..	..	11800	3000	52000	Corée, République de
..	1586	13679	..	..	..	..	..	Koweït
..	6	5	..	..	..	..	163000	Kirghizistan
..	..	..	..	..	..	..	232000	Rép. dém. pop. lao
760	..	..	..	..	..	..	7000	Lettonie
..	..	..	..	..	..	..	2000	Liban
..	..	..	..	..	..	..	28000	Libéria
..	1491	5350	..	..	..	..	..	Jamah. arabe libyenne
..	..	64	..	..	..	..	5000	Lituanie
..	1	..	5	35	..	..	321000	Madagascar
..	..	..	..	..	8800	..	15000	Malawi
..	2480	365	..	..	..	..	230000	Malaisie
..	..	..	..	..	..	..	12000	Mali
..	..	..	..	..	..	..	150	Maurice
..	412	1847	..	0	1300	525	135000	Mexique
..	..	..	*42	..	46200	15700	56000	Mongolie
..	2	0	8167	..	..	..	12000	Maroc
..	127	..	..	..	..	..	95000	Mozambique
..	485	7	286	..	..	..	342000	Myanmar
..	..	..	..	..	..	..	733000	Népal
..	1256	11	..	..	..	..	1000	Pays-Bas
..	..	..	..	..	..	..	2000	Nouvelle-Calédonie
0	30	7	3	..	..	..	46000	Nouvelle-Zélande
..	..	..	..	..	..	..	33000	Nicaragua
..	..	..	..	..	180500	45000	3000	Niger
..	5150	4823	..	91	..	..	43000	Nigéria
7015	2358	1202	..	..	..	..	560000	Norvège,Svalbd,J.May
..	829	746	..	..	..	..	..	Oman
..	807	40	..	..	..	..	480000	Pakistan
..	..	..	..	..	..	..	26000	Panama
..	428	31	..	..	..	..	175000	Papouasie-Nvl-Guinée
200	..	..	..	..	..	..	130000	Paraguay
..	338	117	..	1	1200	1300	1577000	Pérou
..	100	5	..	..	..	..	47000	Philippines
2300	75	16	7	..	..	..	23000	Pologne
..	..	..	..	..	7000	1450	32000	Portugal
..	25633	1852	..	..	..	..	..	Qatar

Table 38

Selected energy resources and reserves
Million metric tons unless otherwise indicated

Country or area Pays ou zone	Bituminous coal / Anthracite Houille bitumineux / Anthracite			Sub-bituminous coal / Lignite Charbon sous bitumineux / Lignite			Peat Tourbe	
	Proved amount in place Quantités avérées en place	Proved recoverable reserves Réserves récupérables avérées	Estimated additional amount in place Quantités additionnelles estimées en place	Proved amount in place Quantités avérées en place	Proved recoverable reserves Réserves récupérables avérées	Estimated additional amount in place Quantités additionnelles estimées en place	Proved amount in place Quantités avérées en place	Proved recoverable reserves Réserves récupérables avérées
Republic of Moldova	..	..	..	..	..	..	..	
Romania	22	12	2143	3884	410	8177	25	1
Russian Federation	194000	49088	200000	124823	107922	200000	17680	1155
Rwanda	..	..	..	..	..	..	..	
Samoa	..	..	..	..	..	..	..	
Saudi Arabia	..	..	..	..	..	..	..	
Senegal	..	..	..	..	..	..	40	2
Serbia	27	6	..	21149	13879	..	..	
Sierra Leone	..	..	..	..	..	..	..	
Slovakia	2	2	..	519	260	..	..	
Slovenia	..	..	..	644	232	40	..	
Solomon Islands	..	..	..	..	..	..	..	
Somalia	..	..	..	..	..	..	..	
South Africa Customs Un.	115000	48248	205253	30	..	100	47	3
Spain	812	200	3000	584	330	1260	94	7
Sri Lanka	..	..	..	..	..	..	5	
Sudan	..	..	..	..	..	..	..	
Suriname	..	..	..	..	..	..	..	
Sweden	..	..	..	4	1	20	700	7
Switzerland	..	..	..	..	..	..	..	
Syrian Arab Republic	..	..	..	..	..	..	..	
T.F.Yug.Rep. Macedonia	..	..	..	..	..	..	..	
Tajikistan	..	..	..	..	..	..	..	
Thailand	..	..	..	2056	1354	2857	..	
Timor-Leste	..	..	..	..	..	..	..	
Togo	..	..	..	..	..	..	..	
Trinidad and Tobago	..	..	..	..	..	..	..	
Tunisia	..	..	..	..	..	..	..	
Turkey	590	449	249	2166	1814	296	..	
Turkmenistan	..	..	..	..	..	..	..	
Uganda	..	..	..	..	..	..	..	
Ukraine	20467	15351	5170	24697	18522	6174	2160	68
United Arab Emirates	..	..	..	..	..	..	..	
United Kingdom	570	155	190	1000	500	..	..	
United Rep.Tanzania	*304	200	*1500	..	..	..	..	
United States	244313	112261	445346	202870	130460	667415	26000	1300
Uruguay	..	..	..	..	..	..	..	
Uzbekistan	..	1000	..	..	2000	..	..	
Venezuela(Bolivar. Rep.)	1328	479	4528	..	..	0	..	
Viet Nam	312	150	..	..	..	..	..	
Yemen	..	..	..	..	..	..	..	
Zambia	..	10	0	69	55	18	..	
Zimbabwe	1535	502	5820	965	..	..	..	

Table 38

Ressources et réserves énergétiques choisies
Million de tonnes métriques sauf ou indiqué

| Peat Tourbe | Proved recoverable reserves Réserves récupérables avérées | | | | Uranium (metric tons) Uranium (tonnes métriques) | | Hydropower (Gross theoretical capability) Energie hydraulique (Capacité brute théorique) (GWH/Year Année) | Country or area Pays ou zone |
Estimated additional amount in place Quantités additionnelles estimées en place	Natural gas (billions cubic metres) Gaz naturel (billions de mètres cubes)	Crude oil and NGL Pétrole brut et LGN	Oil shale Schiste bitumineux	Bituminous sands Sables bitumineux	Reasonably assured resources Ressources raisonnablement assurées	Estimated additional resources Ressources additionnelles estimées		
..	..	..	..	..	..	..	2000	Rép. de Moldova
10	121	53	0	1	3100	3608	70000	Roumanie
168320	47820	10027	35470	4513	131700	40700	2295000	Fédération de Russie
2000	57	..	..	..	..	..	2000	Rwanda
..	..	..	..	..	..	..	140	Samoa
..	6848	34550	..	..	..	..	..	Arabie saoudite
52	11	..	..	..	..	..	11000	Sénégal
..	48	11	..	..	..	..	37000	Serbie
..	..	..	..	..	..	..	11000	Sierra Leone
..	15	1	..	..	1800	..	10000	Slovaquie
..	..	..	..	..	1200	5500	19000	Slovénie
..	..	..	..	..	..	..	3000	Iles Salomon
..	6	..	..	..	4900	2500	2000	Somalie
..	31	3	19	..	438200	184800	107000	Un.douan.d'Afr.mérid
..	3	21	40	..	4900	6400	150000	Espagne
46	..	..	..	..	..	..	18000	Sri Lanka
..	113	864	..	..	..	..	48000	Soudan
..	..	17	..	..	..	..	32000	Suriname
0	..	..	875	..	4000	6000	130000	Suède
..	..	..	..	..	..	..	125000	Suisse
..	298	335	..	..	..	..	11000	Rép. arabe syrienne
..	..	..	..	..	..	..	9000	L'ex-RY Macédoine
..	6	2	..	..	..	..	527000	Tadjikistan
..	304	51	916	..	5	5	41000	Thaïlande
..	..	0	..	..	..	..	..	Timor-Leste
..	..	..	..	..	..	..	4000	Togo
..	532	81	..	1	..	..	..	Trinité-et-Tobago
..	92	69	..	..	..	..	1000	Tunisie
..	15	165	284	..	7400	3220	433000	Turquie
..	2860	74	1100	..	..	..	24000	Turkménistan
..	..	..	..	..	..	..	18000	Ouganda
1846	787	151	600	..	66700	23100	45000	Ukraine
..	6071	12555	..	..	..	..	..	Emirats arabes unis
..	481	516	501	12	..	..	40000	Royaume-Uni
..	24	..	..	..	..	..	47000	Rép. Unie de Tanzanie
11102	5866	3691	301566	3	342000	..	4485000	Etats-Unis
46	..	..	40	..	..	..	32000	Uruguay
..	1850	70	1200	..	76900	38600	88000	Ouzbékistan
..	4315	11269	..	9310	..	..	320000	Venezuela(Rép. bolivar.)
..	365	413	..	..	1000	5435	300000	Viet Nam
..	479	384	..	..	..	..	..	Yémen
..	..	..	..	..	..	..	53000	Zambie
..	..	..	..	..	1350	..	44000	Zimbabwe